The **Rough Guide** to

South Ind

written and researched by

David Abram, Nick Edwards, Mike Ford, Devdan Sen and Beth Wooldridge

ROUGH GUIDES

NEW YORK • LONDON • DELHI

www.roughguides.com

Contents

◄◄ Kerala backwaters, ◄ Mumbai bazaar

3

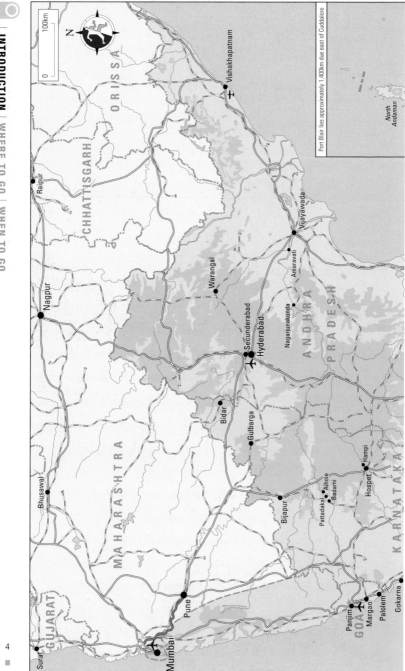

Port Blair lies approximately 1,400km due east of Cuddalore

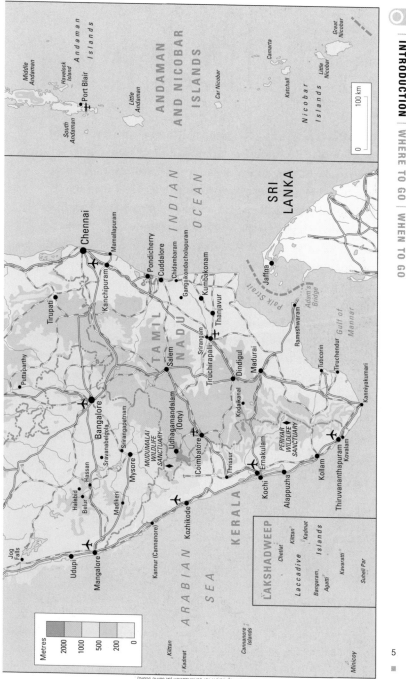

See inset map below for continuation (at same scale)

5

Introduction to

South India

Though its borders are uncertain, there's no doubt that South India, the tapering tropical half of this mighty peninsula, differs radically from the landlocked north. Stepping off a winter flight from foggy Delhi into the greenhouse humidity of Chennai or Thiruvananthapuram (Trivandrum), you enter a world far removed from the muted hues of the great Indian river plains. In the south, the coconut groves seem a deeper green and the rice paddies positively luminescent, the faces are a darker brown and the vermilion caste marks smeared over them arrestingly red. The region's heavy rainfall means that lush paddy fields and palm groves patchwork the volcanic soils during all but the hottest months. But under a sun whose rays feel concentrated by a giant magnifying glass, the ubiquitous colours of South India – of silk saris, shimmering classical dance costumes, roadside political posters and frangipani flowers – radiate with a life of their own.

South India's three mightiest rivers – the Godavari, the Krishna and the Kaveri – and their countless tributaries, flow east across a low, fertile alluvial basin that has been inhabited as long as anywhere in the subcontinent. Separated from the prehistoric Indus valley civilizations of the northwest by tracts of barren hills, the earliest South Indian societies are thought to have evolved independently of their northern cousins. Periodic invasions left their marks on the territory referred to in some of India's oldest inscriptions as **Dravidadesa**, "Land of the Dravidians". But neither the Moghuls, Portuguese, French nor British were ever fully able to subjugate the south. As a result, traditions, languages and ways of life have endured intact here for more than two thousand years – a fact that lends to any journey into the region a unique resonance.

▲ Kailasanatha temple, Kanchipuram

The persistence of a distinctly Dravidian culture in part accounts for the **regionalism** that has increasingly dominated the political and cultural life of the South since Independence in 1947. With the exception of Goa, a former Portuguese colony, and the Andaman and Nicobar Islands, the borders of the states covered in this book – Karnataka, Kerala, Tamil Nadu and Andhra Pradesh – were drawn along linguistic lines. Each state boasts its own distinctive styles of music, dance, architecture and cuisine, not to mention religious cults and dress. Moreover, attempts by New Delhi to homogenize the country by imposing Hindi, the most widely spoken language in the North, as the medium of education and government, have consistently met with resistance, stimulating support for the regional parties whose larger-than-life leaders beam munificently from giant hoardings in every major town and city.

More pervasive even than the power of politics in South India is the influence of **religion**, which, despite the country's resolutely secular constitution, still permeates every aspect of life. Of the four major faiths, **Hinduism** is by far the most prevalent, practised by around eighty percent of the population. If the sacred peaks of the Himalayas are Hinduism's head, and the Ganges its main artery, then the temple complexes of the South are its spiritual heart and soul. Soaring high above every urban skyline, their colossal towers are emblematic of the awe with which the deities enshrined inside them have been held for centuries. Some, like the sea-washed temple at Tiruchendur in Tamil Nadu, are thought to be as old as human speech itself; others, such as the Sabarimala forest shrine in Kerala, are less ancient, but attract greater numbers of pilgrims than even Mecca. For foreign visitors, however,

7

Meals Ready

Many people come to India expecting the rich, meaty cuisine served up in British curry houses, but the reality turns out to be a lot more exciting: vegetarians, in particular, will find southern cooking a delight. Wander into almost any restaurant or canteen displaying a "Meals Ready" sign, and you'll have a tin tray with little cups, or a fresh green banana leaf, spread in front of you. In (or on) to this, legions of busy waiters will spoon a variety of rice, fresh vegetables and bean preparations, dhals, breads, yoghurt, pickles, poppadums and sauces, each flavoured with a different blend of spices, lime juice, coconut milk and sour mango. And, at the first sign that you're making any headway with this bewildering quantity of food, they'll slop another ladleful on.

Each region has its own distinctive style of set leaf or plate meal; the one thing they have in common is that they'll fill you to bursting point and cost next to nothing. For the ultimate "Meals Ready" experience, head for any branch of *Saravana Bhavan* in Chennai (see p.462), *Fry's Village Restaurant* in Kochi (see p.411), or just about anywhere that's doing a brisk trade.

the most extraordinary of all have to be the colossal Chola shrines of Tamil Nadu. Joining the crowds that stream through Madurai's Meenakshi-Sundareshwar temple or Shri Ramalingeshwara in Rameshwaram will take you to the very taproot of the world's last surviving classical culture, some of whose hymns, prayers and rites predate the Egyptian pyramids.

By comparison, **Islam**, South India's second religion, is a fledgling faith, first introduced by Arab traders along the coast in the twelfth century. Later, offshoots of the Muslim dynasties that ruled the North carved out feudal kingdoms beyond the Godavari, establishing a band of Islamic culture across the middle of the Deccan plateau. Other elements in the great South Indian melting pot include a dozen or more denominations of **Christianity**, ranging from the ancient Syrian Orthodoxy believed to have been introduced by the apostle St Thomas, to the Roman Catholicism of Old Goa's Portuguese Jesuits. The

▼ Thanjavur

region also harbours sites sacred to **Jains**, followers of the prophet Mahavira, a contemporary of Buddha, while in Kochi, Kerala, a vestigial population of **Jews** is all that remains of a once thriving mercantile community.

Since Independence, these diverse groups have coexisted more or less peacefully, rarely succumbing to the waves of communal blood-letting that have often blighted life in the northern cities. In the 1990s, supposedly as a reaction to the rise of Hindu extremist parties, bombs and riots erupted around the Muslim ghettos of Mumbai (Bombay) and Coimbatore (in western Tamil Nadu), but these are widely viewed as isolated flare-ups rather than a growing trend. The last decade has seen a dramatic rise in **caste violence**, however. The age-old hierarchy introduced by the Aryans more than three thousand years ago still forms the backbone of South Indian society, crossing all religious and ethnic divides. But recent political reforms have enabled members of disadvantaged minorities to claim a fairer share of government jobs

> **If the sacred peaks of the Himalayas are Hinduism's head, and the Ganges its main artery, then the temple complexes of the South are its spiritual heart and soul**

and university places, as well as political posts, and this has generated widespread resentment, strengthening the very divisions positive discrimination was intended to dissolve.

South India, though, remains one of the most relaxed and congenial parts of Asia to explore. It is also among the easiest. In all but the remotest districts, accommodation is plentiful, clean and inexpensive by Western standards. Freshly cooked, nutritious food is nearly always available. Getting

Masala movies

Emblematic of modern India at its most highly charged and lurid are the huge, hand-painted hoardings that tower over city intersections. Featuring blood-splattered macho men, curvaceous heroines in various states of distress (and undress), chubby, bulging-eyed bad guys and explosions a-plenty, they give you a pretty good taste of the kind of movies churned out by the record-beating film industries of Mumbai and Chennai. In either Hindi or Tamil, all follow formulaic hero-gets-the-girl plots, interrupted at frequent intervals by sweeping song-and-dance sequences whose ubiquitous soundtracks crackle out of cassette machines from Kashmir to Kerala. Catch the latest box-office smash at one of the big-city cinema houses, primed by our background accounts on "Bollywood" (p.139) and the Tamil film industry (p.456).

around is usually straightforward, although the sheer size and problematic geography of the South means journeys can be long. The region's extensive rail network moves vast numbers of people at all times of the day and night, and if a train isn't heading where you want to go, a bus probably will be. Furthermore, the widespread use of English makes communication relatively easy. South Indians are the most garrulous and inquisitive of travellers, and train rides are always enlivened by conversations that invariably begin with the refrain of "Coming from?" or "Your native place?"

The extent to which you enjoy travelling in South India will probably depend less on your luck with **Modern and traditional thrive side by side. Walking through downtown Bangalore, you could brush shoulders with a software programmer one moment and a saffron-clad ascetic the next**

hotels, restaurants and transport than your reaction to the country itself. Many people expect some kind of exotic time warp, and are surprised to find a consumer culture that's as unashamedly materialistic as anywhere. It is a credit to the South Indians' legendary capacity for assimilating new ideas, however, that the modern and traditional thrive side by side. Walking through downtown Bangalore, you could brush shoulders with a software programmer one moment and a saffron-clad ascetic the next, while bullock carts and stray cattle mingle with Japanese luxury cars. There are, of course, the usual travel hassles: interminable queues, packed buses and constant encroachments on your personal space. Yet, just when your nerves feel stretched to breaking point, South India always offers something that makes the effort worthwhile: a glimpse of a wild elephant from a train window; a sumptuous vegetarian meal delicately arranged on a fresh banana leaf; or a hint of fragrant cardamom in your tea after an all-night Kathakali recital.

Where to go

South India's boundaries vary according to whom you're talking to: while some regard the River Krishna, the upper limit of India's last Hindu empire, as the real north–south divide, others place the subcontinent's main cultural fault line at the River Godavari or, further north still, at the Vindhya Hills, the barrier of arid table-topped mountains bounding the Ganges Basin. In this guide we've started with **Mumbai**, a hot, congested city which is the arrival point for most international flights. Mumbai gets a pretty bad press, and most people pass straight through, but those who stay find themselves witness to the reality of modern-day India, from the deprivations of the city's slum-dwellings to the glitz and glamour of Bollywood movies.

The other principal gateway is **Chennai**, capital of **Tamil Nadu**, in the deep south, which is a slightly less stressful point of entry. Although it's another major metropolis bursting at the seams, hidden under its surface are artful gems such as regular public performances of classical music

▲ Mahamastakabhisheka ceremony, Sravanabelgola

Teyyattam

From late October to May, archaic ritual dances known as *teyyattam* take place in over 400 villages and temples along the north Malabar coast. Performances often last all night, and provide a spectacular way of discovering the traditions that lie at the heart of Kerala. Each community nurtures an allegiance to a popular deity; the body and expression of the dancer, the *theyyam*, becomes a vessel for the deity to connect with their devotees. According to tradition, a *theyyam* must come from a low-caste family, but while they perform, their humble status is eliminated and social equality reigns. The *theyyam* starts to learn the art when he is 9 years old and will, for the next eight years, receive training in dance, martial arts and massage. Some *theyyam* are required to dance deft steps while wearing a headdress (*mudi*) almost twice their size; there are also particularly rare and dangerous *teyyattam* where the dancer dons a headdress the height of a coconut tree. For more on tracking down *teyyattam*, see p.435.

▲ Pao bhaji breakfast, Goa

and dance. With regular flights and ship departures to Port Blair, Chennai is also the major springboard for the **Andaman Islands**, a remote archipelago ringed by coral reefs and crystal-clear seas, 1000km east of the mainland in the Bay of Bengal.

The majority of visitors' first stop after Chennai is **Mamallapuram**, an ancient port littered with weatherworn sculpture sites, including the famous Shore temple. To get right off the beaten track you only have to head inland to **Kanchipuram**, whose innumerable Hindu shrines span the golden age of the illustrious Chola kingdom, or to **Tiruvannamalai**, where one of the region's massive temple complexes rises dramatically from the base of a sacred mountain, site of countless ashrams and meditation caves. Back on the coast, the former French colony of **Pondicherry** retains a distinctly Gallic feel, particularly in its restaurants, where you can order *coq au vin* and a bottle of Burgundy before a stroll along the promenade. The Kaveri (Cauvery) Delta, further south, harbours astonishing crops of monuments, some of the most impressive of which are around **Thanjavur** (Tanjore), the Cholas' former capital, dominated by the awesome Brihadishwara temple. You could profitably spend days exploring the town's watery hinterland, hunting out bronze-casting villages, crumbling ruins and other forgotten sacred sites among the web of rivers and irrigation canals. Most travellers press on south to **Madurai**, the region's most atmospherically charged city, where the mighty Meenakshi-Sundareshwar temple presides over a quintessentially Tamil swirl of life.

The two other most compelling destinations in Tamil Nadu are the island of **Rameshwaram**, whose main temple features a vast enclosure of pillared corridors, and **Kanniyakumari**, the auspicious southernmost tip of India, where the Bay of Bengal, Indian Ocean and Arabian Sea flow together. The dark shadows visible on the horizon from here mark the start of the **southern and western Ghats**, which stretch for more than 1000km in a virtually unbroken chain all the way to Mumbai, forming a sheer barrier between Tamil Nadu and neighbouring Kerala. Covered in immense forests and windswept grasslands, the mountains rise to the highest peaks in peninsular India, with sides sculpted by tea terraces, coffee plantations and cardamom groves. The hill stations of **Udhagamandalam** (or Ooty, as it's still better known) and **Kodaikanal**, established by India's former colonial rulers as retreats from the summer heat of the plains, attract hordes of Indian visitors in the run-up to the rains, but see plenty of foreign tourist traffic during the winter, too.

Neighbouring **Kerala**'s appeal lies less in its religious monuments, many of which remain off-limits to non-Hindus, than its infectiously easy-going, tropical ambience. Covering a long thin coastal strip backed by a steep wall of

▲ North Goa beach

▶ Puram Festival, Thrissur

hills, this is the wettest and most densely populated state in the south. It is also the most distinctive, with a culture that sets it squarely apart. Its ritualized theatre (Kathakali), faintly Southeast Asian architecture and ubiquitous communist graffiti (Kerala was the first place in the world to gain a democratically elected communist government) are perhaps the most visual expressions of this difference. But spend a couple of days exploring the spicy backstreets of old **Kochi** (Cochin), the jungles of the **Cardamom Hills** around the Periyar Wildlife Sanctuary or the hidden aquatic world of the coastal backwaters, and you'll see why many travellers end up staying here a lot longer than they originally intended. If you're not pushed for time and find yourself crossing northern Kerala during the winter, set aside a few days to search for Teyyattam, a spectacular masked dance form unique to the villages around Kannur.

A short ride across the mountains takes you to **Mysore** in **Karnataka**, whose opulent maharaja's palace, colourful markets and comfortable California-like climate have made it among South India's most popular tourist destinations. **Bangalore**, the hectic modern capital, is not one of the highlights of the state, which are for the main part scattered over a vast area of rolling, granite-boulder-strewn uplands. Most, such as the richly carved Hoysala temples of **Belur** and **Halebid**, or the extraordinary Jain colossus at **Sravanabelgola**, are religious monuments. Amongst other extraordinary sights are the mausolea, mosques and Persian-style palaces of **Bijapur**, Karnataka, often dubbed the "Agra of the South". Almost unsurpassable, however, is the awesome scale and faded splendour of the Vijayanagar ruins at **Hampi**, on the River Tungabhadra. Until it was ransacked by a confederacy of Muslim sultanates in 1565, this was the magnificent capital of South India's last Hindu empire, encompassing most of the peninsula.

Only one day's journey to the west, the palm-fringed, white-sand beaches of **Goa** offer a change of scenery from the rocky terrain of the Deccan. Succumbing to the hedonistic pleasures of warm seawater, constant sunshine and cheap drinks, many travellers find it hard to tear themselves away from the coast. Further east, a string of smaller former dynastic capitals punctuate the journey across the heart of the Deccan plateau to **Hyderabad**, capital of **Andhra Pradesh**, whose principal landmarks are the Charminar and Golconda fort. Andhra's other attractions, by contrast, lie much further off the beaten track. Comparatively few Western visitors ever reach them, but **Puttaparthy**, the ashram of India's most famous living saint, Sai Baba, and **Tirupati**, whose temple receives more pilgrims than anywhere else on earth, are essential stops for South Indians.

When to go

The relentless tropical sun aside, the source of South India's irrepressible fecundity lies in its high **rainfall**. Unlike the north of the country, which sees only a single deluge in the summer, most of peninsular India receives **two annual monsoons** – one sucked in from the Arabian Sea in the southwest, and the other on stormy northwesterly winds off the Bay of Bengal. The heaviest rains are reserved for the Western Ghats, a chain of mountains running parallel with the southwest coast. Cloaked for the most part in dense forest, these form a curtain that impedes the path of the first summer monsoon, which breaks in June and lasts through October. In a nutshell, you should, when planning a trip to South India, avoid the rainy seasons. The novelty of torrential downpours and the general mayhem

▲ View from Palani temple

that attend the annual deluges wears off very quickly. Road blockages, landslides and burst riverbanks can interrupt the best-laid travel plans, not to mention the discomfort of being wet through for days on end; the widespread flooding is also none too healthy, emptying the sewers and polluting reservoirs. Broadly speaking, rule out the period between April and September, when the southwest monsoon is in full swing

across the whole peninsula. From late October until April, the weather is perfect in Karnataka and Goa, but less reliable in Kerala, where, by November, the "retreating", or northwest monsoon means constant grey skies and showers. Being on the eastern side of the mountains, Tamil Nadu gets even heavier rains at this time. To enjoy the far south and the Andaman Islands at their best, come between January and March, before the heat starts to build up again. Late April and May are simply insufferable for anyone not accustomed to intense tropical heat.

Average temperatures and rainfall

	Jan	Feb	Mar	Apr	May	June	July	Aug	Sept	Oct	Nov	Dec
Bangalore (Kar)												
Av daily max (°C)	28	31	33	34	33	30	28	29	28	28	27	27
Rainfall (mm)	4	14	6	37	119	65	93	95	129	195	46	16
Chennai (TN)												
Av daily max (°C)	29	31	33	35	38	37	35	35	34	32	29	28
Rainfall (mm)	24	7	15	25	52	53	83	124	118	267	309	139
Hyderabad (AP)												
Av daily max (°C)	29	31	35	37	39	34	30	29	30	30	29	28
Rainfall (mm)	2	11	13	24	30	107	165	147	163	71	25	5
Kochi (Ker)												
Av daily max (°C)	31	31	31	31	31	29	28	28	28	29	30	30
Rainfall (mm)	9	34	50	139	364	756	572	386	235	333	184	37
Madurai (TN)												
Av daily max (°C)	31	31	31	31	31	29	28	28	28	29	30	30
Rainfall (mm)	26	16	21	81	59	31	48	117	123	179	161	143
Mumbai (M)												
Av daily max (°C)	31	32	33	33	33	32	30	29	30	32	33	32
Rainfall (mm)	0	1	0	0	20	647	945	660	309	17	7	1
Panjim (Goa)												
Av daily max (°C)	31	32	32	33	33	31	29	29	29	31	33	33
Rainfall (mm)	2	0	4	17	18	580	892	341	277	122	20	37

32

things not to miss

It's not possible to see everything that South India has to offer in one trip – and we don't suggest you try. What follows is a selective taste of the region's highlights: outstanding buildings, natural wonders, spectacular festivals and unforgettable journeys. They're arranged in five colour-coded categories, which you can browse through to find the very best things to see and experience. All highlights have a page reference to take you straight into the guide, where you can find out more.

01 Jog Falls Page **294** • India's highest waterfall offers awesome views and refreshingly wet walks.

02 Tamil sculpture Page **527** • The great Tamil shrines of the Kaveri Delta writhe with sensuous stone sculpture, such as this exquisite *apsara* at Srirangam's Ranganathaswamy shrine.

03 Feni Page **73** • The ultimate tropical cocktail base, Goan *feni*, is distilled from coconut sap collected twice daily by teams of toddy tappers. Sample a drop of the hard stuff yourself at Palolem or Benaulim.

05 Cricket Page **81** • The nation's favourite sport is played everywhere, from street corners to the Oval Maidan in Mumbai.

04 Old Goa Page **184** • Belfries and Baroque church facades loom over trees on the banks of the Mandovi, all that remains of a once-splendid colonial city.

06 Boating on the backwaters Page **378** • Hire a *kettu vallam* (rice barge) or take the local ferryboat through Kerala's teeming Kuttanad backwater region – South India at its most luxuriant.

07 Palolem beach Page **227** • Far from a secret, but still breathtakingly beautiful despite the hordes who winter here.

08 Golgumbaz tomb Page **327** • The finest of the many sublime Islamic monuments which litter the Deccan regions of Karnataka.

09 Keralan ritual theatre Page **712** • Kerala is the place to experience Kathakali, the state's unique and flamboyant form of ritual theatre.

10 Mamallapuram Page **475** • Popular fishing and stone-carving village, with magnificent boulder friezes, shrines and the sea-battered Shore Temple.

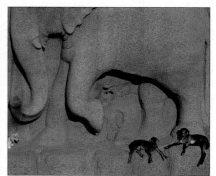

12 **Drum orchestras** Page **710** • Ear-splitting Keralan drum orchestras are one of the key ingredients of Kerala's uniquely intense temple festivals.

11 **Scuba diving** Page **624** • The remote Andaman Islands lie in some of the richest, clearest seawater in the world, offering wonderful diving opportunities.

13 **Periyar Wildlife Sanctuary** Page **387** • One of the region's foremost reserves, set in the tropical Cardamom Hills and home to abundant wildlife, including a rare (and rarely spotted) population of tigers.

14 **Fishing villages** Page **362** • Experience beach life as few Western tourists see it in the Muslim fishing villages around Kovalam.

15 **The Nilgiri Blue Mountain Railway** Page **567** • The bone-shaking ride up to Ooty on one of Asia's last steam railways is a must for Raj-philes, and worth it for the views alone.

16 **Ayurvedic massage** Page **47** • Experience holistic Indian healthcare at its most indulgent with a traditional Ayurvedic massage, at Kovalam or Varkala.

18 **Elephants** Pages **387, 396 & 435** • Spot elephants in the wild in Kerala's Periyar, Erivikulam and Tholpetty national parks.

17 **Meenakshi Temple, Madurai** Page **535** • One of South India's greatest temples, surmounted by soaring *gopuras* and home to a range of spectacular festivals.

19 **Kochi** Page **397** • Atmospheric colonial settlement, suffused with contrasting Portuguese, British and Keralan influences.

20 **Christmas in Kerala** Page **343** • Attend Christmas Eve mass in Kerala for a glimpse of one of the oldest surviving Christian traditions in Asia.

21 **Ashrams** Page **84** • Brush up on your yoga *asanas* and meditation technique at one of South India's many ashrams.

22 **Chariot festivals** Page **522** • Among the great spectacles of southern India are temple chariot (*rath*) festivals, such as this one at Thiruvarur in Tamil Nadu.

23 **Gokarna** Page **296** • The beautiful beaches on the edge of this temple town are popular with budget travellers fleeing the commercialism of nearby Goa.

24 Chola bronzes Page **521** • The Nayak Durbar Hall Art Museum in Thanjavur holds India's finest collection of Chola bronzes, while you can see contemporary casters at work at Swamimalai.

25 Dussehra Page **77** • Giant effigies of the demon Ravana are stuffed with firecrackers and burnt for the Dusshera festival (Sept–Oct). Mumbai's Shivaji Park hosts one of the biggest events.

26 Sravanabelgola Page **274** • This mystical Jain colossus at Sravanabelgola forms the centrepiece of southern Karnataka's most atmospheric pilgrimage town.

27 Hampi Page **308** • The great ruined capital of the Vijayanagar dynasty, its superb monuments scattered over boulder-strewn plains around the Tungabhadra River.

28 Golconda Fort Page **589** • The former capital of the Qutb Shahi dynasty, this dramatic fort sits on a hilltop just outside Hyderabad.

30 Kalarippayat martial art Page **351** • Kerala's unique martial art, practised in gyms throughout the state.

31 Elephanta Caves Page **133** • These ancient caves, cut from solid rock in Mumbai harbour, offer the perfect escape from the madness of the Maharashtran capital.

29 Sacred art Page **385** • Vibrant murals, such as this sixteenth-century mural from Mahadeva temple in Ettumanur, form part of the South's rich repertoire of sacred art.

32 Venkateshvara Temple, Tirumala Page **600** • The world's most visited religious site, attracting more pilgrims than Mecca.

Basics

Basics

Getting there

Most visitors to South India fly into the major international gateways of either Mumbai (Bombay) or Chennai (Madras). Non-stop flights from London reach Mumbai in just nine hours and Chennai in ten hours. Travelling from North America, you're on the opposite side of the globe and will have at least one change of plane ahead of you. Nor are there any direct flights from New Zealand or Australia; the quickest route is via Southeast Asia.

Airfares worldwide always depend on the **season**, with the highest being from roughly November to March, when the weather in India is best; fares drop during the shoulder seasons – April to May and August to early October – and you'll get the best prices during the low season, June and July. The most expensive fares of all are those coinciding with Diwali in November, when demand peaks as Indian emigrants travel home for holidays with their families.

You can often cut costs by going through a specialist flight agent – either a **consolidator**, who buys up blocks of tickets from the airlines and sells them at a discount, or a **discount agent**, who in addition to dealing with discounted flights may also offer special student and youth fares and a range of other travel-related services such as travel insurance or tours. Some agents specialize in **charter flights**, which may be cheaper than anything available on a scheduled service, but again departure dates are fixed and withdrawal penalties are high. For destinations such as Goa and Kerala, you may even find it cheaper to pick up a bargain **package deal** from one of the tour operators listed on p.28 and p.29, and then find your own accommodation when you get there. Indian law prohibits the sale of flight-only tickets by charter companies, but operators sometimes get around this by tacking budget "bunk-house" accommodation to their tickets, which (if it exists at all) travellers ditch on arrival. Note also that charter tickets to India are not allowed to cover more than 28 days. If you wish to stay in the country for longer than that, you have to take a scheduled flight. Nor is it possible to fly in on a charter and out on a scheduled flight, or vice versa.

If India is only one stop on a longer journey, you might want to consider buying a **Round-the-World** (RTW) ticket. Some travel agents can sell you an "off-the-shelf" RTW ticket that will have you touching down in about half a dozen cities (Delhi and Mumbai are on many itineraries); others will have to assemble one for you, which can be tailored to your needs but is apt to be more expensive. Figure on £950/$1400–£1500/$2400 for a RTW ticket including India, open for one year.

However you fly to South India, shop around for the most convenient **arrival times**; nearly all of the cheaper flights land in the middle of night, and it can be well worth shelling out a little extra to avoid passing through the airport in darkness, particularly if this is your first trip to India.

Booking flights online

Many airlines and discount travel websites offer you the opportunity to book your tickets **online**, cutting out the costs of agents and middlemen. Good deals can often be found through discount or auction sites, as well as through the airlines' own websites.

Online booking agents

ⓦ travel.yahoo.com (US and Canada), ⓦ www .cheapflights.com (UK and Ireland), ⓦ www .cheapflight.com (US), ⓦ www.cheapflights .ca (Canada), ⓦ www.cheapflights.com.au (Australia). Flight deals, details of travel agents, and links to other travel sites.
ⓦ www.cheaptickets.com Discount flight specialists (US only) whose search engine claims to dig up the lowest possible fares worldwide; the one drawback is the cumbersome log-in procedure.
ⓦ www.counciltravel.com If you're travelling

from the US and you've some flexibility, this site can come up with competitive deals.

ⓦ www.etn.nl/discount.htm A hub of consolidator and discount agent Web links, maintained by the nonprofit European Travel Network.

ⓦ www.expedia.com (US), ⓦ www.expedia.co.uk (UK), ⓦ www.expedia.ca (Canada). Discount airfares, all-airline search engine and daily deals.

ⓦ www.flights4less.co.uk ABTA-bonded site (a subsidiary of ⓦ www.lastminute.com) offering access to a vast range of discounted flights worldwide.

ⓦ www.flynow.com Simple to use independent travel site offering good-value fares.

ⓦ www.hotwire.com Bookings from the US only. Last-minute savings of up to forty percent on regular published fares. Travellers must be at least 18 and there are no refunds, transfers or changes allowed. Log-in required. If you're looking for the cheapest possible scheduled flight, this is probably your best bet.

ⓦ www.lastminute.com (UK), ⓦ www.lastminute.com.au (Australia). Good last-minute holiday package and flight-only deals.

ⓦ www.qixo.com A comparison search engine that trawls through other ticket sites – including agencies and airlines – to find the best deals.

ⓦ www.skyauction.com Bookings from the US only. Auctions tickets and travel packages using a "second bid" scheme, just like eBay. You state the maximum you're willing to pay, and the system will bid only as much as it takes to outbid others, up to your stated limit.

ⓦ www.ticketplanet.com California-based site that claims to be the first to sell consolidator fares over the Web. Especially good for circle-Pacific and round-the-world fares.

ⓦ www.travelocity.com (US), ⓦ www.travelocity.ca (Canada) and ⓦ www.travelocity.co.uk (UK and Ireland). Hot Web fares and deals for car hire, accommodation and lodging, as well as fares. Provides access to the travel agent system SABRE, the most comprehensive central reservations system in the US.

ⓦ www.travelshop.com.au Australian website offering discounted flights, packages, insurance and online bookings.

Packages

A large number of operators run **package holidays** to India, covering activities such as trekking and safaris as well as sightseeing and sunbathing. Specialist minority-interest tours range from steam locomotives and textiles to religion, food and wildlife.

In addition, many companies will arrange **tailor-made tours**, and can help you plan your own route.

Of course, any package holiday is a lot easier than going under your own steam, particularly if you only have a short time and don't want to use it up on making your own travel bookings. On the other hand, a typical sightseeing tour can rather isolate you from the country, shutting you off in air-conditioned hotels and buses. Specialist trips such as trekking and tailor-made tours will work out rather expensive, compared to what you'd pay if you organized everything independently, but they do cut out a lot of hassle. However, late-availability Goa beach holidays and packages to Kovalam in Kerala offered by UK-based companies can sometimes work out cheaper than a normal flight.

Specialist tour operators

In the UK

Abercrombie and Kent ☏ 0845/070 0610, ⓦ www.abercrombiekent.co.uk. Upmarket sightseeing and trekking and wildlife trips; tailor-made holidays also available.

Andrew Brock/Coromandel ☏ 01572/821330 ⓦ www.coromandelabt.com. Car itineraries, textile trips to village craft workshops, plus David Sayer's botanical and horticultural tours.

Audley Travel ☏ 01869/276218 ⓦ www.audleytravel.com. Privately guided, tailor-made itineraries using interesting accommodation (homestays, tented camps and heritage properties); they're also strong on wildlife.

Bales ☏ 0870/241 3208, ⓦ www.balesworldwide.com. Sixteen escorted tours covering most of South India.

Blazing Trails UK ☏ 01293/533338, ⓦ www.blazingtrails.com. Escorted motorcycle tours (on Enfields) in Goa and Kerala.

Cox & Kings ☏ 020/7873 5000, ⓦ www.coxandkings.com. Tailor-made itineraries with an operator established in India since 1758.

Discovery Initiatives ☏ 01285/643333 ⓦ www.discoveryinitiatives.co.uk. Nature tour specialist offering small groups or tailor-made trips with an emphasis on conservation and ecology.

Essential India ☏ 01225/868544, ⓦ www.essential-india.co.uk. Courses in India on a wide range of subjects, from writing, painting and pottery to Buddhism and outdoor pursuits, for individuals or groups. They favour low-impact travel and use local companies wherever possible.

Exodus ☎020/8675 5550, ⓦwww.exodustravels
.co.uk. Experienced specialists in small-group
itineraries, treks and overland tours.
High Places ☎0114/275 7500, ⓦwww
.highplaces.co.uk. Biking and boating in Kerala.
Jewel in the Crown ☎01293/533338, ⓦwww
.jewelholidays.com. Established Goa and Kerala
specialist, offering a wide range of holidays in both
states; they also run motorcycle tours on Enfields.
Kambala ☎01803/732488. One of the few
operators specializing in very small group tours for the
over-50s. General sightseeing and "hobby" holidays
(eg textiles and painting) in rural Kerala.
Kerala Connections ☎01892/722440, ⓦwww
.keralaconnect.co.uk. South India specialists,
offering itineraries in Tamil Nadu, Karnataka and
Lakshadweep, as well as Kerala, for a wide range of
budgets.
Pettitts India ☎01892/515966, ⓦwww.pettitts
.co.uk. Tailor-made holidays off the beaten track.
SD Enterprises ☎020/8903 0392, ⓦwww
.indiarail.co.uk. Run by Indian rail experts, SD
Enterprises put together complex itineraries for
independent travellers wanting to explore India by
train, as well as budget packages to Goa and Kerala.
Soul of India ☎020/8901 7320, ⓦwww
.soulofindia.com. Guided tours (set or tailor-
made, and for individuals or groups) of sacred
India, including the Hindu and Christian south, and
landmarks associated with the Buddha.
Trans Indus Travel ☎020/8566 2729, ⓦwww
.transindus.co.uk. Specialists in wildlife, fishing and
trekking offering fixed and tailor-made tours from
various Indian cities.
Voyages Jules Verne ☎020/7616 1000, ⓦwww
.vjv.co.uk. Fourteen classic India-wide heritage tours,
including some by rail.
Western & Oriental Travel ☎0870/499 1111,
ⓦwww.westernoriental.com. Award-winning
upmarket agency with tailor-made itineraries covering
all of India, but favouring Goa and Kerala.

In the US and Canada

Adventure Center ☎1-800/228-8747, ⓦwww
.adventurecenter.com. Trekking and cultural tours.
Butterfield & Robinson ☎1-800/678-1147 or
1-510/654-1879, ⓦwww.butterfield.com. Bespoke
tours, with an emphasis on cycling and walking.
Geographic Expeditions ☎1-800/777-8183,
ⓦwww.geoex.com. Remote mountain treks and
unusual tours including sea kayaking in the Andamans.
Myths and Mountains ☎1-800/670-6984 or
775-832-5454, ⓦwww.mythsandmountains.com.
Special-interest trips, tailor-made or group, with an
emphasis on culture, crafts, religion and traditional
medicine.

Nature Expeditions International ☎1-800/
869-0639 or 503/484-6529, ⓦwww.naturexp
.com. Upscale wildlife viewing, "soft adventure" and
cultural tours.
Wilderness Travel ☎1-800/368-2794, ⓦwww
.wildernesstravel.com. Their seventeen-day
"Treasures of South India" tour takes in the highlights
of Tamil Nadu and coastal Kerala.
Worldwide Quest Adventures ☎1-800/387-
1483, ⓦwww.worldwidequest.com. Sightseeing
plus trekking, cycling, camel safaris and cultural tours.

In Australia and New Zealand

Abercrombie and Kent Australia ☎02/9241
3213, New Zealand ☎0800/441638, ⓦwww
.abercrombiekent.com.au. Specialist in individual
mid- and upmarket holidays away from the main
tourist trails.
Classic Oriental Tours Australia ☎02/9657
2020, ⓦwww.classicoriental.com.au. Wide choice
of tours ranging from three-day city breaks to 22-day
itineraries, with some adventure options.
Peregrine Adventures Australia ☎03/9663 8611,
ⓦwww.peregrine.net.au. Trekking specialists with a
wide range of tailored group and individual tours.
San Michele Travel Australia ☎02/9299 1111 &
1800/222244, ⓦwww.asiatravel.com.au. Budget
and upmarket air and accommodation packages, rail
tours and tailor-made land excursions for groups or
individual travellers.
Travel.com.au Australia ☎02/9249 6000,
ⓦwww.travel.com.au. Agent for a broad range of
tour operators. You can select set itineraries or tailor-
make your own packages on their website.

Flights from the UK and Ireland

It takes between eight-and-a-half and eleven hours to **fly from the UK** direct to India. However, most airlines route passengers through their hub city on the way, which can double the total travelling time. By and large you get what you pay for. Economy airlines may offer rock-bottom fares from as low as £350 (or less), but you'll invariably find this means a tediously long wait at obscure airports well off the direct route, and departure and arrival times at unsociable hours of the night. At the other end of the scale, a ticket costing upwards of £600 with British Airways, Emirates or Air India should get you there non-stop from London by a more civilized hour. Flight-only deals with charters go for as little as £250 low season (and sometimes even less), or around £450–650 over Christmas and New Year.

Airlines

Air France UK ☎0845/084 5111, ⓦwww
.airfrance.co.uk; Republic of Ireland ☎01/605
0383, ⓦwww.airfrance.com/ie.
Air India ☎020/8560 9996 or 8745 1000,
ⓦwww.airindia.com.
Alitalia UK ☎0870/544 8259, Republic of Ireland
☎01/677 5171; ⓦwww.alitalia.co.uk.
Biman Bangladesh Airlines ☎020/7629 0252,
ⓦwww.bimanair.com.
British Airways UK ☎0870/850 9850, Republic
of Ireland ☎1800/626747; ⓦwww.ba.com.
EgyptAir UK ☎020/7734 2343 or 7734 2395,
ⓦwww.egyptair.com.eg.
Emirates Airlines UK ☎0870/243 2222, ⓦwww
.emirates.com.
Gulf Air UK ☎0870/777 1717, ⓦwww.gulfairco
.com.
Jet Airways ☎020/8970 1525, ⓦwww
.jetairways.com.
KLM Royal Dutch Airlines ☎08705/074074,
ⓦwww.klm.com.
Lufthansa UK ☎08457/737747, Republic of
Ireland ☎01/844 5544; ⓦwww.lufthansa.co.uk.
Pakistan International Airlines UK ☎020/7499
5500, ⓦwww.piac.com.pk.
Qantas ☎08457/747767, ⓦwww.quantas.com.
Royal Brunei Airlines UK ☎020/7584 6660,
ⓦwww.bruneiair.com.
Royal Jordanian UK ☎020/7878 6333, Republic
of Ireland ☎061/712874; ⓦwww.rja.com.jo.
Sahara Airlines UK☎0870/127 1000, ⓦwww
.airsahara.net.
SriLankan Airlines UK ☎020/8538 2000,
ⓦwww.srilankan.lk.
Swiss UK ☎0845/601 0956, ⓦwww.swiss.com.
Thai Airways International UK ☎0870/606
0911, ⓦwww.thaiair.com.
United Airlines UK ☎0845/844 4777, ⓦwww
.unitedairlines.co.uk.
Virgin Atlantic Airways UK ☎01293/747747,
ⓦwww.virgin.com/atlantic.

Flight and travel agents

UK

Arrowguide Ltd 29 Dering St, London W1
☎020/7629 9516, ⓦwww.arrowguide.co.uk. Long-
established and reliable consolidator specializing in
cheap flights to India.
Bridge the World ☎0870/814 4400, ⓦwww
.bridgetheworld.com. Specializing in round-the-world

tickets, with good deals aimed at the backpacker
market.
Co-op Travel Care ☎0870/112 0085, ⓦwww
.travelcareonline.com. Award-winning agent, offering
flights and holidays around the world.
Flightbookers ☎0870/010 7000, ⓦwww
.ebookers.com. Low fares on an extensive selection
of scheduled flights.
North South Travel ☎01245/608291, ⓦwww
.northsouthtravel.co.uk. Friendly, competitive travel
agency offering discounted fares worldwide – profits
are used to support projects in the developing world,
especially the promotion of sustainable tourism.
Rosetta Travel Northern Ireland ☎028/9064 4996,
ⓦwww.rosettatravel.com. Flight and holiday agent.
STA Travel ☎0870/160 0599, ⓦwww.statravel
.co.uk. Worldwide specialists in low-cost flights
and tours for students and under-26s, though other
customers welcome.
Top Deck ☎020/8879 6789, ⓦwww
.topdecktravel.co.uk. Long-established agent dealing
in discount flights.
Trailfinders ☎0845/058 5858, ⓦwww
.trailfinders.co.uk. One of the best-informed and
most efficient agents for independent travellers;
they produce a very useful quarterly magazine worth
scrutinizing for round-the-world routes.
Travel Bag ☎0800/082 5000, ⓦwww.travelbag
.co.uk. Discount flights to Australia, New Zealand,
USA and the Far East; official Qantas agent.

Republic of Ireland

Apex Travel ☎01/241 8000, ⓦwww.apextravel
.ie. Family-owned company and agents for flights
worldwide.
Aran Travel International ☎091/562595,
ⓦhomepages.iol.ie/~arantvl/aranmain.htm. Good-
value flights to all parts of the world.
CIE Tours International ☎01/703 1888, ⓦwww
.cietours.ie. General flight and tour agent.
Joe Walsh Tours ☎01/241 0888, ⓦwww
.joewalshtours.ie. General budget fares agent.
Lee Travel ☎021/277111, ⓦwww.leetravel.ie.
Flights and holidays worldwide.
McCarthy's Travel ☎021/427 0127, ⓦwww
.mccarthystravel.ie. General flight agent.
Trailfinders ☎01/677 7888, ⓦwww.trailfinders
.ie. See UK listing above.
usit NOW ☎01/602 1600 (Northern Ireland
☎028/9032 7111), ⓦwww.usitnow.ie. Student and
youth specialists for flights and trains.

Flights from the US and Canada

India is on the other side of the planet
from the **US** and **Canada**. If you live on

the East Coast it's somewhat shorter to go via Europe, while from the West Coast it's quicker via the Pacific, but either way it's a long haul, involving one or more intermediate stops. You'll arrive fresher and less jet-lagged if you can manage to fit in a few days' layover somewhere en route.

From the East Coast, you'll stop over somewhere in Europe (most often London), the Gulf, or both. Figure on at least eighteen hours' total travel time. Prices are most competitive out of **New York**, where the cheapest low-season consolidated fares to Mumbai hover around $1250 (rising to $1600 in high season). From Washington or Miami, figure on $1600 in low season, $1850 in high season; from Chicago $1600/$2000; and from Dallas/Fort Worth $1800 /$3000.

From the West Coast, it works out slightly quicker to fly west rather than east – a minimum of 22 hours' total travel time – and if you're booking through a consolidator there may not be much difference in price. From **Los Angeles** or **San Francisco** you're looking at a minimum of $1300 to fly to Mumbai in low season, and up to $1700 in high season.

The only direct flight **from Canada** to India is from Vancouver to Delhi on Air Canada (via London, and taking just under 20hr. All other routings involve a plane change and more layover time. A discount agent will probably break the journey into two, using one of dozens of carriers for the transatlantic (or trans-Pacific) leg. Typical discounted low and high season fares to Mumbai from Montreal, Toronto and Vancouver are CDN$2000/$2600.

Airlines in North America

Aeroflot US ☎1-888/340-6400, Canada ☎416/642-1653; @www.aeroflot.com.
Air Canada ☎1-888/247-2262, @www .aircanada.ca.
Air France US ☎1-800/237-2747, @www .airfrance.com; Canada ☎1-800/667-2747, @www.airfrance.ca.
Air India ☎1-800/223-7776 or 212/751-6200, @www.airindia.com.
Alitalia US ☎1-800/223-5730, Canada ☎1-800/361-8336; @www.alitalia.com.
All Nippon Airways ☎1-800/235-9262, @www .fly-ana.com.
Asiana Airlines ☎1-800/227-4262, @www .flyasiana.com.

Biman Bangladesh Airlines ☎1-888-702-4626 or 212/808-4477, @www.bimanair.com.
British Airways ☎1-800/247-9297, @www .ba.com.
Cathay Pacific ☎1-800/233-2742, @www .cathay-usa.com.
Czech Airlines US ☎1-877/359-6629 or 212/765-6022, Canada ☎416/363-3174; @www .czechairlines.com.
Delta Air Lines Domestic ☎1-800/221-1212, international ☎1-800/241-4141, @www.delta.com.
EgyptAir US ☎1-800/334-6787, Canada ☎416/960-0009; @www.egyptair.com.eg.
Emirates Air ☎1-800/777-3999, @www .emirates.com.
Gulf Air ☎1-888/359 4853, @www.gulfairco .com.
Jet ☎1-925/866 1205, @www.jetairways.com.
KLM Royal Dutch Airlines/Northwest Domestic ☎1-800/225-2525, international ☎1-800/447-4747, @www.nwa.com, @www.klm.com.
Kuwait Airways ☎212/659-4200, @www .kuwait-airways.com.
Lufthansa US ☎1-800/645-3880, Canada ☎1-800/563-5954; @www.lufthansa-usa.com.
Malaysia Airlines ☎1-800/552-9264, @www .mas.com.my.
Northwest/KLM Royal Dutch Airlines Domestic ☎1-800/225-2525, international ☎1-800/447-4747, @www.nwa.com, @www.klm.com.
Pakistan International Airlines ☎1-800/221-2552 or 212/760-8484, @www.piac.com.pk.
Polynesian Airlines ☎1-800/644-7659, @www .polynesianairlines.com.
Qantas Airways ☎1-800/227-4500, @www .qantas.com.
Royal Jordanian Airlines ☎1-800/223-0470 or 212/949-0050, @www.rja.com.jo.
Royal Nepal Airlines ☎1-800/266-3725, @www.royalnepal.com.
Sahara US ☎212/685 5456, Canada ☎416/966 4825; @www.airsahara.net.
Singapore Airlines ☎1-800/742-3333, @www .singaporeair.com.
SriLankan Airlines ☎1-877/915-2652, @www .srilankan.lk.
Swiss ☎1-877/359-7947, @www.swiss.com.
Thai Airways International US ☎1-800/426-5204, Canada ☎1-800/668-8103; @www.thaiair .com.
TWA Domestic ☎1-800/221-2000, international ☎1-800/892-4141, @www.twa.com.
United Airlines Domestic ☎1-800/241-6522, international ☎1-800/538-2929, @www.ual.com.
Virgin Atlantic Airways ☎1-800/862-8621, @www.virgin.com/atlantic.

Travel agents, consolidators and travel clubs in the US and Canada

Air Brokers International ☎ 1-800/883-3273, 🖳 www.airbrokers.com. Consolidator and specialist in round-the-world and Circle Pacific tickets.

Airtech ☎ 212/219-7000, 🖳 www.airtech.com. Standby seat broker; also deals in consolidator fares and courier flights.

Airtreks.com ☎ 1-877/247-8735, 🖳 www .airtreks.com. Round-the-world and Circle Pacific tickets. The website features an interactive database that lets you build and price your own round-the-world itinerary.

Educational Travel Center ☎ 1-800/747-5551 or 608/256-5551, 🖳 www.edtrav.com. Student/youth discount agent.

STA Travel US ☎ 1-800/781-4040, Canada 1-888/427-5639; 🖳 www.statravel.com. Worldwide specialists in independent travel; also student IDs, travel insurance, car rental, rail passes etc.

Student Flights ☎ 1-800/255-8000 or 480/951-1177, 🖳 www.isecard.com. Student/youth fares, student IDs.

TFI Tours ☎ 1-800/745-8000 or 212/736-1140, 🖳 www.lowestairprice.com. Consolidator.

Travel Cuts Canada ☎ 1-866/246-9762, US ☎ 1-800/952-2887; 🖳 www.travelcuts.com. Canadian student-travel organization.

Travelers Advantage ☎ 1-877/259-2691, 🖳 www.travelersadvantage.com. Discount travel club; annual membership fee required (currently $1 for 3 months' trial).

Flights from Australia and New Zealand

There are no non-stop flights to India from either **Australia** or **New Zealand**; you have to make at least one change of plane in a southeast Asian hub city (usually Kuala Lumpur, Singapore or Bangkok). The choice of routes and airlines is bewildering, and most agents will combine two or more carriers to get the best price.

Flying west, the main, and cheapest, South Indian gateway city tends to be Chennai (Madras), with Mumbai (Bombay) not far behind. As a rule of thumb, the best-value tickets from Australia are on departures from the east coast. Flying from Perth to Chennai in low/shoulder season (Feb 1–Nov 21) costs A$1100–1700 depending on the airline, and a couple of hundred dollars more in peak season.

Flying **from New Zealand**, the cheapest fares to India from Auckland are around NZ$2000–2250; add on approximately NZ$150 for flights from Wellington and Christchurch.

Round-the-World fares from Australia and New Zealand can take in India. Round-the-World tickets including Delhi or Mumbai with Thai Airways, Air New Zealand, Qantas and Malaysia Airlines start from around A$2200/NZ$2600.

Airlines in Australia and New Zealand

Air France Australia ☎ 02/9244 2100, New Zealand ☎ 09/308 3352; 🖳 www.airfrance.com.au.

Air India Australia ☎ 02/9299 2022, New Zealand ☎ 09/303 1301; 🖳 www.airindia.com.

Air New Zealand Australia ☎ 132476, New Zealand ☎ 0800 247764; 🖳 www.airnewzealand .com.

British Airways Australia ☎ 1300/767177, New Zealand ☎ 09/966 9777; 🖳 www.ba.com.

Cathay Pacific Australia ☎ 131747, New Zealand ☎ 09/379 0861; 🖳 www.cathaypacific.com.

KLM Royal Dutch Australia ☎ 1300/303747, New Zealand ☎ 09/302 1792; 🖳 www.klm.com.

Lufthansa Australia ☎ 1300/655727, New Zealand ☎ 09/303 1529 or 0800/945220; 🖳 www .lufthansa.com.

Malaysia Airlines Australia ☎ 132627, New Zealand ☎ 0800/777747 or 649/379 3743; 🖳 www.malaysiaairlines.com.

Qantas Australia ☎ 131313, New Zealand ☎ 09/357 8900 or 0800/808767; 🖳 www.qantas .com.

Singapore Airlines Australia ☎ 131011 or ☎ 02/9350 0262, New Zealand ☎ 09/379 3209; 🖳 www.singaporeair.com.

SriLankan Airlines Australia ☎ 02/9244 2234, New Zealand ☎ 09/308 3353; 🖳 www.srilankan.lk.

Swiss Australia ☎ 1300/724666, New Zealand ☎ 09/977 2238; 🖳 www.swiss.com.

Thai Airways Australia ☎ 1300/651960, New Zealand ☎ 09/377 3886; 🖳 www.thaiair.com.

Travel agents in Australia and New Zealand

Flight Centre Australia ☎ 133133 or 02/9235 3522, 🖳 www.flightcentre.com.au; New Zealand ☎ 0800/243544 or 09/358 4310, 🖳 www .flightcentre.co.nz. Discount flight agents.

Holiday Shoppe New Zealand ☎ 0800/808480, 🖳 www.holidayshoppe.co.nz. General travel agent with deals updated daily.

STA Travel Australia ☎ 1300/733035 or 02/9212 1255, ⊛ www.statravel.com.au; New Zealand ☎ 0508/782872 or 09/309 9273, ⊛ www.statravel .co.nz. Worldwide specialists in independent travel; also student IDs, travel insurance, car rental, rail passes etc.

Trailfinders Australia ☎ 9247 7666 or 1300/780212, ⊛ www.trailfinders.com.au. One of the best-informed and most efficient agents for independent travellers; especially strong on round-the-world routes.

Visas and red tape

Gone are the days when Commonwealth nationals could stroll visa-less into India and stay for as long as they pleased: today, everyone except citizens of Nepal and Bhutan needs a visa.

If you're going to India on business or to study, you'll need to apply for a special student or business visa; otherwise, a **standard tourist visa** will suffice. These are **valid for six months** from the date of issue (not of departure from your home country or entry into India), and cost £30/US$60/CDN$62/A$55/NZ$90. As you're asked to specify whether you need a single-entry or a **multiple-entry visa**, and the same rates apply to both, it makes sense to ask for the latter, just in case you decide to make a side trip to Nepal or another neighbouring country.

Much the best place to get a visa is in your country of residence, from the embassies and high commissions listed on pp.34–35; you should be able to download forms from the embassy and consulate websites. In Britain and North America you'll need a passport valid for at least six months, two passport photographs and an application form, obtainable in advance by post or on the day; address applications to the **Postal Visa Section** of the consulate in question. In Australia and New Zealand, one passport-sized photo and your flight/travel itinerary are

required, together with the visa application form. As a rule, visas are issued in a matter of hours, although embassies in India's neighbouring countries often drag their feet, demand letters of recommendation from your embassy (expensive if you are, for example, British), or make you wait and pay for them to send your application to Delhi. In the US, postal applications take a month as opposed to a same-day service if you do it in person – check with your nearest embassy, high commission or consulate. Make sure that your visa is signed by someone at the embassy, as you may be refused entry into the country otherwise.

In many countries it's also possible to pay a **visa agency** (or "visa expediter") to process the visa on your behalf, which in the UK costs £30–35 (plus the price of the visa). This is an option worth considering if you're not able to get to your nearest India High Commission, embassy or consulate yourself. Prices vary a little from company to company, as do turna-round times. Three working days is about standard, but you can get a visa in as little as 24 hours if you're prepared to pay premium

---

Indian public holidays: a warning

Wherever you intend to get your visa from, bear in mind that your nearest high commission, embassy or consulate will observe **Indian public holidays** (as well as most of the local ones), and that it might therefore be closed. Always check opening hours in advance by phone, or via the website, beforehand.

rates (typically £60 on top of the cost of your visa). For a full rundown of services, check the company websites below, from where you can usually download visa application forms and confirm requirements. In **Britain**, try The Visa Service (☎08708/900185, ⓦwww.visaservice.co.uk); Gold Arrow (☎0870/165 7412, ⓦwww.goldarrow.info); or Visa Express (☎020/7251 4822, ⓦwww.visaexpress.com). In **North America**, where you can expect to pay anywhere between US$140–260 to obtain a visa within two weeks, reliable expediters include Travel Document Systems (☎202/638 3800, ⓦwww.traveldocs.com) and Visa Connection (ⓦwww.visaconnection.com) – the latter has offices in Vancouver, Calgary, Ottawa and Toronto, as well as in the US.

Visa extensions

It is no longer possible to **extend a visa** in India, though exceptions may be made in special circumstances. Most people whose standard six-month tourist visas are about to expire head for Bangkok or neighbouring capitals such as Colombo in Sri Lanka or Kathmandu in Nepal, and apply for a new one. However, in recent years this has been something of a hit-and-miss business, with some tourists having their requests turned down for no apparent reason. The Indian High Commission in Kathmandu is particularly notorious for this; you can telephone them or visit their website to check their current policy, but the online advice is confused and you shouldn't, in any case, expect the story to be the same when you arrive. Try to find out from other travellers what the visa situation is, and always allow enough time on your current permit to re-enter India and catch a flight out of the country in case your request is refused.

If you do stay more than 180 days you are supposed to get a **tax clearance certificate** before you leave the country, available at the foreigners' section of the income-tax department in every major city. They are free, but you should take bank receipts to show you have changed your money legally. In practice, tax clearance certificates are rarely demanded, but you never know.

For details of other kinds of visas – five-year visas can be obtained by foreigners of Indian origin, business travellers and even students of yoga – contact your nearest Indian embassy.

In addition to a visa, **special permits** may be required for travel to the Andaman Islands and Lakshadweep. Arriving by plane, you'll be issued them at the airport, but tourists travelling to the Andamans by ship may have to obtain permits before leaving the port of origin (Chennai, Calcutta or Vishakapatnam; see p.466 and p.599).

Indian embassies

Afghanistan Embassy: Malalai Wat, Shahre-Nau, Kabul, Afghanistan ☎873-76/309 5560, eindembkabul@nic.in.
Australia High Commission: 3–5 Moonah Place, Yarralumla, Canberra, ACT 2600 ☎02/6273 3999, ⓔhcicouns@bigpond.com. Consulates: Level 27, 25 Bligh St, Sydney, NSW 2000 ☎02/9223 9500, ⓦwww.indianconsulatesydney.org; 15 Munro St, Coburg, Melbourne, Vic 3058 ☎03/9384 0141. Honorary Consulates: Level 1, Terrace Hotel, 195 Adelaide Terrace, East Perth, WA 6004, Australia (mailing address: PO Box 6118, East Perth, WA 6892, Australia) ☎08/9221 1485, ⓔindia@vianet.net.au.
Bangladesh High Commission: House 120, Rd 2, Dhanmondi Residential Area, Dhaka ☎02/865373, ⓦwww.hcidhaka.org. Consulate: 1253–1256 Nizam Rd, Mehdi Bagh, Chittagong ☎031/654201.
Bhutan Embassy of India, India House Estate, Thimphu ☎09752/22162, ⓔloplg@druknet.net.bt.
Burma (Myanmar) Embassy: Oriental Assurance Building, 545–547 Merchant St (PO Box 751), Yangon (Rangoon) ☎01/82550.
Canada High Commission: 10 Springfield Rd, Ottawa, ON K1M 1C9 ☎613/744 3751, ⓦwww.hciottawa.ca. Consulates: 2 Bloor St W, #500, Toronto, ON M4W 3E2 ☎416/960 0751, ⓦcgitoronto.ca; 325 Howe St, 2nd floor, Vancouver, BC V6C 1Z7 ☎604/662 8811, ⓦwww.cgivancouver.com.
China Embassy: Ri Tan Dong Lo, Beijing ☎01/532 1908, ⓦwww.indianembassy.org.cn. Consulate: 1008, Shanghai International Trade Centre, 2200 Yan An (West) Rd, Shanghai ☎021/275 8885, ⓦwww.indianembassy.org.cn.
Japan Embassy: 2–11, Kudan Minami 2-Chome, Chiyoda-ku, Tokyo 102 ☎03/3262 2391, ⓔindembjp@gol.com.
Malaysia High Commission: 2 Jalan Taman Dlita, off Jalan Duta (PO Box 10059), 50704 Kuala Lumpur ☎03/253 3504, ⓔhoc@po.jaring.my.
Nepal Embassy: Lainchaur, off Lazimpath (PO Box

92), Kathmandu ℡ 01/441 0900, ⓦ www
.south-asia.com/Embassy-India.

The Netherlands Embassy: Buitenrustweg-2,
2517 KD, The Hague ℡ 070/346 9771, ⓦ www
.indianembassy.nl.

New Zealand High Commission: 180 Molesworth
St (PO Box 4005), Wellington ℡ 04/473 6390,
ⓦ www.hicomind.org.nz.

Pakistan High Commission: G-5, Diplomatic
enclave, Islamabad ℡ 051/220 69501. Consulate:
India House, 3 Fatima Jinnah Rd (PO Box 8542),
Karachi ℡ 021/522275.

Singapore Embassy: India House, 31 Grange
Rd (PO Box 9123), Singapore 0923 ℡ 737 6777,
ⓦ www.embassyofindia.com.

Sri Lanka High Commission: 36–38 Galle Rd,
Colombo 3 ℡ 011 242 1605, ⓦ www.indiahcsl.org.
Consulate: 31 Rajapihilla Mawatha (PO Box 47),
Kandy ℡ 081 224 563.

Thailand Embassy: 46 Soi 23 (Prasarn Mitr),
Sukhumvit Rd, Bangkok 10110 ℡ 02/258 0300,
ⓔ indiaemb@mozart.inet.co.th. Consulate:
113 Bumruangrat Rd, Chiang Mai 50000
℡ 053/243066, ⓕ 247879.

UK High Commission: India House, Aldwych, London
WC2B 4NA ℡ 020/7836 8484, ⓦ www.hcilondon
.net. Consulates: 20 Augusta St, Jewellery Quarter,
Hockley, Birmingham B18 6GL ℡ 0121/ 212 2782,
ⓦ www.cgibirmingham.org; 17 Rutland Square,
Edinburgh EH1 2BB ℡ 0131/229 2144.

USA Embassy of India (Consular Services): 2107
Massachusetts Ave NW, Washington DC 20008
℡ 202/939-7000. Consulates: 3 East 64th St, New
York, NY 10021 ℡ 212/774-0600, ⓦ www.indiacgny
.org; 540 Arguello Blvd, San Francisco, CA 94118
℡ 415/668-0683, ⓦ www.indianconsulate-sf.org;
455 North Cityfront Plaza Drive, Suite 850, Chicago
Il 60611 ℡ 312/595 0405 (ext 22 for visas),
ⓦ http://chicago.indianconsulate.com; 201 St Charles
Ave, New Orleans, LA 70170 ℡ 504/582-8106; 2051
Young St, Honolulu, HI 96826 ℡ 808/947-2618.

Vietnam Embassy of India, 58–60 Tran,
Hung Dao, Hanoi ℡ 04/824 4989, ⓔ india
@netnam.org. Consulate General of India, 49
Tran Quoc Thao St, 3rd District, Ho Chi Minh City
℡ 08/231539.

Foreign consulates in South India

Australia 16th Floor, Maker Tower, E Block, Cuffe
Parade, Colaba, Mumbai ℡ 022/2218 1071 or
2204 2044.

Canada 4th Floor, Maker Chambers VI, J Bajaj
Marg, Nariman Point, Mumbai ℡ 022/2287 6027.

France 2nd Floor, Datta Prasad Bldg, 10 NG Cross
Rd, Cumballa Hill, Mumbai ℡ 022/2495 0948; 40
College Rd, Chennai, ℡ 044/2826 6651.

Germany 10th Floor, Hoechst House, Nariman
Point, Mumbai ℡ 022/2283 2422.

Ireland Royal Bombay Yacht Club Chambers, Apollo
Bunder, Mumbai ℡ 022/2202 4607.

Netherlands Forbes Bldg, Chiranjit Rai Marg, Fort,
Mumbai ℡ 022/2201 6750; Catholic Centre, Ist
Floor, 64 Armenian St, Chennai, ℡ 044/2538 4894,
2538 5829.

New Zealand 132 Cathedral Rd, Chennai 600086
℡ 044/2811 2472; 1st Floor, 5 Altamount Rd,
Mumbai 400026, ℡ 022/2384 0022.

South Africa Gandhi Mansion, 20 Altamount Rd
℡ 022/2389 3725.

UK Maker Chambers IV, 2nd Floor, 222 Jamnalal
Bajaj Rd, Nariman Point, Mumbai 400021
℡ 022/2283 0517; 20 Anderson Rd, Chennai
(Madras) 600006, Tamil Nadu ℡ 044/5219 2151;
13/14 Dempo Towers, Patto Plaza, Panjim, Goa
℡ 0832/243 8734, ⓔ bcagoa@sancharnet.in,
ⓦ www.ukinindia.com.

USA Lincoln House, 78 Bhulabhai Desai Rd,
Cumballa Hill, Mumbai 022/2363 3611 or 2811
3611; Gemini Circle, 220 Anna Salai, Chennai
600006, Tamil Nadu ℡ 044/2811 2000, ⓦ chennai
.usconsulate.gov.

Information, websites and maps

The Indian government maintains a number of tourist offices abroad, whose staff are usually helpful and knowledgeable. Other sources of information include the websites of Indian embassies and tourist offices, travel agents (though their advice may not always be totally unbiased), and the Indian Railways representatives listed on p.56.

Inside India, both national and local governments run **tourist information offices**, providing general travel advice and handing out an array of printed material, from city maps to glossy leaflets on specific destinations. The Indian government's tourist department (Ⓦwww.india-tourism.com), whose main office is opposite Churchgate railway station in Mumbai, has branches in most regional capitals. These, however, operate independently of the **state government information counters** and their commercial bureaux run by the state tourism development corporations, usually referred to by their initials (eg KSTDC in Karnataka and TTDC in Tamil Nadu), which offer a wide range of travel facilities, including guided tours, car rental and their own hotels (identified with the relevant acronyms throughout this book).

Just to confuse things further, the Indian government's tourist office has a go-ahead corporate wing too. The **Indian Tourism Development Corporation (ITDC)** is responsible for the Ashok chain of hotels and operates tour and travel services, frequently competing with its state counterparts.

Indian government tourist offices overseas

Australia Level 2, Piccadilly, 210 Pitt St, Sydney NSW ☏02/9264 4855, ✉indtour@ozemail.com.au; Level 1, 17 Castlereagh St, Sydney, NSW 2000 ☏02/9232 1600.
Canada 60 Bloor St (West), #1003, Toronto, ON M4W 3B8 ☏416/ 962-3787, ✉indiatourism@bellnet.ca.
Netherlands Rokin 9–15, 1022 KK, Amsterdam ☏020/620 8991, Ⓦwww.indiatourismamsterdam.com.
Singapore 20 Karamat Lane, 01–01A United House, Singapore 0922 ☏065/235 3800, ✉singapore@tourismindia.com.

Thailand Singapore Airlines Bldg, 3rd floor, 62/5 Thaniya Rd (Silom), Bangkok ☏02/235 2585 & 235 6670, ☏236 8411.
UK 7 Cork St, London W1X 2LN ☏020/7437 3677, Ⓦwww.incredibleindia.org.
USA 3550 Wilshire Blvd, Suite #204, Los Angeles, CA 90010 ☏213/380-8855, ✉la@tourismindia.com; Suite 1808, 1270 Ave of Americas, New York NY 10020 ☏212/586 4901, eny@itony.com.

Indian State Tourist Office websites

States not listed below (namely the Andaman and Nicobar islands) do not yet have a website.
Andhra Pradesh Ⓦwww.aptourism.com
Goa Ⓦwww.goatourism.org
Karnataka Ⓦkstdc.nic.in
Kerala Ⓦwww.keralatourism.org
Lakshadweep Ⓦwww.lakshadweeptourism.com
Maharashtra Ⓦwww.maharashtratourism.gov.in
Tamil Nadu Ⓦwww.tamilnadutourism.org

South India online

India has one of the highest levels of IT awareness on the planet, and this has helped fuel the growth of home-grown resources on the **Internet**. There are several excellent South India-specific websites and portals covering a vast range of topics. We list relevant websites throughout the Guide; the recommendations below are more general, and are a good place to start exploring.

General

Ⓦ**www.britannicaindia.com** Highly informative general site on India, part of the famous encyclopedia chain.
Ⓦ**www.indiamike.com** Popular travel forum run out of a bedroom in New Jersey by inveterate India-phile Mike Szewczyk. Lively chat rooms, bulletin

boards, photo archives and banks of members' travel articles, as well as a daily news feed.

Ⓦ **www.rediff.com** Another leading India-specific portal with great search facilities and a site plan that stretches from news to travel.

Ⓦ **www.travelintelligence.net/wsd/articles /artbyplce_143.html** A huge selection of top-quality, inspiring travelogues by India experts including William Dalrymple, Sue Carpenter and Justine Hardy.

News and media

Ⓦ **www.guardian.co.uk/india** High-quality news features are the meat of this "Special Report" section of the *Guardian's* award-winning website, which also has links to its archived India articles and an excellent dossier on Kashmir. Access is free.

Ⓦ **http://in.news.yahoo.com** India-related news from Yahoo.

Ⓦ **www.samachar.com** One of the best news gateway sites, featuring headlines and links to leading Indian newspapers.

Ⓦ **www.tehelka.com** Alternative news magazine (in)famous for exposing corruption scandals in government.

Ⓦ **timesofindia.indiatimes.com**; Ⓦ **www .hinduonline.com**; Ⓦ **www.hindustantimes .com**; Ⓦ **www.deccanherald.com** The websites of some of India's leading daily papers, with detailed national coverage. The *Deccan Herald* site has a fast-loading text-only format.

Travel advice

Ⓦ **www.fco.gov.uk/travel** The British Foreign Office website is useful for checking potential or actual dangerous areas.

Ⓦ **travel.state.gov** The US State Department's travel advice regarding potential hot spots.

Culture

Ⓦ **www.artindia.net** Portal for India's performing arts.

Ⓦ **www.themusicmagazine.com** A music e-zine with an incredible range, from Bob Dylan to *ghazal*.

Ⓦ **www.carnaticmusic.com** Very well-organized site which explores Carnatic (South Indian) classical music.

Ⓦ **www.planetbollywood.com** Bollywood portal where you can gorge yourself on gloss from the Hindi film world.

Ⓦ **www.sruti.com** The online version of a very informative and in-depth music and dance magazine devoted to India's performing arts.

Ⓦ **www.stardustindia.com** First stop for Bollywood gossip.

Ⓦ **www.geocities.com/Athens/Acropolis /1863/kolam.html** Tutorial that teaches you how to draw *kollam* (or *rangoli*, as they're known in the north) – the rice-flour patterns with which women decorate floors and thresholds. For further inspiration, go to Ⓦ www.angelfire.com/cantina/visithra ("Vortex of Kollams").

Religion

Ⓦ **www.sacredsites.com** The India section of this website features scholarly background on India's most holy places, with quality images.

Ⓦ **www.hinduweb.org** Amazingly comprehensive site featuring diverse topics such as Hindu art, history, religion and philosophy, with links to other sites created by users.

Ⓦ **www.hindulinks.org** Portal with nearly 30,000 links to a multitude of India-related matters.

Ⓦ **www.jainnet.com** Site dedicated to Jainism, featuring a concise introduction, devotional songs and e-cards.

Sport

Ⓦ **sify.com/sports** India's best sports site, especially strong on cricket – as you'd expect.

South India

Ⓦ **www.bangalorenet.com**
Ⓦ **www.chennaidirectory.com**
Ⓦ **www.hyderabad.co.uk**
Ⓦ **www.mangalore.com**
Ⓦ **www.mumbai-central.com**
Ⓦ **www.pondicherry.com**
Besides our own extensive site on India (Ⓦ www .roughguides.com), these are some useful websites on South Indian cities, some with search engines, listings and news. Ⓦ www.explocity.com has comprehensive city listings for Bangalore, Hyderabad and Mumbai among other places.

Ⓦ **www.aponline.gov.in**
Ⓦ **www.goacom.com**
Ⓦ **www.karnataka.com**
Ⓦ **www.kerala.com**
Ⓦ **www.cs.utk.edu/~siddhart/tamilnadu**
Ⓦ **www.anislands.com**
Useful state-wide websites with search engines and some good links.

Maps

Even allowing for a bit of bias here, we think you'll find the Rough Guide's South India **map** to be the most user friendly on the market. Drawn at a scale of 1:1,200,000, it features clear modern mapping and bang up-to-date research, and is printed on plastic paper so it won't tear (and should even survive a dip in the Arabian Sea). It's also been tested and proofed on the road by the authors of this guide.

Another excellent map of South India is the Nelles' India 4 (South) 1:1,500,000, which shows colour contours, road distances, inset city plans and even the tiniest places. Ttk, a Chennai-based company, publishes basic state maps, which are widely available in India and in some specialized travel and map shops in the UK such as Stanfords (see below). Regional Automobile Associations based in Mumbai and Chennai produce books of road maps which are useful for those planning overland routes across India. For basic state-by-state and city road maps try @http://mapsofindia.com/maps. The Indian Railways map at the back of the publication *Trains at a Glance* is useful for planning railway journeys.

If you need larger-scale city maps than the ones we provide in this book – which are keyed to show recommended hotels and restaurants – try Eicher's excellent City Map series, featuring Mumbai, Chennai and Bangalore.

Book and map outlets

In the UK and Ireland

Stanfords @www.stanfords.co.uk; 12–14 Long Acre, London WC2E 9LP ⊕020/7836 1321; 29 Corn Street, Bristol BS1 1HT ⊕0117/929 9966; 39 Spring Gardens, Manchester M2 2BG ⊕0161/831 0250.

Blackwell's Map and Travel Shop @maps .blackwell.co.uk/index.html. Branches all over the UK; check the website for details.

Easons Bookshop 40 Lower O'Connell St, Dublin 1 ⊕01/858 3800, @www.eason.ie, plus other branches around Ireland; call or check the website for details.

John Smith & Son Glasgow Caledonian University Bookshop, 70 Cowcaddens Rd, Glasgow G4 0BA ⊕0141/332 8173, @www.johnsmith.co.uk. For details of other branches in Scotland and England, call or check the website.

The Map Shop 30a Belvoir St, Leicester LE1 6Q(H) ⊕0116/247 1400, @www.mapshopleicester.co.uk.

National Map Centre 22–24 Caxton St, London SW1H 0QU ⊕020/7222 2466, @www.mapstore .co.uk.

Ordnance Survey Ireland Phoenix Park, Dublin 8 ⊕01/8025 300, @www.irlgov.ie/osi.

Ordnance Survey of Northern Ireland Colby House, Stranmillis Ct, Belfast BT9 5BJ ⊕028/9025 5755, @www.osni.gov.uk.

The Travel Bookshop 13–15 Blenheim Crescent, London W11 2EE ⊕020/7229 5260, @www .thetravelbookshop.co.uk.

In the US and Canada

Book Passage 51 Tamal Vista Blvd, Corte Madera, CA 94925 ⊕1-800/999-7909, @www .bookpassage.com.

Complete Traveller Bookstore 199 Madison Ave, New York, NY ⊕212/685-9007, @www .completetravellerbooks.com.

Distant Lands 56 S Raymond Ave, Pasadena, CA 91105 ⊕1-800/310-3220, @www.distantlands .com.

Elliot Bay Book Company 101 S Main St, Seattle, WA 98104 ⊕1-800/962-5311, @www .elliotbaybook.com.

Globe Corner Bookstore 28 Church St, Cambridge, MA 02138 ⊕1-800/358-6013, @www.globecorner.com.

Map Link 30 S La Patera Lane, Unit 5, Santa Barbara, CA 93117 ⊕805/692-6777 or 1-800/962-1394, @www.maplink.com.

Rand McNally @www.randmcnally.com; 595 Market St, San Francisco, CA 94105-2803 ⊕415-777-3131; Galleria I, Houston, TX 77056, ⊕713-960-9846.

The Travel Bug Bookstore 3065 W Broadway, Vancouver V6K 2G2 ⊕604/737-1122, @www .travelbugbooks.ca.

World of Maps 1235 Wellington St, Ottawa, ON K1Y 3A3 ⊕1-800/214-8524, @www.worldofmaps.com.

In Australia and New Zealand

The Map Shop 6–10 Peel St, Adelaide, SA 5000 ⊕08/8231 2033, @www.mapshop.net.au.

Mapland 372 Little Bourke St, Melbourne, Victoria 3000, ⊕03/9670 4383, @www.mapland.com.au.

MapWorld 173 Gloucester St, Christchurch ⊕03/374 5399 or 0800/627967, @www .mapworld.co.nz.

Travel insurance

In the light of the potential health risks involved in a trip to South India – see p.40 – travel insurance is too important to ignore. In addition to covering medical expenses and emergency flights, travel insurance also insures your money and belongings against loss or theft.

Before paying for a new policy, however, it's worth checking to see whether you are already covered: some all-risks home insurance policies may cover your possessions when overseas, and many private medical schemes include cover when abroad. In Canada, provincial health plans usually provide partial **medical cover** for mishaps overseas, while holders of official student/teacher/youth cards in Canada and the US are entitled to – albeit meagre – accident coverage and hospital in-patient benefits. Students will often find that their student health coverage extends during the vacations and for one term beyond the date of last enrolment.

After exhausting the possibilities above, you might want to contact a specialist **travel insurance company**, or consider the travel insurance deal offered by Rough Guides (see box below). A typical travel insurance policy usually provides cover for the loss of baggage, tickets and – up to a certain limit – cash or cheques, as well as cancellation or curtailment of your journey. Most of them exclude so-called dangerous sports unless an extra premium is paid: in India this can mean scuba-diving, whitewater rafting, windsurfing and trekking with ropes, though probably not jeep safaris. Many policies can be chopped and changed to exclude coverage you don't need – for example, sickness and accident benefits can often be excluded or included at will. If you do take medical coverage, ascertain whether benefits will be paid as treatment proceeds or only after return home, and whether there is a 24-hour medical emergency number. When securing baggage cover, make sure that the per-article limit – typically under £500 – will cover your most valuable possession. If you need to make a claim, you should keep receipts for medicines and medical treatment, and in the event you have anything stolen, you must obtain an official statement from the police.

Rough Guides travel insurance

Rough Guides has teamed up with Columbus Direct to offer you **travel insurance** that can be tailored to suit your needs.

Readers can choose from many different travel insurance products, including a low-cost **backpacker** option for long stays; a **short break** option for city getaways; a typical **holiday package** option; and many others. There are also annual **multi-trip** policies for those who travel regularly, with variable levels of cover available. Different sports and activities (trekking, skiing, etc) can be covered if required on most policies.

Rough Guides travel insurance is available to the residents of 36 different countries with different language options to choose from via our website – ⓦwww.roughguidesinsurance.com – where you can also purchase the insurance.

Alternatively, UK residents should call ☏0800/083 9507; US citizens should call ☏1-800/749-4922; Australians should call ☏1 300/669999. All other nationalities should call ☏+44 870/890 2843.

Health

A lot of visitors get ill in South India just as in the rest of the country, and some of them get very ill. However, if you are careful, you should be able to get through the region with nothing worse than a mild dose of "Madras belly". The important thing is to keep your resistance high and to be very aware of health risks such as poor hygiene, untreated water, mosquito bites and undressed open cuts.

What you **eat** and **drink** is crucial: a poor diet lowers your resistance. Ensure you eat a balance of protein, energy, vitamins and minerals. Meat and fish are obvious sources of protein for non-vegetarians in the West, but not necessarily in India, though in southern India the fish bought along the coast should be fresh and safe. Eggs, pulses (lentils, peas and beans), rice and curd are all protein sources, as are nuts. Overcooked vegetables lose a lot of their vitamin content; eating plenty of peeled fresh fruit – provided this is fruit you have peeled yourself – helps keep up your vitamin and mineral intake. With all that sweating, too, make sure you get enough salt – put a bit extra on your food – and drink enough water. This is especially important in the consistently hot and humid south. It's also worth taking daily multivitamin and mineral tablets with you. Above all, make sure you eat enough – an unfamiliar diet may reduce the amount you eat – and **get enough sleep** and rest: it's easy to get run down if you're on the move a lot, especially in a hot climate.

It's worth knowing, if you are ill and can't get to a doctor, that almost any medicine can be bought over the counter without a prescription.

Medical resources for travellers

For up-to-the-minute information, make an appointment at a **travel clinic**. These clinics also sell travel accessories, including mosquito nets and first-aid kits. Information about specific diseases and conditions, drugs and herbal remedies is provided by the websites below; you could also consult the *Rough Guide to Travel Health* by Dr Nick Jones.

Health-related websites

ⓦ **www.cdc.gov/travel** US Department of Health and Human Services travel health and disease control department, listing precautions, diseases and preventive measures by region.

ⓦ **health.yahoo.com** Information on specific diseases and conditions, drugs and herbal remedies, as well as advice from health experts.

ⓦ **www.fitfortravel.scot.nhs.uk** UK NHS website carrying information about travel-related diseases and how to avoid them.

ⓦ **www.istm.org** The website of the International Society for Travel Medicine, with a full list of clinics worldwide specializing in travel health.

ⓦ **www.tmvc.com.au** Contains a list of all travellers' medical and vaccination centres throughout Australia, New Zealand and Southeast Asia, plus general information on travel health.

ⓦ **www.travelvax.net** Everything you ever wanted to know about diseases and vaccines.

ⓦ **www.tripprep.com** Travel Health Online provides an online-only comprehensive database of necessary vaccinations for most countries, as well as destination and medical service provider information.

Travel clinics

In the UK and Ireland

British Airways Travel Clinics 213 Piccadilly, London W1G 9HQ (Mon–Fri 9.30am–5.30pm, Sat 10am–4pm, no appointment necessary); 101 Cheapside, London EC2 (Mon–Fri 9am–4.30pm, appointment required; ☏ 0845/600 2236); ⓦ www.britishairways.com/travel/healthclinintro. Vaccinations, tailored advice from an online database and a complete range of travel healthcare products. **Glasgow Travel Clinic** 3rd floor, 90 Mitchell St, Glasgow G1 3NQ ☏ 0141/221 4224. Advice and vaccinations; walk-in clinics Wed–Fri 10am–6pm, otherwise appointments.

Hospital for Tropical Diseases Travel Clinic 2nd floor, Mortimer Market Centre, off Capper

St, London WC1E 6AU (Mon–Fri 9am–5pm by appointment only; ☎020/7388 9600, ⊛www .thehtd.org). A consultation costs £15, which is waived if you have your injections here. A recorded health line (☎0906/133 7733; 50p per min; fax-back service ☎0906/991992; £1.50 per min) gives hints on hygiene and illness prevention, as well as listing appropriate immunizations.

Liverpool School of Tropical Medicine Pembroke Place, Liverpool L3 5QA ☎0151/708 9393 or premium-rate helpline ☎09067/010095, ⊛www.liv.ac.uk/lstm. Walk-in clinic (Mon–Fri 9am–noon); appointment required at other times.

MASTA (Medical Advisory Service for Travellers Abroad) Forty regional clinics – call ☎0870/606 2782 for your nearest branch; ⊛www .masta.org. Also operates a prerecorded 24hr Travellers' Health Line (UK ☎0906/550 1402; £1 per min), giving written information tailored to your journey by return of post.

Nomad Pharmacy (⊛www.nomadtravel.co.uk) Surgeries at 52 Grosvenor Gdns, Victoria, London SW1W 0AG ☎020/78323/5823; 43 Bernard St, London WC1N 1LE ☎020/7833 4114; and 3–4 Wellington Terrace, Turnpike Lane, London N8 0PX ☎020/8889 7014; all have walk-in and appointment clinics from Monday to Saturday.

Trailfinders Immunization clinic (no appointments necessary) at 194 Kensington High St, London W8 7RG (Mon–Fri 9am–5pm except Thurs to 6pm, Sat 10am–5.15pm; ☎020/7938 3999).

Travel Medicine Services 16 College St, Belfast BT1 6BT ☎028/9031 5220. Offers pre-trip medical advice and help afterwards in the event of a tropical disease.

Tropical Medical Bureau Grafton Buildings, 34 Grafton St, Dublin 2 ☎01/671 9200, plus locations all around Ireland; call ☎1850/487674 or visit ⊛tmb.exodus.ie for details. Advice and vaccinations.

In the US and Canada

Canadian Society for International Health 1 Nicholas St, Suite 1105, Ottawa, ON K1N 7B7 ☎613/241-5785, ⊛www.csih.org. Distributes a free pamphlet, *Health Information for Canadian Travellers*, containing an extensive list of travel health centres in Canada.

Centers for Disease Control 1600 Clifton Rd NE, Atlanta, GA 30333 ☎1-800/311-3435 or 404/639-3534, ⊛www.cdc.gov. Publishes outbreak warnings, suggested inoculations, precautions and other background information for travellers. There's also an International Travelers Hotline on ☎1-877/FYI-TRIP.

International Association for Medical Assistance to Travellers (IAMAT) 1623 Military Rd, #279, Niagara Falls, NY 14302 ☎716/754-4883, ⊛www.iamat.org; and 1287 St Clair Avenue West, Suite #1, Toronto, ON M6E 1B8 ☎416/652-0137. A non-profit organization supported by donations, it can provide climate charts and leaflets on various diseases and inoculations.

International SOS Assistance 3600 Horizon Blvd, Suite 300, Trevose, PA 19053, USA 19053-6956 ☎1-800/523-8930, ⊛www.intsos.com. Members receive pre-trip medical referral info, as well as overseas emergency services designed to complement travel insurance coverage.

A travellers' first-aid kit

Below are items you might want to take, especially if you're planning to go trekking – all are available in India itself, for a fraction of the price you might pay at home:

- ❏ Antiseptic cream
- ❏ Insect repellent and cream such as Anthisan for soothing bites
- ❏ Plasters/band aids
- ❏ A course of Flagyl antibiotics
- ❏ Water sterilization tablets or water purifier
- ❏ Lint and sealed bandages
- ❏ Knee supports
- ❏ Imodium (Lomotil) for emergency diarrhoea treatment
- ❏ A mild oral anaesthetic such as Bonjela for soothing ulcers or mild toothache
- ❏ Paracetamol/aspirin
- ❏ Multivitamin and mineral tablets
- ❏ Rehydration sachets
- ❏ Hypodermic needles and sterilized skin wipes

MEDJET Assistance ☎ 1-800/963-3528, ⓦ www .medjetassistance.com. Annual membership programme for travellers that, in the event of illness or injury, will fly members home or to the hospital of their choice in a medically equipped and staffed jet.
Travel Medicine ☎ 1-800/TRAVMED, ⓦ www .travmed.com. Sells first-aid kits, mosquito netting, water filters, reference books and other health-related travel products; there's a travel clinic directory, too on the website.

In Australia and New Zealand

Travellers' Medical and Vaccination Centres ⓦ www.tmvc.com.au. Vaccination and general travel health advice, plus disease alerts. Call ☎ 1-300/658-844 for details of travel clinics countrywide.

Precautions

The lack of sanitation in India can be exaggerated; it's not worth getting too worked up about, or you'll never enjoy anything. A few **common-sense precautions**, however, are in order, bearing in mind that things such as bacteria multiply far more quickly in a tropical climate, and your body will have little immunity to Indian germs.

For details on the water, see the box opposite. When it comes to **food**, it's quite likely that tourist restaurants and Western dishes will bring you grief. Be particularly wary of prepared dishes that have to be reheated – they may have been on display in the heat and the flies for some time. Anything that is boiled or fried (and thus sterilized) in your presence is usually all right, though meat can sometimes be dodgy, especially in towns or cities where the electricity supply (and thus refrigerators) frequently fails. Any food that has been left out for any length of time is definitely suspect. Raw unpeeled fruit and vegetables should always be viewed with suspicion, and you should avoid salads unless you know they have been soaked in an iodine or potassium permanganate solution. Wiping down a plate before eating is sensible, and avoid straws as they are usually dusty or secondhand. As a rule of thumb, stick to cafés and restaurants that are doing a brisk trade, and where the food is thus freshly cooked, and you should be fine.

Be vigilant about **personal hygiene**. Wash your hands often, especially before eating. Keep all cuts clean – treat them with iodine

or antiseptic – and cover them up to prevent infection. Be fussier than usual about sharing things like drinks and cigarettes, and never share a razor or toothbrush. It is also inadvisable to go around barefoot – and best to wear flip-flop sandals, including in the shower.

Advice on avoiding **mosquitoes** is offered under the section on malaria on p.44. If you do get bites or itches try not to scratch them: it's hard, but infection and tropical ulcers can result if you do. Tiger balm, calamine lotion, antihistamine cream and even dried soap may relieve the itching.

Finally, especially if you are going on a long trip, have a **dental check-up** before you leave home – you don't want to go down with unexpected tooth trouble in India. If you do, and it feels serious, head for Mumbai, Chennai or Bangalore, and ask a foreign consulate to recommend a dentist.

Vaccinations

No **inoculations** are legally required for entry into India, but meningitis, typhoid and hepatitis A jabs are recommended, and it's worth ensuring that you are up to date with tetanus, polio and other boosters. All vaccinations can be obtained in Mumbai, Chennai and other major cities if necessary; just make sure the needle is new or provide your own.

Hepatitis A is not the worst disease you can catch in India, but the frequency with which it strikes travellers makes a strong case for immunization. Transmitted through contaminated food and water, or through saliva, it can lay a victim low for several months with exhaustion, fever and diarrhoea – and may cause liver damage. The Havrix vaccine has been shown to be extremely effective; though expensive, it lasts for up to ten years. The protection given by gammaglobulin, the traditional serum of hepatitis antibodies, wears off quickly and the injection should therefore be given as late as possible before departure: the longer your planned stay, the larger the dose.

Symptoms by which you can recognize hepatitis include a yellowing of the whites of the eyes, nausea, general flu-like malaise, orange urine (though dehydration could also cause that) and light-coloured stools. If you think you have it, avoid alcohol, try

What about the water?

One of the chief concerns of many prospective visitors to India is whether the water is safe to drink. To put it simply, it's not, though your unfamiliarity with Indian micro-organisms is generally more of a problem rather than any great virulence in the water itself.

As a rule, it is not a good idea to drink **tap water**, although in big cities it is usually chlorinated. However, you'll find it almost impossible to avoid untreated tap water completely: it is used to make ice, which may appear in drinks without being asked for, to wash utensils and so on.

Bottled water, available in all but the most remote places these days, may seem like the simplest and most cost-effective solution, but it has some major drawbacks. The first is that the water itself might not always be as safe as it seems. Independent tests carried out in 2003 on major Indian brands revealed levels of **pesticide** concentration up to 104 times higher than EU norms. Top sellers Kinley, Bisleri and Aquaplus were named as the worst offenders.

The second downside of bottled water is the **plastic pollution** it causes. Visualize the size of the pile you'd leave behind you after getting through a couple of bottles per day, and imagine that multiplied by millions, which is the amount of non-biodegradable land-fill waste generated each year by tourists alone.

The best solution from the point of view of your health and the environment is to purify your own water. **Chemical sterilization** is the cheapest method. **Iodine** isn't recommended for long trips, but **chlorine** is completely effective, fast and inexpensive, and you can remove the nasty taste it leaves with neutralizing tablets or lemon juice.

Alternatively, invest in some kind of **purifying filter** incorporating chemical sterilization to kill even the smallest viruses. An ever-increasing range of compact, lightweight products are available these days through outdoor shops and large pharmacies, but anyone who's pregnant or suffers from thyroid problems should check that iodine isn't used as the chemical sterilizer.

---

to avoid passing it on and get lots of rest. More serious is **hepatitis B**, passed on like AIDS through blood or sexual contact. There is a vaccine, but it is only recommended for those planning to work in a medical environment, or in rural areas. **Typhoid**, also spread through contaminated food or water, is endemic in India, but rare outside the monsoon. It produces a persistent high fever with malaise, headaches and abdominal pains, followed by diarrhoea. Vaccination can be by injection (two shots are required, or one for a booster), giving three years' cover, or orally – tablets, which are more expensive but easier on the arm.

Most medical authorities now recommend vaccination against **meningitis** too. Spread by airborne bacteria (through coughs and sneezes for example), it attacks the lining of the brain and can be fatal. Symptoms include fever, a severe headache, stiffness in the neck and a rash on the stomach and back. If you think you may have meningitis, seek immediate medical attention.

You should have a **tetanus** booster every ten years whether you travel or not. Tetanus (or lockjaw) is picked up through contaminated open wounds and causes severe muscular spasms; if you cut yourself on something dirty and are not covered, get a booster as soon as you can.

Assuming that you were vaccinated against **polio** in childhood, only one (oral) booster is needed during your adult life. Immunizations against mumps, measles, TB and rubella are a good idea for anyone who wasn't vaccinated as a child and hasn't had the diseases.

Rabies is a problem in India. The best advice is to give dogs and monkeys a wide berth, and not to play with animals at all, no matter how cute they might look. A bite, a scratch or even a lick from an infected animal could spread the disease; wash any such wound immediately but gently with soap or detergent, and apply alcohol or iodine if possible. Find out what you can about the animal and swap addresses with the owner (if there is one) just in case. If the animal might be infected, or the wound begins to tingle and fester, act immediately to get treatment – rabies is invariably fatal once symptoms appear. There is a vaccine, recommended if you plan to work in rural areas, but it is expensive and only effective for a maximum of three months.

Malaria

Protection against **malaria** is absolutely essential. The disease, caused by a parasite carried in the saliva of female Anopheles mosquitoes, is endemic everywhere in South India and is nowadays regarded as the big killer in the subcontinent. It has a variable incubation period of a few days to several weeks, so you can become ill long after being bitten. Programmes to eradicate the disease by spraying mosquito-infested areas and distributing free preventative tablets have proved disastrous; within a short space of time, the Anopheles mosquitoes develop immunities to the insecticides, while the malaria parasite itself constantly mutates into drug-resistant strains, rendering the old cures ineffective.

It is vital for travellers to take **preventative tablets** according to a strict routine, and to cover the period before and after your trip. The drug most usually used is **chloroquine** (trade names include Nivaquin, Avloclor and Resochin), and you usually take two tablets weekly, but India has chloroquine-resistant strains, and you'll need to supplement it with daily **proguanil** (Paludrine) or weekly **Maloprim**.

Malarone is the newest addition to the armoury against the deadlier *Plasmodium falciparum* strain, and is increasingly prescribed for people travelling to areas of the world, like Goa, where chloriquine- and other drug-resistant forms of malaria are present. Being a relative newcomer, there's less evidence available on its long-term effects, but initial studies have claimed it to be 98 percent effective and to have relatively few side-effects. The main drawback is that it's expensive and is only licensed for use for 28 days (although in practice it's probably safe for longer). Malarone is taken once daily with food or milk, starting two days before entering a malaria risk area and continuing daily until seven days after leaving the area. Children can also take it.

A weekly drug, **mefloquine** (Lariam), was supposed to replace cholriquine and proguanil, but during its first year on the market many travellers complained of serious side-effects, notably acute depression, and few doctors now recommend it.

As the malaria parasite can incubate in your system without showing symptoms for more than a month, it is essential that you continue to take preventative tablets for at least four weeks after you return home: the most common way of catching malaria is when travellers forget to do this. **Side-effects** of anti-malaria drugs may include itching, rashes, hair loss and sight problems. In the case of Larium some people may experience disorientation, depression and sleep disturbance; if you're intending to use Larium you should begin to take it two weeks before you depart to see whether it will agree with your metabolism, though normally you only need to begin taking anti-malaria medication a week before your departure date. Chloroquine and quinine are safe during pregnancy, but Malarone, Maloprim, Fansidar, mefloquine and tetracycline should be avoided.

Symptoms of malaria

The first **signs of malaria** are remarkably similar to a severe flu, and may take months to appear: if you suspect anything, go to a hospital or clinic immediately. The shivering, burning fever and headaches are like severe flu and come in waves, usually beginning in the early evening. Anyone who develops such symptoms should get to a doctor for a blood test as soon as possible. Malaria is not infectious, but some strains are dangerous and can occasionally be fatal when not treated promptly, in particular, the choloquine-resistant **cerebral malaria**. This virulent and lethal strain of the disease, which affects the brain and often proves fatal if left untreated, is treatable, but has to be diagnosed early. Erratic body temperature, lack of energy and aches are the first key signs, and if you get diagnosed at such an early stage, you have a much better chance of being treated without complications and the onset of more unpleasant symptoms.

Preventing mosquito bites

The best way of avoiding malaria, of course, is to **avoid mosquito bites**. Sleep under a **mosquito net** if possible – one which can hang from a single point is best (you can usually find a way to tie a string across your room to hang it from). Burn mosquito coils, which are readily available in South India, but tend to break in transit (there are some question marks over health risks if coils are used in a room with poor ventilation, and they should be avoided if you suffer from asthma). Increasingly common are plug-in **vapour mats**. When out after dusk, smother yourself in mosquito **repellent**: an Indian brand of repellent, Odomos, is widely available, very effective and has a pleasant lemon scent, though most travellers bring their own from home, usually one containing the noxious but effective compound DEET. DEET can cause rashes, and a strength of more than thirty percent is not advised for those with sensitive skin. The new wrist and ankle bands are as effective as spray and a good alternative for sensitive skin. Although they are active from dusk till dawn, female Anopheles mosquitoes prefer to bite in the evening, so be especially careful at that time. Wear long sleeves, skirts and trousers, avoid dark colours, which attract mosquitoes, and put repellent on exposed skin. A more natural alternative for those with sensitive skin is **citronella** or Mosi-guard Natural, made in the UK from a blend of **eucalyptus oils**. In India, the New Age centre, Auroville, produces its own herbal coils, incense and spray, available in all traveller ghettos.

Dengue fever and Japanese encephalitis

Another illness spread by mosquito bites is **dengue fever**, whose symptoms are similar to those of malaria, with the additional symptom of aching bones. There is no vaccine available and the only treatment is complete rest, with drugs to assuage the fever. **Japanese encephalitis** (yet another mosquito-borne viral infection causing fever, muscle pains and headaches) has been on the increase in recent years in wet, rural rice-growing areas. However, there have been no reports of travellers catching the disease, and you shouldn't need the vaccine (which is expensive and has several potentially nasty side-effects) unless you plan to spend much time around paddy fields during and immediately after the monsoons.

Intestinal troubles

Diarrhoea is the most common bane of travellers. When mild and not accompanied by other major symptoms, it may just be your stomach reacting to unfamiliar food. Accompanied by cramps and vomiting, it could well be food poisoning. In either case, it will probably pass of its own accord in 24–48 hours without treatment. In the meantime, it's essential to replace the fluids and salts you're losing, so take lots of water with oral **rehydration salts** (commonly referred to as ORS, or called Electrolyte in India). If you can't get ORS, use half a teaspoon of salt and eight of sugar in a litre of water. If you are too ill to drink, seek medical help immediately. Travel clinics and pharmacies sell double-ended moulded plastic spoons with the exact ratio of sugar to salt.

While you are suffering, it's a good idea to avoid greasy food, heavy spices, caffeine and most fruit and dairy products. Some say bananas and pawpaws are good, as are *kitchri* (a simple dhal and rice preparation) and rice soup and coconut water, while curd or a soup made from Marmite or Vegemite (if you happen to have some with you) are forms of protein that can be easily absorbed by your body when you have the runs. Drugs like Lomotil or Immodium simply plug you up – undermining the body's efforts to rid itself of infection – though they can be useful if you have to travel. If symptoms persist for more than a few days, a course of antibiotics may be necessary; this should be seen as a last resort, and only used following medical advice.

Sordid though it may seem, it's a good idea to look at what comes out when you go to the toilet (and it makes an endless topic of polite meal-time conversation with your fellow travellers). If your diarrhoea contains blood or mucus and if you are suffering other symptoms including rotten-egg belches and farts, the cause may be dysentery or giardia. With a fever, it could well be caused by **bacillic** dysentery, and may clear up without treatment. If you're sure you need it, a course of antibiotics such as tetracycline should sort you out, but they also destroy "gut flora" in your intestines (which help protect you – curd can replenish them to some extent). If you start a course, be sure to finish it, even after the symptoms have gone. Similar symptoms, without fever, indicate **amoebic dysentery**, which is much more serious, and can damage your gut if untreated. The usual cure is a course of Metronidazole (Flagyl) or Fasigyn, both antibiotics which may themselves make you feel ill, and must not be taken with alcohol; avoid caffeine, too. Symptoms of **giardia** are similar – including frothy stools, nausea and constant fatigue – for which the treatment again is Metronidazole. If you suspect that you have any of these, seek medical help, and only start on the Metronidazole (750mg three times daily for a week for adults) if there is blood in your diarrhoea and it is impossible to see a doctor.

Finally, bear in mind contraceptive that oral drugs, such as malaria pills and the contraceptive pill, are likely to be largely ineffective if taken while suffering from diarrhoea.

Bites and creepy-crawlies

Worms may enter your body through skin (especially the soles of your feet) or food. An itchy anus is a common symptom, and you may even see them in your stools. They are easy to treat: if you suspect you have them, get some worming tablets such as Mebendazole (Vermox) from any pharmacy.

Biting insects and similar animals other than mosquitoes may also aggravate you. The obvious ones are **bed bugs** – look for signs of squashed ones around cheap hotel beds. An infested mattress can be left in the hot sun all day to get rid of them, but they often live in the frame or even in walls or floors. Other notorious culprits, particularly bothersome in parts of the Andaman Islands, are **sandflies**, whose bites can become unbearably itchy. Head and body **lice** can also be a nuisance, but medicated soap and shampoo (preferably brought with you from home) usually see them off. Avoid

scratching bites, which can lead to infection, sometimes in dangerous forms such as **septicaemia** or **tropical ulcers**. Bites from ticks and lice can spread **typhus**, characterized by fever, muscle aches, headaches and, later, red eyes and a measles-like rash. If you think you have it, seek treatment (Tetracycline is usually prescribed – for adults, a single 1g dose followed by 300mg four times daily for five days).

Snakes are unlikely to bite unless accidentally disturbed, and most are harmless in any case. To see one at all, you will need to search stealthily – if you walk heavily, they usually oblige by disappearing. If you do get bitten, remember what the snake looked like (kill it if you can), try not to move the affected part and seek medical help: antivenoms are available in most hospitals. A few **spiders** have poisonous bites too. **Leeches** may attach themselves to you in jungle areas. Remove them with salt or a lit cigarette; never just pull them off.

Heat trouble

The sun and the heat can cause a few unexpected problems, especially in the tropical south. Many people get a bout of **prickly heat** rash before they've acclimatized – an infection of the sweat ducts caused by excessive perspiration that doesn't dry off. A cool shower, zinc oxide powder (sold in India) or talcum powder and loose cotton clothes should help. **Dehydration** is another possible problem, so make sure you're drinking enough liquid, and drink rehydration salts frequently, especially when hot and/or tired. The main danger sign is irregular urination (only once a day for instance). Dark urine probably means you should drink more, although it could also indicate hepatitis (see p.42).

The **sun** can burn, or even cause sunstroke, and a high-factor sunblock is vital on exposed skin, especially when you first arrive, and on areas newly exposed by haircuts or changes of clothes. A light hat is also a very good idea, especially if you're doing a lot of walking around.

Finally, be aware that overheating can cause **heatstroke**, which is potentially fatal. Signs are: a very high body temperature without a feeling of fever, accompanied by headaches and disorientation. Lowering body temperature (a tepid shower for example) and resting in an air-conditioned room is the first step in treatment.

HIV and AIDS

The rapidly increasing presence of **AIDS** has only recently been acknowledged by the Indian government as a national problem. The reluctance to address the issue is partly due to the disease's association with sex, a traditionally closed subject in India. As yet only NGOs and foreign agencies such as the WHO have embarked on awareness and prevention campaigns. As elsewhere in the world, high-risk groups include prostitutes and intravenous drug users. It is extremely unwise to contemplate casual sex without a condom – carry some with you (preferably brought from home, as Indian ones may be less reliable; also, be aware that heat affects the durability of condoms), and insist on using them.

Should you need an injection or a transfusion in India, make sure that new,

---

Ayurvedic medicine

Ayurveda, a Sanskrit word meaning the "knowledge for prolonging life", is a five-thousand-year-old holistic medical system which is widely practised in India and especially popular in the South, where Kerala is a particular stronghold. Ayurvedic doctors and clinics in large towns deal with foreigners as well as their usual patients, and some pharmacies specialize in Ayurvedic preparations, including toiletries such as soaps, shampoos and toothpaste.

Ayurveda assumes the fundamental sameness of self and nature and as such it is a sister science to yoga, stemming from the same period of Vedic philosophy. It places great importance on the harmony of mind, body and spirit and acknowledges the psychosomatic causes behind many diseases. Unlike the allopathic medicines of the West, which depend on finding out what's ailing you and then killing it, Ayurveda looks at the whole patient: disease is regarded as a symptom of imbalance, so it's the imbalance that's treated, not the disease.

Ayurvedic theory holds that the body is controlled by three *doshas* (forces), themselves made up of the basic elements of space, fire, water, earth and air, which reflect the forces within the self. The three *doshas* are: *pitta*, the force of the sun, which is hot and rules the digestive processes and metabolism; *kapha*, likened to the moon, the creator of tides and rhythms, which has a cooling effect, and governs the body's organs and bone structure; and *vata*, wind, which relates to movement, circulation and the nervous system. People are classified according to which *dosha* or combination of them is predominant. The healthy body is one that has the three forces in the correct balance for its type. To diagnose an imbalance, the Ayurvedic doctor not only goes into the physical complaint but also into family background, daily habits and emotional traits.

Imbalances are typically treated with herbal remedies designed to alter whichever of the three forces is out of whack. This commonly involves the application of oils or ingestion of specially prepared medicines. Made according to traditional formulae and using indigenous plants, Ayurvedic medicines are cheaper than branded or imported ones. Traditional, strictly vegetarian diets are also advised for long-term benefits. In addition, the doctor may prescribe various forms of yogic cleansing to rid the body of waste substances. To the uninitiated, these techniques will sound rather off-putting – for instance, swallowing a long strip of cloth, a short section at a time, and then pulling it back up again to remove mucus from the stomach.

Many places advertising Ayurvedic treatments in the more touristy spots are just glorified massage parlours using a few herbal oils and traditional techniques; however, even these can provide welcome relaxation. Those who seek out more bona fide clinics for lengthier purification regimes, or for the treatment of individual ailments, are often full of praise for the efficacy of these ancient methods.

sterile equipment is used; any blood you receive should be from voluntary rather than commercial donor banks. Try to bring needles from home in your first-aid kit. If you have a shave from a barber, make sure he uses a clean blade, and don't submit to processes such as ear-piercing, acupuncture or tattooing unless you can be sure that the equipment is sterile.

Getting medical help

Pharmacies can usually advise on minor medical problems, and most **doctors** in India speak English. Many hotels also have a doctor on call. Basic medicaments are made to Indian Pharmacopoea (IP) standards, and most medicines are available without prescription – although always check the sell-by date. **Hospitals** vary in standard. Private clinics and mission hospitals are often better than state-run ones, but may not have the same facilities. Hospitals in the big cities are generally pretty good; university and medical-school hospitals are best of all. Private hospitals may require patients (even emergency cases) to buy necessities such as medicines, plaster casts and vaccines and to pay for X-rays before procedures can be carried out, though costs are a fraction of private health care in the West (be sure to keep all original documents and receipts to claim money back on insurance if need be). However, government hospitals provide all surgical and aftercare services free of charge, and in most other state medical institutions, charges are usually so low that for minor treatment the expense may well be lower than the initial "excess" on your insurance. You will need a companion to stay, or you'll have to come to an arrangement with one of the hospital cleaners, to help you out in hospital – relatives are expected to wash, feed and generally take care of the patient. Addresses of foreign consulates (who will advise in an emergency), and of clinics and hospitals can be found in the Listings sections for major towns in this book.

Costs, money and banks

For visitors, India is still one of the least expensive countries in the world; a little foreign currency can go a long way. You can be confident of getting good value for your money, whether you're setting out to keep your budget to a minimum or to enjoy the opportunities that spending a bit more brings.

While we attempt below to suggest the kind of sums you can expect to pay for varying degrees of comfort, it's vital not to make a rigid assumption at the outset of a long trip that whatever money you bring to India will last for a certain number of weeks or months. On any one day it may be possible to spend very little, but cumulatively you won't be doing yourself any favours if you don't make sure you keep yourself well rested and properly fed. As a foreigner in India, you will find yourself penalized by double-tier entry prices to museums and historic sites (see box opposite) as well as in upmarket hotels and air fares, both of which are levied at a higher rate and in dollars.

What you spend depends on you: where you go, where you stay, how you get around, what you eat and what you buy. You can manage on a budget of as little $11/£6 (Rs500) per day if you eat in local *dhabas* and don't move about too much; double that, and you'll be able to afford comfortable mid-range hotels, as well as meals in smarter restaurants, regular rickshaw or taxi rides and entrance fees to monuments. If you're happy spending $30–35/£15–18 (around Rs1500) per day, however, you can really pamper yourself; to spend much more than that, you'd have to be doing a lot of air-conditioned travelling, consistently staying in swish hotels and eating in the top restaurants. Five-star luxury in India is cheap by Western standards but, particularly with all the extra government taxes it incurs, can soon send your budget spiralling.

Accommodation ranges from as little as $3/£2 per night upwards (see p.62), while a no-frills vegetarian **meal** in an ordinary restaurant will typically cost less than half that. Long-distance **transport** can work out to be phenomenally good value if you stick to state buses and standard second-class non-a/c trains, but soon starts to add up if you opt for air-conditioned carriages on the superfast intercity services. The twelve-hour, 500-kilometre trip from Mumbai to Goa, for example, can cost anywhere from Rs300 ($6.50/£3.70) to Rs2400 ($54/£30), depending on the level of comfort.

Where you are also makes a difference: Mumbai is notoriously pricey, especially for accommodation, while tourist enclaves like the Goa beaches are more expensive for things like food, as well as having more souvenirs to tempt you. Out in the sticks, on the other hand, and particularly away from your fellow tourists, you'll find things incredibly cheap, though your choice will obviously be more limited.

Some independent travellers tend to indulge in wild and highly competitive **penny-pinching**, which Indian people find rather pathetic – they know how much an air ticket to Delhi or Mumbai costs, and they have a fair idea of what you can earn at home. Bargain where appropriate, but don't begrudge a few rupees to someone who's worked hard for them: consider what their services would cost at home, and how much more valuable the money is to them than it is to you. Even if you get a bad deal on every rickshaw journey you make, it will only add a minuscule fraction to the cost of your trip. Remember, too, that every pound or dollar you spend in India goes that much further, and luxuries you can't afford at home become possible here: sometimes it's worth spending more simply because you get more for it. At the same time, don't pay well over the odds for something if you know what the going rate is. Thoughtless extravagance can, particularly in remote areas that see a disproportionate number of tourists, contribute to inflation, putting even basic goods and services beyond the reach of local people.

Currency

India's unit of currency is the **rupee**, usually abbreviated "Rs" and divided into a hundred **paise**. Almost all money is paper, with notes of 10, 20, 50, 100, 500 and, recently, 1000 rupees; a few notes of 1, 2 and 5 rupees are still in circulation. Coins start at 10 paise range up to 20, 25 and 50 paise, and 1, 2 and 5 rupees.

Banknotes, especially lower denominations, can get into a terrible state. Don't accept **torn banknotes**, since no one else will be prepared to take them and you'll be left saddled with the things unless you can be bothered to change them at the Reserve

Entrance fees

In 2000, the Archeological Survey of India announced a **double-tiered entry system**, with foreign visitors (including non-resident Indians) required to pay $5–20 or its rupee equivalent to enter major archeological sites. This means that foreigners can find themselves paying forty times the entrance fee levied to domestic visitors. Due to an outcry from tour agencies and tourists, the Indian government is currently reviewing this policy, and discount pass schemes may emerge; ask at a Government of India tourist office for the latest.

Foreign visitors may be charged in either dollars or rupees; where, as is the case at some sites, foreigners are charged in dollars, we give the dollar rate current at the time of going to press (although it's normal for foreigners to pay the dollar price in rupees at that day's exchange rate), so bear in mind that this may fluctuate. Throughout the Guide, we list the price for Indian visitors in square brackets.

Bank of India or large branches of other big banks. Don't pass them on to beggars; they can't use them either, so it amounts to an insult.

Large denominations can also be a problem, as **change** is usually in short supply. Many Indian people cannot afford to keep much lying around, and you shouldn't necessarily expect shopkeepers or rickshaw-wallahs to have it (and they may – as may you – try to hold onto it if they do). Paying for your groceries with a Rs100 note will probably entail waiting for the grocer's errand boy to go off on a quest to try and change it. Larger notes – like the Rs500 note – are good for travelling with and can be changed for smaller denominations at hotels and other suitable establishments. A word of warning – the Rs500 note looks remarkably similar to the Rs100 note.

At the time of writing, the **exchange rate** was approximately Rs81 to £1 and Rs42 to $1.

Travellers' cheques, credit cards and ATMs

In addition to your cash, carry some **travellers' cheques** to cover all eventualities, with a few small denominations for the end of your trip, and for the odd foreign-currency purchase such as tourist-quota rail tickets, which can be bought with American Express travellers' cheques. US dollars are the easiest **currency** to convert, with pounds sterling a close second. Major hard currencies can be changed easily in tourist areas and big cities, less so elsewhere. If you enter the country with more than $10,000 or the equivalent, you are supposed to fill in a currency declaration form.

Travellers' cheques aren't as liquid as cash, but obviously more secure (and you get a slightly better exchange rate for them at banks). Not all banks, however, accept them, and those that do can be quirky about exactly which ones they will change. Well-known brands such as Thomas Cook and American Express are your best bet, but in some places even American Express is only accepted in US dollars and not as pounds sterling.

A **credit card** is a handy back-up, as an increasing number of hotels, restaurants,

large shops and tourist emporia, as well as airlines and train companies, now take plastic; American Express, Mastercard and Visa are the most commonly accepted brands. If you have a selection of cards, take them all. You'll get much the same exchange rate as you would in a bank, and bills can take a surprisingly long time to be charged to your account at home. The Bank of Baroda and Standard Chartered Grindlays issue rupees against a Visa card at all their branches. Remember that all cash advances are treated as loans, with interest accruing daily from the date of withdrawal; there may be a transaction fee on top of this. However, you may be able to make withdrawals from ATMs in India using your **debit card**, which is not liable to interest payments, and the flat transaction fee is usually quite small – your bank will be able to advise on this. Make sure you have a personal identification number (PIN) that's designed to work overseas.

A compromise between travellers' cheques and plastic is **Visa TravelMoney**, a disposable prepaid debit card with a PIN which works in all ATMs that take Visa cards. You load up your account with funds before leaving home, and when they run out you simply throw the card away. Up to nine cards can be purchased to access the same funds – useful for couples or families travelling together – and it's a good idea to buy at least one extra as a back-up in case of loss or theft. The card is available in most countries from branches of Thomas Cook and Citicorp. For more information, check the Visa TravelMoney website at ⓦwww.usa.visa.com/personal/cards/prepaid/visa_travel_money.html.

Several banks now have **ATM** machines, but they are only found in cities and not all will accept foreign cards even if they sport Visa and Mastercard signs; it's best to enquire first before sticking your card into the slot. Delhi and Mumbai branches of the Hong Kong Bank and Bank of America have 24hr ATMs that take Visa and Mastercard, while some of Standard Chartered Grindlays banks also have foreigner-friendly ATM machines.

It is illegal to carry rupees (besides spending money) into India, and you won't get them at a particularly good rate in the West anyhow (though you might in Thailand, Malaysia or Singapore). It is also illegal to take any rupees out of the country.

Travellers' cheques and credit card contacts

Both American Express and Thomas Cook have offices in other major cities throughout India; see the relevant accounts in the Guide and collect a full list when you purchase your **travellers' cheques**.

American Express

ⓦ www.americanexpress.com.
Lost and stolen cards/cheques ☎ 011/2614 5920 or 2687 5050 (open 24hr).
Bangalore Janardhan Tower, 2 Residency Rd ☎ 080/2248 1800.
Chennai G-17, Spencer Plaza, 768–769 Anna Salai, ☎ 044/2851 5800.
Mumbai Regal Cinema Building, Chhatrapati Shivaji Maharaj Rd, Colaba ☎ 022/2497 9800 or 989/260 0800.

Thomas Cook

ⓦ www.thomascook.co.in
Lost and stolen cards/cheques ☎ 0044-1733/318949.
Bangalore 70 Mahatma Gandhi Rd and 55 Mahatma Gandhi Rd ☎ 080/2558 8028.
Chennai Ceebros Centre, 45 Montieth Rd, Egmore ☎ 044/2855 3276 or 2336 8560.
Mumbai Dr Dadabhai Naoroji Rd, Fort ☎ 022/2204 8556–7.

Banks

Changing money in regular banks, especially government-run banks such as the State Bank of India (SBI), can be a time-consuming business, involving lots of form-filling and queuing at different counters, so change substantial amounts at any one time. Banks in main cities are likely to be most efficient, though not all change foreign currency and some won't take **travellers' cheques** or currencies other than dollars or sterling (banks usually charge a percentage of the transaction, while Grindlays charge a flat Rs200). You'll have no such problems with **private companies** such as Thomas Cook and American Express who have offices in most state capitals.

Major cities and main tourist centres usually have several **licensed currency**

exchange bureaux; rates usually aren't as good as at a bank, but transactions are generally a lot quicker and there's less paperwork to complete. Note that if you arrive at a minor airport you may not be able to change anything except cash US dollars or sterling.

Outside **banking hours** (Mon–Fri 10am till 2–4pm, Sat 10am–noon), large hotels may change money, probably at a lower rate, and exchange bureaux have longer opening hours. Banks at Mumbai and Chennai **airports** stay open 24 hours, but neither is very conveniently located.

Hold on to **exchange receipts** ("encashment certificates"); they will be required if you want to change back any excess rupees when you leave the country, and to buy air tickets and reserve train berths with rupees. The State Bank of India now charges for tax clearance forms (see p.34 to find out if you'll need one.)

Wiring money

Having **money wired** from home using one of the companies listed below is never convenient or cheap, and should be considered a last resort.

Money-wiring companies

Thomas Cook ⓦ www.thomascook.com
US ☎ 1-800/287-7362; Canada ☎ 1-888/823-4732; Great Britain ☎ 01733/318922; Northern Ireland ☎ 028/9055 0030; Republic of Ireland ☎ 01/677 1721.
Travelers Express MoneyGram ⓦ www.moneygram.com.
US ☎ 1-800/955-7777; Canada ☎ 1-800/933-3278; UK ☎ 0800/018 0104; Republic of Ireland ☎ 1850/205800; Australia ☎ 1800/230100; New Zealand ☎ 0800/262263.
Western Union ⓦ www.westernunion.com.
US and Canada ☎ 1-800/325-6000; UK ☎ 0800/833833; Republic of Ireland ☎ 1800/395395; Australia ☎ 1800/501500; New Zealand ☎ 0800/270000.

Baksheesh

As a presumed-rich sahib or memsahib, you will, like wealthy Indians, be expected to be liberal with the **baksheesh**, which takes three main forms. The most common is **tipping**: a small reward for a small service, which can encompass anyone from a waiter or porter to someone who lifts your bags onto the roof of a bus or keeps an eye on your vehicle for you. Large amounts are not expected – ten rupees should satisfy all the aforementioned. Taxi drivers and staff at cheaper hotels and restaurants do not necessarily expect tips, but always appreciate them, of course, and they can keep people sweet for the next time you call. Some may take liberties in demanding baksheesh, but it's often better just to acquiesce rather than spoil your mood and cause offence over trifling sums.

More expensive than plain tipping is paying people to **bend the rules**, many of which seem to have been invented for precisely that purpose. Examples might include letting you into a historical site after hours, finding

you a seat or a sleeper on a train that is "full", or speeding up some bureaucratic process. This should not be confused with bribery, a more serious business with its own risks and etiquette, which is best not entered into.

The last kind of baksheesh is **alms giving**. In a country without a welfare system, this is an important social custom. People with disabilities and mutilations are the traditional recipients, and it seems right to join local people in giving out small change to them. Kids demanding money, pens, sweets or the like are a different case, pressing their demands only on tourists. In return for a service it is fair enough, but to yield to any request encourages them to go and pester others.

Getting around

Inter-city transport in South India may not be the fastest or the most comfortable in the world, but it's cheap, goes more or less everywhere and generally gives you the option of train or bus, sometimes plane, and occasionally even boat. Transport around town comes in even more permutations, ranging from cycle rickshaws just about everywhere to double-decker buses in Mumbai.

Whether you're on road or rail, public transport or your own vehicle, India offers the chance to try out some classics: narrow-gauge railways, steam locomotives, the Ambassador car and the Enfield Bullet motorbike, they're all here. Indeed some people come to India for these alone.

By train

Travelling by **train** is one of the great experiences of South India. It's a system which looks like chaos, but it works, and works well. Trains are often late of course, sometimes by hours rather than minutes, but they do run, and with amazing efficiency too: when the train you've been waiting for rolls into the station, the reservation you made halfway across the country several weeks ago will be on a list pasted to the side of your carriage, and when it's time to eat, the

packed meal you ordered down the line will be ready at the next station, put on the train and delivered to your seat.

It's worth bearing in mind, with journeys frequently lasting twelve hours or more, that an overnight train can save you a day's travelling and a night's hotel bill, assuming you sleep well on trains. While sleeper carriages can be more crowded during the day, between 9pm and 6am anyone with a bunk reservation is entitled to exclusive use of their bunk. When travelling overnight, however, always padlock your bag to your bunk – metal attachments or chains are usually provided under the lower bunk.

Routes and classes

The rail network covers almost the whole of South India; only a few places (such as some parts of the Ghats) are inaccessible by train. **Inter-city trains**, called "**express**" or "**mail**", vary a lot in the time taken to cover the same route. Slow by Western standards, they're still much faster than local "**passenger**" trains, which you need only use to get right off the beaten track. There is also an increasing number of special "**super-fast**" a/c trains, usually named Rajdhani or Shatabdi Express, which cover routes between major cities in as little as half the normal time. Note that express and mail trains cost a fair amount more than ordinary passenger trains, so if travelling unreserved you must buy the right ticket to avoid being fined.

Most lines are either metre-gauge or broad-gauge (1.676m, or 4ft 6in), the latter being faster; many metre-gauge lines are now being converted to broad-gauge. The only narrow-gauge line (often referred to as "the toy train") in the South, runs to Ootacamund (Ooty), and you will only find **steam locomotives** in routinely scheduled service on the steep sections of this narrow-gauge mountain railway. All other trains are now hauled by diesel engines.

Classes of train travel

Indian Railways (Ⓦ www.indianrail.gov.in) distinguishes between no fewer than seven **classes of travel**, though you'll seldom have more than the following four to choose from on mainline services: second-class unreserved, second-class sleeper, first and a/c first (or a/c two- or three-tier sleeper class). In general, most travellers (not just those on low budgets) choose to travel second class, and prefer not to be in a/c compartments; an open window keeps you cool enough, and brings you into contact with the world outside, while air-conditioning by definition involves being sealed away behind glass, which is often virtually opaque. Doing without a sleeper on an overnight journey is, however, a false economy. Bed rolls (sheet,

At the end of each chapter in this book, you'll find a **Travel details** section summarizing major transport connections in the relevant state. In addition, "Moving on" boxes at the end of each major city give details of onward transport from that city.

blanket and pillow) are available in first class and a/c second for that extra bit of comfort – book these with your ticket, or before you board the train.

Second-class unreserved is painfully crowded and noisy with no chance of a berth overnight, but incredibly cheap: Rs103 (that's just over $2 or around £1.40) for a thousand-kilometre journey. However, the crush and hard wooden seats (if you are lucky or nifty enough to get one) make it viable only for short hops or for the extremely hardy. Far more civilized and only around fifty percent more expensive is **second-class sleeper** (from Rs190 for 1000km), which must be booked in advance even for daytime journeys. If you have an unreserved ticket and travel in a sleeper carriage, even if it is not full, you will be charged a Rs60 fine as well as the difference in fare. Second-class sleepers can be pretty crowded during the day but never lack activity, with peanut-, chai- and coffee-sellers, travelling musicians, beggars or sweepers passing through the carriages. Overnight trips in second-class sleeper compartments are reasonably comfy (provided the berths are foam and not wooden).

First class, in comfortable if ageing compartments of two to four berths, used mainly by English-speaking business travellers, costs about 3.5 times as much as sleeper class (from Rs990 for 1000km on express and mail trains). Not always available on passenger trains and gradually being phased out, first class insulates you to a certain extent from the chaotic hustle and bustle.

Air-conditioned travel, unavailable on "passenger trains", falls into five categories but only one or two will be available on any particular service, except for the Rajdhani, which has three. The best value is the **a/c chair car** (often denoted as CC), with comfortable reclining seats at only twice the price of second-class sleeper class. The "super-fast" Shatabdi expresses are exclusively chair car but come in two classes – ordinary a/c chair car and, for double the price, an executive a/c chair car. Very occasionally, a/c chair cars appear on express or mail trains. **Air-conditioned three-tier sleepers** (3AC) cost slightly less than normal first class but cost more on the Rajdhani. Three-tier can feel a bit cramped, especially with loads of luggage, but represents good value (Rs845 for 1000km); they are, however, not as common as the **a/c two-tier sleepers** (2AC) which cost half as much again as first class – Rs1350 for 1000km, and more for Rajdhani. Top of the tree is **a/c first class** (1AC), which offers shared compartments for two or four and has a little more luxury with carpeting and more presentable bathrooms, but at Rs2630 for 1000km and more on the Rajdhani, this is not much cheaper than flying. Bed linen is provided free on most a/c services while meals are also included on Rajdhani and Shatabdi trains.

Ladies' compartments exist on all over-night trains for women travelling on their own or with other women; they are usually small and can be full of noisy kids, but can give untold relief to women travellers who otherwise have to endure incessant staring in the open section of the carriage. They can be a good place to meet Indian women, particularly if you like (or are with) children. Some stations also have ladies-only waiting rooms.

Timetables and tickets

Indian Railways publish an annual **timetable** of all mail and express trains – in effect, all the trains you are likely to use. Called *Trains at a Glance*, it is available from information counters and newsstands at all main stations, and from IR agents abroad. You can also consult rail timetables and fares, and check availability, at ⓦ www.indianrail.gov.in.

All rail **fares** are calculated according to the exact distance travelled. *Trains at a Glance* prints a chart of fares by kilometres, and also gives the distance in kilometres of stations along each route in the timetables, making it possible to calculate what the basic fare will be for any given journey.

Each individual train has its own **name and number**, prominently displayed in station booking halls. When buying a second-class ticket, it makes sense to pay the tiny extra fee to reserve a seat or sleeper (the fee is already included in the price of the higher classes). To do so, you fill in a form specifying the train you intend to catch, its number, your date of travel, and the stations you are travelling to and from, plus your age and sex (this helps conductors to determine who you are). Most stations have **computerized booking counters** (these are listed in *Trains at a Glance*), and you will be told immediately whether or not seats are available.

Reserving tickets

Reservation offices in the main stations are often in a separate building and generally

Rail records

Comprising 42,000 miles (over 60,000km) of track and 14,000 locomotives that daily transport an average of 12 million passengers, India's **rail network** is the second largest in the world. It's also the biggest employer on the planet, with a workforce of around 1.6 million.

One record the country's transport ministers are somewhat less proud of, however, is the **accident rate**. Four to five hundred crashes occur annually in India, causing between seven and eight hundred fatalities, which makes this the most dangerous rail network in the world, by a long chalk.

The country's worst rail disaster took place in Ferozabad, near Delhi, in 1995, when a cyclone blew a train off a bridge, killing 800. In August 1999, another 350 passengers died when two trains – carrying a total off 2500 people – collided head on in West Bengal. On both occasions, as in sixty percent of Indian rail accidents, human error was cited as the cause. In reality, lack of adequate training, maintenance and investment at government level are the real roots of the problems facing India's ageing network.

Train passengers, however, can take solace in the fact that travelling by rail in India is considerably safer than using the buses. An average of 233 people die on the country's roads every day (that's 85,000 annually).

Tatkal tickets

Indian Railways recently introduced a late-availability reservation system for train travellers called **Tatkal**, which has been controversial in India, but looks set to be a great help for foreign tourists. A quota of ten percent of places on most trains is reserved under this scheme, bookable at any computerized office. Tickets are released from 8am on the day before the train departs, and there's an extra charge of Rs150 in sleeper or chair car, and Rs300 in first or a/c sleepers. The real catch, however, is that you also have to pay for the entire length of the journey from originating to terminating station, however much or little of the ride you do, so Tatkal is obviously not worth it if you want to get on, say, the Guwahati–Kanniyakumari Express between Trichy and Madurai. If you're covering most of the route, though, you're pretty well guaranteed to find a place, especially if you get in the day before, as a lot of resident Indians have been put off by the price hike.

One of the routes on which Tatkal is most likely to be helpful to foreign travellers is **Mumbai–Goa**, on the Konkan Railway, where standard tickets sell out weeks in advance and are thus not available to tourists newly arrived in the country (unless they've booked at premium rates via Indian Railways agents abroad – see p.56).

open from Monday to Saturday from 8am to 8pm, and on Sunday to 2pm. In larger cities, the major stations have special **tourist sections** to cut the queues for foreigners and Indian citizens resident abroad, with helpful English-speaking staff; however, if you don't pay in pounds sterling or dollars (travellers' cheques or cash), you must produce an encashment certificate to back up your rupees. Elsewhere, buying a ticket can often involve a long wait, though women get round this at ticket counters which have **"ladies' queues"**; travelling in a mixed group or couple, a woman will find it easier to get a ticket. Some stations also operate a number system of queuing, allowing you to repair to the chai stall or check the timetable until your number is called. Alternatively, many travel agents will secure tickets for a reasonable Rs25–50 fee. Failure to buy a ticket at the point of departure will result in a stiff penalty when the ticket controller (known as the "TC") finds you.

It's important to plan your train journeys in advance, as demand often makes it impossible to buy a long-distance ticket on the same day that you want to travel (although the new **Tatkal** quota system – see the box above – has made life a little easier if you're happy to pay extra). Travellers following tight itineraries tend to buy their departure tickets from particular towns the moment they arrive, to avoid having to trek out to the station again. At most large stations, it's

possible to reserve tickets for journeys starting elsewhere in the country. You can even book tickets for specific journeys before you leave home, with Indian Railways representatives abroad (see p.56). They accept bookings up to six months in advance, with a minimum of one month for first class, and three months for second.

If there are no places available on the train you want, you have a number of choices. First, some seats and berths are set aside as a **"tourist quota"** – ask at the tourist counter if you can get in on this, or else try the stationmaster. This quota is available in advance but usually only at major or originating stations. Failing that, other **special quotas**, such as one for "emergencies", only released on the day of travel, may remain unused – however, if you get a booking on the emergency quota and a pukka emergency or VIP turns up, you lose the reservation. Alternatively, you can stump up extra cash for a **Tatkal** ticket (see box above), which guarantees you access to a special ten percent quota on most trains, though certain catches and conditions apply.

RAC – or "Reservation Against Cancellation" – tickets are another option, giving you priority if sleepers do become available – the ticket clerk should be able to tell you your chances. With an RAC ticket you are allowed onto the train and can sit until the conductor can find you a berth. The worst sort of ticket to have is a **wait-listed** one – identifiable by the letter "W" prefixing your passenger number – which will allow you onto the train but not in a reserved compartment; in this case go and see the ticket inspector as soon as possible to persuade him to find you a place if one is free: something usually is, but you'll be stuck in unreserved if it isn't. Wait-listed ticket holders are not allowed onto Shatabdi and Rajdhani trains. Finally, and as a last resort if you get on where the train starts its journey, **baksheesh** may persuade a ticket controller to "reserve" you an unreserved seat or, better still, a luggage rack where you can stretch out for the night. You could even fight your way on and grab one yourself, although your chances are slim. As for attempting to **travel unreserved**, for journeys of any length it's too uncomfortable to be worth considering on any major route.

Indian Railways sales agents abroad

Australia Adventure World, 73 Walker St (PO Box 480), North Sydney, NSW 2059 ℡ 02/9956 7766, Ⓦ www.adventureworld.com.au.

UK SD Enterprises Ltd, 103 Wembley Park Drive, Wembley, Middx HA9 8HG ℡ 020/8903 3411, Ⓦ www.indiarail.co.uk.

Cloakrooms

Most stations in India have **cloakrooms** (sometimes called "parcel offices") for passengers to leave their baggage. These can be extremely handy if you want to go sightseeing in a town and move on the same day. In theory, you need a current train ticket or Indrail pass to deposit luggage, but they don't always ask; they may however refuse to take your bag if you can't lock it. Losing your reclaim ticket causes problems; the clerk will be assumed to have stolen the bag if he can't produce it, so there'll be untold running around to obtain clearance before you can get your bag without it. Make sure, when checking baggage in, that the cloakroom will be open when you need to pick it up. The standard charge is currently Rs10 for the first 24 hours.

Indrail passes

Indrail passes are available for periods ranging from half a day to ninety days. Passes cover all fares and reservation fees and are valid on all trains; they're available only to foreigners and Indians resident abroad. Even if you travel a lot, passes work out considerably more expensive than buying your tickets individually (especially in second class), but they will save you queuing for tickets, allow you to make and cancel reservations with impunity (and without charge), and generally smooth your way in, for example, finding a seat or berth on a "full" train (passholders get priority for tourist quota places). Indrail passes are available, for sterling or US dollars, at main station tourist counters in India, and outside the country at IR agents (see above). If you're travelling **from Britain**, Dr Dandapani of **SD Enterprises Ltd** (see above) is an excellent contact, providing information on all aspects of travel on Indian railways.

	a/c First Class Sleeper, or a/c Chair car		First Class or a/c		Second Class	
	Adult	Child	Adult	Child	Adult	Child
1 day*	$95	$48	$43	$22	$19	$10
4 days*	$220	$110	$110	$55	$50	$25
7 days	$270	$135	$135	$68	$80	$40
15 days	$370	$185	$185	$95	$90	$45
21 days	$396	$198	$198	$100	$100	$50
30 days	$495	$248	$248	$125	$125	$63
60 days	$800	$400	$400	$200	$185	$95
90 days	$1060	$530	$530	$265	$235	$120

Children under 5 travel free

*For sale outside India only; half-day and two-day pass also available.

Indian Railways online

Online ticket reservation is now available across the network via Indian Railways' website, Ⓦ **www.indianrail.gov.in**. However, at the time of writing, you need an Indian bank account (with HFDC, Citibank or the State Bank of India) to make payments. Other disincentives include a lengthy sign-up and login process, and the overall unreliability of the Indian postal system by means of which tickets are delivered. Basically, foreign travellers are better off either purchasing tickets in person or paying a travel agent to do so on their behalf. That said, the website is extremely useful as a means of **checking fares**, **timetables** and the **availability of berths** – information that you would normally have to travel to a station and queue to obtain – although a fast connection and a good pop-up blocker are needed to browse the site comfortably.

By air

Though obviously more expensive than going by train or bus, **flying** can save a lot of time: Mumbai–Chennai, for example, can take around thirty hours' hard travelling by train compared to a mere 1hr 45min by plane. Delays and cancellations can whittle away the time advantage, especially over small distances, but if you're short of time and plan to cover a lot of ground, you should definitely consider flying.

India's national domestic carrier is **Indian Airlines**, or IA (Ⓦwww.indian-airlines.nic.in), which serves over 140 routes countrywide, including all major cities in the south. In addition, **Air India** (Ⓦwww.airindia.com) runs feeder services from across the region to its hub, Mumbai, to connect with its international flights. **Jet Airways** (Ⓦwww.jetairways.com) flies many of the major routes covered by IA, and generally provides a more efficient and slicker service than the national airline. Among the smaller private airlines, **Sahara** (Ⓦwww.airsahara.net) operates a reliable, expanding network that now reaches most corners of southern India (and beyond). The real success story of the past few years, however, has been India's first low-cost airline, **Air Deccan** (Ⓦwww.airdeccan.net) which has slashed fares across the board by adopting the "no-frills" approach. They fly to many destinations in South India, often for ludicrously small amounts of money: you can, for example, pick up tickets for Delhi–Mumbai for as little as Rs500, though these special deals tend to be in short supply and sell out well in advance. The rock-bottom fares mean all their flights tend to be fully

booked, so you'll have to buy your tickets well ahead of departure; this is easy enough to do, even from abroad, via the Air Deccan website, which accepts foreign credit and debit cards.

Hot on the heels of Air Deccan, other private, low-cost carriers have joined the fray, notably **Kingfisher** airlines (Ⓦwww .flykingfisher.com), launched in May 2005 by flamboyant beer tycoon Vijay Mallya. With the slogan "Fly the Good Times", Kingfisher offers a flashier experience than the competition, calling its planes "funliners" and kitting them out with designer white and red upholstery and exclusively female cabin crews of so-called "flying models". **Spicejet** (Ⓦwww .spicejet.com) is more in the mould of Air Deccan, prioritizing low prices over frills.

The domestic airlines all have a number of **special deals**. IA offers 25 percent discount for under-30s and students, and 50 percent for over-65s, while Jet Airways and Air Deccan offer multi-flight passes and discounts (see box on p.58). Unless you book online, one major drawback with flying inside India (particularly with the less efficient Indian Airlines) is that you tend to have to spend a considerable amount of time queuing at the airline office to get a **reservation**; it's often quicker to book through a hotel or travel agent, which is the norm for booking on private carriers. Finally, whichever airline you're travelling on, always reconfirm 72 hours before your flight.

Airlines have offices or representatives in all the places they fly to, listed in this book in the relevant city sections. IA tickets must be paid for in hard currency or with a **credit**

Multi-flight deals

For details of deals offered by low-cost airlines, visit their respective websites.

Air Deccan
Ⓦ www.airdeccan.net
Value Flier Multi-ticket discount: 14 flights for Rs24,000 (£276/$520).

Air Sahara
Ⓦ www.airsahara.net
Sixer Six tickets for Rs36,000 (£445/$780).

Indian Airlines
Ⓦ www.indian-airlines.nic.in
Discover India Fare Unlimited travel on all internal flights: 7 days $400; 15 days $600; 21 days $850 (no single route twice).
India Wonderfare Seven days' travel in one given region; $320.

Jet Airways
Ⓦ www.jetairways.com
Visit India Fare Unlimited travel on their routes: 7 days $400; 15 days $630; 21 days $895; 7 days regional fare (either North or South India) $320.

---

card (not accepted in smaller towns). Children under twelve pay half fare, and under-twos (one per adult) pay ten percent. There are no **cancellation charges** if you pay in foreign currency, but tickets are not replaceable if lost.

By bus

Although generally less comfortable than travelling by train, **buses** fill in the gaps in the rail network, as well as serving places which are awkward to reach by train or where road transport is simply faster (as in most places without broad-gauge track). Buses go almost everywhere, and more frequently than trains (though mostly in daylight hours). There are state-government-operated services everywhere, and plenty of private firms besides.

Buses vary somewhat in price and standards. Ramshackle **government-run** affairs, packed to the gunnels with people, livestock and luggage, cover both short and very long

distances. In more widely travelled areas there usually tend to be additional **private** buses offering more leg-room and generally travelling faster – not necessarily a plus point when you consider the dilapidated state of the vehicles.

Some clue as to comfort can be gained from the description given to the bus. "**Ordinary**" buses usually have minimally padded fixed upright seats. "**Deluxe**", "**luxury**" and even "**super-deluxe**" are fairly interchangeable terms and when applied to government buses may hardly differ from "ordinary". Usually they refer to private services, though, and should then guarantee a softer, sometimes reclining, individual seat. You can check this out when booking, and it's also worth asking if your bus has a video or music system, as their deafening noise ruins any chances of sleep. The south generally has fewer smart private buses, and those available are aimed primarily at foreigners. However, smaller private bus companies may be only semi-legal and have little backup in case of breakdown or accident. You should also bear in mind that even luxury coaches can have broken seats, recliners that don't recline and windows that don't close, so be prepared, and always try to avoid the back seats – they accentuate bumpy roads, launching you into the air several times a minute. Try to sit in the middle of the bus for safety.

Luggage travels in the hatch on private buses, sometimes at a small extra charge, but you can usually squeeze it into an unobtrusive corner inside state-run vehicles, although you may sometimes be requested to have it travel on the roof (you may be able to travel up there yourself if the bus is too crowded, though it's dangerous and illegal); check that it's well secured (ideally, lock it there yourself or watch it being tied on) and not liable to get squashed. Baksheesh is in order for whoever puts it up there for you.

Buying a bus ticket is usually less of an ordeal than buying a train ticket, although at large city bus stations there may be twenty or so counters, each assigned to a different route. When you buy your ticket you'll be given the registration number of the bus and, sometimes, a seat number. As at railway stations, there is usually a separate, quicker, ladies' queue, although it may not be signed in English. You can always get on ordinary state buses without a ticket, while at bus stands outside major cities you can usually only pay on board, so you have to be sharp to secure a seat. Prior booking is usually available and preferable for express and private services and it is a good idea to check with the agent exactly where the bus will depart from. You can usually pay on board private buses, too, though that reduces your chances of a seat.

By boat

Apart from flat-bottomed river ferries, which are common along the Konkan coast (particularly in Goa), the **boat services** you're most likely to use in South India are those plying the backwaters of **Kerala**, where the majority of settlements are still most easily reached by water. Foreign visitors generally stick to the route connecting the area's two main towns, Alappuzha and Kollam, along which the local tourist office operates popular sightseeing boats, but it can be fun to catch run-of-the-mill village ferries to smaller, less developed areas.

The other region of South India still heavily reliant on ferries is the **Andaman Islands**, around 1000km east of Chennai in the Bay of Bengal. A new road runs the length of this remote archipelago, crossing larger estuaries by means of small river ferries, but to reach any of the offshore islands you'll have to wait around in the capital, Port Blair, for one of the sporadic government ferry services. If you can't afford the air fare (or can't get a ticket on the over-subscribed flight), boats – from Chennai, Vishakapatnam and Kolkata – are the only other way to reach the Andamans. The crossing is frequently uncomfortable and lasts three or four days (see p.614).

For more detailed information on the routes outlined above, see the relevant chapters of the guide. At the time of writing, these were the only ferry services in operation in South India. Sri Lanka can for the moment only be reached by air, while the scheduled ship cruise to the Lakshadweep Islands from Kochi (Kerala) is very expensive.

By car or motorbike

It's much more usual for tourists in South India to be driven than it is for them to drive; car rental firms operate on the basis of supplying **chauffeur-driven vehicles**, and taxis are available at cheap daily rates. Arranged through tourist offices, local car rental firms, a chauffeur-driven car will run to about £20/US$32 per day. On longer trips, the driver sleeps in the car. The big international chains, Hertz, Budget and Europcar, are the best bet for **self-drive car** rental; in India they charge around the same as chauffeur-driven, with a Rs1000 deposit against damage, though if you pay in your home country it can cost a whole lot more. In one or two places, **motorbikes** or **mopeds** may be rented out for local use, but for biking around the country, it's a much better idea to buy one (see p.61).

Driving in India is not for beginners. If you do drive yourself, expect the unexpected, and count on other drivers taking whatever liberties they can get away with. Traffic circulates on the left, but don't expect road regulations to be obeyed. Traffic in the cities is heavy and undisciplined; vehicles cut in and out without warning, and pedestrians, cyclists and cows wander nonchalantly down the middle of the road as if you don't exist. In the country the roads are narrow, in terrible repair and hogged by overloaded Tata trucks that move aside for nobody, while something slow-moving like a bullock cart or a herd of goats can easily take up the whole road. To overtake, sound your horn – the driver in front will signal if it is safe to do so; if not, he will wave his hand, palm downwards, up and down. A huge number of potholes don't make for a smooth ride either. Furthermore, during the monsoon, roads can become flooded and dangerous; rivers burst their banks and bridges get washed away. Ask local people before you set off, and proceed with caution, sticking to main highways if possible.

You should have an **international driving licence** to drive in India, but this is often overlooked if you have your licence from home (but beware of police in Goa, who are quick to hand out fines). Insurance is compulsory, but not expensive. Car seatbelts and motorcycle crash-helmets are not compulsory but very strongly recommended; helmets are best brought from home. Accident rates are high, and you should be on your guard at all times. It is very dangerous to drive at night – not everyone uses lights, and bullock carts don't have any. If you have an **accident**, it might be an idea to leave the scene quickly and go straight to the police to report it; mobs can assemble fast, especially if pedestrians or cows are involved.

Fuel is reasonably cheap, but the state of the roads will take its toll, and mechanics are not always very reliable, so a knowledge of **vehicle maintenance** is a help, as is a check-over every so often to see what all those bone-shaking journeys are doing to your car. Luckily, if you get a flat tyre, puncture-wallahs can be found almost everywhere.

To **import a car or motorbike** into India, you'll have to show a *carnet de passage*, a document intended to ensure that you won't sell the vehicle illegally. These are available from foreign motoring organizations such as the AA. It's also worth bringing a few basic spares, as spare parts for foreign makes can be hard to find in India, although low-quality imitations are widely available. All in all, the route is arduous, and bringing a vehicle to India something of a commitment.

The classic Indian automobile is the Hindustan Ambassador (basically a Morris Oxford), nowadays largely superseded by more modern vehicles such as the Japanese-style Maruti Suzuki: these two are likely options if you're renting a car. If you're interested in buying one, the Ambassador is not famed for its mod cons or low mpg, but has a certain style and historical interest, and buying a later model makes little sense as prices are higher and quality lower than in the West.

By motorbike

Buying a motorbike is a much more reasonable proposition and, again, if it's an old British classic you're after, the Enfield Bullet (350 model), sold cheapest in Pondicherry on the coast of Tamil Nadu, leads the field. If low price and practicality are your priorities, however, a smaller model, perhaps even a moped or a scooter, might better fit the bill. Many Japanese bikes are now made in India, as are Vespas and Lambrettas, and motorbikes of various sorts can easily be bought new or secondhand. Garages and repair shops are a good place

to start; Bales Road in Chennai is particularly renowned. Obviously, you will have to haggle for the price, but you can expect to pay half to two-thirds the original price for a bike in reasonable condition. Given the right bargaining skills, you can sell it again later for a similar price – perhaps to another foreign traveller – by advertising in hotels and restaurants. A certain amount of bureaucracy is involved in transferring vehicle ownership, but a garage should be able to put you on to a broker ("auto consultant") who, for a modest commission (around Rs500), will help you find a seller or a buyer, and do the necessary paperwork. A motorbike can be taken in the luggage car of a train for the same price as a second-class passenger fare. You could, of course, bring your own bike all the way **overland** from Europe but remember it is that much further again to the south of India and you will need to consider spares. Helmets are best brought from home, even if you are planning to get a bike once in India.

Some **knowledge of mechanics** is necessary to ensure that you are not being sold a pup so, if you are not too savvy yourself, make sure you take someone with you to give the engine, forks, brakes and suspension the once-over. Bear in mind that experienced overlanders often claim that making sure the seat is comfy is the crucial element to an enjoyable trip. Beside the appalling road conditions encountered (see p.59) and the ensuing fatigue, **renting a bike**, unless you are well versed in maintenance, can be a bit of a nightmare, with breakdowns often occurring in the most inconvenient places. If you do break down in the middle of nowhere, you may need to flag down an empty truck to transport the bike to the nearest town for repairs. Motorbike rental is available in some tourist towns and handy for local use, but the quality of the bikes can't be relied upon.

If you're unsure of negotiating the purchase of your own bike or travelling around on your own you could join one of the **motorbike tours** offered by Blazing Trails (UK ☎01293/533338, ⓦwww.jewelholidays .com) or by Classic Bike Adventure, "Casa Tres Amigos", Assagao (near Anjuna, Goa) (☎0832/224 4467, ⓦwww.classic-bike -india.com).

By bicycle

Ever since Dervla Murphy's *Full Tilt*, a steady but increasing trickle of travellers has either done the overland trip by **bicycle**, or else bought a bike in India and ridden it around the country. In many ways the bicycle is the ideal form of transport, offering total independence without any loss of contact with local people. You can camp out, though there are cheap lodgings in almost every village – take the bike into your room with you – and, if you get tired of pedalling, you can put it on top of a bus as luggage, or transport it by train (it goes in the luggage van: get a form and pay a small fee at the station luggage office).

Bringing a bike from abroad requires no *carnet* or special paperwork, but spare parts and accessories may be of different sizes and standards in India, and you may have to improvise. Bring basic spares and tools and a pump. Panniers are the obvious thing for carrying your gear, but fiendishly inconvenient when not attached to your bike, and you might consider sacrificing ideal load-bearing and streamlining technology for a backpack you can lash down on the rear carrier.

Buying a bike in India presents no great difficulty; most towns have cycle shops and even cycle markets. The advantages of a local bike are that spare parts are easy to get, locally produced tools and parts will fit and your vehicle will not draw a crowd every time you park it. Disadvantages are that Indian bikes tend to be heavier and less state-of-the-art than ones from abroad – bikes with gears, let alone mountain bikes, are virtually unheard of. Selling should be quite easy: you won't get a tremendously good deal at a cycle market, but you may well be able to sell privately, or even to a rental shop.

Bicycles can be **rented** in most towns, usually for local use only: this is a good way to find out if your legs and bum can survive the Indian bike before buying one. The going rate is Rs10–30 per day or Rs2–3 per hour, occasionally more in tourist centres, and you may have to leave a deposit, or even your passport, as security.

As for **contacts**, International Bicycle Fund, 4887 Columbia Drive S, Seattle, WA 98108-1919 (T 206/767-0848, W www.ibike.org), publishes information, offers advice on bicycle travel around the world, and maintains a useful website.

City transport

City transport takes various forms, with buses the most obvious. These are usually single-decker, though double-deckers (some articulated) exist in Mumbai and elsewhere. City buses can get unbelievably crowded, so beware of pickpockets, razor-armed pocket-slitters and "Eve-teasers" (see p.93); the same applies to **suburban trains** in Mumbai (Chennai is about the only other place where you might want to use trains for local city transport).

You can also take **taxis**, usually rather battered Ambassadors (painted black and yellow in Mumbai). With any luck, the driver will agree to use the meter; in theory you're within your rights to call the police if he doesn't, but the usual compromise is to agree a fare for the journey before you get in. Naturally, it helps to have an idea in advance of what the fare should be, though any figures quoted in this or any other book should be treated as being the broadest of guidelines only. From places such as main stations, you may be able to find other passengers to share a taxi to the town centre; many stations, and certainly most airports, operate prepaid taxi schemes with set fares that you pay before departure; more expensive prepaid limousines are also available.

The **auto-rickshaw**, that most Indian of vehicles, is the front half of a motor-scooter with a couple of seats mounted on the back. Cheaper than taxis, better at nipping in and out of traffic, and usually metered (again, in most places they probably won't use them and you should agree a fare before setting off), auto-rickshaws are a little unstable and their drivers often rather reckless, but that's all part of the fun. In major tourist centres rickshaws can, however, hassle you endlessly on the street, often shoving themselves right in your path to prevent you ignoring them, and once they've got you on board, they may take you to several shops before reaching your destination. Moreover, agreeing a price before the journey will not necessarily stop your rickshaw-wallah reopening discussion when the trip is under way, or at its end. In general it is better to hail a rickshaw than to take one that's been following you, and to avoid those that hang around outside posh hotels.

Lots of towns and cities in South India also have larger versions of auto-rickshaws known as **tempos**, with six or eight seats behind, which usually ply fixed routes at flat fares.

Slower and cheaper still is the **cycle rickshaw** – basically a glorified tricycle with a large raised seat behind. In spite of the fact that this remains the most common form of public taxi in many provincial south Indian towns, foreign visitors often feel uncomfortable being pedalled around by someone half their size for what by Western standards are

tiny sums. In the end, though, to deny them your custom on those grounds is spurious logic; cycle rickshaw drivers will earn even less if you don't use them, and there's nothing to stop you from tipping them extra for their pains (even if, as is likely, you'll already have been charged more than the locals' rate). Bear in mind, too, that cycle rickshaws are a far more environmentally sound way of travelling than the alternatives.

To see a variety of places around town, consider hiring a taxi, rickshaw or auto-rickshaw for the day. Find a driver who speaks English reasonably well, and agree a price beforehand. You will probably find it a lot cheaper than you imagine: the driver will invariably act as a guide and source of local knowledge, and tipping is usually in order.

Accommodation

There are far more Indians travelling around South India at any one time – whether for holidays, on pilgrimages or for business – than there are foreign tourists, and a vast infrastructure of hotels and guesthouses caters for their needs. On the whole, accommodation for foreign tourists, like so many other things in South India, provides extremely good value for money, though in the major cities, especially, prices soar for luxury establishments providing Western-style comforts and service.

Inexpensive hotels

While accommodation prices in India are generally on the up, there's still an abundance of **cheap hotels**, catering for backpacking tourists and less well-off Indians. Most charge Rs150–250 for a double room, and some outside the big cities have rates below Rs100. Even cheaper still are *dharamshalas*, hostels run by religious establishments and pilgrim guesthouses (see p.65).

Budget accommodation varies from filthy fleapits to homely guesthouses and, naturally, tends to be cheaper the further you get off the beaten track; it's most expensive in Mumbai, where prices are at least double those for equivalent accommodation in most other cities.

Cold showers or "bucket baths" are the order of the day – not really a problem in most of India for most of the year – and it's always wise to check out the state of the bathrooms and toilets before taking a room. Bed bugs and mosquitoes are other things to check for – splotches of blood around the bed and on the walls where people have squashed them are tell-tale signs.

If a taxi driver or rickshaw-wallah tells you that the place you ask for is full, closed or has moved, it's more than likely that it's because he wants to take you to a hotel that pays him commission – added, in some cases, to your bill. **Hotel touts** operate in some major tourist spots, working for commission from the hotels they take you to; this can become annoying, but sometimes paying the little extra can be well worth it, especially if you arrive alone in a new place at night. One way to avoid the hassle is to stay put – some airports have retiring rooms, and so do most of the larger railway stations.

Mid-range hotels

Even if you value your **creature comforts**, you don't need to pay through the nose for them. A large clean room, freshly made bed, your own spotless (often sit-down) toilet, and hot and cold running water can still cost under Rs350 (£5/$7). Extras that bump up the price include local taxes, TV, mosquito nets, a balcony and, above all, **air-conditioning**. Abbreviated in this book and in India itself as **a/c**, air-conditioning is not necessarily the advantage you might expect – in some hotels you can find yourself paying double for a system that is so dust-choked, wheezy and noisy as to preclude any possibility of sleep – but providing it entitles a hotel to consider itself mid-range. Some also offer a halfway-house option known as **air-cooled** – noisy and not as effective as full-blown a/c, but better than nothing in severe heat – which is found only in drier climes as coolers do not work in areas of extreme humidity such as along the coasts of South India. Many medium-priced hotels also have attached restaurants, and even room service.

New hotels tend to be lined inside, on floors and walls, with marble (or some imitation), which can make them feel totally character-less. They are, however, much cleaner than older hotels, where dirt and grime clings to cracks and crevices, and damp quickly devours paint. Some mid-range hotels feel compelled to furnish their rooms with wall-to-wall carpeting, which often smells due to humidity and damp.

Most state governments run their own "**tourist bungalows**", similar to mid-range hotels, but often also offering pricier a/c rooms and cheaper dorms. They are usually good value, though they vary a lot from state to state and even within states. Tamil Nadu's, for example, tend to be rather run-down, whereas Karnataka's are, as a rule, very well kept, and some of those in Kerala are positively luxurious. We've indicated such places throughout this guide by including the state acronym in the name – eg KTDC Palace. The "TDC" stands for Tourist Development Corporation and most states have one. Bookings for state-run hotels can be made in advance by telephone, or through the state tourist offices throughout the country.

Upmarket hotels

Most **luxury hotels** in India fall into one of two categories: old-fashioned institutions brimming with class, and modern jet-set chain hotels, largely confined to large cities and tourist resorts.

The faded grandeur of the Raj lingers on in the venerable edifices of British imperial

Accommodation price codes

All **accommodation prices** in this book are **coded** using the symbols below. The prices given are for a double room; in the case of dorms, we give the per person price in rupees. Most mid-range and all expensive and luxury hotels charge a luxury tax of around ten to fifteen percent and a local tax of around five percent. All taxes are included in the prices we quote.

India doesn't have a **tourist season** as such, and most accommodation keeps the same prices throughout the year. Certain resorts, however, and some spots on established tourist trails do experience some variation and will be more expensive, or less negotiable, when demand is at its peak. For the hill stations, this will be in the summer (April–July); for Goa and other beach resorts in the south, it'll be the winter, especially around Christmas and New Year. We indicate such fluctuations in the Guide where appropriate.

❶ up to Rs150	❹ Rs500–700	❼ Rs1500–2000
❷ Rs150–300	❺ Rs700–1000	❽ Rs2000–3000
❸ Rs300–500	❻ Rs1000–1500	❾ Rs3000 and upwards

hangouts such as Mumbai (Bombay) and the hill stations of the Nilgiri Hills in the far south. These can be well worth seeking out for their old-world charm, and their knack of being somehow more quintessentially British than the British ever managed. In addition, some former princely palaces or aristocratic seats in the region (notably in Karnataka and Goa) have been converted into **heritage hotels** where you can sample grand period architecture at close quarters

Modern deluxe establishments – slicker, brighter and far more businesslike – tend to belong to **chains**, as often Indian as international. The *Taj Mahal Palace and Tower* in Mumbai, for example, the country's grandest hostelry, is part of a chain that includes former palaces in Rajasthan; some Taj hotels rank among the best and certainly the most expensive in the world. Other chains include Oberoi, Hilton, Hyatt and Marriott and the India Tourist Development Corporation's Ashok chain. You'll find such hotels in most state capitals and some resorts favoured by rich Indian and foreign tourists. It's becoming more common for these to quote tariffs in US dollars, starting at $80 and rising to a hefty $500. In palaces and heritage hotels, however, you'll still get excellent value for money, with rates only just beginning to approach those of their counterparts back home.

Bookings for many of the larger hotel chains can be made in offices around the world and via email; we've included website addresses for hotels that have them throughout the Guide. Only the standard "rack rates" will be offered to you if you walk into a hotel direct, though special reductions are available online. You may also find **discounts** through travel agencies such as the Travel Corporation of India, which offer up to sixty percent off certain luxury hotels, depending on the season.

Other options

Many **railway stations** have **retiring rooms** where passengers can sleep – if they can put up with station noises. These rooms can be particularly handy if you're catching an early morning train, but tend to fill up quickly. They vary in price, but generally charge roughly the same as a budget hotel,

and have large, clean, if somewhat institutional rooms; dormitories, where you can bank on being woken at the crack of dawn by a morning chorus of throat-clearing, are often available, too. Occasionally you may come across a main station with an air-conditioned room, in which case you will have found a real bargain. Retiring rooms cannot be booked in advance and are allocated on a first-come-first-serve basis; just turn up and ask if there's a vacancy.

In one or two places, it's possible to rent rooms in people's **homes**. In Mumbai and Kerala the local tourist offices run **"paying guest"** or **"homestay schemes"** to place tourists with families offering lodging. **Servas** (ⓦ www.servasindia.org) represents some 626 hosts in India; you have to join before travelling by applying to the local Servas secretary (see the website) – you then get a list of hosts to contact in the place you are visiting. Some people provide free accommodation, others are just day hosts. There is no guarantee a bed will be provided – it's up to the individual.

Camping is possible, too, although in most of the country it's hard to see why you'd want to be cooped up in a tent overnight when you could be sleeping on a cool *charpoi* (a sort of basic bed) on a roof terrace for a handful of rupees – let alone why you'd choose to carry a tent around India in the first place. Except possibly on treks, it's not usual simply to pitch a tent in the countryside, though many hotels allow camping in their grounds. The YMCA runs a few sites, as do state governments (Maharashtra in particular), and the Scouts and Guides.

YMCAs and **YWCAs**, confined to big cities, are plusher and pricier than mid-range hotels. They are usually good value, but are often full, and some are exclusively single-sex. Official and non-official youth hostels, some run by state governments, are spread haphazardly across the country. They give HI cardholders a discount, but rarely exclude non-members, nor do they usually impose daytime closing. Prices match the cheapest hotels; where there is a youth hostel, it usually has a dormitory and may well be the best budget accommodation available – which goes especially for the **Salvation Army** ones.

Accommodation practicalities

Check-out time is often noon, but confirm this when you arrive: some places expect you out by 9am, but many others operate a 24-hour system, under which you are simply obliged to leave by the same time as you arrived. Some places let you use their facilities after the official check-out time, sometimes for a small charge, others won't even let you leave your baggage after check-out unless you pay for another night.

Unfortunately, not all hotels offer **single rooms**, so it can often work out more expensive to travel alone; in hotels that don't, you may be able to negotiate a slight discount. It's not unusual to find rooms with three or four beds, however – great value for families and small groups.

In cheap hotels and hostels, you needn't expect any additions to your basic bill, but as you go up the scale you'll find **taxes** and **service charges** creeping in, sometimes adding as much as a third on top of the original tariff. Service is generally ten percent, but taxes are a matter for local governments and vary from state to state.

Like most other things in India, the price of a room may well be open to **negotiation**. If you think the price is too high, or if all the hotels in town are empty, try haggling. You may get nowhere – but nothing ventured, nothing gained.

Finally, religious institutions, particularly Sikh **gurudwaras**, offer accommodation for pilgrims and visitors, and may put up tourists; a donation is often expected, and certainly appreciated, but some of the bigger ones charge a fixed, nominal fee. Pilgrimage sites, especially those far from other accommodation, also have **dharamshalas** where visitors can stay – they're very cheap and very simple, usually with basic, communal washing facilities; some charitable institutions have rooms with simple attached bathrooms. *Dharamshalas*, like *gurudwaras*, offer accommodation either on a donations system or charge a nominal fee, which can be as low as Rs20.

Eating and drinking

India's aromatic and delicious food has a richly deserved reputation throughout the world, and food in the south is some of the finest in the subcontinent, with a range of cuisines reflecting the region's broad spectrum of cultures. As well as offering wonderful fresh fish, South India can be particularly special if you're a vegetarian, and even the most confirmed meat-eaters will find themselves tucking into delicious veg curries with relish.

For the first-time visitor, South India's bewildering range of regional cuisines can challenge all preconceptions of Indian food. What Westerners call a curry covers a variety of dishes, each made with a different *masala,* or mix of spices. The word **curry** probably originates from the *karhi* leaf, a type of laurel, found in much of Indian cooking especially in the South. Curry powder does not exist in India, the nearest equivalent being the northern *garam masala* ("hot mix"), a combination of dried, ground black pepper and other spices, added to a dish at the last stage of cooking to spice it up. Commonly used **spices**, mostly grown along the lush spice belt of the Western Ghats particularly in Kerala, include pepper, cardamom, cloves, cinnamon, chilli, turmeric, garlic, ginger, coriander – both leaf and seed – cumin and saffron. Some are used whole, so beware of chewing on them.

It's the Indian penchant for **chilli** that alarms many Western visitors, though if you have a fondness for the hotter curries served in Indian restaurants in Britain, you may find those in India mild on the whole. The majority of newcomers develop a tolerance for it, but if you don't, stick to mild dishes and eat rice and plenty of *dahi* (curd) to counter the effects. Fresh lime squeezed onto hot curries also tends to reduce the fire. Curd rice, a typical southern dish, is calming and good for an upset stomach, as is tender coconut water. Beer is one of the best things for washing chilli out of your mouth; the essential oils that cause the burning sensation dissolve in alcohol, but not in water. A softer option – a *lassi* (sweet or salty curd drink) – to accompany your meal can also help cool things down.

Most religious Hindus, and a large majority of people in the far south, do not eat meat, while some orthodox Brahmins will not eat food cooked by anyone outside their household (or onions or garlic, as they inflame the baser instincts). Jains are even stricter and will go as far as shunning tomatoes, which remind them of blood. **Veganism** as such is not common, however, so if you're vegan keep your eyes open for dairy products which are prevalent in all forms of cooking, from sweets to ghee (the unclarified butter often used in more elaborate cuisine).

Many eating places state whether they are vegetarian or non-vegetarian – **"veg"** and **"non-veg"**. Sometimes, especially in the South, you will come across restaurants advertising both veg and non-veg, indicating they have two separate kitchens and, often, two distinct parts to the restaurant so as not to contaminate and offend their vegetarian clientele. You'll also see **"pure veg"** advertised, which means that no eggs or alcohol are served. As a rule, meat-eaters should exercise caution in India: even when meat is available, especially in the larger towns, its quality is not assured and you won't get much in a dish anyway – especially in railway canteens where it's mainly there for flavouring. Note, what is called "mutton" is in fact goat. Hindus, of course, do not eat beef, and Muslims shun pork, so you'll only find those in a few Christian enclaves such as the beach areas of Goa, in the few Tibetan communities and among the Kodavas of the Kodagu (Coorg) hill country of Karnataka, who love pork. In Kerala, due to a liberal mix of religions and cultures, attitudes to food can be more relaxed, and both beef and pork appear on the same menu. Fish, especially along the coast, is popular and is consumed by most, except strict vegetarians.

Set **"meals"** – rather more plain food usually served on a banana leaf instead of a plate – are served all over South India, the equivalent of a North Indian thali. After the meal, the banana leaf is either assigned to compost or as fodder for cows. In some circles, tradition is so entrenched that the banana leaf is preferred even in an urban environment. "Meals" restaurants are usually found clustered around major bus stations and busy bazaars; they serve endless quantities of rice and vegetables and are normally excellent value. Not all "meals" restaurants are vegetarian. Some serve chicken and fish, and a good way of approaching a "meal" is to order a vegetarian meal, with fish or chicken on the side. Most "meals" restaurants often come with a plain canteen and a more upmarket section, some with air-conditioning. You may even encounter "meals" restaurants that come with vegetarian and non-vegetarian sections. Occasionally found along main highways, though more prevalent in north India, *dhabas* are a Punjabi tradition and cater mainly to truck drivers serving basic but delicious wholesome food including dhal (lentil soup pronounced "da'al") and *roti* (oven-baked unleavened bread).

In the South – perhaps even more so than elsewhere – **eating with your fingers** is *de rigueur* (you want to feel the food as well as taste it), and cutlery may not always be available. Wherever you eat, however, remember to use only your right hand (see p.86), and wash your hands before you start. Use the tips of your fingers to avoid getting food on the palm of your hand.

Restaurants vary in price and quality, and offer a wide variety of dishes. If you're in a group, order a variety of dishes and sample each one. Deluxe restaurants, such as those in five-star hotels, are expensive by Indian standards, but they offer the chance to sample top-quality classic Indian cuisine: rich, subtle and mouthwatering, at a fraction of the price you'd pay at home – assuming you could find Indian food that good. Try one out at least once but avoid the wine, which is invariably overpriced.

An alternative type of eating-place – catering specifically for foreign travellers with unadventurous tastebuds, or simply a hankering for home – is the **tourist restaurant**, found in beach resorts, hill stations and travellers' centres. Here you can get Western food galore: pancakes and fritters, omelettes and toast, chips, fried prawns, cereal and fruit salad. They tend to be a bit pricey and are not, of course, authentically Indian.

Finally, should you be lucky enough to be invited into someone's **home**, you will get to taste the most authentic Indian food of all. Most Indian women are expert cooks, trained from childhood by mothers, grandmothers and aunties, and aided by daughters and nieces. They can quite easily spend a whole day cooking – grinding and mixing the spices themselves – and using only the freshest ingredients.

South Indian food

Occasionally, a sweeping generalization is made, that the cuisine of North India is rich and spicy, while that of the South is plain. Considering the incredible **regional variety**, ranging from the rich northern-style Mughlai cooking, developed within the opulent courts of Muslim Hyderabad, to more simple vegetarian dishes in Tamil Nadu, this generalization is quite simply not true. The street food of Mumbai is renowned; Goan cuisine reflects strong Portuguese influences; and Karnataka draws heavily from the plain cooking of its southern neighbours as well as from the rich, aromatic cooking of Hyderabad. Kerala's cuisine is remarkably varied. Tamil Nadu, the most vegetarian and perhaps the most austere state, however, offers pockets

For advice on **water** in India, see box on p.43 and for a **glossary** of dishes and cooking terms, see p.744.

of variety in regions such as Chettinad – with its memorable version of fried chicken – and the small, diminishing Franco–Indian population of Pondicherry – whose unique cuisine, now rare outside the family home, threatens to disappear altogether.

Most quintessential of all South Indian food are *iddlis* (steamed rice cakes), *vadas* (deep-fried lentil cakes) and *dosas* (rice pancakes), which come either with filling (masala) or plain (*sada*) – dished up with *sambar* (lentil soup) and coconut chutney. They are served as breakfast, snacks and frequently as part of "meals" dishes throughout South India.

Those with a penchant for North Indian food and tandoori (clay oven) preparations will find dishes such as chicken *tikka* (boneless cubes of **tandoori** chicken, marinated with yoghurt, spices and herbs) and other favourites feature on the menus of more upmarket restaurants and five-star hotels.

Goan cuisine

The hot-and-sour **vindaloo** curry, found on menus in Indian restaurants worldwide, is possibly the most famous of all **Goan** dishes. *Vindaloo* originates from the Portuguese *vinho d'alho*, literally "garlic wine", and consists of meat or fish seasoned with vinegar, but is traditionally made with pork. Goan food is particularly distinctive in that it uses palm vinegar, a Portuguese introduction, in many of its preparations. In fact, the **Portuguese influence** spread far beyond the borders of their once colonial enclave, when they introduced vegetables and spices from the New World. These included green and red peppers – chillies – which eventually replaced black pepper as the source of heat in Indian cooking.

Pork specialities from Goa include: *chouriço* (red sausages), *leitao* (suckling pig) and *balchao* (pork in a rich brown sauce). Essentially a *vindaloo*, *sarpotel* (pork with liver and heart, vinegar, chillies, spices and tamarind) combines the best of both Portuguese and Indian influences, as does *assado* (a spicy, pan-cooked beef preparation, usually served with salad and potatoes). Although meats like pork and beef feature heavily in Goan cuisine, being a coastal region, its seafood is exceptional. Much like the food of Kerala, Goan cooking relies heavily on coconuts, especially ground coconut, an ingredient that appears in assorted dishes, from fish curries to cakes. Best prepared with *pomfret*, a flat fish found in coastal waters throughout India, the classic Goan fish curry is cooked with spices mixed with coconut and tamarind, and is usually served with plain, boiled rice. For another fish curry, *caldeen*, the fish is marinated in vinegar before being cooked in a spicy sauce made with coconut and chillies. Goa's wonderfully fresh seafood includes shellfish such as clams, lobster and prawn cooked in a variety of ways. Specialities are hot curries and soups such as *sopa de camarão*, a prawn soup cooked with puréed potatoes, egg yolk and milk, and *apa de camarão*, a spicy prawn pie with a rice and semolina crust. Goa is also celebrated for its cakes and desserts such as *bebinca*, a custard made with *gram* (chickpea) flour, eggs and coconut milk.

Hyderabadi haute cuisine

Some connoisseurs may argue, and not without a certain justification, that the haute cuisine originating from **Hyderabad** in Andhra Pradesh represents the pinnacle of all **Indian Muslim cooking**. Although the grandeur of a once luxurious court has faded, traditions still linger on and if you find yourself in the city, a culinary tour will leave indelible impressions. Many Hyderabadi dishes will already be familiar to visitors. Preparations such as *korma* (an aromatic but mild and creamy curry), *pilaf* (aromatic fried rice; also known as *pilau*) and *biryani* (aromatic baked rice) feature prominently in India and are recognized worldwide.

During the height of the Nizam's rule (nineteenth/early twentieth century) Hyderabad attracted Muslims from all over India and abroad, who left their influence on food preparation in the region. Spice mixtures present in some preparations are derived from Persian recipes, and these are combined with indigenous ingredients from the spice belts of the nearby Malabar Coast to give a uniquely rich and aromatic cuisine. With the help of tamarind and local spices, Persian dried lamb with beans is re-created as the delicious *dalcha*, and the fiery *til ki chutney*, inspired by the Middle Eastern *tahini*, is made of sesame seeds. Common ingredients used in Hyderabadi cuisine include: cassia buds, *karhi* leafs, chillies, cinnamon, cardamom, tamarind, peanuts, coconut milk and curds (*dahi*). Mixing these spices is a high art, best illustrated by *potli ka masala*, an unusual mixture consisting of *khas* (vetivert) and dried rose petals, ground and sprinkled onto prepared food, and sometimes present on meat dishes such as *nahari* (a slow cooked stew of lamb with tongue and trotters). Other meat dishes include *lukmi*, which is a type of deep-fried ravioli, and *chippe ka gosht*, where lamb, marinated in yoghurt and coconut, is cooked slowly in an earthenware pot to give it its distinctive earthy flavour.

As with Muslim cooking everywhere, Hyderabadi cuisine is heavily meat-orientated, with a large variety of kebabs and meat preparations. There are also delicious **vegetarian** dishes however, such as *bagheri baingan*, also known as *Hyderabadi baingan* (small aubergines cooked with peanut paste), as well as several rice preparations including *khichari* (rice cooked with lentils and *ghee*), which is traditionally served at breakfast.

Food from Karnataka

Sandwiched between the meat-loving Muslim enclaves of Hyderabad and the central Deccan, and the lush, rice-eating coastal regions to the south, **Karnataka** enjoys the best of both worlds in terms of food. In restaurants in Bangalore you can eat the most sumptuous chicken *biryanis* inspired by Andhra Pradesh cuisine and served on banana leafs, while your neighbour on the next table tucks into a vegetarian "meal" complete with unlimited quantities of vegetables, *sambar* (lentil soup), rice and *rasam* (pepper water).

By far the most famous of all of Karnataka's cooking comes from the town of **Udupi**, to the north of Mangalore, where the Udupi Brahmins have gained a legendary reputation as excellent restaurateurs and hotel-keepers, and for their vegetarian cuisine which developed, in part, through making offerings to their famous Krishna temple. Udupi Brahmin food has become synonymous with quality, and throughout the south restaurants and hotels boast they are "Udupi-run". Udupi food is presented as a classic banana-leaf "meal", but complemented with excellent rice preparations and a variety of delicious vegetable curries, liberally sprinkled with ghee (clarified butter) and accompanied by pickle. Udupi "meals" restaurants are well worth seeking out, not just because of their legendary food, but also for their excellent value. Their restaurants are also good for the *iddlis*, *vadas* and *dosas* – it's said that the ubiquitous masala *dosa*, wrapped around a filling of potatoes and vegetables, was invented by an Udupi Brahmin.

While Bangalore offers the most choice, a visit to **Mysore** provides an opportunity to sample a good selection of Karnatakan cuisine, offering a handful of good Andhra and Udupi restaurants. The city's best-known dish is its Mysore *pak*, a sweet made from a rich, crumbly mixture of maize flour and *ghee*. Regional variety within Karnataka includes the meat-dominated specialities of the Kodavas (see p.279) and the North Indian-style food of the central Deccan in the north of the state, where spicy curries are accompanied by *joleata roti*, a *chapati* (unleavened flat bread) made from a locally grown maize.

Keralan cooking

Colourful communities living in close proximity to each other have given **Kerala** a legacy of a rich and varied cuisine, complemented by the great spice belts along the Western Ghats and plentiful **fish** from along the Malabar Coast and the Kuttanad backwaters. Kerala has always been a key centre for the **spice trade**, and has attracted traders throughout history from all over the world. These different cultures, including Arabs, Phoenicians, Egyptians, Greeks, Romans and Chinese, were all instrumental in the development of Keralan cuisine. Syrian Christians and an ancient Iraqi Jewish community, along with indigenous Keralan Christians, Hindus and Muslims have, more recently, helped create a tolerant and liberal atmosphere that is reflected in the food

– Kerala is, in fact, the only state in India where the slaughter of beef is tolerated. A veritable hothouse enclosed by a lush mountain range and the highest tea estates in the world, Kerala offers a huge variety of vegetables, from beans to bitter gourds, and fruit, including mangoes, bananas and jackfruit, which lie at the heart of the diverse cuisine of this region.

One dish that is universally Keralan is **appam** – rice pancakes mixed with coconut, and cooked in a wok, known as *cheena chatti* (Chinese pot), to give it a soft centre and crisp edges which can make it look like a large fried egg. Variously known as *kallappam* or *wellayappam*, *appam* is traditionally served with an "*eshtew*" (a stew) of chicken and potatoes in a creamy white mild sauce, flavoured with spices such as pepper and cloves and complemented with coconut milk. While the *eshtew* may or may not have been inspired by European imports, the Malabar pudding – made of sago and topped with liquid jaggery and coconut milk instead of sugar and cream – has far more obvious European roots.

The most famous of all Keralan dishes, however, is its wonderful **fish curry**, or *molee*, cooked in a delicious cream of tomatoes, ground coconut and coconut milk. The coastal waters contain a huge variety of seafood including marlin and shark, and the day's catch is proudly displayed on the stands of the seaside tourist restaurants of Kovalam and Varkala. Some of the best fish comes from the backwaters, where the black *karimeen*, a flat sole-like fish that hugs the muddy bottoms, is justifiably prized. Also known as fish tamarind, *kodampoli* (*Garcinia indica*) provides the distinctive flavour in the fiery fish curry *meen vevichathu*, which is cooked in an earthenware pot. Muslim fishermen of the Mopla community favour shellfish, as well as beef, while the Christian fishing communities around Kovalam specialize in catching pomfret, mackerel, squid, prawns and other seafood, which they then sell on the beach to the highest bidder.

Rice features heavily in various forms in the Keralan diet. The *pilaf* (aka *pulau*) is especially popular among Muslims, and is served with seafood, especially prawns along the coast; occasionally tapioca, known locally as *kappa*, appears as an alternative staple to accompany coastal fish curries or is served as deep-fried chips.

Snacks and street food

Feeling peckish should never be a problem, with all sorts of **snack meals** and **finger food** to choose from. Served in restaurants and cafés throughout the South, *vadas*, *iddlis* and *dosas* are the most popular snacks. *Appams*, offered along the seafront at Kochi, are served by vendors from portable stands, and are a favoured regional snack.

Street food includes *bhel puris* (a Mumbai speciality consisting of puffed rice, finely chopped vegetables and spices, and small *puris* stuffed with tamarind sauce), *pani puris* (the same *puris* dunked in peppery and spicy water – only for the seasoned), *bhajis* (deep-fried cakes of vegetables in chickpea flour), *samosas* (meat or vegetables in a pastry triangle, fried) and *pakoras* (vegetables or potato dipped in chickpea flour batter and deep-fried). Kebabs are common in the north and around Hyderabad, most frequently *sheekh kebab* (minced lamb grilled on a skewer) but also *shami kebab* (small minced lamb cutlets). With all street snacks, though, remember that food left lying around attracts germs – make sure it's freshly cooked. Be especially careful with snacks involving water

such as *pani puris* and cooking oil, which is often recycled. Generally, it's a good idea to acclimatize to Indian conditions before you start eating street snacks.

You won't find anything called "Bombay mix" in India, but there's no shortage of dry spicy snack mixes, often referred to as *channa chur*. Jackfruit chips are sometimes sold as a savoury snack, though they are rather bland; cashew nuts are a real bargain. Peanuts, also known as "monkey nuts", usually come roasted and unshelled. Look out for *gram* vendors who sell dry roasted chickpeas – known as *gram*. Another sweeter street snack seen throughout the south in bright yellow piles is banana chips fried in coconut oil.

Non-Indian food

Chinese food has become widespread in towns all over the country, where it is generally cooked by Indian chefs and not what you'd call authentic. However, India does have a small Chinese population, and there's some very good Chinese cuisine in Mumbai, Bangalore and Chennai. Chinese communities tend to adapt their cooking to their environment and, in India, Chinese food comes with a hint of spice.

Outside of upmarket hotels, **Western food** is often dire, and expensive compared with

Paan

You may be relieved to know that the red stuff people spit out all over the streets – predominantly in the North and major cities in the South – isn't blood, but juice produced by chewing **paan** (also known as *paan masala*), a digestive, commonly taken after meals, and also a mild stimulant.

A paan consists of chopped or shredded nut (always referred to as *betel* nut, though in fact it comes from the areca palm), wrapped in a leaf (which *does* come from the betel tree). It may be prepared with ingredients such as *katha* (a red paste), *chuna* (slaked white lime, to activate the betel), *mitha* masala (a mix of fennel seeds, sweet spices, and other flavourings) and *zarda* (chewing tobacco, not to be swallowed on any account, especially if made with *chuna*). The triangular package thus formed is wedged inside your cheek and chewed slowly, and in the case of *chuna* and *zarda paans*, spitting out the juice as you go. Paan is an acquired taste; novices should start off, and preferably stick with, the sweet and harmless *mitha* variety, which is the most benign form and easier to ingest.

Paan is sold by paan-wallahs, often from tiny stalls squeezed between shops. Paan-wallahs develop big reputations and some of the more extravagant concoctions come with silver and, in some rare cases, even gold foil; these are often produced at weddings.

Indian food, although the international chains serve the same standard fare as elsewhere in the world at much cheaper prices. Branches of *Pizza Hut*, *Domino's*, *KFC* and *McDonald's* can be found in Mumbai, Chennai and Bangalore in ever-increasing numbers. *Wimpy's*, home-grown chains such as *Kwality's* and independently owned fast-food cafés like *Pizza Corner* can be found in most cities and large towns. Tourist centres, however, such as Goa, Pondicherry and Kovalam offer a reasonable choice of Western food, from patisseries serving cakes and croissants to restaurants offering lasagne on candle-lit terraces. Small cheese factories are beginning to emerge, providing an alternative to the dreary processed cheese produced by Amul; cheeses and breads made at Auroville are sold throughout the South. Cities such as Bangalore and Mumbai also offer a choice of **Tex-Mex**, **Thai**, **Japanese**, **Italian** and **French** cuisine, but these are often only available in the restaurants of luxury hotels.

Breakfast

Westerners seem to get especially homesick around **breakfast** time, but getting your fry-ups and hash browns is likely to be a problem. Each region has its own traditional way of greeting the day and in the South *iddli*, *vada*, *dosa* and *uppma* (semolina and nuts) is the most common equivalent, while members of the *India Coffee House* chain can be depended upon for some decent coffee and toast.

In those towns which have established a reputation as hangouts for "travellers", budget hotels and restaurants serve up the usual hippy fare – banana pancakes, muesli, etc – as well as omelettes, toast, porridge (not always oatmeal), cornflakes and even bacon and eggs.

Sweets

Most Indians have rather a sweet tooth and Indian **sweets**, usually made of milk, can be very sweet indeed. Although the emphasis on milk products is stronger in the North than in the South, sweets, including regional specialities, are popular throughout the country, with sweet shops thriving in all cities and large towns.

Of the more solid type, **barfi**, a kind of fudge made from boiled-down and condensed milk, varies from moist and delicious to dry and powdery. It comes in various flavours, from plain, creamy white to livid green *pista* (pistachio), and is often sold covered with silver leaf (which you eat). Smoother-textured, round *pedha* and thin diamonds of *kaju katri*, plus moist *sandesh* and the harder *paira*, are among many other sweets made from boiled-down milk. Numerous types of gelatinous **halwa** are especially popular in Hyderabad, all of which are totally different in taste and texture to the Middle Eastern variety. Of the regional varieties, Mysore *pak*, made from a rich crumbly mixture of maize flour and ghee, is one South Indian sweet that is exported to the rest of India.

Getting softer and stickier, those circular orange tubes, dripping syrup in sweet-shop windows, called *jalebis*, and made of deep-fried treacle, are as sickly as they look. *Gulab jamuns* (deep-fried cream cheese sponge balls soaked in syrup) are just as unhealthy. Common in both the North and the South, *laddu* consists of balls made from semolina flour with raisins and sugar, and sometimes made of other grains and flour.

Chocolate is improving rapidly in India, and Cadbury's and Amul bars are available everywhere. None of the indigenous brands of imitation Swiss and Belgian chocolates appearing on the cosmopolitan markets are worth eating.

Among the large **ice-cream** vendors, Kwality, Vadilal's, Gaylord and Dollops stand out. Uniformed men push carts of ice cream around and the bigger companies have many, usually quite obvious, imitators. Some have no scruples – stay away from water ices unless you have a seasoned constitution. Now common throughout southern towns and cities, ice-cream parlours selling elaborate concoctions including sundaes have really taken off. When travelling, especially around coastal Karnataka and parts of Kerala, look out for a local variation known as *gad-bad* (literally "mix-up"), where layers of ice cream come interspersed with chopped nuts and dried and glacéd fruit. Be sure to try *kulfi*, a pistachio or mango- and cardamom-flavoured frozen-milk preparation which is India's answer to ice cream. *Bhang kulfi*, not available everywhere but popular during the festival of Holi, is laced with cannabis, so has an interesting kick to it, but should be approached with caution.

Fruit

What **fruit** is available varies with region and season, but there's always a fine choice. Ideally, you should peel all fruit, including apples, or soak it in a strong iodine or potassium permanganate solution for thirty minutes. Roadside vendors sell fruit which they often cut up and serve sprinkled with salt and even masala. Don't buy anything that looks as if it's been hanging around for a while.

Mangoes are usually on offer, but not all are sweet enough to eat fresh – some are used for pickles or curries. Indians are picky about their mangoes, which they feel and smell before buying; if you don't know the art of choosing the fruit, you could be sold the leftovers. Among the varieties appearing at different times in the season – from spring to summer – look out for Alphonso, which is grown in the vicinity of Mumbai, and Langra, which is grown all over South India. Oranges and tangerines are generally easy to come by, as are sweet melons and thirst-quenching watermelons, although the South is famous for its numerous kinds of **bananas**, on sale all year round. Some bananas, such as the *nendrakai* variety of Kerala, come raw and are meant for cooking. Try the delicious red bananas of Kovalam, or the *nanjangod* variety grown in the vicinity of Mysore, which are considered by many Mysore city-dwellers as the best and most extravagant at around Rs5 per fruit! Certainly, while travelling on the buses through southern India, bananas provide a good fallback in places where safe, nourishing and hygienic food might not otherwise be readily available. They're especially good for upset or sensitive stomachs, complemented by tender-coconut water.

Tropical fruits such as coconuts, papayas (pawpaws) and pineapples are common, while things such as lychees and pomegranates are very seasonal. Among less familiar fruit, the *chiku*, which looks like a kiwi and tastes a bit like a pear, is worth a mention, as is the watermelon-sized jackfruit (*chakkai* in

Malayalam), a favourite with Keralans, whose spiny green exterior encloses sweet, slightly rubbery yellow segments, each containing a seed. The custard apple, a knobbly green case housing a scented white pulp with large black seeds, is another interesting seasonal fruit.

Drinks

South India is home to some of the world's prime coffee-growing areas, and **coffee** is as common as tea, or more so in some spots. South Indian coffee is traditionally prepared with sugar and topped with large quantities of milk to produce a distinctive taste. A whole ritual is attached to the drinking of milky Keralan coffee, poured in flamboyant sweeping motions between tall glasses to cool it down. One of the best places to get a decent cup of South Indian coffee is at a branch of the India Coffee House co-operative chain, found in every southern town. Good vacuum-packed filter coffee from Coorg (Kodagu) in Karnataka is now available but is yet to have an impact in cafés and restaurants.

India's undisputed national drink, however, is **tea** (or **chai**) – grown in Darjeeling and Assam in the north and in the Nilgiri Hills in South India and sold by chai-wallahs on just about every street corner. It's traditionally prepared in a different way to in the West, with lots of milk and sugar (though if you're quick off the mark you can usually get them to hold the sugar – ask for "sugar separate"). Ginger, pepper and/or cardamoms may also often added to make a *masala chai*. English tea it isn't, but many travellers find it an irresistible brew and the rest get used to it: "Just don't think of chai as tea," advise some waverers. Sometimes, especially in tourist spots and upmarket hotels, you might get a pot of European-style "tray" tea, generally consisting of a tea bag in lukewarm water – you'd do better to stick to the pukka Indian variety, unless you are in a traditional tea-growing area. In some of the highest estates in the world, on the borders of Kerala and Tamil Nadu, the tea gardens of the Nilgiris produce fine, strong tea with a full flavour and, in some cases, a high price tag.

With **bottled water** so widely available, you may have no need of **soft drinks**. These have long been surprisingly controversial in India. Coca-Cola and Pepsi returned to India in the early 1990s after being banned from the country for seventeen years. That policy was originally instigated, in part, to prevent the expatriation of profits by foreign companies; since their return, militant Hindu groups such as the RSS have threatened to make them the focus of a new boycott campaign against multinational consumer goods. The absence of Coca-Cola and Pepsi spawned a host of Indian colas such as Campa Cola (innocuous), Thums Up (not unpalatable), Gold Spot (fizzy orange) and Limca (rumoured to have dubious connections to Italian companies and to contain additives banned there). All contain a lot of sugar but little else adverts for Indian soft drinks have been known to boast "Absolutely no natural ingredients!" None will quench your thirst for long.

More recommendable are straight water (treated, boiled or bottled; see also box on p.43) and cartons of Frooti Jumpin, Réal and similar brands of fruit juice drinks, which come in mango, guava, apple and lemon varieties. Avoid cartons which look at all mangled, as they may have been recycled. Tender-coconut water from **green coconuts**, common around coastal areas, are cheaper than any of these, and sold on the street by vendors who will hack off the top of the coconut for you with a machete and give you a straw to suck up the coconut water (you then scoop out the flesh and eat it).

India's greatest cold drink, **lassi** – originally from the north but now available throughout India – is made with beaten curd and drunk either salted, sweetened with sugar or mixed with fruit. It varies widely from smooth and delicious to insipid and watery, and is sold at virtually every café, restaurant and canteen in the country. Freshly made milk shakes are also common at establishments with blenders, as are fruit juices, which usually contain fruit, water and sugar (or salt) liquidized and strained; street vendors selling fresh fruit juice in less than hygienic conditions are apt to add salt and garam masala. In central and northern cities, especially in Hyderabad, Middle Eastern-inspired *sharbat* – flavoured drinks made with sugar, fruit and, often, rose essence – remain popular, especially among Muslims.

With all such drinks, however appetizing they may seem, exercise great caution in deciding where to drink them, unless you're confident your body has acclimatized; find out where the water is likely to have come from and hold the ice.

Alcohol

Prohibition, once widespread in India, is now only partially enforced in a few states, including Tamil Nadu, which retains some semblance of prohibition in the form of "dry" days, high taxes, restrictive licences and health warnings on labels ("Liquor – ruins country, family and life"). Kerala's licensing laws have also resulted in restrictive licences and prohibitive fees to all except the government agencies, such as the Kerala Tourist Development Corporation, who have a virtual monopoly on beer parlours throughout the state.

Except for the new pub scene in cosmopolitan cities such as Bangalore, most Indians drink to get drunk as quickly as possible and this trend has had a terrible toll on family life, especially among the working classes and peasantry. Because of this, politicians searching for votes have from time to time played the prohibition card. In states like Tamil Nadu, which persist with draconian drinking policies, the illicit trade in liquor flourishes, and every now and then papers report cases of mass contamination from illicit stills leading to extraordinary numbers of deaths.

Beer is widely available, if rather expensive by local standards. Prices vary from state to state, but you can usually expect to pay Rs40–80 for a 650ml bottle. Kingfisher and Black Label are the leading brands, but there are plenty of others. All lagers, which tend to contain chemical additives including glycerine, are usually pretty palatable if you can get them cold. In certain places, notably unlicensed restaurants in Tamil Nadu, beer comes in the form of "special tea" – a teapot of beer, which you drink from a teacup to disguise the contents. A cheaper, and often delicious, alternative to beer in Kerala and one or two other places is *toddy* (palm wine).

Spirits usually take the form of "Indian Made Foreign Liquor" (IMFL), although the recently legitimized foreign liquor industry is expanding rapidly. Some Scotch, such as Seagram's Hundred Pipers, is now being bottled in India and sold at a premium; Smirnoff vodka is also available, along with other foreign brands such as Southern Comfort and Bacardi rum (though they're made to different recipes in India, and don't taste much like their Western counterparts). Some types of Indian whisky aren't too bad, and are affordable in comparison; gin and brandy can be pretty rough,

while Indian rum is sweet and distinctive. Goan *feni* is a spirit distilled from coconut or cashew fruit. Steer well clear of illegally distilled *arak*, however, which often contains methanol (wood alcohol) and other poisons. A look through the press, especially at festival times, will soon reveal numerous cases of blindness and death as a result of drinking bad hooch (or "spurious liquor" as it's called). Licensed country liquor, sold in several states under such names as *bangla*, is an acquired taste.

Telephones, mail and Internet access

There is no need to be out of touch with the rest of the world while you're in India. The mail service is pretty reliable if a little slow; international phone calls are surprisingly easy; and Internet access is widely available.

Telephones

Privately run **phone services** with international **direct dialling** facilities are very widespread. Advertising themselves with the acronyms **STD/ISD** (standard trunk dialling/international subscriber dialling), they are extremely quick and easy to use; some stay open 24 hours. Both national and international calls are dialled direct. To call abroad, dial the international access code (00), the code for the country you want – 44 for the UK, for example – the appropriate area code (leaving out any initial zeros), and the number you want; then you speak, pay your bill, which is calculated in seconds, and leave. Prices vary between private places and are slightly cheaper at official telecommunications offices; many have fax machines too. Calling from hotels is usually more expensive. "Call back" (or "back call", as it's often known) is possible at most phone booths and hotels, although check before you call and be aware that, in the case of booths, this facility rarely comes without a charge of Rs3–10 per minute.

Direct dialling **rates** are very expensive during the day – Monday to Saturday 8am to 7pm – but fall by half on Sundays, national holidays, and daily from 7am to 8am and 7pm to 8.30pm, after which the charge is reduced further.

Home country direct services are now available from any phone to the UK, the US, Canada, Ireland, Australia, New Zealand and a growing number of other countries. These allow you to make a collect or telephone credit card call to that country via an operator there. If you can't find a phone with home country direct buttons, you can use any phone toll-free, by dialling 000, your country code, and 17 (except Canada which is 000-127).

To **call India** from abroad, dial your country's international access code, followed by 91 for India, the local code minus the initial zero, then the number you want.

Internet joints in India's big metropolitan cities have started to offer **Net2Phone** services, which allow you to make telephone calls over the web for incredibly low rates: typically Rs2–3 for calls to the UK and US. At the time of writing, services were limited to international calls. We've listed where you

International dialling codes

	From India	To India
UK	℡00 44	℡00 91
Irish Republic	℡00 353	℡00 91
US and		
Canada	℡00 1	℡011 91
Australia	℡00 61	℡0011 91
New Zealand	℡00 64	℡00 91

can access Net2phone in the Guide, but more providers are popping up each month, so keep you eyes peeled for the logo.

Mobile phones

Call charges to and from **mobile phones** are far lower in India than Western countries, which is why lots of foreign tourists opt to sign up to a local network while they're travelling. To do this you'll need to buy an Indian SIM card from a mobile phone shop; these cost around Rs150, plus the price of a top-up card (varying from Rs150–500). Your retailer will help you get connected. They'll also advise you on which company to use. Different states tend to be dominated by one or other of the main firms – Airtel, BPL or !dea (formerly AT&T). If you intend to stay inside their designated coverage area, charges for texts and calls are cheap. However, to use your phone outside your company's coverage you'll need to shell out extra for a roaming facility – otherwise, you'll have to buy a new SIM card each time you change states. Note that when roaming, both you and your caller pay for incoming calls.

Internet and email

All large cities and many tourist towns have places offering **Internet** and **email** access – these are usually cybercafés, but also include many hotels and STD booths. Charges range from Rs10 to Rs60 per hour for reading mail and browsing, and extra for printing; most cybercafés offer membership deals which can cut costs. In the main cities and resorts faster ISDN/broadband connections are now common, though they cost twice the price of standard dial-up connections. Shops which offer Internet access alongside

unrelated business concerns are cheaper, but you have to send and receive mail through their own private account, which means your messages are open to public scrutiny, and the service is invariably slow.

Mail

Mail can take anything from three days to four weeks to get to or from India, depending largely on where exactly you are; ten days is about the norm. Stamps aren't expensive, and aerogrammes and postcards cost the same to anywhere in the world. Ideally, you should have mail franked in front of you. Most post offices are open Monday to Friday 10am to 5pm and Sat 10am to noon, but big city GPOs, where the poste restante is usually located, keep longer hours (Mon–Fri 9.30am–6pm, Sat 9.30am–1pm). You can also buy stamps at big hotels.

Poste restante (general delivery) services throughout the country are pretty reliable, though exactly how long individual offices hang on to letters is more or less at their own discretion; for periods of longer than a month, it makes sense to mark mail with your expected date of arrival. Letters are filed alphabetically; in larger offices, you sort through them yourself. To avoid misfiling, your name should be printed clearly, with the surname in large capitals and underlined, but it's still a good idea to check under your first name, too, just in case. Have letters addressed to you c/o Poste Restante, GPO (if it's the main post office you want), and the name of the town and state. American Express offices also keep mail for holders of their charge card or travellers' cheques.

Having parcels sent out to you in India is not such a good idea – chances are they'll go astray. If you do have a parcel sent, have it registered. Sending a parcel out of India can be quite a performance. First you have to get it cleared by customs at the post office (they often don't bother, but check), then you take it to a tailor and agree a price to have it wrapped in cheap cotton cloth (which you may have to go and buy yourself), stitched up and sealed with wax. In big city GPOs, people offering this service will be at hand. Next, take it to the post office, fill in and attach the relevant customs forms (it's best to tick the box marked "gift" and give its value as less than Rs1000 or "no commercial value" to avoid bureaucratic entanglements), buy your stamps, see them franked, and dispatch it. Parcels shouldn't be more than a metre long or weigh more than 20kg. Surface mail is incredibly cheap, and takes an average of three months to arrive – although delivery times vary wildly, and it may take anything from six weeks or a year. It's a good way to dump excess baggage and souvenirs, but don't send anything fragile.

As in Britain, North America and Australasia, books and magazines can be sent more cheaply, unsealed or wrapped around the middle, as printed papers ("book post"). Alternatively, there are numerous **courier** services, although they're not as reliable as they should be, and there have been complaints of packages going astray – it's safest to stick to known international companies such as DHL or Fedex, which have offices in all the state capitals. Packages sent by air are expensive. Remember that all packages from India are likely to be suspect at home, and searched or X-rayed: don't send anything dodgy.

Media

With over one billion people and a literacy rate of around fifty percent, India produces a staggering 4700 daily papers in over 300 languages and another 39,000 journals and weeklies. There are a large number of English-language daily newspapers, both national and regional. The most prominent of the nationals are the Hindu, the Statesman, the Times of India, the Independent, the Economic Times and the Indian Express (usually the most critical of the government). All are pretty dry and sober, and concentrate on Indian news, though their flowery prose can be entertaining. Asian Age, published simultaneously in India, London and New York, is a conservative tabloid that sports a motley collection of colourful stories. All the major Indian newspapers have websites (see p.37), with the Times of India, The Hindu and the Hindustan Times providing the most up-to-date and detailed news services.

India's press is among the freest in Asia, and attacks on the government can be quite outspoken. That said, most papers form an active part of the political establishment and are unlikely to print anything that might upset the "national consensus" – particularly when it comes to Pakistan, the Kashmir conflict and foreign affairs generally.

In recent years, a number of *Time/Newsweek*-style **news magazines** have hit the market, with a strong emphasis on politics. The best of these are *India Today*, published independently, and *Frontline*, published by *The Hindu*. Others include *Outlook*, which presents the most readable broadly themed analysis, *Sunday* and *The Week*. As they give more of an overview of stories and issues than the daily papers, you will probably get a better idea from them of what is going on in Indian politics, and most tend to have a higher proportion of international news, too. *Business India* is more financially orientated, and the *India Magazine* more cultural. Film fanzines and gossip mags are very popular (*Screen* and *Filmfare* are the best, though you'll have to be reasonably *au fait* with Indian movies to follow a lot of the coverage), but magazines and periodicals in English cover all sorts of popular and minority interests, so it's worth having a look through what's available. One publication of special interest is *Amar Chitra Katha*'s series of Hindu legends, Indian history and folk tales in comic form for children.

Foreign publications such as the *International Herald Tribune*, *Time*, *Newsweek*, *The Economist* and the international edition of the British *Guardian* are all available in the main cities and in the most upmarket hotels, but they're rather expensive, particularly considering that you can now read most of them online for free. Expat-orientated bookstalls stock slightly out-of-date and expensive copies of magazines like *Vogue* and *NME*.

BBC World Service radio can be picked up on short wave, although reception quality is highly variable. The wavelength also changes at different times of day. In the morning, try 5965Khz (49m/5.95–6.20Mhz) or 9605Khz (31m/9.40–9.90Mhz); in the afternoon, 9740Khz (31m/9.40–9.90Mhz) or 11750 (25m/11.70Mhz). A full list of the World Service's many frequencies appears on the BBC website (🌐www.bbc.co.uk/worldservice).

The government-run **TV** company, Doordarshan, which broadcasts a sober diet of edifying programmes, has tried to compete with the onslaught of mass access to cable and **satellite TV** but is losing ground fast. The main broadcaster in English is Rupert Murdoch's **Star TV** network, which incorporates the BBC World Service. Zee TV (with Z News) presents a progressive blend of Hindi-orientated chat, film, news and music programmes. Star Sports and ESPN churn out a mind-boggling amount of cricket with occasional forays into other sports – ESPN broadcasts Premier and Champions League football, for example. Others include CNN, the Discovery Channel, National Geographic, MTV, the immensely popular Channel V hosted by scantily clad Mumbai models and DJs, and an increasing number of reasonable film channels like Star Movies, HBO and AXN. Most hotels from the top end of the budget range upwards have cable TV these days, but exactly how many channels you will get in any particular location is rather hit and miss.

Festivals and holidays

Virtually every temple in every town or village across the country has its own festival. While mostly religious in nature, merrymaking rather than solemnity are generally the order of the day, and onlookers are usually welcome. Indeed, if you are lucky enough to coincide with a local festival, it may well prove to be the highlight of your trip. Music and dance, originally nurtured within the temple environment, are often key features of temple festivals and, in winter, multi-day music festivals known as "conferences" spring up in most major southern cities where you can hear the cream of Carnatic classical music.

The biggest and most splendid of festivals, such as Madurai's three annual festivals and Mysore's celebrated **Dussehra** festival, are major attractions. In Karnataka and Tamil Nadu, the focus of a temple festival is usually a rath (chariot) in which the deities are borne aloft in procession through the streets. However, in Kerala, instead of a *rath*, the deity is carried on a pageant of elephants. A few festivals feature **elephant** races while others, especially along the coast of Kerala, host spectacular **boat races** and regattas.

A list of the main national and regional celebrations is given in the box on pp.78–80. Hindu, Sikh, Buddhist and Jain festivals follow the Indian **lunar calendar** and their dates therefore vary from year to year against the plain old Gregorian calendar. Determining them more than a year in advance is a highly complicated business best left to astrologers.

Principal South Indian festivals

India has only four national public holidays: January 26 (Republic Day); August 15 (Independence Day); October 2 (Gandhi's birthday); and December 25 (Christmas Day). Each state, however, has its own calendar of public holidays; most businesses close on the major holidays of their own religion, marked with an asterisk below. The Hindu calendar months are given in brackets below, as most of the festivals listed are Hindu.

Key: **B**=Buddhist; **C**=Christian; **H**=Hindu; **J**=Jain; **M**=Muslim; **N**=non-religious; **P**=Parsi; **S**=Sikh.

Jan–Feb (Magha)

(H) Pongal (1 Magha) Tamil harvest festival celebrated with decorated cows, processions and *rangolis* (chalk designs on the doorsteps of houses). *Pongal*, a sweet porridge made from newly harvested rice, is eaten by all, including the cows. The festival is also known as Makar Sankranti and is celebrated in Karnataka, Andhra Pradesh and the east of India.

(H) Vasant Panchami (5 Magha) One-day spring festival in honour of Saraswati, the goddess of learning, celebrated with kite-flying, yellow saris and the blessing of schoolchildren's books and pens by the goddess.

(C) Feast of Mar Thoma A colourful procession of decorated carts leads to this ancient site where St Thomas first landed.

(N) Republic Day (Jan 26)*

(N) Goa Carnival Goa's own Mardi Gras features float processions and *feni*-induced mayhem in the state capital, Panjim.

(H) Floating Festival (16 Magha) at Madurai (Tamil Nadu).

(N) Elephanta Music and Dance Festival (Mumbai).

(H) Elephant Festival Thiruvananthapuram's Shiva temple hosts a spectacular elephant procession.

Feb–March (Phalguna)

(B) Losar (1 Phalguna) Tibetan New Year celebrations among Tibetan communities throughout India including Karnataka.

(H) Shivratri (10 Phalguna) Anniversary of Shiva's *tandav* (creation) dance and his wedding anniversary. Popular family festival, but also a *sadhu* festival of pilgrimage and fasting, especially at important Shiva temples.

(H) Holi (15 Phalguna)* Water festival held during *Dol Purnima* (full moon) to celebrate the beginning of spring, most popular in North India but heartily celebrated in Mumbai and parts of northern Karnataka, where you can expect to be bombarded with water, paint, coloured powder and other mixtures.

(C) Carnival (Mardi Gras) The last day before Lent, forty days before Easter, is celebrated in Goa, as in the rest of the Catholic world.

(H) Puram, Guruvayur (Kerala) Although the temple here is off-limits to non-Hindus, the elephant procession with over forty elephants and the elephant race are well worth the visit.

March–April (Chaitra)

(H) Ramanavami (9 Chaitra)* Birthday of Rama, the hero of the Ramayana, celebrated with readings of the epic and discourses on Rama's life and teachings.

(C) Easter* Celebration of the resurrection of Christ. Good Friday is a particularly celebrated day.

(P) Pateti Parsi new year, also known as Nowroz, celebrating the creation of fire. Feasting, services and present-giving.

(P) Khorvad Sal (a week after Pateti) Birthday of Zarathustra (aka Zoroaster).

(H) Chittirai, Madurai (Tamil Nadu) Elephant-led procession.

(H) Arat Festival, Thiruvananthapuram Held again during Oct/Nov, this festival celebrates the deities of the rajas of Travancore, who are led to the sea in a procession of elephants.

April–May (Vaisakha)

(HS) Baisakhi (1 Vaisakha) To the Hindus, it's the solar new year, celebrated with music and dancing; to the Sikhs, it's the anniversary of the foundation of the *Khalsa* (Sikh brotherhood).

(J) Mahavir Jayanti (13 Vaisakha)* Birthday of Mahavira, the founder of Jainism. The main Jain festival of the year.

(H) Puram Festival, Thrissur (Kerala) Frenzied drumming and elephant parades.

(B) Buddha Jayanti (16 Vaisakha)* Buddha's birthday. He was born, attained *nirvana* and died on the same date.

July–Aug (Shravana)

(H) Naag Panchami (3 Shravana) Snake festival in honour of the *naga* snake deities. Mainly celebrated in Rajasthan and Maharashtra.

(H) Raksha Bandhan/Narial Purnima (16 Shravana) Festival to honour the sea god Varuna. Brothers and sisters exchange gifts, the sister tying a thread known as a *rakhi* to her brother's wrist. Brahmins, after a day's fasting, change the sacred thread they wear.

(N) Independence Day (15 Aug)* India's biggest secular celebration, on the anniversary of its Independence from Britain.

Aug–Sept (Bhadraparda)

(H) Ganesh Chaturthi (4 Bhadraparda) Festival dedicated to Ganesh, especially celebrated in Maharashtra. In Mumbai, huge processions carry images of the god to immerse in the sea.

(H) Onam Keralan harvest festival, celebrated with snake-boat races. The Nehru Trophy snake-boat race at Alappuzha (held on the second Saturday of August) is the most spectacular, with long boats each crewed by 150 rowers.

(H) Janmashtami (23 Bhadraparda)* Krishna's birthday, an occasion for feasting and celebration, especially in Vaishnava centres like Udupi and in Mumbai.

(H) Avani Mula Festival, Madurai (Tamil Nadu) Celebration of the coronation of Shiva.

Sept–Oct (Ashvina)

(H) Dussehra (1–10 Ashvina)* Ten-day festival (usually two days' public holiday) associated with vanquishing demons, in particular Rama's victory over Ravana in the Ramayana, and Durga's over the buffalo-headed Mahishasura. Dussehra celebrations include performances of the *Ram Lila* (life of Rama). Best seen in the South in Mysore (Karnataka).

(N) Mahatma Gandhi's Birthday (2 Oct)* Rather solemn commemoration of Independent India's founding father.

Oct–Nov (Kartika)

(H) Diwali (Deepavali) (15 Kartika)* Festival of lights, especially popular in the north but celebrated everywhere, to mark Rama and Sita's homecoming in the Ramayana. Festivities include the lighting of oil lamps and firecrackers and the giving and receiving of sweets.

Principal South Indian festivals   *Cont...*

(J) Jain New Year (15 Kartika) Coincides with Diwali, so Jains celebrate alongside Hindus.

(S) Nanak Jayanti (16 Kartika)* Guru Nanak's birthday marked by prayer readings and processions around Sikh *gurudwaras.*

(N) Hampi Festival (Karnataka) Government-sponsored music and dance festival.

Dec–Jan (Pausa)

(CN) Christmas (Dec 25)* Popular in Christian areas of Goa and Kerala, and in big cities.

(N) Carnatak Music Festivals, Chennai For around a month every year, the city hosts thirteen or so large music programmes called "conferences", each lasting several days.

(N) Mamallapuram Dance Festival Colourful dance and music festival which runs for several days on a stage in front of the famous shore temple.

(N) Kerala Kalamandalam Festival, Cheruthuruthy The annual festival of music and dance serves as a showcase for this leading arts institution, featuring the best Keralan performers and attracting musicians and dancers from all over the country.

Moveable

(M) Ramadan (first day: Sept 24, 2006; Sept 14, 2007) The start of a month during which Muslims may not eat, drink or smoke from sunrise to sunset, and should abstain from sex. Towards the end of the month it takes its toll, so be gentle with Muslims you meet at this time.

(M) Id ul-Fitr (Oct 24, 2006; Oct 13, 2007)*: Feast to celebrate the end of Ramadan, after the lunar month is complete.

(M) Id ul-Zuha Pilgrimage festival to commemorate Abraham's preparedness to sacrifice his son Ismail. Celebrated with the slaughtering and consumption of sheep.

(M) Muharram Festival to commemorate the martyrdom of the (Shi'ite) Imam, the Prophet's grandson and popular saint, Hussain.

Each lunar cycle is divided into two *paksas* (halves): "bright" (waxing) and "dark" (waning), each consisting of fifteen *tithis* ("days" – but a *tithi* might begin at any time of the solar day). The *paksa* starts respectively with the new moon (*ama* or *bahula* – the first day of the month) and the full moon (*purnima*). Lunar festivals, then, are observed on a given day in the "light" or "dark" side of the month. The lunar calendar adds a leap month every two or three years to keep it in line with the seasons. Muslim festivals follow the **Islamic calendar**, whose year is shorter and which thus loses about eleven days per annum against the Gregorian. Christianity – following the Gregorian calendar – is especially strong in Goa and Kerala where the feasts of saints are celebrated and carols are sung in churches packed to the brim during Christmas.

Sports and outdoor pursuits

India is not perhaps a place that most people associate with sports – they won only one silver medal at the Athens Olympics in 2004. However, cricket, hockey and football (soccer) all have their place.

Spectator sports

Cricket is by far the most popular of these, and a fine example of how something quintessentially English has become something quintessentially Indian. Travellers to India will find it hard to get away from cricket – it's everywhere and enjoys extensive coverage on television. Cricketing heroes such as the maestro batsman Sachin Tendulkar are held in the highest esteem and live under the constant scrutiny of the media and public. Expectations are high and disappointments acute; India versus Pakistan matches are especially emotive. In 1999, the right-wing Hindu group Shiv Sena threatened to disrupt Pakistan's tour of India and even dug up the pitch in Delhi, but to no avail. Tests were suspended during the Kashmir-related hostilities of the early 2000s, but recommenced again in 2005. Inter-state cricket is easy to catch – the most prestigious competition is the Ranji Trophy. Besides spectator cricket, you'll see games being played on open spaces all around the country. Occasionally, you may even come across a match blocking a road, and will have to be patient as the players grudgingly let your vehicle continue.

Horseracing can be a good day out, especially if you enjoy a flutter. There are several racecourses around the south, mostly in larger cities such as Mumbai, Hyderabad, Mysore and Bangalore; look in local newspapers, such as *Bangalore Today*, and any local listings magazine to find out when race meetings are being held. Polo, originally from upper Kashmir, was taken up by the British to become one of the symbols of the Raj. Rajasthan princes were considered the best polo players in the world from the 1930s to the 1950s, but since the 1960s, when their privy purses were cut off, they have been unable to maintain their stables and the tradition of polo has declined. Today, it's mainly the army which plays polo, so you may catch a game near a major southern cantonment.

After years in the doldrums, Indian **hockey**, which used regularly to furnish India with Olympic medals, is making a strong comeback. The haul of medals dried up in the 1960s when international hockey introduced astro-turf – still a rare surface in India. However, hockey is still very popular, especially in schools and colleges and, interestingly, among the tribal girls of Orissa, who supply the Indian national team with a regular influx of players. Indian **athletics** are improving all the time, and India bagged 36 medals at the 2002 Asian Games (although none at the 2004 Athens Olympics – apart from a single silver in the double-trap shooting).

Football (soccer) has similarly large fan base, with a keenly contested national championship. The best teams are based in Kolkata (Calcutta), but Goa and Kerala are two of the areas with most interest in the world's favourite sport after that.

Tennis in India has always been a sport for the middle-classes and is increasing in popularity as that class expands. The country boasts a player or two of world-class standing, such as the duo of Bhupati and Paes, who briefly achieved a world number-one ranking in mens' doubles in 1999.

Among the contact sports unique to India, **kushti**, a form of Indian wrestling, has a small but dedicated following and is a favourite of devotees of the monkey god, Hanuman. However, the most dramatic and ferocious of all is the popular Keralan martial art of **kalarippayat** (see p.351), which involves both hand-to-hand combat and the use of weapons. **Kabadi**, where two teams of seven try to "tag" each other in an enclosed court, to continuous cries of "kabadikabadikabadi", is another traditional Indian pastime. Although still an amateur sport, kabadi is taken very seriously, with state and national championships and a slot in the Asian Games – however, it's not as popular in South India as it is further north.

Trekking

Although there are far more **trekking** possibilities in the mountainous north, low-level treks are available in the Western Ghats and Nilgiri Hills, which most people should have no trouble with. It isn't necessary to have any specialized gear for such low altitudes but it is a good idea to have the following equipment: clothes to wear in layers, sturdy shoes or boots, a waterproof jacket, backpack, compass and map, pocket knife, sleeping bag, sunblock, toiletries and toilet paper, torch, water bottle, basic medical kit and some emergency provisions. It's usually best to take a guide if you are planning to get off the beaten track. Suggestions on specific routes are given in the relevant chapters.

Scuba diving and snorkelling

Served by well-equipped and reputable diving centres, the Andaman islands and Lakshadweep offer world-class **scuba diving** on a par with just about anything in Asia. Don't come here expecting rock-bottom prices though. Compared with Thailand, India's dive schools are pricey, typically charging around Rs15,000 ($350) for a four-day PADI-approved open-water course.

For independent travellers, the most promising destination for both scuba diving and **snorkelling** is the **Andaman islands**, an isolated archipelago ringed by gigantic coral reefs whose crystal-clear waters are teeming with tropical fish and other marine life. Given the prohibitively high cost of diving courses, most visitors stick to snorkelling, but if you already have your PADI permit, it's well worth renting equipment from one of the two dive schools in the islands (see p.624). If you want to do an open-water course, book ahead as places can be in short supply during the peak season, between December and February.

The other group of Indian islands surrounded by clear seas and abundant marine life is **Lakshadweep**, a classic coconut-palm-covered atoll, some 400km west of Kerala in the Arabian Sea. The shallow lagoons, extensive coral reefs and exceptionally good visibility make this a perfect option for both first-timers and more experienced divers. The catch is that permit restrictions mean foreigners are only allowed to visit one island, Bangaram, where accommodation is confined to a single, phenomenally expensive five-star resort. There's no way around this problem as you have to have pre-booked a room in the hotel in order to procure the necessary permit.

For anyone on a limited budget, a better option is **Goa**. Visibility is not so great along this stretch of coast, but you can escape the worst of the silt by heading further out to sea by boat, where a handful of islands and two wrecks shelter prolific marine life. Most of the dive sites are shallow (between 10m and 20m), and thus ideal for beginners.

As with other countries, qualified divers should take their current certification card and/or log book; if you haven't used it for one year or more, you may have to take a short test costing around Rs300 ($7).

Yoga, meditation and ashrams

Of all India's exports, the ancient techniques of yoga and meditation, refined over more than two thousand years and still widely practised as part of everyday religious life in the subcontinent, have arguably been the most influential. The source of many Western stereotypes about the "mystic east", they have also ensured a steady supply of spiritual questers over the centuries – particularly since Allen Ginsberg's drug-fuelled visions in Varanasi and the Beatles' much-publicized sojourn with Maharishi Yogi in Rishikesh.

The West's long-standing obsession with Indian gurus and godmen doubtless says more about the shortcomings of occidental culture than the essence of the subcontinent, but modern India remains – despite the rampant materialism that has taken hold in the late twentieth century – a land of countless living saints, wandering *sadhus* and *yogis* with mysterious powers. This is particularly true of the south, which, even more than the famous religious sites of the Ganges plains, has always attracted foreigners seeking spiritual nourishment. While you may not be tempted to don saffron and disappear into the forest for a decade, a short spell in an ashram learning yoga and meditation can, if nothing else, be an ideal antidote to the chaos and pollution of the southern cities, or the overt hedonism of beach life.

Yoga is taught virtually everywhere in the South and, in addition, there are several internationally known yoga centres where you can train to become a teacher. **Meditation** is similarly practised all over the region and specific courses are available in temples, meditation centres and monasteries. South India also has innumerable **ashrams** — communities where people work, live and study together, drawn by a common (usually spiritual) goal. The most established of these is the Sri Aurobindo Ashram in Pondicherry, but there are dozens of others dotted around the southern states, from the headquarters of India's most famous living holy man, Sai Baba, in Andhra Pradesh, to the home of the celebrated "Hugging Guru", Amritanandamayi, in the backwaters of Kerala.

Details of yoga and meditation courses and ashrams are provided throughout the Guide section of the book. Most centres offer courses that you can enrol on at short notice; however, many of the more popular ones listed below need to be booked well in advance.

Yoga

The word **"yoga"** literally means "to unite" and the aim of the discipline is to help the practitioner unite his or her individual consciousness with the Divine. This is achieved by raising awareness of one's self through spiritual, mental and physical discipline. *Hatha* yoga is based on physical postures called *asanas*, and although the most popular form in the West, it is traditionally just the first step leading on to more subtle stages of meditation which commence when the energies of the body have been awakened and sensitized by stretching and relaxing. Other forms of yoga include *raja* yoga, which includes moral discipline, and *bhakti* yoga, the yoga of devotion, which entails a commitment to one's guru or teacher. Traditional centres for yoga in the South include Mysore, in Karnataka (see p.84) and Tiruvanammalai in Tamil Nadu (see p.84), but numerous institutions throughout the region have good teachers and advanced practitioners. In many of the travellers' haunts, such as Goa and Kovalam, posters in cafés advertise local teachers.

Meditation

Meditation is often practised after a session of yoga, when the energy of the body has been awakened, and is an essential part of Hindu and Buddhist practices. It is considered the most powerful tool for understanding the true nature of mind and self, an essential step on the path to enlighten-ment. **Vipassana** meditation is a technique originally taught by the Buddha, whereby practitioners learn to become more aware of physical sensations and mental processes. Courses last for a minimum of ten days and are austere, involving 4am kick-offs, around ten hours of meditation a day, no solid food after noon, segregation of the sexes and no talking for the duration (except with the leaders of the course). Courses are free for all first-time students to allow everyone an opportunity to learn and benefit from the technique. Vipassana is taught in more than 25 centres throughout India including ones in Bangalore, Chennai and Hyderabad.

Courses and ashrams

Ashrams range in size from several thou-sand people to just a handful, and their rules, regulations and restrictions vary enor-mously. While some offer on-site accom-modation, charge Western prices and have set programmes, others will require you to stay in the nearest town or village, operate through donations and only offer guidance and teaching as and when requested.

The following well-known establishments routinely welcome foreign visitors:

Astanga Yoga Nilayam 235 8th Cross, 3rd stage, Gokulam, Mysore 570002, Karnataka ⓦwww.ayri .org. Run by Pattabhi Jois, one of India's great yoga innovators. Courses in dynamic yoga affiliated with martial arts last at least a month and need to be booked in advance.

Osho Commune International 17 Koregaon Park, Pune, Maharashtra 411001 ⓣ020/612 6655, ⓦwww.osho.com. Established by the enigmatic Osho, who generated a huge following of both Western and Indian devotees, this centre is set in 31 acres of beautifully landscaped gardens and offers a variety of courses in personal therapy, healing and meditation. For full details, see p.159. There are numerous other Indian and international centres dedicated to Osho's teachings.

Prasanthi Nilayam Puttaparthy, Andhra Pradesh ⓣ08555/87236, ⓦwww.saionline.org. The ashram of Satya Sai Baba, one of India's most revered and popular gurus, who has a worldwide following of millions despite the deaths of four followers at the ashram in mysterious circumstances in 2000. The ashram is four or five hours by bus from Bangalore and visitors sometimes comment on the strict security staffing and rigid rules and regulations. Cheap accommodation is available in dormitories or "flats" for four people. There is no need to book in advance though you should phone to check availability; see p.604 for more details. Sai Baba also has a smaller ashram in Bangalore and one in Kodaikanal.

Saccidananda Ashram Thanneepalli, Kullithalai, near Tiruchirapalli, Tamil Nadu ⓣ04323/22260, ⓦwww.bedegriffiths.com. Also known as Shantivanam (meaning Peace Forest in Sanskrit), the ashram is situated on the banks of the sacred River Cauvery. Founded by Father Bede Griffiths, a visionary Benedictine monk, it presents a curious but sympathetic fusion of Christianity and Hinduism. Visitors can join in the services and rituals or just relax here. Accommodation is in simple huts dotted around the grounds and meals are communal. Very busy during the major Christian festivals.

Sivananda Yoga Vedanta Dhanwanthari Ashram PO Neyyar Dam, Thiruvananthapuram Dist, Kerala 695576 ⓣ0471/273493, ⓦwww .sivananda.org. An offshoot of the original Divine Life Society, a yoga-based ashram where yoga postures (*asanas*), breathing techniques (*pranayama*) and meditation are taught. They also run teacher-training programmes.

Vipassana International Academy The Vipassana movement (ⓦwww.dhamma.org) has three regional centres in South India: Dhamma Khetta, Nagarjan Sagar Rd, Kusum Nagar Vanasthali Puram, Hyderabad 500070, Andhra Pradesh ⓣ040/402 0290; 73 Netaji Subhashchandra Bose Rd, Sowcarpet, Chennai 600079, Tamil Nadu ⓣ044/2535 8316; Bangalore Vipassana Centre, Dhamma Sumana, c/o Bharat Silks, no. 185, 1st floor, 4th Cross, Lalbagh Rd, Bangalore 560027 Karnataka ⓣ080/2222 4330.

Crime and personal safety

In spite of the crushing poverty and the yawning gulf between rich and poor, India is on the whole a very safe country in which to travel. As a tourist, however, you are an obvious target for the tiny number of thieves (who may include some of your fellow travellers). Given that you stand to face serious problems if you do lose your passport, money and ticket home, common sense suggests a few precautions.

If you can tolerate the encumbrance, carry valuables in a money belt or in a pouch around your neck at all times. In the latter case, the cord should be hidden under your clothing and not be easy to cut through (a metal guitar string is good). Beware of **crowded locations**, such as packed buses or trains, in which it is easy for pickpockets to operate – slashing pockets or bags with razor blades is not unheard of in certain locations – and don't leave valuables unattended on the beach when you go for a swim. Backpacks in dormitory accommodation are also obvious targets.

Budget travellers would do well to carry a **padlock**, as these are usually used to secure the doors of cheap hotel rooms and it's reassuring to know you have the only key; strong combination locks are ideal. You can also lock your bag to seats or racks in trains, for which a length of chain also comes in useful. Don't put valuables in your luggage for bus or plane journeys: keep them with you at all times. If your baggage is on the roof of a bus, make sure it is well secured. On trains and buses, the prime time for theft is just before you leave, so keep a particular eye on your gear then, beware of deliberate diversions and don't put your belongings next to open windows. Remember that routes popular with tourists tend to be popular with thieves too.

However, don't get paranoid. Crime levels in India are a long way below those of Western countries, and violent crime against tourists is extremely rare. Virtually none of the people who approach you on the street intend any harm: most want to sell you something (though this is not always made apparent immediately), some want to

practise their English, others (if you're a woman) to chat you up, while more than a few just want your address in their book or a snap taken with you. Anyone offering wonderful-sounding money-making schemes, however, is almost certain to be a con artist.

Be wary of **credit-card fraud**; a credit card can be used to make duplicate forms to which your account is then billed for fictitious transactions, so don't let shops or restaurants take your card away to process – insist they do it in front of you. Even **monkeys** rate a mention here: it is not unknown for them to steal things from hotel rooms with open windows or even to snatch bags from unsuspecting shoulders. It's not a bad idea to keep US$100 or so separately from the rest of your money, along with your travellers' cheque receipts, insurance policy number and phone number for claims and a photocopy of the pages in your passport containing personal data and your Indian visa. This will cover you in case you do lose all your valuables.

If the worst happens and you get robbed, the first thing to do is **report the theft** as soon as possible to the local police. They are very unlikely to recover your belongings, but you need a report from them in order to claim on your travel insurance. Dress smartly and expect an uphill battle; city cops in particular tend to be jaded from too many insurance and travellers' cheque scams.

Losing your passport is a real hassle, but does not necessarily mean the end of your trip. First, report the loss immediately to the police, who will issue you with the all-important "complaint form" you'll need to travel around and check into hotels, as well as claim back any expenses incurred in replacing your passport from your insurer. A complaint form, however, will not allow you to change money or travellers' cheques. If you've run out of cash, your best bet is to ask your hotel manager to help you out (staff will have seen your passport when you checked in, and the number will be in the register, and you should be able to exchange travellers' cheques on the strength of it). The next thing to do is telephone your nearest embassy or consulate in India (see pp.34–35). Normally, passports have to be applied for and collected in person, but if you are stranded, it is usually possible to arrange to receive the necessary forms in the post. However, you still have to go to the embassy or consulate to pick it up. "Emergency passports" are the cheapest form of replacement, but are normally only valid for the few days of your return flight. If you're not sure when you're leaving India, you'll have to obtain a more costly "full passport"; these can only be issued by embassies and larger consulates in Mumbai, and not those in Chennai or Panjim.

Cultural hints and etiquette

Cultural differences extend to all sorts of little things, and while allowances will usually be made for foreigners, visitors unacquainted with Indian customs may need a little preparation to avoid causing offence or making fools of themselves. The list of dos and don'ts here is hardly exhaustive: when in doubt, watch what the Indian people around you are doing.

Eating and the right-hand rule

The biggest minefield of potential faux pas has to do with **eating**. This is usually done with the fingers, and requires practice to get absolutely right. Rule one is: eat with your **right hand only**. In India, as right across Asia, the left hand is for wiping your bottom, cleaning your feet and other unsavoury functions (you also put on and take off your shoes with your left hand), while the right hand is for eating, shaking hands, and so on.

Quite how rigid individuals are about this tends to vary, with brahmins and southerners likely to be the strictest. While you can hold a cup or utensil in your left hand, and you can usually get away with using it to help tear your chapati, you should not eat, pass food or wipe your mouth with your left hand. The best thing is to keep it out of sight below the table.

This rule extends beyond food. In general, do not pass anything to anyone with your left hand or point at anyone with it either, and Indians definitely won't be impressed if you put it in your mouth. In general, you should accept things given to you with your right hand – though using both hands is a sign of respect.

The other rule to beware of when eating or drinking is that your lips should not touch other people's food – *jhutha* or sullied food is strictly taboo. Don't, for example, take a bite out of a chapati and pass it on. When drinking out of a cup or bottle to be shared with others, don't let it touch your lips, but rather pour it directly into your mouth. This custom also protects you from things like hepatitis. It is customary to wash your hands before and after eating.

Temples and religion

Religion is taken very seriously in South India; it's important always to show due respect to religious buildings, shrines, images and people at prayer. When entering a temple or mosque, remove your shoes and leave them at the door (socks are acceptable and protect your feet from burning-hot, stony ground). Some temples – Jain ones in particular – do not allow you to enter wearing or carrying leather articles and forbid entry to menstruating women. **Dress conservatively** (see below), and try not to be obtrusive; cover your head with a cap or cloth when entering a *dargah* (Sufi shrine) or Sikh *gurudwara*. At a mosque, you'll not normally be allowed in at prayer time and women are sometimes not let in at all. In a Hindu temple, you are often not allowed into the inner sanctum. At a Buddhist stupa or monument, you should always walk round clockwise (with the stupa on your right). Hindus are very superstitious about taking **photographs** of images of deities and inside temples; if in doubt, resist. Do not take photos of funerals or cremations.

Dress

Indian people are very conservative about **dress**. Women are expected to dress modestly, with legs and shoulders covered. Trousers are acceptable, but shorts and short skirts are offensive to many. Men should not walk around bare-chested and should avoid wearing shorts (a sign of low caste), except around the obvious beach resorts. These rules are doubly important in temples and mosques.

Never mind sky-clad Jains or *naga sadhus*, **nudity** is not acceptable in India. The mild-mannered people of Goa may not say anything about nude bathing (though it is in theory prohibited), but you can be sure they don't like it.

In general, Indians find it hard to understand why rich Western sahibs should wander round in ragged clothes or imitate the lowest ranks of Indian society, who would love to have something more decent to wear. Staying well groomed and dressing "respectably" vastly improves the impression you make on local people, and reduces sexual harassment too.

Other possible gaffes

Kissing and **embracing** are regarded in India as part of sex: do not do them in public. It is not even a good idea for couples to hold hands, though Indian men can sometimes be seen holding hands as a sign of "brotherliness". Be aware of your feet. When entering a private home, you should normally remove your shoes (follow your host's example); when sitting, avoid pointing the soles of your feet at anyone. Accidental contact with someone's foot is always followed by an apology.

Indian English can be very formal and even ceremonious. Indian people may well call you "sir" or "madam", even "good lady" or "kind sir". At the same time, you should be aware that your English may seem rude to them. In particular, **swearing** is taken rather seriously in India, and casual use of the F-word is likely to shock.

Meeting people

Westerners have an ambiguous status in Indian eyes. In one way, you represent the rich sahib, whose culture dominates the world, so the old colonial mentality has not completely disappeared. On the other hand, as a non-Hindu, you are an outcaste, your presence in theory polluting to an orthodox or high-caste Hindu, while to members of all religions, your morals and your standards of spiritual and physical cleanliness are suspect. Even if you are of Indian origin, you may be considered to suffer from Western corruption, and people may test you out on that score.

As a traveller, you will constantly come across people who want to strike up a **conversation**. English not being their first language, they may not be familiar with the conventional ways of doing this, and thus their opening line may seem abrupt if at the same time very formal. "Excuse me gentleman, what is your mother country?" is a typical one. It is also the first in a series of questions for asking Western tourists that Indian men seem sometimes to have learnt from a single book. Some of the questions may baffle at first – "What is your qualification?" "Are you in service?" – some may be queries about the ways of the West or the purpose of your trip, but mostly they will be about your family and your job.

You may find it bewildering or even intrusive that complete strangers should want to know that sort of thing, but these subjects are considered polite conversation between strangers in India and help people place one another in terms of social position. Your family, job, even income, are not considered "personal" subjects in India, and it is completely normal to ask people about them. Asking the same questions back will not be taken amiss – far from it. Being curious does not have the "nosy" stigma in India that it has in the West.

Things that Indian people are likely to find strange about you are: lack of religion (you could adopt one), travelling alone, leaving your family to come to India, being an unmarried couple (letting people think you are married

can make life easier) and travelling second class or staying in cheap hotels when, as a tourist, you are relatively rich. You will probably end up having to explain the same things many times to many different people; on the other hand, you can ask questions too, so you could take it as an opportunity to ask things you want to know about India. English-speaking Indians, and members of the large and growing middle class in particular, are usually extremely well informed and well educated and often far more *au fait* with world affairs than Westerners, so you may be drawn into conversations in which you find yourself way out of your depth.

Shopping

So many beautiful and exotic souvenirs are on sale in South India, at such low prices, that it's sometimes hard to know what to buy first. On top of that, all sorts of things (such as made-to-measure clothes) that would be vastly expensive at home are much more reasonably priced. Even if you lose weight during your trip, your baggage might well put on quite a bit – unless of course you post some of it home.

Where to shop

Quite a few items sold in tourist areas are made elsewhere and, needless to say, it's more fun (and cheaper) to pick them up at source. The best local buys are noted in the relevant sections of the guide, along with a few specialities that can't be found outside their regions. South India is awash with street and beach **hawkers**, often very young kids. Although they can be annoying and should be dealt with firmly if you are not interested, do not write them off completely as they sometimes have decent souvenirs at lower than shop prices and are open to hard bargaining.

Virtually all the state governments in India run handicraft "**emporia**". There is also an exceptionally well-stocked Central Cottage Industries Emporium in Mumbai. Goods in these places are generally of a high quality, even if their fixed prices are a little expensive,

and they are worth a visit to get an idea of what crafts are available and how much they should cost.

Other famous places to shop in South India include the weekly flea market in **Anjuna**, Goa, where goods from all over the country are sold alongside the latest fluoro rave gear and techno tapes, and **Kovalam**, in southern Kerala, where vendors import handicrafts from northern states such as Rajasthan and Gujarat. For sheer variety, however, **Mumbai** is hard to beat. With its tourist-oriented streetside boutiques, swish CD and fashion shops, antique markets and huge *khadi* store, this is the perfect place to stock up on souvenirs before you leave.

Bargaining

Whatever you buy (except food, household items and cigarettes), you will almost always be expected to **haggle** over the price. Bargaining is very much a matter of personal style, but should always be light-hearted, never acrimonious. There are no hard and fast rules – it's really a question of how much something is worth to you. It's a good plan, however, to have an idea of how much you want, or ought, to pay. "Green" tourists are easily spotted, so try and look as if you know what you are up to, even on your first day, or leave it till later.

Don't worry too much about initial prices. Some guidebooks suggest paying a third of the opening price, but it's a flexible guideline depending on the shop, the goods and the shopkeeper's impression of you. You may not be able to get the seller much below the first quote; on the other hand, you may end up paying as little as a tenth of it. If you bid too low, you may be hustled out of the shop for offering an "insulting" price, but this is all part of the game, and you'll no doubt be welcomed as an old friend if you return the next day.

Don't start haggling for something if you know you don't want it, and never let any figure pass your lips that you are not prepared to pay. It's like bidding at an auction. Having mentioned a price, you are obliged to pay it. If the seller asks you how much you would pay for something, and you don't want it, say so.

Metalware and jewellery

South Indian artisans have been casting **bronze statues** of Hindu deities for over two thousand years – notably in the Kaveri (Cauvery) Delta of Tamil Nadu, where the Chola dynasty took the form to heights never since surpassed. Traditionally, bronzes were commissioned by wealthy temples, but today the casters are kept busy by demand from rich NRIs (Non-Resident Indians) and tourists who can afford to pay the huge sums for these striking metal icons. The images are produced by the "lost-wax" process, used since medieval times, in which a model is first carved out of beeswax, then surrounded in clay, and finally fired. The wax melts to leave a terracotta mould. Top quality images will have finely detailed fingers and eyes, and the metal should not have pits or spots. Still the best place to watch bronze casters

in action is the village of **Swamimalai**, near Kumbakonam in Tamil Nadu (see p.514), where showrooms display awesome dancing Shivas and other Chola-style bronzes. Some Chola bronzes are priceless, such as those in the temples of Tamil Nadu, but affordable miniatures are available direct from the artisans. For more on Chola bronzes, see p.689.

Brass and **copperware** can be exquisitely worked, with trays, plates, ashtrays, cups and bowls among the products available. **Bidri** work (see box on p.333), named after Bidar (Karnataka), where it originated, is a method of inlaying a gunmetal alloy with fine designs in brass or silver, then blackening the gunmetal with sal ammoniac, to leave the inlay work shining. *Bidri* jewellery boxes, dishes, bracelets and hookah pipes, among other things, are widely sold, particularly in Karnataka and Andhra Pradesh. **Stainless steel** is less decorative and more workaday: *thali* sets, tiffin and spice tins are all possible buys, available throughout the region.

Among precious metals, silver is generally a better buy than **gold**. The latter is usually 22 carat and very yellow, but relatively expensive due to taxes; added to this is its investment value – women traditionally keep their wealth in this form, and a bride's jewellery is an important part of her dowry. **Silver** varies in quality, but is usually reasonably priced, with silver jewellery generally heavier and rather more folksy than gold. Gold and silver are usually sold by weight, the workmanship costing very little. While silversmiths are ubiquitous in South India, goldsmiths are thinner on the ground, with the largest single concentration around the Kapalishvara temple in the Mylapore district of Chennai (see p.459) and in Kozikhode in northern Kerala. Mylapore is also a prime place to spot the gaudy but distinctively Tamil **dance jewellery** worn by Bharat Natyam performers. Made from gold-coated silver, studded with artificial rubies, the most striking items are the headpiece, or *thalasaman*, the *adigay*, a long chain worn around the neck with a large floral or peacock-shaped pendant known as a *padakkam*, and the heavy ornamental belt, or *odyanan*.

Gemstones can be something of a minefield; scams abound, and you would be most unwise even to consider buying gems for resale or as an investment without a basic knowledge of the trade. That said, some precious and semi-precious stones can be a good buy in India, particularly those which are indigenous, such as garnets, black stars and moonstones.

Woodwork and stone carving

Ornate carvings of gods and goddesses are a speciality of Mysore, where members of the *gudigar* caste work with fragrant **sandalwood**, their preferred medium for a thousand years or more. At one time, deities could only be carved from this rare wood, but dwindling forests have forced the price up, and these days fake sandalwood – cheaper soft wood that's been rubbed with essential oil – is almost as common as the real thing. In Kerala, deep-red **rosewood**, inlaid with lighter coloured woods to create geometric patterns, is used for carving elephants and heavy furniture, samples of which are to be found at most state-run emporia. For more authentic Kathakali masks and old wooden jewellery boxes, however, the bric-a-brac and antiques market in the former Jewish quarter of Kochi (Fort Cochin) is the best place to look. Embossed with brass, these traditionally contained a woman's dowry goods. Metal trunks have largely superseded them, but Keralan cabinet-makers still turn out reproductions for the tourist market.

The fishing village of Mamallapuram, just south of Chennai, is renowned as India's **stone-carving** capital. Countless workshops line its sandy lanes, and the sound of chisels chipping granite is a constant refrain from dawn until well into the night. Pieces range from larger-than-life-size icons for temples to pocket-size gods sold to the many tourists who pour through every day. Whatever their size, though, the figures are always precisely carved according to measurements meticulously set out in ancient canonical texts, which explains why little innovation has taken place over the centuries. The only recent developments in Mamallapuram's stone carving has been in the design of *chillums*, and small pendants, bought wholesale for the summer festival hippy market back in Europe.

Textiles and clothing

Textiles are so much a part of Indian culture that Gandhi wanted a spinning wheel put on the flag. The kind of cloth he had in mind was the plain white homespun material worn by Nehru, whose style of hat, jacket and *dhoti* are still worn by many politicians to this day to demonstrate their affinity with "the common man". Homespun, handloom-woven, hand-printed cloth is called **khadi**, and is sold all over India in government shops called Khadi Gramodyog. Methods of dying and printing this and other cloth vary from the tie-dying (*bandhini*) of Rajasthan to block printing and screen printing of calico (from Calicut – now Kozhikode, Kerala), cotton and silk.

Saris are normally made of cotton for everyday use, although **silk** is used for special occasions (worn more frequently throughout the south). Western women are notoriously inept at wearing this most elegant of garments – it takes years of practice to carry one off properly – but silk is usually a good buy in India, provided you're sure it is the real thing. The best silk in India comes from **Kanchipuram** (see p.485), in northern Tamil Nadu, whose hallmarks are contrasting borders (known as Ganga–Jamuna borders after India's two most sacred rivers) and ornate designs featuring *gopurams* (temple gate towers). Kanchi's weavers are also famous for **brocade** – top-quality silk hand-woven with expensive gold or silver thread.

In Andhra Pradesh, cloth is more likely to be patterned using the **ikat** technique, where yarn is resist- or tie-dyed before being woven. The geometric images of flowers, animals and birds that result have attractive blurred, or "flame", edges that conjure up Southeast Asia, to where *ikat* was exported in the medieval era.

Less expensive cloth to look out for, especially in Goa, includes that touted by the **Lamanis** – the semi-nomadic low-caste minority from northern Karnataka who traditionally lived by transporting salt across the Deccan Plateau. These days, the women and girls make most of the family money through the sale of textiles carefully tailored for the tourist trade. Their rainbow cloth, woven with geometric designs and inlaid with cowrie shells or fragments of mirror and mica, is fashioned into shoulder bags, caps and money belts. If you haggle hard and can put up with all the shouting and tugging that inevitably accompanies each purchase, you can usually pick stuff up at bargain prices.

From Tamil Nadu, an authentic souvenir to take home is the kind of **Madras-check lunghis** worn by most of the men (at least in the countryside); Keralans tend to prefer jazzier varieties, with day-glo colours rendered on polyester. Particularly beautiful and high-quality **lunghis** of creamy cotton or **calico** are to be found in **Kozhikode**, Kerala (see p.429). Indeed the town's former name of Calicut came about because of its trade in the material. For women, **salwar kamise**, the elegant pyjama suits worn by Muslims, unmarried girls and middle-class students, make ideal travel outfits, although in the sticky heat of the far south you may find them too heavy. Long loose shirts – preferably made of khadi and known as *kurta* or *panjabi* – are more practical. Tourist shops sell versions in various fabrics and colours. Block-printed bedsheets, as well as being useful, make good wall-hangings. You will find every region has its own fabrics, its own methods of colouring them and making them up – the choice is endless.

On top of this, with **tailoring** so cheap in India, you can choose the fabric you want, take it to a tailor, and have it made into whatever you fancy. For formal Western-style clothes, you'll want to see quite a posh tailor in a big city, but tailors in almost every village in the country can run you up a shirt or a pair of pyjama-type trousers in next to no time. Many tailors will also copy a garment you already have.

Carpets and rugs

South India is generally less renowned for its **carpets** than the north, but the former Muslim kingdoms of the Deccan, notably around Eluru and Warangal in Andhra Pradesh, have retained weaving traditions dating from the seventeenth century, when Moghul artisans drifted south in the wake of their conquering armies. They brought with them techniques and designs from medieval Persia, and these still feature prominently in today's flat-weave durries. The colours tend to be pale pastels, with floral motifs overlaid on cameo backgrounds. In accordance with an old Persian tradition, each design is named after a patron of the weaving industry. The carpets themselves are hard to come by – they are only produced in small numbers by a few families – but you can usually track some down in the Muslim bazaars of Hyderabad.

A little visited spot which has a lively handloom and weaving industry is Tasara, near Kozhikode (Calicut) in Kerala (see p.431). There you can not only watch the artisans at work but actually design your own rug or wall-hanging and learn how to make it. For everyday domestic use, **rag rugs**, made from recycled clothing, are good buys. Available just about everywhere, they cost little enough in Europe and North America, but in India are fantastically cheap; many visitors buy large ones and post them home by surface mail.

Of course, you don't have to go all the way north to buy a **Kashmiri** rug or carpet. Many Kashmiris have set up shop in the main tourist centres of the south and you can find high-quality goods, though not all the dealers are known for their scruples and it is best to learn something about what you are trying to buy before you lay out a lot of cash. A pukka Kashmiri carpet should have a label on the back stating that it is made in Kashmir, what it is made of (wool, silk or "silk touch", the latter being wool combined with a little cotton and silk to give it a sheen), its size, density of knots per square inch (the more the better) and the name of the design. To tell if it really is silk, scrape the carpet with a knife and burn the fluff – real silk shrivels to nothing and has a distinctive smell. Even producing a knife should cause the seller of a bogus silk carpet to demur.

Paintings and antiques

The former Chola capital of Thanjavur (Tanjore), in the Kaveri (Cauvery) Delta area of Tamil Nadu, is famous throughout the south for its school of religious painting, which emerged in the nineteenth century under patronage from the local maharaja. "**Painting**" is actually something of a misnomer, as the images are partly raised in low plaster relief, and inlaid with precious stones, glass pieces, pearls, mica and ivory. The Tanjore school's preferred subject is Balakrishna (Krishna as a crawling baby stealing butter balls), and depictions of Vishnu's other incarnations. You'll come across these all over the region, but only in **Thanjavur** itself (see p.575) are you likely to see the artists in action. Prices range from Rs2000 to Rs200,000 depending on the size, the quality of the painting and the value of the inlays and gold leaf.

The villages of Machilipatnam and Kala-hasti, southeast of Vijayawada in Andhra Pradesh, are the source of a rare kind of devotional painting known as **Kalamkari**. Stylized images of deities and mythologi-cal scenes are outlined in black on lengths of thick cotton and coloured with beautiful natural dyes. Ochre, russet, blue-green, soot black and red are the predominant colours of the ornate hangings, which were tradition-ally produced for temples.

At the opposite end of the market, **leaf skeleton paintings** from southern Kerala are widely available in handicraft and souve-nir shops, though they too vary somewhat in quality.

When it comes to **antiques**, if they really are genuine – and, frankly, that is unlikely – you'll need a licence to export them, which is virtually impossible to get.

Toys and puppets

Wooden **toys** crop up in various craft villages around Andhra Pradesh, among them Kondapalli, near Vijayawada, and Ettikopakka in the Vishakapatnam district, where brightly coloured figures, thought to have originally been made for temple rituals, are produced on lathes. Sticks of lac dye (a kind of hard lacquer applied to turned wood in colour bands, and then polished) are used to decorate them; the heat generated by friction as the crayons are pressed against the revolving wood causes the pigment to melt. When this dries it forms a hard, bright shell. A similar technique has been refined in the village of Chennapatna, between Mysore and Bangalore in Karnataka, where artisans fashion toy replicas of buses, trains, planes and everyday household objects for children to play with.

Shadow puppets (*tolu bommalaatam* in Tamil) are another traditional South Indian way of amusing and instructing kids. Made of translucent leather, dyed and decorated with geometric perforations, they are manipulated with bamboo sticks by teams of puppet-eers seated behind a back-lit cloth screen – a technique that was exported by medieval Tamil traders and which has subsequently taken root in parts of Indonesia, including Bali. Music and percussion accompanies the performances of mythological epics such as the Ramayana and Mahabharata. Squeezed out by cinema, puppetry is sadly a dying art in South India these days, but you can still see performances at the Dakshina Chitra folk museum near Chennai (see p.484), while souvenir-sized shadow puppets are sold at most government emporia in Tamil Nadu.

Odds and sods

Of course, not everything typically Indian is old or traditional. **CDs and audio cassettes** of Hindustani classical, Carnatic, *Bhangra*, *filmi* and Western music are available in most major towns and cities for a fraction of what you'd pay back home. By far the best-stocked stores are in Mumbai, Bangalore and Chennai.

Books are also excellent buys in India, whether by Indian writers (see Contexts, p.718) or writers from the rest of the English-speaking world. Once again, they are usually much cheaper than at home, if not so well printed or bound. Hardback volumes of Indian sacred literature are particularly good value.

Bamboo flutes are incredibly cheap, while other **musical instruments** such as tabla, sitar and *sarod* are sold in music shops in the larger cities. The quality is crucial; there's no point going home with a sitar that is virtually untunable, even if it does look nice. Students of music purchase their instruments from master craftsmen or established shops. A good place to start looking is Chennai, where you can pick up quality Carnatic percussion instruments such as *mridangam*, the double-headed drum that gives South Indian music its distinctive rhythms; *vinas*, the southern cousin of the sitar; and *nadasvaram*, a kind of over-sized oboe used in temple rituals. For more on Carnatic music, see Contexts on p.703.

Other possible souvenirs include kitchen implements like tiffin boxes, wind-up clockwork tin toys, film posters, tea (especially Orange Pekoe from the plantations of the Nilgiri mountains), essential oils (such as eucalyptus, citronella or sandalwood) from Coonor in Tamil Nadu, spices and peacock feather fans (though these are considered unlucky).

Things not to bring home include ivory and anything made from a rare or protected species, including snakeskin and turtle products. As for drugs – don't even think about it.

Women travellers

South India doesn't offer any huge obstacles to women travellers – petty annoyances are more the order of the day. In the days of the Raj, upper-class eccentrics started a tradition of lone women travellers, taken up enthusiastically by the flower children of the hippy era. Women today still do it, and most come through the challenge perfectly unscathed. However, few women get through their trip without any hassle, and it's good to prepare yourself to be a little thick-skinned.

South Indian streets are almost without exception male-dominated – something that may take a bit of getting used to, particularly when you find yourself subjected to incessant **staring**. This can usually be stopped by ignoring the gaze and quickly moving on, or by firmly telling the offender to stop looking at you. Most of your fellow travellers on trains and buses will be men, and some may start up unwelcome conversations about sex, divorce and the freedom of relationships in the West. These cannot often be avoided, but demonstrating too much enthusiasm to discuss such topics can lure men into thinking that you are easy about sex, and the situation could become threatening. At its worst, in larger cities, all this can become very tiring. You can get round it to a certain extent by joining women in public places, and you'll notice an immense difference if you join up with a male travelling companion. In this case, however, expect Indian men to approach him (assumed, of course, to be your husband – an assumption it is sometimes advantageous to go along with – you could even consider wearing a wedding ring) and talk to him about you quite happily as if you were not there. Beware, however, if you are (or look) Indian with a non-Indian male companion: this may well cause you grief

and harassment, as you will be seen to have brought shame on your family by adopting the loose morals of the West.

In addition to staring and suggestive comments and looks, outright sexual harassment, or "**Eve teasing**" as it is bizarrely known, is likely to be a nuisance, but not generally a threat. Expect to get groped in crowds, and to have men "accidentally" squeeze past you at any opportunity. This tends to be worse in cities than in small towns and villages but, wherever you are, being followed can be a real problem.

In time you'll learn to gauge a situation – sometimes wandering around on your own may attract so much unwanted attention that you may prefer to stay in one place until you've recharged your batteries or your male fan club has moved on. It's always best to dress modestly whenever in public – a *salwar kamise* is perfect, or baggy clothing – and refrain from smoking and drinking in public, which only reinforces suspicions that Western women are "loose" and "easy".

Returning an unwanted touch with a punch or slap is perfectly in order (Indian women often become aggressive when offended), and does serve to vent a little frustration. It should also attract attention and urge someone to help you, or at least deal with the offending man – a man transgressing social norms is always out of line, and any passer-by will want to let him know it. If you feel someone getting too close in a crowd or on a bus, brandishing your left shoe in his face can be very effective.

Going to watch a Bollywood movie at the cinema is a fun and essential part of your trip to India, but unfortunately such an occasion is rarely without hassle. The crowd is predominantly male and mostly young at that. If you do go and see a film, go with a group of people and/or sit in the balcony area – it's a bit more expensive but the crowd is much more sedate up there.

Violent sexual assaults on tourists are extremely rare, but unfortunately the number of reported cases of rape is rising. Though no assault can be predicted, you can take **precautions**: at night avoid quiet, dimly lit streets and alleys; if you find a trustworthy rickshaw/taxi driver in the day keep him for the night journey; and try to get someone to accompany you to your hotel whenever possible. While Indian women are still quite timid about reporting rape – it is considered as much a disgrace to the victim as to the perpetrator – Western victims should always report it to the police, and before leaving the area try to let other tourists, or locals, know, in the hope that pressure from the community may uncover the offender and see him brought to justice. At present there's nowhere for tourists who've suffered sexual violence to go for sanctuary; most victims seek support from other travellers, or go home.

The **practicalities of travel** take on a new dimension for lone women travellers. Often you can turn your gender to your advantage. For example, on buses the driver and conductor will often take you under their wing, watch out for you and buy you chai at each stop, and there will be countless other instances of kindness wherever you travel. You'll also be more welcome in some private houses than a group of Western males, and may find yourself learning the finer points of Indian cooking round the family's clay stove. Women frequently get preference at bus and train stations where they can join a separate "ladies' queue", and use ladies' waiting rooms. On overnight trains you can aim for the enclosed ladies' compartments, which are peaceful havens – unless filled with noisy children – or share a berth section with a family so as to draw you into the security of the group, making you less exposed to lusty gazing. In hotels watch out for "peep-holes" in your door (and in the common bathrooms), be sure to cover your window when changing and when sleeping, and avoid the sleazy permit-room hotels of the southern cities.

Lastly, bring your own supply of tampons, not widely available outside Indian cities.

Womens' organizations in India

Forum against the Oppression of Women 29 Bhatia Bhawan, Babrekan Rd, Gokale Rd (North), Dadar, Mumbai 400028 ☎022/2422 2436. Support centre which also organizes workshops.

Streelekha (International Feminist Bookshop and Information Centre), 15/55, 1st floor, Cambridge, Jeevan Kendra Layout, Bangalore 560008, Karnataka. Stocks books, journals and posters, and provides space for women to meet.

Gay travellers

Homosexuality is not generally open or accepted in India, and "carnal intercourse against the order of nature" (anal intercourse) is a ten-year offence under article 377 of the penal code. Laws against "obscene behaviour" are used to arrest gay men for cruising or liaising anywhere that could be considered a public place. The same law could in theory be used against lesbians.

The homosexual scene in India was brought into the spotlight in 1998 with the nationwide screening of the highly controversial film *Fire* by Deepa Mehta, about two sisters-in-law living together under the same roof who become lesbian lovers. Flying in the face of the traditional emphasis on heterosexual family life, the film created a storm. Right-wing extremists attacked cinemas that showed it, and in the wake of the attacks, many gays and lesbians came out for the first time to hold candlelit protest vigils in Delhi, Mumbai, Kolkata (Calcutta), Chennai and Bangalore.

For **lesbians**, making contacts is rather difficult; even the Indian Women's Movement does not readily promote lesbianism as an issue that needs confronting. The only public faces of a hidden scene are the organizations listed below. Meeting places for **gay men** are marginally easier to find, with established gay bars cropping up in more Westernized cities such as Mumbai and Bangalore. Contact the organizations listed given below, and they will tell you about gay events and parties.

Gay contacts

Write in advance for information – most addresses are PO boxes:

Bombay Dost 105A Veena-Beena Shopping Centre, Bandra Station Rd, Bandra (West), Mumbai 400050, ⓦ www.bombaydost.com. Publishes a newsletter and has contacts nationwide.

Gay Bombay ⓦ www.gaybombay.org. Informal support, chat, background and guides to gay Mumbai.

Gay Info Centre c/o Owais, PO Box 1662, Secunderabad HPO 500003, Andhra Pradesh. Provides literature, contacts and resources on homosexuality in India.

Good As You 201 Samaraksha, 2nd Floor Royal Corner, 1–2 Lalbang Rd, Bangalore ☏ 080/547 5571, ⓦ www.geocities.com/goodasyoubangalore. Gay support group.

Humsafar Trust ⓦ www.humsafar.org. Website set up to promote safe sex among gay men, with lots of links and up-to-date information.

Saathi PO Box 571, Putlibowli PO, Hyderabad, Andhra Pradesh. Gay support group.

Disabled travellers

Disability is common in India, and many conditions that would be treatable in the West, such as cataracts, are permanent disabilities because people can't afford the treatment. Disabled people are unlikely to get jobs, and the choice is usually between staying at home being looked after by your family and going out on the street to beg for alms.

For the **disabled traveller**, this has its advantages: disability and disfigurement, for example, do not get the same embarrassed reaction from Indian people that they do from some able-bodied Westerners. On the other hand, you'll be lucky to see a state-of-the-art wheelchair or a loo for the disabled (major airports usually have both, though the loo may not be in a usable state), and the streets are full of all sorts of obstacles that would be hard for a blind or wheelchair-bound tourist to negotiate independently. Kerbs are often high, pavements uneven and littered, and ramps non-existent. There are potholes all over the place and open sewers. Some of the more expensive hotels have ramps for the movement of luggage and equipment, but if that makes them accessible to wheelchairs, it is by accident rather than design.

If you walk with difficulty, you will find street **obstacles** and steep stairs hard going. Another factor that can be a problem is the constant barrage of people proffering things at you (hard to wave aside if you are for instance on sticks or crutches), and all that queuing, not to mention heat, will take it out of you if you have a condition that makes you tire quickly. A light, folding camp-stool is one thing that could be invaluable if you have limited walking or standing power.

Then again, Indian people are likely to be very helpful if, for example, you need their help getting on and off buses or up stairs. Taxis and rickshaws are easily affordable and very adaptable; if you rent one for a day, the driver is certain to help you on and off, and perhaps even around the sites you visit. If you employ a guide, they may also be prepared to help you with steps and obstacles.

If complete independence is out of the question, going with an able-bodied companion might be on the cards. Contact one of the specialist organizations listed below for further advice on planning your trip. Otherwise, some package tour operators try to cater for travellers with disabilities – Bales and Somak among them – but you should always contact any operator and discuss your exact needs with them before making a booking. You should also make sure you are covered by any insurance policy you take out.

Contacts for disabled travellers

Britain and Ireland

Irish Wheelchair Association Blackheath Drive, Clontarf, Dublin 3 ☏01/818 6400, ⓦwww.iwa.ie. Useful information provided about travelling abroad with a wheelchair.

RADAR (Royal Association for Disability and Rehabilitation) 12 City Forum, 250 City Rd, London EC1V 8AF ☏020/7250 3222, minicom ☏020/7250 4119, ⓦwww.radar.org.uk. A good source of advice on holidays and travel.

Tripscope The Vassall Centre, Gill Ave, Bristol BS16 2QQ ☏0845/7758 5641 ⓦwww.tripscope.org.uk. This registered charity provides a national telephone information service offering free advice on UK and international transport for those with a mobility problem.

US and Canada

Access-Able ⓦwww.access-able.com. Online resource for travellers with disabilities.

Directions Unlimited 123 Green Lane, Bedford Hills, NY 10507 ☏1-800/533-5343 or 914/241-1700. Travel agency specializing in bookings for people with disabilities.

Mobility International USA 45 W Broadway, Eugene, OR 97401 ☏541/343-1284, ⓦwww.miusa.org. Information and referral services, access guides, tours and exchange programmes. Annual membership $35 (includes quarterly newsletter).

Society for the Advancement of Travelers with Handicaps (SATH) 347 5th Ave, New York, NY 10016 ☎ 212/447-7284, 🖳 www.sath.org. Non-profit educational organization that has actively represented travellers with disabilities since 1976.
Wheels Up! ☎ 1-888/38-WHEELS, 🖳 www .wheelsup.com. Provides discounted airfares, tour and cruise prices for disabled travellers, publishes a free monthly newsletter and has a comprehensive website.

Australia and New Zealand

ACROD (Australian Council for Rehabilitation of the Disabled) PO Box 60, Curtin ACT 2605; Suite 103, 1st floor, 1–5 Commercial Rd, Kings Grove 2208; ☎ 02/6282 4333, TTY ☎ 02/6282 4333, 🖳 www.acrod.org.au. Provides lists of travel agencies and tour operators for people with disabilities.

Disabled Persons Assembly 4/173–175 Victoria St, Wellington, New Zealand ☎ 04/801 9100 (also TTY), 🖳 www.dpa.org.nz. Resource centre with lists of travel agencies and tour operators for people with disabilities.

India

India Rehabilitation Co-ordination A–2 Rasadhara Co-operation Housing Society, 385 SVP Rd, Mumbai 400004 ☎ 040/2402 2143. Mumbai-based support group.
Timeless Excursions 9 Bhikaji Cama Place, New Delhi ☎ 011/2616 1198, 🖳 www .timelessexcursions.com. International tour operator that offers a 13-day wheelchair holiday from Delhi to Goa, via Agra, Jaipur and Mumbai.

Travelling with children

Travelling with kids can be both challenging and rewarding. Indians are very tolerant of children so you can take kids almost anywhere without restriction, and they always help break the ice with strangers.

The main problem with **children**, especially small ones, is their vulnerability. Even more than their parents, they need protecting from the sun, unsafe drinking water, heat and unfamiliar food. All that chilli in particular may be a problem, even with older kids, if they're not used to it. Remember too, that **diarrhoea**, perhaps just a nuisance to you, could be dangerous for a child: rehydration salts (see p.45) are vital if your child goes down with it. Make sure too, if possible, that your child is aware of the dangers of rabies; keep children away from **animals**, and consider a rabies jab. Advice on malaria is given on p.44.

For babies, **nappies** (**diapers**) and places to change them can be a problem. For a short visit, you could bring disposable ones with you; for longer journeys, consider going over to washables. A changing mat is another necessity, and if your baby is on powdered

milk, it might be an idea to bring some of that too; you can certainly get it in India, but it may not taste the same. Dried baby food could also be worth taking; mix it with hot (boiled) water – any café or chai-wallah should be able to supply you with some.

For touring, hiking or walking, **child-carrier backpacks** are ideal; they start at around £40 and can weigh less than 2kg. If the child is small enough, a fold-up buggy is also well worth packing – especially if they will sleep in it (while you have a meal or a drink). If you want to cut down on long journeys by flying, remember that under 2s travel for ten percent of the adult fare (or less in some cases), and under-12s for half price.

For a lively account of a successful trip to India with kids in tow, complete with advice on packing and other essentials, go to 🖳 travel.guardian.co.uk/activities/family /story/0,7447,511603,00.html.

Voluntary organizations

While in India, you may consider doing some voluntary charitable work. Several charities welcome volunteers on a medium-term commitment for a couple of months or so.

If you do want to spend your time working for an **NGO (Non-Government Organization)**, you should make arrangements well before you arrive by contacting the body in question, rather than on spec. Special visas are generally not required unless you intend to work for longer than six months.

Voluntary work resources

Charities Aid Foundation (CAF) Kings Hill, West Malling, Kent ME19 4TA, UK ☎01732/520000, ⓦ www.cafonline.org/cafindia/i_search.cfm. Can provide the contact details and aims of 2350 voluntary organizations in India.

India Development Information Network The British Council, 17 Kasturba Gandhi Marg, New Delhi 110001 ☎011/2371 1401, ⓦ www .indev.org. INDEV is another huge databank, accessed through their website, with over 1000 Indian NGOs.

Peace Corps of America ☎1-800/424 8580, ⓦ www.peacecorps.gov. The US-government sponsored aid and voluntary organization, with projects all over the world.

Voluntary Service Overseas (VSO) 317 Putney Bridge Rd, London SW15 2PN, UK ☎020/8780 7200, ⓦ www.vso.org.uk. A British government-funded organization that places volunteers on various projects around the world and in India.
Voluntary Service Overseas (VSO) ⓦ www .vsocanada.org. Canada 806-151 Slater Street, Ottawa, ON K1P 5H3 Canada ☎1-888-VSO-2911. Canadian-based organization affiliated to the British VSO.

Charities

Basic Needs India Trust 114 4th Cross OMBR Layout, Banaswadi, Bangalore 560043 ☎080/545 9235, ⓦ www.basicneeds.org.uk. Works with the mentally ill in their communities, reaching a large number of people in a way that conventional institutional-based care cannot.
Janodaya No.3 9th Cross, 5th Main, Jayamahal Extension, Bangalore 560046. Works with oppressed women in disadvantaged communities.
IRCDES PO 7, 6 Namakkal Ramalingam Street, Rajajipuram, Tiruvallur 602001. Organization set up to promote community-based rehabilitation among disabled children and adults in rural areas.

Directory

AIRPORT DEPARTURE TAX There is a standard departure tax of either Rs750 – for most international flights – or Rs210, for domestic flights and flights to Pakistan, Bangladesh, Nepal, Sri Lanka, Myanmar (Burma), the Maldives and Afghanistan. The tax is now included in the ticket price of all flights, wherever purchased, but there is no harm in double-checking that it has been covered when you reconfirm your flight. This tax also applies to international sea departures.

CIGARETTES Indian cigarettes, such as Wills, Gold Flake, Four Square and Charms, are OK once you get used to them, and hardly break the bank (Rs10–30 per pack), but if you find them too rough, stock up on imported brands such as Marlboro and Benson and Hedges, or some rolling tobacco, available in the bigger towns, cities and tourist resorts. One of the great smells of India is the *beedi*, the country's cheapest smoke, made of a single low-grade tobacco leaf. If you smoke roll-ups, stock up on good papers as Indian Capstan cigarette papers are thick and don't stick very well and Rizlas, where available, are pretty costly.

DUTY-FREE ALLOWANCE Anyone over 17 can bring in one US quart (0.95 litre – but nobody's going to quibble about the other 5ml) of spirits, or a bottle of wine and 250ml spirits; plus 200 cigarettes, or 50 cigars, or 250g tobacco. You may be required to register anything valuable on a Tourist Baggage Re-export Form to make sure you can take it home with you, and to fill in a currency declaration form if carrying more than US$10,000 or the equivalent.

ELECTRICITY Generally 220V 50Hz AC, though direct current supplies also exist, so check before plugging in. Most sockets are triple round-pin (accepting European-size double round-pin plugs). British, Irish and Australasian plugs will need an adaptor, preferably universal; American and Canadian appliances will need a transformer, too, unless multi-voltage. Power cuts and voltage variations are very common; voltage stabilizers should be used to run sensitive appliances such as laptops.

INITIALS AND ACRONYMS Widely used in Indian English. Thus, the former prime minister, Vishwanath Pratap Singh, was always "VP", and many middle-class Indian men bear similar monikers. Likewise, Andhra Pradesh (not Arunchal Pradesh) is AP and MG Road anywhere you go means Mahatma Gandhi Road. State and national or state organizations such as ITDC, KSTDC and so on are always known by their acronyms.

LAUNDRY In India, no one goes to self-service laundries: if they don't do their own, they send it out to a *dhobi*-wallah. Wherever you are staying, there will either be an in-house *dhobi*-wallah or one very close by to call on. The *dhobi*-wallah will take your dirty washing to a *dhobi ghat*, a public clothes-washing area (the bank of a river for example), where it is shown some old-fashioned discipline: separated, soaped and given a damn good thrashing to beat the dirt out of it. Then it's hung out to dry in the sun and, once dried, taken to the ironing sheds where every garment is endowed with razor-sharp creases and then matched to its rightful owner by hidden cryptic markings. Your clothes will come back from the *dhobi*-wallah absolutely spotless, though this kind of violent treatment does take it out of them: buttons get lost and eventually the cloth starts to fray. If you'd rather not entrust your Saville Row made-to-measure to their tender mercies, there are dry-cleaners in large towns.

NUMBERS A hundred thousand is a *lakh* (written 1,00,000); ten million is a *crore* (1,00,00,000). The words "million", and "billion" are not in common use.

OPENING HOURS Standard shop opening hours in India are Mon–Sat 9.30am–6pm. Most big stores, at any rate, keep those

Things to take

Most things are easy to find in India and cheaper than at home, but here is a list of useful items worth bringing with you:

- ☐ Padlock and chain (to lock rooms in budget hotels, and attach your bag to train fittings)
- ☐ Universal electric plug adapter and a universal sink plug (few sinks or bathtubs have them)
- ☐ Mosquito net
- ☐ Sheet sleeping bag (made by sewing up a sheet – so you don't have to worry about the state of the ones in your hotel room)
- ☐ Pillowcase
- ☐ Washing line
- ☐ Quick-dry towel
- ☐ Hat
- ☐ Small flashlight
- ☐ Earplugs (for street noise in hotel rooms and music on buses)
- ☐ High-factor sunblock
- ☐ Pocket alarm clock
- ☐ Inflatable neck-rest or pillow, to help you sleep on long journeys
- ☐ Multipurpose penknife
- ☐ Needle and some thread (but dental floss is better than cotton for holding baggage together)
- ☐ Plastic, or nylon, bags (to sort your baggage, make it easier to pack and unpack, and keep out damp and dust)
- ☐ Small umbrella (local ones tend not to retract)
- ☐ Tampons
- ☐ Condoms
- ☐ First-aid kit
- ☐ Multivitamin and mineral tablets

hours, while smaller shops vary from town to town, religion to religion and one to another, but usually keep longer hours. Government tourist offices are open in principle Mon–Fri 9.30am–5pm, Sat 9.30am–1pm, though these may vary slightly; state tourist offices are likely to be open Mon–Fri 10am–5pm, but sometimes operate much longer hours.

PHOTOGRAPHY Beware of pointing your camera at anything that might be considered "strategic", including airports, anything military and even bridges, train stations and main roads. Remember too that some people prefer not to be photographed, so it is wise to ask before you take a snapshot of them. More likely, you'll get people, especially kids, volunteering to pose. Camera film, sold at average Western prices, is widely

available in India (but check the date on the box, and note that false boxes containing outdated film are often sold – Konica have started painting holograms on their boxes to prevent this). It's fairly easy to get films developed, though they don't always come out as well as they might at home. Konica studios through South India have hi-tech equipment and process film in one hour (Rs200–250). If you're after slide film, buy it in the big cities, and don't expect to find specialist brands such as Velvia. Also, remember to guard your equipment from dust.

TIME India is all in one time zone: GMT+5hr 30min. This makes it 5hr 30min ahead of London, 10hr 30min ahead of New York, 13hr 30min ahead of LA, 4hr 30min behind Sydney and 6hr 30min behind NZ; however, summer time in those places will vary the difference by an hour.

TOILETS A visit to the loo is not alway one of India's more pleasant experiences: public toilets are often filthy and stink, particuarly those in bus and train stations. They are also major potential breeding grounds for disease. In addition, there is the squatting position to get used to, as the traditional Asian toilet has a hole in the ground, with two small platforms either side for feet instead of a seat. Indians use a jug of water and their left hand instead of paper, a method you may also come to prefer, but if you do use paper, keep some handy – it isn't usually supplied, and it might be an idea to stock up before going too far off the beaten track as it is not available everywhere.

Guide

Guide

1

Mumbai and southern Maharashtra

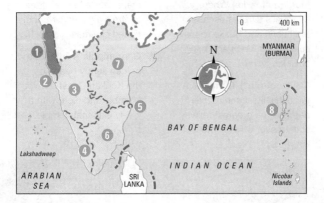

CHAPTER 1   # Highlights

* **The Gateway of India** The departure-point for the last British troops leaving India, now a favourite spot for an evening stroll. See p.121

* **Chhatrapati Shivaji Museum** A fine collection of priceless Indian art, from ancient temple sculpture to Moghul armour, displayed in splendid Raj-era surroundings. See p.123

* **Maidans (parks)** Where Mumbai's citizens escape the hustle and bustle to play cricket, eat lunch and hang out. See p.126

* **CS ("Victoria") Terminus** A fantastically eccentric pile, perhaps the greatest railway station ever built by the British. See p.128

* **The bazaars** A labyrinth of packed streets selling everything from gold wedding jewellery to junk left over from the Raj. See p.131

* **Elephanta Island** A magnificent rock-cut Shiva temple on an island in Mumbai harbour. See p.133

* **Bollywood blockbusters** Check out the latest Hindi mega movie in one of the city centre's gigantic air-conditioned cinemas. See p.139

* **Ganpatipule** A little-visited golden sandy beach on the Konkan Coast between Mumbai and Goa, with a lovely Ganapati temple. See p.152

△ Gateway of India

Mumbai and southern Maharashtra

E ver since the opening of the Suez Canal in 1869, the principal gate-way to the Indian subcontinent has been **MUMBAI (Bombay)**, the city Aldous Huxley famously described as "the most appalling . . . of either hemisphere". Travellers tend to regard time spent here as a rite of passage to be survived rather than savoured. But as the powerhouse of Indian business, industry and trade, and the source of its most seductive media images, the Maharashtran capital can be a compelling place to kill time. Whether or nor you find the experience enjoyable, however, will depend largely on how well you handle the heat, humidity, hassle, traffic fumes, relentless crowds and appalling poverty of India's most dynamic, westernized city.

First impressions of Mumbai tend to be dominated by its chronic **shortage of space**. Crammed onto a narrow spit of land that curls from the swamp-ridden coast into the Arabian Sea, the city has, in less than five hundred years since its "discovery" by the Portuguese, metamorphosed from an aboriginal fishing settlement into a sprawling megalopolis of over sixteen million people. Being swept along broad boulevards by endless streams of commuters, or jostled by coolies and hand-cart pullers in the teeming bazaars, you'll continually feel as if Mumbai is about to burst at the seams.

The roots of the population problem and attendant poverty lie, paradoxically, in the city's enduring ability to create **wealth**. Mumbai alone contributes one-third of the national tax revenue, its port handles half the country's foreign trade, its movie industry is the biggest in the world, while a massive $20bn development programme currently being implemented by the city authority (involving a slum clearance project which will render nearly half-a-million people homeless by 2010) should give it even more economic muscle. Symbols of this prosperity are everywhere – from the phalanx of office blocks clustered on Nariman Point, Maharashtra's Manhattan, to the expensively dressed teen-agers posing in Colaba's trendiest nightspots – while real estate prices are the eighth highest in the world.

The flip side to the success story is the city's much chronicled **poverty**. Each year, around 100,000 economic refugees pour into Mumbai from outside Maharashtra. Some find jobs and secure accommodation; many more end up living on the already overcrowded streets, or amid the squalor of Asia's largest

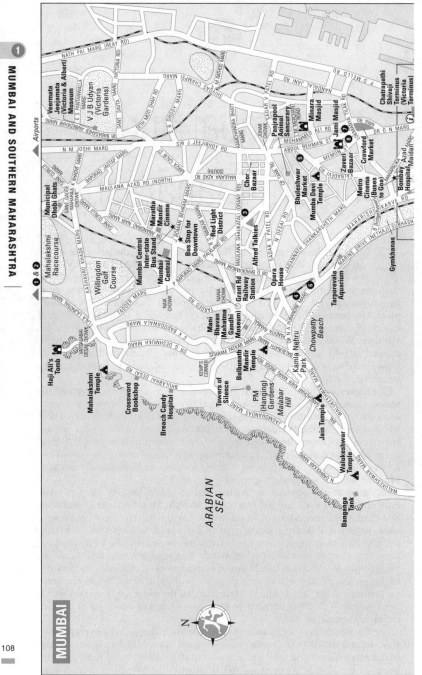

MUMBAI

Airports

❶ & ❷

Veermata Jeejamata (Victoria & Albert) Museum

V J B Udyan (Victoria Gardens)

Municipal Dhobi Ghats

Mahalakshmi Racecourse

Willingdon Golf Course

NATH PAI MARG (REAY RD)

N M JOSHI MARG

SIR J JEEJIBHOY RD

MAULANA AZAD RD (SOUTH)

MAULANA AZAD RD (NORTH)

Panjrapool Animal Sancurary

Minara Masjid

Jami Masjid ❼

Zaveri Bazaar ❽

Crawford Market

Chatrapathi Shivaji Terminus (Victoria Terminus)

Chor Bazaar

Bhuleshwar Market ❺

Mumba Devi Temple

Metro Cinema (Buses to Goa)

Bombay Azad Hospital Maidan

Maratha Mandir Cinema

Bus Stop for Downtown

Mumbai Central Inter-state Bus Stand

Mumbai Central

Red Light District

Alfred Talkies ❸

Opera House

Grant Rd Railway Station

❹

❻

Tarporevala Aquarium

Gymkhanas

Mahalakshmi Temple

Haji Ali's Tomb

Crossword Bookshop

Breach Candy Hospital

Mani Bhavan (Mahatma Gandhi) Museum

Bulbunath Mandir Temple

Towers of Silence

PM (Hanging) Gardens

Malabar Hill

Kamla Nehru Park

Chowpatty Beach

Jain Temple

Walukeshwar Temple

Banganga Tank

ARABIAN SEA

N

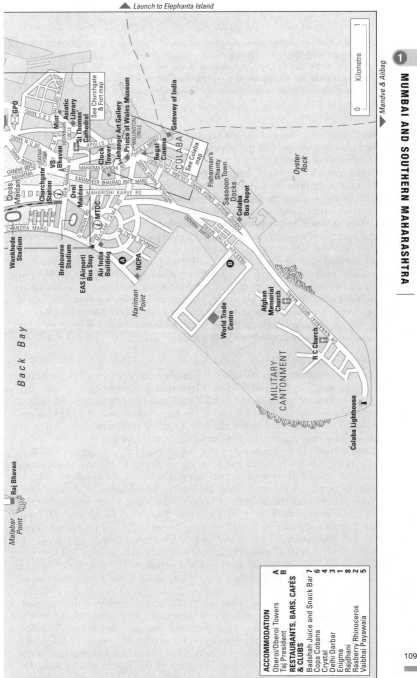

Launch to Elephanta Island

Mandve & Alibag

0   Kilometre   1

ACCOMMODATION
Oberoi/Oberoi Towers   A
Taj President   B
RESTAURANTS, BARS, CAFÉS & CLUBS
Badshah Juice and Snack Bar 7
Copa Cobana   6
Crystal   4
Delhi Darbar   3
Enigma   1
Rajdhani   8
Rasberry Rhinoceros   2
Vaibhai Payawaia   5

Back Bay

Malabar
Point

Raj Bhavan

Oyster
Rock

MILITARY
CANTONMENT

Wankhede
Stadium

Brabourne
Stadium

EAS (Airport)
Bus Stop

Air India
Building

NCPA

Nariman
Point

World Trade
Centre

Afghan
Memorial
Church

R C Church

Colaba Lighthouse

GPO

Mint
Asiatic
Library

St Thomas'
Cathedral

See Churchgate
& Fort map

VS?

Bhavan

Clock
Tower

Jehangir Art Gallery

Prince of Wales Museum

Gateway of India

Cross
Maidan

Churchgate
Station

Oval
Maidan

MTDC

Regal
Cinema

COLABA

See Colaba
map

Fisherman's
Shanty

Sassoon Town

Colaba
Docks

Colaba
Bus Depot

CHANDRA MARG

MAHARISHI KARVE RD

MAHATMA GANDHI RD

APOLLO ST.

WELLINGTON
CIRCLE

HORNIMAN
CIRCLE

109

Mumbai/Bombay

In 1996 Bombay was renamed **Mumbai**, as part of a wider policy instigated by the ultra-right-wing Shiv Sena Municipality to replace names of any places, roads and features in the city that had connotations of the Raj. Mumbai is the Marathi title of the local deity, the mouthless "Maha-amba-aiee" (Mumba for short), who is believed to have started her life as an obscure aboriginal earth goddess.

slums, reduced to rag-picking and begging from cars at traffic lights. It has been estimated that around half the population currently live in less than one-tenth of the city's total space.

However, while it would definitely be misleading to downplay its difficulties, Mumbai is far from the ordeal some travellers make it out to be. Once you've overcome the major hurdle of finding somewhere to stay, you may begin to enjoy its frenzied pace and crowded, cosmopolitan feel.

Many travellers bypass **southern Maharashtra** completely en route to Goa and points further south, but a number of places are worth a visit in their own right and certainly break up an otherwise tedious journey. On the coast two places stand out, the relaxed village of **Murud-Janjira**, with its impressive fort, and the pilgrimage temple and beach resort of **Ganpatipule**. The Western Ghats conceal the delights of wooded **Matheran**, the ancient cave temples around **Lonavala** and the pleasant hill station of **Mahabaleshwar**. The largest city in this region, most famous for the Osho International Meditation Resort, is the surprisingly absorbing **Pune**, while **Kolhapur** makes a good stop for those on their way to northern Karnataka.

Some history

Mumbai originally consisted of seven **islands**, inhabited by small Koli fishing communities. The town of Puri on **Elephanta** is thought to have been the major settlement in the region, until King Bimba, or Bhima, sited his capital at Mahim on one island, at the end of the thirteenth century. In 1534, Sultan Bahadur of Ahmedabad ceded the land to the **Portuguese**, who felt it to be of little importance, and concentrated development in the areas further north instead. They handed over the largest island to the English in 1661, as part of the dowry when the Portuguese infanta Catherine of Braganza married Charles II; four years later Charles received the remaining islands and the port, and the town took on the anglicized name of Bombay (the name derives from the Mumba Devi deity who resided here long before the Portuguese came and corrupted it to "Bom Bahia", or "Good Bay". This was the first part of India that could properly be termed a colony; elsewhere on the subcontinent the English had merely been granted the right to set up "factories", or trading posts. Because of its natural safe harbour and strategic position for commerce, the **East India Company**, based at Surat, wanted to buy the land; in 1668 a deal was struck, and Charles leased Mumbai to them for a pittance.

The English set about an ambitious programme of fortifying their outpost, living in the area known today as Fort. However, life was not easy. There was a fast turnover of governors, and malaria and cholera culled many of the first settlers. **Gerald Aungier**, the fourth governor (1672–77), began planning "the city which by God's assistance is intended to be built", and by the start of the eighteenth century the town was the capital of the East India Company. He is credited with encouraging the mix that still contributes to the city's success, welcoming Hindu traders from Gujarat, Goans, Muslim weavers and, most visibly, the business-minded Zoroastrian **Parsis**.

Much of the British settlement in the old Fort area was destroyed by a devastating fire in 1803. The arrival of the **Great Indian Peninsular Railway** half a century or so later improved communications, encouraging yet more immigration from elsewhere in India. This crucial artery, coupled with the cotton crisis in America following the Civil War, gave impetus to the great Bombay cotton boom and established the city as a major industrial and commercial centre. With the opening of the Suez Canal in 1869, and the construction of enormous docks, Bombay's access to European markets improved further. **Sir Bartle Frere**, governor from 1862 to 1867, oversaw the construction of the city's distinctive colonial-Gothic buildings; the most extravagant of all, **Victoria Terminus** railway station – now officially Chhatrapati Shivaji Terminus or CST – is a fitting testimony to this extraordinary age of expansion.

As the most prosperous city in the nation, Bombay was at the forefront of the Independence struggle; Mahatma Gandhi used a house here, now a museum, to co-ordinate the struggle through three decades. Fittingly, the first British colony took pleasure in waving the final goodbye to the Raj, when the last contingent of British troops passed through the Gateway of India in February 1948. Since Independence, Mumbai has prospered as India's commercial and cultural capital and this period has seen the population grow tenfold to more than thirteen million.

However, the resultant overcrowding has done little to foster relations between the city's various minorities and the past two decades have seen repeated outbursts of communal tensions among the poorer classes. Strikes and riots paralysed the metropolis throughout the 1980s and early 1990s as more and more immigrants from other regions of the country poured in. The mounting discontent fuelled the rise of the extreme right-wing Maharashtran party, the **Shiv Sena**, founded in 1966 by the former cartoonist, Bal "the Saheb"

Festivals in Mumbai

Mumbai has its own versions of all the major Hindu and Muslim **festivals**, plus a host of smaller neighbourhood celebrations imported by its immigrant communities. Exact dates vary from year to year; check in advance at the government tourist office.

Makar Sankranti (Jan). A celebration of prosperity, when sweets, flowers and fruit are exchanged by all, and kites are flown in the parks as a sign of happiness.

Elephanta Music and Dance Festival (Feb). MTDC-organized cultural event including floodlit performances by classical artists with the Shiva cave temple as a backdrop.

Gokhulashtami (July/Aug). Riotous commemoration of Krishna's birthday; terracotta pots filled with curd, milk-sweets and cash are strung from tenement balconies and grabbed by human pyramids of young boys.

Nowroz (July/Aug). The Parsi New Year is celebrated with special ceremonies in the Fire Temples, and feasting at home.

Ganesh Chathurthi (Aug/Sept). Huge effigies of Ganesh, the elephant-headed god of prosperity and wisdom, are immersed in the sea at Chowpatty Beach in a ritual originally promoted by freedom-fighters to circumvent British anti-assembly legislation. Recently it has seemed in danger of being hijacked by Hindu extremists such as the Shiv Sena, tingeing it more with chauvinism than celebration.

Nariel Purnima (Sept). Koli fishermen launch brightly decorated boats to mark the end of the monsoon.

The Dons

Criminals have always been a part of Mumbai's life, but the 1980s saw an intensification of **organized crime** in the city. Previously, gangsters had confined their activities to small-scale racketeering in poor neighbourhoods. After the post-1970s real-estate boom, however, many petty "landsharks" became powerful godfather figures, or **dons**, with drug- and gold-smuggling businesses as well as involvement in extortion and prostitution. Moreover, corrupt politicians who employed the gangs' muscle-power to rig elections had become highly placed political puppets with debts to pay – a phenomenon dubbed **criminalization**. The dividing line between the underworld and politics grew increasingly blurred during the 1990s – in 1992, no fewer than forty candidates in the municipal elections had criminal records.

The gangs have also become integral in the dirty war between India and Pakistan, with Karachi-based Dawood Ibrahim heavily implicated with the Pakistani security services – he is thought to be behind the bombings of 1993 – and Bombay's leading don, Chhota Rajan, with the Indian forces. In fact, many see the bungling of Rajan's subsequent extradition from Thailand, and escape from a guarded hospital room (he drugged his Thai police guards and climbed out of the window using his bed sheets), as payment for services rendered.

The late 1980s saw the entrance of the dons into **Bollywood**, when the rise of video and TV made regular film financiers nervous of investing in the industry. Mob money poured in and it's an open secret that the film industry is one of the favoured forms of money-laundering with the dons – rival films mysteriously put back their release dates in order to give mob-backed movies a clear run at the box office. In 2000, however, the authorities began to take action, and Bollywood mogul Bharat Shah (who usually has around ten billion rupees invested in films at any one time) was imprisoned for two years for financial links to the Dawood Ibrahim gang.

However, Mumbai is still the playground for mafia gangs, each with their own personalities and legends. If you read any newspapers while you're in the city you won't escape this phenomenon; the media revels in the shocking and bloodthirsty exploits of the gangsters, and the unfolding sagas run like a Bollywood blockbuster.

Thackery, a self-confessed admirer of Hitler. Many people blamed Sena cadres for orchestrating the appalling attacks on Muslims that followed in the wake of the Babri Masjid destruction in Ayodhya in 1992–93, when thousands were murdered by mobs as the city descended into anarchy for ten days.

Just as Mumbai was regaining its composure, disaster struck again. On March 12, 1993, ten massive **bomb blasts** ripped through the heart of the city, destroying key buildings (such as the Stock Exchange and Air India HQ) and killing 260 people. No one claimed responsibility, but the involvement of Muslim godfather Ibrahim Dawood and the Pakistani secret service was suspected. The finger of blame pointed in the same direction eleven years later when – on August 25, 2003 – a **car bomb** exploded near a crowded concourse next to the **Gateway of India**; 107 people died and hundreds more were injured. Police arrested four suspects soon after, but the identity of their backers remains a subject of speculation.

After both bombing attacks, the city bounced back with characteristic ebullience, and in the popular imagination continues to be identified less with terrorist outrages than with the glamour purveyed by its movie and satellite-TV industries: Bollywood starlets, VJs and playboy heirs to industrial fortunes provide the staple for the gossip columns and fanzines lapped up across the country, while dozens of Hindi blockbusters are shot in its streets and suburban studios each month.

Arrival and information

Unless you arrive in Mumbai by train at **Chhatrapati Shivaji Terminus** (formerly Victoria Terminus), be prepared for a long slog into the centre. The international and domestic **airports** are north of the city, way off the map, and ninety minutes or more by road from the main hotel areas, while from **Mumbai Central** train or **bus station** you face a laborious trip across town. Finding a place to stay can be even more of a hassle; phone around before you set off into the traffic.

By air

Mumbai's busy **international airport, Chhatrapati Shivaji** (30km north), is divided into two "modules", one for Air India flights and the other for foreign airlines. Once through customs and the lengthy immigration formalities, you'll find a 24hr State Bank of India exchange facility, government (ITDC) and state (MTDC) tourist information counters, car rental kiosks, cafés and a prepaid taxi stand in the arrivals concourse. There's also – very usefully – an **Indian Railways booking office** which you should make use of if you know your next destination; it'll save you a long wait at the reservation offices downtown. If you're on one of the few flights to land in the afternoon or early evening – by which time most hotels tend to be full – it can be worth paying on the spot for a room at the **accommodation booking desk** in the arrivals hall. All of the domestic airlines also have offices outside the main entrance, and there's a handy 24hr **left luggage** "cloakroom" in the car park nearby (Rs60 per day, or part thereof; maximum duration 90 days).

Many of the more upmarket hotels, particularly those near the airport, send out **courtesy coaches** to pick up their guests. **Taxis** are not too extravagant. To avoid haggling over the fare or being duped by the private taxi companies outside the airport, pay the "Pre-Paid" taxi desk in the arrivals hall. The price on the receipt, which you hand to the driver on arrival at your destination, is slightly more than the normal meter rate (around Rs350 to Colaba or Nariman Point, or Rs150 to Juhu), but at least you can be sure you'll be taken by the most direct route. Taxi-wallahs sometimes try to persuade you to stay at a different hotel from the one you ask for. Don't agree to this; their commission will be added onto the price of your room.

Internal flights land at Mumbai's **domestic airport** (26km to the north of downtown), formerly called "Santa Cruz" but, somewhat confusingly, renamed Chhatrapati Shivaji, like its international counterpart. It is divided into separate terminals: the cream-coloured one (Module 1A) for Indian Airlines, and the blue-and-white (Module 1B) for private carriers. If you're transferring directly from here to an international flight take the free "fly-bus" that shuttles every fifteen minutes between the two. The Indian government and MTDC both have 24hr information counters in the arrivals hall, and there's a foreign exchange counter and accommodation desk tucked away near the first-floor exit. The official "Pre-Paid" taxi counter on the arrivals concourse charges around Rs350 to Colaba.

Malaria warning

Due to the massive slum encampments and bodies of stagnant water around the **airports**, both Chhatrapati Shivaji and Santa Cruz are major **malaria** blackspots. Clouds of mosquitos await your arrival in the car park, so don't forget to smother yourself with strong insect repellent before leaving the terminal.

Don't be tempted by the cheaper fares offered by touts outside, and avoid **auto-rickshaws** altogether, as they're not allowed downtown and will leave you at the mercy of unscrupulous taxi drivers on the edge of vile-smelling Mahim Creek, the southernmost limit of their permitted area.

By train

Trains to Mumbai from most central, southern and eastern regions arrive at **Chhatrapati Shivaji Terminus** or **CST** (formerly **Victoria Terminus**, or VT), the main railway station at the end of the Central Railway line. From here it's a ten- or fifteen-minute ride to Colaba; taxis queue at the busy rank outside the south exit, opposite the new reservation hall.

Mumbai Central, the terminus for Western Railway trains from northern India, is a half-hour ride from Colaba; take a taxi from the forecourt, or flag one down on the main road outside.

Some trains from South India arrive at more obscure stations. If you find yourself at **Dadar**, way up in the industrial suburbs, and don't want to shell out on a taxi (Rs500), cross the Tilak Marg road bridge onto the Western Railway and catch a suburban train into town (remembering to purchase a ticket at the hatch on platform 1 beforehand). **Kurla** station, where a few Bangalore trains pull in, is even further out, just south of the domestic airport; taking a suburban train for Churchgate is the only reasonable alternative to a taxi (Rs300). From either, it's worth asking at the station when you arrive if there is another long-distance train going to Churchgate or CST (Victoria Terminus) shortly after – it's far preferable to trying to cram into either a suburban train or bus.

By bus

Nearly all interstate **buses** arrive at **Mumbai Central** bus stand, a stone's throw from the railway station of the same name. You have a choice between municipal black-and-yellow taxis, the BEST buses (#66, #70 & #71), which run straight into town from the stop on Dr DN Marg (Lamington Road), two minutes' walk west from the bus station, or a suburban train from Mumbai Central's local platform over the footbridge.

Most **Maharashtra State Road Transport Corporation** (MSRTC) buses terminate at Mumbai Central, though those from Pune, Nasik (and surrounding areas) end up at the **ASIAD** bus stand, a glorified parking lot near the railway station in **Dadar**.

Information

The best source of **information** in Mumbai is the excellent **Government of India tourist office** (Mon–Fri 8.30am–6pm, Sat 8.30am–2pm; ☏022/2203 3144, ⊛www.tourismofindia.com) at 123 M Karve Rd, opposite Churchgate station's east exit. The staff here are exceptionally helpful and hand out a wide range of leaflets, maps and brochures both on Mumbai and the rest of the country. There are also 24hr tourist **information counters** at Chhatrapati Shivaji International (☏022/2682 9248) and Domestic (☏022/2615 6920) airports.

The Maharashtra State Tourism Development Corporation (**MTDC**) office, on Madam Cama Road (Mon–Sat 8.30am–7pm; ☏022/202 6731), opposite the LIC Building in Nariman Point, can reserve rooms in MTDC resorts and also sells tickets for city sightseeing tours (see opposite).

If you need detailed **listings**, the most complete source is Mumbai's *Time Out*, which carries full details of what's on and where, just like its London and New York counterparts. Alternatively, check out "The List" section of

Mid-Day (Mumbai's main local rag), the "Metro" page in the *Indian Express*, or the "Bombay Times" section of the *Times of India*. All are available from street vendors around Colaba and the downtown area.

City transport

Transport congestion has eased slightly since the opening of the huge flyover that now scythes straight through the heart of the city from just north of CST station. During peak hours, however, gridlock is the norm and you should brace yourself for long waits at junctions if you take to the roads by taxi, bus or auto. Local **trains** get there faster, but can be a real endurance test even outside rush hours.

Tours

MTDC's "City" tour (Tues–Sun 2–6pm; Rs75, not including admission charges) is a good way to cram downtown Mumbai's touristic highlights into a half day, with stops at the Prince of Wales Museum, Marine Drive, Chowpatty Beach, the Hanging Gardens and Mani Bhavan. The trip starts at the company's main office on Madam Cama Road (see opposite), where you can also purchase tickets in advance. A more leisurely alternative, focusing on architecture and history, are the guided walks organized by the Mumbai Heritage Walks Society on the last Sunday of each month (except during the monsoons). The tours cost Rs100 (or Rs50 for students on production of a student ID card) and last ninety minutes. Get further details on ☏022/2281 0123 or 2834 4622, or ✉heritagewalks@hotmail.com.

Buses

BEST (Brihanmumbai Electric Supply and Transport; ☏022/2285 6262; ⓦwww.bestundertaking.com) operates a **bus** network of labyrinthine complexity, extending to the furthest-flung corners of the city. Unfortunately, neither its website, route booklets, maps nor "Point to Point" guides (which you can consult at the tourist office or at newsstands) make things any clearer. Finding out which buses you need is difficult enough. Recognizing them in the street can be even more problematic, as the numbers are written in Marathi (although in English on the sides). Aim, wherever possible, for the "Limited" services, which stop less frequently, and avoid rush hours at all costs. Tickets should be bought from the conductor on the bus.

Trains

Mumbai's local **trains** carry millions of commuters each day between downtown and the sprawling suburbs in the north. One line begins at CST (VT), running up the east side of the city as far as Thane. The other leaves Churchgate, hugging the curve of Back Bay as far as Chowpatty Beach, where it veers north towards Mumbai Central, Dadar, Santa Cruz and Vasai, beyond the city limits. Services depart every few minutes from 5am until midnight, stopping at dozens of small stations. Carriages remain packed solid virtually the whole time, with passengers dangling precariously out of open doors to escape the crush, so start to make your way to the exit at least three stops before your destination. Peak hours (approximately 8.30am–10am & 4–7pm) are the worst of all. Women are marginally better off in the "ladies carriages"; look for the crowd of saris and *salwar kamises* grouped at the end of the platform.

Taxis

With rickshaws banished to the suburbs, Mumbai's ubiquitous black-and-yellow **taxis** are the quickest and most convenient way to nip around the city centre. In theory, all should have meters and a current "tariff card" (to convert the amount shown on the meter to the correct fare); in practice, particularly at night or early in the morning, many drivers refuse to use them. If this happens, either flag down another or haggle out a fare. As a rule of thumb, expect to be charged Rs8 per kilometre after the minimum fare of around Rs15, together with a small sum for heavy luggage (Rs5 per article). The latest addition to Mumbai's hectic roads is the **cool cab**, a blue taxi that boasts air conditioning, and charges higher rates for the privilege (T022/2824 6216).

Boats

Ferryboats regularly chug out of Mumbai harbour, connecting the city with the far shore and some of the larger islands in between. The most popular with visitors is the **Elephanta Island** launch (see p.133), which departs from the Gateway of India. Boats to **Mandve** (9 daily; 6.30am–6.15pm; 90min; Rs45), for Alibag, the transport hub for the rarely used **coastal route south**, leave from the Gateway of India.

Car rental

Cars with drivers can be rented per eight-hour day (Rs900–1250 for a non-a/c Ambassador, upwards of Rs1450 for more luxurious a/c cars), or per kilometre, from ITDC. They have an (occasionally) staffed counter at the Government of India tourist office and on the eleventh floor of the Nirmal Building at Nariman Point. Otherwise, go through any good travel agent (see p.144). Ramniranjan Kedia Tours and Travels (T022/2437 1112, W www.rnk .com) are recommended if you want to book a vehicle on arrival at Chhatrapati Shivaji international airport.

Accommodation

Finding **accommodation** at the right price when you arrive in Mumbai may be a real problem. Budget travellers, in particular, can expect a hard time: standards at the bottom of the range are grim and room rates exorbitant. The best of the relatively inexpensive places tend to fill up by noon, which can often mean a long trudge in the heat with only an overpriced fleapit at the end of it, so you should really phone ahead as soon as (or preferably well before) you arrive. Prices in upmarket places are further inflated by the state-imposed "**luxury tax**" (between four and thirty percent depending on how expensive the room is), and "**service charges**" levied by the hotel itself; such charges are included in the price symbols used in the following reviews.

Colaba, down in the far southern end of the city, is where the majority of foreign visitors head first. A short way across the city centre, **Marine Drive**'s accommodation is generally a little more expensive, but more salubrious, with Back Bay and the promenade right on the doorstep. If you're arriving by train and plan to make a quick getaway, a room closer to **CST** (VT) station is worth considering. Alternatively, **Juhu**, way to the north near the airports, hosts a string of flashy four- and five-stars, with a handful of less expensive places behind the beach. For those who just want to crawl off the plane and straight into bed, a handful of overpriced options are also available in the suburbs around the **airports**, a short taxi ride from the main terminal buildings.

Finally, if you would like to **stay with an Indian family**, ask at the government tourist office in Churchgate, or at their information counters in the airports about the popular **"paying guest" scheme**. Bed and breakfast-style accommodation in family homes, vetted by the tourist office, is available throughout the city at rates ranging from Rs500 to Rs1350.

Colaba

A short ride from the city's main commercial districts, railway stations and tourist office, **Colaba** makes a handy base. It also offers more in the way of food and entertainment than neighbouring districts, especially along its busy main thoroughfare, **"Colaba Causeway"** (Shahid Bhagat Singh – SBS – Marg). The streets immediately south and west of the Gateway of India are chock-full of accommodation, ranging from grungy guesthouses to India's most famous five-star hotel, the *Taj Mahal Palace & Tower*. Avoid at all costs the nameless lodges lurking on the top storeys of wooden-fronted houses along **Arthur Bunder Road** – the haunts of touts who depend on commission to finance their heroin habits.

The hotels below are marked on the **map** of Colaba on p.122, except for the *Taj President*, which is on the main Mumbai map (pp.108–109).

Aga Bheg's & Hotel Kishan Ground & 2nd Floor, Shirin Manzil, Walton Rd ☏ 022/2284 2227. *Aga Bheg's* has lurid pink walls and little wooden blue beds, though it's clean, cool and quiet. *Hotel Kishan's* more comfy a/c rooms are better value. ⑤–⑥

Ascot 38 Garden Rd ☏ 022/2284 0020 or 2287 2105, ⊛www.ascothotel.com. One of the oldest hotels in Mumbai, now sporting a state-of-the-art designer look. Very comfortable, and a bargain for a three-star in this area. All rooms en suite and a/c. ⑧

Bentley's 17 Oliver Rd ☏ 022/2284 1474, ⊛www.bentleyshotel.com. Dependable old favourite in four different colonial tenements, all on leafy back-streets. Well maintained, secure and good value, with spacious rooms opening onto rear gardens. ⑥

Fariyas 25 Arthur Rd ☏ 022/2204 2911, ⊛www.fariyas.com. Compact luxury hotel, overlooking the Koli fishing *bastee* on one side, with all the trimmings of a five-star but none of the grandeur. Doubles from $175. ⑨

Godwin Jasmine Building, 41 Garden Rd ☏ 022/2287 2050, ⊛www.cybersols.com/godwin. Top-class three-star with great views from upper floors (ask for 804, 805 or 806 when you book). The *Garden* (☏ 022/2283 1330, ☏ 2204 4290), next door, is similar but slightly inferior. Both ⑧

Gorden House 5 Battery St, Apollo Bunder ☏ 022/2287 1122, ⊛www.ghhotel.com. Ultra-chic designer place behind the Regal cinema. Each floor is differently themed: "Scandinavian" (the easiest to live with), "Mediterranean" and

"American Country"; CD players in every room, but no pool. ⑨

Lawrence 3rd Floor, 33 Sri Sai Baba Marg (Rope Walk Lane), off K Dubash Marg, behind *TGI's* ☏ 022/2284 3618 or 5633 6107. Arguably Mumbai's best-value cheap hotel, close to the Jehangir Art Gallery. Six well-scrubbed doubles (one single) with fans, and not-so-clean shared shower-toilet. Breakfast included in the price. Advance booking essential. ③

Moti International 10 Best Marg ☏ 022/2202 1654. British-era building that's quiet and clean, though frayed around the edges, with original painted wood-work. The rooms range from non-attached doubles (Rs650) to deluxe with a/c, fridges and TVs. ④–⑥

Red Shield Red Shield House, 30 Mereweather Rd, near the *Taj* ☏ 022/2284 1824 or 2282 4613. Rock-bottom bunk beds (Rs135) in cramped, stuffy dorms (lockers available), or larger good-value doubles (Rs600 without a/c, Rs900 with), recently refurbished and fully en suite. Rates include three meals, served in a sociable travellers' canteen. Priority given to women, but your stay is limited to one week or less. ①–④

Regent 8 Best Rd ☏ 022/2287 1854, ✉hotelregent@vsnl.com. Smart, international-standard hotel on a small scale; the rooms aren't large, but good value in this bracket. ⑧

Sea Palace Kerawalla Chambers, 26 PJ Ramchandani Marg ☏ 022/2284 1828, ⊛www.seapalacehotel.com. Comfortable, recently reno-vated hotel at the quiet end of the harbour front. Sea views cost extra. All rooms a/c. ⑧

Sea Shore 4th Floor, 1-49 Kamal Mansion, Arthur Bunder Rd ☎ 022/2287 4237. Among the best budget deals in Colaba. The sea-facing rooms with windows (Rs520) are much nicer than the airless cells on the other side. Friendly management and free, safe baggage store. Common baths only, though some rooms have a/c. If it's full try the wooden-partitioned rooms at the less salubrious *India* (☎ 022/2283 3769; ④–⑤) or the grubby but bearable *Sea Lord* (☎ 022/2284 5392; ④–⑥) in the same building. ⑤–⑦

Shelley's 30 PJ Ramchandani Marg ☎ 022/2284 0229, ⓦ www.shelleyshotel.com. Charmingly old-fashioned hotel in the colonial mould despite renovations to the rooms. Worth paying the extra Rs300 for sea-facing rooms. ⑦

Taj Mahal Palace & Tower PJ Ramchandani Marg ☎ 022/5665 3366, ⓦ www.tajhotels.com. The stately home among India's top hotels (see p.121), and the haunt of Mumbai's *beau monde*, with 546 luxury rooms, shopping arcades, a huge outdoor pool, nine bars and restaurants, plus one of the city's favourite nightclubs (*Insomnia*). Views vary according to price. If your budget can stretch to it, go for a sea-facing suite in the old wing, where rates are $400–500; in the *Tower*, count on $300–380. ⑨

Taj President 90 Cuffe Parade, ☎ 22/5665 0808, ⓦ www.tajhotels.com. Modern, business-oriented five-star occupying an 18-floor skyscraper just south of Colaba. A much more competitively priced option than its sister concern, the *Taj Mahal Palace & Tower*, though lacking old-world style and atmosphere. The pool is outdoors and large, with a multi-gym and steam room adjacent. ⑨

YWCA 18 Madam Cama Rd ☎ 022/2202 5053, ⓦ www.ywcaic.info. Relaxing, secure and quiet hostel with spotless dorms (Rs35 per bed), doubles (recently renovated and with windows from Rs600, or Rs900 a/c) or family rooms (sleeping 3 to 6). Rates include membership, breakfast and filling buffet dinner. One month's advance booking (by money order) advisable. ⑦

Marine Drive and Nariman Point

At the western edge of the downtown area, Netaji Subhash Chandra Marg, or **Marine Drive**, sweeps from the skyscrapers of Nariman Point in the south to Chowpatty Beach in the north. Along the way, four- and five-star hotels take advantage of the panoramic views over Back Bay and the easy access to the city's commercial heart, while a couple of inexpensive guesthouses are worth trying if Colaba's cheap lodges don't appeal.

The hotels below are marked on the **map** on p.127, apart from the *Oberoi*, which is marked on pp.108–109.

Ambassador VN Rd ☎ 022/2204 1131, ⓦ www .ambassadorindia.com. Ageing four-star whose scruffy concrete exterior and slightly worn furnishings are redeemed by its choice location, close to the sea and main shopping and café strip. Even if you're not staying, pop up to the revolving *Pearl in the Orient* restaurant for the matchless city views. ⑨

Bentley 3rd Floor, Krishna Mahal, Marine Drive ☎ 022/2281 5244. Not to be confused with *Bentley's* in Colaba (see p.117), this small, friendly guesthouse is across town on the corner of D Rd/Marine Drive, near the cricket stadium. It had a major face lift in 2004 and now offers great value for money. The rooms are marble-lined and most share shower-toilets, but they're kept immaculately clean. Rates (from Rs700) include breakfast. ⑤

Chateau Windsor 5th Floor, 86 VN Rd ☎ 022/2204 4455, ⓦ www.chateauwindsor.com. Impeccably neat and central, with unfailingly polite staff and a choice of differently priced rooms in 1950s style. Very popular, so reserve well in advance. ⑦–⑧

Intercontinental 135 Marine Drive ☎ 022/3987 9999, ⓦ www.intercontinental.com. Ultra-chic "boutique" hotel that's currently one of India's most stylishly modern addresses. The rooms have large sea-facing windows and state-of-the-art gadgets (including 42" plasma screens, DVD players, safes with laptop rechargers and broadband connections), while the bars and restaurants rank among Mumbai's most fashionable. Doubles from $335. ⑨

Marine Plaza 29 Marine Drive ☎ 022/2285 1212, ⓦ www.sarovarparkplaza.com. Ritzy but small luxury hotel on the seafront, with retro-Art-Deco atrium lobby, glass-bottomed rooftop pool, and the usual 5-star facilities. Rooms from around $330. ⑨

Oberoi/Oberoi Towers Nariman Point ☎ 022/2232 5757, ⓦ www.oberoihotels.com. India's largest hotel, where Bill Clinton stayed on his state visit, enjoys a prime spot overlooking Back Bay. There's little difference between the two sections, which form a single complex. Glitteringly opulent throughout, and the first choice of business travellers, though lacking the heritage character of the *Taj*. Rooms from $365 to $2500 per night. ⑨

Around Victoria (Chhatrapati Shivaji) Terminus

Arriving in Mumbai at **CST** (VT) after a long train journey, you may not feel like embarking on a room hunt around Colaba. Unfortunately, the area around the station and the nearby GPO, though fairly central, has little to recommend it. The majority of places worth trying are mid-range hotels grouped around the crossroads of P D'Mello (Frere) Road, St George's Road and Shahid Bhagat Singh (SBS) Marg, immediately southeast of the post office (5min on foot from the station). CST (VT) itself also has **retiring rooms** (Rs150), although these are invariably booked up by noon. The following are all marked on the Churchgate and Fort map on p.127.

City Palace 121 City Terrace ☎022/2261 5515, Ⓔhotelcitypalace@vsnl.net. Large and popular hotel bang opposite the station. "Ordinary" rooms are tiny and windowless, but have a/c, are perfectly clean and proudly sport "electronic push button telephone instruments". The pricier ones higher up the building have great views over Nagar Chowk. And there's a reliable left luggage facility for guests. ⑥–⑦

Grand 17 Shri S R Marg, Ballard Estate ☎022/5658 0500, ⓌQwww.grandhotelbombay.com. British-era place out near the old docks and former financial district. Their rooms are huge and a bit institutional but have plenty of 1940s period feel, which some may consider worth the extra. ⑧–⑨

Oasis 276 SBS Marg ☎022/5637 6521 or 2269 7887, Ⓔhoteloasis@satyam.net.in. The best-value budget place in this area. Non a/c doubles from under Rs700: good beds, clean linen, all en suite and with TVs, and very well placed for CST station. ⑤

Prince 34 Walchand Hirachand Rd, near Red Gate ☎022/2261 2809, ⒻP2265 8049. The best fallback if *Oasis* is full: nothing special, but neat and respectable. Avoid the airless partition rooms upstairs. ④–⑦

Railway 249 P D'Mello Rd ☎022/2261 6705 or 2262 0775, Ⓦwww.hotelrailway.com. Spacious, clean and friendly, and the pick of the mid-range bunch around CST (VT), though correspondingly pricey and with no a/c options. ⑦–⑧

Around the airports

Hotels in the congested area around Chhatrapati Shivaji and Santa Cruz **airports** cater predominantly for transit passengers and flight crews, at premium rates. If you can face the half-hour drive across town, head for **Juhu**, one of the city's swisher suburbs, which faces the sea and is a lot less hectic. With its palm trees, glamorous seaside apartment blocks and designer clothes stores, Juhu is Mumbai's answer to Sunset Boulevard, though sunbathing and swimming are out of the question, thanks to an oily slick of raw sewage that seeps into the Arabian Sea from the slum *bastis* surrounding Mahim Creek to the south. Wherever you stay, bookings should be made well in advance, by phone, fax or email, and re-confirmed a couple of days before your arrival. Nearly all the hotels below have courtesy buses to and from the terminal building, or at worst can arrange for a car and driver to meet you (in which case check the tariff beforehand). Travellers on lower budgets who need to overnight close to the airport might also consider one of the Government of India's Paying Guest addresses, available via email: Ⓔgitobest@bom5.vsnl.net.in or Ⓔindiatourism@vsnl.com.

Bawa International Vile Parle (East) ☎022/2611 3636, Ⓔbawaintl@vsnl.com. Nothing special, but spotlessly clean, efficient, modern and right next to the domestic airport. Doubles from Rs4400. ⑨

Holiday Inn Balraj Sahani Marg, Juhu ☎022/2693 4444, Ⓦwww.holidayinnbombay.com. Formulaic five-star – exactly what you'd expect from a *Holiday Inn*, and slap on the beach, with a decent-sized swimming pool. Rooms from around $200. ⑨

Lotus Suites Andheri Kurla Road, International Airport Zone, Andheri (East) ☎022/2827 0707, Ⓦwww.lotussuites.com. An "Eco-Four-Star at Three-Star prices" is how this environment-friendly hotel describes itself. A very comfortable option for under $100 if you book online. ⑨

Midland Jawaharlal Nehru Road, Santa Cruz (East) ☎022/2611 0413, Ⓦwww.hotelmidland.com. Dependable, welcoming two-star with well

furnished twin-bedded rooms. Rates (from Rs2300) include courtesy bus and breakfast. **7**
Orchid 70-C Nehru Rd, Vile Parle (East) ☎022/2616 4040, ⓦwww.orchidhotel.com. Award-winning "Eco-Five-Star", built with organic or recycled materials and non-VOC paints. Every effort is made to minimize waste of natural resources, with a water recycling plant and "zero garbage" policy. Even the coat hangers are made of compressed sawdust. Rooms from around $300. **9**

Samrat 3rd Rd, Khar, Santa Cruz (East), near Khar railway station ☎022/2648 5441, ⓔhotelsamrat@vsnl.com. Basic budget transit hotel in a quiet suburban backstreet. No courtesy bus. **6**
Sea Princess Juhu Tara Rd, Juhu ☎022/2661 1111, ⓦwww.seaprincess.com. The nicest of the five-stars overlooking Juhu beach. Cosy, recently refitted rooms (some with sea views) and a smart restaurant, in addition to a small pool. Doubles from $175. **9**

The City

Nowhere reinforces your sense of having arrived in Mumbai quite as emphatically as the **Gateway of India**, which, alongside its grandly gabled and domed neighbour, the *Taj Mahal Palace & Tower*, stands as the city's defining landmark. Crowds of trippers congregate here on evenings and weekends, but early morning before the heat builds is the best time to be at the adjacent boat jetty if you're planning a trip across the harbour to the ancient rock-cut Shiva temple on **Elephanta Island**. Only a five-minute walk north, the **Prince of Wales Museum** (or the Chhatrapati Shivaji Vastu Sanghralaya, as it was recently re-named) should be next on your list of sightseeing priorities, as much for its flamboyantly eclectic exterior as for the art treasures inside. The museum provides a foretaste of what lies in store just up the road, where the cream of Bartle Frere's Bombay – the University and High Court – line up with the open *maidans* on one side, and the boulevards of **Fort** on the other. The commercial hub of the city, Fort is a great area for aimless wandering, with plenty of old-fashioned cafés, department stores and street stalls crammed between the pompous Victorian piles. The innumerable banks and other financial institutions at the east end of Fort around **Horniman Circle** – site of the British era's oldest buildings, **St Thomas' Cathedral** and the old **town hall** – stand as reminders of the cotton boom prosperity of the late-nineteenth century. But for the fullest sense of why the city's founding fathers declared it *Urbs Prima in Indis*, you should visit **Victoria Terminus** (now re-named Chhatrapati Shivaji Terminus), the high watermark of India's Raj architecture.

Few visitors venture much further north than here unless they have to, but teeming **central Mumbai** certainly has its appeal. Beginning at **Crawford Market**, a quirky British structure crammed with fresh produce, you can press north into the thick of the intense **bazaar** district to visit the Mumba Devi temple from which the city took its name. Beyond lie the Muslim neighbourhoods, which encompass some of Mumbai's most interesting backstreet bazaars, as well as a serene little **Jain animal sanctuary**.

When the crush of city's central districts gets too much, an evening stroll along **Marine Drive**, bounding the western edge of the downtown area, is the ideal antidote. From there you can skirt Mumbai's most affluent enclave, Malabar Hill, to reach two important religious sites, the Hindu **Lakshmi temple** and Muslim **tomb of Haji Ali**.

One incentive to break out of Mumbai altogether is the thousand-year-old **Kanheri Cave** complex, carved from a forested hillside, which you can get to within striking distance of by train.

Colaba

At the end of the seventeenth century, **Colaba** was little more than the last in a straggling line of rocky islands extending to the lighthouse that stood on Mumbai's southernmost point. Today, the original outlines of the promontory (whose name derives from the Koli who first lived here) have been submerged under a mass of dilapidated colonial tenements, hotels, bars, restaurants and handicraft emporia. If you never venture beyond the district, you'll get a very distorted picture of Mumbai. In spite of being the main tourist enclave and a trendy hangout for the city's rich young things, Colaba has retained the sleazy feel of the port it used to be, with touts, dealers and pimps hissing at passers-by from the kerbsides.

The Gateway of India

Commemorating the visit of King George V and Queen Mary in 1911, India's own honey-coloured Arc de Triomphe, the **Gateway of India**, was built in 1924 by George Wittet, the architect responsible for many of the city's grandest constructions. Blending indigenous Gujarati motifs with high Victorian pomp, it was originally envisaged as a ceremonial disembarkation point for passengers alighting from the P&O steamers, but – ironically – is today more often remembered as the place the British chose to stage their final departure from the country. On February 28, 1948, the last batallion of troops remaining on Indian soil slow marched under the arch to board the waiting ship back to Tilbury. Nowadays, the only boats bobbing about at the bottom of its stone staircase are the launches that ferry tourists across the harbour to Elephanta Island (see p.133).

The Gateway made international headlines more recently when, on August 25, 2003, a car bomb exploded at the taxi rank in front of it; 107 people were killed in the attack. No one claimed responsibility, but four suspects believed to have links with Islamic militant groups were arrested soon after.

Behind the Gateway

Directly behind the Gateway, the older hotel in the **Taj Mahal Palace & Tower** complex (see p.118) stands as a monument to local pride in the face of colonial oppression. Its patron, the Parsi industrialist J.N. Tata, is said to have built the old *Taj* as an act of revenge after he was refused entry to what was then the best hotel in town, the "whites only" *Watson's*. The ban proved their undoing. *Watson's* disappeared long ago, but the *Taj*, with its grand grey-and-white stone facade and red-domed roof, still presides imperiously over the seafront, the preserve of visiting diplomats, sheikhs, businessmen and aircrew on expense accounts, and Mumbai's jet set. Lesser mortals are allowed in to sample the tea lounge, shopping arcades and vast air-conditioned lobby (a good place to cool down if the heat of the harbourfront has got the better of you).

From the *Taj*, you can head down the promenade, PJ Ramchandani Marg, better known as **Apollo Bunder** (the name is a colonial corruption of the Koli words for a local fish, *palav*, and quay, *bunda*), taking in the sea breezes and views over the busy harbour. Alternatively, Shivaji Marg heads northwest towards **Wellington Circle** (SPM Chowk), the hectic roundabout in front of the Art Deco Regal cinema. The latter route takes you past the old **Bombay Yacht Club**, another idiosyncratic vestige of the Raj. Very little seems to have changed here since its smoky common rooms were a bolt hole for the city's *burra-sahibs*. Behind its half-timbered gabled facade, dusty sporting trophies and models of clippers and dhows stand in glass cases lining the corridors, polished from time to time by bearers in cotton tunics. If you want to look around, seek permission from the club secretary.

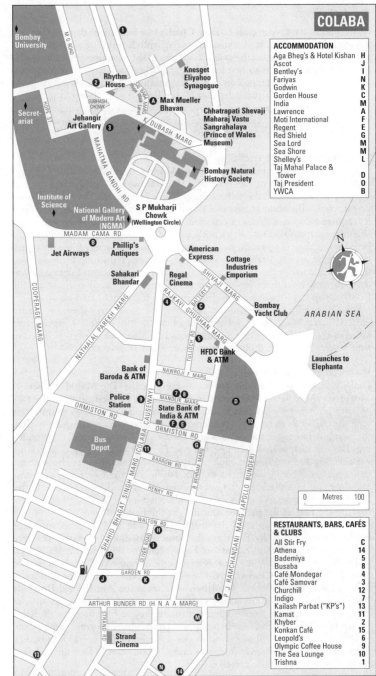

Southwards along Colaba Causeway

Reclaimed in the late nineteenth century from the sea, the district's main thoroughfare, **Colaba Causeway** (this stretch of Shahid Bhagat Singh Marg), leads south towards the military cantonement. Few tourists stray much further down it than the claustrophobic hawker zone at the top of the street, but it's well worth doing so, if only to see the neighbourhood's earthy **fresh produce market**, a couple of blocks south of the Strand cinema, which provides an unexpected splash of rustic colour amid the urban surroundings. From here, return to the main road and turn left to reach the gates of Mumbai's wholesale seafood market, **Sassoon Docks**. Photographed to powerful effect by Sebastião Salgado in his book, *Work*, the docks are at their most vigorous in the hour after sunrise, when coolies haul the night's catch in crates of crushed ice over gangplanks to the quayside, while Koli women, their saris hitched up *dhoti*-style, wash and pile the fish into baskets for sale. The stench, as overpowering as the noise, comes mostly from bundles of one of the city's traditional exports, "**Bombay duck**", drying on the trawlers' rigging. Note that **photography** is strictly forbidden, as the docks are adjacent to a sensitive navy area.

Hop on any bus heading south down Colaba Causeway (#3, #11, #47, #103, #123 or #125) through the cantonment to reach the **Afghan Memorial Church of St John the Baptist**, built (1847–54) as a memorial to the British victims of the First Afghan War. With its tall steeple and tower, the pale yellow church wouldn't look out of place in Worcester or Suffolk. If the door is unlocked, take a peep inside at the battle-scarred military colours on the wall and marble memorial plaques to officers who died in various campaigns on the Northwest Frontier.

Downtown Mumbai

The critic and travel writer Robert Byron (of *Road to Oxiana* fame), although a wholehearted fan of New Delhi, was unenthusiastic about the architecture of **downtown Mumbai**, which he described as "that architectural Sodom". Today, the massive monuments of Empire and Indian free enterprise appear not so much ugly as intriguing. Between them, you'll occasionally come across still more curious buildings, with facades flanked by what appear to be Meso-potanian griffins. These are old Zoroashtrian (Parsi) **fire temples** – or *agiaries* – erected by wealthy worthies in the late nineteenth century. Few attract more than a trickle of ageing worshippers, and as a non-Parsi you won't be allowed inside, but they're a definitive Mumbai spectacle.

The area immediately north of Colaba, centred on the crescent of MG Road and Subhash Chowk, is known as **Kala Ghoda** ("Black Statue"), after the large equestrian statue of King Edward VII which formerly stood in its main square. Flanked by the city's principal museum and art galleries, the district has in recent years been re-launched as a "cultural enclave" – as much in an attempt to preserve its many historic buildings as to promote the contemporary visual arts that have thrived here since the 1950s. Fancy stainless-steel interpretative panels now punctuate the district's walkways, and on Sundays in December and January, the **Kala Ghoda Fair** sees portrait artists, potters and *mehendi* painters plying their trade in the car park fronting the Jehangir Art Gallery.

Chhatrapati Shivaji Museum (Prince of Wales Museum)

Set back from Mahatma Gandhi (MG) Road in its own grounds, the **Prince of Wales Museum of Western India** (Tues–Sun 10.15am–6pm; Rs300, Rs6 for students and Indian nationals, camera Rs30 – no tripods or flash), recently renamed as the tongue-twisting **Chhatrapati Shivaji Maharaj Vastu Sangrahalaya,** ranks among the city's most distinctive Raj-era constructions. Crowned by a massive white Moghul-style dome, it houses a superb collection of paintings and sculpture that you'll need several hours, or a couple of visits, to get the most out of. The building was designed by George Wittet, of Gateway of India fame, and is the epitome of the hybrid **Indo-Saracenic** style – regarded in its day as an "educated" interpretation of fifteenth- and sixteenth-century Gujarati architecture, mixing Islamic touches with typically English municipal brickwork.

To justify the hefty entrance fee demanded from foreigners, the museum's curators recently introduced an **audio tour** (included in the ticket price), which you collect at the admissions kiosk inside. Given the haphazard nature of the exhibitions and absence of contextual information, this would have been a welcome initiative if the commentary were up to scratch, but you'll probably find it does little to enhance your visit. The heat and humidity inside the building can also be a trial. For breaks, the institutional tea-coffee kiosk in the ground-floor garden is a much less congenial option than the *Café Samovar* outside (for a review, see p.135), but to exit the museum and re-enter (which you're entitled to do) you'll have to get your ticket stamped in the admissions lobby first.

The **Key Gallery** in the central hall provides a snapshot of the collection's treasures. Highlights here include the richly bejewelled Rewa dagger, a few choice Moghul paintings, an exquisitely enamelled Lucknowi hookah and – to the right of the entrance – stucco Buddhist figures dating from the fifth century AD. These were unearthed by the archeologist Henry Cousens in 1909 at Mirapur Khas, an early Gupta stupa that was bricked over soon after construction, which explains why the pieces remain so well preserved: traces of black and red paint are still visible on some of them. The standing figure, thought to represent a donor disciple, is the most recognizable of the group, his high rank denoted by non-matching earrings and a gracefully held lotus flower.

The main **sculpture room** on the **ground floor** displays some fine fourth- and fifth-century heads and figures from the Buddhist state of Gandhara, a former colony of Alexander the Great (hence the Greek-style features). Important Hindu sculptures include a seventh-century Chalukyan bas-relief from Aihole depicting Brahma seated on a lotus, and a sensuously carved torso of Mahisasuramardini, the goddess Durga, with tripod raised ready to skewer the demon buffalo.

Once past a missable mezzanine gallery dominated by facsimiles of prehistoric artefacts and Assyrian bas-reliefs, the main attraction on the **first floor** has to be the famous collection of **Indian painting**. Most of it was amassed by the Peshwa diplomat, Nana Phadnis (1741–1800), from distress sales of aristocratic heirlooms during the breakup of the Moghul empire. Featured here are pages of Akbar's own lavish edition of the Panchatantra – the Moghul equivalent of Aesop's fables – and an equally well-known portrait of Shah Jehan in old age. More fine medieval miniatures are housed in the recently inaugurated **Karl & Meherbai Khandalavala Gallery**, on the renovated east wing of this floor. Around a contemporary mock-courtyard made of rubber and wood, objects collected by a wealthy Parsi lawyer and his wife, former curators of the museum, are displayed to great effect. They include priceless pieces of Ghandaram sculpture, a splendid devotional wall hanging from Nathdwara in Rajasthan, Chola bronzes (see p.689) and some of the country's finest surviving examples of medieval Gujarati wood carving.

Himalayan *thangkas*, deities and ritual objects dating from the thirteenth century onwards form the backbone of the **Buddhist gallery**, also on the first floor. The final, **second floor** showcases a vast array of Oriental ceramics and glassware, and some European art gifted by wealthy Parsi benefactors, including a minor Titian and a Constable. Finally, among the grizzly **weapons** and pieces of armour stored in a small side gallery at the top of the building are a cuirass, helmet and jade dagger which the museum only recently discovered belonged to the Mughal emporer Akbar – the Persian inscription on the breast-plate hinted at its provenance, but wasn't translated until a few years ago.

Kala Ghoda Art Galleries

Technically in the same compound as the Prince of Wales Museum, though approached from further up MG Road, the **Jehangir Art Gallery** (daily 11am–7pm; free) is Mumbai's oldest-established venue for contemporary art, with five small halls specializing in twentieth-century arts and crafts from

Dabawallahs

Mumbai's size and inconvenient shape create all kind of hassles for its working population – not least having to stew for over four hours each day in slow municipal transport. One thing the daily tidal wave of commuters does not have to worry about, however, is where to find an inexpensive and wholesome home-cooked lunch. In a city with a wallah for everything, it will find them. The members of the **Nutan Mumbai Tiffin Box Suppliers Charity Trust**, known colloquially, and with no little affection, as "**dabawallahs**", see to that. Every day, around 1000 *dabawallahs* deliver freshly cooked food from 160,000 suburban kitchens to offices in the downtown area. Each lunch is prepared early in the morning by a devoted wife or mother while her husband or son is enduring the crush on the train. She arranges the rice, dhal, *subzi*, curd and *parathas* into cylindrical aluminium trays, stacks them on top of one another and clips them together with a neat little handle. This **tiffin box**, not unlike a slim paint tin, is the lynchpin of the whole operation. When the runner calls to collect it in the morning, he uses a special colour code on the lid to tell him where the lunch has to go. At the end of his round, he carries all the boxes to the nearest railway station and hands them over to other *dabawallahs* for the trip into town. Between leaving the wife and reaching its final destination, the tiffin box will pass through at least half a dozen different pairs of hands, carried on heads, shoulder-poles, bicycle handlebars and in the brightly decorated handcarts that plough with such insouciance through the midday traffic. Tins are rarely, if ever, lost – a fact recently reinforced by the American business magazine, *Forbes*, which awarded Mumbai's *dabawallahs* a 6-Sigma performance rating, the score reserved for companies who attain a 9.99999 percentage of correctness. This means that only one tiffin box in 6 million goes astray, in efficiency terms putting the illiterate *dabawallahs* on a par with bluechip firms such as Motorola.

To catch them in action, head for **CST (VT)** or **Churchgate** stations around late morning, when the tiffin boxes arrive in the city centre. The event is accompanied by a chorus of "*lafka! lafka!*" – "hurry! hurry!" – as the *dabawallahs*, recognizable in their white Nehru caps and baggy pyjama trousers, rush to make their lunch-hour deadlines. Nearly all come from the same small village near Pune and are related to one another. They collect Rs150 from each customer, or around Rs5000 per month in total – not a bad income by Indian standards. One of the reasons the system survives in the face of competition from trendy fast-food outlets is that *daba* lunches still work out a good deal cheaper, saving precious paise for the middle-income workers who use the system.

around the world. You never know what you're going to find – most exhibitions last only a week and exhibits are often for sale.

On the opposite side of MG Road, facing the museum and Mukharji Chowk, stands the larger **National Gallery of Modern Art** (Tues–Sun 10am–5pm; Rs20), housed in a converted concert hall. It holds a mix of permanent and temporary exhibitions on three storeys, charting the development of modern Indian art from its beginnings in the 1950s to the present day. The installations, in particular, tend to be a lot more adventurous than those you'll find in the Jehangir across the road.

Around Oval Maidan

Some of Mumbai's most important Victorian buildings flank the eastern side of the vast green **Oval Maidan**, where impromptu cricket matches are held almost every day (foreign enthusiasts are welcome to take part, but should beware the *maidan*'s demon bowlers and less-than-even pitches). The dull yellow **Old Secretariat** now serves as the City Civil and Sessions Court. Indian civil servant G.W. Forrest described it in 1903 as "a massive pile whose main features have been brought from Venice, but all the beauty has vanished in transhipment". Inside, you can only imagine the originally highly polished interior, which no longer shines, but buzzes with activity. Lawyers in black gowns, striped trousers and white tabs bustle up and down the staircases, whose corners are emblazoned with expectorated paan juice, and offices with perforated swing-doors give glimpses of textbook images of Indian bureaucracy – peons at desks piled high with dusty beribboned document bundles.

Across AS D'Mello Road from the Old Secretariat, two major buildings belonging to **Mumbai University** (established 1857) were designed in England by Sir Gilbert Scott, who had already given the world the Gothic extravaganza of London's St Pancras railway station. Access through the main gates is monitored by caretakers who only allow you in if you say you're visiting the library. Funded by the Parsi philanthropist Cowasjee "Readymoney" Jehangir, the **Convocation Hall** greatly resembles a church. The **library** (daily 10am–10pm) is beneath the 79.2-metre-high **Rajabhai Clock Tower** which is said to be modelled on Giotto's campanile in Florence. Until 1931, it chimed tunes such as "*Rule Britannia*" and "*Home Sweet Home*". You can scale the grand staircase from the lobby to enter the magnificent vaulted reading room, whose high Gothic windows and stained glass still evoke a reverential approach to learning.

Hutatma Chowk (Flora Fountain)

A busy five-point intersection in the heart of the Fort area, the roundabout formerly known as **Flora Fountain** has been renamed **Hutatma Chowk** ("Martyr's Square") to commemorate the freedom fighters who died to establish the state of Maharashtra in the Indian Union. The *chowk* centres on a statue of the Roman goddess **Flora**, erected in 1869 to commemorate Sir Bartle Frere. It's hard to see quite why they bothered – the Raj architecture expert, Philip Davies, was not being unkind when he said, "The fountain was designed by a committee, and it shows."

Horniman Circle and the Town Hall

Horniman Circle, formerly Elphinstone Circle, is named after a pro-Independence newspaper editor. It was conceived in 1860 as a centrepiece of a newly planned Bombay by the then Municipal Commissioner, Charles Forjett, on the site of Bombay "Green". Forjett, a Eurasian, had something of a peculiar

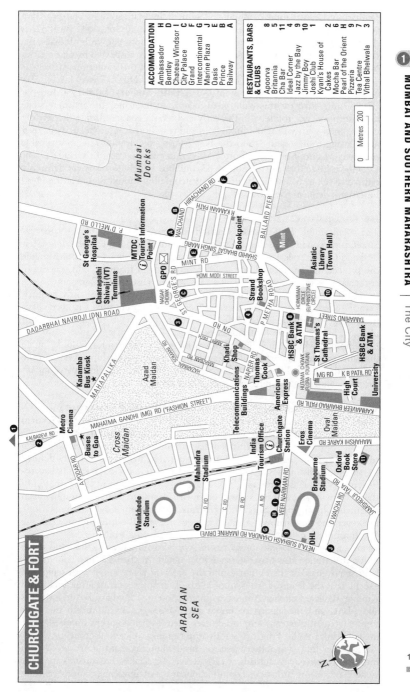

CHURCHGATE & FORT

ACCOMMODATION

Ambassador	H
Bentley	D
Chateau Windsor	I
City Palace	C
Grand	F
Intercontinental	G
Marine Plaza	J
Oasis	E
Prince	B
Railway	A

RESTAURANTS, BARS & CLUBS

Apoorva	8
Britannia	5
Cha Bar	11
Ideal Corner	4
Jazz by the Bay	9
Jimmy Boy	10
Joshi Club	1
Kyani's House of Cakes	2
Mocha Bar	6
Pearl of the Orient	H
Pizzeria	7
Tea Centre	9
Vithal Bhelwala	3

0 Metres 200

ARABIAN SEA

Mumbai Docks

reputation; he was fond of disguising himself in "native" dress and prowling about certain districts of the city to listen out for seditious talk. In 1857, at the time of the First War of Independence (as it is now known by Indians; the British call it the Indian Mutiny), Forjett fired on two suspected revolutionaries from a cannon on the Esplanade (roughly the site of the modern *maidans*).

Flanking the east side of the circle, the impressive Doric Town Hall on SBS Marg houses the vast collection of the **Asiatic Society Library** (Mon–Sat 10am–7pm). Save for the addition of electricity, little has changed here since the institution was founded in the early eighteenth century. Inside the reading rooms, lined with wrought-iron loggias and teak bookcases, scholars pour over mouldering tomes dating from the Raj. Among the 10,000 rare and valuable manuscripts stored here is a fourteenth-century first edition of Dante's *Divine Comedy*, said to be worth around $3 million, which the Society famously refused to sell to Mussolini. Visitors are welcome but should sign in at the Head Librarian's desk on the ground floor.

St Thomas' Cathedral

The small, simple **St Thomas' Cathedral** (daily 6.30am–6pm), on Tamarind Street, is reckoned to be the oldest British building in Mumbai, blending Classical and Gothic styles. After the death of its founding father, Governor Aungier, the project was abandoned; the walls stood 5m high for forty-odd years until enthusiasm was rekindled by a chaplain to the East India Company in the second decade of the eighteenth century. It was finally opened on Christmas Day 1718, complete with the essential "cannon-ball-proof roof". In those days, the seating was divided into useful sections for those who should know their place, including one for "Inferior Women".

St Thomas' whitewashed and polished brass-and-wood interior looks much the same as when the staff of the East India Company worshipped here in the eighteenth century. Lining the walls are memorial tablets to British parishioners, many of whom died young, either from disease or in battle.

Victoria Terminus (Chhatrapati Shivaji Terminus)

Inspired by St Pancras station in London, F.W. Stevens designed **Victoria Terminus**, the most barmy of Mumbai's buildings, as a paean to "progress". Built in 1887 as the largest British edifice in India, it's an extraordinary amalgam of domes, spires, Corinthian columns and minarets that was succinctly defined by the journalist James Cameron as "Victorian-Gothic-Saracenic-Italianate-Oriental-St Pancras-Baroque". In keeping with the current re-Indianization of the city's roads and buildings, this icon of British imperial architecture has been renamed **Chhatrapati Shivaji Terminus**, in honour of a Maratha warlord. However, the new name is a bit of a mouthful and the locals mostly still use **VT** (pronounced "vitee" or "wee tee") when referring to it.

Few of the two million or so passengers who fill almost a thousand trains every day notice the mass of decorative detail. A "British" lion and Indian tiger stand guard at the entrance, and the exterior is festooned with sculptures executed at the Bombay Art School by the Indian students of John Lockwood Kipling, Rudyard's father. Among them are grotesque mythical beasts, monkeys and plants and medallions of important personages. To minimize the sun's impact, stained glass was employed, decorated with locomotives and elephant images. Above it all, "Progress" stands atop the massive central dome.

An endless frenzy of activity goes on inside: hundreds of porters in red with impossibly oversize headloads; TTEs (Travelling Ticket Examiners) in black jackets and white trousers clasping clipboards detailing reservations; spitting checkers busy handing out fines to those caught in the act; chai-wallahs with trays of tea; trundling magazine stands; crowds of bored soldiers smoking *beedis*; and the inexorable progress across the station of sweepers bent double. Amid it all, whole families spread out on the floor, eating, sleeping or just waiting and waiting.

Marine Drive and Chowpatty Beach

Netaji Subhash Chandra Marg, better known as **Marine Drive**, is Mumbai's seaside prom, an eight-lane highway with a wide pavement built in the 1920s on reclaimed land. Sweeping in an arc from the skyscrapers at Nariman Point in the south, the route ends at the foot of Malabar Hill and Chowpatty Beach. The whole stretch is a favourite place for a stroll; the promenade next to the sea has uninterrupted views virtually the whole way along, while the apartment blocks on the land side are some of the most desirable and expensive addresses in the city.

Just beyond the huge flyover at its northern end are a series of cricket pitches known as **gymkhanas**, where there's a good chance of catching a match any day of the week. A number are exclusive to particular religious communities. The first doubles as a swanky outdoor wedding venue for Parsi marriages; others include the Catholic, Islamic and Hindu pitches, the last of which has a classic colonial-style pavilion.

Chowpatty Beach

Chowpatty Beach is a Mumbai institution, which really comes to life at night and on Saturday. People do not come here to swim (the sea is foul) but to wander, sit on the beach, let the kids ride a pony or a rusty Ferris wheel, have a massage, get ears cleaned or picnic on *bhel puri* and cups of *kulfi*. For the last century or so, Gupta Bhelwallas's *bhel puri* stall has satisfied the discerning Mumbai palate with a secret concoction of the sunset snack; you'll find it amid the newly constructed "shacks" to which the *bhel* wallahs were recently moved as part of the Municipality's bid to clean the beach up.

Once a year in September the **Ganesh Chathurthi** festival (see box p.111) draws gigantic crowds to participate in the immersion of idols, both huge and small, of the elephant-headed god Ganesh.

Mani Bhavan Mahatma Gandhi Museum

A ten-minute walk north from the middle of Chowpatty Beach (along P Ramabai Marg), **Mani Bhavan**, at 19 Laburnum Rd (daily 9.30am–6pm), was Gandhi's Bombay base between 1917 and 1934. Set in a leafy upper-middle-class road, the house is now a permanent memorial to the Mahatma with an extensive research library. Within the lovingly maintained polished-wood interior, the walls are covered with photos of historic events and artefacts from the man's extraordinary life – the most disarming of which is a friendly letter to Hitler suggesting world peace. Gandhi's predictably simple sitting room-cum-bedroom is preserved behind glass. Laburnum Road is a few streets along from the Bharatiya Vidya Bhavan music venue on KM Munshi Marg – if coming by taxi ask for the nearby Gamdevi Police Station.

North of Chowpatty

Two of Mumbai's most popular religious sites, one Hindu, the other Muslim, can be reached by following Bhulabhai Desai Road **north from Chowpatty** as far as Prabhu Chowk, through the exclusive suburb of Breach Candy (bus

△ Ganesha festival, Mumbai

#132 from Colaba). Alternatively, make for Mumbai Central and head due northwest to Vatsalabai Desai Chowk (also bus #132).

Mahalakshmi Mandir is joined to Bhulabhai Desai Road by an alley lined with stalls selling puja offerings and devotional pictures. Mumbai's favourite *devi*, **Lakshmi**, goddess of beauty and prosperity – the city's most sought-after attributes – is here propitiated with coconuts, sweets, lengths of shimmering silk and giant lotus blooms. Gifts pile so high that the temple *pujaris* run a money-spinning sideline reselling them. Their little shop, to the left of the entrance, is a good place to buy cut-price saris and brocades infused with lucky Lakshmi-energy. While you're here, find out what your future holds by joining the huddle of devotees pressing rupees onto the rear wall of the shrine room. If your coin sticks, you'll be rich.

Occupying a small islet in the bay just north of the Mahalakshmi is the mausoleum of the Muslim saint, Afghan mystic **Haji Ali Bukhari**. The tomb is connected to the mainland by a narrow concrete **causeway**, only passable at low tide. When not immersed in water, its entire length is lined with beggars who change one-rupee pieces into ten-paise coins for pilgrims. The prime sites, closer to the snack bars that flank the main entrance, near the small mosque, and the gateway to the **tomb** itself, are allocated in a strict pecking order. If you want to make a donation, spare a thought for the unfortunates in the middle. After all the commotion, the tomb itself comes as something of a disappointment. Its white Moghul domes and minarets look a lot less exotic close up than when viewed from the shore, silhouetted against the sun as it drops into the Arabian Sea.

The central bazaars

Lining the anarchic jumble of streets north of Lokmanya Tilak (formerly Carnac) Road, Mumbai's teeming **central bazaars** are India at its most intense. You could wander around here for days without seeing the same shop front twice. In practice, most visitors find a couple of hours mingling with the crowds in the heat and din quite enough. Nevertheless, the market districts form a fascinating counterpoint to the wide and Westernized streets of downtown, even if you're not buying.

In keeping with traditional divisions of guild, caste and religion, most streets specialize in one or two types of merchandise. If you lose your bearings, the best way out is to ask someone to wave you in the direction of **Mohammed Ali Road**, the busy road through the heart of the district (now surmounted by a gigantic flyover), from where you can hail a cab.

Crawford Market

Crawford (aka Mahatma Phule) **Market**, ten minutes' walk north of CST (VT) station, is an old British-style covered market dealing in just about every kind of fresh food and domestic animal imaginable. Thanks to its pompous Norman–Gothic tower and prominent position at the corner of Lokmanya Tilak Road and Dr DN Marg, the Crawford Market is also a useful landmark and a good place to begin a foray into the bazaars.

Before venturing inside, stop to admire the **friezes** wrapped around its exterior – a Victorian vision of sturdy-limbed peasants toiling in the fields designed by Rudyard Kipling's father, Lockwood, as principal of the Bombay School of Art in 1865. The **main hall** is still divided into different sections: pyramids of polished fruit and vegetables down one aisle, sacks of nuts or oil-tins full of herbs and spices down another. Around the back of the market, in the atmospheric wholesale wing, the pace of life is more hectic. Here, noisy crowds of coolies mill about with large reed-baskets held high in the air (if they are looking for work) or on their heads (if they've found some).

One place animal-lovers should definitely steer clear of is Crawford Market's **pet** and **poultry** section, on the east side of the building. You never quite know what creatures will turn up here, cringing in rank-smelling, undersized cages.

North of Crawford Market

The streets immediately **north of Crawford Market** and west of **Moham-med Ali Road**, form one vast bazaar area. Ranged along both sides of narrow **Mangaldas Lane**, the cloth bazaar, are small shops draped with lengths of bright silk and cotton. Low doorways on the left open onto a colourful **covered market** area, packed with tiny stalls.

Eastwards along Mangaldas Lane from Carnac Road, the pale green-washed domes, arches and minarets of the **Jami Masjid**, or "Friday Mosque" (c.1800), mark the start of the Muslim neighbourhoods. **Memon Street**, cutting north from the mosque, is the site of the **Zaveri Bazaar**, the jewellery market where Mumbaikars come to shop for dowries and wedding attire.

By the time the gleaming golden spire that crowns the **Mumba Devi temple**'s cream-and-turquoise tower appears at the end of the street, you're deep in a maze of twisting lanes hemmed in by tall, wooden-balconied buildings. One of the most important centres of Devi worship in India, the temple was built early in the nineteenth century, when the deity was relocated from her former home to make way for CST (VT) station. Mumba Devi's other claim to fame is that her name is the original root of the word "Bombay", as well as the official, Maharashtran version, "**Mumbai**".

Bear left at the temple and keep heading along the main bazaar for ten or fifteen minutes and you'll arrive at another important Hindu enclave, **Bhuleshwar**. The district is famous throughout the city for its colourful **phool galli** (flower lane), where temple goers buy luxurious garlands, lotus bundles and marigolds heaped in huge baskets. Of the 85 shrines said to be crammed into its lanes the most important is the **Bhola Ishtwar Mandir**, the ancient Shiva temple around which this district is believed to have first grown up in the eighteenth century. Its odd mix of Gujarati, Rajasthani and Konkan architectural styles reflect the origins of the neighbourhood's first immigrants. Jain merchants also settled here from the northwest, erecting a pair of finely carved white marble temples – **Shantinath** and **Parshavanath** – tucked away down a narrow lane just off the nest crossroads, Jayamber Chowk. Animal lovers should ask the way here to the nearby **Panjarapool animal sanctuary**, where around four hundred beautiful brown *gir* cows are cared for, along with a menagerie of pigeons, rabbits, chickens and ducks. You can purchase donatory bowls of grain and *ladoo* balls to feed them at reception, where stern-faced Jain attendants enforce the strict no photography rule.

Chor Bazaar, Mutton Road and the red-light district

Jump in a taxi at the junction just down the lane from the Mumba Devi temple for the two-kilometre trip north to the other concentration of markets around **Johar Chowk**, just north of SP Patel Road. The most famous of these, **Chor** (literally "thieves") **Bazaar** (where vendors peevishly insist the name is a corruption of the Urdu *shor*, meaning "noisy"), is the city's largest **antiques**-cum-flea market. Friday, the Muslim holy day, is the best day to be here. From 9am onwards, the neighbourhood is cluttered with hawkers and handcarts piled high with bric-a-brac and assorted junk. At other times, the antique shops down on **Mutton Road** are the main attraction. Once, you could hope to unearth real gems in these dark, fusty stores, but your chances of finding a genuine bargain nowadays are minimal. Most of the stuff is pricey Victoriana – old gramophones, chamber pots, chipped china – salvaged from the homes of Parsi families on the decline. The place is also awash with **fakes**, mainly small bronze votive statues, which make good souvenirs if you can knock the price down.

Press on north through Chor Bazaar and you'll eventually come out onto **Grant Road** (Maulana Shaukatali Road). Further north and west, in the warren of lanes below JB Behram Marg, lies the city's infamous **red-light district. Kamathipura**'s rows of luridly lit, barred shop fronts, from where an estimated 25,000 prostitutes ply their trade, are one of Mumbai's more degrading and unpleasant spectacles. Many of these so-called "**cage girls**" are young teenagers from poor tribal areas, and from across the border in Nepal, who have been sold by desperate parents into **bonded slavery** until they can earn the money to pay off family debts.

Elephanta

An hour's boat ride from Colaba, the island of **ELEPHANTA** offers one of the more atmospheric escapes from the seething claustrophobia of the city – as long as you time your visit to avoid the weekend deluge of noisy day-trippers. Populated only by a small fishing community, it was originally known as **Gharapuri**, the "city of Ghara priests", until the island was renamed in the sixteenth century by the Portuguese in honour of the carved elephant they found at the port. Its chief attraction is its unique **cave temple**, whose massive **Trimurti** (three-faced) **Shiva sculpture** is as fine an example of Hindu architecture as you'll find anywhere.

"**Deluxe**" **boats** set off from the Gateway of India (Oct–May hourly 9am–2.30pm; Rs100 return including government guide); book through the kiosks near the Gateway of India. Ask for your guide at the cave's ticket office on arrival – they take about thirty minutes. **Ordinary ferries** (Rs80 return), also from the Gateway of India, don't include guides, and are usually packed. The journey takes about an hour on either boat.

Cool drinks and souvenir stalls line the way up the hill, and at the top, the MTDC *Chalukya* restaurant offers food and beer, and a terrace with good views out to sea, but you cannot stay overnight on the island.

The Cave

Elephanta's impressive excavated eighth-century **cave** (9.30am–4pm; $5 [Rs5]), covering an area of approximately 5000 square metres, is reached by climbing more than one hundred steps to the top of the hill. Inside, the massive columns, carved from solid rock, give the deceptive impression of being structural. To the right, as you enter, note the panel of **Nataraj**, Shiva as the cosmic dancer. Though spoiled by the Portuguese who, it is said, used it for target practice, the panel remains magnificent; Shiva's face is rapt, and in one of his left hands he removes the veil of ignorance. Opposite is a badly damaged panel of Lakulisha, Shiva with a club (*lakula*).

Each of the four entrances to the simple square main **shrine** – unusually, it has one on each side – is flanked by a pair of huge fanged *dvarpala* guardians (only those to the back have survived undamaged), while inside a large *lingam* is surrounded by coins and smouldering joss left by devotees. Facing the northern wall of the shrine, another panel shows Shiva impaling the demon Andhaka, who wandered around as though blind, symbolizing his spiritual blindness. The panel behind the shrine on the back wall portrays the marriage of Shiva and Parvati. A powerful six-metre bust of **Trimurti**, the three-faced Shiva, who embodies the powers of creator, preserver and destroyer, stands nearby, and to the west a sculpture shows Shiva as **Ardhanarishvara**, half male and half female. Near the second entrance on the east, another panel shows Shiva and Parvati on **Mount Kailasha** with Ravana about to lift the mountain. His curved spine shows the strain.

The outskirts: Kanheri Caves

Overlooking the suburb of Borivli, 42km out at the northern limits of Mumbai's sprawl, are the Buddhist **Kanheri Caves** (daily 9am–5.30pm; $2 [Rs5]), ranged over the hills in virtually unspoilt forest. It's an interminable journey by road, so catch one of the many **trains** (50min) on the suburban line from Churchgate (marked "BO" on the departure boards; "limited stop" trains are 15min faster) to Borivli East. When you arrive, take the Borivli East exit, where a **bus** (for Kanheri Cave via SG Parles; Rs14), **auto-rickshaw** (about Rs75) or **taxi** (about Rs100) will take you the last 15km. Bring water and food as the stalls here only sell warm soft drinks.

Kanheri may not be as spectacular as other cave sites, but some of its sculpture is superb – though to enjoy the blissful peace and quiet that attracted its original occupants you should **avoid the weekends**. Most of the caves, which date from the second to the ninth century AD, were used simply by monks for accommodation and meditation during the four months of the monsoon, when an itinerant life was impractical. They are connected by steep winding paths and steps; engage one of the friendly local guides at the entrance to find your way about, but don't expect any sort of lecture as their English is limited. The risk of muggings in some of the remoter caves means it is not advisable to venture off the beaten track alone.

In **Cave 1**, an incomplete *chaitya* hall (a hall with a stupa at one end, an aisle and row of columns at either side), you can see where the rock was left cut, but unfinished. Two stupas stand in **Cave 2**; one was vandalized by a certain N. Christian, whose carefully incised Times-Roman graffiti bears the date 1810. A panel shows seated Buddhas, portrayed as teachers. Behind, and to the side, is the *bodhisattva* of compassion, Padmapani, while to the right the *viharas* feature rock-cut beds.

Huge Buddhas, with serenely joyful expressions and unfeasibly large shoulders, stand on either side of the porch to the spectacular **Cave 3**. Between them, you'll see the panels of "donor couples", thought to have been foreigners that patronized the community.

The sixth-century **Cave 11** is a large assembly hall, where two long "tables" of rock were used for the study of manuscripts. Seated at the back, in the centre, is a figure of the Buddha as teacher, an image repeated in the entrance, to the left, with a wonderful flight of accompanying celestials. Just before the entrance to a small cell in **Cave 34**, flanked by two standing Buddhas, an unfinished ceiling painting shows the Buddha touching the earth. There must be at least a hundred more Buddha images on panels in **Cave 67**, a large hall. On the left side, and outside in the entrance, these figures are supported by *nagas* (snakes representing *kundalini*, yogic power).

Eating

In keeping with its cosmopolitan credentials, Mumbai is crammed with interesting **eating places**, whether you fancy splashing out on a buffet lunch-with-a-view

Street food

Mumbai is renowned for distinctive street foods – and especially **bhel puri**, a quintessentially Mumbai masala mixture of puffed rice, deep-fried *vermicelli*, potato, crunchy *puri* pieces, chilli paste, tamarind water, chopped onions and coriander. More hygienic, but no less ubiquitous, is **pao bhaji**, a round Portuguese-style bread roll stuffed with griddle-fried, spicy lentil stew, and **kanji vada**, savoury doughnuts soaked in fermented mustard and chilli sauce. And if all that doesn't appeal, a pit stop at one of the city's hundreds of **juice bars** probably will. There's no better way to beat the sticky heat than with a glass of cool milk shaken with fresh pineapple, mango, banana, *chikoo* (small brown fruit that tastes like a sweet pear) or custard apple. Just make sure they hold on the ice – made, of course, with untreated water.

from a flashy five-star restaurant, or simply tucking into piping-hot roti kebab by gaslight in the street.

Restaurants, bars and cafés are listed by district. **Phone numbers** have been given where we recommend you reserve a table for dinner; and beware of **service charges** levied on your bill by some of the more expensive places.

Colaba and Kala Ghoda

Colaba and Kala Ghoda's cafés, bars and restaurants encompass just about the full range of modern Mumbai's gastronomic possibilities, from no-frills kerbside kebab joints and old Irani cafés to exclusive air-conditioned restaurants patronized by Bollywood stars and politicians. The majority – among them the popular travellers' haunts, *Leopold's* and the *Café Mondegar* – are up at the north end of the Causeway. The following all feature on our Colaba map, p.122.

All Stir Fry *Gorden House Hotel.* Build-your-own wok meal from a selection of fresh veg, meat, fish, noodles and sauces, flash-cooked in front of you (Rs250–350 per bowl). Trendy white, minimalist decor, glacial a/c, and snappy service.

Bademiya Behind the *Taj* on Tulloch Rd. Legendary Colaba kebab-wallah serving delicious flame-grilled chicken, mutton and fish steaks, wrapped in paper-thin, piping hot *rotis*, from benches on the sidewalk. Rich families from uptown drive here on weekends, eating on their car bonnets, but there are also little tables and chairs if you don't fancy a takeaway.

Busaba 4 Mandlik Marg ☎022/2204 3779. Sophisticated bar-restaurant specializing in Far-Eastern cuisine – Thai, Korean, Burmese, Vietnamese and Tibetan staples, with exotic salads (green mango and glass noodle). One of *the* places to be seen (if you can't quite afford to eat at *Indigo* next door). Count on Rs750–1000 per head for the works.

Café Samovar Jehangir Art Gallery, MG Rd ☎022/2284 8000. Very pleasant, peaceful semi-al-fresco café opening onto the museum gardens, with a good-value lunch menu (Rs50) featuring *pulaos*, stuffed *parathas* and biriyanis, as well as plenty of à la carte choices (prawn curry, roti

kebabs, and fresh salads and dhansak. They also served delicious chilled guava juice and beer (Rs90), but note no drinks are served 1–3pm.

Churchill 103 Colaba Causeway. Tiny 26-seater Parsi diner, with a bewildering choice of curious dishes, mostly meat based and served in mild gravies alongside a blob of mash and boiled veg – ideal if you've had your fill of spicy food. No alcohol. Main courses around Rs150.

Indigo 4 Mandlik Marg ☎022/2236 8999. Currently the city's most fashionable restaurant, and for once deserving of the hype. The cooking's Italian-based with a Konkan–Keralan twist (eg Kochi oysters with saffron ravioli). House flambée is extremely popular, as much for its head-turning potential as anything else. Count on Rs1000-plus for three courses. Reservations essential.

Kailash Parbat ("KP's") 1 Pasta Lane, near the Strand cinema. Uninspiring on the outside, but the *aloo parathas* for breakfast, pure veg nibbles, hot snacks and sweets (across the road) are worth the walk. A Colaba institution – try their famous *makai-ka* (corn) *rotis*.

Kamat Colaba Causeway. Friendly little eatery serving unquestionably the best South Indian breakfasts in the area, as well as the usual range of southern snacks (*iddli-vada-sambar*), delicious spring *dosas* and (limited) thalis for Rs30–85. The best option in the area for budget travellers with big appetites.

Khyber opposite Jehangir Art Gallery, Kala Ghoda ☎022/2267 3227. Opulent Arabian Nights interior and uncompromisingly rich "Northwest Frontier" cuisine, served by black-tie waiters. The chicken tikka is legendary, but their tandoori dishes and kebab platter are superb too. Count on Rs800–1000.

Konkan Café *Taj President Hotel*, Cuffe Parade ☎022/5665 0808. This is the place to push the boat out: a sophisticated five-star hotel restaurant serving fine regional cuisine from coastal Maharashtra, Goa, Karnataka and Kerala – at reasonable prices. You can choose from their thali platters (Rs375–475), or go à la carte: the crab in butter pepper garlic is to die for, as is the tiger prawn in *kokum* garlic and *meen pollichattu* (red snappers steamed Keralan-style in banana leaves). Quite simply some of the most mouthwatering South Indian food you'll ever eat.

Leopold's Colaba Causeway. Colaba's most famous – and overpriced – café-bar is determinedly Western, with a clientele to match. Three hundred items on the menu from scrambled eggs to "chilly chicken", washed down with cold beer (Rs120). There's also a bar upstairs.

Olympia Coffee House 1 Colaba Causeway. *Fin-de-siècle* Irani café with marble tabletops, wooden wall panels, fancy mirrors and a mezzanine floor for "ladies". Waiters in Peshwari caps and *salwar kamises* serve melt-in-the-mouth kebabs, flavoured with subtle spices and delicious curd-based dips. For dessert, go for the "custard". A quintessential Bombay experience. Inexpensive.

The Sea Lounge *Taj Mahal Hotel*. Spacious 1930s-style lounge café on the first floor of the *Taj*. Come for afternoon tea or a late breakfast with a backdrop of the Gateway and harbour. Worth splashing out on for the atmosphere. Opens at 7am for breakfast; closes at midnight. Pastries Rs200–300; coffees and teas Rs125–200.

Trishna 7 Sai Baba Marg (Ropewalk Lane), Kala Ghoda ☎022/2270 1623. Visiting dignitaries and local celebs from the President of Greece and Imran Khan to Bollywood stars have eaten here (as photos attest). Wonderful fish dishes in every sauce going, and prices to match the clientele (main courses from Rs450). Butter pepper garlic crab is their signature dish, but the pomfret stuffed with green masala is great too. Very small, so book in advance.

Downtown: Fort, CST (VT) and Dhobi Talao

Don't be discouraged by the heat and traffic from venturing outside Colaba for a meal. A short walk or taxi ride north are some of the best cafés and restaurants in the city, among them Mumbai's last surviving traditional Parsi diners, whose menus and decor have changed little over three or four generations. The places listed below are all marked on the Churchgate and Fort map on p.127.

Apoorva Vasta House (Noble Chambers), SA Brelvi Rd ☎022/2287 0335. Currently the city's most rated Mangalorean, hidden up a side street off Horniman Circle (look for the tree trunk wrapped with fairy lights). The cooking's completely authentic and the seafood – simmered in spicy coconut-based gravies – fresh off the boats each day. Try their definitive Bombay Duck or sublime prawn *gassi*, served with perfect *sanna* and *appams*. Women should note the ground floor doubles as a bloke-ish bar in the evenings.

Britannia & Co Opposite the GPO, Sprott Rd, Ballard Estate. Quirky little Parsi restaurant, famous as much for its quaint period atmosphere as its wholesome Irani food. Most people come for the sublime "*berry pulao*" (chicken, mutton or vegetable), made with deliciously tart dried berries imported from Tehran (Rs150, but portions are gigantic). For afters, there's the house "caramel custard". One of the city's unmissable eating experiences. Open 11.30am–3.30pm.

Ideal Corner 12 F/G Hornby View, Gunbow St ☎022/2262 1930. Another Parsi café with a cult following, but more in the thick of things than *Britannia* and less old world since its recent facelift. Go for one of their delicious homemade Parsi specialities: *kchchidi* prawn, lamb dhansak or chicken *farcha*, rounded off with the legendary *lagan* custard (a nutty crème caramel served chilled in little foil tubs). Most mains Rs45–60. Closed evenings and Sun.

Jimmy Boy 11 Bank St, Vikas Bldg, off Horniman Circle ☎022/2270 0880. Among the few places left in Mumbai where you can sample pukka Parsi wedding food (albeit in rather inauthentic a/c surroundings, to a Shania Twain soundtrack). Go for the Rs225 fixed menu (pomfret and green chilli sauce steamed in a banana leaf/mutton *pulao* with dhansak dhal/dessert).

Joshi Club 31-A Narottamwadi, Kalbadevi Rd ☎022/2205 8089. Also known as *The Friends Union Joshi Club*, this eccentric thali canteen serves what many aficionados regard as the most genuine and tasty Gujarati-Marwari meals in the city, dished up on unpromising Formica tables against a backdrop of grubby walls. Rs70 buys you unlimited portions of four vegetables, dhals and up to four different kinds of bread, with all the trimmings (and banana custard). Extra *farsan* and sweets cost Rs20. Finding it requires some effort: walk or catch a cab to the bottom of Kalbadevi Rd (opposite the Metro cinema; see map p.000); head north across Vardhaman Chowk, and continue up Kalbadevi Rd for 5min until you see a signboard on your right for "Bhonalaya", below a first-floor window. The locals will know where it is.

Kyani's "House of Cakes" Bakery opposite Metro cinema, Dhobi Talao. The most dated and authentic Parsi joint in the city, worth a visit more for the atmosphere than for the food – neither of which has altered in over ninety years since the café first opened. They serve freshly baked biscuits and cakes, "bun-*maska*" (basically warm buttered rolls) and good strong chai in china cups.

Vithal Bhelwala 5 AK Naik Marg (Baston Rd), close to CST (VT). Mumbai's favourite *bhel puri* outlet, open since 1875 and still doing a roaring trade. No fewer than 25 kinds of *bhel* are on offer, including one pitched at British palates, with "boiled veg and cornflakes". They also do delicious potato cutlets, served with crunchy *puri* and yoghurt. Handy for the movie houses and the station.

Churchgate and Nariman Point

The restaurants listed below are marked on the Churchgate and Fort map on p.127.

Cha Bar Oxford Bookstore, 3 Dinsha Vaccha Rd, Churchgate. Very chic a/c café accessed via the city's top book store, popular mainly with well-heeled students. They serve an exhaustive range of single-estate and regional teas and coffees, from high-fired Darjeeling to Kashmiri *kawa* and Ladhaki butter tea, as well as trendy ayurvedic brews and house "tea cocktails"; and there's a tempting menu of (pricy) light snacks and toasties. Open 10am–10pm.

Mocha Bar VN Rd. Chilled terrace café where swarms of north Mumbai bratpackers order American-style coffees, Mediterranean mezes and outrageously expensive New World wines, crashed out on bolster cushions smoking fruit-flavoured tobacco on a hookah pipe: very much the zeitgeist.

The Pearl of the Orient *Ambassador Hotel*, VN Rd ☏ 022/229 1131. Revolving Oriental restaurant in this four-star hotel. The cooking's nothing special (and expensive at around Rs750 for three courses), but the views over the city are extraordinary.

The Pizzeria corner of Veer Nariman and Marine Drive. Delicious, freshly baked pizzas served on newly renovated terrace overlooking Back Bay, or to take away. Plenty of choice, and moderate prices (Rs175–295 per pizza).

The Tea Centre Resham Bhavan, 78 VN Rd. Another vestige of colonial days which, despite a lavish new refit, has retained its Raj-era charm, with paddle fans, comfy furniture and waiters wearing old-style *pugris*. Fine tea is its *raison d'être*, but they also serve delicious Continental snacks (try their fluffy cheese omlettes) and cakes, as well as a good-value "Executive Lunch" (Rs200).

Crawford Market and the central bazaars

The restaurants listed below are marked on the main Mumbai map on pp.108–109.

Badshah Juice and Snack Bar Opposite Crawford Market, Lokmanya Tilak Rd. Mumbai's most acclaimed *falooda* joint also serves delicious kulfi, ice creams and dozens of freshly squeezed fruit juices. The ideal place to round off a trip to the market, though expect to have to queue for a table.

Delhi Darbar Corner of Maulana Shaukatali Rd (Grant Rd) and PB Marg (Falkland Rd), opposite Alfred Talkies. On the fringes of the red light district, but a must for lovers of authentic Mughlai cuisine. Waiters in Peshawari caps serve up superb flame-grilled chicken and mutton *sheekh* kebabs, biriyanis, *pulaos* and the house speciality, chicken tikka, rounded off with the creamiest lassis in Mumbai. Most dishes only Rs50–150.

Rajdhani Mangaldas Rd (in the silk bazaar opposite Crawford Market). Outstanding, eat-till-you-burst Gujarati thalis. Very cramped and more expensive than usual (Rs150 on weekdays, and Rs195 for the "Special" Sunday lunch), but they don't stint on quality. Closed Sun evenings.

Vaibhai Payawala 45 Guzer St, Bohri Mohalla. Aficionados of the "full English breakfast" should sample its Muslim Mumbaikar equivalent, the *bara handi.* Slow-cooked overnight in twelve pots sealed with flour dough, the dishes are all traditional meat delicacies, prepared the same way here for four generations. Enjoy them with rice or smoky-flavoured *lamba pau* bread from the adjacent bakery. Jump in a cab to Bohri Mohalla and ask the way when you get there. Inexpensive.

Chowpatty Beach

The restaurant listed below is marked on the main Mumbai map on pp.108–109.

Crystal 19 Chowpatty Seaface, near Wilson College. Chowpatty is crammed with snack joints and cheap restaurants, but this one stands out – not that you'd ever know it from the grimy decor. Homesick Punjabis and lovers of pukka north Indian home cooking travel here from across the city to eat the wholesome dhal *makhini, alu jeera* and other spicy vegetarian dishes, served from a soot-blackened kitchen. A hot contender for Mumbai's best budget restaurant, with most mains under Rs50. And don't miss the lightly chilled *kir* for dessert.

Nightlife and entertainment

Mumbai never sleeps. No matter what time of night you venture out, there are bound to be others going about some business or other. The city has always led the **nightlife** scene in India and there are bars and clubs to suit every taste: jazz dens compete with salsa, tabla-dance fusions and funk. Mumbai's alternative but decidedly yuppie crowd meet at the *Ghetto Bar* before heading down to the gay, glitzy or groovy clubs around Colaba and Juhu.

Of course, Mumbai is also a cultural centre, attracting the finest **Indian classical music** and **dance** artists from all over the country. There are frequent concerts and recitals at venues such as: Bharatiya Vidya Bhavan, KM Munshi Marg (☎022/2363 0224), the headquarters of the international cultural (Hindu) organization; and the National Centre for the Performing Arts, Nariman Point (NCPA; ☎022/2288 3838).

Bars

Mumbai has an unusually easy-going attitude to **alcohol**; popping into a bar for a beer is very much accepted (for men at least) even at lunchtime. Chowpatty Beach and Colaba Causeway, where you'll find *Leopold's* and the *Café Mondegar*, form the focus of the travellers' social scene, but if you want to sample the pulse of the city's nightlife, venture up to Bandra and Juhu.

Laughter clubs

On the principle that laughter is the best medicine, Mumbai doctor Madan Kataria has created a new kind of therapy: *hasya* (laughter) yoga. There are now over 300 **Laughter Clubs** in India and many more worldwide; around 50,000 people joined the Laughter Day celebrations in Mumbai in January 2003.

Fifteen-minute sessions start with adherents doing yogic breathing whilst chanting "Ho ho ha ha", which develops into spontaneous "hearty", "silent" and "swinging" laughter. Sessions mostly take place between 6am and 7am, a time that, according to the good doctor, "keeps you in good spirits throughout the day, energizes your body and charges you with happiness". There are many clubs in Mumbai itself: look for semi-circles of people holding their hands in the air and laughing on Juhu beach, or go to ⊛www.laughteryoga.org for the full story.

For anyone brought up on TV, it's hard to imagine the power that **movies** continue to wield in India. Every village has a cinema within walking distance and, with a potential audience in the hundreds of millions, the Indian film industry is the largest in the world, producing around 900 full-length features each year. Regional cinema, catering for different language groups (in particular the Tamil cinema of Chennai), though popular locally, has little national impact. Only Hindi film – which accounts for one-fifth of all the films made in India – has crossed regional boundaries to great effect, most particularly in the north. The home of the Hindi blockbuster, the "all-India film", is Mumbai, famously known as **Bollywood**.

To overcome differences of language and religion, the Bollywood movie follows rigid conventions and genres; as in myth, its characters have predetermined actions and destinies. Knowing a plot need not detract from the drama and, indeed, it is not uncommon for Indian audiences to watch films numerous times. Unlike the Hollywood formula, which tends to classify each film under one genre, the Hindi film follows what is known as a **"masala format"**, and includes during its luxurious three hours a little bit of everything, especially romance, violence and comedy. Frequently the stories feature dispossessed male heroes fighting evil against all odds with a love interest thrown in. The sexual element has tended to be repressed, with numerous wet sari scenes and dance routines featuring the tensest pelvic thrusts, but strictly no kissing. Other typical **themes** include male bonding and betrayal, family melodrama, separation and reunion and religious piety. Dream sequences are almost obligatory, too, along with a festival or celebration scene – typically Holi, when people shower each other with paint – a comic character passing through, and a depraved, alcoholic and mostly Western "cabaret", filled with strutting villains and lewd dancing.

Recent blockbusters have also seen the introduction of a new stock character, the returning emigrant or "NRI" (Non-Resident Indian). This is one element in a more general trend sweeping Bollywood at the moment, as the big studios seek to pull in Hindi-speaking audiences in the UK, US and Canada. Overseas tickets typically cost ten times what they do in the flashiest of Mumbai's cinemas, and together with videos and DVD sales now account for forty percent of the industry's revenues. Budgets, production standards and on-screen sauciness have all been on the rise as a result, with more and more films using foreign locations, smaller spangly miniskirts and MTV-style choreography. A memorable recent example was the big first dance sequence in the smash hit *Kal Ho Naa Ho*, starring Shahrukh Khan and Preity Zinta, which takes place on the streets of Manhattan, featuring a multicultural cast of dancers in outlandish outfits waving little American flags.

Audiences may be growing in New York and London, but there has been a thirty percent drop in cinema receipts at home with the new pro-Western trends. Many pundits now warn that in its scramble for crossover hits, Bollywood is becoming perilously detached from the tastes of its less sophisticated audiences in India.

Visitors to the city should have ample opportunity to sample the delights of a Hindi movie, traditional or otherwise. To make an educated choice, buy *Bombay* magazine, which contains extensive **listings** and reviews. Alternatively, look for the biggest, brightest hoarding, and join the queue. Seats in a comfortable air-conditioned cinema cost Rs50–75, or less if you sit in the stalls (not advisable for women). Of the two hundred or so **cinemas**, only eight regularly screen **English-language** films. The most central and convenient are the Regal in Colaba, the gloriously Art Deco Eros opposite Churchgate station, the Sterling, the New Excelsior and the New Empire, which are all a short walk west of CST (VT) station.

Café Mondegar Colaba Causeway (see map p.122). Draught beer by the glass or pitcher (both imported and Indian) and deliciously fruity cocktails in a small café-bar. The atmosphere is very relaxed, the music tends towards rock classics and the clientele is a mix of Westerners and students;

murals by a famous Goan cartoonist give the place a cheerful ambience.

Copa Cobana 39-D Dariya Vihar, Chowpatty Beach (see map pp.108–109). A small, trendy tapas bar in a great location.

Czar Bar *Hotel Intercontinental*, 135 Marine Drive. Trendy vodka bar with chic, minimalist decor, clever lighting and 24 brands on offer (from Rs200/shot), plus a full range of other drinks and cocktails. The music's lounge until around 11pm, then picks up.

Quiet on weekday nights, but popular on weekends.

Indigo 4 Mandlik Rd, Colaba (see map p.122). One of the coolest hangouts in south Mumbai, popular with young media professionals and wine buffs. Its funky, stripped-bare decor set a new trend in the city.

Leo's Square 1st Floor, *Leopold's*, Colaba Causeway. Pretty much the same menu and prices as *Leopold's* downstairs, but here you can enjoy a/c, black-lighting and a quality sound system.

Nightclubs

The **nightclub** scene in Mumbai is the best in India and the late 1990s saw the rise of a funkier, groovier scene as the moneyed jet set began to hear the latest house, trance, fusion and funk that was hitting the decks in Goa and the West.

Most discos and clubs charge per couple on the door (with a portion of the entrance cost redeemable at the bar), and in theory have a "couples-only" policy. In practice, if you're in a mixed group or don't appear sleazy you won't have any problems. At the five-star hotels, entry can be restricted to hotel guests and members. Closing times vary; the Municipality recently slapped a 1.30am finish time on nightclubs, but – in spite of fears that this would kill Mumbai's booming nightlife – the ruling is routinely ignored.

Athena 41–44 Minoo Desai Marg, behind Radio Club, Colaba (see map p.122). Along with *Insomnia*, south Mumbai's most talked about nightspot: an all-white affair with a high-end restaurant, various lounges and a huge wine list (the owner is an Indian wine magnate). The music's mainstream R&B and Hindi pop, with the odd trance number. Rs1000 per couple. Closes at 1.30am, when there's a general exodus over to *Insomnia*.

Enigma *JW Marriott Hotel*, Juhu Tara Rd (see map pp.108–109). If you want to see what Hindi film stars and hip young Indian millionaires do for kicks, this is the place to come: the sexiest outfits, latest dance music (including plenty of *filmi* hits), most gorgeous decor and stiffest entrance cost (Rs1500 per couple).

Insomnia *Taj Mahal Palace & Tower*. Well-heeled yuppies and their NRI relatives strut their stuff

in this warren of light-up bars, hardwood dance floors and chill-out spaces beneath the *Taj*, featuring one of the city's heftiest sound systems. Open to non-members, but you'll have to look your best. Cover Rs1000 per couple. Punters start arriving at 11pm and it usually stays open until 3am.

Polly Esther's *Gorden House Hotel*, Battery St, Colaba. Retro club with brightly coloured theme decor, leather upholstery and a 1990s night on Thursdays; pop, rock, disco and Motown on the weekend. Rs750 per couple.

Rasberry Rhinoceros *Juhu Hotel*, Juhu Beach (see map pp.108–109). The most famous nightspot in the city, with a live head-banging rock band on Thursdays and a heavy metal sound system the rest of the time. Rs800 per couple.

Shopping

Mumbai is a great place to shop, whether for last-minute souvenirs, or essentials for the long journeys ahead. Locally produced **textiles** and export-surplus clothing are among the best buys, as are **handicrafts** from far-flung corners of the country. With the exception of the swish arcades in the five-star hotels, prices compare surprisingly well with other Indian cities. In the larger shops, rates are fixed and **credit cards** are often accepted; elsewhere, particularly dealing with street-vendors, it pays to haggle. Uptown, the **central bazaars** – see p.131 – are better for spectating than serious shopping, although the **antiques** and Friday flea market in the Chor, or "thieves" bazaar, can sometimes yield the odd bargain. The **Zaveri** (goldsmiths') **bazaar** opposite Crawford Market is the place to head for new gold and silver jewellery. The city features a number of swish modern **shopping centres**, including India's largest, Crossroads, at 28 Pandit MM Rd near the Haji Ali mosque. **Tea** lovers should check out the *Tea Centre* on VN Road (reviewed on p.137), which sells a wide range of quality tea, including the outrageously expensive "fine tippy golden Orange Pekoe" (Rs1000 per 250g).

Opening hours in the city centre are Monday to Saturday, 10am to 7pm. The Muslim bazaars, quiet on Friday, are otherwise open until around 9pm (or through the night during Ramadan).

Antiques

The **Chor Bazaar** area, and Mutton Street in particular, is the centre of Mumbai's **antique trade**. For a full account, see p.132. Another good, if much more expensive, place is **Phillip's** famous antique shop, on the corner of Madam Cama Road, opposite the Regal cinema in Colaba, which was in the middle of a major re-fit on our last visit. Brass, bronze and wood Hindu sculpture, silver jewellery, old prints and aquatints form the mainstay of its collection. Most of the stuff on sale dates from the twilight of the Raj – a result of the Indian government's ban on the export by foreigners of items more than a century old.

In the **Jehangir Art Gallery** basement, a branch of the antiques chain Natesan's Antiqarts offers a tempting selection of antique (and reproduction) sculpture, furniture, paintings and bronzes.

Clothes, textiles and household goods

Mumbai produces the bulk of India's **clothes**, mostly the lightweight, light-coloured "shirtings and suitings" favoured by droves of uniformly attired office-wallahs. For cheaper Western clothing, you can't beat the long row of stalls on the pavement of MG Road, opposite the Mumbai Gymkhana. "**Fashion Street**" specializes in reject and export-surplus goods ditched by big manufacturers, selling off T-shirts, jeans, leggings, summer dresses, and trendy sweatshirts. Better-quality cotton clothes (often stylish designer-label rip-offs) are available in shops along **Colaba Causeway**, such as Cotton World, down Mandlik Marg.

If you're looking for **traditional Indian clothes,** head for the Khadi Village Industries Emporium at 286 Dr DN Marg, near the Thomas Cook office. As Whiteaway & Laidlaw, this rambling Victorian department store used to kit all the newly arrived *burra-sahibs* out with pith helmets, khaki shorts and quinine tablets. These days, its old wooden counters, shirt and sock drawers stock dozens of different hand-spun cottons and silks, sold by the metre or made up as vests, *kurtas* or block-printed *salwar kamises*. Other items include the ubiquitous white Nehru caps, *dhotis*, Madras-check *lunghis* and fine brocaded silk saris.

Mumbai is one of the cheapest places in the world to buy **soft furnishings** and **household goods**, and if you know where to shop you could save the cost of your flight in an afternoon. For tablecloths, cotton and silk quilts, rattan blinds and upholstery fabric, try Chunilal Mulchand & Co, at the Indian Mercantile Mansion on Madame Cama Road, close to the Prince of Wales Museum. They'll copy **loose covers** for sofas and lounge chairs in a week.

Malabar, at the *Taj Mahal Palace & Tower*, is much pricier, but stocks some exquisite beaded cushion covers and throws in traditional Indian textiles. For other designer home furnishings – everything from cutlery to curtain panels – Contemporary Arts & Crafts, at 19 Jagmohandas Marg (Napean Sea Road) up in the exclusive Malabar Hill area, is a must.

Handicrafts

Regionally produced **handicrafts** are marketed in assorted state-run emporia at the World Trade Centre, down on Cuffe Parade, and along Sir PM Road, Fort. The quality is consistently high – as are the prices, if you miss out on the periodic holiday discounts. The same goes for the **Central Cottage Industries Emporium**, 34 Shivaji Marg, near the Gateway of India in Colaba, whose size and central location make it the single best all-round place to hunt for souvenirs. Downstairs you'll find inlaid furniture, wood- and metal-work, miniature paintings and jewellery, while upstairs specializes in toys, clothing and textiles – Gujarati appliqué bedspreads, hand-painted pillowcases and Rajasthani mirror-work, plus silk ties and Noel Coward dressing-gowns. **Mereweather Road**, directly behind the *Taj*, is awash with Kashmiri handicraft stores stocking overpriced papier-mâché pots and bowls, silver jewellery, woollen shawls and rugs. Avoid them if you find it hard to shrug off aggressive sales pitches.

Perfume is essentially a Muslim preserve in Mumbai. Down at the south end of Colaba Causeway, around Arthur Bunder Road, shops with mirrored walls and shelves are stacked with cut-glass carafes full of syrupy, fragrant essential oils. **Incense** is hawked in sticks, cones and slabs of sticky *dhoop* on the sidewalk nearby (check that the boxes haven't already been opened and their contents sold off piecemeal). For bulk buying, the hand-rolled, cottage-made bundles of incense sold in the Khadi Village Industries Emporium on Dr DN Marg (see p.141) are a better deal; it also has a handicraft department where, in addition to furniture, paintings and ornaments, you can pick up glass bangles, block-printed and calico bedspreads, and wooden votive statues produced in Maharashtran craft villages.

Books

Mumbai's excellent English-language **bookshops** and bookstalls are well stocked with everything to do with India, and a good selection of general classics, pulp fiction and travel writing. Indian editions of popular titles cost a fraction of what they do abroad and include lots of interesting works by lesser-known local authors. If you don't mind picking through dozens of trigonometry textbooks, back issues of *National Geographic* and salacious 1960s paperbacks, the **street stalls** between Flora Fountain and Churchgate station can also be good places to hunt for secondhand books.

Chetana 34 Dubash Rd (Rampart Row). Exclusively religion and philosophy.

Crossword Mahalakshmi Chambers, 22 Bhulabhai Desai Rd, Breach Candy ☎022/2492 2458. Mumbai's largest reputable retailer, a bus ride (#132) from the downtown area, near Mahalakshmi temple/Haji Ali's tomb. Open Mon–Fri 10am–8pm, Sat & Sun 10am–9pm.

Nalanda Ground floor, *Taj Mahal*. An exhaustive range of coffee-table tomes and paperback literature, though at top prices.

Oxford Bookstore Apeejay House, 3 Dinsha Vacha Rd, Churchgate. Not quite as large as Crossword, but almost, and much more easily accessible if you're staying downtown or in Colaba. It also has a very cool a/c café.

Pustak Bharati Bharatiya Vidya Bhavan, KM Munshi Marg. Excellent small bookshop specializing in Hindu philosophy and literature, plus details of Bhavan's cultural programmes.

Shankar Book-Stand Outside the *Café Mondegar*, Colaba Causeway. Piles of easy-reads, guidebooks, classic fiction, and most of the old favourites on India, at competitive rates.

Strand Next door to the Canara Bank, off PM Rd, Fort. The best value bookshop in the city centre, with the full gamut of Penguins and Indian literature, sold at amazing discounts.

Music

The most famous of Mumbai's many good **music shops** are near the Moti cinema along SV Patel Road, in the central bazaar district. Haribhai Vishwanath, Ram Singh and RS Mayeka are all government-approved retailers of traditional

Indian instruments, including sitars, sarods, tablas and flutes. For **cassettes and CDs** the best outlet by far is Rhythm House, Subhash Chowk, next to the Jehangir Art Gallery. This is a veritable Aladdin's cave of classical, devotional and popular music from all over India, with a reasonable selection of Western rock, pop and jazz, as well as DVDs of classic and contemporary Hindi movies.

Listings

Airlines, domestic Indian Airlines, Air India Building, Nariman Point (Mon–Sat 8.30am–7.30pm, Sun 10am–1pm & 1.45–5.30pm); ☏022/2202 3031); counter at the airport ☏022/2682 9328; Jet Airways, Amarchand Mansion, Madam Cama Rd ☏022/2285 5788; Sahara Airlines, Unit 7, Ground Floor, Tulsiani Chambers, Nariman Point ☏022/2283 6000.

Airlines, international Aeroflot, Ground Floor, 14 Tulsiani Chambers, Free Press Journal Rd, Nariman Point ☏022/2285 6648; Air France, Maker Chambers VI, 1st Floor, Nariman Point ☏022/2202 4818; Air India, Air India Building, Nariman Point ☏022/2202 4142; Air Lanka, 12-D, Raheja Centre, Nariman Point ☏022/2282 3288; Alitalia, Industrial Insurance Building, VN Rd, Churchgate ☏022/5663 0800; British Airways, 202-B Vulcan Insurance Building, VN Rd, Churchgate ☏022/2282 0888; Cathay Pacific, Bajaj Bhavan, 3rd Floor, 226 Nariman Point ☏022/2202 9561; Delta, Taj Mahal, Colaba ☏022/2288 5652; Egypt Air, Oriental House, 7 J Tata Rd, Churchgate ☏022/2282 4088; Emirates, 228 Mittal Chambers, Nariman Point ☏022/2287 1645; Gulf Air, Maker Chamber V, Nariman Point ☏022/2202 4065; Japan Airlines, Raheja Centre, Nariman Point ☏022/2283 3136; KLM, 7th Floor, 712 Acme Plaza, Andheri–Kurla Rd, opp. Sangam cinema ☏022/5697 5959; Kuwait Airways, 86 VN Rd, Churchgate ☏022/2204 5351; Lufthansa, 1st Floor, Express Towers, Nariman Point ☏022/5630 1940; Qantas Airways, 2nd Floor, Godrej Bhavan, Home St ☏022/2200 7440; Royal Nepal Airlines, 222 Maker Chamber V, Nariman Point ☏022/2283 6197; SAS and Thai Airways, Oberoi Towers, 11th Floor, Room 1120, Nariman Point ☏022/2230 8725; Saudia, 3rd Floor, Express Towers, Nariman Point ☏022/2202 0199; South African Airways, Podar House, 10 Marine Drive, Churchgate ☏022/2284 2242; Syrian Arab Airlines, 7 Brabourne Stadium, VN Rd, Churchgate ☏022/2282 6043; TWA, Amarchand Mansion, M Carve Rd ☏022/2282 3080.

Airport enquiries Chhatrapati Shivaji International Airport ☏022/2682 9000. Chhatrapati Shivaji Domestic Airport ☏022/2615 6600.

Ambulance ☏101 for general emergencies; but you're nearly always better off taking a taxi. See also "Hospitals" below.

Banks and currency exchange The logical place to change money when you arrive in Mumbai is at the State Bank of India's 24hr counter in Chhatrapati Shivaji International Airport. Rates here are standard but you may have to pay for an encashment certificate – essential if you intend to buy tourist-quota train tickets or an Indrail pass at the special counters in Churchgate or CST (VT) stations. All the major state banks downtown change foreign currency (Mon–Fri 10.30am–2.30pm, Sat 10.30am–12.30pm); some (eg the Bank of Baroda) also handle credit cards and cash advances. Most now have 24hr ATMs that can handle international transactions, usually Visa, Delta and Mastercard. It's worth noting that there's often a limit on how much you can take out; it can be as low as Rs4000. For the location of large branch ATM machines downtown, see our maps. The most convenient if you're staying in Colaba is the Bank of Baroda's at the north end of SBS Marg (Colaba Causeway). The fast and efficient American Express office (daily 9.30am–6pm; ☏022/2204 8291), on Shivaji Marg, around the corner from the Regal cinema in Colaba, offers all the regular services (including poste restante) to travellers' cheque- and card-holders and is open to anyone wishing to change cash. Thomas Cook's big Dr DN Marg branch (Mon–Sat 9.30am–7pm; ☏022/2204 8556), between the Khadi shop and Hutatma Chowk, can also arrange money transfers from overseas.

Consulates and high commissions Although the many consulates and high commissions in Mumbai can be useful for replacing lost travel documents or obtaining visas, most of India's neighbouring states, including Bangladesh, Bhutan, Burma, Nepal and Pakistan, only have embassies in New Delhi and/or Kolkata (Calcutta) – see relevant city account. All of the following are open Mon–Fri: Australia, 16th Floor, Maker Tower "E", Cuffe Parade (9am–5pm; ☏022/2218 1071); Canada, 41/42 Maker Chambers VI, Nariman Point (9am–5.30pm; ☏022/2287 6027); China, 1st floor, 11 ML Dahanukar Marg (10am–4.30pm; ☏022/2282 2662); Denmark, L & T House, Narottam Moraji Marg, Ballard Estate (10am–12.45pm; ☏022/2261 4462); France, 2nd Floor, Datta Prasad, N Gamadia Cross Rd (9am–1pm & 2.30–5.30pm; ☏022/2495 0948); Germany,

10th Floor, Hoechst House, Nariman Point (8–11am; ☎022/2283 2422); Indonesia, 19 Altamount Rd, Cumbala Hill (10am–4.30pm; ☎022/2380 0940); Republic of Ireland, Royal Bombay Yacht Club Chambers, Apollo Bunder (9.30am–1pm; ☎022/2202 4607); Netherlands, Forbes Bldg, Chiranjit Rai Marg, Fort (9am–5pm; ☎022/2201 6750); Norway, Navroji Mansion, 31 Nathelal Parekh Marg (10am–1pm; ☎022/2284 2042); Philippines, 61 Sakhar Bhavan, Nariman Point (10am–1pm; ☎022/2202 4792); Singapore, 10th Floor, Maker Chamber IV, 222 Jamnal Bajaj Marg, Nariman Point (9am–noon; ☎022/2204 3205); South Africa, Gandhi Mansion, 20 Altamount Rd (9am–noon; ☎022/2389 3725); Spain, Ador House, 3rd floor, 6 K Dubash Marg, Kala Ghoda (10.30am–1pm; ☎022/2287 4797); Sri Lanka, Sri Lanka House, 34 Homi Modi St, Fort (9.30am–11.30am; ☎022/2204 5861); Sweden, 85 Sayani Rd, Subash Gupta Bhawan, Prabhadevi (10am–12.30pm; ☎022/2436 0493); Switzerland, Maker Chamber IV, 10th floor, Nariman Point (8am–10am; ☎022/2288 4563); Thailand, Malabar View, 4th floor, Dr Purandure Marg, Chowpatty Sea Face (9–11.30am; ☎022/2363 1404); United Kingdom, 2nd Floor, Maker Chamber IV, Nariman Point (8am–11.30am; ☎022/2283 0517); USA, Lincoln House, 78 Bhulabhai Desai Rd (8.30am–11am; ☎022/2363 3611).

Hospitals The best hospital in the centre is the private Bombay Hospital (☎022/2206 7676, ⓦwww.bombayhospital.com), New Marine Lines, just north of the government tourist office on M Karve Rd. Breach Candy Hospital (☎022/2363 3651, ⓦwww.breachcandyhospital.org) on Bhulabhai Desai Rd, near the swimming pool, is also recommended by foreign embassies.

Internet access A couple of cramped 24hr places (Rs40/hr) can be found in Colaba, just round the corner from *Leopold's* on Nawroji F Marg, though it's worth paying the Rs5 extra at Access Infotech, located down a small alley further down Colaba Causeway on the left, which is faster and more comfortable. At the time of writing, neither offered broadband services.

Left luggage If your hotel won't let you store bags with them, try the cloakrooms at the airports (see p.113), or the one in CST (VT) station (Rs7–10 a day). Anything left here, even rucksacks, must be securely fastened with a padlock and can be left for a maximum of one month.

Libraries Asiatic Society (see p.128), SBS Marg, Horniman Circle, Ballard Estate (Mon–Sat 10.30am–7pm); British Council (for British newspapers), A Wing, 1st Floor, Mittal Tower, Nariman Point (Tues–Sat 10am–6pm); Alliance Française de Mumbai, Theosophy Hall, 40 New Marine Lines; Max Mueller Bhavan, Prince of Wales Annexe, off MG Rd (Mon–Fri 9.30am–6pm). The KR Cama Oriental Institute, 136 Mumbai Samachar Marg (Mon–Fri 10am–5pm, Sat 10am–1pm), specializing in Zoroastrian and Irani studies, has a public collection of 22,000 volumes in European and Asian languages. Mumbai Natural History Society, Hornbill House (Mon–Fri 10am–5pm, Sat 10am–1pm, closed 1st & 3rd Sat of the month), has an international reputation for the study of wildlife in India. Visitors may become temporary members which allows them access to the library, natural history collection, occasional talks and the opportunity to join organized walks and field trips.

Pharmacies Bombay Chemist, 39–40 Kakad Arcade, opposite Bombay Hospital, New Marine Lines (☎022/2207 6171) opens daily 8am–11pm. Kemps in the Taj Mahal also opens late.

Photographic studios and equipment The Javeri Colour Lab, opposite the Regal cinema in Colaba, stocks colour-print and slide film, as do most of the big hotels. A small boutique behind the florists in the Sahakari Bhandar covered market does instant Polaroid passport photographs.

Police The main police station in Colaba (☎022/2285 6817) is on the west side of Colaba Causeway, near the crossroads with Ormiston Rd.

Postal services The GPO (Mon–Sat 9am–8pm, Sun 9am–4pm) is around the corner from CST (VT) Station, off Nagar Chowk. Its poste restante counter (Mon–Sat 9am–6pm, Sun 9am–3pm) is among the most reliable in India, although they trash the letters after four weeks. The much less efficient parcel office (10am–4.30pm) is behind the main building on the first floor. Packing-wallahs hang around on the pavement outside. DHL (☎022/2850 5050) has eleven offices in Mumbai, the most convenient being the 24hr one under the *Sea Green Hotel* at the bottom of Marine Drive (turn south off the western end of VN Rd and it's a short way on your right).

Telephones and faxes STD/ISD booths abound in Mumbai. For rock-bottom phone and fax rates, however, head for Videsh Sanchar Bhavan (open 24hr), the swanky government telecom building on MG Marg, where you can make reverse charge calls to destinations such as the UK, US and Australia. Receiving incoming calls costs a nominal Rs10. Numbers in the city change constantly, so if you can't get through after several attempts, try directory enquiries on ☎197.

Travel agents The following travel agents are recommended for booking domestic and international flights, and long-distance private buses where specified: Cox and Kings India Ltd, 271/272, Dr DN Marg ☎022/2207 3065, ⓦwww.coxkings.com; Sita World Travels Pvt Ltd, 8 Atlanta Building, Nariman Point ☎022/2286 0684, ⓔbom@sitaincoming.com; Thomas Cook (see p.51).

Moving on from Mumbai

Most visitors feel like getting out of Mumbai as soon as they can. Fortunately, the city is equipped with "super-fast" services to arrange or confirm **onward travel**. All the major international and domestic **airlines** have offices in the city, the railway networks operate special tourist counters in the main reservation halls, and dozens of **travel agents** and road transport companies are eager to help you on your way by **bus**.

Travel within India

Mumbai is the nexus of several major internal flight routes, train networks and highways, and is the main transport hub for traffic heading towards South India. The most travelled trails lead north up the Gujarati coast to **Rajasthan** and **Delhi**; northwest into the **Deccan** via Aurangabad and the caves at Ellora and Ajanta; and south towards **Goa** and the **Malabar Coast**.

By plane

Indian Airlines and other **domestic carriers** – such as the more efficient Jet Airways and Sahara Airlines – fly out of Chhatrapati Shivaji domestic airport (formerly Santa Cruz) to destinations all over India. Availability on popular routes should never be taken for granted. Check with the airlines as soon as you arrive; **tickets** can be bought directly from their offices (see p.57), via the Internet, or through any reputable travel agent.

In theory, it is also possible to book domestic air tickets abroad when you buy your original long-haul flight. However, as individual airlines tend to have separate agreements with domestic Indian carriers, you may not be offered the same choice (or rates) as you will through agents in Mumbai. Note, too, that Indian Airlines is the only company offering 25 percent discounts (on all flights) to customers under the age of thirty.

By train

Three main networks converge on Mumbai: the **Western Railway** (Ⓦ www .westernrailway.com) runs to north and west India; the **Central Railway** (Ⓦ www.centralrailway.com) connects Mumbai to central, eastern and southern regions; and the **Konkan Railway** (Ⓦ www.konkanrailway.com) winds south down the coast to Goa, Mangalore and Kerala.

Nearly all services to Gujarat, Rajasthan, Delhi and the far north leave from **Mumbai Central** station, in the mid-town area. Second-class tickets can be booked here through the normal channels, but the quickest place for foreign nationals to make reservations is at the efficient tourist counter (no. 28) on the first floor of the **Western Railway's booking hall**, next door to the Government of India tourist office in **Churchgate** (Mon–Fri 9.30am–4.30pm, Sat 9.30am–2.30pm; ☏022/2209 7577). This counter, at the far (bottom) end of the booking hall, also has access to special "tourist quotas", which are released the day before departure if the train leaves during the day, or the morning of the departure if the train leaves after 5pm. If the quota is "closed" or already used up, and you can't access the "Emergency quota" (always worth a try), you will have to join the regular queue. Periods before major national holidays (notably **Diwali**, when half of India is on the move) should be avoided at all costs. But if you do find yourself having to travel when there don't seem to be any tickets left, bear in mind you can pay extra for a special *tatkal* seat (see p.55 for full details on these) – an option well worth considering, for example, if you want to get to Goa on the oversubscribed Konkan Railway route.

Recommended trains from Mumbai

The services listed below are the most direct and/or the fastest. This list is by no means exhaustive and there are numerous slower trains that are often more convenient for smaller destinations. All the details listed below were correct at the time of writing, but departure times, in particular, should be checked when you purchase your ticket, or in advance via the Indian Railways website: ⑩ www.indianrail.gov.in.

Destination	Name	No.	From	Frequency	Departs	Total time
Agra	Punjab Mail	#2137/38	CST	Daily	7.10pm	24hr 15min
Aurangabad	Devgiri Express	#1003	CST	Daily	9.05pm	7hr 05min
Bangalore	Udyan Express	#6529	CST	Daily	8am	25hr
Bhopal	Punjab Mail	#2137	CST	Daily	7.10pm	14hr
Chennai	Mumbai–Chennai Express	#6011	CST	Daily	2.10pm	26hr 35min
Delhi	Rajdhani Express	#2951	MC	Daily	4.55pm	17hr
	Golden Temple Mail	#2903	MC	Daily	9.25pm	21hr 35min
Goa	Mumbai–Madgaon Express	#KR0111	CST	Daily	11pm	11hr 45min
Hyderabad	Hussainsagar Express	#7001	CST	Daily	9.50pm	15hr
Jaipur	Mumbai–Jaipur Express	#2955	MC	Daily	6.50pm	18hr
Jodhpur	Ranakpur Express	#4708	Bandra	Daily	3pm	19hr 25min
Kochi* (Cochin)	Netravati Express	#6345	LTT (Kurla)	Daily	11.40am	26hr 40min
Kolkata (Calcutta/ Howrah)	Gitanjali Express	#2859	CST	Daily	6am	31hr 35min
	Mumbai–Howrah Mail	#2809	CST	Daily	8.40pm	33hr 45min
Mysore	Sharavathi Express	#1035	Dadar	Tues	10.45pm	23hr 45min
Pune	Udyan Express	#6529	CST	Daily	8.40am	3hr 35min
Thiruvanan-thapuram (Trivandrum)	Netravati Express	#6345	LTT (Kurla)	Daily	11.40am	31hr 40min
Udaipur	Saurashtra Express**	#9215	MC	Daily	7.55am	23hr 45min
Varanasi	Mahanagiri Express	#1093	CST	Daily	12.10pm	28hr 20min

*details also applicable for Ernakulam Junction
**change at Ahmedabad to the Delhi Sarai Rohila Express #9944

Mumbai's other "Tourist Ticketing Facility" is in the snazzy air-conditioned **Central Railway booking office** to the rear of **CST** (VT) (Mon–Sat 8am–1.30pm & 2–3pm, Sun 8am–2pm; ☎022/2262 2859), the departure point for most trains heading east and south. Indrail passes can also be bought here, and there's an MTDC tourist information kiosk in the main concourse if you need help filling in your reservation slips.

Tickets for seats on the **Konkan Railway** can be booked at either Churchgate or CST booking halls; for more info on getting to Goa by rail, see box on pp.148–149.

Just to complicate matters, some Central Railway trains to **South India** – notably those running via the Konkan Railway to **Kerala** – do not depart from CST at all, but from **Kurla station** (aka Lokmanya Tilak Terminus, or **LTT**), up near the airports. Others leave from **Dadar**, also way north of the centre. Getting to either on public transport can be a major struggle, though many long-distance trains from CST (VT) or Churchgate stop there and aren't as crowded. Much the easiest way is to jump in a cab.

Wherever you're heading, a good investment for anyone planning to do much rail travel is Indian Railway's indispensable *Trains at a Glance*, available from most station bookstalls for Rs30. You can also access **timetables** via the Indian Railways website at ⓦ www.indianrail.gov.in, and even book tickets online.

By bus

The main departure point for long-distance **buses** leaving Mumbai is the frenetic **Central bus stand** on JB Behram Marg, opposite Mumbai Central railway station. States with bus company counters here (daily 8am–8pm; ☎022/2307 6622) include Maharashtra, Karnataka, Madhya Pradesh, Goa and Gujarat. Few of their services compare favourably with train travel on the same routes. Reliable timetable information can be difficult to obtain, reservations are not available on standard buses, and most long-haul journeys are gruelling overnighters. Among the exceptions are the deluxe buses run by MSRTC to Pune, Nasik and Kolhapur; the small extra cost buys you more leg-room, fewer stops and the option of advance booking. The only problem is most leave from the ASIAD bus stand in Dadar, thirty minutes or so by road or rail north of Mumbai Central.

Other possibilities for road travel include the "super-fast" **luxury coaches** touted around Colaba. Most are run by private companies, guaranteeing break-neck speeds and possible long waits for the bus to fill up. ITDC also operates similarly priced services to the same destinations, which you can book direct from their main offices downtown or through the more conveniently situated Government of India tourist office, 123 M Karve Rd, Churchgate. Two night buses leave Nariman Point every evening for the twelve-hour trip to **Aurangabad**, and there are morning departures to **Nasik** and **Mahabaleshwar**, which take six and seven hours respectively.

Leaving India

In spite of its prominence on trans-Asian flight routes, Mumbai is no longer the bargain basement for **international air tickets** it used to be. Discounted fares are very hard to come by – a legacy of Rajiv Gandhi's economic reforms of the 1980s. If you do need to book a ticket, stick to one of the tried and tested agents listed on p.144.

All the major airlines operating out of Mumbai have offices downtown where you can buy scheduled tickets or confirm your flight; see p.143 for a list of addresses. The majority are grouped around Veer Nariman Road, opposite the *Ambassador Hotel*, or else on Nariman Point, a short taxi ride west of Colaba.

Since the inauguration of the Konkan Railway, the best-value way to travel the 500km from Mumbai to Goa has been by **train**. However, tickets for the twelve-hour ride down the coast tend be in short supply, and virtually impossible to obtain at short notice, so it's best to try and book at home before setting off. Otherwise, you'll probably find yourself having to shell out for a **flight**. Considering how hellish the bus ride can be, and how hard getting hold of train tickets is, it's well worth paying the extra to travel by plane, which could save you days waiting around in Mumbai. Alternatively, consider heading south in stages, via Pune or southern Maharashtra.

By plane
Between ten and twelve flights shuttle daily between Mumbai and Dabolim airport in Goa. The cheapest fares, by far, are offered by low-cost airline Air Deccan (🌐www .airdeccan.net/airdeccan), which sells tickets on its website from as little as Rs550, though the normal rate is more like $60. Flying with Indian Airlines (🌐www.indian -airlines.nic.in) will set you back $95, or $100 with Sahara (🌐www.airsahara.net) or Jet (🌐www.jetairways.com). In addition, Air India (🌐www.airindia.com) operates a service to Mumbai (also for $100) which few people seem to know about, so you can nearly always get a seat (the one drawback is that you have to check in three hours before departure as Air India is an international carrier). At the time of writing, two more low-cost carriers – Kingfisher Airlines (🌐www.flykingfisher.com) and SpiceJet (🌐www.spicejet.com) – were also poised to enter the fray, and will be worth checking for competitive fares.

Demand for seats can be fierce around Diwali and Christmas/New Year, when you're unlikely to get a ticket at short notice. At other times, one or other of the carriers should be able to offer a seat on the day you wish to travel. If you didn't pre-book when you purchased your international ticket, check availability with the airlines as soon as you arrive; tickets can be bought directly from their offices (see "Listings" on p.143), through any reputable travel agent in Mumbai (bearing bear in mind that an agent may charge you the dollar fare at a poorer rate of exchange than that offered by the airline company), by phone or direct via the Internet (the best way in the case of the low cost airlines).

All Goa flights leave from Chhatrapati Shivaji Domestic Airport, 30km north of the city centre.

By train
The Konkan Railway line runs daily express trains from Mumbai to Goa. **Fares** for the twelve-hour journey from CST start at Rs293 for standard sleeper class, rising to

Southern Maharashtra

Most tourists heading south from Mumbai skip southern Maharashtra, but if you have a little time you can break up the journey. **Pune** retains its Maratha character, in the old quarter at least, and also boasts a unique museum; some may also be attracted by its much-derided Osho Commune. Hill stations such as **Matheran** and **Mahabaleshwar** provide coolness, wooded walks and fine views, while the **Konkan coast** has little-visited beaches and forts that make a pleasant journey down to Goa. From **Lonavala**, you can get to see the earliest Buddhist rock-cut art in the western Deccan, while **Kolhapur**, the last major

Rs1242 for II class a/c or Rs2345 for luxurious I class a/c. However, these services are not always available at short notice from the booking halls at CST and Churchgate. If you're certain of your travel dates in advance (ie if you're flying into Mumbai and want to catch the train to Goa soon after arriving), consider **booking online** (at ⓦwww.konkanrailway.com). There are downsides to this: you're only entitled to relatively expensive three-tier a/c fares (Rs1242 one-way) and must make your booking between seven and two days before your date of departure – but all in all, online reservation is a much more convenient way to secure a seat than leaving it until you arrive in Mumbai. Alternatively, you could make the reservation through an Indian Railways agent in your home country; for more on how to do this, see Basics on p.56.

Don't be tempted to travel "unreserved" class on any Konkan service as the journey as far as Ratnagiri (roughly midway) is overwhelmingly crushed. The most convenient of the Konkan services is the overnight Mumbai–Madgaon Express #KR0111 (11pm; 12hr) which departs from CST. The other, only slightly faster train is the Mandovi Express #KR0103, leaving at 7am (also from CST).

By bus

The Mumbai–Goa bus journey ranks among the very worst in India. Don't believe travel agents who assure you it takes thirteen hours. Depending on the type of bus you get, appalling road surfaces along the sinuous coastal route make eighteen to twenty hours a more realistic estimate.

Fares start at around Rs300 for a push-back seat on a beaten-up Kadamba (Goan government) or MSRTC coach. Tickets for these services are in great demand in season with domestic tourists, so book in advance at Mumbai Central or Kadamba's kiosks on the north side of Azad Maidan, near St Xavier's College (just up from CST station; ☎022/2262 1043). More and more private overnight buses (around 25 daily) also run to Goa, costing around Rs375–400 for a noisy front-engined Tata bus, Rs400–450 for an a/c bus with pneumatic suspension and on-board toilet, and Rs600–675 for a service with coffin-like sleeper compartments which quickly become unbearably stuffy. Tickets should be booked at least a day in advance through a reputable travel agent (see p.144), though it's sometimes worth turning up at the car park opposite the Metro cinema, Azad Maidan, where most buses leave from, on the off-chance of a last-minute cancellation. Make sure, in any case, that you are given both your seat and the bus registration number, and that you confirm the exact time and place of departure with the travel agent, as these frequently vary between companies.

city before Karnataka to the south, or Goa to the southwest, is a town with more traditional atmosphere than most and some striking Raj-era architecture.

Matheran

The little hill station of **MATHERAN**, 108km east of Mumbai, is set on a narrow north–south ridge, at an altitude of 800m in the Sahyadri Range. From viewpoints with such names as Porcupine, Monkey and Echo, at the edge of sheer cliffs that plunge into deep ravines, you can see way across the hazy plains – on a good day, so they say, as far as Mumbai. The town itself, shrouded in thick mist for much of the year, has, for the moment, one unique attribute: cars, buses,

Note that when phoning towns within 200km of Mumbai, such as Matheran or Murud-Janjira, you should replace the initial 0 of the area code with 95 in order to be charged a lower local rate.

motorbikes and auto-rickshaws are prohibited. That, added to the journey up, on a **miniature train** that chugs its way through spectacular scenery to the crest of the hill, gives the town an agreeably quaint, time-warped feel.

Matheran (literally "mother forest") has been a popular retreat from the heat of Mumbai since the nineteenth century. These days, however, few foreign visitors venture up here, and those that do only hang around for a couple of days, to kill time before a flight or to sample one of India's most charming colonial-style hotels, **Lord's Central Hotel**. The tourist season lasts from mid-September to mid-June (at other times it's raining or misty), and is at its most hectic between November and January, in April and May, and over virtually any weekend. There's really nothing up here to do but relax, wander the woods on foot or horseback, and enjoy the fresh air and views.

As the crow flies, Matheran is only 6.5km from Neral on the plain below, but the train climbs up on 21km of track with no fewer than 281 curves, said to be among the sharpest on any railway in the world. After 1907, the demanding haul was handled by four complex steam engines. Sadly, they puffed their last in 1980 and were replaced by cast-off diesels from Darjeeling, Shimla and Ooty. The two-hour train ride is a treat, especially if you get a window seat, but be prepared for a squash and hard benches.

In 1974, the All India Rail Strike cut Matheran off. To combat the situation, the track from Neral was made passable for Jeeps and finally in 1984 was sealed up to Dasturi Naka, 2km from the town, though any attempts to extend it through the town have been thwarted by the encouragingly ecofriendly local authorities.

Practicalities

To reach Matheran by **train**, you must first get to **Neral Junction**, easily done by taking the hourly suburban train from **Mumbai** (CST or Dadar) to Kargat, which stops there (2hr 15min). Otherwise, the daily Deccan Express #1007 (7.15am) or Sahyadri Express #1023 (5.50pm) are both considerably quicker and also leave from CST. From **Pune** (2hr 30min–3hr), the same two trains – Sahyadri Express #1024 (7am) and Deccan Express #1008 (3.30pm) stop at Neral. Note that later services in each direction do not connect with the toy train. A good alternative from Pune is to travel to Karjat and pick up the suburban service to Mumbai.

Narrow-gauge trains up from **Neral** to **Matheran** (2hr) depart at 9am, 10.45am and 5pm (also 7.30am April to mid-June) on weekdays and there are a couple of extra services at weekends. All trains are timed to tie in with incoming mainline services, so don't worry about missing a connection if the train you're on is delayed – the toy train service should wait. Matheran **station** is in the centre of town on MG Road, which runs roughly north–south. Leaving town, there is a little halt on the miniature railway near the Dasturi Naka taxi stand, but, unless you've already booked a seat, you won't be allowed on.

All **motor transport**, including shared taxis and minibuses from Neral (Rs50 per person, Rs250 for car), parks at the taxi stand next to the MTDC *Holiday Camp* at Dasturi Naka, 2km north of the town centre. From here you can walk with a porter (Rs50–60), be led by horse (Rs80), or take a hand-pulled rickshaw (Rs120). If you're happy to carry your own bags, follow the rail tracks, which cut straight to the middle of Matheran, rather than the more convoluted dirt road. However you arrive, you must pay a **toll** (Rs25) to enter the town, valid for your entire stay.

A small **tourist information** booth (daily 10am–6pm) opposite the railway station has maps and can help you get your bearings – otherwise, you can buy maps (Rs2) of the town at *Prince's Cafe*. To **change money**, The Union Bank near the station can cash travellers' cheques only but the rates are poor; the larger hotels accept credit cards.

Accommodation and eating

Matheran has plenty of **hotels**, though few could be termed cheap. Most are close to the railway station on MG Road and on the road behind it, Kasturba Bhavan. Reduced rates of up to fifty percent often apply to midweek or long stays, and during the rainy off-season (when many places close down). Most operate a 10am or 11am checkout. Virtually all the hotels provide **full** or **half board** at reasonable rates, but if you want to eat out, or are on a tight budget, try one of the numerous thali joints around the station or tasty meat dishes at *Hookahs'N'Tikkas*, also on MG Road.

Gujarat Bhavan Maulana Azad Rd
T 02148/230278 or Mumbai T 022/2203 0876. Clean and comfortable pure-veg Jain resort hotel, with a range of rooms and cottages (some a/c with TV), playground and swimming pool. Full board only. **7**–**8**

Hope Hall MG Rd T 02148/230253, opposite *Lord's Central*. The best budget option: large, clean en-suite rooms arranged around a secluded yard with badminton and table tennis at the quiet end of town. Run by very friendly brother–sister duo. **2**

Lord's Central MG Rd T 02148/230228, W www .lordsmatheran.com Matheran's most characterful landmark, near the railway station. Genteel (non-a/c) Raj-era cottages with terraces, and superb views across the Western Ghats from a relaxing garden. Excellent veg and non-veg menu including Parsi and British food. Full board only, booking recommended. **8**–**9**

Madhumalti Just north of railway station
T 02148/230144. Basic but clean lodge with

attached rooms among the enclave just below the tracks. Best budget option if *Hope Hall* is full. **3**

MTDC Holiday Camp Dasturi Naka
T 02148/230540, F 230566 or Mumbai
T 022/2202 6713. "Cottage-style" rooms in a large old colonial house, plus a simple open-air restaurant. A 40min walk from the centre of town but a good option. **4**–**6**

Rugby Vithalrao Kotwal Marg T 02148/230291, W www.rugbyhotel.com. Two minutes' walk up the road opposite the railway station. Old hotel, recently renovated and expanded, offering a range of rooms around a garden, with a multi-cuisine restaurant (complete with Raj-era decor) and a good bakery attached. **7**–**9**

The Verandah in the Forest 2km southwest of station T 02148/230296, W www.neemranahotels .com. Set in woods a short way above Charlotte Lake, this tastefully restored colonial house, with elegant rooms and a huge verandah, rivals *Lord's Central* as Matheran's classiest hotel. **8**–**9**

The Konkan Coast: Murud-Janjira

Despite the recent appearance of a string of upscale resorts pitched at wealthy urbanites, the coast stretching south from Mumbai, known as the **Konkan** region, remains relatively unspoilt. Empty beaches, backed by casuarina and areca trees and coconut plantations, regularly slip in and out of view, framed by the distant Ghats, while little fortified towns preserve a distinct coastal culture, with its own dialect of Marathi and fiery cuisine. The number of rivers and estuaries slicing the coast meant that for years this little explored area was difficult to navigate, but the Konkan railway, which winds inland between Mumbai and Kerala via Goa, now renders it easily accessible.

The first interesting place to break the journey south is the quiet port of **MURUD-JANJIRA**, 165km south of Mumbai. A traditional trade centre formerly belonging to the Siddis of Janjira, it still features plenty of attractive wood-built houses, some brightly painted and fronted by pillared verandas. The gently shelving beach is wide and safe for swimming, though the sand is cleaner and softer 3km north in **Kashid**. Five kilometres south, an imposing sixteenth-century **fort**, built on an island in the river, was one of the few the Marathas failed to penetrate. You can reach it by local *hodka* boat (around Rs50) from the jetty at the southern end of town – an excellent excursion – or by *tempo*. The 1661 Kasa Fort sits in the open sea 2km off the beach but cannot be visited, nor can the impressive nineteenth-century palace of the last Nawab, which dominates the northern end of the bay. Fine views of the bay and surrounding countryside can be had, however, from the hilltop **Dattatreya Temple**, sporting an Islamic-style tower but dedicated to the triple-headed deity comprising Brahma, Vishnu and Shiva.

Murud-Janjira practicalities

There is a **ferry** service from the Gateway of India in Mumbai to **Rewas** (hourly 6am–5.30pm; 1hr 30min), from where you have to get a local bus that trundles through the coastal villages from Alibag to Murud. Most direct **buses** from Mumbai Central take five hours; there are two faster ASIAD services (5.45am & 11am; 4hr), which must be booked in advance. Don't jump out prematurely at the inland bus stand but continue to Murud's main street, Durbar Road, parallel to the coast, where you'll find the tiny post office, covered market, a handful of basic restaurants and the town's accommodation.

Most **hotels** are overpriced for what you get, one exception being the basic *Sea Shore Resort* (☎02144/274223; ❷–❸), which has a pleasant courtyard and one sea-facing room; it's almost directly opposite the smart, new *Club Leisure Shoreline* (☎02144/274640; ❺–❼), which has well-appointed rooms. Further north up Durbar Rd are the *Mirage Holiday Homes* (☎02144/276744; ❺–❻), in an attractive colonial-style building, and the luxury concrete bungalows of the *Golden Swan Beach Resort* (☎02144/274078, ⓦ www.goldenswan.com; ❻–❾), some only inches from the virtually deserted beach; its restaurant serves local Malvani cuisine.

Other reasonable places to **eat** on Durbar Rd include the shady garden of the *Anand Vatika*, south of the *chowk*, which serves South Indian veg snacks and fuller north Indian meals, and the *Hotel Vinayak*, whose menu is more extensive in theory than practice. A row of seafront stalls south of the *chowk* dish up tasty seafood and veg snacks.

Ganpatipule

Two hundred and fifteen kilometres south of Marud-Janjira lies the Konkan coast's other commendable stopover, **GANPATIPULE**, a tiny village with a long, golden sandy beach and a very fine **Ganapati temple**. Although attracting thousands of Indian pilgrims each year, this sleepy place sees relatively few foreign visitors, with most of the tourists being honeymooners from Mumbai. The temple is built around a Ganapati *omnar*, a naturally formed – though not strictly accurate – image of the elephant god. **Accommodation** is available at the swanky MTDC *Resort* (☎02357/235248, Ⓕ235328; ❹–❽), which has very comfortable and mostly a/c rooms, as well as cheaper tent accommodation – all a stone's throw from the beach. Two cheaper options, both on the approach road to the beach and offering good discounts out of season, are the *Shri Ganesh Kripa* (☎02357/235229; ❹), with basic attached rooms, and the

Shreesagar (☎02357/235145; ➎), which has clean compact doubles with TV. For **food**, there's decent Nepalese cooking at the MTDC resort, a Punjabi menu at the *Shri Ganesh Kripa*, or *dhabas* at the bottom of the village towards the main road.

To get to Ganpatipule, either make your way to Ratnagiri (on the Konkan railway and well connected by state and private buses) and take a local bus (10 daily; 1–1hr 30min) the last 32km, or take one of the direct MSRTC services from Mumbai, Pune or Kolhapur. All the buses stop outside the MTDC resort.

Lonavala and around

Just thirty years ago, the town of **LONAVALA**, 110km southeast of Mumbai, and 62km northwest of Pune, was a quiet retreat in the Sahyadri hills. Since then, the place has mushroomed to cope with hordes of holiday-makers and second-home owners from the state capital, and is now only of interest as a base for the magnificent **Buddhist caves** of **Karla**, **Bhaja** and **Bedsa**, some of which date from the Satavahana period (second century BC).

Frequent buses arrive at Lonavala's central **bus stand**, just off the old Mumbai–Pune Road, but the train is infinitely preferable. Lonavala is on the main railway line between Mumbai (3hr) and Pune (1hr 30min), and most express trains stop here. The **railway station** is on the south side of town, a ten-minute walk from the bus stand area; take the path right at the end of platform 1 to get there. With a car, or by taking an early train, it's just about possible to take in the caves as a day-trip from Mumbai, but it's better to allow yourself a full day to get around. There's a UTI Bank **ATM** before the bridge across the railway lines, left off the Mumbai–Pune Road, and just before the corner leading to it is the Ritz Cyber Café (Rs40/hr).

Accommodation

Lonavala has a wide range of **accommodation**, from moderately cheap to five-star; many of its hotels lower their rates out of season (Oct–March) or for longer stays or weekdays. Budget and mid-range places are concentrated in the centre, by the bus and railway stations.

Adarsh Behind the bus stand on Shivaji Rd ☎02114/272353. Spotless a/c and non-a/c rooms, some overlooking a central courtyard. Dependable mid-range option, but the management isn't very welcoming and early mornings are noisy. ➏–➑
Chandralok Opposite the bus stand on Shivaji Rd ☎02114/272294, ℗272921. Tucked just off the busy road, this mid-range place has comfortable rooms, some a/c, and a good Gujarati thali restaurant. ➌–➎
Duke's Retreat Mumbai–Pune Rd, Khandala ☎02114/269201, ⓦwww.dukesretreat.com. Superb position overlooking a ravine around 6km from town, with a prize-winning garden and a pool (Rs150 for

non-residents). Comfortable rooms and cottages, with its own outdoor café, a/c restaurant and bar. Weekend packages include breakfast and dinner. ➑–➒
MTDC Karla Resort Mumbai–Pune Rd ☎02114/282230, ℗282370. On the Lonavala–Karla bus route, 3km from Malavli railway station and 7km out of town. Range of comfortable accommodation (some a/c) in cottages, suites and economy doubles in a tranquil setting. ➍–➑
Shahani Holiday Home DJ Shahani Rd, 5min walk east of the railway station ☎02114/272784. Lonavala's best budget option: large, immaculate rooms in a modern block tucked down a suburban backstreet. ➌

Eating

Most of Lonavala's hotels lay on full board or have very good **restaurants**, while a number of smaller restaurants and snack bars on the main street cater for the brisk through trade. You'll also come across dozens of shops selling the local sweet speciality, **chikki** – a moreish amalgam of dried fruit and nuts set in rock-solid honey toffee. *Super Chikki* on the main street allows you to sample the many varieties before you buy. Their main competitors, *National Chikki*, further down, is also recommended; this is also the best place to stock up on delicious deep-fried nibbles (*namkeen*), the other local speciality.

China Blue Before bridge over railway. Sparkling, colourfully decorated a/c lounge upstairs serving above average Chinese favourites.
Diamond Mumbai–Pune Rd, opposite the *Kumar Resort*. Garden restaurant specializing in Punjabi and Chinese food, with fairly high prices but a relaxing atmosphere.
Guru Krippa Mumbai–Pune Rd. Sparkling, clean pure-veg joint on the main street:

piping-hot South Indian snacks, cheese toasties, and inexpensive thalis with Chinese and Punjabi main meals. Also a good selection of ice creams, *kulfi* and full-on *faloodas*. Recommended.
Shabri *Hotel Rama Krishna*, Mumbai–Pune Rd. The well-heeled Mumbaikar favourite. Spacious and clean, serving a wide range of north and South Indian dishes and chilled beer.

The Buddhist caves of Karla, Bhaja and Bedsa

The three cave sites of **Karla**, **Bhaja** and **Bedsa** comprise some of the finest rock-cut architecture in the northwest of the Deccan region. Though not in the same league as Ajanta and Ellora, they harbour some beautifully preserved ancient sculpture, and are definitely worth a look if you are passing.

The three sites lie some way from each other, all to the east of Lonavala. Covering Karla and Bhaja under your own steam by bus and/or train is manageable in a day, if you are prepared for a good walk, but if you want to get out to Bedsa, too, the easiest option is to rent an **auto-rickshaw** (around Rs300–400) or **car** (Rs500–600 for 4hr) for the tour (usually found at Lonavala railway station). Finally, if you want to see the caves at their best, avoid the weekends, when they are inundated with busloads of rowdy day-trippers.

Karla

KARLA (also Karli) is 3km north of **Karla Caves Junction** on the Mumbai–Pune Road and 11km from Lonavala. Take any bus or tempo to the junction (from where it's a Rs30 rickshaw ride), or there are five daily **buses** (6am, 9am, 12.30pm, 3pm & 6.30pm) that head for the caves directly from Lonavala, with the last bus returning from Karla at 6.30pm.

The rock-cut Buddhist **chaitya** hall at Karla (daily 8.30am–6pm; $2 [Rs5]), reached by steep steps that climb 110m, is the largest and best preserved in India, dating from the first century AD. As you approach across a large courtyard, itself hewn from the rock, the enormous fourteen-metre-high facade of the hall towers above, topped by a horseshoe-shaped window and with three entrances below, one for the priest and the others for devotees. To the left of the entrance stands a *simhas stambha*, a tall column capped with four lions.

In the porch of the cave, dividing the three doorways, are panels of figures in six couples, presumed to have been the wealthy patrons of the hall. Two rows of octagonal columns with pot-shaped bases divide the interior into three, forming a wide central aisle and, on the outside, a hall that allowed devotees to circumambulate the monolithic stupa at the back. Above each pillar's fluted capital kneels a finely carved elephant mounted by two riders, one with arms draped over the other's shoulders. Amazingly, perishable remnants survive from the time when the hall was in use. Full views of the main entrance are obscured by the much later accretion, to the right, of a Hindu shrine to **Ekviri**, a goddess-oracle revered by Koli fishing communities.

Bhaja

Although the eighteen **caves** (daily 8.30am–6pm; $2[Rs5]) at **BHAJA** may not be as elaborate as those at Karla, they are more atmospheric. They lie 3km south of Karla Caves Junction, reached by following a path up from the village square near the railway station at Malavli, just 1.5km away. Hourly passenger **trains** call here, and are the cheapest and most convenient way to get back to Lonavala if you're not travelling by rented rickshaw or car.

The caves are among the oldest in India, dating from the late second to early first century BC, during the earliest, Hinayana, phase of Buddhism. Most consist of simple halls – *vihara* – with adjoining cells that contain plain shelf-like beds; many are fronted by rough verandas. Bhaja's apsidal *chaitya* hall, **Cave 12**, which contains a stupa, but no figures, has 27 plain bevelled pillars which lean inwards, mimicking the style of wooden buildings. Sockets in the stone of the exterior arch reveal that it once contained a wooden gate or facade. Further south, the last cave, **Cave 19**, a *vihara*, is decorated with superb carvings. Mysteriously, scholars identify the figures as the Hindu gods, **Surya** and **Indra**, who figure prominently in the *Rig Veda* (c. 1000 BC).

Bedsa

It's quite possible that you won't encounter anyone else when visiting the caves at **BEDSA** (daily 8.30am–6pm; $2 [Rs5]), which is one of its great attractions. Once you reach the village, 12km beyond Bhaja on NH-4, or a three-kilometre bus ride from Kamshet, the nearest railway station, you'll have to ask the way to the unsigned path. The village kids hanging around might scramble up the steep hillside with you, for a fee.

Bedsa's *chaitya* hall, excavated later than that at Karla, is far less sophisticated. The entrance is extremely narrow, leading from a porch which appears to be supported, though of course it is not, by four octagonal pillars more than 7m high, with pot-shaped bases and bell capitals; bulls, horses and elephants rest on inverted, stepped slabs on top. Inside, 26 plain octagonal columns lead to an unadorned monolithic stupa.

Pune (Poona)

At an altitude of 598m, **PUNE**, Maharashtra's second largest city, lies close to the Western Ghat mountains (known here as the Sahyadri hills), on the edge of the Deccan plains as they stretch away to the east. Capital of the Marathas' sovereign state in the sixteenth century, Pune was – thanks to its cool, dry climate – chosen by the British in 1820 as an alternative headquarters for the Bombay Presidency. Their military cantonment in the northwest of town is still used by the Indian army, and a number of British buildings, such as the Council Hall and Deccan College, survive. Since colonial days, Pune has continued to develop as a major industrial city and a centre for higher education. But to most outsiders, it is notorious as the home of the **Osho International Meditation Resort**, founded in 1970 by the charismatic Bhagwan Rajneesh, or Osho (1931–90), whose syncretic and, to many Indians, scandalous philosophy of life lured thousands of followers from Europe and America. The city is now linked to Mumbai by the three-lane NH-4 motorway, which is planned to extend all the way to Bangalore eventually.

Arrival and information

From Pune's Lohagaon **airport**, 10km northeast of the centre, prepaid taxis (around Rs200), auto-rickshaws (Rs120–130) and regular "Ex-Servicemen" buses (Rs25) are on hand for the fifteen-minute trip to the city centre. Pune is an important staging point on southern express-train routes from Mumbai (3hr 30min–4hr 30min); the main **railway station** is in the centre of town, south of the river. Auto-rickshaws and tourist taxis wait outside the station – locals often use shared long-distance taxis to get to Mumbai (see box p.161). Of the three main **bus stands**, the City bus stand, next to the railway station, is split into two sections, one serving the city itself (with signs and timetables only in Marathi), the other opposite serving some destinations south and west, including Goa, Lonavala and Mumbai. Swargate Bus Stand, about 5km south, close to Nehru Stadium, services Karnataka and some of the same destinations as City,

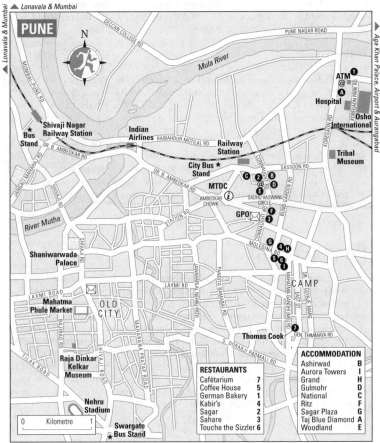

▲ Lonavala & Mumbai

PUNE

RESTAURANTS
Cafétarium	7
Coffee House	5
German Bakery	1
Kabir's	4
Sagar	2
Sahare	3
Touche the Sizzler	6

ACCOMMODATION
Ashirwad	B
Aurora Towers	I
Grand	H
Gulmohr	D
National	C
Ritz	F
Sagar Plaza	G
Taj Blue Diamond	A
Woodland	E

▼ Mahabaleshwar & Kolhapur

while the stand next to Shivaji Nagar Railway Station, 3km west of the centre, runs buses to towns in the north, including Nasik and Aurangabad. To establish which station you require for your destination, ask at the enquiries hatch of the City bus stand.

You can get general information, make MTDC resort reservations and seek advice about bus services at the **MTDC Tourist Office** (Mon–Sat 10am–5.30pm; ☎0212/2612 6867, ℱ2611 9434), inside "I" block of Central Building (enter between Ambedkar Chowk and Sadhu Vaswani Circle). Similar services are available at the **Information Counter** (allegedly Mon–Fri 10am–6pm & Sat 10am–1pm; closed 2nd & 4th Sat of month) opposite the railway station's first-class booking office.

One of the best places to **change money** is Thomas Cook, at 13 Thacker House, just off General Thimmaya Road (Mon–Sat 9.30am–6pm; ☎0212/613 8188); the State Bank of India on Laxmi Road will do the same, only more slowly and without any commission. There is a Citibank **ATM** next to the *German Bakery* near the Osho ashram. The very efficient **GPO** is on Connaught Road. The Modern Bookshop, on General Thimmaya Road, stocks an impressive array of fiction and a good selection of Indian maps and guidebooks. Manney's Booksellers, 7 Moledina Rd, Clover Centre, and Crossword, Sohrab Hall, 1st floor (behind the railway station), are two alternatives. You can access the **Internet** in many places, including the superfast Dishnet, five minutes' walk from the railway station on Connaught Road (Rs25/hr), and the Hub near the Osho ashram (Rs30/hr), which also has Net2phone facilities.

Accommodation

Pune is well supplied with **hotels**, though in keeping with most big cities prices are quite high for what you get. Most of the budget accommodation can be found in the area south of the railway station around Connaught Road. The station itself also has better-than-average **retiring rooms** (Rs100–200). For information on staying at the *Osho International Meditation Resort*, see p.159.

Ashirwad 16 Connaught Rd ☎0212/2612 8585, ℮hotelash@vsnl.com. Newish hotel near the station. Some smart a/c rooms with balconies and TV. Good veg restaurant, room service, exchange and travel desk. ❼–❽

Aurora Towers 9 Moledina Rd ☎0212/2613 1818, ⓦwww.auroratowers.com. High-rise luxury hotel 2km from railway station, offering smart rooms with full amenities, 24hr room service and coffee shop, two good Indian and Chinese restaurants, shops and pool. ❾

Grand MG Rd, near Dr Ambedkar Statue ☎0212/2636 0728, opposite *Aurora Towers*. Single wood-partition rooms with common bathrooms or simple but spacious en-suite doubles in an old colonial townhouse. Relaxing veranda, beer garden, restaurant and fast-food outlet, cats and friendly management. ❸

Gulmohr 15A/1 Connaught Rd ☎0212/2612 2773, ℮gulmohr@vsnl.com. Clean mid-range hotel near the railway station. Good value rooms, all with attached bathroom and cable TV, some a/c. ❹–❻

National 14 Sassoon Rd, two minutes' walk from the railway station ☎0212/2612 5054. Rooms, some a/c, with wooden verandas and attached bathrooms in a dilapidated old building, while others are in basic modern "cottages". Popular with budget travellers. ❸–❺

Ritz Connaught Rd ☎0212/2612 2995. Former travellers' hangout revamped into mostly a/c hotel with swish marble interiors and prices to match. There are two restaurants – thankfully still serving their legendary Gujarati thalis – and a travel centre. ❻–❽

Sagar Plaza 1 Bund Garden Rd ☎0212/2612 2622, ⓦwww.sarovarparkplaza.com. Medium-sized, flashy four-star, 1km from railway station, with ritzy restaurant, 24hr coffee shop, bar, health club, bookshop and swimming pool. ❾

Taj Blue Diamond 11 Koregaon Rd ☎0212/2612 5555, ⓦwww.tajhotels.com. Five-star Taj group hotel, 2km northeast of railway station near the Osho ashram. Classy rooms with plush carpets and furniture. Facilities include posh Indian and Thai restaurants, 24hr coffee shop, swimming pool, and shops. ❾

Woodland Sadhu Vaswani Circle ☎ 0212/2612 6161, ⓦ www.tghotels.com. Reasonable value rooms of decent size and comfort, mostly a/c, ten minutes' walk from the railway station. Veg restaurant, travel desk and foreign exchange. ⑦–⑧

The City

Pune centre is bordered on the north by the **River Mula** and to the west by the **River Mutha** – the two join in the northwest to form the Mutha-Mula, at Sangam Bridge. The principal shopping area, and the greatest concentration of restaurants and hotels, is in the streets south of the railway station, particularly Connaught and, further south, **MG Road**. The old Peshwa part of town, by far the most interesting to explore, is towards the west between the fortified **Shaniwarwada Palace** and fascinating **Raja Dinkar Kelkar Museum**; old wooden *wadas* – palatial city homes – survive on these narrow, busy streets, and the Victorian, circular **Mahatma Phule Market** is always a hive of activity.

Raja Dinkar Kelkar Museum

Dinkar Gangadhar Kelkar (1896–1990), aside from being a celebrated Marathi poet, published under the name Adnyatwass, spent much of his life travelling and collecting arts and crafts from all over the country. In 1975, he donated his collection to the Maharashtran government for the creation of a museum dedicated to the memory of his son, Raja, who had died at the age of 12. Housed in a huge old-town mansion, the **Raja Dinkar Kelkar Museum** (daily 9.30am–5.30pm; Rs100 [Rs12]) on 1378 Shukrawar Peth (buses #72 or #74 from the railway station to Mahatma Phule Market), is a wonderful pot-pourri in which beauty and interest is found in both artistic and everyday objects. Paraphernalia associated with *paan*, the Indian passion, includes containers in every conceivable design, made from silk, wood, brass and silver: some mimic animals or fish, or are egg-shaped and in delicate filigree; others are solid, heavy-duty boxes built to withstand constant use. Also on show are musical instruments, superb Marathi textiles and costumes, toys, domestic shrines and furniture, beauty accessories and a model of Shaniwarwada Palace.

Shaniwarwada Palace

In the centre of the oldest part of town, only the imposing high walls of the **Shaniwarwada Palace** (daily 8am–noon & 2–6pm; Rs100 [Rs5]) survived three fires in the eighteenth and nineteenth centuries. Founded by the Peshwa ruler Bajrao I in 1730 and the chief residence of the Peshwas until the British arrived in 1817, the building has little to excite interest today, though there's a daily **Sound and Light** show in English (7pm; Rs100). The entrance is through the Delhi gate on the north side, one of five set into the perimeter wall, whose huge teak doors come complete with nasty elephant-proof spikes. The interior of the palace is now grassed over, the seven-storey building entirely absent. Only one of the guides, usually available in the afternoons, speaks English. Bus #3 runs the 2km southwest from the railway station to the palace.

Aga Khan Palace and Gandhi Memorial

In 1942, Mahatma Gandhi, his wife Kasturba and other key figures of the freedom movement were interned at the **Aga Khan Palace** (daily 9am–5.30pm; Rs100 [Rs5]), which is set in quiet leafy gardens across the River Mula, 5km northeast of the centre (buses #1, #158 & #156). The Aga Khan donated the palace to the state in 1969, and it is now a small Gandhi museum, typical of many all over India, with captioned photos and simple rooms unchanged since they were occupied by the freedom fighters. A memorial behind the house commemorates Kasturba, who died during their imprisonment. A small *khadi* shop sells hand-loom cloth and products made by village co-operatives.

Tribal Museum

The Tribal Research and Training Institute, which runs the **Tribal Museum**, Koregaon Road (daily 10am–5pm; free), 2km east of the railway station, is dedicated to the protection and documentation of Maharashtra's numerous tribal groups, such as the Wagdheo, Bahiram, Danteshwari and Marai, who number more than five million. The museum's faded photos, costumes and artefacts serve as an excellent introduction to this little-known world, but the highlights are the wonderful collections of dance masks and Worli wedding paintings. Talk to the director of the museum if you're interested in guided (but culturally sensitive) **tours** to tribal areas.

Osho Commune International

Pune is the headquarters of Bhagwan Rajneesh's avowedly nonreligious **Osho International Meditation Resort**, 17 Koregaon Park Road (☎0212/2401 9999, ⓦ www.osho.com), 2km east of the railway station. Calling itself a "tasteful and classy resort", the commune celebrates the sniping of critics, proudly displaying the *Wall Street Journal*'s description of it as a "spiritual Disneyland for disaffected First World yuppies".

With a considerable daily income during peak season (Dec–March) and years of dedicated help from volunteers, the commune has transformed its twenty acres into a dreamy playground of cafés, swimming pool, sauna and clinics, with a shop selling Osho's enormous list of books, videos and cassettes. The faithful have erected space-age, air-conditioned buildings, landscaped the gardens, bored tube wells for water, planted trees to improve air quality and grow organic vegetables. Courses at its Multiversity, mostly one to three days in duration (around Rs2500 per day), are offered in a variety of New Age and traditional techniques. Forty-five-minute lunchtime demos are also available if you want to try before you buy. Osho's own brand of jargon is extensive; tennis, for example, is here played as Zennis, which helps you "get out of your body's way, bring the outer and the inner together" in "a unique synthesis of tennis and meditation". There are a host of other courses ranging from primal screaming to meditation techniques and more offbeat therapies.

This ecofriendly bubble follows a strict door policy: visitors who wish to spend longer than the ten minutes of the guided tours (daily 9.45am–noon & 2–3.30pm; Rs10) must produce two passport photos and an HIV-negative certificate no less than thirty days old. If you don't have one and still want to stay there, you'll have to take an HIV test at the ashram clinic as part of your induction – the registration, HIV test and initial day-pass package costs Rs1160 for foreigners (Rs460 for Indians), after which it's Rs330 per day. You'll also need two robes (maroon for daywear, white for evenings), which cost Rs300 inside the ashram or Rs150 from stalls outside. If you want to actually stay inside the ashram, the smart but simply furnished guesthouse will set you back $60 a night for a double, $57 a single.

Eating

In addition to the hotel restaurants, there are numerous reasonably priced cafés and fast-food outlets around **Connaught** and **Moledina** roads, always busy in

Bhagwan Rajneesh

It is more than thirty years since the first disciple was initiated into the **Bhagwan Rajneesh** cult, latterly renamed Osho Commune International, an evolving philosophy of Buddhism, Sufism, sexual liberationism, Tantric practices, Zen, yoga, hypnosis, Tibetan pulsing, disco and unabashed materialism. The first Rajneesh ashram was founded in Pune in 1974. It rapidly attracted droves of Westerners and some Indians, who adopted new Sanskrit names and a uniform of orange or maroon cottons and a bead necklace (*mala*) with an attached photo of the enlightened guru, in classic style, sporting long white hair and beard. This immediately identified the wearer as a *sannyasin* (borrowing from Shaivistic tradition, a renunciating mendicant who has attained a state of holiness).

Few early adherents denied that much of the attraction lay in Rajneesh's novel approach to fulfilment. His dismissal of Christianity ("Crosstianity") as a miserably oppressive obsession with guilt struck a chord with many, as did the espousal of liberation through sex. Rajneesh assured his devotees that material comfort was not to be shunned. Within a few years, satellite ashrams were popping up throughout Western Europe, and by 1980 an estimated 200,000 devotees had liberated themselves in 600 meditation centres across 80 countries.

To protect itself from pollution, nuclear war and the AIDS virus, the organization poured money into a utopian project, **Rajneeshpuram**, on 64,000 acres of agricultural land in Oregon, USA. It was at this point that the tabloids and TV documentary teams really got interested in Rajneesh, now a multimillionaire. Infiltrators leaked stories of strange goings-on at Rajneeshpuram and before long its high-powered female executives became subject to police interest. Charges of tax evasion, drugs, fraud, arson and a conspiracy to poison several people in a neighbouring town to sway the vote in local elections provoked further sensation. Although he claimed to know nothing of this, Rajneesh pleaded guilty to breaches of US immigration laws and was deported in 1985. Following protracted attempts to resettle in 21 different countries, and now suffering complications of the chronic fatigue, ME, the Valium-addicted Rajneesh returned home to Pune, where he died in 1990, aged 59.

The ashram went through a period of internal squabbles and financial trouble in the 1990s. At his death, Rajneesh appointed an inner circle to manage the group, though several departed and the Osho "brand" – with around 4 million books sold each year (supplemented by tapes, paintings and photos) – is now controlled from Zurich and New York. Pune wasn't seeing enough of this to meet its costs and consequently prices have been hiked, changing the pattern of life at the ashram; whereas in its heyday an average stay was three to six months, today people typically stay no more than two weeks and few followers live on site. This has led to a labour shortage, with non-Osho locals brought in to keep the place afloat, and a dismantling of the sense of community that was the source of its attraction.

the evening. A sociable place to round off the day is on Dr Ambedkar Road, running east from the GPO, where, from dusk until around 10pm, a string of pavement cafés serve up spicy snacks, cold drinks and fresh juices to young punters.

Cafétarium Sunder Plaza, MG Rd. Smart coffee shop in the atrium round the corner from Thomas Cook, serving from mid-morning until 11pm. The place for a cappuccino, light lunch or cosmopolitan meal.

Coffee House 2 Moledina Rd. A relaxing, upmarket South Indian snack joint that serves the best coffee, *dosas* and breakfasts in Pune. It's also a/c, and a good spot to beat the heat.

German Bakery 291 Koregaon Park. One of the infamous chain of cafés providing safe Western meals, pastry snacks and home-made breads for homesick travellers and Oshoites.

Kabir's 6 Moledina Rd. Good selection of north

Indian dishes for around Rs50–90, including lots of tasty tandoori options. Try to get a table outside in the garden. Serves beer.

Sagar Sassoon Rd, opposite the railway station. Large and busy, serving tasty, Indian and Chinese food in clean, no-smoking surroundings. The place to head for if you are staying at the *National* or have a long wait for a train.

Sahare 5 Connaught Rd. Outstanding Gujarati/ Rajasthani unlimited thalis served in spotless airy surroundings opposite the GPO. Costs a little more than the average thali, but well worth it.

Touche the Sizzler 7 Moledina Rd. Great fast food: chicken and lamb "sizzlers" and burgers, and plenty of Punjabi-style veg dishes. Popular with Pune's bright young things, and a little pricey.

Moving on from Pune

By air

Indian Airlines runs two daily **flights** to Delhi, one travelling via Mumbai, and one flight to Bangalore via Goa; Jet Airways has two daily flights to Mumbai, one of which continues to Kolkata (Calcutta), one flight to Delhi and one to Chennai via Bangalore. Sahara operates two daily flights to Delhi, one to Bangalore and one to Kolkata via Hyderabad. IA's office is at Airline House on Dr Ambedkar Rd (℡0212/2612 6451), Jet Airways at 39 Dr Ambedkar Rd (℡0212/2613 7181) and Sahara at 21 Sassoon Rd (℡0212/2605 9003).

By train

As Pune is one of the last stops for around twenty long-distance **trains** bound for or Mumbai, rail services are excellent. Many depart early morning, however, and some terminate at Dadar, so always check first – an information service is run through the Railway Enquiries Office (℡131/133). The most convenient, if crowded, options for Mumbai CST are Deccan Queen Express #2124 (7.15am), Pragati Express #1026 (7.50am) and Deccan Express #2124 (3.30pm), which all take around four hours. Direct express trains from Pune also run to Hyderabad (Mumbai–Hyderabad Express #7031; daily 4.40pm), New Delhi (Jhelum Express #1077; daily 5.35pm), Chennai (Mumbai–Chennai Express #6011; daily 6.05pm), Bangalore (Udyan Express #6529; daily 11.40am) and Thiruvananthapuram (Kanniyakumari Express #1081; daily 3.45pm). Reservations for all trains should be made at the new **Reservation Centre** next to the station (Mon–Sat 8am–2pm & 2.15–8pm, Sun 8am–2pm).

By bus and taxi

Private luxury buses to Ahmedabad, Indore, Goa, Aurangabad and Ratnagiri can be booked through Prasanna Tours & Travels, Shivaji Nagar Terminus (℡0212/2553 9358) or Swargate Terminus (℡0212/2444 4139, ⓦwww.prasanna tours.com). Recommended **travel agents** in the centre of town for the above are Abhay Travels, 42 Karve Rd (℡0212/2543 6463), and Bulsara Tours & Travels, 14 Sadhu Vaswani Rd (℡0212/2612 3137). Seek advice from the MTDC Tourist Information Counter at the railway station or call ℡0212/2612 6218 for the latest information on **state bus** services; the bus stands display no information in English. Services from the long-distance section of the City stand next to Pune station head south and west, to Mahabaleshwar, Kolhapur, Goa and Lonavala. ASIAD buses to Mumbai also leave here every fifteen minutes between 5.30am and 11.30pm. Additional services in these directions leave from the Swargate stand 5km south. If you're heading up to Nasik or Aurangabad, you'll have to travel across the river to the Shivaji Nagar terminus. There are several excellent-value 24-hour **taxi agencies** near the City bus stand that drive the three to four hours to Dadar in Mumbai, charging per person – try Cool Cabs (℡0212/2612 1090; non-a/c Rs255, a/c Rs315)

See "Travel Details" at the end of this chapter for more information on journey frequencies and durations.

Mahabaleshwar and around

MAHABALESHWAR, 250km southeast of Mumbai and rivalling Matheran as the most visited hill resort in Maharashtra, is easily reached from Pune, 120km northeast. The highest point in the Western Ghats (1372m), it is subject to extraordinarily extreme **weather** conditions. The start of June brings heavy mists and a dramatic drop in temperature, followed by a deluge of biblical proportions: up to seven metres of rain can fall in the hundred days up to the end of September. As a result, tourists only come here between November and May; during April and May, at the height of summer, the place is packed. There is a Rs10 per head entry fee for visitors, collected at toll booths at each end of town.

For most foreign visitors, Mahabaleshwar's prime appeal is its location midway between Mumbai and Goa, but it holds enough good **hiking trails** to keep walkers here for a few days, with tracks through the woods to waterfalls and assorted vantage points overlooking the peaks and plains. You can also take **boats** out on the central **Yenna Lake**, and **shop** for strawberries, raspberries, locally made jams and honey in the lively market. One commendable short route is the walk to **Wilson's Point**, the highest spot on the ridge, which you should aim to reach well before dusk. To pick up the (driveable) trail, head south through the bazaar (away from the bus stand) and straight over the crossroads at the end past the *Mayfair* hotel; ten minutes' further up the hill, you reach a red-and-white sign pointing left off the road. Wilson's Point lies another stiff ten minutes' up, crowned by a gigantic radio transmitter that is visible for miles. The sunset **panoramas** from here can be breathtaking.

Practicalities

The central **State bus stand** at the northwest end of the bazaar serves Pune (hourly; 3hr 30min), the most convenient railhead, as well as Kolhapur (7 daily; 7hr) and Satara (every two hours; 1hr), which is 17km from Satara Road railway station, connected to Mumbai via Pune and Goa via Miraj. There are five daily buses from Mumbai, the best option being the MSRTC semi-luxury bus which departs from the Mumbai Central bus stand at 7am (7hr). The single daily direct service to Panaji in Goa departs at 9am (12hr). There are a couple of unreliable **Internet** joints in the bazaar, where you can also **change money** at the Bank of Maharashtra.

As in many hill stations, despite an abundance of hotels, prices in Mahabaleshwar are well above average. The cheapest **places to stay** are on the Main Bazaar (officially Dr Sabne Rd) and the road parallel to it, Murray Peth; with a little haggling, you can pick up rooms for under Rs300 midweek or off season. Accommodation is scarce during the monsoon (mid-June to mid-Sept), when most hotels close, and during peak times like Diwali and over Christmas and New Year, when tariffs double. Apart from the hotel restaurants and ubiquitous thali joints, two worthwhile **eateries** on the Main Bazaar are *Dragon Chinese Den* and *Tinklers-The Taste Bud*, which does excellent if slightly pricey. South Indian and other snacks.

Hotels

Blue Star 114 Dr Sabne Rd ☎02168/260678. Plenty of peeling plaster but adequate; offers as good off-peak deals as you'll find for a basic attached room with TV. ③–④

Deluxe Dr Sabne Rd ☎02168/260202. Clean modern lodge above a fabrics shop. One of the better budget deals. ②–④

Dreamland Directly below the State bus stand ☎02168/260228, ⊛www.hoteldreamland.com. Large, established resort hotel in extensive gardens. Rooms range from simple chalets ("cottages") to new a/c poolside apartments with stupendous views. The congenial garden café serves decent espresso and the restaurant fine Indian, Continental, Mexican and Chinese cooking. ❼

MTDC Holiday Camp 2km west of the centre ☎02168/260318, ℱ 260300 or Mumbai ☎022/2202 6713. Wide range of good-value no-frills accommodation, including cottages to sleep four, doubles and group accommodation.

Better than average restaurant and beer bar. ❹–❻

Paradise International Main Rd, near bus stand ☎02168/260084. Ramshackle but acceptable mid-range lodge whose saving grace is a pleasant courtyard. ❹–❺

Rahil International 292 Murray Peth ☎02168/260639. One of a string of dependable, clean and essentially characterless places on this street. Good deals on full board. ❻

Pratapgadh

An hour's bus ride away from Mahabaleshwar, or a hike of 24km, the seventeenth-century **fort** of **PRATAPGADH** (daily dawn–dusk; free) stretches the full length of a high ridge. Reached by five hundred steps, it is famously associated with the Maratha chieftain, **Shivaji**, who lured the Moghul general Afzal Khan here from Bijapur to discuss a possible truce. Neither, it would seem, intended to keep to the condition that they should come unarmed. Khan attempted to knife Shivaji, who responded by killing him with the gruesome *wagnakh*, a set of metal claws worn on the hand. Modern visitors can see Afzal Khan's tomb, a memorial to Shivaji, and views of the surrounding hills. The easiest way to reach the fort is on MSRTC's daily half-day tour (9.30am–1.30pm; Rs60).

Kolhapur

KOLHAPUR, on the banks of the River Panchaganga 225km south of Pune, is thought to have been an important centre of the Tantric cult associated with Shakti worship since ancient times. The town probably grew around the sacred site of the present-day **Mahalakshmi temple**, still central to the life of the city, although there are said to be up to 250 other temples in the area. With a population of more than 500,000, Kolhapur has become a major industrial centre, but the city has retained enough Maharashtran character to make it worthy of a stopover.

Former capital of the Chhatrapatis (descendants of Shivaji, who made this their capital in 1708), Kolhapur later played an important role in the development of the so-called **Indo-Saracenic** style of British colonial architecture. The architect Major Charles Mant, under the auspices of the maharaja, blended Western styles with Islamic, Jain and Hindu ones, resulting in buildings that would prove profoundly influential. Mant's work, which can be seen all over the city, includes the High School and Town Hall; the General Library; the Albert Edward Hospital; and the New Palace, now a museum.

The **Mahalakshmi temple**, whose cream-painted sanctuary towers embellish the western end of town, is thought to have been founded in the seventh century by the Chalukyan king Karnadeva. However, what you see today probably dates from the early eighteenth century. It is built from bluish-black basalt on the plan of a cross, with the image of the goddess Mahalakshmi beneath the eastern and largest of five domed towers. Presiding over the square just up the road from the Mahalakshmi temple, the **Rajwada**, or Old Palace, is still occupied by members of the Chhatrapati family. Visitors can see the entrance hall (daily 10am–6pm; free) by passing under a pillared porch which extends out into the town square.

Kolhapur is famous as a centre for traditional wrestling, or *kushti*. On leaving the palace gates, turn right and head through the low doorway in front of you, from where a path picks its way past a couple of derelict buildings to the sunken *motibaug*, or **wrestling ground**. Come here between 5.30am and 5.30pm, and you can watch the wrestlers training. The main season is between June and September, the coolest time of year, but you may see them active at other times. Hindus and Muslims train together, and it's fine to take photographs.

The maharaja's **New Palace** (Tues–Sun 9.30am–1pm & 2.30–6pm; Rs20), 2km north of the centre, was built in 1884, following a fire at the Rajwada. Designed by Major Mant, its style fuses Jain and Hindu influences from Gujarat and Rajasthan and local touches from the Rajwada while remaining indomitably Victorian, with a prominent clock tower. The present maharaja lives on the first floor, while the ground floor holds an absorbing collection of costumes, weapons, games, jewellery, embroidery and paraphernalia such as silver elephant saddles.

Practicalities

Two direct express **trains** leave Mumbai CST for Kolhapur via Pune (9hr) each evening: the Mahalaxmi Express #1011 (8.25pm; 11hr 20min) and the Sahyadri Express #1023 (5.50pm; 12hr 45min). Heading in the other direction, the Mahalaxmi Express, bound for Pune and Mumbai, leaves Kolhapur at 7.15pm. The **railway station** is 500m from the **bus stand** on Station Road, near the centre of town. A five-minute walk from here (turn right) brings you to the **MTDC tourist office**, in the Kedar Complex on Station Road (Mon–Sat 8.30am–6.30pm; ☎0231/269 2935), where you can sign up for a guided **tour** of Kolhapur (Mon–Sat 10am–5.30pm; Rs60). The only place in Kolhapur to **exchange** travellers' cheques is at the State Bank of India at Dasara Chowk Bridge, near Shahamahar railway station, though there's a UTI Bank **ATM** on Station Rd. If you need to get online, Balaji Net Café (Rs20/hr), on Station Road between the bus stand and railway station, is reliable.

There's no shortage of decent, reasonably priced **accommodation** in Kolhapur, most within easy reach of the bus stand along Station Road. the *Maharaja*, 514 Station Rd (☎0231/265 0829; ❸), is a basic lodge, directly opposite the bus stand, with dozens of good-value, simple, clean rooms, and a veg restaurant. If it's full, try the *Sony* (☎0231/265 8585; ❷–❸), diagonally across the square inside the Mahalaxmi Chambers complex. Opposite the railway station, the *Rajpurush* (☎0231/266 4888, ✉hotelrajpurush@yahoo.com; ❷–❸) also offers good-value, clean rooms, with TV and attached bathrooms. One of the best options, though, is in a peaceful suburb a five-minute rickshaw drive away: *Hotel Woodlands*, 204E Tarabai Park (☎0231/265 0941, ⓕ263 3378; ❺–❻), has a range of a/c and non-a/c rooms with TV, plus a 24-hour coffee shop, multi-cuisine restaurant, garden and bar.

Outside the hotels, the best **food** is to be had in *Subraya* at the top of Station Square, a comfortable a/c restaurant with a varied menu including good Maharashtran thalis, breakfast and cheaper South Indian-style snacks such as tasty *dosas*, *vada pao* and filling *pani puris*.

Travel details

Trains

Mumbai to: Agra (4 daily; 23hr 15min–27hr); Ahmedabad (4 daily; 7hr 10min–12hr); Aurangabad (2 daily; 7hr 45min); Bangalore (3 daily; 26hr 10min); Bhopal (4 daily; 14hr); Chennai (3 daily; 24–29hr); Delhi (11 daily; 17–33hr); Hyderabad (2 daily; 15–17hr); Indore (1 daily; 14hr 35min); Jaipur (2 daily; 18–23hr); Jodhpur (1 daily; 19hr 25min; change at Ahmedabad); Kolhapur (3 daily; 11–12hr); Kolkata (Calcutta) (4 daily; 32–40hr); Nagpur (4 daily; 14–15hr); Nasik (15 daily; 4hr); Pune (25 daily; 3hr 25min–5hr); Thiruvananthapuram (2 daily; 42hr); Udaipur (1 daily; 24hr 40min; change at Ahmedabad); Ujjain (1 daily; 12hr 25 min); Varanasi (2 daily; 29–36hr).

Pune to: Bangalore (3–4 daily; 19hr 15min–22hr 40min); Chennai (3 daily; 20hr–25hr 45min); Delhi (3 daily; 26hr 30min–29hr 15min); Hyderabad (3–5 daily; 11hr 25min–14hr); Jalgaon (2–3 daily; 9hr 45min–11hr); Kolhapur (4 daily; 7hr 30min–7hr 50min); Mumbai (20–23 daily; 3hr 25min–5hr 10min); Nagpur (1–2 daily; 17hr 20min–19hr).

Buses

Only state bus services are listed here; for details of private buses, see p.147.

Mumbai (ASIAD Dadar) to: Kolhapur (4 daily; 10hr); Nasik (17 daily; 5hr); Pune (half-hourly; 4hr).

Mumbai (Mumbai Central) to: Aurangabad (2 daily; 10hr); Bangalore (3 daily; 24hr); Bijapur (3 daily; 12hr); Goa (2 daily; 18–19hr); Indore (2 daily; 16hr); Ujjain (1 daily; 17hr).

Pune to: Aurangabad (10 daily; 5hr); Bijapur (1 daily; 11–12hr); Goa (4 daily; 15–16hr); Kolhapur (4 daily; 6–7hr); Mahabaleshwar (9 daily; 3hr 30min–4hr); Mumbai (every 15min; 4hr–4hr 30min); Nasik (every 30min; 3–4hr).

Flights

For a list of airline addresses and travel agents, see p.143. In the listings below IA is Indian Airlines, AI Air India, JA Jet Airways, and SA Sahara Airlines.

Mumbai (Chhatrapati Shivaji Domestic Airport) to: Ahmedabad (AI, IA, JA 5–7 daily; 1hr); Aurangabad (IA, JA 3 daily; 45min); Bangalore (AI, IA, JA, SA 10–12 daily; 1hr 30min); Bhopal (IA, JA 2 daily; 2hr 05min); Bhubaneshwar (IA 3 weekly; 2hr); Bhuj (IA, JA daily; 1hr 15min); Chennai (AI, IA, JA 6–8 daily; 1hr 45min); Cochin (see "Kochi"); Delhi (AI, IA, JA, SA 33–36 daily; 1hr 55min); Coimbatore (SA 1 daily; 2hr); Goa (AI, IA, JA, SA 7–8 daily; 45min–1hr); Hyderabad (IA, JA, SA 8–15 daily; 1hr 15min); Indore (IA, JA 3 daily; 1hr 05min); Jaipur (IA, JA 4 daily; 1hr 35min); Jodhpur (IA, JA 2 daily; 2hr 10min); Kochi (AI, IA, SA 2–4 daily; 1hr 45min); Kolkata (Calcutta; AI, IA, JA, SA 9–10 daily; 2hr 40min); Madurai (IA 1 daily; 3hr 20min); Mangalore (IA, JA 2–3 daily; 1hr 15min); Nagpur (IA, JA 3 daily; 1hr 55min); Pune (IA, JA, SA 5 daily; 35min); Thiruvananthapuram (AI, IA, JA 2–3 daily; 2hr); Udaipur (IA 2–3 daily; 1hr 10min); Varanasi (IA, SA 2 daily; 4hr 55min).

Pune to: Bangalore (2 daily; 1hr 20min–2hr 25min); Chennai (1 daily; 2hr 45min); Delhi (5 daily; 2hr 5min–3hr 20min); Hyderabad (1 daily; 1hr); Kolkata (Calcutta) (2 daily; 2hr 55min–3hr 30min); Mumbai (3 daily; 30–35min).

Goa

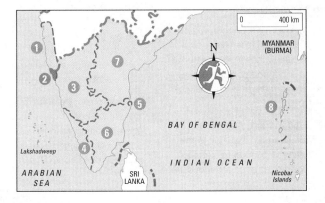

CHAPTER 2 # Highlights

✳ **Old Goa** The belfries and Baroque church facades looming over the trees on the banks of the Mandovi are all that remains of this once splendid colonial city. See p.184

✳ **Beach shacks** Tuck into a fresh kingfish, tandoori pomfret or lobster, washed down with a *feni* cocktail or an ice-cool Kingfisher beer. See p.198

✳ **Ingo's Night Bazaar, Arpora** Cooler and less hassly than the flea market, with better quality goods on sale and heaps more atmosphere. See p.199

✳ **Flea market, Anjuna** Goa's famous tourist bazaar is the place to pick up the latest party gear, shop for souvenirs, and watch the crowds go by. See p.203

✳ **Nine Bar, Vagator** The epicentre of hip Goa, where trance music accompanies the sunsets over the beach. See p.206

✳ **Arambol** An alternative resort with exquisite beaches and some of Asia's best budget restaurants. See p.215

✳ **Perreira-Braganza House, Chandor** The region's most extravagant colonial-era mansion, crammed with period furniture and fittings. See p.221

✳ **Sunset stroll, Palolem** Tropical sunsets don't come much more romantic than at this idyllic palm-fringed cove in the hilly deep south. See p.227

△ Arambol beach

2

Goa

I f one word could be said to encapsulate the essence of **GOA**, it would have to be the Portuguese *sossegarde*, meaning "carefree". The pace of life in this former colonial enclave, midway down India's southwest coast, has picked up over the past twenty years, but in spite of the increasing chaos of its capital, beach resorts and market towns, Goa has retained the laid-back feel that has traditionally set it apart from the rest of the country. Its 1.4 million inhabitants are unequivocal about the roots of their distinctiveness; while most of the subcontinent was colonized by the stiff-upper-lipped British, Goa's European overlords were the **Portuguese**, a people far more inclined to enjoy the good things in life than their Anglo-Saxon counterparts.

Goa was Portugal's first toe-hold in Asia, and served as the linchpin for a vast trade network for over 450 years. However, when the Lusitanian empire began to founder in the seventeenth century, so too did the fortunes of its capital. Cut off from the rest of India by a wall of mountains and hundreds of miles of un-navigable alluvial plain, it remained resolutely aloof from the wider subcontinent – while India was tearing itself to pieces in the run-up to Independence in 1947, the only machetes being wielded here were cutting coconuts. Not until 1961, after exasperated Prime Minister Jawaharlal Nehru gave up trying to negotiate with the Portuguese dictator Salazar and sent in the army, was Goa finally absorbed into India.

Those who visited in the late 1960s and 1970s, when the overland travellers' trail wriggled its way south from Bombay, found a way of life little changed in centuries: Portuguese was still very much the lingua franca of the well-educated elite, and the coastal settlements were mere fishing and coconut cultivation villages. Relieved to have found somewhere inexpensive and culturally undemanding to recover from the travails of Indian travel, the "freaks" got stoned, watched the mesmeric sunsets over the Arabian Sea and partied madly on full-moon nights, giving rise to a holiday culture that soon made Goa synonymous with hedonistic **hippies**.

Since then, the state has largely shaken off its reputation as a drop-out zone, but hundreds of thousands of visitors still flock here each winter, the vast majority to relax on Goa's beautiful **beaches**. Around two dozen stretches of soft white sand indent the region's coast, from spectacular 25-kilometre sweeps to secluded palm-backed coves. The level of development varies wildly; while some are lined by ritzy Western-style resorts, the most sophisticated structures on others are palm-leaf shacks and old wooden outriggers that are heaved into the sea each afternoon.

Wherever you travel in Goa, vestiges of former Portuguese domination are ubiquitous, creating an ambience that is at once exotic and strangely familiar.

The festivals of Goa

Some of Goa's **festivals** are on fixed dates each year; ask at a tourist office for dates of the others. The biggest celebrations take place at Panjim and Margao.

Festa dos Reis (Jan 6). Epiphany celebrations include a procession of young boys decked out as the Three Kings to the Franciscan chapel of Reis Magos, near Panjim on the north bank of the Mandovi, 3km east of Fort Aguada. Other processions are held at Cansaulim and Chandor.

Carnival (Feb/March). Three days of *feni*-induced mayhem, centring on Panjim, to mark the run-up to Lent.

Shigmo (Feb/March). The Goan version of Holi is celebrated with big parades and crowds; drum and dance groups compete and huge floats, which threaten to bring down telegraph wires, trundle through the streets.

All Saints (March). On the fifth Monday in Lent, 26 effigies of saints, martyrs, popes, kings, queens and cardinals are paraded around the village of Velha Goa, near Panjim. A fair also takes place.

Igitun Chalne (May). *Dhoti*-clad devotees of the goddess Lairya enter trances and walk over hot coals at the village of Sirigao, Bichloim.

Sanjuan (June 24). The festival of St John is celebrated all over Goa, but is especially important in the coastal villages of Arambol and Terekol. Youngsters torch straw dummies (representing St John's baptism, and thus the death of sin), while revellers in striped pants dive into wells after drinking bottles of *feni*.

International Film Festival of India (late Nov to early Dec). The powers that be haven't decided whether or not Panjim is to become the permanent venue for this Bollywood bash (see box on p.177), but it looks more than likely. Hundreds of movies – both foreign and Indian – are shown over a fortnight, on huge beachside screens and in Panjim's two major venues, the Innox multiplex and Kala Academy. For more, see p.177.

Christmas (Dec 24–25). Celebrated everywhere in Goa. Late-night Mass is usually followed by music, dancing and fireworks.

Siolim Zagor (first Sun after Christmas). Processions, dance dramas and satirical songs mark this unusual festival at Siolim, in northern Goa near Chapora, which is ostensibly Christian but celebrated with equal enthusiasm by local Hindus.

This is particularly true of Goan **food** which, blending the Latin love of meat and fish with India's predilection for spices, is quite unlike any other regional cuisine in Asia. Equally unique is the prevalence of **alcohol**. Beer is cheap, and six thousand or more bars around the state are licensed to serve it, along with the more traditional tipple, *feni*, a rocket-fuel spirit distilled from cashew fruit or coconut sap.

Travelling around the Christian heartland of central Goa, with its white-washed churches and wayside shrines, it's all too easy to forget that **Hinduism** remains the religion of more than two-thirds of the state's population. Unlike in many parts of the country, however, religious intolerance is rare here, and traditional practices mingle easily with more recently implanted ones. Faced by the threat of merger with neighbouring states, Goans have always put regional cohesion before communal differences at the ballot box. A potent stimulus for regional identity was the campaign through the 1980s to have **Konkani**, the language spoken by the vast majority of Goans, recognized as an official state language, which it eventually was in 1992. Since then, the **immigration** issue has come to dominate the political agenda. Considerably more prosperous than neighbouring states, Goa has been deluged over the past couple of decades with economic refugees, stirring up fears that the region's cultural distinctiveness will disappear. Among the main employers of migrant labour in recent years has been the **Konkan Railway**, completed in 1997 to form a super-fast land link with Mumbai – another conduit of economic prosperity that has brought lasting changes.

Which beach you opt for when you arrive largely depends on what sort of holiday you have in mind. More developed resorts such as **Calangute** and **Baga** in the north, and **Colva** and **Benaulim** in the south, offer more "walk-in" accommodation and tourist facilities than elsewhere. Even if you're looking

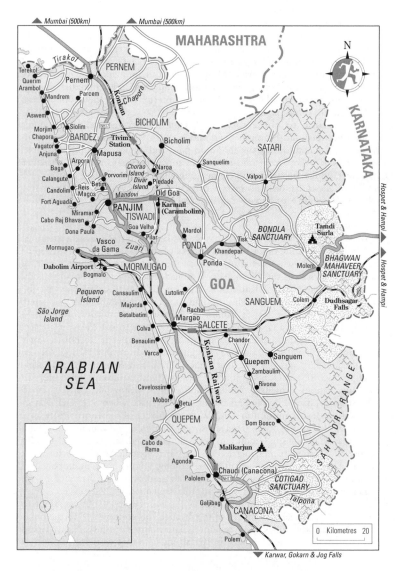

for a less touristy scene, it can be worth heading for these centres first, as finding places to stay in less commercialized corners is often difficult. **Anjuna**, **Vagator** and **Chapora**, where accommodation is generally more basic and harder to come by, are the beaches to aim for if you've come to Goa to party. However, the bulk of budget travellers taking time out from tours of India end up in **Palolem**, in the far south, or **Arambol**, both beyond the increasingly long reach of the charter buses. That said, Palolem, in particular, has become a major resort in its own right, with thousands of long-stay visitors in peak season.

Some 10km from the state capital, **Panjim**, the ruins of the former Portuguese capital at **Old Goa** are foremost among the attractions away from the coast – a sprawl of Catholic cathedrals, convents and churches that draw crowds of Christian pilgrims from all over India. Another popular day excursion is to Anjuna's Wednesday **flea market**, a sociable place to shop for souvenirs and dance wear. Further inland, the thickly wooded countryside around **Ponda** harbours numerous temples, where you can experience Goa's peculiar brand of Hindu architecture. The district of Salcete, and its main market town, **Margao**, is also littered with Portuguese mansions, churches and seminaries. Finally, wildlife enthusiasts may be tempted into the interior to visit the nature reserve at **Cotigao** in the far south.

The best **time to come** to Goa is during the dry, relatively cool winter months between mid-November and mid-March. At other times, either the sun is too hot for comfort, or the monsoon rains and clouds make life miserable. During peak season, from mid-December to the end of January, the weather is perfect, with temperatures rarely nudging above 32°C. Finding a room or a house to rent at that time, however – particularly over Christmas and New Year when tariffs double, or triple – can be a real hassle.

Some history

Goa's sheer inaccessibility by land has always kept it out of the mainstream of Indian history; on the other hand, its control of the seas and the lucrative spice trade made it a much-coveted prize for rival colonial powers. Until a century before the arrival of the Portuguese, Goa had belonged for over a thousand years to the kingdom of **Kadamba**. They, in turn, were overthrown by the Karnatakan Vijayanagars, the Muslim Bahmanis, and Yusuf Adil Shah of Bijapur, but the capture of the fort at Panjim by **Afonso de Albuquerque** in 1510 signalled the start of a Portuguese occupation that was to last 451 years.

As Goa expanded, its splendid capital (now Old Goa) came to hold a larger population than Paris or London. Though Ismail Adil Shah laid siege for ten months in 1570, and the Marathas under Shivaji and later chiefs came nail-bitingly close to seizing the region, the greatest threat was from other European maritime nations, principally Holland and France. Meanwhile, conversions to **Christianity**, started by the Franciscans, gathered pace when St Francis Xavier founded the **Jesuit** mission in 1542. With the advent of the **Inquisition** soon afterwards, laws were introduced censoring literature and banning any faith other than Catholicism. Hindu temples were destroyed, and converted Hindus adopted Portuguese names, such as da Silva, Correa and de Sousa, which remain common in the region. Thereafter, the colony, whose trade monopoly had been broken by its European rivals, went into gradual decline, hastened by the unhealthy, disease-ridden environment of its capital.

Despite a certain liberalization, such as the restoration of Hindus' right to worship and the final banishment of the dreaded Inquisition in 1820, the nineteenth century saw widespread civil unrest. During the British Raj many Goans moved to Bombay, and elsewhere in British India, to find work.

The success of the post-Independence Goan struggle for freedom owed as much to the efforts of the Indian government, which cut off diplomatic ties with Portugal, as to the work of freedom fighters such as **Menezes Braganza** and **Dr Cunha**. After a "liberation march" in 1955 resulted in a number of deaths, the state was blockaded. Trade with Bombay ceased, and the railway was cut off, so Goa set out to forge international links, particularly with Pakistan and Sri Lanka. That led to the building of Dabolim airport, and a determination to improve local agricultural output. In 1961, Prime Minister Jawaharlal Nehru finally ran out of patience with his opposite number in Lisbon, the right-wing dictator Salazar, and sent in the armed forces. Mounted in defiance of a United Nations resolution, **"Operation Vijay"** met only token resistance, and the Indian army overran Goa in two days. Thereafter, Goa (along with Portugal's other two enclaves, Daman and Diu) became part of India as a self-governing **Union Territory**, with minimum interference from Delhi.

Since Independence, Goa has continued to prosper, bolstered by iron-ore exports and a booming tourist industry. Dominated by the issues of statehood, the status of Konkani and the ever-rising levels of immigration, its political life

Police, drugs and nudism

While the vast majority of visitors to Goa never encounter any **trouble**, tourism-related crime is definitely more prevalent here than in other parts of the country. **Theft** is the most common problem – usually of articles left unattended on the beach. Don't assume your valuables are safe in a padlocked house or hotel room, either; break-ins, particularly on party nights, are on the increase. The most secure solution is to rent a deposit box at your hotel or guesthouse, or from a private locker shop.

The other eventuality to avoid, at all costs, is getting on the wrong side of the law. **Drugs** are the most common cause of serious trouble. Many travellers imagine that, because of Goa's free-and-easy reputation, drug use is legal: it isn't. Possession of even a small amount of cannabis is a criminal offence, punishable by large fines or prison sentences. If you're approached by anyone offering you narcotics, whether foreign or Indian, ignore them; and bear in mind that numerous arrests in the past three or four years have followed tip-offs from the dealers themselves, who are paid a cut of the resulting bribe taken by the police as a reward, or have been obliged to inform on their customers in order to operate free from police interference. A couple of seasons ago, several foreigners were also admitted to Panjim hospital with life-threatening conditions resulting from having smoked *charas* (cannabis resin), bought from Kashmiri dealers, which had been cut with something very nasty.

Though violent crime is rare, women should think twice before wandering down deserted beaches and dark tracks on their own. **Sexual harassment** usually takes the form of unsubtle ogling, but there have also been several incidents of **rape** in recent years. So, wherever you're staying, take the same commonsense precautions as you would at home: keep to the main roads when travelling on foot or by bicycle, avoid dirt tracks and unfrequented beaches (particularly on party nights) unless you're in a group, and when you're in your hotel or guesthouse after dark, ensure that all windows and doors are locked.

Bikinis and, increasingly, topless bathing are the norm on Westerner-dominated beaches, but expect to attract plenty of attention if you walk around under-dressed in front of Indian visitors from out of state, or in less developed parts of Goa. Such behaviour isn't likely to cause offence, but will provoke staring and possibly hassle. The best policy for women is to cover up with a sarong or *lunghi* when you see families or groups of Indian men approaching. Total **nudism** is never acceptable, and technically illegal.

has been dogged by chronic **instability**. In the 1990s, no fewer than twelve chief ministers held power over a succession of shaky, opportunistic coalitions, which saw standards of government plummet to depths hitherto unseen in the region.

Among the main beneficiaries of the ongoing chaos have been the extreme right-wing Hindu fundamentalists, the **BJP**. In the past, their advocacy of merger with Maharashtra made them unpopular with the Goan electorate – even Hindus – despite the party's dominance in the national arena. But with one-quarter of the seats in the Goan assembly, the BJP dominated the state government between 2000 and 2004. Chief Minister **Manohar Parrikar** made himself popular with middle class urban voters after he initiated improvements to buildings and roads in the capital, and brought the International Film Festival of India to Panjim. But life for him and his party became more difficult after the elections of May 2004, when Congress won a majority in the State Legislature.

Pressure started to build after a series of tit-for-tat political sackings and appointments created the Goan equivalent of a hung parliament, and sent

Getting around

White Maruti van **taxis** serve as the main means of travelling between resorts. You'll find them lined up outside most charter hotels, where a board invariably displays "fixed rates" to destinations in and around the region. These fares only apply to peak season, however, and at other times you should be able to negotiate a hefty reduction.

By ferry

Although gradually being superseded by road bridges, flat-bottomed **ferries** are Goa's quintessential mode of transport. Crammed with cars, buses, commuters on scooters, fisherwomen and clumps of overheated tourists, these rusting blue-painted hulks are incredibly cheap, and run from the crack of dawn until late in the evening. The most frequented river crossings in Goa are Panjim to **Betim**, across the Mandovi (every 15min); **Old Goa** to Divar Island (every 15min); Querim to **Terekol**, over the River Terekol (every 30min); and **Cavelossim**, in the far south of Salcete, to Assolna (every 20–30min).

By train

The **Konkan Railway** serves as Goa's principal long-distance transport artery, although it's rarely convenient for shorter journeys within the state. The relative infrequency of services and distance of the line from most of the resorts means you're invariably better off catching the bus. The one trip it really is worth catching the train for is the two-hour ride south to the temple town of Gokarna, in neighbouring Karnataka.

By bus

The Goan transport corporation, **Kadamba**, runs long-distance services throughout the state from their main stands at Panjim, Mapusa and Margao. Private buses, serving everywhere else (including the coastal resorts) are cheap, frequent and more relaxed than many in India, although you should still brace yourself for a crush on market days and when travelling to major towns and tourist centres. Details on how to get around by bus are listed in the relevant accounts, and on p.233.

By motorcycle taxi

Goa's unique pillion-passenger **motorcycle taxis**, known locally as **"pilots"**, are ideal for nipping between beaches or into town from the resorts. Bona fide operators ride black bikes with yellow mudguards and white number plates. Fares, which should leaders of both parties scurrying to the Governor's residence to request permission to form a government. With both Congress and the BJP trying to engineer defections from one side to the other, the situation soon spiralled into chaos. Eventually, in March 2005 – barely three hours after the Congress narrowly won a vote of confidence (the third in thirty days) – New Delhi stepped into the breach and declared **President's Rule**. At the time of writing, a new round of elections was planned to break the deadlock, but it seems unlikely that Goa's political life will stabilize in the medium to long term.

Panjim and central Goa

Stacked around the sides of a lush terraced hillside at the mouth of the River Mandovi, **PANJIM** (also known by its Marathi name, **Panaji** – "land that

be settled in advance, are comparable with auto-rickshaw rates: roughly Rs7 per kilometre.

By rented motorcycle

Renting a motorcycle in Goa gives a lot of freedom but can be perilous. Every season, an average of one person a day dies on the roads; many are tourists on two-wheelers. Make sure, therefore, that the lights and brakes are in good shape, and be especially vigilant at night: Goan roads can be appallingly pot-holed and unlit, and stray cows, dogs and bullock carts can appear from nowhere.

Officially, you need an **international driver's licence** to rent, and ride, anything more powerful than a 25cc moped. Owners and rental companies rarely enforce this, but some local **police** use the rule to extract baksheesh from tourists. If you don't have a licence with you, the only way around the problem is to avoid big towns such as Panjim, Margao and Mapusa (or Anjuna on market day), and only to carry small sums of money when driving. If you are stopped for not having the right papers, it's no big deal, though police officers may try to convince you otherwise; keep cool, and be prepared to negotiate. Some unlicensed operators attempt to rent out machines to unwary visitors; always make sure you get some evidence of rental and insurance.

Rates vary according to the season, the vehicle, and how long you rent it for; most owners also insist on a deposit and/or passport as security. The range is pretty standard, with the cheapest choice a step-through style scooter such as a **Honda Kinetic 100cc** (Rs150–200 per day); with automatic gears, this is a good first-time choice and arguably the best all-rounder. To travel any significant distance, however, you should consider renting an **Enfield Bullet 350cc** (upwards of Rs250 per day), popular mainly for its pose value, or a smaller, lighter and generally more reliable **Yamaha 100cc** or **Bajaj Pulsar 180cc** (both around Rs200/250 per day, respectively).

Tours

On paper, guided **tours** (daily; Rs150) run by the local tourism authority **GTDC** (⊛www.goa-tourism.com) from Panjim, Margao, Calangute and Colva seem like a good way of getting around Goa's highlights in a short time. However, they're far too rushed for most foreign tourists, appealing essentially to Indian families wishing to combine a peek at the resorts with a whistle-stop puja tour of the temples around Ponda. Most also include a string of places inland that you wouldn't otherwise consider visiting. Leaflets giving full itineraries are available at any GTDC office.

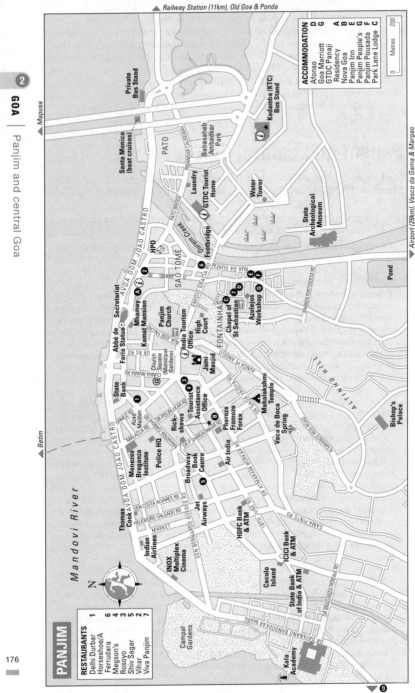

Railway Station (11km), Old Goa & Ponda

▲ Mapusa

▲ Betim

Mandovi River

N

ACCOMMODATION
Afonso	D
Goa Marriott	G
GTDC Panaji Residency	A
Nova Goa	B
Panjim Inn	E
Panjim People's	G
Panjim Pousada	F
Park Lane Lodge	C

0   Metres   200

Airport (29km), Vasco da Gama & Margao ▶

PANJIM

RESTAURANTS
Delhi Durbar	1
Horseshoe/A	6
Ferrudara	4
Megson's	3
Rosoyo	5
Shiv Sagar	2
Vihar	
Viva Panjim	7

Private Bus Stand

Santa Monica (boat cruises)

Kadamba (KTC) Bus Stand

Babasaheb Ambedkar Park

PATO

MANDOVI CAUSEWAY

PATO BRIDGE

Laundry

GTDC Tourist Home

Water Tower

State Archeological Museum

Pond

Footbridge

HPO

Ouem Creek

SAO TOME

RUA DA OUREM

Secretariat

Abbé de Faria Statue

Mhamay Kamat Mansion

Panjim Church

India Tourism Office

Church Square (Municipal Gardens)

EMIDIO GRACIA

High Court

FONTAINHAS

Chapel of St Sebastian

Azulejos Workshop

ALTINHO HILL

Bishop's Palace

ALBUQUERQUE RD

AVDA DOM JOAO CASTRO

State Bank

Azad Maidan

MALACCA RD

Police HQ

Thomas Cook

Menezes Braganza Institute

Jami Masjid

India Tourism Office

Rick-shaws

Tourist Assistance Office

Pheroze Framoze Forex

Mahalakshmi Temple

Vaca de Boca Spring

AVENIDA FE ANGELO

DR DADA VAIDYA RD

GEN COSTA ALVARES RD

HELIODORO SALGADO RD

MARKET

GEN BERNARDO GUEDES RD

Indian Airlines

INOX Multiplex Cinema

Broadway Book Centre

Jet Airways

Air India

HDFC Bank & ATM

ICICI Bank & ATM

Caculo Island

State Bank of India & ATM

Campal Gardens

Kala Academy

DR ATMARAM BORKAR RD

DR DANANAND BANDODKAR MARG

DR BRAGANZA PEREIRA RD

GAMA PINTO RD

ALBUQUERQUE RD

does not flood") was for centuries little more than a minor landing stage and customs house, protected by a hilltop fort and surrounded by stagnant swampland. It only became state capital in 1843, after the port at Old Goa had silted up and its rulers and impoverished inhabitants had fled the plague. Although the last Portuguese viceroy managed to drain many of Panjim's marshes, and erect imposing public buildings on the new site, the town never emulated the grandeur of its predecessor upriver – a result, in part, of the Portuguese nobles' predilection for erecting their mansions in the countryside rather than the city. Panjim expanded rapidly in the 1960s and 1970s, without reaching the unmanageable proportions of other Indian capitals. After Mumbai, or even Bangalore, its uncongested streets seem easy-going and pleasantly parochial. Sights are thin on the ground, but the backstreets of the old quarter, **Fontainhas**, have retained

Goan to the movies

Goa's state capital ground to a total halt for three days in February 2003 when it was commandeered by the makers of **The Bourne Supremacy**, starring Hollywood star Matt Damon. Although the chase scene that opened the movie started at a location you might recognize as Palolem beach, it cut straight to Panjim, and then to Nerul bridge, near Candolim, via a dramatic car chase through the normally sleepy streets of Fontainhas.

This brush with international cinema celebrity was the perfect preamble to the 35th **International Film Festival of India** (IFFI), held for the first time in Goa the following year. In the months leading up to the event, Panjim enjoyed a multi-crore makeover: main roads and buildings around the city were spruced up and the formerly broken walkway along the riverbank became a revamped promenade, complete with 2000 ornamental street lamps and fountains specially imported from Belgium. Three controversial lights (costing more than £27,000) were also installed to illuminate the temporary wooden jetty behind the festival's main venue, the Kala Academy, where delegates and guests alighting from launches from the *Taj Fort Aguada* hotel would arrive. The stage was thus set for superstars from across the world to pose for photocalls along Panjim's waterfront, "à la Cannes". Hollywood was conspicuous by its absence, but a bevy of Bollywood's top names, including Amir Khan, Sanjay Dutt and the "Big B" himself, Amitabh Bachchan, loyally turned up, to the obvious delight of the local dignitaries and politicians hosting the event.

In total, 169 films from 55 countries were shown over the course of the fortnight, among them the Indian premiere of *Vanity Fair*, introduced by its director, Mira Nair. But the biggest splash was reserved for *filmi* score supremo, A.H. Rahman, who performed a live outdoor concert.

Although some dissenting voices in the Goan media deemed the whole exercise a colossal waste of time and money, most people in Panjim were flattered by the profile it gave the town, and greeted the news that Goa would host the 2005 IFFI with great enthusiasm, amid hopes that the state would become a permanent venue for the event.

If it does, expect a stiff hike in hotel rates around the end of November to early December, and an acute shortage of rooms. Rather than stay in town to catch the films, therefore, consider travelling down from one or other of the resorts up the coast. In addition to the big open-air venues along the Mandovi in Campal, movies are screened in Panjim's state-of-the-art new multiplex, the Innox (see "Listings", p.183); tickets can be purchased in advance from the festival box office at the Old Goa Medical College Heritage precinct, Dayanand Bandodkar (DB) Marg. For listings and previews of the films on show, pick up a festival programme from the festival office (opposite the Inox cinema, Old Goa Medical College Heritage precinct, Dayanand Bandodkar (DB) Marg), or at the Kala Academy.

a faded Portuguese atmosphere, with colour-washed houses, Catholic churches and shopfronts sporting names such as De Souza and Pinto.

Some travellers see no more of Panjim than its noisy bus terminal – which is a pity. Although you can completely bypass the town when you arrive in Goa, either by jumping off the train or coach at Margao (for the south), or Mapusa (for the northern resorts), or by heading straight off on a local bus, it's definitely worth spending time here – if only a couple of hours en route to the ruined former capital at Old Goa.

The area **around Panjim** attracts far fewer visitors than the coastal resorts, yet its paddy fields and wooded valleys harbour several attractions worth a day or two's break from the beach. **Old Goa** is just a bus ride away, as are the unique temples around **Ponda**, an hour or so southeast, to where Hindus smuggled their deities during the Inquisition. Further inland still, the forested lower slopes of the Western Ghats, cut through by the main Panjim–Bangalore highway, shelter the impressive **Dudhsagar falls**, which you can only reach by four-wheel-drive Jeep.

Arrival, information and local transport

European charter planes and domestic flights arrive at **Dabolim airport** (℡0832/254 0788), 29km south of Panjim on the outskirts of Vasco da Gama, Goa's second city. Prepaid taxis into town (45min; Rs475), booked at the counter in the forecourt, can be shared by up to four people.

There's no **train** station in town itself; the nearest one, on the Konkan Railway, is at **Karmali** (11km east of Panjim at Old Goa; ℡0832/228 5798). State buses to central Panjim await arrivals.

Long-distance and local **buses** pull into Panjim's busy Kadamba bus stand, 1km east of the centre in the district of Pato. Ten minutes' walk, across Ourem

---

Dabolim airport

Dabolim, Goa's airport, lies on top of a rocky plateau, 4km southeast of the industrial town of Vasco da Gama. A large new civilian terminal has been constructed at this naval aerodrome to accommodate Goa's rapidly increasing air traffic, but long delays are still common.

Facilities in the terminal buildings include a post office, counters for domestic airlines and State Bank of India **foreign exchange desks** (check exchange certificates and cash carefully before leaving, as there have been reports of short-changing). There's also a handy pre-paid **taxi counter** outside the main exit. Fixed fares to virtually everywhere in the state are displayed behind the desk; pay here and give the slip to the driver when you arrive.

Facilities in Dabolim's first floor **departures hall** include another pint-size State Bank of India (Mon, Tues, Thurs & Fri 10.30am–1.30pm, Sat 10.30am–noon), a sub-post-office and branches of several domestic airlines: Indian Airlines (daily 7.15am–2pm; ℡0832/251 2788), Sahara Airlines (daily 9.30am–5pm; ℡0832/251 0043) and Jet (daily 9.30am–5pm; ℡0832/254 0029). There's a very ordinary and overpriced cafeteria, too, but it doesn't open in time for early morning domestic departures, so if you're looking for a filling breakfast, head across the road from the front of the terminal building to the staff canteen, where you can grab piping hot pau bhaji and batata wada for a few rupees.

Anyone **visiting** the airport, or meeting arrivals, should note that a Rs20 visitor ticket (on sale at the hatch next to the main ground-floor exit) will buy you entrance to the foyer of the air-conditioned arrivals hall.

Creek to Fontainhas, brings you to several budget hotels. For the more modern west end of town, flag down a motorcycle taxi or jump into an auto-rickshaw at the rank outside the station concourse (Rs20–25).

GTDC's **information** counter, inside the concourse at the main Kadamba bus stand (daily 9.30am–1pm & 2–5pm; ℡0832/222 5620, Ⓦwww.goa-tourism .org) is useful for checking train and bus timings, but little else. The more efficient **India Tourism office** is across town on Church Square (Mon–Fri 9.30am–6pm, Sat 9.30am–1pm; ℡0832/222 3412, Ⓦwww.tourismofindia.com).

Auto-rickshaws are the most convenient way of **getting around** Panjim; flag one down at the roadside or head for one of the ranks around the city.

Accommodation

The majority of Goa's Indian visitors prefer to stay in Panjim rather than the coastal resorts, which explains the huge number of **hotels** and **lodges** crammed into the town centre, especially its noisy, more modern west end. Foreigners spending the night here instead of on the coast, on the other hand, tend to do so primarily to sample the atmosphere of the old quarter, Fontainhas. Finding a room is only a problem during the festival of St Francis (Nov 24–Dec 3), Dusshera (Sept/Oct) and during peak season (mid-Dec to mid-Jan); the codes below apply to October through March, excluding the above periods, when prices can double or triple. Note that **checkout times** vary wildly; find out what yours is as soon as you arrive, or your hard-earned lie-in could end up costing you an extra day's rent.

Afonso St Sebastian Chapel Square, Fontainhas ℡0832/222359. This refurbished colonial-era house in a picturesque backstreet is your best bet if you can't afford the *Panjim Inn* down the road. Spotlessly clean, cool en-suite rooms, friendly owners and rooftop terrace with views. Single occupancy available. Rates soar to Rs800 at Christmas, but are otherwise low for the level of comfort and location. ❹

Goa Marriott Miramar beach ℡0832/243 7001, Ⓦwww.marriott.com. Huge five-star out on the edge of town, facing the mouth of the Mandovi. Predictably formulaic, and not a great location for a package holiday (despite what the brochures might suggest), but large and luxurious, with all the mod cons you'd expect, and the management hosts complimentary cocktail parties each week for guests' feedback. ❾

GTDC Panaji Residency Avda Dom Joao Castro ℡0832/223396, Ⓦwww.goa-tourism.com. Spacious rooms in an amorphous government-run hotel next to the main road and river. Not at all inspiring, but good value. ❺

Nova Goa Dr Atmaram Borkar Rd ℡0832/227 7226, Ⓦwww.hotelnovagoa.com. Panjim's brightest, newest top-class hotel in the heart of the shopping area and with the usual comforts, plus bath tubs and a pool. Popular mainly with visiting Portuguese and corporate clients. ❽

Panjim Inn E-212, 31 Janeiro Rd, Fontainhas ℡0832/243 5628, Ⓦwww.panjiminn.com. Grand 300-year-old townhouse, now managed as a homely heritage hotel, with period furniture, sepia family photos, balconies and a common veranda where meals and drinks are served to guests. The same family runs the even more beautiful *Panjim Pousada* (same phone number; ❻), across the road, an old Hindu house which gives you the chance sample what Panjim must have felt like a century ago; ask for a room on the first floor, where a lovely wooden balcony, shaded by a breadfruit tree, overlooks the inner courtyard. ❻

Panjim Peoples 31 Janeiro Rd, Fontainhas ℡0832/222 1122, Ⓦwww.panjiminn.com. The *Panjim's Inn*'s latest "heritage" venture, opposite the original house (see above) occupies a former high school. It's more upmarket than their other two wings, but no less appealing for that. The rooms are huge, fitted with antique rosewood furniture, gilded pelmets and lace curtains, and the bathrooms feature the Sukhija family's hallmark crazy-mosaic tiling. Tariffs mid-season start at around Rs5000 per night. ❾

Park Lane Lodge near the Chapel of St Sebastian ℡0832/222 7154, Ⓔpklaldg@sancharnet.in. Cramped but clean and friendly family guesthouse in a rambling 1930s house. Pepper and coffee plants add atmosphere to a narrow communal terrace, and there's a TV lounge upstairs; also safe deposit facilities, Internet access and a laundry service. Rates are ambitious in season, but at other times you get discounts. ❹

The Town

The leafy rectangular park opposite the India Government tourist office, known as **Church Square** or the **Municipal Gardens**, forms the heart of Panjim. Presiding over its southeast side is the town's most distinctive and photogenic landmark, the toothpaste-white Baroque facade of the **Church of Our Lady of the Immaculate Conception**. Flanked by rows of slender palm trees, at the head of a crisscrossing laterite walkway, the church was built in 1541 for the benefit of sailors arriving here from Lisbon. The weary mariners would stagger up from the quay to give thanks for their safe passage before proceeding to the capital at Old Goa – the original home of the enormous bell that hangs from its central gable.

Running north from the church, Rua José Falcao brings you to the riverside, where Panjim's main street, Avenida Dom Joao Castro, holds the town's oldest surviving building. With its sloping tiled roofs, carved-stone coats of arms and wooden verandas, the stalwart **Secretariat** looks typically colonial. Yet it was originally the summer palace of Goa's sixteenth-century Muslim ruler, the Adil Shah. Later, the Portuguese converted it into a temporary rest house for the territory's governors (who used to overnight here en route to and from Lisbon) and then a residence for the viceroy. Today, it accommodates the Goan State Legislature – hence shiny chauffeur-driven Ambassador cars outside and the armed guards at the door.

A hundred metres east, a peculiar statue of a man holding his hands over the body of an entranced reclining woman shows **Abbé de Faria** (1755–1819), a Goan priest who emigrated to France to become one of the world's first professional hypnotists.

Just behind the esplanade, 500m west of the Abbé de Faria statue, stands another grand vestige of the colonial era, the **Menezes Braganza Institute**. Now the town's Central Library (Mon–Fri 9.30am–1pm & 2–5.30pm), this Neoclassical building was erected as part of the civic makeover initiated by the Marquis of Pombal and Dom Manuel de Portugal e Castro in the early nineteenth century. Its entrance lobby on Malacca Road is lined with panels of blue-and-yellow-painted ceramic tiles, known as **azulejos**, depicting scenes from Luis Vaz Camões' epic poem, *Os Luisiades*.

Fontainhas

Panjim's oldest and most interesting district, **Fontainhas**, spreads from the banks of Pato creek opposite the bus stand – a dozen or so blocks of Neoclassical houses rising up the sides of leafy Altinho Hill. Many have retained their traditional coat of ochre, pale yellow, green or blue – a legacy of the Portuguese insistence that every Goan building (except churches, which had to be white) should be colour-washed after the monsoons. While some (notably the Portuguese **Fundacão Oriente** building at the south end of the neighbourhood, and the three wings of the *Panjim Inn*) have been restored, most remain in a state of charismatic decay.

The whitewashed **Chapel of St Sebastian**, still holding to the old colonial decree, stands at the centre of Fontainhas, at the head of a small square where the Portuguese-speaking locals hold a lively annual street *festa* to celebrate their patron saint's day in mid-November. The eerily lifelike crucifix inside the chapel, brought here in 1812, formerly hung in the Palace of the Inquisition in Old Goa. Unusually, Christ's eyes are open – allegedly to inspire fear in those being interrogated by the Inquisitors.

Just off the bottom of the square is a small workshop where you can watch traditional Goan *azulejos* being made. The main sales room, **Galeria Velha Goa**, is a couple of blocks away, next door to the *Panjim Inn*.

Grander colonial-era buildings are to found up on **Altinho Hill**, which can be reached via the flight of steps beginning alongside the *Park Lane Lodge*. The first one you come to at the top of the steps is the High Court of Goa, a splendid example of late-nineteenth-century Portuguese municipal architecture. Ten minutes' walk further south, occupying the highest point in Panjim, the **Archishop's Palace**, a long, white, double-storeyed building with an imposing facade, is still occupied by Goa's highest ranking prelate, hence the whitewash.

The State Archeological Museum

The most noteworthy feature of Panjim's **State Archeological Museum** (Mon–Fri 9.30am–1.15pm & 2–5.30pm; Rs20; Ⓦ www.goamuseum.nic.in) is its impressive size, which stands in glaringly inverse proportion to the collections inside. In their bid to erect a structure befitting a state capital, Goa's bureaucrats ignored the fact that there was precious little to put in it. The only rarities to be found amid the lame array of temple sculpture, hero stones and dowdy colonial-era artefacts are a couple of beautiful Jain bronzes rescued by Customs and Excise officials from smugglers and, on the first floor, the infamous Italian-style table used by Goa's Grand Inquisitors, complete with its original, ornately carved tall-backed chairs.

The Houses of Goa Museum

Across the river, near the new hilltop suburb of **Porvorim**, renowned local architect Gerard de Cunha and colleagues recently set up the quirky **Houses of Goa Museum** (Tues–Sun 10am–7.30pm; Rs25; Ⓦ www.archgoa.org). Its general aim is to showcase the region's way of life as it used to be before the protective shield of Portuguese rule was lifted in 1961.

The triangular building itself resembles a modern ark, with themed displays divided between four levels interconnected by spiral staircases. After a whistlestop graphic résumé of Goan history, the exhibitions are largely given over to domestic houses, described as "the prime expression of Goan identity". Pieces of traditional colonial-era houses – from wonderful old doors and oyster-shell windows, to carved railings, ceramic tiles, furniture and masonry – are assembled to explain construction processes and changes in decor and style. Architectural features that were adapted in a uniquely Goan way, such as colour schemes, ornamental gateposts, verandas and false ceilings, are also highlighted, and interactive computer exhibits let you delve more deeply into the subjects covered.

Only 5km from Panjim, the House of Goa museum is most easily reached by taxi or auto-rickshaw. With your own transport, head north over the Mandovi bridge and keep going until you reach the big Alto-Porvorim Circle roundabout. Take a right here and follow the road until it forks, then bear left and head straight on for 750m or so, until you reach a second fork, where you bear left again: the museum is next to Nisha's Play School. By bus, you can travel as far as the Alto-Porvorim circle on any Panjim–Mapusa service from the Kadamba stand: get down at *O Coqueiro* restaurant (infamous as the place where international jewel thief and suspected serial killer **Charles Sobhraj** was captured by police in 1987), which is just north of the roundabout, then walk the remaining 2km, or jump in an auto if there's one hanging around.

Eating and drinking

Catering for the droves of tourists who come here from other Indian states, as well as more price-conscious locals, Panjim is packed with good **places to eat,**

Goan food and drink

Not unnaturally, after 450 years of colonization, Goan **cooking** has absorbed a strong Portuguese influence – palm vinegar (unknown elsewhere in India), copious amounts of coconut, garlic, tangy tamarind and fierce local chillies all play their part. Goa is the home of the famous *vindaloo* (from the Portuguese *vinho d'alho*, literally "garlic wine"), originally an extra-hot and sour pork curry, but now made with a variety of meat and fish. Other **pork** specialities include *chouriço* red sausages, *sorpotel*, a hot curry made from pickled pig's liver and heart, *leitao*, suckling pig and *balchao*, pork in a rich brown sauce. Delicious alternatives include mutton *xacutti*, made with a sauce of lemon juice, peanuts, coconut, chillies and spices. The choice of **seafood**, often cooked in fragrant masalas, is excellent – clams, mussels, crab, lobster, giant prawns – while **fish**, depending on the type, is either cooked in wet curries, grilled, or baked in tandoor clay ovens. *Sanna*, like the South Indian *iddli*, is a steamed cake of fermented rice flour, but here made with palm toddy. Sweet tooths will adore *bebinca*, a rich, delicious solid egg custard with coconut.

As for **drinks**, locally produced wine, spirits and beer are cheaper than anywhere in the country, thanks to lower rates of tax. The most famous and widespread **beer** is Kingfisher, which tastes less of glycerine preservative than it does elsewhere in India, but you'll also come across pricier Fosters, brewed in Mumbai and nothing like the original. Goan **port**, a sweeter, inferior version of its Portuguese namesake, is ubiquitous, served chilled in large wine glasses with a slice of lemon. Local **spirits** – whiskies, brandies, rums, gins and vodkas – come in a variety of brand names for less than Rs30 a shot, but, at half the price, local speciality **feni**, made from distilled cashew or from the sap of coconut palms, offers strong competition. Cashew *feni* is usually drunk after the first distillation, but you can also find it double-distilled, flavoured with ginger or cumin to produce a smooth liqueur.

from hole-in-the-wall fish-curry-rice joints to swish air-conditioned restaurants serving top-notch Mughlai cuisine. In a week you could feasibly attempt a gastronomic tour of the subcontinent without straying more than five minutes from the Municipal Gardens. Vegetarians are best catered for at the numerous *udipi* canteens dotted around town, most of which open around 7am for South Indian **breakfasts**. Beer, *feni* and other spirits are available in all but the purest "pure veg" places.

Delhi Durbar behind the *Hotel Mandovi*. A provincial branch of the famous Mumbai restaurant, and the best place in Panjim – if not all Goa – to sample traditional Mughlai cuisine of mainly meat steeped in rich, spicy sauces (try their superb *rogan josh* or melt-in-the-mouth chicken tikka). Most main dishes are around Rs175–200, but this place is well worth a splurge.

Horseshoe/A Ferrudara Rua de Ourem, Fontainhas. The town's only Portuguese restaurant, serving a limited, but reasonably priced, menu of old standards such as *canja de galinha*, *caldo verde*, *feijoada*, soup, chicken piri piri, fish *balchao* and grilled sardines. The food is not as good as at *Viva Panjim*, but the decor and atmosphere make this a worthwhile option, plus it's air-conditioned. Most mains around Rs100.

Megson's 18th June Rd. The state's top deli, with a great selection of traditional Goan foods: spicy sausages, prepared meats, tangy cheese from the Nilgiris, olive oil, and the best *bebinca* you can buy (ask for *Linda* brand).

Rosoyo 18th June Rd. Run by *Megson's*, this busy little fast-food joint is *the* place to sample tasty, hygienic Mumbai-style street food: crunchy *bhel puri* or delicious *pau bhaji*. They also serve Gujarati snacks such as *thepla* – chapatis griddle-cooked with curry leaves and cumin, and served with South Indian *chatni* – plus a range of shakes and ice creams. You'll be hard pushed to spend Rs50.

Shiv Sagar Mahatma Gandhi Rd. Smarter than average snack-café that does a brisk trade with the city's middle classes, offering consistently fresh, delicious pan-Indian food and fresh fruit juices. The northern dishes aren't so great, but their South Indian menu is superb (try the delicious *palak dosa*, made with spinach). A/c "family" mezzanine upstairs. No alcohol.

Vihar 31 Janeiro Rd. Arguably the best budget *udipi* in Panjim; try their super tasty *rawa* masala *dosas*.

Viva Panjim 31 Janeiro Rd, Fontainhas. Traditional Goan home cooking – millet-fried mussels, *xacutis*, vindaloo, prawn *balchao*, *cafreal*, *amotik* and delicious freshly grilled fish – served by a charming local lady in atmospheric colonial-era backstreet. This place should be your first choice for dinner if you're staying in Fontainhas for a taste of old colonial Goa. Get there early for one of the half-dozen tables outside in the alley. Most mains under Rs150.

Listings

Airlines Air France, Air Seychelles, American Airlines, Biman Bangladesh, Gulf Air, Kenyan Airways, Royal Jordanian, Sri Lankan Airlines, all c/o Jetair, Rizvi Chambers, 1st Floor, H. Salgado Rd ☎0832/222 0122 or 222 6154; Air India, Colvakar Centaur, Campal ☎0832/222 4081 or 222 5172; Alitalia, Globe Trotters International, G-7 Shankar Parvati Building, 18th June Rd ☎0832/243 8950–52; British Airways, DKI Airlines Service, 2 Excelsior Chambers, MG Rd ☎0832/222 4573 or 243 8055–57; Indian Airlines, Dempo House, Dr D. Bandodkar Rd ☎0832/242 8787 or 223 7826; Jet Airlines, Sesa Ghor, ECD Plaza, next to GTDC *Panjim Residency*, Pato ☎0832/243 8792 or 222 1476; Sahara Airlines, Ground Floor, Livein Appts, General Bernard Guedes Rd ☎0832/223 7346 or 223 0237.

Banks and ATMs The most efficient places to change money are: Thomas Cook, near the Indian Airlines office at 8 Alcon Chambers, Devanand Bandodkar Rd (Mon–Sat 9am–6pm, Oct–March also Sun 10am–5pm); and the Pheroze Framroze Exchange Bureau on Dr P. Shirgaonkar Rd (Mon–Sat 9.30am–7pm & Sun 9.30am–1pm). The latter's rates are competitive and they don't charge commission on either currency or travellers' cheques. The HDFC Bank on 18th June Rd is one of several major banks in the centre with a handy 24hr ATM, where you can make withdrawals using Visa or Mastercard. Changing money in the regular, government-run banks tends to take a lot longer: the Bank of Baroda (where you can draw money on Visa cards at its Bobcard counter) is on Azad Maidan.

Books The best selection of Goa-related books is at the Broadway Book Centre on 18th June Rd, opposite Gulf Supermarket, which sells a great range of old stuff in facsimile editions and lots of architecture and photographic tomes in hardback at discounted prices.

British Consular Assistant The British High Commission of Mumbai has a Tourist Assistance Office in Panjim, run by Ms Shilpa Caldeira – a useful contact for British nationals who've lost passports, get into trouble with the law or need help dealing with a death. It's over near the Kadamba bus stand at 13/14 Dempo Towers, Patto Plaza ☎0832/243 8734, ✉bcagoa@sancharnet.in, ✇www.ukinindia.com. In emergencies only, Ms Caldeira may be reached on her mobile number ☎9822/102428.

Cinema Panjim's swanky new multiplex, the 1272-seater Inox, is in the northwest of town on the site of the old Goa Medical College, Dayanand Bandodkar (DB) Marg (☎0832/242 0999, ✇www.inoxmovies.com). Designed by the Kiwi architects, Walkers, and opened for the first International Film Festival of India in 2004, the complex screens all the latest Hindi blockbusters, and some English-language Hollywood movies; see the local press or the Inox website for listings and booking details (Internet ticketing was in the pipeline when we last checked).

Hospital The state's main medical facility is the new Goa Medical College, aka GMC (☎0832/245 8700–07), 7km south on NH17 at Bambolim, where there's also a 24hr pharmacy. Ambulances (☎102) are likely to get you there a lot less quickly than a standard taxi. Conditions are grim by Western standards; relatives sleep on the wards to provide food for patients. Less serious cases can receive attention at the Vintage Hospital, next to Fire Brigade Headquarters in Panjim's St Inez district (☎0832/564 4401–05).

Internet access Hotels and guesthouses, including the *Park Lane Lodge* and *Panjim Inn* (see p.179), offer Internet access to guests. Otherwise, the little Net café on the west side of Church Square has an ISDN connection.

Music and dance Regular recitals of classical Indian music and dance are held at Panjim's school for the performing arts, the Kala Academy in Campal (✇www.kalaacademy.org), at the far west end of town on Devanand Bandodkar Rd. The building, originally designed by award-winning Goan achitect Charles Correa, enjoyed a major facelift ahead of the 2004 film festival, in the hope that it would provide a permanent venue for the event. For details of forthcoming concerts, consult the boards in front of the auditorium or the listings page of local newspapers.

Pharmacies Panjim's best pharmacy is Hindu Pharma, next to the *Hotel Aroma* on Church Square, which stocks Ayurvedic, homeopathic and allo-pathic medicines.

Police Police Headquarters is on Malacca Rd, central Panjim (☏0832/222 5360 or 222 4997).

Post Panjim's reliable poste restante counter (Mon–Sat 9.30am–1pm & 2–5.30pm) is in the Head Post Office, 200m west of Pato Bridge. To get your stamps franked, walk around the back of the building and ask at the office behind the second door on the right. For parcel stitching, ask at Deepak Stores on the corner of the next block north.

Travel agent AERO Mundial, Ground Floor, *Hotel Mandovi*, Dr D. Bandodkar Rd ☏0832/222 3773.

Old Goa

A one-time byword for splendour with a population of several hundred thousand, Goa's erstwhile former capital, **OLD GOA**, was virtually abandoned following malaria and cholera epidemics from the seventeenth century onwards. Today you need considerable imagination to picture the once-great capital as it used to be. The maze of twisting streets, piazzas and ochre-washed villas has gone, and all that remains is a score of cream-painted churches and convents. Granted World Heritage Status by UNESCO, Old Goa today attracts busloads of foreign tourists from the coast, and Christian pilgrims from around India, in roughly equal numbers. While the former come to admire the gigantic facades and gilt altars of the beautifully preserved churches, the main attraction for the latter is the tomb of **St Francis Xavier** (see p.187), the legendary sixteenth-century missionary, whose remains are enshrined in the **Basilica of Bom Jesus**.

If you're staying on the coast and contemplating a day-trip inland, this is the most obvious and accessible option. Just thirty minutes by road from the state capital, Old Goa is served by buses every fifteen minutes from Panjim's Kadamba bus stand; alternatively, hop into an auto-rickshaw (Rs75–100), or rent a taxi (Rs250-300). The best **place to eat** on the site, where all the taxi drivers go, is *Sanjay's Café*, which serves wholesome vegetarian and Goan fish-curry-rice thalis. To find it, head east along the main road through Old Goa and across the roundabout towards Karmali Station; the café is on the right (north) side of the road.

Arch of the Viceroys and the Church of St Cajetan

On arriving at the river landing stage to the north, seventeenth-century visitors passed through the **Arch of the Viceroys** (1597), constructed to commemorate

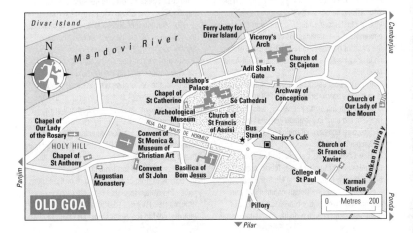

Vasco da Gama's arrival in India and built from the same porous red laterite as virtually all Old Goa's buildings. Above it a Bible-toting figure rests his foot on the cringing figure of a "native", while its granite facade, facing the river, holds a statue of da Gama himself. It's hard to imagine today that these overgrown fields and simple streets with a few cool-drinks stands were once the focus of a lively market, with silk and gem merchants, horse dealers and carpet weavers. The one surviving monument, known as **Adil Shah's Gate**, predates the Portuguese and possibly even the Muslim period. Hindu in style, it consists simply of a lintel supported by two columns in black basalt, to which are attached the remains of perforated screens. You can find it by turning left at the crossroads immediately above the Arch of the Viceroys.

A short way up the lane from the Gate, the distinctive domed **Church of St Cajetan** (1651) was modelled on St Peter's in Rome by monks from the Theatine order. While it does boast a Corinthian exterior, you can also spot certain non-European elements in the decoration, such as the cashew-nut designs in the carving of the pulpit. Hidden beneath the church is a crypt where the embalmed bodies of Portuguese governors were once kept in lead coffins before they were shipped back to Lisbon. Forgotten for over thirty years, the last batch (of three) was only removed in 1992 on the eve of the state visit to Goa of Portuguese president Mario Soares.

The Sé (St Catherine's Cathedral)

The Portuguese viceroy Redondo (1561–64) commissioned the **Sé**, or **St Catherine's Cathedral**, southwest of St Cajetan's, to be "a grandiose church worthy of the wealth, power and fame of the Portuguese who dominated the seas from the Atlantic to the Pacific". Today it stands larger than any church in Portugal, although it was beset by problems, not least a lack of funds and Portugal's temporary loss of independence to Spain. It took eighty years to build and was not consecrated until 1640.

On the Tuscan-style exterior, the one surviving tower houses the **Golden Bell**, cast in Cuncolim (south Goa) in the seventeenth century. During the Inquisition, its tolling announced the start of the gruesome *auto da fés* that were held in the square outside, when suspected heretics were subjected to public torture and burned at the stake. The scale and detail of the Corinthian-style interior is overwhelming; no fewer than fifteen altars are arranged around the walls, dedicated among others to Our Ladies of Hope, Anguish and Three Needs. An altar to St Anne treasures the relics of the **Blessed Martyrs of Cuncolim**, whose failed mission to convert the Moghul emperor Akbar culminated in their murder, while a chapel behind a highly detailed screen holds the **Miraculous Cross**, which stood in a Goan village until a vision of Christ appeared on it. Said to heal the sick, it is kept in a box; a small opening on the side allows devotees to touch it. The staggeringly ornate gilded main **altar** comprises nine carved frames and a splendid crucifix. Panels depict episodes from the life of St Catherine of Alexandria (died 307 AD), including an interchange of ideas with the pagan Roman emperor Maxim, who wished to marry her, and her subsequent flogging and martyrdom.

The Archbishop's Palace

Adjoining the Sé Cathedral, with which it is an exact contemporary, the **Archbishop's Palace** is unique as the last surviving civil building of colonial Goa's golden era. Though in a lamentable state of disrepair, its steeply inclined roofs and white facade still perfectly embody the solidity and imposing strength of the so-called "chã" style of architecture, derived from military constructions of the day, of which the most extreme example was the Viceroy's Fortress Palace (Palacio da Fortaleza), which has since vanished without trace. Presenting their most austere aspect to the river, these two fortified palaces formerly dominated the skyline of the waterfront, appropriately enough for a city perennially under threat of attack.

Nineteenth-century photos show that the city-facing side of the building was originally enfolded by a low wall, which surrounded a garden. This has long been dismantled, but the two grand **entrance porches** remain intact. The one on the right (as you look at the building) is original, complete with red decorative frescoes lining the side walls, among the last remaining paintings of their kind left in Goa. During the Portuguese heyday, guards in blue livery would have stood on its steps, as they did in the Viceroys' palace and most *hidalgo* (noble) houses.

The palace is officially closed to visitors so if you want to have a nose around, you'll have to persuade the ASI caretaker.

The Church of St Francis of Assisi and Archeological Museum

Southwest of the Cathedral is the ruined **Palace of the Inquisition**, in operation up until 1774, while to the west stands the **Convent of St Francis of Assisi**, built by Franciscan monks in 1517 and restored in the mid-eighteenth century. Today, the core of its **Archeological Museum** (daily except Fri 10am–5pm; Rs5) is a gallery of **portraits** of Portuguese viceroys, painted by local artists under Italian supervision. Other exhibits include coins, domestic Christian wooden sculpture, and downstairs in the cloister, pre-Portuguese Hindu sculpture. Next door, the **Church of St Francis** (1521) features fine decorative frescoes, *hidalgos'* tombstones in the floor paving, and paintings on wood showing the life of St Francis of Assisi.

Basilica of Bom Jesus

Close to the convent of St Francis, the 1605 church of **Bom Jesus**, "Good" or "Menino Jesus" (Mon–Sat 9am–6.30pm, Sun 10am–6.30pm), is known principally for the **tomb of St Francis Xavier**. In 1946, it became the first church in India to be elevated to the status of Minor Basilica. On the west, the three-storey Renaissance facade encompasses Corinthian, Doric, Ionic and Composite styles.

The interior is entered beneath the choir, supported by columns. On the northern wall, in the centre of the nave, is a cenotaph in gilded bronze to **Dom Jeronimo Mascarenhas**, the Captain of Cochin and benefactor of the church. The main altar, extravagantly decorated in gold, depicts the infant Jesus under the protection of St Ignatius Loyola (founder of the Jesuit Order); to each side are subsidiary altars to Our Lady of Hope and St Michael. In the southern transept, lavishly decorated with twisted gilded columns and floriate carvings, stands the **Chapel and Tomb of St Francis Xavier**. Constructed of marble and jasper in 1696, it was the gift of the Medici, Cosimo III, the Grand Duke of Tuscany; the middle tier contains panels detailing the saint's life. An ornate domed reliquary in silver contains his remains; for a week around his feast day, December 3, tens of thousands of pilgrims – Hindus as well as Christians – queue for *darshan* (ritual viewing) of the casket before attending open-air Mass in the square outside.

Holy Hill

A number of other important religious buildings and a museum stand opposite Bom Jesus on **Holy Hill**. The **Convent of St Monica**, constructed in 1627,

St Francis Xavier

Francis Xavier, the "Apostle of the Indies", was born in 1506 in the old kingdom of Navarre, now part of Spain. After taking a masters' degree in philosophy and theology at the University of Paris, where he studied for the priesthood until 1535, he was ordained two years later in Venice. He was then recruited by (Saint) **Ignatius Loyola** (1491–1556) along with five other priests into the new "Society of Jesus", which later became known as the **Jesuits**.

When the Portuguese king, Dom Joao III (1521–57), received reports of corruption and dissolute behaviour among the Portuguese in Goa, he asked Ignatius Loyola to despatch a priest who could influence the moral climate for the better. In 1541 Xavier was sent to work in the diocese of Goa, constituted seven years earlier, and comprising all regions east of the Cape of Good Hope. Arriving after a year-long journey, he embarked on a busy programme throughout southern India. Despite frequent obstruction from Portuguese officials, he founded numerous churches, and is credited with converting 30,000 people and performing such miracles as raising the dead and curing the sick with a touch of his beads. Subsequently he took his mission further afield to Sri Lanka, Malacca (Malaysia), China and Japan, where he was less successful.

When Xavier left Goa for the last time, it was with the ambition of evangelizing in China; however, he contracted dysentery aboard ship and died on the island of San Chuan (Sancian), off the Chinese coast, where he was buried. On hearing of his death, a group of Christians from Malacca exhumed his body – which, although the grave had been filled with lime, they found to be in a perfect state of preservation. Reburied in Malacca, it was later removed and taken to Old Goa, where it has remained ever since, enshrined in the Basilica of Bom Jesus.

However, Saint Francis' incorruptible corpse has never rested entirely in peace. Chunks of it have been removed over the years by relic hunters and curious clerics: in 1614, the right arm was dispatched to the Pope in Rome (where it allegedly wrote its name on paper), a hand was sent to Japan, and parts of the intestines to southeast Asia. One Portuguese woman, Dona Isabel de Caron, even bit off the little toe of the cadaver in 1534; apparently, so much blood spurted into her mouth, it left a trail to her house and she was discovered.

Every ten years, the saint's body is carried in a three-hour ceremony from the Basilica of Bom Jesus to the Sé Cathedral, where visitors file past, touch and photograph it. During the 2004–5 "**exposition**", around 256,000 pilgrims flocked for *darshan* or ritual viewing of the corpse, these days a shrivelled and somewhat unsavoury spectacle.

destroyed by fire in 1636 and rebuilt the following year, was the only Goan convent at the time and the largest in Asia. It housed around a hundred nuns, the Daughters of St Monica, and also offered accommodation to women whose husbands were called away to other parts of the empire. The **church** adjoins the convent on the south. As they had to remain away from the public gaze, the nuns attended mass in the choir loft and looked down upon the congregation. Inside, a **Miraculous Cross** rises above the figure of St Monica at the altar. In 1636, it was reported that the figure of Christ had opened his eyes, motioned as if to speak, and blood had flowed from the wounds made by his crown of thorns. The last Daughter of St Monica died in 1885, and since 1964 the convent has been occupied by the Mater Dei Institute for nuns.

Next door to the Chapel of the Miraculous Cross stands Goa's foremost **Museum of Christian art** (daily 9.30–5pm; Rs15), moved here from the Rachol Seminary in 2002. Exhibits include processional crosses, ivory ornaments, damask silk clerical robes and some finely sculpted wooden icons dating from the sixteenth and seventeenth centuries, among them an unusual statue of John the Baptist wearing a tiger-skin wrap (in the style of the Hindu god Shiva).

Nearby, the **Convent of St John of God**, built in 1685 by the Order of Hospitallers of St John of God to tend to the sick, was rebuilt in 1953. At the top of the hill, the **Chapel of Our Lady of the Rosary**, built in 1526 in the Manueline style (after the Portuguese king Manuel I, 1495–1521), features Ionic plasterwork with a double-storey portico, cylindrical turrets and a tower that commands fine views across the river from the terrace where Albuquerque surveyed the decisive battle of 1510. Its cruciform interior is unremarkable, except for the marble tomb of **Catarina a Piró**, believed to have been the first European woman to set foot in the colony. A commoner, she eloped here to escape the scandal surrounding her romance with Portuguese nobleman Garcia de Sá, who later rose to be governor of Goa. Under pressure from no less than Francis Xavier, Garcia eventually married her, but only *in articulo mortis* as she lay on her deathbed. Her finely carved tomb, set in the wall beside the high altar, incorporates a band of intricate Gujarati-style ornamentation, probably imported from the Portuguese trading post of Diu.

Ponda and around

Characterless, chaotic **Ponda**, 28km southeast of Panjim and 17km northeast of Margao, is Ponda district's administrative headquarters and main market town. Straddling the busy Panjim–Bangalore highway (NH-4), it's not a place to spend any time. However, scattered among the lush valleys and forests **around Ponda** are a dozen or so **Hindu temples** founded during the seventeenth and eighteenth centuries, when this hilly region was a Christian-free haven for Hindus fleeing persecution by the Portuguese. Although the temples are fairly modern by Indian standards, their deities are ancient and held in high esteem by both local people and thousands of pilgrims from Maharashtra and Karnataka.

The temples are concentrated in two main clusters: the first to the north of Ponda, on the NH-4, and the second deep in the countryside, around 5km west of the town. Most people only manage the **Shri Manguesh** and **Shri Mahalsa** (Ⓦ www.mahalsa.org), between the villages of **Mardol** and **Priol**. Among the most interesting temples in the state, they lie just a stone's throw from the main highway and are passed by regular **buses** between Panjim and Margao via Ponda. The others are farther off the beaten track, although they are not hard to find on motorbikes; locals will wave you in the right direction if you get lost.

Mardol and Priol

Although the **Sri Manguesh** temple originally stood in a secret location in Cortalim, and was moved to its present site between **MARDOL** and **PRIOL** during the sixteenth century, the structure visitors see today dates from the 1700s. A gateway at the roadside leads to a paved path and courtyard that gives onto a water tank, overlooked by the white temple building, raised on a plinth. Also in the courtyard is a seven-storey *deepmal*, a tower for oil lamps. Inside, the floor is paved with marble, and bands of decorative tiles emblazon the white walls. Flanked by large *dvarpala* guardians, embossed silver doorways with floriate designs lead to the sanctum, which houses a *shivalingam*.

Two kilometres south, the **Mahalsa Marayani** temple was also transferred from its original site, in this case Salcete *taluka* further south, in the seventeenth century. Here, the *deepmal* is exceptionally tall, with 21 tiers rising from a figure of Kurma, the tortoise incarnation of Vishnu. Original features include a marble-floored wooden *mandapa* (assembly hall) with carved pillars, ceiling panels of parakeets and, in the eaves, sculptures of the incarnations of Vishnu.

Dudhsagar waterfalls

Measuring a mighty 600m from head to foot, the famous **Dudhsagar water-falls**, on the Goa–Karnataka border, are some of the highest in India, and a spectacular enough sight to entice a steady stream of visitors from the coast into the rugged Western Ghats. After pouring across the Deccan plateau, the headwaters of the Mandovi River form a foaming torrent that fans into three streams, then cascades down a near-vertical cliff face into a deep green pool. The Konkani name for the falls, which literally translated means "sea of milk", derives from clouds of foam kicked up at the bottom when the water levels are at their highest. Overlooking a steep, crescent-shaped head of a valley carpeted with pristine tropical forest, Dudhsagar is set amid breathtaking **scenery** that is only accessible on foot or by Jeep; the recently upgraded Margao–Castle Rock railway actually passes over the falls on an old stone viaduct, but services along it are infrequent.

One you've reached Dudhsagar, there's little to do beyond enjoying the views and clambering over the rocks below the falls in search of pools to swim in. The **best time to visit** is immediately after the monsoons, from October until mid-December, when water levels are highest, although the falls flow well into April. Unfortunately, the train line only sees two services per week in each direction, neither of them returning the same day. As a result, the only practicable way to get there and back is by four-wheel-drive **Jeep** from **Colem** (reachable by train from Vasco, Margao and Chandor, or by taxi from the north coast resorts for around Rs1250). The cost of the onward thirty- to forty-minute trip from Colem to the falls, which takes you across rough forest tracks and two or three river fords, is Rs350–400 per person; the drive ends with an enjoyable fifteen-minute hike, for which you'll need a sturdy pair of shoes. Finding a Jeep-wallah is easy; just turn up in Colem and look for the "Controller of Jeeps" near the station. However, if you're travelling alone or in a couple, you may have to wait around until the vehicle fills up, or else fork out to cover the cost of hiring the whole Jeep yourself. Note that it can be difficult to arrange transport of any kind from Molem crossroads, where regular taxis are in short supply.

North Goa

Beyond the mouth of the Mandovi estuary, the Goan coast sweeps **north** in a near-continuous string of beaches, broken only by the odd saltwater inlet, rocky headland, and three tidal rivers – the most northerly of which, the Arondem, still has to be crossed by ferry. Development is concentrated mainly behind the seven-kilometre strip of white sand that stretches from the foot of **Fort Aguada**, crowning the peninsula east of Panjim, to Baga creek in the north. Encompassing the resorts of **Candolim**, **Calangute** and **Baga**, this is Goa's prime charter belt and an area most independent travellers steer clear of.

Since the advent of mass tourism in the 1980s, the alternative "scene" has drifted progressively north away from the sunbed strip to **Anjuna** and **Vagator** – now predominantly Israeli rave enclaves boasting some of the region's loveliest beaches – and scruffier **Chapora**, a workaday fishing village on the riverside which has in the last few seasons been colonized by Russians. Further north still, **Arambol** has thus far escaped any large-scale development, despite the completion of the new road bridge across the Chapora River. What little extra traffic there is since the new road link tends to focus on the low-key resorts just south of Arambol, namely **Aswem** and **Mandrem**, where facilities remain basic by modern standards.

North Goa's market town, **Mapusa**, is this area's main jumping-off place, with bus connections to most resorts on the coast. If you're travelling here by train via the **Konkan Railway**, get off the train at **Tivim** (☏0832/229 8682), 19km west of Margao, from where you'll have to jump in a bus or taxi for the remaining leg.

Mapusa

MAPUSA (pronounced *Map*sa) is the district headquarters of Bardez *taluka*. A dusty collection of dilapidated, mostly modern buildings ranged around a busy central square, the town is of little more than passing interest, although it does host a lively **market** on Friday mornings. Anjuna's market may be a better place to shop for souvenirs, but Mapusa's is much more authentic. Local specialities include strings of spicy Goan sausages (*chouriço*), bottles of *toddy* (fermented palm sap) and large green plantains from nearby Moira.

Practicalities

Tivim, the nearest railway station to Mapusa, is 12km east in the neighbouring Bicholim district. Buses should be on hand to transport passengers into town, from where you can pick up local services to Calangute, Baga, Anjuna, Vagator, Chapora and Arambol. These leave from the **Kadamba bus stand**, five minutes' walk west of the main square, where all state-run services from Panjim also pull in. **Motorcycle taxis** hang around the square to whisk lightly laden shoppers and travellers to the coast for around Rs40–50. **Taxis** charge considerably more (Rs125–150), but you can split the fare with up to five people.

The Konkan Railway's Konkan–Kanya Express (#KR0111) arrives in Tivim at around 9.30am, leaving plenty of time to find **accommodation** in the coastal resorts west of Mapusa. It's best to avoid staying in the town if possible, but if you can't, try GTDC's *Mapusa Residency* (☏0832/226 2794, ⓦwww .goa-tourism.com; ❹), on the roundabout below the square, which has spacious and clean rooms and a Goa **tourist information** counter. Best of the **eating** options on or around the main square are the *Ruchira*, within the *Hotel Satya-heera* on the north side of the main square, which serves a standard multi-cuisine menu and cold beer. For quick, authentically Goan food, you won't do better than the beguilingly dated *FR Xavier* café over in the Municipal Market, which has been here (and changed little) since the Portuguese era. The waiters leave heaped baskets of fresh veg patties and beef samosas on your table, billing you for what you eat at the end.

Candolim and Fort Aguada

Compared with Calangute, 3km north along the beach, **CANDOLIM** (from the Konkani kandoli, meaning "dykes", in reference to the system of sluices that the area's first farmers used to reclaim land from nearby marshes) is a surprisingly sedate resort, attracting mainly middle-aged package tourists from the UK and Scandinavia. Over the past five years or so, however, its ribbon development of hotels and restaurants has sprouted a string of multistorey holiday complexes, and during peak season the few vestiges of authentically Goan culture that remain here are drowned in a deluge of Kashmiri handicraft stalls, luridly lit

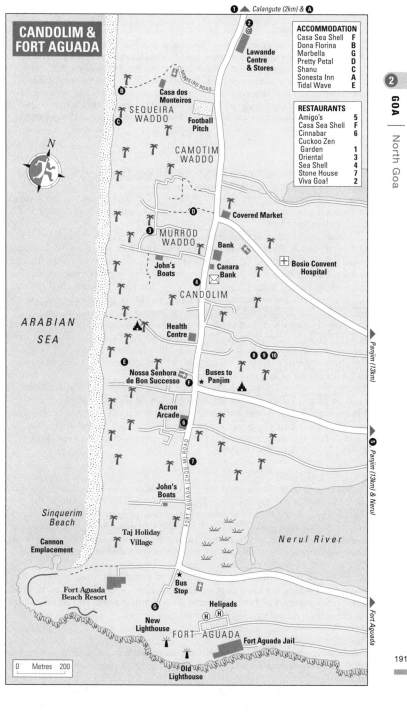

CANDOLIM & FORT AGUADA

Calangute (2km) & **A**

Lawande Centre & Stores

Panjim (13km)

Panjim (13km) & Nerul

Fort Aguada

ACCOMMODATION
Casa Sea Shell	F
Dona Florina	B
Marbella	G
Pretty Petal	D
Shanu	C
Sonesta Inn	A
Tidal Wave	E

RESTAURANTS
Amigo's	5
Casa Sea Shell	F
Cinnabar	6
Cuckoo Zen Garden	1
Oriental	3
Sea Shell	4
Stone House	7
Viva Goa!	2

GOA | North Goa

Casa dos Monteiros

MONTEIRO ROAD

SEQUEIRA WADDO

Football Pitch

CAMOTIM WADDO

Covered Market

MURROD WADDO

Bank

Canara Bank

Bosio Convent Hospital

John's Boats

CANDOLIM

N

ARABIAN SEA

Health Centre

Nossa Senhora de Bon Successo

Buses to Panjim

Acron Arcade

John's Boats

Sinquerim Beach

Taj Holiday Village

Nerul River

Cannon Emplacement

Fort Aguada Beach Resort

Bus Stop

Helipads

New Lighthouse

FORT AGUADA

Fort Aguada Jail

Old Lighthouse

0 Metres 200

terrace cafés and shopping arcades. On the plus side, Candolim has lots of pleasant places to stay, many of them tucked away down quiet sandy lanes and better value than comparable guesthouses in nearby Calangute, making this a good first stop if you've just arrived in Goa and are planning to head further north after finding your feet.

Immediately south, **Fort Aguada** crowns the rocky flattened headland at the end of the beach. Built in 1612 to protect the northern shores of the Mandovi estuary from Dutch and Maratha raiders, the bastion encloses several natural springs, the first source of drinking water available to ships arriving in Goa after the long sea voyage from Lisbon. The ruins of the fort can be reached by road; follow the main drag south from Candolim as it bears left, past the turning for the *Taj Holiday Village*, and keep going for around 1km until you see a right turn, which runs uphill to a small car park. Nowadays, much of the site serves as a prison, and is therefore closed to visitors. It's worth a visit, though, if only for the superb views from the top of the hill where a four-storey Portuguese **lighthouse**, erected in 1864 and the oldest of its kind in Asia, looks down over the vast expanse of sea, sand and palm trees.

From the base of Fort Aguada on the northern flank of the headland, a rampart of red-brown laterite juts into the bay at the bottom of picturesque **Sinquerim Beach** (in effect the southernmost reach of Calangute beach). This was among the first places in Goa to be singled out for upmarket tourism. Taj Group's *Fort Aguada* resorts, among the most expensive hotels in India, lord over the sands from the slopes below the battlements.

Practicalities

Buses to and from Panjim stop every ten minutes or so at the stand opposite the *Casa Sea Shell*, in the middle of Candolim. A few continue south to the *Fort Aguada Beach Resort* terminus, from where services depart every thirty minutes for the capital via Nerul village; you can also flag down buses from anywhere along the main drag to Calangute. **Taxis** are ubiquitous. During the season, however, there is often a shortage of **motorcycles for rent** here, and you may find yourself having to search for a bike in Calangute.

You can **change money** at any number of private exchange places dotted around Candolim, but their rates are unlikely to be as competitive as those on offer in Calangute. For **Internet** access, I-Way, at the north end of the village on the main road, offers a fast broadband connection.

Accommodation

Candolim is charter-holiday land, so **accommodation** tends to be expensive for most of the season. That said, if bookings are down you can find some great bargains here.

Casa Sea Shell Fort Aguada Rd, near *Bom Successo* ☎0832/247 9879 or 277 6131, ✉seashellgoa@hotmail.com. A newish block with its own pool, picturesquely situated beside a small chapel. The rooms are large, with spacious tiled bathrooms, and the staff and management welcoming and courteous. If they're full ask for a room in the identical and slightly cheaper (but pool-less) *Sea Shell Inn* (☎0832/228 1555) up the road. ❺

Dona Florina Monteiro Rd ☎0832/275051 or 227 7398. Large, ten-year-old guesthouse in a superb location, overlooking the beach in the most secluded corner of the village. Well-heeled *sanyasins* from the Rajneesh ashram in Pune have long been its mainstay, hence the higher than usual rates – worth paying if you want idyllic sea views. No car access. ❹

Marbella Sinquerim ☎0832/247 9551, ✉marbella_goa@yahoo.com. Individually styled suites and spacious rooms (from Rs1550) in a beautiful house built to resemble a traditional Goan mansion. The decor, fittings and furniture are gorgeous, especially in the top-floor "Penthouse" (Rs2500), and the whole place is screened by a giant mango tree. Unashamedly romantic and well worth splashing out on. ❼–❽

Pretty Petal Camotim Waddo ☎0832/276184, ⓦwww.prettypetalsgoa.com. Not as twee as it sounds: very large, modern rooms, all with fridges and balconies, and relaxing, marble-floored communal areas overlooking lawns. The top-floor apartment, with windows on four sides and a huge balcony, is the best choice, though more expensive. ❺–❻

Shanu Escrivao Waddo ☎0832/227 9606, ✉shanu_goa@yahoo.com. Good-sized, well-furnished rooms with narrow balconies right on the dunes, some of them with uninterrupted views of the sea (a real rarity). Ask the hospitable owners, Shanu and Peter Mascarenhas, for #120 (or failing that #118, #111, #110 or #107). Breakfast served in your room. ❹–❺

Sonesta Inn Escrivao Waddo ☎0832/222 7688, ⓦwww.sonestainns.com. Smart package hotel, a 2-min walk from the sea, ranged around a large central pool. Most of the comforts of a 4-star, but on a smaller scale. ❽

Tidal Wave Vaddy Candolim, just down the lane from *Casa Sea Shell* ☎0832/227 6884, ✉newmanwarren@rediffmail.com. Lovely sea-facing rooms in a recent construction right behind the beach. Those in the newest block are more spacious and have kitchenettes for long lets. ❹

Eating and drinking

Candolim's numerous beach **cafés** are a cut above your average seafood shacks, with pot plants, posh sound systems and prices to match. The further from the *Taj* complex you venture, the more realistic the prices become.

Amigo's 3km east of Candolim at Nerul bridge ☎0832/240 1123, or 9822/104920. Well off the beaten track, this rough-and-ready riverside shack, tucked away under the bridge Matt Damon sped off in *The Bourne Supremacy*, is famous locally for its superb fresh seafood, served straight off the boats. *Tamoso* (red snapper) is their speciality, but they also do stuffed pomfret, calamari chilli-fry, red snapper and, best of all, Jurassic-sized crabs in butter-garlic sauce (to order the day before). Count on Rs250 for the works, with drinks.

Casa Sea Shell *Casa Sea Shell* hotel. This is the place to head for top-notch tandoori (from a pukka charcoal-fired oven) and north Indian dishes, although they also offer a good choice of Chinese and European food, served on a hotel patio next to an illuminated fountain. Excellent service and moderate prices. Don't miss the to-die-for Irish coffee.

Cinnabar Acron Arcade, south Candolim. Hip new café, with Italian-style glass- and wood-panelled interior, stone vases and Indian curios, serving what we reckon is Goa's best cappuccino.

Occasional DJs add to the ambience. Opens at 8am for cooked breakfasts.

Cuckoo Zen Garden 1.5km north of Candolim. Authentic Taiwanese and Japanese evening meals, including melt-in-the-mouth (and scrupulously hygienic) sushi, miso and tofu, made with imported ingredients and served on Oriental porcelain against a backdrop of low light and chilled music. Go for a seat on the rooftop. It's difficult to find: turn down the lane just south of *Bob's Inn* (towards the sea), and then first right, and first left after that. Most mains Rs150–200. Closed Sat.

Oriental next to *Surfside Holiday Home*, Murrod Waddo. Sumptuous Thai cuisine prepared by Master Chef Chawee, who turns out eighteen house sauces to accompany choice cuts of seafood, meat and poultry, as well as plenty of vegetarian options. Be sure to try their signature starter, *soom tham* (papaya salad). At around Rs500–600 for three courses, it's superb value for cooking of this standard.

Sea Shell at the *Sea Shell Inn*, Fort Aguada Rd. A congenial terrace restaurant in front of an old, double-fronted colonial-era *palacio* decked with green fairy lights. Sizzlers, spaghetti bolognaise and beef steaks are their specialities, but they do a range of seafood and Indian dishes, as well as delicious cocktails. Not at all as pricey as it looks, either (with most mains Rs175–300). Wine by the bottle or glass.

Stone House Fort Aguada Rd. Lively, low-lit bar-restaurant, spread in front of a gorgeous bare-laterite Goan house. Prime cuts of beef and kingfish, served with scrumptious baked potatoes, are their most popular dishes. It's run by a blues aficionado; enthusiasts will want to come just for the CD collection. Most mains under Rs200.

Viva Goa! Fort Aguada Rd. Succulent, no-nonsense Goan food fresh from the market – mussel fry, barramundi (*chonok*), lemon fish (*modso*) and sharkfish steaks fried *rechead* style in chilli paste or in millet (*rawa*) – served on a roadside terrace. Tourists are welcome, but it's essentially a locals' place – with local prices.

Calangute

In the 1970s and early 1980s, Indian visitors flocked by the busload to **CALANGUTE**, a 45-minute ride up the coast from Panjim, in order to giggle at the tribes of dreadlocked Westerners lying naked on the vast white sands. All but a handful of die-hard hippies moved off long ago, but this remains the state's busiest resort, and continues to attract streams of Indian tourists from out of state – which ensures large, noisy bus parties of paddlers on the beach (especially at weekends) and relentlessly heavy traffic during the day. As a consequence, the main drag through the village has become a shambles of hastily erected shops and market stalls, clogged with itinerant vendors, day labourers and stray animals – much to the amazement of the few package tourists who book holidays here after seeing brochure pictures of the beach (out of season).

Each year, as another crop of construction sites blossoms into resort complexes, what little charm Calangute has retained gets steadily more submerged under ferroconcrete. Its all too evident pollution problems are compounded by an absence of adequate provision for waste disposal and sewage treatment, and ever-increasing water-consumption levels. One worrying sign that the village has already started to stew in its own juices has been a dramatic rise in **malaria** cases: virex, and the more serious falciparum strain, are now both endemic here, and rife during the early part of the season.

In short, this isn't somewhere to consider for a lengthy stay, even though it does hold several outstandingly good value guesthouses. If you're staying somewhere else, the only reasons to endure the chaos are to shop for essentials in the well-stocked market, change money, and to eat: Calangute boasts some of the best **restaurants** in the whole state.

Practicalities

Buses from Mapusa and Panjim pull in at the small bus stand-cum-market square in the centre of Calangute. Some continue to Baga, stopping at the crossroads behind the beach en route.

The best place to **change money** and travellers' cheques is Wall Street Finances (Mon–Sat 8.30am–7pm, Sun 10am–2pm), opposite the petrol pump. For Visa encashments, go to the Bank of Baroda (Mon–Fri 9.30am–2.30pm, Sat 9.30am–noon, Sun 9.30am–2pm), just north of the temple and market area; a commission fee of Rs100, plus one percent of the amount changed, is levied on all Visa withdrawals. The ICICI Bank, on the main street, is one of several banks in the market with a 24-hour **ATM** (all the usual cards accepted). There are innumerable cafés scattered around town offering broadband **Internet** access, notably Sify-I-Way, marked on our map.

One of Goa's best **book shops**, The Oxford Bookstore, stands on the south side of town, directly opposite St Anthony's Chapel on the main Candolim road.

Accommodation

In spite of the encroaching mayhem, plenty of budget travellers return to Calangute year after year, staying in little family guesthouses in the fishing *waddo* where the pace of life remains remarkably unchanged.

Arabian Retreat Gauro Waddo ☎0832/227 9053, Ⓦwww.arabianretreat.com. Swathed in greenery and shaded by areca palms, this new block has large rooms with balconies on both sides (those on the first floor are best), and some have a/c. Much loved by frequent returners are Simba the cat and Foxy the dog. Only Rs700 per double, but rising to Rs1200 from December to mid-January. ❹

Camizala 5-33B Maddo Waddo ☎0832/227 9530 or 9822/986544. Lovely, breezy little place with only four rooms, common verandas and sea views. About as close to the beach as you can get, and the *waddo* is very quiet. Cheap considering the location. ❷–❸

CoCo Banana 1195 Umta Waddo ☎0832/227 6478 or 227 9068, Ⓦwww.cocobanana.com. Very comfortable, spacious chalets, all with bathrooms, fridges, mosquito nets, extra-long mattresses and verandas, around a central garden – but no a/c. Down the lane past *Meena Lobo's* restaurant, it's run by a very sorted Swiss–Goan couple, Walter and Marina Lobo, who have been here for nearly twenty years. Rates double at Christmas. ❺

Gabriel's Gauro Waddo ☎0832/227 9486, Ⓔfele@rediffmail.com. A congenial, quiet guesthouse midway between Calangute and Candolim, run by a gorgeous family who go out of their way to help guests. Shady garden, pleasant views from the rear side across the *toddi*

dunes, a top little restaurant and very close to the beach. ❸

Golden Eye Gauro Waddo ☎0832/227 7308, Ⓦwww.hotelgoldeneye.com. Situated on the sand; no pool, but the rooms are attractively done out and some have sea views from their balconies. ❻–❼

Indian Kitchen behind Our Lady of Piety Church ☎0832/227 7555, Ⓔikitchen@satyam.net.in. Jazzily decorated guesthouse with crazy mosaic tiling, brightly patterned walls and lanterns. The rooms, all en suite, have fridges and music systems. ❸–❹

Kerkar Retreat Gauro Waddo ☎0832/227 6017, Ⓦwww.subodhkerkar.com. Colour-themed "boutique hotel", artfully decorated with original paintings (by local artist and owner, Subodh Kerkar), Goan *azulejos* and designer furniture creating an effect that's modern, but definably Goan. The only downside is the roadside location. ❼

Pousada Tauma Porba Waddo ☎0832/227 9061, Ⓦwww.pousada-tauma.com. Small-scale luxury resort complex, comprising double-storey laterite villas ranged around a pool, near the middle of Calangute, but screened from the din by lots of vegetation. Understated decor and repro-antique furnishings, and a very exclusive atmosphere, preserved by five-star prices. Their big draw is a first-rate Keralan Ayurvedic health centre (open to non-residents). From $200 per night. ❾

Eating and drinking

Ever since *Souza Lobo* opened on the beachfront to cater for Goan day-trippers in the 1930s, Calangute has been somewhere people come as much to eat as for a stroll on the beach, and even if you stay in resorts elsewhere you'll doubtless be tempted down here for a meal.

After Eight Gauro Waddo. Midway between Calangute and Candolim, down a lane leading west off the main road, between the Lifeline Pharmacy and a small chapel, this is a superb gourmet restaurant in a quiet garden, run by two ex-*Taj* (Mumbai) whizz kids. Steaks are their most popular dish, but seafood is equally sublime, served with original, delicate sauces blending Bengali and Italian influences (try the *rahu*, a local river fish, in balsamic vinegar and mustard); there's baby-corn *millefeuilles* for veggies, and they do a memorable chocolate mousse. Main courses Rs175–225.

A Reverie Gauro Waddo ☎0832/228 2597. Set up by the cofounders of *After Eight*, with even more romantic and extravagant menu and decor, but within

reach of most budgets (around Rs500 per head, plus drinks – a steal given the quality of the food). The dishes are all original, with eclectic influences, and beautifully presented: try the cappuccino of mushrooms with marjoram and fresh parsley sauce, or chicken breast stuffed with pistachio mousseline.

Florentine's 4km inland from Calangute church at Saligao, opposite Ayurvedic Natural Health Centre. Well worth the trip inland to taste Florence D'Costa's legendary chicken *cafreal*, made to a jealously guarded family recipe that pulls in crowds of locals and tourists from across north Goa. The restaurant's a down-to-earth Goan-style place, with prices to match, serving only chicken, some seafood and vegetarian snacks.

Gabriel's *Gabriel's* guesthouse, Guara Waddo. Authentic Goan cooking (pork *sorpotel*, chicken *xacuti*, stuffed squid and prawn masala), and very popular Italian dishes (with homemade pasta) served on a cosy roof terrace well away from the main road. A tiny bit pricier than average for a budget place (most mains around Rs100) but worth it, and the espresso coffee is excellent.

Infantaria Pastelaria Baga Rd, next to St John's Chapel. Roadside terrace café run by *Souza Lobo's* that gets packed out for its stodgy croissants, freshly baked apple pie and traditional Goan sweets (such as *dodol* and house-made *bebinca*). Top of the savoury list, though, are the prawn and veg patties, which locals buy by the boxload.

Plantain Leaf near Vanessa cinema, Calangute market. The best *udipi* restaurant outside Panjim, serving the usual range of delicious dosas and other spicy snacks in a clean, cool, marble-lined canteen, with relentless background *filmi* music. Try their tasty *iddli*-fry – South India's answer to chips – or the filling thalis (Rs50).

Souza Lobo Beachfront. A Calangute institution, even though the food – served on gingham tablecloths by legions of fast-moving waiters in matching Madras-checked shirts – isn't always what it used to be. Stuffed crab, whole baby kingfish and crêpe Souza are the house specialities. Main dishes Rs100–150.

Nightlife

Calangute's **nightlife** is surprisingly tame for a resort of its size. All but a handful of the bars wind up by midnight, leaving punters to prolong the short evenings back at their hotels, find a shack that's open late, or else head up to Baga (see below).

Down on the south edge of Calangute in Gauro Waddo, the **Kerkar Art Gallery** (℡0832/227 6017, ⓦwww.subodhkerkar.com) hosts evenings of **classical music and dance** (Tues 6.45pm; Rs300), held in the back garden on a sumptuously decorated stage, complete with incense and evocative candlelight. The recitals, performed by students and teachers from Panjim's Kala Academy, are kept comfortably short for the benefit of Western visitors, and are preceded by a short introductory talk. You can also attend performances of authentic Keralan **Kathakali** at a small venue next to the roundabout on the beach road (see map opposite); make up starts at 6pm, and the performance lasts from 7–8pm. Both their explanations of this arcane form of ritual theatre, and the dancing, get positive reviews from readers.

Baga

BAGA, 10km west of Mapusa, is basically an extension of Calangute; not even the locals agree where one ends and the other begins. Lying in the lee of a rocky, wooded headland, the only difference between this far northern end of the beach and its more congested centre is that the scenery here is marginally more varied and picturesque. A small creek flows into the sea at the top of the village below a broad spur of soft white sand, from the opposite bank of which a stoney path winds around the promontory towards Anjuna.

Since the package boom, Baga has developed more rapidly than anywhere else in the state and today looks less like the Goan fishing village it still was in the early 1990s than a small-scale resort on one the Spanish Costas, with a predominantly young, charter-tourist clientele to match. But if you can steer clear of the lager louts, Baga boasts distinct advantages over its neighbours: a crop of excellent **restaurants** and a **nightlife** that's consistently more full-on than anywhere else in the state, if not all India.

Accommodation

Accommodation is harder to arrange on spec in Baga than in Calangute, as most of the hotels have been carved up by the charter companies; even rooms in smaller guesthouses tend to be booked up well before the season gets under

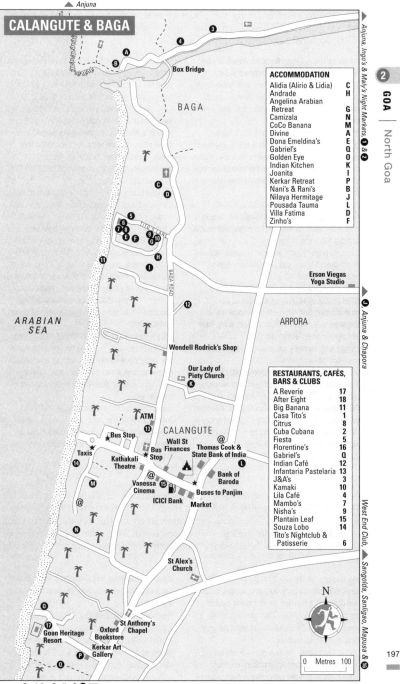

CALANGUTE & BAGA

▲ Anjuna

BAGA

Box Bridge

A R A B I A N S E A

ARPORA

Erson Viegas Yoga Studio

Wendell Rodrick's Shop

Our Lady of Piety Church

ATM

Bus Stop

CALANGUTE

Taxis

Wall St Finances

Bus Stop

Thomas Cook & State Bank of India

Kathakali Theatre

Bank of Baroda

Vanessa Cinema

Buses to Panjim

ICICI Bank

Market

St Alex's Church

N

Goan Heritage Resort

St Anthony's Chapel

Oxford Bookstore

Kerkar Art Gallery

0 Metres 100

Candolim, Panjim & ⑱ ▼

ACCOMMODATION	
Alidia (Alirio & Lidia)	C
Andrade	H
Angelina Arabian Retreat	G
Camizala	N
CoCo Banana	M
Divine	A
Dona Emeldina's	E
Gabriel's	Q
Golden Eye	O
Indian Kitchen	K
Joanita	I
Kerkar Retreat	P
Nani's & Rani's	B
Nilaya Hermitage	J
Pousada Tauma	L
Villa Fatima	D
Zinho's	F

RESTAURANTS, CAFÉS, BARS & CLUBS	
A Reverie	17
After Eight	18
Big Banana	11
Casa Tito's	1
Citrus	8
Cuba Cubana	2
Fiesta	5
Florentine's	16
Gabriel's	Q
Indian Café	12
Infantaria Pastelaria	13
J&A's	3
Kamaki	10
Lila Café	4
Mambo's	7
Nisha's	9
Plantain Leaf	15
Souza Lobo	14
Tito's Nightclub & Patisserie	6

Anjuna, Ingo's & Mak's Night Markets ① & ②

Anjuna & Chapora

West End Club, Sangolda, Saniiago, Mapusa & ⑯

way. The majority of family-run places lie around the north end of the beach, where night-times have been a lot more peaceful since Goa's premier club, *Tito's*, acquired soundproofing.

Alidia (Alirio & Lidia) Baga Rd, Saunta Waddo ☏0832/227 6835, ✉alidia@goaworld.com. Attractive, modern chalet rooms with good-sized verandas looking onto the dunes and double or twin beds. Quiet, friendly and the best deal in this area. ❹

Andrade ("Rita") just south of Tito's Lane ☏0832/227 9087. Half a dozen sea-facing rooms, built in 2002. Those on the lower floor are smaller, but with larger verandas than the much nicer top-storey ones. Friendly management, and close to the liveliest stretch of beach. ❸

Angelina Saunta Waddo ☏0832/227 9145, ✉angelinabeachresort@rediffmail.com. Spacious, well-maintained rooms with large tiled bathrooms and big balconies, in the thick of things off Tito's Lane. Particularly good value out of peak season, and owners Stanley and Lisa D'Sa are perfect hosts. A/c available. ❸

Divine near *Nani's & Rani's*, north of the river ☏0832/227 9546. Run by a couple of hospitable, animal-loving Gulf returners, the rooms are on the small side, but impeccably clean; some have attached shower-toilets; and there's a lovely upper terrace with sunbeds and shades. Advance booking essential. ❸

Dona Emeldina's Sauto Waddo ☏0832/227 6880. Pleasantly old-fashioned cottages with verandas opening onto lawns, run by an extrovert Portuguese-speaking lady from Canada. A bargain in low and mid-season (Rs575–675), but pricey over Christmas, due to its proximity to the party enclave – a dubious distinction. ❻

Joanita Baga Rd ☏0832/227 7166. Clean, airy rooms with attached baths and some double beds, around a quiet garden. A good choice if you want to be in the village centre but off the road. ❷–❸

Nani's & Rani's north of the river ☏0832/227 6313, ✉gizellaferns@yahoo.com. A handful of red-tiled, whitewashed budget cottages in a secluded garden behind a huge colonial-era house. Fans, some attached bathrooms, well water, outdoor showers and Internet facility. ❸–❹

Nilaya Hermitage Arpora Bhati ☏0832/227 6793, ⓦwww.nilayahermitage.com. Set on the crest of a hilltop 6km inland from the beach, with match-less views over the coastal plain, this place ranks among India's most exclusive hotels, patronized by a very rich international jet set (Richard Gere, Gior-gio Armani and Kate Moss have all stayed here). The complex is a fantasy of rich Indian colours, fiddly ironwork and gilded pillars, opening onto a dreamy pool. Room tariffs include use of the steam room, gym, clay tennis court, and a restaurant. Rooms from around $295 for two (or $450 over Christmas–New Year), including meals and airport transfers. ❾

Villa Fatima Baga Rd ☏0832/227 7418, ✉villa .fatima@sympatico.ca. Thirty-two en-suite rooms in a large, three-storey hotel centred on a sociable garden terrace. Rates are reasonable, varying with room size. Popular mainly with young backpack-ers. ❷–❸

Zinho's 7/3 Saunta Waddo ☏0832/227 7383. Tucked away off the main road, close to *Tito's*. Seventeen modest-sized, clean rooms above a family home; those in the new a/c block are a bit overpriced. ❺–❻

Eating

Nowhere else in the state offers such a good choice of quality eating as Baga. Restaurateurs – increasing numbers of them European expats or refugees from upper-class Mumbai – vie with each other to lay on the trendiest menus and most romantic, stylish gardens or terraces. It's all a very far cry indeed from the rough-and-ready beach-shack culture that held sway only seven or eight years ago.

Big Banana on the beach, at the end of CSM Lane. We tend not to recommend shacks, but this one deserves a mention for its superb steaks: try the house speciality, Chateaubriand, which is enough for two. They also do the usual range of local seafood specialities.

Citrus Tito's Lane. The first pure-vegetarian fine-dining restaurant in Goa. Starters include deli-cious cashew rissoles with satay sauce; creamed

pumpkin croquettes and roquefort brik are pick of the mains (from Rs175). Real Italian coffee is also available.

Fiesta Tito's Lane ☏0832/227 9894. Baga's most extravagantly decorated restaurant enjoys a perfect spot at the top of a long dune, with sea views extending from the veranda of a 1930s house. The Mediterranean–Portuguese menu is delectable – try their buffalo mozzarella salad or smoked aubergine paté for starters, followed by paella, moussaka or the wonderful house pizzas. Most mains around Rs200–250.

Indian Café Baga Rd. Traditional home-cooked South Indian snacks – dosas, *iddlis* and *vadas*, with fiery sambar, green chutney and delicious fresh fruit lassis – dished up on the veranda of an old Goan house. A lot more relaxing than the *Plantain Leaf* in Calangute, and much cheaper.

J&A's Anjuna Rd ℡ 0832/227 5274, ⓦ www .littleitalygoa.com. Mouthwatering, authentic Italian food (down to the imported Parmesan, sun-dried tomatoes and olive oil) served in the gorgeous candlelit garden of an old fisherman's cottage. There's an innovative range of salads and antipasti (the carpaccio of beef is sublime), a choice of sumptuous pasta dishes, wood-fired pizzas and tender steaks (in port and rosemary sauce) for mains, though their signature dish, seafood lasagna, is hard to beat. For dessert, go for the melt-in-the-mouth hot chocolate soufflé to round things off. Most mains Rs275–300; count on at least Rs550 per head for three courses, plus drinks.

Lila Café Baga Creek. Laid-back bakery-cum-terrace-café with white and purple decor run by a German couple who've been here for decades. Their healthy homemade breads and cakes are great, and there's an adventurous lunch menu featuring spinach à la crème, aubergine paté and smoked water buffalo ham.

Nisha's Tito's Lane ℡ 0832/227 7588. This little restaurant, occupying a sandy terrace just down from *Tito's*, can't be beaten for simply prepared seafood – snapper, kingfish, tiger prawns and lobster – flame-grilled or tandoori-baked to perfection in front of you. Freshness counts more here than fancy sauces. For starters, try calamari in chilli oil with lemon. Most mains are a reasonable Rs250–300.

Tito's Patisserie Tito's Lane. Relaxed little a/c café that couldn't be further from the headlong atmosphere of *Tito's* by night. Their chilled pastries – including toffee and apple tart, banoffi pie and lemon cheesecake – are delicious, as is the freshly ground espresso and cappuccino; and it's only a skip from the beach.

Nightlife

That Baga's **nightlife** has become legendary in India is largely attributable to one club, *Tito's*. Lured by TV images of sexy dancewear and a thumping sound-and-light system, hundreds of revellers descend on its long narrow terrace each night to drink, shuffle about and watch the action, the majority of them men from other states who've come to Goa as an escape from the moral confines of life at home. For Western women, in particular, this can sometimes make for an

---

Saturday Night Bazaars

One of the few genuinely positive improvements to the north Goa resort strip in recent times has been **Ingo's Saturday Night Bazaar**, held on a plot midway between Baga and Anjuna. The brainchild of an expat German, it's run with great efficiency and a sense of fun that's palpably lacking these days at the Anjuna Flea Market. The balmy evening temperatures and pretty lights are also a lot more conducive to relaxed browsing than the broiling heat of mid-afternoon on Anjuna beach; moreover, the laid-back ambience is preserved with a "three-strikes-and-out" ban on hassling customers, which means you can even walk past the normally full-on Lamani women unmolested.

Although far more commercial than its predecessor in Anjuna, many old Goa hands regard this as far truer to the original spirit of the flea market. A significant proportion of the stalls are taken up by foreigners selling their own stuff, from reproduction Indian pop art to antique photos, the latest trance-party designer wear, hand-polished coconut shell art and techno DJ demos. There's also a mouthwatering array of ethnic food to choose from and a stage featuring live music from around 7pm until midnight, when the market winds up. Admission is free.

Somewhat confusingly, a **rival but inferior market** in much the same mould, called **Macy's**, has opened nearby, closer to Baga by the riverside. Spurned by the expatriate designers and stallholders, this one's not a patch on its rival, though, no matter what your taxi driver may tell you.

uncomfortably loaded atmosphere, although since a recent facelift (and a hike in door charges), *Tito's* seems to have put the era of Kingfisher-fuelled brawls behind it. New theme bars and clubs are also popping up each year, offering increasingly sophisticated alternatives.

For anyone who's been travelling around the rest of the country, Baga by night – complete with drunken karaoke, toga parties and all the garishness of a Saturday in British clubland – can come as an unpleasant shock. So, too, can the traffic congestion on Fridays and Saturdays; if you venture down here by motorbike on the weekend, park well away from Tito's Lane or you might find yourself literally jammed in until the small hours.

For more on the area's nightlife, see our accounts of Calangute (p.194) and Anjuna (below).

Bars and clubs

Casa Tito's Arpora, opposite Ingo's Night Market. Chic Italian gastro-lounge bar in an old Portuguese-era house, with designer furniture, cocktails and gourmet food. Perfect post-Ingo's chill-out spot.

Cuba Cubana 82 Xim Waddo, Arpora Hill ⓦwww .clubcubana.net. Glam nightclub on a forested hilltop inland from Baga, spread around an underlit open-air pool. Its high entrance charge (Rs500 for men, Rs400 for women) buys you unlimited drinks from a well-stocked bar – a policy intended to keep out the low-spending riff-raff from down on the strip. R&B, hip hop and garage (they purposely stay well away from techno) played on a twin-storey, a/c dance floor. Fri, Sat & Sun 9.30pm–5am.

Kamaki Tito's Lane, Saunta Waddo. Big screen sports and a state-of-the-art karaoke machine account for the appeal of this a/c, Brit-dominated bar just up the lane from *Tito's*. Rs100 cover charge sometimes applies.

Mambo's Tito's Lane, Saunta Waddo. Large, semi-open-air place with wooden decor and a big circular bar that gets packed out most nights in season with a lively, mixed crowd. Once again, karaoke is the big draw, though drinks cost well above average, and they slap on a Rs200 admission charge after 11pm.

Tito's Tito's Lane, Saunta Waddo. Occasional cabarets, fashion shows and guest DJs feature throughout the season at India's most famous nightclub. Red upholstery and uniformed waiters set the tone; music policy is lounge grooves till 11pm, and hip hop, house, salsa and trance thereafter. See the notice board for retro and other theme nights. Admission prices vary for men (from Rs400–450, or Rs300 for couples); no charge for women. At Christmas, prices can soar to Rs800 or more depending on the attraction. Open 8–late Nov–Dec; and until 11pm out of season.

Anjuna

With its fluorescent-painted palm trees and famous full-moon parties, **ANJUNA**, 8km west of Mapusa, is Goa at its most "alternative". Fractal patterns and day-glo lycra may have superseded cotton kaftans, but most people's reasons for coming are the same as they were in the 1970s: drugs, dancing and lying on the beach slurping tropical fruit. Depending on your point of view, you'll find the hedonism a total turn-off or heaven-on-sea. Either way, the scene looks here to stay, despite government attempts to stamp it out, so you might as well get a taste of it while you're in the area, if only from the wings, with a day-trip to the famous **flea market**.

The season in Anjuna starts in early November, when most of the long-staying regulars show up, and peters out in late March, when they drift off again. Young Israelis – fresh out of the army and full of devil-may-care attitudes to drugs and other people's sleep – are the village's mainstay these days, much to the chagrin of the locals. Outside peak season, however, Anjuna has a surprisingly simple, unhurried atmosphere – due, in no small part, to the shortage of places to stay. Most visitors who come here on market day or for the parties travel in from other resorts.

Yoga in north Goa

Whether you're a complete beginner, improver or budding yogi, Goa is the perfect place to brush up on your yoga, as several first-rate teachers set up small schools here in the winter.

Down in **Candolim**, the **Goa Iyengar Yoga School** (℡0832/249 7245, mobile 9326/12373, ℗www.yogamaggieh.com) is run by Maggie Hughes, an Iyengar-certified teacher with twenty-plus years' experience. She works from her first-floor studio, opposite *Sonesta Inn* – heading south, take the turning on the right between Davidair and *Bob's Inn* (there's a sign pointing the way). Drop-in classes start at 8am (or sometimes an hour later), last for ninety minutes, and cost Rs300. Beginners are welcome. Maggie also hosts teacher training courses in January and February, lasting ten or thirty days (for more details see her website).

Another Iyengar-qualified teacher is **Erson Viegas** (℡0832/227 7993), whose studio is a couple of kilometres inland from Calangute at Arpora. Erson charges Rs250–300 per session for individual tuition and slightly less if you attend one of his group classes.

In **Anjuna**, the **Purple Valley Yoga Centre** (℡0832/226 9643, mobile ℡098/2309 9788, ℗www.yogagoa.net) specializes in Ashtanga yoga, as taught in Mysore by Sri K. Pattabhi Jois. They have world-class teachers in residence at their main studio in the garden of *Granpa's Inn* (see p.202), but all levels of ability are catered for. Drop-in classes cost Rs400, or Rs3000 if you book ten in advance, and they also offer two-week retreats in a purpose-built *shala* (yoga studio) in some nearby woods.

Between Aswem and Arambol, look out for signs advertising classes by Iyengar-qualified **Sharat** (℗www.hiyogacentre.com), a highly respected direct student of BKS Iyengar who holds five-day classes at his centre on the beach (Rs1250). Prospective students usually have to sign up by Tuesday at 2pm; courses start on Fridays. Sharat also hosts month-long intensives, as well as teacher training courses (full details on the website).

The **beach** is no great shakes by Goan standards, with a dodgy undertow and even dodgier groups of whiskeyed-up Indian men in constant attendance. North of the market ground, the sand broadens, running in an uninterrupted kilometre-long stretch to a low red cliff. A small, pretty and better-sheltered cove at its opposite southern end is where Anjuna's mostly Israeli, frisbee-throwing tourists hang out during the day, techno thumping away from the shacks behind it.

Practicalities

Buses from Mapusa and Panjim drop passengers at various points along the tarmac road across the top of the village, which turns north towards Chapora at the main Starco's crossroads. If you're looking for a room, get off here as it's close to most of the guesthouses. The crossroads has a couple of small **stores**, a **motorcycle taxi** rank, and functions as a de facto village square and **bus stand**.

The *Manali* guesthouse (see p.203) and Oxford Stores **change money** (at poor rates). The Bank of Baroda on the Mapusa Road will make encashments against Visa cards, but doesn't do foreign exchange, nor is it a good place to leave valuables, as thieves have previously climbed through an open window and stolen a number of "safe custody" envelopes. The **post office**, on the Mapusa road near the bank, has an efficient poste restante counter. The *Manali* guest-house also offers broadband **Internet access** (Rs40/hr), as does Space Ride, next to Speedy Travel.

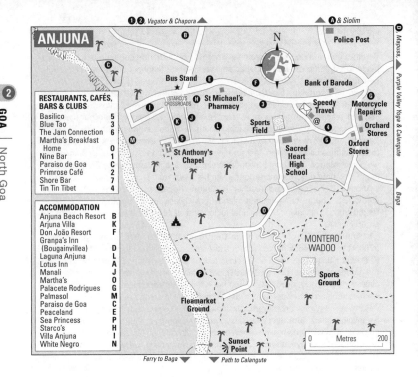

Map legend:

RESTAURANTS, CAFÉS, BARS & CLUBS

Basilico	5
Blue Tao	3
The Jam Connection	6
Martha's Breakfast Home	0
Nine Bar	1
Paraiso de Goa	C
Primrose Café	2
Shore Bar	7
Tin Tin Tibet	4

ACCOMMODATION

Anjuna Beach Resort	B
Arjuna Villa	K
Don João Resort	F
Granpa's Inn (Bougainvillea)	D
Laguna Anjuna	L
Lotus Inn	A
Manali	J
Martha's	O
Palacete Rodrigues	G
Palmasol	M
Paraiso de Goa	C
Peaceland	E
Sea Princess	P
Starco's	H
Villa Anjuna	I
White Negro	N

Ferry to Baga ▼   ▼ *Path to Calangute*

Accommodation

Most of Anjuna's **accommodation** consists of small unfurnished **houses**, although finding one is a problem at the best of times – in peak season it's virtually impossible. By then, all but a handful have been let to long-staying regulars who book by post several months in advance, and budget travellers hoping to find one on spec will probably have to make do with a room in a guesthouse at first. Since the recent construction of a couple of classy designer hotels, higher spending visitors are spoiled for choice.

Anjuna Beach Resort De Mello Waddo ☏ 0832/227 4499, ✉ fabjoe@sancharnet.com. Fifteen spacious, comfortable rooms with balconies, fridges, attached bathrooms and solar hot water in a new concrete building. Those on the upper floor are best. There's also a newly constructed block of apartments for long stayers (④). Both options are very good value. ③

Anjuna Villa House #681/1 D'Mello Waddo, 4th Lane ☏ 0832/227 4590 or 227 4591, ✉ dogfreymathia@hotmail.com. Basic but pleasant budget rooms with tiled floors and high ceilings, opening on to a deep common veranda (again, those on the upper storey are much nicer). Floodlit badminton a speciality. ④

Don João Resort Soronto Waddo ☏ 0832/227 4325 or 222 2147, ⊛ www.travelingoa.com /donjoaoresorts. Large former charter hotel, slap in

the middle of the village, with a pool. A bit shabby around the edges, but comfortable enough and very good value in this bracket. ④–⑤

Granpa's Inn Gaunwadi ☏ 0832/227 3270, ⊛ www.goacom.com/hotels/granpas. Formerly known as *Bougainvillea*, a lovely 200-year-old house set in half an acre of lush gardens, with a pool and shady breakfast terrace. The en-suite rooms are large and have high ceilings; the suites are even nicer. Ashtanga yoga on site; and there's a billiards table. Very popular, so book well ahead. ⑤–⑥

Laguna Anjuna De Mello Waddo ☏ 0832/227 4305, ⊛ www.lagunaanjuna.com. Alternative "boutique resort", comprising 25 colourfully decorated, domed laterite cottages with wooden rafters and terracotta tiles, grouped behind a convoluted pool. Restaurant, pool tables and bar. Doubles

The Anjuna flea market

Anjuna's Wednesday **flea market** is the hub of Goa's alternative scene, and *the* place to indulge in a spot of souvenir shopping. A decade or so ago, the weekly event was the exclusive preserve of backpackers and the area's semi-permanent population, who gathered here to smoke chillums, and to buy and sell clothes and jewellery they probably wouldn't have the nerve to wear anywhere else: something like a small pop festival without the stage. These days, however, everything is more organized and mainstream. Pitches are rented out by the metre, drugs are banned and the approach roads to the village are choked solid all day with a/c buses and Ambassador cars ferrying in tourists from resorts further down the coast.

The range of **goods** on sale has broadened, too, thanks to the high profile of migrant hawkers and stallholders from other parts of India. Each region or culture tends to stick to its own corner. At one end, Westerners congregate around racks of fluorescent party gear and designer beachwear. Nearby, hawk-eyed Kashmiris sit cross-legged beside trays of silver jewellery and papier-mâché boxes, while trendily dressed Tibetans preside over orderly rows of prayer wheels, turquoise bracelets and sundry Himalayan curios. Most distinctive of all are the Lamani women from Karnataka, decked from head to toe in traditional tribal garb, and selling elaborately woven multicoloured cloth, which they fashion into everything from jackets to money belts, and which makes even the Westerners' party gear look positively funereal. Elsewhere, you'll come across dazzling Rajasthani mirrorwork and block-printed bedspreads, Keralan woodcarvings and a scattering of Gujarati appliqué.

What you end up paying for this exotic merchandise largely depends on your ability to **haggle**. Lately, prices have inflated as tourists not used to dealing in rupees will part with almost anything. Be persistent, though, and cautious, and you can usually pick things up for a reasonable rate. Even if you're not spending, the flea market is a great place to sit and watch the world go by. Mingling with the sun-tanned masses are bands of strolling musicians, religious mendicants, performing monkeys, snake-charmers and holy cows.

from $125 mid-season, rising to $225 for Christmas–New Year. **9**

Lotus Inn Zor Waddo ☎0832/227 4015, ⓦwww .lotusinngoa.com. On the leafy northern limits of Anjuna, tucked away down a maze of narrow lanes: eleven swish suites (**9**) and six double rooms (on the small side for the Rs1500 tariff), all with a/c and centred around a good-sized pool (Rs100 for non-residents). There's also a trendy Italian poolside restaurant, and parties hosted on Sundays. **7**

Manali south of Starco's Crossroads ☎0832/227 4421, ⓔmanali@goatelecom.com. Anjuna's best all-round budget guesthouse has simple rooms (shared toilets) opening onto a yard, fans, safe deposit, money-changing, library, Internet connection, and sociable terrace-restaurant. Good value, so book in advance. **2**

Martha's 907 Montero Waddo ☎0832/227 4194, ⓔmpd8650@hotmail.com. Eight immaculate en-suite rooms run by a friendly family. Basic amenities include kitchen space, fans and running solar-heated water. Two pleasant houses also available. **4**

Palacete Rodrigues near Oxford Stores, Mazal Waddo ☎0832/227 3358, ⓦwww .palaceterodrigues.com. Two-hundred-year-old residence converted into an upmarket guesthouse, with carved wood furniture and a relaxed, traditional-Goan feel. Single occupancy available. The three economy options in a separate block around the back are good value. **4–5**

Palmasol Guest House Praia de St Anthony ☎0832/227 3258. Huge, comfortable rooms in an immaculately kept old house very near the beach. The larger ones have running water, verandas, cooking space and a relaxing garden; cheaper alternatives are in the back yard. **3**

Peaceland Soronto Waddo ☎0832/227 3700. Simple en-suite rooms in two blocks, run by a charming local couple with the help of a pair of friendly dogs. All have high-clay-tiled roofs, mozzie nets, rucksack racks, hammocks, clothes hangers and other nice homely touches that make this easily the best value place in its class. **3**

Sea Princess House #649 Goenkar Waddo, Dando ☎0832/227 4499, ⓔfabjoe@sancharnet .com. Newish guesthouse in a prime position in the middle of the beach, near the *Shore Bar*. The rooms are spacious and well maintained, and all have bathrooms with dependable plumbing. Hard to beat in terms of location and value for money in this mid-range bracket. ❸–❹

Starco's Starco's Crossroads. No phone. Some of the cheapest rooms in Anjuna: very basic, but well maintained, clean and screened from the racket outside. Excellent value if you're happy with bare-bones amenities. ❷

Villa Anjuna near Anjuna beachfront ☏0832/227 3443, ⓦwww.anjunavilla.com. Modern, efficient

resort hotel close to the beachfront area, on the main road through the village. Amenities include a good-sized pool and Jacuzzi. Popular with party lovers who can't afford *Laguna* as it's a short stagger from *Paradiso* (so noisy at night). ❼

White Negro 719 Praia de St Anthony, south of the village ☏0832/227 3326, ⓔmjanets@goatelecom.com. A row of twelve spotless back-to-back chalets catching the sea breeze, all with attached bathrooms, tiled floors, safe lockers and mozzie nets. Quiet, efficient and good value. ❺

Eating and drinking

Anjuna's beach shacks tend to be overpriced by comparison with those elsewhere in the state (especially on flea market days, when they hike their prices) but many will feel the location is worth paying for. Responding to the tastes of its many "alternative" visitors, the village also boasts a crop of quality wholefood **cafés** serving healthy veg dishes and juices. If you're hankering for a taste of home, call in at the **Orchard Stores** on the eastern side of the village, which, along with its rival **Oxford Stores**, directly opposite, serves the expatriate community with pricey imported delights such as digestive biscuits, Marmite and extra-virgin olive oil. They also offer delicious coffee and fresh croissants.

Basilico D'Mello Waddo ☏0832/227 3721. Cool, Italian-run garden restaurant, hidden away down one of the village's quieter lanes. The pizzas and pasta dishes are authentic, the service efficient and the atmosphere relaxed. Most mains around Rs150–175.

Blue Tao on the main road through the village. Another Italian-run place, this time an "alternative health restaurant" that offers some of Goa's most delicious breakfasts (sour-dough and wholemeal breads, herbal teas, tahini and spirulina spreads). In addition to a full menu of main courses (Rs100–150), they also do an excellent range of juices, including wheatgrass, ginseng and ayurvedic concoctions. Non-smoking and child-friendly.

The Jam Connection near Oxford Stores, opposite *Tin Tin Tibet*. Fresh, interesting salads (with real organic rocket and garden herbs), mocha and espresso coffee, homemade ice cream and all-day breakfasts, served in a lovely garden. You can lounge on bamboo easy chairs or on tree platforms. Daily except Wed 11am–7pm.

Martha's Breakfast Home *Martha's* guesthouse, 907 Montero Waddo. Secluded, very friendly breakfast garden serving fresh Indian coffee, crepes and delicious waffles.

Tin Tin Tibet near *Oxford Stores*. Well-established budget café, serving the usual budget-travellers' grub, plus Tibetan specialities (*momos* and *thukpa*), and some Israeli dishes. Worth a try if only for the fried banana with cashew nuts.

Nightlife

Anjuna's **nightlife** scene has calmed down considerably over the past few years (see box opposite), but there are now a couple of pay-to-enter clubs have that, unlike illegal free parties, are above board and thus less prone to being shut down by the police. First stop for confirmed techno heads should be the **Paraiso de Goa**, aka **Paradiso**, at the far north end of Anjuna beach. Partly owned by the government, it epitomizes the new, more above-board face of Goa Trance. Presiding over a dance space surrounded by spacey statues of Hindu gods and Tantric symbols, visiting DJs spin textbook tunes for a mainly Israeli crowd.

It's all a bit commercial, but even the now-legendary Goa Gill, one of the leading free-party hosts of the 1980s and 1990s, has given the club his seal of approval by playing here. *Paradiso* keeps to a sporadic timetable, but should

Hedonism has figured prominently in European images of Goa from the mid-sixteenth century, when mariners and merchants returned to Lisbon with tales of unbridled debauchery among the colonists. The French traveller François Pyrard was first to chronicle this as moral decline, in a journal peppered with accounts of wild parties and sleaze scandals.

Following the rigours of the Inquisition, a semblance of morality was restored, which prevailed through the Portuguese era. But traditional Catholic life in Goa's coastal villages sustained a rude shock in the 1960s with the first influx of **hippies** to Calangute and Baga beaches. Much to the amazement of the locals, the preferred pastime of these would-be *sadhus* was to cavort naked on the sands together on full-moon nights, amid a haze of *chillum* smoke and loud rock music blaring from makeshift PAs. The villagers took little notice of these bizarre gatherings at first, but with each season the scene became better established, and by the late 1970s the **Christmas and New Year** parties, in particular, had become huge events, attracting thousands of foreign travellers.

In the late 1980s, the local party scene received a dramatic facelift with the coming of acid house and techno. Ecstasy became the preferred dance drug as the dub-reggae scene gave way to rave culture, with ever greater numbers of young clubbers pouring in for the season on charter flights. Goa soon spawned its own distinctive brand of psychedelic music, known as **Goa Trance**. Distinguished by its multilayered synth lines and sub-bass rhythms, the hypnotic style combines the darkness of hard techno with an ambient sentiment. Cultivated by artists such as Goa Gill, Juno Reactor and Hallucinogen, the new sound was given wider exposure when big-name DJs Danny Rampling and Paul Oakenfold started mixing Goa Trance in clubs and on national radio back in the UK, generating a huge following among music lovers who previously knew nothing of the place which had inspired it.

The **golden era** for Goa's party scene, and trance, was in the early 1990s, when big raves were held two or three times a week in beautiful locations around Anjuna and Vagator. UV and flouro gear appeared and for a few years no one bothered about the growing scene. Then, quite suddenly, the plug was pulled by the local authorities. For years, drug busts and bribes had provided the notoriously corrupt Goan cops with a lucrative source of baksheesh. But after a couple of drug-related deaths, a series of sensational articles in the local press and a decision by Goa Tourism to promote upmarket over backpacker tourism, the police began to demand impossibly large bribes – sums that the organizers (many of them drug dealers) could not hope to recoup. Although the big New Year and Christmas events continued unabated, smaller parties, hitherto held in off-track venues such as "Disco Valley" behind Middle Vagator beach, started to peter out, much to the dismay of local people, many of whom had become financially dependent on the raves and the punters they pulled in to the villages.

Against this backdrop, news of the Y2K **amplified-music ban** between 10pm and 7am seemed to sound the death knell for Goa's party scene. Reports in the international media that India's rave era was at an end were, however, premature. Five years on, the scene survives, albeit in a more mainstream style, with a batch of large new clubs – notably the **Nine Bar** see p.206 and **Paradiso** (see opposite) – providing permanent venues and big sound systems for the first time in Goa.

All the same, if you've come here expecting an Indian equivalent of Ko Pha Ngan or Ibiza-on-the-Arabian-Sea, you'll be sorely disappointed. Only over Christmas and New Year do really big parties take place, and these are a far cry from the free-and-easy events that once filled the beaches and bamboo groves of Anjuna on full-moon nights.

be open most nights from around 10pm; admission charges are Rs300–500, depending on the night. Along similar lines, but with free admission, is the **Nine Bar**, above Vagator beach, and the nearby **Primrose Café** (see p.207).

Down on the beach proper, the **Shore Bar** used to be *the* place to hang out after the flea market, attracting hundreds of people for sunset, but it has fallen out of favour over the past couple of years and now lacks the atmosphere of the Nine Bar.

Vagator

Barely a couple of kilometres of clifftops and parched grassland separate Anjuna from the southern fringes of its nearest neighbour, **VAGATOR**. Spread around a tangle of leafy lanes, this is a more chilled, undeveloped resort that appeals, in the main, to Israeli and northern European trance-heads, who hole up for the full season in ramshackle old Portuguese bungalows or cheap guesthouses.

With the red ramparts of Chapora fort looming above it, Vagator's broad sandy **beach** – known as **Big Vagator** – is undeniably beautiful. However, a peaceful swim or lie on the sand is out of the question here as it's a prime stop for bus parties of domestic tourists, which ensures a steady stream of whisky-swilling Maharashtran men. Far better, then, to head to the next cove south. Backed by a steep wall of crumbling palm-fringed laterite, **Ozran** (or "Little") **Vagator beach** is more secluded and much less accessible than either of its neighbours. To get there, walk ten minutes' south from Big Vagator, or drive to the end of the lane off the main Chapora–Anjuna road, from where a footpath drops sharply down to the wide stretch of level white sand (look for the mopeds and bikes parked at the top of the cliff). The Israeli- and Italian-dominated scene revolves around a string of large, well-established shacks behind Little Vagator, at the end of which a face carved out of the rocks – staring serenely skywards – is the most prominent landmark. Relentless racquetball, trance sound systems and a particularly big herd of stray cows are this beach's other defining features.

Practicalities

Buses from Panjim and Mapusa, 9km east, pull in every fifteen minutes or so at the crossroads on the far northeastern edge of Vagator, near where the main road peels away towards Chapora. From here, it's a one-kilometre walk over the hill and down the other side to the beach, where you'll find most of the village's accommodation, restaurants and cafés. The *Primrose Café*, on the south side of the village, has a **foreign exchange** licence (for cash and travellers' cheques) but their rates are less competitive than those on offer at Jackie's Daynite shop on the south side of the village. For **Internet** access, go to *Bethany Inn* (Rs50/hr).

Accommodation

Accommodation in Vagator consists of family-run budget guesthouses, a couple of pricey resort hotels and dozens of small private properties rented out

---

Petrol pumps in north Goa

The main Calangute **petrol pump** was closed down in 2000 when it was found to be bulking out its supply with solvents. As a result, you'll either have to travel up to the one between **Anjuna and Vagator** to refill, or else head into **Mapusa**. There's also a station just north of **Arambol** on the Kerim–Terekol road, but the locals claim it laces its petrol too. As ever, ensure the attendants reset the pumps to zero before serving you – they often don't, in order to overcharge and pocket the extra.

for long periods. **Water** is in very short supply here, and you'll be doing the villagers a favour if you use it frugally at all times.

Bethany Inn Chapora crossroads ☎0832/227 3731, ⓔbethany@goatelecom.com. Seven immaculately clean rooms with fridges, balconies and attached bathrooms. Tastefully furnished, and efficiently managed. ④–⑤

Boon's Ark near *Bethany Inn* ☎0832/227 4045. Pleasant, clean and efficient place with recently built rooms opening on to small verandas and a well-tended little garden. ④

Dolrina Vagator Beach Rd ☎0832/227 4896. Nestled under a lush canopy of trees near the beach, Vagator's largest budget guesthouse is run by a friendly Goan couple and features attached or shared bathrooms, a sociable garden café, individual safe deposits and roof space. Single occupancy rates, and breakfasts available. ③

Garden Villa Vagator Beach Rd ☎0832/227 3571, ⓔgarden@goatelecom.com. Two categories of rooms: the older ones are better value than the ones in the newer block. All are spacious and cool, with tiled floors and large bathrooms, and there's a friendly café showing video movies daily at 7.30pm. ③

Jolly Jolly Lester Vagator Beach Rd ☎0832/227 3620. Eleven pleasant doubles with tiled bathrooms set in a lovingly kept garden and surrounded by woodland. Small restaurant on site; single occupancy is possible. ③

Jolly Jolly Roma Vagator Beach Rd ☎0832/227 3620.Very smart, good-sized chalet rooms with verandas; laundry, exchange facilities and a small library for guests. ④

Julie Jolly south side of the village ☎0832/227 3357. Recently revamped and now one of the most pleasant places in Vagator, set on the edge of a leafy belt and within easy reach of Ozran beach. All rooms tiled and well aired; self-caterers can stay in larger suites with sitting rooms and kitchenettes. ②–③

L'Amour north side of village, on hillside above Chapora ☎0832/277 4180. Immaculately clean, tiled en-suite rooms in a block tucked away in the woods above Chapora. Quiet, well run and fantastic value. ②

Leoney Resort on the road to Disco Valley ☎0832/227 3634, ⓦwww.leoneyresortgoa .com. Comfortable option, with swish chalets and pricier (but more spacious) octagonal "cottages" on the sleepy side of village, ranged around a very nice little pool. Restaurant, laundry, lockers and foreign exchange facilities. No advance bookings Dec–Jan. ⑦–⑧

Eating, drinking and nightlife

Vagator boasts an eclectic batch of **restaurants**, with wildly varying menus and prices, and an equally dramatic turnover of chefs. Western tourists tend to stick to the pricier ones lining the road through the village, while Indian visitors frequent the more impersonal, cheaper places down on the beach itself. For a sundown drink, head to *Nine Bar*, encircled by a fortress-style laterite wall that opens onto a great chill-out terrace and the sea on one side. Big trance sounds attract a fair-sized crowd for sunset, especially on Wednesdays after the flea market; the dancing starts after dark and keeps going until the bar closes around 10pm. At this point, there's a general exodus over to the nearby *Primrose Café*, which offers much the same atmosphere, without the views.

Bean Me Up near the petrol pump. India's one and only American-run tofu joint – the last word in Goan gourmet healthy eating. Main courses (around Rs175–225) come with steamed spinach, fresh brown bread and hygienically washed salads; try their delicious Thai-style *tempeh* in spicy cashew sauce. There's also a tempting range of vegan desserts – the banana pudding with soya whip is a winner.

China Town Chapora Crossroads, next to *Bethany Inn*. This small roadside restaurant, tucked away just south of the main drag, is the village's most popular budget eating place, serving particularly tasty seafood dishes in addition to a large Chinese selection, as well as all the usual Goa-style travellers' grub.

Le Bluebird on the road out to *Nine Bar*. Tucked away in the most appealing corner of the village is Vagator's renowned French-run restaurant, which serves classier-than-average Gallic food – pepper steak in brandy sauce, prawns in coconut, squid in white wine and garlic – at traveller-friendly prices (around Rs300–400 for 3 courses, plus wine). Seafood is their strong point, but they offer a better range of veg dishes than you'd find in a real French restaurant, as well as crepes, Bordeaux claret and champagne (around Rs2000 per bottle).

Nine Bar above Ozran beach. Boasting a crystal trance sound system, this clifftop café enjoys a prime location, with fine sea views from its terrace through the palm canopy, where Nepali waiters serve up cold beer and the usual range of budget travellers' grub to a generally spaced-out clientele.
Primrose Café on the southern edge of the village. Goa's posiest café-bar livens up around 10pm.

Tasty German wholefood snacks, light meals and cakes are on offer, as well as drinks.
Tibet O-Live Main Road. Run by a team of friendly young lads from Darjeeling, this place shuttles between Manali in the summer and Goa in the winter, and has earned a strong reputation in both for its ultra-tasty, inexpensive pizzas. There's also top-fried *momos* (the spinach and cheese ones are best).

Chapora

Huddled in the shadow of a Portuguese fort on the opposite, northern side of the headland from Vagator, **CHAPORA**, 10km from Mapusa, is a lot busier than most north coast villages. Dependent on fishing and boat-building, it has,

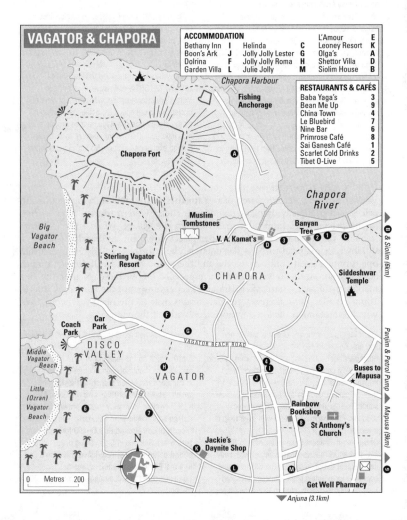

VAGATOR & CHAPORA

ACCOMMODATION

Bethany Inn	I	Helinda	C	L'Amour
Boon's Ark	J	Jolly Jolly Lester	G	Leoney Resort
Dolrina	F	Jolly Jolly Roma	H	Olga's
Garden Villa	L	Julie Jolly	M	Shettor Villa
				Siolim House

(L'Amour E, Leoney Resort K, Olga's A, Shettor Villa D, Siolim House B)

RESTAURANTS & CAFÉS

Baba Yaga's	3
Bean Me Up	9
China Town	4
Le Bluebird	7
Nine Bar	6
Primrose Café	8
Sai Ganesh Café	1
Scarlet Cold Drinks	2
Tibet O-Live	5

Siolim Zagor

While much of India has had to learn to live with the spectre of religious violence, Goa's Christians and Hindus, despite the sabre-rattling of their respective right-wing politicians, manage to coexist peacefully and in a spirit of mutual respect unsurpassed on the subcontinent. Emblematic of this communal harmony, and indeed of the richness of Goa's melting-pot culture in general, is the extraordinary **Zagor festival**, held in Siolim, just east of Chapora, on the first Sunday after Christmas.

Although ostensibly a Christian celebration, coinciding with the feast day of Nossa Senhora de Guia, the night-long event blends together elements from both religions. It centres on a small Hindu shrine, housed under *peepal* tree down a lane near the ferry ramp. This sacred spot is associated with an important local deity called **Zagoryo**, believed to be the guardian of the village dams (*bunds*) which hold the river off the rice paddy. During the festival, each household makes offerings to Zagor to give thanks and ensure the village is protected from flooding over the coming year: Christians give candles, Hindus give oil and both offer cakes of pressed rice called *pohe*.

The festivities, however, start with a sombre candle-lit **procession** through Siolim, in which an effigy of Zagor is carried around the various *waddos* of the village, stopping at wayside crosses and shrines along the way to receive offerings. Everyone then gathers at a *mand*, or sacred arena, in a Catholic house for a **dance drama**. The actors in this ancient ritual, assuming hereditarily assigned roles, are always drawn from two old Siolim families: the Shirodkars (Hindus) and D'Souzas (Catholics); it enacts stories from the legend of the Zagor deities. At dawn, when the play is complete and the priests have recited mantras and Christian scriptures to invoke the god's protection, Zagor is carried amid much pomp back to his shrine, where offerings of roasted maize, *feni* and fermented rice pikelets (called *sanna*) are placed before his small domed shrine.

Traditionally, local satirists used to take over at this point, performing **zupatteos**: songs poking fun at politicians, priests and anyone else who deserved to be taken down a peg or two. These days, however, the culmination of Zagor tends to be Konkani *tiatr* play, followed by a set of crowd-pleasing Konkani classics from local rock star, Remo Fernandes, who was born and still lives in Siolim.

Aside from being a model of religious tolerance, Zagor is a great spectacle and enormous fun. Surprisingly few tourists participate, but foreigners are welcomed enthusiastically, both to the religious dance drama and resolutely secular, *feni*-fuelled party that succeeds it.

to an extent, retained a life of its own independent of tourism. That said, the recent relaxation of Goa's drug laws combined with the influx of long-staying Russians have made a significant impact here over the past three or four years. Whereas the main street used to retain a workaday indifference to the annual invasion of foreigners, now it's largely given over to Amsterdam-style coffee shops and budget travellers' cafés, with everyone spliffing up in public at sunset time. Even so, it's unlikely Chapora will ever develop into a major resort; tucked away under a dense canopy of trees on the muddy southern shore of a river estuary, it lacks both the space and the white sand that have pulled crowds to Calangute and Colva. The main drawback to staying here, though, is the general grubbiness of the accommodation on offer, which tends to be booked for long periods to a mixture of hard-drinking, heavy-smoking hippies and dodgy-looking Muscovites with tattoos.

Chapora's chief landmark is its venerable old **fort**, most easily reached from the Vagator side of the hill. At low tide, you can also walk around the bottom of the headland, via the anchorage and the secluded coves beyond it to Big Vagator, then head up the hill from there. The red-laterite bastion, crowning the rocky bluff, was built by the Portuguese in 1617 on the site of an earlier Muslim structure (thus the village's name – from *Shahpura*, "town of the Shah"). Deserted in the nineteenth century, it lies in ruins today, although the **views** up and down the coast from the weed-infested ramparts are still superb.

Also worth a visit is the village's busy little **fishing anchorage**, where you can buy delicious calamari fresh off the boats most evenings.

Practicalities

Direct **buses** arrive at Chapora three times daily from Panjim, and every fifteen minutes from Mapusa, with departures until 7pm from various points along the main road. **Motorcycle taxis** hang around the old banyan tree at the far end of the main street, near where the buses pull in. Air, train and bus **tickets** may be booked or reconfirmed at Soniya Tours and Travels, next to the bus stand. For **medical attention**, contact Dr Jawarhalal Henriques at Zorin, near the petrol pump (℡0832/227 4308).

If you want to check into a cheap guesthouse while you sort out more permanent **accommodation**, best bet is the basic but good-value *Shettor Villa* (℡0832/227 4335; ❷–❸), off the west side of the main street. Nearly all its rooms, ranged around a sheltered back yard, come with fans and running water. Otherwise, try the *Helinda* (℡0832/227 4345; ❷–❸), at the opposite end of the village, which has rock-bottom options and a couple of more comfortable rooms with attached shower-toilets; or *Olga's* (℡0832/227 4355; ❷), a rudimentary but clean and quiet little guesthouse on the west side of the village towards the fishing anchorage.

The only luxury place hereabouts is *Siolim House* (℡0832/227 2138, ⓦwww .siolimhouse.com; ❾), 5km inland from Chapora along the south bank of the river, in **Siolim** village. Housed in a recently restored *palacio*, the hotel captures the period feel of the Portuguese era: its luminous, simply furnished rooms (from $70), ranged around a central pillared courtyard, have typical oyster-shell windows and carved, four-poster beds. There's also a twelve-metre pool in the garden, and an unpretentious restaurant serving fine Goan food.

Finding cheap **meals** in Chapora itself is easy: just take your pick from the crop of inexpensive little cafés and restaurants on the main street. *Baba Yaga's* caters for the Russians, with signs and menus in Cyrillic script, while for snacks and juices *Scarlet Cold Drinks* and the *Sai Ganesh Café*, both a short way east of the main street, are safe bets, knocking up deliciously cool fresh fruit milkshakes and travellers' grub for as long as there are customers to serve.

The far north

Bounded by the Chapora and Arondem (aka "Terekol") rivers, **Pernem** is Goa's northernmost district. Apart from the fishing village of **Arambol**, which, during the winter, plays host to a large contingent of hippy travellers seeking a less pretentious alternative to Anjuna and Vagator, the beautiful Pernem coastline remains the quietest stretch of shoreline in the state. Catch the tide right, and it is possible to walk in a couple of hours all the way from the sandy spit at **Morjim**, on the opposite side of the river mouth from Chapora, to Arambol, via the villages of **Aswem** and **Mandrem**, where facilities for visitors are limited to a handful of shacks and small hut camps. In the far north, **Terekol fort**, on the Maharashtran border, makes a good target for a day-trip by motorbike or taxi.

Travelling north from **Siolim**, on the south bank of the River Chapora, the entry point to Pernem proper is the far side of the new road bridge at **Chopdem**.

Head straight on for 200m or so until you arrive at a T-junction. A right turn here will take you along the quick route to Arambol; bear left, and you'll head along one of the few stretches of undeveloped coastline remaining in Goa – an area that looks, since the completion of the bridge, to be living on borrowed time.

Morjim

Viewed from Chapora fort, **MORJIM** (or **Morji**) appears as a dramatic expanse of empty sand sweeping north from a spoon-shaped spit to the river mouth – one of Goa's last remaining nesting site for Olive Ridley turles (see box on p.212). Behind it, broken dunes are backed by a dense patch of palms and casuarina trees, sheltering a mixed Hindu-Christian village whose inhabitants still live predominantly from in-shore fishing and rice farming. Bypassed completely by the main road north, their settlement has remained a relative backwater. Only in the past three or four years, since the completion of the Siolim bridge, has it started to see many tourists, the majority of them young Russians (whose early-morning fitness routines on the beach are still regarded with puzzled amusement by the straw-hatted handnet fishers working the foreshore).

Practicalities

Half a dozen **buses** per day connect Morjim with Panjim, the first at 7am; heading the other way, you can pick up a direct bus from Panjim at 5pm, and there are frequent services from Mapusa via Siolim. They'll drop you on the main road, five minutes' walk from the beachfront area at **Vithaldas Waddo**. If you're planning to stay anywhere else, keep your eyes peeled for the roadside signboards or you could be in for a long walk – rickshaws are few and far between this far north.

The main turning for Vithaldas Waddo, 1km back from the beach, is where you'll find Morjim's **Internet café**, Amigo's; access (on a slow dial-up connection but with good new computers) costs Rs40/hour. They also have telephone and fax facilities, and are licensed to **change money** (albeit at poor rates).

For **food**, you won't do better than *Britto's*, a small, family-run shack five minutes' walk down the beach, where millet-fried mussels, clams in spicy coconut sauce, vegetable fried rice and Chapora calamari in lime are the specialities; they also serve stupendously good lassis and fresh fruit juices. The shack is decorated with **murals** by the Welsh artist Andrea Davies.

Accommodation

Most of the **accommodation** in Morjim is in private houses which get snapped up early in the season, or even the previous one by entrepreneurial Muscovites who then sublet them at inflated rates. But you can usually find vacant rooms in one or other of the small guesthouses that have opened close to the beach; and a couple of higher-end places have recently sprung up beyond the northern limits of the village, on the road to Aswem.

Britto's Vithaldas Waddo ☎0832/224 4245. Friendly guesthouse back in the palm grove. The rooms are a bit institutional, but cheap, and the fun family atmosphere more than compensates. To find it, turn left down a sandy track 30m before the main beachfront road swings to the right (a blue signboard marks the spot); or else walk down the beach. ❷

Camp 69 Vithaldas Waddo ☎0832/224 4458. The oldest established place on the beachfront,

now boasting large, well-spaced "log cabins", fitted with beds, sofas, fans and en-suite bathrooms. They also run a relaxing little terrace restaurant shaded by palms and flowering trees. ❹

Hard Rock ("Gilbert's") Temb Waddo ☎9822/581928, ✉bobmarley_gilbert@hotmail .com. Local lad Gilbert Fernandes has converted a wing of his family home, behind the southernmost

The turtle wind

When a strong and steady on-shore breeze blows through the night in early November at Morjim – the long, empty beach west of the ferry ramp at Chopdem – the locals call it a **turtle wind** because such weather normally heralds the arrival of Goa's rarest migrant visitors: the **Olive Ridley marine turtles** (*Lepidochelys olivacea*).

For as long as anyone can remember, the spoon-shaped spit of soft white sand at **Temb**, the far southern end of the beach, has been the nesting ground of these beautiful sea reptiles. Each winter, a succession of females emerges from the surf during the night and, using their distinctive flippers, crawls to the edge of the dunes to lay their annual clutch of 105–115 eggs. Just over two months later, the fresh hatchlings clamber out and crawl blinking over their siblings to begin the perilous trek back to the water, guided into the sea by reflected moonlight. Little more is known about how these enigmatic creatures spend the rest of their long lives (turtles frequently live for over a century), but it is thought that the females return to the beaches where they were born to lay their own eggs. Some have been known to travel as far as 4500km to do this.

Once a thriving species, with huge populations spread across the Pacific, Atlantic and Indian oceans, the Olive Ridley is nowadays endangered. Aside from a wealth of traditional predators (such as crows, ospreys, gulls and buzzards, who pick off the hatchlings during their dash for the sea), the newborns and their parents are vulnerable to a host of man-made threats. In Morjim, as in most of Asia, the eggs are traditionally considered a delicacy and local villagers collect them to sell in Mapusa market. Many (perhaps as many as 35,000 worldwide) are killed accidentally by fisherman, caught up in fine shrimp nets or attracted by squid bait used to catch tuna. Floating litter, which the hapless turtles mistake for jellyfish, has also taken its toll over the past two decades, as have tar balls from oil spills, which coat the animals' digestive tracks and hamper the absorption of food. The growth of tourism poses an additional danger: electric lights behind the beaches throw the hatchlings off course as they scuttle towards to sea, and sand compressed by sunbathers' trampling feet damages nests, preventing the babies from digging their way out at the crucial time. On average, only two out of a typical clutch of more than one hundred survive into

part of the beach inland from the shacks, with very stylish oxide floors and ochre-washed walls. Comfortable, secluded and retaining plenty of local Goan atmosphere. ❸

Montego Bay Vithaldas Waddo ☎ 0832/224 4222, ⓦwww.montegobaygoa.com. A dozen or so plush Rajasthani tents, stylishly equipped with driftwood beds, fans, coir mats and running-water bathrooms, at a breezy spot in the dunes under coconut trees. The most comfortable option bang on the beach, though overpriced for the area. Breakfast included. ❼

Morjim Beach Resort Temb Waddo ☎ 9822/481480. This recently built guesthouse is a long plod south down the beach, midway between the village centre and sandy spit at the end: basically, you'll need at least a bicycle to stay here. But it is perfectly situated and well set up, with proper rooms as well as leaf huts. Signposted off the road. ❸

Nifa 480 Mardi Waddo ☎ 0832/224 4635 or 9822/135333, ⓔhotelnifa@yahoo.com. Charming,

peaceful guesthouse on the coast road, run by a welcoming Iranian–Swiss couple. They've made a real effort with the rooms, which are spacious and have mozzie nets, floaty curtains and hot showers in the bathrooms. Also worth singling out is the restaurant and the views from their pleasant garden terrace. ❼

Papa Jolly's House #749/A, Morjim–Aswem Road, Mardi Waddo. A self-styled "Spiritual Holiday Resort", complete with ethnically furnished rooms and lovely curved pool. The new laterite building is pleasant enough, as is the location, but the tariffs – sweetened with lots of soothing New Age blurb on the website – are ludicrous: Rs6730 (roughly $125) for a double room, rising to Rs8775 at Christmas. ❾

Tequila Sunset Hideout Vithaldas Waddo ☎ 9822/588003. Large, new rooms, with attached bathrooms (closets) and big tiled balconies overlooking a beachfront plot. A first-floor café-restaurant is in the pipeline, which will have great sea views. ❹

adulthood to reproduce. In Goa, the resulting decline has been dramatic. Of the 150 nesting females that used to return each year to Morjim, for example, only thirteen showed up in 1999.

However, under the auspices of the Forest Department, a scheme has been launched to revive turtle populations. Locals are employed to watch out for the females' arrival in November, and guard the nests after the eggs have been laid until they hatch. You'll see them camped under palm-leaf shades on the beach, with the nests fenced in and marked by Forest Department signs. One of the main reasons the fishing families at Temb have so enthusiastically espoused the initiative is that its success promises to bring about the creation of an official **nature sanctuary** at Morjim, blocking forever plans to build unwanted tourist resorts on their beach.

So far, the government-led conservation attempt seems to have been successful, although after an initial leap in hatchling figures, recent results have shown a marked dip, which the Forest Department ascribes to an increase in tourist activity. Over the winter of 2003–04, 927 eggs were laid in nine nests on Morjim, of which 558 hatched (as against a total of 2500 hatchlings in 2001–02). A further 922 baby turtles survived at Goa's other main nesting site, Galjibag, in the south (see p.232), and 213 more in Agonda.

Watching the nesting turtles is an unforgettable experience, although one requiring a certain amount of dedication, or luck. No one knows for sure when an Olive Ridley female will turn up, but with a strong turtle wind blowing at the right time, the chances are good. Much more predictable are the appearances of the hatchlings, who emerge exactly 54 days after their mothers laid the eggs. If you ask one of the wardens looking after the nests, they can tell you when this will be.

For more on international attempts to save marine turtles, including the massive synchronized *arribida* (arrival) of around 200,000 at the Bhita Kanika Sanctuary, Orissa, on the east coast of India, visit the website of the World Wildlife Fund (🌐www .wwf.org), which tells you how you can join environmental groups such as the Marine Conservation Society.

Aswem

A solitary whitewashed crucifix rises from the rocks dividing Morjim from **ASWEM**, the next village north. Aside from the odd German nudist or two, you should have the sands pretty much to yourself until you arrive at the burgeoning cluster of shacks and hut camps midway along the beach. Huddled under the canopy of a beautiful coconut *mand*, this ad hoc tourist settlement started to snowball after a couple of French restaurateurs from Baga opened a chic beach café here (*La Plage* – see p.214). Their business excepted, amenities remain basic (leaf huts are the norm as the local council has vigorously enforced the Coastal Protection Zone building ban), but the beach is all the more appealing for that. It's clean, quiet for most of the season and, outside the full-moon period, safe for kids to swim off. Only at the far northern end, where a tidal creek periodically prevents you from continuing north towards Arambol, has package tourism made any discernable inroads: Maruti vans deposit punters here to overnight in purpose-built hut camps on the shoreline, but the setup is very low-key.

Practicalities

Sporadic **buses** from Panjim and Mapusa cover the quiet stretch of road running parallel to the beach inland, from where a five-minute walk across the paddy fields brings you to the shacks (signboards indicate the paths). Other than the cafés, there are no facilities whatsoever here. Nearly everyone who stays rents a scooter from somewhere else to get to and around Aswem. The nearest Internet access and shops are at Morjim, an idyllic half-hour plod south.

For **food**, head to *La Plage* (T9850/258543; closed evenings), where light Gallic–Mediterranean, heat-beating snacks and drinks (chilled asparagus soup, mint lassis, Moroccan salads, fresh strawberries and cream), along with sumptuous chargrilled seafood and barbequed main courses, are dished up by Nepalis in black *lunghis* against a diaphanous backdrop of floaty white muslin. It's a surreal counterpoint to the fishing *waddo* down the beach, but a very pleasant breakfast or lunch venue nonetheless.

Accommodation

Change Your Mind T0832/224 4790 or 9822/389290. Basic huts and treehouses behind a lively shack. ❷–❸

Gopal T0832/224 4431, 224 7030 or 9822/147416, Egopal@ingoa.com/258543. In much the same mould as *Change Your Mind*, at identical rates. ❷–❸

Little Goa T9822/383795. Classier than average huts – with comfier beds and fans – and an unusually well-stocked bar, though you pay dearly for the frills. ❹

Palm Grove T0832/224 7440. Pick of the bunch: further up the beach from the others, and with large treehouses that are not only well spaced but also have perfect sea views. The best option if you're here to escape the tourist scene. ❹

Mandrem

A magnificent, and largely empty, beach stretches north of Aswem towards Arambol, uninterrupted save for a couple of large-scale hut camps and a single package hotel. Whether or not **MANDREM** can continue to hold out against the rising tide of tourism remains to be seen, but for the time being, nature still has the upper hand. Olive Ridley marine turtles nest on the quietest stretch, and you're more than likely to catch a glimpse of one of the white-bellied fish eagles that live in the casuarina trees – their last stronghold in Pernem. If you can afford it, the best spot from which to savour this last unspoilt strip of the Goan coast is Denzil Sequeira's exclusive beachhouse *Elsewhere* (see below), nestled in the dunes just north of the creek and unquestionably the most beautiful hideaway hereabouts. The rest of this area's accommodation is tucked away inland at **Junasa Waddo**, where a handful of small guesthouses and hotels have sprung up.

Practicalities

Public transport is thin on the ground. Visitors walk or rent scooters for the five-minute ride to **Madlamaz–Mandrem**, a typically north-Goan market village straddling the main road inland. Parsekar Stores holds an Anjuna-style stock of tourist-oriented food and drink – including muesli, olive oil and Nilgiri cheese – and natural cosmetics; and there's a tiny **laundry** above a jeweller's shop in the small courtyard just to the east of the main road.

Accommodation

Dunes T0832/224 7219 or 224 7071, Wwww .dunesgoa.com. Huge "holiday village" of twin-bedded, yellow-painted leaf huts. They're a notch too close together for comfort and brightly lit, spoiling the aspect of the beach at night, but this is an efficiently run outfit that fills up in peak season. Pricier en suite available. ❸–❹

Elsewhere T022/2373 8757 or 9820/037387, Wwww.aseascape.com. Goan fashion photographer Denzil Sequeira converted his grandfather's hot-season retreat into a dream getaway, retaining its colonial-era character with a gorgeous sea-facing veranda and traditional wood furniture, yet incorporating modern elements (a fridge, two cobalt-blue bathrooms and luminous white cotton drapes that catch the breezes). Flanked by the beach on one side and a creek on the other, it's romantic and exclusive, but affordable if you get a group together (the three bedrooms sleep six). From £670 per week; includes services of an on-site cook. ❾

Flying Carpet ☎ 0832/244 7104 or 9822/140996. A dozen neatly furnished holiday rooms in a new block on the lane through Junasa Waddo. ❸

Otter Creek ☎ 022/2373 8757 or 9820/037387, ⓦ www.aseascape.com. Three beautiful luxury tents, each with their own bamboo four-posters, bathroom, colour-washed sitout and jetty on the river; you have to cross a rickety foot bridge to get there, or walk over the dunes from the beach. Rs3320 per night. ❾

Riva Resort ☎ 0832/224 7088 or 224 7612, ⓦ www.rivaresorts.com. The other big hut camp next to *Dunes*. This one's more upmarket, with swisher huts and higher rates (Rs400–800 depending on the level of comfort, rising to a hefty Rs1500–2000 at Christmas.) The site centres on a huge bar-restaurant that hosts DJ nights and has big-screen video/DVD. ❸–❺

Villa River Cat ☎ 0822/224 7928, ⓦ www .villarivercat.com. Quirky riverside hotel, screened from the beach by the dunes, with distinctive hippy-influenced decor and furniture. The 16 rooms are all individually designed: mosaics, shells, devotional sculpture and hammocks set the tone. Some have balconies, and there's a great sunset roof terrace and rear garden for lounging in. Host Rinoo Seghal is an animal lover, so brace yourself for a menagerie of cats and dogs, which some will enjoy. ❺

Arambol (Harmal)

The largest coastal village in Pernem district is **ARAMBOL** (sometimes called **Harmal**), 32km northwest of Mapusa. If you're happy with basic amenities but want to stay somewhere lively, this might be your best bet. The village's two beaches are beautiful and still relatively unexploited – thanks to the locals, who a few years back managed to block proposals put forward by a local landowner to site a sprawling five-star resort here. The majority of foreigners who stay in Arambol tend to do so for the season, and over time a close-knit expat community (of mostly ageing hippies who've been coming here for years) has grown up, with its own alternative health facilities, paragliding school, yoga gurus and wholefood cafés.

Modern Arambol is scattered around an area of high ground west of the main coast road. From here, a bumpy lane runs downhill to the more traditional fishing quarter, clustered under a canopy of widely spaced palm trees. The main **beach** lies 200m further along a lane that the predominantly British, festival-going tourist population call Glastonbury Street. Strewn with dozens of old wooden boats and a line of tourist café-bars, the gently curving bay is good for bathing, but much less picturesque than its neighbour around the corner, **Paliem** or "**Lakeside**" **beach**. To reach this, follow the track over the headland to the north; beyond a rather insalubrious-smelling, rocky-bottomed cove, the trail emerges to a broad strip of soft white sand hemmed in on both sides by steep cliffs. Behind it, a small **freshwater lake** extends along the bottom of the valley into a thick jungle. Hang around the banks of this murky green pond for long enough, and you'll probably see a fluorescent-yellow human figure or two appear from the bushes at its far end. Fed by boiling hot springs, the lake is lined with sulphurous mud, which, when smeared over the body, dries to form a surreal, butter-coloured shell. The resident hippies swear it's good for you and spend much of the day tiptoeing naked around the shallows like refugees from some obscure tribal initiation ceremony – much to the amusement of Arambol's Indian visitors.

Practicalities

Buses to and from Panjim (via Mapusa) pull into Arambol every half-hour until noon, and every 90min thereafter, at the small bus stop on the main road. A faster private **minibus** service from Panjim arrives daily opposite the chai

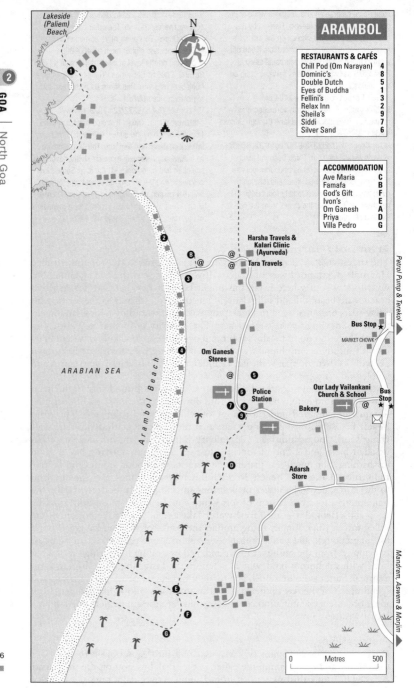

ARAMBOL

Lakeside (Paliem) Beach

N

RESTAURANTS & CAFÉS

Chill Pod (Om Narayan)	4
Dominic's	8
Double Dutch	5
Eyes of Buddha	1
Fellini's	3
Relax Inn	2
Sheila's	9
Siddi	7
Silver Sand	6

ACCOMMODATION

Ave Maria	C
Famafa	B
God's Gift	F
Ivon's	E
Om Ganesh	A
Priya	D
Villa Pedro	G

Petrol Pump & Terekol

Harsha Travels & Kalari Clinic (Ayurveda)

Tara Travels

Bus Stop

MARKET CHOWK

ARABIAN SEA

Arambol Beach

Om Ganesh Stores

Police Station

Our Lady Vailankani Church & School

Bus Stop

Bakery

Adarsh Store

Mandrem, Aswem & Morjim

0   Metres   500

stalls at the beach end of the village. Lots of signs around the village advertise **motorcycle and scooter rental**; rates are standard. The **post office**, next to the church, has a poste restante box; there are also several places offering **Internet access** in the village, the cheapest of them just past the junction on the main road. Reliable **money changers** include Harsha Travels, on the east side of the main road, and Tara Travels, directly opposite, where you can also reconfirm and book air tickets.

Accommodation

Standards of tourist accommodation in Arambol lag well behind the rest of the state, although there are signs of improvement, with a crop of new, family guesthouses beginning to appear on the south side of the village in **Modlo** and **Girkar Waddos**. This area is much more peaceful, but you have to walk down the beach to get there – not such a great idea at night if you're female. The warren of narrow sandy lanes behind the north end of the beach, known as **Khalcha Waddo**, is busier, but – with the exception of those listed below – its guesthouses are uniformly cramped and grotty.

Ave Maria House #22, Modlo Waddo ☎0832/229 7674, ⓔavemaria_goa@hotmail.com. Arambol's largest guesthouse offers good-value rooms, with or without bathrooms, and a sociable rooftop restaurant in a three-storey modern building. Tricky to find: turn left onto a *kutchha* track where the main road through the south side of the village makes a sharp right bend. ❷

Famafa Khalcha Waddo ☎0832/229 2516, ⓦwww.travelingoa.com/famafa. Large, ugly concrete place just off Glastonbury Street; popular with Israelis, and correspondingly rowdy, but it usually has vacancies and is very close to the beach. ❸

God's Gift House #411, Girkar Waddo ☎0832/222 9239. Variously priced, sizeable rooms, all tiled and with comfortable verandas; some also have living rooms and kitchens. Rates are good and the proprietors friendly. ❷

Ivon's Girkar Waddo ☎0832/229 2672 or 9822/127398. The pick of the bunch, with immaculately clean, tiled rooms, all with attached bathroom and fronted by good-sized tiled balconies

opening onto a well-groomed family compound or the dunes. ❸

Om Ganesh in the cove between the village and Lakeside beach; book at the Om Ganesh stores, near *Double Dutch Café* on the main drag ☎0832/229 7657 or 0832/229 7619. Nicest of the "cottages" stacked up the cliffside just south of Lakeside beach. The sea views from their verandas are superb, but some may find the Israeli chillum scene in the nearby cafés a bit of a disincentive. Rates vary wildly according to demand, and advance booking (with a deposit) is all but essential by mid-season. ❹

Priya Modlo Waddo ☎0832/229 2661, ⓔzdmello@hotmail.com. Welcoming ten-roomed guesthouse, which is the best fallback if nearby *Ave Maria* is full. ❷

Villa Pedro Girkar Waddo ☎0832/229 7689. Small family guesthouse just beyond *God's Gift*, amid the toddy grove just in from the beach – thus well placed if you want to be near the sea, but a fair way away from the village. The rooms are clean and pleasant, and some have sea views. Good value. ❷

Eating

Thanks to its annually replenished pool of expatriate gastronomic talent, Arambol harbours a handful of unexpectedly good **restaurants** – not that you'd ever guess from their generally lacklustre exteriors. The village's discerning hippy contingent cares more about flavours than fancy decor, and prices reflect the fact that most of them eke out savings to stay here all winter. If you're on a really rock-bottom budget, stick to the "rice-plate" shacks at the bottom of the village. Tasty thalis at *Sheila's* and *Siddi* come with *puris*, and both have a good travellers' breakfast menu of pancakes, eggs and curd. *Dominic's*, also at the bottom of the village (near where the road makes a ninety-degree bend), is renowned for its fruit juices and milkshakes, while *Sai Deep*, a little further up the road, does generous fruit salads with yoghurt.

Chill Pod (aka "Om Narayan") on the beach, midway down the shacks. Great for inexpensive north-Indian vegetarian: go for the *malai kofta*, cheese *nan* and veg *makhanwala*.

Double Dutch Main Street, halfway down on the right (look for the yellow signboard). Spread under a palm canopy in the thick of the village, this laid-back café is the hub of alternative Arambol. Renowned for its melt-in-the-mouth apple pie (possibly the best in the world), it also does a tempting range of home-baked buttery biscuits, cakes (Buddha's Dream's a winner), healthy salads and sumptuous main meals (from Rs120), including fresh buffalo steaks and the perennially popular "mixed stuff" (stuffed mushrooms and capsicums with sesame pesto).

Fellini's Glastonbury Street. Italian-run restaurant serving delicious wood-fired pizzas (Rs80–140),

and authentic pasta or gnocchi with a choice of over twenty sauces. It gets horrendously busy in season, so be here early if you want snappy service.

Relax Inn Arambol beach. Top-quality seafood straight off the boats and unbelievably authentic pasta (you get even more of the expat Italians in here than at *Fellini's*). Try the vongole clam sauce. Inexpensive, but expect a wait as they cook to order.

Silver Sand opposite Arambol chapel. At the south side of the village, this is another deceptively ordinary streetside café specializing in fresh seafood (including Chapora calamari), home-made pasta, ratatouille for vegans and popular chocolate cake, baked daily. The espresso's top-notch, too, and there can be queues at breakfast for the home-made pineapple jam.

Terekol

North of Arambol, the sinuous coast road climbs to the top of a rocky, undulating plateau, then winds down through a swathe of thick woodland to join the River Arondem (or Terekol), which it then follows for 4km through a landscape of vivid paddy fields, coconut plantations and temple towers protruding from scruffy red-brick villages. The tiny enclave of **TEREKOL**, the northernmost tip of Goa, is reached via a clapped-out car ferry (every 30min; 5min) from the hamlet of Querim, 42km from Panjim. If the tide is out and the water levels are too low for the ferry to run, you can either backtrack 5km, where there's another one, or arrange for the boatman at the jetty to run you across (for a negotiable fee).

Set against the backdrop of a filthy iron-ore complex, the old **fort** that dominates the estuary from the north – an ochre-painted building with turreted ramparts that wouldn't look out of place in coastal Portugal – was built by the Marathas at the start of the eighteenth century, but taken soon after by the Portuguese. These days, it serves as a low-key luxury heritage **hotel**, *The Fort Tiracol* (T 0832/226 8258; ●), created by the owners of the swish *Nilaya Hermitage* at Arpora (see p.198). The seven rooms are all decorated in traditional ochre and white, with black-oxide floors, black-tiled drench showers and rustic wood and wrought-iron furniture; tariffs start at $180 per night. Non-residents are welcome to visit the restaurant and stylish lounge bar, where you can eat chargrilled tiger prawns while enjoying what must rank among the finest seascapes in southern India.

South Goa

Beyond the unattractive port city of Vasco da Gama and its nearby airport, Goa's southern reaches are fringed by some of the region's finest **beaches**, backed by a lush band of coconut plantations, and green hills scattered with attractive villages. An ideal first base if you've just arrived in the region is **Benaulim**, 6km west of Goa's second city, **Margao**. The most traveller-friendly resort in the area, Benaulim stands slap in the middle of a spectacular 25-kilometre stretch of pure white sand. Although increasingly carved up by Mumbai time-share companies, low-cost accommodation here is plentiful and of a consistently high standard. Nearby Colva, by contrast, has degenerated over the past decade into an insalubrious charter resort. Frequented by huge numbers of day-trippers, and boasting few discernible charms, it's best avoided.

With the gradual spread of package tourism down the coast, **Palolem**, a couple of hours' south of Margao down the main highway, has emerged as the budget travellers' preferred resort, despite its relative inaccessibility. Set against a backdrop of forest-cloaked hills, its beach is spectacular and development restrained, although the numbers of visitors can feel overwhelming in high season.

Margao (Madgaon) and around

The capital of prosperous Salcete *taluka*, **MARGAO** – referred to in railway timetables and on some maps by its official government title, **Madgaon** – is Goa's second city. Surrounded by fertile farmland, the town has always been an important agricultural market, and was once a major religious centre, with dozens of wealthy temples and *dharamshalas* – however, most of these were destroyed when the Portuguese absorbed the area into their Novas Conquistas ("New Conquests") during the seventeenth century. Today, Catholic churches still outnumber Hindu shrines, but Margao has retained a cosmopolitan feel due to a huge influx of migrant labour from neighbouring Karnataka and Maharashtra.

If you're arriving in Goa on the Konkan Railway from Mumbai or South India, you'll almost certainly have to pause in Margao to pick up onward transport by road. The other reason to come here is to shop at the town's **market**. Stretching from the south edge of the main square to within a stone's throw of the old railway station, the bazaar centres on a labyrinthine covered area where you'll find everything from betel leaves and sacks of lime paste to baby clothes and cheap Taiwanese toys. When the syrupy air gets too stifling, explore the

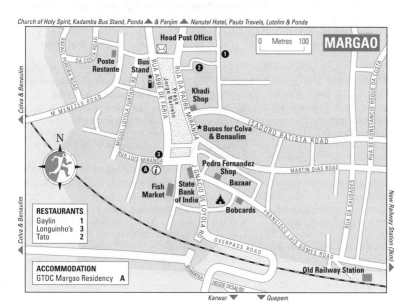

Church of Holy Spirit, Kadamba Bus Stand, Ponda ▲ & Panjim ▲ Nanutel Hotel, Paulo Travels, Lutolim & Ponda

streets around the market, among which is one given over to cloth merchants and tailors. Also worth checking is the excellent little government-run **Khadi Gramodyog** shop, on the main square (near the *Kamat*), which sells quality hand-spun cottons and raw silk by the metre, as well as ready-made traditional Indian garments.

A rickshaw ride north, the **Church of the Holy Spirit** is the main landmark in Margoa's dishevelled colonial enclave. Built by the Portuguese in 1675, it ranks among the finest examples of late-Baroque architecture in Goa, its interior dominated by a huge gilt reredos dedicated to the Virgin. Just northeast of it, overlooking the main Ponda road, stands one of the state's grandest eighteenth-century *palacios*, **Sat Banzam Ghor** ("Seven Gables house"). Only three of its original seven high-pitched roof gables remain, but the mansion is still an impressive sight, its facade decorated with fancy scroll work and huge oyster-shell windows.

For more of Goa's wonderful vernacular colonial architecture, you'll have to head **inland from Margao**, where villages such as **Lutolim**, **Racaim** and **Rachol** are littered with decaying old Portuguese houses, most of them empty – the region's traditional inheritance laws ensure that old family homes tend to be owned by literally dozens of descendants, none of whom are willing or can afford to maintain them.

Another reason to head into Margao is to catch a movie in South Goa's principal **cinema**, the Osia Multiplex (℡0832/270 1717), out in the north of town near the Kadamba bus stand. It screens Hollywood as well as Bollywood releases; tickets cost Rs50–70.

Practicalities

Margao's new **railway station** lies 3km south of the centre, its reservation office (Mon–Sat 8am–4.30pm, Sun 8am–2pm; ℡0832/271 2940) divided between the ground and first floor. Tickets for trains to Mumbai are in short supply, so make your reservation as far in advance as possible. If you're catching the twice-weekly train to Hospet (en route to Hampi) get here early to avoid long queues. Several of the principal trains that stop in Margao do so at unsociable times of night, but there's a 24-hour information counter (℡0832/271 2790), and a round-the-clock prepaid auto-rickshaw and taxi stand outside the exit.

Local private buses to Colva and Benaulim leave from in front of the *Kamat Hotel*, on the east side of Margao's main square. Arriving on long-distance government services you can get off either here or at the main **Kadamba bus stand**, 3km further north, on the outskirts of town. The latter is the departure point for interstate services to Mangalore, via Chaudi and Gokarn, and for services to Panjim and north Goa. Paulo Travel's deluxe coach to and from Hampi works from a lot next to the *Nanutel Hotel*, 1km or so south of the Kadamba bus stand on Padre Miranda Road.

GTDC's **information office** (Mon–Fri 9.30am–5.30pm; ℡0832/222 5528), which sells tourist maps and keeps useful lists of current train and bus times, is inside the lobby of the *GTDC Margao Residency*, on the southwest corner of the main square. Exchange facilities are available at the State Bank of India off the west side of the square, which also has a 24-hour **ATM**; the Bobcard office in the market sub-branch of the Bank of Baroda, on Francisco Luis Gomes Road, does Visa encashments. The GPO is at the top of the central municipal gardens, although its poste restante is in a different building, 200m west on the Rua Diogo da Costa. For the central **police** station, on the west side of the main square near the GPO, ℡0832/270 5095.

For visitors in need of medical attention, Margao's two main **hospitals** are: the Hospicio (☎0832/270 5664 or 270 5754), Rua De Miranda and the Apollo Victor Hospital, in the suburb of Malbhat (☎0832/272 8888 or 272 6272).

With Colva and Benaulim a mere twenty-minute bus ride away, it's hard to think of a reason why anyone should choose to **stay** in Margao. If you do get stuck here, however, the safest choice is the *GTDC Margao Residency* (☎0832/271 5528; ❹), a comfortable mid-range place that recently had a major face-lift.

In terms of **eating**, most visitors make a beeline for *Longuinho's* on Rua Luis Miranda. The long-established hangout of Margao's English-speaking middle classes, it's a relaxing, old-fashioned café serving a reasonable selection of moderately priced meat, fish and veg mains, freshly baked savoury snacks (including Portuguese prawn *rissois* and veg puffs), cakes and drinks. The food isn't up to much these days, and the old Goan atmosphere has been marred by the arrival of satellite TV, but it's a pleasant enough place in which to catch your breath over a beer. South Indian snacks are available all over town, but the best place is *Tato*, tucked away up an alley off the east side of the Municipal Gardens square; the breakfast samosas are especially good, and they do masala *dosas* from midday on. *Gaylin*, behind Grace Church, serves a good selection of Cantonese and Szechuan dishes (mostly steeped in hot red Goan chilli paste) in a smart air-conditioned dining room.

Chandor

Thirteen kilometres east of Margao across Salcete district's fertile rice fields lies sleepy **CHANDOR** village, a scattering of tumbledown villas and farmhouses ranged along shady tree-lined lanes. The main reason to venture out here is the splendid **Perreira-Braganza/Menezes-Braganza house** (daily except holidays, no set hours; recommended donation Rs100), regarded as the grandest of Goa's colonial mansions. Dominating the dusty village square, the house, built in the 1500s by the wealthy Braganza family for their two sons, has a huge double-storey facade, with 28 windows flanking its entrance. Braganza de Perreira, the great-grandfather of the present owner, was the last knight of the king of Portugal; more recently, Menezes Braganza (1879–1938), a journalist and freedom fighter, was one of the few Goan aristocrats actively to oppose Portuguese rule. Forced to flee Chandor in 1950, the family returned in 1962 to find their house, amazingly, untouched. The airy tiled interiors of both wings contain a veritable feast of **antiques**.

The house is divided into two separate wings, owned by different branches of the old family. Both are open to the public, though there are no set hours as such – just turn up between 10am and noon or 3 to 5pm, go through the main entrance, up the stairs and knock at either of the doors. You'll be expected to leave a donation of at least Rs100. Furniture enthusiasts, and lovers of rare Chinese porcelain, in particular, will find plenty to drool over in the Menezes-Braganza wing (to the right as you face the building), which has preserved the famous journalist's library. Next door in the Perreria-Braganza portion, an ornate oratory enshrines St Francis Xavier's diamond-encrusted toenail, recently retrieved from a local bank vault. The house's most famous feature, however, is its ostentatiously grand ballroom, or **Great Salon**, where a pair of matching high-backed chairs, presented to the Perreira-Braganzas by King Dom Luís of Portugal, occupy pride of place.

Colva

A hot-season retreat for Margao's moneyed middle classes since long before Independence, **COLVA** is the oldest and largest – but least appealing – of south

Cobra warning

You'll rarely see a Benaulim villager crossing a rice field at night. This is because paddy is prime territory for snakes, especially **cobras**. If you do intend to cut across the fields after dark, take along a strong flashlight, make plenty of noise and hit the ground ahead of you with a stick to warn any lurking serpents of your approach.

Goa's resorts. Its outlying *waddos*, or wards, are pleasant enough, dotted with colonial-style villas and ramshackle fishing huts, but the beachfront is dismal: a lacklustre collection of concrete hotels, souvenir stalls and fly-blown snack bars strewn around a bleak central roundabout. The atmosphere is not improved by heaps of rubbish dumped in a rank-smelling ditch that runs behind the beach, nor by the stench of drying fish wafting from the nearby village. Benaulim, only a five-minute drive further south, has a far better choice of accommodation and range of facilities, and is altogether more salubrious.

Benaulim

According to Hindu mythology, Goa was created when the sage Shri Parasurama, Vishnu's sixth incarnation, fired an arrow into the sea from the top of the Western Ghats and ordered the waters to recede. The spot where the shaft fell to earth, known in Sanskrit as Banali ("place where the arrow landed") and later corrupted by the Portuguese to **BENAULIM**, lies in the dead centre of Colva Beach, 7km west of Margao. Twenty years ago, this atmospheric fishing and rice-farming village, scattered around the coconut groves and paddy fields between the main Colva–Mobor road and the dunes, had barely made it onto the backpackers' map. Since the completion of the nearby Konkan railway, however, big-spending middle-class Indians have started to holiday here, in the luxury resorts and time-share apartment complexes that have mushroomed in the rice fields. As a result, the village has lost some of its famously *sossegarde* feel. Even so, if you time your visit well (avoiding Diwali and the Christmas peak season), Benaulim is still hard to beat as a place to unwind. Its tourist scene is neither particularly "alternative" nor alcohol-driven. The seafood is superb, accommodation and motorbikes cheaper than anywhere else in the state, and the beach breathtaking, particularly around sunset, when its brilliant white sand and churning surf reflect the changing colours to magical effect. Shelving away almost to Cabo da Rama on the horizon, the beach is also lined with Goa's largest, and most colourfully decorated, fleet of wooden outriggers, and these provide welcome shade during the heat of the day.

Practicalities

Buses from Margao and Colva roll through Benaulim every fifteen minutes or so, dropping passengers at the Maria Hall crossroads. Ranged around this busy junction are two well-stocked general stores, a couple of café-bars, a bank, pharmacy, laundry and the taxi and auto-rickshaw rank, from where you can pick up **transport** to the beach, 1.5km west.

Signs offering **motorbikes** for rent are dotted along the lane leading to the sea: rates are standard, descending in proportion to the length of time you keep the vehicle. Worth bearing in mind if you're planning to continue further south is that motorbikes are much cheaper to rent (and generally in better condition) here than Palolem, where there's a relative shortage of vehicles. **Petrol** is sold by the litre from a table at the roadside, two minutes' walk south down the

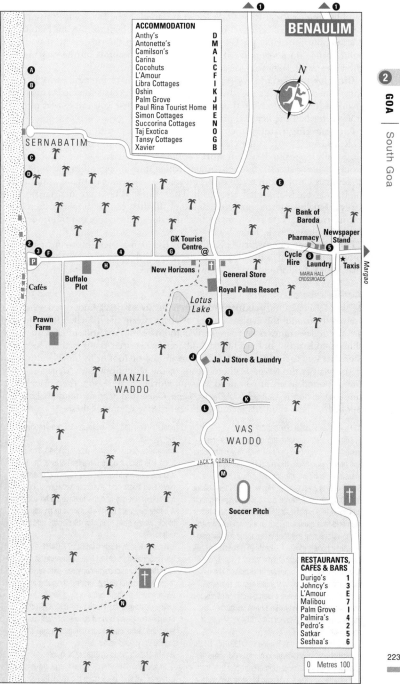

BENAULIM

N

ACCOMMODATION

Anthy's	D
Antonette's	M
Camilson's	A
Carina	L
Cochuts	C
L'Amour	F
Libra Cottages	I
Oshin	K
Palm Grove	J
Paul Rina Tourist Home	H
Simon Cottages	E
Succorina Cottages	N
Taj Exotica	O
Tansy Cottages	G
Xavier	B

SERNABATIM

Bank of Baroda

Newspaper Stand

Pharmacy

GK Tourist Centre @

Cycle Hire

Laundry

Taxis

Margao

MARIA HALL CROSSROADS

New Horizons

General Store

Royal Palms Resort

Cafés

Buffalo Plot

Lotus Lake

Prawn Farm

Ja Ju Store & Laundry

MANZIL WADDO

VAS WADDO

JACK'S CORNER

Soccer Pitch

RESTAURANTS, CAFÉS & BARS

Durigo's	1
Johncy's	3
L'Amour	E
Malibou	7
Palm Grove	I
Palmira's	4
Pedro's	2
Satkar	5
Seshaa's	6

0   Metres   100

O, Varca Cavelossim, Mobor & Palolem

road leading to *Royal Palm Beach Resort*, but tends to be laced with solvent and smokes badly. Local boys will try to get you to pay them to fill your bike up in Margao, but invariably pocket half of the money in the process, so if you've a valid licence do it yourself (Margao's main petrol pump is on the west side of the Praça Jorge Barreto – see map on p.223).

Bicycles cost around Rs50 per day to rent. If you're intending to stay for a long time, it might be worth buying one. Several cycle shops in Margao sell standard Indian-style Hero models for Rs2000–25,000; you can expect to resell it again for half the original price.

For **changing money**, the most convenient places offering the best rates are G.K. Tourist Centre, at the crossroads in the village centre, and New Horizons, diagonally opposite. It's often worth comparing the two. Down at the beach-front, *L'Amour* also has a forex counter which in principle offers the same rates as Thomas Cook. With a Visa card, you can also make encashments at the Bank of Baroda on Maria Hall crossroads. The nearest **ATMs** are in Margao and Colva. Finally, international and domestic **flights** can be booked, altered or reconfirmed at New Horizons, which also does deluxe bus and train ticketing for cities elsewhere in India.

For **Internet access**, try G.K. Tourism (Rs40/hr). New Horizons has been promising to install a broadband connection for the past couple of seasons, and may well have done so by the time you read this.

Accommodation

Most of Benaulim's **accommodation** consists of small budget guesthouses, scattered around the lanes 1km or so back from the beach. The majority are featureless annexes of spartan tiled rooms with fans and, usually, attached shower-toilets; the only significant difference between them is their location. The best way to find a vacancy is to hunt around on foot or by bicycle, although if you wait at the Maria Hall crossroads or the beachfront with luggage, someone is bound to ask if you need a room. During peak season, the village's few mid-range hotels (namely *L'Amour*, *Palm Grove* and *Carina*) tend to be fully booked, so reserve in advance if you want to stay in one of these.

Anthy's Sernabatim ☏ 0832/277 1680, ⓔ anthysguesthouse@rediffmail.com. Well-maintained rooms right on the sea, with tiny bathrooms and breezy verandas; there's a Keralan ayurvedic massage centre on site too. ❸

Antonette's Jack Corner, House #1695 Vas Waddo ☏ 0832/277 0358. Not a particularly inspiring location (next to a crossroads where all the local fishermen and lads hang out), but in a peaceful corner of the village and the rooms are large for the price, plus they have fridges – a rarity in this bracket. ❷

Camilson's Sernabatim ☏ 0832/277 1582, ⓦ www.camilsons.com. Well-maintained rooms, with private terraces, in a small resort set very close to the beach amid a lush garden, well away from the village. If they don't have vacancies, try the less welcoming *Xavier's* (☏ 0832/227 1489) next door. Both ❺–❻

Carina Tamdi-Mati, Vas Waddo ☏ 0832/277 0413, ⓔ carinabeachresort@yahoo.com. Good-value, if somewhat lackadaisical, upmarket hotel in a tranquil location on the south side of Benaulim, with a pool, garden and bar-restaurant. Some rooms have a/c. ❺–❻

Cocohuts Sernabatim ☏ 9822/101398. The only bona fide budget option this far north of the village, a stone's throw from the beach. Its eight leaf huts have tiled floors and attached bathrooms, but heat up in the day and the beds are a bit ropey. A better prospect is the six rooms in an adjacent block, which have high clay-tiled roofs and partition toilets. ❸

L'Amour Beach Road ☏ 0832/277 0404, ⓕ 277 0578. Benaulim's oldest hotel comprises a comfortable thirty-room cottage complex, with terrace restaurant, travel agent, money-changing and some a/c rooms. No single occupancy. ❺–❻

Libra Cottages Vas Waddo ☏ 0832/277 0598. Spartan but clean budget rooms, all with fans, attached bathrooms, sound plumbing and Western toilets. Very good value. ❷

Oshin Mazil Waddo ☏ 0832/277 0069, ⓔ inaciooshin@rediffmail.com. Large, triple-storey complex set well back from the road. Its rooms are spacious and clean, with en-suite bathrooms and balconies; those on the top floor afford views over the tree tops. A notch above most places in this area, and very good value, but quite a walk from the beach. ❹

Palm Grove Tamdi-Mati, 149 Vas Waddo ☎0832/277 0059, ⊛www.palmgrovegoa.com. Secluded hotel surrounded by beautiful gardens, offering two classes of room (Rs600–800), some of them a/c; plus there's one of Benaulim's better restaurants on site. A bike-ride back from the beachfront, but by far the most pleasant place in its class, and the management is very helpful. ❺

Paul Rina Tourist Home Beach Rd ☎0832/277 0595. Nice big rooms, secluded balconies and attached shower-toilets in a modern house next to the beach road. A little better than the standard budget places, so good value. If full, try the cheaper *Caroline Guest House* (☎0832/277 0590) next door. Both ❷

Simon Cottages Sernabatim Ambeaxir ☎0832/277 1839. Currently among the best

budget deals in Benaulim: huge rooms on three storeys, all with shower-toilets and verandas, opening onto a sandy courtyard in a quiet spot at the unspoilt north side of the village. ❷

Succorina Cottages 1711/A Vas Waddo ☎0832/277 0365. Immaculate rooms in a newish, pink-coloured house, 1km south of the crossroads in the fishing village, offering glimpses of the sea across the fields. A perfect place to get away from the tourist scene, and a 5-min walk from the quietest stretch of beach. Telephone bookings accepted. ❷

Tansy Cottages Beach road ☎0832/277 0574. Various sized appartments, from rooms with self-catering kitchenettes (for Rs500) to one- and two-bedroom flats in a three-storey block (Rs700–1000). The balconies could be more private, but you get lots of space indoors for your money, plus fridges and cooking utensils, and guesthouse owner Libby Fernandes is very welcoming. ❹–❻

Eating and drinking

Benaulim's proximity to Margao market, along with the presence of a large Christian fishing community, means its **restaurants** serve some of the most succulent, competitively priced seafood in Goa. The best shacks flank the beachfront area, where *Johncy's* catches most of the passing custom. However, you'll find better food at lower prices at places further along the beach, which seem to change chefs annually; the only way to find out which ones offer the best value for money is to wander past and see who has the most customers. An enduring favourite is *Domnick's,* whose gregarious owner hosts bonfire parties one night per week (traditionally on Tuesdays), featuring a live band; prices here are on the high side. *Pedro's* on the beachfront is marginally better value and also puts on gigs, mostly on Saturday nights.

Durigo's Sernabatim, 2km north of Maria Hall. This is the locals' favourite place to eat, serving traditional Goan seafood of a kind and quality you rarely find in the shacks: try their succulent mussels, lemon fish (*modso*) or barramundi (*chonok*), marinated in spicy, sour *rechead* sauce and pan-fried in millet. They also serve delicious local coconut *feni,* as well as the usual range of bottled beers. Some may find the atmosphere a bit rough and ready, in which case follow the example of the village's middle classes and order a takeout.

L'Amour *L'Amour* hotel. Just about the slickest restaurant in Benaulim, serving an exhaustive multi-cuisine dinner menu (mains Rs100–150), as well as drinks. With background noise limited to chinking china and hushed voices, it's also a relaxing place for breakfast: fresh fruit, muesli, yoghurt and pancakes.

Malibou Vas Waddo, near *Palm Grove*. Cosy little corner café-restaurant that's also a popular late-night drinking spot. Attentive service, fresh seafood,

and a tandoor to bake pomfret, kebabs and spicy chicken. Mains from Rs75.

Palmira's Beach Road. Benaulim's best tourist breakfasts: wonderfully creamy, fresh set curd, copious fruit salads with coconut, real espresso coffee, warm local bread (*bajri*) and smiling service.

Palm Grove *Palm Grove* hotel. Mostly Goan seafood, with some Indian and Continental options, served in a smart new garden pagoda, against a backdrop of illuminated trees. Main courses Rs100–150.

Satkar Maria Hall Crossroads. No-frills locals' *udipi* canteen that's the only place in the village where you can order regular Indian snacks – samosas, masala *dosas,* hot *pakoras* and spicy chickpea stew (*channa*) – at regular Indian prices. And the *pau bhaji* breakfast here is a must.

Seshaa's Maria Hall Crossroads. Gloomy and rather cramped local lads' café, but great for pukka Goan *channa bhaji* and, best of all, deliciously flaky veg or beef patties.

The far south: Canacona

Ceded to the Portuguese by the Raja of Sund in the Treaty of 1791, Goa's **far south** – **Canacona** district – was among the last parts of the territory to be absorbed into the Novas Conquistas, and has retained a distinctly Hindu feel. The area also boasts some of the state's most outstanding scenery. Set against a backdrop of the jungle-covered Sahyadri hills (an extension of the Western Ghat range), a string of pearl-white coves and sweeping beaches scoop its indented coastline, enfolded by laterite headlands and colossal piles of black boulders.

With the exception of the village of **Palolem**, whose near-perfect beach attracts a deluge of travellers during high season, coastal settlements such as **Agonda**, a short way north, remain rooted in a traditional fishing and *toddy*-tapping economy. However, the red gash of the **Konkan Railway** threatens to bring its days as a tranquil rural backwater to an end. For the last few years, it has been possible to reach Canacona by direct "super-fast" express trains from Mumbai, Panjim and Mangalore: the developers' bulldozers and concrete mixers are sure to follow.

The region's main transport artery is the NH-17, which crawls across the Sahyadri and Karmali ghats towards Karnataka via the district headquarters, **Chaudi**; travellers jump off here for Palolem, a few kilometres across the fields, and the small market is a useful source of essentials. Bus services between here and Margao are frequent; off the highway, however, bullock carts and bicycles still outnumber motor vehicles. The only way to do the area justice, therefore, is by motorcycle, although you'll have to rent one further north (Benaulim's your best bet for this) and drive it down here, as few are available in situ.

Agonda

AGONDA, 10km north of Chaudi, can only be reached along the sinuous coast road connecting Cabo da Rama with NH-17 at Chaudi. No signposts mark the turning, and few of the tourists that whizz past en route to Palolem pull off here, but the beach is superb – albeit with a strong undertow that weak swimmers should be very wary of (head for the safer cove at the far southern end of the beach, where the fishing boats are moored).

Facilities for visitors are basic, but adequate, and well spaced apart: Agonda never gets too congested, even in peak season. **Places to stay and eat** are dotted along the road behind the beach, and over the past couple of seasons a handful of small guesthouses and treehouse camps have also opened up at the northern end, beyond the church. If you're only overnighting here en route to or from Palolem, *Dercy's* should probably be your first choice, not least because its terrace restaurant offers the best seafood in the village: groaning fillets of butter-garlic rockfish straight off the boat, served with piles of chips. For a sundowner, the aptly named *Sun Set Bar*, up on a bluff just south of *Dercy's* surveying the bay, is hard to beat.

Accommodation

Dercy's south end of the beach, on the roadside ☎0832/264 7503. Exceptionally clean and comfortable, with tiled floors and good sized bathrooms. Those on the first floor (front side) have a common sea-facing veranda that catches the breezes; you can lie in bed and hear the waves crashing only 100m away. Proprietor Inacio also runs a couple of rows of beach huts on the opposite side of the lane. ❸

Dunhill Beach Resort A short way down the lane beyond *Dercy's* ☎0832/264 7604, Ⓔdunhill -resort@rediffmail.com. All the rooms here are en suite with small verandas opening onto a sandy enclosure, where you can eat locally caught fish (the pan-fried *rawa* mackerel is delicious). The family also offer Internet access for guests. ❸

Jelicia north end of the beach, 100m before *Sea*

View; no phone. A couple of simple budget rooms, with coconut wood rafters and clay tile roofs, plus three huts on the beach. ❶–❷

Maria Paul just north of *Dercy's* towards the church ☎0832/264 7606. Big new pink building on the roadside (look for the disconcerting "Welcome Aboard" life-ring), with six large, cool, marble-floored rooms. A bigger and slightly more anonymous guesthouse than the others in the village, which some might prefer. ❹

Palm Beach Lifestyle Resort Behind *Dercy's* ☎0832/214 7783. Swish, purpose-built chalets that have nice wooden decks and sea views. The most comfortable option in Agonda. ❻

Sami near the church ☎9850/453805. Most appealing of the village's small hut camps, right on the beach. Larger than average huts that are far enough apart, with painted balconies. Bikes for rent. Also worth trying is the nearby *Madhu* (☎0832/264 7116, ✉shekhar1303@sify.com). Both ❷

Sea View at the far north end of the beach ☎0832/264 7548. The quietest option: three lovely mud-and-thatch huts with cow-dung floors (a lot more fragrant than they may sound) and decent beds, run by the friendly Fatima Fernandes. They're ultra basic, but clean and secluded, and slap on the sand. ❷

Palolem

Nowhere else in peninsula India conforms so closely to the archetypal image of a paradise beach as **PALOLEM**, 35km south of Margao. Lined with a swaying curtain of coconut palms, the bay forms a perfect curve of golden sand, arcing north from a giant pile of boulders to the spur of Sahyadri Ghat, which tapers into the sea draped in thick forest. For those foreigners who found their way here before the mid-1990s, however, Palolem is most definitely a paradise lost these days. With the rest of Goa largely carved up by package tourism, this is the first-choice destination of most independent travellers, and the numbers can feel overwhelming in peak season, when literally thousands of people spill across the beach. Behind them, an unbroken line of shacks and Thai-style bamboo- and palm-leaf huts provide food and shelter that grows more sophisticated (and less Goan) with each season – not least because many of the businesses here are now run, if not owned, by expatriates. Thanks to a local law forbidding the construction of permanent buildings close to the beach, development has been restrained, but it's still a far cry from the idyll of only a few years ago.

Palolem in full swing is the kind of place you'll either love at first sight or want to get away from as quickly as possible. If you're in the latter category, try

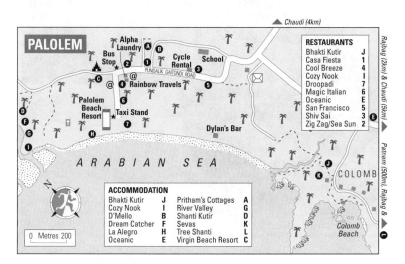

PALOLEM

▲ *Chaudi (4km)*

RESTAURANTS
Bhakti Kutir	J
Casa Fiesta	1
Cool Breeze	4
Cozy Nook	1
Droopadi	7
Magic Italian	6
Oceanic	E
San Francisco	5
Shiv Sai	3
Zig Zag/Sea Sun	2

ACCOMMODATION
Bhakti Kutir	J	Pritham's Cottages	A
Cozy Nook	I	River Valley	G
D'Mello	B	Shanti Kutir	D
Dream Catcher	F	Sevas	K
La Alegro	H	Tree Shanti	L
Oceanic	E	Virgin Beach Resort	C

A R A B I A N S E A

Dylan's Bar

COLOMB

Colomb Beach

Rajbag (2km) & Chaudi (5km)

Patnem (500m), Rajbag &

Alpha Laundry · Bus Stop · Cycle Rental · School · Rainbow Travels · PUNDALIK GAITONDI ROAD · Palolem Beach Resort · Taxi Stand

0 Metres 200

△ Boat on Palolem beach

Water shortages in Palolem

The vast increase in Palolem's visitor numbers has led, in part, to the severe water shortages that have afflicted Canacona district over the past three years. The municipality seems unwilling or unable to do anything about the problem, so the onus falls on tourists to **use as little water as possible** during their stay. One of the most effective ways you can do this is to **avoid water toilets**, which dump a colossal quantity of untreated sewage into often poorly manufactured septic tanks below the ground. Traditional pig loos, still common in the village, are a far cleaner, greener option.

smaller, less-frequented **Patnem** beach, a short walk south, where the shack scene is more subdued and the sand emptier. Further south still, **Rajbag**, around half-an-hour's walk from Palolem, used to be one of Goa's last deserted beaches until a vast, seven-star luxury resort was recently built slap behind it.

Practicalities

Frequent **buses** run between Margao and Karwar (in Karnataka) via Chaudi (every 30min; 2hr), from where you can pick up an **auto–rickshaw** (Rs50) or **taxi** (Rs75) for the 2km journey west to Palolem. Alternatively, get off the bus at the Char Rastay ("Four-Way") crossroads, 1.5km before Chaudi, and walk the remaining kilometre or so to the village. Hourly buses also go all the way to Palolem from Margao; these stop at the end of the lane leading from the main street to the beachfront.

The last bus from Palolem to Chaudi/Margao leaves at around 4.30pm; check with the locals for the precise times, as these change seasonally. **Bicycles** may be rented from a stall halfway along the main street for the princely sum of Rs5 per hour (with discounts for longer periods). The village has a dozen or more STD/ISD **telephones**; avoid the one in the *Beach Resort*, which charges more than double the going rate for international calls, and head for the much cheaper booths 100m down the lane (next to the bus stop). This is also where you'll find several **Internet cafés**; others are dotted around the village, and there are three or four over in Patnem. Rates are pretty standard at around Rs40/hr.

You can **change money** at any number of agents advertising their services along the lanes through Palolem and on the beach road, though it's worth shopping around for the best rates; LKP Forex in the *Palolem Beach Resort* (on the beachfront behind the taxi stand) was the most competitive when we last checked. The nearest **ATM** (for Visa and Mastercard withdrawls) is in Chaudi. For those wishing to stash valuables, Lalita Enterprises, on the main beach road, offer lockers for Rs15 per day.

Accommodation

Local resistance to large-scale development explains why most of the village's **accommodation** consists of simple palm-leaf huts or tree houses. With the exception of the more snazzily set up places listed below, there's very little difference between most of the camps: check in to the first that takes your fancy and investigate the rest of the beach at leisure when you've found your feet. The other option is to look for a room in a family home. The majority, though not all, of these also have limited shared washing facilities, and sometimes pig toilets. The easiest way to find a place is to walk around the palm groves behind the beach with a rucksack; sooner or later someone will approach you. Rates vary depending on the size of the room, levels of comfort and the time of year.

At the time of writing, some of the best set up and situated places were at the far north end of the beach, just behind *Cozy Nook* on the banks of the estuary (see map p.227). At the southern end, there are several good places in the *waddo* of Colomb, which we cover below.

Bhakti Kutir Colomb ☎0832/264 3469 or 264 3472, ⊛www.bhaktikutir.com. Ecofriendly, Indian-village-style "Eco Huts" equipped with Western amenities (including completely biodegradable chemical toilets), set amid mature gardens five minutes' walk from the south end of Palolem beach, on the headland above the fishing village. Beautifully situated, discreet and sensitively designed to blend with the landscape by its German–Goan owners. The new double-storey units (❻), aimed at families, offer more space; and there's a quality ayurvedic healing centre on site. ❻

Cozy Nook north end of the beach, near the island ☎0832/264 3550. One of the most attractive setups in the village, comprising 25 bamboo huts (sharing seven toilets, but with good mattresses, mozzie nets, safe lockers and fans) opening onto the lagoon on one side and the beach on the other – an unbeatable spot, which explains the higher than average tariffs. ❺

D'Mello Pundalik Gaitondi Rd ☎0832/264 3057. A mix of en-suite and shared-bathroom rooms on three storeys, some in a concrete annexe set back from the main road. Well maintained, and most have balconies. ❸

Dream Catcher north end of the beach behind *Cozy Nook* ☎0832/264 4873 or 9822/137446, ⓔlalalandjackie7@yahoo.com. Individually styled huts, with more space, better mattresses, nicer textiles, bigger windows and sturdier foundations than most, in a plum position by the riverside. The welcoming Keralan–Liverpudlian couple who run it have also built shaded yoga *shala* for classes, and there's a "chillout-ambient bar". ❹–❺

La Alegro north side of the beach ☎0832/264 4261. En-suite rooms right on the beach. Very basic and not all that private, but the location's great. The same owner also has five more (cheaper) identikit rooms around the back, as well as a clutch of slightly larger ones on Pundalik Gaitondi Rd. ❸

Oceanic Tembi Waddo ☎0832/264 3059, ⊛www.hotel-oceanic.com. A relative newcomer that, strictly speaking, is in Colomb, a 10-min walk inland from the beach; you can also get here via the back-road to Chaudi. Owned and managed by a resident British couple, its rooms are tastefully fitted-out, with large mosquito nets, blockprinted bedspreads and bedside lamps. There's also a brand new pool on a wooded terrace behind, and a quality restaurant. ❹

Pritham's Cottages down a lane north of Pundalik Gaitondi Rd ☎0832/264 3320. Quiet two-storey block of budget rooms in the centre of the village: they're bigger than average (all with attached bathrooms) and share a common veranda. ❷

River Valley north end of beach behind *Cozy Nook* ☎9822/155502, ⓔsrmh2141@hotmail.com. This small hut camp and its hospitable young owner, Manju, consistently get rave reviews. Named after sacred Indian rivers, the ten bamboo huts (sharing three toilets) are in a nice open compound with beautiful views across the estuary to the hills and forest. Good value for the location, which is a lot more relaxing than comparable sites on the beach. A sound budget choice. ❷

Sevas Colomb ☎0832/231 7408 or 9326/117674, ⓔsevasmicho@yahoo.com. A cheaper, less sophisticated version of *Bhakti Kutir*, but beautifully done all the same, and the site is peaceful. The "ethnic" cabañas have traditional rice-straw roofs, mud and dung floors, hygienic squat-style loos and bucket baths. Also on offer are massages and yoga classes, and there's a pleasant restaurant serving very good thalis for only Rs50. ❹

Shanti Kutir north end of beach behind *River Valley* and *Dream Catcher* ☎9422/450392 or 9822/183631, ⓔshantikutirgoa@yahoo.co.in. Keralan-run hut camp that's pleasantly secluded and well sited on the river. Thirty comfortable huts (some en-suite) on stilts. Rates vary according to proximity to the water. ❷–❸

Tree Shanti Colomb ☎0832/264 4460, ⓔsaritagita7@rediffmail.com. Seven basic rooms and three huts in a lovely spot under dense tree cover, ten minutes' walk south of Palolem in Colomb. Run by the feisty Komarpant sisters, this is a fun and lively place to stay with a full-on family atmosphere. ❷

Virgin Beach Resort Palolem village ☎0832/264 3451. Swanky new tiled rooms, in modern three-storey block near the lane. Not exactly the kind of architecture that enhances the village's natural feel, but it's an out-of-the-way spot and some may consider the comfort and security a good trade-off. ❷

Eating and drinking

Palolem's **restaurants** and **bars** reflect the cosmopolitan make-up of its visitors. Each year, a fresh batch of innovative, ever more stylish places open, most of them managed by expats – and both standards, and prices, have increased greatly as a consequence. For those on tight budgets, there are a couple of cheap and cheerful **bhaji stalls** outside the landmark *Palolem Beach Resort*, and a pair of local cafés along the road running parallel with the beach – the Hindu *Shiv Sai* and Christian *San Francisco* – which serve filling breakfasts of *pau bhaji*, fluffy bread rolls, omelettes and chai for next to nothing, and equally inexpensive fish-currry-rice meals and samosas from lunchtime. Again, you'll find several good options in the *waddo* of Colomb, just south of Palolem.

Bhakti Kutir Colomb. Laid-back terrace café-restaurant with rustic wooden tables and an Indo–European fusion menu: sunny tomato and mozzarella salad (with fresh basil), fish from the bay and north Indian vegetarian dishes, all made with local and organically produced ingredients.

Casa Fiesta Pundalik Gaitondi Rd. Funky expat-run place on the main drag, offering an eclectic menu of world cuisine: hummus, Greek salad, Mexican specialities and fish *pollichatu*; mains (mostly under Rs175) come with delicious roast potatoes.

Cool Breeze Beach Rd. This is one of the classiest restaurants in the village. The steaks, tandoori chicken and seafood, in particular, have set new standards for Palolem, and the prices are reasonable. Come early, or you could face a long wait for a table – and leave room for the banoffi pie dessert. Most mains around Rs150–200.

Cozy Nook far north end of the beach. Wholesome Goan-style cooking served on a small terrace that occupies a prime position opposite the island at the end of the bay. The filling four-course set dinners (7–9pm; Rs150) are deservedly popular, offering imaginative and carefully prepared dishes such as pan-fried fish, aubergine with shrimps and fresh beans. They also put a tasty veg equivalent (Rs100), as well as a full seafood and north Indian curry, and there's a popular, hygienic salad bar (eat all you like for Rs100).

Droopadi on the beachfront. This place enjoys both a top location and Palolem's best Indian chef, who specializes in rich, creamy Mughlai dishes and tandoori fish. Go for the superb *murg makhini* or one of the *paneer* options. With most main courses around Rs125, prices are low considering the quality of the cooking.

Magic Italian Beach Rd. South Goa's number one Italian restaurant, on the busy approach to the seafront, serving home-made ravioli and tagliatelle, along with scrumptious wood-fired pizzas (Rs130–175).

Oceanic Tembi Waddo, Colomb. Chilled terrace restaurant, set well back from the beach but worth the walk for the better-than-average food and background music (the owner is an ex-Womad sound man). North and South Indian dishes are the chef's forte (especially *dum aloo* Kashmiri and butter chicken), but there are also great red and green Thai curries, tempting desserts, including lemon-and-ginger cheesecake and banoffi pie, and coffee liqueur. Check the specials board for dishes of the day. Occasional live music.

Zig Zag/Sea Sun Pundalik Gaitondi Rd. A Keralan–British co-project, particularly strong on South Indian food (a rarity in Palolem), in addition to veg, meat and fish dishes prepared with light, mild sauces and fresh herbs. Mains under Rs150. Some confusion surrounds the name, so look for both.

South of Palolem: Colomb, Patnem and Rajbag

Once across the creek and boulder-covered spur bounding the south end of Palolem beach, you arrive at **COLOMB**, a largely Hindu fishing village scattered around a series of rocky coves. Dozens of long-stay rooms, leaf huts and houses are tucked away under the palm groves and on the picturesque headland running seawards from the *Boom Shankar Bar*, at the bottom of the bay. This is the best place in the village to start an accommodation hunt – the lads will know of any vacant places; but be warned that most of the rooms here are very basic indeed and may not have running water, let alone toilets. Alternatively, there are several good guesthouses reviewed along with Palolem's accommodation (opposite).

A string of small hut camps and shacks line the next beach south, **PATNEM**, but the scene is altogether more subdued here than in Palolem. The beach, curving for roughly a kilometre to a steep bluff, is broad, with little shade, and shelves quite steeply at certain phases of the tide, though the undertow rarely gets dangerously strong. There are plenty of good **accom-modation** options, ranging from no-frills leaf huts with shared toilets to fully en-suite rooms with verandas. At the top of the range, *Home*, in the centre of the beach (☎0832/264 3916, ✉homeispatnem@yahoo.com; ❸), is a cut above your average beachfront guesthouse, run by a Swiss–English couple who've fitted out an annexe of en-suite rooms with attractive textiles, lampshades and other cosy little touches to justify higher than usual tariffs. They also run Patnem's best café-restaurant, serving *mezes*, fresh salads, Italian espresso and wonderful desserts (such as banoffi pie, warm apple tart with fresh cream, chocolate-and-walnut cake). A notch cheaper, but another place that's made an untypically Goan effort with interior design, is *Mountain Palms* (no phone; ❷), whose bargain huts are kitted out with big four-posters, pink mosquito nets, silky drapes and floral curtains. Among the string of camps behind the beach shacks, *Namaste* (☎9850/925821; ❷) is another depend-able, fun budget option, run by the aimiable Satay, most of whose clientele comes back season after season. He offers two categories of shack, ranging from Rs150–350 depending on size and time of year. *Magic View*, tucked at the far north end of the beach, serves the best cappuccinos for miles, choco-late pastries for breakfast, good salads and pastas, though its pizzas (evenings only) get mixed reviews. With main courses from Rs100–140, prices are a bit above average for the area, but the view over the beach is as lovely as its name suggests.

Most of the **buses** between Palolem and Margao pass through Patnem (roughly 20min later), stopping at regular intervals along the lane running parallel with the beach.

At low tide, you can walk around the bottom of the steep-sided headland dividing Patnem from neighbouring **RAJBAG**, another kilomtre-long sweep of white sand. Sadly, its remote feel has been entirely submerged by the massive five-star *Goa Grand Intercontinental* (⊛www.intercontinental.com; ❾), recently erected on the land behind it – much to the annoyance of the locals, who campaigned for four years to stop the project.

It's possible to press on even further **south from Rajbag**, by crossing the Talpona River via a hand-paddled ferry, which usually has to be summoned from the far bank (fix a return price in advance and only pay once you've completed both legs of the trip, as the boatmen are rumoured to have been holding wealthy tourists from the *Goa Grand* to ransom by refusing to paddle them back unless they hand over huge "tips"). Once across, a short walk brings you to **Talpona Beach**, backed by low dunes and a line of straggly palms. From there, assuming you haven't already succumbed to sunstroke and dehydration, you can cross the headland at the end of the beach to reach **Galjibag**, a totally wild white-sand bay that's a protected nesting site for Olive Ridley marine **turtles**. A strong undertow means swimming isn't safe here.

Cotigao Wildlife Sanctuary

The **Cotigao Wildlife Sanctuary**, 12km southeast of Palolem, was established in 1969 to protect a remote and vulnerable area of forest lining the Goa–Karna-taka border. Encompassing 86 square kilometres of mixed deciduous woodland, the reserve is certain to inspire tree lovers, but less likely to yield many wildlife sightings: its tigers and leopards were hunted out long ago, while the gazelles, sloth bears, porcupines, panthers and hyenas that allegedly lurk in the woods rarely appear. You do, however, stand a good chance of spotting at least two species of monkey, a couple of wild boar and the odd gaur (the primeval-looking

Indian bison), as well as plenty of exotic birdlife, including hornbills. Best visited between October and March, Cotigao is a peaceful and scenic park that makes a pleasant day-trip from Palolem. Any of the buses running south on the NH-14 to Karwar via Chaudi will drop you within 2km of the gates. However, to explore the inner reaches of the sanctuary, you really need your own transport. The wardens at the reserve's small **Interpretative Centre** at the main gate, where you have to pay your entry fees (Rs15, plus Rs75 for a car, Rs20 for motorbike, Rs40 for camera permit) will show you how to get to a 25-metre-high tree-top watchtower, overlooking a **waterhole** that attracts a handful of animals around dawn and dusk. You can also **stay** in a rather unprepossessing little room (❷) in the compound behind the main reserve gates; it's rented out on a first-come first-served basis. Food and drink may be available by prior arrangement, and there's a **shop** at the nearest village, 2km inside the park.

More inspiring accommodation is to be found at a secluded riverside location on the edge of Cotigao. Hidden away in a working spice plantation, *Pepper Valley* (☏0832/264 2370; ❸) comprises a row of simple huts on the riverbank, shaded by a canopy of areca palms, with cashew bushes and yam plants growing around. Facilities are basic for the money, but this is lovely spot to chill out for an evening. To find it, turn left at the Cotigao Interpretative Centre then follow the road for 500m until you see a signboard indicating a motorable track off to the right.

Travel details

Trains

Margao to: Chaudi (3 daily; 50min); Colem (3 weekly; 55min); Delhi (1–2 daily; 26–35hr); Ernakulam/Kochi (4 weekly; 12–15hr 40min); Gokarna (2 daily; 1hr 50min); Hospet (3 weekly; 8hr); Hubli (3 weekly; 5hr 30min); Mangalore/Kanakadi (5 daily; 4–6hr); Mumbai (4–5 daily; 12hr); Pune (1 weekly; 13hr 40min); Thiruvananthapuram (1–2 daily; 16hr); Udupi (4 daily; 3hr 40min).

Buses

Benaulim to: Cavelossim (hourly; 20min); Colva (every 30min; 20min); Margao (every 30min; 15min); Mobor (hourly; 25min).
Chaudi to: Gokarna (2 daily; 3hr); Karwar (every 30min; 1hr); Margao (every 30min; 1hr 40min); Palolem (2 daily; 15min); Panjim (hourly; 2hr 15min).
Mapusa to: Anjuna (hourly; 30min); Arambol (12 daily; 1hr 45min); Baga (hourly; 30min); Calangute (hourly; 45min); Chapora (every 30min; 30–40min); Mumbai (6 daily; 13–17hr); Panjim (every 15min; 25min); Vagator (every 30min; 25–35min).
Margao to: Agonda (4 daily; 2hr); Benaulim (every 30min; 15min); Cavelossim (8 daily; 30min);

Chandor (hourly; 45min); Chaudi (every 30min; 1hr 40min); Colva (every 15min; 20–30min); Gokarna (2 daily; 4hr 30min); Hampi (1 nightly; 10hr); Karwar (every 30min; 2hr); Mangalore (5 daily; 7hr); Mapusa (10 daily; 2hr 30min); Mobor (8 daily; 35min); Mumbai (2 daily; 16–18hr); Panjim (every 30min; 50min); Pune (1 daily; 12hr).
Panjim to: Arambol (12 daily; 1hr 45min); Aurangabad (1 daily; 16hr); Baga (every 30min; 45min); Bijapur (7 daily; 10hr); Calangute (every 30min; 40min); Candolim (every 30min; 30min); Chaudi (hourly; 2hr 15min); Gokarna (2 daily; 5hr 30min); Hampi (2 daily; 9–10hr); Hospet (3 daily; 9hr); Hubli (hourly; 6hr); Hyderabad (1 daily; 18hr); Kolhapur (hourly; 8hr); Mahabaleshwar (1 daily; 12hr); Mangalore (4 daily; 10hr); Mapusa (every 15min; 25min); Margao (every 15min; 55min); Morjim (6 daily; 1hr 30min–2hr); Mumbai (6 daily; 14–18hr); Mysore (2 daily; 17hr); Old Goa (every 15min; 20min); Ponda (hourly; 50min); Pune (7 daily; 12hr).

Flights

For a list of **airline addresses and websites,** see p.57. In the listings on p.70 IA is Indian Airlines, AI Air India, JA Jet Airways, SA Sahara Airlines and AD Air Deccan.

Seats on planes from Goa can be in short supply at certain times of year, especially around Diwali and Christmas. Wherever possible, try and book flights directly through the airline, as private agents charge the dollar fare at poor rates of exchange; addresses of airline offices in Panjim are listed on p.183. Seats on all **Konkan Railway** services can be booked at the KRC reservation office on the first floor of Panjim's Kadamba bus stand (Mon–Sat 8am–8pm, Sun 8am–2pm) or at KRC's main reservation hall in Margao station (Mon–Sat 8am–4.30pm, Sun 8am–2pm; ☎0834/271 2780). Make your bookings as far in advance as possible, and try to get to the offices soon after opening time – the queues can be horrendous (at the KRC office in Panjim, touts monopolize queue numbers early in the day, and then charge what they think they can get away with to wait on your behalf). Seats on the Konkan Railway from Goa to Mumbai are in notoriously short supply as the lion's share of the quotas goes to longer-distance travellers from Kerala, with the result that peak periods tend to be reserved up to two months in advance. One way around this is to **book online** at ⓦwww.konkanrailway.com, though bear in mind if you do you'll only be eligible for the relatively expensive three-tier a/c fares (Rs1250 one-way) and must make your booking between seven and two days before your date of departure.

Kadamba **bus tickets** can be bought in advance at their offices in Panjim and Mapusa bus stands (daily 9–11am & 2–5pm); private companies sell theirs through the many travel agents immediately outside the bus stand in Panjim, and at the bottom of the square in Mapusa. **Information** on all departures and fares is available from Goa Tourism's counter inside Panjim's bus stand (see p.178).

For a full rundown of destinations reachable from Goa by bus, train and plane, see Travel details at the end of this chapter.

To Mumbai

If you're heading north to **Mumbai**, the quickest and easiest way is **by plane**. Between eight and ten flights leave Goa's Dabolim airport daily. One-way fares range from $60 or less with the low-cost Internet airline Deccan Air (ⓦwww.airdeccan .net) to $95 with Indian Airlines (ⓦwww.indian-airlines.nic.in), or $100 with Sahara (ⓦwww.airsahara.net) or Jet (www.jetairways.com). In addition, Air India (☎www .airindia.com) operates a service to Mumbai which few people seem to know about, so you can nearly always get a seat (the one drawback is that you have to check in three hours before departure as Air India is an international carrier).

Two services run daily on the **Konkan Railway**, the most convenient being the overnight Konkankanya Express (#0112), which departs from Margao at 6pm, arriving at CST (still commonly known as "Victoria Terminus", or "VT") at 5.50am the following day. The other fast train from Margao to Mumbai CST is the Mandvi Express (#0104), departing at 10.10am and arriving at 9.45pm.

The cheapest, though most nightmarish, way to get to Mumbai is by **night bus**, which takes fourteen to eighteen hours, covering 500km of rough road at often terrifying speeds. Fares vary according to levels of comfort, and luxury buses arrive two or three hours sooner. Book Kadamba bus tickets at their offices in the Panjim and Mapusa bus stands (daily 9–11am & 2–5pm); private companies sell theirs through the many travel agents immediately outside the bus stand in Panjim, and at the bottom of the square in Mapusa. The most popular private service to Mumbai, and the most expensive, is the 24-seater run by a company called Paulo Travels. A cramped berth on this bus (which bizarrely you may have to share) costs Rs650, and it is worth pointing out that women travellers have complained of harassment during the journey. For tickets, contact Paulo Holiday Makers, near the Kadamba bus stand, Panjim (☎0832/222 3736) or at *Hotel Nanutel*, opposite Club Harmonia, Margao (☎0834/272 1516). Information on all departures and fares is available from

Goa Tourism's counter inside Panjim's bus stand (see Arrival, information and local transport, p.178).

To Hampi

Much the least stressful wasy to reach Hampi from Goa is by **train**. Three services each week leave Vasco (at 7.10am) and Margao (7.35am) on Wednesdays, Saturdays and Sundays, arriving in Hospet – the nearest railhead to Hampi – just over eight and a half hours later at 4pm. Tickets can be bought on the day at either point of departure. This is a wonderful rail journey, taking you along one of the wildest stretches of the Western Ghats, including the Dudhsagar Falls area (see p.178). Travelling in the other direction, trains leave Hospet at 8.50am on Mondays, Thursdays and Fridays, and arrive in Margao at 6.23pm. Tickets cost Rs700 for two-tier a/c, Rs450 for a/c three-tier and Rs170 in standard sleeper class.

The **bus** journey covering the same route is no cheaper than the train (sleeper class) and is far more gruelling. Two or three clapped-out government services leave Panjim's Kadamba stand (platform 9) each morning for Hospet, the last one at 10.30am. Brace yourself for a long, hard slog; all being well, it should take nine or ten hours, but delays and breakdowns are frustratingly frequent. **Tickets** for Kadamba and KSRTC (Karnatakan State Road Transport Corporation) services should be booked at least one day in advance at the hatches in the bus stand.

From Margao, you can also travel to Hampi on a swish **night bus**, complete with pneumatic suspension and berths. The service, operated by Paulo Travels, leaves at 6pm from a lot next to the *Nanutel Hotel* on Margao's Rua da Padre Miranda, arriving in Hampi early the next morning. Tickets cost around Rs450 and can be bought from most reputable travel agents around the state. Although the coach is comfortable enough, the coffin-like berths can get very hot and stuffy, making sleep very difficult; moreover, there have been complaints from women of harassment during the night on this service.

To Gokarna, Jog Falls, Mangalore and southern Karnataka

From Goa, the fastest and most convenient way to travel down the coast to Gokarna is via the **Konkan Railway**. At 2.10pm, the Verna–Mangalore Passenger leaves Margao, passing through Chaudi at 2.50pm en route to Gokarna Road, the town's railhead, where it arrives at around 4pm. The station lies 9km east of Gokarna itself, but a minibus is on hand to shuttle passengers the rest of the way. As this is classed as a passenger service, you don't have to buy tickets in advance; just turn up at the station 30min before the departure time and pay at the regular ticket counter. As ever, it is a good idea to **check timings** in advance, through any tourist office or travel agent, or via the KRC's website (@www.konkanrailway.com).

Buses take as much as two-and-a-half hours longer to cover the same route. A direct service leaves Margao's interstate stand in the north of town daily at 1pm. You can also get there by catching any of the services that run between Goa and Mangalore, and jumping off either at **Ankola**, or at the Gokarna junction on the main highway, from where frequent private minibuses and tempos run into town.

The Konkan highway is straightforward by **motorcycle**, with a better-than-average road surface, and frequent fuel stops along the way. Travelling on a rented bike also gives you the option of heading down sandy side lanes to explore some of the gorgeous beaches glimpsed from the road. Aside from the obvious dangers involved in motorcycling on Indian highways, the main drawback is **crossing the border**, which can involve a baksheesh transaction.

For **Jog Falls**, the easiest route is to catch a train on the Konkan Railway to **Hona-var** (two stations south of Gokarna Road; 2hr 15min), from where seven daily buses run up the *ghats* to Jog.

Moving on from Goa — *Contd...*

To Delhi

The Konkan Railway has also improved train services to **Delhi**, which can now be reached on the superfast Rajdhani Express #2431 in a little over 26 hours (Weds & Fri only). A slower daily service, the Vasco–Nizamuddin Express (#2779) takes nearly 38 hours to cover the same distance. Alternatively, you can fly to the capital with Indian Airlines or Jet in 2hr 45min from around $249 one-way.

Dabolim airport (Vasco da Gama) to: Bangalore (2 daily; 1hr 30min–2hr 25min); Chennai (Madras) (2 weekly; 3hr 15min); Cochin (Kochi) (2 weekly; 1hr); Delhi (IA, SA 2 daily; 2hr 35min–3hr 45min); Hyderabad (DA, JA 2 daily; 1hr 40min–3hr 15min); Kolkota (Calcutta) (AS 2 daily; 3hr 30min); Mumbai (AI, IA, DA, JA, SA 8–10 daily; 40–50min).

GOA | Travel details

Karnataka

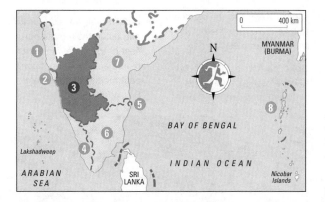

CHAPTER 3   # Highlights

* **Mysore** The sandalwood city has bundles of old-fashioned charm and lots to see, including the opulent Maharaja's Palace. See p.254

* **Halebid & Belur** Two wonderfully ornate Hoysala temples, set in the slow-paced Karnataka countryside. See p.270 & p.272

* **Jog Falls** India's highest waterfalls offer fresh air, superb views and the chance to take a dip after the downhill hike. See p.294

* **Gokarna** A quiet Hindu holy town, blessed with a series of exquisite crescent beaches, ideal for serious unwinding. See p.296

* **Hampi** Home to the remains of the Vijayanagar kingdom, scattered among fertile plantations punctuated by weird rock formations. See p.308

* **Bijapur** Known as the "Agra of the South" for its splendid Islamic architecture, most famously the vast dome of the Golgumbaz. See p.324

* **Bidar** Rarely visited Muslim outpost in the remote northeast of the state, famed for its *bidri* metalwork and magnificent medieval monuments See p.331

△ Maharaja's Palace, Mysore

3

Karnataka

Created in 1956 from the princely state of Mysore, **KARNATAKA** – the name is a derivation of the name of the local language, Kannada, spoken by virtually all of its 53 million inhabitants – marks a transition zone between northern India and the Dravidian deep south. Along its border with Maharashtra and Andhra Pradesh, a string of medieval walled towns, studded with domed mausoleums and minarets, recalls the era when this part of the Deccan was a Muslim stronghold, while the coastal and hill districts that dovetail with Kerala are quintessential Hindu South India, profuse with tropical vegetation and soaring temple *gopuras*. Between the two are scattered some of the peninsula's most extraordinary historic sites, notably the ruined Vijayanagar city at Hampi, whose lost temples and derelict palaces stand amid an arid, boulder-strewn landscape of surreal beauty.

Karnataka is one of the wettest regions in India, its **climate** dominated by the seasonal monsoon, which sweeps in from the southwest in June, dumping an average 4m of rain on the coast before it peters out in late September. Running in an unbroken line along the state's palm-fringed coast, the **Western Ghats**, draped in dense deciduous forests, impede the path of the rain clouds east. As a result, the landscape of the interior – comprising the southern apex of the triangular Deccan trap, known here as the **Mysore Plateau** – is considerably drier, with dark volcanic soils in the north, and poor quartzite-granite country to the south. Two of India's most sacred rivers, the Tungabhadra and Krishna, flow across this sun-baked terrain, draining east to the Bay of Bengal.

Broadly speaking, Karnataka's principal attractions are concentrated at opposite ends of the state, with a handful of lesser-visited places dotted along the coast between Goa and Kerala. Road and rail routes dictate that most itineraries take in the brash state capital, **Bangalore**, a go-ahead, modern city which epitomizes the aspirations of the country's new middle classes, with glittering malls, fast-food outlets and a nightlife unrivalled outside Mumbai. The state's other major city, **Mysore**, appeals more for its old-fashioned ambience, nineteenth-century palaces and vibrant produce and incense markets. It also lies within easy reach of several important historical monuments. At the nearby fortified island of **Srirangapatnam** – site of the bloody battle of 1799 that finally put Mysore State into British hands, with the defeat of the Muslim military genius **Tipu Sultan** – parts of the fort, a mausoleum and Tipu's summer palace survive.

A cluster of other unmissable sights lies further northwest, dotted around the dull railway town of **Hassan**. Around nine centuries ago, the Hoysala kings sited their grand dynastic capitals here, at the now middle-of-nowhere villages of **Belur** and **Halebid**, where several superbly crafted temples survive intact. More impressive still, and one of India's most extraordinary sacred sites, is the

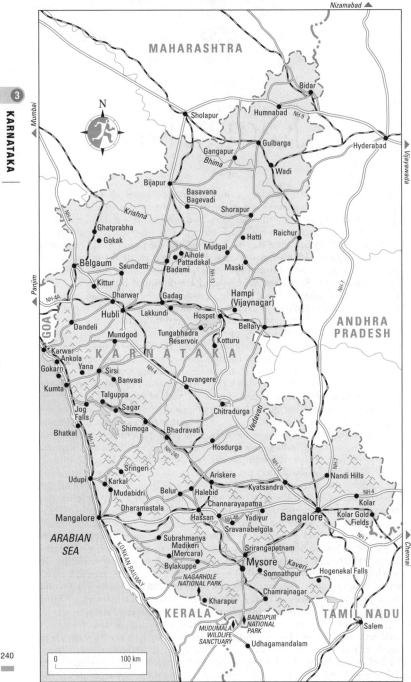

eighteen-metre Jain colossus at **Sravanabelgola**, which stares serenely over idyllic Deccan countryside.

West of Mysore, the Ghats rise in a wall of thick jungle cut by deep ravines and isolated valleys. You can either traverse the range by rail, via Hassan, or explore some of its scenic backwaters by road. Among these, the rarely visited coffee- and spice-growing region of **Kodagu** (**Coorg**) has to be the most entrancing, with its unique culture and lush vistas of misty wooded hills and valleys. Most Coorgi agricultural produce is shipped out of **Mangalore**, the nearest large town, of little interest except as a transport hub. Situated midway between Goa and Kerala, it's also a convenient – if uninspiring – place to pause on the journey along Karnataka's beautiful **Karavali coast**. Interrupted by countless mangrove-lined estuaries, the state's 320-kilometre-long red-laterite coast has always been difficult to navigate by land, and traffic along the recently revamped highway remains relatively light. Although there are plenty of superb beaches, facilities are, with rare exceptions, nonexistent, and locals often react with astonishment at the sight of a foreigner. Few Western tourists visit the famous Krishna temple at **Udupi**, an important Vaishnavite pilgrimage centre, and fewer still venture into the mountains to see India's highest waterfalls at **Jog Falls**, set amid some of the region's most spectacular scenery. However, atmospheric **Gokarna**, further north up the coast, is an increasingly popular beach hideaway for budget travellers. Harbouring one of India's most famous *shivalinga*, this seventeenth-century Hindu pilgrimage town enjoys a stunning location, with a high headland dividing it from a string of exquisite beaches.

Winding inland from the mountainous Goan border, NH-4A and the rail line comprise sparsely populated **northern Karnataka**'s main transport arteries, linking a succession of grim industrial centres. This region's undisputed highlight is the ghost city of Vijayanagar, better known as **Hampi**, scattered around boulder hills on the south banks of the Tungabhadra River. The ruins of this once splendid capital occupy a magical site, while the ancient bazaar is a great spot to hole up for a spell. The jumping-off place for Hampi is **Hospet**, from where buses leave for the bumpy journey north across the rolling Deccani plains to **Badami**, **Aihole** and **Pattadakal**. Now lost in countryside, these tiny villages were once capitals of the **Chalukya** dynasty (sixth to eighth centuries), and the whole area is littered with ancient rock-cut caves and finely carved stone temples.

Further north still, in one of Karnataka's most remote and poorest districts, craggy hilltop citadels and crumbling wayside tombs herald the formerly troubled buffer zone between the Muslim-dominated northern Deccan and the Dravidian-Hindu south. The bustling, walled market town of **Bijapur**, capital of the Bahmanis, the Muslim dynasty responsible for the eventual downfall of Vijayanagar, harbours South India's finest collection of Islamic architecture, including the world's second-largest freestanding dome, the Golgumbaz. The first Bahmani capital, **Gulbarga**, site of a famous Muslim shrine and theological college, has retained little of its former splendour, but more isolated **Bidar**, to which the Bahmanis moved from Gulbarga in the sixteenth century, definitely deserves a detour en route to or from Hyderabad, four hours to the east by bus. Perched on a rocky escarpment, its crumbling red ramparts harbour Persian-style mosaic-fronted mosques, mausoleums and a sprawling fort complex evocative of Samarkand and the great silk route.

Some history

Like much of southern India, Karnataka has been ruled by successive Buddhist, Hindu and Muslim dynasties. The influence of Jainism has also been marked;

India's very first emperor, **Chandragupta Maurya**, is believed to have converted to Jainism in the fourth century BC, renounced his throne, and fasted to death at Sravanabelgola, now one of the most visited Jain pilgrimage centres in the country.

During the first millennium AD, this whole region was dominated by power struggles between the various kingdoms, such as Vakatakas and the Guptas, who controlled the western Deccan and at times extended their authority as far as the Coromandel coast in Tamil Nadu. From the sixth to the eighth centuries, briefly interrupted by thirteen years of Pallava rule, the **Chalukya** kingdom included Maharashtra, the Konkan coast on the west, and the whole of Karnataka. The **Cholas** were powerful in the east of the region from about 870 until the thirteenth century, when the Deccan kingdoms were overwhelmed by General Malik Kafur, a convert to Islam.

By the medieval era, Muslim incursions from the north had forced the hitherto warring and fractured Hindu states of the south into close alliance, with the mighty **Vijayanagars** emerging as overlords. Founded by the brothers Harihara and Bukka, their lavish capital, Vijayanagar, ruled an empire stretching from the Bay of Bengal to the Arabian Sea, and south to Cape Comorin. The Muslims' superior military strength, however, triumphed in 1565 at the Battle of Talikota, when the **Bahmanis** laid siege to Vijayanagar, reducing it to rubble and plundering its opulent palaces and temples.

Thereafter, a succession of Muslim sultans held sway over the north, while in the south of the state the independent **Wadiyar Rajas** of Mysore, whose territory was comparatively small, successfully fought off the Marathas. In 1761, the brilliant Muslim campaigner Haider Ali, with French support, seized the throne. Haider Ali and his son, Tipu Sultan, turned Mysore into a major force in the south, before Tipu was killed by the British at the **battle of Srirangapatnam** in 1799.

Following Tipu's defeat, the British restored the Wadiyar family to the throne, which they kept until riots in 1830 led the British to appoint a commission to rule in their place. Fifty years later, the throne was once more returned to the Wadiyars, who remained governors until Karnataka was created by the merging of the states of Mysore and the Madras Presidencies in 1956. In the years since its creation, the state has been spared the excesses of communal and political unrest, although the scene can be volatile. Following Independence the political scene was largely dominated by the Congress party until it was routed in the 1990s – first by a reunited Janata Dal, and subsequently by a fundamentalist BJP alliance – although it returned to power in the most recent state elections.

Bangalore

Once across the Western Ghats, the cloying air of Kerala and the Konkan coast gradually gives way to the crisp skies and dry heat of the dusty **Mysore Plateau**. The setting for E.M. Forster's acclaimed Raj novel, *A Passage to India*, this southern tip of the Deccan – a vast, open expanse of gently undulating plains dotted with wheat fields and dramatic granite boulders – formed the heartland of the region's once powerful princely state. Today it remains the political hub of the region, largely due to the economic importance of **BANGALORE**, Karnataka's capital, which, with a population racing towards eight million is one of the fastest-growing cities in Asia. A major scientific research centre at the cutting edge of India's technological revolution, Bangalore has a trendy high-speed self-image, quite unlike anywhere else in South India.

In the 1800s, Bangalore's gentle climate, broad streets, and green public parks made it the "Garden City". Until well after Independence, senior figures, film stars and VIPs flocked to buy or build dream homes amid this urban idyll, which offered such unique amenities as theatres, cinemas and a lack of restrictions on alcohol. However, for well over a decade, Bangalore has undergone a massive transformation. The wide avenues, now dominated by tower blocks, are teeming with traffic, and water and electricity shortages have become the norm. Even the climate has been affected and pollution is a real problem.

The city's excellent transport connections mean that many foreigners turn up in Bangalore without really knowing why they've come. Some pass through on their way to see Satya Sai Baba at his ashram in **Puttaparthy** in Andhra Pradesh, or at his temporary residence at the **Whitefield** ashram on the outskirts of the city. What little there is to see is no match for the attractions elsewhere in the state, and the city's very real advantages for Indians are two-a-penny in the West. That said, travellers who have been in India for a while may enjoy the novelty of spending some time in a relaxed, cosmopolitan and westernized Indian city with good shopping, eating and hotels, while Bangalore is also the only place in the subcontinent to boast anything resembling at a pub culture. You may even

The silicon rush

Many visitors are surprised to learn that India is the second-largest exporter of computer software after the US. Generating sales of approaching one billion dollars per year, the centrepiece of this hi-tech boom was the Electronic City Industrial Park on the outskirts of Bangalore, dubbed **Silicon Valley** by the Indian press. Today, due to the meteoric rise of Hyderabad in neighbouring Andhra Pradesh as the new computer capital of India, and to Bangalore's own growth pangs, the city is losing some of its attraction to new investors.

Bangalore's meteoric industrial rise began in the early 1980s. Fleeing the crippling costs of Mumbai and Delhi, a group of hi-tech Indian companies relocated here, lured by the comparatively cool climate and an untapped pool of highly skilled, English-speaking labour (a consequence of the Indian government's decision to concentrate its telecommunications and defence research here in the 1960s). Within a decade, Bangalore had become a major player in the software market, and a magnet for multinationals such as Motorola and Texas Instruments (who have their own satellite link with their head offices in Dallas).

For a while, Bangalore revelled in a spending frenzy that saw the centre of the city sprout gleaming skyscrapers, swish stores and shopping malls. Soon, however, the price of prosperity became apparent. At the height of the boom, millions of immigrants poured in, eager for a slice of the action – it's estimated that in less than five years the population more than doubled to 7.5 million. However, too little municipal money was invested in infrastructure, and today Bangalore is buckling under the weight of numbers and suffering rocketing levels of traffic **pollution**. Although **power cuts**, which became routine in the late 1990s, have been cut back by increasing the output of the city's power grid, the new-found problems had an adverse effect on business and industry. The chaos played a big part in the decision of several multinationals to decamp to India's latest software capital, Hyderabad, but although Bangalore's economy was hit hard by the departure of so many high-spending expats and computer whiz-kids, it has bounced back in the past few years with rapid growth in the international telecom and call-centre sector – AOL has a help desk here, for example. Meanwhile, old Bangaloreans wonder what happened to their beloved "Garden City".

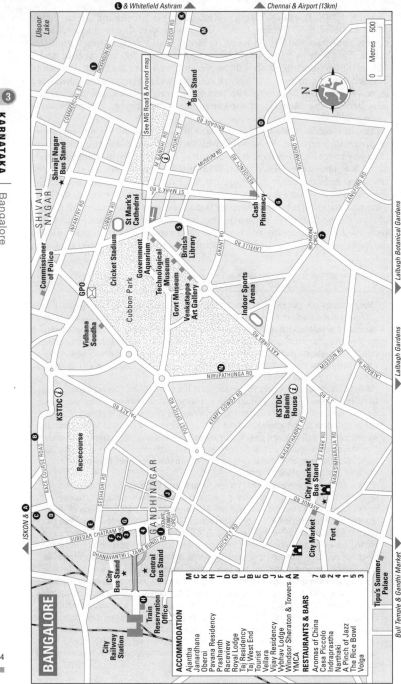

BANGALORE

Ulsoor Lake

❶ & Whitefield Ashram ▲   ▲ Chennai & Airport (13km)

ISKON & Ⓐ ◀

Mysore ▼

Bull Temple & Gandhi Market ▼

Lalbagh Gardens ▼

Lalbagh Botanical Gardens ▼

City Railway Station

Train Reservation Office

City Bus Stand ★

Central Bus Stand ★

SUBEDAR CHATRAM RD

DHANAVANTRI RD

TANK BUND RD

RACE COURSE ROAD

Racecourse

KSTDC ⓘ

SESHADRI RD

PALACE RD

POST OFFICE RD

GANDHINAGAR

KEMPE GOWDA RD

KEMPE GOWDA CIRCLE

CHICKPET RD

AVENUE RD

NARASIMHARAJA RD

NRUPATHUNGA RD

City Market Bus Stand ★

City Market

Fort

S J P RD

S J PARK RD

J C RD

MISSION RD

LALBAGH RD

Tipu's Summer Palace

KSTDC Badami House ⓘ

N

Vidhana Soudha

GPO

Commissioner of Police

INFANTRY RD

SHIVAJI NAGAR

Shivaji Nagar Bus Stand ★

COMMERCIAL ST

CUBBON RD

Cricket Stadium

Cubbon Park

Government Aquarium

Technological Museum

Govt Museum

Venkatappa Art Gallery

St Mark's Cathedral

ST MARK'S RD

GRANT RD

LAVELLE RD

Indoor Sports Arena

KASTURBA RD

British Library

M GANDHI RD

MG Road & Around map

See MG Road & Around map

DICKENSON RD

ULSOOR RD

CHURCH ST

BRIGADE RD

Bus Stand ★

MUSEUM RD

RESIDENCY RD

RICHMOND RD

RICHMOND CIRCLE

LANGFORD RD

Cash Pharmacy

ⓘ

❶ ❶ ❺ ❻ ❼

Ⓐ Ⓑ Ⓒ Ⓓ Ⓔ Ⓕ Ⓖ Ⓗ Ⓘ Ⓙ Ⓚ Ⓛ Ⓜ Ⓝ Ⓞ

0 Metres 500

N

ACCOMMODATION

Ajantha	M
Janardhana	C
Oberoi	K
Pavana Residency	H
Prashanth	I
Raceview	D
Royal Lodge	G
Taj Residency	L
Taj West End	B
Tourist	E
Vellara	O
Vijay Residency	J
Vybhav Lodge	F
Windsor Sheraton & Towers	A
YMCA	N

RESTAURANTS & BARS

Aromas of China	7
Casa Piccolo	6
Indraprastha	2
Narthaki	4
A Pinch of Jazz	1
The Rice Bowl	5
Volga	3

appreciate the lack of cows in large parts of the city – another indication of its Western orientation.

Some history

Bangalore began life as the minor "village of the half-baked *gram*" and to this day *gram* (beans) remain an important local product. In 1537, Magadi **Kempe Gowda**, a devout Hindu and feudatory chief of the Vijayanagar empire, built a mud fort and erected four watchtowers outside the village, predicting that it would, one day, extend that far; the city now, of course, stretches way beyond. During the first half of the seventeenth century, Bangalore fell to the Muslim sultanate of Bijapur and changed hands several times before being returned to Hindu rule under the Wadiyar rajas of Mysore. In 1758, Chikka Krishnaraja Wadiyar II was deposed by the military genius Haider Ali, who set up arsenals here to produce muskets, rockets and other weapons for his formidable anti-British campaigns. Both he and his son, **Tipu Sultan**, greatly extended and fortified Bangalore, but Tipu was overthrown by the British in 1799. They then set up a cantonment, which made the city an important military station, and passed the administration over to the Maharaja of Mysore in 1881. After Independence, the erstwhile maharaja became governor of Mysore state. Bangalore was designated capital in 1956, and retained that status when Karnataka state was created in 1973.

Arrival, information and city transport

Recently expanded and revamped to accommodate increased traffic and planned international flights, **Bangalore airport**, 13km north of the city centre, serves cities in South India and beyond; for details of departures, see box on pp.254–255. The **KSTDC desk** in the arrivals hall (daily 7.30am–1.30pm & 2–7.30pm; ☎080/2526 8753) stocks leaflets on Karnataka and can book hotel rooms. Branches of the State Bank of Mysore (daily 8am–7pm) and Vijaya Bank (daily 8.30am–12.30pm) **change money**. You can get into the city by **taxi** (Rs160–200; book at the prepaid desk), on one of the **auto-rickshaws** (Rs80–100) that gather outside, or by **bus** – numerous local services run along the main road only several hundred metres from the terminal.

Bangalore City railway station is west of the centre, near Kempe Gowda Circle, and across the road from the main bus stands (for the north of the city, get off at Bangalore Cantonment railway station). As you come into the entrance hall from the platforms, the far left-hand corner holds an **ITDC booth** (daily 8am–4pm; ☎080/2220 4277), where you can rent cars and book tours; they will book you a hotel for a fee of ten percent of the day's room rate. The **KSTDC tourist information office** (daily 7am–8pm; ☎080/2287 0068), to the right, also books tours and can provide useful advice. You'll find a rank of metered taxis outside; alternatively, prepaid auto-rickshaws charge Rs25–40 for the trip to MG Road, depending on the time of day.

Innumerable **long-distance buses** arrive at the big, busy **Central (KSRTC) Bus Stand**, opposite the railway station. There's a comprehensive timetable in English in the centre of the concourse. A bridge divides it from **City Bus Stand**, used by local services.

Information

For information on Bangalore, Karnataka and neighbouring states, go to the excellent **India Tourism office** (Mon–Fri 9.30am–6pm, Sat 9am–1pm; ☎080/2558 5417, ⓦwww.india-tourism.com), in the KSFC Building, 48

Church Street (parallel to MG Road between Brigade and St Mark's roads). You can pick up a free city map here and the staff are very useful in helping you put together tour itineraries. Apart from their desks at Bangalore City railway station and airport (see p.245), **Karnataka State Tourist Development Corporation (KSTDC)** has two city offices. One is at Badami House, NR Square (daily 6.30am–10pm; ☎080/2227 5883), where you can book the tours outlined below; the other is their head office on the second floor of Khanija Bhavan, Race Course Road (Mon–Sat 9am–5.30pm, closed second Sat of month; ☎080/2235 2901, ⓦwww.kstdc.nic.in). They share these smart new offices with Karnataka Tourism, who aren't great at providing face-to-face information for visitors but do have a decent website (ⓦwww .karnatakatourism.com). For up-to-the-minute information about **what's on**, plus details about local restaurants and shops, check the ad-sponsored listings magazine *City Info* (ⓦwww.explocity.com), distributed free at the larger hotels and India Tourism.

If you're planning to visit any of Karnataka's **national parks**, call in at the Wildlife Office, Forest Department, Aranya Bhavan, Malleswaram (☎080/2334 1993) for information, or approach Jungle Lodges & Resorts, Floor 2, Shrungar Shopping Centre, off MG Road (☎080/2559 7021, ⓦwww.junglelodges .com). A quasi-government body, Jungle Lodges promotes so-called ecotourism through several upmarket forest lodges, including the much lauded *Kabini River Lodge* near Nagarhole.

City transport

The easiest way of getting around Bangalore is by metered **auto–rickshaw**; fares start at Rs10 for the first kilometre and Rs5 per kilometre thereafter. Most meters do work and drivers are usually willing to use them, although you'll occasionally be asked for a flat fare, especially during rush hours.

Bangalore's extensive **bus** system, run by the Bangalore Metropolitan Transport Corporation (BMTC), radiates from the City (Kempe Gowda) Bus Stand (☎080/2222 2542), near the railway station. Most buses from platform 17 travel past MG Road. Along with regular buses, BMTC also operates a deluxe express service, Pushpak, on a number of set routes (#P109 terminates at Whitefield ashram) as well as a handful of night buses. Other important city bus stands include the KR Market bus stand (☎080/2670 2177), to the south of the railway station, and Shivajinagar (☎080/2286 5332), to the north of Cubbon Park – the #P2 Jayanagar service from here is handy for the Lalbagh Botanical Gardens.

You can book **chauffeur-driven cars and taxis** through several agencies including the Cab Service, Sabari Complex, 24 Residency Rd (☎080/2558 6121) and the 24hr Dial-a-Car service (☎080/2526 1737, ⓔdialacar@hotmail .com). Typical rates for car rental are around Rs150 per hour, Rs400 for four hours (which includes 40km), and Rs550 for eight hours (including 80km); the extra mileage charge is around Rs5 per kilometre. Note that most taxi companies start calculating their time and distances from when the car leaves their depot. If you need a taxi for a one-way journey, be prepared to pay for the return fare as well. A metered taxi system is planned for the future, which will make hiring a cab simpler. See Listings, pp.252–253, for details of self-drive car rental.

For **long-distance car rental** and **tailor-made itineraries**, try Gullivers Tours & Travels, South Black, 201–202 Manipal Centre, 47 Dickenson Road (☎080/2558 8001); Clipper Holidays, 406 Regency Enclave, 4 Magrath Road (☎080/2559 9032); or any KSTDC office or the ITDC booth at the railway station.

Guided tours

KSTDC operates a selection of guided **tours** from Bangalore. Though rushed, these can be handy if you're short of time. The twice-daily **city tour** (7.30am–1.30pm or 2–7.30pm; Rs85) calls at the museum, Vidhana Soudha, Ulsoor Lake, Lalbagh Gardens, Bull Temple and Tipu Sultan's palace and winds up with a long stop at the government handicrafts emporium. The **New Bangalore tour** (Wed–Sun 7.15am–8pm; Rs150) gets you to the "seven new wonders" of the city, including the ISKCON temple, planetarium and musical fountain. "**Outstation**" **tours** include a long day-trip to Srirangapatnam/Mysore and another to Belur/Halebid/Sravanabelgola, but they aren't recommended unless you're happy to spend at least eight hours on the bus.

Accommodation

Rooms in Bangalore often fill up, especially the smarter places, though the 24hr checkout system operated by most hotels means openings always crop up; still, there's no harm phoning ahead. **Budget accommodation** is concentrated around the railway station (which itself has good-value, but often full, retiring rooms for Rs100–400) and Central Bus Stand. Standards in this area can be very low, however; the better options are on the east side of the station, dotted around Dhanavantri (Tank Bund) Road and the parallel Subedar Chatram Road. **Mid-range** and **expensive hotels** are more scattered; some are located around the racecourse, a short rickshaw trip northeast of the station; others are in the MG Road area.

Around Bangalore City railway station and Central Bus Stand

Pavana Residency 88 RBDGT Charities Building ☎080/2228 6681, ✉hotelpavan@hotmail.com. Sizeable rooms of varying standards, some with a/c. It's rather overpriced, but as close to the railway station as you can be, yet quiet. ④–⑥

Prashanth 21 E Tank Bund Rd ☎080/2287 4041, ⓦwww.prasanth_hotel.com. Among the better hotels opposite Central Bus Stand, and all rooms are well lit, with shower-toilets. The Mayura nearby is the best fall-back. ③–④

Royal Lodge Subedar Chatram Rd ☎080/2226 3740–2. Large, clean and efficient lodge. Most rooms are compact en-suite doubles with cable TV. ②–③

Tourist Ananda Rao Circle ☎080/2226 2381–8. A short walk from the station, this is one of Bangalore's best all-round budget lodges, with small rooms, long verandas, and friendly family management. No reservations are accepted, however, and it fills up quickly. ②

Vijay Residency 18 3rd Cross, Main Road ☎080/2220 3024, ⓦwww.vijayresidency.net. Within striking distance of the railway station, this Comfort Inn franchise is plush and comfortable, if a bit ostentatious, with central a/c, foreign currency exchange and a quality restaurant. ⑦–⑧

Vybhav Lodge 60 Subedar Chatram Rd ☎080/2287 3997. Good, clean budget lodge offering small en-suite rooms with TV, dotted around a little courtyard. Decent value, especially for singles. ③

Around the Racecourse and Cubbon Park

Janardhana Kumara Krupa Rd ☎080/2225 4444, ⓕ2225 8708. Neat, clean and spacious rooms with balconies and baths. Well away from the chaos, and good value at this price (despite hefty service charges). ③–⑤

Raceview 25 Race Course Rd ☎080/2220 3401. Run-of-the-mill mid-range hotel whose upper front rooms overlook the racecourse. Facilities include safe deposit, foreign exchange and some a/c. ④–⑤

Taj West End Race Course Rd ☎080/2225 5055, ⓦwww.tajhotels.com. Dating back to 1887, with fabulous gardens and long colonnaded walkways. The most characterful rooms (from $260) are in the old wing, where deep verandas overlook acres of grounds. ⑨

Windsor Sheraton & Towers 25 Golf Course Rd ☎080/2226 9898, ⓦwww.sheraton.com. Ersatz palace run by Starwood as a luxurious five-star, mainly for overseas businesspeople, with rates

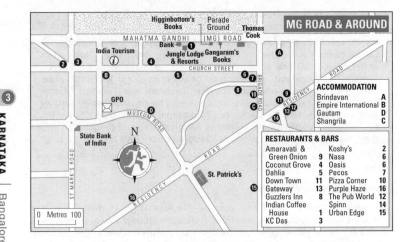

MG ROAD & AROUND

ACCOMMODATION

Brindavan	A
Empire International	B
Gautam	D
Shangrila	C

RESTAURANTS & BARS

Amaravati & Green Onion	9	Koshy's	2
Coconut Grove	4	Nasa	6
Dahlia	5	Oasis	6
Down Town	11	Pecos	7
Gateway	13	Pizza Corner	10
Guzzlers Inn	8	Purple Haze	16
Indian Coffee House	1	The Pub World	12
		Spinn	14
KC Das	3	Urban Edge	15

from \$270. Facilities include voicemail, modems, gym, jacuzzis and pool. ❾

YMCA Nirupathanga Rd, Cubbon Park, midway between the bus stand and MG Rd ☎080/2221 1848. Large, clean rooms and cheaper dorm beds for students only. Economical rates, but often full. ❸

Around MG Road

Brindavan 40 MG Rd ☎080/558 4000. Old-style budget to mid-range hotel with some a/c rooms, set slightly off the main road. Good value, especially for singles. ❸–❺

Empire International 36 Church St ☎080/2559 3743, ⓦwww.hotelempireinternational.com. Smart new hotel with very comfortable rooms boasting modern decor and good facilities. ❻–❼

Gautam 17 Museum Rd ☎080/558 8764. Large, characterless concrete block of standard rooms, but there's lots of space so it's a good fallback if other places are full. The quiet street is a bonus. ❹

Shangrila 182 Brigade Rd ☎080/5112 1622. Welcoming Tibetan-run lodge right in the thick of things; the comfy standard rooms are as good value as anywhere in the area. ❹–❻

The City

The **centre** of modern Bangalore lies around **MG Road**, about 4km east of Kempe Gowda Circle and the principal train and bus stations. On MG Road you'll find most of the mid-range accommodation, restaurants, shops, tourist information and banks. Leafy **Cubbon Park**, with its less-than-exciting museums, lies to the west, while the oldest, most "Indian" part of the city extends south from Bangalore City railway station, a warren of winding streets at their most dynamic in the hubbub of the **City** and **Gandhi markets**. Bangalore's tourist attractions are spread out; monuments such as **Tipu's Summer Palace** and the **Bull Temple** are some way south of the centre. Most, if not all, can be seen on a half-day tour, but if you plan to explore on foot, be warned that Bangalore has some of the worst pavements in India.

Cubbon Park and around

A welcome green space in the heart of the city, shaded by massive clumps of bamboo, **Cubbon Park** is entered from the western end of MG Road, presided over by a statue of Queen Victoria. On Kasturba Road, which runs along its southern edge, the poorly labelled and maintained **Government Museum** (Tues–Sun 10am–5pm; Rs4) features prehistoric artefacts, Vijayanagar, Hoysala and Chalukya sculpture, musical instruments, Thanjavur paintings and Deccani and Rajasthani miniatures. It includes the adjacent **Venkatappa Art Gallery**, which exhibits twentieth-century landscapes, portraits, abstract art, wood sculpture and occasional temporary art shows. Next door, the **Technological and Industrial Museum** (daily 10am–6pm; Rs10) is geared towards kids. Further towards the junction with MG Road, the octagonal **Government Aquarium** (Tues–Sun except 2nd Tues of month 10am–5.30pm; Rs5) contains a few murky tanks downstairs and some more visible tropical fish upstairs.

Northwest of Cubbon Park, Bangalore's vast State Secretariat, **Vidhana Soudha**, built in 1956, is the largest civic structure of its kind in the country. K. Hanumanthaiah, chief minister at the time, wanted a "people's palace" which, following the transfer of power from the royal Wadiyar dynasty to a legislature, would "reflect the power and dignity of the people". In theory, its design is entirely Indian, combining local models from Bangalore, Mysore and Somnathpur with features from Rajasthan and the rest of India. Its overall effect, however, is not unlike bombastic colonial architecture, built in the so-called Indo-Saracenic style – incorporating onion-domes and oriental features.

Lalbagh Botanical Gardens

Inspired by the splendid gardens of the Moghuls and the French botanical gardens at Pondicherry in Tamil Nadu, Sultan Haider Ali set to work in 1760 laying out the **Lalbagh Botanical Gardens** (daily 8am–8pm; Rs15 before 6pm, free after 6pm), 4km south of the centre. Originally covering forty acres, just beyond his fort – where one of Kempe Gowda's original watchtowers can still be seen – the gardens were expanded under Ali's son Tipu, who introduced numerous exotic species of plants, and today they house an extensive horticultural seedling centre. The British brought in gardeners from Kew in 1856 and – naturally – built a military bandstand and a glasshouse, based on London's Crystal Palace, which hosts wonderful flower shows. Now spreading over 240 acres, the gardens are pleasant to visit during the day, but tend to attract unsavoury characters after 6pm. Great sunsets and views of the city to the north are to be had from the central hill, topped by a small shrine.

Tipu's Summer Palace and Bull Temple

A two-storey structure built in 1791, mostly of wood, **Tipu's Summer Palace** (daily 9am–5pm; $2 [Rs5]), southwest of the City Market and 3km from MG Road, is similar to the Daria Daulat Palace at Srirangapatnam (see p.262), but in a far worse state, with most of its painted decoration destroyed. Next door, the **Venkataramanaswamy temple**, dating from the early eighteenth century, was built by the Wadiyar rajas. The *gopura* entranceway was erected in 1978.

Continuing south from the summer palace, about 6km south of the City Bus Stand (bus #34 & #37) in the Basavanagudi area, Kempe Gowda's sixteenth-century **Bull Temple** (open to non-Hindus; daily 7.30am–1.30pm & 2.30–8.30pm) houses a massive monolithic Nandi bull, its grey granite made black by the application of charcoal and oil. The temple is approached along a path lined with mendicants and snake charmers; inside, for a few rupees, the priest will offer you a string of fragrant jasmine flowers. For more information on Kempe Gowda, the city's founder, see p.245.

ISKCON temple

A hybrid of ultra-modern glass and vernacular South Indian temple architecture, the gleaming new temple of the ISKCON (International Society of Krishna Consciousness), the **Sri Radha Krishna Mandir**, Hare Krishna Hill, Chord Road (daily 7am–1pm & 4pm–8.30pm), 8km from the centre, is a fantastic and lavish showpiece crowned by a gold-plated dome. Barriers, designed with huge crowds in mind, guide visitors on a one-way journey through the huge well-organized complex to the inner sanctum, where images of the god Krishna and his consort Radha are displayed. Collection points throughout, and inescapable merchandizing, are evidence of ISKCON's highly successful commercialization. Regular **buses** to the temple depart from both the City and Shivajinagar bus stands.

Eating

With unmissable sights thin on the ground, but tempting cafés and restaurants on every corner, you could easily spend most of your time in Bangalore **eating**. Nowhere else in South India will you find such gastronomic variety. Around **MG Road**, pizzerias (including *Pizza Hut*), ritzy ice-cream parlours and gourmet French restaurants stand cheek by jowl with regional cuisine from Andhra Pradesh and Kerala, Mumbai *chaat* cafés and snack bars where, in true Bangalorean style, humble thalis from as little as Rs30 masquerade as "executive mini-lunches".

Amaravati Residency Road Cross, MG Rd. Excellent Andhra cooking with "meals" served on banana leaves and specialities including biriyanis and fried fish. Hectic at lunchtime, but well worth any wait.

Aromas of China G3–4 Shiva Shankar Plaza, 19 Lalbagh Rd, Richmond Circle. One of the city's top Chinese restaurants offering delicacies including quality dim sum, duck and sharkfin soup, as well as above-average versions of all the usual Chinese favourites, albeit at above-average prices.

Casa Piccolo Devata Plaza, 131 Residency Rd. A dozen different tasty pizzas and big portions of Wiener Schnitzel, steaks, fried chicken and ice cream, but no alcohol. Tables outside on the basement patio and flower baskets give the place a European ambience.

Coconut Grove Church St. Mouthwatering and moderately priced gourmet Keralan coastal cuisine: vegetarian, fish and meat preparations served in traditional copper thalis on a leafy terrace. Try their tender coconut juice cocktail, thala chickory bom.

Dahlia Brigade Gardens, Church St. Japanese café, tucked in a modern business complex, serving authentic dishes at reasonable prices.

Gateway 66 Residency Rd ☎080/2558 4545. The Northern Gate serves a fairly undistinguished selection of Mughlai and other North Indian dishes, while the Karavalli specializes in west coast dishes from Goa to Kerala, including seafood and veg, and has a very attractive setting in traditional southern style; there are also tables outside under an old tamarind tree. Reservations essential. Expensive.

Green Onion Next door to the Amaravati, this small, modern triangular-shaped establishment offers a tasty range of kebabs, curries, Chinese food and sweets at fair prices in a café-style atmosphere.

Indian Coffee House MG Rd. The usual cheap south Indian snacks, egg dishes and good filter coffee served by waiters in turbans and cummerbunds. Best for breakfast.

Indraprastha Subedar Chatram Rd. Excellent cheap South Indian snacks, including their wonderful special masala *dosa*, and other veg dishes. One of the best options around the train and bus stations.

KC Das 38 Church St (corner of St Mark's Rd). Part of the legendary chain of Bengali sweet shops serving traditional steam-cooked sweets, many soaked in syrup and rosewater. Try their definitive *rasgullas*. Eat in or take away.

Koshy's St Mark's Rd, next to British Library. Bangalore's most congenial meeting place, this spacious, old-style café with cane blinds, pewter teapots and cotton-clad waiters serves full meals, snacks and alcohol.

Narthaki Just off Subedar Chatram Rd. The best restaurant in the station/bus stand area. Filling Andhra meals are served on the first floor, while the second-floor restaurant-bar has a full menu of Indian and Chinese dishes. The chicken chilli is a belter.

Pizza Corner Brigade Rd. The most central location of this popular chain. Quality pizza (with curry toppings available of course) and other fast food items.

Rice Bowl 40/2 Lavelle Rd. Plush a/c Chinese restaurant; try the chop suey, followed by lychees and ice cream. Evenings only.

Volga Subedar Chatram Rd. Revamped restaurant with an breezy roof garden and a plasticky indoor dining room. Serves good portions of the usual Indian and Chinese fare.

Nightlife

The big boom may be over, but Bangalore's bright young things still have money to spend, and **nightlife** in the city is thriving. A night on the town generally kicks off with a bar crawl along **Brigade Road**, **Residency Road** or **Church Street**, where there are scores of swish **pubs**, complete with MTV, lasers and thumping sound systems. Drinking alcohol does not have the seedy connotations here as it does elsewhere in India, and you'll even see young Indian women enjoying a beer with their mates. Pubs close at 11pm but, once in, you generally get served till later. For quiet, elegant drinking head for the bars of five-star **hotels** such as the *Jockey Club* at the *Taj Residency*, the *Polo Club* at the *Oberoi* or, for a taste of colonial grandeur, the *Colonnade* at the *Taj West End*.

Local listings magazines (see below) carry details of Bangalore's small but steady stream of **live music** and **theatre**, some of which is homegrown; there are also a handful of **discos**, though these usually follow a couples-only policy. Bangalore is also a major centre for **cinema**, with a booming industry and dozens of theatres showing the latest releases from India and abroad. Check the listings page of the *Deccan Herald*, the *Evening Herald*, the free listings monthly, *Trail Blazer*, and *Bangalore Fortnightly*, to find out what's on. Western movies are often dubbed into Hindi, although their titles may be written in English; check the small print in the newspaper. Cinema fans should head for **Kempe Gowda Circle**, where you'll find the Majestic and Triveni cinemas along with posters, hoardings and larger-than-life-size cardboard cutouts of the latest stars, strewn with spangly garlands. To arrange a visit to a local movie studio, phone Chamundeshwari Studio (☎080/2226 8642) or Shree Kanteera Studio (☎080/2337 1008).

Pubs and clubs

Down Town Next to Galaxy Cinema, Residency Road. Large pub that also serves food and wine, and has a couple of pool tables at the back.

Guzzlers Inn 48 Rest House Rd, off Brigade Rd. Popular and established pub offering MTV, Star Sport, snooker, pool and draught beer.

Nasa 1/4 Church St, next to Oasis. Sci-fi décor, featuring lasers and a mock space shuttle, and the usual combination of karaoke, big-screen MTV and in-your-face music.

Oasis Church St, next to Nasa. The chill-out option, with low light and an unobtrusive sound-system.

Pecos Rest House Rd, off Brigade Rd. Small and relaxed pub on two floors with 1960s and 1970s music; popular with a mixed arty set.

A Pinch of Jazz The Central Park, 47 Dickenson Rd. Upmarket jazz café serving Cajun cuisine and live soft-jazz covers.

Pub World Opposite Galaxy Cinema, Residency Rd. A well-presented newish place popular with trendy young professionals. Actually four pubs from different regions under one roof. The usual high-volume music and sports on TV.

Purple Haze Residency Rd. Still one of the trendiest of the downtown pubs with a smart but jumping upstairs bar sporting Jimi Hendrix-themed graphics. More chance of decent rock here than most places.

Spinn 80 3rd Cross, Residency Rd. Funk house and other dance music in old colonial house with hi-tech add-ons. No shorts. Open late.

Urban Edge 131 Brigade Rd. Hopping disco with an E-zone, games and regular theme nights.

Shopping

Bangalore has many fine shops, particularly if you're after **silk**. A wide range of silk is available at Karnataka Silk Industries Corporation and Vijayalakshmi Silk Kendra, both on Gupte Market, Kempe Gowda Road, and at Deepam Silk Emporium on MG Road. **Handicrafts** such as soapstone sculpture, brass, carved sandalwood and rosewood are also good value; emporia include: Central Cottage Industries Emporium, 144 MG Rd; the expensive Cottage Industries

Exposition Ltd, 3 Cunningham Rd; Gulshan Crafts, 12 Safina Plaza, Infantry Rd, and Karnataka's own state emporium, Cauvery, at the MG Road and Brigade Road crossing. For **silver**, try looking on and around Commercial Street (north of MG Road) and at KR Market on Residency Road, as well as at Jewels de Paragon between MG Road and Kasturba Road. The long-established Natesan's Antiqarts, 64 MG Rd, sells antiques and beautifully made reproduction sculpture, furniture and paintings at international art-house prices. If you want to take a look at expensive Indian haute couture try Ffolio at Embassy Chamber, Vittal Mallya Road, which features the work of several well-known Indian designers.

Bangalore is also a great place for **bookshops**. The first floor of Gangarams, 66 MG Rd, offers a wide selection on India (coffee-table art books and academic) plus the latest paperback fiction, and a great selection of Indian greetings cards. Another good option is Higginbotham's, 72 MG Rd, and you can browse in air-conditioned comfort at LB Publishers, 91 MG Rd. The shop belonging to established publishers Motilal Banarsidas at 16 St Mark's Rd, close to the junction with MG Road, offers a superb selection of heavyweight Indology and philosophy titles. Sankars at 15/2 Madras Bank Rd is an airy new shop with a good range of fiction, plus art, educational and religious books. Further afield in Gandhinagar, the Sapna Book House in the Thunga Complex opposite Tribhuvan Cinema is a massive 32,000 square-foot bibliophile's paradise. The best **music** shops in the city centre, selling Indian, Western and World music, are Music World and Planet M, both on Brigade Road, and Rhythms, at 14 St Mark's Rd, beneath the *Nahar Heritage* hotel.

Listings

Airlines (domestic) Air Deccan ☎98457 77008; Indian Airlines, Cauvery Bhavan, Kempe Gowda Rd ☎080/2297 8423 airport 2522 6233, enquiries ☎1407; Jet Airways, 1–4 M Block, Unity Building, JC Rd ☎080/2522 1929, airport 2522 0688; Sahara Airlines, 35 Church St ☎080/2558 3957, airport 2522 0065.

Airlines (international) Air France, Sunrise Chambers, 22 Ulsoor Rd ☎080/2558 9397; Air India, Unity Building, JC Rd ☎080/2227 7747; Alitalia, 44 Safina Plaza, Infantry Rd ☎080/2559 1936; American, 22 Sunrise Chambers, Ulsoor Rd ☎080/2559 4240; Austrian, 22 Sunrise Chambers, Ulsoor Rd ☎080/2559 4240; Biman Bangladesh, 22 Sunrise Chambers, Ulsoor Rd ☎080/2559 4240; British Airways, 7 Sophia's Choice, St Mark's Rd ☎080/2227 1205; Delta, Park View, 17 Curve Rd, Tasker Town ☎080/2286 7873; Gulf Air, Sunrise Chambers, 22 Ulsoor Rd ☎080/2558 4702; KLM/Northwest Airlines Taj West End, Race Course Rd ☎080/2226 5562; Lufthansa, 44/2 Dickenson Rd ☎080/2558 8791; Malaysian Airlines, Richmond Circle ☎080/2212 2991; Pakistan International Airlines, 108 Commerce House, 911 Cunningham Rd ☎080/2226 0667; Qantas, Westminster, Cunningham Rd ☎080/2226 4719; Singapore Airlines, Park View, 17 Curve Rd, Tasker Town ☎080/2286 7873; Swiss Air, Park View, 17 Curve Rd, Tasker Town ☎080/2286 7873; Thai Airways, G-5 Imperial Court, Cunningham Rd ☎080/5112 4333; United Airlines, 17–20 Richmond Towers, 12 Richmond Rd ☎080/2224 4620.

Banks and exchange Reliable places to change money include Thomas Cook, 55 MG Rd, on the corner of Brigade Rd; Weizmann Forex Ltd, 56 Residency Rd; and Wall Street Finances, 3 House of Lords, 13/14 St Mark's Rd (all Mon–Sat 9.30am–6pm). Better rates are still to be had at banks, however, of which the State Bank of Mysore on MG Rd is most convenient. There are an increasing number of ATMs dotted around the city, especially around MG Rd.

Car rental You can find self-drive car rental at Avis, The Oberoi, 37–39 MG Rd ☎080/2558 5858, ⓦ www.avis.com; and Hertz, Unit 12, Raheja Plaza, 17 Commissariat Rd ☎080/2559 9408, ⓦ www .hertz.com; both also have offices at the airport. Charges are from around Rs1000 per day.

Hospitals Victoria, near City Market ☎080/2670 1150; Sindhi Charitable, 3rd Main St, SR Nagar ☎080/2223 7318.

Internet access At the last count Bangalore had a staggering 700 email/Internet bureaus – charges are usually around Rs10–30 per hour and places open for most, if not all, 24 hours of the day. The Cyber Café, 13–15 Brigade Rd, is one of the most popular; coffee is available, but they don't encourage more than one person per computer. Alternatives include Cyber Craft, 33 Rest House Rd; and Cyber Den, first floor, S112A Manipal Centre, Dickenson Rd. There's a superfast DSL service at Hub, in the forecourt of Bangalore City railway station. A number of Internet joints also have Net2Phone facilities, such as the one outside Hotel Brindavan, off MG Rd.

Libraries The British Council (English-language) library, 23 Kasturba Rd Cross (Mon–Sat 10.30am–6.30pm; ☎080/2221 3485), has newspapers and magazines which visitors are welcome to peruse in a/c comfort, as does the Alliance Française (French), 16 GMT Rd (☎080/2225 8762), and Max Mueller Bhavan (German), 3 Lavelle Rd (☎080/2227 5435).

Pharmacies The following are open all night: Al-Siddique Pharma Centre, opposite Jami Masjid near City Market; Janata Bazaar, in the Victoria Hospital, near City Market; Sindhi Charitable Hospital, 3rd Main SR Nagar. During the day, head for Santoshi Pharma, 46 Mission Rd.

Photographic equipment Adlabs, Mission Rd, Subbaiah Circle, stocks transparency film. GG Welling, 113 MG Rd, and GK Vale, 89 MG Rd, sell transparency and Polaroid film.

Police ☎100.

Post office On the corner of Raj Bhavan Rd and Cubbon St, at the northern tip of Cubbon Park, about ten minutes' walk from MG Road (Mon–Sat 10am–7pm, Sun 10.30am–1.30pm).

Swimming pools The only luxury hotel pool open to non-residents (including sauna, jacuzzi and health club) is at the Taj West End (Rs500).

Travel agents For flight booking and reconfirmation and other travel necessities, try Gullivers Tours & Travels, South Black, 201/202 Manipal Centre, 47 Dickenson Rd ☎080/2558 8001; Merry Go Round Tours, 41 Museum Rd, next to the Empire International hotel ☎ & ☎080/2558 6946; Marco Polo Tours, Janardhan Towers, 2 Residency Rd ☎080/2227 4484, ☎2223 6671; and Sita Travels, 1 St Mark's Rd ☎080/2558 8892.

Around Bangalore

Bangalore is surrounded by some very pleasant countryside, which includes good walking country in the Nandi Hills to the north and the Bannerghatta National Park to the south. The **Janapada Loka Folk Arts Museum**, between Bangalore and Mysore, gives a fascinating insight into Karnataka culture, while anyone wishing to see or study classical dance in a rural environment should check out the **Nrityagram Dance Village**.

Janapada Loka Folk Arts Museum

The **Janapada Loka Folk Arts Museum** (daily 9am–6pm; free), 53km south-west of Bangalore on the Mysore road, includes an amazing array of Karnatakan agricultural, hunting and fishing implements, weapons, ingenious household gadgets, masks, dolls and shadow puppets, carved wooden *bhuta* (spirit-worship) sculptures and larger-than-life temple procession figures, manuscripts, musical instruments and *Yakshagana* theatre costumes. In addition, an incredible 1600 hours of **audio and video recordings** of musicians, dancers and rituals from the state are available for viewing on request.

To get to the museum, take one of the many slow Mysore buses (not the non-stop ones) from Bangalore; after the town of Ramanagar, alight at the 53-kilometre stone by the side of the road. The museum complex has a small **restaurant** serving simple food, and dorm **accommodation** (❶). For more details, contact the Karnataka Janapada Trust, 7 Subramanyaswami Temple Road, 5th Cross, 4th Block, Kumara Park West, Bangalore.

Nrityagram Dance Village

Nrityagram Dance Village (Tues–Sun 10am–5.30pm; Rs20) is a delightful purpose-built model village, 30km west of Bangalore, designed by the award-winning architect Gerard de Cunha and founded by the late Protima Gauri. The school attracts pupils from all over the world and hosts regular performances and

Bangalore is South India's principal transport hub. Fast and efficient computerized booking facilities make **moving on** relatively hassle-free, although the availability of seats should never be taken for granted; book as far in advance as possible. For an overview of travel services to and from Bangalore, see "Travel details" on pp.334–335.

Bangalore's modern **airport** is the busiest in South India, with international and domestic departures. The most frequent flights are to **Mumbai**, **Delhi** and **Chennai**, with at least ten daily flights to each operated by Air Deccan, Air India, Jet Airways, Indian Airlines and Sahara. For a full rundown of destinations, see "Travel details" on pp.334–335; addresses of airline offices and recommended travel agents appear in Listings on pp.252–253.

Most of the wide range of long-haul **buses** from Central Bus Stand can be booked in advance at the computerized counters near Bay 13 (7.30am–7.30pm). Aside from KSRTC, state bus corporations represented include Andhra Pradesh, Kerala, Maharashtra, Tamil Nadu and the Kadamba (Goa) Transport Corporation. Timings and ticket availability for the forthcoming week are posted on a large board left of the main entrance. For general enquiries, call ℡080/2287 3377. Several private bus companies run luxury coaches to destinations such as Mysore, Bijapur, Ooty, Chennai, Kochi/Ernakulam, Thrissur, Kollam and Thiruvananthapuram. Agencies opposite the bus stand sell tickets for private coach companies such as Sharma (℡080/2652 1924), National (℡080/2225 7202) and Shama (℡080/2670 3186), which all advertise overnight deluxe buses to **Goa** (Rs350) as well as sleeper coaches (Rs450) and services to **Mumbai** for Rs550 and **Chennai** for Rs250–450. The most reliable of the private bus companies is Vijayanand Travels, which has a branch at *Sri Saraswathi Lodge*, 3rd Main 2nd Cross, Gandhinagar (℡080/2228 7222) and several others throughout the city; their distinctive yellow-and-black luxury coaches run to destinations such as Mangalore and Hospet for Hampi.

While Southern Railways completes the conversion to broad gauge, the **line** from Hassan to Mangalore remains closed. Check the situation when you arrive. Bangalore City station's reservations office (Mon–Sat 8am–2pm & 2.15–8pm, Sun 8am–2pm; reservations 132) is in a separate building, east of the main station (to the

lectures on Indian mythology and art, as well as offering courses in different forms of Indian dance. **Guided tours** of the complex cost Rs850 per person (minimum 6), including lunch and a demonstration. **Accommodation** (❼) for longer stays promises "oxygen, home-grown vegetables and fruits, no TV, telephones, newspapers or noise". Contact their Bangalore office (℡080/2846 6313).

Mysore

A centre of sandalwood-carving, silk and incense production, 159km southwest of Bangalore, **MYSORE**, the erstwhile capital of the Wadiyar Rajas, is one of South India's most-visited places. Considering the clichés that have been heaped upon the town, however, first impressions can be disappointing. Like anywhere else in the region, visitors stumbling off the bus or train aren't greeted by the scent of jasmine blossom or gentle wafts of sandalwood but by the usual cacophony of careering auto-rickshaws and noisy buses, bullock carts and tongas. Nevertheless, Mysore is a charming, old-fashioned and undaunting town, dominated by the spectacular **Maharaja's Palace**, around which the boulevards of the city radiate. Just up the road from Mysore, **Srirangapatnam** still harbours architectural gems left as you approach). Counter 14 is for foreigners. If you have an Indrail Pass, go to the Chief Reservations Supervisor's Office on the first floor (turn left at the top of the stairs), where "reservations are guaranteed". There are two 24hr telephone information lines; one handles timetable enquiries (☎131), the other reels off a recorded list of arrivals and departures (☎133).

Recommended trains from Bangalore

The following trains are recommended as the fastest and/or most convenient from Bangalore.

Destination	Name	No.	Departs	Total time
Chennai	Shatabdi Express*	#2008	daily except Tues 4.25pm	5hr
	Lalbagh Express	#2608	daily 6.30am	5hr 30min
Delhi	Rajdhani Express*	#2429	4 weekly 6.35pm	34hr 40min
	Karnataka Express	#2627	daily 6.30pm	41hr 40min
Ernakulam (for Kochi)	Kanniyakumari Express	#6526	daily 9.45pm	11hr 50min
Hospet (for Hampi)	Hampi Express	#6592	daily 10.05pm	9hr 35min
Mumbai	Udyan Express	#6530	daily 8pm	23hr 55min
Mysore	Shatabdi Express*	#2007	daily except Tues 11am	2hr
	Tipu Express	#6206	daily 2.15pm	2hr 30min
	Chamundi Express	#6216	daily 6.15pm	3hr
Secunderabad (Hyderabad)	Rajdhani Express*	#2429	4 weekly 6.35pm	12hr 5min
Thiruvanan-thapuram	Kanniyakumari Express	#6526	daily 9.45pm	17hr

*= a/c only

from the days of the great Indian hero, Tipu Sultan, and the magnificent Hoysala temple of **Somnathpur** lies little more than an hour's drive away.

In the tenth century, Mysore was known as "Mahishur" – "the town where the demon buffalo was slain" (by the goddess Durga). Presiding over a district of many villages, the city was ruled from about 1400 until Independence by the Hindu **Wadiyars**, and its fortunes were inextricably linked with those of Srirangapatnam, which became the Wadiyar headquarters from 1616 (see p.262). Their rule was only broken from 1761, when the Muslim Haider Ali and his son Tipu Sultan took over. Two years later, the new rulers demolished the labyrinthine old city to replace it with the elegant grid of sweeping, leafy streets and public gardens that survives today. However, following Tipu Sultan's defeat in 1799 by the British colonel Arthur Wellesley (later the Duke of Wellington), Wadiyar power was restored. As the capital of Mysore state, the city thereafter dominated a major part of southern India. In 1956, when Bangalore became capital of newly formed Karnataka, its maharaja was appointed governor.

Arrival and information

Six or seven daily trains from the state capital arrive at the **railway station**, 1.5km northwest of the centre, with connections to and from Chennai. Mysore has three **bus** stands: major long-distance KSRTC services pull in to **Central**, near the heart of the city, where there's a friendly KSTDC booking counter for their tours, also good for information regarding bus times. The **Private** stand has moved to a new location on Sayaji Rao Rd, about 1km northwest. Local buses, including services for Chamundi Hill and Srirangaptnam, stop at the **City** stand, next to the northwestern corner of the Maharaja's Palace.

Five minutes' walk east of the railway station, on a corner of Irwin Road in the Old Exhibition Building, is the helpful **tourist reception centre** (daily 10am–5.30pm; ☎0821/422096), whose staff do their best to answer queries and can arrange transport, as well as give out brochures and maps. The **KSTDC office** (daily 6.30am–8.30pm; ☎0821/242 3652), at the hotel *Mayura Hoysala*, 2 Jhansi Lakshmi Bai Rd, is of little use except to book one of their **tours**. The whistle-stop city tour (7.30am–8.30pm; Rs160) makes for a long day, covering Jaganmohan Palace Art Gallery, the Maharaja's Palace, St Philomena's Cathedral, the Zoo, Chamundi Hill, Somnathpur, Srirangapatnam and Brindavan Gardens. It only leaves with a minimum of ten passengers, so you may not know for sure whether it will run when you buy your ticket. Their long-distance tour to Belur, Halebid and Sravanabelgola (7.30am–9pm; Rs250) isn't recommended, as it's too long for a single day and you spend far too much time on the bus; it's a similar story with their Ooty tour (7.30am–9pm; Rs300). However, their **car rental** rates, at Rs4.50 per kilometre (for a minimum of 250km per day), are quite reasonable if you want to put together your own itinerary. The private Tourist Corporation of India office, inside *Rajabhadra Lodge* on Gandhi Square (☎0821/526 0294), acts as a KSTDC agent and arranges tours and car rental.

The main **post office** (which handles poste restante) is on the corner of Ashoka and Irwin roads (Mon–Sat 10am–7pm, Sun 10.30am–1.30pm). If you need to **change money**, there's a State Bank of Mysore on the corner of Sayaji Rao and Sardar Patel Road, and an Indian Overseas Bank, Gandhi Square, opposite *Dasaprakash Hotel*. There are a couple of **ATMs** around Harding Circle and an Oriental Bank one at the station. For **Internet access**, try Netzone (Rs20 per hour), opposite the *Sangeeth Hotel*, or Internet Online (Rs30 per hour), on Chandragupta Road near *Mannars Hotel*.

Accommodation

The city has plenty of **hotels** to suit all budgets, and finding a room is only a problem during Dussehra, when popular places are booked up weeks in advance. Most foreigners stay near the Maharaja's Palace, on or around **Sri Harsha Road**, which has a range of accommodation to suit all budgets. Other pricier hotels are more spread out, but a good place to start is **Jhansi Lakshmi Bai Road**, which runs south from the railway station. If you're looking for total opulence, then head straight for the *Lalitha Mahal Palace*.

Inexpensive

Govardhan Opposite the Opera cinema, Sri Harsha Rd ☎0821/243 4118, ⊛www .hotelgovardhan.com. Basic budget rooms (some a/c) close to the palace. Frayed around the edges, but clean enough. ❷–❹

Indra Bhavan Dhanavantri Rd ☎0821/242 3933, Ⓕ242 2290, ⓔhotelindrabhavan@rediffmail.com. Dilapidated and characterful old lodge popular with Tibetans, with en-suite singles and doubles. Their "ordinary" rooms are a little grubby, but the good-value "deluxe" have clean tiled floors and open onto a wide common veranda. ❷

KSTDC Yatri Niwas 2 Jhansi Laxmi Bai Rd ☎0821/242 3492, ⊛www.kstdc.nic.in. The government-run Mayura Hoysala's economy wing, offering simple rooms around a central garden, plus dorm beds for Rs75. ❷

Mannars Lodge Chandragupta Rd ☎0821/244 8060. Deservedly popular backpackers hotel near the bus stand and Gandhi Square. No frills, though the deluxe rooms have TV. ❷

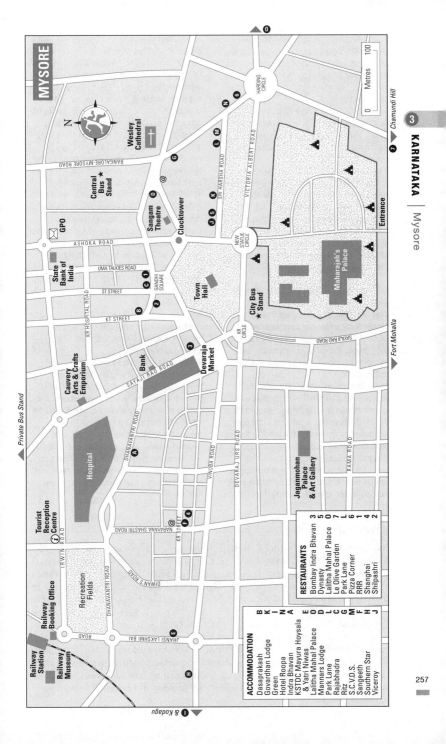

MYSORE

Wesley Cathedral

Central Bus Stand

GPO

State Bank of India

Sangam Theatre

Clocktower

Town Hall

Cauvery Arts & Crafts Emporium

Bank

Devaraja Market

Hospital

Tourist Reception Centre

Railway Booking Office

Railway Station

Railway Museum

Recreation Fields

Maharajah's Palace

City Bus Stand

Jaganmohan Palace & Art Gallery

HARDING CIRCLE

BANGALORE-MYSORE ROAD

ASHOKA ROAD

UMA TALKIES ROAD

ST STREET

GANDHI SQUARE

KT STREET

KR HOSPITAL ROAD

SAYAJI RAO ROAD

DHANAVANTRI ROAD

NARAYANA SHASTRI ROAD

KR STREET

DIWAN'S ROAD

VINOBA ROAD

DEVARAJ URS ROAD

RAMA ROAD

VICTORIA ALBERT ROAD

SRI HARSHA ROAD

NEW STATUE CIRCLE

KR CIRCLE

SAYAJI RAO ROAD

IRWIN ROAD

DHANAVANTRI ROAD

JHANSI LAKSHMI BAI ROAD

Entrance

Fort Mohalla

▲ Chamundi Hill

▲ Private Bus Stand

▲ Kodagu

Metres
0   100

N

ACCOMMODATION

Dasaprakash	B
Govardhan Lodge	K
Green	I
Hotel Roopa	N
Indra Bhavan	A
KSTDC Mayura Hoysala & Yatri Niwas	E
Lalitha Mahal Palace	O
Manmars Lodge	D
Park Lane	L
Rajabhadra	C
Ritz	G
S.C.V.D.S.	M
Sangeeth	F
Southern Star	H
Viceroy	J

RESTAURANTS

Bombay Indra Bhavan	3
Dynasty	5
Lalitha Mahal Palace	7
Le Olive Garden	L
Park Lane	L
Pizza Corner	6
RRR	1
Shanghai	4
Shilpashri	2

Park Lane Sri Harsha Rd ℡0821/243 4340, ℻242 8424. Eight pleasant clean rooms backing onto a popular beer-garden/restaurant. Just about the best deal going, but can get noisy and has some dodgy plumbing. Avoid room 8 (it's next to the generator). ❶

Rajabhadra Gandhi Square ℡0821/526 0152. Best value of several look-a-like lodges on the square. The front rooms are great if you don't mind being in the thick of things. Also has some singles. ❶

Ritz Bangalore–Nilgiri Rd ℡0821/242 2668, ℗hotelritz@rediffmail.com. Wonderful colonial-era hotel a stone's throw from the Private Bus Stand. Only four rooms, though, so book ahead. ❸

Sangeeth 1966 Narayana Shastry Rd, near the Udipi Krishna temple ℡0821/242 4693. One of Mysore's best all-round budget deals: bland and a bit boxed in, but friendly and very good value, and now with a new rooftop restaurant. ❷

Moderate to expensive

Dasaprakash Gandhi Square ℡0821/244 2444, ℗hoteldasaprakash@sancharnet.in. Slightly faded large hotel complex arranged round a spacious courtyard. It's busy, clean and efficient, though lacking character, and has some a/c rooms, cheap singles and a veg restaurant. ❸–❺

Green Chittaranjan Palace, 2270 Vinoba Rd, Jayalakshmipuram ℡0821/251 2536, ⓦwww.greenhotelindia.com. On the western outskirts of the city, this former royal palace has now been refurbished as an elegant, eco-conscious two-star set in large gardens. There are spacious rooms, lounges, verandas, a croquet lawn and well-stocked library, and all profits go to charities and environmental projects. Their auto-rickshaw will pick you up with prior arrangement. They can also

be contacted through the Charities Advisory Trust in London ℡020/7794 9835. ❼–❾

Lalitha Mahal Palace T Narasipur Rd ℡0821/247 0470, ⓦwww.lalithamahalpalace.com. On a slope overlooking the city, and visible for miles around, this white, Neoclassical palace was built in 1931 to accommodate the maharaja's foreign guests. It's now a Raj-style fantasy, popular with tour groups. Tariffs are astronomical by Indian standards, ranging from $70 turret rooms to $750 per night for the "Viceroy Suite". The tea lounge, restaurant and pool (Rs150) are open to non-residents, and there's a free snooker table in bar. ❾

KSTDC Mayura Hoysala 2 Jhansi Laxmi Bai Rd ℡0821/242 5349, ⓦwww.kstdc.nic.in. Reasonably priced rooms and suites in a colonial-era mansion with a terrace restaurant and beer garden. Good value, but the food is uninspiring. ❸–❺

Hotel Roopa 2724c Bangalore–Nilgiri Rd ℡0821/244 3770, ⓦwww.hotel-roopa.com. Sparkling new hotel block with compact but comfy rooms at surprisingly reasonable prices. Very handy for the palace. ❸–❺

S.C.V.D.S. Sri Harsha Rd ℡0821/242 1379, ℻242 7580. Newish lodge with cable TV in most rooms and some a/c. Very friendly, and offers a Rs50 discount to foreigners. ❸–❹

Southern Star Vinobha Rd ℡0821/242 6426, ⓦwww.ushashriramhotels.com. Modern and comfortable monolithic hotel, affiliated to Quality Inn, with all facilities, including two restaurants, a bar and a swimming pool. Rooms from Rs4200. ❾

Viceroy Sri Harsha Rd ℡0821/242 8001, ⓦwww.theviceroymysore.com. Snazzy new business-oriented hotel, with most mod-cons and views over the park to the palace from front rooms. Mostly a/c but generally rather overpriced, although there's a quality restaurant on ground floor. ❻–❼

The City

In addition to its official tourist attractions, chief amongst them the **Maharaja's Palace**, Mysore is a great city simply to stroll around. The characterful, if dilapidated, pre-Independence buildings lining market areas such as **Ashoka Road** and **Sayaji Rao Road** lend an air of faded grandeur to the busy centre, teeming with vibrant street life. The best place to get a sense of what's on offer is the Government Cauvery Arts and Crafts Emporium, Sayaji Rao Road (closed Thurs), which stocks a wide range of local crafts, which can be shipped overseas. Elsewhere, souvenir stores spill over with the famous **sandalwood**. The city's famous **Devaraja Market**, on Sayaji Rao Road, is one of South India's most atmospheric produce markets: a giant complex of covered stalls bursting with bananas (the delicious *nanjangod* variety), luscious mangoes, blocks of sticky jaggery and conical heaps of lurid *kumkum* powder.

Silk weaving in Mysore

As an important centre of silk production, Mysore has several silk factories, the most prestigious of which is the Karnataka Silk Industries Corporation's **Silk Weaving Factory** (Mon–Sat 10am–noon & 2–4pm) on HD Kote Road, 4km from the centre. Visitors are welcome and the showroom offers silk – mostly saris – at fixed but competitive prices. You will need a chit from the office to enter the complex; there are no conducted tours. The large factory, founded in the 1920s by the Maharaja of Mysore, runs in shifts signalled by wailing sirens, and consists of huge workshops filled with automated machines. You can see the silk being loomed, some batches with pure gold thread, before it goes into the dyeing process. The machine tenders are happy to explain the operation to you but, with the machines working flat out, you'll be lucky if you can hear a word over the deafening din. They also have a show-room at *KSTDC Yatri Niwas* hotel.

Maharaja's Palace

Mysore centre is dominated by the walled **Maharaja's Palace** (daily 10am–5.30pm; Rs12), a fairy-tale spectacle, topped with a shining brass-plated dome surmounting a single tower; it's especially magnificent on Sunday nights and during festivals, when it is illuminated by no fewer than five thousand light bulbs. Designed in the hybrid Indo-Saracenic style by Henry Irwin, the British consultant architect of Madras state, it was completed in 1912 for the 24th Wadiyar raja, on the site of the old wooden palace that had been destroyed by fire in 1897. Twelve temples surround the palace, some of them of much earlier origin. Although there are six gates in the perimeter wall, entry is on the south side only. Shoes and cameras must be left at the cloakroom inside.

An extraordinary amalgam of styles from India and around the world crowds the lavish **interior**. Entry is through the Gombe Thotti, or **Dolls' Pavilion**, once a showcase for the figures featured in the city's lively Dussehra celebrations and now a gallery of European and Indian sculpture and ceremonial objects. Halfway along the pavilion, the brass **Elephant Gate** forms the main entrance to the centre of the palace, through which the maharaja would drive to his car park. Decorated with floriate designs, it bears the Mysore royal symbol of a double-headed eagle, now the state emblem. To the north, past the gate, are dolls dating from the turn of the century, a wooden *mandapa* glinting with mirrorwork and, at the end, a ceremonial wooden elephant *howdah* (frame to carry passengers). Elaborately decorated with 84kg of 24-carat gold, it appears to be inlaid with red and green gems – in fact, the twinkling lights are battery-powered signals to let the *mahout* know when the maharaja wished to stop or go.

Walls leading into the octagonal **Kalyana Mandapa**, the royal wedding hall, are lined with a meticulously detailed frieze of oil paintings illustrating the great Mysore Dussehra festival of 1930, executed over fifteen years by four Indian artists. The hall itself is magnificent, a cavernous space featuring cast-iron pillars from Glasgow, Bohemian chandeliers and multicoloured Belgian stained glass arranged in peacock designs in the domed ceiling. A mosaic of English floor tiles repeats the peacock motif. Beyond here lie small rooms cluttered with grandiose furniture, including a pair of silver chairs and others of Belgian cut-crystal made for the maharaja and Lord Mountbatten, the last Viceroy of India. One of the rooms has a fine ceiling of Burma teak carved by local craftsmen.

Climbing a staircase with Italian marble balustrades, past an unnervingly realistic life-size plaster-of-Paris figure of Krishnaraja Wadiyar IV, lounging

Mysore Dussehra festival

Following the tradition set by the Vijayanagar kings, the ten-day festival of **Dusse-hra** (Sept/Oct), commemorating the goddess Durga's slaying of the demon buffalo, Mahishasura, is celebrated in grand style at Mysore. Scores of cultural events occur, including concerts of South Indian classical (Carnatic) music and dance perform-ances, in the great Durbar Hall of the Maharaja's Palace. On Vijayadasmi, the tenth and last day of the festival, a magnificent procession of mounted guardsmen on horseback and caparisoned elephants – one carrying the palace deity, Chaamun-deshwari, on a gold *howdah* – marches 5km from the palace to Banni Mantap. There's also a floating festival in the temple tank at the foot of Chamundi Hill and a procession of chariots around the temple at the top. A torchlight parade takes place in the evening, followed by a massive firework display and much jubilation in the streets.

comfortably with his bejewelled feet on a stool, you come into the **Public Durbar Hall**, an Orientalist fantasy often compared to a setting from *A Thousand and One Nights*. A vision of brightly painted and gilded colonnades, open on one side, the massive hall affords views out across the parade ground and gardens to Chamundi Hill. The maharaja gave audience from here, seated on a throne made from 280kg of solid Karnatakan gold. These days, the hall is only used during the Dussehra festival, when it hosts classical concerts. Paintings by the celebrated artists Shilpi Siddalingaswamy and Raja Rama Varma, from the Travancore (Kerala) royal family, adorn the walls. The whole is crowned by white marble, inlaid with delicate floral scrolls of jasper, amber and lapis lazuli in the Moghul style. Somewhat out of sync with the opulence are a series of ceiling panels of Vishnu, painted on fire-proof asbestos, dating from the 1930s. The smaller **Private Durbar Hall** features especially beautiful stained glass and gold-leaf painting. Before leaving you pass two embossed silver doors – all that remains of the old palace.

Nearby, behind the main palace building but within the same compound, a line of tacky souvenir shops leads to a small **museum** (same hours; Rs20) run by the royal family which shows paintings from the Thanjavur and Mysore schools, some inlaid with precious stones and gold leaf. After a lengthy judicial tussle, in 1998 the courts decided in favour of formally placing the main palace in the hands of the Karnataka state government, but the royal family, who still hold a claim, are set to appeal.

Jaganmohan Palace: Jayachamarajendra Art Gallery

Built in 1861, the **Jaganmohan Palace** (daily 8am–5pm; Rs10; no cameras), 300m west of the Maharaja's Palace, was used as a royal residence until it was turned into a picture gallery and museum in 1915 by Maharaja Krishnaraja Wadiyar IV. Most of the "contemporary" art on show dates from the 1930s, when a revival of Indian painting was spearheaded by E.B. Havell and the Tagore brothers Rabrindrath and Gaganendranath in Bengal.

On the ground floor, a series of faded black-and-white photos of ceremo-nial occasions shares space with elaborate imported clocks. Nineteenth- and twentieth-century paintings dominate the first floor; among them is the work of the pioneering oil painter Raja Ravi Varma who, although not everyone's cup of tea, has been credited with introducing modern techniques to Indian art. Inspired by European masters, Varma gained a reputation in portraiture and also depicted epic Indian themes from the classics, such as the demon king Ravana absconding with Rama's wife Sita. Games on the upper floor include circular *ganjeeb* playing cards illustrated with portraits of royalty or deities and board games delicately inlaid with ivory. There's also a cluster of musical instruments, among them a brass *jaltarang* set and glass xylophone, and harmonicas and clarinet played by Krishnaraja Wadiyar IV himself. Another gallery, centering on a large wooden Ganesh seated on a tortoise, is lined with paintings, including Krishnaraja Wadiyar sporting with the "inmates" of his *zenana* (women's quarter of the palace) during Holi.

Chamundi Hill

Chamundi Hill, 3km southeast of the city, is topped with a temple to the chosen deity of the Mysore Rajas: the goddess Chamundi, or Durga, who slew the demon buffalo Mahishasura. It's a pleasant, easy bus trip (#201 from the City Bus Stand) to the top: sit on the left side for the best views; the walk down, past a huge Nandi – Shiva's bull – takes about thirty minutes. Pilgrims, of course, make the trip in reverse order. The walk isn't very demanding, but by the end of it, after more than a thousand steps, your legs are likely to be a bit wobbly. Take plenty of drinking water, especially if you're walking in the middle of the day.

Don't be surprised if, at the top of the hill, which is dominated by the temple's forty-metre *gopura*, you're struck by a feeling of déjà vu: as one of the displays at the **Godly Museum** at the summit states, "5000 years ago at this time you had visited this place in the same way you are visiting now. Because world drama repeats itself identically every 5000 years." Another exhibit goes to the heart of our "problematic world: filthy films, lack of true education, blind faith, irreligiousness, bad habits and selfishness". Suitably edified, proceed along a path from the bus stand, past trinket and tea stalls, to the temple square. Immediately to the right, at the end of this path, are four bollards painted with a red stripe; return here after visiting the temples, when you want to take the path back down the hill.

Non-Hindus can visit the twelfth-century **temple** (daily 7am–2pm, 3.30–6pm & 7–9pm), staffed by friendly priests who will plaster your forehead in vermilion paste. The Chamundi figure inside is solid gold; outside, in the courtyard, stands a fearsome if gaily coloured statue of the demon Mahishasura. On leaving, if you continue by the path instead of retracing your steps, you can return to the square via two other temples and various buildings storing ceremonial paraphernalia and animal figures used during Dussehra. You'll also come across loads of scampering monkeys and the odd dreadlocked *sadhu*, who will willingly pose for your holiday snaps – for a consideration. The magnificent five-metre **Nandi**, carved from a single piece of black granite in 1659, is an object of worship himself, adorned with bells and garlands and tended by his own priest. Minor shrines, dedicated to Chamundi and the monkey god Hanuman among others, line the side of the path and, at the bottom, a little shrine to Ganesh lies near a chai-shop. From here it's usually possible to pick up an auto-rickshaw or bus, back into the city, but at weekends the latter are often full. If you walk on towards the city, passing a temple on the left, with a big water tank (the site of the floating festival during Dussehra), you come after ten minutes to the main road between the *Lalitha Mahal Palace* and the city; there's a bus stop, and often auto-rickshaws, at the junction.

Eating

Mysore has scores of **places to eat**, from numerous South Indian "meals" joints dotted around the market to the opulent *Lalita Mahal Palace*, where you can work up an appetite for a gourmet meal by swimming a few lengths of the pool. To sample the celebrated Mysore *pak*, a sweet, rich, crumbly mixture made of ghee and maize flour, queue at *Guru Sweet Mart*, a small stall at KR Circle, Savaji Rao Road, which is considered the best sweet shop in the city. Another speciality from this part of the world is *malligi iddli*, a delicate light fluffy *iddli* usually served in the mornings and at lunch at several of the downtown "meals" restaurants.

Bombay Indra Bhavan Savaji Rao Rd. Comfortable and popular veg restaurant that serves both south and north Indian cuisine and sweets. Their other branch on Dhanavantri Road (see p.256) is equally popular and also has an a/c section.
Dynasty Palace Plaza hotel, Sri Harsha Rd. Dark but nicely decorated restaurant/bar serving Indian, Chinese and Continental veg and non-veg dishes. The same menu is also available at the roof garden restaurant.
Lalitha Mahal Palace T Naraispur Rd. Sample the charms of this palatial five-star with an expensive hot drink in the atmospheric tea lounge, or an à la carte lunch in the grand dining hall, accompanied by live sitar music. The old-style bar also boasts a full-size billiards table.
Le Olive Garden Near the bottom of Chamundi Hill, 2km southeast of the city. Leafy garden restaurant serving tandoori, Chinese and Western dishes. Occasional live entertainment. Moderately expensive.
Park Lane Sri Harsha Rd. Congenial courtyard restaurant-cum-beer garden, with moderately priced veg and non-veg food (meat sizzlers are a speciality), pot plants and live Indian classical music every evening. Popular with travellers and Indians alike, and there's a ladies and family balcony upstairs.
Pizza Corner Bangalore-Nilgiri Rd, near Harding Circle. New branch of the Bangalore chain serving high-quality pizza in bright plastic Western decor.
RRR Gandhi Square. A plain "meals" restaurant in front with a small but plush a/c room at the back which gets packed at lunchtimes and at weekends. Well worth the wait for its excellent set menus on banana leaves, chicken biriyani and fried fish.
Shanghai 1487 Shivrampet. Fine Chinese and Japanese fare served in an elongated dining room. Teppan yaki dishes feature among the better known faves.
Shilpashri Gandhi Square. Quality north Indian-style food, with particularly tasty tandoori (great chicken tikka) plus plenty of good veg options, including lots of dhals and curd rice. Serves alcohol.

Around Mysore

Mysore is a jumping-off point for some of Karnataka's most popular destinations. At **Srirangapatnam**, the fort, palace and mausoleum date from the era of Tipu Sultan, the "Tiger of Mysore", a perennial thorn in the side of the British. To the southeast, the superb **Hoysala temple** of **Somnathpur** is an architectural masterpiece, while the little-visited hilltop Jain shrine at **Gomatagiri** is a veritable oasis of tranquillity northwest of the city.

If you're heading south towards Ooty, **Bandipur National Park**'s forests and hill scenery offer another escape from the city, although your chances of spotting any rare animals are quite slim. The same is true of **Nagarhole National Park**, three hours southwest of Mysore towards the Kerala border.

Srirangapatnam

The tiny island of **Srirangapatnam**, in the Kaveri (Cauvery) River, 14km north of Mysore, measures only 5km by 1km. Long a site of Hindu pilgrimage, it is named for its tenth-century Sriranganathaswamy Vishnu temple, which in 1133 served as a refuge for the philosopher Ramanuja, a staunch Vaishnavite, from the Shaivite Cholas in Tamil Nadu. The Vijayanagars built a fort here in 1454, and in 1616 it became the capital of the Mysore Wadiyar rajas. However, Srirangapatnam is more famously associated with **Haider Ali**, who deposed the Wadiyars in 1761, and even more so with his son, **Tipu Sultan**. During Tipu's

If you're contemplating a long journey from Mysore, the best way to travel is by **train**, usually with a change at **Bangalore**. Six or seven express services and six passenger trains leave Mysore each day for the Karnatakan capital. The fastest of these, the a/c Shatabdi Express (#2008; daily except Tues 2.20pm; 1hr 55min), continues on to Chennai; most of the others terminate in Bangalore, where you can pick up long-distance connections to a wide range of Indian cities (see box on pp.254–255). **Reservations** can be made at Mysore's computerized booking hall inside the station (Mon–Sat 8am–2pm & 2.15–8pm, Sun 8am–2pm). There are four services daily to **Hassan**, of which the Shimoga Express (#268; 10.15am; 2hr 5min) is substantially faster than the other passenger trains.

Given the number of trains between Mysore and Bangalore, you shouldn't ever have to do the trip by **bus**, which takes longer and is a lot more terrifying. Most destinations within a day's ride of Mysore can only be reached by road. Long-distance services operate out of Central Bus Stand, where you can book computerized tickets up to three days in advance. English timetables are posted on the wall inside the entrance hall, and there's a helpful enquiries counter in the corner of the compound. Regular buses leave here for **Hassan** (3–4hr), jumping-off place for the Hoysala temples at **Belur** and **Halebid**, for Channarayapatna/**Sravanabelgola** (2hr 30min–3hr) and for **Hubli** (for Hospet/**Hampi**). Heading south to **Ooty** (5hr), there's a choice of eight buses, all of which stop at **Bandipur National Park**. Direct services to several cities in Kerala, including **Kannur**, **Kozhikode** and **Kochi**, also operate from Mysore. The only way to travel direct to **Goa** is on the 4pm or 5pm overnight buses that arrive at **Panjim** at 9am and 10am respectively. Most travellers, however, break this long trip into stages, heading first to **Mangalore** (7hr), and working their way north from there, usually via **Gokarna** – which you can also reach by direct bus (14hr) – or **Jog Falls**. Mangalore-bound buses and coaches tend to pass through **Madikeri**, capital of Kodagu (Coorg), which is also served by hourly buses, most of which travel through the Tibetan enclave of **Bylakuppe**. For details of services to **Somnathpur** and **Srirangapatnam**, see the relevant accounts below. A host of tour agents can make bookings for **private buses** to many destinations – the Tourist Corporation of India at the *Rajabhadra Lodge* is one of the best.

Mysore doesn't have an **airport** (the nearest one is at Bangalore), but you can confirm and book Indian Airlines flights at their office in the KSTDC *Mayura Hoysala* (Mon–Sat 10am–1.30pm & 2.15–5pm; ☎0821/242 1846).

seventeen-year reign – which ended with his death in 1799, when the future Duke of Wellington took the fort at the bloody battle of Seringapatnam – he posed a greater threat than any other Indian ruler to British plans to dominate India.

Tipu Sultan and his father were responsible for transforming the small state of Mysore into a major Muslim power. Born in 1750, of a Hindu mother, Tipu Sultan inherited Haider Ali's considerable military skills. However, unlike his illiterate father, he was an educated, cultured man who introduced radical agricultural reforms. His burning, life-long desire to rid India of the hated British invaders naturally brought him an ally in the French. He obsessively embraced his popular name of the **Tiger of Mysore**, surrounding himself with symbols and images of tigers; much of his memorabilia is decorated with the animal or its stripes, and, like the Romans, he is said to have kept tigers for the punishment of criminals.

Tipu Sultan's Srirangapatnam was largely destroyed by the British, but parts of the fort area in the northwest survive, including gates, ramparts, arsenals, the

Wildlife sanctuaries around Mysore

In addition to Bandipur and Nagarhole (see p.266 & p.268), two lesser wildlife sanctuaries lie within striking distance of Mysore. The closer, some 2km southwest of Srirangapatnam, is the **Ranganathittu Bird Sanctuary** (daily 9am–6pm; Rs60 [Rs20]). It's a must for ornithologists, especially during October and November, when the lake, fed by the Kaveri River, attracts huge flocks of migrating birds. At other times it's a tranquil spot to escape the city, with boat rides (Rs25) available through the backwaters to look for crocodiles, otters and dozens of species of resident waders, wildfowl and forest birds. The easiest way to get there is by **rickshaw** from Srirangapatnam.

The **Biligiri Rangaswamy Wildlife Sanctuary**, 90km to the east of Mysore, lies in an unspoiled corner of the state inhabited by the Soliga tribe. Covering an area of 525 square kilometres, the deciduous forests spread over the picturesque Biligiri Rangaswamy Hills harbour myriad forms of wildlife, including elephant, panther, tiger, wild dog, sloth bear and several species of deer. Despite the thick cover, the sanctuary is a bird-watcher's dream, with over 270 species, including the majestic crested hawk eagle. Accessible by bus via Nanjangod and Chamarajnagar, the sanctuary is being promoted by Jungle Lodges & Resorts, Bangalore (℡080/2559 7021, www .junglelodges.com), a government-sponsored organization which aims to promote wildlife in the state through comfortable, upmarket camps and resorts. Their luxurious *K Gudi* widerness camp at the sanctuary charges Indian visitors Rs1000 per person per night and foreigners US$50 for an all-inclusive stay, including elephant ride and forest walks.

grim dungeons (where chained British prisoners were allegedly forced to stand neck-deep in water) and the domed and minareted Jami Masjid mosque. The former summer palace, the **Daria Daulat Bagh** (daily except Fri 10am–5pm; $2 [Rs5]), literally meaning "wealth of the sea", is situated 1km east of the fort and was used to entertain Tipu Sultan's guests. At first sight, this low, wooden colonnaded building set in an attractive formal garden fails to impress because most of it is obscured by sunscreens. However, the superbly preserved interior, displaying ornamental arches, tiger-striped columns and floral decoration on every inch of the teak walls and ceiling, is remarkable. A much-repainted mural on the west wall relishes every detail of Haider Ali's victory over the British at Pollilore in 1780. Upstairs, a small collection of Tipu Sultan memorabilia, European paintings, Persian manuscripts on handmade paper and a model of Srirangapatnam are on show.

An avenue of cypress trees leads from an intricately carved gateway to the **Gumbaz mausoleum** (daily except Fri 9am–5pm; free), 3km east of the palace. Built by Tipu Sultan in 1784 to commemorate Haider Ali, and to serve as his own resting place, the lower half of the grey granite edifice is crowned by a dome of whitewashed brick and plaster. Ivory-inlaid rosewood doors lead to the tombs of Haider Ali and Tipu Sultan, each covered by a pall (tiger stripes for Tipu), while an Urdu tablet records Tipu Sultan's martyrdom. The interior walls are also painted in striking tiger colours.

At the heart of the fortress, the great temple of **Sriranganathaswamy** still stands proud and virtually untouched by the turbulent history that has flowed around it, and remains, for many devotees, the prime draw. Developed by succeeding dynasties, the temple consists of three distinctive sanctuaries and is entered via an impressive five-storey gateway and a hall built by Haider Ali. The innermost sanctum, the oldest part of the temple, open to all, contains an image of the reclining Vishnu.

Practicalities

Frequent buses from Mysore City bus stand (including #313 and #316) and all Mysore–Bangalore trains pull in near the temple and fort. Srirangapatnam is a small island, but places of interest are quite spread out; tongas, auto-rickshaws and bicycles are available on the main road near the bus stand. The KSTDC hotel-cum-restaurant, *Mayura River View* (℡08236/252114; ❹–❺), occupies a pleasant spot beside the Kaveri, 3km from the bus stand. Another good option is the smart and elegant *Fort View Resorts* (℡08236/252777; ❺–❻), set in its own grounds not far from the fort entrance.

Gomatagiri

Eighteen kilometres to the northwest of the city near the small town of Betta-door is the hill of **Gomatagiri**, where a monolithic five-metre-high statue of **Gomateshvara** stands gazing serenely over the surrounding countryside from atop a rocky granite outcrop. Also known as Bahubali, the son of the first Jain *tirthankara*, Gomateshvara is shown here, as he is in sites all over southern Karnataka, naked and in a state of deep meditation, with his arms limp by his sides. An idyllic spot among eucalyptus groves, Gomatagiri sees no tourists. The only other building here besides the temple on top of the hill is the Jain guest-house where the welcoming caretaker-cum-priest lives; he will gladly open the temple for you.

Small shrines litter the base of the outcrop and house the footprints of the 24 Jain *tirthankaras*. Steps hewn out of rock lead up to the temple and the eleventh-century temple, with distant views out towards the Brindavan Gardens and the Krishnaraja Sagar dam on the Kaveri River. The only time the peace of the place is at all disturbed is during the **Mastakabhisheka ceremony** around September every year, when the statue is anointed with a nectar of milk.

If you're tempted to stay here, **accommodation** is limited to the very basic rooms of the guesthouse (❶), none of which have beds, so bring a mat. Bus #264 from Mysore's City Bus Stand runs past Gomatagiri five times a day, with the first bus at 6.30am and the last at 6.30pm. The journey takes one hour and the bus continues to a village a short distance past Gomatagiri, then after a short break heads back to Mysore the way it came.

Somnathpur

Built in 1268 AD, the exquisite **Keshava Vishnu temple** (daily 9am–5pm; $2 [Rs5]), in the sleepy hamlet of **SOMNATHPUR**, was the last important temple to be constructed by the Hoysalas; it is also the most complete and, in many respects, the finest example of this singular style (see box on p.273). Somnathpur itself, just ninety minutes from Mysore by road, is little more than a few neat tracks and some attractive simple houses with pillared verandas.

Like other Hoysala temples, the Keshava is built on a star-shaped plan, but, as a triple shrine, it represents a mature development from the earlier construc-tions. ASI staff can show you around and also give you permission to clamber up onto the enclosure walls to get a marvellous bird's-eye view of the modestly proportioned structure. It's best to do this as early in the day as possible, as the stone gets very hot to walk on in bare feet.

The temple is in the style of a *trikutachala* or "three-peaked hill", with a tower on each shrine – a configuration also seen in certain Chalukya temples and in the three temples on Hemakuta Hill at Vijayanagar (Hampi; see p.315). Each shrine, sharing a common hallway, is dedicated to a different form of Vishnu. In order of "seniority" they are Keshava in the central shrine, Venugopala to the right and Jagannath to the left. The Keshava shrine features a very unusual *chandrasila* ("moonstone") step at its entrance and, diverging from the usual semicircular Hoysala style, has two pointed projections.

The Keshava's high plinth (*jagati*) provides an upper ambulatory, which on its outer edge reproduces the almost crenellated shape of the structure and allows visitors to approach the upper sections of the profusely decorated walls. Among the many superb images here are an unusually high proportion of Shaivite figures for a Vishnu temple. As at Halebid, a lively frieze details countless episodes from the Ramayana, *Bhagavata Purana* and Mahabharata. Intended to accompany circumambulation, the panels are "read" (there is no text) in a clockwise direction. Unusually, the temple is autographed; all its sculpture was the work of one man, named Malitamba.

Outside the temple stands a *dvajastambha* column, which may originally have been surmounted by a figure of Vishnu's bird-vehicle Garuda. The wide ground-level ambulatory that circles the whole building is edged with numerous, now empty, shrines.

Practicalities

There are no direct **buses** from Mysore to Somnathpur. Buses from the Private Bus Stand run to **T Narasipur** (1hr), from where there are regular buses to Somnathpur (20min). Everyone will know where you want to go, and someone will show you which scrum to join. Alternatively, join one of KSTDC's guided tours (see p.256). There's nowhere to stay near the temple and the only **food** available is in the shape of biscuits or maybe a samosa at one of the chai stalls or fruit from a street-seller; you'll have to go back to the cheap "meals" hotels at T Narasipur for anything more substantial.

Tucked in the backwaters of a dammed section of the Cauvery, a further 25km southeast, the exquisite *Talakadu Jaladhana* **resort** (☎0821/271197, ✉jaladhana@hotmail.com; ➒) offers secluded cottages, some with rooftop hot tubs and herb gardens, and full board for Rs1770 per person. Boating and sports activities are available, and it can be reached by direct private bus from Mysore.

National parks around Mysore

Mysore lies within striking distance of three major wildlife sanctuaries: **Bandipur**, **Nagarhole** and **Mudumalai**, across the border in Tamil Nadu – all of which are part of the vast **Nilgiri Biosphere Reserve**, one of India's most extensive tracts of protected forest. The parks are once again fully open to tourists, since the bandit Veerappan (see p.574), who terrorized the region for years until being killed in October 2004. A few upmarket private "resorts" on the edge of the parks and one or two tourist complexes allow visitors to experience the delights of an area renowned for its **elephants**. Forest Department accommodation at Bandipur (see opposite) and Nagarhole (see p.268) must be booked as far in advance as possible through their offices at Aranya Bhavan, Ashokapuram (☎0821/248 0901), 6km south of the centre of Mysore, on bus #61 from the City Bus Stand, or at Aranya Bhavan, 18th Cross, Malleswaram, Bangalore (☎080/2334 1993). For information on Mudumalai see p.574.

Bandipur National Park

Situated among the broken foothills of the Western Ghat mountains, **Bandipur National Park**, 80km south of Mysore, covers 880 square kilometres of dry deciduous forest south of the River Kabini. Created in the 1930s from the local maharaja's hunting lands and expanded in 1941, Bandipur – in spite of its good accommodation and well-maintained metalled jeep tracks – is a disappointment as a wildlife-viewing destination. Glimpses of anything more exciting than a langur or spotted deer are rare outside the core area, which is off limits, while the noisy diesel bus laid on by the Forest Department to transport tourists around the accessible areas of park scares off what little fauna remains.

On the plus side, Bandipur is one of the few reserves in India where you stand a good chance of sighting wild **elephants**, particularly in the wet season (June–Sept), when water and forage are plentiful and the animals evenly scattered. Later in the monsoon, huge herds congregate on the banks of the River Kabini, in the far north of the park, where you can see the remnants of an old stockade used by one particularly zealous nineteenth-century British hunter as an elephant trap.

Bandipur also boasts some fine scenery: at **Gopalswamy Betta**, 9km from the park reception centre, a high ridge looks north over the Mysore Plateau and its adjoining hills, while to the south, the **Rolling Rocks** afford sweeping views of the craggy, 260-metre-deep **Mysore Ditch**.

Practicalities

The **best time to visit** is during the rainy season (June–Sept); unlike neighbouring parks, Bandipur's roads do not get washed out by the annual deluge, and elephants are more numerous at this time. By November/December, however, most of the larger animals have migrated across the state border into Mudumalai, where water is more plentiful in the dry season. **Avoid weekends**, as the park attracts busloads of noisy day-trippers.

Getting to Bandipur by bus is easy; all regular KSRTC services to Ooty from Mysore's Central Bus Stand (12 daily; 2hr 30min) pass through the reserve (the last one back to Mysore leaves at 5pm), stopping outside the Forest Department's reception centre same (daily 9am–4.30pm). If you miss the last bus from Mysore you can change at Gundulapet, 18km away, from where you can also take a taxi to the main reception centre (Rs220). There's a Rs150 [Rs50] **entrance fee**, plus Rs20 per camera.

You can confirm **accommodation** bookings in the sanctuary at the Forest Department's reception centre. Comfort varies from beds in large, institutional dorms to the "VIP" *Gajendra Cottages*, which have en-suite bathrooms and verandas. Upmarket options include *Tusker Trails*, a **resort** run by members of the royal family of Mysore, at Mangala village, 3km from Bandipur (bookable through their office at Hospital Cottage, Bangalore Palace, Bangalore; ℡080/2353 0748, ℻2334 2862; ❾), which has cottages, a swimming pool and a tennis court and organizes trips into the forest; *Bush Betta*, off the main Mysore highway (bookable through Gainnet, Raheja Plaza, Richmond Road, Bangalore; ℡080/2551 2631; ❾), offers comfortable cottages and guided tours; and Jungle Lodges & Resorts' *Bandipur Safari Lodge* (℡080/2559 7021, Ⓦwww .junglelodges.com; ❾), where foreigners pay a somewhat overpriced $50 per person per night for comfortable but not particularly luxurious facilities.

Unless you have your own vehicle or are booked on to an upmarket hotel tour, the only **transport around the park** is the hopeless Forest Department bus, which makes two tours daily (6–9am & 4–6pm; Rs25). You may see a deer or two, but nothing more, on the half-hour **elephant ride** (Rs50) around the reception compound. Visitors travelling to Gopalswamy Betta should note that car rental is not available at Bandipur; you can get a car at Gundulapet, but operators will try and charge a lot more than the official Rs500. You must exit the park before nightfall.

Nagarhole National Park

Bandipur's northern neighbour, **Nagarhole** ("Snake River") **National Park**, extends 640 square kilometres north from the River Kabini, dammed to form a picturesque artificial lake. During the dry season (Feb–June) this perennial water source attracts large numbers of animals, making it a potentially prime spot for sighting wildlife. The forest here is of the moist deciduous type – thick jungle with a thirty-metre-high canopy – and more impressive than Bandipur's drier scrub.

However, disaster struck Nagarhole in 1992, when friction between local pastoralist "tribals" and the park wardens over grazing rights and poaching erupted into a spate of arson attacks during which thousands of acres of forest were burned to the ground. The trees have grown back in places, but it will be decades before animal numbers completely recover. An added threat to the region's fragile jungle tracts is a notorious female gang of wood smugglers from Kerala, who have developed a fearsome and almost mythical reputation. Meanwhile, Nagarhole is only worth visiting at the height of the dry season, when its muddy riverbanks and grassy swamps, or *hadlus*, offer better chances of sighting gaur (Indian bison), elephant, *dhole* (wild dog), deer, boar, and even the odd tiger or leopard, than any of the neighbouring sanctuaries.

Practicalities

Nagarhole is open year-round, but avoid the monsoons, when floods wash out most of its dirt tracks and leeches make hiking impossible. To get there from Mysore, catch one of the two daily **buses** from the Central Bus Stand to **Hunsur** (3hr), 10km from the park's north gate, where you can pick up transport to the Forest Department's two rest houses (②–⑤). The **rest houses** have to be booked well in advance through the Forest Department offices in Mysore or Bangalore (see Bandipur, p.267). Turn up on spec, and you'll be told that accommodation isn't available. It's also essential to arrive at the park gates well before dusk, as the road through the reserve closes at 6pm and is prone to "elephant blocks". The Nagarhole **visitor centre** charges a Rs150 [Rs50] entrance fee plus Rs20 per camera. They organize elephant rides (Rs50) and schedule bus tours round the sanctuary (6–9am & 3.30–6pm; Rs50).

Other **accommodation** around Nagarhole includes the highly acclaimed and luxurious *Kabini River Lodge* (book through Jungle Lodges & Resorts in Bangalore; ☏080/2559 7021; ⑨), approached via the village of Karapura, 3km from the park's south entrance. Set in its own leafy compound on the lakeside, this former maharaja's hunting lodge offers expensive deals for $110 per person per night that include meals, transport around the park with expert guides. It's impossible to reach by public transport, so you'll need to rent a car to get there, and you'll also have to book well in advance. Another upmarket option, though not quite in the same league, is the *Jungle Inn* at Veerana Hosahalli (☏08222/252781; ⑨; bookable through their Bangalore office ☏080/2224 3172), which is close to the park entrance and arranges wildlife safaris, with a very hefty surcharge for foreign visitors. Some tour groups prefer the luxury of *Orange County* (see p.284) near the town of Siddapura in Kodagu 75km to the north, despite the long drive.

Hassan and around

Unprepossessing **HASSAN**, 118km northwest of Mysore, is visited in disproportionately large numbers because of its proximity to the Hoysala temples at

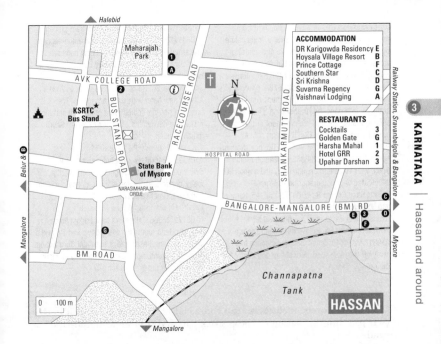

Belur and Halebid, both northwest of the town, and the Jain pilgrimage site of Sravanabelgola to the southeast. Some travellers end up staying a couple of nights, killing time in neon-lit thali joints and dowdy hotel rooms, but with a little forward planning you shouldn't have to linger here for longer than it takes to get on a bus somewhere else. Set deep in the serene Karnatakan countryside, Belur, Halebid and Sravanabelgola are much more congenial places to stay.

Practicalities

Hassan's **KSRTC bus stand** is in the centre of town, at the northern end of Bus Stand Road, which runs south past the post office to **Narsimharaja Circle**. Here you'll find most of the town's accommodation and also the State Bank of Mysore, where you can change money, but not Thomas Cook travellers' cheques. Local auto-rickshaws operate without meters and charge a minimum of Rs10. The friendly and informative **tourist office** (Mon–Sat 10am–5.30pm; ☏08172/268862) is under five minutes' walk from the bus stand at AVK College Road. The **railway station**, served by one express and three slow passenger trains a day from Mysore, is a further 2km down the road. Note that the route from here across the Ghats to Mangalore on the coast is still suspended due to engineering work involved with gauge conversion.

Accommodation

Considering the number of tourists who pass through, Hassan is oddly lacking in good **accommodation**. Most of the budget options are of a pitiful standard: the few exceptions are within walking distance of the bus stand, around **Narsimharaja Circle**. Wherever you stay, call ahead, as most hotels tend to be full by early evening.

DR Karigowda Residency BM Rd, 1km from the railway station ℡ 08172/264506. Immaculate budget hotel: friendly, comfortable and amazing value. Single occupancy rates, but no a/c. ❷
Hoysala Village Resort Belur Rd, 6km northwest of the centre ℡ 08172/256764, ⓦ www.karnatakatourism.com. Government-run luxury cottages in a peaceful rural setting. Fine multi-cuisine restaurant and the only pool in the area open to non-residents (Rs75 per hr). ❼–❽
Mahaveer Abhiruchi Lodge BM Rd, near Narsimharaja Circle ℡ 08172/268885. Cleanish rooms (most with TVs and mosquito nets) and a good but dilapidated veg restaurant, the *Abhiruchi*. ❷
Palika Race Course Rd ℡ 08172/267145. Large and somewhat characterless block with sizeable rooms; the cheaper ones are good value. ❷–❸
Prince Cottage BM Rd, behind Bhanu Theatre ℡ 08172/234740. Small, neat guesthouse tucked away off the main road. Very cheap and handy for the railway station. ❶

Southern Star BM Rd, 500m from train station ℡ 08172/251816, ⓦ www.ushashriramhotels.com. The smartest place in town, this new hotel has all mod-cons. It's part of the Quality Inn chain, but better value than most. ❻–❼
Sri Krishna BM Rd ℡ 08172/263240, ⓕ 260195. A large new hotel with some a/c rooms. The spacious non-a/c rooms are a great deal and the restaurant downstairs produces excellent South Indian cooking. ❸–❺
Suvarna Regency PB 97, BM Rd ℡ 08172/264006, ⓦ www.hotelsuvarna.com. Swish place with lots of lights, a shiny marble lobby, comfortable rooms (some a/c) and a rooftop barbecue. Great value. ❸–❹
Vaishnavi Lodging Harsha Mahal Rd ℡ 08172/263885. Hassan's best budget lodge, with big clean rooms (all with phone and TV) and a veg restaurant. Reservations essential. Turn left out of the bus stand, right onto Church Rd and it's on the corner of the first left turn. ❷

Eating

Most of the **hotels** listed above have commendable restaurants, or you can take your pick from the string of cheap snack bars and thali joints outside the bus stand.

Cocktails BM Rd near Krishna. A new multistorey development with a terraced restaurant and bar offering a run-of-the-mill but varied menu.
Golden Gate Suvarna Regency, PB 97, BM Rd. Plush restaurant and bar with a garden extension, and the best food Hassan has to offer, though the varied menu – including Indian, Chinese and Western dishes – is not cheap.
Harsha Mahal Below the Harsha Mahal Lodge, Harsha Mahal Rd. No-nonsense veg canteen

serving freshly cooked *iddli* and *dosa* breakfasts from 7.30am.
Hotel GRR Opposite the bus stand. Traditional, tasty and filling "mini-meals" served on plantain leaves, with a wide choice of non-veg dishes and some ice creams.
Upahar Darshan BM Rd. Cheap South Indian restaurant serving good "meals" and fresh *dosas* and *iddlis*.

Halebid

Now little more than a scruffy hamlet of brick houses and chai stalls, **HALEBID**, 32km northwest of Hassan, was once the capital of the powerful Hoysala dynasty, which held sway over south Karnataka from the eleventh until the early fourteenth centuries. Once known as **Dora Samudra**, the city's name was changed to *Hale-bidu*, or "Dead City", in 1311 when Delhi Sultanate forces under the command of Ala-ud-Din-Khilji swept through and reduced it to rubble. Despite the sacking, several large Hoysala temples survive, two of which, the Hoysaleshvara and Kedareshvara, are covered in exquisite carvings. A small **archeological museum** (daily except Fri 10am–5pm; free) next to the Hoysaleshvara temple houses a collection of Hoysala art and other finds from the area.

The Hoysaleshvara temple

The **Hoysaleshvara** temple (daily sunrise–sunset; free) was started in 1141, and after some forty years of work was left unfinished, which possibly accounts for

Moving on from Hassan

Hassan is well connected to most points in southwest Karnataka, with frequent **buses** to Mysore from the KSRTC bus stand. Hassan lies midway on the main bus route between Mangalore (180km) and Bangalore (187km), serviced by several ordinary and occasional luxury buses, plus more comfortable private buses, of which Vijayananda Travels, *Suvarna Regency*, PB 97, BM Road (☏08172/265807), which runs the private VRL service, is by far the best.

Apart from taking a tour, the only way to see Sravanabelgola (53km), Belur (37km) and Halebid (30km) in one day is **by car**, which some visitors share; most of the hotels can fix this up (around Rs1000 per day or Rs4.50 per kilometre for a minimum of 250km). Travelling **by bus**, you'll need at least two days. Belur and Halebid can be comfortably covered in one day; it's best to take the first (6am) of the hourly buses to Halebid (1hr) and move on to Belur (30min; 16km), from where services back to Hassan during the evening are more frequent (6.30am–6.15pm; 1hr 10min). **Sravanabelgola**, however, is in the opposite direction, and not served by direct buses; you have to head to **Channarayapatna** aka "CR Patna" (from 6.30am; 1hr) on the main Bangalore highway and pick up one of the regular buses (30min) or any number of minibuses from there. If you want to get to Sravanabelgola in time to visit the site and move on the same day (to Mysore or Bangalore), aim to catch one of the private luxury buses to Bangalore that leave from the road just below the *Vaishnavi Lodge* before dawn (5.30–6am); they all stop briefly in Channarayapatna. Bear in mind, too, that there are places to stay in both Belur and Halebid; arrive in Hassan early enough, and you can travel on to the temple towns before nightfall, although you should phone ahead to check rooms are available.

For more on public transport from Hassan, see "Travel details", p.334.

the absence of the type of towers that feature at Somnathpur. It is no longer known which deities were originally worshipped here, though the double shrine is thought to have been devoted at one time to Shiva and his consort. In any event, both shrines contain *shivalingams* and are adjoined by two linked, partly enclosed *mandapa* hallways in which stand Nandi bulls.

Like other Hoysala temples, the Hoysaleshvara is raised on a high plinth (*jagati*) which follows the star-shaped plan and provides an upper ambulatory; the *mandapas* are approached by flights of steps flanked by small, free-standing, towered shrines. Inside, the lower portions of the black polished stone pillars were lathe-turned, though the upper levels appear to have been hand-carved to reproduce the effect of turning.

Hoysaleshvara also features many Vaishnavite images. The **sculptures**, which have a fluid quality lacking in earlier work at Belur, include Brahma aboard his swan-vehicle, Hansa; Krishna holding up Mount Govardhana; Krishna playing the flute; and Vishnu (Trivikrama) bestriding the world in three steps. One of the most remarkable images is of the demon king **Ravana** shaking Shiva's mountain abode, Mount Kailash. The mountain is populated by numerous animals and figures, and Shiva is seated atop with Parvati. Secular themes, among them dancers and musicians, occupy the same register as the gods, and you'll come across the odd erotic tableau featuring voluptuous, heavily bejewelled maidens. A narrative frieze, on the sixth register from the bottom, follows the length of the Nandi *mandapas* and illustrates scenes from the Bhagavata Gita, Vishnu *Puranas*, Mahabharata and Ramayana.

The Jain bastis and the Kedareshvara temple

About 600m south of the Hoysaleshvara, a group of Jain *bastis* (temples) stands virtually unadorned; the only sculptural decoration consists of ceiling friezes inside the *mandapas* and elephants at the entrance steps, where there's an impressive donatory plaque. The thirteenth-century temple of **Adi Parshwanatha**, marked by a large entrance *mandapa*, is dedicated to the 23rd *tirthankara*, while the newer **Vijayanatha**, built in the sixteenth-century and easily recognized by its predominant *manasasthamba* pillar in front, is dedicated to the *tirthankara* Shantinatha. The *chowkidar* at the Parshwanatha temple will demonstrate various tricks made possible by the carved pillars' highly polished surfaces; some are so finely turned they sound metallic when struck.

To the east, there's a smaller Shiva temple, **Kedareshvara** (1217–21), also built on a stellate plan. Unfortunately, due to instability, it's not possible to go inside. Many fine images decorate the exterior, including an unusual stone Krishna dancing on the serpent demon Kaliya – more commonly seen in bronze and painting.

Practicalities

Frequent **buses** run between Halebid (the last at 8.30pm) and Hassan, and then on to Belur (the last at 8pm). The private **minibuses** that leave from the crossroads outside the Hoysaleshvara temple take a lot longer and only leave when crammed to bursting.

The monuments lie within easy walking distance of each other, but if you fancy exploring the surrounding countryside, rent a **bicycle** from the stalls by the bus stand (Rs3 per hour). The road running south past the temples leads through some beautiful scenery, with possible side-hikes to hilltop shrines, while the road to Belur (16km) makes for another pleasant bicycle ride. **Accommodation** in the village is limited to the KSTDC *Mayura Shantala* (℡08177/773224; ❷), opposite the main temple, which has two comfortable doubles with verandas, plus a four-bedded room – all should be booked in advance. This is also the only place to eat after 6pm, when the chai stalls at the crossroads have shut.

Belur

BELUR, 37km northwest of Hassan, on the banks of the Yagachi, was the Hoysala capital – prior to Halebid – during the eleventh and twelfth centuries. Still in use, the **Chennakeshava temple** (7.30am–8.30pm; free) is a fine and early example of the singular Hoysala style (see box opposite). The temple was built by King Vishnuvardhana in 1117 to celebrate his conversion from Jainism, victory over Chola forces at Talakad and independence from the Chalukyas. Today, its grey-stone *gopura* (gateway tower) soars above a small, bustling market town – a popular pilgrimage site from October to December, when busloads of Ayappan devotees stream through en route to Sabarimala (see p.392). The **car festival** held around March or April takes place over twelve days and has a pastoral feel, attracting farmers from the surrounding countryside, who conduct a bullock-cart procession through the streets to the temple. If you have time to linger, Belur, with marginally better facilities than those found at Halebid, is a far better place to base yourself in order to explore the Hoysala region.

Built on a star-shaped plan, Chennakeshava stands in a huge walled courtyard, surrounded by smaller shrines and columned *mandapa* hallways. Lacking any form of superstructure, and terminating at the first floor, it has the appearance of having a flat roof. If it ever had a tower, it would have disappeared by the Vijayanagar (sixteenth-century) period; above the cornice, a plain parapet, presumably added at the same time as the east entrance *gopura*, shows a typically Vijayanagar Islamic influence. Both the sanctuary and *mandapa* are raised on the

Hoysala temples

The **Hoysala** dynasty ruled southwestern Karnataka between the eleventh and thirteenth centuries. From the twelfth century, after the accession of King Vishnu Vardhana, they built a series of distinctive temples centred primarily at three sites: **Belur** and **Halebid**, close to modern Hassan, and **Somnathpur**, near Mysore.

At first sight, and from a distance, Hoysala temples appear to be modest structures, compact and even squat. On closer inspection, however, their profusion of fabulously detailed and sensuous sculpture, covering every inch of the exterior, is astonishing. Detractors are prone to class Hoysala art as decadent and overly fussy, but anyone with an eye for craftsmanship is likely to marvel at these jewels of Karnatakan art.

The intricacy of the carvings was made possible by the material used in construction: a soft stearite soapstone that on oxidization hardens to a glassy, highly polished surface. The level of detail, similar to that seen in sandalwood and ivory work, became increasingly freer and more fluid as the style developed, and reached its highest point at Somnathpur. Beautiful bracket figures, often delicate portrayals of voluptuous female subjects, were placed under the eaves, fixed by pegs top and bottom. A later addition (except possibly in the Somnathpur temple), these serve no structural function.

Another technique more usually associated with wood is the unusual treatment of the massive stone **pillars**: lathe-turned, they resemble those of the wooden temples of Kerala. They were probably turned on a horizontal plane, pinned at each end, and rotated with the use of a rope. It may be no coincidence that, to this day, wood turning is still a local speciality. Only the central shaft of each pillar seems to have been turned; in the base and capitals, a less precise, presumably handworked imitation of turning is evident.

The architectural style of the Hoysala temples is commonly referred to as **vesara**, or "hybrid" (literally "mule") rather than belonging to either the northern, *nagari*, or southern Dravidian styles. However, they show great affinity with *nagari* temples of western India and represent another fruit of contact, like music, painting and literature, facilitated by the trade routes between the north and the south. All Hoysala temples share a star-shaped plan, built on high plinths (*jagati*) that follow the shape of the sanctuaries and *mandapas* to provide a raised surrounding platform. Such northern features may have been introduced by the designer and artists of the earliest temple at Belur, who were imported by Vishnu Vardhana from further north in Andhra Pradesh. Also characteristic of the Hoysala style is the use of *ashlar* masonry, without mortar. Some pieces of stones are joined by pegs of iron or bronze, or mortice and tenon joints. Ceilings inside the *mandapas* are made up of corbelled domes, looking similar to those of the Jain temples of Rajasthan and Gujarat; in the Hoysala style they are only visible from inside.

usual plinth (*jagati*). Double flights of steps, flanked by minor towered shrines, afford entry to the *mandapa* on three sides; this hallway was originally open, but in the 1200s pierced stone screens carved with geometric designs and scenes from the *Puranas* were inserted between the lathe-turned pillars. The main shrine opens four times a day for worship (8.30–10am, 11am–1pm, 2.30–5pm & 6.30–8.30pm) and it's worth considering using one of the guides who offer their services at the gates (Rs40) to explain the intricacies of the carvings.

The quantity of **sculptural decoration**, if less mature than in later Hoysala temples, is staggering. Carvings on the plinth and lower walls, in successive and continuous bands, start at the bottom with depictions of elephants, followed by garlands and arches with lion heads. As you progress, the carvings illustrate stylized vegetation with dancing figures; birds and animals; pearl garlands; projecting niches containing male and female figures and seated *yakshas*, or spirits; miniature pillars alternating with female figures dressing or dancing; miniature temple towers interspersed with dancers; and, above them, lion heads. Above the screens, a series of 42 figures, added later, shows celestial nymphs hunting, playing music, dancing and beautifying themselves.

Columns inside, each unique, feature extraordinarily detailed carving, with more than a hundred deities on the central **Narasimha pillar**. The inner sanctum contains a black image of Chennakeshava, a form of Krishna who holds a conch (*shankha*, in the upper right hand), discus (*chakra*, upper left), lotus (*padma*, lower right) and mace (*gada*, lower left). He is flanked by consorts Shri Devi and Bhudevi. Within the same enclosure, the **Kappe Channigaraya temple** has some finely carved niche images and a depiction of Narasimha (Vishnu as man-lion) killing the demon Hiranyakashipu. Further west, fine sculptures in the smaller **Viranarayana** shrine include a scene from the Mahabharata of Bhima killing the demon Bhaga.

Practicalities

Buses from Hassan and Halebid pull into the small bus stand in the middle of town, ten-minutes' walk along the main street from the temple; some through buses don't bother to pull into the bus stand but stop on the highway next to it. There are auto-rickshaws available, but a good way to explore the area, including Halebid, is to rent a **bicycle** (Rs3 per hour) from one of the stalls by the bus stand. The **tourist office** (Mon–Sat 10am–5pm), located within the KSTDC *Mayuri Velapuri* compound near the temple, has all the bus times and other useful local information.

The KSTDC *Mayuri Velapuri* (☎08177/722209; ❷) is the best **place to stay**, with immaculately clean and airy rooms in its new block, or dingy ones in the older wing. The two dorms are rarely occupied (Rs35 per bed), other than between March and May, when the hotel tends to be block-booked by pilgrims. Down the road, the *Annapurna* (☎08177/722039; ❷) has adequate if dull rooms over an uninspiring restaurant; the *Swagath Tourist Home* (☎08177/722159; ❶), further up the road towards the temple, is extremely basic, boxed in and doesn't have hot water, but is fine as a fall-back. Of the hotels around the bus stand, the *Vishnu Lodge* (☎08177/722263; ❷–❸), above a restaurant and sweet shop, is the best bet, with spacious rooms (some with TV) but tiny en-suite bathrooms where hot water is only available in the mornings.

The most salubrious **place to eat** is at KSTDC *Mayuri Velapuri*'s restaurant, but the menu is limited. There are several other options, many located beneath hotels strung along the main road, in addition to the veg *dhabas* by the temple, and the *Indian Coffee House* on the main road by the temple gates. If you have a weakness for Indian sweets, head for *Poonam's* below the *Vishnu Lodge*.

Sravanabelgola

The sacred Jain site of **SRAVANABELGOLA**, 49km southeast of Hassan and 93km north of Mysore, consists of two hills and a large tank. On one of the hills, Indragiri (also known as Vindhyagiri), stands an extraordinary eighteen-metre-high monolithic statue of a naked male figure, **Gomateshvara**. Said to be the largest free-standing sculpture in India, this tenth-century colossus, visible for miles around, as well as the nearby *bastis* (Jain temples), make Sravanabelgola a key pilgrimage centre, though surprisingly few Western travellers find their way out here. Spend a night or two in the village, however, and you can climb Indragiri Hill before dawn to enjoy the serene spectacle of the sun rising over the sugar-cane fields and outcrops of lumpy granite that litter the surrounding plains – an unforgettable sight.

Sravanabelgola is linked in tradition with the Mauryan emperor Chandragupta, who is said to have starved himself to death on the second hill in around 300 BC, in accordance with a Jain practice. The hill was renamed Chandragiri, marking the arrival of Jainism in southern India. At the same time, a controversy regarding the doctrines of Mahavira, the last of the 24 Jain **tirthankaras** (literally "crossing-makers", who assist the aspirant to cross the "ocean of rebirth"), split Jainism into two separate branches. *Svetambara*, "white-clad" Jains, are more common in North India, while *digambara*, "sky-clad", are usually associated with the south. Truly ascetic *digambara* devotees go naked, though few do so away from sacred sites.

All the *tirthankaras* are represented as naked figures, differentiated only by their individual attributes: animals, inanimate objects (such as a conch shell), or symbols (such as the *swastika*). Each of the 24 is also attached to a particular *yaksha* (male) or *yakshi* (female) spirit; such spirits are also evident in Mahayana Buddhism, suggesting a strand of belief with extremely ancient origins. *Tirthankaras* are represented either sitting cross-legged in meditation – resembling images of the Buddha, save for their nakedness – or *kayotsarga*, "body upright", where the figure stands impassive; here Gomateshvara stands in the latter, more usual, posture.

The monuments at Sravanabelgola probably date from no earlier than the tenth century, when a General Chamundaraya is said to have visited Chandragiri in search of a Mauryan statue of Gomateshvara. Failing to find it, he decided to have one made. From the top of Chandragiri he fired an arrow across to Indragiri Hill; where the arrow landed, he had a new Gomateshvara sculpted from a single rock.

Indragiri Hill

Gomateshvara is approached from the tank between the two hills by 620 steps, cut into the granite of **Indragiri Hill**, which pass numerous rock inscriptions on the way up to a walled enclosure. Shoes must be deposited at the stall to the left of the steps, and you can leave bags at the site office nearby. Anyone unable to climb the steps can be carried up by a chair known as a *dholi*. Take plenty of water, especially on a hot day, as there is none available on the hill. Entered through a small wagon-vaulted *gopura*, the **temple** is of the type known as *betta*, which, instead of the usual *garbhagriha* sanctuary, consists of an open courtyard enclosing the massive sculpture. Figures and shrines of all the *yaksha* and *yakshi* spirits stand inside the crenellated wall, but the towering figure of Gomateshvara dominates. With his elongated arms and exaggeratedly wide shoulders, his proportions are decidedly non-naturalistic. The sensuously smooth surface of the white granite "trap" rock is finely carved, particularly the hands, hair and serene face. As in legend (see box on p.276), ant-hills and snakes sit at his feet and creepers appear to grow on his limbs.

Bhandari Basti and monastery (math)

The road east from the foot of the steps at Chandragiri leads to two interesting Jain buildings in town. To the right, the **Bhandari Basti** (1159), housing a shrine with images of the 24 *tirthankaras*, was built by Hullamaya, treasurer of the Hoysala Raja Narasimha. A high wall encloses the temple, forming a plain ambulatory which contains a well. Two *mandapa* hallways, where naked *digambara* Jains may sometimes be seen discoursing with devotees clad in white, lead to the shrine at the back. Pillars in the outer *mandapa* feature

Gomateshvara and Mahamastakabhisheka

Gomateshvara, or Bahubali, who was the son of the legendary King Rishabdev of Ayodhya (better known as Adinath, the first *tirthankara*), had a row with his elder brother, Bharat, over their inheritance. After a fierce fight, he lifted his brother above his head, and was about to throw him to the ground when he was gripped by remorse. Gently setting Bharat down, Gomateshvara resolved to reject the world of greed, jealousy and violence by meditating until he achieved *moksha*, release from attachment and rebirth. This he succeeded in doing, even before his father.

As a *kevalin*, Gomateshvara had achieved **kevalajnana**, or "sole knowledge", acquired through solitude, austerity and meditation. While engaged in this non-activity, he stood "body upright" in a forest. So motionless was he that ants built their nest at his feet, snakes coiled happily around his ankles, and creepers began to grow up his legs.

Every twelve years, at an auspicious astrological conjunction of certain planets, the Gomateshvara statue is ritually anointed in the **Mahamastakabhisheka ceremony** – this last took place in late 2005, and the next ceremony will be in 2017. The process lasts for several days, culminating on the final morning when 1008 *kalashas* (pots) of "liberation water", each with a coconut and mango leaves tied together by coloured thread, are arranged before the statue in a sacred diagram (mandala), on ground strewn with fresh paddy. A few priests climb scaffolding, erected around Gomateshvara, to bathe him in milk and ghee. After this first bath, prayers are offered. Then, to the accompaniment of temple musicians and the chanting of sacred texts, a thousand priests climb the scaffold to bathe the image in auspicious unguents, including the water of holy rivers, sandalwood paste, cane juice, saffron and milk, along with flowers and jewels. The ten-hour 1993 ceremony reached a climax when a helicopter dropped 20kg of gold leaf and 200 litres of milk on the colossus, along with showers of marigolds, gem stones and multi-hued powders. The residue formed a cascade of rainbow colours down the statue's head and body, admired by lakhs of devotees, Jain *sadhus* and *sadhvis* (female *sadhus*), and the massed cameras of the world. A satellite township, Yatrinagar, provides accommodation for 35,000 during the festival, and eighteen surrounding villages shelter pilgrims in temporary *dharamshalas*.

carvings of female musicians, while mythical beasts adorn the entrance to the inner, *navaranga*, hallway.

At the end of the street, the *math* (monastery) was the residence of Sravana-belgola's senior *acharya*, or guru. Thirty male and female monks, who also "go wandering in every direction", are attached to the *math*; normally a member of staff will be happy to show visitors around. Among the rare palm-leaf manuscripts in the library, some more than a millennium old, are works on mathematics and geography, and the *Mahapurana*, hagiographies of the *tirthankaras*. Next door, a covered, walled courtyard contains a number of shrines; the entrance is elaborately decorated with embossed brass designs of *yali* mythical beasts, elephants, a two-headed eagle and an image of Parshvanath, the 23rd *tirthankara*, shown here as Padmavati. Inside, the courtyard is edged by a high platform on three sides, on which a chair is placed for the *acharya*. A collection of tenth-century bronze *tirthankara* images is housed here, and vibrant murals detail the various lives of Parshvanath. The hills where the *tirthankaras* stood to gain *moksha* are represented in a model, somewhat resembling a jelly mould, with tacked-on footprints.

Chandragiri Hill

Leaving your shoes with the keeper at the bottom, take the rock-cut steps to the top of the smaller **Chandragiri Hill**. Miraculously, the sound of radios and rickshaws down below soon disappears. Fine views stretch south to Indragiri and, from the north on the far side, across to a river, paddy and sugar-cane fields, palms and the village of **Jinanathapura**, where there's another ornate Hoysala temple, the Shantishvara *basti*.

Rather than a single large shrine, as at Indragiri, Chandragiri holds a group of *bastis* in late Chalukya Dravida style, within a walled enclosure. Caretakers will take you around and open up the closed shrines. Save for pilasters and elaborate parapets, all the temples have plain exteriors. Named after its patron, the tenth-century **Chamundaraya** is the largest of the group, dedicated to Parshvanath. Inside the **Chandragupta** (twelfth century), superb carved panels in a small shrine tell the story of Chandragupta and his teacher Bhadrabahu. Traces of painted geometric designs survive and the pillars feature detailed carving. Elsewhere in the enclosure stands a 24-metre-high *manastambha*, or "pillar of fame", decorated with images of spirits, *yakshis* and a *yaksha*. No fewer than 576 inscriptions dating from the sixth to the nineteenth centuries are dotted around the site, on pillars and on the rock itself.

Practicalities

Sravanabelgola, along with Belur and Halebid, features on **tours** from Bangalore and Mysore (see box on p.247 & p.256). However, if you want to look around at a civilized pace, it's best to come independently (see box on p.271). The **tourist office** (Mon–Sat 10am–5.30pm; ☎08176/657254), at the bottom of the steps, has little to offer and the management committee office next door only serves to collect donations and hand out tickets for the *dholis*.

If you want **accommodation**, there are plenty of **dharamshalas**, managed by the temple authorities, offering simple, scrupulously clean rooms, many with their own bathrooms and sit-outs, ranged around gardens and courtyards, and most costing less than Rs150 per night. The 24hr accommodation office (☎08176/657258) is located inside the *SP Guest House*, next to the bus stand (look for the clock tower); they will allocate you a room here. *Yatri Niwas* (❷), which is close by and also booked through the accommodation office, is about as expensive as it gets, but is only marginally better than the best of the guesthouses. *Hotel Raghu*, opposite the main tank, houses the best of the many small local **restaurants**.

Crisscrossed by winding back roads, the idyllic (and mostly flat) countryside around Sravanabelgola is perfect cycling terrain. **Bicycles** are available for hire (Rs3 per hour) at Saleem Cycle Mart, on Masjid Road, opposite the northeast corner of the tank or stalls on the main road. If you're returning to Hassan, you'll have to head to **Channarayapatna**, aka "CR Patna", by bus or in one of the shared vans that regularly ply the route and depart only when bursting; change at CR Patna for a bus to Hassan.

Kodagu (Coorg)

The hill region of **Kodagu**, formerly known as **Coorg**, lies 100km west of Mysore in the Western Ghats, its eastern fringes merging with the Mysore Plateau. Comprising rugged mountain terrain interspersed with cardamom jungle, coffee plantations and swathes of lush rice paddy, it's one of South India's most beautiful areas. Little has changed since Dervla Murphy spent a few months here with her daughter in the 1970s (the subject of her classic travelogue, *On a Shoestring to Coorg*), and was entranced by the landscape and people, with their distinctive customs, language and appearance.

Today tourism is still very low-key, and the few travellers who pass through rarely venture beyond **Madikeri** (Mercara), Kodagu's homely capital. However, if you plan to cross the Ghats between Mysore and the coast, the route through Kodagu is definitely worth considering. Most of the area around Kodagu is swathed in lush coffee plantations. Some coffee-plantation owners open their doors to visitors; to find out more contact the Codagu Planters Association, Mysore Road, Madikeri (☎08272/229873). A good time to visit is during the festival season in early December or during the **Blossom Showers** around March and April, when the coffee plants bloom with white flowers, although some find the strong scent overpowering.

Kodagu is relatively undeveloped, and "sights" are few, but the country-side is idyllic and the climate refreshingly cool, even in summer. A growing trickle of visitors now come to Kodagu to **trek** through the unspoilt forest tracts and ridges which fringe the district (see box on p.282). On the east-ern borders of Kodagu on the Mysore Plateau, large **Tibetan settlements** around Kushalnagar have transformed a once barren countryside into fertile

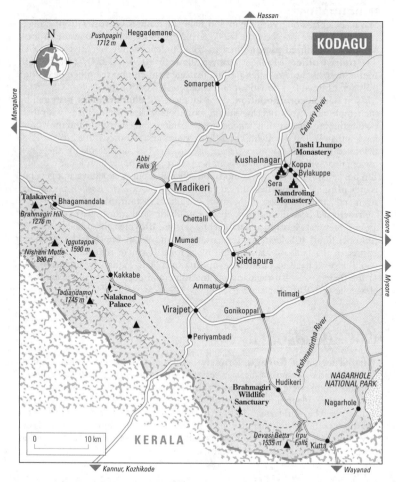

The Kodavas

Theories abound as to the origins of the **Kodavas**, or **Coorgis**, who today comprise less than one-sixth of the hill region's population. Fair-skinned and with their own language and customs, they are thought to have migrated to southern India from Kurdistan, Kashmir and Rajasthan, though no one knows exactly why or when. One popular belief holds that this staunchly martial people, who since Independence have produced some of India's leading military brains, are descended from Roman mercenaries who fled here following the collapse of the Pandyan dynasty in the eighth century; some even claim connections with Alexander the Great's invading army. Another theory is that the Kodavas were originally from Arabia, having been pushed out by the early Muslims and made to flee into exile.

Whatever their origins, the Kodavas have managed to retain a distinct identity apart from the freed plantation slaves, Moplah Muslim traders and other immigrants who have settled here. More akin to Tamil than Kannada, their language is Dravidian, yet their religious practices, based on ancestor veneration and the worship of nature spirits, differ markedly from those of mainstream Hinduism. Land tenure in Kodagu is also quite distinctive, with taxation based on type of land and, unlike in some other traditional societies, women have a right to inheritance and ownership; they are also allowed to remarry. Kodava martial traditions are grounded in the family where, according to custom, one son was raised to work the land while another joined the army. Even today, they are allowed to carry weapons without licence.

Spiritual and social life for traditional Kodavas revolves around the **Ain Mane**, or ancestral homestead. Built on raised platforms to overlook the family land, these large, detached houses, with their beautiful carved wood doors and beaten-earth floors, generally have four wings and courtyards to accommodate various branches of the extended family, as well as shrine rooms, or **Karona Kalas**, dedicated to the clan's most important forebears. Key religious rituals and rites of passage are always conducted in the Ain Mane, rather than the local temple. However, you could easily travel through Kodagu without ever seeing one, as they are invariably away from roads and shrouded in thick forest.

You're more likely to come across traditional Kodava **costume**, which is donned for all auspicious occasions, such as marriages, funerals, harvest celebrations and clan get-togethers. The men wear dapper knee-length coats called *kupyas*, bound at the waist with a scarlet and gold cummerbund, and daggers (*peechekathis*) with ivory handles. Most distinctive of all, though, is the unique flat-bottomed turban; sadly, the art of tying these is dying, and most men wear ready-made versions (which you can buy in Madikeri bazaar). Kodava women's garb is even more stunning, comprising long, richly coloured silk saris, pleated at the back and with a *pallav* draped over their shoulders, enlivened by heaps of heavy gold and silver jewellery, along with precious stones. Women also wear headscarves, in the fields as well as for important events, tying the corners behind the head, Kashmiri style.

The Kodava diet is heavily carnivorous, their favourite meat being pork: an important dish at festive occasions where it is often served as a dryish dish known as *pandi curry*, but sometimes substituted by *nooputtakoli curry* made with chicken, and usually accompanied with a rice preparation, *tumbuttu pandi*. Their traditional breakfast, consisting of a type of chapati known as *aki oti* served with honey and *pajji*, a chutney, is far lighter.

Like all traditional Indian cultures, this one is on the decline, not least because young Kodavas, predominantly from well-off land-owning families, tend to be highly educated and move away from home to find work, weakening the kinship ties that have for centuries played such a central role in the life of the region. However, in recent years there has been a rekindling of Kodava pride, with calls for a state separate from Karnataka.

farmland dotted with busy monasteries, some of which house thousands of monks.

Some history

Oblique references to Kodagu crop up in ancient Tamil and Sanskrit scriptures, but the first concrete evidence of the kingdom dates from the eighth century, when it prospered from the salt trade passing between the coast and the cities on the Deccan Plateau. Under the Hindu **Haleri Rajas**, the state repulsed invasions by its more powerful neighbours, including Haider Ali and his son Tipu Sultan, the infamous Tiger of Mysore. A combination of hilly terrain, absence of roads (a deliberate policy on the part of defence-conscious Kodagu kings) and the tenacity of its highly trained army, ensured that Kodagu was the only Indian kingdom never to be conquered.

Peace and prosperity prevailed through the 1700s, when the state was ruled by a line of eccentric rajas, among them the paranoid Dodda Vira (1780–1809), who reputedly murdered most of his relatives, friends, ministers and palace guards. The monarchy was more accountable during the reign of his successor, Chickavirarajah Rajendra, known as **Vira Raja**, but eventually lapsed into decadence and corruption. Emulating his father's brutal example, Vira Raja imprisoned or assassinated his rivals and indulged his passion for women and spending. The king's ministers eventually appealed to the British Resident in Mysore for help to depose the despot. Plagued by threats from Vira Raja, the colonial administration was eager for an excuse to intervene; they got it in 1834 when the unruly raja killed his cousin's infant son. Accusing him of maladministration, the British massed troops on the border and forced a short siege, at the end of which Vira Raja (and what remained of his family) fled into exile.

Thereafter, Kodagu became a princely state with nominal independence, which it retained until the creation of Karnataka in 1956. During the Raj, **coffee** was introduced and, despite plummeting prices on the international market, this continues to be the linchpin of the local economy, along with pepper and cardamom. Nowadays Kodagu is Karnataka's wealthiest region, though despite providing the highest level of revenue to the state, it does not reap the rewards, a fact which – coupled with the distinct identity and fiercely independent nature of the Kodavas – has resulted in the Kodagu freedom movement, known as **Kodagu Rajya Mukti Morcha**, which seeks its own statehood. Methods used by the KRMM include cultural programmes and occasional strikes, known as *bandhs*, designed to close down all commercial activity in protest.

Madikeri (Mercara) and around

Nestling beside a curved stretch of craggy hills, **MADIKERI** (**Mercara**), capital of Kodagu, undulates around 1300m up in the Western Ghats, roughly midway between Mysore and the coastal city of Mangalore. It's a pleasant enough town, with red-tiled buildings and undulating roads that converge on a bustling bazaar, and is gradually attracting an increasing number of foreigners.

The **Omkareshwara Shiva** temple, built in 1820, features an unusual combination of red-tiled roofs, Keralan Hindu architecture, Gothic elements and Islamic-influenced domes. The fort and palace, worked over by Tipu Sultan in 1781 and rebuilt in the nineteenth century, now serve as offices and a prison. Also worth checking out are the huge square **tombs of the Rajas** which, with their Islamic-style gilded domes and minarets, dominate the town's skyline. **St Mark's Church** holds a small **museum** (Tues–Sun 9am–5pm, closed second Sat of the month; free) of British memorabilia, Jain, Hindu and village deity figures and weapons. At the western edge of town, **Rajas' Seat**, next to KSTDC *Hotel Mayura Valley View*, is a belvedere, said to be the Kodagu kings' favoured place to watch the sunset.

Madikeri is the centre of the lucrative coffee trade, and although auto-rickshaws will take you there and back for around Rs185, a walk to **Abbi Falls** (8km) is a good introduction to coffee-growing country. The pleasant road, devoid of buses, winds through the hill country past plantations and makes for a good day's outing. At the littered car park at the end of the road, a gate leads through a private coffee plantation sprinkled with cardamom sprays and pepper vines to the bottom of the large stepped falls – most impressive during and straight after the monsoons.

Practicalities

You can only reach Madikeri by road, a scenic three-hour **bus** ride via **Kushalnagar** from **Mysore**, 120km southeast (unless you mistakenly get on one of the few buses that goes via Siddapura, which take more than an hour longer). Regular services, including deluxe buses, also connect Madikeri with **Mangalore**, 135km northwest across the Ghats. The KSTRC state **bus stand** is at the bottom of town, below the main bazaar; private buses from villages around the region pull into a parking lot at the end of the main street.

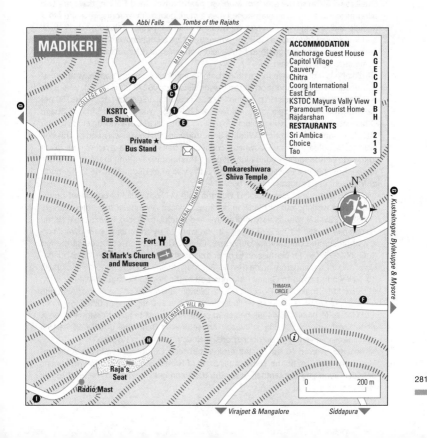

The small local **tourist office** (Mon–Sat 10.30am–5.30pm, closed second Sat of the month; ☎08272/228580) stands five minutes' walk along the Mysore road, below Thimaya Circle, next to the *PWD Travellers' Bungalow*, and can suggest itineraries, but is otherwise quite limited. There's **Internet** access at Paramount Cyber Zone (Rs30 per hour), near Chowk in the heart of the bazaar, and Cyber Land (Rs20 per hour), opposite the bus stand.

Accommodation and eating

Accommodation in Madikeri isn't usually hard to come by, except occasionally in the budget range, most of which is concentrated around the bazaar and

Trekking in Kodagu

The finest of Kodagu's **treks** lie to the south of the region along the Keralan border, where an ancient path snakes through forests and across mountain ridges linking **Nagarhole to Talakaveri** in the southwest. The trek, which takes around a week, starts at the entrance to Nagarhole National Park and continues, with tempting diversions, to Talakaveri. Passing by the Shri Ramneshwarna Temple, with a side-trip through forest to the Irpu Falls, the trail runs to Nalaknod Palace, an old hunting lodge now used as a camp and for bee-keeping, then continues to the hill temple of Nishani Motte before arriving at Brahmagiri Hill and Talakaveri (see p.285). From **Kakkabe**, a small town 50km to the south of Madikeri near the Nalaknod Palace, there are two alternative routes to Talakaveri – one takes a more gentle, lower route while the other tackles challenging high ground over Kodagu's highest peak, **Tadiandamol** (1745m), and the peak of **Iggutappa** (1590m), where there are a couple of old temples. You are best advised to take a guide to help avoid elephants, and for route-finding through sometimes difficult terrain.

Kakkabe is a good base for climbing both Tadiandamol and Iggutappa, with excellent accommodation and food at the *Palace Estate* (☎08272/238446; ⑧), where Mr A.P. Poonamma will assist in planning treks and negotiating guides (around Rs150 per day). Several direct buses leave Madikeri for Kakkabe every morning from 6.30am. Other possible treks in Kodagu include a climb to the hill of Devasi Betta close to Irpu Falls, through the **Brahmagiri Wildlife Sanctuary**, for which you will need permission from the sanctuary office. Elsewhere, connecting trails from Talakaveri can be taken to the top of Kodagu's second highest peak, **Pushpagiri** (1712m), to the north of the region. Pushpagiri can also be climbed via the village of Heggademane to the north of Madikeri, and is accessible by bus.

Walking routes are best explored with the help of the handful of **specialist agencies**, some working out of Madikeri, such as Ganesh Aiyanna at the *Hotel Cauvery* (☎08272/225492), who is very informative and helpful, or Coorg Travels, next to the *Rajdarshan Lodge* (☎08272/225817). If you want to try to arrange your own itinerary, approach the Conservator of Forests, Deputy Commissioner's Office, at the fort (☎08272/225708), for permission to enter the forests and to stay at their forest bungalows, and for a mandatory guide (Rs150–300/day). Even if you intend to do it yourself, it's well worth talking to Ganesh Aiyanna and to the helpful Kodagu Wildlife Society, PO Box 111, Chain Gate Road (☎08272/223505), 2km east of the centre. Although not local, experienced Clipper Holidays, with offices in Bangalore (☎080/2559 9032) and Cochin (☎0484/236 4443), has been organizing forest treks in Kodagu for years, while Madhushudan Shukla at Woody Adventures in Bangalore (☎080/2225 9159) specializes in a variety of outdoor sports, including trekking in Kodagu.

The best **season** to trek in the area is between October and March; April and May aren't quite as hot as some other parts of Karnataka, but avoid the monsoons between June and September, when the trails can get muddy and the leeches are rampant.

bus stand. The better-class places (and some of the budget hotels) generally have **restaurants**, and some also have bars. The *Choice Hotel* on School Road is a restaurant only, serving breakfast items and a decent range of veg and non-veg dishes. *Tao*, up near the fort, is an authentic Chinese place and the adjacent *Sri Ambica* serves wholesome veg snacks and meals. Traditional Kodagu food is very meat oriented, with scrumptious dishes like *pandi curry* (rich, spicy pork), although *akki otti* (rice flour *puris*) and the sweet *tambittu* should appeal to vegetarians.

Anchorage Guest House Kohinoor Rd
℡08272/228939. On a quiet side street close to the bus stand, with absolutely no-frills en-suite rooms. ❷
Capitol Village ℡08272/225975. Six kilometres east of the centre and booked through the *Cauvery* in Madikeri, this is the best place to stay in the area, but you'll need your own transport. The "village" consists of a cottage complex surrounded by splendid flowerbeds on the edge of a coffee plantation. It's quiet and secluded and excellent value, with a lakeside dorm (Rs250). ❺
Cauvery School Rd ℡08272/225492, ℱ225735. Below the private bus stand, this large and friendly place is almost hidden behind their excellent Capitol restaurant. ❸
Chitra School Rd ℡08272/225372, ℱ225191. Best value in town, with neat, well-kept rooms, the slightly pricier ones with cable TV. There's an excellent non-veg restaurant-cum-bar downstairs. ❸
Coorg International Convent Rd ℡08272/228071, ℱ228073. Ten minutes by rickshaw west of the centre, this large but slightly characterless hotel is one of the few upmarket options in Madikeri, with comfortable Western-style rooms, a multi-cuisine restaurant, exchange facilities and shops. ❽–❾
East End General Thimaya Rd (aka Mysore Rd) ℡08272/229996. A large, plain, tiled-roof colonial bungalow turned into a hotel with a hint of character, but more renowned for its popular bar and restaurant. ❹
KSTDC Hotel Mayura Valley View ℡08272/228387. Well away from the main road, past Rajas' Seat, and with excellent views. The rooms are huge and the restaurant serves beer. Hail a rickshaw to get there, as it's a stiff twenty-minute uphill walk from the bus stand. ❸
Paramount Tourist Home School Rd ℡08272/221880. Simple but neat rooms, marginally cheaper than most other places round the bazaar. ❸
Rajdarshan ℡08272/229142. Modern and salubrious place just below Raja's Seat, with a landscaped garden, good restaurant and bar. ❺–❻

Tibetan settlements around Sera

Madikeri provides an excellent base from which to explore the delights of Kodagu, including the **Tibetan settlements** that straddle the district border to the east. Cooperatives line the Madikeri–Mysore highway, and maroon-clad monks ride tractors to work the fields around the town of **Kushalnagar**, 30km from Madikeri, and the Tibetan villages, known as "camps", scattered around **Bylakuppe**, 6km away across the district border. Although the term "camp" suggests a sense of transition, the Tibetans who first settled here as refugees in the 1960s make up one of the largest settlements outside their homeland and have adapted remarkably well to a starkly different environment. There are now around eight thousand monks out of a total Tibetan population in the area of over 18,000, mostly in the vicinity of **SERA**, 5km to the south of the main highway.

Several monasteries punctuate the landscape: chief amongst them the great *gompa* of **Sera**, a huge complex which acts as a university for the monks. At the centre of Sera is a large main hall built on three floors, designed to accommodate the vast congregation of monks who gather here for instruction and ceremony. Despite the colossal image of the Buddha Shakyamuni at the head of the hall, there's nothing especially attractive about the rather functional monastery, although the village has a buzz and the monks are welcoming. The newer buildings of nearby **Sera Me** are almost as impressive. Halfway towards Sera from the main road is another wonderful monastery of the Nyingmapa sect,

Namdroling, also known as the Golden Temple, which has peaceful grounds around a huge colourful prayer hall housing three enormous gilt Buddhas and two startling dragon columns.

The only transport to and from the Madikeri–Mysore highway is on the **auto-rickshaws** that regularly ply the route; the turn-off to Sera Je is at **Koppa**, midway between Bylakuppe and Kushalnagar. Another important monastery in the vicinity of Bylakuppe is **Tashi Lhunpo**, which is 1km off the main road past the police station. Tashi Lhunpo is much smaller than Sera Je but is renowned as the seat of the Panchen Lama, Tibet's second most revered spiritual leader after the Dalai Lama. If you're arriving by bus from Mysore, ask to be let down at Bylakuppe, recognizable by the Tibetan farm cooperatives, for Tashi Lhunpo, or Koppa for Namdroling and Sera. If you're coming from the west, however, you'll reach Kushalnagar first, where there are more auto-rickshaws available at the bus stand. If you want an auto-rickshaw all to yourself, it will cost Rs30 to Sera, or you can share one for Rs10 per head.

The only places **to stay** around Bylakuppe are the monastery guesthouses, but the government has recently began to more strictly enforce the require-ment that visitors have a PAP (protected area permit) in order to stay there. You officially need one even to enter the area, but daytime visits rarely seem to be monitored. Permits can be obtained free from Delhi but usually take months to come through, so don't really suit the casual visitor. If you really want to stay with the Tibetans, it's best to check the current situation by phoning the friendly *Theckchen Khangsar Guest House*, just before the *mons* in Sera (T08223/258135; ❶). The best place for **food** is the *Olive Restaurant*, popular with young monks, which is just beyond Namdroling monastery on the Sera road. The welcoming proprietors are a fount of local information, and they serve great *thukpas*, *momos*, *shabhaleys*, *mothuk* and fried rice. *Dawa's* nearby, on the opposite side of the road, does similarly fine fare. The only food on the main highway at Bylakuppe is at basic meals joints like the *Green Land Hotel*.

There's more accommodation at Kushalnagar; the most comfortable of the **hotels** is the *Kannika International* (T08276/274728, Ekannika@rediffmail .com; ❹–❺), set back from the main road near the bus stand, with its own garden, a restaurant and bar with tables on the porch, and airy rooms with TV. Cheaper options on the main road around the bus stand include the basic *Ganesh* (T08276/274528; ❷). For a bit more quiet, follow the lane along the side of the bus stand past the communications tower to the *Mahalaxmi Lodge* (T08276/274622; ❷). **Eating** options are limited to the usual sprinkling of meals places and snack stalls. Kushalnagar is well connected **by bus** to Manga-lore (via Madikeri), Bangalore, Mysore and Hassan, as well as to several destina-tions in Kerala. Bus times are posted in English and deluxe and express buses stop here as well.

Siddapura

The sleepy coffee town of **SIDDAPURA**, on the banks of the River Kaveri (Cauvery), lies 32km to the south of Madikeri in the heart of coffee country and offers the chance to stay on a plantation – a delightful, if pricey, experience. Across the river, the **Dubare Reserve Forest** offers good short exploratory treks with the chance of seeing wildlife and the occasional elephant; contact the Conservator of Forests in Madikeri (see box on p.282) for more information and take a guide.

The **Orange County** resort (T08274/258481; bookings through their Bangalore office on T080/2558 2380; ❾), at Karadigodu, 3km from Siddapura, is the most luxurious place to stay in the whole of Kodagu. The resort lies at the edge of a wealthy estate and is approached by a small road which winds through lush plantations. Accommodation is in mock-Tudor cottages set in a manicured estate, and activities include treks and horse-riding; there's also a pleasant pool (residents only) and a good restaurant with a varied menu, including some Kodava dishes. The resort also provides a base from which to visit Nagarhole National Park, 75km to the south (see p.268). It's popular with affluent Indians and tour groups, however, so book in advance.

Bhagamandala and Talakaveri

A good bus excursion from Madikeri takes you to the quiet village of **BHAGAMANDALA** (35km west), and from there to the sacred site of **TALAKAVERI**, which is said to be the source of the holy River Kaveri (Cauvery). The hill scenery is superb, and you can opt to walk part of the way on blissfully quiet country roads. Wear something warm, and take the 6.30am bus from Madikeri's private stand to Bhagamandala. You should arrive around 8am, with just enough time to grab a good breakfast of *parathas* and local honey at the *Laxmi Vilas* tea shop, next to the bus stop from which the bus to Talakaveri leaves at 8.30am. At Bhagamandala, the holy spot where the Kaveri merges with two streams, Kanike and Sujyothi, the **Bhagandeshwara Temple** is a fine example of Keralan-style architecture, with tiled roofs and courtyards.

At Talakaveri, the bus stops on the slopes of Brahmagiri Hill by the entrance to the sacred tank and **temple**. During **Kaveri Shankrama** in October, thousands of pilgrims come here to witness a spring – thought to be the goddess Kaveri, known as Lopamudra, the local patron deity – suddenly spurting into a small well. To bathe in the tank at this time is considered especially sin-absolving. The belief is that if the spring dries up, all the rivers of southern India will dry up too. Whenever you come, you're likely to find wild-haired *sadhus* and bathing pilgrims, and the surrounding walls swathed in drying *dhotis* and saris. Two small shrines stand at the head of the tank, one containing an image of Ganesh and the other a metal *lingam* with a *naga* snake canopy. Steep granite steps to the right lead up to the peak of **Brahmagiri Hill**, which affords superb 360 degree views over Kodagu.

Mangalore

Many visitors only come to **MANGALORE** on their way somewhere else. As well as being fairly close to Madikeri and the Kodagu (Coorg) hill region, it's also a stopping-off point between Goa and Kerala, and is the nearest coastal town to the Hoysala and Jain monuments near Hassan, 172km east.

Mangalore was one of the most famous ports of South India, renowned overseas as early as the sixth century as a major source of pepper; the fourteenth-century Muslim writer Ibn Battuta noted its trade in pepper and ginger and the presence of merchants from Persia and the Yemen. In the mid-1400s, the Persian ambassador Abdu'r-Razzaq saw Mangalore as the "frontier town" of the Vijayanagar empire, which was why the Portuguese captured it in 1529. In Haider Ali's time, during the eighteenth century, the city became a shipbuilding centre. Nowadays, the modern port, 10km north of the city proper, is principally known for the processing and export of coffee and cocoa (much of which comes from Kodagu), and cashew nuts from Kerala and Karnataka, as well as granite – it's also a centre for the production of *beedi* cigarettes. Mangalore's heady ethnic mix lived more or less in harmony until 1998, when communal

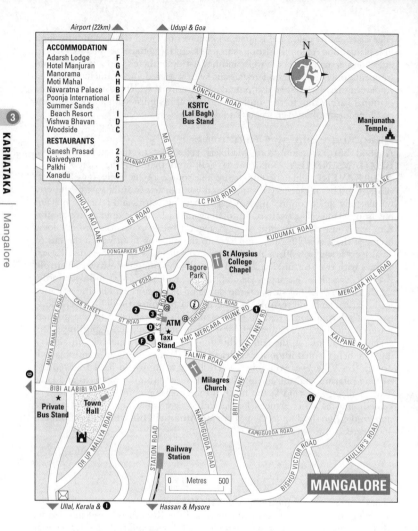

ACCOMMODATION

Adarsh Lodge	F
Hotel Manjuran	G
Manorama	A
Moti Mahal	H
Navaratna Palace	B
Poonja International	E
Summer Sands Beach Resort	I
Vishwa Bhavan	D
Woodside	C

RESTAURANTS

Ganesh Prasad	2
Naivedyam	3
Palkhi	1
Xanadu	C

Airport (22km)

Udupi & Goa

KONCHADY ROAD

★ KSRTC (Lal Bagh) Bus Stand

Manjunatha Temple

N

MG ROAD

MANNAGUDDA RD

PINTO'S LANE

LC PAIS ROAD

BHOJA RAO LANE

BS ROAD

KUDUMAL ROAD

DONGARKERI ROAD

St Aloysius College Chapel

Tagore Park

MERCARA HILL ROAD

VT ROAD

A

B   C

HILL ROAD

LIGHTHOUSE

KSR RAO ROAD

CAR STREET

GT ROAD

2   3

ATM

D

F   E   Taxi Stand

KMC MERCARA TRUNK RD

BALMATTA NEW RD

KALPANE ROAD

MUKYA PRANA TEMPLE ROAD

FALNIR ROAD

Milagres Church

BRITTO LANE

G

BIBI ALABIBI ROAD

Town Hall

★ Private Bus Stand

H

DR UP MALLYA ROAD

STATION ROAD

NANDIGUDDA ROAD

KAPRIGUDDA ROAD

BISHOP VICTOR ROAD

MULER'S ROAD

Railway Station

0   Metres   500

MANGALORE

Ullal, Kerala &

Hassan & Mysore

riots saw sections of the large Christian community in the city attacked by right-wing Hindu fundamentalists.

Arrival and information

Mangalore's busy **KSRTC Bus Stand** (known locally as the "Lal Bagh" bus stand) is 2km north of the town centre, Hampankatta, at the bottom of Kadri Hill. Private buses arrive at the much more central stand near the Town Hall. **Bajpe airport**, 22km north of the city (bus #22 or 47A, Indian Airlines city bus or taxis for Rs250–300), is served by both Indian Airlines/Alliance and Jet Airways from Mumbai and Bangalore, and by Air Deccan from the latter. The **railway station**, on the south side of the city centre, sees daily services from cities all over India, including Delhi, Agra, Hyderabad, Bangalore, Chennai and Thiruvananthapuram. Hampankatta, close to the amenities of Lighthouse Hill

Road, acts as the city's traffic hub, from where you can catch **city buses** and **auto-rickshaws**, although their drivers prefer not to use their meters.

The **tourist office** (Mon–Sat 10am–1.30pm & 2.30–5.30pm; ☎0824/244 2926), on the ground floor of the *Hotel Indraprastha* on Light House Hill Road, is helpful for general information and some bus times, but carries no information on trains, for which you'll need to go to the railway station. You can **change money** at Trade Wings, Light House Hill Road (Mon–Sat 9.30am–5.30pm; ☎0824/426817), who also cash travellers' cheques; and at Wall Street Interchange (same hours; ☎0824/242 1717), 1st Floor, Utility Royal Towers, KS Rao Road. The State Bank of India (Mon–Fri 10.30am–2.30pm & Sat 10.30am–12.30pm), near the Town Hall on Hamilton Circle, is somewhat slower. There's a CorpBank **ATM** opposite the *Mangalore International* hotel on KS Rao Road.

Mangalore's **post office** (Mon–Sat 10am–7pm, Sun 10.30am–1.30pm) is a short walk from the centre, at Shetty Circle. For **Internet** access, try the friendly and popular Kohinoor Computer Zone, Plaza Towers, Light House Hill Road (Rs25 per hr), down the road from the tourist office; or Cyber Zoom, 1st Floor, Utility Royal Towers, KS Rao Road (Rs20per hr).

Accommodation

Mangalore's **accommodation** standards are forever improving; it even has a modern five-star hotel. The main area for hotels, **KS Rao Road**, runs south from the bus stand and has an ample choice to suit most pockets. You can also stay out of town by the beach in **Ullal**.

Adarsh Lodge Market Rd ☎0824/244 0878. Decent-value, especially for singles, with compact but clean rooms, all en suite. Convenient for the Private Bus Stand. ❷

Hotel Manjuran Old Port Rd, 2km west of the railway station ☎0824/242 0420, ℻242 0585. Modern business hotel belonging to the Taj group. Some rooms have sea views, and all have a/c, and facilities include a travel desk, currency exchange, pool, bar, two classy restaurants and a 24hr coffee shop. ❻–❾

Manorama KS Rao Rd ☎0824/244 0306. A 65-room concrete block with spartan, large and very clean rooms (some a/c). Good value, though there are better central options. ❸–❺

Moti Mahal Falnir Rd ☎0824/244 1411. Large hotel with some a/c rooms, 24hr room service, coffee shop, bar, pool, shops, currency exchange and travel desk. The Mangala (non-veg) and Madhuvan (veg) restaurants serve Indian, Chinese and Western food. ❹–❻

Navaratna Palace KS Rao Rd ☎0824/244 1104, ℮nish77772000@yahoo.com. Preferable to its adjacent older sister Navaratna, with better rooms

(some a/c) for not much extra, plus two good a/c restaurants, the Heera Panna and Palimar (pure veg). ❸–❺

Poonja International KS Rao Rd ☎0824/244 0171, ℅www.hotelpoonjainternational.com. Smart, mostly a/c high-rise with all facilities and stunning views from the upper floors. Buffet South Indian breakfast included. ❹–❽

Summer Sands Beach Resort Chota Mangalore, Ullal, 10km south of the city ☎0824/246 7690, ℅www.summer-sands.com. This recommended place has spacious rooms and cottages (some a/c) near the beach, with a pool and a bar-restaurant serving local specialities, plus Indian and Chinese food. Currency exchange for guests. Take bus #44A from town. ❺–❾

Vishwa Bhavan KS Rao Rd ☎0824/244 0822. The best of the real cheapies, with cheap, plain rooms (some en suite) set around a courtyard and close to all amenities. ❶

Woodside KS Rao Rd ☎0824/244 0296. Old-fashioned hotel offering a range of rooms (some a/c; the economy doubles are the best deal), but "no accommodation for servants". ❸–❺

The city and beaches

Mangalore's strong Christian influence can be traced back to the arrival further south of St Thomas (see p.676). Some 1400 years later, in 1526, the Portuguese

Kambla

If you're anywhere between Mangalore and Bhatkal from October to April and come across a crowd gathering around a water-logged paddy field, pull over and spend a day at the races – Karnatakan style. Few Westerners ever experience it, but the unique and spectacular rural sport of **kambla**, or **bull racing**, played in the southernmost district of coastal Karnataka (known as Dakshina Kannada), is well worth seeking out.

Two contestants, usually local rice-farmers, take part in each race, riding on a wooden plough-board attached to a pair of prize bullocks. The object is to reach the opposite end of the field first, but points are also awarded for style, and riders gain extra marks – and roars of approval from the crowd – if the muddy spray kicked up from the plough-board splashes the special white banners, or *thoranam*, strung across the course at a height of 6 to 8m.

Generally, race days are organized by wealthy landowners on fields specially set aside for the purpose. Villagers flock in from all over the region, as much for the fair, or *shendi*, as the races themselves: men huddle in groups to watch cock fights (*korikatta*), women haggle with bangle sellers and kids roam around sucking sticky *kathambdi goolay*, the local bon-bons. It is considered highly prestigious to be able to throw such a party, especially if your bulls win any events or, better still, come away as champions. Known as *yeru* in Kannada, racing bulls are thoroughbreds who are rarely, if ever, put to work. Pampered by their doting owners, they are massaged, oiled and blessed by priests before big events, during which large sums of money are often won and lost.

founded the **Most Holy Rosary Church**, one of the earliest churches on the coast, although the present building, close to the old port and with a dome based on St Peter's in Rome, dates only from 1910. Fine restored fresco, tempera and oil murals, the work of an Italian artist, Antonio Moscheni, adorn the Romanesque-style **St Aloysius College Chapel**, built in 1885, on Lighthouse Hill Road, near the centre.

At the foot of Kadri Hill, 3km north and served by numerous city buses, Mangalore's tenth-century **Manjunatha Temple** is an important centre of the Shaivite and Tantric Natha-Pantha cult. Thought to be an outgrowth of Vajrayana Buddhism, the cult is a divergent species of Hinduism, similar to certain cults in Nepal. Enshrined in the sanctuary, a number of superb **bronzes** include a 1.5-metre-high seated Lokeshvara (Matsyendranatha), made in 958 AD and considered the finest southern bronze outside Tamil Nadu. To see it close up you'll have to visit at *darshan* times (6am–1pm & 4–8pm), although the bronzes can be glimpsed through the wooden slats on the side of the sanctuary. If possible, time your visit to coincide with **mahapooja** at 8am, noon or 8pm, when the priests give a fire blessing to the accompaniment of raucous music. Manjunatha's square and towered sanctuary, containing an unusual *lingam*, is surrounded by two tiled and gabled colonnades with louvred windows, showing strong affinity with the temple complexes further south in Kerala. Nine water tanks adjoin the temple. Opposite the east entrance, steps lead via a laterite path to a curious group of minor shrines. Beyond this complex stands the **Shri Yogishwar Math**, a hermitage of Tantric *sadhus* set round two courtyards, one of which contains shrines to Kala Bhairava (a form of Dakshinamurti, the southern aspect of Shiva and deity of death), Durga and god of fire, Agni. Nearby, cut into the side of the hill, a tiny unadorned cave is credited with being one of the "night halts" for the Pandava brothers from the Mahabharata.

If you're looking to escape the city for a few hours, head out to the village of **ULLAL**, 10km south, whose long sandy **beach**, backed by wispy fir trees, stretches for miles in both directions. It's a deservedly popular place for a stroll, particularly in the evening when families and courting couples come out to watch the sunset, but a strong undertow makes swimming difficult, and at times unsafe. You're better off using the pool at the excellent *Summer Sands Beach Resort* (see p.287), immediately behind the beach (Rs100 for non-residents). A further 2km past the *Summer Sands*, a banyan-lined road leads to the Shiva temple of **Someshwar**, built in Keralan style, overlooking a rocky promontory, and another popular beach which is subject to gangs of gawking youths. Towards the centre of Ullal, and around 700m from the main bus stand, is the *dargah* (burial shrine) of **Seyyid Mohammad Shareeful Madani**, a sixteenth-century saint who is said to have come from Medina in Arabia and floated across the sea on a handkerchief. The extraordinary nineteenth-century building with garish onion-domes houses the saint's tomb, which is one of the most important sufi shrines in southern India. Visitors are advised to follow custom and cover their heads and limbs and wash their feet before entering. Local **buses** (#44A) run to Ullal from the junction at the south end of KS Rao Road. As you cross the Netravathi River en route, look out for the brick chimney-stacks clustered on the banks at the mouth of the estuary. Using quality clay shipped downriver from the hills, these factories manufacture the famous terracotta red **Mangalorean roof tiles**, which you see all over southern India.

Eating

The best **places to eat** are in the bigger hotels. If you're on a tight budget, try one of the inexpensive café-restaurants opposite the bus stand, or the excellent canteen inside the bus stand itself, which serves great *dosas* and other South Indian snacks. Also recommended for delicious, freshly cooked and inexpensive "meals" is the *Ganesh Prasad*, down the lane alongside the uninspiring *Vasanth Mahal*. The rooftop *Palkhi* on Mercara Trunk Road is an airy family restaurant with a wide menu. For something a little more sophisticated, head for the a/c *Xanadu*, at the *Woodside Hotel*, also on KS Rao Road, which offers classy non-veg cuisine and alcohol. It's too dingy for lunch, but fine for dinner, when its kitsch fish tanks and resident ducks are illuminated. One of the best of the hotel restaurants, however, is the pure-veg *Naivedyam* at the *Mangalore International*, also on KS Rao Road, which has a plush a/c plus a comfortable non-a/c section.

Around Mangalore

Although the most famous of all the **Jain bastis** (temples) is at Sravanabelgola on the outskirts of Hassan (see p.274), the greatest concentration of these shrines lies to the east and northeast of Mangalore. The *bastis* of **Mudabidri**, **Karkala** and **Dharamastala**, some of which date back to the ninth century, continue to form part of a pilgrimage circuit attracting Jains from all over India, and can be taken in on day-trips from Mangalore.

Of the important Hindu pilgrimage centres near Mangalore, the great *matha* (a centre of pilgrimage and learning), at **Sringeri** to the east, continues to play a pivotal role in ongoing developments in Hindu theology.

Mudabidri

The most extensive of the *bastis* can be found in the small and quiet town of **MUDABIDRI**, 35km north of Mangalore. According to legend, a Jain

Mangalore is a major crossroads for tourist traffic heading along the Konkan coast between Goa and Kerala, and between Mysore and the coast. The city is also well connected **by air** to **Mumbai**, **Bangalore** and **Chennai**. The Indian Airlines office is at Airlines House, Hathill Rd, Lalbagh (℡0824/245 1046) and the Jet Airways office at DS Ram Bhavan Complex, Kodiabail (℡0824/244 1181). Note that Air Deccan can only be contacted by mobile or online (℡98457 77008, www.airdeccan.net).

By train

With the inauguration of the single-track coastal **Konkan Railway**, services have opened up north to Goa and Mumbai, although note that through services do not pass through the city terminus itself. A better choice of train connections for the Konkan Railway in both directions can be had from **Kankanadi**, around 10km north, or **Kasargode**, an easy bus ride across the Kerala border. From Mangalore itself, the fast #KR2 *Verna Passenger* departs Mangalore at 7.10am and travels north along the coast to **Margao** in Goa (6hr 10min) via Udupi and **Gokarna** (3hr 50min). The *Matsyagandha Express* (#2620), which departs at 2.40pm, is slightly faster to Gokarna (3hr 5min) and Margao in Goa (5hr 45min); it continues on to Mumbai (Lokmanya Tilak station; 13hr 55min).

Heading south, the service is good and, if you're travelling to Kerala, far quicker and more relaxing than the bus. Two services leave Mangalore station every day for **Thiruvananthapuram**, via **Kozhikode**, **Ernakulam/Kochi**, **Kottayam** and **Kollam**. Leaving at the red-eyed time of 4.15am, the *Parsuram Express* (#6350) is the faster of the two, but the *Malabar Express* (#6330), which leaves at 5.50pm, is convenient as an overnight train to Thiruvananthapuram, arriving there at 9.25am. For those travelling to **Chennai**, the overnight Mangalore–Chennai mail (#6602) departs at 12.30pm and follows the Kerala coast till Shoranur where it turns east to **Palakaad** before journeying on to **Erode** and arriving at Chennai at 6.25am. Note that conversion work on the line inland to Hassan for Mysore and Bangalore has been further delayed, but there's no harm checking on its progress.

By bus

The traditional way to travel on to **Goa** was always by **bus**, though that is being usurped by the Konkan Railway. Only two buses now leave the KSRTC Lal Bagh stand daily, taking around 10hr 30min to reach Panjim. You can jump off at Chaudi (for Palolem) en route. Tickets should be booked in advance (preferably the day before) at KSRTC's well-organized computer booking hall (daily 7am–8pm), or at the Kadamba office on the main concourse. KSRTC also has a central office (daily 8.30am–8.30pm) on the ground floor of Utility Royal Towers, KS Rao Road. The Goa buses are also good for **Gokarna**; hop off at **Kumta** on the main highway, and catch an onward service from there. The only direct bus to Gokarna leaves Mangalore at 1.30pm. There are plenty of state buses heading north to **Udupi** and south along the coast towards **Kerala**, though it's easier to pick up the more numerous private services to those places.

For **Mysore**, **Bangalore** and **Hassan**, you're restricted to the bus until the railway line reopens, but there are plenty of services, both state and private. **Madikeri** is only reachable by road: the hourly buses to Mysore stop there, as do some luxury services to Bangalore. The best private bus service to Bangalore is on the distinctive yellow luxury coaches of VRL; two buses leave nightly at 10pm (7–8hr); tickets are available through Vijayananda Travels, PVS Centenary Building, Kodiyalbail, Kudmulranga Rao Road (℡0824/249 3536). Agents along Falnir Road include Anand Travels (℡0824/244 6737) and Ideal Travels (℡0824/242 4899), who also run luxury buses to Bangalore (6–7hr) and two buses to **Ernakulam** (8pm & 9pm; 9–10hr).

ascetic settled here in the eighth century when he saw a tiger playing with a cow. Most of the eighteen *bastis* and several *mathas* (monasteries) at Mudabidri were built between the fifteenth and sixteenth centuries. The most impressive, close to the town centre, is the **Chandranatha Basti**, completed in 1430 AD and known as Tribhuvana Tilaka Chudamani Basti, or more commonly as the "thousand-pillar hall". Approached by an imposing entrance gate and fronted by a tall, multistorey stone lamp, the main temple consists of two large interconnected columned halls. The surrounding veranda has stone columns supporting a sloping stone roof that is, in turn, crowned by a roof coated with copper tiles supported by carved wooden angle brackets.

Karkala

An eighteen-kilometre bus ride north of Mudabidri, the small town of **KARKALA** is famous for the thirteen-metre high statue of **Gomateshvara**, standing placid and naked atop a rocky granite outcrop 1km from the town centre. Steps hewn out of rock lead up to the dramatic freestanding image, which was built in 1432 by Veerapandyadeva, a local ruler, and inspired by the monolith at Sravanabelgola. At the bottom of the hill lies the **Chaturmukha Basti**, built in 1586 and so called because of its identical four (*chatur*) faces (*mukha*) or directions. The main object of the symmetry is the columned hall where four doors punctuate the porch, each with a view of three deities within the inner sanctum. By circumambulating the sanctuary, the devotee is thus able to take in twelve *tirthankaras* in all.

Dharamastala

A popular Hindu pilgrimage town set against a pleasant backdrop of paddy fields, wooded hills and plantations, **DHARAMASTALA**, 75km east of Mangalore, has another monolithic stone image of **Gomateshvara**, completed in 1973 by the artist Ranjal Gopal Shenoy. Although impressive, the fourteen-metre-high statue, which borrows heavily from its predecessors and took five years to create, lacks the refinement of those at Karkala and Sravanabelgola. It stands on a hill, above the frenetically busy **Manjunatha Temple** (daily 6.30am–1pm & 7–8pm), where both Hindus and Jains worship. An important Shaivite shrine, managed by Vaishnava priests, the temple was founded in 1780 by the influential Hegdes, a family of Jains who still run the temple and were responsible for the statue of Gomateshvara. According to custom, pilgrims to Dharamastala bathe in the **Netravati River**, 3km away.

Sringeri

On the banks of the River Tunga, the scenic village of **SRINGERI**, on the edge of coffee plantations 100km northeast of Mangalore, is notable for its ancient *matha*, established in the ninth century by the great Hindu reformer and theologian Shankara, who is supposed to have spent twelve years of his life in Sringeri. The village itself has been at the centre of religious and social events, formerly exerting a strong influence over the Vijayanagar empire based at Hampi. During the festival of Navaratri, held each September/October, which commemorates the goddess Sharada's triumph over evil, the village swells with the influx of pilgrims.

The modern **Sharada temple** at Sringeri, devoted to a form of the goddess Saraswati, receives a steady stream of pilgrims. Steps lead down to the River Tunga, where devotees congregate to feed the sacred fish. More interesting architecturally is the sixteenth-century **Vidyashankara temple**, a short distance to the south of the Sharada temple, on a picturesque location above the river. Built on a high plinth decorated with friezes of animals, figures and gods, the temple enshrines a *lingam* that is considered to be the *samadhi* (memorial) to Shankara. The twelve pillars of the *mandapa* support a set of heavy ceiling-slabs and feature lavish details including riders on mythical beasts, representing each of the twelve signs of the zodiac. The walls of the temple are richly adorned with carvings depicting the gods, while the niches hold various aspects of Shiva and the incarnations of Vishnu, including Krishna playing the flute.

Practicalities

Regular buses from the KSRTC Bus Stand in Mangalore run to Dharamastala, Mudabidri and Karkala, the latter can also be approached directly from Udupi to the northwest. Several buses continue on to Sringeri, but if you miss these you can change at Karkala. The road between Karkala and Sringeri is particularly beautiful, as it passes through a lush belt of forest on its way up the Western Ghats. Mudabidri and Karkala can be taken in as long day-trips from Mangalore. At both places, **accommodation** is limited to the form of basic government-run *Tourist Cottages* (❷), bookable through the tourist office in Mangalore. Both Dharamastala and Sringeri have **room reservation offices** located near the temple entrances, which will assign you temple-run rooms (❶). These are usually excellent value and can range from very basic rooms with shared bathrooms to comfortable doubles with attached baths. Private accommodation (❶–❸) is available near the bus stands, where you'll also find basic "meals" restaurants.

North of Mangalore: coastal and western Karnataka

Whether you travel the **Karnatakan (Karavali) coast** on the recently opened Konkan Railway or along the busy NH-14, southern India's smoothest highway, the route between Goa and Mangalore ranks among the most scenic anywhere in the country. Crossing countless palm- and mangrove-fringed estuaries, the recently upgraded road, dubbed by the local tourist board as "The Sapphire Route", scales several spurs of the Western Ghats, which here creep to within a stone's throw of the sea, with spellbinding views over long, empty beaches and deep blue bays. Highlights are the pilgrim town of **Udupi**, site of a famous Krishna temple, and **Gokarna**, a bustling village which provides access to exquisite unexploited beaches. A couple of bumpy back roads wind inland through the mountains to **Jog Falls**, India's highest waterfall, more often approached from the east. Infrequent buses crawl from the coast through rugged jungle scenery to this spectacular spot, but you'll enjoy the trip more by motorbike; it's possible to rent one in Goa and ride down the coast from there, stopping off at secluded beaches, falls and viewpoints en route.

Just across the Ghats from the coast are several places worth visiting: the temple towns of **Sirsi**, with its unique Kavi art, and ancient **Banvasi** both offer quiet escapes from the main tourist trail, while the **Dandeli Wildlife Sanctuary** is renowned for its population of black panthers. Workaday **Hubli**, the area's main transport hub, offers varied side-trips for those with time to spare.

Udupi

UDUPI (also spelt Udipi), 60km north of Mangalore, is one of South India's holiest Vaishnavite centres. The Hindu saint **Madhva** (1238–1317) was born here, and the **Krishna temple** and *mathas* (monasteries) he founded are visited by *lakhs* of pilgrims each year. The largest numbers congregate during the late winter, when the town hosts a series of spectacular **car festivals** and gigantic, bulbous-domed chariots are hauled through the streets around the temple. Even if your visit doesn't coincide with a festival, Udupi is a good place to break the journey along the Karavali coast. Thronging with *pujaris* and pilgrims, its small sacred enclave is wonderfully atmospheric, and you can take a boat from the nearby fishing village at **Malpé beach** to **St Mary's Island**, the deserted outcrop of hexagonal basalt where Vasco da Gama erected a crucifix prior to his first landfall in India.

Incidentally, Udupi also lays proud claim to being the birthplace of the nationally popular **masala dosa**; these crispy stuffed pancakes, made from fermented rice flour, were first prepared and made famous by the Udupi brahmin hotels.

The Krishna temple and maths

Udupi's **Krishna temple** lies five minutes' walk east of the main street, surrounded by the eight **maths** founded by Madhva in the thirteenth century. Legend has it that the idol enshrined within was discovered by the saint himself after he prevented a shipwreck. The grateful captain of the vessel concerned offered Madhva his precious cargo as a reward, but the holy man asked instead for a block of ballast, which he broke open to expose a perfectly formed image of Krishna. Believed to contain the essence (*sannidhya*) of the god, this deity draws a steady stream of pilgrims and is the focus of almost constant ritual activity. It is cared for by *acharyas*, or pontiffs, from one or other of the *maths*. The only people allowed to touch the idol, they perform pujas (5.30am–8.45pm) that are open to non-Hindus; men are only allowed in the main shrine barechested. As the *acharya* approaches the shrine, the crowd divides to let him through, while brahmin boys fan the deity with cloths, accompanied by a cacophony of clanging bells and clouds of incense smoke.

A stone tank adjacent to the temple, known as the **Madhva Sarovara**, is the focus of a huge festival every two years (usually January 17–18), when a new head priest is appointed. Preparations for the **Paryaya Mahotsava** begin thirteen months in advance, and culminate with the grand entry of the new *acharya* into the town at the head of a huge procession. Outside in the street, a window in the wall affords a view of the deity; according to legend, this is the spot where a Harijan, or "untouchable" devotee, denied entry due to his caste, was worshipping Krishna from outside when the deity turned to face him. A statue of the devotee stands opposite. Nearby, there's a magnificent gold-painted wooden temple chariot (*rath*), carved in the distinctive Karnatakan style, its onion-shaped tower decked with thousands of scraps of paper, cloth and tinsel.

Staff at the **Regional Resources Centre for the Performing Arts** in the MGM College can tell you about local festivals and events that are well off the tourist trail; the centre's collection includes film, video and audio archives. The pamphlet *Udupi: an Introduction*, on sale in the stalls around the sacred enclave, is another rich source of background detail on the temple and its complex rituals.

Malpé, Thottam and St Mary's Island

Udupi's weekend picnic spot, **Malpé beach**, 5km north of the centre, is disappointing, marred by a forgotten concrete structure that was planned to be a government-run hotel. After wandering around the smelly fish market at the harbour, you could haggle to arrange a boat (around Rs800) to take you out to **St Mary's Island**, an extraordinary rock face of hexagonal basalt. Vasco da Gama is said to have placed a cross here in the 1400s, prior to his historic landing at Kozhikode in Kerala. From a distance, the sandy beach at **Thottam**, 1km north of Malpé and visible from the island, looks tempting; in reality it's an open sewer.

Practicalities

Udupi's three **bus stands** are dotted around the amorphous square in the centre of town: the KSRTC and private stands form a practically indistinguishable gathering spot for the numerous services to Mangalore and more long-distance buses to Mysore, Bangalore, Gokarna, Jog Falls, and other towns between northern Kerala and Goa. The City Bus Stand lies down some steps to the north and handles private services to nearby villages, including Malpé. Udupi's **railway station** is at Indrali on Manipal Road 3km from the centre and there are at least five trains in each direction daily. The modest tourist office is near the temple in the Krishna Building, Car Street (Mon–Sat 10am–5.30pm; ☎0820/252 9718). You can **change money** at the KM Dutt branch of Canara Bank on the main road just south of the bus stands; at UA Exchange (Mon–Sat 9.30am–6pm, Sun 9.30am–1pm; ☎0820/228 6655); or the CorpBank ATM on the south side of the square. **Internet** access is available nearby on the central square – Netpoint (Rs30 per hour) is one of several outlets here.

Accommodation and eating

Udupi has a good choice of **places to stay** to suit all budgets, most within a few minutes' walk of the temple and city centre. As you might expect of the birthplace of the masala dosa, there are many simple but fine South Indian **restaurants** where you can sample veg favourites, such as *Adarsha*, below the *Janardhana*. For non-veg or alcohol, you'll have to try a posh hotel, such as the *Pisces* at the *Sriram Residency*.

Durga International Just west of City Bus Stand ☎0820/253 6977, ✉durga-hotel@yahoo.com. Airy and efficient lodge with a variety of rooms, all en suite with TV and some a/c, on the upper storeys of a modern block. ❸–❻

Janardhana South of the KSRTC Bus Stand ☎0820/252 3880, ⊠252 3887. Fairly mundane hotel with simple en-suite rooms of varying sizes, most with cable TV. ❷–❹

Hotel Sharada International 2km out of town on the NH-17 ☎0820/252 2910. Mid-range place with a variety of rooms from singles to carpeted a/c doubles, as well as veg and non-veg restaurants and a bar. ❸–❻

Sri Vidyasamudra Choultry Opposite Krishna temple ☎0820/252 0820. Basically for pilgrims, but foreigners are welcome. It's ultra-basic, but the front rooms overlooking the temple and bathing tank are incredibly atmospheric ❶

Sriram Residency Opposite the Head Post Office ☎0820/253 0761, ✉sriramresidency@indiatimes .com. Plushest place in the centre, with a smart lobby, comfortable a/c rooms, two restaurants and a bar. ❸–❼

Vyavahar Lodge Kankads Rd ☎0820/252 2568. Basic but friendly and clean lodge between the bus stands and temple. ❷

Jog Falls

Hidden in a remote, thickly forested corner of the Western Ghats, **Jog Falls** (Rs2; rate varies for vehicles), 240km northeast of Mangalore, are the highest **waterfalls** in India. These days, they are rarely as spectacular as they were before the construction of a large dam upriver, which impedes the flow of the River Sharavati over the sheer red-brown sandstone cliffs. However, the surrounding scenery is spectacular at any time, with dense scrub and jungle carpeting sparsely populated, mountainous terrain. The views of the falls from the opposite side of the gorge is also impressive, unless, that is, you come

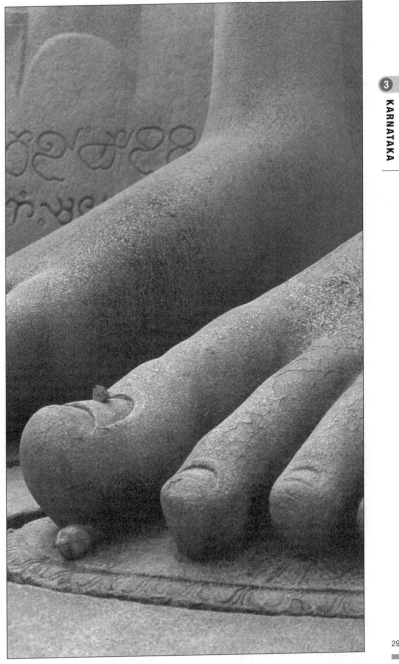

△ Statue, Sravanabelgola

here during the monsoons, when mist and rain clouds envelop the cascades. Another reason not to come here during the wet season is that the extra water, and abundance of leeches at this time, make the excellent **hike** to the floor valley a trial. So if you can, head up here between October and January. The trail starts just below the bus park and winds steeply down to the water, where you can enjoy a refreshing dip. The whole area opposite the falls has now been landscaped, with appealing viewing platforms and an impressive entrance gate.

Practicalities

Getting to Jog Falls by **bus** is now a lot easier thanks to the completion of the NH-206 across the Ghats. There are buses to the falls from **Honavar** (6 daily; 2hr 30min), on the Konkan Railway; from **Kumta** (4 daily; 3hr), which is reachable by bus from Gokarna; from **Udupi** and **Mangalore** (both 2 daily; 5hr 30min/7hr); from **Shimoga** (hourly; 1hr), which is reachable by bus from Hospet and Hampi; from **Panaji** (1 daily; 7hr); and from **Bangalore** (2 daily; 10hr). Better connections can be had at nearby **Sagar** (30km southeast), which is linked by bus to Shimoga, Udupi, Mysore, Hassan and Bangalore. With a **car or motorbike**, you can approach the falls from the coast along one of several scenic routes through the Ghats. The **tourist office** (Mon–Sat 10am–1.30pm & 2–5pm), upstairs at the new reception centre, opens rather erratically but can supply info on transport and vehicle hire.

Accommodation is limited and is largely a monopoly of the KSTDC (Ⓣ08186/244732), which runs the ugly concrete *Mayura Shraravathi* (❸), which has vast rooms with fading plaster and bathrooms with rickety plumbing (but good views), and the humbler *Tunga Tourist Home*, nearer the reception centre, with basic en-suite doubles (❷). On the opposite side of the road the Karnataka Power Corporation also rent out their four comfy a/c rooms (Ⓣ08186/244742; ❹) when available, as does the Shimoga District *PWD Inspection Bungalow* (Ⓣ08186/244333; ❸), whose a/c rooms are nicely situated on a hillock about 400m west of the falls' reception centre. The youth hostel (Ⓣ08186/244251; ❶), ten minutes' walk down the Shimoga road, has undergone renovation but is still very basic. If you can get in, the *PWD Inspection Bungalow*, on the north side of the gorge, has great views from its spacious, comfortable rooms, but is invariably full and has to be booked in advance through the Assistant Engineer's office in Siddapur (Ⓣ08389/222103; ❶–❷).

Apart from the KSTDC *Jaladarshini* canteen next to the *Tunga Tourist Home*, which offers the usual adequate but uninspiring fare, the only other **food** options are at the enclave of small chai stalls and shops at the reception centre – *Hotel Rashmita* is the best of the bunch.

Gokarna

Set behind a broad white-sand beach, with the forest-covered foothills of the Western Ghats forming a blue-green backdrop, **GOKARNA** (also spelled Gokarn), a seven-hours bus ride north of Mangalore, is among India's most scenically situated sacred sites. Yet this compact little coastal town – a Shaivite centre for more than two millennia – remained largely undiscovered by Western tourists until a little under a decade ago, when it began to attract dreadlocked and didgeridoo-toting travellers fleeing the commercialization of Goa. Now, it's firmly on the tourist map, although the Hindu pilgrims pouring through still far outnumber the foreigners who flock here in winter.

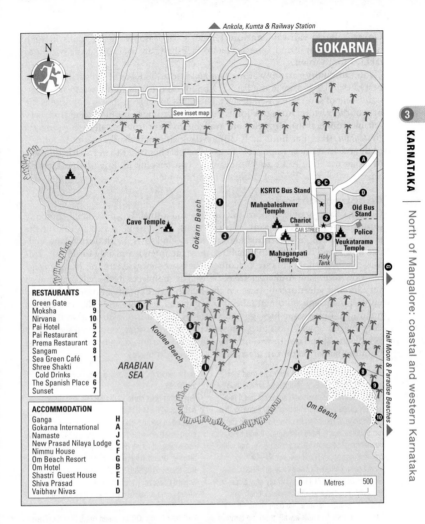

GOKARNA

See inset map

KSRTC Bus Stand

Mahabaleshwar
Temple

Old Bus
Stand

Chariot

CAR STREET

Police

Veukatarama
Temple

Mahaganpati
Temple

Holy
Tank

Cave Temple

Gokarn Beach

Kootlee Beach

*ARABIAN
SEA*

Om Beach

RESTAURANTS

Green Gate	B
Moksha	9
Nirvana	10
Pai Hotel	5
Pai Restaurant	2
Prema Restaurant	3
Sangam	8
Sea Green Café	1
Shree Shakti Cold Drinks	4
The Spanish Place	6
Sunset	7

ACCOMMODATION

Ganga	H
Gokarna International	A
Namaste	J
New Prasad Nilaya Lodge	C
Nimmu House	F
Om Beach Resort	G
Om Hotel	B
Shastri Guest House	E
Shiva Prasad	I
Vaibhav Nivas	D

0	Metres	500

Even if you're not tempted to while away weeks on isolated beaches, Gokarna is well worth a short detour from the coastal highway. Like Udupi, it's an old-established pilgrimage place with a markedly traditional feel: shaven-headed brahmins sit cross-legged on their verandas murmuring Sanskrit verses, while Hindu pilgrims file through a bazaar crammed with religious paraphernalia to the sea for a holy dip.

Arrival and information

The **KSRTC Bus Stand** lies 300m from Car Street and within easy walking distance of Gokarna's limited accommodation. You may well find that your bus, especially coming from major tourist points like Goa and Hampi, deposits you at the new police checkpost on the way into town, where you have to register; this is a new measure against beach crime and nothing to get het up about.

Gokarna Road **railway station**, served by at least two daily trains in each direction, is 9km inland; buses and auto-rickshaws are available at the station to take you into town.

You can **change money** at the *Om Hotel* near the KRSTC bus stand but the best rates to be had are at the Pai STD booth on the road into town near the bus stand, one of several licensed dealers. The tiny Om bureau almost opposite is the best of the various **Internet** joints (all Rs40 per hour), though none have very reliable connections. **Bicycles** are available for rent from a stall next to the *Pai Restaurant*, (Rs3 per hour or Rs30 per day), although thanks to the roughness of the tracks it's near impossible to cycle to beaches other than the town beach, or along the long route to Om beach. If you become ill, English-speaking Dr Shastri (℡08386/256220) is highly recommended.

Accommodation

Gokarna has a couple of bona fide **hotels** and a small but reasonable choice of **guesthouses**. As a last resort, you can nearly always find a bed in one of the pilgrims' hostels, or **dharamshalas**, dotted around town. With dorms, bare, cell-like rooms and basic washing facilities, these are intended mainly for Hindu visitors, but Western tourists are welcome if there are vacancies: try the *Prasad Nilaya*, just down the lane from *Om Hotel*. As well as the places in the village, there's a very limited selection of places on the **beach** (see opposite). Some people end up sleeping rough on the beaches, but nights can be chilly and robberies are not unknown. Leave your luggage and valuables behind in Gokarna if you plan to sleep on the beach (most guesthouses will store your stuff for a small fee), and if you plan to spend any time on the beaches, consider investing in a cheap mattress from the bazaar – you can always sell it when you leave.

Gokarna International On the main road into town ℡08386/256622, ℮hotelgokarn@yahoo .com. Gokarna's newest and smartest hotel is a friendly place and offers unbeatable value, with a good range of rooms from cheap singles to deluxe a/c doubles; some have bathtubs, TV and balconies overlooking the palms. The restaurants, one with bar, are less appealing, however. ❷–❹

New Prasad Nilaya Lodge Near the KRSTC Bus Stand ℡08386/257135. A relatively new place, very reasonably priced and offering clean, bright and spacious rooms with attached bathrooms. ❶–❷

Nimmu House A minute's walk from the temples towards Gokarna beach ℡08386/256730, ℮nimmuhouse@yahoo.com. Gokarna's best budget guesthouse, run by the friendly and helpful lady whose name it bears, with clean rooms (some en suite). The new block has very reasonable doubles and there are reliable left-luggage

and Internet facilities, plus a peaceful yard to sit in. ❶–❷

Om Hotel Just north of the KRSTC Bus Stand ℡08386/256445. Conventional economy hotel pitched at middle-class Indian pilgrims, with plain, good-sized en-suite rooms, overpriced a/c, and two restaurants (though one is more of a bar). ❷–❺

Shastri Guest House 100m east of the KRSTC Bus Stand ℡08386/256220. Tucked behind the Shastri Clinic on the main road, this quiet place offers some en-suite rooms and rock-bottom single rates. ❷

Vaibhav Nivas Off the main road, less than five minutes from the bus stand ℡08386/256714. Friendly, cheap and justifiably popular place, despite some tiny rooms – was undergoing renovations at the time of writing to make all rooms en suite. Internet and left-luggage facilities available. ❶–❸

The Town

Gokarna **town**, a hotchpotch of wood-fronted houses and red terracotta roofs, is clustered around a long L-shaped bazaar, its broad main road – known as **Car Street** – running west to the town beach, a sacred site in its own right. Hindu mythology identifies it as the place where Rudra (an early name for Shiva) was reborn through the ear of a cow from the underworld after a period of penance. Gokarna is also the home of one of India's most powerful *shivalingam*

– the **pranalingam**, which came to rest here after being carried off by Ravana, the evil king of Lanka, from Shiva's home on Mount Kailash in the Himalayas. Sent by the gods to reclaim the sacred object, Ganesh, with the help of Vishnu, tricked Ravana into letting him look after the *lingam* while he prayed, knowing that if it touched the ground it would take root and never be moved. When Ravana returned from his meditation, he tried to pick the *lingam* up, but couldn't, because the gods had filled it with "the weight of three worlds".

The *pranalingam* resides in Gokarna to this day, enshrined in the medieval **Shri Mahabaleshwar Temple**, at the far west end of the bazaar. It is regarded as so auspicious that a mere glimpse of it will absolve a hundred sins, even the murder of a brahmin. Local Hindu lore also asserts that you can maximize the *lingam's* purifying power by shaving your head, fasting and taking a holy dip in the sea before *darshan*, or ritual viewing of the deity. For this reason, pilgrims traditionally begin their tour of Gokarna with a walk to the beach. They are aided and instructed by their personal *pujari* – one of the bare-chested priests you see around town, wearing sacred caste threads and with single tufts of hair sprouting from their shaven heads – whose job it is to guide the pilgrims. Next, they visit the **Shri Mahaganpati Temple**, a stone's throw east of Shri Mahabaleshwar, to propitiate the elephant-headed god Ganesh. Sadly, owing to some ugly incidents involving insensitive behaviour by a minority of foreigners, tourists are now banned from the temples, though you can still get a good view of proceedings in the smaller Shri Mahaganpati from the entrance. En route, check out the splendid **rath**, or chariot, that stands at the end of the bazaar next to the Mahaganpati temple. During important festivals, notably Shiva's "birthday", **Shivratri** (Feb), deities are installed inside this colossal carved-wood cart and hauled by hand along the main street, accompanied by drum bands and watched by huge crowds.

The beaches

Notwithstanding Gokarna's numerous temples, shrines and tanks, most Western tourists come here for the beautiful **beaches** situated south of the more crowded town beach, beyond the lumpy laterite headland that overlooks the town. Many lounge around here for weeks, taking advantage of relatively lax attitudes towards the smoking of herb and imbibing of potent *bhang lassis*.

To pick up the trail, head along the narrow alley opposite the south entrance to the Mahaganpati temple, and follow the path uphill through the woods. After twenty minutes, you drop down from a sun-baked rocky plateau to **Kootlee beach** – a wonderful kilometre-long sweep of pure white sand sheltered by a pair of steep-sided promontories. Despite appearances, locals consider the water here to be dangerous. The palm-leaf chai stalls and seasonal cafés that spring up here during the winter give some respite from the heat of the midday sun, and some offer very basic accommodation in huts. Two places have more solid, lockable brick or mud huts but are likely to be booked out by long-term visitors: the *Ganga*, to the right as you first approach the beach (T08386/257195; ❶), and *Shiva Prasad* at the far end (T08386/257150; ❶). *The Spanish Place* (owned by a lady from Spain), set behind a line of neatly planted palms midway down the beach, serves good pasta, sandwiches, sweets and creamy lassis in a relaxed atmosphere, while the nearby *Sunset* offers seafood, tasty sizzlers and other more basic meals. Fresh water has been a perennial problem, but bottled water is widely available. A couple of places even have (slow) Internet connections.

It takes around twenty minutes more to hike over the headland from Kootlee to exquisite **Om beach**, so named because its distinctive twin crescent-shaped bays resemble the auspicious Om symbol. The construction of a dirt road from town means the coves are now frequented by a more diverse crowd than the hard-core hippy fringe whose exclusive preserve it used to be until the late-1990s. Hammocks and basic huts still fills the palm groves, and about a dozen laid-back chai houses such as *Sangam*, *Nirvana* and *Moksha* provide ample food and drink, but the nicely landscaped *Namaste* (℡08386/257141; ❶–❷) has the best restaurant and only solid accommodation until Cgh Earth open up their luxury resort behind the beach. Five kilometres inland in the hills, the new *Om Beach Resort* (℡08386/257052, ✉ombeachresort@info.com; ❽) costs Rs1500 per person for full board in smart a/c suites with sitouts.

Aforementioned developments notwithstanding, it's unlikely the concrete mixers will ever reach Gokarna's two most remote beaches, which lie another twenty- to forty-minute walk over the hill east of Om beach **Half-Moon** and **Paradise** beaches, are, despite the presence of one or two chai houses on each and the occasional shack, mainly for intrepid sun-lovers happy to pack in their own supplies. If you're looking for near-total isolation, this is your best bet.

Eating and drinking

Gokarna town offers a good choice of **places to eat**, with a string of busy "meals" joints along Car Street and the main road. Being Karnataka, **beer** is freely available and fairly cheap, both in town and on the beaches. Look out for the local sweet speciality, *gad-bad*, several layers of different ice creams mixed with chopped nuts and chewy dried fruit.

Green Gate Om Hotel, near the KRSTC bus stand. The Om Hotel's pleasant upstairs eatery offers a range of Mexican, Italian and Israeli dishes, as well as fish and sizzlers. The restaurant downstairs is more of a drinking den, though it serves good spicy Indian food; the courtyard is a more pleasant place to eat.

Pai Hotel Car St. A favourite meeting spot for travellers, this tiny joint has excellent veg snacks and delicious milky coffee.

Pai Restaurant Main Rd. Excellent spot for fresh and tasty veg thalis, masala dosas, crisp *wadas*, teas and coffees. Open until late.

Prema Restaurant Near the beach end of Car St. Standard traveller-friendly menu of pasta, sandwiches and bland Indian, plus the best *gadbad* in town.

Sea Green Café Just behind the main town beach. Tibetan and Nepali food in a breezy courtyard, and a good place to enjoy the sunset over a beer.

Shree Shakti Cold Drinks Car Street. Homemade peanut butter and fresh cheese, both made to American recipes, and the latter served with rolls, garlic and tomato; also serves filling toasties. Follow this up with ice cream or wash it all down with a creamy lassi.

Moving on from Gokarna

Gokarna is well connected by direct daily **bus** to Panjim in Goa (5hr), and several towns in Karnataka, including Bangalore (13hr), Hospet/Hampi (10hr) and Mysore (14hr), via Mangalore (7hr) and Udupi (6hr). Although there are only three direct buses north along the coast to Karwar (2hr), close to the border with Goa, you can change at Ankola on the main highway for more services. For more buses to Hospet and Hampi and the best connections to Jog Falls, change at Kumta; **tempos** regularly ply the route between Gokarna and Kumta (32km), as well as Ankola. The KSRTC counter in the new bus stand is helpful for information about current bus timings.

Gokarna Road railway station now has at least two daily stopping **trains** in each direction. The Verna Passenger heads north to Margao at 11.14am (#KR2) and south to Mangalore at 3.29pm (#KR1), while the Matsyagandha Express runs north to Goa and Mumbai at 6.15pm (#2620) and south to Mangalore (#2619) at the inconvenient time of 1.45am. A couple of weekly expresses also stop here, but you'll get better connections to Goa, Mangalore, Udupi and Kerala by heading first to either Kumta or Ankola.

For more on public transport from Gokarna, see "Travel details", p.334.

Sirsi and around

The large, bustling administrative centre of **SIRSI**, 83km east of Gokarna, sees few visitors but provides a good stop on long journeys to and from the coast, and also has onward connections to the Tibetan settlements of Mundgod and Hubli in the north, Jog Falls to the south, and Hospet to the east. The town's main point of interest is the striking **Marikamba temple**, but the chief reason for stopping here is to visit the fascinating temple complex at nearby **BANVASI**.

The Town

Marikamba temple, 500m from the bus stand in Sirsi, sees a steady stream of devotees coming to propitiate Durga, the ferocious multi-armed goddess who, as usual, is depicted astride a tiger and slaying a demon. The temple is at its most frenetic in the evenings, but is best seen during the day when it's easiest to appreciate the remarkable murals, some of the finest surviving examples of **Kavi art**. A rare form of wall-art once prevalent throughout the coastal Konkan region of west Karnataka but now practically extinct, Kavi art uses an unusual technique whereby a top layer of plaster, dyed with a blood-red pigment, is etched away to create detail revealed by the lower white layer of plaster.

An imposing nineteenth-century facade, finished in red, leads into a grand courtyard with the temple at its centre; the cloisters are lavishly decorated with gods and goddesses. Parts of the inner sanctum, which houses an image of Durga, date back to the sixteenth century, but numerous additions hide any traces of the original structure. Marikamba's **rath festival**, during which the deity is placed on a *rath* (chariot) and paraded through the town, is held here once every other year in February and is one of the grandest in Karnataka. The next festival here will be held in 2007.

Banvasi

The ancient town of **BANVASI**, 22km southeast of Sirsi, dates back to the third century BC when it was a centre of Buddhist learning. Little remains from that period, however, and the brick stupas that once graced the banks of the River Varada have all but disappeared. From the fourth century onwards, under the Kadambas, a dynasty that ruled the region for around two hundred years, Banvasi became the capital of Kannada, the forerunner of modern Karnataka, and is still held in high esteem as the home of the Kannada script.

The **Madhukeshvara Temple**, at the far end of Banvasi's winding Car Street, 1.5km from the bus stand, is still in use today. It dates back to the Kadamba period, although most of the major additions are attributed to the late Chalukya period of the twelfth century. The inner sanctum of the main temple – dedicated to Shiva as the lord (*ishvara*) of the bees (*madhuka*), who is represented here with a honey-coloured *lingam* – is said to date back to the fourth century, and the adjoining pillared stone hall to the sixth century. To the right of the inner sanctum stands a marble image of Datatreya, a three-headed combination representing the Hindu trinity of Brahma the creator, Vishnu the preserver and Shiva the destroyer. A most imposing Nandi, Shiva's bull and vehicle, sits outside in ever-faithful attendance facing the *lingam*.

The entrance hall (*mukhamandapa*) has numerous pillars, all unique in style except for the four highly polished reflective granite pillars that surround the stone dance circle, now no longer in use. In the middle chamber, a stone throne with lavishly carved pillars, built in 1628, is still used to hold idols during special occasions such as Vasant Utsava, the summer festival held around April every year.

Immediately to the right of the main temple is a temple dedicated to Parvati, built in the late twelfth century. The extensive courtyard has an interesting collection of stone images, including gods known as the Ashtadigpalakas (the guardians of the eight directions), each with his own animal vehicle. The Ashtadigpalakas, who date back to the Vedic period, include Indra (east) on his elephant; Agni (southeast) on his ram; Yama, the god of death (south) on his buffalo; Niraruti (southwest), whose vehicle is a man; Varuna (west) on a crocodile; Yayu (northwest) on a deer; Kubera (north) on a horse, and Ishana, one of the prototypes of Shiva (northeast), on his bull. Each of the gods is shown with his consort. At one side of the courtyard stands a small temple dedicated to Ganesh.

A small **museum** by the main gates holds a collection of sculpture from around Banvasi, including a striking fifteenth-century image of the Jain Gomateshvara and Buddhist plaques from the second century. Outside the main temple stands the majestic temple *rath* (chariot), built in 1608 and used to transport the gods during Vasant Utsava. A path opposite the temple entrance leads down between some shacks to the river and is a favourite picnic spot for visiting pilgrims.

Practicalities

Several **buses** travel between Sirsi and Banvasi, though services stop after 6pm. Buses from Sirsi's KSRTC bus stand, which is over 1km north of the centre, usually also call at the old stand in town and connect it to numerous destinations including Gokarna (via Kumta), Hospet, Jog Falls, Karwar, Mundgod and Hubli. Private companies operate deluxe buses from near the old bus stand to destinations such as Hubli and Bangalore.

The best way of getting around town is an **auto-rickshaw**; **taxis** are available near the old bus stand, although if you book one through a hotel, you may find it cheaper. **Hotels** in Sirsi are good value. Ignore the dives around the bus stand and head 2km out to College Road, where you'll find a handful of good options, including the *Madhuvana* (℡08384/237496, ⓔhotelmadhuvana@hotmail.com; ②–③), a large, clean and well-run hotel with excellent-value suites and a very good vegetarian restaurant. The *Samrat*, next door (℡08384/236278; ①–②), has simple, slightly faded rooms, including some sleeping up to five. The poshest of Sirsi's hotels, the *Panchavati* on Yellapur Road (℡08384/236755, ⓕ238301; ③–⑥), is 4km from the centre but well worth the ride. Set in large, pleasant grounds on the edge of town, it offers good facilities, including a restaurant and some a/c rooms. Note that there is no accommodation in Banvasi. Of the dingy bars serving non-veg **food** in the vicinity of College Road, the *Parijata*, just round the corner towards the bus stand in Hospet Road, is the most salubrious.

Dandeli Wildlife Sanctuary

Lying between Hubli 75km to the east and Panjim 145km to the west, the scruffy town of **DANDELI**, on the banks of the River Kali in Uttar Kanada (Northern Karnataka), provides access to the **Dandeli Wildlife Sanctuary** (best Dec–April, closed June–Sept 6–8am & 4–6pm; Rs150 [Rs50]), an extensive, unspoiled forest on the edge of the Deccan Plateau. Despite its close proximity to Goa and its situation at a major crossroads on the route to Hampi via Hubli, the sanctuary sees few visitors except for occasional jeeploads from nearby Maharashtra, and remains a low-key and undeveloped wildlife destination.

Spread across 834 square kilometres, the large, mixed-deciduous forest, famed for its teak, spills over the lip of the Deccan Plateau where it gives way to the hills, ravines and deep river valleys of the Western Ghats. At the heart of the forest, 22km from the entrance gate, the 100-metre-high **Cyntheri Rock** rises out of the **River Kanari**. The river provides an excellent vantage point for observing animals. The sanctuary is famous for its black panthers, but sightings are rare, especially with the deep cover; you stand a better chance of seeing sambar deer, spotted deer, flying squirrels, wild boar and Indian bison – distinguished by distinctive white bands across parts of their body. Dandeli also shelters elephants, sloth bears and a small handful of tigers, while the rivers, including the **River Kali**, which sweeps past the town of Dandeli, is home to mugger crocodiles. **Sunset Point**, 6km from the gate, and remote **Sykes Point** provide sweeping views of the jungle-covered ridges of the Western Ghats.

The main Hubli–Karwar highway, which passes by Dandeli, is one of the most beautiful in Karnataka as it descends through the verdant **Anasi National Forest**, which forms part of the same forest-belt as that of the Dandeli Wildlife Sanctuary. Travelling through the area you may notice the striking features of the **Siddhis**, a group of African descent who live in the region and maintain their own customs and language; they were brought over in the nineteenth century by a local raja to act as bodyguards.

Practicalities

Dandeli's **KSRTC Bus Stand**, in the centre of town, is well connected, with frequent buses to Hubli and to Karwar on the coast; in addition, the two daily KSRTC buses between Panjim in Goa and Hubli stop here. The forest checkpost, at the gate of the wildlife sanctuary, is around 18km from town; you will need to arrange your own vehicle, either privately or through the Forest Department in Dandeli, before getting here (jeeps cost from Rs150 per hour). If you want to stay at any of the Forest Department's **resthouses** (❶–❷) in the sanctuary you'll also need to contact their office (☎08284/231585, ℻230300), which is located on the main Karwar road, near the Kali River.

Cheap, simple **accommodation** is available around the bus stand, but for a little more comfort try the popular, but often full, *Government Guest House* nearby (☎08284/231299; ❷), which has attractive, clean rooms. The Forest Department's *Nature Camp* (❶), located at the forest gates next to the inter-pretation centre, has permanent tented accommodation costing Rs150 for a four- to five-person tent, although it's mainly geared up to accommodate groups of schoolchildren. Across the River Kali from Dandeli lies Jungle Lodges & Resorts' *Kali Wilderness and Adventure Resort* (☎080/559 7021, ⓦwww .junglelodges.com; ❾), with ten spacious rooms in the main concrete building and nine luxurious tents with attached baths along the river – bring plenty of mosquito repellent and be aware that as a foreigner you'll be paying an inflated price of $50 a night, though the package does include accommodation, entrance fees, jeep safari and a coracle ride along the River Kali. Their safaris and food, served in an open thatched restaurant, are both excellent, however. The *Bison River Resort* (☎08383/246539; ❽), on the other side of the sanctu-ary at Bangur Nagar, has luxury cabins which are offered at half-price during the off-season, when the park is closed – fine for a pampered break, though of course you can't go and see any animals.

Hubli and around

Karnataka's second most industrialized city, **HUBLI**, 418km northwest of Bangalore, has little to offer tourists except for its transport connections to Mumbai, Goa, the coast of Uttar Kanada (Northern Karnataka), Hampi and

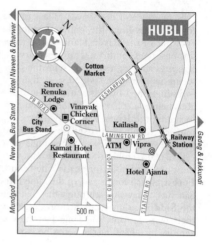

other points in the interior. It does, however, make a convenient base from which to explore the various sites in the area. These include the large Tibetan monastery of **Drepung** on the outskirts of the town of Mundgod, 48km south of Hubli. Improbably located in the rolling countryside of central Karnataka, where summer temperatures can soar well above 40°C – a stark contrast with the cold climate of Tibet – the busy and rarely visited complex at Drepung is home to several hundred monks. Representing the ancient scholastic monastery that once flourished outside Lhasa, along with the Sera monasteries at Bylakuppe (see p.283), Drepung is one of the most important Tibetan monasteries in India. The environs of Drepung, as around Bylakuppe, have been settled by Tibetan refugees, who have industriously farmed the once barren land since the 1960s. Although few travellers come this way, visitors are welcome.

Some 10km to the west of Hubli, the leafy university town of **DHARWAR** is far less polluted than Hubli itself and, although it attracts few foreigners, is nationally renowned for its Hindustani classical music connections, being home to several famous musicians and vocalists. In musical terms, this region marks the watershed between the Carnatic classical music of South India, and the Hindustani music of North India (see Contexts, p.703). The main concert season is in the winter, and performances are held at various venues around Dharwar and Hubli; check local papers for listings.

Travelling east towards Hospet and Hampi, the cotton town of **GADAG**, 53km east of Hubli, is an important stop on the train line (for connections to Badami and Bijapur – when conversion is complete). During the cotton season, between February and June, the town is a hive of activity, but at other times returns to its quiet ways. Few travellers stop here, but for those with the time and inclination, Gadag and its environs make a good diversion from the well-travelled route to and from Hampi, with a handful of rarely visited Chalukya temples dating back to the eleventh century. The best of the Gadag monuments are the **Trikuteshwara** and **Saraswati** temples, which share a compound in the southern part of the town. The inner sanctum of the Trikuteshwara temple houses a triple *lingam*; the adjoining Saraswati temple shares the same hall and boasts a porch with impressive carvings. You may find parts of the complex locked, in which case you'll need to look for the priest, who will unlock it for you.

Gadag's other temples are in a terrible state of repair, and travelling to the village of **LAKKUNDI**, a further 11km east along the Hospet highway, is more rewarding. Less threatened by urban growth, Lakkundi's Chalukya temples, from the same period as those in Gadag, include a **Jain** *basti*, dominating the north of the village, with an impressive tower and sanctuary walls. A short distance away, the **Kashi Vishwanatha Temple**, dedicated to Shiva as lord of Kashi (Varanasi), consists of two temples facing each other and sharing the same plinth. Unfortunately, the connecting porch has collapsed, but the animal and flower friezes along the plinth are impressive, as are the carvings along the doorways and pillars. Close to the bus stand, a square stepped bathing tank with a columned bridge halfway through was designed to provide privacy for women bathers.

Practicalities

Hubli's **railway station**, close to the town centre and within walking distance of several of the hotels, is well connected to Bangalore, Mumbai, Pune and Hospet (see box on p.306). The line to Goa has now been converted but there still aren't trains every day, so the bus is still the best option. Hubli's efficient new **KSRTC Bus Stand**, over 2km south of town, has regular services linking the city with Goa, coastal Karnataka, Badami, Hospet, Mumbai and Bangalore. It can be reached by numerous buses from the chaotic City Bus Stand, about 1km west of the railway station, and by others from outside the station itself. There are more buses than trains for Hospet, numerous buses to Dharwar and several to Dandeli and Karwar. Many buses connect Lakkundi to Gadag as well as to Hospet. Most long-distance services are overnight; private operators can be found across the main road from the bus stand. Janata Travel (☎0836/235 4968) operates buses for Mumbai and Pune. Perhaps the most reputable of the private outfits, Vijayananda Travels (☎0836/235 0630), distinguishable by their yellow-and-black signs, operate luxury buses to Mumbai, Pune, Gulbharga, Bijapur, Sirsi and Bangalore. For Drepung, there are several buses from the KSRTC Bus Stand to Mundgod; alternatively, head for the *Modern Lodge*, opposite the railway station, where the Tibetan community congregates and from where two or three shared jeeps depart every morning. The best way of getting around the city is by **auto-rickshaw**; these have meters, but there's also an efficient pre-paid booth outside the railway station.

Accommodation around the railway station includes the huge *Hotel Ajanta* on JC Nagar (☎0836/236 2216; ❷–❸), which has small plain rooms, including very cheap singles with shared bathroom, and rickety plumbing. Opposite the City Bus Stand, the large and well-organized *Shree Renuka Lodge* (☎0836/225 1384; ❷–❸) offers a range of reasonable budget rooms. Between the railway station and the bus stand, Lamington Road has a few more options, including the pleasant *Kailash* (☎0836/235 2235, ⓦwww.hotelkailash.com; ❸–❹), an efficient business hotel, which has good-value a/c rooms and a plain restaurant. *Vipra*, opposite, is a good deal cheaper, with a range of simple rooms (☎0836/236 2336, ⓔvipratravels@satyam.net.in; ❶–❷). For a lot more comfort, *Naveen* at Unkal (☎0836/237 2283, ⓕ237 2730; ❼–❾), 6km west of the centre, despite its lavish use of concrete, is quite attractive, with cottages, a pleasant lakeside setting and a swimming pool; transport can be laid on from the railway station or bus stand by prior arrangement.

Most hotels have their own **restaurants** – the *Shree Renuka*, for example, has two sections, one serving South Indian vegetarian food and the other Chinese and North Indian cuisine. The best of the independent restaurants is the ever-reliable vegetarian chain *Kamat Hotel*, by the traffic island at the head of Lamington Road towards the bus stand. The downstairs restaurant serves excellent South Indian food, while the plush restaurant upstairs, *Kosher*, serves vegetarian North Indian and Chinese dishes; there's another branch opposite the railway station. *Vinayak Chicken Corner*, opposite the city bus stand, is a good spot for inexpensive non-veg and beer. ICICI Bank has an **ATM** at the railway station and another one halfway along to the City Bus Stand. For **Internet** access, head to Netzone (Rs30 per hour) in JC Nagar, almost opposite the *Ajanta*.

Recommended trains from Hubli

The services listed below are the **most convenient** and/or the **fastest**. This list is by no means exhaustive and there are numerous slower trains which are often more convenient for smaller destinations – see p.334.

Destination	Train	Number	Frequency	Departs	Total Time
Bangalore	Hubli–Bangalore Siddhaganga Inter City Express	#2726	Daily	6.20am	7hr 30min
Hospet	Hubli–Bangalore Hampi Express	#6591	Daily	5pm	2hr 55min
Mumbai	Bangalore–Mumbai Chalukya Express/ Mysore–Mumbai Sharavathi Express	#1018/1036	Daily	2.40pm	16hr 50min*
Mysore	Dhanwar-Mysore Express	#6202	Daily	8.15pm	9hr 55min

* Stops in Pune

Hospet

Charmless **HOSPET**, ten hours by bus east of Goa, is of little interest except as a transport hub and, in particular, as the jumping-off place for the extraordinary ruined city of Hampi (Vijayanagar), 13km northeast. If you arrive late, or want somewhere fairly comfortable to sleep, it makes sense to stay here and catch a bus or taxi out to the ruins the following morning. Otherwise, hole up in Hampi, where the setting more than compensates for the basic facilities.

Practicalities

Hospet's **railway station**, 1.5km north of the centre, is served by the overnight Hampi Express (#6592) from Bangalore and services from Hyderabad, via Guntakal Junction. The line continues west to Hubli for connections to the coast and Goa. For connections to Badami and Bijapur, travel to Gadag and change onto the slow single track running north. Auto-rickshaws are plentiful or you can get into town by cycle rickshaw (Rs10), or by foot if unencumbered. The **long-distance bus stand** is in the centre, just off MG (Station) Road, which runs south from the railway station. The most frequent services are from Bangalore and Hubli, and there are daily arrivals from Mysore, Badami, Bijapur, Hassan, Gokarna (via Kumta), Mangalore and Goa. For a summary of services see "Travel details" on p.334. **Bookings** for long-distance routes can be made at the ticket office on the bus stand concourse (daily 8am–noon & 3–6pm), where there's also a **left luggage** facility.

The **tourist office** at the Rotary Circle (Mon–Sat: June–March 10am–5.30pm; April & May 8am–1.30pm; ☎08394/228537) offers limited information and sells tickets for KSTDC tours (see p.308). You can **change** travellers' cheques and cash at the State Bank of Mysore (Mon–Fri 10.30am–2.30pm & Sat 10.30am–12.30pm), next to the tourist office, and cash only at the State Bank of India (same hours) on Station Road. Full exchange facilities are available at the *Hotel Malligi*, while Sneha Travels (☎08394/225838) at the Elimanchate Complex, next to the *Hotel Priyadarshini* on MG Road, also changes any currency and travellers' cheques, and advances money on credit cards. They also

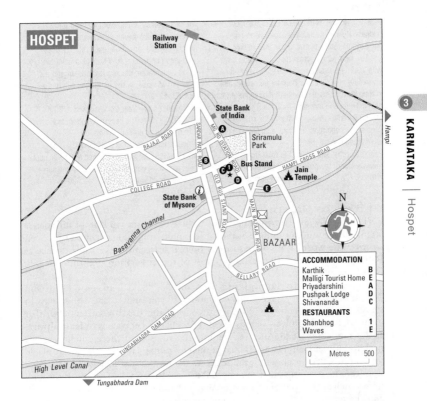

HOSPET

Railway
Station

State Bank
of India

Sriramulu
Park

Bus Stand

Jain
Temple

State Bank
of Mysore

Basavanna Channel

BAZAAR

ACCOMMODATION
Karthik   B
Malligi Tourist Home   E
Priyadarshini   A
Pushpak Lodge   D
Shivananda   C
RESTAURANTS
Shanbhog   1
Waves   E

0   Metres   500

High Level Canal

Tungabhadra Dam

book airline and train tickets, have cars for hire and run private **luxury buses
to Goa**, which are operated by Paulo Travels (℡08394/225867) next door.
Their sleeper coach departs at 7pm, costs Rs450 and takes ten hours to reach
Panjim. Luxury buses are also available for Bangalore (10hr; Rs200) departing
between 10pm and 11pm at night. There's **Internet** access at Cybernet (Rs40
per hour), next to the *Shivananda* hotel.

Accommodation and eating

Accommodation in Hospet, concentrated around MG Road, ranges from
budget to mid-price. There's little to do in Hospet, so you'll probably spend
a fair amount of time **eating and drinking**. Many of the hotels have good
dining rooms, but in the evening, the upmarket but affordable *Waves*, a terrace
restaurant within the *Malligi* hotel complex, is the most congenial place to
hang out, serving tandoori and chilled beer from 7pm to 11pm (bring lots of
mosquito repellent). *Shanbhog*, an excellent little Udupi restaurant next to the
bus station, is a perfect pit stop before heading to Hampi, and opens early for
breakfast.

Karthik Pampa Villa, off MG Rd ℡0839/424938,
℉420028. A new, characterless block featuring
unremarkable rooms but with a surprise around the
back in the form of an extraordinary nineteenth-
century stone villa housing two huge suites. ③–⑦

Malligi Tourist Home 6/143 Jambunatha
Rd, 2min walk east of MG Rd (look for the
signs) and the bus stand ℡0839/428101,
©malligihome@hotmail.com. This friendly, well-
managed hotel is by far the most popular place

to stay in Hospet, with something to suit most budgets. Options includes cheaper, clean and comfortable rooms (some a/c) in the old block, and two new wings across the immaculate lawn, with luxurious a/c rooms. There's also a great new swimming pool (Rs25per hour for non-residents) in their Waves complex beneath the restaurant/bar. plus billiards and massage facilities. The al fresco Madhu Paradise restaurant/bar in the old block serves great veg food, and they also have an efficient travel service. ❷–❻
Priyadarshini MG Rd, up the road from the bus stand, towards the railway station ☎0839/428838, ⓦwww.priyainnhampi.com.

Various rooms ranging from rock-bottom singles to doubles with TV and a/c (some with balconies). It's large and bland, but spotless and very good value, and they also have two good restaurants: the veg Naivedyam and the non-veg Manasa, in the garden, which has a bar. ❸–❻
Pushpak Lodge Near the bus stand, MG Rd ☎0839/421380. The best rock-bottom lodge, with basic but clean en-suite rooms. ❷
Shivananda Beside the bus stand, ☎0839/420700. Well-maintained hotel with spotless rooms, all en suite with cable TV and some a/c. Very good value. ❷–❸

Getting to Hampi

KSTDC's daily guided **tour** only stops at three of the sites in Hampi and spends an inordinate amount of time at the far less interesting Tungabhadra Dam. Even so, it can be worth it if you're short of time. It leaves from the tourist office at Rotary Circle (Taluk Office Circle), east of the bus station (9.30am–5.30pm; Rs100 including lunch).

Frequent **buses to Hampi** run from the bus stand between 6.30am and 7.30pm; the journey takes thirty minutes. If you arrive late, either stay in Hospet, or take a taxi (Rs120–150) or one of the rickshaws (Rs60–80) that gather outside the railway station. It's also possible to catch a bus to **Kamalpura**, at the south side of the site, and explore the ruins from there, catching a bus back to Hospet from Hampi Bazaar at the end of the day. **Bicycles** are available for rent at several stalls along the main street, but the trip to, around, and back from the site is a long one in the heat. **Auto-rickshaws**, best arranged through hotels such as the *Malligi* or *Priyadarshini*, will also take you to Hampi and back and charge around Rs50–60 per hour. For the adventurous, Bullet **motorbikes** are available to rent (and buy) from Bharat Motors (☎08394/224704) near *Rama Talkies*. Finally, some hotels in Hospet can also organize for you to hook up with **trained guides** in Hampi; ask at the *Malligi* or *Priyadarshini*.

Hampi (Vijayanagar)

The city of Bidjanagar [Vijayanagar] is such that the pupil of the eye has never seen a place like it, and the ear of intelligence has never been informed that there existed anything to equal it in the world... The bazaars are extremely long and broad... Roses are sold everywhere. These people could not live without roses, and they look upon them as quite as necessary as food... Each class of men belonging to each profession has shops contiguous the one to the other; the jewellers sell publicly in the bazaars pearls, rubies, emeralds and diamonds. In this agreeable locality, as well as in the king's palace, one sees numerous running streams and canals formed of chiselled stone, polished and smooth... This empire contains so great a population that it would be impossible to give an idea of it without entering into extensive details.

Abdu'r-Razzaq, the Persian ambassador who visited Vijayanagar in 1443

The ruined city of **Vijayanagar** (City of Victory) – better known as **HAMPI**, the name of the main local village – spills from the south bank of the River

Tungabhadra, littered among a surreal landscape of golden-brown granite boulders and leafy banana fields. According to Hindu mythology, the settlement began its days as Kishkinda, the monkey kingdom of the Ramayana, ruled by the monkey kings Bali and Sugriva, and their ambassador, Hanuman; the weird rocks – some balanced in perilous arches, others heaped in colossal, hill-sized piles – are said to have been flung down by their armies in a show of strength.

Between the fourteenth and sixteenth centuries, this was the most powerful Hindu capital in the Deccan. Travellers such as the Portuguese chronicler Domingo Paez, who stayed for two years after 1520, were astonished by its size and wealth, telling tales of markets full of silk and precious gems, beautiful, bejewelled courtesans, ornate palaces and joyous festivities.

However, in the second half of the sixteenth century, the dazzling city was devastated by a six-month Muslim **siege**, thanks to which most of Hampi's monuments are in disappointingly poor shape, appearing a lot older than their four or five hundred years. Yet the serene riverine setting and air of magic that lingers over the site, sacred for centuries before a city was ever founded here, make it one of India's most extraordinary locations. Even so, mainstream tourism has thus far made little impact: along with streams of Hindu pilgrims and tatty-haired *sadhus* who hole up in the more isolated rock crevices and shrines, most visitors are budget travellers straight from Goa. Many find it difficult to leave, and spend weeks chilling out in cafés, wandering to whitewashed hilltop temples and gazing at the spectacular sunsets.

The **best time to come** to Hampi, weather-wise, is from late October to early March, when daytime temperatures are low enough to allow long forays on foot through the ruins. The village starts to get busy over Christmas and New Year, however, and for a month or so from early January the site is swamped by an exodus of travellers from Goa. If you want to enjoy Hampi at its best, come outside peak season.

Some history

This was an area of minor political importance under the Chalukyas, but the rise of the **Vijayanagar empire** seems to have been a direct response, in the first half of the fourteenth century, to the expansionist aims of Muslims from the north, most notably Malik Kafur and Muhammad-bin-Tughluq. Two Hindu brothers from Andhra Pradesh, **Harihara** and **Bukka**, who had been employed as treasury officers in Kampila, 19km east of Hampi, were captured by the Tughluqs and taken to Delhi, where they supposedly converted to Islam. Assuming them to be suitably tamed, the Delhi sultan despatched them to quell civil disorder in Kampila, which they duly did, only to abandon both Islam and allegiance to Delhi shortly afterwards, preferring to establish their own independent Hindu kingdom. Within a few years, they controlled vast tracts of land from coast to coast. In 1343, their new capital, Vijayanagar, was founded on the southern banks of the River Tungabhadra, a location long considered sacred by Hindus. The city's most glorious period was under the reign of **Krishna Deva Raya** (1509–29), when it enjoyed a near monopoly on the lucrative trade in Arabian horses and Indian spices passing through the coastal ports.

Thanks to its natural features and massive fortifications, Vijayanagar was virtually impregnable. In 1565, however, following his interference in the affairs of local Muslim sultanates, the regent Rama Raya was drawn into a battle with a confederacy of Muslim forces, 100km away to the north, which left the city open to attack. At first, fortune appeared to be on the side of the Hindu forces, but there were as many as 10,000 Muslims in their number, and loyalties

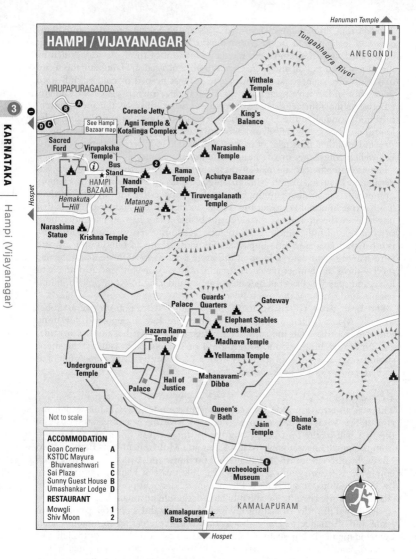

HAMPI / VIJAYANAGAR

Hanuman Temple

Tungabhadra River

ANEGONDI

VIRUPAPURAGADDA

Vitthala
Temple

Coracle Jetty

King's
Balance

Agni Temple &
Kotalinga Complex

See Hampi
Bazaar map

Sacred
Ford

Virupaksha
Temple

Narasimha
Temple

Bus
Stand

Rama
Temple

Achutya Bazaar

HAMPI
BAZAAR

Nandi
Temple

Tiruvengalanath
Temple

Hemakuta
Hill

Matanga
Hill

Narashima
Statue

Krishna Temple

Guards'
Quarters

Palace

Gateway

Elephant Stables

Hazara Rama
Temple

Lotus Mahal

Madhava Temple

Yellamma Temple

"Underground"
Temple

Mahanavami-
Dibba

Palace

Hall of
Justice

Queen's
Bath

Bhima's
Gate

Jain
Temple

Not to scale

Archeological
Museum

KAMALAPURAM

N

ACCOMMODATION

Goan Corner	A
KSTDC Mayura	
Bhuvaneshwari	E
Sai Plaza	C
Sunny Guest House	B
Umashankar Lodge	D

RESTAURANT

| Mowgli | 1 |
| Shiv Moon | 2 |

Kamalapuram
Bus Stand

Hospet

may well have been divided. When two Vijayanagar Muslim generals suddenly
deserted, the army fell into disarray. Defeat came swiftly; although members of
his family fled with untold hoards of gold and jewels, Rama Raya was captured
and suffered a grisly death at the hands of the sultan of Ahmadnagar. Vijayanagar
then fell victim to a series of destructive raids, and its days of splendour were
brought to an abrupt end.

Practicalities

Buses from Hospet terminate close to where the road joins the main street
in Hampi Bazaar, halfway along its dusty length. A little further towards the

Virupaksha Temple, the **tourist office** (daily except Fri 10am–5.30pm; ☎08394/241339) can put you in touch with a **guide** (Rs500 per day) but not much else. Most visitors coming from Hospet organize a guide from there (see p.308).Rented **bicycles**, available from stalls near the lodges, cost Rs5 per hour or Rs30–40 for a 24hr period, although they can be hard work on the bumpy roads, so consider a motorized two-wheeler. **Motorbikes and scooters** can be rented for around Rs150 per day from the Raju stall, round the corner from the tourist office. Sneha Travels, whose main office is at D131/11 Main Street (daily 9am–9pm; ☎08394/241590), can **change money** (at poorish rates), advance cash on credit cards and book airline and **train tickets**, as well as **luxury buses** to Bangalore and sleeper coaches to Goa and Gokarna; although these drop people off right in Hampi Bazaar, you have to pick them up from Hospet thanks to the powerful taxi/rickshaw mafia (and note that, whatever you are told, the Gokarna bus involves a transfer at Ankola in the small hours). There are at least a dozen **Internet** outlets, which have fixed a universally high rate of Rs60 per hour.

Run by Shri Swamy Sadashiva Yogi, the **Shivananda Yoga Ashram** overlooking the river, past the site of the new footbridge and coracle crossing, offers courses in **yoga and meditation** as well as homeopathic treatment, magnetotherapy and **Ayurvedic treatment**, in particular for snakebites.

Accommodation

If you're happy to make do with basic amenities, Hampi is a far more enjoyable place to stay than Hospet, with around fifty congenial **guesthouses** and plenty of cafés to hang out in after a long day in the heat. Staying in the village also means you can be up and out early enough to catch the sunrise over the ruins – a mesmerizing spectacle. Some travellers shun Hampi Bazaar for the fast-growing **Virupapuradadda** across the river, which has become extremely popular with Israelis. Outside **high season**, which lasts for six weeks starting around Christmas, you may well get a substantial discount on the room rates quoted below. Note there is generally a 10am check-out.

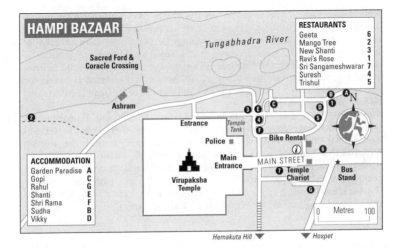

Hampi Bazaar

Garden Paradise Far east end of village ☎08394/241954. Four cramped but cute huts (shared bathrooms) in an excellent riverside location and with a chilled-out restaurant. ②

Gopi Guest House A short walk down the lanes behind Shanti ☎08394/241695, ✉gopiguesthouse93@yahoo.co.in. Ten rooms with attached baths (though they cost more than most in peak season) and a pleasant rooftop café with temple view. ③

Rahul Guest House South of Main St, near the bus stand ☎08394/241648. Now has some new en-suite rooms in addition to the small and spartan old ones, which share rudimentary washing and toilet facilities, along with a pleasant shaded café. ①–③

Shanti Guest House Just north of the Virupaksha Temple ☎08394/241568. This is a real favourite, comprising a dozen or so twin-bedded cells ranged on two storeys around a leafy inner courtyard. It's basic (showers and toilets are shared) but spotless, and all rooms have fans and windows. ①

Shri Rama Guest House Next to the Virupaksha temple ☎08394/241219, ✉venkannaj@yahoo.com. Rock-bottom en-suite rooms mainly for Hindu pilgrims, but foreigners are also welcome. Also has a rooftop restaurant. ①

Sudha Guest House At the east end of the village ☎08394/241451. Very friendly and pleasantly situated family operation, with cool en-suite rooms downstairs and smaller ones with shared facilities upstairs. Good value, and mozzie nets are provided. ①–③

Vikky At the end of the lane furthest northeast from the temple ☎08394/241694. Friendly place with small clean rooms, some en suite, and a popular rooftop restaurant. ②–③

Virupapuragadda and Kamalapuram

Goan Corner 500m east of the coracle crossing ☎94487 18951. Large complex amidst the paddy fields and near the rocks, with a lively restaurant and a range of rooms and huts, some with attached bathrooms. ①–②

KSTDC Mayura Bhuvaneshwari Kamalapuram, 2.5km from Hampi Bazaar ☎08394/241574. The only remotely upmarket place to stay within reach of the ruins, with clean en-suite rooms and competitively priced a/c rooms – and fixed goverment rates mean there are no peak season price hikes. There's a pleasant garden, a good restaurant and a bar serving cold beers, but it feels detached from Hampi Bazaar and the village lacks charm. ②–③

Sai Plaza ☎08533/287017, ✉santoshgvt@yahoo.com. Attractive huts with bathrooms, set around a pleasant landscaped garden, with swing beds outside. ②

Sunny Guest House ☎08533/287005. Nicely landscaped gardens with a row of compact rooms and somewhat roomier huts. ②–③

Umashankar Lodge ☎08533/287067. One of the better places to stay across the river. Small but clean en-suite rooms (though the upstairs ones are rather overpriced) set round a leafy courtyard. ①–③

The site

Although spread over 26 square kilometres, the ruins of Vijayanagar are mostly concentrated in two distinct groups: the first lies in and around **Hampi Bazaar** and the nearby riverside area, encompassing the city's most sacred enclave of temples and *ghats*; the second centres on the **royal enclosure** – 3km south of the river, just northwest of **Kamalapuram** village – which holds the remains of palaces, pavilions, elephant stables, guard houses and temples. Between the two stretches a long boulder-choked hill and swathes of banana plantations, fed by ancient irrigation canals.

Frequent buses run from Hospet to Hampi Bazaar and Kamalapuram, and you can start your tour from either; most visitors prefer to set out on foot or bicycle from the former. After a look around the soaring **Virupaksha Temple**, work your way east along the main street and river bank to the beautiful **Vitthala Temple**, and then back via the **Achyutaraya** complex at the foot of Matanga Hill. From here, a dirt path leads south to the royal enclosure, but it's easier to return to the bazaar and pick up the tarred road, calling in at **Hemakuta Hill**, a group of pre-Vijayanagar temples, en route.

On KSTDC's whistle-stop **guided tour** (see p.308) it's possible to see most of the highlights in a day. If you can, however, set aside at least two or three days to explore the site and its environs, crossing the river by **coracle** to **Anegondi** village, with a couple of side-hikes to hilltop viewing points: the west side of Hemakuta Hill, overlooking Hampi Bazaar, is best for sunsets, while **Matanga Hill**, though plagued by thieves in recent years, offers what has to be one of the world's most exotic sunrise vistas.

Hampi Bazaar, the Virupaksha Temple and around

Lining Hampi's long straight main street, **Hampi Bazaar**, which runs east from the eastern entrance of the Virupaksha temple, you can still make out the remains of Vijayanagar's ruined, columned bazaar, partly inhabited by today's lively market. Landless labourers live in many of the crumbling 500-year-old buildings.

Dedicated to a local form of Shiva known as Virupaksha or Pampapati, the still-functioning **Virupaksha Temple** (daily 8am–12.30pm & 3–6.30pm; Rs2) dominates the village, drawing a steady flow of pilgrims from all over southern India. Also known as **Sri Virupaksha Swami**, the temple is free for all who come for *arati* (worship; daily 6.30–8am & 6.30–8pm), when the temple has the most atmosphere For a rupee you can receive a blessing from the temple elephant, Lakshmi. The complex consists of two courts, each entered through a *gopura*. The larger gateway, on the east, is approximately 56m high, topped by a single wagon-vault and *kalasha*, a pot-shaped finial. In the southwest corner, a water channel runs along a large columned *mandapa*.

A colonnade surrounds the inner court, usually filled with pilgrims dozing and singing religious songs; in the middle, the principal temple is approached through a *mandapa* hallway whose carved columns feature rearing animals. Rare Vijayanagar-era paintings on the *mandapa* ceiling show aspects of Shiva, a procession with the sage Vidyaranya, the ten incarnations of Vishnu and scenes from the Mahabharata; the style of the figures is reminiscent of local shadow puppets. Faced by a brass image of Nandi, a *shivalingam* is housed in the small sanctuary, its entrance decorated with painted *makaras*, semi-aquatic mythical animals whose bodies end with foliage instead of a tail. Blue water spouts from their mouths, while above them flicker yellow flames. Just outside the main temple's wall, immediately to the north, is a small earlier temple, thought to have been the "ancestor" of the Virupaksha.

The sacred **ford** in the river is reached from the Virupaksha's north *gopura*; you can also get there by following the lane around the impressive temple **tank**. A *mandapa* overlooks the steps that originally led to the river, now some distance away. **Coracles** ply from this part of the bank, just as they did five centuries ago,

Festivals in Hampi

Vijayanagar's main **festivals** include, at the Virupaksha Temple, a **car festival** with street processions each April, and, in December, the marriage ceremony of the deities, accompanied by drummers and dances. The **Hampi Festival** (Nov 3–5), organized by the tourist department, features classical music and dance from both Carnatic and Hindustani (North Indian) traditions performed on temple stages and at Anegondi. The festival, which is beginning to attract well-known musicians and dancers, has been growing in size and prestige, and hotels in the area can get booked up well in advance. The national **Shivaratri** festival in February or March also draws thousands of pilgrims to the Virupaksha temple.

ferrying villagers to the fields and tourists to the increasingly popular enclave of **Virupapuragadda** on the other side. The road left through the village eventually loops back towards the hilltop Hanuman shrine, about 5km east, and on to Anegondi – a recommended circular walk described opposite.

The place to head for sunrise is the boulder hill immediately east of Hampi Bazaar. From the end of the main street, an ancient paved pathway winds up a rise, at the top of which the magnificent **Tiruvengalanatha Temple**. The views improve as you progress up **Matanga Hill**, at whose summit a small stone temple provides an extraordinary vantage point. The problem of muggings early in the morning along this path seems to have waned, but it's probably still a good idea to be vigilant if there are only one or two of you.

To reach the Vitthala Temple, walk east from the Virupaksha along the length of Hampi Bazaar, at the end of which a monolithic **Nandi** statue gazes from afar at the main temple from its shrine. You can also nip into the Cauvery Crafts Shop and small photo gallery on the left-hand side of the colonnade here. Just before you reach them, a path on the left, patrolled at regular intervals by conch-blowing *sadhus* and an assortment of other ragged mendicants, follows the river past a couple of cafés and numerous shrines, including a Rama temple – home to hordes of fearless monkeys. Beyond at least four Vishnu shrines, a paved and colonnaded **bazaar** leads due south to the **Achyutharaya Temple**, whose beautiful stone carvings – among them some of Hampi's famed erotica – are being restored by the ASI. Back on the main path again, make a short detour across the rocks leading to the river to see the little-visited waterside **Agni Temple**; next to it, the Kotalinga complex consists of 108 (an auspicious number) tiny *lingas*, carved on a flat rock. As you approach the Vitthala temple, to the south is an archway known as the **King's Balance**, where the rajas were weighed against gold, silver and jewels to be distributed to the city's priests.

Vitthala temple

Although the area around the **Vitthala Temple** (daily 6am–6pm; $5 [Rs10]; ticket is also valid for the Lotus Mahal on the same day) doesn't show the same evidence of early cult worship as that around the Virupaksha, the ruined bridge to the west probably dates from before Vijayanagar times. The bathing *ghat* may be from the Chalukya or Ganga period, but as the temple has fallen into disuse, it seems that the river crossing (*tirtha*) here has not had the same sacred significance as the Virupaksha site. Now designated a World Heritage Monument by UNESCO, the Vitthala Temple was built for Vishnu, who according to legend was too embarrassed by its ostentation to live there. The tower of the principal Vishnu shrine is made of brick – unusual for South India – capped with a hemispherical roof; in front is an enclosed *mandapa* with carved columns, the ceiling of which has partly collapsed. Two doorways lead to a dark passageway surrounding the sanctuary.

The open *mandapa* features slender monolithic granite **musical pillars** which were constructed so as to sound the notes of the scale when struck. Today, due to vandalism and erosion from being repeatedly beaten, heavy security makes sure that no one is allowed to play them. Guides, however, will happily demonstrate the musical resonance of other pillars on an adjacent structure. Outer columns sport characteristic Vijayanagar rearing horses, while friezes of lions, elephants and horses on the moulded basement display sculptural trickery – you can transform one beast into another simply by masking one portion of the image.

In front of the temple, to the east, a stone representation of a wooden processional **rath**, or chariot, houses an image of Garuda, Vishnu's bird-vehicle. Now cemented, at one time the chariot's wheels revolved. The three *gopura* entrances, made of granite at the base with brick and stucco multistorey towers, are now badly damaged.

Anegondi and beyond

With more time, and a sense of adventure, you can head across the Tungabhadra to **ANEGONDI**, a fortress town predating Vijayanagar and the city's fourteenth-century headquarters. The most pleasant way to go is to take a **putti**, a circular rush-basket coracle, from the ford 1500m east of the Vitthala temple; the *puttis*, which are today reinforced with plastic sheets, also carry bicycles. At the time of writing a new road bridge was nearing completion, which will almost certainly put this coracle crossing out of business.

Forgotten temples and fortifications litter Anegondi village and its quiet surroundings. The ruined **Huchchappa-matha Temple**, near the river gateway, is worth a look for its black stone lathe-turned pillars and fine panels of dancers. **Aramani**, a ruined palace in the centre, stands opposite the home of the descendants of the royal family; also in the centre, the **Ranganatha temple** is still active. A huge wooden temple chariot stands in the village square. You can get basic **snacks** at the *Hoova Café*.

To complete a five-kilometre loop back to Hampi from here, head left (west) along the turning just north of the village, which winds through sugar cane fields and eventually comes out near Virupapuragadda – this is the simplest route if you have wheels. En route you can visit the sacred **Pampla Sarovar**, signposted down a dirt lane to the left. The small temple above this square bathing tank, tended by a *swami* who will proudly show you photos of his pilgrimage to Mount Kailash, is dedicated to the goddess Lakshmi and holds a cave containing a footprint of Vishnu. If you are staying around Anegondi, this quiet and atmospheric spot is best visited early in the evening during *arati* (worship).

Another worthwhile detour from the road is the hike up to the tiny whitewashed **Hanuman Temple**, perched on a rocky hilltop north of the river, from where you gain superb views over Hampi, especially at sunrise or sunset. The steep climb up to it takes around half an hour An alternative walking route back involves following the path a further 2km until you reach an impressive old **stone bridge** dating from Vijayanagar times. The bridge no longer spans the river, but just beyond it to the west, another coracle crossing returns you to a point about halfway between the Vitthala Temple and Hampi bazaar. This rewarding round walk can, of course, be completed in reverse. Whichever loop you choose – and especially if you attempt it on foot, which requires at least three hours – take plenty of water.

Hemakuta Hill and around

Directly above Hampi Bazaar, **Hemakuta Hill** is dotted with pre-Vijayanagar temples which probably date from between the ninth and eleventh centuries (late Chalukya or Ganga). Three are of the *trikutachala* (three-peaked hills) type, with three shrines facing into a common centre. Aside from the architecture, the main reason to clamber up here is to admire the **views** of the ruins and surrounding countryside. Looking across miles of boulder-covered terrain and banana plantations, the sheer western edge of the hill is Hampi's prime sunset spot, attracting a crowd of blissed-out tourists most evenings, along with a couple of entrepreneurial chai-wallahs.

A couple of interesting monuments lie on the road leading south towards the main, southern group of ruins. The first of these, a walled **Krishna temple** complex to the west of the road, dates from 1513. Although dilapidated in parts, it features some fine carving and shrines. On the opposite side of the road, a fifty-metre-wide processional path leading east through what's now a ploughed field, with stray remnants of colonnades straggling on each side, is all that remains of an old market place.

Hampi's most-photographed monument stands just south of the Krishna temple in its own enclosure. Depicting Vishnu in his incarnation (*avatar*) as the Man-Lion, the monolithic **Narasimha** statue, with its bulging eyes and crossed legs strapped into meditation pose, is one of Vijayanagar's greatest treasures.

The southern and royal monuments

The most impressive remains of Viyayanagar, the city's **royal monuments**, lie some 3km south of Hampi Bazaar, spread over a large expanse of open ground. Before tackling the ruins proper, it's a good idea to get your bearings with a visit to the small **Archeological Museum** (daily except Fri 10am–5pm; free) at Kamalapuram, which can be reached by bus from Hospet or Hampi. Turn right out of the Kamalapuram bus stand, take the first turning on the right and the museum is on the left – two minutes' walk. Among the sculptures, weapons, palm-leaf manuscripts and paintings from Vijayanagar and Anegondi, the highlight is a superb scale-model of the city, giving an excellent bird's-eye view of the entire site.

To walk into the city from the museum, go back to the main road and take the nearby turning marked "Hampi 4km". After 200m or so, you reach the partly ruined massive **inner city wall**, made from granite slabs, which runs 32km around the city, in places as high as 10m. The outer wall was almost twice as long. At one time, there were said to have been seven city walls; coupled with areas of impenetrable forest and the river to the north, they made the city virtually impregnable.

Just beyond the wall, the **citadel area** was once enclosed by another wall and gates, of which only traces remain. To the east, the small *ganigitti* (oil-woman's) fourteenth-century **Jain temple** features a simple stepped pyramidal tower of undecorated horizontal slabs. Beyond it is **Bhima's Gate**, once one of the principal entrances to the city, named after the Titan-like Pandava prince and hero of the Mahabharata. Like many of the gates, it is "bent", a form of defence that meant anyone trying to get in had to make two 90 degree turns. Bas-reliefs depict episodes such as Bhima avenging the attempted rape of his wife, Draupadi, by killing the general Kichaka. Draupadi vowed she would not dress her hair until Kichaka was dead; one panel shows her tying up her locks, the vow fulfilled.

Back on the path, to the west, the plain facade of the fifteen-metre-square **Queen's Bath** belies its glorious interior, open to the sky and surrounded by corridors with 24 different domes. Eight projecting balconies overlook where once was water; traces of Islamic-influenced stucco decoration survive. Women from the royal household would bathe here and umbrellas were placed in shafts in the tank floor to protect them from the sun. The water supply channel can be seen outside.

Continuing northwest brings you to **Mahanavami–Dibba**, or "House of Victory", built to commemorate a successful campaign in Orissa. A twelve-metre pyramidal structure with a square base, it is said to have been where the king gave and received honours and gifts. From here he watched the magnificent parades, music and dance performances, martial art displays, elephant fights and animal sacrifices that made celebration of the ten-day Dussehra festival famed throughout the land (the tradition of spectacular Dussehra festivals is continued at Mysore; see box on p.260). Carved reliefs of dancers, elephant fights, animals and figures decorate the sides of the platform. Two huge mono-lithic doors on the ground nearby may have once been part of a building atop the platform, of which no signs remain. To the west, another platform – the largest at Vijayanagar – is thought to be the basement of the **King's Audi-ence Hall**. Stone bases of a hundred pillars remain, in an arrangement that has caused speculation as to how the building could have been used; there are no passageways or open areas.

The two-storey **Lotus Mahal** (daily 6am–6pm; $5 [Rs10]; ticket is also valid for the Vitthala Temple on the same day), a little further north and part of the **zenana enclosure** (women's quarters), was designed for the pleasure of Krishna Deva Raya's queen: a place where she could relax, particularly in summer. Displaying a strong Indo-Islamic influence, the pavilion is open on the ground floor, whereas the upper level (no longer accessible by stairs) contains windows and balcony seats. A moat surrounding the building is thought to have provided water-cooled air via tubes.

Beyond the Lotus Mahal, the **elephant stables**, a series of high-ceilinged, domed chambers, entered through arches, are the most substantial surviving secular buildings at Vijayanagar – a reflection of the high status accorded to elephants, both ceremonially and in battle. An upper level, with a pillared hall, is capped with a tower at the centre; it may have been used by the musicians who accompanied the royal elephant processions. There are usually tender coconuts on sale under the shade of a nearby tree. East of here, recent archeological exca-vations have revealed what are thought to have been the foundations of a series of Vijayapuragadda administration offices, which until 1990 had remained buried under earth deposited by the wind.

Walking west of the Lotus Mahal, you pass two temples before reaching the road to Hemakuta Hill. The rectangular enclosure wall of the small **Hazara Rama** (One Thousand Ramas) temple, thought to have been the private palace temple, features a series of medallion figures and bands of detailed friezes show-ing scenes from the Ramayana. The inner of two *mandapas* contains four finely carved polished black columns. Many of the ruins here are said to have been part of the Hazara Rama Bazaar, which ran northeast from the temple. Much of the so-called **Underground Temple**, or Prasanna Virupaksha, lies below ground level and is filled with rainwater spends for part of the year. Turning north (right) onto the road that runs west of the Underground Temple will take you back to Hampi Bazaar, via Hemakuta Hill.

Eating

Hampi has a plethora of traveller-oriented chai stalls and **restaurants** – many of the most popular are attached to guesthouses, such as *Rahul, Gopi, Vikki* and *Sudha*, all in the bazaar, or the growing row of joints in Virupapuragadda. As a holy site, the whole village is supposed to be strictly vegetarian and alcohol-free, but one or two places bend the rules for inveterate carnivores and even more are happy to supply a surreptitious beer or two.

Geeta On the main bazaar. Old favourite not far from the bus stand, serving wholesome Western snacks, Indian veg, *momos* and ravioli.

Mango Tree 300m beyond the sacred ford. Wonderfully relaxed riverside hangout – a great place to linger over a simple snack or drink.

Mowgli Virupapuragadda. At the far west end of the strip, this popular lodge-restaurant has plenty of space to lounge on mattresses beside the rice paddies bordering the river, though the food – Indian, Israeli and Western – is mostly bland.

New Shanti On the path from the Virupaksha Temple down to river. Best known for its delicious cakes and breads, but also does standard Indian and continental dishes.

Ravi's Rose East end of the village. Newish

rooftop restaurant that (unlike many tourist places) can actually make spicy dishes. Good sounds and a line in special lassis.

Shiv Moon On the riverside path east of the village. A good place to break the journey to or from the Vitthala Temple, serving pastas and standard curries.

Sri Sangameshwarar On the main bazaar. One of the more genuine Indian places, with the best thalis and masala dosas in the village, as well as the odd Western snack.

Suresh On the path from the Virupaksha Temple down to the river. Established joint specializing in tuna, Goan dishes and *momos*.

Trishul On the lane beside the tourist office. Offers one of the widest menus in the village, including chicken, tuna, lasagne, pizza and desserts such as scrumptious apple crumble. Beer available too.

Badami and around

Now quiet villages, **BADAMI**, **AIHOLE** and **PATTADAKAL** in northwest Karnataka were once the capital cities of the **Chalukyas**, who ruled much of the Deccan between the fourth and eighth centuries. The astonishing profusion of **temples** in the area beggars belief, and it is hard to imagine the kind of society that can have made use of them all. Most visitors use Badami, which can offer a few basic lodges, as a base; Aihole boasts a single resthouse, but there's no accommodation at Pattadakal. The **best time to visit** is between October and early March; in April and May, most of this part of northwest Karnataka becomes much too hot and government offices only open between 8am and 1pm.

Badami and Aihole's cave temples, stylistically related to those at Ellora, are some of the most important of their type. The many free-standing temples include some of the earliest in India and, uniquely, it is possible to see both northern (*nagari*) and southern (*Dravida*) architectural styles side by side. Clearly much experimentation went on, as several other temples (commonly referred to, in art historical terms, as "undifferentiated") fit into neither system.

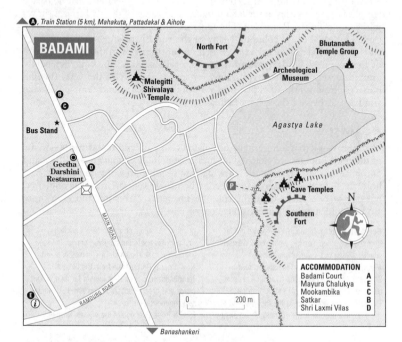

Although some evidence of **Buddhist** activity around Badami and Aihole exists, the earliest cave and structural temples are assigned to the period of the Chalukya rise to power in the mid-sixth century, and are mostly **Hindu**, with a few Jain examples. The first important Chalukyan king was Pulakeshin I (535–66), but it was Pulakeshin II (610–42) who captured the Pallava capital of Kanchipuram in Tamil Nadu and extended the empire to include Maharashtra to the north, the Konkan coast on the west and the whole of Karnataka. Although the Pallavas subsequently briefly took most of his territory, including the capital Badami, at the end of his reign, Pulakeshin's son Vikramaditya I (655–81) later recovered it, and the Chalukyas continued to reign until the mideighth century. Some suggest that the incursion of the Pallavas accounts for the southern elements seen in the structural temples.

Badami and around

Surrounded by a yawning expanse of flat farmland, **BADAMI**, capital of the Chalukyas from 543 AD to 757 AD, extends east into a gorge between two red sandstone hills, topped by two ancient fort complexes. The south is riddled with cave temples, while to the north stand early structural temples. Beyond Badami, to the east, is an artificial lake, **Agastya**, said to date from the fifth century. The (small) selection of places to stay and restaurants makes Badami an ideal base from which to explore the Chalukyan remains at Mahakuta, Aihole and Pattadakal, as well as the temple village of Banashankari on the outskirts of town. The whole Badami area is also home to numerous troupes of **monkeys**, especially around the monuments, and you're likely to find the cheeky characters all over you if you're unwise enough to produce any comestibles.

Practicalities

Badami **bus stand** – in the centre of the village on Main (Station) Road – sees frequent daily services to Gadag (2hr), Hospet (5hr), Hubli (3hr), Bijapur (4hr) and Kolhapur, and local buses to Aihole and Pattadakal. The **railway station** is 5km north, along a road lined with *neem* trees; tongas (Rs30 or Rs5 per head shared) as well as buses and auto-rickshaws are usually available for the journey into town. The slow metre-gauge line connecting Badami to Bijapur in the north, and to Gadag in the south was being converted at the time of writing, and only the sector from Bagalkot via Badami to Gadag was operational, with three trains daily.

The new and friendly **tourist office** (Mon–Sat: June–March 10am–5.30pm; April & May 8am–1pm; ☏08357/220414), on Ramdurg Road next to the KSTDC *Hotel Mayura Chalukya*, can put you in touch with a **guide**. If you need to **change money**, *Hotel Mookambika* opposite the bus stand will change US dollars and sterling (but not travellers' cheques) at poor rates; alternatively, try the *Hotel Badami Court*.

Ambika Tours & Travels at *Hotel Mookambika* runs **tours** in Ambassador taxis taking in Badami, Mahakuta, Aihole and Pattadakal for a reasonable Rs700. One of the best ways of exploring the closer sites, including Mahakuta and the temple village of Banashankari, is to rent a **bicycle** (Rs3 per hour) from stalls in front of the bus stand, but cycling to Aihole and Pattadakal is a challenge.

Accommodation and eating

Of Badami's handful of **places to stay** and **eat**, by far the most comfortable is the *Hotel Badami Court* (☏08357/220230, ✉badamicourt@nivalink.com; ⑥–⑧), 2km north of town towards the railway station. Ranged around a garden on two storeys, its 27 en-suite rooms are plain but spacious. Meals and expensive beer are available, and their swimming pool is open to non-residents for Rs80 per hour. The far cheaper KSTDC *Hotel Mayura Chalukya* (☏08357/220046; ❷), on the south side of town on Ramdurg Road, has ten basic rooms with decrepit plumbing and peeling plaster but, despite fearless scavenging monkeys, the gardens are pleasant and there's a restaurant. Opposite the bus stand, the *Mookambika Deluxe* (☏08357/220067, ℻220106; ❸–❻) is the best option in the centre of town, with simple doubles on the ground floor and comfortable new a/c rooms upstairs. Other options include the recently upgraded *New Satkar Delux* (☏08357/220417; ❷–❺) and the extremely basic *Shri Laxmi Vilas* (☏08357/220077; ❶), which also has a reasonable restaurant.

For food and especially breakfast, try the *Geetha Darshini* (closed Sun), 100m south of the bus stand, whose *iddlis*, *vadas* and *dosas* are out of this world. Otherwise the *Mookambika Deluxe*'s plain upstairs restaurant and livelier *Kanchan* bar and restaurant next door share the same kitchen and provide a wide menu of excellent veg and non-veg Indian and Chinese food.

Southern Fort cave temples

Badami's earliest monuments, in the Southern Fort area, comprise a group of sixth-century **caves** (daily sunrise–sunset; $2 [Rs5]) cut into the hill's red sandstone, each connected by steps leading up the hillside. About 15m up the face of the rock, **Cave 1**, a Shiva temple, is probably the earliest. Entrance is through a triple opening into a long porch raised on a plinth decorated with images of Shiva's dwarf attendants, the *ganas*. Outside, to the left of the porch, a *dvarpala* door guardian stands beneath a Nandi bull. On the right is a striking 1.5-metre-high image of a sixteen-armed dancing Shiva. He carries a stick-zither-type *vina*, which may or may not be a *yal*, a now-extinct musical instrument, on which the earliest Indian classical music theory is thought to have been developed. In the antechamber, a panel on the left shows Harihara (Shiva and Vishnu combined), accompanied by consorts Lakshmi and Parvati and the gods' vehicles Nandi and Garuda. On the right, Ardhanarishvara (Shiva combined with Parvati; half-male, half-female) is accompanied by Nandi and the skeleton Bringi. Ceiling panels include a coiled Naga snake deity, flying couples and Shiva and Parvati. Inside, a columned hall, divided into aisles, leads to a small, square sanctuary at the back, containing a *lingam*.

A little higher, the similar **Cave 2**, a Vishnu shrine, is approached across a courtyard with two *dvarpala* door guardians at the end. The porch contains a panel to the left of Varaha, the boar incarnation of Vishnu, and, to the right, of Trivikrama, Vishnu as a dwarf brahmin who grows miraculously in size to cross the earth in three steps. On the ceiling nearby, Vishnu is shown riding Garuda. A central square of the ceiling features a lotus encircled by sixteen fish; other decoration includes swastika designs and flying couples. Traces of painting show how colourful the caves originally were.

Steps and slopes lead on upwards, past a natural cave containing a smashed image of the Buddhist *bodhisattva*, Padmapani (he who holds the lotus), and steps on the right in a cleft in the rock lead up to the fort. **Cave 3** (578 AD) stands beneath a thirty-metre-high perpendicular bluff. The largest of the group, with a facade measuring 21m from north to south, it is also considered the finest on account of the quality of its sculptural decoration. Eleven steps lead up to the plinth decorated with dwarf *ganas*. The treatment of the pillars is extremely elaborate, featuring male and female figures, lotus motifs and medallions portraying amorous couples.

To the east of the others, a Jain temple, **Cave 4**, overlooks Agastya Lake and the town. This much simpler shrine, carved from striped rock, dates from the sixth century. Figures, both seated and standing, of the 24 *tirthankaras*, mostly without their identifying emblems, line the walls.

After seeing the caves, you can climb up to the fort and walk east where, hidden in the rocks, a carved panel shows Vishnu reclining on the serpent Adisesha, attended by a profusion of gods and sages. Continuing, you can skirt the gorge and descend on the east to the Bhutanatha temples at the lakeside. Before you get to them, there's another rock carving of a reclining Vishnu and his ten incarnations.

North Fort

North of **Lake Agastya** lie a number of structural temples and the small **Archeological Museum** (daily except Fri 10am–5pm; Rs2), which contains sculpture from the region. Although now dilapidated, the **Upper Shivalaya Temple** is one of the earliest Chalukyan buildings here. Scenes from the life of Krishna decorate the base and various images of him can be seen between pilasters on the walls. Only the sanctuary and tower of the **Lower Shivalaya** survive. Perched on a rock, the **Malegitti Shivalaya** (late seventh century) is the finest southern-style early Chalukyan temple. Its shrine is adjoined by a pillared hallway with small windows hewn out of stone and a single image on each side: Vishnu on the north and Shiva on the south.

Banashankari

A pleasant excursion by foot, bicycle or rickshaw is to the temple village of **BANASHANKARI**, 5km to the northwest of Badami; it is believed to date back to the sixth century, although much of it was built during the Maratha period of the eighteenth century. Banashankari is worth a visit more for its peaceful atmosphere than for its architectural interest. Dedicated to Shiva's consort Parvati, the shrine, with a large bathing tank, is the most important living temple of the region and attracts a steady stream of devotees throughout the year, especially during the *rath* (chariot) festival (held either in January or February), when the deity is led through the streets in procession. At this time, the usually quiet village is overtaken by the fun and excitement of a large and hectic country fair, complete with circus acts, stalls selling everything from toys to food and a colourful cattle fair down the road towards Badami.

Mahakuta

Another crop of seventh-century Chalukyan temples lies 15km out of Badami on the route to Pattadakal at **MAHAKUTA**, a temple village which attracts local devotees, pilgrims and a sprinkling of *sadhus* – it may only be a minor league Chalukyan architectural sight, but it does have a timeless atmosphere, enhanced by its brooding banyan trees. Four buses a day and the occasional shared tempo run to the site, but the two- to three-hour **walk**, via an ancient, paved pilgrim trail, is well worthwhile, although it can get very hot; take plenty of water and an umbrella to keep off the sun.

The path starts a short way beyond the Archeological Museum, just before you reach the first temple complex and tank. Peeling left up the hill, it winds past a series of crumbling shrines, gateways and old watercourses and peters out into the flat plateau. The turning down to Mahakuta is easy to miss: look for a stone marker-post that reads "RP", which leads you to a steep, roughly paved stairway. At the bottom, the main temple complex is ranged around a crystal-clear spring-fed tank, popular with bathers (it's open to all) and offering an enjoyable spot for a dip at the end of a hot walk. On a rise above the tank, next to a shady courtyard dominated by a huge banyan tree, stands the whitewashed **Mahakutesvara Temple** with its silver-crowned lingam. Around the base of the temple are wrapped some fine stone friezes – those on the southwest corner, depicting Shiva and Parvati with Ravana, the demon king of Lanka, are particularly accomplished. More carvings adorn the entrance and ceilings of the **Mallikarjuna Temple** on the opposite side of the tank, while in the clearing outside the nearby **Sangameshwar Temple** stands a gigantic stone-wheeled chariot used during the annual festival in May.

There are a couple of teashops but no official guesthouse; if you want **to stay**, you may be able to negotiate to use one of the very basic rooms outside the temple gates.

Aihole

No fewer than 125 temples, dating from the Chalukyan and the later Rashtrakuta periods (sixth–twelfth centuries) can be found in the tiny village of **AIHOLE** (Aivalli), near the banks of the River Malaprabha. Lying in clusters within the village, in surrounding fields and on rocky outcrops, many of the temples are remarkably well preserved, despite being used as dwellings and cattle sheds. Reflecting both its geographical position and spirit of architectural experimentation, Aihole boasts northern (*nagari*) and southern (*Dravida*) temples, as well as variants which failed to survive subsequent stylistic developments.

Two of the temples are rock-cut caves dating from the sixth century. The Hindu **Ravanaphadigudi**, northeast of the centre, a Shiva shrine with a triple entrance, contains fine sculptures of Mahishasuramardini, a ten-armed Nateshan (the precursor of Shiva Nataraja) dancing with Parvati, Ganesh and the Sapta Matrikas (Seven Mothers). A central lotus design, surrounded by mythical beasts, figures and foliate decoration, adorns the ceiling. Near the entrance is Gangadhara (Shiva with the River Ganga in his hair) accompanied by Parvati and the skeleton Bringi. A two-storey cave, plain save for decoration at the entrances and a panel image of Buddha in its upper veranda, can be found partway up the hill to the southeast, overlooking the village. At the top of that hill, the Jain **Meguti Temple**, which may never have been completed, bears an inscription on an outer wall dating it to 634 AD. The porch, *mandapa* hallway and upper storey above the sanctuary, which contains a seated Jain image, are later additions. You can climb up to the first floor for fine views of Aihole and surrounding country.

The late seventh to early eighth century **Durga Temple** (daily 6am–6pm; $2 [Rs5]), one of the most unusual, elaborate and large in Aihole, stands close to others on open ground in the Archeological Survey compound, near the centre of the village. It derives its name not from the goddess Durga, but from the Kannada *durgadagudi*, meaning "temple near the fort". Its apsidal-ended sanctuary shows influence from earlier Buddhist *chaitya* halls; another example of this curved feature, rare in Hindu monuments, can be seen in one of the *rathas* at Mamallapuram in Tamil Nadu. Here the "northern"-style tower is probably a later addition, and is incongruously square-backed. The temple is raised on a plinth featuring bands of carved decoration. A series of pillars – many featuring amorous couples – forms an open ambulatory that continues from the porch around the whole building. Other sculptural highlights include the decoration on the entrance to the *mandapa* hallway and niche images on the outer walls of the now-empty semicircular sanctum. Remains of a small and early *gopura* gateway stand to the south. Nearby, a small **Archeological Museum** (daily except Fri 10am–5pm; free) displays early Chalukyan sculpture and sells the booklet *Glorious Aihole*, which includes a site map and accounts of the monuments.

Further south, beyond several other temples, the **Ladh Khan** (the name of a Muslim who made it his home) is perhaps the best known of all at Aihole. Now thought to have been constructed at some point between the end of the sixth century and the eighth, it was dated at one time to the mid-fifth century and was seen as one of the country's temple prototypes. The basic plan is square, with a large adjoining rectangular pillared porch. Inside, twelve pillars support a raised clerestory and enclose a further four pillars; at the centre stands a Nandi bull. A small sanctuary containing a *shivalingam* is next to the back wall. Both the *lingam* and Nandi may have been later additions, with the original inner sanctum located at the centre.

Practicalities

Six daily **buses** run to Aihole from Badami (1hr 30) via Pattadakal (45min) from 5.30am to 9pm; the last bus returns around 6pm. The only place to **stay and eat** (apart from a few chai shops) in Aihole is the small, clean and spartan KSTDC *Tourist Rest House* (☎0835/134541; **①**), about five minutes' walk up the main road north out of the village, next to the ASI offices. They have a "VIP" room, two doubles with bath, plus two doubles and four singles without. Simple, tasty food is available by arrangement – and by candlelight during the frequent power cuts. The *Kiran Bar* on the same road, but in the village, serves beer and spirits and has a restaurant.

Pattadakal

The village of **PATTADAKAL**, on a bend in the River Malaprabha 22km from Badami, served as the site of Chalukyan coronations between the seventh and eighth centuries; in fact, it may only have been used for such ceremonials. Like Badami and Aihole, Pattadakal boasts fine Chalukyan architecture, with particularly large and mature examples, and, as at Aihole, both northern and southern styles can be seen. Pattadakal's main group of monuments (daily 6am–6pm; $5 [Rs10]) stands in a well-maintained compound, next to the village, and has recently been declared a World Heritage Site.

Earliest among the temples, the **Sangameshvara**, also known as **Shri Vijayeshvara** (a reference to its builder, Vijayaditya Satyashraya; 696–733), shows typical southern features, such as the parapet lined with barrel-vaulted miniature roof forms and walls divided into niches flanked by pilasters. To the south, both the **Mallikarjuna** and the enormous **Virupaksha**, side by side, are in the southern style, built by two sisters who were successively the queens of Vikramaditya II (733–46). The temples were inspired by the Pallava Kailashanatha temple at Kanchipuram in Tamil Nadu, complete with enclosure wall with shrines and small *gopura* entranceway. Along with the Kanchi Temple, the Virupaksha was probably one of the largest and most elaborate in India at the time. Interior pillars are carved with scenes from the Ramayana and Mahabharata, while in the Mallikarjuna the stories are from the life of Krishna. Both temples have open Nandi *mandapa* hallways and sanctuaries housing black polished stone *lingams*.

The largest northern-style temple, the **Papanatha**, further south, was probably built after the Virupaksha in the eighth century. It features two long pillared *mandapa* hallways adjoining a small sanctuary with a narrow internal ambulatory. Outside walls feature reliefs (some of which, unusually, bear the sculptors' autographs) from the Ramayana, including, on the south wall, Hanuman's monkey army.

About 1km south of the village, a fine **Rashtrakuta** (ninth–tenth century) **Jain temple** is fronted by a porch and two *mandapa* hallways with twin carved elephants at the entrance. Inexplicably, the sanctuary contains a *lingam*. In the first *mandapa*, on the right, a stone staircase leads up to the roof, where there's a second, empty sanctuary. The porch is lined with bench seats interspersed with eight pillars; the doorway is elaborately decorated with mythical beasts.

Pattadakal is connected by regular state **buses** and hourly private buses to Badami (45min) and Aihole (22km; 45min). Aside from a few tea shops and cold drinks and coconut stalls, there are no facilities. For three days at the end of January, Pattadakal hosts an annual **dance festival** featuring dancers from all over the country.

Bijapur and the north

Boasting some of the Deccan's finest Muslim monuments, **BIJAPUR** is often billed as "The Agra of the South". The comparison is partly justified: for more than three hundred years, this was the capital of a succession of powerful rulers whose domed mausoleums, mosques, colossal civic buildings and fortifications recall a lost golden age of unrivalled prosperity and artistic refinement. Yet there the similarities between the two cities end. A provincial market town of just 220,000 inhabitants, modern Bijapur is a world away from the urban frenzy of Agra. With the exception of the mighty **Golgumbaz**, which attracts bus loads of day-trippers, its historic sites see only a slow trickle of tourists, while the ramshackle town centre is surprisingly laid-back, dotted with peaceful green spaces and colon-naded mosque courtyards. The best **time to come** here is between November and early March; in summer, Bijapur gets unbearably hot, and in April and May offices shut at 1pm. On February 6 and 7, Bijapur hosts an annual **music festival** which attracts well-known musicians from both the Carnatic (South Indian) and the Hindustani (North Indian) classical music traditions.

Some history

Bijapur began life in the tenth century as **Vijayapura**, the Chalukyas' "City of Victory". Taken by the Vijayanagars, it passed into Muslim hands for the first time in the thirteenth century with the arrival of the Sultans of Delhi. The Bahmanis administered the area for a time, but it was only after the local rulers, the **Adil Shahis**, won independence from Bidar by expelling the Bahmani garrison and declaring this their capital, that Bijapur's rise to prominence began.

Burying their differences for a brief period in the late sixteenth century, the five Muslim dynasties that issued from the breakdown of Bahmani rule – based at Golconda, Ahmednagar, Bidar and Gulbarga – formed a military alliance to defeat the Vijayanagars. The spoils of this campaign, which saw the total destruction of Vijayanagar (Hampi), funded a two-hundred-year building boom in Bijapur, during which the city acquired its most impressive monu-ments. However, old enmities between rival Muslim sultanates on the Deccan soon resurfaced, and the Adil Shahis' royal coffers were gradually squandered on fruitless and protracted wars. By the time the British arrived on the scene in the eighteenth century, the Adil Shahis were a spent force, locked into a decline from which they and their capital never recovered.

Arrival, information and city transport

State and interstate **buses** from as far afield as Mumbai and Aurangabad pull into the KSRTC bus stand on the southwest edge of the town centre; ask at the enquiries desk for exact timings, as the timetables are all in Kannada. For a full run down of destinations, see "Travel details", p.334. Most visitors head off to

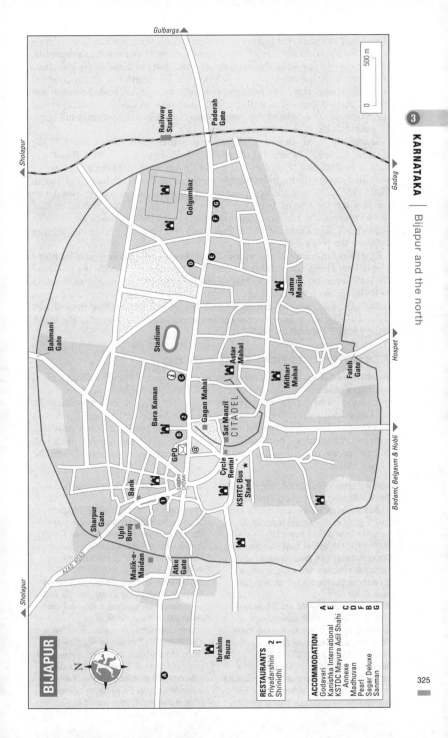

BIJAPUR

N

Gulbarga

Sholapur

Sholapur

Gadag

Hospet

Badami, Belgaum & Hubli

Railway Station

Paderah Gate

Golgumbaz

Jama Masjid

Bahmani Gate

Stadium

Astar Mahal

Mithari Mahal

Fateh Gate

Bara Kaman

Gagan Mahal

Sat Manzil

CITADEL

GPO

GANDHI CHOWK

Cycle Rental

KSRTC Bus Stand

Bank

Sharpur Gate

Upli Buruj

Malik-e-Maidan

Atke Gate

AZAD ROAD

Ibrahim Rauza

F G
E
D
B 2

0   500 m

RESTAURANTS
Priyadarshini   2
Shrinidhi   1

ACCOMMODATION
Godavari   A
Kanishka International   E
KSTDC Mayura Adil Shahi   C
Annexe
Madhuvan   D
Pearl   F
Sagar Deluxe   B
Sanman   G

their hotel in (unmetered) auto-rickshaws, though there are also horse-drawn tongas for about the same price. Just a stone's throw away from the Golgumbaz, outside the old city walls, the **railway station**, 3km northeast of the bus stand, is a more inspiring point of arrival. Since the line north has been converted to broad guage, there are now three trains weekly from both Mumbai and Yesvantpur (Bangalore), as well as a daily passenger service to Hyderabad and three more as far as Solapur, for more connections. The line south was still being converted at the time of writing.

Besides the usual literature, the **tourist office** (Mon–Sat 10am–5.30pm; ☎08352/250359), behind the *Hotel Adil Shahi Annexe* on Station Road, can help with arranging itineraries and guides. If you need to **change money** (or travellers' cheques), the most reliable service is at Girikand Tours and Travels (☎08352/220510) on the first floor at Nishant Plaza, Rama Mandir Road; you can also use the Canara Bank, on nearby Azad Road, but you'll need to take photocopies of the relevant pages of your passport. **Internet** access is available at Friends Cyber Zone and Cyber Park (both Rs25 per hr), next to one another opposite the post office.

Bijapur is flat, relatively uncongested, and generally easy to negotiate by **bicycle**; rickety Heros are available for rent from several stalls outside the bus stand for Rs3 per hour. **Auto-rickshaws** don't have meters and charge a minimum of Rs10; although most of Bijapur is covered by a fare of Rs30, they are a much more expensive way of getting around the monuments, when they charge around Rs200 for a four-hour tour. **Taxis**, available from near the bus stand, charge Rs5.50 per kilometre.

Accommodation and eating

Accommodation standards are pretty low in Bijapur, although finding a room is rarely a problem. Such hotels as exist are also fairly widely spread out, so it's not a bad idea to decide where you want to stay in advance. **Eating** possibilities are largely confined to the hotels – try the *New Empire* at the *Pearl*. The town's odd independent eating establishments are invariably pure veg, unless you brave a dingy drinking den. The *Shrinidhi Hotel* on Gandhi Chowk serves good South Indian vegetarian food, as does the *Priyadarshini*, across the main road from the Gagan Mahal.

Godavari Athani Rd ☎08352/253105, 🖷256225. This monolithic but fading hotel is something of a landmark, though its prices have been pegged back to reflect its very average status. ②–⑤
Kanishka International Station Rd ☎08352/223788, 🖳www.kanishkabijapur.com. One of the better value places, providing comfy rooms with most mod-cons and good service at decent rates, plus fine veg and non-veg restaurants. ③–⑤
KSTDC Mayura Adil Shahi Annexe Station Rd ☎08352/250401. The only surviving state-run establishment in town with large, dowdy rooms (some a/c), but no restaurant. ③–④
Madhuvan Station Rd ☎08352/255571, 🖷256201. The smartest place in town, with a variety of rooms from overpriced ordinary doubles to more comfortable a/c "deluxe" options. The restaurant serves good-value thalis at lunchtime,

and there are money-changing facilities for residents. ⑤–⑥
Pearl Station Rd ☎08352/256002, 🖷243606. Bright modern hotel with clean, sizeable rooms. The front ones have balconies and those at the top give views of Golgumbaz. Better value than the Madhuvan, and with an excellent restaurant too. ③–⑤
Sagar Deluxe Next to Bara Kaman, Busreshwar Chowk ☎08352/259234. Centrally located hotel with unremarkable but cheap doubles and some deluxe and a/c rooms. ①–③
Sanman Opposite the Golgumbaz, Station Rd ☎08352/251866. Best value among the budget places, and well placed for the railway station. The good-sized rooms all have mozzie nets and clean bathrooms (and some have a/c). The Udupi canteen is used as a stop for bus parties, so their south Indian snacks are all freshly cooked. ②–④

The Town

Unlike most medieval Muslim strongholds, Bijapur lacked natural rock defences and had to be strengthened by the Adil Shahis with huge **fortified walls**. Extending some 10km around the town, these ramparts, studded with cannon emplacements (*burjes*) and watchtowers, are breached in five points by *darwazas*, or strong gateways, and several smaller postern gates (*didis*). In the middle of the town, a further hoop of crenellated battlements encircled Bijapur's **citadel**, site of the sultans' apartments and durbar hall, of which only fragments remain. The Adil Shahis' **tombs** are scattered around the outskirts, while most of the important **mosques** lie southeast of the citadel.

It's possible to see Bijapur's highlights in a day, although most people stay for three or four nights, taking in the monuments at a more leisurely pace. Our account covers the sights from east to west, beginning with the **Golgumbaz** – which you should aim to visit at around 6am, before the bus parties descend – and ending with the exquisite **Ibrahim Rauza**, an atmospheric spot to enjoy the sunset.

The Golgumbaz

The vast **Golgumbaz** mausoleum (daily 6am–6pm; $2 [Rs5]), Bijapur's most famous building, soars above the town's east walls, visible for miles in every direction. Built towards the end of the Adil Shahis' reign, the Golgumbaz is a fitting monument to a dynasty on its last legs – pompous, decadent and ill-proportioned, but conceived on an irresistibly awesome scale.

The cubic tomb, enclosing a 170-square-metre hall, is crowned with a single hemispherical **dome**, the largest in the world after St Peter's in Rome (which is only 5m wider). Spiral staircases wind up the four seven-storey octagonal towers that buttress the building to the famous **Whispering Gallery**, a three-metre-wide passage encircling the interior base of the dome from where, looking carefully down, you can get a real feel of the sheer size of the building. Get here just after opening time and you can experiment with the extraordinary acoustics; by 7am, though, the cacophony generated by bus-loads of whooping and clapping tourists means you can't hear yourself think, let alone make out whispering 38m away. A good antidote to the din is the superb **view** from the mausoleum's ramparts, which overlook the town and its monuments to the dark-soiled Deccan countryside beyond, scattered with minor tombs and ruins.

Set on a plinth in the centre of the hall below, are the gravestones of the ruler who built the Golgumbaz, **Muhammed Adil Shahi**, along with those of his wife, daughter, grandson and favourite courtesan, Rambha. At one corner of the grounds stands the simple gleaming white shrine to a sufi saint of the Adil Shahi period, **Hashim Pir**, which around February attracts *qawwals* (singers of devotional *qawwali* music) to the annual *urs*, lasting three days.

The Jami Masjid

A little under 1km southwest of the Golgumbaz, the **Jami Masjid** (Friday Mosque) presides over the quarter that formed the centre of the city during Bijapur's nineteenth-century nadir under the Nizam of Hyderabad. It was commissioned by Ali Adil Shahi, the ruler credited with constructing the city walls and complex water-supply system, as a monument to his victory over the Vijayanagars at the Battle of Talikota in 1565, and is widely regarded as one of the finest mosques in India. As it is still in use, you should cover your head and limbs when entering.

Approached via a square *hauz* (ablutions tank), the main **prayer hall** is surmounted by an elegantly proportioned central dome, with 33 smaller shallow domes ranged around it. Simplicity and restraint are the essence of the colon-naded hall below, divided by gently curving arches and rows of thick plaster-covered pillars. Aside from the odd geometric design and trace of yellow, blue and green tile-work, the only ornamentation is found in the mihrab, or Mecca-facing prayer niche, which is smothered in gold leaf and elaborate calligraphy. The marble floor of the hall features a grid of 2500 rectangles, known as *musal-lahs* (after the *musallah* prayer mats brought to mosques by worshippers). These were added by the Moghul emperor Aurangzeb, allegedly as recompense for making off with the velvet carpets, long golden chain and other valuables that originally filled the prayer hall.

The Mithari and Asar Mahals

Continuing west from the Jami Masjid, the first monument of note is a small, ornately carved gatehouse on the south side of the road. Although of modest size, the delicate three-storey structure, known as the **Mithari Mahal**, is one of Bijapur's most beautiful buildings, with ornate projecting windows and mina-rets crowning its corners. Once again, Ali Adil Shahi erected it, along with the mosque behind, using gifts presented to him during a state visit to Vijayanagar. The Hindu rajas' generosity, however, did not pay off. Only a couple of years later, Adil Shahi and his four Muslim allies sacked their city, plundering its wealth and murdering most of its inhabitants.

The lane running north from opposite the Mithari Mahal brings you to the dilapidated **Asar Mahal**, a large open-fronted hall propped up by four green-painted pillars and fronted by a large stagnant step-well. Built in 1646 by Muhammed Adil Shahi as a Hall of Justice, it was later chosen to house hairs from the Prophet's beard, thereby earning the title **Asar-i-Sharif** (place of illustrious relics). In theory, women are not permitted inside to view the upper storey, where fifteen niches are decorated with mediocre, Persian-style pot-and-foliage murals, but, for a little *baksheesh*, one of the girls who hang around the site will unlock the doors for you.

The citadel

Bijapur's **citadel** stands in the middle of town, hemmed in on all but its north side by battlements. Most of the buildings inside have collapsed, or have been converted into government offices, but enough remains to give a sense of how imposing this royal enclave must once have been.

The best-preserved monuments lie along, or near, the citadel's main north–south artery, Anand Mahal Road, reached by skirting the southeast wall from the Asar Mahal, or from the north side via the road running past the defunct KSTDC *Mayura Adil Shahi Hotel*. The latter route brings you first to the **Gagan Mahal**. Originally Ali Adil Shahi's "Heavenly Palace", this now-ruined hulk later served as a durbar hall for the sultans, who would sit in state on the platform at the open-fronted north side, watched by crowds gathered in the grounds opposite. West off Anand Mahal Road, the five-storey **Sat Manzil** was the pleasure palace of the courtesan Rambha, entombed with Muhammed Adil Shahi and his family in the Golgumbaz. In front stands an ornately carved water pavilion, the **Jal Mandir**, now left high and dry in an empty tank.

Bara Kaman

Just north of the citadel on the far side of the main road, a quiet lane leads to one of Bijapur's less-visited sights, the peaceful **Bara Kaman**. Another mauso-leum, for Ali Rauza, its construction was commenced in 1658 but the building remained uncompleted after his death in 1673. However, many chunky stone columns, some still linked by arches, remain to this day. They surround a central courtyard with a single tomb in the middle, set upon a huge square plinth that rises high above tranquil landscaped gardens.

Malik-i-Maidan and Upli Burj

Guarding the principal western entrance to the city is one of several bastions (*burje*) that punctuate Bijapur's battlements. This one, the Burj-i-Sherza (Lion Gate), sports a colossal cannon, known as the **Malik-i-Maidan**, literally "Lord of the Plains". It was brought here as war booty in the sixteenth century, and needed four hundred bullocks, ten elephants and an entire battalion to haul it up the steps to the emplacement. Inscriptions record that the cannon, whose muzzle features a relief of a monster swallowing an elephant, was cast in Ahmednagar in 1551.

A couple more discarded cannons lie atop the watchtower visible a short walk northwest. Steps wind around the outside of the oval-shaped **Upli Burj** (Upper Bastion), to a gun emplacement that affords unimpeded views over the city and plains.

The Ibrahim Rauza

Set in its own walled compound less than 1km west of the ramparts, the **Ibrahim Rauza** represents the highpoint of Bijapuri architecture (daily 6am–6pm; $2 [Rs5]). Whereas the Golgumbaz impresses primarily by its scale, the appeal of this tomb complex lies in its grace and simplicity. Beyond the reach of most bus parties, it's also a haven of peace, with cool colonnaded verandas and flocks of iridescent parakeets careering between the mildewed domes, minarets and gleaming golden finials.

Opinions differ over whether the tomb was commissioned by Ibrahim Adil Shah (1580–1626), or his favourite wife, Taj Sultana, but the former was the first to be interred here, in a gloomy chamber whose only light enters via a series of exquisite pierced-stone (*jali*) windows. Made up of elaborate Koranic inscriptions, these are the finest examples of their kind in India. More amazing stonework decorates the exterior of the mausoleum and the equally beautiful **mosque** opposite, the cornice of whose facade features a stone chain carved from a single block. The two buildings, bristling with minarets and domed cupolas, face each other from opposite sides of a rectangular raised plinth, divided by a small reservoir and fountains. Viewed from on top of the walls that enclose the complex, you can see why its architect, Malik Sandal, added a self-congratulatory inscription in his native Persian over the tomb's south doorway, describing his masterpiece as "A beauty of which Paradise stood amazed".

Moving on from Bijapur

Moving on from Bijapur is getting easier with efficient private companies such as VRL, recognizable by their distinctive yellow-and-black luxury coaches, travelling to Bangalore (3 buses from 7pm) and operating other overnight services to Mangalore via Udupi and Mumbai. Seats on VRL services can be booked through Vijayanand Travel, Terrace floor, Shastri Market, Gandhi Circle (℡08352/251000) or at their other branch just south of the bus stand. KSRTC also runs deluxe buses to Bangalore, Hubli, Mumbai and Hyderabad (via Sholapur). Heading to Badami, it's often quicker to take the first bus to Bagalkot and change there. For train info, see arrival, above; for more on public transport from Bijapur, see "Travel details", p.334.

Gulbarga

GULBARGA, 165km northeast of Bijapur, was the founding capital of the Bahmani dynasty and the region's principal city before the court moved to Bidar in 1424. Later captured by the Adil Shahis and Moghuls, it has remained a staunchly Muslim town, and bulbous onion-domes and mosque minarets still soar prominently above its ramshackle concrete-box skyline. The town is also famous as the birthplace of the *chisti*, or saint, Hazrat Bandah Nawaz Gesu Daraz (1320–1422), whose tomb, situated next to one of India's foremost Islamic theological colleges, is a major shrine.

In spite of Gulbarga's religious and historical significance, its **monuments** pale in comparison with those at Bijapur, and even Bidar. Unless you're particularly interested in medieval Muslim architecture, few are worth breaking a journey to see. The one exception is the tomb complex on the northeast edge of town, known as the **Dargah**. Approached via a broad bazaar, this marble-lined enclosure, plastered in mildew-streaked limewash, centres on the tomb of Hazrat Gesu Daraz, affectionately known to his devotees as **Bandah Nawaz**, or "the long-haired one who brings comfort to others". The saint was spiritual mentor to the Bahmani rulers, and it was they who erected his beautiful double-storey mausoleum, now visited by hundreds of thousands of Muslim pilgrims each year. Women are not allowed inside, and must peek at the tomb – which is surrounded by a mother-of-pearl inlaid wooden screen and draped with green silk – through the pierced-stone windows. Men, however, can enter to leave offerings and admire the elaborate mirror-mosaic ceiling. The same gender bar applies to the neighbouring tomb, whose interior has retained its exquisite Persian paintings. The Dargah's other important building, open to both sexes, is the **madrasa**, or theological college, founded by Bandah Nawaz and enlarged during the two centuries after his death. The syllabus here is dominated by the Koran, but the saint's own works on sufi mysticism and ethics are also still studied.

After mingling with the crowds at the Dargah, escape across town to Gulbarga's deserted **fort**. Encircled by sixteen-metre-thick crenellated walls, fifteen watchtowers and an evil-smelling, stagnant moat, the great citadel now lies in ruins behind the town's artificial lake. Its only surviving building is the beautiful fourteenth-century **Jami Masjid**, whose elegant domes and arched gateways preside over a scrubby wasteland. Thought to have been modelled by a Moorish architect on the great Spanish mosque of Cordoba, it is unique in India for having an entirely domed prayer hall.

Practicalities

Daily KSRTC **buses** from Bijapur, Bidar and Hospet pull in to the state bus stand on the southwest edge of town. Private minibuses work from the roadside opposite, their conductors shouting for passengers across the main concourse. Don't be tempted to take one of these to Bidar; they only run as far as the fly-blown highway junction of Humnabad, 40km short, where you'll be stranded for hours. Gulbarga's main-line **railway station**, with services to and from Mumbai, Pune, Hyderabad, Bangalore and Chennai, lies 1.5km east of the bus stand, along **Mill Road**. **Station Road**, the town's other main artery, runs due north of here past the lake, to the busy **Chowk** crossroads, at the heart of the bazaar.

Gulbarga's main sights are well spread out, so you'll need to get around by **auto-rickshaw**; fix fares in advance. For medical help, head for the town **hospital**, east of the centre next door to the *Hotel Santosh*, which has a well-stocked pharmacy. There is a Syndicate Bank **ATM** on Station Road, which accepts foreign cards.

Accommodation and eating

Gulbarga is well provided with good-value **accommodation**, and even travellers on tight budgets should be able to afford a clean room with a small balcony. All the hotels listed below have **restaurants**, mostly pure-veg places with a no-alcohol rule. *Kamat*, the chain restaurant, has several branches in Gulbarga, including a pleasant one at Station Chowk, specializing in vegetarian "meals" as well as *iddlis* and *dosas*; try *joleata roti*, a local bread cooked either hard and crisp or soft like a chapati. Several hole-in-the-wall spots on the road up from the station sell freshly-fried chicken and fish.

Adithya 2-244 Station Rd, opposite Public Gardens ☎08472/224040, ☏235661. Upmarket a/c rooms plus non-a/c ones for almost the same price. Their impeccably clean pure-veg Udupi restaurant, Pooja, on the ground floor, does great thalis and snacks. ❹–❺

Pariwar Station Rd, 10min walk from the station ☎08472/221522, ✉hotelpariwar@yahoo.com. One of the town's more established hotels, but not especially great value. The Kamakshi Restaurant serves quality vegetarian south Indian food, but no beer. Some a/c. ❸–❺

Hotel Prashant first lane on right leaving the station ☎08472/221456. Decent rooms of varying size and amenities, and surprisingly quiet. ❷–❹

Preetam Lodge Mill Rd ☎08472/221673. Head and shoulders above the rest of the places in the vicinity of the bus stand, with clean, spacious rooms in a new block. ❷–❹

Raj Rajeshwari Vasant Nagar, Mill Rd ☎08472/225881. A five-minute walk from the bus stand, this place is friendly and better value than the Pariwar set in a well-maintained modern building with large en-suite rooms with balconies. Also has a reasonable veg restaurant, but strictly no alcohol. ❸–❹

Southern Star Near the Fort, Super Market ☎08472/224093. Comfortable place with two restaurants, a bar and some a/c rooms. ❷–❺

Bidar

In 1424, following the break-up of the Bahmani dynasty into five rival factions, Ahmad Shah I shifted his court from Gulbarga to a less constricted site at **BIDAR**, spurred, it is said, by grief at the death of his beloved spiritual mentor, Bandah Nawaz Gesu Daraz (see opposite). Revamping the town with a new fort, splendid palaces, mosques and ornamental gardens, the Bahmanis ruled from here until 1487, when the Barid Shahis took control. They were succeeded by the Adil Shahis from Bijapur, and later the Moghuls under Aurangzeb, who annexed the region in 1656, before the Nizam of Hyderabad finally acquired the territory in the early eighteenth century.

Lost in the far northwest of Karnataka, Bidar, 284km northwest of Bijapur, is nowadays a provincial backwater, better known for its fighter-pilot training base than the monuments gently decaying in and around its medieval walls. Yet the town, half of whose 140,000 population are still Muslim, has a gritty charm, with narrow red-dirt streets ending at arched gates, which provide vistas across the plains. Littered with tile-fronted tombs, rambling fortifications and old mosques, it merits a visit if you're travelling between Hyderabad (150km east) and Bijapur, although expect little in the way of Western comforts, and more than the usual amount of curious approaches from locals. Lone women travellers, especially, may find the attention more hassle than it's worth.

Practicalities

Bidar lies on a branch line of the main Mumbai–Secunderabad–Chennai rail route, and can only be reached by slow passenger **train**. The few visitors that come here invariably arrive **by bus**, at the KSRTC bus stand on the far north-western edge of town, which has hourly direct services to Hyderabad (3hr 30min) and Gulbarga (3hr), and several a day to Bijapur (7hr) and Bangalore (12hr). There is no tourist office or currency exchange facilities, although there are several **Internet** outlets such as *Swamy's Cyber Café* (9am–10pm; Rs40 per hr), 100m southeast of the bus stand on Udgir Road.

Bidar's sights are too spread out to be comfortably explored on foot. Auto-rickshaws tend to be thin on the ground away from the main streets, however, and are reluctant to wait while you look around the monuments, so it's a good idea to rent a **bicycle** for the day from Rouf's, 50m east of the bus stand next to the excellent *Karnatak Juice Centre*.

Most **places to stay** are an auto-rickshaw ride away in the centre, so it makes sense to opt for the new *Hotel Mayura* (⊕08482/228142; ❷–❹) opposite the bus stand, which is one of the two best in Bidar and has large rooms with optional a/c. The other decent hotel is its older sister, the *Ashoka* (⊕08482/227621; ❷–❹), 1.5km from the bus stand past Dr Ambedkar Chowk, which has comfortable, good-value deluxe rooms, some with a/c. If you don't mind a bit of grubbiness, there's the budget *Hotel Kailash* (⊕08482/227727; ❶), on Udgir Road in the centre of town.

Finding somewhere good to **eat** is not a problem in Bidar, again thanks to the restaurants at the *Mayura* and *Ashoka*, which both offer a varied selection of North Indian veg and meat dishes (try the *Mayura*'s pepper chicken) and cold beer. Also recommended, and much cheaper, is the popular *Udupi Krishna* restaurant, overlooking the *chowk*, which serves up unlimited pure-veg thalis for lunch; they have a "family room" for women, too, and open early (around 7.30am) for piping hot South Indian breakfasts. The *Jyothi Udupi*, opposite the KRSTC bus stand, is another classic south Indian joint.

The old town

The heart of Bidar is its medieval **old town**, encircled by crenellated ramparts and eight imposing gateways (*darwazas*). This predominantly Muslim quarter holds many Bahmani-era mosques, *havelis* and *khanqahs* – "monasteries" set up by the local rulers for Muslim cleric-mystics and their disciples – but its real highlight is the impressive ruin of **Mahmud Gawan's Madrasa**, or theological college, whose single minaret soars high above the city centre. Gawan, a scholar and Persian exile, was the *wazir*, or prime minister, of the Bahmani state under Muhammed Bahmani III (1463–82). A talented linguist, mathematician and inspired military strategist, he oversaw the dynasty's expansion into Karnataka and Goa, bequeathing this college as a thank-you gift to his adoptive kingdom in 1472. The distinctively Persian-style building, originally surmounted by large bulbous domes, once housed a world-famous library. However, this burnt down after being struck by lightning in 1696, while several of the walls and domes were blown away when gunpowder stored here by Aurangzeb's occupying army caught fire and exploded. Today, the *madrasa* is little more than a shell, although its elegant arched facade has retained large patches of the vibrant Persian glazed tile-work that once covered most of the exterior surfaces. This includes a beautiful band of Koranic calligraphy, and striking multicoloured zigzags wrapped around the base of the one remaining *minar*, or minaret.

The fort

Presiding over the dark-soiled plains from atop a sheer-faced red laterite escarp-ment, Bidar's **fort**, at the far north end of the street running past the *madrasa*, was founded by the Hindu Chalukyas and strengthened by the Bahmanis in the

Bidri

Bidar is celebrated as the home of a unique damascene metalwork technique known as **bidri**, developed by the Persian silversmiths who came to the area with the Bahmani court in the fifteenth century. These highly skilled artisans engraved and inlaid their traditional Iranian designs onto a metal alloy composed of lead, copper, zinc and tin, which they blackened and polished. The resulting effect – swirling silver floral motifs framed by geometric patterns and set against black backgrounds – has since become the hallmark of Muslim metalwork in India.

Bidri objets d'art are displayed in museums and galleries all over the country. If you want to see pukka bidri-wallahs at work, take a walk down Bidar's **Siddiq Talim Road**, which cuts across the south side of the old town, where skull-capped artisans tap and burnish vases, goblets, plates, spice boxes, betel-nut tins and ornamental hookah pipes, as well as less traditional objects – coasters, ashtrays and bangles – that crop up (at vastly inflated prices) in silver emporiums as far away as Delhi and Kolkata (Calcutta).

early fifteenth century. Despite repeated sieges, it remains largely intact, encircled by 10km of ramparts that drop away in the north and west to three-hundred-metre cliffs. The main southern entrance is protected by equally imposing man-made defences: gigantic fortified gates and a triple moat formerly crossed by a series of drawbridges. Once inside, the first building of note (on the left after the third and final gateway) is the exquisite **Rangin Mahal**. Mahmud Shah built this modest "Coloured Palace" after an unsuccessful uprising of Abyssinian slaves in 1487 forced him to relocate to a safer site inside the citadel. The palace's relatively modest proportions reflect the Bahmanis' declining fortunes, but its interior comprises some of the finest surviving Islamic art in the Deccan, with superb wood-carving above the door arches and Persian-style mother-of-pearl inlay on polished black granite surfaces. If the doors to the palace are locked, ask for the keys at the nearby ASI **museum** (daily 8am–1pm & 2–5pm; free), which houses a missable collection of Hindu temple sculpture, weapons and Stone Age artefacts.

Opposite the museum, an expanse of gravel is all that remains of the royal gardens. This is overlooked by the austere **Solah Khamb** mosque (1327), Bidar's oldest Muslim monument, whose most outstanding feature is the intricate pierced-stone *jali* calligraphy around its central dome. From here, continue west through the ruins of the former royal enclosure – a rambling complex of half-collapsed palaces, baths, *zenanas* (women's quarters) and assembly halls – to the fort's west walls. You can complete the round of the **ramparts** in ninety minutes, taking time out to enjoy the views over the red cliffs and across the plains.

Ashtur: the Bahmani tombs

As you look from the fort's east walls, a cluster of eight bulbous white domes floats alluringly above the trees in the distance. Dating from the fifteenth century, the mausoleums at **Ashtur**, 3km east of Bidar (leave the old town via Dulhan Darwaza gate), are the final resting places of the Bahmani sultans and their families, including the son of the ruler who first decamped from Gulbarga, Alauddin Shah I. His remains by far the most impressive **tomb**, with patches of coloured glazed tiles on its arched facade and a large dome whose interior surfaces writhe with sumptuous Persian paintings. Reflecting sunlight onto the ceiling with a small pocket mirror, the *chowkidar* picks out the highlights, among them a diamond, barely visible among the bat droppings.

The tomb of Allaudin's father, the ninth and most illustrious Bahmani sultan, Ahmad Shah I, stands beside that of his son, decorated with Persian inscriptions. Beyond this are two more minor mausoleums, followed by the partially collapsed tomb of Humayun the Cruel (1458–61), cracked open by a bolt of lightning. Continuing along the line, you can chart the gradual decline of the Bahmanis as the mausoleums diminish in size, ending with a sad handful erected in the early sixteenth century, when the sultans were no more than puppet rulers of the Barid Shahis.

Crowning a low hillock halfway between Ashtur and Bidar, on the north side of the road, the **Chaukhandi of Hazrat Khalil Ullah** is a beautiful octagonal-shaped tomb built by Allaudin Shah for his chief spiritual adviser. Most of the tiles have dropped off the facade, but the surviving stonework and calligraphy above the arched doorway, along with the views from the tomb's plinth, deserve a quick detour from the road.

The Badri Shahi tombs

The **tombs of the Shahi** rulers, who succeeded the Bahmanis at the start of the sixteenth century, stand on the western edge of town, on the Udgir road, 200m beyond and visible from the bus stand. Although not as impressive as those of their predecessors, the mausoleums, mounted on raised plinths, occupy an attractive site. Randomly spaced rather than set in a chronological row, they are surrounded by lawns maintained by the ASI. The most interesting is the tomb of **Ali Barid** (1542–79), whose Mecca-facing wall was left open to the elements. A short distance southwest lies a mass grave platform for his 67 concubines, who were sent as tribute gifts by vassals of the Deccan overlord from all across the kingdom. The compound is only officially open for afternoon promenading (daily 4.30–7.30pm; $2 [Rs5]), but the gateman may let you in earlier if he's around.

Travel details

Trains

When this book went to press, the changeover from metre- to broad-gauge track was largely completed, but the Mangalore–Hassan and Bijapur–Gadag sections were still not fully operational; check the current situation with Indian Railways.

Bangalore to: Chennai (5–7 daily; 5hr–7hr 40min); Delhi (2–4 daily; 34hr 40min–49hr 40min); Gulbarga (2–3 daily; 11hr 35min–12hr 20min); Hospet (1 daily; 9hr 35min); Hubli (2–4 daily; 7–13hr); Hyderabad (Secunderabad) (1–3 daily; 12hr 15min–14hr 10min); Kochi (Ernakulam) (1–2 daily; 12hr–13hr 5min); Kolkata (Calcutta) (3 weekly; 37hr 10min); Mumbai (2–3 daily; 23hr 25min–25hr); Mysore (6–7 daily; 2–3hr 15min); Pune (2–4 daily; 19hr 20min–21hr 30min); Thiruvananthapuram (1–2 daily; 17hr–17hr 55min).

Hassan to: Mysore (4 daily; 2hr 10min–3hr 55min).

Hospet to: Bangalore (1 daily; 10hr 30min); Gadag (3 daily; 1hr 15min–1hr 35min); Hubli (3 daily; 2hr 30min–3hr 20min).

Mangalore to: Chennai (1 daily; 17hr 55min); Kochi (Ernakulam) (2 daily; 9hr 30min–10hr 5min); Margao, Goa (2 daily; 5hr 45min–6hr 10min); Gokarna (2 daily; 3hr 5min–3hr 50min); Kollam (2 daily; 12hr 50min–13hr 30min); Thiruvananthapuram (2 daily; 14hr 40min–15hr 35min).

Mysore to: Bangalore (6–7 daily; 1hr 55min–3hr 30min); Hassan (4 daily; 2hr 10min–4hr).

Buses

Bangalore to: Bidar (2 daily; 16hr); Bijapur (4 daily; 13hr); Chennai (hourly; 8hr); Coimbatore (2 daily; 9hr); Goa (4 daily; 14hr); Gokarna (2 daily; 13hr) Gulbarga (6 daily; 15hr); Hassan (every 30min; 4hr); Hospet (3 daily; 8hr); Hubli (3 daily; 9hr); Hyderabad (6 daily; 16hr); Jog Falls (1 daily; 8hr); Karwar (3 daily; 13hr); Kochi (Ernakulam) (6 daily; 12–13hr); Kodaikanal (1 nightly; 13hr); Madikeri (hourly; 6hr); Madurai (2 daily; 12hr);

Mangalore (evry 30min–1hr; 10hr); Mumbai (2 daily; 24hr); Mysore (every 15min; 3hr); Ooty (6 daily; 7hr 30min); Pondicherry (2 daily; 9–10hr).

Bijapur to: Aurangabad (4 daily; 12hr); Badami (4 daily; 4hr); Bangalore (5 daily; 13hr); Bidar (4 daily; 8hr); Gulbarga (hourly; 4hr); Hospet (12 daily; 5hr); Hubli (hourly; 6hr); Hyderabad (6 daily; 10hr); Mumbai (10 daily; 12hr); Pune (10 daily; 8hr).

Hassan to: Channarayapatna, for Sravanabelgola (hourly; 1hr); Halebid (hourly; 1hr); Hospet (1 daily; 10hr); Mangalore (hourly; 4hr); Mysore (every 30min; 3hr).

Hospet to: Badami (3 daily; 5hr); Bangalore (3 daily; 8hr); Bidar (2 daily; 10hr); Gokarna (2 nightly; 9–10hr); Hampi (every 30min; 20min); Hyderabad (4 daily; 12hr); Margao (4 daily; 9hr); Mysore (2 daily; 10–11hr); Panjim (4 daily; 10hr); Vasco da Gama (4 daily; 10–11hr).

Mangalore to: Bangalore (every 30min–1hr; 8hr); Bijapur (1 daily; 16hr); Chaudi (2 daily; 8hr); Gokarna (1 daily; 7hr); Kannur (hourly; 3hr); Karwar (9 daily; 8hr); Kasargode (every 30min–1hr; 1hr);

Kochi (Ernakulam) (1 daily; 9hr); Madikeri (hourly; 3hr 30min); Mysore (hourly; 7hr); Panjim (2 daily; 10–11hr); Udupi (every 10 min; 1hr).

Mysore to: Bangalore (every 15min; 3hr); Channarayapatna (every 30min; 2hr); Jog Falls (via Shimoga) (every 90min; 7hr); Kannur (8 daily; 7hr); Kochi (6 daily; 12hr); Kozhikode (6 daily; 5hr); Madikeri (hourly; 3hr); Mangalore (hourly; 7hr); Ooty (10 daily; 5hr); Srirangapatnam (every 15min; 20min).

Flights

Bangalore to: Chennai (11–12 daily; 45min–1hr); Delhi (11–12 daily; 2hr 30min–3hr 30min); Goa (3 daily; 1hr–2hr 30min); Hyderabad (7–9 daily; 1hr–1hr 30min); Kochi (Ernakulam) (3 daily; 55min–1hr 20min); Kolkata (Calcutta; 4–5 daily; 2hr 20min–3hr 30min); Mangalore (1 daily; 1hr 5min); Mumbai (15–17 daily; 1hr 30min–1hr 45min); Pune (3 daily; 1hr 20min); Thiruvanthapuram (1 daily; 2hr).

Mangalore to: Bangalore (2 daily; 1hr 5min–1hr 15min); Mumbai (3 daily; 1hr 15min).

Kerala

CHAPTER 4 # Highlights

* **Varkala** Chill out in a cliff-top café, sunbathe on the beach or soak up the atmosphere around the village's busy temple tank. See p.367

* **The backwaters** Explore the beautiful waterways of this densely populated coastal strip on a traditional *kettu vallam* boat, following the narrow, overgrown canals right into the heart of the villages. See p.378-379

* **Plantations** Head to the tea plantations of Munnar, or into the lush hills around Kumily, where the air is heady with the smell of cloves, cardamom and coffee. See p.391 & p.392

* **Fort Cochin** This atmospheric peninsula, strung with Chinese fishing nets, draws on Jewish, Portuguese, British and Keralan culture. See p.406

* **Kathakali performance** An essential part of the Kerala experience, this noisy and colourful ritualized drama is stunning; arrive early to watch the characters come alive as intricate make-up is applied. See p.408

* **Wildlife** The wildlife sanctuaries of Periyar, Eravikulam and Tholpetty offer plenty of opportunities to spot elephants, buffalo, boar, deer and – if you're extremely lucky – the elusive tiger. See p.387, p.396 & p.435

△ Kathkali billboard, Fort Cochin

Kerala

A sliver of dense greenery sandwiched between the Arabian Sea and the forested Western Ghat mountains, the state of **KERALA** stretches for 550km along India's southwest coast, and is just 120km wide at its broadest point. It's blessed with unique geographical features, and the lush tropical landscape, fed by two annual monsoons, and beautiful backwaters intoxicate every newcomer. Equally, Kerala's arcane rituals and spectacular festivals stimulate even the most jaded imagination, continuing centuries of tradition that has never strayed far from the realms of magic.

Small scale and relatively relaxed, Kerala's cities and towns are all within easy reach of each other. The most popular tourist destination is undoubtedly the great port of **Kochi** (formerly Cochin), where Kerala's extensive history of peaceful foreign contact is evident in the atmospheric old quarters of Mattancherry and Fort Cochin – hubs of a still-thriving tea and spice trade. The capital, **Thiruvananthapuram** (aka Trivandrum), almost as far south as you can go, and a gateway to the nearby palm-fringed beaches of **Kovalam**, provides varied opportunities to sample Kerala's rich cultural and artistic life.

More than anywhere else in India, the greatest joy of exploring Kerala is in the travelling itself, especially by **boat**. Ferries, cruisers, wooden longboats and even houseboats ply the **backwaters**, slowly meandering through the spellbinding **Kuttanad** region near historic **Kollam** (Quilon) and **Alappuzha** (Alleppey), on the southern tip of the huge **Vembanad Lake** that stretches northwards to **Kochi**. Drifting between swathes of palm trees and past tiny villages in the humid heat, you cannot fail to be lulled by the unhurried pace of life.

The only way to escape the humidity of the lowlands is to head for the **hills**. Roads wind through landscapes dotted with churches and temples and past spice, tea, coffee and rubber plantations, as well as natural forest, en route to wildlife reserves such as **Tholpetty** and **Periyar**, where sightings of wild elephants are virtually guaranteed. Further highland options include the former British hill station of **Munnar**, surrounded by endlessly rolling fields of tea, **Palakkad**, with its spice plantations, and the beautiful forested district of **Wayanad** with its indigenous tribal population.

Kerala is short on the historic monuments prevalent elsewhere in India, and furthermore the ancient temples that remain today are still in use, and usually closed to non-Hindus. Following an unwritten law, few buildings in Kerala, whether palaces, houses or temples, are higher than the trees, often creating the illusion of clean and green cities. Typical features of both domestic and temple architecture include long, sloping tiled and gabled roofs that minimize the excesses of both rain and sunshine, and pillared verandas. The definitive example

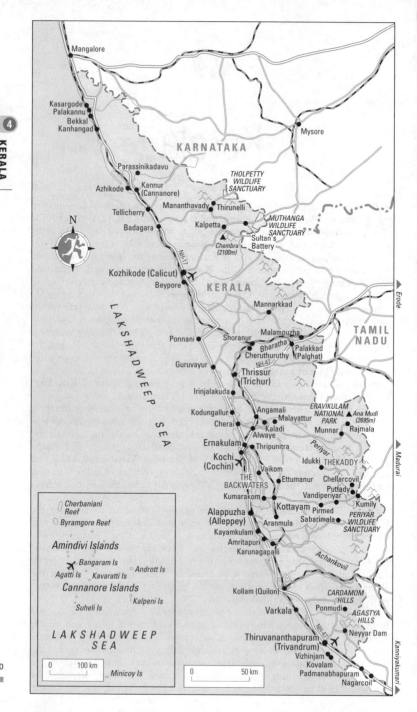

Keralan buses

Kerala must be the only Indian state where the state **buses** are superior to and safer than the private ones. There's not a lot of difference in degrees of discomfort – both rate extremely highly – but the state buses have slightly more leg room, tend not to allow as many passengers on board and are generally safer, displaying marginally fewer suicidal tendencies than their private counterparts.

Both state and private buses in Kerala reserve at least three rows of three seats (state buses at the back, private buses at the front) for **women only**. Men are only allowed to sit on them if there are no women on board – if a woman shows up, men must ignominiously vacate their seats and join the scrimmage in the aisle. However, as the signs designating women-only seats are in Malayalam, you'll have to ask to find out where they are.

Finally, do not be fooled by the **"limited stop"** signs on the windscreen of every private bus; buses will stop whenever anybody wants to get on or off, and in practice this usually means the bus will stop every twenty metres or so. It's worth bearing in mind that though express buses stop less frequently, "limited stop" services tend to go faster in between stops to maintain healthy competition.

of such architecture is **Padmanabhapuram Palace**, just over the border in Tamil Nadu, and easily reached from Thiruvananthapuram.

Phenomenal amounts of money are lavished upon the many, varied and often all-night **entertainments** based in Kerala's temples. Fireworks fill the sky, while processions of gold-bedecked elephants are accompanied by some of the loudest (and deftest) drum orchestras in the world. The famous **Puram** festival in Thrissur is the most extravagant, but smaller events take place throughout the state.

Theatre and **dance** styles abound in Kerala; not only the region's own female classical dance form, **Mohinyattam** (dance of the enchantress), but also the martial-art-influenced **Kathakali** dance-drama, which has for four centuries brought gods and demons from the Mahabharata and Ramayana to Keralan villages (see p.714). Its 2000-year-old predecessor, the Sanskrit drama **Kutiyattam**, is still performed by a handful of artists, while localized rituals known as **Theyyam**, in which dancers wearing tall masks become "possessed" by temple deities, continue to be a potent ingredient of village life in northern Kerala. Few visitors ever witness these extraordinary all-night performances first hand, but between November and May it is possible to spend weeks travelling between colourful village festivals, experiencing a way of life that has altered little in centuries.

Travelling around is relatively easy as the state is so compact – Kerala amounts to just over one percent of India's total landmass. There are efficient rail services from the main coastal towns to the rest of the country, but local passenger trains are not necessarily the most efficient method of travelling within the state itself. Most visitors will use local ferries, buses and the odd taxi to get around. Although a bus journey doesn't have the charm of a Kuttanad boat ride, you will remember it all the same – Kerala's bus drivers, both private and state-employed, are very competitive and often reach sickening speeds in the most improbable of places along the coastal highway.

The **best time to visit** Kerala is between December and April and during August and September, when the skies are clear and humidity at its least debilitating. From May, the humidity becomes uncomfortable in the pre-monsoon build up, and the rains usually hit the coast in early June. This is considered the auspicious time to begin a course in Ayurvedic treatment if you want to really experience the benefits, but a beach holiday is out as the sand often disappears under the high tides and crashing waves. The second annual monsoon that sweeps through Tamil Nadu from October to December leaves Kerala overcast, a definite problem if working on a golden tan is your main priority.

Some history

The god **Parasurama**, or "Rama with the battleaxe", the sixth incarnation of Vishnu, is credited with creating Kerala. Born a brahmin, he set out to re-establish the supremacy of the priestly class, whose position had been usurped by arrogant *kshatryas*, the martial aristocracy. Brahmins were forbidden to engage in warfare, but despite this he embarked upon a campaign of carnage which only ended when Varuna, the all-seeing god of the sea, gave him the chance to create a new land from the ocean, where brahmins could live in peace. Its limits were defined by the distance Parashurama could throw his axe; the waves duly receded up to the point where it fell. Fossil evidence suggests that the sea once extended to the Southern Ghats, so the legend reflects a geological truth.

Ancient Kerala is mentioned as the land of the Cheras in a third-century BC Ashokan edict, and also in the Ramayana (the monkey king Sugriva sent emissaries here in search of Sita), and the Mahabharata (a Chera king sent soldiers to the Kurukshetra war). The Tamil *Silappadikaram* ("The Jewelled Anklet") was composed here and provides a valuable picture of life around the time of Christ. Early foreign accounts, such as those by Pliny and Ptolemy, testify to thriving trade between the ancient port of Muziris (now known as Kodungallur) and the Roman Empire.

Little is known about the early history of the **Cheras**; their dominion covered a large area, but their capital, Vanji, has not been identified. Other contemporary rulers included the Nannanas in the north and the Ay chieftains in the south, who battled with the Pandyas from Tamil Nadu in the eighth century. At the start of the ninth century, the Chera king Kulashekhara Alvar – a poet-saint of the Vaishnavite *bhakti* movement known as the *alvars* – established his own dynasty. His son and successor, Rajashekharavarman, is thought to have been a saint of the parallel Shaivite movement, the *nayannars*. Eventually, the prosperity acquired by the Cheras through trade with China and the Arab world proved too much of a temptation for the neighbouring **Chola** empire; at the end of the tenth century, they embarked on a hundred years of sporadic warfare with the Cheras. Around 1100, the Cheras lost their capital at Mahodayapuram in the north, and shifted south to establish a new capital at Kollam (Quilon).

When the **Portuguese** ambassador and general Vasco da Gama and his fleet first arrived in India in 1498, people were as much astounded by their recklessness in sailing so close to Calicut during monsoon as by their physical and sartorial strangeness. Crowds filled the streets of Calicut to see them, and a Moroccan found a way to communicate with them. Eager to meet the king – whom they believed to be a Christian – the Portuguese were escorted in torrential rain to his palace. However, Vasco da Gama soon established that the gifts he had brought from the king of Portugal had not made the good impression he had hoped for. The *zamorin* (raja) wanted silver and gold, not a few silk clothes and a sack of sugar.

Vasco da Gama, after such diplomatic initiatives as the kidnapping, mutilation and murder of assorted locals, came to an agreement of sorts with the *zamorin*, after which he pressed on to demand exclusive rights to the **spice trade**. He was determined to squeeze out the Keralan Muslim (Mappila) traders who for centuries had been a respected section of the community – acting as middlemen between local producers and traders in the Middle East. Exploiting an existing enmity between the royal families of Cochin and Calicut, Vasco da Gama turned to Cochin, which became the site of India's first Portuguese fortress in 1503. The city's strategic position enabled the Portuguese to break the Middle Eastern monopoly of trade with western India. They introduced new agricultural products such as cashew and tobacco, and turned coconut into a cash crop, having recognized the value of its by-products: coir rope and matting.

Festivals of Kerala

Catching one of the numerous festivals – **Utsavam** – held throughout the year makes a visit to Kerala all the more rewarding. Kerala's festivals are too numerous to list here, but local tourist offices have current information, and the state tourist department publishes a useful little annual booklet, *Fairs and Festivals of Kerala*, which is available from all offices.

Perhaps one of the greatest spectacles of the festivals are the **elephant processions**, which feature particularly strongly in temple festivals known as **Puram** – the celebration of local deities, usually a goddess. One of the highlights of the elephant parades is the *Kudamattom* ritual, when the colourful parasols atop the elephants are changed in synchronized motion. The Puram festivals originate from the tradition of carrying the local deity in a procession, accompanied by drums and fanfare, to receive offerings at the end of the harvest period. The most remarkable of all the *Puram* festivals are held in the town of **Thrissur** (April/May), when deities from the surrounding countryside are brought together in celebration. *Puram* festivals are not exclusive to Thrissur: they are held in several towns and villages throughout central Kerala including Cherai on the northern outskirts of Kochi/Ernakulam, and in and around Palakkad. The annual eight-day elephant procession at Ernakulam's Shiva temple (Jan/Feb) is not to be missed, nor is the **Arat** festival held in Thiruvananthapuram, when the deity is led to sea escorted by elephants (March/April & Oct/Nov). An **elephant race** is held at Guruvayur (Feb/March); although the temple itself is off-limits to non-Hindus, the public part of the festival showcases over forty elephants. **Onam**, the annual harvest festival found throughout Kerala (Aug/Sept), also features elephant processions and water carnivals – one of the best of these is at **Aranmula**, near the town of Kottayam, which holds a **snakeboat race** consisting of long boats each with two lines of rowers. The most famous and spectacular of all the snakeboat races, the **Nehru Trophy Boat Race**, is held at Alappuzha (Aug) and, unlike the light-hearted festival spirit of Aranmula, is taken very seriously.

Many Keralan festivals feature **classical music** and **dance**, and provide an excellent opportunity to catch a **Kathakali** performance in a genuine setting (see p.714 for further details on Kathakali dance). The **Shri Purnatrayisa temple**, in the small town of Thripunitra near Kochi, runs an all-night Kathakali show during its annual festival (Oct/Nov), while the royal family of Travancore are great patrons of the arts and hold a yearly **Carnatic music** festival at the Puttan Malika Palace in Thiruvananthapuram. Probably the best place to experience one of the numerous performing art forms of Kerala and other regions of South India, however, is at **Cheruthuruthy** near Thrissur, where an annual performing arts festival is held every year towards the end of December.

Christmas, when the climate is pleasant, is also a good time to travel in Kerala. Of Fort Cochin's several churches, the historic St Francis' hosts an extremely popular carol service where the congregation spills onto the street. Another notable Christian festival is held yearly in early January at Mar Thoma Pontifical Shrine near Kodungallur; here, devotees process to the ancient site with colourfully decorated carts laden with gifts.

No smoking

In 2003 Kerala became the first state in India to **ban smoking** from all public places, including streets, parks and beaches. Unlike such laws in the West, though, the ban doesn't include restaurants or bars, where it remains at the owner's discretion. There's a Rs200 on-the-spot fine for offenders, though the law seems to be more strictly enforced in larger cities than rural areas. Of course, you won't receive a ticket if busted, so it's a handy extra source of baksheesh for the Keralan coppers.

The rivalry between Cochin and Calicut allowed other colonial powers to move in: both the **Dutch**, who forcibly expelled the Portuguese from their forts, and the **British**, in the shape of the East India Company, firmly established themselves early in the seventeenth century. During the 1700s, first Raja Marthanda Varma, then Tipu Sultan of Mysore, carved out independent territories, but the defeat of Tipu Sultan by the British in 1792 left them in control right up until Independence.

Kerala today can claim some of the most startling **radical** credentials in India. In 1957 it was the first state in the world to elect a communist government democratically and, despite having one of the lowest per capita incomes in the country, it currently has the most equitable land distribution, due to uncompromising reforms made during the 1960s and 1970s. In 1996, the Left Democratic Front, led by the Communist Party of India (Marxist), retook the state from the Congress-led United Democratic Front, which had been in power for five years; however, the UDF were returned after the 2001 election, when they gained a comfortable two-thirds majority. Poverty is not absent, but it appears far less acute than in other parts of India. Kerala is also justly proud of its reputation for healthcare and education, with a literacy rate that stands, officially at least, at one hundred percent. Industrial development is negligible, however, with potential investors from outside tending to fight shy of dealing with such a politicized workforce. Many Keralans now work in the Gulf and the resultant influx of petro-dollars has led to greater wealth and spending power for the itinerant workers and their families. As you explore the state, you'll see massive white mansions on the outskirts of every village – bought by Gulf petro-dollars – but you'll see plenty of the hammer and sickle, too.

Thiruvananthapuram

Kerala's capital, the coastal city of **THIRUVANANTHAPURAM** (still widely and more commonly known as **Trivandrum**), is set on seven low hills, 87km from the southern tip of India. Despite its administrative importance – demonstrated by wide roads, multistorey office blocks and gleaming white colonial buildings – it's a decidedly easy-going city, with a mix of narrow backstreets and traditional red-tiled gabled houses, and acres of palm trees and parks breaking up the bustle of its modern concrete centre.

Although it has few monuments as such, Thiruvananthapuram, as a window on Keralan culture, is an ideal first stop in the state. The oldest and most interesting part of town is the **Fort** area in the south, around the **Shri Padmanabhaswamy temple** and **Puttan Malika Palace**, while the **Shri Chitra Art Gallery** and **Napier Museum**, important showcases for painting, crafts and sculpture, stand together in a park in the north. In addition, schools specializing

The city of the snake Anantha

Thiruvananthapuram was the capital of the kingdom of Travancore from 1750 until 1956, when the state of Kerala was created. Its name – formally readopted to replace "Trivandrum" – derives from *thiru-anantha-puram*, or "the holy city of Anantha", the **coiled snake** on which the god Vishnu reclines in the midst of the cosmic ocean.

Vishnu is given a special name for this non-activity – Padma-nabha (lotus-navel) – and is invariably depicted lying on the sacred snake with a lotus growing from his navel. The god Brahma sits inside the lotus, which represents the beginning of a new world era. Padmanabha is the principal deity of the royal family of Travancore and of Thiruvananthapuram's Shri Padmanabhaswamy temple.

in the martial art Kalarippayat and the dance/theatre forms of Kathakali and Kutiyattam offer visitors an insight into the Keralan obsession with physical training and skill.

Most travellers choose to pass straight through Thiruvananthapuram, lured by the promise of Kovalam's palm-fringed beaches (see p.355). A mere twenty-minute bus ride south, this popular resort is close enough to use as a base to see the city, although the recent upsurge in package tourism means it's far from the low-key, inexpensive travellers' hangout it used to be.

Arrival, information and tours

Connected to most major Indian cities, as well as Sri Lanka, the Maldives and the Middle East, **Beemapalli airport** is 6km southwest of town and serviced by an airport bus and bus #14 to and from the City Bus Stand. Auto-rickshaws will run you into the centre for around Rs50 and there's also a handy prepaid taxi service. There are tourist information and foreign exchange facilities at the airport.

The long-distance KSRTC **Thampanoor Bus Stand** (☏0471/232 3886) and **railway station** (☏0471/232 1622) face each other across Station Road in the southeast of the city, a short walk east of Overbridge Junction on MG Road. **Local buses** (including Kovalam) depart from **City Bus Stand**, in East Fort, ten minutes' walk south from the KSRTC and railway stations. **Auto-rickshaws** run to Kovalam for Rs80–100, while **taxis** charge around Rs150 – but beware of overcharging scams.

Information and tours

All the **tourist offices** at the **airport** are open during flight times. **India Tourism's** counter (☏0471/250 1498) offers general information regarding Kerala and adjacent states, while the **Kerala Department of Tourism** has two counters, one at the domestic terminal (☏0471/250 1085) and the other at the international terminal (☏0471/250 2298), offering Kerala-specific information (on backwater cruises, for example). The Kerala Department of Tourism also has a booth at the **Thampanoor Bus Stand** (Mon–Sat 10am–5pm; ☏0471/232 7224), which is good for general information and maps, and at the **railway station** (☏0471/233 4470). Their main visitor centre is 150m south of the Napier Museum on Museum Road (open 24hr; ☏0471/232 6812, @www.keralatourism.org).

The **Kerala Tourist Development Corporation** (KTDC), the best organized of all the Indian state tourist corporations, is designed primarily to sell its own products and promote cultural events. KTDC's main visitor reception

▲ Kollam, Kochi & NH-47

THIRUVANANTHAPURAM (TRIVANDRUM)

VELLAYAMBALAM

RESTAURANTS

Amma	8
Ananda Bhavan	3
Arya Niwas	6
Food World	2
Indian Coffee House (I)	1
Indian Coffee House (II)	2
Indian Coffee House (III)	9
Kalavara	5
Kerala House & Akash Ganga	4
KTDC Chaithram	N
Prime	7

ACCOMMODATION

Greenland Lodging	M
Highland	L
Horizon	G
Jas	I
KTDC Chaithram	N
KTDC Mascot	A
Navratana	E
Pankaj	D
Prasanth	H
Residency Tower	F
The South Park	B
Sree Devi	K
Sukhvas	J
YWCA	C

Indian Airlines
Sri Chitra Art Gallery
Natural History Museum
Kanakakumu Palace
Air India
Zoo
Museum of Science & Technology
Kerala Dept. of tourism
Napier Museum, Open Air Theatre & Natural History Museum
Library
Stadium
VAZHUTHAKAD

KUNNUKUZHI

Connemara Market
SPENCER JCTN
BAKERY JCTN
ATM
DC Books
Secretariat
STATUE RD
Telegraph Office
YMCA RD
British Library
Foreigners Registration Office
VANCHIYUR
GPO
Aries Travel
PRESS ROAD
THYCAUD
Swastik Tours
Ayurveda College
COLLEGE JCTN
ARISTO ROAD
New Theatre
Tourist Reception Centre
KSRTC Thampanoor Bus Stand
STATION ROAD
Railway Station
THAMPANOOR
OVERBRIDGE JUNCTION
THAKARAPARAMBU ROAD
POWER HOUSE ROAD
PADMAVILASAM ROAD
FORT
Tank
City & Local Bus Stand
CHENTITTA
Sri Padmanabhaswamy Temple
Puttan Malika Palace
Wall Street Finances
CHALAI
City Bus Stand (Kovalam Buses)
CHALAI BAZAAR ROAD
MAHATMA GANDHI RD
MANJALIKULAM ROAD
SS COIL ROAD
TAKKAD HOSPITAL RD
VAZHUTHACUD ROAD
CHETTIKULANGARA ROAD

◄ Kochi
◄ Airport (6 km)
◄ Beemapalli Airport (6 km)

N

0   250 m

▼ Kovalam & Kanniyakumari

centre, next to their *KTDC Chaitram* hotel on Station Rd (☎0471/233 0031, ⓦwww.ktdc.com), can book accommodation in their good-value **hotel** chain and sells tickets for various **guided tours**. Most of these, including the city tours (daily 8.30am–7pm, Rs130; half-day 8.30am–1pm or 2–7pm; Rs70/80), are far too rushed, but if you're pushed for time try the **Kanniyakumari** tour (daily 7.30am–9pm; Rs250), which takes in Padmanabhapuram Palace (except Mon), Suchindram temple, and Kanniyakumari. They also offer their **backwater cruises** with flexible itineraries. Several smaller independent companies are starting backwater cruises within striking distance of Thiruvananthapuram, which are worth considering if you don't have time to explore the much more rewarding Kuttanad region; try Island Queen at Pazhikkara, Pachalloor (☎0471/248 1559).

Accommodation

Thiruvananthapuram's mid-range and expensive **hotels** are, in general, cheaper than in most state capitals, but are not concentrated in any one district. Budget hotels are grouped mainly in the streets around **Station Road**. Good areas to start looking are **Manjalikulam Road**, five minutes' walk west from the railway station, or the lanes off **Aristo Road**, just north of the railway station, but note that the best of the budget places tend to be full by late afternoon. If you prefer to base yourself at the beach, head for **Kovalam** (see p.355).

Greenland Lodging Aristo Rd, Thampanoor ☎0471/232 8114. Large and efficient budget lodge with spotless rooms with attached bathrooms – the best option in the vicinity of the bus stand and railway station. Book ahead or arrive before noon. ❷

Highland Manjalikulam Rd ☎0471/233 3200, ⓦwww.highland-hotels.com. Dependable mid-range option, well managed and a short walk from the stations, with a range of clean non-a/c and a/c rooms. It's in a multistorey block, and the easiest place in the area to find. ❸–❻

Horizon Aristo Rd ☎0471/232 6888, ⓔhotelhorizon@vsnl.com. Plush and efficient business hotel near the railway station offering smart rooms and suites with central a/c, plus two restaurants – one on the leafy rooftop – and a bar. Rates include breakfast. ❼–❾

Jas Thycaud, Aristo Junction ☎0471/232 4881, ⓦwww.jashotel.com. Reasonable two-star, in a quiet central location near the bus and railway stations, with a range of decent non-a/c and a/c rooms, all with cable TV and smart bathrooms. ❺–❽

KTDC Chaithram Station Rd ☎0471/233 0977, ⓦwww.ktdc.com. Large tower-block hotel very close to the railway station and Thampanoor Bus Stand, with spacious rooms (some a/c), a/c veg restaurant, bank, travel agent, car rental, beauty parlour, cybercafé, bookshop and bar. ❹–❻

KTDC Mascot Mascot Junction, near Indian Airlines office ☎0471/231 8990, ⓦwww .ktdc.com. KTDC's upmarket hotel occupies an atmospheric period building with long corridors and huge non-a/c and a/c rooms. There are a swimming pool, bar and restaurant, and it's conveniently located near all the museums. ❽–❾

Navaratna YMCA Rd, southeast of Secretariat ☎0471/233 1784, ⓔvantnam@yahoo.com. Run-of-the-mill place in the centre of town offering pleasant enough a/c and non-a/c rooms. The restaurant is reasonably priced and serves everything from beef and pork to duck. ❸–❻

Pankaj MG Rd, opposite the Secretariat ☎0471/246 4645, ⓦwww.hotelpankaj.com. Stylish and well-maintained three-star hotel. Some rooms have beautiful views over the trees, as does the good Keralan restaurant. Tariff includes buffet breakfast. ❼–❾

Prasanth Aristo Rd ☎0471/232 7180. One of a crop of rock-bottom and very basic family-run guesthouses near the station. The non-a/c rooms have attached bathrooms and are ranged around a courtyard. The *Sajin* and *Salrah* next door are similar. ❷

Residency Tower Press Rd ☎0471/233 1661, ⓦresidencytower.com. A centrally located, top-end business hotel with reasonable a/c rooms, rooftop restaurant and cocktail bar. ❽–❾

The South Park MG Rd ☎0471/233 3333, ⓦwww.thesouthpark.com. Comfortable, business-oriented Welcomgroup four-star with central a/c, an efficient travel agency, multi-cuisine restaurant and 24hr coffee shop. Popular with tour groups and flight crews so book in advance. ❽–❾

Sree Devi Off Aristo Rd ☎ 0471/233 7195. Small budget hotel within easy reach of the railway station, offering very basic but clean en-suite rooms. ❶
Sukhvas Manjalikulam Rd ☎ 0471/233 1967. Nothing special, but a reliable and cheaper back-up if the nearby *Highland* is full. Small rooms with TV and attached bathroom, and some singles available. ❸

YWCA Spencer Junction ☎ 0471/247 7308. Spotless en-suite doubles on the fourth floor of an office block. Friendly, safe and central with neat non-a/c rooms, but the puritanical order and quiet is slightly overwhelming and the place is locked at 10.30pm sharp. Primarily for women, but couples and men welcome. ❸

The City

Thiruvananthapuram's centre can be explored easily on foot, though you might be glad of a rickshaw ride (around Rs20) back from the museums and parks, close to the top end of MG Road. The historical and spiritual heart of town is in the **Fort area**, at the southern end of **MG Road**, which encloses the Shri Padmanabhaswamy Vishnu temple. Following MG Road north leads you through the main shopping district, which is busy all day, and especially choked when one of the frequent, but generally orderly, political demonstrations converges on the grand colonial **Secretariat** building halfway along.

Fort area

A solid but unremarkable fort gateway leads from near the Kovalam Bus Stand at East Fort to the **Shri Padmanabhaswamy temple**, which is still controlled by the Travancore royal family. Unusually for Kerala, it's built in the Dravidian style of Tamil Nadu, with a tall *gopura* gateway, but it's surrounded by high fortress-like walls, and is closed to non-Hindus. Most of Padmanabhaswamy's buildings date from the eighteenth century, added by Raja Marthanda Varma to the much older shrine within. According to legend, the temple was founded after Vishnu – disguised as a beautiful child – merged into a huge tree in the forest, which immediately crashed to the ground. There it transformed into an image of the reclining Vishnu, a full 13km long. Divakara, a sage who witnessed this, was frustrated by his limited human vision, and prayed to Vishnu to assume a form that he could view in its entirety. Vishnu complied, and the temple appeared.

The area in front of Shri Padmanabhaswamy, where devotees bathe in a huge tank, is lined with stalls selling religious souvenirs such as shell necklaces, puja offerings, jasmine and marigolds, as well as the ubiquitous plaster-cast models of Kathakali masks. As you approach the main entrance, the red-brick CVN Kalari Sangam, a **Kalarippayat martial arts** gymnasium, is on the left. From 6.30am to 8am (Mon–Sat) you can watch the students practising Kalarippayat fighting exercises. Foreigners may join courses in the gym, arranged through the head teacher, although prior experience of martial arts and/or dance is a prerequisite; three-month courses are also available for Rs500, but you'll have to find your own accommodation. You can also come here for a traditional **Ayurvedic massage**, and to consult the gym's expert Ayurvedic doctors (Mon–Sat 10am–1pm & 5–7.30pm, Sun 10am–1pm).

Along the north side of the tank, the path that leads past the temple entrances makes for an atmospheric walk, particularly in the early morning and at dusk, when devotees make their way to and from prayers (a closed iron gate bars the northern side, but everybody climbs through the gap). During the days of Kerala's extraordinarily strict caste system, this was a "no go" area for some members of the community – possibly on pain of death.

Behind the temple on West Fort, set back from the road across open ground, the Margi school of **Kathakali** dance/drama and **Kutiyattam** theatre (see

Festivals of Thiruvananthapuram

The annual **Nishangandi Dance and Music festival** (February 22–27) is held at Kanakakannu Palace, just to the east of the public gardens, originally built as a cultural venue for the maharajas of Tiruvananthapuram. A large amphitheatre in the formal gardens is a pleasant place to take in an evening of classical dances and music by Indian artists. Ask at a KTDC Tourist Office for details.

The **Arattu** festival, centred around the Shri Padmanabhaswamy temple, takes place biannually, in Meenam (March/April) and Thulam (Oct/Nov). Each time, ten days of festivities inside the temple (open to Hindus only) culminate in a procession through the streets of the city, taking the deity, Padmanabhaswamy, to the sea for ritual immersion. Five caparisoned elephants, armed guards, a *nagaswaram* (double-reed wind instrument) and *tavil* drum group are led by the maharaja of Travancore, in his symbolic role as *kshatrya*, the servant of the god. Instead of the richly apparelled figure that might be expected, the maharaja (no longer officially recognized) wears a simple white *dhoti*, with his chest bare save for the sacred thread. Rather than riding, he walks the whole way, bearing a sword. To the accompaniment of a 21-gun salute and music, the procession sets off from the east gate of the temple at around 5pm, moving at a brisk pace to reach Shankhumukham Beach at sunset, about an hour later. The route is lined with devotees, many of whom honour both the god and the maharaja. After the seashore ceremonies, the cavalcade returns to the temple at about 9pm, to be greeted by another gun salute. An extremely loud firework display rounds off the day.

For ten days in March, Muslims celebrate **Chandanakudam Maholsavam** at the Beemapalli mosque, 5km southwest of the city on the coastal road towards the airport. The Hindu-influenced festival commemorates the anniversary of the death of Beema Beevi, a woman revered for her piety. On the first, most important, day, pilgrims converge on the mosque carrying earthenware pots decorated with flowers and containing money offerings. Activities such as the sword form of *daharamuttu* take place inside the mosque, while outside there is dance and music. In the early hours of the morning, a flag is brought out from Beema Beevi's tomb and taken on a procession, accompanied by a *panchavadyam* drum and horn orchestra and capari-soned elephants, practices normally associated with Hindu festivals. Once more, the rest of the night is lit up with fireworks.

The great Keralan festival of **Onam** (late August or September) takes place through-out the state over ten days during the coolest time of year, when Keralans remember the reign of King Mahabali, a legendary figure who, it is believed, achieved an ideal balance of harmony, wealth and justice during his tenure. Unfortunately, the gods became upset and envious at Mahabali's success and so Vishnu came to pack him off to another world. However, once a year the king was allowed to return to his people for ten days, and Onam is a joyful celebration of the royal visit. Families display their wealth, feasts and boat races are held and, in Tiruvananthapuram, there's a week-long cultural festival of dance and music culminating in a colourful street carnival Check with any KTDC office for further details and dates.

p.717) is housed in Fort High School. With prior notice you can watch classes; this is the place to ask about authentic Kathakali performances.

Puttan Malika Palace

The **Puttan Malika Palace** (Tues–Sun 8.30am–12.30pm & 3–5.30pm; Rs20, camera Rs15), immediately southeast of the temple, became the seat of the Travancore rajas after they left Padmanabhapuram at the end of the nineteenth century. To generate funds for much-needed restoration, the Travancore royal family has opened the palace to the public for the first time in more than two hundred years. Although much of it remains off-limits, you can wander around some of the most impressive wings, which have been converted into a **museum**. Cool chambers, with highly polished plaster floors and lined with delicately carved wooden screens, house a crop of dusty Travancore heirlooms. Among the predictable array of portraits, royal regalia and weapons are some genuine treasures, such as a solid crystal throne given by the Dutch, and some fine murals. The real highlight however, is the elegant Keralan architecture itself. Beneath sloping red-tiled roofs, hundreds of wooden pillars, carved into the forms of rampant horses, prop up the eaves, with airy verandas projecting onto the surrounding lawns. The royal family have always been keen patrons of the arts, and the tradition is upheld with an open-air **Carnatic music festival**, held in the grounds during the festival of Navaratri (Oct/Nov). Performers sit on the palace's raised porch, flanked by the main facade, with the spectators seated on the lawn. For details, ask at the KTDC tourist office.

MG Road: markets and shopping

An assortment of **craft shops** along **MG Road**, north of Station Road, sell sandalwood, brass and Keralan bell-metal oil lamps (see box on p.424). The Gandhian **Khadi Gramodyog**, between Pazhavangadi and Overbridge junctions, stocks handloom cloth (dig around for the best stuff), plus radios and cassette machines manufactured by the Women's Federation. **Natesan's Antique Arts**, further up, is part of a chain that specializes in paintings, temple wood-carvings and so forth. Prices are high, but they usually have some beautiful pieces, among them some superb reproduction Thanjavur paintings and traditional inlaid chests for Kathakali costumes.

At first glance most of the **bookstores** in the area seem largely intended for exam entrants, but some, such as the a/c **Continental Books** on MG Road, stock a good choice of titles in English – mostly relating to India – and a fair selection of fiction too. Smaller, but with a wide array of English-language fiction and assorted subjects, such as philosophy, history and music, **DC Books**, on Statue Road, on the first floor of a building above Statue Junction, is well worth a browse. Other bookshops along MG Road include the chain store **Higginbothams** and **Paico Books**.

Almost at the top of MG Road, on the right-hand side, the excellent little **Connemara Market** is the place to pick up odds and ends, such as dried and fresh fish, fruit, vegetables, coconut scrapers, crude wooden toys, coir, woven winnowing baskets and Christmas decorations. The workshops of several **tailors** are within the market.

The Napier Museum and Shri Chitra Art Gallery

A minute's walk east from the north end of MG Road, opposite the KTDC Visitors Centre, brings you to the entrance to Thiruvananthapuram's **Public Gardens**. As well as serving as a welcome refuge from the noise of the city – its lawns are usually filled with courting couples, students and picnicking families – the park holds an eminently missable zoo and the city's best museums. Give the dusty and uninformative Natural History Museum a miss and head instead for the extraordinary **Napier Museum** of arts and crafts (Tues–Sun 10am–5pm; Rs6). Designed at the end of the nineteenth century by architect Robert Fellowes Chisolm (1840–1915), it was an early experiment in what became known as the "Indo-Saracenic" style, with tiled, double-storey gabled roofs, garish red-, black- and salmon-patterned brickwork, and, above the main entrance, a series of pilasters forming Islamic arches. The spectacular interior boasts stained-glass windows, a wooden ceiling and loud turquoise, pink, red and yellow stripes on the walls. The architect, Robert Fellowes Chisolm, set out to incorporate Keralan elements into colonial architecture; the museum was named after his employer, Lord Napier, the governor of the Madras Presidency. Highlights of the collection include fifteenth-century Keralan woodcarvings from Kulathupuzha, gold necklaces and belts, minutely detailed ivory work, a carved temple chariot (*rath*), wooden models of Guruvayur temple and an oval temple theatre (*kuttambalam*), plus twelfth-century Chola and fourteenth-century Vijayanagar bronzes.

The attractive **Shri Chitra Art Gallery** (Tues–Sun 10am–5pm; Rs5), opposite, with its curved veranda and tiled roof, houses some splendid paintings from the Rajput, Moghul and Tanjore schools, as well as China, Tibet and Japan. The works by Raja Ravi Varma (1848–1906), who is widely credited with having introduced oil painting to India, have been criticized for their sentimentality and Western influence, but his treatment of Hindu mythological themes is both dramatic and beautiful. Also on display are paintings by the Russian artist-philosopher and mystic, Nicholas Roerich, who arrived in India at the turn of the twentieth century. His spiritually oriented, strongly coloured Himalayan landscapes reflect his love of the region. Roerich lived out his latter years in Nagar (in the Kulu valley), where he died in 1947.

Away from the centre

The **Chachu Nehru Children's Museum** (Tues–Sun 10am–5pm; free), in Thycaud in the east of the city, serves as a rather dusty testament to the enthusiasm of an anonymous collector back in the 1960s. One room contains ritual masks, probably from Bengal, Rajasthan and Orissa, while the rest of the place is taken up with stamps, health-education displays and over two thousand dolls

Kalarippayat

Started in the thirteenth-century, **Kalarippayat** is a ferocious Keralan martial art which uses hand-to-hand combat and weapons. It is believed to have been developed by the bodyguards of medieval warlords and chieftains, though there are many other theories surrounding its origins, including a legend that the martial art was introduced by the warrior sage **Parasuram**, who reclaimed the land of Kerala from the ocean by throwing his *mazhu* (battle axe) into the ocean. Others believe that **Lord Shiva** himself was the founder of Kalarippayat, and that Parasuram and **Agasthya** (another illustrious sage linked to the form) were Shiva's disciples. Yet another theory among the practitioners of Kalarippayat is that **Bodhi Dharma**, the Buddhist monk from South India, took the form to China and the Far East, when he made his epic journey to spread the faith.

In the eighteenth century Kalarippayat was banned by the British, but it has since made a strong comeback. Kalarippayat has two distinct **schools** – the southern system and the northern system. The southern system places particular emphasis on footwork and the use of hands in combat, involving a complicated range of moves, blows and locks. The northern system is more complex and uses four basic stages of training for battle. The first stage, **Meythari**, is a series of twelve levels of body exercise. The second stage, **Kothari**, uses wooden replica weapons. The third stage, **Ankathari**, involves training with real medieval weapons such as the *udaval* (sword), *paricha* (shield), *kadaras* (dagger), *kuntham* (spear), *gadha* (mace) and *urumi* (a long flexible sword). The final stage, **Verum Kaythari**, involves barehanded combat against an armed enemy and is for advanced practitioners only. Kalarippayat demonstrations are never dull, and injuries, although rare, do happen. Traditionally practised by the martial Nair caste, Kalarippayat is popular today with Hindus, Muslims and Christians alike. For details of a place to learn Kalarippayat, see p.348 & p.352.

featuring figures in Indian costume, American presidents, Disney characters and British Beefeaters.

Also on the eastern side of town, visitors can, by arrangement, watch classes in the martial art of **Kalarippayat** (see box on p.351), at the PS Balachandran Nair Kalari **martial arts gymnasium**, Kalariyil, TC 15/854, Cotton Hill, Vazhuthakad (daily 6–8am & 6–7.30pm). Built of stone in 1992 along traditional lines, the *kalari* fighting pit is overlooked from a height of 4m by a viewing gallery. Students (some as young as eight) train both in unarmed combat and in the use of weapons. The school arranges short courses in Kalarippayat, and can also provide guides for forest trekking.

Eating

Thiruvananthapuram offers menus for all tastes and budgets, although smart **restaurants** specializing in Keralan cuisine are thin on the ground. Most of the mid- to top-range hotels include a few local dishes in their standard multi-cuisine menus, and the *Pankaj* and *Horizon* both have pleasant rooftop restaurants, while the *South Park* hotel's restaurant occasionally has live Carnatic music. For full-flavoured Keralan meals or cheap *dosa*-type snacks, eat with the locals in the numerous small *udipi* cafés dotted around town.

Moving on from Thiruvananthapuram

Thiruvananthapuram is the main transport hub for traffic along the coast and cross-country. Towns within a couple of hours of the capital – such as Varkala and Kollam – are most quickly and conveniently reached by **bus**. For longer hauls, though, you're better off travelling by **train**, as buses tend to hurtle along the coastal highway at terrifying speeds; they're also more crowded. JAICO produces an excellent monthly guide with timetables and comprehensive travel details for Kerala and beyond; it's available from bookshops, Thampanoor bus stand and the railway station for Rs10.

For an overview of transport from Thiruvananthapuram, see "Travel details", p.438.

By air

From Thiruvananthapuram's **airport**, there are Jet Airways, Indian Airlines and Air India flights to **Bangalore, Chennai, Delhi, Mumbai and Trichy**. Indian Airlines and Air Maldives also fly daily to **Malé** in the **Maldives**, with additional services on Fridays and Sundays. SriLankan Airlines operates one or two flights daily to **Colombo** in Sri Lanka.

By bus

From the KSRTC **Thampanoor Bus Stand** (☎0471/232 3886), frequent services run north through Kerala to Kollam, Alappuzha to Ernakulam/Kochi. Two buses a day go up to Thekkady for the Periyar Wildlife Reserve and there are six buses daily to Kanniyakumari. Most state buses heading eastwards or southwards are operated by the Tamil Nadu State Road Transport Corporation (TNSRTC; ☎0471/232 7756) and include eight daily buses to Chennai via Madurai. **Tickets** for all the services listed above may be booked in advance at the reservations hatch on the main bus stand concourse; note that the TNSRTC has its own counter. Numerous private bus companies also run inter-state services; many of the agents are on Aristo Road near the *Greenland Lodging*.

By train

Kerala's capital is well connected **by train** with other towns and cities in the country, although getting seats at short notice on long-haul journeys can be a problem.

Amma Station Rd. Blissful a/c and conveniently near the stations, offering the usual South Indian snacks and no less than seven different types of *uttappam* (rice pancake).

Ananda Bhavan MG Rd. Cheap, simple restaurant offering fresh regional veg meals.

Arya Niwas *Arya Niwas* hotel, Aristo Junction, Thampanoor. Excellent Indian vegetarian food served in a spotless dining room on the hotel's ground floor. Hugely popular with locals and justifiably so.

Food World Anna's Arcade, Spencer Junction, MG Rd. Bakery-cum-supermarket where you can buy tasty savoury and sweet pastries and cakes. No seating.

Indian Coffee House (I) LMS Junction. Opposite the entrance to the Public Gardens, this is a clean and busy place to down a refreshing cold coffee after visiting the museums. Also does excellent omelettes and South Indian snacks, and low-cost meals are available all day.

Indian Coffee House (II) Spencer Junction, MG Rd. All the usual Indian Coffee House fare in a small, colonial-style building set back from the road.

Indian Coffee House (III) Station Rd. Next to the bus station and unbeatable for breakfast or a quick snack. Turbaned waiters serve *dosas*, *vadas*, omelettes and hot drinks in a bizarre spiral building. Obligatory cultural and gastronomic pit-stop, and very cheap too.

Kalavara Press Rd. Situated on the same stretch as several bookshops, *Kalavara* is an upstairs restaurant which features a mixed menu and local cuisine, including pork and beef dishes.

Kerala House & Akash Ganga Statue Rd. Good-value Keralan cuisine in the basement *Kerala House*, and more upmarket local dishes and good views at *Akash Ganga* on the rooftop.

KTDC Chaithram Station Rd. Two moderately priced restaurants, one pure veg and the other Mughlai-style. The former, a tastefully decorated

Reservations should be made as far in advance as possible from the efficient computerized booking office at the station (Mon–Sat 8am–2pm & 2.15–8pm, Sun 8am–2pm). Sleepers are sold throughout Kerala on a first-come, first-served basis, not on local stations' quotas.

The following trains are recommended as the **fastest** and/or **most convenient** from Thiruvananthapuram.

Recommended trains from Thiruvananthapuram

Destination	Name	Number	Frequency	Departs	Total time
Bangalore	Kanniyakumari–Bangalore Express	#6525	daily	12.55pm	18hr
Chennai	Triv'–Chennai Mail*	#2624	daily	2.30pm	16hr 30min
Delhi	Rajdhani Express**	#2431	Tues & Thurs	7.15pm	42hr 35min
	Kerala Express	#2625	daily	11.30am	52hr 30min
Ernakulam (Kochi)	Kerala Express	#2625	daily	11.30am	4hr
Kanniyakumari	Kanniyakumari Exp	#1081	daily	9.55am	2hr
Kollam	Kerala Express	#2625	daily	11.30am	1hr 5min
Kozhikode	Triv'–Kannur Exp	#6347	daily	8.45pm	10hr 30min
Madgaon (Goa)	Netravati Express	#6346	daily	10am	20hr 20min
Mangalore	Parasuram Exp***	#6349	daily	6.10am	15hr
	Malabar Express***	#6329	daily	6.20pm	15hr 30min
Mumbai	Netravati Exp***	#6346	daily	10am	30hr 55min

* via Kollam, Kottayam, Ernakulam and Palakkad
** a/c only
*** via Kollam, Ernakulam, Thrissur, Kozhikode, Kannur, Kasargode

air-cooled place, is the better of the two, offering good-value Keralan specialities and a standard range of rice-based North Indian dishes.

Prime Restaurant Prime Square, near the bus station. A tiny, cheap *dhaba*-style restaurant with tasty North and South Indian dishes.

Listings

Airlines Air India, Museum Rd, Vellayambalam Circle ☎0471/231 0310 (airport ☎0471/250 1426); Air Maldives, Spencer Rd ☎0471/24 6341; British Airways, Vellayambalam ☎0471/232 6604; Gulf Air, Vellayambalam ☎0471/232 8003; Indian Airlines, Air Centre, Mascot Junction ☎0471/231 6870 (airport ☎0471/250 1542); Jet Airways, Akshaya Towers, 1st Floor, Sasthamangalam Junction ☎0471/272 1018 (airport ☎0471/250 0710); KLM/Northwest, Spencer Junction ☎0471/246 3531; SriLankan Airlines, Spencer Building, Palayam, MG Rd ☎0471/247 1815.

Ayurvedic health centres Contact the Ayurvedic Medical College Hospital, MG Rd ☎0471/246 0823. For Kayachikitsa or traditional Ayurvedic massage and foot therapy, contact Agastheswara, Ayurvedic Health Centre, Jiji Nivas, Killi, Kattakkada ☎0471/229 1270.

Banks and exchange The State Bank of India, near the Secretariat on MG Rd, changes travellers' cheques and currency. The State Bank of Travancore, at Statue Junction and the domestic airport terminal accepts travellers' cheques, cash, Visa and Mastercard. Thomas Cook has a counter at the airport and an office at Tourindia, MG Rd. There's a Central Reserve Bank branch and Andhra Bank ATM at the *KTDC Chaitram* and an Idbi Bank ATM near the Secretariat on MG Rd.

Car rental Nataraj Travels, Thampanoor ☎0471/232 3034; Swastik Travels, MG Rd ☎0471/233 1770; Travel India, opposite the Secretariat, MG Rd ☎0471/247 8208.

Dance and drama For Kathakali and Kutiyattam check with the Margi School (see p.348) or the tourist office on Station Rd (see p.345), which can also supply info on the Nishagandi Festival at the open-air Nishagandhi Auditorium in the first week of April.

Hospitals General Hospital, near Holy Angels Convent, Vanchiyur ☎0471/244 3870; Ramakrishna Mission Hospital, Sastamangalam ☎0471/232 2123.

Internet access Of the many outlets, the most efficient is at the *KTDC Chaithram* hotel on Station Rd (Rs30 per hr). Alternatively, try Megabyte on MG Rd or Tandem Communications at Statue Junction.

Pharmacies Central Medical Stores, amongst others, at Statue Junction, MG Rd.

Post office The main post office, with poste restante (daily 8am–6pm), is on MG Rd, south of the Secretariat.

Travel agents Airtravel Enterprises (good for air tickets), New Corporation Building, MG Rd, Palayam ☎0471/232 3900; Aries Travels (specialists for tours to the Maldives), Ayswarya Building, Press Rd ☎0471/233 0964; Tourindia (pioneering cruise and tour operators), MG Rd ☎0471/233 0437.

Yoga The Sivananda Yoga Ashram at 37/1929 Airport Rd, Palkulangara, West Fort (☎0471/245 0942), holds daily classes at various levels. Better still, head for Neyyar Dam (see box on p.366), 28km east of town, where the world-famous Dhanwanthari ashram offers excellent two-week introductory courses amid idyllic mountain surroundings.

South of Thiruvananthapuram

Despite the fact that virtually the entire 550-kilometre length of the **Keralan coast** is lined with sandy beaches, rocky promontories and coconut palms, **Kovalam** is one of the only places where swimming in the sea is not considered eccentric by locals, and which offers accommodation to suit all budgets. To experience the slow rhythms of daily life away from the exploits of the Kovalam beach scene, you can take an easy wander through the shady toddy groves to villages such as **Pachalloor** and **Vizhinjam**. A finely preserved example of Keralan architecture is also within easy reach of Thiruvananthapuram; 63km to the south is the magnificent palace of **Padmanabhapuram**, former capital of the kingdom of Travancore.

Kovalam

The coastal village of **KOVALAM** may lie just 14km south of Thiruvananthapuram but, as Kerala's most developed **beach resort**, it's a world away from the rest of the state. Each year greater numbers of Western visitors – budget travellers and package tourists alike – arrive in search of sun, sea and palm-fringed beaches. For many travellers it has become, with Goa and Mamallapuram, the third essential stop on a triangular tour of tropical South Indian "paradises" – or indeed another leg of the trail along the coasts of South Asia. Europeans have been visiting Kovalam since the 1930s, but no hotels were built until hippies started to colonize the place some thirty years later. As the resort's popularity began to grow, more and more paddy fields were filled and the first luxury holiday complexes sprang up. These soon caught the eye of European charter companies scouting for "undiscovered" beach hideaways to supplement their Goa brochures, and since the mid-1990s plane loads of package tourists have flown here direct from Europe. This influx has had a dramatic impact on Kovalam, with rocketing prices and burgeoning numbers of Kashmiri souvenir shops and pricey fish restaurants. Taller than the palm-trees, the concrete hotels certainly detract from Kovalam's original charm, and these, together with tenacious touts strutting their irritating stuff, have led to Kovalam's detractors calling it "the Costa del Kerala".

Arrival, information and getting around

Buses (20min; marked in English) from platform #9 (the furthest south) at Thiruvananthapuram's East Fort loop through Kovalam and stop at the gates to the *Kovalam Beach Resort* complex, on the promontory between Hawah and Kovalam beaches. If you're not intending to stay here or on Samudra Beach get off the bus just past *Hotel Blue Sea* where the road forks – the left road leads down to Hawah Beach. It's also possible to take an **auto-rickshaw** or **taxi** all the way from Thiruvananthapuram; auto-rickshaws cost between Rs80 and Rs100 but will try to get away with a lot more, while taxis charge around Rs150. There are a lot of commission-seeking touts working in Kovalam, so if you've already got a hotel in mind, give them a wide berth – walking round the back paths is a good ploy.

The friendly **tourist facilitation centre** (daily 10am–5pm, closed Sun in low season; ☏0471/248 0085), just inside the *Kovalam Beach Resort* gates, has plenty of leaflets to give out and up-to-date advice about cultural events. They also run a small **reading room** next door (same hours) which holds British and American newspapers and novels.

There are plenty of places to **change money** in Kovalam, but private exchange rates can vary so it's best to check beforehand. The Central Bank of India is at the *Kovalam Beach Resort* and the Andhra Bank at KTDC *Samudra*. Reliable private operators include Pheroze Framroze Foreign Exchange (daily 9.30am–7pm) near the bus stand, and *Wilson's* hotel (see p.359).

Western Travels (daily 8am–8pm; ☏0471/248 1334) near the bus stand is a reliable agent for flight confirmations and ticketing, and can arrange **car rental**. Voyager Travels, near the police station (☏0471/2481993) specializes in **motorbike rental** (Enfield Bullet Rs350–500 per day; scooter Rs250) at competitive rates. **Surfboards** can be rented on Lighthouse Beach for an extortionate Rs250 per hour, or boogie boards for Rs50. Alternatively, for around Rs300 you can also take a ride on a traditional **kettumaran** (*kettu* meaning tied; *maran* logs), which gave the catamaran its name. Widely used by the fishermen of Kovalam, the rudimentary boat consists of five logs tied together, and feels fairly fragile in a choppy sea.

Keralan Ayurvedic treatments

The ancient system of **Ayurvedic herbal medicine**, dating back to the sixth century BC, has been experiencing a healthy resurgence over the last few decades (see p.47), and nowhere more so than in Kerala. Institutes such as the Ayurvedic Medical College on MG Road in Thiruvananthapuram have been making tremendous steps with their research, which has resulted in Keralan Ayurveda being well regarded in medical circles.

Ayurveda, which aims to eliminate the toxic imbalances that cause the body to become susceptible to ill-health, concentrates on the well-being of the individual as a whole and not just the affected part. The best time for treatment is during the monsoon from June till November, when the atmosphere remains cool and free of dust. The most common form of Ayurveda in Kerala is **massage**, which uses oils and herbs in a course of treatment, either for rejuvenation or as remedies. Rejuvenation therapy, or *Rasayan Chikitsa*, advocates face and head massage using medicated oils and creams, body massage using hands and feet, and medicated baths. *Kayaka-lpachikitsa*, whose primary objective is to control the ageing process, concentrates on diet. *Sweda Karma*, used in the treatment of certain rheumatic illnesses, uses medicated steam baths to improve tone and reduce fat. Other therapeutic treatments include *Dhara*, for mental disorders, and *Pizhichil*, for the treatment of rheumatic diseases and nervous disorders; both involve courses of between seven and twenty-one days. Among numerous remedies available in Keralan Ayurveda, *Snehapanam* prescribes medicated ghee and is aimed at curing osteoarthritis and leukaemia.

Ayurvedic massage is advertised everywhere in Kovalam. "Ayurvedic centres" offer cheap massages, usually costing Rs250–500, and you'll constantly be approached by men professing to be well-qualified Ayurvedic practitioners – they even show you impressive certificates. However, most of the so-called Ayurvedic centres along Lighthouse Beach are seasonal, as are the "doctors" and "masseurs", and there have been an increasing number of complaints about sexual harassment during sessions, serious skin reactions to dodgy Ayurvedic oils and post-massage pains and problems. For genuine Ayurvedic massages, the safest bet is to head for the more reputable hotels who offer Ayurveda, such as *KTDC Samudra, Kovalam Beach Resort* and the *Blue Sea*, or talk with other travellers and go by word of mouth. Alternatively, contact the Ayurveda College in Thiruvanathapuram (℡0471/246 0823) for a recommended practitioner in Kovalam.

Throughout Kerala, you'll find that almost all upmarket hotels have an Ayurvedic massage centre, and many offer designer all-inclusive "Ayurvedic rejuvenation programmes", which range from five days to a month and include special food and a consultancy with an Ayurvedic doctor. The doctors at such establishments are likely to be pukka (ask to see their qualifications), as the reputation of the hotel is at stake. Otherwise, Thiruvananthapuram (see "Listings" on p.354) and Kochi (p.397) both have well-established Ayurvedic hospitals where they'll point you in the direction of a reliable local practitioner.

Plenty of places offer **Internet** access for around Rs40–50 per hour. Kovalam doesn't have a major **bookshop**, but many of the tailors and clothes stalls supplement their trade by dealing in the usual hit-and-miss selection of second-hand books.

Accommodation

Kovalam is crammed with **accommodation**, ranging from budget to five-star hilltop chalets. Only decent rock-bottom rooms are hard to find, as all but a handful of the many budget travellers' guesthouses have been upgraded to suit the large number of package tourists who flock here over Christmas and the

New Year. This also means that hotels are often block-booked weeks in advance, so it's a good idea to make a reservation before you arrive, which also spares you from the tenacious touts who hang around the bus stand. The main concentration of mid-range hotels is around the **Lighthouse Beach** area, while quieter **Samudra Beach** has a couple of upmarket places and few simple ones. The best of the resorts, such as *Lagoona Davina* (see p.361) and *Surya Samudra* (see box, p.359), are a little further away and require transport.

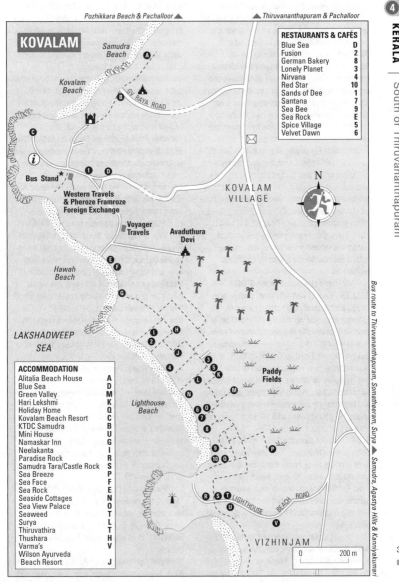

Pozhikkara Beach & Pachalloor ▲   ▲ Thiruvananthapuram & Pachalloor

KOVALAM

Samudra Beach

Kovalam Beach

GV RAYA ROAD

Bus Stand ★

Western Travels & Pheroze Framroze Foreign Exchange

Voyager Travels

Avaduthura Devi

Hawah Beach

KOVALAM VILLAGE

N

LAKSHADWEEP SEA

Paddy Fields

Lighthouse Beach

VIZHINJAM

LIGHTHOUSE BEACH ROAD

RESTAURANTS & CAFÉS	
Blue Sea	D
Fusion	2
German Bakery	8
Lonely Planet	3
Nirvana	4
Red Star	10
Sands of Dee	1
Santana	7
Sea Bee	9
Sea Rock	E
Spice Village	5
Velvet Dawn	6

ACCOMMODATION	
Alitalia Beach House	A
Blue Sea	D
Green Valley	M
Hari Lekshmi	K
Holiday Home	Q
Kovalam Beach Resort	C
KTDC Samudra	B
Mini House	U
Namaskar Inn	G
Neelakanta	I
Paradise Rock	R
Samudra Tara/Castle Rock	S
Sea Breeze	P
Sea Face	F
Sea Rock	E
Seaside Cottages	N
Sea View Palace	O
Seaweed	T
Surya	L
Thiruvathira	H
Thushara	V
Varma's	
Wilson Ayurveda Beach Resort	J

0   200 m

Bus route to Thiruvananthapuram, Somatheeram, Surya ▲ Samudra, Agastya Hills & Kanniyakumari

Prices are extortionate compared with the rest of Kerala, almost doubling in peak season (Dec to mid-Jan), when you'll be lucky to find a basic room for less than Rs300. At other times, haggling should bring the rate down by twenty to fifty percent, especially if you stay for more than a week. The codes below are for high-season prices.

Alitalia Beach House Samudra Beach ⊤0471/248 0042. Away from the razzmatazz of Lighthouse Beach, this is the cheapest option on Samudra. Characterful and clean, with a great roof terrace and four octagonal rooms arranged around a courtyard with a palm tree in the middle. ❺

Blue Sea 100m before junction to Hawah Beach ⊤0471/248 1401, ⓦwww.hotelbluesea .net. Friendly hotel with homely atmosphere and aesthetically pleasing architecture: the best rooms are in unusual circular towers set amidst lovely gardens. Also has a swimming pool, Ayurvedic treatments, good restaurant and free airport pick-ups. ❸–❽

Green Valley Lighthouse Beach ⊤0471/248 0636, ⓔindira_ravi@hotmail.com. Set amid paddy fields, this is one of the best budget places in Kovalam, with pleasant en-suite rooms ranged around leafy and secluded courtyards. Great value singles, but a bit of a mozzie problem. ❹

Hari Lekshmi Lighthouse Beach ⊤0471/248 1341. Small guesthouse offering four spotless, good-value white-painted rooms with attached bathrooms, and there's a relaxing communal veranda. ❸

Holiday Home Lighthouse Beach ⊤0471/248 6382. Two rows of well-appointed cottage-like rooms, built in traditional Keralan style with spacious individual wooden verandas and set in a quiet little garden. No sea views, but good value. ❸

Kovalam Beach Resort On the headland overlooking Kovalam Beach ⊤0471/248 0101, ⓦwww .kovalamhotel.com. Four complexes of chalets and "cottages" in Charles Correa's award-winning hilltop block. Bars, restaurants, pools, yoga centre and tennis courts make this Kovalam's swankiest option, but it's swarming with VIP security personnel and tour groups. Rooms $125–175. ❾

KTDC Samudra Samudra Beach ⊤0471/248 0089, ⓦwww.ktdc.com. Posh government-run three-star, set away from other hotels in manicured gardens overlooking Kovalam Beach. All rooms (from Rs3000) are sea-facing, with hammocks outside, and there's a lovely swimming pool, as well as a restaurant and a good Ayurvedic massage centre. ❾

Mini House Lighthouse Beach Rd ⊤0471/248 0867, ⓔnaswara@hotmail.com. Six large non-a/c rooms with balconies in a great location right over the rocks and the breaking sea. The nicest of the

cluster of places around this road, if a bit over-priced. ❺–❻

Namaskar Inn Hawah Beach ⊤0471/248 1903, ⓔnamaskar@yahoo.co.in. Two choice rooms occupying an entire floor – both are sunny, tastefully decorated and have two walls of windows looking out to sea. The other rooms are standard en-suite doubles with no views to speak of. ❺–❼

Neelakanta Behind Lighthouse Beach ⊤0471/248 1321, ⓦwww.neelakantakovalam.com. Slightly more tasteful than the other big resorts: all rooms have private balconies and sea views, and there's an Ayurvedic centre on site. ❻–❾

Paradise Rock Lighthouse Beach Rd ⊤0471/248 0658, ⓔvisitindia@eth.net. Clean, inexpensive and welcoming place with just four rooms, variously priced according to size and views. ❷–❸

Samudra Tara/Castle Rock Lighthouse Beach Rd ⊤0471/248 1608, ⓔkarithjoshy@msn.com. Three-storey concrete block set above the beach, with comfortable rooms and private balconies. ❹–❻

Sea Breeze Lighthouse Beach ⊤0471/248 0024, ⓦwww.seabreezeayurvedicresort.com. Quiet and secluded place, located in a coconut grove, with large and sunny communal balconies overlooking a tropical garden. Most of the clean and simple rooms are non a/c with attached bathrooms. ❷–❸

Sea Face Hawah Beach ⊤0471/248 1835, ⓦwww.seaface.com. An ugly modern block with three-star pretensions and comfortable rooms, starting at Rs3000; its saving grace is the good swimming pool. ❽–❾

Sea Rock Hawah Beach ⊤0471/248 0422. One of Kovalam's oldest hotels (and much better value than *Sea Face*) with a block of rooms, with or without sea views, right on the seafront and a popular open-air restaurant. ❼–❽

Seaside Cottages Lighthouse Beach ⊤0471/248 1934, ⓔmjnair@asianetindia.com. The least expensive place to stay right on the beach, with simple rooms in a row, each with a small sea-facing balcony. ❸

Sea View Palace Lighthouse Beach ⊤0471/248 1599, ⓔhotelseaviewpalace@hotmail.com. Set back from the beach but with unobstructed sea views. The eighteen identical rooms have tasteful wooden furniture and common balconies set on three floors. ❺

Seaweed Lighthouse Beach Rd ⊤0471/248 0391, ⓦwww.hotelseaweed.com. Neat, clean and

Two of the most luxurious of Kovalam's resorts lie around 8km to the south by road. The *Surya Samudra* at **Pulinkudi** (☎0471/248 0413, ⓦwww.suryasamudra.com; ⑨) consisting of 21 beautifully presented antique Keralan wood cottages (7 with a/c; $180–520), which spread discreetly along a rocky hillside and look down onto two small beaches. There's also an on-site Ayurvedic centre and an extraordinary swimming pool cut into the rock. Nearby, *Somatheeram*, at Chowera (☎0471/226 8101, ⓦwww.somatheeram.com; ⑧–⑨), was formerly an Ayurvedic hospital and now offers high-quality massage and Ayurvedic treatment in four-star surroundings; comfortable cottages and apartments ($59–227) in exquisite Keralan houses spill down its landscaped hillside to a private beach. If it's full, try its sister concern around the corner, *Manaltheeram* (☎0471/248 1610, ⓦwww.manaltheeram.com; ⑨), which has a narrower range of accommodation ($80–101) and shares the same Ayurvedic facilities. Next to *Surya Samudra*, the *Bethsaida Hermitage* (☎0471/248 1554, ⓦwww.bethsaida-c.org; ⑧–⑨) prides itself as being an ecofriendly beach resort, built without sacrificing a single tree. Set in a superb location, the resort is made up of pleasant but small cottages ($65–120), built in traditional style, and has its own beach and a great restaurant which serves both South and North Indian dishes; Ayurvedic treatment and yoga are also available. The resort belongs to a Christian trust and a percentage of the profits goes to various charitable projects.

For a bit of quiet, head south to **Poovar** at the mouth of the River Neyyar, 20km south of Kovalam (taxis charge Rs200). Here, the *Treasure Island* resort (☎0471/221 2063, ⓕ221 0019; ⑦–⑧), pre-booked through *Wilson Tourist Home* in Kovalam (☎0471/248 0051), occupies a very secluded spot on a palm-studded island. Set in a coconut plantation, the cottages are pleasantly simple but stylish, and there's a swimming pool and the chance to explore this beautiful stretch of the coastline by boat or on foot.

breezy hotel that claims to "get away from all the madness". Some of the 43 rooms ranged around the leafy courtyard have a/c; as usual, those with views cost extra. There's also a pleasant rooftop restaurant. ④–⑥

Surya Lighthouse Beach ☎0471/248 1012, ⓔkovsurya@yahoo.co.in. One of a clutch of iden-tikit, no-frills places tucked behind the main beach, with small but clean rooms, a roof terrace but no views. ②–③

Thiruvathira Lighthouse Beach Rd ☎0471/248 0787. En-suite rooms with private verandas; the more expensive ones have a/c and limited sea views. The comfortable non-a/c rooms at the back are cheaper and offer better value. ③–⑤

Thushara Behind Lighthouse Beach ☎0471/248 1694, ⓦwww.hotelthushara.net. Small, smart midrange hotel where the rooms have private balconies, but no views. There a pool, and rates include continental breakfast. ⑤–⑥

Varma's Lighthouse Beach Rd ☎0471/248 0478, ⓔvarnabeach@hotmail.com. Modern hotel, furnished in traditional Keralan style. The tasteful rooms (a/c costs little extra) feature carved wood, tiles and sea-facing balconies. ⑧

Wilson Ayurveda Beach Resort Lighthouse Beach ☎0471/248 0051. Popular place, worth the extra rupees for its spacious en-suite rooms (some a/c), balconies (some with swinging chairs), garden and friendly staff. Ayurvedic treatments available. ③–⑥

The beaches

Kovalam consists of four, fairly small, stretches of sand; the southernmost, known for obvious reasons as **Lighthouse Beach**, is where most visitors spend their time. It takes about ten minutes to walk from end to end, either along the sand or on the concrete pathway (patrolled by lots of touts) which fronts a long strip of resorts, guesthouses and restaurants. You can hire surfboards, venture out to sea in wooden outriggers (see p.355) or hire beach chairs and parasols for the day. The red-and-white **lighthouse**, on the promontory at the southern end of

Warning: swimming safety

Due to unpredictable rip currents and a strong undertow, especially during the monsoons, **swimming** from Kovalam's beaches is not always safe. The introduction of blue-shirted lifeguards has reduced the annual death toll, but at least a couple of tourists still drown here each year, and many more get into difficulties. Follow the warnings of the safety flags at all times and keep a close eye on children. There's a first-aid post midway along Lighthouse Beach.

the beach, is the area's most prominent landmark and affords superb views, but it's closed to the public.

On the other side of a small rocky headland, **Hawah Beach** functions as a base for local fishermen, who hand-haul their massive nets through the shallows each morning, singing and chanting as they scoop up thrashing multi-hued minnows and coil endless piles of coir rope – the *Sea Rock* terrace (see p.358) is the best vantage point to watch them in action. North of the headland which holds the *Kovalam Beach Resort*, and in full view of its distinctive sloping terraces, is **Kovalam Beach**. Home to a small mosque, it's also used by local fishermen and is the preferred domain of domestic tourists; to get there follow the road just beyond the bus terminus. The next beach north, **Samudra**, is very small, especially at high tide, with a glut of new package-tour resorts surrounding the tiny temple.

If you want to escape the beach scene, head into the cool and shaded **coconut groves** behind Lighthouse Beach's hotel strip. Here, ladies gossip in shrill Malayalam while they wash both clothes and children in the village tank, sewing machines whirr as tailors make hippy gear from unlikely looking materials and children play innovative versions of cricket with coconut shells and sticks. Bear in mind that although the sight of Westerners in skimpy bathing suits on the beach has become relatively normal for locals, it's only polite to dress in a respectful manner when walking in the coconut groves or near Kovalam Beach's mosque.

Eating, drinking and nightlife

Lighthouse Beach is lined with identikit cafés and restaurants specializing in **seafood**: you pick from the fresh fish such as blue marlin, sea salmon, barracuda and delicious seerfish, as well as lobster, tiger prawns, crab and mussels. All are put out on display, then weighed, grilled over a charcoal fire or cooked in a tandoor (traditional clay oven), and served with rice, salad or chips. Meals are **pricey** by Indian standards – typically around Rs150 per head for fish, and double that for lobster or prawns – and service is often painfully slow, but the food is generally very good and the ambience of the beachfront terraces convivial. For **breakfast** you can chose from any number of typical budget-traveller cafés offering the usual brown bread, fruit salad and pancakes, or try the traditional breakfast of *iddli* and *sambar* at one of the cheap cafés along the main road and near the bus stand.

Nightlife in Kovalam is pretty laid-back, and revolves around the beach, where Westerners chill when the restaurants close. Beer, spirits and local *feni* are served in most restaurants, albeit very discreetly due to tight liquor restrictions, to a background of reggae or Pink Floyd. The rave scene that you see in Goa and Gokarn has so far failed to take off in Kovalam, although some restaurants organize beach parties at Christmas and New Year. Several restaurants also run **movie nights**, screening pirate copies of just-released hits. The *Kingfisher*, at the northern end of Lighthouse Beach, occasionally hosts **classical Indian music**, as does the *Blue Sea* hotel, while the *Hotel Neptune*, behind the midpoint of Lighthouse Beach, has regular **kathakali** performances (Mon, Wed & Sat; make-up 5pm, dance 6.45pm).

During your stay in Kovalam you may be offered *charas*, but bear in mind that cannabis is illegal in Kerala, as everywhere else in India, and that the local police occasionally conduct raids.

Blue Sea 100m before junction to Hawah Beach. Well worth the five-minute walk up the hill to sample their excellent garlic prawns or tandoori chicken and to enjoy the Escher-esque architecture.

Fusion Lighthouse Beach. Currently the funkiest place in Kovalam, with three menus (eastern, western and fusion), a fine selection of drinks, the best music on the beach and a toilet that has to be seen to be believed.

German Bakery Lighthouse Beach. Rooftop terrace serving tasty Western food, lots of tempting cakes (try the waffles with chocolate sauce) and fruit lassis. Breakfasts include full English and French (croissants with espresso and a cigarette) options.

Lonely Planet Lighthouse Beach. Congenial, generally inexpensive, veg restaurant tucked away in the paddy fields and overlooking a pond (bring mosquito repellent in the evening). Wide selection of Indian food, including breakfast *iddli*. Thursday evenings see a cultural show with all-you-can-eat buffet (7–9pm; Rs150).

Nirvana Lighthouse Beach. Relaxed seafront restaurant with a wide variety of fish, as well as other Indian, Chinese and continental dishes.

Red Star Lighthouse Beach. Popular with budget travellers, this small shack near the lighthouse offers inexpensive breakfasts, South Indian snacks, lassis and Keralan meals, including fiery fish curries.

Sands of Dee Main Rd, near the bus stand. Large restaurant, colourfully illuminated at night, catering predominantly for domestic tourists with a menu of Indian and Chinese cuisine at mid-range prices.

Santana Lighthouse Beach. One of the best seafood joints with a great barbecue, tandoori fish and chicken, and better music than most.

Sea Bee Lighthouse Beach. Tasty curries and seafood, a nice ambience and a background track of top Indian fusion music. There's usually strong beer available too.

Sea Rock Hawah Beach. Superb seafront location, best enjoyed in the morning when the local fishermen gather on the sand.

Spice Village Behind Lighthouse Beach, next to *Hari Lekshmi*. Set back in a secluded palm grove under a thatched roof and serving good food in a pleasant atmosphere.

Velvet Dawn Lighthouse Beach. One of Kovalam's top fish and seafood places, where you can wash down your meal with a decent beer while watching the beams of the lighthouse revolve.

Pozhikkara beach and Pachalloor village

If you need a break from the rampant commercialism of Kovalam, head north along Samudra Beach for around 4km, passing through a string of fishing hamlets before arriving at a point where the sea merges with the backwaters to form a salt-water lagoon. Although only thirty minutes' walk from the *Kovalam Beach Resort*, the sliver of white sand, known as **Pozhikkara beach**, is a world away from the headlong holiday culture of Kovalam. Here, the sands are used primarily for landing fish and fixing nets, while the thick palm canopy shelters a mixed community of Hindu fishermen and Christian coir makers.

The tranquil village of **PACHALLOOR**, behind the lagoon, is a good alternative base to Thiruvananthapuram or Kovalam. There are two guesthouses here, including the idyllic *Lagoona Davina* (☏0471/238 0049, ⊛www .lagoonadavina.com; ➒), with twenty individually decorated en-suite rooms ($77–137) close to the water. Lazing in a hammock under the palm trees, you can watch fishermen paddling past in their dug-outs and sand-wallahs diving to collect silt. The **food** served in the restaurant – a fusion of authentic Keralan village dishes and European *nouvelle cuisine* – is exceptional, and they organize **backwater trips** (Rs350 per head for 2hr); accompanied by a knowledgeable guide, you're punted around the neighbouring villages, with stops to see coir being made and to identify an amazing wealth of tropical fruit trees, spices and birds. You can also have an Ayurvedic massage or take yoga lessons with the resident doctor. If you book in advance, you'll be met at the airport; otherwise take a taxi 6km along the highway towards Kovalam, and bear right along the "bypass" where the road forks, just after the Thiruvallam bridge. After another 1km or so, a sign on the right-hand side of the road points through the trees to the guesthouse. The other guesthouse at Pachalloor, the *Beach and Lake Resort* (℡0471/238 2086, ✉beachandlake@yahoo.com; ❸), lies across the water from *Lagoona Davina,* has just five rooms and less atmosphere.

Vizhinjam

A tightly packed cluster of thatched fishers huts, the unassuming village of **VIZHINJAM** (pronounced "Virinyam"), on the opposite (south) side of the headland from Lighthouse Beach, was once the capital of the Ay kings, the earliest dynasty in south Kerala. During the ninth century the Pandyans fought to control it, and it was the scene of major Chola–Chera battles in the eleventh century. A number of simple small shrines survive from those times, and can be made the focus of a pleasant afternoon's stroll through coconut groves, best approached from the centre of the village rather than the coast road – brace yourself for the sharp contrast between hedonistic tourist resort and simple fishing village. A modern pink **mosque** on the promontory overlooks the village. For centuries, the Muslim fishermen here were kept at arm's length by orthodox Hindus, being perpetually forced into debt by the combination of low prices for their produce and exorbitant interest – as much as ten percent per day – charged by moneylenders on loans for boats and nets. The tensions resulted in a series of violent riots in the early 1990s, which resulted in the deaths of numerous local people, but things have calmed down somewhat since then, with cooperatives established to provide interest-free loans and to sell fish – at favourable prices – on behalf of individual fishermen. Nonetheless, some antipathy still persists between the two communities.

On the far side of the fishing bay in the village centre, fifty metres down a road opposite the police station, a small unfinished eighth-century **rock shrine** features a carved figure of Shiva with a weapon. The **Tali Shiva** temple nearby, reached by a narrow path from behind the government primary school, may mark the original centre of Vizhinjam. The simple shrine is accompanied by a group of *naga* snake statues, a reminder of Kerala's continuing cult of snake worship that survives from pre-brahminical times.

Toward the sea, ten minutes' walk from the village's main road along Hidy-atnagara Road, the grove known as **Kovil Kadu** ("temple forest") holds a square Shiva shrine and a rectangular one dedicated to the goddess **Bhagavati**. Thought to date from the ninth century, these are probably the earliest struc-tural temples in Kerala, although the Bhagavati shrine has been renovated.

Padmanabhapuram

Although now officially in Tamil Nadu, **PADMANABHAPURAM**, 63km southeast of Thiruvananthapuram, was the capital of Travancore between 1550 and 1750, and maintains its historic links with Kerala, from where it is still administered. For anyone with even a minor interest in Keralan architecture, the small **Padmanabhapuram Palace** (Tues–Sun 9am–4.30pm; Rs50 [Rs20], cameras Rs20), whose design represents the high watermark of regional build-ing, is an irresistible attraction. Avoid weekends, however, when the complex gets overrun with bus parties. It's a pleasant ten- to fifteen-minute walk to the palace from the bus station: cross the main road outside the station, turn left and follow the road on the right. Once through the paddy fields, you'll emerge at a village that backs onto the substantial palace compound walls.

Set in neat, gravelled grounds against a backdrop of steep-sided hills, the palace's predominantly wooden exterior displays a perfect combination of clean lines and gentle angles, with the sloping tiled roofs of its various interconnecting buildings broken by triangular projecting gables that enclose delicately carved screens. The palace is well maintained by the Archaeological Survey of India.

In the **entrance hall** (a veranda), a brass oil lamp hangs from an ornate teak, rosewood and mahogany ceiling and is carved with ninety different lotus flowers. Beautifully ornamented, the revolving lamp inexplicably keeps the position in which it is left, seeming to defy gravity, while in fact demonstrating a perfect centre of gravity. The raja rested from the summer heat on the cool, polished-granite bed in the corner. On the wall is a collection of *onamvillu* (ceremonial bows) decorated with images of Padmanabha – the reclining form of Vishnu (see box below) – which local chieftains would present to him during the Onam festival.

Directly above the entrance hall, on the first floor, is the **mantrasala** (council chamber), gently illuminated by the light filtering through panes of coloured mica. Herbs soaking in water were put into the boxed bench seats along the front wall, as a natural air-cooling system. The highly polished black floor is made from a now-lost technique using burnt coconut, sticky sugar-cane extract, egg whites, lime and sand. The oldest part of the complex is the **Ekandaman-dapam**, or "lonely place". Built in 1550, it was used for rituals for the goddess Durga and typically employed elaborate floor paintings known as *kalam ezhuttu* (see p.691). A loose ring attached to a column is a tour de force of the carpenter: both ring and column are carved from a single piece of jackwood. Nearby is a *nalekettu*, a four-sided courtyard found in many Keralan houses, open to the sky and surrounded by a pillared walkway. A trapdoor once served as the entrance to a secret passageway leading to another palace, since destroyed.

The Pandya-style stone-columned **dance hall** stands directly in front of a shrine to the goddess of learning, Saraswati. The women of the royal household had to watch performances through screens on the side, and the staff through holes in the wall from the gallery above. Typical of old country houses, steep, wooden ladder-like steps, ending in trapdoors, connect the floors. Belgian mirrors and Tanjore miniatures of Krishna adorn the chamber forming part of the **women's quarters**, where a swing hangs on plaited iron ropes. A four-poster bed, made from sixteen kinds of medicinal wood, dominates the **raja's bedroom**. Its

Travancore and the servants of Vishnu

In front of a depiction of the god in the meditation, or prayer, room at Padmanabhapuram Palace lies a sword. In 1750, **Raja Marthanda Varma** symbolically presented this weapon to Padmanabha – the god Vishnu – who reclines on the sacred serpent Anantha in the midst of the cosmic ocean, thereby dedicating the kingdom of Travancore to Vishnu. From that day, the raja took the title of Padmanabhadasa ("servant of Padmanabha"), and ruled as a servant of the god.

Thus Travancore belonged to Vishnu, and the raja was merely its custodian – a spiritual, and presumably legal, loophole that is said to have proved invaluable in restricting the power of the British in Travancore. Travancore, therefore, remained under direct control of the raja, with the British presence restricted to that of a resident only.

elaborate carvings depict a mass of vegetation, human figures, birds and, as the central motif, the snake symbol of medicine, associated with the Greek physician deity Asclepius. The **murals** for which the palace is famous – alive with detail, colour, graceful form and religious fervour – adorn the walls of the **meditation room** directly above the bedroom, which was used by the raja and the heirs apparent. Unfortunately, this is now closed to preserve the murals, which have already been damaged by generations of hands trailing along the walls.

Further points of interest in the palace include a **dining hall** intended for the free feeding of up to two thousand brahmins, and a 38-kilo stone which, it is said, every new recruit to the raja's army had to raise above his head 101 times.

Practicalities

Frequent **buses** run to Padmanabhapuram from Thiruvananthapuram's Thampanoor station; hop on any service heading south towards Nagercoil or Kanniyakumari and get off at **Thakkaly** (sometimes written Thuckalai). If you're determined to see Padmanabhapuram and Kanniyakumari (see p.362 & p.551) in one day, leave Thiruvananthapuram early to arrive when the palace opens at 9am. Heading back, two express buses leave Thakkaly at 2.30pm and 3.30pm for Thiruvananthapuram. Another way to see Padmanabhapuram is on KTDC's Kanniyakumari tour from Thiruvananthapuram (daily 7.30am–9pm; Rs250).

The small stalls inside the outer walls of the palace are the best place to get **snacks** and **drinks**, as the area around the bus station is noisy and dirty.

North of Thiruvananthapuram

When it gets too hot at sea level, **Ponmudi** and the **Peppara Wildlife Sanctuary**, just northeast of Thiruvananthapuram, make a refreshing overnight break: in a couple of hours you can be walking through rubber and cardamom plantations and endless slopes of green tea bushes in refreshingly cool air. Alternatively, the richly forested **Agastya Hills** are 25km northeast of Thiruvananthapuram and make a pleasant day-trip, forming a beautiful backdrop to the **Neyyar Dam**, on the banks of which is the excellent **Sivananda Yoga Centre**. Just before you turn off to the Agastya Hills, it's well worth visiting the fascinating **Koikkal Kottaram** at Nedumangod. This palace is the epitome of traditional Keralan architectural elegance, and is open to the public as a museum of local archeology, history and culture.

If you want to stick to the coastline, head up to the quiet and relaxed village of **Varkala**, popular with Hindu pilgrims and western sun-worshippers. A little further north, the busy town of **Kollam** is one of the main departure points for boat trips through the unforgettable Keralan **backwaters**.

Koikkal Kottaram

The beautiful palace of **Koikkal Kottaram** (Tues–Sun 10am–5pm; Rs3, cameras Rs10), 20km northeast of Thiruvananthapuram and just short of the turning to Neyyar Dam and Agastya Hills, sits on the outskirts of the lively market town of Nedumangod, 1km north of the KSTRC bus station. This little-known palace is cared for by the Archaeological Survey of India, who provide knowledgeable guides to take you around the collections and exhibits; the guides are free but a tip is appreciated.

The palace was originally constructed for Umyamma Rani, a local queen who reigned from 1677 until 1684. It retains all the distinctive features of traditional

Keralan architecture: a bowed tiled roof, intricately carved teak features outside and in, cool stone floors and dark rooms, a private central courtyard for the ladies and a wonderfully effective natural air-conditioning system using sloping wooden slats. There is also a secret passage leading out from the courtyard that the queen could use as an escape when her enemies laid siege to the palace, a common military tactic in seventeenth-century Kerala. A maze of trees is being cultivated in the beautiful manicured gardens around the palace.

The **ground-floor** rooms contain a vast coin collection that is imaginatively displayed to chart the development of international trade along the Malabar coastline. Most were discovered during archeological excavations in the area and include Roman Pinari coins, tiny punch-marked coins with the royal seals of local rajas, and more modern British examples from the Victorian period. Other rooms around the courtyard contain Keralan household and farming implements dating from the eighteenth and nineteenth centuries, as well as three ornamental palanquins for carrying the royal ladies.

Upstairs, the make-up and costumes for Kathakali, Ottan Thullal and *theyyam* (see p.717) dance performances are displayed on ferocious-looking models, and there is an exquisite *kettuvialaku* (platform) for the goddess Durga which is carried around town during local spring festivities. Also displayed are the musical instruments and implements used in the colourful and archaic rituals that frequently take place in Keralan temples, such as the iron weaponry employed to represent aspects of deities and the elaborate jewellery worn by officiating priests.

Agastya Hills

Within easy distance of Kovalam, 25km to the northeast and feasible on a day-trip, the jagged, forested **AGASTYA HILLS** form a verdant backdrop to the **Neyyar Dam** (signs warn you not to take photographs of the dam for security reasons). In an idyllic position on the banks of the dam, the **Sivananda Yoga Vedanta Dhanwanthari Ashram** (see box on p.366) is one of the country's leading **yoga** ashrams. Nearby are **ornamental gardens**, boasting outsize, garishly painted plaster images of gods and heroes. A tiny, two-acre **safari park** on a corner of the dam, approached by boats from near the Forest Department, is home to seven lions, whose roars during feeding time at sunset echo through the hills. You are strongly advised not to swim in the dammed waters as they're infested with **crocodiles**.

Across the dam the forest beckons. The only way to enter the Agastya Hills reserve, however, is through the Forest Department, who will, on request, organize a **boat** and an obligatory **guide**. The guide service is free but you should have prior permission to **trek** in the park from the Forest Department offices at Vazhuthacud in Thiruvananthapuram. On occasions, the local range officer does give permission, especially if you arrange it through the manager at the tourist bungalow, KTDC *Agastya House* (see below). Longer treks into the forest can be arranged through the department or through the *Agastya Garden Hill Resort* (see p.366).

Practicalities

Buses from the KSRTC Thampanoor bus stand in Thiruvananthapuram depart every half-hour for the Neyyar Dam. The only decent **accommodation** at Neyyar Dam is the KTDC *Agastya House* (℡0471/227 2160; ❸), which has huge rooms and verandas (with views), and a decent restaurant serving South Indian meals and snacks. During the weekend, avoid the rooms upstairs as the popular beer bar below gets noisy. For a bit more comfort, head for **Kalipara**,

Sivananda Yoga Vedanta Dhanwantari

Located amid the serene hills and tropical forests around **Neyyar Dam**, 28km east of Thiruvananthapuram, the **Sivananda Yoga Vedanta Dhanwantari** (ⓦ www.sivananda .org) is one of India's leading **yoga** ashrams. It was founded by Swami Sivananda – dubbed the "Flying Guru" because he used to pilot light aircraft over war-stricken areas of the world, scattering flowers and leaflets calling for peace – as a centre for meditation, yoga and traditional Keralan martial arts and medicine. Sivananda was a renowned exponent of Advaitya Vedanta, the philosophy of non-duality, as espoused by the Upanishads and promoted later by Shankara in the eleventh century.

Aside from training teachers in advanced raja and hatha yoga, the ashram offers excellent **introductory courses** for beginners. These comprise four hours of intensive tuition per day (starting at 5.30am), with background lectures that provide helpful theory and a good practical start. During the course, you have to stay at the ashram and comply with a regime that some Western students find fairly strict (no sex, drugs, rock'n'roll, no smoking, pure veg diet and early morning starts), as well as join in Hindu devotional worship. Some people have also noted strained relations with the local villagers, whom ashramites are discouraged from mixing with or even buying goods from. For more details, contact the ashram itself (☎0471/229 0493), or their branch in Thiruvananthapuram at 37/1929 Airport Rd, West Fort (☎0471/245 0942). For more information look at their publication, *Sivananda Yoga Life*, published by the Sivananda Yoga Vedanta Centre, 51 Felsham Rd, London SW15 1AZ (☎020/8780 0160).

the large, black, rocky hill with a small temple on top. The *Agastya Ayurveda Garden* resort (☎0471/227 3151; ⑦–⑧) has comfortable, though rather expensive, mock-rustic cottages with incredible views. The resort has introduced treks in the Agastya Hills reserve forest, and boat tours, but with a dearth of competition, these are vastly overpriced.

Ponmudi and Peppara Wildlife Sanctuary

In the tea-growing region of the **Cardamom** (or Ponmudi) **Hills**, about 60km northeast of Thiruvananthapuram and 77km from Kovalam, at an altitude of 1066m, lies the hill station of **PONMUDI**, comprising a range of cottages, rooms and a restaurant on the top of a hill commanding breathtaking views out across the range as far as the sea. The main reason to come up here is that Ponmudi serves as the only practical base for visits to the 53 square kilometres of forest set aside as the **Peppara Wildlife Sanctuary**, which protects elephants, *sambhar*, lion-tailed macaques, leopards and other assorted wildlife. Although Peppara is theoretically open all year, the main season is from January until May; check before you go with the District Forest Officer, Thiruvananthapuram Forest Division, Thiruvananthapuram (☎0471/232 0674).

The beautiful drive up, via the small towns of Nedumangad and Vithura, runs along very narrow roads past areca nut, clove, rubber and cashew plantations, with first the Kavakulam and then the River Kallar close at hand. The bridge at **Kallar Junction** marks the start of the real climb. Twenty-two hairpin bends (numbered at the roadside) lead slowly up, starting in the foothills, heading up past great lumps of black rock and thick clumps of bamboo (*iramula*), then through the Kallar teak forest. Finally you wind through the tea plantations; the temperature is noticeably cooler and, once out of the forest, the views across the hills and the plains below become truly spectacular – on a clear day you can see the sea. There really is very little to do up here, but the high ridges and tea estates make good rambling country.

Practicalities

Six daily **buses** run from Thiruvananthapuram to Ponmudi, via Vithura; the first is at 5.30am and the last at 3.30pm. The nearest **tourist office** is currently in Thiruvananthapuram, where information on Ponmudi is readily available. The *Government Guest House* (T0472/289 0230; ❸) has 24 rooms and seven cottages, all with attached bathrooms and hot water. Simple and inexpensive but delicious meals have to be ordered a couple of hours in advance; otherwise the cold drinks and snack shop is open daily until 4pm, or you can walk down the road to the teashop on the bend (400m from the hotel). The main building, which originally belonged to the raja of Travancore, has lost any charm it may once have possessed, and the huge plate-glass windows of its canteen-like restaurant rattle disconcertingly in the wind, but the views across the hills and misty valleys from the terrace make up for all that. Weekends get relatively lively, thanks to the beer parlour (daily 10am–6pm).

Varkala

Long renowned by Hindus as a place of pilgrimage, **VARKALA**, 54km northwest of Thiruvananthapuram, with its beautiful sands and cliffs, is these days a considerably more appealing – and somewhat less full on – beach destination than Kovalam. Centred on a clifftop row of budget guesthouses and palm-thatch cafés, the tourist scene is still relatively low-key, although the arrival in recent years of the first charter groups and luxury hotels may well be the harbinger of full-scale development. Building inland and at both ends of the beach is already proceding apace. The best time to visit is from October to early March; during the monsoons the beach is virtually unusable.

Arrival and information

Varkala's railway station, 2.5km east of the village, is served by express and mail **trains** from Thiruvananthapuram, Kollam (hourly; 45min), and most other Keralan towns on the main line. An auto-rickshaw to the beach costs around Rs40. Regular **buses** also run from Thiruvananthapuram's Thampanoor stand, and from Kollam (1hr 30min). A few go all the way to the beach, but most stop in the village centre, a five-minute auto-rickshaw ride away. If you can't get a direct bus, take any "superfast" or "limited stop" bus along the main NH-47 highway to **Kallamballam**, 15km from Varkala, from where you can get a local bus to Varkala, or an auto-rickshaw (Rs80–100) or taxi (Rs120–150).

The new **Kerala Department of Tourism** office (Mon–Sat 10am–5pm; T0470/260 2227) is in the same complex as their *Guest House*, behind the *Taj Garden Retreat*. You can hire **two-wheelers** everywhere in Varkala: the going rate for a scooter is Rs200–250, Rs300 for a motorbike, and Rs350 for an Enfield. Travel agents may also try to sell you expensive "day-long" elephant rides in a nearby forest, which last an hour. The official government rate is Rs350 per hour per person, plus a taxi to the forest (Rs50 return).

There are numerous places to **change money** on the clifftop and also at Nikhil's hotel on Beach Road. The many **Internet** centres in Varkala charge Rs35–40, with a minimum charge of Rs20.

Accommodation

Varkala has a reasonable range of **places to stay**, from basic rooms with shared bathrooms to comfortable mid-range resorts. The hotels along Beach Road are a good bet for late arrivals, but the places on the cliff-top have more inspiring views and vibes. Auto-rickshaws from the railway station and village tank go as far as the helipad or round the back to North Cliff; it's worth stopping on the way to see if the wonderful *Government Guest House* has vacancies. Accommodation is tight in **peak season** (late Nov–Jan), when it's worth booking in advance.

Akshay Beach Resort Beach Rd ☎0470/260 2668, ⓔakshay-varkala@yahoo.co.in. Clean guesthouse 100m from the beach with a wide range of en-suite rooms (some with a/c and private balconies) and helpful management. ②–⑦

Bamboo Village North Clifftop ☎0470/261 0732. A very popular place with a congenial social scene

of its own. Accommodation is in an assortment of bamboo huts with little balconies and rooms, all en suite; the huts are cuter but the rooms are better value. ②–③

Clafouti North Clifftop ☎0470/260 1414, ⓕ260 0494. Spotless tiled rooms ranged around a courtyard, all with private

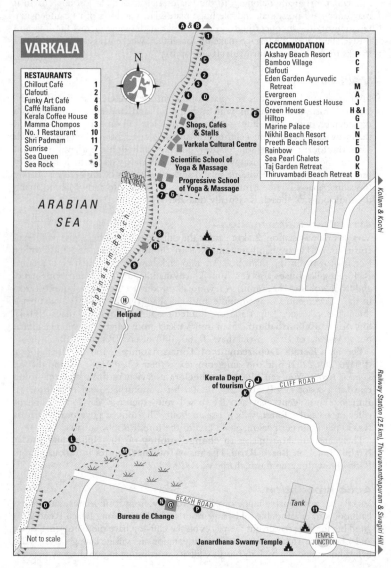

VARKALA

RESTAURANTS
Chillout Café	1
Clafouti	2
Funky Art Café	4
Caffé Italiano	6
Kerala Coffee House	8
Mamma Chompos	3
No. 1 Restaurant	10
Shri Padmam	11
Sunrise	7
Sea Queen	5
Sea Rock	9

ACCOMMODATION
Akshay Beach Resort	P
Bamboo Village	C
Clafouti	F
Eden Garden Ayurvedic Retreat	M
Evergreen	A
Government Guest House	J
Green House	H & I
Hilltop	G
Marine Palace	L
Nikhil Beach Resort	N
Preeth Beach Resort	E
Rainbow	D
Sea Pearl Chalets	O
Taj Garden Retreat	K
Thiruvambadi Beach Retreat	B

ARABIAN SEA

Papanasam Beach

Shops, Cafés & Stalls
Varkala Cultural Centre
Scientific School of Yoga & Massage
Progressive School of Yoga & Massage

Helipad

Kerala Dept. of tourism ⓘ
CLIFF ROAD

Bureau de Change
BEACH ROAD
Tank

Janardhana Swamy Temple
TEMPLE JUNCTION

Not to scale

▲ Kollam & Kochi

▶ Railway Station (2.5 km), Thiruvananthapuram & Sivagiri Hill balconies; the more expensive ones have sea views. ❸–❹

Eden Garden Ayurvedic Retreat Off Beach Rd ☎0470/260 3910, ⓦwww.eden-garden.net. Popular place situated in the paddy fields behind the beach, with twelve non a/c rooms with verandas arranged round a fishpond (beware of mosquitoes). Offers Ayurvedic treatments (Rs450–750) and food (but no cricket). ❸–❻

Evergreen North Clifftop ☎0470/260 3257. Mid-range option at the quiet end of Varkala with rooms and plusher cottages (both a/c and non a/c). ❺–❼

Government Guest House Cliff Rd ☎0470/260 2227, ⓦwww.keralatourism.org. Five minutes' walk north of the temple, behind the *Taj* hotel, this is a former maharajah's holiday palace converted into a characterful guesthouse. Two of the nine rooms are enormous and fantastic value; the others are in a modern building in the same grounds and are much more ordinary. Meals available on request. ❷–❸

Green House Clifftop ☎0470/260 4659, ⓔgreenhousecliff@hotmail.com. Only two minutes' walk from the cliff edge, behind a small temple in an unhurried and friendly hamlet. The rooms are basic, and the cheapest ones share a common bathroom, but it's a popular place with a nice vibe. A small new block right on the cliff top (❺) offers more comfortable rooms. ❷

Hilltop North Clifftop ☎0470/260 1237, ⓦwww.hilltopvarkala.com. A great spot, with pleasant, breezy rooms (with attached shower-toilets) and a relaxing terrace restaurant. The cheaper rooms are at the back, while the more expensive ones upstairs have sea views; cottages are also available. Ayurveda treatments available. ❸–❼

Marine Palace Off Beach Rd ☎0470/260 3204. En-suite rooms in a large white building; the pricier wooden cottages at the front have sea views and balconies; those in the thatched annexe, where there's a congenial restaurant, are cheaper. Good value. ❷–❺

Nikhil Beach Resort Beach Rd ☎0470/260 5191, ⓦwww.nikhil-resort.com. Reasonable range of rooms (a/c and non a/c), and good facilities including Internet access and foreign exchange. ❷–❻

Preeth Beach Resort North Clifftop area, off Cliff Rd ☎0470/260 0942, ⓦwww.preethbeachresort.com. Large, well-maintained complex shaded by a palm grove, with a range of well-appointed rooms (some a/c), each with a private balcony, and more expensive cottages. There's also a swimming pool, pleasant grounds and a restaurant. ❹–❽

Rainbow North Clifftop ☎0470/309 0825. Friendly family house with three clean and compact rooms with small balconies, less than 100m behind the clifftop. ❸

Sea Pearl Chalets South Beach ☎0470/260 260 5875. Attractive circular cottages with good amenities set in a quiet location south of Beach Rd. ❸–❻

Taj Garden Retreat Cliff Rd ☎0470/260 3000, ⓦwww.tajhotels.com. Very comfortable rooms with central a/c, a good restaurant and bar, fitness and Ayurveda centre, terraced gardens and a pleasant swimming pool – though it's all a bit ostentatious for a laid-back place like Varkala. The tariff ($125–160) includes breakfast and dinner buffets. ❾

Thiruvambadi Beach Retreat North Clifftop ☎0470/260 1028. Set back from the cliffs in a palm grove at the quiet northern end of Varkala, with four sea-facing rooms and cheaper inner rooms, hammocks in the garden and a restaurant. The non a/c rooms are expensive, however. ❺–❻

The beach and village

Known in Malayalam as Papa Nashini ("sin destroyer"), Varkala's beautiful white-sand **Papanasam Beach** has long been associated with ancestor worship. Devotees come to the beach after praying at the **Janardhana Swamy Temple** (said to be over 2000 years old), to bring the ashes of departed relatives for their "final rest". Non-Hindus are not permitted to enter the inner sanctum of the temple but are welcome in the grounds. A small government hospital at the north end of the temple, opened by Indira Gandhi in 1983, was set up to benefit from being built on the same site as three **natural springs**, and to take advantage of the sea air, which is said to boost the health of asthma sufferers.

Backed by sheer red laterite cliffs and drenched by rolling waves off the Arabian Sea, the coastline is imposingly scenic and the beach relatively peaceful, despite the usual presence of hawkers. The religious significance of the beach means attitudes to (especially female) public nudity are markedly less liberal than other coastal resorts in India, and stripping off here is clearly inappropriate. Western sun-worshippers tend to congregate at the northern end of the beach, where they are tolerated and serviced by the local "hello pineapple coconut" vendors. Whistle-happy lifeguards ensure the safety of swimmers by enforcing the no-swim zones beyond the flags, where the undercurrent is strong. **Dolphins** are often seen swimming quite close to the coast, and, if you're lucky, you may be able to swim with them by arranging a ride with a fishing boat. Sea otters are also occasionally seen playing on the cliffs by the sea.

Few of Varkala's Hindu pilgrims make it as far as the decadent **clifftop area**, a very different world from the village below (be aware that the rope used to cordon off the precipitous cliff edge is flimsy, and actually extends beyond the edge in places where the cliff has crumbled). The cliff can be reached directly from the beach by several steep flights of steps cut into the sandy cliff, along the gentler path that starts behind the *Marine Palace* restaurant, and by the metalled road that winds its way up from the village and was built to service the helipad in advance of Indira Gandhi's visit. She didn't come here to study yoga but many Westerners do, and there are two **schools** on the clifftop that will bend over backwards to match your needs. The Scientific School of Yoga & Massage, offers **Ayurvedic massage** (Rs400 per session), **meditation courses**, courses in **yoga** (Rs1000 for a week, Rs2000 for an unlimited number of lessons) and fortnight-long courses in **massage** (Rs10,000). The school also runs a small shop, Prakrithi Stores, which stocks local honey, essential oils, herbs and handmade soaps, as well as books on yoga, meditation and massage. The Progressive School of Yoga and Massage also offers massage sessions (Rs400) and short courses in **reiki**, **reflexology**, yoga and Ayurvedic massage. As in Kovalam, many non-qualified masseurs have jumped on the Ayurveda bandwagon, so it's wise to look around, and talk with other travellers to get their recommendations before going for a treatment (see p.356).

Aimed unashamedly at the tourist market, the **Varkala Cultural Centre** (℡0470/608793), behind the *Sunrise* restaurant on North Clifftop, holds daily **Kathakali** and **Bharatanatyam** dance performances (make-up 5pm; performance 6.30-8pm; Rs150). It's a pleasant enough introduction to the two types of dance, especially if you're not going to make it to Kochi. If you want to learn more, the centre also offers short courses on make-up.

Eating

Seafood lovers will enjoy Varkala's crop of clifftop **café-restaurants**, which dish up delicious baked, steamed or coconut-curried freshly caught shark, marlin or butterfish, as well as pasta, pizza and, if you're lucky, some Indian dishes too. Prices are fairly high: expect to pay around Rs50 for a simple veggie curry, Rs50-100 for pizza or pasta, and over Rs100 for a fresh fish dish. Service, though, can be very slow here, but the superb location more than compensates, especially in the evenings when the sea twinkles with the lights of distant fishing boats.

Due to Kerala's antiquated licensing laws, which involve huge amounts of tax, a lot of cafés choose to serve **beer** discreetly; a teapot-full costs Rs75-90. The *Taj Garden Retreat*'s licensed bar is nice but far more expensive.

Caffé Italiano Clifftop. Authentic Italian menu starring several varieties of pizza and pasta, and very good – but pricey – cappuccino.

Chillout Café North Clifftop. Simple thatched café with a limited menu, but you can't beat the Rs40 breakfast specials.

Clafouti North Clifftop. Wonderful French bakery offering real croissants, *pain aux raisins*, baguettes and sweet pies, served at little tables under rustling palm trees. There's a range of moderately priced multi-cuisine options, including seafood

dishes, and a set three-course evening menu (Rs150).

Funky Art Café North Clifftop. Trendiest place at the northern end of the beach, with good music and a selection of Indian and western fare.

Kerala Coffee House Clifftop. The funkiest place on the clifftop, pleasingly close to the edge, with great music, a friendly atmosphere and a more extensive Indian menu than at many places hereabouts. Expect to pay Rs50-80 for a main course.

Mamma Chompos North Clifftop. Pizzeria with

Indian and Chinese dishes, too, and seating either at ground level or on the sturdy wooden balcony.
No. 1 Restaurant Beach Rd. Illuminated by atmospheric fairy lights at night and with an extensive menu featuring the usual travellers' favourites.
Sea Queen North Clifftop. Good views and plenty of fish, calamari, mussel and prawn dishes amongst the pizza and pasta – only the wine is missing. The adjacent *Gnosh* is very similar.
Sea Rock Clifftop, next to the helipad. A fairly standard range of Indian and Continental cuisine

plus good Indian music and film screenings.
Shri Padmam Varkala village. This grubby-looking café might seem unpromising, but the veg food is cheap and delicious, and the location is very atmospheric, with a large rear terrace affording views of the temple tank.
Sunrise North Clifftop. Great-value Israeli, French, Italian, English and South Indian set breakfasts, good fruit juices and an evening Keralan speciality of fish with coconut and spices, steamed in a banana leaf and served with rice.

Kollam (Quilon) and around

One of the Malabar coast's oldest ports, **KOLLAM** (pronounced "Koillam", and previously known as Quilon), 74km northwest of Thiruvananthapuram and 85km south of Alappuzha, was once at the centre of the international spice trade. The port flourished from the very earliest times, trading with the Phoenicians, Arabs, Persians, Greeks, Romans and Chinese – the sixteenth-century Portuguese writer Duarte Barbossa described it as a "very great city with a right good haven" visited by "Moors, Heathen and Christians in great numbers".

Nowadays, Kollam is chiefly of interest as one of the entry or exit points to the backwaters of Kerala (see box pp.378–379), and most travellers simply stay overnight en route to or from Alappuzha. The **town** itself, sandwiched between the sea and Ashtamudi ("eight inlets") Lake, is less exciting than its history might suggest. It's a typically sprawling Keralan market community, with a few characterful old tiled wooden houses and winding backstreets, kept busy by the local trade in coir, cashew nuts (a good local buy), pottery, aluminium and fish. The reputable Santhigiri Janakanthi **Ayurvedic Centre** (☎0474/276 3014, ⓔjanakanthi@sify.com) is situated on the shore of Ashtamudi Lake.

Arrival, information and tours

The **railway station** lies east of the clocktower which marks the centre of town. Numerous daily trains run from Ernakulam and Thiruvananthapuram and beyond. On platform 4, the tiny **District Tourism Promotion Council** (DTPC) tourist information counter will book hotels; you have to pay one night in advance, but the only extra charge is for the phone call. They also have a tourist office (daily 9am–6pm; ☎0474/274 5625, ⓦwww.dtpckollam.com) at the **boat jetty** on the edge of Ashtamudi Lake, but only provide details on their own tourist ferry service. The local **Allapuzha Tourism Development Council** (ATDC; daily 7am–9pm; ☎0474/276 7440) office on the opposite side of the road also has information on tourist and local ferry services. The DTPC and ATDC run cruises on alternate days from Kollam to Alappuzha, which depart at 10.30am and take eight hours (Rs300), with stops for lunch and tea. While the cruise is popular, you may find that you get a far better impression of backwater life by hopping between villages on the very cheap local ferries. Tickets for both the DTPC and ATDC ferries can be bought on the morning of the trip from any agent and some of the hotels; tickets for the local ferries are purchased at the booth on the jetty. Both companies also offer exclusive overnight *kettu vallam* cruises (see box on p.379 for details), and the DTPC organizes half-day trips to nearby **Monroe Island** (9am–1pm; 2–6.30pm; Rs300), which provide a fascinating glimpse of village life in this unique – and very scenic – waterlogged region.

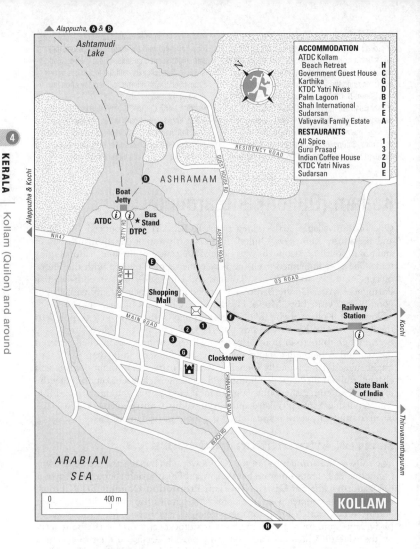

ACCOMMODATION
ATDC Kollam	
Beach Retreat	H
Government Guest House	C
Karthika	G
KTDC Yatri Nivas	D
Palm Lagoon	B
Shah International	F
Sudarsan	E
Valiyavila Family Estate	A

RESTAURANTS
All Spice	1
Guru Prasad	3
Indian Coffee House	2
KTDC Yatri Nivas	D
Sudarsan	E

KOLLAM

The jetty and KSRTC **bus stand** are close together on the edge of Ashtamudi Lake. Bookable express **buses** leave for Thiruvananthapuram (1hr 45min) and Kochi (3hr) via Alappuzha (2hr) every fifteen minutes or so; the express services are much better than the "limited stop" buses. Note that most Thiruvananthapuram-bound **trains** do not stop in Varkala. Useful **facilities** such as exchange bureaux, ATMs and Internet outlets are to be found in the smart modern shopping mall, just south of the main road between the jetty and the clocktower.

Accommodation and eating

The most congenial **places to stay** are outside the town, across Ashtamudi Lake from the DTPC boat jetty; they're reachable by ferry (Rs20) or auto-rickshaw (Rs20). Places to **eat** include the *Indian Coffee House* on Main Road, for omelettes, rice, dhal, simple veg dishes and coffee, or *Guru Prasad*, a little further along the same road, which serves a wide range of great South Indian veg food. In the hotels, the *Sudarsan* has a good, upmarket air-conditioned restaurant serving Indian food, but most travellers end up at the congenial lakeside restaurant at the KTDC *Yatri Nivas*, where various tasty fish dishes are available. *All Spice*, on the road south of the shopping mall above a good bakery, is a brightly lit cafeteria serving authentic Chinese and reasonable Western food.

Hotels and guesthouses

Government Guest House Ashtamudi Lake, Ashramam, 3km northeast of town ☏0474/274 3620, Ⓦwww.keralatourism.org. This old colonial building and former British Residency is full of character, with gracious verandas, original furniture and a curved tiled roof – very popular, so book in advance. The six rooms in the main building have more character than those in the newer annexe. Meals and backwater cruise tickets are available. ❷–❸

Karthika Off Main Rd, near the mosque ☏0474/275 1821. Large and popular budget hotel in a central location with clean, plain rooms (some a/c) ranged around a courtyard in which the centrepiece is, rather unexpectedly, three huge nude figures. Rooms with TV cost extra, and some also have a/c. ❷–❹

Kollam Beach Retreat 3.5km south of centre ☏0474/275 276 3793, Ⓦwww.kollambeach retreat.com. ATDC hotel with comfortable rooms and a restaurant, the only place to stay on the town beach. ❸–❹

KTDC Yatri Nivas Ashramam ☏0474/274 5538, Ⓦwww.ktdc.com. Modern, clean rooms with bathrooms and nice balconies in a great location overlooking the lake; the best fall-back if the *Government*

Guest House is full. The restaurant is very popular with travellers, and there's also a beer parlour. ❸–❺

Palm Lagoon Vellimon West ☏0474/254 8974, Ⓦwww.palmlagoon.com. In a beautiful location on Ashtamudi Lake, 18km from town, with pleasant thatched cottages and breakfast or full board. Good Ayurvedic treatment facilities available, and the opportunity to explore the backwaters. Book directly or through the DTPC for directions and a discount. ❺–❻

Shah International Chinnakkada Rd ☏0474/274 2362, Ⓔhotelshah@hotmail.com. A modern hotel block with surprisingly large, clean and bright rooms and suites, some with a/c and cable TV. ❸–❻

Sudarsan Parameswar Nagar ☏0474/274 4322. Central and popular, but definitely not as palatial as the posh foyer would lead you to believe. There's a wide range of rooms, some with a/c and cable TV, and a ground floor a/c restaurant (watch out for hidden taxes). ❸–❽

Valiyavila Family Estate Ashtamudi Lake ☏474/270 1546, Ⓔvaliyavali1@rediffmail.com. Four lovely rooms (and one cheaper outhouse) with teak furniture, in a stylish marble villa right on the lakeshore. Will collect from airport or town. ❺–❽

Around Kollam

KAYAMKULAM, served by local buses from Kollam and Alappuzha, was once the centre of its own small kingdom, which after a battle in 1746 came under the control of Travancore's king Marthanda Varma. In the eighteenth century, the area was famous for its spices, particularly pepper and cinnamon. The Abbé Reynal claimed that the Dutch exported some two million pounds of pepper each year, one-fifth of it from Kayamkulam. At this time, the kingdom was also known for the skill of its army, made up of 15,000 Nayars (Kerala's martial caste).

Set in a tranquil garden, the dilapidated eighteenth-century **Krishnapuram Palace** (Tues–Sat 10am–4.30pm; Rs3, camera Rs15) is imbued with Keralan grace, constructed largely of wood with gabled roofs and rooms opening out onto shady internal courtyards. It's now a museum, but unlike the palace at Padmanabhapuram (see p.362), with which it shares some similarities, the whole place is in need of restoration and the collection inside is poorly labelled and neglected. The best way to learn about the palace and its exhibits is to hire one of the unofficial **guides** hanging around the palace entrance. They are knowledgeable but, despite their claim to "accept no money", they will expect a tip.

A display case contains puja ceremony utensils and oil lamps, some of which are arranged in an arc known as a *prabhu*, placed behind a temple deity to provide a halo of light. Fine miniature *panchaloha* ("five-metal" bronze alloy, with gold as one ingredient) figures include the water god Varuna, several Vishnus and a minuscule worshipping devotee. Small stone columns carved with serpent deities were recovered from local houses.

The prize exhibit is a huge **mural** of the classical Keralan school, in muted ochre-reds and blue-greens, which covers more than fourteen square metres. It depicts **Gajendra Moksha** – the salvation of Gajendra, king of the elephants. In the tenth-century Sanskrit *Bhagavata Purana*, the story is told of a Pandyan king, Indrayumna, a devotee of Vishnu cursed by the sage Agastya to be born again as an elephant. One day, while sporting with his wives at the edge of a lake, his leg was seized by a crocodile whose grip was so tight that Gajendra was held captive for years. Finally, in desperation, the elephant called upon his chosen deity Vishnu, who immediately appeared, riding his celestial bird-man vehicle, Garuda, and destroyed the crocodile. The centre of the painting is dominated by a dynamic portrayal of Garuda about to land, with huge spread wings and a facial expression denoting *raudra* (fury), in stark contrast to the compassionate features of the multi-armed Vishnu. Smaller figures of Gajendra in mid-trumpet, and of his assailant, are shown to the right. As with all paintings in the Keralan style, every inch is packed with detail. Bearded sages, animals, mythical beasts and forest plants surround the main figures. The outer edges are decorated with floriate borders, which at the bottom form a separate triptych-like panel showing Balakrishna, the child Krishna, attended by adoring females.

In **KARUNAGAPALLI**, 23km north of Kollam on NH-47 towards Alappuzha, it's possible to see traditional **kettu vallam**, or "tied boats", being built and repaired. These long cargo boats, a familiar sight on the backwaters, are built entirely without the use of nails. Each jackwood plank is **sewn** to the next with coir rope, and then the whole is coated with a caustic black resin made from boiled cashew kernels. With careful maintenance they last for generations. If you want to buy a *vallam* you'll need around two *lakh* (200,000) rupees; a far cheaper alternative is to hire these boats by the day or on longer overnight trips (see p.379).

Karunagapalli is best visited as a day-trip from Kollam; regular **buses** pass through on the way to Alappuzha. One daytime **train**, #6525, leaves Kollam at 2.25pm, arriving in Karunagapalli half an hour later, but you have to get a bus back. On reaching the bus stand or railway station, take an auto-rickshaw 1km north along the national highway, then turn left into a lane for 4km to the riverside village of **Alumkattaru**, and the boatyard of the *vallam asharis*, the boat carpenters, who are generally friendly and happy to let visitors watch them work. In the shade of palm trees at the edge of the water, some weave palm leaves, others twist coir strands into rope and craftsmen repair the boats. Soaking in the shallows nearby are palm leaves, used for thatch, and coconut husks for coir rope.

Alappuzha

Under its former appellation of Alleppey, **ALAPPUZHA** is another romantic and historic name from Kerala's past. Roughly midway between Kollam (85km south) and Kochi (64km north), Alappuzha was one of the best-known and wealthiest ports along the Malabar Coast, to the extent that successful British traders who had settled here during the Raj were loath to leave at Independence. A sizeable community of British expats remained here until the 1950s, enticed by thriving trading opportunities; their luck ran out in 1957, however, when the newly elected communist government clamped down on private businesses and they were forced to return to Britain. With such a long trading history, tourist literature is fond of referring to Alappuzha as the "Venice of the East", but while it may be full of interconnecting **canals**, there the resemblance ends. Alappuzha has a bustling, messy centre of ramshackle wood and corrugated iron-roofed houses, although some suburban parts are quiet and leafy. The town is chiefly significant in the coir industry, which accounts for much of the traffic on its sludgy waterways.

Despite its insalubrious canals, Alappuzha is prominent on the tourist trail as one of the major centres for **backwater boat trips** on public ferries and private tourist boats to and from Kollam and Kottayam. Most visitors stay just one night, catching a boat or bus out early the next morning. There is little to see here, but the bazaar along the main street, **Mullakal Road**, is worth a browse, with a good selection of lurid Keralan *lunghis*. However, if you do have an afternoon to spare, a ten-minute walk northeast of the centre takes you to the **lakeside**, shaded under a canopy of palm trees.

Alappuzha really comes alive on the second Saturday of August, in the middle of the monsoon, when it serves as the venue for one of Kerala's major spectacles – the **Nehru Trophy snakeboat race**. This event, first held in 1952, is based on the traditional Keralan enthusiasm for racing magnificently decorated longboats, with raised rears designed to resemble the hood of a cobra. Each boat carries 25 singers, and 100–130 enthusiastic oarsmen power the craft along, all rowing to the rhythmic *Vanchipattu* (song of the boatman). There are a number of prize categories, including one for the women's race; sixteen boats compete for each prize. The atmosphere is tremendous as Alappuzha is packed with thousands of cheering spectators all dressed in their Sunday best, out to enjoy the colourful pre-race pageant in the morning as much as the races themselves. Similar races can be seen at Aranmula (p.384), and at Champakulam, 16km by ferry from Alappuzha. The ATDC information office (see below) will be able to tell you the dates of these other events, which change every year.

There are a number of fascinating **temples** in villages dotted along the main coast road south of Alappuzha, but it's only really practical to visit them if you rent a taxi for the morning (they close in the afternoons). Ask the driver to take you to **Ambalapuzzha** for the Sri Krishna Temple, the state's most important Krishna temple after Guruvayur (see p.425), then on to **Mannarsala** for the Nagaraja Temple, dedicated to the snake-god; the temple is particularly powerful in helping childless couples to conceive. You can complete the tour with a stop at **Harippad** for the Subramanya Swami temple. The temples are all impressive in their own right and have the added attraction that you are very unlikely to see another tourist.

Arrival and information

The KSRTC **bus stand**, on the east of town, is served by half-hourly buses to Kollam, Thiruvananthapuram and Ernakulam; less frequent buses run to Kottayam, Thrissur and Palakkad. The **boat jetty** is just one minute's walk west from the bus stand. The daily tourist ferry to Quilon leaves at 10.30am from the jetty, and public ferry services to Kottayam at 7.30am, 9.45am, 11.15am, 1pm and 2.30pm (Rs10; 2hr 30min). The **railway station** is 3km southwest of the jetty. The most useful services north from Alappuzha include the Jan Shatabdi Express (#2076; 8.20am) to Ernakulam, and the Alleppey–Chennai Express (#6042; 3pm), which stops at Ernakulam Junction before continuing to Thrissur, Palakkad and Chennai. For points further north along the coast including Mangalore, changing at Ernakulam will give you far more options. Few trains continue south beyond Alappuzha. The best trains to Thiruvananthapuram are the Ernakulam–Trivandrum Express (#6341; 7.20am) and Jan Shatabdi (#2075; 6.33pm).

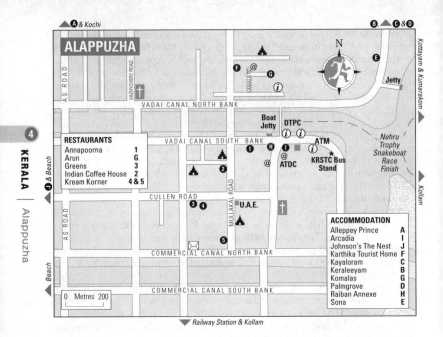

ALAPPUZHA

Kottayam & Kumarakom

Kollam

Jetty

VADAI CANAL NORTH BANK

Boat
Jetty

DTPC

VADAI CANAL SOUTH BANK

Nehru
Trophy
Snakeboat
Race
Finish

ATM

ATDC

KRSTC Bus
Stand

RESTAURANTS

Annapoorna	1
Arun	G
Greens	3
Indian Coffee House	2
Kream Korner	4 & 5

CULLEN ROAD

U.A.E.

COMMERCIAL CANAL NORTH BANK

ACCOMMODATION

Alleppey Prince	A
Arcadia	I
Johnson's The Nest	J
Karthika Tourist Home	F
Kayaloram	C
Keraleeyam	B
Komalas	G
Palmgrove	D
Raiban Annexe	H
Sona	E

0 Metres 200

COMMERCIAL CANAL SOUTH BANK

Railway Station & Kollam

Alappuzha has several rival **tourist departments**. The main ATDC tourist information office (daily 8am–8pm; ☎0477/224 3462, ⓦwww.atdcalleppey .com) is opposite the jetty on the second floor of the Municipal Shopping Complex, and they also have a smaller office just off Komala Road. The DTPC office (daily 7.30am–9pm; ☎0477/225 1796), at the jetty, handles **hotel bookings** for all KTDC and private hotels throughout Kerala and in other parts of South India for the charge of the telephone call and on receipt of one night's room rate. The ATDC and DTPC both sell tickets for their **ferries**, **backwater cruises** and charter boats. The Kerala Department of Tourism office, also at the DTPC jetty (Mon–Sat 10am–5pm; ☎0477/226 0722, ⓦwww.keralatourism .org), is good for general travel information. Other ferry and charter organizations include Kerala Backwaters at Choondapally Buildings, near the Nehru Trophy finishing point (☎0477/224 1693); Alappuzha Tour Co, Punchiri Building, Jetty Road (☎0477/226 2931); and Cruisors, Komala Road (☎0477/226 4777).

The best place to **change money** is UAE on Mullakal Road (Mon–Sat 9.30am–6.30pm, Sun 9.30am–1pm); there's an ATM on the same block. The State Bank of India is on Beach Road; the Canara Bank is next to the Zion Food Shop, near the jetty. **Internet** access is widely available for Rs25–35 per hour, with several outlets along the road facing the boat jetty and one near *Hotel Komala*.

Accommodation

Alappuzha's town-centre **lodgings** are uninspiring, but there are some great places to stay if you are willing to travel into the outskirts and pay a bit more.

Alleppey Prince AS Rd (aka Ernakulam Rd or NH-47), 2km north of the jetty ☎0477/224 3752, ⓔprincehotel@satyam.net.in. The poshest option close to the town centre, though past its prime,

with a/c rooms, private backwater trips, and classical music and Kathakali by the pool. ⑥–⑧

Arcadia Vadai Canal South Bank, by the KSRTC Bus Stand ☎0477/225 1354,

@www.arcadiakerala.com. Soulless place with clean rooms (some a/c) close to the jetty; the restaurant serves excellent fish. Overpriced but popular, as it's so convenient for the ferry. ②—⑤

Coir Village Lake Resort Thrikunnapuzha ℗0477/223 1145, @www.coirvillage.com. ATDC resort 35km south of Allapuzha, with seventeen water-facing a/c cottages and some houseboats, all Rs3450. ⑨

Johnson's The Nest Lalbagh, Convent Square, 2km west of the centre ℗0477/224 5825, @johnsongilbertlk1@hotmail.com. Wonderful and extremely friendly homestay in an attractive colonial building ten minutes' walk from the beach. Some of the rooms are huge, with spacious balconies, and there are also some smaller ones in the house opposite. Home-cooked food on request. ②—④

Karthika Tourist Home Mullakal Rd, across the canal and opposite the jetty ℗0477/224 5524. Plain rooms, some with attached bathrooms and wicker chairs (no. 31, with its large bay windows, is particularly good value) – the budgie aviary is a nice touch. ②

Kayaloram Punnamada Kayal ℗0477/223 2040, ℻225 2918. Twelve cool wooden cottages built in Keralan style (complete with open-air showers) and set in an incredible location in a grove of palms with views onto the lake. Ayurvedic courses and daily sunset cruises are available, and there's a pool. Book through the resort's city office at Punchiri Buildings, Jetty Rd (℗0477/226 2931) and you'll be taken there by boat from the Nehru Trophy jetty. $70 including breakfast. ⑨

Keraleeyam Nehru Trophy Rd, Thathampally ℗0477/223 1468, @www.keraleeyam.com.

Situated on the Nehru Trophy channel (and reachable by boat from the jetty), this traditional Keralan house has oodles of character and elegant rooms arranged around a communal living area, as well as lovely cottages (some with a/c). It has been an Ayurvedic centre for sixty years, and tailor-made rejuvenation courses are available. ⑥—⑧

Komalas Zilla Court Ward ℗0477/224 3631. A five-minute walk across the canal from the bus stand, with a good range of clean rooms (some with a/c) and a decent South Indian restaurant. ②—⑤

KTDC Yatri Nivas AS Rd, near *Alleppey Prince* ℗0477/224 4460, @www.ktdc.com. Immaculate rooms (the larger ones with a/c), a restaurant and a male-oriented beer parlour. ②—⑤

Palmgrove Punnamada Kayal, Punnamada ℗0477/223 5004. Some 2.5km from the jetty, and reachable by bus or boat, this place has quaint and very simple bamboo huts dotted around a manicured palm grove, with attached open-air bathrooms. The restaurant is in an open hut, serving South Indian food only. This place isn't in the same league as some other resorts along the backwaters, but then it is a lot more affordable. ⑤

Raiban Annexe Vadai Canal South Bank ℗0477/226 1017. Budget hotel set back from the canal in a communal courtyard. Small rooms but reasonable value. ②—③

Sona Lakeside, Thathampally ℗0477/223 5211, @www.sonahome.com. Lovely old Keralan home, set in a beautiful garden, with four rooms with mosquito nets, plenty of family atmosphere and home cooking. The hospitable owners love to share their knowledge of the history of the town and backwaters. ③—④

Eating

Alappuzha has plenty of decent, inexpensive places to **eat**. For a splurge, catch a rickshaw out to the *Alleppey Prince*, whose a/c *Vembanad* restaurant offers the town's classiest menu, and beer by the pool. The KTDC *Yatri Nivas* round the corner is a lot cheaper and also serves beer.

Annapoorna Vadai Canal South Bank. Very good, inexpensive veggie restaurant – highlights of the menu include delicious Keralan coconut curries.
Arun *Komalas Hotel*, Zilla Court Ward. Tasty Chinese noodles and Indian veg (including delicious *dal makhini*, *malai kofta* and *subzis*) at reasonable prices, but avoid the Continental food. One of the most popular places in town; if it's busy, settle in for a wait.
Greens Cullen Rd. Cheap, clean and popular restaurant, with a little garden out front and a menu of fresh South Indian snacks and

all-you-can-eat thalis, mainly veg, but also some with meat and fish.
Indian Coffee House Mullakal Rd. Part of the all-India chain of cooperatives, with a predictable, inexpensive menu of reliable filter coffee, omelettes, *dosas* and *iddlis*, as well as some meat dishes.
Kream Korner Mullakal Rd. Non-veg restaurant-cum-ice-cream parlour. Mains centre on chicken and mutton, and there's a selection of snacks, milkshakes and ice creams. There's a second, smaller branch next to *Greens*.

One of the most memorable experiences for travellers in India – even those on the lowest of budgets – is the opportunity to take a boat journey on the **backwaters of Kerala**. Immortalized as the setting for Arundhati Roy's Booker-prize-winning novel *The God of Small Things*, the area known as **Kuttanad** stretches for 75km from Kollam in the south to Kochi in the north, sandwiched between the sea and the hills. This bewildering labyrinth of shimmering waterways, composed of lakes, canals, rivers and rivulets, is lined with dense tropical greenery and preserves rural Keralan lifestyles that are completely hidden from the road.

Views constantly change, from narrow canals and dense vegetation to open vistas and dazzling green paddy fields. Homes, farms, churches, mosques and temples can be glimpsed among the trees, and every so often you might catch the blue flash of a kingfisher, or the green of a parakeet. Pallas fishing eagles cruise above the water looking for prey and cormorants perch on logs to dry their wings. If you're lucky enough to be in a boat without a motor, at times the only sounds are birds chattering and occasional film songs drifting across from distant radios. Some families live on tiny pockets of land, with just enough room for a simple house, yard and boat. They bathe and wash their clothes – sometimes their buffaloes, too, muddy from plough-ing the fields – at the water's edge. Traditional Keralan longboats, *kettu vallam*, glide along, powered by gondolier-like boatmen with poles and sails, with the water often lapping perilously close to the edge. Fishermen work from tiny dugout canoes, long rowing boats and operate massive Chinese nets on the shore.

Coconut trees at improbable angles form shady canopies, and occasionally you pass under simple curved bridges. Here and there basic drawbridges can be raised on ropes, but major bridges are few and far between; most people rely on boatmen to ferry them across the water to connect with roads and bus services, resulting in a constant crisscrossing of the waters from dawn until dusk (a way of life beautifully represented in the visually stunning film *Piravi*, by Keralan director Shaji). Poles stick-ing out of the water indicate dangerous shallows.

Threats to the ecosystem

The **African moss** that often carpets the surface of the narrower waterways may look attractive, but it is actually a menace to small craft traffic and starves underwater life of light. It is also a symptom of the many serious **ecological problems** currently affecting the region, whose population density ranges from between two and four times that of other coastal areas in southwest India. This has put growing pressure on land, and hence a greater reliance on fertilizers, which eventually work their way into the water causing the build-up of moss. Illegal land reclamation, however, poses the single greatest threat to this fragile ecosystem. In a little over a century, the total area of water in Kuttanad has been reduced by two-thirds, while mangrove swamps have been decimated by pollution and the spread of towns and villages around the edges of the backwater region. Tourism is now adding to the problem, as the film of oil from motorized ferries and houseboats spreads through the waters, killing yet more fish, which has in turn had to a reduction of over fifty percent in the number of bird species found in the region. Some of the tourist agencies are trying to lessen the impact of visitors by introducing more ecofriendly vessels.

Routes and practicalities

There are numerous backwater **routes** to choose from, on vessels ranging from local ferries, through chauffeur-driven speedboats offered by the KTDC, to customized *kettu vallam* and rice boat cruises. The most popular excursion is the full-day journey between **Kollam** and **Alappuzha**. All sorts of private hustlers offer their services, but the principal boats are run on alternate days by the Alleppey Tourism Development Co-op (ATDC) and the District Tourism Promotion Council (DTPC) – see p.371 for contact details. The double-decker boats leave from both Kollam and Alappuzha daily, departing at 10.30am (10am check-in); tickets cost Rs300 and can be bought in advance or on the day at the ATDC/DTPC counters, other agents and some hotels. Both companies make three stops during the 8hr journey, including one for lunch, and another at the renowned **Mata Amritanandamayi Mission** at Amritapuri, around three hours north of Kollam. Foreigners are welcome to stay at the ashram (℡0476/289 6399, ⓦwww.amritapuri.org; ➊), which is the home of the renowned female guru, Shri Amritanandamayi Devi, known as "hugging Mama" because she gives each of her visitors and devotees a big, power-imparting hug during the daily *darshan* sessions. Rs150 a day gets you simple meals and a basic room in the startling high-rise block.

Although it is by far the most popular backwater trip, many tourists find the Alappuzha–Kollam route too long and at times uncomfortable, with crowded decks and intense sun. There's also something faintly embarrassing about being cooped up with a crowd of fellow tourists madly photographing any signs of life on the water or canal banks, while gangs of kids scamper alongside the boat screaming "one pen, one pen". You can sidestep the tourist scene completely by catching **local ferries**. These are a lot slower and more crowded, but you'll gain a more intimate experience of life on the backwaters. The trip from Alappuzha to Kottayam (5 daily; Rs10) is particularly recommended. The first ferry leaves at 7.30am; arrive early to get a good place with uninterrupted views. There are also numerous daily ferries that ply routes between local villages, allowing you to hop on and off as you like. The scenery on these routes is often more varied than that between Alappuzha and Kollam, beginning with open lagoons and winding up on narrow canals through densely populated coconut groves and islands – and the tickets cost a fraction of the tourist boats. Whichever boat you opt for, take a sun hat and plenty of water. **Check the departure times** in advance, as these can vary from year to year.

Groups of up to ten people can charter a *kettu vallam* moored at **Karunagapalli** (see p.374) for a day's **cruise** on the backwaters. Boats have comfortable cane chairs and a raised central platform where passengers can laze on cushions; there are bathrooms on board plus food and drinks. Whether powered by local gondoliers or by sail, the trip is as quiet and restful as you could possibly want. Starting at Rs4000 for the day, including lunch, the luxury is well worth it.

Almost every mid- to top-range hotel near the backwaters has its own private *kettu vallum* boat available for residents to hire, while the DTPC and ATDC, along with many *kettu vallam* operators in both Alleppey and Kollam, can arrange a trip if you turn up on spec. One of the more reliable private operators is Southern Backwaters (℡0474/274 6037, ⓦwww.southernbackwaters.com) in Kollam or Tharavad Boats (℡0477/224 4599, ⓔalleppeytharavad@sify.com) in Alleppey. However, these overnight *kettu vallam* cruises are not cheap – expect to pay Rs4000–10,000 for two people for a 24hr cruise, depending on the distance travelled, though you may be able to haggle the price down in the low season.

Although backwater life may seem idyllic, there have been recent reports of theft, especially during the night when the crew sleep on land and windows are left open – so take care of your belongings at all times; lock them away if possible or, at the very least, keep them away from the windows. Also insist that your boat isn't moored near one with a generator that may run all night.

As Alappuzha isn't on the main railway network, but on a branch line, the choice of **trains** servicing the town is limited. There are, however, train connections to Thiruvananthapuram and Kollam in the south, and to Kochi/Ernakulam, Thrissur, Palakkad and other points in the north. **Bus** connections are adequate, especially to Kochi/Ernakulam, where there is a greater choice of trains to northern destinations and Tamil Nadu. Although buses travel to Kollam, the best way of getting there is by **boat**. Regular ferry services connect to Kottayam from where you can get buses to Periyar, as well as several destinations along the coastal highway. For more on public transport from Alappuzha, see "Travel details", p.438.

By bus

The shambolic KSRTC bus stand, on the east side of town and a minute's walk from the boat jetty, is served by half-hourly buses to **Kollam** (2hr), **Thiruvananthapuram** (3hr–3hr 30min) and **Kochi/Ernakulam** (1hr 30min). Less frequent buses run to **Kottayam** (4hr) and **Thrissur** (8hr).

By boat

Tourist boats travel regularly to **Kollam**, with the ATDC and DTPC boats operating a similar schedule departing at 10.30am and arriving in Kollam at 6.30pm. Much cheaper local **ferries** travel to **Kottayam**, there are five services between 7.30am and 2pm. Ferries run later but it will be too dark for photos and the mosquitoes will be out.

By train

As the backwaters prevent trains from continuing directly south beyond Alappuzha, only a few major daily services and a handful of passenger trains depart from the railway station, 3km southwest of the jetty. For points further north along the coast including **Mangalore**, take an early train and change at Ernakulam, as the afternoon Alleppey–Cannanore Express (#6307), which continues to **Kozhikode** and **Kannur**, arrives at those destinations rather late at night.

The following trains are recommended as the **fastest** and/or **most convenient** from Alappuzha.

Recommended trains from Alappuzha

Destination	Name	Number	Frequency	Departs	Total time
Ernakulam/	Jan Shatabdi Exp.	#2076	daily	8.20am	1hr 25min
Kochi	*Alleppey–Chennai Exp.	#6042	daily	3pm	1hr 10min
Chennai	*Alleppey–Chennai Exp.	#6042	daily	3pm	15hr 5min
Thiruvanan-thapuram	Ernakulam–Trivandrum Exp.	#6341	daily	7.20am	3hr 5min
	Jan Shatabdi Exp.	#2075	daily	6.33pm	2hr 48min

* this train also travels to Thrissur and Palakkad

Kottayam and around

Some 76km southeast of Kochi and 37km northeast of Alappuzha, the busy commercial centre of **KOTTAYAM** is strategically located between the back-waters and the stunning Lake Vembanad to the west, and the spice, tea and rubber plantations, forests and mountains of the Western Ghats to the east. Most visitors come here on their way somewhere else – foreigners take short backwater trips to Alappuzha or set off to Periyar Wildlife Sanctuary, while Ayappa devotees pass through en route to the forest temple at Sabarimala (see p.392).

Kottayam's long history of **Syrian Christian** settlement is reflected by the presence of two thirteenth-century churches on a hill 5km northwest of the centre, which you can get to by rickshaw. Two eighth-century Nestorian stone crosses with Pahlavi and Syriac inscriptions, on either side of the elaborately decorated altar of the **Valliapalli** ("big") church, are probably the earliest solid evidence of Christianity in India. The visitors' book contains entries from as far back as the 1890s, including one by the Ethiopian king, Haile Selassie, and a British viceroy. The interior of the nearby **Cheriapalli** ("small") church is covered with lively paintings, thought to have been executed by a Portuguese artist in the sixteenth century. If the doors are locked, ask for the key at the church office (9am–1pm & 2–5pm).

Practicalities

Kottayam's KSRTC **bus stand**, 500m south of the centre on TB Road (not to be confused with the private stand for local buses on MC Road), is an important stop on routes to and from major towns in South India. Four of the frequent buses to Kumily/Periyar (3–4hr) continue daily on to Madurai in Tamil Nadu (7hr), and there are regular services to Thiruvananthapuram, Kollam and Ernakulam. The **railway station**, 2km north of the centre, sees a constant flow of traffic between Thiruvananthapuram and points north. **Ferries** from Alappuzha and elsewhere dock at the weed-clogged jetty, 2km south of town. For details of backwater trips from Kottayam, see p.379.

There's a tiny DTPC tourist office at the jetty (daily 9am–5pm; ☎0481/256 0479). The best place to **change money** is Muthoot Bankers (Mon–Sat 9.30am–1pm & 1.30–5pm) on KK Road, and there's a CorpBank ATM near the corner of KK Rd and Gandhi Square. **Internet** facilities are available at Intimacy (Rs25 per hour) on KK Rd and Brain Net (Rs15 per hour), just north of the KSRTC Bus Stand.

Accommodation and eating

Kottayam has a good choice of mid-range **hotels**; if you're in search of utter luxury, head out to one of the five-star resorts that nestle on the banks of the nearby Vembanad lake (see p.382) in Kumarakom.

There are basic **restaurants** in the centre of Kottayam, especially around the bus station on TB Road, and an *Indian Coffee House* on TB Road, while the best spot for non-veg grub such as burgers plus Indian and Chinese favourites is *JobGees* on MC Road. Hotel eateries include the good veg and fish restaurant at the *Homestead* and the *Vembanad Lake Resort*, where you eat Indian, Western and Chinese dishes, including seafood, either in a lakeside garden or on a moored *kettu vallam*, making for a special evening out.

Hotels and guesthouses

Aida TB Junction, MC Rd ☎0481/256 8391, ⓦwww.aidahotel.com. Large, friendly hotel with a wide range of rooms, including some with a/c, plus reasonably priced singles. Facilities include a good restaurant, bar, money-changing facilities and a travel agency. ④–⑤

Aiswarya International Off Temple Rd ☎0481/258 1440, ⓕ258 1254. Seven-storey property with large, light and airy rooms with TV. ④–⑤

Ambassador KK Rd ☎0481/256 3293. A well-run economy hotel with clean rooms, some with big TVs and balcony. Chocolate delicacies for sale in reception. ②–④

Green Park Kurian Uthup Rd, Nagampadam, near the railway station ☎0481/256 3311, ⓔgreenparkhotel@yahoo.com Modern and

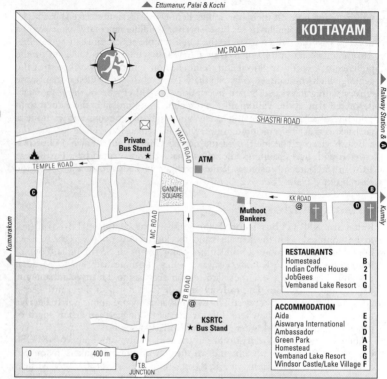

▲ Ettumanur, Palai & Kochi

KOTTAYAM

MC ROAD

SHASTRI ROAD

Private Bus Stand ★

ATM

TEMPLE ROAD

GANDHI SQUARE

Muthoot Bankers

KK ROAD

KSRTC ★ Bus Stand

0 — 400 m

T.B. JUNCTION

Railway Station & 🅰

Kumily

Kumarakom

RESTAURANTS

Homestead	B
Indian Coffee House	2
JobGees	1
Vembanad Lake Resort	G

ACCOMMODATION

Aida	E
Aiswarya International	C
Ambassador	D
Green Park	A
Homestead	B
Vembanad Lake Resort	G
Windsor Castle/Lake Village	F

▼ Boat Jetty, ⓘ, 🅵, 🅶, Thiruvananthapuram & Alappuzha

efficient business hotel, with decent non-a/c and a/c rooms, a bar and two restaurants. Good value. ③–⑤
Homestead KK Rd ☎0481/256 0467. Well-appointed, central hotel with a range of options from clean budget to comfortable a/c rooms. Good veg and fish restaurant. ③–⑥
Vembanad Lake Resort Kodimatha, 3km from the centre of town and a five-minute walk from ferry ☎0481/236 0866, ⓦwww.vembanadlakeresort .com. Western-style motel beside an inlet of Lake Vembanad. The ten old rooms are close to the

noisy road, but the newer wing near the water is pleasant. ④–⑥
Windsor Castle/Lake Village Kodimatha, just before *Vembanad Lake Resort* ☎0481/230 3622, ⓦwww.thewindsorcastle.com. This place comprises two distinct sections: a white tower-block of characterless luxury rooms (the "castle" part), and the far nicer "Lake Village", made up of comfortable a/c chalets ($135) on a lagoon, with a pool and a very pleasant open-air restaurant specializing in Keralan cuisine. ⑧–⑨

Around Kottayam

Some of Kerala's most attractive scenery lies within easy reach of Kottayam. Probably the ideal destination for a day-trip – although it also has some wonderful accommodation – is the beautiful **Kumarakom Bird Sanctuary**, in the backwaters to the west. **Aranmula**, to the south, is one of the last villages still making *kannady* metal mirrors, and has a Krishna temple which organizes a ritual "non-competitive" boat race. The Mahadeva temple at **Ettumanur**, a short way north of Kottayam, is known to devotees as the home of a dangerous and wrathful Shiva and to art lovers as a sublime example of temple architecture, adorned with wood-carvings and murals. A short way northeast of Ettumanur is the little town of **Palai**, where the beautiful Church of St Thomas boasts exquisite eighteenth-century frescoes.

Kumarakom

KUMARAKOM, 16km west of Kottayam, is technically an island on Vembanad Lake. Although right in the thick of a tangle of lush tropical waterways, it can be reached quite easily by bus from Kottayam (every 10min). The best time to visit the **Bird Sanctuary** (daily dawn–dusk; Rs45) is between November and March when it serves as a winter home for many migratory birds, some from as far away as Siberia. Species include the darter or snake bird, little cormorant, night heron, golden-backed woodpecker, crow pheasant, white-breasted water hen and tree pie. Dawn is the quietest and best time for viewing, when the first rays of sunlight filter through the lush tropical canopy. Although the island is quite small, a guide is useful; you can arrange one through *Water Scapes* (see p.384) or the other luxury hotels.

Next to the sanctuary, set in waterside gardens, a refurbished colonial bungalow that once belonged to a family of Christian missionaries and rubber planters forms the nucleus of a luxury **hotel**, the *Taj Garden Retreat* (☎0481/252 5711, ⓦ www.tajhotels.com; ⑨), which consists of eighteen cottages ($190–230) in a landscaped garden around a private lagoon, plus a *kettu vallam* houseboat ($250–300). However, it's not nearly as impressive as the *Coconut Lagoon Hotel* (☎0481/252 4491, ⑤252 4495; ⑨), 1km northwest on the edge of Vembanad

Arundhati Roy

Published in 1997, Arundhati Roy's remarkable novel, **The God of Small Things**, is set in a riverside village on the outskirts of Kottayam. It earned her the Booker Prize as well as the ire of certain sections of the local populace who reacted strongly to her description of small-town Kerala. The intricate, haunting and intensely personal tale gives a glimpse of social tensions in Keralan life, and has an astutely observed interplay of character and environment. Roy was brought up in the same village as Ayemenem, the protagonist, and some of her family are still living there. Although the house in Ayemenem in the book is fictional, one of the most obvious landmarks in the book is the so-called "History house", sitting right on the shore of Vembanad lake in Kumarakom. This was where the central characters, the twins, watched the local police beat up their friend Velutha, an untouchable servant. The "History house", built by British colonial settlers, was where Arundhati Roy played as a child and it now forms the central body of the *Taj Garden Retreat Hotel*.

An architect by training, Roy comes from a proactive family; in the 1990s her mother, Mary Roy, fought and won a landmark legal battle to secure the right for Christian women in Kerala to divorce their husbands. Arundhati Roy is a dedicated supporter of low-caste Keralan poets and writers who write in the state vernacular, Malayalam. In 1998, she became an important spokesperson for the anti-nuclear campaign that followed the "blast" – India's nuclear tests – and wrote a passionate pamphlet, *For the Greater Common Good*, on the issue. Her profile as a campaigner for social and environmental issues became global after she was **arrested** in January 2000 during protests over the Narmada valley hydroelectric dam project in central India which, if plans come to fruition, will result in the displacement of some 33 million people. After demonstrating against the decision to give the go-ahead to the project in late 2000, Roy was accused of inciting violence and attacking a court official, and faced a contempt of court charge in summer 2001. Found guilty at a March 2002 hearing of India's Supreme Court, she was sentenced to a day's "symbolic imprisonment".

Lake and reached by launch (you can telephone for the boat from a kiosk at the canalside). Superbly crafted from fragments of ruined Keralan palaces, with beautiful woodcarvings and brass work, the building alone merits a visit. It was designed in traditional Keralan style, and even if you can't afford to stay here (rooms start at $230), you could try the wonderful Keralan specialities at the **restaurant**.

Another alternative for those with deep pockets is the *Kumarakom Lake Resort* (T0481/252 4900, Wwww.klresort.com;), 3km from the village and just before the *Taj*. This ostentatious place comprises two beautiful 300-year-old palaces recovered and reconstructed on site, and ultra-luxurious cottages ($210–280) made up from bits of old Keralan houses, each with an outdoor bathroom in the lush tropical garden. The Ayurveda centre has two doctors and four massage rooms; the swimming pool boasts a jacuzzi, its water lapping the edge of the lake.

Nearby, KTDC *Water Scapes* (T0481/252 5861, Wwww.ktdc.com;) sits right on the lake and consists of comfortable a/c cottages (from Rs5500) built on stilts; few have a decent view over the lake and the ugly metal walkways further detract, but it's significantly cheaper than its competitors and convenient for the bird sanctuary. You can drift across the lake on one of the luxury *kettu vallams* moored here. If you're on a budget, the excellent *Moolappura Guest House* (T0481/252 5980;), 200m before the bus stand at the *Taj*, has three rooms with attached bathrooms. The family is very welcoming and offers rides on its dugout boats, personal tours in the bird sanctuary, and has a professional chef, who conjures up Keralan and continental dishes.

Besides the hotels, the only other place to **eat** is KTDC's uninspiring café at the *Tourist Complex* near where the bus from Kottayam pulls in, close to the *Taj* hotel gates.

Aranmula

The village of **ARANMULA** offers another appealing day-trip from Kottayam (start early), 30km to the south, and 10km beyond Chengannur. Its ancient temple is dedicated to Parthasarathy, which was the divine name under which Krishna acted as Arjuna's charioteer during the bloody Kurekshetra war recorded in the Mahabharata, and the guise in which he expounded the Bhagavad Gita. About 1800 years old, the temple is a major site on the Vishnaivite pilgrimage trail in Kerala, and, as Vishnu is represented here in the form of Annadanaprabhu ("One Who Gives Food"), it is said that no pilgrim worshipping at the temple will go hungry. Each year, towards the end of the Onam festival (Aug/Sept), a **Snakeboat Regatta** is celebrated as part of the temple rituals, and crowds line the banks of the Pampa River to cheer on the thrusting longboats (similar to those seen at Alappuzha; see p.374).

Aranmula is also known for the manufacture of extraordinary *kannady* **metal mirrors** (called Aranmula *kannadi*), produced using the "lost wax" technique (see p.689) with an alloy of copper, silver, brass, lead and bronze. Once a prerequisite of royal households, these ornamental mirrors are now exceedingly rare; only two master craftsmen, Subramanian Achary and Arjun Achary and their families, still make them. The most modest models cost around Rs300, while custom-made mirrors can cost up to Rs50,000.

The **Vijana Kala Vedi Cultural Centre** in Aranmula offers ways of "experiencing traditional India through the study of art and village life". Introductory courses are offered in Kathakali, Mohiniattam and Bharatnatyam dance, woodcarving, mural painting, cooking, Kalarippayat, Ayurvedic medicine and several Indian languages. Courses cost upwards of US$200 per week and are booked by writing to the Director, Vijana Kala Vedi Cultural Centre, Tarayil Mukku Junction, Aranmula, Kerala 689533.

Ettumanur

The magnificent Mahadeva temple at **ETTUMANUR**, 12km north of Kottayam on the road to Ernakulam, features a circular shrine, fine woodcarving and one of the earliest (sixteenth-century) and most celebrated of Keralan **murals**. The deity is Shiva in one of his most terrible aspects, described as *vaddikasula vada*, "one who takes his dues with interest" and is "difficult to please". His predominant mood is *raudra* (fury). Although the shrine is open to Hindus only, foreigners can see the courtyard murals, which may be photographed after obtaining a camera ticket (Rs20; video Rs50) from the counter on the left in the temple courtyard. The four-metre mural depicts Nataraja – Shiva – executing a cosmic *tandava* dance, trampling evil underfoot in the form of a demon. Swathed in cobras, he stands on one leg in a wheel of gold, with his matted locks fanning out amid a mass of flowers and snakes, while devotees gather round. Musical accompaniment is provided by Krishna on flute, three-headed Brahma on cymbals and, playing the ancient sacred Keralan *mizhavu* drum, Shiva's special rhythm expert Nandikesvara.

Ettumanur's ten-day **annual festival** (Feb/March) reflects the wealth of the temple, with elaborate celebrations including music. On the most important days, the eighth and tenth, priests bring out the temple's golden elephants – seven large specimens, each fashioned from 95 kilos of gold, and a smaller one half the weight – which were presented in the eighteenth century by Marthanda Varma, the raja of Travancore.

Palai

The small town of **PALAI**, 30km northeast of Kottayam, is home to the **Church of St Thomas**, a stunning Portuguese-style building that features a wall of beautiful **frescoes**. Well off the tourist trail, Palai is best visited as a daytrip, although there are several ultra-basic lodges if you want to stay. Buses from Kottayam and Kochi pull in and leave Palai frequently from the KSRTC **bus stand** next to the bell tower in the centre of town. From here the church is a two-kilometre walk or auto-rickshaw ride east along the main road and over a small bridge; turn right into a lane which leads to St Thomas's.

A chapel – modelled along the lines of a Hindu temple – was built to service the spiritual needs of the five Christian families resident in the Parish of St Thomas in 1003. In the sixteenth century this was destroyed and a new building erected, but it was burned down a century later during a protracted conflict with local Muslim settlers. The present structure, built in the eighteenth century, has a soaring and startlingly white ornamental facade, and a squat spire and nave.

Inside the church is a bizarre spiral pulpit, carved from a single piece of teak that was mysteriously found already cut and floating down a river nearby; the ceilings are richly painted with gold leaf. An elaborate altar dating back to 1853, is home to some plastic flowers and three rather kitsch models of St Thomas, the Virgin Mary and Jesus, complete with flashing lights. However, to see the *pièce de resistance*, hidden behind the altar, you'll need to ask the resident caretaker for a candle. Extraordinarily well preserved in the darkness is a wall of exquisite eighteenth-century frescoes painted with plant pigments, depicting the life of St Thomas and Jesus as the Lamb of God.

The larger and modern church alongside was built in 1981; the local congregation has swelled to 1000 members in a parish of 7000 Marthoma Christians.

The history of Kerala's **Christians** – who today represent 21 percent of the population – is said to date back to the first century AD, some three centuries before Christianity received official recognition in Europe. These days there are five main branches among a bewildering assortment of churches. They are **Nestorians** (confined mainly to Thrissur and Ernakulam), **Roman Catholics** (found throughout Kerala), **Syrian Orthodox Church** (previously known as the Jacobite Syrians), **Marthoma Syrians** (a splinter group of the Syrian Orthodox) and the Anglican **Church of South India**.

A legend, widely believed in Kerala but the object of academic scepticism, states that **St Thomas** the Apostle – "Doubting Thomas" – landed on the Malabar Coast in 52AD, where he converted several brahmins and others and founded seven churches. Muziris, his first port of call, has been identified as **Kodungallur** (see p.423); the traditional accounts of Jews who later arrived there in 68AD state that they encountered a community of Christians known as **Nazranis**, or "followers of the Nazarene" (Jesus). The Nazranis found little opposition from the largely Hindu population, and were able to amalgamate some age-old indigenous Hindu practices into their newfound religion.

In the fourth century, their number was augmented by an influx of **Syrian Christians** belonging to seven tribes from Baghdad, Nineveh and Jerusalem, who were under the leadership of the merchant **Knayi Thoma** (Thomas of Cana). Assisted by the development of commerce, the Syrian Christians were to play a vital role in the spread of Christianity in Kerala. As they went around building churches, the Syrians introduced architectural conventions from the Middle East, and so incorporated the nave and chancel with a gabled facade, which resulted in a distinctive style of Keralan Christian church. They also absorbed some architectural styles from the Nazranis by retaining the *dhwajastamba* (flag mast), the *kottupura* (gate house) and the *kurisuthara* (altar with a mounted cross).

A significant faction of the Syrian Christian community, the **Nestorians** (after Nestorius, the patriarch of Constantinople) were the dominant Christian group in Kerala after the sixth century and at one stage had centres in various parts of India. However, the assertive spread of **Portuguese Catholicism** centuries later reduced the Nestorians to a small community, which survives today in Thrissur (see p.417).

Christians gradually came to the forefront as traders, and eventually gained special privileges from the local rulers. The early communities followed a liturgy in the **Syriac language** (a dialect of Aramaic). Latin was introduced by missionaries who visited Kollam in the Middle Ages, and once the Portuguese turned up, in 1498, a large community of **Latin Christians** developed, particularly on the coast, and came under the jurisdiction of the pope. In the middle of the seventeenth century, with the ascendancy of the Dutch, part of the Church broke away from Rome, and local bishops were appointed through the offices of the Jacobite patriarch in Antioch.

During the nineteenth century, the Anglican Church amalgamated with certain "free" churches, to form the **Church of South India**. At the same time, elements in the Syrian Church advocated the replacement of Syriac with the local language of Malayalam. The resultant schism led to the creation of the new **Marthoma Syrian Church**.

Today, numerous roadside shrines known as *kurisupalli*, or "chapels of the cross", and large and popular churches bear testimony to the continuing strength of the Christian communities throughout the state. **Christmas** is an important festival in Kerala; during the weeks leading up to December 25, innumerable star-shaped lamps are put up outside shops and houses, illuminating the night and identifying followers of the faith.

A finger-bone relic of St Thomas is kept here and brought out for public viewing once a year on the Feast of the Magi (mid October).

Periyar Wildlife Sanctuary and around

One of the largest and most visited wildlife reserves in India, the **Periyar Wildlife Sanctuary** occupies 777 square kilometres of the Cardamom hills region of the Western Ghats. The majority of its visitors come in the hope of seeing **tigers** and **leopards** – and most leave disappointed, as the few that remain very wisely keep their distance, and there's only a slight chance of a glimpse even at the height of the dry season (April/May). However, there are plenty of other animals: elephant, *sambhar*, Malabar giant squirrel, gaur, stripe-necked mongoose, wild boar and over 260 species of birds including Nilgiri wood pigeon, purple-headed parakeet, tree pie and flycatchers. Located close to the Kerala–Tamil Nadu border, the park makes a convenient place to break the long journey across the Ghats between Madurai and the coast. It's also a good base for day-trips into the Cardamom hills, with a couple of tea factories, spice plantations, the trailhead for the Sabarimala pilgrimage (see p.392), and viewpoints and forest waterfalls within striking distance.

Just over 100km east of Kottayam, and centred on a vast artificial **lake** created by the British in 1895 to supply water to the drier parts of neighbouring Tamil Nadu, Periyar lies at altitudes of 900m to 1800m and is correspondingly cool: temperatures range from 15°C to 30°C. The royal family of Travancore, anxious to preserve favourite hunting grounds from the encroachment of tea plantations, declared it to be a forest reserve, and built the Edapalayam Lake Palace to accommodate their guests in 1899. It expanded as a wildlife reserve in 1933, and once again when it became part of **Project Tiger** in 1979 (see Contexts, p.696).

Seventy percent of the protected area, which is divided into core, buffer and tourist zones, is covered with evergreen and semi-evergreen forest. The **tourist zone** – logically enough, the part accessible to casual visitors – surrounds the lake, and consists mostly of semi-evergreen and deciduous woodland interspersed with grassland, both on hilltops and in the valleys. Although excursions on the lake are the standard way to experience the park, you can get much more out of a visit by **walking** with a local guide in a small group, or, especially, staying in basic accommodation in the sanctuary (see p.391) away from the crowd. However, avoid the period immediately after the monsoons, when **leeches** make hiking virtually impossible. The **best time to visit** is from December until April, when the dry weather draws animals from the forest to drink at the lakeside.

Getting to Periyar

The base for exploring Periyar is the village of **Kumily**, north of the main park entrance at **Thekkady**. The road that winds up through the undulating hills from Ernakulam and Kottayam makes for a slow drive but provides wonderful views across the Ghats. The route is dotted with churches and roadside shrines to St Francis, St George and the Virgin Mary – a charming Keralan blend of ancient and modern. Once you've climbed through the rubber-tree plantations into Idukki District, the mountains become truly spectacular, and the wide-floored valleys are carpeted with lush tea and cardamom plantations. **Buses** from Kottayam (every 30min; 4hr), Ernakulam

(10 daily; 6hr), and Madurai in Tamil Nadu (at least hourly; 5hr 30min) pull in to the scruffy bus stand east of Kumily's bazaar. **Auto-rickshaws** will run you from the bus stand to the visitor centre inside the park for around Rs35, stopping at the park entrance for you to pay the fee. Remember the gates close at 6pm, after which you will have to show proof of accommodation booking before they will let you in. If you are staying at the KTDC *Lake Palace*, the last boat is officially at 4pm but the hotel will arrange a boat during daylight hours.

The **entrance fee** to the park is Rs12 for Indians and Rs150 for foreigners for the first day, Rs50 on subsequent days. If you're staying inside the park you must buy a new pass for each day you stay, either from the entrance gate or from the Forest Information Centre by the jetty. KTDC's hectic and uncomfortable **weekend tours** to Periyar from Kochi, calling at Kadamattom and Idukki Dam en route (Sat 7.30am–Sun 8pm), are not recommended unless you're really pushed for time.

Kumily

As beds inside the sanctuary are in short supply, most visitors stay in **KUMILY**, which is now built up the full 1.5km south to the park gates. Here tourism runs side by side with the spice trade as the main source of income. Almost every shop on the town's main street sells freshly collected spices; just walking along the street and breathing in air filled with the scent of cloves, nutmeg, cinnamon and cardamom is a heady experience. In the middle of the bazaar stands the main **cardamom sorting** area, where you can watch tribal women sifting through the fragrant green pods in heart-shaped baskets.

There's a new Idduki State **tourist office** (Mon–Sat 10am–5pm; ☎04869/222620) just south of the bus stand. Besides offering information on the district itself, they organize conducted tours, including a "spice valley" trip (6.30am–9.30pm; Rs250) which takes in Munnar and several spice plantations. The other source of information is the **TTDC office** inside the *Rolex Tourist Home* (☎04869/222081).

As well as the attraction of the wildlife sanctuary, **tea factory** and **spice plantation tours** are a big draw here: every hotel and tourist agency in Kumily offers similar packages at very competitive rates. Unfortunately, some places, such as Abraham's Plantation, have become heavily

Kottayam ◢ ◣ ◢ **A** ◢ Munnar

0   300 m

Bazaar

Bus Stand

KUMILY

Madurai

TTDC Tourist Office

Mangaladevi

THEKKADY ROAD

Forest Checkpost & Gate

THEKKADY

N

ACCOMMODATION	
Ambadi	J
Coffee Inn	L
Green View	G
Hornbill Cottages	K
KTDC Aranya Niwas	O
KTDC Lake Palace	P
KTDC Periyar House	N
Kumily Gate	D
Maliackal Tourist Home	B
Mickey's Cottage	H
Rolex Tourist Home	C
Shalimar Spice Garden	A
Spice Village	F
Taj Garden Retreat	I
White House	M
Woodlands Prime Castle	E

RESTAURANTS	
Aayam	1
Chrissie's Café	2
Coffee Inn	L
Pepper Garden Coffee House	3
Spice Village	E

Periyar Lake

Forest Department Visitors' Centre

Jetty

PERIYAR

commercialized and expensive, so it's worth shopping around; often the best way to organize a tour is to ask at your hotel – most of the staff will have a relative who has a good plantation. Expect to pay Rs250–500 per person (depending on numbers; maximum group size is five) for a three-hour tour with guide and vehicle.

Both the State Bank of Travancore, near the bus stand, and the Muthoot bureau on Thekkady Road can **change money**; there's an ATM at the former. **Internet** facilities are available around Thekkady Junction for about Rs40 per hour. Although hilly, this is good cycling territory and **bicycle rental** is available from stalls in the market. For entertainment, Mudra Kathakali, near *Woodlands* hotel, put on daily shows at 4pm and 7pm.

Accommodation and eating

Kumily has **accommodation** to suit all pockets, and new hotels and resorts emerge each season. Thankfully, most places are well outside the noisy bazaar area, dotted along the Thekkady Road leading to the park. **Rooms in family houses** are popular options; some hosts will cook for you, while others provide kitchen facilities. Most of them are in Rosapukandam, ten minutes' walk from the bus stand.

Ambadi Next to turn-off for Mangaladevi temple, Thekkady Rd ☎04869/222193, ⓦwww .hotelambadi.com. Pleasant hotel with decent rooms sporting coir mats and wood carvings, and some cottages. The *Adhithi* restaurant serves good chicken. ❺–❻

Coffee Inn Thekkady Rd ☎04869/222763, ⓔcoffeeinn@sancharnet.in. A handful of simple rooms (one en suite) around a covered terrace and garden. Their "Wild Huts" annexe, in an attractive enclosed garden just along the road, has a small but eclectic selection of accommodation, including tree houses and huts, all with shared showers and toilet. ❶–❸

Green View By-pass Rd ☎04869/211015. Pleas-ant, quiet and great value homestay with en-suite rooms. ❷–❸

Hornbill Cottages Rosapukandam, south of By-pass Rd ☎04869/222889. Homestay with clean rooms, some en suite, and kitchen facilities. ❷–❸

Kumily Gate Behind the bus stand ☎04869/222279, ⓔkumilygate@yahoo.co.in. Modern block with large, clean rooms, a restaurant and a popular, noisy bar. Expensive for what it is, but good for late arrivals. Try for a discount. ❺–❼

Maliackal Tourist Home Thekkady Rd ☎04869/222589. Handy for the bus stand but near a mosque, so expect to be woken up early. Good clean rooms, some with cable TV and balco-nies (but no views). ❷–❹

Mickey's Cottage By-pass Rd ☎04869/222196, ⓦwww.mickeyscottage.com. One of the best homestays in Kumily, with lovely rooms and cottages, all with balconies and some with swing-ing basket chairs. ❷–❸

Rolex Tourist Home Thekkady Rd ☎04869/222465, ⓦwww.thekkadytours.com. Smart new block with a range of en-suite rooms and good views from the upper floors. ❷–❹

Shalimar Spice Garden Murikaddy ☎04869/222132, ⓦwww.shalimarkerala .com. Beautiful and tranquil Italian-run place in a secluded spot on the edge of a cardamom and pepper estate, 5km from Kumily (Rs50 by jeep). Accommodation is in beautiful cottages ($130–160) built using teak in traditional Kerala style; there's also a pool and a good restaurant. ❾

Spice Village Thekkady Rd ☎04869/222315, ⓦwww.cghearth.com. Thatched huts and tradi-tional Keralan wood cottages (from $220) in immaculate grounds boasting every imaginable spice and species of tree. Great restaurant and a pool, Keralan cookery classes available, and lots of activities on offer. Book ahead. ❾

Taj Garden Retreat Amalambika Rd ☎04869/222273, ⓦwww.tajhotels.com. Luxuri-ous, pseudo-rustic cottages ($165) built to emulate a jungle lodge with great views. There's an elegant restaurant and a pool. ❾

White House Thekkady Rd ☎04869/222987. A mixed but very good-value bag of bamboo huts, tree houses and rooms, handily placed for the park gates. ❷–❸

Woodlands Prime Castle Thekkady Rd ☎04869/222077. Two separate blocks which share a reception. The *Tourist Bhavan* on the left is cheap and very rudimentary, although clean enough for a short stay (it also has a Rs75 dorm). The main block is a good mid-range option, with en-suite rooms and some a/c. ❶–❻

Eating

Nearly every Kumily hotel has its own **café–restaurant**, ranging from the *Taj Garden Retreat's* smart à la carte, to the more traveller-oriented *Coffee Inn*.

Aayam *Lake Queen* hotel, Main Rd. Good veg restaurant in the basement, better than the non-veg *Ginger* upstairs.

Chrissie's Café By-pass Rd. Fine rooftop restaurant serving pizza, pasta, brownies and the like.

Coffee Inn Thekkady Rd. Well-established café serving delicious, if slightly overpriced, home-made backpacker nosh. With a pleasant wooden terrace and garden, it's a popular place for a lingering breakfast after the early morning boat ride in the sanctuary.

Pepper Garden Coffee House By-pass Rd. Wonderful coffees, teas (both grown in the garden), lassis and excellent breakfasts, as well as good, inexpensive thalis and some Chinese and South Indian dishes.

Spice Village Thekkady Rd. Superb restaurant that caters primarily for the tour groups and rich Indian visitors who stay at the hotel; the accent is on multi-cuisine, but the chef's speciality is Keralan food.

The sanctuary

Vehicles are allowed in to the Periyar sanctuary dailyfrom 7am to 6pm. Tickets for the **boat trips** on the lake (daily at 7am, 9.30am, 11.30am, 2pm & 4pm; 2hr; Rs55 for the lower deck, Rs100 for the upper deck, which is less cramped and has a better view) are sold through the Forest Department at their hatch just above the main **visitor centre** (daily 7am–6pm; ℡04869/222027, Ⓦwww .periyartigerreserve.org) at the end of the road into the park. Those on a tight budget should ask at the centre about spaces on the boat run by the Forestry Commission boat (same times; Rs15) – but if there are seats, they'll be on the lower deck.

Although it's unusual to see many animals from the boats – engine noise and the presence of a hundred other people make sure of that – you might spot a group of elephants, wild boar and *sambhar* by the water's edge. Upper decks are best for game viewing, although the seats are often block-booked by the upmarket hotels. To maximize your chances of seeing wildlife, take the 7am boat (wear warm clothing) – the early morning mist is very atmospheric, too.

The birds of Periyar

Although animals are not often visible due to the dense forest cover, **birds** are plentiful in Periyar, with over 260 species recorded in the sanctuary. The most notable amongst these are the darters, which are also known as snakebirds due to the snake-like appearance of their necks while swimming. They belong to the cormorant family, and can be seen perching on top of dead tree trunks protruding from the water, sometimes allowing boats to get quite close. Other common aquatic birds include the cormorant, grey heron, squat and tailless little grebe – also known as dabchick. Of the several types of kingfisher, the lesser pied kingfisher has distinctive white flashes around its neck, and the blue-eared and storkbilled kingfishers are both a more common blue. The osprey or fish hawk is often seen, cruising above the water. Occasionally, you may be fortunate enough to see a grey-headed fishing eagle, recognizable by its white body, which contrasts with its deep brown back and wings. Other common birds of prey in Periyar include the brahminy kite, which is a handsome gold bird with a regal, white neck and crest. Amongst many of Periyar's other birds are the Nilgiri wood pigeon, purple-headed parakeet, tree pie, laughing thrushes and flycatchers, the woolly-necked stork and the white cattle egret. If you're lucky, you might catch sight of the great Indian hornbill, a majestic multicoloured bird with a large yellow beak.

Chances of good sightings lessen after heavy rain, as the animals only come to the lake when water sources inside the forest have dried up.

Trekking in the sanctuary (3hr; departures at 7am, 11am & 1pm; Rs500 per group, maximum five people) is arranged through the visitor centre. Private guides, who operate more flexibly, will approach you in Kumily or near the park gates at Thekkady, but some have proven to be unreliable, so it's best to go by word of mouth. The Forest Department also offers full day treks (8am–6pm; Rs750 per person) and a nighttime "Jungle Patrol" (7pm, 10pm & 1am; Rs500 per person) around the forest fringe, but it's more appealing for the general atmosphere rather than for any chance of seeing much apart from the odd watchful eye reflecting your torch beam. **Elephant rides** into the park are a bargain at Rs30 for two people (30min), but the pachyderms are often out of commisson.

Accommodation and eating in the sanctuary

For the *Lake Palace*, *Periyar House* and the *Aranya Nivas* you should book in advance at the KTDC offices in Thiruvananthapuram or Ernakulam – essential if you plan to come on a weekend, a public holiday, or during **peak season** (Dec–March), when rooms are often in short supply.

Forest Department Rest Houses Reserve in advance at the Forest Department's visitor centre in Thekkady. Fairly basic and overpriced accommodation in the woods on the far side of the lake, either at Edappalayam (six rooms) or Mankavala (two rooms). Bring your own food (though there are no cooking facilities). An unforgettable experience, despite the price – but you'll be lucky to get in on a weekend or in December. ⑤

Forest Department Bamboo Grove & Jungle Inn Reserve in advance at the Forest Department's visitor centre in Thekkady. Rather overpriced and cramped, though these places have slightly more facilities than the rest houses and the price includes supper, breakfast, boating and trekking. ⑦

KTDC Aranya Nivas Near the boat jetty, Thekkady ☎04869/222023, ⓦwww.ktdc.com. Plusher than *Periyar House*, this colonial manor has some huge rooms ($100–160), a pleasant garden, a great swimming pool, an excellent multi-cuisine restaurant, a cosy bar and plenty of marauding wild monkeys to keep you entertained. Full board and upper-deck tickets for two boat trips are included in the tariff. ⑨

KTDC Lake Palace Across the lake from the visitor centre ☎04869/222023, ⓦwww.ktdc .com. The sanctuary's most luxurious hotel, with six suites in a converted maharajah's game lodge surrounded by forest, with wonderful views. Rooms are charmingly old-fashioned, and there's great food and a lovely lawn – this has to be one of the few places in India where you stand a chance of spotting tiger and wild elephant while sipping tea on your own veranda. Full-board only at $190 per double room. ⑨

KTDC Periyar House Midway between the park gates and the boat jetty, Thekkady ☎04869/222026, ⓦwww.ktdc.com. Close to the lake, with a restaurant, bar and balcony overlooking the monkey-filled woods leading down to the waterside. Not as nice a location as the neighbouring *Aranya Niwas*, but a lot cheaper. Ask for a lake-facing room. ⑤–⑦

Around Periyar and Kumily: the Cardamom Hills

Nestled amid mist-covered mountains and dense jungles, Periyar and Kumily are convenient springboards from which to explore Kerala's beautiful **Cardamom Hills**. Guides will approach you at Thekkady with offers of trips by jeep; if you can get a group together, these are good value. Among the more popular destinations is the **Mangaladevi temple**, 14km east of Kumily. The rough road to this tumbledown ancient ruin deep in the forest is sometimes closed due to flood damage, but when it is open the round trip takes about five hours. With a guide, you can also reach remote waterfalls and mountain viewpoints offering panoramic vistas of the Tamil Nadu plains. Rates vary according to the season, but expect to pay around Rs500 for a jeep-taxi, and an additional Rs150 for a guide. An easy day-trip by bus (or as part of a local plantation tour) from Kumily is to the grand viewpoint of **Chellarcovil**, right on the edge of the mountains, with the endless green plains of Tamil Nadu falling away below. To get here, take a bus or Jeep to the village of Anakkara, 15km north of Kumily, and jump on a rickshaw for the last 4km through the paddy fields to Chellarkovil; hang onto your driver if you don't want to walk back to the bus.

High Range Tea Factory

Of places that can be visited under your own steam, the fascinating **High Range Tea Factory** (T04868/277038) at Puttady (pronounced "Poo-*tee*-dee"), 19km north of Kumily, is a rewarding diversion on the road to Munnar. Regular buses leave from Kumily bus stand; get off at the Puttady crossroads, and pick up a rickshaw from there to the factory. Driven by whirring canvas belts, old-fashioned English-made machines chop, sift and ferment the leaves, which are then dried in wood-fired furnaces and packed into sacks for delivery to the tea auction rooms in Kochi. The affable owner, Mr P.M. James, or one of his clerks, will show you around; you don't have to prearrange a visit, but it's a good idea to phone ahead to check if they are open.

Sabarimala

The other possible day-trip from Kumily, though one that should not be undertaken lightly (or, because of Hindu lore, by pre-menopausal women), is to the Sri Ayappan forest shrine at **Sabarimala** (see opposite). This remote and sacred site can be reached in a long day-trip, but you should leave with a pack of provisions, as much water as you can carry and plenty of warm clothes in case you get stranded. Jeep-taxis wait outside Kumily bus stand to transport pilgrims to the less frequented of Sabarimala's two main access points at a windswept mountaintop 13km above the temple (2hr; Rs50 per person if the jeep is carrying ten passengers). Peeling off the main Kumily–Kottayam road at **Vandiperiyar**, the route takes you through tea estates to the start of an appallingly rutted forest track. After a long and spectacular climb, this emerges at a grass-covered plateau where the jeeps stop. You proceed on foot, following a well-worn path through superb old-growth jungle, complete with hanging creepers and monkeys crashing through the high canopy, to the temple complex at the foot of the valley – a surreal spread of concrete sheds and walkways in the middle of the jungle. Allow at least two hours for the descent, and an hour or two more for the climb back up to the roadhead, for which you'll need plenty of drinking water. The alternative route from Kumily to Sabarimala involves a jeep ride on a forest road to **Uppupara** (42km), with a final walk of 6km through undulating country. Given the very real risks involved with missing the last jeep back to Kumily (the mountaintop is prime elephant and tiger country), it's advisable to get a group together and rent a 4WD for the day (about Rs900 including waiting time).

Munnar and around

MUNNAR, 130km east of Kochi and 110km north (four-and-a-half hours by bus) of the Periyar Wildlife Sanctuary, is the centre of Kerala's principal tea

The Ayappa cult

During December and January, Kerala is packed with huge crowds of men wearing black or blue *dhotis*; you'll see them milling about train stations, driving in overcrowded and gaily decorated jeeps and cooking a quick meal on the roadside by their tour bus. These men are all pilgrims on their way to the Shri Ayappa forest temple (also known as Hariharaputra or Shasta) at **Sabarimala**, in the Western Ghat mountains, around 200km from both Thiruvananthapuram and Kochi. The **Ayappa devotees** can seem disconcertingly ebullient, chanting "*Swamiye Sharanam Ayappan*" ("give us protection, god Ayappa") in a call and response style reminiscent of English football fans.

Although he's primarily a Keralan deity, Ayappa's appeal has spread phenomenally in the last thirty years across South India, to the extent that this is said to be the **second largest pilgrimage in the world**, with as many as a million devotees each year. A curious story relates to the birth of Ayappa. One day, when the two male gods, Shiva and Vishnu, were together in a pine forest, Shiva asked to see Vishnu's famed female form Mohini, the divine enchantress. Vishnu refused, having a fair idea of what this could lead to. However, Shiva was undeterred, and used all his powers of persuasion to induce Vishnu to transform. As a result of the inevitable passionate embrace, Vishnu became pregnant, and the baby Ayappa emerged from his thigh.

Pilgrims are required to remain celibate, abstain from intoxicants, and keep to a strict vegetarian diet for a period of 41 days prior to setting out on the four-day walk through the forest from the village of **Erumeli** (61km, as the crow flies, northwest) to the shrine at Sabarimala. Rather less devoted devotees take the bus to the village of Pampa, and join the five-kilometre queue. When they arrive at the modern temple complex, pilgrims who have performed the necessary penances may ascend the famous eighteen **gold steps** to the inner shrine. There they worship the deity, throwing donations down a chute that opens onto a subterranean conveyor belt, where the money is counted and bagged for the bank. In recent years, the mass appeal of the Ayappa cult has brought an abundance of rupees to the temple, which now numbers among India's richest, despite being open for only a few months each year. Funds also pour in from the shrine's innumerable spin-off businesses, such as the sale of coconut oil and milk (left by every pilgrim) to a soap manufacturer.

The pilgrimage reaches a climax during the festival of **Makara Sankranti** when massive crowds of over 1.5 million congregate at Sabarimala. On January 14, 1999, 51 devotees were buried alive when part of a hill crumbled under the crush of a stampede. The devotees had gathered at dusk to catch a glimpse of the final sunset of *makara jyoti* ("celestial light") on the distant hill of Ponnambalamedu.

Although **males** of any age and even of any religion can take part in the pilgrimage, **females** between the ages of nine and fifty are barred. This rule, still vigorously enforced by the draconian temple oligarchy, was contested in 1995 by a bizarre court case. Following complaints to local government that facilities and hygiene at Sabarimala were substandard, the local collector, a 42-year-old woman, insisted she be allowed to inspect the site. The temple authorities duly refused, citing the centuries-old ban on women of menstrual age, but the High Court, who earlier upheld the gender bar, was obliged to overrule the priests' decision. The collector's triumphant arrival at Sabarimala soon after made headline news, but she was still not allowed to enter the shrine proper.

For advice on how to visit Sabarimala, via a back route beginning at Kumily near the Periyar Wildlife Sanctuary, see opposite.

growing region. Although billed as a "hill station", it is less a Raj-style resort than a scruffy settlement of corrugated iron-roofed cottages and factories, surrounded by vast swathes of rolling green **tea plantations**. Nonetheless, the town still has something of a colonial look about it, with the odd veranda-ed British bungalow clinging to a side of the valley and the famous **High Range Club** perched on the southeast edge of town, with lovely flowerbeds and a golf course (open to non-residents). Beyond the club sprawl some of Munnar's vast plantations, most of which are owned by the industrial giant Tata. You can wander freely in the plantations but not visit the factories, although the recently opened **Tea Museum** (Tues–Sun 9am–4pm; Rs50), 2km northwest of the centre on Nallathany Rd, contains lots of machinery and information on production techniques.

It's easy to see why the pioneering Scottish planters who first developed this hidden valley in the 1900s felt so at home here. At an altitude of around 1600m, the town enjoys a refreshing climate, with crisp winter mornings and relentlessly heavy rain during the monsoons. Hemmed in by soaring mountains – including peninsular India's highest peak, **Ana Mudi** (2695m) – it also boasts a spectacular setting; when the river mist clears, the surrounding summits form a wild backdrop to the carefully manicured plantations carpeting the valley floor and sides.

Munnar's greenery and cool air mainly draws well-heeled honeymooners from Mumbai and Bangalore. However, more and more foreigners are stopping here for a few days, enticed by the spell-binding bus ride from Periyar, which takes you across the high ridges and lush tropical forests of the Cardamom Hills, or for the equally spectacular climb across the Ghats from Madurai. Munnar has become popular with the young **off-road cycling** posse. There are no official routes, just miles and miles of hills to climb up and speed down. You can **rent** gearless bicycles (Rs10 per hour) in the market or proper mountain bikes from either the DTPC office (around Rs250 per day) or KTDC *Tea County* (see p.396) – their top-notch bikes are officially for residents but it's worth enquiring if any are available. The **hiking** scene is also growing as the countryside around Munnar offers walks for all levels of fitness, from gentle rambles through the tea fields to mountain climbing, including the scenic hamlet of **Top Station**.

Arrival and information

Munnar can be reached by **bus** from Kochi, Kottayam, Kumily and Madurai. State-run and private services all pull into the Town Bus Stand in the modern main bazaar, near the river confluence and Tata headquarters; state ones continue through town, terminating at the bus stands nearly 3km south. For most hotels you should ask to be dropped off at **Old Munnar**, 2km south of the centre, near the ineffectual DTPC **tourist office** (daily 8.30am–7pm; ☎04865/231516). A better source of **information** on transport, accommodation and day-trips, including to Eravikulam, is the helpful **Joseph Iype**, who runs the **Tourist Information Service** (no set hours; ☎04865/230349) from a small office in the main bazaar. Immortalized in Dervla Murphy's book *On a Shoestring to Coorg*, this self-appointed tourist officer has become something of a legend. He has some useful **maps** and newspaper articles, can arrange **transport** for excursions, and may well bombard you with background on the area. A few metres north is the **Munnar Tourist Information Centre** (daily 10am–8pm; ☎04865/230552), a government-sponsored body whose primary concern appears to promote its own guided tour (daily 9am–5pm; Rs250). Designed mainly for Indian tourists, the tour takes in a spice plantation, boating, a dairy farm, view points and Top Station in the morning, and Rajmalai Wildlife

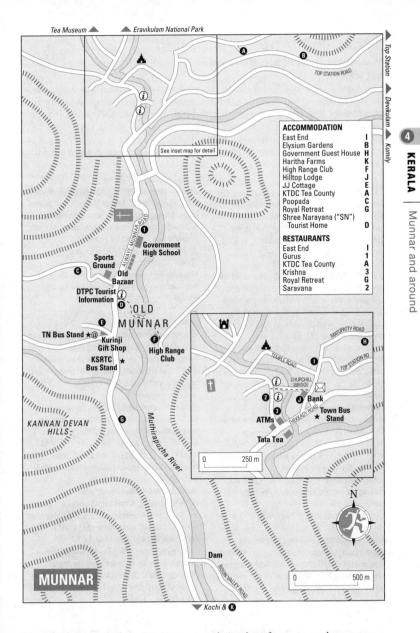

Tea Museum ▲▲   ▲ Eravikulam National Park

▶ Top Station
▶ Devikulam
▶ Kumily

4

KERALA | Munnar and around

Ⓐ
Ⓑ
TOP STATION ROAD

See inset map for detail

ACCOMMODATION

East End	I
Elysium Gardens	B
Government Guest House	H K
Haritha Farms	K
High Range Club	F
Hilltop Lodge	J
JJ Cottage	E A C
KTDC Tea County	
Poopada	C
Royal Retreat	G
Shree Narayana ("SN") Tourist Home	D

RESTAURANTS

East End	I
Gurus	1 A
KTDC Tea County	
Krishna	3 G
Royal Retreat	2
Saravana	

ALWAYE–MUNNAR ROAD

Ⓘ Ⓞ
Government
High School

Sports
Ground
Ⓒ Old
Bazaar
DTPC Tourist Ⓘ
Information
Ⓓ   OLD

Ⓔ   MUNNAR

TN Bus Stand ★@
Ⓕ
Kurinji
Gift Shop   High Range
Club
KSRTC ★
Bus Stand

*KANNAN DEVAN
HILLS*

Ⓖ

Muthirapuzha River

MATUPATTY ROAD
Ⓗ
TEMPLE ROAD
Ⓘ
TOP STATION RD
CHURCHILL
BRIDGE
Ⓘ
Ⓘ
2
Ⓘ   Ⓙ Bank
3
ATMs
THEKKADY ROAD
Town Bus
★ Stand
Tata Tea

0   250 m

N

Dam

BISON VALLEY ROAD

0   500 m

MUNNAR

▼ *Kochi &* Ⓚ

Sanctuary, waterfalls, an amusement park in the afternoon and sunset at a viewpoint.

You can **change money** at the State Bank of Travancore, the State Bank of India or the two ATMs facing each other on Gandhi Road. **Internet** access is available from a couple of places around town, such as Alpha Computer Centre (Rs50 per hour), next to the Tamil Nadu Bus Stand.

395

Accommodation and eating

Munnar has plenty of **accommodation**, although budget options are limited and are unfortunately too close to the Town Bus Stand for a peaceful sleep. The *Royal Retreat* and *KTDC Tea County* have excellent restaurants with eclectic menus and attentive service, while *Gurus*, in the old bazaar opposite the government high school, is a characterful old-style coffee shop serving South Indian snacks. *Saravana* in the main market serves good vegetarian food, while *East End*'s plush, mid-range restaurant is the best in the town centre, with an extensive Indian menu. For a tasty pastry or cake, check out *Krishna* fast food on Gandhi Road.

Hotels and guesthouses

East End Temple Rd, across the river from the bus stand ☏04865/230451, ⊛www.edasserygroup .com. Immaculate upmarket hotel close to the centre of town, with Raj-style "cottages" in a big garden and a good restaurant. ❼–❽

Elysium Gardens Top Station Rd ☏04865/232620, ℮elysium@sify.com. Quiet and pleasant location with a choice of large cottages and good rooms, all with cable TV and hot water. Decent South Indian restaurant and a massive sign above the reception warning that "the Lord promotes, not man". ❸–❽

Government Guest House Mattupaty Rd ☏04865/230385. Near the main bazaar, on the far side of the river, this characterful old British bungalow has just six well-refurbished and comfortable rooms; meals by arrangement. Nice garden and location. ❻

Haritha Farms Kadalikad, off the Muvattupuzha–Thodupuzha Rd ☏04865/260216, ⊛www .harithafarms.com. In the foothills over halfway to Kochi, around 70km from Munnar, this organic farm has four en-suite cottages for rent. Delicious home-cooked food is included in the rates, and cooking classes and local sightseeing tours are available. ❻–❽

High Range Club Kannan Devan Hills ☏04865/230253, ℮hrcmunnar@sify.com. A renowned members' club for a hundred years, now offering cosy rooms in the large Raj-era clubhouse hung with hunting trophies. Knock back the gins, play billiards, golf, tennis, squash, or just read a good book in the beautiful gardens. Full board only. ❺–❼

Hilltop Lodge Corner of Temple Rd and Thekkady Rd ☏04865/230655. One of Munnar's best budget deals, offering small, clean rooms with attached bathrooms (blankets and hot water extra), but with a constant racket of traffic outside. ❷

JJ Cottage Near the KSRTC bus stand ☏04865/230104. Excellent and very friendly homestay with rooms of varying sizes; the posh two front ones have stunning views of the hills. ❸–❹

KTDC Tea County Off Mattupathy Rd ☏04865/230460, ⊛www.ktdc.com. The grandest address in Munnar, with a range of luxurious chalet style rooms and suites ($90–140) ranged along a hilltop, affording views across the valley. There's a good Indian restaurant, a bar, and a range of sporting and adventure activities, including paragliding and rock climbing. ❾

Poopada Kannan Devan hills, on the Manukulam Rd ☏04865/230223, ⊛www.poopada.com. The front looks a bit dilapidated, but the good-sized en-suite rooms are clean, there's a good cheap restaurant and it's set in a secluded location, with fine valley views. Booking recommended at weekends. ❺–❻

Royal Retreat Kannan Devan Hills ☏04865/230240, ℮royalretreat@sify.com. Pleasant, sunny yellow complex at the south end of town with spacious and comfortable rooms, some with brick fireplaces and cane furniture. ❺–❼

Shree Narayana ("SN") Tourist Home Kannan Devan hills, on the main road near the tourist office ☏04865/230212. A popular and cheerful lodge by a river, offering slightly shabby en-suite rooms with hot water. ❹

Eravikulam National Park and Top Station

Encompassing 100 square kilometres of moist evergreen forest and grassy hilltops in the Western Ghats, the **Eravikulam National Park** (daily 7am–6pm; Rs50 [Rs10]), 13km northeast of Munnar, is the last stronghold of one of the world's rarest mountain goats, the **Nilgiri tahr**. Its innate friendliness made the tahr pathetically easy prey during the hunting frenzy of the colonial era. During a

Trekking to Kodaikanal

A superb **trek**, probably best done with a guide, takes around three days and follows the forested hill country from Munnar to the hill station of **Kodaikanal**, 85km to the southeast in Tamil Nadu. Joseph Iype of the Tourist Information Service in Munnar (see p.394) will be happy to assist with organization, and several agencies such as Clipper Holidays (℡0484/236 4443) and Trio Travels (℡0484/236 9571), both in Kochi, will also organize the trek.

break in his campaign against Tipu Sultan in the late 1790s, the future Duke of Wellington reported that his soldiers were able to shoot the unsuspecting goats as they wandered through his camp. By Independence the tahr was virtually extinct; today, however, numbers are healthy, and the animals have regained their tameness, largely thanks to the efforts of the American biologist Clifford Rice, who studied them here in the early 1980s. Unable to get close enough to observe the creatures properly, Rice followed the advice of locals and attracted them using salt, and soon entire herds were congregating around his camp. The tahrs' salt addiction also explains why so many hang around the park gates at **Vaguvarai**, where visitors – despite advice from rangers – slip them salty snacks.

Another popular excursion is the 34-kilometre uphill climb by bus through the subcontinent's highest tea estates to **TOP STATION**, a tiny hamlet on the Kerala–Tamil Nadu border with superb views across the plains. It's renowned for the very rare **Neelakurunji plant** (*Strobilatanthes*), which grows in profusion on the mountainsides but only flowers once every twelve years, when crowds descend to admire the cascades of violet blossom spilling down the slopes. The next flowering is due in October–November 2006. Top Station is accessible by **bus** from Munnar (10 daily starting at 5.30am; 1hr 30min), and jeep-taxis do the round trip for Rs700. Joseph Iype in Munnar (see p.394) organizes Ambassador trips taking in Eravikulam, Chinnar, Indira Gandhi sanctuary, waterfalls and a view of Anamudi (maximum 4 people; Rs1000 per car).

Kochi (Cochin) and around

The venerable city of **KOCHI** (long known as Cochin) is Kerala's prime tourist destination, spreading across islands and promontories in a stunning location between the Arabian Sea and the backwaters. Its main sections – modern **Ernakulam** and the old peninsular districts of **Mattancherry** and **Fort Cochin** to the west – are linked by a complex system of ferries, and distinctly less romantic bridges. Although many visitors opt to stay in the more convenient Ernakulam, increasing numbers are now basing themselves in Fort Cochin itself, where Kochi's complex history is reflected in an assortment of architectural styles. Exotic spice markets, Chinese fishing nets, a synagogue, Portuguese palace, India's first European church, Dutch homes, and a village green that could have been transported from England's Home Counties can all be found within an easy day's walk. Kochi is also one of the few places in Kerala where you are guaranteed **Kathakali dance** performances, both in authentic and abridged tourist versions. Around Kochi, a 12km auto-rickshaw or bus ride southeast of Ernakulam, the colonial-style hill palace at **Thripunitra** is now an eclectic museum which stages a music and dance festival in October or November.

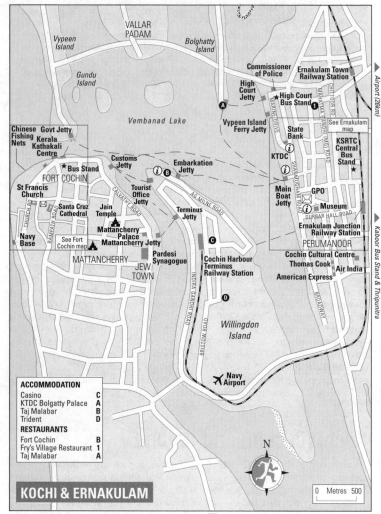

Map: KOCHI & ERNAKULAM

VALLAR PADAM

Vypeen Island

Bolghatty Island

Gundu Island

Commissioner of Police

Ernakulam Town Railway Station

High Court Jetty

★ High Court Bus Stand

Marine Drive

Airport (26km) ▸

Vembanad Lake

Vypeen Island Ferry Jetty

State Bank

Chinese Fishing Nets

Govt Jetty

Kerala Kathakali Centre

KTDC

KSRTC Central Bus Stand ★

See Ernakulam map

Customs Jetty

Embarkation Jetty

★ Bus Stand

FORT COCHIN

Tourist Office Jetty

AG MILNE ROAD

Main Boat Jetty

GPO

Museum

St Francis Church

Santa Cruz Cathedral

Jain Temple

Terminus Jetty

DURBAR HALL ROAD

Ernakulam Junction Railway Station

Navy Base

See Fort Cochin map

Mattancherry Palace

Mattancherry Jetty

PERUMANOOR

MATTANCHERRY

Pardesi Synagogue

Cochin Harbour Terminus Railway Station

Cochin Cultural Centre

Thomas Cook

Air India

JEW TOWN

INDIRA GANDHI ROAD

American Express

BROADWAY

Kaboor Bus Stand & Thripunitra ▸

Willingdon Island

BRISTON ROAD

✈ Navy Airport

N

ACCOMMODATION
Casino — C
KTDC Bolgatty Palace — A
Taj Malabar — B
Trident — D

RESTAURANTS
Fort Cochin — B
Fry's Village Restaurant — 1
Taj Malabar — A

0 Metres 500

KOCHI & ERNAKULAM

▾ Alappuzha & Thiruvananthapuram

Kochi sprang into being in 1341, when a flood created a natural safe port which swiftly replaced Muziris (Kodungallur, 50km north) as the chief harbour on the Malabar Coast. The royal family transferred here from Muziris in 1405, after which the city grew rapidly, attracting Christian, Arab and Jewish settlers from the Middle East. The name probably derives from *kocchazhi*, meaning the new, or small, harbour. The history of **European** involvement in Kochi from the early 1500s onwards is dominated by the aggression of the Portuguese, Dutch and British, who successively competed to control the port and its lucrative spice trade. In 1800, the state of Cochin became part of the British Madras Presidency, and from 1812 until Independence in 1947 it was administered by a succession of *diwans*, or finance ministers. In the 1920s, the British expanded the port to accommodate modern ocean-going ships, and Willingdon Island, between Ernakulam and Fort Cochin, was created by extensive dredging.

Arrival and local transport

Kochi's **international airport** is at Nedumbassery, near Alwaye (aka Alua), 26km to the north of Ernakulam – a prepaid taxi into town costs Rs 350–375. There are two main **railway stations** – Ernakulam Junction (☎0484/237 6131) near the centre, and Ernakulam Town (☎0484/239 5198), 2km further north. No trains run to Fort Cochin or Mattancherry. The Cochin Harbour Terminus, on Willingdon Island, serves the island's luxury hotels.

The KSRTC **central bus stand** (☎0484/237 2033), beside the rail line east of MG Road and north of Ernakulam Junction, is for state-run long-distance services. There are also two stands for private services (see box on p.414): the **Kaloor Stand** (rural destinations to the south and east) is across the bridge from Ernakulam Town railway station on the Alwaye Road; while the **High Court Stand** (buses to Kumily, for Periyar Wildlife Reserve, and north to Thrissur, Guruvayur and Kodungallur) is opposite the High Court ferry jetty. The Fort Cochin bus stand serves tourist buses and local services to Ernakulam.

Kochi by ferry

Half the fun of visiting Kochi is getting about on the cheap **local ferries**, which depart from the four jetties marked on the map opposite. A pamphlet giving exact ferry timings is available from the ticket hatches by the jetties and from the helpful tourist desk at the Main Boat Jetty in Ernakulam.

Ernakulam to Bolghatty Island
From Ernakulam (High Court Jetty); 6.30am–9pm; journey time 10min. There are also speedboat taxis (Rs25; free if you're staying at the *Bolgatty Palace* hotel).

Ernakulam to Fort Cochin
From Ernakulam (Main Jetty) to Fort Cochin (Customs Jetty). Pick up a free timetable at the tourist desk for exact times. Every 20–55min; 5.55am–9.30pm; journey time 15min. A less frequent express service runs from Ernakulam's High Court Jetty to Government Jetty in Fort Cochin.

Ernakulam to Mattancherry
From Ernakulam (Main Jetty) via Fort Cochin (Customs Jetty) and Willingdon Island (Terminus Jetty) to Mattancherry (Mattancherry Jetty). Every 1hr 30min; 7.10am–5.40pm.

Ernakulam to Vypeen
From Ernakulam (Main Jetty). This service has two routes: one to Willingdon Island (Embarkation Jetty; 25min), and a fast one to Vypeen (Government Jetty; 15min). Every 30min–1hr; 7am–9.30pm.

Fort Cochin to Vypeen
From Fort Cochin (Government Jetty) to Vypeen (Government Jetty). Every 10min; 6.30am–9pm; journey time 10min.

Willingdon Island to Fort Cochin
From the Tourist Office Jetty (Willingdon Island) to Customs Jetty (Fort Cochin). Every 30min; 6.30am–6.15pm; journey time 10min.

△ Holy Cross Church, Kochi

Although **auto-rickshaws** are plentiful and reliable in Ernakulam, expect to pay well over the odds across the water in Mattancherry and Fort Cochin. Kochi's excellent **ferry system** (see box on p.399) provides a relaxing way to reach the various parts of town. **Bicycles** can be rented from many of the hotels and guest houses in Fort Cochin (see p.403).

Tours and backwater trips

KTDC's half-day **Kochi boat cruise** (daily 9am–12.30pm & 2–5.30pm; Rs100) is a good way to orient yourself but doesn't stop for long in either Mattancherry or Fort Cochin, so give it a miss unless you're pushed for time. Departing from the Sealord Jetty on Shanmugham Road, Ernakulam, it calls at Willingdon Island, the synagogue, Mattancherry Dutch Palace, St Francis Church, the Chinese fishing nets and Bolghatty Island. There's also a daily sunset tour (5.30–7pm; Rs40) around the harbour. Book at the KTDC Reception Centre on Shanmugham Road (☎0484/235 3234).

The KTDC tourist office and a couple of private companies also operate popular all-day **backwater trips** (see p.378) out of Kochi. Taking in a handful of coir-making villages north of the city, these offer a leisurely and enjoyable way to experience rural Kerala from small hand-punted canoes. KTDC's daily tours cost Rs350, including the car or bus trip to the departure point, 30km north, and a knowledgeable guide. Better value is the excellent trip run by the **tourist desk** (see below) at the Main Boat Jetty (daily 8.30am–5pm; Rs550), which includes hotel pick-up, transfer, a morning cruise on the open backwaters, a village tour, excellent Keralan lunch buffet on board the *kettu vallam* and an afternoon trip through narrow waterways in a much smaller boat.

Information

If you're based on Willingdon Island, head for the helpful **India Tourism** office (Mon–Fri 9am–5.30pm, Sat 9am–noon; ☎0484/266 8352, ⓦwww .india-tourism.com), between the *Taj Malabar Hotel* and Tourist Office Jetty. They offer information on Kerala and beyond, and can provide reliable guides; they also have a desk at the airport. KTDC's **reception centre**, on Shanmugham Road, Ernakulam (daily 8am–7pm; ☎0484/235 3234, ⓦwww.ktdc .com) reserves accommodation in their hotel chain and organizes sightseeing and backwater tours (see p.379); they also have a counter at the airport. The **Kerala Department of Tourism** has a new office (Mon–Sat 10.15am–5pm; no phone, ⓦwww.keralatourism.com), which hands out excellent maps of the town and backwaters, by the Government Jetty in Fort Cochin. The tiny, independent, award-winning **tourist desk** (daily 8am–6.30pm; ☎0484/237 1761, etouristdesk@satyam.net.in) at the entrance to the Main Boat Jetty in Ernakulam is very friendly and helpful and the best place to check ferry and bus times or pick up free city and state maps. A mine of information on ritual theatre and temple festival dates around the state, the office also publishes a useful South India information guide, arranges daily boat tours, accommodation on houseboats, and runs (and takes bookings for) two excellent guesthouses, one near Kannur and the other in Wayanad. They have a subsidiary office (same hours; ☎0484/221 6129) on Tower Road in Fort Cochin.

Useful local **publications** include the monthly *Jaico Timetable* (Rs10) and the bimonthly *Hello Cochin* (free), both with comprehensive details of bus, train, ferry and flight times. KTDC publishes an excellent free walking tour map and guide to Fort Cochin (available from all KTDC tourist offices), which includes a brief history of the area and most important buildings in the fort area.

Accommodation

The romantic atmosphere of **Fort Cochin** is being rashly exploited, and the growing number of budget guesthouses and upmarket hotels is altering the face of this quaint area. The biggest crisis however, is the **shortage of clean water**, something which hits locals very hard, especially in the high season; if you do stay in Fort Cochin, keep your daily water consumption to a minimum. To help preserve the fort area, you could opt to stay in **Ernakulam**, which lacks the old-world ambience, but is far more convenient for travel connections and has lots of choice; however its guesthouses and hotels often fill up by late afternoon, so book in advance. The eighteenth-century Dutch palace on the tip of **Bolghatty Island** is a congenial three-star complex, although years of endless renovation have eroded almost all its once grand charm.

Hotels in Ernakulam and Fort Cochin are marked on their respective maps (p.409 & p.407); those on Willingdon and Bolghatty islands appear on the main Kochi/Ernakulam map (p.398).

Ernakulam

Abad Plaza MG Rd ☎0484/238 1122, ⓦwww .abadhotels.com. Comfortable and pleasant business-style high-rise in the centre of Ernakulam, with restaurant and bar, swimming pool and health club (Rs150 for non-residents). ❼–❽

Aiswarya Jos Junction ☎0484/2364454. Mid-range hotel with good-value non a/c rooms, and a/c rooms on the top floors with balconies, plus a good restaurant downstairs. ❸–❺

Avenue Regent MG Rd ☎0484/237 7977, ⓦwww.avenueregent.com. Very comfortable four-star Best Western affiliate, close to the railway station and main shopping area, with a restaurant, 24hr coffee shop and bar. Expect only the highest standards, as this place doubles as a well-respected hotel-management training college. ❽–❾

Basoto Lodge Press Club Rd ☎0484/235 2140, Ⓔtouristplanet@yahoo.com. Dependable backpackers' lodge with twelve basic non-a/c rooms. Useful information on offer, but no restaurant. ❶

Bharat Gandhi Square, Durbar Hall Rd ☎0484/235 3501, ⓦwww.bharathotel.com. Large, modern hotel with comfortable rooms (non-a/c ones are relatively inexpensive), Internet access and two restaurants (the *Sulabh* restaurant has tribal decor and excellent cheap food) and a 24hr coffee shop. ❺–❼

Biju's Tourist Home Corner of Cannonshed and Market roads ☎0484/238 1881, ⓦwww.bijutourist home.com. Pick of the budget bunch, with thirty clean and spacious rooms (some with a/c and TV) and a cheap same-day laundry service. Friendly and very popular. ❸–❺

Cochin Tourist Home Chavar Rd ☎0484/237 7577. Cleanest of the cheap hotels lined up outside Ernakulam Junction station, but often full of noisy families and pilgrim groups. There's a dingy organic restaurant in the basement. ❷–❸

Excellency Nettipadam Rd, Jos Junction ☎0484/237 8251, ⓦwww.hotelexcellency.com. Smart, modern mid-range place, better value than most, with 49 rooms, most a/c, 24hr coffee shop and good multi-cuisine restaurant with some worthy Keralan specialities. ❹–❺

Grand MG Rd ☎0484/238 2061, ⓦwww.grand hotelkerala.com. Smart hotel, recently upgraded to three-star, where the spacious rooms have wooden flooring, a/c and cable TV. There is a multi-cuisine restaurant and bar on site. ❼–❽

Grand Residency St Benedict Rd ☎0484/239 8081. Comfortable non a/c hotel with 43 rooms. Convenient for Ernakulam Town station. ❸–❹

Hakoba Shanmugham Rd ☎0484/236 9839. Conveniently located midway between Main and High Court Jetties. It's dowdy, but all the rooms (some with a/c) have cable TV and there's a trendy new coffee bar below the hotel on the ground floor. ❸–❺

Maple Guest House XL/271 Cannonshed Rd ☎0484/235 5156. This is the best deal in the district, with cheap, clean non-a/c rooms and a good location very close to the main boat jetty. ❷

Meluvallil Tourist Home GS Building, Market Rd ☎0484/236 0355. New budget place, tucked away in an arcade and offering clean non-a/c rooms with TV. ❷

Metropolitan Chavar Rd ☎0484/237 5412, ⓦwww.metropolitancochin.com. Smart business hotel near Ernakulam Junction station – good for late-night arrivals and early-morning departures – with a multi-cuisine restaurant, 24hr coffee shop and bar. ❻–❼

Modern Guest House XL/6067 Market Rd ☎0484/235 2130. Popular place above a (noisy)

Keralan veg restaurant, with simple non-a/c en-suite rooms. If full try the annexe, the *Modern Rest House* (℡0484/236 1407), which has sixteen plain but pleasant – and slightly more expensive – rooms. ❷

Paulson Park Carrier Station Rd ℡0484/237 8240, ⓦwww.paulsonpark.com. Good-value place close to Ernakulam Junction, with large, well-appointed rooms set around a huge and quirky atrium featuring some surreal sculptures. ❹–❻

Saas Tower Cannonshed Rd ℡0484/236 5319, ⓦwww.saastower.com. Dependable four-storey block, handy for the Main Jetty, with average a/c and non-a/c rooms. ❸–❺

Sangeetha 36/1675 Chittoor Rd, near Ernakulam Junction station ℡0484/237 6123, ⓦwww .gaanamhotels.com. Comfortable rooms, if small for the price; the non-a/c ones can be stuffy. A complimentary breakfast is included, and there's a left-luggage store and foreign exchange. ❺–❻

Sealord Shanmugham Rd ℡0484/238 2472, ⓦwww.sealordhotels.com High-rise hotel near High Court jetty with central a/c. Standard rooms are excellent value (the best are on the top floor) and there's a rooftop restaurant, bar and foreign exchange. ❻–❼

Taj Residency Marine Drive ℡0484/237 1471, ⓦwww.tajhotels.com. Ernakulam's top business hotel, in a prime location overlooking the harbour, with luxury a/c rooms, an impressive greenhouse-like café, and good restaurant. If you want a pool and more leisure space, however, head over to the *Taj Malabar* on Willingdon Island. $85–200. ❾

Woodlands Woodlands Junction, MG Rd ℡0484/238 2052, ⓔwoodland1@vsnl.com. Primarily aimed at Indian tourists, with cosy a/c and non-a/c rooms and spotless marble bath-rooms. Excellent vegetarian restaurant. ❺–❻

Yuvarani Residency Jos Junction, MG Rd ℡0484/237 7040, ⓦwww.yuvaniresidency.com. Comfortable, central and well-managed three-star hotel with a choice of carpeted or tiled rooms, all with TV. There's also an excellent seafood restau-rant, a well-stocked bar and a coffee shop. ❺–❼

Fort Cochin

Adams Old Inn Burgher St ℡0484/221 7595, ⓔadamsoldinn@hotmail.com. Great family-run guesthouse in a well-restored period building. Rooms are modern (one has a/c and a balcony) and there's also a decent rooftop dorm (Rs100) and a small rooftop terrace. ❷–❸

Ann's Residency 1/307A Bishop Joseph Kuree-thara Rd ℡0484/221 8024, ⓦwww.annsresidency .com. Spacious rooms, stylishly decorated, some with baths and balconies, in a classy mansion

with a garden restaurant in the attractive grounds. ❻–❼

Brunton Boatyard Bellar Rd, next to Fort Cochin Jetty ℡0484/221 8221, ⓦwww.cghearth.com. Luxury chain hotel, built on the site of an eighteenth-century British boatyard; the look is Keralan carved wood and whitewash, with beautifully designed, breezy a/c rooms and balconies overlooking the bay. Facilities include three speciality restaurants and a pool edging onto the lake. $200–275. ❾

Chiramel Residency 1/296 Lilly St ℡0484/221 7310, ⓦwww.chiramelhomestay.com. A great seventeenth-century heritage homestay, with welcoming owners and five carefully restored rooms set around a congenial communal sitting room. The lofty non-a/c rooms all have big wooden beds, teak floors and modern bathrooms; some also have balconies. ❺–❻

Delight Ridsdale Rd, opposite the Parade Ground ℡0484/221 7658, ⓦwww.delightfulhomestay .com. Run by a friendly and helpful family, this attractive homestay has seven spacious, comfort-able and airy rooms (a couple a/c) and a pleasant, leafy courtyard garden. Breakfast available. ❸–❼

Elite Princess St ℡0484/221 5733. Several floors of basic but clean and cheap non-a/c rooms, plus a few with a/c, all en suite. There's also a very popular restaurant, a pleasant rooftop garden and foreign-exchange facilities. ❷–❺

Fort Avenue Tower Rd ℡0484/221 5219, ⓔfortavenue@yahoo.com. Family house in a quiet but convenient location with six small but pleasant non-a/c rooms. ❸

Fort Heritage 1/283 Napier St ℡0484/221 5333, ⓦwww.fortheritage.com. Restored seventeenth-century Dutch mansion, with comfortable, airy a/c rooms, a restaurant and loads of character – albeit a little pricey at $69–95 a night. ❾

Fort House 2/6A Calvathy Rd ℡0484/221 7103, ⓦwww.forthousecochin.com. Pleasant non a/c rooms and bamboo huts (with mozzie screens and nets) ranged around an interesting if eccentric compound, littered with pots and statues. The café serves delicious seafood. ❻

Kapithan Inn 1/931 KL Bernard Rd ℡0484/221 6560, ⓦwww.kapithaninn.com. Small clean, pleas-ant rooms in friendly homestay behind Santa Cruz basilica, plus some posh new a/c cottages. ❹–❽

Malabar House Residency 1/268 Parade Rd ℡0484/221 6666, ⓦwww.malabarhouse.com. Beautiful, historic mansion renovated with a highly successful mix of old-world charm and delightful European designer chic. The Keralan temple-style pool in the minimalist courtyard is stunning, and there's an excellent restaurant. Tariff includes breakfast. $150–250. ❾

Seagull Calvathy Rd ℡ 0484/221 8128, ℮ shih_ab@yahoo.co.uk. Assorted rooms with attached bathrooms, a couple with a/c, though none makes the most of the waterside location. ❸–❹

Spencer Home 1/298 Parade Rd ℡ 0484/221 5049. Characterful place set in an old, rambling Portuguese house, with eleven large and spotless a/c and non-a/c rooms, all facing the pretty communal garden. ❹–❻

Walton's Homestay Princess St ℡ 0484/221 5309, ℮ cewalton@rediffmail.com. Excellent homestay run by a philosophical gentleman in a centuries-old Dutch house. Facilities include a book-swap library, and communal breakfast is available for Rs50. ❺–❻

Willingdon and Bolghatty islands

Casino Willingdon Island, 2km from Navy Airport, close to Cochin Harbour Terminus railway station ℡ 0484/266 8221, ℗ www.cghearth.com. Efficient deluxe place, but utterly characterless and shut in by the grey docks. Facilities include a small pool, travel agent, foreign exchange and two excellent restaurants. Very popular with tour groups, so book ahead. $100–190. ❾

KTDC Bolgatty Palace Bolghatty Island ℡ 0484/275 0500, ℗ www.ktdc.com. Extensively renovated palace in a beautiful location, a short hop from High Court Jetty. The main building, built by the Dutch in 1744 and later home of the British Resident, is now a three-star hotel with twenty deluxe rooms; there are also six "honeymoon" cottages on stilts right at the water's edge. Reserve through any KTDC tourist office and come armed with mosquito repellent. At weekends, the adjacent KTDC canteen and bar is noisy with day-trippers. ❽–❾

Taj Malabar Willingdon Island, by Tourist Office Jetty ℡ 0484/266 6811, ℗ www.tajhotels.com. Pink-orange tower block in a superb location on the tip of the island with sweeping views of the bay; the old "heritage" wing, waterfront gardens and pool have been extensively refurbished, and the whole place oozes *Taj* style and quality. $170–220. ❾

Trident Bristow Rd, Willingdon Island ℡ 0484/266 6816, ℗ www.tridentcochin.com. Despite the grey dockyard environs, this new hotel is the most intimate and congenial of the five-stars on the island, with interesting displays of Keralan tribal and household artefacts, a pool in a tropical oasis, a restaurant, bar and a range of luxurious rooms. Officially $120–170, but discounts often available. ❾

Mattancherry and Fort Cochin

With high-rise development restricted to Ernakulam, across the water, the old-fashioned character of **Mattancherry** and **Fort Cochin** remains intact, with glimpses of Kochi's past greeting you at virtually every turn. Approaching Mattancherry jetty by ferry, the shoreline, with its tiled roofs and pastel-coloured buildings, offers a view that can't have changed for centuries. Despite the revenue brought in by tourism, traditional trade is still the most important activity here. Barrows loaded with sacks of produce trundle between *godowns* (warehouses), and there are numerous little shops where dealers negotiate prices for tea, jute, rubber, chillies, turmeric, cashew, ginger, cardamom and pepper.

Jew Town

The road heading left from Mattancherry Jetty leads into the district known as **Jew Town**, where N.X. Jacob's tailor shop and the offices of J.E. Cohen, advocate and tax consultant, serve as reminders of a once-thriving Jewish community. The area is now occupied by a sizeable population of Kashmiris, entrepreneurial as always and quite aggressive in touting for trade. The hassle-factor is partially defused by the sheer variety of goods on sale: antiques, Hindu and Christian wood-carvings, oil lamps, masks, spice boxes and other bric-a-brac, plus some tempting coffee-table books.

Turning right at the India Pepper & Spice Trade Building, usually resounding with the racket of dealers shouting the latest prices, and then right again, brings you into Synagogue Lane. The **Pardesi (White Jew) Synagogue** (daily except Sat 10am–noon & 3–5pm; Rs2) was founded in 1568 and rebuilt in 1664.

The Jews of Kochi

According to tradition, the **Myuchasim** ("black") **Jews**, who were the first to arrive on the Malabar coast, were fleeing from the occupation of Jerusalem by Nebuchadnezzar, in 587 BC. However another legend claims that the first Jews arrived in the eleventh century BC, as part of King Solomon's trading fleet. Whatever the truth, the Jews settled in Cranganore, just north of Cochin, to trade in spices. They remained respected members of Keralan society and even had their own ruler until the arrival of the Portuguese Inquisition in the early sixteenth century.

At that time, when Jews were being burned at the stake in Goa and evicted from their settlements elsewhere along the coast, the raja of Cochin gave them a parcel of land adjoining the royal palace in Mattancherry. A new Jewish community was created in the area now known as Jew Town, and a synagogue built. The Jews were in demand as they spoke Malayalam, and trading was in their blood; the community thrived during the great trading period under the more liberal and supportive Dutch and later British rule.

There were three distinct groups of Jews in Kerala. The **Black** Jews were employed as labourers in the spice business, and their community of thousands resulted from the earliest Jewish settlers marrying and converting Indians; **Brown** Jews are thought to have been slave converts. **White** (Pardesi) Jews considered both groups inferior to themselves; they were orthodox and married only among themselves. However, by the early 1950s, most of Kochi's Jews emigrated when they were given free passage to Israel. The White Jews' traditional ways of life are on the verge of disappearing – only seven families survive, and their ideals and values have inevitably moved with the times.

Its interior is an attractive, if incongruous, hotchpotch; note the floor, paved with hand-painted eighteenth-century blue and white tiles from Canton, each unique, depicting a love affair between a mandarin's daughter and a commoner. The nineteenth-century glass oil-burning chandeliers suspended from the ceiling were imported from Belgium. Above the entrance, a gallery supported by slender gilt columns was reserved for female members of the congregation. Opposite the entrance, an elaborately carved Ark houses four scrolls of the *Torah* (the first five books of the Old Testament), encased in silver and gold, on which are placed gold crowns presented by the maharajas of Travancore and Cochin, testifying to good relations with the Jewish community. The synagogue's oldest artefact is a fourth-century copperplate inscription from the Raja of Cochin.

An attendant is usually available to show visitors around and answer questions; his introductory talk features as part of the KTDC guided tour (see p.401). Outside, in a small square, several antique shops are worth a browse – but don't expect any bargains.

Draavidia, on Jew Street, is a small but active art **gallery** with an emphasis on contemporary work. Live "Sadhana" Indian **classical music** concerts are staged here daily (6–7pm; Rs100).

Mattancherry Palace and around

Mattancherry Palace (daily except Fri 10am–5pm; Rs2) stands on the left side of the road a short walk from the Mattancherry Jetty in the opposite direction from Jew Town. The gateway on the road is, in fact, the back entrance, but is the most accessible way from the ferry. Known locally as the Dutch Palace, the two-storey building was actually erected by the Portuguese, as a gift to the raja of Cochin, Vira Keralavarma (1537–61) – though the Dutch did add to the complex. While its squat exterior is not particularly striking, the interior is captivating.

The **murals** that adorn some of its rooms are among the finest examples of Kerala's much underrated school of painting friezes illustrating stories from the Ramayana, on the first floor, date from the sixteenth century. Packed with detail and gloriously rich colour, the style is never strictly naturalistic; the treatment of facial features is pared down to the simplest of lines for the mouths, and characteristically aquiline noses. Downstairs, the women's bedchamber holds several less complex paintings, possibly dating from the 1700s. One shows Shiva dallying with Vishnu in his female form, the enchantress Mohini; a second portrays Krishna holding aloft Mount Govardhana; another features a reclining Krishna surrounded by *gopis*, or cowgirls. His languid pose belies the activity of his six hands and two feet, intimately caressing adoring admirers. While the paintings are undoubtedly the highlight of the palace, the collection also includes interesting Dutch maps of old Cochin, coronation robes belonging to past maharajas, royal palanquins, weapons and furniture. Without permission from the Archaeological Survey of India, **photography** is strictly prohibited.

A few hundred metres west of the palace, on Gujarati Rd, lies the peaceful **Jain temple**, boasting a pair of airy marble sanctuaries with some delicate carving. The temple's peaceful atmosphere is broken daily at noon when one devotee rings a bell loudly to announce the feeding of the local pigeons. At this point the courtyard turns into a mini-Trafalgar Square, and anyone around is encouraged to help dish out grain to the hungry birds.

Fort Cochin

Moving northwest from Mattancherry Palace along Bazaar Road, you pass wholesale emporia with traders sitting surrounded by sacks of aromatic spices. Walking in a northerly direction, over the canal and then westwards, you'll eventually reach **Fort Cochin**, some three kilometres from Mattancherry Palace. The architecture of the quiet streets in this enclave is very definitely European, with fine houses built by wealthy British traders, and Dutch cottages with split farmhouse doors. If you've been travelling around India for a while, the sedate and sleepy streets, the look of the houses and village atmosphere is enough to induce a sense of culture shock at the familiarity of it all.

Just north of the Chinese fishing nets (see opposite) is the bus stand and Government Jetty, while behind them are several food and drinks stalls in Vasco da Gama Square. This area and nearby Princess Street, where many budget and mid-range hotels can be found, attracts backpackers and local touts. To fully appreciate the idiosyncratic nature of Fort Cochin, try the excellent **Fort Cochin: Walking Tour Map and Guide**, produced by Kerala Tourism, and available for free at the KTDC tourist office (see p.401). The tour takes you around some of the more important houses, the Dutch Cemetery, the Bishop's House and other strategic landmarks that make up the Fort area's unique and colourful past. Today, Fort Cochin is home to a unique community of Eurasians, commonly known as **Anglo-Indians**, who have developed a distinct and lively culture, although the development of tourism and the opening of new guesthouses are threatening the fragile infrastructure of this community and altering the face of the area.

Fort Cochin has a small but active **arts scene** based around the interesting and lively *Kashi Art Café* (daily 8.30am–7.30pm) on Burgher Street, which has a gallery exhibiting contemporary art, occasional classical Indian musical performances, news of local events and a relaxed café space. The Kerala Kathakali Centre at the Cochin Aquatic Club (by the Chinese fishing nets) organizes performances of **Kathakali** every evening (see box on p.408), as does the Cochin Cultural Centre next to the *Seagull* hotel.

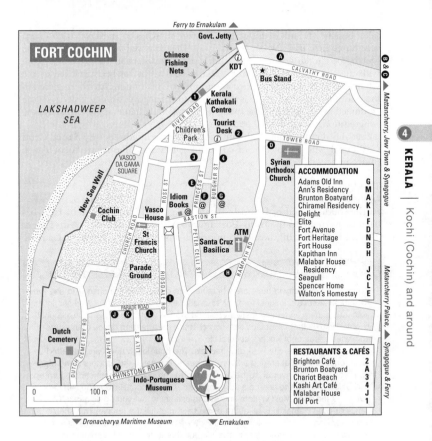

FORT COCHIN

Ferry to Ernakulam

Govt. Jetty

Chinese
Fishing
Nets

KDT

CALVATHY ROAD

Bus Stand

A

B & C

Mattancherry, Jew Town & Synagogue

Kerala
Kathakali
Centre

RIVER ROAD

LAKSHADWEEP
SEA

Children's
Park

Tourist
Desk

TOWER ROAD

D

VASCO
DA GAMA
SQUARE

New Sea Wall

BURGHER ST

Syrian
Orthodox
Church

4

KERALA | Kochi (Cochin) and around

Cochin
Club

Vasco
House

Idiom
Books

PRINCESS ST

BASTION ST

E

F   G

Matancherry Palace,

St
Francis
Church

CHURCH ROAD

Santa Cruz
Basilica

ATM

PETER CELLI ST

RAMPATH RD

H

Parade
Ground

RIDSDALE RD

Seagull
Spencer Home
Walton's Homestay

ACCOMMODATION
Adams Old Inn   G
Ann's Residency   M
Brunton Boatyard   A
Chiramel Residency K
Delight   I
Elite   F
Fort Avenue   D
Fort Heritage   N
Fort House   B
Kapithan Inn   H
Malabar House
  Residency   J
Seagull   C
Spencer Home   L
Walton's Homestay   E

Synagogue & Ferry

PARADE ROAD

J K   L

Dutch
Cemetery

DUTCH CEMETERY RD

NAPIER ST

LILY ST

M

N

N

ELPHINSTONE ROAD

Indo-Portuguese
Museum

0   100 m

RESTAURANTS & CAFÉS
Brighton Café   2
Brunton Boatyard   A
Chariot Beach   3
Kashi Art Café   4
Malabar House   J
Old Port   1

Dronacharya Maritime Museum

Ernakulam

Chinese fishing nets

The huge, elegant **Chinese fishing nets** lining the northern shore of Fort Cochin add grace to an already characterful waterside view, and are probably the single most familiar photographic image of Kerala. Traders from the court of Kublai Khan are said to have introduced them to the Malabar region. Known in Malayalam as *cheena vala*, they can also be seen throughout the backwaters further south. The nets, which are suspended from arced poles and operated by levers and weights, require at least four men to control them. You can buy fresh fish from the tiny market here and have it grilled with sea salt, garlic and lemon at one of the ramshackle stalls nearby (but don't go for fried fish, as the oil used is often old).

St Francis Church and around

South of the Chinese fishing nets on Church Road (the continuation of River Road) is the large, typically English village green, known locally as the **Parade Ground**, where local lads brush up their cricketing skills.

Overlooking it is the **Church of St Francis**, the first built by Europeans in India. Its exact age is not known, though the stone structure is thought to date back to the early sixteenth century; the land was a gift of the local raja, and the title deeds, written on palm leaf, are still kept inside. The facade, with its multi-curved sides, became the model for most Christian churches in India. Vasco da Gama was buried here in 1524, but his body was later removed to Portugal. Under the Dutch, the church was renovated and became Protestant in 1663, then Anglican with the advent of the British in 1795; since 1949 it has been attached to the Church of South India. Inside, various tombstone inscriptions have been placed in the walls, the earliest of which is from 1562. One hangover from British days is the continued use of *punkahs*, large swinging cloth fans on frames suspended above the congregation, operated by a "punkah-wallah".

East of St Francis church, the interior of the twentieth-century **Santa Cruz Cathedral** will delight fans of colourful, gaudy Indo-Romano-Rococo style of decoration.

The Indo-Portuguese museum and Dronacharya Maritime Museum

At the southern end of Ridsdale Road, the grand Bishop House of 1557 has been converted into the **Indo–Portuguese Museum** (Tues–Sun 9am–1pm & 2–6pm; Rs25 [Rs10]), hosting a none-too-impressive assortment of Catholic

---

Kathakali in Kochi

Kochi is the only city in the state where you are guaranteed the chance to see live **Kathakali**, Kerala's unique form of ritualized theatre (see p.714). Whether in its authentic setting, in temple festivals held during the winter or at the shorter tourist-oriented shows that take place year-round, these mesmerizing dance dramas are an unmissable feature of Kochi's cultural life.

Four venues in the city hold daily recitals. The hour-long shows are preceded by an introductory talk at around 6.30pm. You can also watch the dancers being made up if you arrive an hour or so before this, and keen photographers should turn up well before the start to ensure a front-row seat. Tickets cost Rs100–150 and can be bought at the door. Most visitors only attend one show, but you'll gain a much better sense of what Kathakali is all about if you take in at least a couple. This should be followed, ideally, with an all-night recital at a temple festival, or at least one of the recitals given by the Ernakulam Kathakali Club. For further details contact the tourist desk at the Main Boat Jetty, Ernakulam. The four principal venues are listed below.

Art Kerala, Kannanthodathu Lane, Valanjambalam ☏0484/237 5238 ✉art_kerala@satyam.net.in. Next door to the See India Foundation, the Kathakali performances here have proved popular with large tour groups, so expect a crowd. Make-up starts at 6pm, performance 7pm.

Cochin Cultural Centre, Manikath Road ☏0484/236 7866. The least commendable option: the dancing at this a/c theatre ("sound-proof, insect-proof, and dust-proof") is accomplished, but performances are short, with only two characters, and you can't see the musicians. Tour groups often monopolize the front seats, and the PA is loud.

Dr Devan's Kathakali, See India Foundation, Kalathiparambil Cross Rd, near Ernakulam railway station ☏0484/236 9471. The oldest-established tourist show in the city, introduced by the inimitable Dr Devan, who steals the show with his lengthy discourse on Indian philosophy and mythology. An excellent introduction.

Kerala Kathakali Centre, Cochin Aquatic Club, River Road, Fort Cochin waterfront. Performances by a company of young graduates of the renowned Kalamandalam Academy. What the actors may lack in expertise, they make up for with enthusiasm. The small, dilapidated performance space, right by the water, adds to the atmosphere but can get very crowded. You usually get to see three characters, and the music is good.

relics, altarpieces and other religious paraphenalia. Some minimal ruins of the fort's foundations can be seen in the basement.

Further southwest, on the coast road, the **Dronacharya Maritime Museum** (Tues–Sun 9.30am–1pm & 2–6pm; Rs10) is strictly for those of a militarist persuasion. Apart from some interesting material on early cultural and trading history, most of the displays are of uniforms and military hardware, such as the ugly missiles in the courtyard, while a blatantly patriotic thirty-minute video covers all the Indo-Pak conflicts since Partition.

Ernakulam and south of the centre

ERNAKULAM presents the modern face of Kerala, with more of a big-city feel than Thiruvananthapuram, but small enough not to be daunting. Other

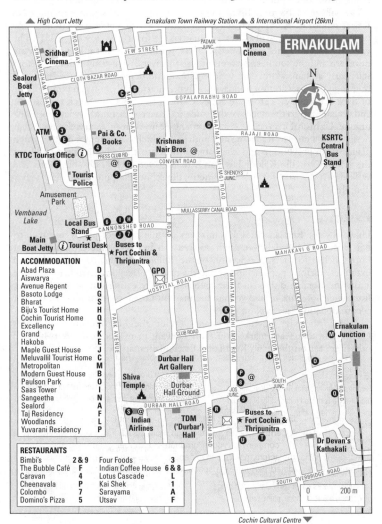

High Court Jetty   Ernakulam Town Railway Station ▲ & International Airport (26km)

ERNAKULAM

N

Sridhar Cinema

JEW STREET

PADMA JUNC.

Mymoon Cinema

BROADWAY

SHANMUGHAM ROAD

CLOTH BAZAR ROAD

Sealord Boat Jetty

MARKET ROAD

GOPALAPRABHU ROAD

MAHATMA GANDHI (MG) ROAD

RAJAJI ROAD

KSRTC Central Bus Stand

ATM

Pai & Co. Books

Krishnan Nair Bros @

KTDC Tourist Office (i)

PRESS CLUB RD

CONVENT ROAD

SHENOYS JUNC.

Tourist Police

Amusement Park

CONVENT ROAD

MULLASSERRY CANAL ROAD

Vembanad Lake

Local Bus Stand

CANNONSHED ROAD

Main Boat Jetty (i) Tourist Desk

Buses to ★ Fort Cochin & Thripunitra

MAHAKAVI G ROAD

KABIKKAMURI ROAD

ACCOMMODATION

Abad Plaza	D
Aiswarya	R
Avenue Regent	U
Basoto Lodge	G
Bharat	S
Biju's Tourist Home	H
Cochin Tourist Home	Q
Excellency	T
Grand	K
Hakoba	E
Maple Guest House	J
Meluvallil Tourist Home	C
Metropolitan	M
Modern Guest House	B
Paulson Park	O
Saas Tower	I
Sangeetha	N
Sealord	A
Taj Residency	F
Woodlands	L
Yuvarani Residency	P

GPO

HOSPITAL ROAD

PARK AVENUE

MAHATMA GANDHI (MG) ROAD

CLUB ROAD

CHITTOOR ROAD

Ernakulam Junction

CHAVAR ROAD

Durbar Hall Art Gallery

Shiva Temple

Durbar Hall Ground

JOS JUNC.

SOUTH JUNC.

@

DURBAR HALL ROAD

Indian Airlines

TDM ('Durbar') Hall

WARRIOM ROAD

Buses to ★ Fort Cochin & Thripunitra

Dr Devan's Kathakali

SOUTH OVERBRIDGE ROAD

RESTAURANTS

Bimbi's	2 & 9	Four Foods	3
The Bubble Café	F	Indian Coffee House	6 & 8
Caravan	4	Lotus Cascade	L
Cheenavala	P	Kai Shek	1
Colombo	7	Sarayama	A
Domino's Pizza	5	Utsav	F

0   200 m

Cochin Cultural Centre ▼

than the contemporary art on display at the small **Durbar Hall Art Gallery** (daily 11am–7pm; free) on Durbar Hall Road, there's little in the way of sights. Along the busy, long, straight **Mahatma Gandhi (MG) Road**, which more or less divides Ernakulam in half, the main activities are shopping, eating and movie-going. Here you can catch up on your emails and phone calls, and choose from an assortment of great places to eat Keralan food. This area is particularly good for cloth, with an impressive selection of colours; whatever the current trend in *lunghis* this year, you'll get it on MG Road.

An eight-day annual **festival** (Jan/Feb) at the Shiva temple, on Durbar Hall Road, features elephant processions and *panchavadyam* (drum and trumpet groups) out in the street. The festival usually features night-time performances of **Kathakali**, and the temple is decorated with an amazing array of electric lights: banks of coloured tubes and sequenced bulbs imitating shooting stars.

The village of Netoor, 10km southeast of the centre, is home to the ENS Kalari school of **Kalarippayat** (℡0484/270 0810, ℮enskalari@eth.net), one of the leading centres of a Keralan martial art form (see box on p.351). The well-organized centre, established in 1954, is unusual in that it blends both the northern and the southern systems of Kalarippayat. Twice-daily training sessions start early at 4am; visitors are welcome to attend demonstrations (6–7pm), and there's an open session on Sundays (3–7pm). Alternatively, you can enrol on one of their Kalarippayat certificate courses, which run from one week to one year and are tailored to the needs of the student. The centre also offers lessons in the unique **Uzhichil massage** – a treatment derived from Ayurvedic medicine, designed as a cure to Kalari-related injuries – which concentrates on the lymph glands to improve tone and circulation. To get to the school take a bus from the KSRTC or the Kaloor bus stands to the Netoor INTUC bus stand, and walk down the road for half a kilometre; the school is opposite the Mahadevar Temple.

Eating

Unusually for Keralan cities, Kochi offers a wide range of places in which to **eat out**, from the delicious fresh-cooked fish by the Chinese fishing nets at Fort Cochin to the sophistication of the *Brunton Boatyard*. Between the two extremes, various popular and modestly priced places in Ernakulam include authentic Keralan dishes on their menus. If you're eating out across the water from your hotel, make sure you are familiar with the ferry timings back to your accommodation (see box on p.399).

Unless otherwise stated, restaurants under the "Ernakulam" and "Fort Cochin" headings are marked on their relevant maps (see p.409 & p.407); all others appear on the main Kochi and Ernakulam map (p.398).

Ernakulam

Bimbi's Shanmugham Rd and Jos Junction. Indian-style fast-food joints. Hugely popular for inexpensive Udupi, north Indian and Chinese snacks and meals, and the tangiest *wada-sambars* in town. They also do a great selection of shakes and ice creams.

The Bubble Café *Taj Residency*, Marine Drive. Luxury coffee shop in a vast conservatory, serving pricey snacks and a particularly good range of Western cakes (Dundee, plum, palmettes and fudge).

Caravan Broadway, near the KTDC tourist office. This air-conditioned ice-cream parlour is a good place to chill out over a banana split or milkshake. Open until midnight.

Cheenavala *Yuvarani Residency*, MG Rd. Restaurant specializing in seafood dishes. The excellent food is accompanied by gentle live fusion music nightly except Tuesday.

Colombo Cannonshed Rd. Very inexpensive fish, meat and egg dishes, with a separate pure veg dining hall round the corner.

Domino's Esplanade Complex, Canal Rd

Sadya: a Keralan feast

Sadya, which means "feast" in Malayalam, is an unforgettable gastronomic affair and an essential part of the Kerala experience. Whether you enjoy it on a longboat on the backwaters, in a family home or at a festival, you will never forget sitting down to a vast array of colourful food displayed on a lush green plantain (a bigger relative of the banana) leaf. True to the all-India fashion of eating the main meal at noon, a *sadya* is invariably a lunch-time meal. There are strict guidelines regarding the placing of food, and the ingredients, the two main ones being tamarind (*muli*), used to give the dish a slightly sour and tangy taste, and coconut, which adds a rich and creamy flavour and takes the edge off the chillies. It is not uncommon for fourteen or so different preparations to be included in a *sadya*, each with a distinctive taste, depending on the combination of freshly ground spices. Most importantly, however, the meal should follow the principles of Ayurveda (see p.356), with a perfect balance between hot, cold, sweet, sour and savoury to enhance digestion and bodily harmony.

The **plantain leaf** is used as a plate and is thrown away at the end of the meal; the tapering end should point to your left. You eat with your right hand and shouldn't get any food on your palm as this is considered inauspicious. To eat with you hands enhances the whole sensory experience of the meal – it's considered just as important to feel the food as it is to taste and smell it. As a guest of honour, your plate must never be empty, and no matter how full you may be, your host will consider it his or her duty to keep giving you more, to avoid appearing stingy or poor. The best way to let the host know that you are full is to stop eating and leave a little food untouched on the plate.

The meal begins with a small cup of **parippu**, a soup made of *gram* (lentils) and coconut. Then comes the **main course**. In Kerala, a Hindu will tend to give you vegetarian dishes, whereas a Muslim or a Christian household will include Kozhi curry (chicken), biriyani and fish and shellfish dishes. First steamed rice is put on the lower half of the leaf. Spoonfuls of condiments such as sweet ginger chutney, coconut chutney and mango and lime pickles, as well as the savoury dishes, are placed in a semicircle on the upper half of the leaf. The essential dish in a *sadya* is **sambar**, a spicy vegetable and lentil stew that you eat with the steamed rice and savouries. The *sambar* is used to combine more dry preparations with rice, so you get a mush that is easy to eat with your hand. There will also be *upperi* – deep-fried plantain chips that have a distinctive taste as they are fried in local coconut oil, and a *pappadam* (poppodom), crumbled into the rice mixture. The other vegetarian dishes may include *pazham* (steamed yellow plantains), *kitchadi* (curd with cucumber or okra, curry leaves and coconut), *mizhukki puratti* (fried green beans and plantains), *thoran* (green vegetables simmered in fresh coconut, red chillies and turmeric), *pulisseri* (yoghurt-based curry), *aviyal* (mixed vegetables, coconut and green chillies), *koottu curry* (potatoes, red and green chillies and coconut) and *olan* (pumpkin with red chickpeas or black-eyed beans in coconut milk).

The third course is the **dessert**, taken on the same banana leaf. You will be served a sweet pancake known as *boli*, or *payasam*, which is a delicious hot, and very sweet, combination of brown molasses, coconut milk, spices, cashew nuts and raisins. There are several varieties of *payasam*, including *lentil payasam*, *jackfruit payasam*, and the rich *apapradhaman payasam*, which comes with rice wafers. *Palppayasam* is made with milk and *ghee*, which makes it sacred and pure. Then, just as you are fit to burst, you are given yet more steamed rice and hot, tangy **rasam**, a watery concoction that is poured on the rice (Mulligatawny soup, the broth so loved by the colonial Brits, is an adaptation of *rasam*).

T 1600-111-123. Pizzas here all come with extra chilli and topping options that reflect Keralan cuisine; deliveries to hotels are free.
Four Foods Shanmugham Rd. Busy, clean and popular roadside restaurant serving veg and non-veg meals, including generous thalis, fish dishes and a good-value "dish of the day". For dessert, try their Mumbai-style *faloodas*, vermicelli steeped in syrup with dried fruits and ice cream.

411

Fry's Village Restaurant Chittoor Rd, next to Mymoor Cinema (see main Kochi map). Moderately priced, ultra-spicy Keralan and other specialities served in style, including the Calicut Muslim delicacy *patthri*, wafer-thin rice pancakes, *idliappam* dumplings and *puthoo* (steamed rice cakes).

Indian Coffee House Branches on the corner of Cannonshed Rd and Park Avenue, and at Jos Junction. The usual excellent coffee, veg and non-veg meals and simple snacks such as *dosa* and omelettes.

Kai Shek Shanmugham Rd. Very smart upmarket restaurant serving excellent Keralan fish dishes, crab specialities, good North Indian cuisine and some continental food.

Lotus Cascade *Woodlands Hotel*, Woodlands Junction, MG Road. Classy veg Indian food, with plenty of tandoori options, at bargain prices and with great service.

Sarayana *Sealord* hotel, Shanmugham Rd. Reasonably priced rooftop restaurant serving good Chinese, Indian and sizzlers. The harbour view is not what it was since the shopping centre opposite was built, but it's still a great spot for a chilled beer.

Utsav *Taj Residency*, Marine Drive. Expensive à la carte Indian restaurant. The Rs320 lunch-time buffets (noon–2.45pm) are better value and you get a matchless view over the harbour and bay at noon. At night, the twinkling lights make this the place for a very romantic dinner.

Fort Cochin

Brighton Café Tower Rd. This simple eatery does fair fish 'n' chips and cheap curries – though no peppermint rock.

Brunton Boatyard Calvathy Rd, next to Fort Cochin Jetty. The expensive menu comprises a broad selection of dishes designed to reflect all the cultural influences that have played a part in the history of Kochi, including Lebanese, Portuguese, British Raj, Dutch, Jewish and, of course, Keralan. Unfortunately, it's à la carte and you end up just wanting to try everything.

Chariot Beach Princess St. Huge variety of seafood and Chinese dishes at reasonable prices, and you can eat alfresco on the small terrace.

Kashi Art Café Burgher St. Great café and exhibition space in a restored old building, with chilled vibes and music. Healthy light meals, cakes, and excellent breakfasts and coffees served all day. Check the noticeboards for details of events and festivals.

Malabar House 1/268 Parade Rd. Superb restaurant where you can wine and dine to live classical music every evening, either at the poolside or at indoor tables. The seafood platter is tastefully arranged and tastes sensational. Not cheap, but excellent value.

Old Port River Rd. Excellent location for a relaxing night right by the Chinese fishing nets. Offers a good range of fish, seafood, beef, pork and veg, both Indian and western style. Surreptitious beer possible.

Willingdon Island

Fort Cochin *Trident Hotel* ℡0484/266 8221. This seafood restaurant is considered the home of some of the best fish dishes in India. You select from a display of the catch of the day, and then choose the style of preparation, which is all done in front of you. Absolutely delicious, but very expensive, and the decor is dull.

Taj Malabar Willingdon Island ℡0484/266 6811. There are two restaurants here: the *Jade Pavilion* for Chinese, and *Rice Boats* serving Western, North Indian and Keralan dishes in a beautiful waterside location. The food is excellent and prices reflect this; the Rs250 lunch-time buffet includes veg and non-veg dishes and is good value.

Listings

Airlines, domestic Indian Airlines, Durbar Hall Rd ℡0484/237 1141, ⊛www.indian-airlines.com; Jet Airways, Bab Chambers, Atlantis, MG Rd ℡0484/235 9212 ⊛www.jetairways.com.

Airlines, international Air France, Old Thevara Rd ℡0484/237 0250; Air India, 35/1301 MG Rd, Ravipuram ℡0484/235 1295; Air Maldives, c/o Spencer & Co, Arya Vaidya Sala Buildings, 35/718 MG Rd ℡0484/238 0517; British Airways, c/o Nijhwan Travels, MG Rd ℡0484/236 4867; Cathay Pacific, c/o Spencer & Co, Arya Vaidya Sala Buildings, 35/718 MG Rd ℡0484/238 0517; Egypt Air, c/o ABC International, Sreekandath Rd ℡0484/235 3457; Gulf Air, c/o Jet Air, Atlantic Junction, MG Rd ℡0484/235 9242; KLM/Northwest, c/o Spencer & Co, Arya Vaidya Sala Buildings, 35/718 MG Rd ℡0484/238 0517; Kuwait Airways, c/o National Travel Service, MG Rd ℡0484/235 9114; Saudi Arabian Airlines, c/o Arafaath Travels, MG Rd ℡0484/235 2689; Singapore Airlines/Silk Air, Aviation Travels, 35/2433 MG Rd, Ravipuram ℡0484/235 8129; SriLankan Airlines, Trans Lanka Ltd, MG Rd ℡0484/236 1215.

Ayurvedic treatment Although widely advertised, the following two come highly recommended: Kerala Ayurveda Pharmacy, Warriom Rd, off MG

Rd ☎0484/236 1202 (Rs350–400 for 1hr 30min massage); and PNVM Shanthigiri, Thrikkakara ☎0484/255 8879 (Rs300 per session), on the northern outskirts of Ernakulam.

Banks Branches on MG Rd in Ernakulam include: ANZ Grindlays; State Bank of India (which also has a branch opposite the KTDC Tourist Reception Centre); and Andhra Bank. To exchange travellers' cheques, the best places are: Thomas Cook (Mon–Sat 9.30am–6pm), near the Air India Building at Palal Towers, MG Rd; or Surana Financial Corporation next door. ATMs can be found in the Ernakulam Syndicate Bank, opposite *Hotel Hakoba*, Shanmugham Rd; at the South India Bank outside *Yuvarani Residency*, MG Rd; in Fort Cochin SBI at *Fort Avenue* homestay; and at the South India Bank next to the Santa Cruz Basilica.

Bookstores The two branches of Idiom (opposite the Synagogue, Jew Town, Mattancherry; and on Bastion St near Princess St, Fort Cochin) are wonderful places to browse for books on travel, Indian and Keralan culture, flora and fauna, religion and art; they also have an excellent range of non-fiction.

Cinemas Sridhar Theatre, Shanmugham Rd, near the *Hotel Sealord*, screens English-language movies daily; check the listings pages of the *Indian Express* or *Hindu* (Kerala edition) to find out what's on. For the latest Malayalam and Hindi releases, head for the comfortable a/c Mymoon Cinema at the north end of Chitoor Rd, or the Saritha Savitha Sangeetha, at the top of Market Rd.

Handicrafts On MG Rd, try Kairali; Khadi Bhavan; Khataisons Curio Palace; Surabhi Kerala State Handicrafts; Coirboard Showroom (for coir carpets). For good quality Keralan, Portuguese and Dutch antiques, head over to Jew St, although you'll have to bargain extremely hard.

Hospitals General, Hospital Rd (☎0484/236 0002); City, MG Rd (☎0484/236 1809); Government, Fort Cochin (☎0484/221 6444).

Internet access There are numerous outlets in travel agencies and hotel receptions along Princess St in Fort Cochin; in Ernakulam, head for Net Park on Convent Rd or Mathsons on Durbar Hall Rd. Rates are around Rs15–30 per hour.

Music stores Sargam, XL/6816 GSS Complex, Convent Rd, opposite the Public Library, stocks the best range of music tapes in the state, mostly Indian (Hindi films and lots of Keralan devotional music), with a couple of shelves of Western rock and pop. Music World, MKV Building, MG Rd is Kochi's answer to a music superstore, with Western pop, classical, compilations, world music and Indian *filmi* music. Sound of Melody, DH Rd, near the Ernakulam Junction station, also has a good selection of traditional South Indian and contemporary Western music.

Musical instruments Manuel Industries, Banerji Rd, Kacheripady Junction, is the best for Indian classical and western instruments. For traditional Keralan drums, ask at Thripunitra bazaar (see below).

Photography City Camera, Lovedale Building, Padma Junction, MG Rd, repairs and sells cameras; Krishnan Nair Bros, Convent Rd, stocks the best range of camera film, including black and white, Kodachrome and Fujichrome and professional colour transparency; Royal Studio, Shanmugham Rd, is also worth a try.

Police The city's tourist police have a counter at the railway station. There is also a counter next to the KTDC Tourist Office at the southern end of Shanmugham Rd.

Post office The GPO is on Hospital Rd, not far from the Main Jetty; the city's poste restante is at the post office behind St Francis Church in Fort Cochin.

Tour and travel agents Clipper Holidays, 40/6531 Convent Rd (☎0484/236 4443), are experienced agents good for wildlife and adventure tours in Kerala and Karnataka. Sita World Travels (☎0484/236 1101) and Travel Corporation of India, MG Rd (☎0484/235 1646), specialize in tours and air-ticketing. The Tourist Desk, Main Jetty (☎0484/237 1761), offers backwater and wildlife tours as well as accommodation in a couple of beautiful locations.

Around Kochi and Ernakulam

Within easy distance of Kochi and Ernakulam are the small suburban town of **Thripunitra**, a former royal seat, and the three-kilometre stretch of sand called **Cherai Beach**, which offers a taste of both beach- and backwater-life. Visitors to Kochi and Ernakulam who really want to get away from it all, however, and have time and a lot of money to spare, could do no better than to head from here for Lakshadweep (see p.416), the "one hundred thousand islands", which lie between 200km and 400km offshore, in the deep blue of the Arabian Sea.

For an overview of travel services to and from Kochi/Ernakulam, see "Travel details" on p.438.

By air

The international airport (☎484/261 0113) at **Nedumbassery**, near Alwaye (aka Alua), is 26km north of Ernakulam and caters predominantly for flights to and from the Gulf. Jet Airways, Indian Airlines and Air India also operate domestic flights from here to Bangalore, Chennai, Delhi, Goa, Mumbai and Thiruvananthapuram. For flights to the **Lakshadweep Islands** contact *Casino Hotel*, Willingdon Island (see p.417). For details of airlines and travel agents, see "Listings" on p.412.

By bus

Buses leave Ernakulam's KSRTC Central bus stand for virtually every town in Kerala, and some beyond; most, but not all, are bookable in advance at the bus station (reservation enquiries ☎0484/237 2033). Travelling south, dozens of buses each day run to **Thiruvananthapuram**; most go via **Alappuzha** and **Kollam**; a few go via **Kottayam**. It's also possible to travel all the way to **Kanniyakumari** (9hr). However, for destinations further afield in Karnataka and Tamil Nadu, you're much better off on the train, although KSRTC's "super express" and private "luxury" buses travel to these destinations. Agents for private buses include Sharma Travels, *Grand Hotel*, Jos Junction, MG Road (☎0484/235 0712); Indira Travels, also near Jos Junction (☎0484/236 0693); Sona Travels (☎0484/262 3984); and SMP Travels (☎0484/235 3080).

By train

Kochi lies on Kerala's main broad-gauge line and sees frequent trains down the coast to Thiruvananthapuram via Kottayam, Kollam and Varkala. Heading north, there are plenty of services to Thrissur, and thence northeast across Tamil Nadu to Chennai, but only a couple run direct to Mangalore. Since the opening of the Konkan Railway, a few superfast trains travel along the coast all the way to Goa and Mumbai, stopping close to Mangalore.

Although most long-distance express and mail trains depart from **Ernakulam Junction**, a couple of key services leave from **Ernakulam Town**. To confuse matters further, a few also start at Cochin Harbour station, so be sure to check the departure point when you book your ticket. The main reservation office, good for trains leaving all three stations, is at Ernakulam Junction (☎131 for general enquiries). For more on Kochi's railway stations, see p.399.

The trains listed below are recommended as the fastest and/or most convenient services from Kochi. If you're heading to **Alappuzha** for the backwater trip to

Thripunitra

Some 12km southeast of Ernakulam and a short bus or auto-rickshaw ride from the bus stand MG Road just south of Jos Junction, the small suburban town of **THRIPUNITRA** is worth a visit for its dilapidated colonial-style **Hill Palace** (Tues–Sun 9am–5pm; Rs10), now an eclectic museum. The royal family of Cochin at one time maintained around forty palaces – this one was confiscated by the state government after Independence, and has slipped into dusty decline over the past decade.

One of the museum's finest exhibits is an early seventeenth-century wooden *mandapa* removed from a temple in Pathanamthitta, featuring excellent carvings of the coronation of the monkey king Sugriva and other themes from the Ramayana. Of interest too are the silver filigree jewel boxes, gold and silver ornaments, and ritual objects associated with grand ceremonies. The **epigraphy**

Kollam, take the bus, as the only train that can get you there in time invariably arrives late.

Recommended trains from Kochi/Ernakulam

Destination	Name	Number	Station	Frequency	Departs	Total time
Bangalore	Kanniyakumari–Bangalore Express	#6525	ET	daily	5.55pm	13hr
Mumbai	Netravati Express	#6346	EJ	daily	2.10pm	26hr 50min
Chennai	Trivandrum–Chennai Mail	#2624	ET	daily	7.05pm	11hr 55min
Delhi	Rajdhani Express*	#2431	EJ	Tues & Thurs	10.50pm	39hr
	Kerala Express	#2625	EJ	daily	3.40pm	48hr 20min
Madgaon/ Margao (Goa)	Rajdhani Express*	#2431	EJ	Tues & Thurs	10.50pm	12hr 35min
	Mangala–Lakshadweep Express	#2617	EJ	daily	12.45pm	14hr 25min
Mangalore	Malabar Express	#6029	ET	daily	11.30pm	10hr 45min
	Parasuram Express	#6349	ET	daily	11.00am	10hr 30min
Thiruvanan-thapuram	Parasuram Express	#6350	ET	daily	1.50pm	5hr 5min
	Ernakulam–Trivandrum Express	#6341	EJ	daily	6.15am	4hr 10min
Varkala	Parasuram Express	#6350	ET	daily	1.50pm	3hr 43min

EJ = Ernakulam Junction
ET = Ernakulam Town
* = a/c only, meals included

gallery contains an eighth-century Jewish Torah, and Keralan stone and copperplate inscriptions. Sculpture, ornaments and weapons in the **bronze gallery** include a *kingini katti* knife, whose decorative bells belie the fact that it was used for beheading, and a body-shaped cage in which condemned prisoners would be hanged while birds pecked them to death. Providing the place isn't crowded with noisy school groups, you could check out the nearby **deer park**, and the garden behind the palace is a peaceful spot to picnic beneath the cashew trees.

Performances of theatre, classical music and dance, including consecutive all-night **Kathakali** performances, are held over a period of several days during the annual festival (Oct/Nov) at the **Shri Purnatrayisa Temple** on the way to the palace. Inside the temple compound, both in the morning and at night, massed drum orchestras perform *chenda melam* in procession with fifteen caparisoned

The Lakshadweep Islands

Visitors to Kochi in search of an exclusive tropical paradise may well find it in **LAKSHADWEEP** (🖥 www.lakshadweep.nic.in), the "one hundred thousand islands" which lie between 200km and 400km offshore in the deep blue of the Arabian Sea. The smallest Union Territory in India, Lakshadweep's 27 tiny, coconut-palm-covered **coral islands** are the archetypal tropical hideaway, edged with pristine white sands and surrounded by calm lagoons where average water temperature stays around 26°C all year. Beyond the lagoons lie the coral **reefs**, home to sea turtles, dolphins, eagle rays, lionfish, parrotfish, octopus and predators like barracudas and sharks. Devoid of animal and bird life, only ten of the islands are inhabited, with a total population of just over 50,000, the majority of whom are Malayalam-speaking Sunni Muslims said to be descended from seventh-century Keralan Hindus who converted to Islam.

The main sources of income are fishing and coconuts. Fruit, vegetables and pulses are cultivated in small quantities but staples such as rice and many other commodities have always had to be imported. The Portuguese, who discovered the value of **coir rope**, spun from coconut husk, controlled Lakshadweep during the sixteenth century; when they imposed an import tax on rice, locals retaliated by poisoning some of the forty-strong Portuguese garrison – and terrible reprisals followed. As Muslims, the islanders enjoyed friendly relations with Tipu Sultan of Mysore, which naturally aroused the ire of the British, who moved in at the end of the eighteenth century and remained until Independence, when Lakshadweep became a Union Territory.

Visiting Lakshadweep

Concerted attempts are being made to minimize the ecological impact of tourism in Lakshadweep. At present, accommodation is available for **non-residents of India** on only two of the islands – Bangaram and Kadmat. Indian tourists are also allowed to visit the neighbouring islands of Kavarattu and Minicoy (both closed to foreigners).

All visits to **Kadmat** must be arranged in Kochi through the Society for Promotion of Recreational Tourism and Sports (SPORTS) on IG Road, Willingdon Island (☎0484/266 8387, 🖥 www.lakshadweeptourism.com). SPORTS offers a six–day package **cruise** to Kadmat ($450 per person for non-a/c, $500 for a/c) on one of their

elephants. At night, the outside walls of the sanctuary are covered with thousands of tiny oil lamps. Although the temple is normally closed to non-Hindus, admittance to appropriately dressed visitors is usually allowed at this time.

Cherai Beach

The closest decent beach to Kochi is **Cherai**, 35km to the north. The beach shelters a backwater and supports an active fishing community, some of whom use Chinese fishing nets (see p.407). The **Sri Goureeswara Temple**, closed to non-Hindus, is dedicated to the deity Sri Subramanya Swami and holds its annual nine-day festival (*utsavam*) in January or February every year. The *utsavam* is a great time to see traditional dance, including Kathakali performances, but the highlight of the festival is on the seventh day, when eighteen caparisoned elephants take to the streets in a spectacular procession.

To get to Cherai Beach you can either get the ferry across to Vypeen Island from Fort Cochin and transfer onto the hourly bus, or catch one of the more frequent buses from opposite the High Court Jetty in Ernakulam. There are a couple of places to **stay** at the beach: the *Sea Men's Cottage* (☎0484/248 9795; ❷–❸) is a quiet place offering a couple of double rooms and a café, which serves up seafood on demand, while the newer *Sea Palace Beach Resort* (☎0484/394 ships; you spend two days at sea and four lying on the beach. All food is included, and permits are taken care of.

The uninhabited, teardrop-shaped 128-acre islet of **Bangaram** welcomes a limited number of foreign tourists at any one time, and expects them to pay handsomely for the privilege. *Bangaram Island Resort* (🌕), bookable in Kochi (see below), accommodates up to thirty couples in thatched cottage rooms, each with a veranda. Cane tables and chairs sit outside the restaurant on the beach, and a few hammocks are strung up between the palms. There's no air-conditioning, TV, radio, telephone, newspapers or shops, let alone discos. Facilities include scuba diving (again expensive at $65 per day plus $30 per dive, or $50 for two), glass-bottomed boat trips to neighbouring uninhabited islands, and deep-sea fishing (Oct to mid-May; $50–75). Kayaks, catamarans and a sailing boat are available free, and it's possible to take a day-trip to Kadmat.

Getting to the islands
At present, the only way for foreigners to reach Bangaram are the expensive flights on small aircraft run by Indian Airlines out of **Kochi** (one daily except Sun; 1hr 35min), bookable through the *Casino Hotel* on Willingdon Island (see p.417). Foreigners pay around $300 for the round trip, which takes an hour and a half. Flights arrive in Lakshadweep at the island of **Agatti**, 8km southwest of Bangaram; the connecting boat journey to Bangaram takes two hours, picking its way through the shallows to avoid corals. During the monsoon (May 16–Sept 15) helicopters are used to protect the fragile coral reefs that lie just under the surface. All arrangements, including flights, accommodation and the necessary entry permit, are handled by the *Casino Hotel*, Willingdon Island, Kochi (☎0484/266 8221, ✉casino@vsnl.net). Some foreign tour operators, however, offer all-in packages combining Lakshadweep with another destination, usually Goa.

Theoretically, it's possible to visit Lakshadweep all year round; the hottest time is April and May, when the temperature can reach 33°C; the **monsoon** (May–Sept) attracts approximately half the total rainfall seen in Kerala, in the form of passing showers rather than a deluge, although seas are rough.

3521, 🌐www.seapaceresorts.com; ❸–❼) offers a wide range of rooms and views of both sea and backwaters. Trio Travels in Ernakulam (☎0484/235 3234) organizes **trips** to the area, including boat trips on the backwaters.

Thrissur

The pleasant town of **THRISSUR** (Trichur), roughly midway between Kochi (74km south) and Palakkad (79km northeast) on the NH-47, is a convenient base for exploring the cultural riches of central Kerala. Conveniently close to the Palghat (Palakkad) Gap – an opening in the natural border made by the Western Ghat mountains – it presided over the main trade route into the region from Tamil Nadu and Karnataka. For years Thrissur was the capital of Cochin State, controlled at various times by both the *zamorin* of Kozhikode and Tipu Sultan of Mysore.

Modern Thrissur dates from the eighteenth century, when Raja Rama Varma (aka the Maharajah Sakthan Thampuran), renowned as the "architect of Thrissur", developed the city, laying out roads and establishing markets with which

Christian merchants were invited to trade. Although a Hindu himself, the Raja helped further ensure the welfare of the Christian communities by establishing Christian enclaves to the east and south of the city centre. The majority of the Christians living here today are Catholic, but there is also a small and unique pocket of Nestorians (see p.386).

Today, Thrissur prides itself as the cultural capital of Kerala and is home to several influential art institutions. The town centres on Kerala's largest temple complex, **Vaddukanatha**, surrounded by a *maidan* (green) that sees all kinds of public gatherings, not least Kerala's most extravagant, noisy and sumptuous festival, **Puram**.

Arrival and information

On the mainline to Chennai and other points in Tamil Nadu, and with good connections to Kochi and Thiruvananthapuram, Thrissur's **railway station** is 1km southwest of Round South, near the KSRTC **long-distance bus stand**. **Priya Darshini Bus Stand** (also known as "North", "Shoranur" and

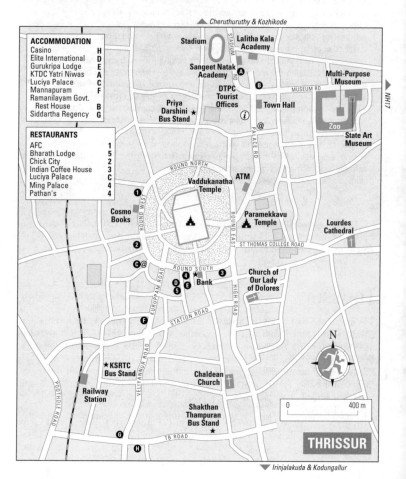

▲ Cheruthuruthy & Kozhikode

ACCOMMODATION
Casino	H
Elite International	D
Gurukripa Lodge	E
KTDC Yatri Niwas	A
Luciya Palace	C
Mannapuram	F
Ramanilayam Govt. Rest House	B
Siddartha Regency	G

RESTAURANTS
AFC	1
Bharath Lodge	5
Chick City	2
Indian Coffee House	3
Luciya Palace	C
Ming Palace	4
Pathan's	4

Stadium

Lalitha Kala Academy

Sangeet Natak Academy

DTPC Tourist Offices

Priya Darshini Bus Stand

Town Hall

Multi-Purpose Museum

MUSEUM RD

NH17

Zoo

State Art Museum

ROUND NORTH

Cosmo Books

ATM

Vaddukanatha Temple

Paramekkavu Temple

Lourdes Cathedral

ST THOMAS COLLEGE ROAD

ROUND SOUTH

Bank

Church of Our Lady of Dolores

HIGH ROAD

STATION ROAD

KURUPPAM ROAD

KSRTC Bus Stand

YELLANNUR ROAD

Chaldean Church

N

POOTHOLE ROAD

Railway Station

Shakthan Thampuran Bus Stand

0   400 m

THRISSUR

TB ROAD

ROUND WEST

ROUND EAST

PALACE RD

▼ Irinjalakuda & Kodungallur

"Wadakkancheri" stand), close to Round North, serves Shoranur (for the Kalamanadalam Academy). The **Shakthan Thampuran Bus Stand**, on TB Road, just over 1km from Round South, serves local destinations south such as Irinjalakuda, Kodungallur and Guruvayur.

The DTPC **tourist office** (Mon–Sat 10am–5pm; ☎0487/232 0800) is on Palace Road, opposite the Town Hall (five minutes' walk off Round East). Run by volunteers, its primary purpose is to promote the Puram elephant festival, but staff also give out maps of Thrissur. KTDC has a small information counter at the *Yatri Niwas* hotel, Stadium Road (☎0487/233 2333). The best place to **change money** and travellers' cheques is UAE Exchange & Financial Services (Mon–Sat 9.30am–6pm, Sun 9.30am–1.30pm) in the basement of the *Casino Hotel* building. The State Bank of India and the Canara Bank on South Road also change money and travellers' cheques, plus there's a conveniently located UTI Bank ATM on Palace Road. The **GPO** is on the southern edge of town, near the *Casino Hotel* off TB Road. **Internet** facilities are available at the excellent Internet Thrissur.Com, 2nd floor, City Centre Shopping Complex, Round West (daily 9am–10pm) and SS Consultants near the *Luciya* hotel (daily 9am–11pm); rates are around Rs30 per hour.

Accommodation

Thrissur has a fair number of mid-price **hotels**, but only a couple of decent budget places. The best deal is the palatial *Ramanilayam Government Rest House*, which offers star-hotel comfort at economy lodge rates, although the constant stream of government officials get priority. Almost all Thrissur's hotels follow a 24hr checkout policy. If you're planning to be here during **Puram**, book well in advance and bear in mind that room rates soar – some of the more upmarket hotels charge up to ten times their normal prices.

Casino TB Rd, near the railway station ☎0487/242 4699, ⓦ www.casinotels.com. Once Thrissur's poshest hotel, but has seen better days; the rooms are decent (non-a/c and a/c) and there's a multi-cuisine restaurant, cocktail bar, lawn and kiddies park, and foreign exchange (residents only). ❸–❻

Elite International Chembottil Lane, off Round South ☎0487/242 1033, ⓔ hoteliteinternational @yahoo.co.in. Pronounced "Ee-light", this big tower block has a mix of standard and deluxe rooms, some with balconies overlooking the green. Staff are friendly, and there's a good restaurant and a great garden. ❸–❼

Gurukripa Lodge Chembottil Lane, off Round South ☎0487/242 1895. A variety of rooms (including several great-value singles) in a large compound; those without a/c are large and simple, with cool tiled floors and attached bathrooms. Some rooms have TV. ❷–❸

KTDC Yatri Niwas Off Museum Rd ☎0487/233 2333, ⓦ www.ktdc.com. Friendly motel-type place with spotless rooms (some a/c and with cable TV), a beer parlour and a restaurant. ❷–❹

Luciya Palace Marar Rd ☎0487/242 4731, ⓔ luciyapalace@hotmail.com. Good mid-range choice with a palatial white-painted exterior. Some a/c rooms, but the standard non-a/c ones, with coir mats and cane furniture, are the best deals. There's a small secluded lawn to the rear. Single rates available. ❹–❻

Mannapuram Kuruppam Rd ☎0487/244 0933, ⓦ www.mannapuramhotels.com. Two-star business hotel with range of rooms with cable TV (some also with a/c), including a few singles, plus a restaurant and coffee bar. ❹–❼

Ramanilayam Government Rest House Palace Rd ☎0471/233 2016. This very good-value place is extremely popular and often full – it's officially for VIPs and they're not obliged to give you a room, but smart clothes will help. Accommodation is in huge, clean and comfortable suites with balconies, or non-a/c and a/c doubles. Breakfast is served daily; other meals by advance order only. ❷–❸

Siddartha Regency Veliyannur Rd, Kokkalai ☎0487/242 4773. ⓔ sregency@md5.vsnl.net.in. In the southwestern corner of town, this comfortable hotel is geared toward Indian visitors, with central a/c and suites with bathtubs. Facilities include a swimming pool, health club, restaurant, bar and gardens. ❺–❻

The Town

The principal point of orientation in Thrissur is the **Round**, a road (subdivided into North, South, East and West) which circles the Vaddukanatha temple complex and *maidan*. Once you've established which side of the Round you're on, you can make short-cuts across the green.

Thrissur's focal point is the central **Vaddukanatha Temple** (closed to non-Hindus) a walled complex of fifteen shrines, dating from the twelfth century or earlier, the principal of which is dedicated to Shiva. Inside, the grassy compound is surprisingly quiet and spacious, with a striking apsidal shrine dedicated to Ayappa (see box on p.393). Sadly, many of the temple's treasures, such as the wood carvings and murals, are not as well maintained as they might be. Once an essential ingredient of the temple's cultural life, but now under-used and neglected, the long, sloping-roofed **Kuttambalam Theatre** (closed to non-Hindus), with carved panels and lathe-turned wooden pillars, serves as a venue for the ancient Sanskrit performance forms of Chakyar Kuttu and Kutiyattam.

The **State Art Museum** and **Zoo** (both Tues–Sun 10am–5pm; Rs6) stand together on Museum Road, ten minutes' walk from the Round in the northeast of town. Although small, the museum has excellent local bronzes, jewellery, fine woodcarvings of fanged temple guardians and a profusion of bell-metal oil lamps. The zoo predictably houses a rather depressing set of tenants, although

Puram

Thrissur is best known to outsiders as the venue for Kerala's biggest annual festival, **Puram**, which takes place on one day in April/May (ask at a tourist office for the exact date). Introduced by the raja of Kochi, Shaktan Tampuran (1789–1803), Puram is today the most extreme example of the kind of celebration seen on a smaller scale all over Kerala, whose main ingredients invariably include **caparisoned elephants**, **drum music** and **fireworks**.

On this day, at the hottest time of year, the centre of Thrissur fills to capacity with a sea of people gravitating towards Round South, where a long wide path leads to the southern entrance of the **Vaddukanatha temple** complex. Two majestic processions, representing the Tiruvambadi and Paramekkavu temples in Thrissur, compete to create the more impressive sights and sounds. They eventually meet, like armies on a battlefield, facing each other at either end of the path. Both sides present fifteen tuskers sumptuously decorated with gold ornaments, each ridden by three brahmins clutching objects symbolizing royalty: silver-handled whisks of yak hair, circular peacock-feather fans and orange, green, red, purple, turquoise, black, gold or patterned silk umbrellas fringed with silver pendants. At the centre of each group, the principal elephant carries an image of the temple's deity. Swaying gently, the elephants stand still much of the time, ears flapping, seemingly oblivious to the mayhem engendered by the crowds, bomb-like firework explosions and the huge orchestra that plays in front of them.

Known as **chenda melam**, this quintessentially Keralan music, featuring as many as a hundred loud, hard-skinned, cylindrical *chenda* drums, crashing cymbals and wind instruments, marks the progress of the procession. Each kind of *chenda melam* is named after the rhythmic cycle (*tala* or, in Malayalam, *talam*) in which it is set. Drummers stand in ranks, the most numerous at the back often playing single beats. At the front, a line of master drummers, the stars of Keralan music, try to outdo each other with their speed, stamina, improvisational skills and showmanship. Facing the drummers, musicians play long double-reed, oboe-like *kuzhals* (similar to the North Indian *shehnai*) and C-shaped *kompu* bell-metal trumpets. The fundamental structure is provided by the *elatalam* – medium-sized, heavy, brass hand-cymbals that resolutely the snakes – king cobra, krait, and viper – are well enough to spit. The peculiar **Multi-Purpose Museum** stands in the same compound, home to an odd hoard of skeletons, stuffed animals, minerals, weapons and costumes.

Next door to the *Yatri Niwas* hotel, the **Kerala Sangeet Natak Academy** (☏0487/233 2134) features a large auditorium that hosts occasional music and dance concerts as well as Keralan theatre, which has an enthusiastic following and tends to be heavily political. Around the corner is the **Lalitha Kala Academy** (☏0487/233 3773), which often exhibits contemporary Indian art.

One of the most important churches for Thrissur's large Christian population is the Syrian Catholic **Lourdes Cathedral**, along St Thomas College Road. Three daily masses serve a regular congregation of nine hundred. Like many of Kerala's Indo-Gothic churches, the exterior of dome and spires is more impressive than the interior, with its unadorned metal rafters and corrugated iron ceiling. Steps lead down from the altar to the crypt, a rather dilapidated copy of the grotto in Lourdes. The **Church of Our Lady of Dolores**, just south of the Round, is another important Catholic church and boasts neo-Gothic spires and the largest interior of any church in South India. Slightly further south, the **Chaldean Church** (services Mon–Sat 7am–9am & Sun 7.30am–9.30am), dedicated to Mary, is the most ancient of all Keralan Christian centres and the focal point of the unique **Nestorian Syrian**

and precisely keep the tempo, essential to the cumulative effect of the music. Over an extended period, the *melam* passes through four phases of tempo, each a double of the last, from a grand and graceful dead slow through to a frenetic pace.

At the arrival of the fastest tempo, those astride the elephants stand, manipulating their feather fans and hair whisks in coordinated sequence, while behind, unfurled umbrellas are twirled in flashes of dazzling colour and glinting silver in the sun. Meanwhile, the cymbals crash furiously, often raised above the head, requiring extraordinary stamina (and causing nasty weals on the hands). The master drummers play at their loudest and fastest, frequently intensified by surges of energy emanating from single players, one after another; a chorus of trumpets, in ragged unison, accompanies the cacophony, creating a sound that has altered little since the festival's origins.

All this is greeted by tremendous firework explosions and roars from the crowd; many people punch the air, while others are clearly *talam branthans*, rhythm "madmen", who follow every nuance of the structure. When the fastest speed is played out, the slowest tempo returns and the procession edges forward, the *mahouts* leading the elephants by the tusk. Stopping again, the whole cycle is repeated. At night, the Vaddukanatha temple entrances are a blaze of coloured lights and a spectacular firework display takes place in the early hours of the morning.

If you venture to Thrissur for Puram, be prepared for packed buses and trains. Needless to say, accommodation should be booked well in advance. An umbrella or hat is recommended for protection from the sun. Unfortunately, Puram has become an excuse for groups of Indian men to get very drunk; women are advised to dress conservatively and only to go in the morning, or to watch with a group of Indian women.

Similar but much smaller events take place in town, generally from September onwards, with most during the summer (April and May). Enquire at a tourist office or your hotel, or ask someone to check a local edition of the newspaper, *Mathrabhumi*, for local performances of *chenda melam*, and other drum orchestras such as *panchavadyam* and *tyambaka*.

community, which also runs a school here. Not much of the original structure remains, as the church was extensively renovated in the nineteenth century. Owing to this renovation, the gabled facade is the most remarkable part of what remains of the original structure. Staff in the friendly and welcoming office by the entrance to the church will open the door to the church for you. Inside, the plain chamber is hung with chandeliers and the extraordinary pulpit is ornately carved in teak.

Shopping

Thrissur is a good place to pick up Keralan **crafts**. The main shopping area is on the Round; on Round West, the **Kerala State Handicraft Emporium** specializes in wood; a one-minute walk from Round East at the top of Palace Road, **Co-optex** sells a good range of hand-loom cloth. At **Chemmanur's**, Round South, near the *Elite Hotel*, you'll find the usual carved wooden-elephant-type souvenirs, and, on the ground floor, a high-kitsch Aladdin's Cave of nodding dogs, Jesus clocks, Mecca table ornaments and parabolic nail-and-string art. **Alter Media** at Utility Building, Nehru Bazaar, Nayarangadi is a small but interesting bookshop devoted to women's studies, while **Cosmos**, on Round West, is a treasure-trove of novels, academic tomes and books on art, drama and culture.

Kuruppam Road, which leads south towards the railway station from the western end of Round South, is one of the best places in Kerala to buy **bell-metal** products, particularly oil lamps made in the village of Nadavaramba, near Irinjalakuda (see p.424). **Nadavaramba Krishna & Sons** and **Bell-metal Craft** both specialize in brass, bronze and bell metal. Lamps cost Rs80–25,000, and "superfine" bell metal is sold by weight, at over Rs250 per kilo. Continuing south on Kuruppam Road to the next junction with Railway Station Road, you'll find a number of small shops selling cheap Christian, Muslim and Hindu pictures etched on metal, and festival accessories, including umbrellas similar to those used for Puram (see box on p.420).

Eating and drinking

Thrissur's big **hotels** offer Indian, Western and Chinese food, and Keralan lunches, while several quality, inexpensive places are clustered near the **Round**. Late at night, on the corner of Round South and Round East, opposite the Medical College Hospital, you'll find a string of chai and omelette stalls, frequented by auto-rickshaw-wallahs, hospital visitors, itinerant mendicants, Ayappa devotees and student revellers.

AFC Round West. Upstairs fast-food joint with Asian as opposed to Kentucky fried chicken, plus tasty burgers and pizza.

Bharath Lodge Chembottil Lane, next door to *Elite Hotel*. Excellent South Indian breakfasts, evening snacks and fixed-price "all you can eat" Keralan meals at lunch time. Inexpensive.

Chick City Round West. Bright ice-cream parlour featuring an astounding array of sundaes with names like cold duck or parrot attack.

Indian Coffee House Round South. Cheap and very popular restaurant serving snacks, Indian meals and excellent filter coffee.

Luciya Palace Marar Rd, just off the southwest

corner of the Round ☎0487/424731. Hotel restaurant serving Indian and Chinese dishes; dinner is served in a pleasant garden illuminated by fairy lights.

Ming Palace Pathan Building, Round South. Inexpensive "Chindian" with dim lighting, cheesy muzak and a menu of chop suey, noodles and lots of chicken and veg dishes.

Pathan's Round South. Deservedly popular veg restaurant, with a cosy a/c family annexe and a large canteen-like dining hall. Generous portions and plenty of choice, including *koftas*, kormas and lots of tandoori options, as well as Keralan thalis and wonderful Kashmiri naan.

Around Thrissur

The chief attraction of the area **around Thrissur** is the opportunity to get to grips with Kerala's cultural heritage. Countless festivals, at their peak before the monsoon hits in May, enable visitors to catch some of the best drummers in the world, **Kathakali** dance-drama and **Kutiyattam**, the world's oldest surviving theatre form.

Irinjalakuda

The village of **IRINJALAKUDA**, 20km south of Thrissur, has a unique temple, five minutes' walk west from the bus stand, dedicated to **Bharata**, the brother of Rama. Visitors are usually permitted to see inside (men must wear a *dhoti*), but, as elsewhere, the inner parts of the temple are closed to non-Hindus. It boasts a superbly elegant tiled *kuttambalam* **theatre** within its outer courtyard, built to afford an unimpeded view for the maximum number of spectators (drawn from the highest castes only), and known for its excellent acoustics. A profusion of painted woodcarvings of mythological animals and stories from the epics decorate the interior. On the low stage, which is enclosed by painted wooden columns and friezes of female dancers, stand two large copper *mizhavu* drums for use in the Sanskrit drama **Kutiyattam** (see p.717), permanently installed in wooden frames into which a drummer climbs to play. Traditionally, *mizhavus* were considered sacred objects; Nandikeshvara, Shiva's rhythm-man, was said to reside in them. The drama for which they provided music was a holy ritual, and in the old days the instrument was never allowed to leave the temple and was only played by members of a special caste, the Nambyars. Since then, outsiders have learned the art of *mizhavu* playing, but the orthodox authorities do not allow them to play inside.

Left of the Bharata temple as you leave, **Natana Kairali** is an important cultural centre dedicated to the performance, protection and documentation of Kerala's lesser-known – but fascinating and vibrant – theatre arts, including Kutiyattam, Nangiar Koothu (female mono-acting), shadow and puppet theatres. The centre is based in the home of one of Kerala's most illustrious acting families, Ammanur Chakyar Madhom (say this name when you ask for directions). Natana Kairali's director, Shri G. Venu (☎0488/282 5559), is a mine of information about Keralan arts, and can advise on forthcoming performances.

Irinjalakuda is best reached by **bus** from the Shakthan Thampuran stand at Thrissur rather than by train, as the railway station is an inconvenient 8km east of town.

Kodungallur

Virtually an island surrounded by backwaters and the sea, the small country town of **KODUNGALLUR** (Cranganore), 35km south of Thrissur, is rich in Keralan history. The dearth of information regarding the modern town contrasts with tales of its illustrious past. Kodungallur has been identified as the site of the ancient cities of **Vanji** (one-time capital of the Chera kingdom), and **Muziris**, described in the first century AD by the Roman traveller Pliny as "*primum emporium Indiae*", the most important port in India. Other accounts describe the harbour as crowded with great ships, warehouses, palaces, temples and *yavanas* (a generic term for foreigners) who brought gold and left with spices, sandalwood, teak, gems and silks. The Romans are said to have built a temple in Kodungallur; nothing remains, but their presence has been shown through finds of coins, the majority of which date from the reigns of Augustus to Nero (27 BC–68 AD).

Its life as a great port was curtailed in 1341 by floods that silted up the harbour, leading to the development of Kochi (Cochin). Today, travellers will find that Kodungallur's "sights", with one exception, require some imagination. The town is best visited in a day-trip by **bus** from Thrissur's Shakthan Thampuran stand (1hr 30min), or en route between Thrissur and Kochi.

Standing on a large piece of open ground at the centre of Kodungallur, the ancient and typically Keralan **Kurumba Bhagavati Temple** is the site of an extraordinary annual event that some residents would prefer didn't happen at all. The **Bharani festival**, held during the Malayalam month of Meenom (March/April), attracts droves of devotees, both male and female, mainly from low-caste communities previously excluded from the temple. Their devotions consist in part of drinking copious amounts of alcohol and taking to the streets to sing Bharani *pattu*, sexually explicit songs about, and addressed to, the goddess Bhagavati, which are considered obscene and highly offensive by many other Keralans. On Kavuthindal, the first day, the pilgrims run en masse around the perimeters of the temple three times at breakneck speed, beating its walls with sticks. Until the mid-1950s, chickens were sacrificed in front of the temple; today, a simple red cloth symbolizes the bloody ritual. An important section of the devotees are the crimson-clad village oracles, wielding scythe-like swords with which they sometimes beat themselves on the head in ecstatic fervour, often drawing blood. Despite widespread disapproval, the festival draws plenty of spectators.

Cheraman Juma Masjid, 1.5km south of Kodungallur centre on NH-17, is thought to be the oldest mosque in India, founded in the seventh century by **Cheraman Perumal**, the legendary Keralan king who converted to Islam, abdicated and emigrated to Mecca. The supposed site of his palace, Cheraman Parambu, is today nothing more than a few broken columns on open ground. The present building, which dates from the sixteenth century, was until recently predominantly made of wood, of a style usually associated with Keralan Hindu temples. Unfortunately, due to weather damage, it has been partly rebuilt, and the facade, at least, is now rather mundane, with concrete minarets. The wooden interior remains intact, however, with a large Keralan oil lamp in the centre. Introduced five centuries ago for group study of the Koran, the lamp has taken on great significance to other communities, and Muslims, Christians and Hindus alike bring oil for the lamp on the auspicious occasion of major family events. In an anteroom, a small mausoleum is said to be the burial place

Nadavaramba bell-metal oil lamps

Keralan nights are made more enchanting by the use of **oil lamps**; the most common type, seen everywhere, is a slim free-standing metal column surmounted by a spike that rises from a circular receptacle for coconut oil, with cloth or banana plant fibre wicks. Every classical theatre performance keeps a large lamp burning centre-stage, all night. The special atmosphere of temples is also enhanced by innumerable lamps, some hanging from chains; others, *deepa stambham*, are multi-tiered and stand metres high.

The village of **Nadavaramba**, near Irinjalakuda, is an important centre for the manufacture of oil lamps and large cooking vessels, known as *uruli* and *varppu*. Alloys made from brass, copper and tin are frequently used, but the best are from **bell metal**, said to be eighty percent copper, and give a sonorous chime when struck. Shops in Thrissur that specialize in Nadavaramba-ware arrange visits to see the craftsmen at work.

of Habib Bin Malik, an envoy sent from Mecca by the convert king Cheraman Perumal. Women are not allowed into the mosque at any time ("they pray at home"), but interested male visitors should contact the assistant *mukhari* (*imam*, or priest), K.M. Saidumohamed, who lives directly opposite and will show you around.

Less than 500m south from the Cheraman Juma Masjid, past a bend in the main highway (NH-17), a wide avenue leads past tall lamps to the **Mahadeva temple**, dedicated to Shiva. It's a fine example of Keralan temple architecture, with access to the outer courtyard via a majestic gateway with a sloping roof and carvings of elephants, protective deities, gods and goddesses. Inside the enclosure, past a large multitiered metal lamp, a porch adorned with carvings dedicated to the heroes of the great Hindu epic, the *Ramayana*, marks the furthest non-Hindus are allowed. Within the restricted enclosure, an impressive columned hall shelters Shiva's ever faithful bull Nandi, while the inner sanctum houses a plain stone *lingam*. Despite the restriction, low retaining walls allow a good view of the extensive complex, which is well worth the short detour. Be careful of the heavy traffic, however, when walking along the narrow highway between the mosque and the temple.

The **Mar Thoma Pontifical Shrine**, fronted by a crescent of Neoclassical colonnades at Azhikode (pronounced "Arikode") Jetty (6km), marks the place where the Apostle Thomas is said to have arrived in India in 52AD. Despite the ugly waterside promenade and the tacky visitor centre it's a moving spot, on the edge of backwaters, but not worth a detour unless you're desperate to see the shard of the saint's wrist bone enshrined within the church.

If you want **to stay** at Kodungallur, the *Hotel Indraprastham*, close to the town centre (☎0488/280 2678; ❸–❺), has standard non-a/c and a/c rooms as well as a cheap "meals" restaurant, an a/c "family" restaurant and a bar.

Guruvayur

Kerala's most important Krishna shrine, the high-walled temple of **GURUVAYUR** (3am–1pm & 4–10pm; closed to non-Hindus), 29km north-west of Thrissur, attracts a constant flow of pilgrims, second only in volume to Ayappa's at Sabarimala (see box on p.392). Its deity, **Guruvayurappan**, has inspired numerous paeans from Keralan poets, most notably Narayana Bhattatiri, who wrote the *Narayaniyam* in the sixteenth century, when the temple, whose origins are legendary, seems to have first risen to prominence.

Guruvayur is one of the richest temples in Kerala and is constantly awash with **pilgrims**, dressed in their best white and old-trim clothes. The market outside is a particularly intense combination of commercial activity, noise and stalls full of glitter and trinkets such as two-rupee plastic Guruvayurappan signet rings, and there's a palpable air of excitement, particularly when events inside spill out into the streets. A temple committee stall outside the main gates auctions off the gifts, including bell-metal lamps, received at the shrine – according to superstition, if you buy any of these items they must be returned to the temple as gifts.

Of the temple's 24 annual **festivals**, the most important are Ekadashi and Ulsavam. The eighteen days of Ekadashi, in the month of Vrischikam (Nov/Dec), are marked by processions of caparisoned elephants outside the temple, while the exterior of the building may be decorated with the tiny flames of innumerable oil lamps. On certain days (check dates with a KTDC office) programmes staged in front of the temple attract the cream of South Indian classical music artists.

The founding of Guruvayur temple

The founding of the **Guruvayur temple** is associated with the end of Krishna's life. After witnessing the massacre of family and compatriots, Krishna returned to his capital, Dvarka, in Gujarat, to end his earthly existence. However, knowing that Dvarka would disappear into the sea on his death, he was concerned that the form of Vishnu there, which he himself worshipped, should be spared its fate.

Krishna invited Brihaspati, also known as Guru, the preceptor of the gods, and a pupil, Vayu, the god of wind, to help him select a new home for Vishnu. By the time they arrived at Dvarka, the sea (Varuna) had already claimed the city, but the wind managed to rescue Vishnu. Krishna, Guru and Vayu travelled south, where they met Parasurama, who had just created Kerala by throwing his axe into the sea. On reaching a beautiful lake of lotuses, Rudratirtha, they were greeted by Shiva and Parvati, who consecrated the image of Vishnu. Guru and Vayu then installed it, the temple was named after them, and so the deity received the title Guruvayurappan ("Lord of Guruvayur").

During Ulsavam, in the month of Kumbham (Feb/March), tantric rituals are conducted inside, an **elephant race** is run outside on the first day, and elephant processions take place during the ensuing six days. On the ninth day, the Palivetta, or "hunt" occurs; the deity, mounted on an elephant, circumambulates the temple accompanied by men dressed as animals, representing human weaknesses such as greed and anger, and are vanquished by the god. The next night sees the image of the god taken out for ritual immersion in the temple tank; devotees greet the procession with oil lamps and throw rice. It is considered highly auspicious to bathe in the tank at the same time as the god.

When not involved in races and other arcane temple rituals, Guruvayur's tuskers are chained at the **Punnathur Kotta Elephant Camp** (daily 9am–6pm; Rs5, cameras Rs25), 4km north of town. Around fifty elephants, aged from 8 to 95, live here, munching for most of the day on specially imported piles of fodder and cared for by their three personal *mahouts*, who wash and scrub them several times a week in the sanctuary pond. Only approach an elephant if a *mahout* allows you, as they can be unpredictable and dangerous.

All the animals are the personal possession of Lord Guruvayur, given to the temple by wealthy patrons from as far afield as Bihar and Assam. All the elephants – apart from the most elderly, who are allowed an honourable retirement – are gainfully employed in local temples, especially at the Guruvayur temple itself. All temples demand pretty elephants for their elaborate festivals, and the competition to rent a particularly favoured pachyderm can become a bitter auction between villages; the standard daily charge of Rs3500 per elephant once reached a record Rs75,000.

Practicalities

Buses from Thrissur (40min) arrive at the main **bus stand** at the top end of East Nada Street, five minutes east of the temple, and the home of most of the **accommodation**. Try the pilgrim-oriented KTDC *Mangalya*, near the entrance of the Krishna temple (℡0487/255 2408; ❸), which large rooms for up to six people and a devotional atmosphere; or the one-star deluxe KTDC *Nandanam* near the railway station (℡0487/255 6266; ❸–❹), which has some a/c rooms. The town is crammed with veg **restaurants**, and there's an *Indian Coffee House* on the southern side of East Nada Street which serves South Indian snacks.

Cheruthuruthy

The village of **CHERUTHURUTHY**, 32km north of Thrissur, is an easy day-trip through green and gently undulating country. It consists of a few lanes and one main street, which runs in a southwards direction from the bank of Kerala's longest river, the **Bharatapuzha** (pronounced "bharatapura"). Considered holy by Hindus, the great river has receded in recent years, leaving a vast expanse of sand. Although of little consolation to locals, who have to deal with the problems of a depleted water supply, it has produced a landscape of incomparable beauty.

Cheruthuruthy is famous as the home of **Kerala Kalamandalam**, the state's flagship training school for Kathakali and other indigenous Keralan performing arts, which was founded in 1927 by the revered Keralan poet Vallathol (1878–1957). At first patronized by the raja of Cochin, the school has been funded by both state and national governments and has been instrumental in the large-scale revival of interest in Kathakali and other unique Keralan art forms. Despite conservative opposition, it followed an open-door recruitment policy, based on artistic merit, which produced "scheduled caste" Muslim and Christian graduates along with the usual Hindu castes, something that was previously unimaginable. During the 1960s, Kalamandalam's dynamic leadership forged international links with cultural organizations. Foreign students were accepted and every attempt was made to modernize, extending into the way in which the traditional arts were presented. Kalamandalam artists perform in the great theatres of the world, many sharing their extraordinary skills with outsiders; luminaries of modern theatre, such as Grotowski and Peter Brook, are indebted to them. Nonetheless, many of these trained artists are still excluded from entering, let alone performing in, temples, a popular venue for Hindu art forms, especially music.

Non-Hindus can see Kathakali, Kutiyattam and Mohiniattam performed in the school's superb **theatre**, which replicates the wooden, sloping-roofed traditional theatres, known as *kuttambalams*, found in Keralan temples. If you're interested in how this extraordinary technique is taught, don't miss the chance to sit in on the training sessions (Mon–Fri 4.30am–5pm; closed on public holidays). A handful of foreigners also come to the Kalamandalam academy each year to attend full-time **courses** in Kathakali and other traditional dance and theatre forms. Short courses last for a minimum of one month, condensed programmes for three to six months and full courses from four to six years. Foreign students with the correct visas can attend a maximum of four years. Applications may be made from abroad (write to the Secretary, Kerala Kalamandalam, Vallathol Nagar, Cheruthuruthy, Thrissur District, Kerala 679531), but it's a good idea to visit before committing yourself, as the training is rigorous. A good time to visit is during their annual week-long festival starting on Christmas Day. For information contact the school office (T04884/262418).

Held at the *kuttambalam* and at their original riverside campus amongst the trees, the festival presents all the art forms of Kerala and is free, although the dearth of accommodation in the area can be a problem. A short walk past the old campus leads to a small but exquisite **Shiva temple** in classic Keralan style. The exterior is lit by candles during the early evening puja making it a particularly rewarding time to visit.

Practicalities

Cheruthuruthy's **accommodation** is limited, with some students staying as guests in private accommodation (phone school for details). Otherwise, the village has a couple of simple guesthouses, and the atmospheric *Government Guest House* (℡04884/262760; ❷–❸), a short distance along the Shoranur road from Kalamandalam, has eight huge but basic rooms, some with Western-style toilets, and all sharing a veranda. For a touch of a/c luxury try the *River Retreat* (℡04884/262922; ❾), in a grand old heritage palace at the banks of the river on Palace Road, which offers deluxe rooms and a smart a/c multi-cuisine restaurant. Other than the *River Retreat*, the only places to **eat** here are the simple *dhabas* in the centre of village such as the vegetarian *Mahatma*.

Buses heading to Shoranur from Thrissur's Wadakkancheri stand pass through, and the nearest **railway station** is Shoranur Junction, 3km south, served by express trains to and from Mangalore, Chennai and Kochi.

Palakkad

Surrounded by paddy fields, **PALAKKAD** (Palghat) lies on NH-47 between Thrissur (79km) and Coimbatore, Tamil Nadu (54km), and on the railway line from Karnataka and Tamil Nadu. Due to the natural twenty-kilometre-wide gap through the Western Ghats here, this area has always been an important entry point into Kerala. The environs are beautiful, but the town itself doesn't warrant a stop other than to break a journey. Palakkad's dry, Deccan-like landscape does, however, give a misleading first impression of Kerala for those who arrive this route.

The well-preserved **fort** (daily 9am–6pm; free), built in 1766 by Haider Ali of Mysore, is the nearest thing to a "sight" and gets plenty of visitors at weekends, despite having little to offer. However, many travellers in search of **Kathakali** performances find themselves directed here as, in April and May particularly, hundreds of one-off events take place in the area. The local Government Carnatic Music College has an excellent reputation, and a small open-air amphitheatre next to the fort often hosts first-class music and dance performances. Ask at the tourist office (see opposite) for details. The landscaped gardens (daily 8am–8pm) and amusement park (daily 11am–9pm; Rs80, includes all rides) at **Malampuzha**, 10km north, are also a popular local attraction at the weekends, when crowds come to ride the cable car or "ropeway". In the same grounds, the fantasy rock garden created by the artist Nek Chand of Chandigarh fame is illuminated on Saturday and Sunday nights (open until 9pm).

Practicalities

Palakkad is well connected to the rest of Kerala and most of the express trains travelling through to Chennai, Bangalore and points further north stop at the town's **railway station**, 6km to the northeast. The KSRTC **bus stand** is right in the middle of Palakkad and the adjacent *Hotel Sarovar* restaurant serves excellent if slightly fiery food.

Accommodation includes the *Ammbadi* (℡0491/253 1244; ❸–❹), on TB Road opposite the town bus stand and 500m from the KSRTC bus stand, which has comfortable rooms (some a/c) and a restaurant serving Indian and Chinese food. The well-managed, modern *Hotel Indraprastha*, English Church Road (℡0491/253 4641, ✉eyepee@md3.vsnl.net.in; ❹–❼), has large rooms (some a/c), a lovely lawn and a dim but blissfully air-conditioned restaurant serving Indian, Western and Chinese cuisine, a well-stocked bar and a 24-hour vegetarian coffee shop. *Fort Palace*, West Fort Road (℡0491/253 4621; ❸–❻), has reasonable rooms, a bar and a huge garden restaurant serving good north and South Indian food; it's particularly nice when lit up in the evening. Another option is to head 10km out of town to KTDC's *Garden House* at Malampuzha (℡0491/281 5217; ❸–❺), which has large non-a/c doubles.

The DTPC's **tourist office**, around the corner from the *Indraprastha* at Fort Maidan (Mon–Sat 9am–5pm, except 2nd Saturday of the month; ☎0491/253 8996), has little more to offer than leaflets and limited travel information. The *Indraprastha* organizes four- and seven-day **tours** of the region, picking up at Coimbatore airport, while tours in the immediate area are on offer from Sahya Eco Tours, 13/530 Farasha, Mankavu (☎0491/253 8832). Both the *Indraprastha* and the *Fort Palace* **change money** (residents only), as does the State Bank of India, next door to the *Indraprastha*.

Nelliampathy

Surrounded by teak forests and estates where tea, coffee, cardamom and oranges grow profusely, the tiny hill station of **NELLIAMPATHY**, 75km south of Palakkad, has made the most of its surroundings by way of several plantations that offer a chance to stay and experience local hospitality, wildlife and scenic beauty. The cool climate, fresh air and heady scents hereabouts make for a very pleasant break from the steamy coastal strip. There's a small DTPC **tourist office** (daily 10am–8pm; ☎0492/234 6266) where **buses** terminate, and most of the plantation resorts will pick you up from here. *ITL Holiday Resorts* (☎0492/234 6357; ❹), an immaculate lodge in nearby Kaikatty, is the cheapest option and also has dorm beds (Rs200). Further upmarket is the *Green Acres Estate* at Palagapandi (☎0492/234 6245; ❹–❻), with rooms in a run-down but atmospheric colonial planter's cottage, and slightly cheaper ones in the newer block. A flat daily rate of Rs300 covers all meals (drinks are extra). The most luxurious option is *Tropical Hill Resorts* in Padagiri (☎0492/234 6238, ✉trophill@sify.com; ❻), which has immaculate double rooms, spacious luxury suites and even a decent dorm (Rs250 per bed) for budget travellers. Horse-riding, whitewater rafting, birdwatching and jungle treks can be arranged.

Kozhikode (Calicut)

Formerly one of Asia's most prosperous trading capitals, the busy coastal city of **KOZHIKODE** (Calicut), 225km north of Kochi, occupies an extremely important place in Keralan legend and history. It's also significant in the history of European involvement on the subcontinent, as Vasco da Gama landed nearby in 1498. Nowadays, with precious few historical remnants, there's little of interest here, and the few foreigners who do come are either lost or merely breaking the long journey between Mysore and Kochi.

Kozhikode's roots are shrouded in myth. According to Keralan tradition, the powerful king Cheraman Perumal is said to have converted from Hinduism to Islam and left for Mecca "to save his soul", never to return. Before he set sail he divided Kerala between his relatives, all of whom had to submit to his nephew, who was given the kingdom of Kozhikode and the title *zamorin*, equivalent to emperor. The city prospered and, perhaps because of the story of the convert king, became the preferred port of Muslim traders from the Middle East in search of spices, particularly pepper. During the Raj, it was an important centre for the export of printed Indian cotton, hence the term "calico", an English corruption of the name Calicut – itself an anglicized version of the city's original Malayalam name, now reinstated. Today Kozhikode is flourishing, thanks to new wealth brought back to the city by locals working in the Gulf.

Arrival and information

The **railway station** (☎0495/270 1234), close to the centre of town, is served by coastal expresses, slower passenger trains, and superfast express trains from Delhi, Mumbai, Kochi and Thiruvananthapuram. There are three **bus stands**. All government-run services from destinations as far afield as Bangalore, Mysore, Ooty, Madurai, Coimbatore and Mangalore pull in at the **KSRTC Bus Stand**, on Mavoor Road (aka Indira Gandhi Road). Private long-distance buses stop at the **New Mofussil Private Stand** (☎0495/272 2823), 500m away on the other side of Mavoor Road – there's a row of agents for booking tickets on these buses on MM Ali Road. The **Palayam Bus Stand** just serves city buses.

Kozhikode's **airport**, at Karippur, 23km south of the city, has flights to Mumbai, Delhi, Coimbatore, Chennai, Goa and various Gulf states. Tickets are available from Century Travels, Bank Road (☎0495/276 6522) or directly from the airlines themselves. Indian Airlines (☎0495/276 6243) and Air India (☎0495/276 6669) are both at the Eroth Centre, 5/2521 Bank Road; Jet Airways are at 29 Mavoor Road (☎0495/274 0052). A taxi from the airport into town will cost around Rs300, but you can save a few rupees by taking an **auto-rickshaw** to the Kozhikode–Palakkad highway and then catching a bus.

The friendly **KTDC tourist information booth** (officially daily 9am–7.30pm; ☎0495/270 0097) at the railway station has info on travel connections and sites around Kozhikode, but opening hours are erratic. The KTDC tourist office (☎0495/272 2391) in the *Malabar Mansion* hotel at the corner of SM Street can supply only limited information about the town and area. There's a **24hr left luggage** facility at the railway station but, as is always the case, they only accept locked luggage. With so much Gulf money floating around, you shouldn't have any difficulty **changing currency** in Kozhikode. A good place for cash or travellers' cheques is PL Worldways, 3rd Floor, Semma Towers, Mavoor Road (daily 9.30am–1.30pm & 2–5.30pm). The Standard Chartered Bank on Town Hall Road and the State Bank of India at Manachira Park also change money, while the Corp Bank on Town Hall Road and Federal Bank on

Kallai Road both have ATMs. **Internet** access is available at The Hub, on the first floor of the block to the right of *Nandhinee Sweets*, MM Ali Road, and at Internet Zone, near *KTDC Malabar Mansion* (both Rs30 per hour).

For **backwater cruises** in the Kozhikode region try the small, friendly and efficient Malabar House Boats (☎0495/245 2045) at 1/335 Purakkatri, Thalakalthur in the northern suburbs. Their *kettu vallam* cruises start at Purakkatri, 12km north of the city, but they can arrange transport to the boat with prior notice. A 24hr cruise costs around Rs7000 for two people, including meals; a day cruise will set you back Rs3500 for up to six people.

The City

Few traces remain of the model fourteenth-century city, which followed a Hindu grid formula based on a sacred diagram containing the image of the cosmic man, Purusha. The axis and energy centre of the diagram was dictated by the position of the ancient **Tali Shiva temple** (closed to non-Hindus), just south of MM Ali Road, which survives to this day. Everything, and everybody, had a place. The district around the port in the northwest was reserved for foreigners: the Chinese community lived in and around Chinese Street (now Silk Street) and the Portuguese, Dutch and British later occupied the area. Keralan Muslims (Mappilas) lived in the southwest. The northeast of the city was a commercial quarter, while the southeast housed Tali temple, a palace and fort; all the military *kalaris* (martial art gymnasia) that stood around the perimeter have now gone.

Considering its history, there is now very little to see in Kozhikode, though it is good for **shopping**. Around SM Street, many good fabric and ready-made clothes shops sell the locally produced cotton cloth, particularly as stylish *lunghis*. You cannot fail to be dazzled by the sheer number of gold jewellery shops, full of ladies spending lavish amounts of the money faithfully sent by relatives in the Gulf. This district is also a good place to try the local *halva* sweets, especially popular with the large Mappila community. Some shops specialize in piping-hot banana chips, straight from the frying pan.

Locals enjoy walking along the **city beach** (3km from the centre) in the late afternoon and early evening. Although not suitable for swimming, it's a relaxing place, where you can munch on freshly roasted peanuts while scanning the seas for dolphins. The northern end towards the pier is distinctly more attractive than the southern stretch, which doubles as a lorry park. After dark it's difficult to find an auto-rickshaw to take you back into town, but there are regular buses back into the centre.

The **Pazhassirajah and Krishnamenon Museums and Art Gallery** (Mon, Tues & Thurs–Sun 10am–12.30pm & 2.30–5pm, Wed 2.30–5pm; free) stand together 5km north of the centre on East Hill. The Pazhassirajah collection includes copies of murals, coins, bronzes and models of the umbrella-shaped, stone megalithic remains peculiar to Kerala, while the museum houses memorabilia associated with the left-wing Keralan politician V.K. Krishnamenon, and a gallery of works by Indian artists.

The experimental handloom centre, the **Tasara Creative Weaving Centre**, is in Beypore North, 7km south of Kozikode, just off the Kozikode–Beypore Road in a compound full of tropical flora. Rugs, bedspreads and wall hangings are produced here as works of art, not simply household furnishings. Visitors are welcome to watch the artists at work, to view the art gallery (daily 9am–6pm; free) and to buy the finished goods – prices range from $15 to $1000. You can also **stay** here and learn the art of the handloom under the tutelage of Mr Vasudevan Balakrishanan (☎0495/241 4832, ⓦwww.tasaraindia.com), with the aim of designing and making your own wall hanging. It costs $750 per person for a month-long course including all food and waving materials,.

The historic beach of **Kappad**, 16km north of Kozhikode, is said to be the landing place of Vasco da Gama and 170 sailors. A small memorial marks the spot, and the small, pleasant and as yet undeveloped beach offers good swimming. **Accommodation** is available at *Beach House*, where Rs2500 gets you the whole house with two rooms, lounge and kitchen (☎0496/268 6427; ❽), and at the new, clean and good-value *Pannu Tourist Home* (☎0496/268 8634; ❸–❹), on a lane behind the seafront. The larger and longer-established *Kappad Beach Resort* was due to reopen at the time of writing; call their Kochi office (☎0484/234 4463) for details. To get to Kappad, take a **bus** from Kozhikode bound for Badagara and get off at Thiruvangoor; the beach is 4km from here and reachable by regular local buses and auto-rickshaws.

Accommodation and eating

Kozhikode's reasonably priced city-centre **hotels**, most of which operate a 24hr check-out, often fill up by midday; the beach area is a quiet alternative. Your best bet for a proper **meal** is to eat at your hotel, though you can get South Indian snacks and great omelette and coffee breakfasts at the dependable *Indian Coffee Houses* on Kallai Road and GH Road. The *Tandoor Prince* on GH Road is a no-nonsense hole-in-the-wall restaurant serving mainly non-veg food. *Nandhinee Sweets*, on MM Ali Road, is an ultra-hygienic sweets, nuts and savoury snacks pit-stop, where you can also get great fresh fruit cocktails, *badam* milk and *falooda* shakes.

Hotels and guesthouses

Alakapuri Guest House MM Ali Rd, near the railway station, 1km from KSRTC Bus Stand ☎0495/272 3451, ⓦwww.alakapurihotels.com. Built around a courtyard, the a/c rooms here have huge bathtubs, polished wood and easy chairs; the cheaper, non-a/c options are rather spartan. There's a bar, restaurant and a lovely lawn, and single rates are available. ❹–❺

Fortune Kannur Rd, 3km north of the centre ☎0495/276 8888, ⓕ276 8111. Welcomgroup hotel for business travellers, with plush rooms and central a/c, plus a rooftop swimming pool, fitness suite and sauna, foreign exchange facilities, bar, 24hr coffee shop and Indian restaurant. The tariff includes a buffet breakfast. ❽

Imperial Kallai Rd ☎0495/270 1291. Large hotel built around a courtyard with basic, very cheap rooms and a branch of *India Coffee House* on the ground floor. ❷

KTDC Malabar Mansion SM St ☎0495/272 2391, ⓦwww.ktdc.com. Good-value modern high-rise hotel near the railway station with a choice of huge a/c suites with cable TV and reasonable non-a/c rooms. There's also a beer parlour and a good South Indian restaurant. ❷–❹

Sasthapuri MM Ali Rd ☎0495/272 3281, ⓦwww.sasthapuri.com. Small budget place with well-maintained non-a/c and a/c rooms and a decent roof garden restaurant and a bar. Good value. ❷–❺

Sea Queen Beach Rd ☎0495/236 6604, ⓔseaqueenclt@sify.com. Quiet, comfortable but ageing middle-class hotel overlooking a rather grim part of the beach – rooms (a/c and non-a/c) are a little dim and stuffed with furniture. There's a popular South Indian restaurant and bar on the ground floor. ❹–❽

Taj Residency PT Usha Rd ☎0495/276 5354, ⓦwww.tajhotels.com. The grandest hotel in town, though it lacks the ubiquitous *Taj* style; nonetheless, the centrally a/c rooms ($80–110) are very comfortable and there's a pool, coffee shop, multi-cuisine restaurant, and health and Ayurvedic centre. ❾

Wayanad

One of the most beautiful regions of Kerala is the hill district of **Wayanad**, situated 70km east of Kozhikode, with tracts of forest covering the western flanks of the Nilgiris. Due to the relative isolation and lack of decent roads, the various tribal groups that populate the area have so far managed to preserve their traditional identities, despite the gradual intrusion of modernization. The scenery is rich and varied, ranging from plantations of tea, spice, coffee and cocoa to the dry scruffy jungles of the **Muthanga Wildlife Sanctuary**. For those with time on their hands, Wayanad makes an alternative and rewarding route between coastal Kerala and Mysore in neighbouring Karnataka, or Ooty in Tamil Nadu.

Travelling from Kozhikode, a beautiful but tortuous road climbs a series of hairpin bends up the Southern Ghats through unspoiled forests, where macaques forage along the roadside, impervious to the groaning, diesel-belching trucks and buses going past. As the road arrives at the lip of the great plateau there are sweeping views back towards the coast of lush, green cover, and you can glimpse the sea in the hazy distance. On the highway to Mysore and Ooty, **Kalpetta**, the district capital, makes a good base from which to discover most of Wayanad, but **Mananthavady**, 27km from Kalpetta, is more convenient for exploring the northern jungles.

Kalpetta and around

Surrounded by plantations and rolling hills, **KALPETTA**, 72km east of Kozhikode, is a quiet market town with little to commend it except its pleasant location on the edge of the Muthanga Wildlife Sanctuary. Along with the settlement of **Vythiri**, 12km to the southwest, Kalpetta provides ample amenities and excellent walking country, including in the ranges around the spectacular **Chembra Peak** (2100m), the highest mountain in Wayanad.

Although not as evocative as Periyar, the **Muthanga Wildlife Sanctuary** (daily 7–10.30am & 3–5.30pm; Rs25 [Rs5]), 40km east of Kalpetta, forms part of the **Nilgiri Biosphere Reserve** along with national parks such as Bandipur and Nagarhole in Karnataka, and Madumalai across the border in Tamil Nadu. Like neighbouring Bandipur National Park, Muthanga, with its dry deciduous forests, is noted for elephants and also shelters deer, wild boar, bear and tiger. The highway from Kalpetta to Mysore and Ooty via the scruffy town of **Sultan's Battery** passes through part of the sanctuary, and provides an opportunity, if you're lucky, to see wild elephants crossing the road on ancient migratory trails.

Accessible from Meppady and 12km south of Kalpetta, **Chembra Peak** (2100m) has soaring ridges and expansive meadows on one side, thick forests on the other. The peak towers over Vythiri, dominating the countryside, and provides stunning views over Wayanad and out to sea. It's a stiff climb, so take plenty of water. To get to Meppady, turn off the main Kozhikode highway at Chundale and follow the Ooty road for a further 8km; you can catch a bus from Kalpetta.

Practicalities

The state **bus** stand in the centre of Kalpeta has connections to Kozhikode (72km; 2hr), Ooty (115km; 3hr 30min), Mysore (125km; 4hr) and Mananthavady (27km; 1hr). **Auto–rickshaws** and **jeeps** are available for local destinations. The DTPC **tourist office** (Mon–Sat 10am–5pm, closed second Sat of each month; ☎04936/202134) is in Kalpetta North, 1km from the bus stand. Although unused to foreign visitors, with a little encouragement they will supply information on buses and the area in general. They can also help with hiring **forest guides** at Rs50 a day, and jeeps (Rs8 per km plus a Rs100 vehicle entrance fee) for those going to the wildlife sanctuaries independently. The Mysore bus passes the **entrance** to Muthanga Sanctuary, near Sultan's Battery. It's cheaper to hire a jeep here than in Kalpetta for trips into the park (Rs200–250).

Accommodation and eating

Kalpetta has ample **accommodation**, most within easy striking distance of the bus stand, including the cheap and basic *Arun Tourist Home* on Main Road (☏04936/202039; ❶). For a bit more comfort, try the rambling modern *Harita Giri*, close by on Emily Road (☏04936/202673; ❹–❼), which offers a wide range of rooms (including singles) from budget to deluxe a/c suites; there's also a garden, bar and a restaurant, and they can arrange tours. By far the best hotel in town, however, is *Green Gates*, above the tourist office on TB Road, Kalpetta North (☏04936/202001; ❻–❽), offering well-appointed standard and a/c rooms and two fine restaurants. For inexpensive **food**, the ever-dependable *India Coffee House*, opposite the tourist office, serves good South Indian snacks, meals and filter coffee.

For a spot of luxury, head out to **VYTHIRI**, 12km southwest of Kalpetta, where there are two excellent **resorts** tucked away on tea, coffee and spice plantations. The first and most accessible is the *Vythiri Resort* (book through Prime Land Holdings ☏0484/235 0249, ⓦwww.vythiriresort.com; ❾); to reach it, turn off the main road which runs south to Kozhikode (adjacent to the spice shop) onto an estate road and continue for 3km; jeeps from Kalpetta charge Rs150. Set in a beautiful seven-acre plot with three boulder-strewn mountain streams flowing through it, *Vythiri* boasts tasteful cottages and rooms ($75–100) and serves exquisite Keralan cuisine in its restaurant. You can also arrange forest and sightseeing tours here, including a visit to the Harrison Malayalam Tea Factory. A further 4km up the same track and only accessible by four-wheel drive (with the final 1.5km on foot), the *Green Magic* nature resort (book via Tourindia, Thiruvananthapuram (☏0471/233 0437, Ⓕ233 1407; ❾) is even more exotic. It consists of luxurious treehouses ($180) nestled under a lush rainforest canopy, each accessed by a unique cane pulley system that uses a counterweight of water to lift you over 20m off the ground. Energy sources include solar power and *gobar* (cow-dung) gas, and meals (included in the rates) are prepared from organically grown vegetables. Several forest trails lead out from the resort offering plenty of opportunities for guided walks; tours of the sanctuaries can also be arranged.

Thirunelli and around

One of Wayanad's most celebrated temples, **Sree Thirunelli**, lies in a remote part of the district 32km north of Kalpetta, off the Kogadu road, in the epony-mous hamlet of Thirunelli. The temple is dedicated to the god Vishnu and is often referred to as the "Kashi of the South", which equates it in veneration with the holy city of Varanasi. An unusual mix of Keralan tiled roofs and north-ern North Indian-style pillared halls, Thirunelli is, like Kashi, considered to be a *tirtha*, or crossing, between the mundane world and the divine. Following tradition, devout pilgrims bathe in the nearby **River Papanasini**, which is said to absolve them of their worldly sins.

More interesting still is the **Valliyurkava Bhagavathi temple**, an unassum-ing Keralan-style temple in a pastoral setting 8km east of Mananthavady and dedicated to the goddess Durga. For the last hundred years, the temple has played host to a tribal labour mart and, although bonded labour is now extinct, the fortnightly **festival** (Feb/Mar) continues as a celebration and attracts tribal people from all over Wayanad. The inner sanctum is closed to non-Hindus. **Accommodation** is available at the brand new, excellent-value *Panchatheertham Rest House* (☏04935/210201; ❶) opposite the Thirunelli temple. Alternatively in **MANANTHAVADY**, the nearest town to the temples, try *Hakson's* (☏04935/240118; ❶–❹), at KT junction on the Kozhikode road, with has clean, good-value doubles (some with bathtubs) and rock-bottom singles. Twelve buses a day travel from Mananthavady to Thirunelli, running from 7.45am until 6.15pm.

Tholpetty

Forming part of the larger Nagarhole National Park, which straddles the Kerala–Karnataka border, **Tholpetty Wildlife Sanctuary** (Rs25 [Rs10]), 40km northeast of Mananthavady, is one of the best parks in South India to see elephants, as well as plentiful bison, boar, *sambhar*, spotted deer, macaques and langurs; tigers also inhabit the park, though they are rarely spotted. There are daily two-hour **jeep safaris** into Tholpetty (7–9am & 3–5pm); these cost Rs300 for up to five people and you also have to pay Rs200 for a guide, though many are a waste of space. Safaris can be arranged through the *Pachyderm Palace* (see below), or just turn up at the sanctuary. It's also possible to **trek** in the park (daily 8am–1pm; Rs750 for up to four people).

   Accommodation is available just outside the park at *Pachyderm Palace* (book through the tourist desk in Kochi on ☏0484/237 1761; ❼), a traditional Keralan bungalow with five comfortable rooms rented on an all-inclusive basis; the authentic Keralan cuisine is delicious, and the welcome is guaranteed to be friendly.

The far north

The beautiful coast **north of Kozhikode** is a seemingly endless stretch of coconut palms, wooded hills and virtually deserted beaches; the towns, though, hold little of interest for visitors, most of whom bypass the area completely. However, this would mean missing out on the chance to see **theyyam**, the extraordinary masked trance dances and oracle readings that take place in villages throughout the region between November and May.

Kannur (Cannanore)

KANNUR (Cannanore), 92km north of Kozhikode, was for many centuries the capital of the Kolathiri rajas, who prospered from the thriving maritime spice trade through its port. In the early 1500s, after Vasco da Gama passed through, the Portuguese took it and erected an imposing bastion, **St Angelo's Fort**, overlooking the harbour, but today this is occupied by the Indian army and closed to visitors. In Kannur itself, the popular town beach can get quite crowded; for a bit more quiet head down to the small **Baby Beach** (4km) in the army's cantonment area (daily access 9am–5pm).

   Most visitors use Kannur as a base while they search out **theyyam** (also known loosely as "*teyyattam*", meaning "performance of *theyyam*"): spectacular spirit-possession rituals, an important feature of town and village life in the area (see p.717). There are over 400 different varieties of *theyyam*, so you could spend days and nights watching the rituals, and never see the same one twice. Locating these events is exciting and an essential part of the whole experience – you can often hear the loud and frenetic drumming miles away, but the temple where the *theyyam* is performed may be hidden deep within the forest or coconut groves. The best way to find them is to ask at the local tourist office or at *Costa Malabari* (see below), which is also a great place to hole up for idyllic beaches. If you're short of time, try the daily rituals at **Parassinikadavu** (see below).

Practicalities

Straddling the main coastal transport artery between Mangalore and Kochi/Thiruvananthapuram, Kannur is well connected by **bus** and **train** to most major towns and cities in Kerala, as well as Mangalore in Karnataka. In addition, buses from here travel to Mysore, turning inland at Thalassery (aka Tellycherry) and climbing the beautiful wooded ghats to Virajpet in Kodagu. The **railway station** is just over 5min by foot southwest of the bus stand. The State Bank of India on Fort Road will **change money** and travellers' cheques, as will UAE Exchange in KVR Tower, 500m east of the bus stand. There's a **DTPC** office near Civil Station (Mon–Sat 10am–5pm; ☎0497/270 6336), and a **tourist information centre** at the railway station (Mon–Sat 10am–5pm; ☎0497/270 3121). **Internet** access is widely available; try Asianet (Rs20 per hr), in an arcade near the station end of Fort Road, or Cyber Valley (Rs30 per hr), just beyond KVR Tower.

Accommodation

Costa Malabari 10km south near Tottada village (book through the Tourist Desk in Kochi ☎0484/237 1761, ⓦwww.costamalabari.com). Hidden deep in cashew and coconut groves, this warm and welcoming guesthouse has five airy and comfortable rooms. There are five pristine golden beaches within ten minutes' walk, and guests are plied with huge portions of excellent Keralan food (meals are included in the rate). The owners will pick up visitors from Kannur for Rs120 by prior arrangement. ❻–❼

Government Guest House Cantonment area ☎0497/270 6426. On a cliff overlooking the sea, with huge, simple non-a/c rooms that catch the breezes; it's primarily for visiting VIPs but there are usually a few spare rooms. ❷–❸

Malabar Residency Thavakkara Rd ☎0497/276 5456, ⓦwww.malabarresidency.com. Smart,

central hotel with comfortable en-suite a/c rooms, two restaurants, including the multi-cuisine *Grand Plaza*, and 24hr coffee shop. ❻–❼

Mascot Beach Resort 300m before Baby Beach ☎0497/270 8445, ⓔmascot_beach_resort@vsnl.com. Perched on the rocky shoreline, offering large well-appointed a/c rooms with views across the cove to the lighthouse. Facilities include a swimming pool, foreign exchange and a good restaurant – but no bar. ❹–❼

Meridian Palace Bellard Rd ☎0497/270 1676. Only two blocks from the station, this compact hotel has a range of comfy rooms and an excellent restaurant serving veg meals and fish.

Sweety International 200m north of railway station ☎0497/270 8283. Standard budget business high-rise with ordinary, executive and a/c rooms, all pretty decent value. ❷–❸

Parassinikadavu

The only place you can be absolutely guaranteed a glimpse of *theyyam* is the village of **PARASSINIKADAVU**, 20km north of Kannur beside the River Valapatanam, where the head priest, or *madayan*, of the **Parassini Madammpura** temple performs every day during winter before assembled devotees. Elaborately dressed and accompanied by a traditional drum group, he becomes possessed by the temple's presiding deity – Lord Muthappan, Shiva, in the form of a *kiratha*, or hunter – and enacts a series of complex offerings. The two-hour ceremony culminates when the priest/deity dances forward to bless individual members of the congregation. Even by Keralan standards, this is an extraordinary spectacle, and well worth taking time out of a journey along the coast for.

Regular local **buses** leave Kannur for Parassinikadavu from around 7am, dropping passengers at the top of the village, ten minutes on foot from the temple. However, if you want to get there in time for the dawn *theyyam*, you'll have to splash out on one of the Ambassador taxis that line up outside Kannur bus stand (around Rs400 round trip). The cabbies sleep in their cars, so you can arrange the trip on the spot by waking one up; you can also arrange a taxi through one of the more upmarket hotels. Either way, you'll have leave around 4.30am. Alternatively, head out to Parassinikadavu for the evening ritual, which starts around 6pm, which more or less commits you to taking a taxi back unless you cut out early. Note that the second performance of the day does not always take place, so it's a good idea to phone to check in advance (T0497/278 0722). There is also a snake park in Parassinikadavu (daily 8.30am–5.30pm) with demonstrations of snake-handling.

Kanhangad

With its range of accommodation and good transport connections, the small town of **KANHANGAD**, straddling NH-17 on the Kannur–Mangalore coastal highway some 60km northwest of Kannur, makes a good base for exploring Kerala's far north. There are a couple of **ashrams** in town – Anand and Nithyanand – and, opposite the *Bekal International* hotel, an excellent **yoga school**, which charges Rs500 for a month-long yoga course. There are also some beautiful **beaches** between Kanhangad and Bekal, though, as this is a staunch Muslim region, sunbathing is not recommended and you're best off swimming fully clothed. If you want to **stay**, the *Bekal International* at 47 TB Road, just behind NH-17 (T04997/202017; ❷–❺), is great value, with large airy rooms where the linen is changed daily, as well as a laundry service, restaurant (but no bar), rooftop terrace and solar-heated water.

Bekal

Just 7km north of Kanhangad, **BEKAL** is popular amongst Indians as a destination for weekend day-trip, with a **fort** (daily 9am–5.30pm; $2 [Rs5]) standing on a promontory between two long, classically beautiful palm-fringed **beaches** (swimming is safe, but dress in suitably modest gear to avoid causing offence). Although this is one of the largest forts in Kerala and has been under the control of various powers including Vijayanagar, Tipu Sultan and the British, it's nothing to get excited about. The bastion's commanding position, with views across the bays to north and south, is impressive enough, but only four watchtowers and the outer walls survive. The small adjacent **Sri Mukhyaprana Hanuman temple** draws a steady stream of visitors. A short walk beyond the main entrance to both temple and fort leads to Bekal's small and pretty useless **tourist information counter** (daily 8am–6pm; T04997/272900).

The most atmospheric place to **stay** at Bekal is the *PWD Rest House* (❶), at the furthest point of the promontory inside the fort – though avoid it at weekends, when bus loads of ghetto-blaster-toting day-trippers hang out on the veranda. To book, try contacting the Kasargode District Collector, Civil Station, Kasargode (T04994/255211), although they are not very reliable. *Eeyam Lodge* at Palakannu, 2km from the fort in the direction of Kasargode (T04997/236343; ❷–❹), is friendly and has decent rooms (some with a/c), a restaurant and money-changing facilities.

Kasargode

The old-fashioned little town of **KASARGODE**, 23km north of Kanhangad toward the Karnataka border, has a predominantly Muslim population and is principally a fishing community – though some say smuggling is not unknown. At present, this is as unexploited an area as you could hope to find, with hardly a beachside café, let alone a five-star hotel. Though the beaches look beautiful, bear in mind the undertow can be dangerously strong in some places, that sunbathing is taboo, and that some stretches of sand serve as communal toilets. The nearest major town is Mangalore, 50km north in Karnataka. Long-distance **buses** usually call at both of Kasargode's bus stands: the KSRTC city bus stand in the centre of town and the private one on the main NH-17 highway. Kasargode's **railway station** is 3km from town.

Near the KRSTC city bus stand, the *Enay Tourist Home* (T04994/221164; ①–③) has some a/c **rooms**, a South Indian restaurant and car rental. At the top (east) end of MG Road, the *City Tower* (T04994/230562; ③–⑤) is Kasargode's fanciest hotel, with reasonably priced doubles, some a/c, and a travel desk, but the restaurant is disappointingly dull.

Travel details

For details of ferry services on the backwaters – primarily between Alappuzha and Kollam – see p.378.

Trains

Kochi/Ernakulam to: Alappuzha (5–7 daily; 1hr 5min–1hr 40min); Bangalore (1–2 daily; 13hr–13hr 15min); Chennai (4–5 daily; 11hr 55min–16hr 20min); Delhi (2–4 daily; 39hr–48hr 20min); Kanniyakumari (2–3 daily; 7hr 25min–7hr 50min); Kollam (13–16 daily; 2hr 50min–4hr 25min); Kottayam (10–12 daily; 1hr 2min–1hr 20min); Kozhikode (5–6 daily; 4hr 25min–5hr 30min); Mumbai (2–3 daily; 26hr 50min–37hr 35min); Thiruvananthapuram (12–16 daily; 4hr 10min–5hr 35min); Thrissur (15–18 daily; 1hr 15min–2hr 30min).

Kozhikode to: Kannur (10–12 daily; 1hr 30min–2hr 10min); Kochi/Ernakulam (5–6 daily; 4hr 15min–5hr 40min); Mangalore (2–4 daily; 5hr 10min–5hr 30min); Mumbai (1 daily; 21hr 35min); Thiruvananthapuram (4–6 daily; 8hr 20min–10hr 30min); Thrissur (7–8 daily; 2hr 40min–3hr 30min).

Thiruvananthapuram to: Alappuzha (3–5 daily; 2hr 30min–3hr 15min); Bangalore (1–2 daily; 18hr–19hr 40min); Chennai (3–4 daily; 16hr 30min–18hr 45min); Delhi (1–3 daily; 42hr 35min–56hr 40min); Kanniyakumari (3–4 daily; 2hr); Kochi/Ernakulam (12–16 daily; 3hr 45min–5hr 20min); Kolkata (Calcutta; 4 weekly; 47hr 40min–47hr 55min); Kollam (13–16 daily; 55min–1hr 30min); Kozhikode (4–6 daily; 8hr 40min–10hr 30min); Madgaon (1–3 daily; 16hr 20min–20hr 20min); Mumbai (2–3 daily; 30hr 55min–42hr 20min); Thrissur (10–12 daily; 5hr 45min–7hr); Varkala (8–10 daily; 33min–55min).

Thrissur to: Chennai (4–5 daily; 10hr–13hr 15min); Kochi/Ernakulam (15–18 daily; 1hr 20min–2hr 15min); Thiruvananthapuram (11–13 daily; 6hr 5min–7hr 10min).

Buses

Kochi/Ernakulam to: Alappuzha (every 30min; 1hr 30min); Kanniyakumari (6 daily; 9hr); Kollam (every 30min; 3hr); Kottayam (every 30min; 1hr 30min–2hr); Kozhikode (hourly; 5hr); Kumily (10 daily; 6–7hr); Munnar (6 daily; 4hr 30min–5hr); Thiruvananthapuram (every 30min; 5–6hr); Thrissur (every 30min; 2hr).

Kozhikode to: Kannur (every 30min; 2–2hr 30min); Kochi/Ernakulam (hourly; 5hr); Mysore (2 daily; 9–10hr); Ooty (4 daily; 6–7hr); Thiruvananthapuram (12–15 daily; 11–12hr); Thrissur (hourly; 3hr 30min–4hr).

Kumily to: Kochi/Ernakulam (10 daily; 6–7hr); Kottayam (every 30min; 3–4hr); Madurai (10 daily; 5hr); Munnar (4 daily; 4hr); Thiruvananthapuram (6 daily; 8–9hr).

Munnar to: Kochi/Ernakulam (6 daily; 4hr 30min–5hr); Kottayam (5 daily; 5hr); Kumily (4 daily; 4hr); Madurai (6 daily; 5hr); Thiruvananthapuram (5 daily; 8–9hr).

Thiruvananthapuram to: Alappuzha (every 30min; 3hr–3hr 30min); Chennai (8 daily; 16–18hr); Kanniyakumari (every 30min–1hr; 2hr); Kochi/Ernakulam (every 30min; 5–6hr); Kollam (every 30min; 1hr 30min–2hr); Kottayam (every 30min; 4hr); Kozhikode (12–15 daily; 11–12hr); Kumily (6 daily; 8–9hr); Madurai (10 daily; 7hr); Munnar (5 daily;

8–9hr); Ponmudi (4 daily; 2hr 30min); Thrissur (hourly; 7–8hr); Varkala (hourly; 1hr 30min).
Thrissur to: Guruvayur (10 daily; 40min); Kochi/ Ernakulam (every 30min; 2hr); Kozhikode (hourly; 3hr 30min–4hr); Mysore (2 daily; 10–11hr); Palakkad (hourly; 2hr); Thiruvananthapuram (hourly; 7–8hr).

Flights

Kochi/Ernakulam to: Bangalore (3 daily; lhr 15min–2hr 15min); Chennai (1–3 daily; 1hr–1hr 55min); Delhi (3 daily; 4hr 25min); Hyderabad (1 daily; 3hr 30min); Kozhikode (1–2 daily; 30min); Lakshadweep (6 weekly; 1hr 35min); Mumbai (5–6 daily; 1hr 45min–3hr); Panjim, Goa (2 weekly; 1hr 10min); Thiruvananthapuram (1 daily; 30min).
Kozhikode to: Chennai (8 weekly; 1hr–2hr 25min); Kochi/Ernakulam (1–2 daily; 30min); Mumbai (3 daily; 1hr 40min–3hr); Panjim, Goa (3 weekly; 1hr 5min); Tiruchirapalli (2 weekly; 55min).
Thiruvananthapuram to: Bangalore (1 daily; 1hr 5min); Chennai (1–2 daily; 1hr 10min–2hr 20min); Colombo, Sri Lanka (1–2 daily; 1hr 25min); Delhi (1 daily; 3hr); Kochi/Ernakulam (1 daily; 30min); Mumbai (2 daily; 1hr 55min–2hr); Tiruchirapalli (4 weekly; 50min).

Chennai

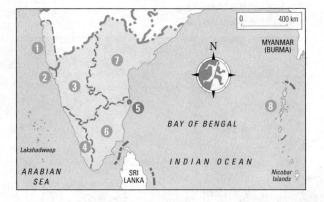

CHAPTER 5 # Highlights

* **Fort St George** The centre of the Madras Presidency during the Raj, this eighteenth-century fort now houses an excellent museum documenting the British occupation. See p.454

* **Shopping** Chennai is a major commercial centre, offering plenty of shopping possibilities from the bazaars of George Town to the modern glitz of Spencer's Plaza, South India's prime mall. See p.455

* **Kapalishvara temple** Chennai's most famous temple, complete with soaring *gopura*, a small complex of temple shops and a water-lily tank. See p.460

* **Theosophical Society Headquarters** Visit the sprawling gardens and fascinating library where Krishnamurti sought to understand divine truth. See p.461

△ Downtown Madras

Chennai

Tucked into the northeastern corner of Tamil Nadu on the Bay of Bengal, **CHENNAI** (still commonly referred to by its former British name, **Madras**) is India's fourth largest city, with a population nudging six million. A hot, frenetic and congested metropolis, it is the major transportation hub of the far south and the eastern coastline, with excellent road, rail and flight connections to the rest of the subcontinent. The major international airport here makes a marginally less stressful entry point to the subcontinent than Mumbai or Delhi – but most travellers stay just long enough to book a ticket for somewhere else. The attractions of the city itself are sparse, though it does boast some fine specimens of Raj architecture, Christian pilgrimage sites connected with the apostle "Doubting Thomas", superb Chola bronzes at its state museum, and plenty of classical music and dance performances.

As capital of Tamil Nadu, Chennai is, like Mumbai and Kolkata (Calcutta), a comparatively modern creation. It was founded by the British East India Company in 1639, on a five-kilometre strip of land between the Cooum and Adyar rivers, a few kilometres north of the ancient Tamil port of **Mylapore** and the Portuguese settlement of **San Thome**, which had been established in 1522. The site had no natural harbour and was selected by **Francis Day**, the East India Company agent, in part because he enjoyed good relations with the local Nayak governor Dharmala Ayyappa, who was able to intercede with the Vijayanagar Raja of Chandragiri, to whom the territory belonged. In addition, the land was protected by water on the east, south and west; cotton could be bought here twenty percent cheaper than elsewhere; and, apparently, Day had a mistress in San Thome.

A fortified trading post, completed on St George's Day in 1640, was named **Fort St George**. By 1700, the British had acquired neighbouring territory including **Triplicane** and **Egmore**, while over the course of the next century, as capital of the **Madras Presidency**, which covered most of south India, the city mushroomed to include many surrounding villages. The French, who had settled a little way down the coastline in Pondicherry, repeatedly challenged the British, and finally managed to destroy most of the city and bring it under their control in 1746. **Robert Clive** ("Clive of India"), then a clerk, was taken prisoner, an experience said to have inspired him to become a military campaigner. Clive was among the first to re-enter Chennai when it was retaken by the British three years later, and continued to use it as his base. Following this, fortifications were strengthened and the British survived a year-long French siege in 1759, completing the work in 1783. By this time, however, Calcutta was in the ascendancy and Madras lost its national importance.

The city's renaissance began after Independence, when it became the centre of the Tamil **movie industry**, and a hotbed of **Dravidian nationalism**. The rise of

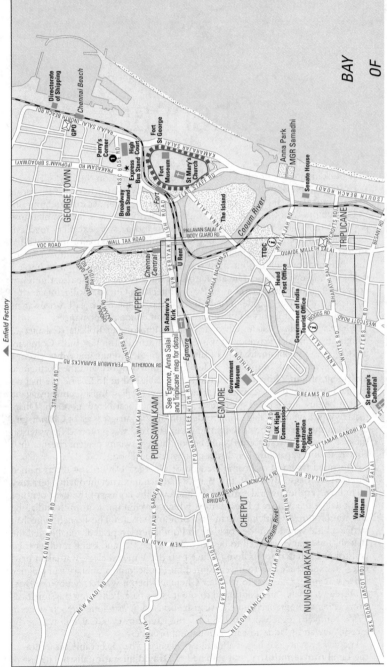

See Egmore, Anna Salai and Triplicane map for detail

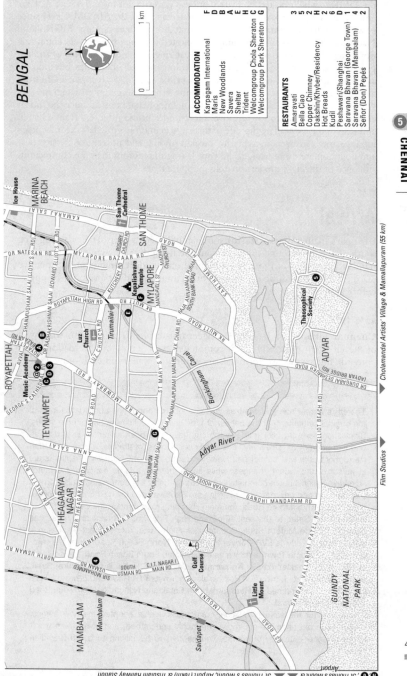

BENGAL

N

0   1 km

Cholamandal Artists' Village & Mamallapuram (55 km)

Film Studios

ACCOMMODATION

Karpagam International	F
Maris	D
New Woodlands	B
Savera	A
Shelter	E
Trident	H
Welcomgroup Chola Sheraton	C
Welcomgroup Park Sheraton	G

RESTAURANTS

Amaravati	3
Bella Ciao	5
Copper Chimney	2
Dakshin/Khyber/Residency	H
Hot Breads	2
Kudil	6
Peshawari/Shanghai	D
Saravana Bhavan (George Town)	1
Saravana Bhavan (Mambalam)	4
Señor (Don) Pepés	2

5

CHENNAI

445

St Thomas's Mount & , St Thomas's Mount &   St Thomas's Mount, Airport (15km) & Tirisulam Railway Station the DMK – which ousted Nehru's Congress government from the state in 1967 and has shared power with its rival pro-Dravidian party, the AIADMK, ever since – owed a lot to its control of the major film studios in Chennai. Later, **MGR**, Tamil Nadu's godlike film-star chief minister, exploited the same mistrust of central rule from New Delhi throughout his eleven-year rule. These days, cutouts of smiling politicians and strings of pennants in party colours are still ubiquitous, but industry and commerce have taken over as the city's prime *raison d'être*. Renamed **Chennai** in 1997 (to assert its pre-colonial identity; the fishing village upon which the city was built was named Chennaipatnam), the metropolis has boomed since the Indian economy opened up to foreign investment under prime ministers Rajiv Ghandi and Rao in the 1990s. The flip side of this rapid economic growth is that Chennai's infrastructure has been stretched to breaking point, and poverty, oppressive heat and pollution are more likely to be your lasting impressions than the conspicuous affluence of the city's modern marble shopping malls.

Arrival

Chennai's main **railway stations** are central, but its **airport** lies a long slog south of the city, around an hour from the hotel districts, while the main **bus** stand is 10km west of the centre. If you're on a budget, finding an inexpensive place to stay can be difficult late at night, so hunt around for a vacancy by phone before arriving.

By air

Chennai airport, at Trisulam in Meenambakkam district, 16km southwest of the city centre on NH-45, is comprehensively served by international and domestic flights; the two terminals are a minute's walk from each other. Out in

---

Name changes

The city's former name of **Madras** was changed **Chennai** (the abbreviated form of the original settlement) at the behest of pro-Dravidian politicians back in the 1990s. Since then several major roads in the city have also been renamed as part of an ongoing attempt to "**Dravidify**" the Tamil capital (most of the new names immortalize former nationalist politicians). However, far from all of Chennai's inhabitants are in favour of the recent changes, while some (notably a large contingent of auto-rickshaw-wallahs) seem completely oblivious to them. The confusing result of this is that both old and new names remain in use. We have used the new ones throughout the chapter. Thus Mount Road, the main shopping road through the centre of town, is now **Anna Salai**; to the east, Triplicane High Road, near *Broadlands Hotel*, has become **Quaide Milleth Salai**; Poonamallee High Road, running east–west across the north of the city, is **EVR Periyar High Road**; North Beach Road, along the eastern edge of George Town is known as **Rajaji Salai**; South Beach Road, the southern stretch of the coastal road, is **Kamarajar Salai**; C-in-C Road, is now **Ethiraj Salai**; south of the centre, Mowbray's Road is also known as **TTK Road** and Edward Elliot's Road has been renamed **Dr Radhakrishnan Salai**; and Nungambakkam High Road **Uttamar Gandhi Salai**.

Although, for the sake of political correctness, we've adopted the new names, many of the old ones are still more commonly understood, and using them won't cause offence – unless, of course, you happen to be talking to a pro-Dravidian activist.

Health warning

It's just as well Chennai boasts some of India's most sophisticated medical facilities, because it is officially one of the unhealthiest places in the world. Exponential, unplanned economic growth, coupled with inadequate investment in the municipal infrastructure, has resulted in chronic pollution problems. Exhaust emissions are the prime cause of **poor air quality**. Over the last decade the number of vehicles clogging Chennai's roads has more than quadrupled, and 75 percent of them are dirty, two-stroke two-wheelers. As a result, carbon monoxide levels are double the permitted maximum, while the amount of "suspended particulate matter" in the air is more than seven times the World Health Organization's prescribed limits. So, if you suffer from asthma or any other respiratory disorders, don't aim to spend long here.

Water quality is equally bad: in a recent survey, eighteen out of twenty groundwater samples collected from around the city were undrinkable due to leakages of untreated sewage from the main waterways into reservoirs. To add to this, there's been a disturbing rise in the incidence of mosquito-borne diseases. Chennai alone accounts for around half of the total number of reported **malaria** cases in Tamil Nadu, with a sixty percent increase over recent years of the number of patients developing the deadly falciparum strain (which can develop into cerebral malaria). There has also been an upsurge in less common diseases such as dengue fever and Japanese encephalitis. So take extra malaria precautions while you're in Chennai – always sleep under a net and cover yourself with repellent – especially during, and immediately after, the monsoons, and take extra care over what you eat and drink.

the main concourse, you'll find a 24-hour post office, Thomas Cook and State Bank of India foreign-exchange counters and a couple of snack bars. It's by no means certain that anyone will be staffing the **Government of Tamil Nadu Tourist Information Centre** booth at the arrivals exit, but if you're lucky you may be able to fix up accommodation from here, or at the "Free Fone" desk nearby. If you plan to leave Chennai by train, note that Southern Railways has a computerized **ticket reservation** counter (Mon–Sat 8am–8pm; Sun 8am–2pm), immediately outside the domestic terminal exit.

There are prepaid minibus and taxi counters at the exit in the international arrivals hall. **Taxis** cost Rs270–300 for the 35-minute ride to the main hotels or railway stations; rickshaws charge Rs150–200, but you'll have to lug your gear out to the main road as they're not allowed to park inside the airport forecourt. A taxi to **Mamallapuram** costs in the region of Rs1000. Shuttle **buses** (Rs50) run to Egmore and Central stations and Thiruvalluvar (Express) bus stand, but they call at several upmarket hotels en route, and are certainly not "Express". The quickest, cheapest and most efficient way to get into town is by suburban **train**. Services run every ten to fifteen minutes (4.30am–11pm) from **Trisulam station**, 500m from the airport on the far side of the road, to Park, Egmore and North Beach stations, taking 30–40 minutes. If you want to leave Chennai straight away by bus, catch local bus #70 or #70a to the new Moffussil bus stand (see p.448).

By train

Arriving in Chennai by train, you come in at one of two **long-distance railway stations**, 1.5km apart on EVR Periyar High Road, towards the north of the city. **Egmore Station**, in the heart of the busy commercial Egmore district, is the arrival point for most trains from Tamil Nadu and Kerala. Other services pull in at **Central Station**, further east, on the edge of George Town, which has a 24-hour left-luggage office (Rs10 per item for 24hr; all luggage must be securely locked) and an excellent Internet centre (also open 24hr) in the concourse. Both stations have STD phone booths outside the exit, as well as poorly staffed, badly equipped information offices, and are served by plenty of metered taxis and auto-rickshaws.

By bus

Long-distance buses arrive at the huge new **Moffussil** bus stand (℡044/2479 4705), inconveniently situated in the suburb of Koyambedu, over 10km west of central Chennai – the chaotic old **Express** and **Broadway** bus stands in the city centre have been amalgamated and are only used for local services. Moffussil is linked to these and other parts of Chennai by a host of city buses from the well-organized platforms outside the main terminal: buses #27, #15b, #15f and #17e go to the Egmore/Central area and Parry's Corner; bus #27b also goes on to Triplicane, while buses #70 and #70a link the bus stand to the airport. Note that most buses from Mamallapuram, Pondicherry and other towns to the south of Chennai stop at Guindy suburban railway station on their way in; you'll save a lot of time by catching a train into the city from here.

Information

The highly efficient and very helpful **India Tourism Office**, at 154 Anna Salai (Mon–Fri 9am–6pm, Sat 9am–1pm; ℡044/2846 0285), has maps and leaflets, and can arrange accommodation. They also have lists of reliable tour agents for car rental and of approved **guides** (see box opposite for rates).

The **Tamil Nadu Tourism Development Corporation** (TTDC) is based in a smart new complex on Wallajah Road, near Anna Park in Triplicane (Mon–Sat 10am–5.30pm; ℡044/2538 3333, Ⓦwww.tamilnadutourism.com), which is where you'll also find the tourist offices of many other states (including that for Kerala ℡044/2536 9789). The TTDC can book you tours or accommodation in their own hotels across the state. The **India Tourist Development Corporation** (ITDC) office at 29 Dr PV Cherian Crescent, Ethiraj Salai (Mon–Fri 10am–5.30pm; ℡044/2827 8884, Ⓔitdc.ros@gems.vsnl.net.in) handles advance bookings for ITDC hotels across the country, and can also arrange tours of the city, state and country.

The long-established *Hallo! Madras* (monthly; Rs10) has useful listings of all the city's services, plus full moon dates (useful for estimating temple festivals), a tourist guide to Tamil Nadu, exhaustive flight and train details, and an outline of Chennai bus timetables. Alternatively, the even more comprehensive quarterly directory *Madura Welcome, Chennai* (Rs50) lists every bus service and route in Chennai, and from Chennai to other towns in the state. Both are available at all book and stationery shops. Unfortunately, neither have a "What's On" section, so for forthcoming music and dance performances, buy the weekly *City Info* (Rs30), consult the events column on page three of the *Hindu*, or try to get hold of a copy of *Chennai: This Fortnight*, available free from all the city's smarter hotels.

City transport

The offices, sights, railway stations and bus stands of Chennai are spread over such a wide area that it's impossible to get around without using some form of **public transport**. Most visitors jump in auto-rickshaws, but outside rush hours you can travel around comfortably by **bus** or suburban **train**.

Incidentally, the city's drastic dry-season water shortage explains the **water carriers** trundling along its congested streets. Watch out for unofficial ones as you cross the road; tractors pull tankers so heavy that they can either topple over or fail to stop when brakes are applied, causing fatal accidents.

Buses

Compared to other parts of India, **buses** in Chennai are regular, inexpensive, and only get cramped during rush hours. On Anna Salai, buses have special stops, but on smaller streets you'll have to flag them down or wait with an obvious crowd of other would-be passengers. Buses in Egmore gather opposite the railway station. The numbers of services to specific places of interest in the city are listed in the relevant accounts; for a full directory of bus routes, buy *Madura Welcome, Chennai* (see opposite). Buses to and from the new Moffussil bus stand are listed opposite.

Trains

If you want to travel south from central Chennai to Guindy (Deer Park), St Thomas Mount or the airport, the easiest way to go is by **train**. Services run every fifteen minutes (on average) between 4.30am and 11pm, prices are minimal, and you can guarantee a seat at any time except rush hour (around 9am & 5pm). First-class carriages substitute padded seats for wooden slatted benches and are a little cleaner; there's always a carriage reserved for ladies, too, which is usually clearly signed. Buy a ticket before boarding.

City trains travel between the following stations: Beach (opposite the GPO), Fort, Park (for Central), Egmore, Nungambakkam, Kodambakkam, Mambalam (for T Nagar and silk shops), Saidapet (for Little Mount Church), Guindy, St Thomas Mount and Trisulam (for the airport).

Taxis and rickshaws

Chennai's yellow-top Ambassador **taxis** gather outside Egmore and Central railway stations and at the airport. All have meters, but drivers often prefer to fix a price before leaving, and invariably charge a return fare whatever the destination, meaning that they're practically pricing themselves out of business – the trip from Central Station to Triplicane, for instance, costs around Rs150. More reliable and economical **radio taxis** are therefore becoming increasingly popular; try Bharati Call Taxi (☎044/2814 2233).

Tours and day-trips

One good way to get around the sights of Chennai is on a TTDC **bus tour** (book at their office; see opposite). The tours are good value, albeit rushed, and the guides can be very helpful. The TTDC **half-day tour** (daily 8am–1pm or 1.30–6.30pm; Rs110 non a/c, Rs160 a/c) starts at their office on EVR Periyar High Road and takes in Fort St George, the Government Museum, the Snake Park, Kapalishvara Temple, Elliot's Beach and Marina Beach (on Friday, the Government Museum is closed, so the tour goes to the Birla Planetarium instead). TTDC also offers good-value **day-trips** to Mamallapuram (including Kanchipuram; daily 6.30am–7pm, non a/c Rs295, a/c Rs420) and Pondicherry/Auroville (Sat & Sun 6.30am–9pm, non a/c Rs315, a/c Rs 490); meals are included in the price in both tours.

Flocks of auto- and cycle-rickshaws wait patiently outside tourist hotels, and not so patiently outside railway stations. **Auto-rickshaw** drivers in Chennai are notorious for demanding high fares from locals and tourists alike. A rickshaw from Triplicane to either of the bus stations, plus Egmore and Central railway stations should cost no more than Rs40. All rickshaws have meters; a few drivers use them if asked, but in many cases you'll save a lot of frustrating bargaining by offering a small sub above the meter-reading (a driver may offer you a rate of "meter plus 5", meaning Rs5 above the final reading). If you need to get to the airport or station early in the morning, book a rickshaw and negotiate the price the night before (the driver may well sleep in his vehicle outside your hotel). Only take **cycle rickshaws** on smaller roads; riding amid Chennai traffic on a fragile seat can be hair-raising.

Car and motorcycle rental

Car rental with driver is available at many of the city's upmarket hotels; through the Government of India Tourist Office (see p.448); or through private companies such as Welcome Tourrs & Travels at 150 Anna Salai (☎044/2846 0908, ⓔwelcome@md2.vsnl.net.in). An ambassador car with driver costs around Rs800–1000 per day (or Rs1100–1200 for a/c) – rates may be negotiable.

Mopeds and **motorcycles** can be rented at U-Rent Services, 1, 1st Main Road, Gandhinagar, Adyar (Mon–Sat 8am–7pm, Sun 9am–6pm; ☎044/2491 0838). Prices range from Rs150 to Rs300 per day, plus a flat Rs200 annual membership fee regardless of how long you rent a bike for.

Accommodation

Finding a **place to stay** in Chennai can be a problem, as hotels are often full by noon and only a couple of places have anything for less than Rs200 (though at least standards in the cheapies are better than in other cities). If you're on a budget, it's advisable to phone and book in advance, at least from the railway station or airport.

Most of the city's mid-range and inexpensive hotels are located around the **railway station**. Other popular areas include **Anna Salai**, which tends to be more expensive, and **Triplicane**, an atmospheric Muslim area boasting some of the city's best budget guesthouses. The bulk of the top hotels are in the south of the city, along Nungambakkam, Dr Radha Krishnan Salai and Cathedral roads; several offer courtesy buses to and from the airport. Almost all hotels have at least one South Indian/multi-cuisine restaurant attached. Due to frequent shortages, visitors should use **water** as sparingly as possible.

Egmore

The following places are marked on the map opposite.

Central Tower 17/2 EVR Periyar High Rd ☎044/2538 1491, ⓕ2536 0522. Ugly modern block in a busy but convenient location almost opposite Central Station. Clean, decent-sized en-suite rooms plus a restaurant. ❹–❺

Chandra Towers 9 Gandhi Irwin Rd ☎044/2514 8137, ⓕ5214 8140. One of the better hotels in the area, under new management and undergoing refurbishment at the time of writing. Central a/c, foreign exchange, 24hr coffee shop, bar and rooftop restaurant. ❺–❻

Howrah 17 EVR Periyar High Rd (reception on 1st floor) ☎044/2536 7445. Clean en-suite rooms close to Central station and slightly cheaper and marginally better value than the adjacent *Central Tower.* ❸–❺

Impala Continental 12 Gandhi Irwin Rd ☎044/2819 1423. Run-of-the-mill lodge but with

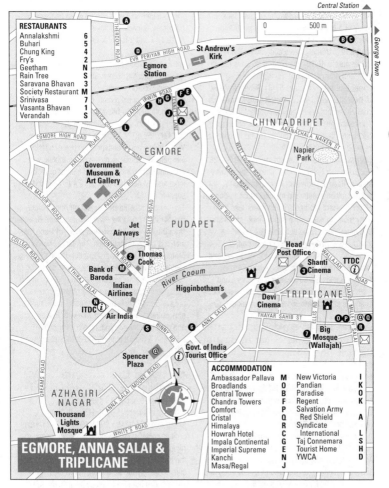

RESTAURANTS

Annalakshmi	6
Buhari	5
Chung King	4
Fry's	2
Geetham	N
Rain Tree	S
Saravana Bhavan	3
Society Restaurant	M
Srinivasa	7
Vasanta Bhavan	1
Verandah	S

ACCOMMODATION

Ambassador Pallava	M	New Victoria	I
Broadlands	O	Pandian	K
Central Tower	B	Paradise	O
Chandra Towers	F	Regent	K
Comfort	P	Salvation Army	
Cristal	Q	Red Shield	A
Himalaya	R	Syndicate	
Howrah Hotel	C	International	L
Impala Continental	G	Taj Connemara	S
Imperial Supreme	E	Tourist Home	H
Kanchi	N	YWCA	D
Masa/Regal	J		

EGMORE, ANNA SALAI & TRIPLICANE

clean non-a/c and a/c en-suite rooms, all with TV and phones. Good value, so often full. ❸–❹

Imperial Supreme 6 Gandhi Irwin Rd ☎044/2819 3954. The best of three sister hotels set in their own enclosed courtyard opposite the station. Has a range of en-suite rooms, including a/c suites, all with TV and phones, and there's also a restaurant and travel services. ❸–❹

Masa 15/1 Kennet Lane ☎044/2819 3344. Variously priced, good-value rooms with attached bathrooms in a clean, modern building, close to the station. The *Regal*, tacked onto the back, is of a similar standard and price. ❷–❹

New Victoria 3 Kennet Lane ☎044/2819 3638. Egmore's smartest option: all rooms have a/c and

hot showers, and rates include breakfast, but it's still a little overpriced. ❻–❼

Pandian 15 Kennet Lane ☎044/2819 1010, Ⓔhotelpandian@vsnl.com. Pleasant, clean and modern mid-scale place within walking distance of the railway station – ask for a room on the Church Park side of the building for green views. Some rooms have a/c, and 24hr Internet access is available (Rs40/hr). ❺–❻

Regent 8 Kennet Lane ☎044/2819 1347, Ⓕ2819 0170. Quiet lodge set around a pleasant courtyard with non-a/c rooms – it's a bit shabby, though the bathrooms are spotless. ❸

Salvation Army Red Shield Guest House 15/31 Ritherdon Rd ☎044/2532 1821,

© redshieldguesthouse@hotmail.com. Tucked away in a leafy backstreet behind the station, this Sally Army lodge has friendly and helpful staff and extremely basic accommodation in either dorms (Rs70) or en-suite doubles (some with a/c). 9am checkout. ②—④

Syndicate International 55/31 Gandhi Irwin Rd ℡044/2819 2919, © contact@hotelsyndicateintl. com. Smart but pricey business-oriented place. The rooms are small and have ethnic cotton-print decor, and there's also a multi-cuisine restaurant, bar and room service. ⑤—⑥

Tourist Home 43–45 Gandhi Irwin Rd ℡044/2819 4679. Popular hotel directly opposite the railway station. Rooms (some a/c) have showers, TV, phones, clean sheets and towels but could do with a spring-clean; the back rooms suffer less from early morning noise. Also has a three- and a six-bed room. Good value but often full. ③—④

YWCA 1086 EVR Periyar High Rd ℡044/2532 4234, © ywca_igh@indiainfo.com. Attractive and friendly hotel in quiet gardens behind Egmore Station. Rooms are spotless and spacious, and there's a safe-deposit and a good restaurant. Book in advance. Rates include a buffet breakfast. ⑤

Anna Salai and Triplicane

The following places are marked on the map on p.451.

Ambassador Pallava 30 Montieth Rd ℡044/2855 4476, © pallava@ambassadorindia.com. Colossal four-star, close to Anna Salai, full of cool white marble and gold-plated mirrors, and with great views from its upper storeys. Also has a sports complex with a pool and health club. Rooms from $85. ⑨

Broadlands 18 Vallabha Agraham St, Triplicane ℡044/2854 5573, © broadlandshotel@yahoo.com. An old whitewashed house, with crumbling stucco and stained glass, ranged around a leafy courtyard – the kind of budget travellers' enclave you either love or loathe. It has a large roof terrace and clean rooms, a few with attached bathrooms, private balconies and views of the mosque. Strict "No Indians" policy. ②—③

Comfort 22 Vallabha Agraham St, Triplicane ℡044/2858 7661, ℻2852 9999. The corridors are long and dimly lit, but the rooms are all en suite and clean, albeit on the small side. ③—④

Cristal 34 CNK Rd, Triplicane ℡044/2858 5605. Friendly place, run by a team of brothers, in a modern building off Quaide Milleth Salai. Rooms are tiled and clean, and all have attached showers. TVs are available for Rs25. As cheap as it gets in Chennai. ①—②

Himalaya 54 Quaide Milleth Salai, Triplicane ℡044/2854 7522, ℻5215 6988. Clean, spacious

rooms (some a/c) with cable TV, hot showers and balconies. Service is efficient, and there's a good restaurant and 24hr Internet access (open to non-residents). ③—⑤

Kanchi 28 Ethiraj Salai ℡044/2827 1100, ⓦwww.hotelkanchi.com. Soulless skyscraper with dingy corridors but with great views from its spacious balconied rooms, plus two restaurants (one rooftop) and a bar. ⑤—⑥

Paradise 17/1 Vallabha Agraham St, Triplicane ℡044/2859 4252, © paradisegh@hotmail.com. Very friendly and a dependable choice, offering inexpensive rooms (including some triples) with attached bathroom (choice of Western or Indian loos) and TV. Also has a large roof terrace and room service. ②—④

Taj Connemara Binny Rd, just off Anna Salai, ℡044/5500 0000, ⓦwww.tajhotels.com. Dating from the Raj era, this whitewashed Art Deco five-star is a Chennai institution. The large "heritage" rooms are the best, with Victorian decor, dressing rooms and verandahs overlooking the pool. The "standard" rooms, by contrast, are modern and a little overpriced. There's a very pleasant poolside area and two excellent restaurants, including the atmospheric al-fresco *Rain Tree* with live music and dance every evening, plus a 24hr coffee shop and a bar. Doubles $200–270, suites from $335. ⑨

Outside the centre

The following places are marked on the map on pp.444–445.

Karpagam International 41 South Mada St, Mylapore ℡044/2495 9984, ℻5210 7925. Fairly ordinary hotel, with reasonable double rooms; the main attraction is the excellent location overlooking the Kapalishvara Temple, and it's also on the right side of the city for the airport, 12km away. Also has some cheap but slightly dingy singles. ③—④

Maris 11 Cathedral Rd ℡044/2811 0541, ℻2811 4847. A 1970s concrete block right next to the *Sheraton* and near the Music Academy. The a/c rooms are a particularly good deal for the area, but there's a distinct lack of atmosphere. You can book TTDC city tours here. ⑤—⑥

New Woodlands 72–75 Dr Radhakrishnan Rd ℡044/2811 3111, www.newwoodlands.com. Sprawling complex of clean, decent-sized rooms and more spacious, self-contained apartments (called "cottages"), plus two restaurants and a swimming pool (Rs70 per day for guests). Rooms ⑥, cottages ⑦—⑧

Savera 146 Dr Radhakrishnan Rd ℡044/2811 4700, © hotsave@md2.vsnl.net.in. Upmarket hotel boasting all mod cons, including a pool, good

The **sabhas** of Chennai – the city's arts societies and venues, of which the most illus-trious is the Chennai Music Academy – stage regular public performances of Carnatic classical music and Bharatanatyam dance. Here, ambitious artists have to undergo the scrutiny of an often fanatical audience and a less-than-generous bevy of news-paper critics, whose reviews can make or break a career. Musicians are expected to correctly interpret the subtleties of any given composition, *raga* or *tala*. The sets of notes that make up a *raga* occupy a place midway between melody and scale; they must be played imaginatively in improvisation, but in strict sequences and with correct emphasis. The worst crime, the sign of an amateur, is to slip accidentally into a different *raga* that might share the same scale. *Tala*, the rhythmic cycle and bedrock of the music, will often be demonstrated by someone on stage, and consists of a series of claps and waves. Unlike in North India, this element is overt in the South and the audience delights in clapping along to keep the often-complex time signatures. The pleasure is heightened during percussion improvisations on the barrel-shaped *mridangam* drum or *ghatam* clay pot that accompany many performances.

The **Chennai Festival** is an annual event held from December 15th until Janu-ary 1st, during which up to five hundred events are staged, primarily at the Music Academy (☎044/2811 2231) on TTK Road. It's a real orgy of classical music and dance recitals, in which many of India's greatest artistes, from all over the country, can be seen at work. **Female vocalists** to look out for include Mani Krishnaswamy, Charumathi Ramachandran, Sudha Raghunathan and Bombay Jayashree; duos such as the Bombay and Hyderabad Sisters are also popular. Top-ranking **male singers**, K.V. Narayanaswamy, B. Rajam Iyer and younger artists like Thrissur Ramachandran and T.N. Seshagopalan should not be missed. Among the best of the **instrumental-ists** are E. Gayatri and Rama Varma on the gentle melodic *vina*, a stringed instrument unique to the South; Ramani on flute; violinists such as T.N. Krishnan, D. Ananda Raman; and N. Ravikiran on *gottuvadyam*, a rare member of the *vina* family, laid flat on the floor and played much like a slide guitar. Carnatic music's answer to John Coltrane is Kadri Gopalnath, whose soaring saxophone and flamboyant dress have made him one of the most distinctive figures on the circuit. Former child prodigy, U. Sriniwas, is a maestro on the electric mandolin. Cassettes and CDs of all the above artistes are available at Music World in Spencer Plaza. For addresses of good musi-cal instrument shops in the city, see Listings, p.465.

The predominant **dance** style is Bharatanatyam, as performed by stars such as Alarmai Valli, and the Dhananjayans. Dance-dramas are also staged by the Kalakshetra Academy, a school of dance and music set in a beautiful hundred-acre compound near the sea in Tiruvanmiyur, on the southern outskirts of the city.

Outside the festival period, to find out about performances of music and dance, ask at the government tourist office on Anna Salai, consult the listings pages of local papers such as *The Hindu*, or have a look in *Chennai: This Fortnight* (see p.448). You may also like to pay a visit to the **Sangita Vadyalaya**, behind the HDFC Bank on Anna Salai (Mon–Fri 9.15am–5.45pm; free), which displays an impressive array of Indian musical instruments. The centre, recently shifted to this new ground-floor building in the centre of town, was set up to preserve and restore antique pieces, but resident artisans also revive rare instruments which are no longer commonly played. You can try your hand at a few of them yourself, and experiment with an amazing horde of old percussion pieces.

---

pastry shop, three bars, excellent South Indian restaurant, plus a rooftop restaurant with great views. ❾
Shelter 19–21 Venkatesa Agraharam St, Mylapore ☎044/2495 1919, ✉shelter@vsnl.com. A stone's

throw from the Kapalishvara Temple, this spar-klingly clean luxury hotel is better value than most upmarket places at this price. ❽–❾
Trident 1/24 GST Rd ☎044/2234 4747, ☎2234 6699. Comfortable five-star hotel in lovely gardens

with luxurious rooms and swimming pool. Near the airport (3km), but a long (12km, albeit complimentary) drive into town. Doubles start around $100. Good restaurants, one of which serves Thai cuisine. ❾

Welcomgroup Chola Sheraton 10 Cathedral Rd ☎ 044/2811 0101, ✉ chola@md2.vsnl.net.in. Palatial five-star in the city centre with all the trimmings, including a pool. The hefty $175–300 plus per night room tariff includes a buffet breakfast and a "cocktail hour". ❾

Welcomgroup Park Sheraton 132 TTK Rd ☎ 044/2499 4101, ✉ writeme@parksheraton .com. Luxury hotel featuring bow-tied valets and all mod cons including swimming pool, health club, a decent business centre, three excellent restaurants, and a 24hr coffee shop. Rooms from $190. ❾

The City

Chennai divides into three main areas: north, central and south. The northern district, separated from the rest by the River Cooum, is the site of the first British outpost in India, **Fort St George**, and the commercial centre, **George Town**, which developed during British occupation. At the southern end of Rajaji Salai is **Parry's Corner**, George Town's principal landmark – look for the tall grey building labelled *Parry's* – it's a major bus stop.

Sandwiched between the Cooum and Adyar rivers and crossed diagonally by the city's main thoroughfare, Anna Salai, **central Chennai** is the modern, commercial heart of the metropolis. To the east, this gives way to the atmospheric old Muslim quarters of **Triplicane** and a long straight **Marina** where fishermen mend nets and set small boats out to sea, and hordes of Indian tourists hitch up saris and trousers for a quick paddle. South of here, near the coast, **Mylapore**, inhabited in the 1500s by the Portuguese, boasts **Kapalishvara Temple** and **San Thome Cathedral**, both tourist attractions and places of pilgrimage. Further out, south of the Adyar river, is the Portuguese church on **St Thomas Mount**.

Fort St George

Quite unlike any other fort in India, **Fort St George** stands amid state offices facing the sea in the east of the city, just south of George Town on Kamaraj Salai. It looks more like a complex of well-maintained colonial mansions than a fort; indeed many of its buildings are used today as offices, a hive of activity during the week as politicians and peons rush between the Secretariat and State Legislature.

The fort was the first structure of Madras town and the first territorial possession of the British in India. Construction began in 1640, but most of the original buildings were replaced later that century after being damaged during French sieges. The most imposing structure is the eighteenth-century colonnaded **Fort House**, coated in deep-slate-grey and white paint. Next door, in the more modestly proportioned **Exchange Building** – site of Madras's first bank – is the excellent **Fort Museum** (daily except Fri 10am–5pm; $2 [Rs5]; video camera Rs25). The collection inside faithfully records the central events of the British occupation of Madras with portraits, regimental flags, weapons, coins minted by the East India Company, medals, stamps and thick woollen uniforms that make you wonder how the Raj survived as long as it did. Some of the most evocative mementos are letters written by figures such as Robert Clive, reporting on life in the colony. The squat cast-iron cage on the ground floor was brought to Madras from China, where for more than a year in the nineteenth century it was used as a particularly sadistic form of imprisonment for a British captain. The first floor, once the public exchange hall where merchants met to gossip and trade, is now an **art gallery**, where portraits of prim officials and their wives sit side by side with fine sketches of the British embarking at Chennai in aristocratic finery, attended by Indians in loincloths. Also on display are etchings by the famous artist **Thomas Daniells**, whose work largely defined British perceptions of India at the end of the eighteenth century.

South of the museum, past the State Legislature, stands the oldest surviving Anglican church in Asia, **St Mary's Church** (daily 9am–5pm), built in 1678 and partly renovated after a battle with the French in 1759. Built with thick walls and a strong vaulted roof to withstand the city's many sieges, the church served as a store and shelter in times of war. It's distinctly English in style, crammed with plaques and statues in memory of British soldiers, politicians and their wives. The grandest plaque, made of pure silver, was presented by Elihu Yale, former governor of Fort St George (1687–96) and founder of Yale University in the USA. A collection of photographs of visiting dignitaries, including Queen Elizabeth II, is on display in the entrance porch. Nearby, **Robert Clive's house** is in a rather sorry state, and is currently used by the Archeological Survey of India as offices.

George Town

North of Fort St George, the former British trading centre of **George Town** (reached on bus #18 from Anna Salai) remains the focal area for banks, offices and shipping companies. This well-ordered grid of streets harbours a fascinating medley of architecture: eighteenth- and nineteenth-century churches, Hindu and Jain temples, and a scattering of mosques, interspersed with grand mansions. However, despite its potential charm, this is Chennai's most chaotic and crowded area, a dirty and uninviting warren clogged by particularly persistent hawkers and thick traffic. Probably the best way to appreciate the area is from its edges. In the east, on Rajaji Salai, the **General Post Office** occupies a robust earth-red Indo-Saracenic building, constructed in 1884. George Town's southern extent is marked by the bulbous white domes and sandstone towers of the **High Court**, and the even more opulent towers of the **Law College**, both showing strong Islamic influence.

It can be fun to take a quick rummage around George Town's **bazaars**, lines of rickety stalls selling clothes, bags, umbrellas, watches, shoes and perfume, concentrated along Rajaji Salai and NSC Bose Road.

Government Museum

Unfortunately the Chennai **Government Museum** (daily except Fri 9.30am–5pm; $5 [Rs10], camera Rs200, video Rs500) has joined the ASI sites in charging a ridiculous rate for foreigners, which is enough to put off all but the most ardent archeological buffs. The museum houses stone sculptures from many of Tamil Nadu's most famous temples, plus an excellent collection of Chola bronzes, although the (much cheaper) museum in Thanjavur also houses a similarly fine collection. If you do decide to visit, hop on bus #11H from Anna Salai for Pantheon Road, south of Egmore railway station.

The deep-red, circular **main building**, fronted by Italian-style pillars and built in 1851, stands opposite the entrance and ticket office. The archeology and geology gallery displays tools, pots, jewellery and weapons from the Stone and Iron Ages, and maps of principal excavations. Later exhibits include a substantial assortment of dismantled panels, railings and statues from the second century AD stupa complex at **Amaravati**, Andhra Pradesh (see p.597). Depicting episodes

Bollywood may be better known, but the film studios of Chennai churn out more movies than any other city in the world – on average, around 900 each year. The movies feature the usual Indian masala mix of fast action, wide-eyed melodrama, romance (with just the hint of a kiss), punch-ups, shoot-outs and, of course, hip-grinding song and dance sequences with as many costume changes as camera angles. They cater for the largely illiterate rural population of Tamil Nadu, although the biggest blockbusters also get dubbed into Hindi and exported north.

One notable difference between the Chennai movie industry and its counterpart in Mumbai (see p.139) is the influence of **politics** on Tamil films – an overlap that dates from the earliest days of regional cinema, when stories, stock themes and characters were derived from traditional folk ballads about low-caste heroes vanquishing high-caste villains. Already familiar to millions, such Robin Hood-style stereotypes were perfect propaganda vehicles for the nascent Tamil nationalist movement, the Dravida Munnetra Kazhagam, or **DMK**. It is no coincidence that the party's founding father, **C.N. Annadurai**, was a top screenplay- and script-writer. Like prominent Tamil Congress leaders and movie-makers of the 1930s and 1940s, he and his colleagues used both popular film genres of the time – "mythologicals" (movie versions of the Hindu epics) and "socials" (dramas set around caste conflicts) – to convey their political ideas to the masses. Audiences were actively encouraged by party workers to boo the villains and cheer each time the proletarian hero, or DMK icons and colours (red and black), appeared on the screen. From this tradition were born the fan clubs, or *rasigar manrams*, that played such a key role in mobilizing support for the nationalist parties in elections.

The most influential fan club of all time was the one set up to support the superstar actor Marudur Gopalamenon Ramachandran, known to millions simply as "**MGR**". By carefully cultivating a political image which mirrored the folk-hero roles he played in films, the maverick matinee idol generated fanatical grass-roots support in the state, especially among women, and rose to become chief minister in 1977. His eleven-year rule is still regarded by liberals as a dark age in the state's history, as chronic corruption, police brutality, political purges and rising organized crime were all rife during the period. Even the fact that his bungled economic policies penalized precisely the rural poor who voted for him never dented MGR's mass appeal. When he suffered a paralytic stroke in October 1984, 22 people cut off limbs, toes and fingers as offerings to pray for his recovery, while more than a hundred followers attempted to burn themselves to death. For the next three years MGR was barely able to speak let alone govern effectively, yet the party faithful and fan club members still did not lose faith in his leadership. When he died in 1988, two million people attended his funeral, and 31 grief-stricken devotees committed ritual suicide. Even today, MGR's statue, sporting trademark sunglasses and lamb's-wool hat, is revered at tens of thousands of wayside shrines across Tamil Nadu.

---

from the Buddha's life and scenes from the *Jataka* stories from ancient Hinayana Buddhist texts, these sensuously carved marble reliefs are widely regarded as the finest achievements of early Indian art, outshining even the Sanchi *toranas*. The **ethnology gallery** shows clothes and weapons, along with photographs of long-gone local tribal societies, while a fascinating display of wind and string instruments, drums and percussion includes the large predecessor of today's sitar and several very old tablas. Wooden doors and window frames from Chettinad, a region near Madurai, exquisitely carved with floral and geometric designs much like those found in Gujarati *havelis*, are also on display.

The museum's real treasure, however, is the world's most complete and impressive selection of **Chola bronzes** (see p.689). Large statues of Shiva,

MGR's political protégé, and eventual successor, was a teenage screen starlet called **Jayalalitha**, a convent-educated brahmin's daughter whom he spotted at a school dance and, despite an age difference of more than thirty years, recruited to be both his leading lady and mistress. The couple would star opposite each other in 25 hit films, and when MGR eventually moved into politics, Jayalalitha followed him, becoming leader of the AIADMK (the party MGR set up after being expelled from the DMK in 1972) after a much publicized power struggle with his widow. Larger-than-life in voluminous silver ponchos and heavy gold jewellery, the now portly Puratchi Thalavi ("Revolutionary Leader") has taken her personality cult to extremes brazen even by Indian standards. On her 46th birthday in 1994, Rs50,000 of public money was spent on giant cardboard cutouts depicting her in academic and religious robes, while 46 of her more fervent admirers rolled bare-chested along the length of Anna Salai. Jayalalitha's spell as chief minister, however, was brought to an ignominious end at the 1996 elections, after allegations of fraud and corruption on an appropriately monumental scale. Despite being found guilty by the High Court, she still managed to bring down the national government and force a general election in 1999 by withdrawing AIADMK support from prime minister Vajpayee's shaky, BJP-led coalition, and later ousted her arch rival, **M. Karunanidhi**, leader of the DMK, to regain her old job as chief minister of Tamil Nadu. One of her first acts was to exact revenge on Karunanidhi, throwing him and one thousand of his supporters into prison on corruption charges. However, she lost a large percentage of her following in the 2004 elections, as voters showed their increasing dissatisfaction with her vindictive and unpopular policies.

Working as an extra

If you've a fervent interest in the Chennai movie industry, you can rub shoulders with today's Tamil movie stars by appearing as an extra in a film at MGR or one of the other major studios on the outskirts of Chennai. Scouts regularly trawl the tourist spots downtown (notably the *Maharaja Restaurant* around the corner from *Broadlands Hotel* in Triplicane) for foreigners to spice up crowd and party scenes. People with long blond hair stand a better chance of getting picked, but being in the right place at the right time is more important. If you're really keen, though, do the rounds of the studios yourself (details available from the Government of India tourist office). If someone does approach you with an offer of work as a movie extra, be sure to check their credentials (scouts always carry laminated cards from the studio with their photos on; you can also ask to see their business card), and the conditions of the job (approximately Rs300 per day, plus meals and transport to and from your hotel are standard). For obvious reasons, it's also advisable to refuse any work offered to one person only, especially if you're female.

Vishnu and Parvati can be seen, along with smaller figurines, including several sculptures of Shiva as **Nataraja**, the Lord of the Dance, encircled by a ring of fire and standing with his arms and legs elegantly poised. One of the finest models is **Ardhanarishvara**, the androgynous form of Shiva (united with Shakti in transcendence of duality); the left side of the body is female and the right male, and the intimacy of detail is astounding. A rounded breast, a delicate hand and a tender bejewelled foot counterpoint the harsher sinewy limbs and torso on the male side of the figure, where the (half) head is also crowned with a mass of matted hair and serpents.

A **children's museum** demonstrates the principles of electricity and irrigation with marginally diverting, semi-functional models, while the magnificent

Indo–Saracenic **art gallery** houses old British portraits of figures such as Clive and Hastings, plus Rajput and Moghul miniatures, and a small display of ivory carvings.

St Andrew's Kirk

Just north-east of Egmore station, off EVR Periyar High Road, **St Andrew's Kirk**, consecrated in 1821, is a fine example of Georgian architecture. Loosely modelled on London's St Martins-in-the-Fields, it's one of just three churches in India which has a circular seating plan, laid out beneath a huge dome painted blue with gold stars and supported by a sweep of Corinthian columns. Marble plaques around the church give a fascinating insight into the kind of people who left Britain to work for the imperial and Christian cause. A staircase leads onto the flat roof, surrounding the dome, from where you can climb further up into the steeple past the massive bell to a tiny balcony affording excellent views of the city.

Valluvar Kottam

In the south of the Nungambakkam district, just off Village Road, the **Valluvar Kottam** is an intriguing construction, built in classical style in 1976 as a memorial to the first-century Tamil poet Thiruvalluvar. Most impressive is the 34-metre-high stone chariot, carved from just three blocks of granite, into a likeness of the great temple car of Thiruvarur. Adjoining this veritable juggernaut is a vast public auditorium, one of the largest in Asia, with a capacity of four thousand. A stroll along the auditorium roof past shallow rectangular ponds brings you to a large statue of the poet-saint, within a shrine carved into the upper reaches of the chariot. Among the many reliefs around the monument, look out for the cat in human pose, reminiscent of the figure at Arjuna's Penance in Mamallapuram.

Marina Beach

One of the longest city beaches in the world, the **Marina** (Kamaraj Salai) stretches 5km from the harbour at the southeastern corner of George Town all the way to San Thome Cathedral. The impulse to transform Chennai's beach into an attractive and sociable esplanade was conceived by Mountstuart Elphinstone Grant-Duff, governor of Madras from 1881to 1886, and numerous buildings have sprung up over the years, along with surreal modern memorials to Tamil Nadu's chief political heroes and freedom fighters.

Today the **beach** itself is a sociable place, peopled by idle paddlers, picnickers and pony-riders; every afternoon crowds gather around the beach market. However, it suffers miserably from being just a little downstream from the port, which belches out waste and smelly fumes, as well as being the local toilet around the areas where the fishermen hang out. Unsurprisingly, swimming and sunbathing are neither recommended nor approved; nor is it advisable to take your shoes off on the beach, as the sand is full of bits of broken glass and rusty bottle tops. Tragically, around two hundred people were killed on Marina Beach by the **tsunami** on the morning of December 26, 2004, including many children who had come here to play cricket. Although the death toll in Chennai was lower than along other stretches of the coast – and much of the city was protected by the sheer width of Marina beach – the high percentage of children who perished here added to the sense of bereavement.

At the northern end of the beach, the **Anna Park** and **MGR Samadhi** parks attract droves of Tamil tourists intent on paying their respects at the shrine of

The Ice House

Over the years, Chennai has seen its fair share of world-shaping moments, but few can have been met with the wonder and unanimous approval that greeted the arrival of an American clipper in the early 1830s. Its cargo, rolled in pine sawdust and steered through the surf in small *masula* boats, had never been seen in peninsular India before, and one can only imagine the amazement of the local coolies when they first felt the weight and burning cold of melting **ice** on their shoulders.

In a little over four months, the ship, the *Tuscany*, had sailed halfway around the world with its precious load, harvested from frozen ponds around Boston. Little technology was required to gather the ice: grappling hooks, lengths of blocks and tackle, a few horse-drawn sleds and one hundred Irish labourers. The real breakthrough that made the trade possible was the discovery, by one Frederic Nathaniel Jarvis, that fresh pine sawdust would insulate ice, even from high tropical temperatures. A few years earlier, his friend, Frederick Tudor Boston, had tried to transport $10,000 dollars worth of New English ice to Martinique in the Caribbean, only to watch the entire cargo melt en route. However, Jarvis's bright idea enabled Boston's **Tudor Ice Company** to export 180 tons of ice to Calcutta in 1833. From that initial shipment enough profit was generated to build warehouses in Bombay and Madras, and thereafter the trade continued to boom for nearly forty years, until the invention of steam-powered ice-making machines put the company out of business.

Overlooking Chennai's sun-scorched Marina Beach, the building erected by the Tudor Ice Company in the 1840s to store their stock still stands as an evocative reminder of this brief, but extraordinary, episode in the city's mercantile history. It was sold to a rich lawyer when the bottom fell out of the trade, and it was with him that the famous Indian philosopher, **Vivekananda**, stayed after his return from the US in 1897, when crowds would gather on the steps outside to hear the sage speak. In memory of this event – and in spite of the fact that it now serves as a hostel for the adjacent Lady Willingdon Teacher Training College – the local municipality has rechristened the building "Vivekananda House", but to everyone else in Chennai, the stalwart old pile, with its peeling yellow-painted walls and distinctive twin circular tiered facade, is still known simply as "**The Ice House**".

the state's most illustrious movie actor and chief minister, **M.G. Ramachandran** (see box on p.456). Nearby is one of the oldest of the city's university buildings, the **Senate House** (1879), an uncharacteristically Byzantine-influenced design by Robert Fellowes Chisholm (1840–1915), one of the British leaders in developing the hybrid Indo-Saracenic style, incorporating Hindu, Jain and Muslim elements along with solid Victorian brickwork.

Continuing south, past the Indo-Saracenic **Presidency College** (1865–71), a number of stolid Victorian university buildings include the **Lady Willingdon Teacher Training College**. Next door, the college's hostel, a huge lump of a building with a semicircular frontage painted white and yellow, was the Madras depot of the Tudor Ice Company (see box above) during the nineteenth century.

Mylapore

Long before Madras came into existence, **Mylapore**, south of the Marina (reached by buses #4, #5 or #21 from the LIC building on Anna Salai), was a major settlement; the Greek geographer Ptolemy mentioned it in the second century AD as a thriving port, and during the Pallava period (fifth to ninth centuries) it was second only to Mamallapuram (see p.475), a little way down the coastline.

An important stop – with Little Mount and St Thomas Mount – on the St Thomas pilgrimage trail, the **San Thome Cathedral** (daily 6am–8pm) marks the eastern boundary of Mylapore, lying close to the sea at the southern end of the Marina. St Thomas is credited as being the first to bring Christianity to the subcontinent in the first century AD. Although the present neo-Gothic structure dates from 1896, San Thome stands on the site of two earlier churches (the first possibly erected by Nestorian Christians from Persia during the tenth century) built over the tomb of St Thomas; his relics are kept inside. Behind the church, a small **museum** (Mon–Sat 10am–5pm; free) houses stones inscribed in Tamil, Sanskrit (twelfth-century Chola) and early Portuguese, and also a map of India dated 1519.

The large **Kapalishvara temple**, less than 1km west of the San Thome Cathedral, is the most famous in Chennai, the principal shrine being dedicated to Shiva. Seventh-century Tamil poet-saints sang its praises, but the present structure probably dates from the sixteenth century. Until then, the temple is thought to have occupied a site on the shore; sea erosion or demolition at the hands of the Portuguese led it to be rebuilt inland. The huge (40m) *gopura* towering above the main east entrance, plastered in stucco figures, was added in 1906. Surrounding an assortment of busy shrines, where priests offer blessings for devotees and non-Hindus alike, the **courtyard** features an old tree where a small shrine to Shiva's consort, Parvati, shows her in the form of a peahen (*mayil*) worshipping a *lingam*. This commemorates the legend that she was momentarily distracted from concentrating on her lord by the enchanting dance of a peacock. Shiva, miffed at this dereliction of wifely duty, cursed her, whereupon she turned into a peahen. To expiate the sin, Parvati took off to a place called Kapalinagar, and embarked upon rigorous austerities. To commemorate her success, the town was named Mayilapore or **Mylapore**. The oldest artefacts in the Kapalishvara temple are the movable bronze images of deities and the 63 Shaivite Nayanmar poet-saints, two of whom came from Mylapore. Unusually, the main shrine faces west, towards a space dominated by an eighteenth-century water-lily tank which appears vast in this cramped suburban district.

Important **festivals** held at Kapalishvara include **Thaipusam** (February; see p.551), when the bronze images of Shiva and Parvati are pulled around the temple tank in a decorated boat to the accompaniment of music. **Brahmotsava** (March/April) celebrates the marriage of Shiva and Parvati; in the afternoon of the eighth day, all 63 bronze images of the Nayanmar saints are clothed, garlanded and taken out in palanquins along the streets to meet the bejewelled images of Shiva and Parvati. **Vasantha** (May/June), the summer festival, is marked by concerts.

In the busy **market streets** that surround the temple, amid stalls selling pots and pans, flowers, religious paraphernalia and vegetables, glittering shops spill over with gold wedding-jewellery. Exquisite saris are unfolded for scrutiny in silk emporia; the finest quality comes from Kanchi and is delicately embroidered with gold and silver thread. Saris of this distinction can add as much as Rs30,000 to the cost of a wedding.

A little further west, before you come to TTK Road, the **Luz Church**, on Luz Church Road, is thought to be the earliest Christian building in Chennai, built by the Portuguese in the sixteenth century. Its founding is associated with a miracle; Portuguese sailors in difficulties at sea were once guided to land and safety by a light which, when they tried to find its source, disappeared. The church, dedicated to Our Lady of Light, was erected where the light left them.

Little Mount Caves

St Thomas is said to have sought refuge from persecution in the **Little Mount Caves**, 8km south of the city centre (bus #18A, #18B, or #52C from Anna Salai), 200m off the road between the Maraimalai Adigal Bridge. Entrance to the caves is beside steps leading to a statue of Our Lady of Good Health. Inside, next to a small natural window in the rock, are impressions of what are believed to be St Thomas' handprints, created when he made his escape through this tiny opening.

Behind the new circular church of Our Lady of Good Health, with its brightly painted replicas of the *Pietà* and Holy Sepulchre, is a natural **spring**, said to have been created when Thomas struck the rock so that the crowds that came to hear him preach could quench their thirst. Even today when Chennai is hit by drought the water level of the well remains unaffected. Samples of its holy water are on sale.

St Thomas Mount

Tradition has it that St Thomas was speared to death (or struck by a hunter's stray arrow) while praying before a stone cross on **St Thomas Mount**, 11km south of the city centre, close to the airport (take a suburban train to Guindy railway station, and walk from there). **Our Lady of Expectation Church** (1523), at the summit of the Mount, can be reached by 134 granite steps marked with the fourteen stations of the Cross, or by a road which curls its way to the top. At the top of the steps, a huge old banyan tree provides shade for devotees who come to fast, pray and sing. Inside the church, St Thomas's cross is rumoured to have bled in 1558, while the altar is said to mark the exact spot of the apostle's death; the painting above the altar of the Madonna and Child is attributed to St Luke. Cold drinks are available in the adjacent Holy Apostle's Convent.

The Theosophical Society Headquarters

The **Theosophical Society** was established in New York in 1875 by American Civil War veteran Colonel Henry S. Olcott, a failed farmer and journalist, and the eccentric Russian aristocrat Madame Helena Petrovna Blavatsky, who claimed occult powers and telepathic links with "Mahatmas" in Tibet. Based on a fundamental belief in the equality and truth of all religions, the Society in fact propagated a modern form of Hinduism, praising all things Indian and shunning Christian missionaries. Needless to say, its two founders were greeted enthusiastically when they transferred their operations to Madras in 1882, establishing their headquarters near Elliot's Beach in Adyar (buses #5, #5C or #23C from George Town/Anna Salai). Even after Madame Blavatsky's psychic powers were proved to be bogus, the society continued to attract Hindus and Western visitors, and its buildings still stand today, sheltering several shrines and an excellent **library** (Mon–Sat 8.30–10am & 2pm–4pm) of books on religion and philosophy. The collection, begun by Olcott in 1886, comprises 165,000 volumes and nearly 200,000 palm-leaf manuscripts from all over the world. A selection is housed in an exhibition room on the ground floor. This includes 800-year-old scroll pictures of the Buddha, a seventeenth-century treatise on embalming bodies from London, rare Tibetan manuscripts written on bark paper, exquisitely illuminated Korans, a giant copy of Martin Luther's *Biblia* printed in Nuremberg three hundred years ago, and a thumbnail-sized Bible in seven languages.

The 270 acres of woodland and gardens surrounding the society's headquarters make a serene place to sit and restore spirits away from the noise and heat of the city streets. In the middle of the grounds, a vast 400-year-old **banyan tree**, said to be the second largest in the world, provides shade for up to 3000 people at a time. J. Krishnamurti and Maria Montessori have both given talks under its tangle of pillar-like root stems, whose growth Theosophists see as symbolizing the spread of the Society itself.

The Enfield factory

India's most stylish home-made motorcycle, the **Enfield Bullet**, is manufactured at a plant on Thiruvottiyur Road in the outskirts of Chennai, 18km north of Anna Salai (bus #1 from LIC Building or Parry's Corner). With its elegant tear-drop tank and thumping 350cc single-cylinder engine, the Bullet has become a contemporary classic – in spite of its propensity to leak oil and break down. Bike enthusiasts should definitely brave the long haul across town to see the **factory**, which is as much a period piece as the machines it turns out. Free guided tours, which last around ninety minutes (Mon–Fri 9.30am–5.30pm; entrance Rs500; ☎044/2573 2622), have to be arranged in advance by telephoning the Enfield's marketing general manager, Mr K. Muralidharan. You can do this yourself, or through the Government of India Tourist Office on Anna Salai.

Eating

Chennai runs on inexpensive indigenous fast-food **restaurants** and "meals" (thali) joints, in particular the legendary *Saravana Bhavan* chain, which serves superb South Indian food for a fraction of the cost of a coffee at one of the five-stars. That said, a minor splurge at *Annalakshmi* on Anna Salai or the *Park Sheraton* on TTK Road is well worth considering. The restaurants listed below are marked on either the Egmore, Anna Salai and Triplicane map on p.451 or the Chennai map on pp.444–445.

Amaravati Corner of Cathedral and TTK roads. One of four dependable options in this complex of regional speciality restaurants, south of the downtown area. This one does excellent Andhran food, including particularly tasty biriyanis.

Annalakshmi 804 Anna Salai. A non-profit making venture run voluntarily by devotees of Swami Shivenanda, where you can enjoy a leisurely and expensive meal in beautiful surroundings. You choose one of several set menus (each with different Ayurvedic properties), and the profits go to charitable works in the community.

Bella Ciao 4 Sree Krishna Enclave, near the Theosophical Headquarters ☎044/2451 1130. Tiny Italian restaurant, under Italian ownership, serving authentic pizza, as well as fresh gnocchi with blue cheese and mushrooms, lamb in red wine, pork chops and eighteen different organic salads (mains cost about Rs200). Add a little tiramisu and Pavarotti to complete the evening. Officially there's no alcohol, although beer can be arranged. Book in advance. Open 11am–3.30pm & 6.30pm–11pm. Closed Tues.

Buhari 83 Anna Salai. Idiosyncratic 1950s-style dining hall overlooking the main street. For some reason, Russian chicken dishes are the house speciality (à la Moscow, Kiev or Leningrad), but they also offer a full tandoori menu, cold beers and freshly baked cakes.

Chung King Anna Salai, Down an alleyway on the left of *Buhari* restaurant. Genuine Chinese cuisine prepared by a pukka Chinese chef.

Copper Chimney 74 St George's Cathedral Rd ☎044/827 5770. Franchise of the famous Mumbai restaurant, offering quality tandoori cuisine, opulent decor and a/c comfort. The meat-eater's equivalent of *Annalakshmi*. Count on Rs200–250 per head.

Dakshin/Khyber/Residency *Welcomgroup Park Sheraton* hotel, 132 TTK Rd ☎044/299 4101. Excellent upmarket hotel restaurants – the *Residency* serves Indian, Western and Chinese, and the *Khyber* offers a meaty poolside barbecue, but best of all is the *Dakshin*, one of the country's top South Indian restaurants, which dishes up a wide choice

The reluctant guru

For a spiritual organization based on principles of inclusiveness and harmony, the Theosophical Society has suffered some acrimonious schisms over the years, particularly after the deaths of its founders Olcott and Blavatsky, when its most prominent personalities clashed in an unseemly power struggle. The most infamous rift of all, though, was one between the Society's mandarins and the young man they identified in 1905 as the "Buddha to Be", **Jiddu Krishnamurti**, a Telegu-speaking brahmin boy brought to Adyar by his father after his mother died. He was first "discovered" by Charles Webster Leadbeater, a leading light in the Theosophical Society who claimed clairvoyant powers. Among the central tenets of the movement was a belief that Lord Krishna and Christ were about to be reborn as a "World Teacher", and from the moment Leadbeater saw the ten-year-old Krishnamurti playing football on the beach at Adyar he knew he had found the "Enlightened One". Jiddu, however, did not initially look the part. Wild, malnourished and sickly, with "crooked teeth . . . and a vacant, almost moronic expression", he seemed more like a street kid than a messiah in the making.

Informed that the "Vehicle" had been identified, **Annie Besant** – the then President of the Theosophical Society – was quick to take the boy under her wing. Over the coming years, Krishnamurti, with the support of the TS and its benefactors, was to receive the best education that money could buy, with places at famous colleges in England and California. Spiritual instruction, meanwhile, came from Leadbeater's own guru, a mystical Buddhist lama who lived in a remote Tibetan ravine and delivered his teachings on the "astral plane".

Not surprisingly, Krishnamurti's father resented Besant's adoption of his son and initiated custody proceedings to prevent the TS from taking him abroad. The High Court of Madras found in Krishnamurti senior's favour, but his decision was overturned after Besant took the case to London (in spite of allegations of "unnatural practices" levelled against Leadbeater). By the time the legal battle had run its course, however, Krishnamurti was legally an adult and already teaching. He'd also matured into an exceedingly handsome, suave young man, with a trademark sweep of jet black hair and a taste for fashionable clothes.

While his teachings were being received with growing enthusiasm, both within India and the US, the fledgling guru was showing definite signs of resenting the role thrust upon him by the Theosophists. Soon, this found expression in criticism of the ritual, mysticism and self-aggrandizing "wise-men" that had become features of the Society's new leadership, some of whom then began to turn against their charismatic detractor, claiming he had been "possessed by black forces". The conflict came to a head when Krishnamurti, addressing a Theosophy camp in the US, formally renounced his position as head for the OSE (Order of the Star in the East), originally formed to promote his teachings. He resigned from the TS soon afterwards, with the famous pronouncement that "Truth is a pathless land . . . you cannot approach it by any path whatsoever, by any religion, by any sect."

For the rest of his life, Krishnamurti – or "K" as he preferred to be known – wandered the world as a individual, lecturing, writing and setting up educational institutions where young people could, as he said, "flower as human beings, without fear, without confusion, with great integrity". When he died in 1986, aged 91, he was one of the most famous philosophers of his generation, but always resisted the label of guru; "mediators", he said, "must inevitably step down the Truth, and hence betray it."

of unusual dishes from the four southern states, including seafood in marinated spices, Karnataka mutton biriyani, and piping-hot *iddiappam* and *appam* made on the spot. Live Carnatic music in the evenings. Expect to pay around Rs600 for a meal with starter and beer.

Fry's Opposite the *Ambassador Pallava* hotel, 30 Montieth Rd. Good, cheap, authentic Keralan food. Open for lunch noon–3.30pm & 6.30pm–11pm.

Geetham *Kanchi Hotel*, 28 Ethiraj Salai. Circular, glass-sided restaurant on the rooftop of this nine-storey tower block. The multi-cuisine menu is surprisingly inexpensive, and the views superb. Open 11am–noon & 7–10pm.

Hot Breads St George's Cathedral Rd. Wholewheat breads, baguettes, fresh quiches and an impressive range of cakes, biscuits and pastries. Decent espresso coffee, too. Eat in or take away.

Kudil Tambaram district, South Chennai, 8km from centre towards Trisulam airport by suburban train ☎044/5571 3659. Acclaimed Keralan restaurant in a pleasant garden setting serving excellent authentic home-cooked food under a traditional thatched roof. Several more intimate tables are dotted around the garden.

Peshawari & Shanghai *Welcomgroup Chola Sheraton* hotel, 10 Cathedral Rd ☎044/2828 0101. Two good restaurants in this upmarket hotel; the *Peshawari* serves lavish (and expensive) north-western frontier food, while the excellent rooftop *Shanghai* specializes in Chinese dishes.

The Rain Tree *Taj Connemara* hotel, Binny Rd ☎044/5500 0000. This excellent and very popular place does superb Chettinad (South Indian) specialities accompanied by live Carnatic music and dance in the evenings. A three-course meal will cost around Rs500–800 (veg/non-veg). Book in advance.

Saravana Bhavan Thanigai Murugan Rathinavel Hall, 77 Usman Rd, T Nagar. This famous South Indian fast-food chain is an institution among the Chennai middle class, with other branches opposite the bus stand in George Town, and in the forecourt of the Shanti cinema at the top of Anna Salai. Try their delicious *rawa iddlis* or one of their range of thalis rounded off with some freshly made *ladoo* or *barfi* from the sweets counter outside.

Señor (Don) Pepés 1st floor, above *Hot Breads*, Cathedral Rd. Swish a/c Tex-Mex joint serving a predictable menu of fajitas, enchiladas, tortillas and burritos, plus so-so pasta dishes (dubbed "Euro-Mex"). Main courses about Rs120.

Society *Ambassador Pallava* hotel, 30 Montieth Rd ☎044/ 2855 4476. Worth a visit for the excellent all-you-can-eat lunchtime buffet (Rs333), with a choice of over twenty veg and non-veg dishes plus a large array of sweets.

Srinivasa Ellis Rd, Triplicane. Excellent South Indian breakfasts – try their *kitchadi* and *vada pongal* – for next to nothing, and the coffee is genuine Coorg. Open the rest of the day for very cheap meals and snacks. There's a separate area for women and families.

Vasanta Bhavan 20 Gandhi Irwin Rd. Easily the best "meals" joint among many around Egmore station, with ranks of attentive waiters and delicious pure veg food – just Rs25 for an unlimited thali. It's busy, spotlessly clean, and their coffee and sweets are delicious too. There are two other branches opposite Egmore station, one specializing in ice cream.

Verandah *Taj Connemara* hotel, Binny Rd ☎044/5500 0000. The ideal venue for a posh Sunday morning breakfast buffet, with crisp newspapers and fresh coffee served in silver pots. The blow-out lunchtime buffets (around Rs400) are also recommended, and they serve à la carte Italian food in the evening.

Listings

Airline offices Air France, Thaper House, 43–44 Montieth Rd ☎044/2855 4916; Air India, 19 Rukmani Lakshmipathy Rd ☎044/2855 4477, airport ☎044/2256 0747; British Airways, Sigma Wing, 177 Anna Salai ☎044/2860 3123; Gulf Air, 52 Montieth Rd ☎044/2855 4417; Indian Airlines, 19 Rukmani Lakshmipathy Rd ☎044/2855 5201; Jet Airways, Thaper House, 43–44 Montieth Rd ☎044/2841 4141; KLM, 10 Montieth Rd ☎044/2852 4427; Lufthansa, 167 Anna Salai ☎044/2854 3500; Malaysia Airlines, Arihant Nico Park, 90 Dr. R.K. Salai ☎044/5219 9999; Qantas, Eldorado Building, 112 Nungambakkam High Rd ☎044/2827 8680; Sahara, D-91 1st Ave, Anna Nagar East ☎044/5208 7070; Singapore Airlines, 108 Dr Radhakrishnan Salai ☎044/2847 3995; SriLankan Airlines, Nagabrahma Towers, 76 Cathedral Rd ☎044/2811 1536; Swissair, 19 Hamid Building, 191 Anna Salai ☎044/2852 4783; Thai Airways, 31 Haddows Rd, Nungambakkam ☎044/5217 3311. For American, Air Canada, Biman, Philippine, Royal Jordanian and TWA, contact JetAir, Apex Plaza, 3 MG Rd ☎044/2859 2564. Most offices are open Mon–Fri 10am–5pm, Sat 10am–1pm.

Banks and currency exchange You should have few difficulties changing money in Chennai: there are plenty of banks, and the major hotels offer exchange facilities (residents only). A conveniently central option is American Express, G-17, Spencer

Plaza, 769 Anna Salai (Mon–Fri 9.30am–5.30pm, Sat 9.30am–2.30pm). Thomas Cook (Mon–Sat 9am–6pm) has offices at the Ceebros Centre, 45 Montieth Rd, Egmore, at the G-4 Eldorado Building, 112 Uttamar Gandhi Salai, and also at the airport (open to meet flights). For cash advances on Visa cards, go to Bobcards, next door to the Bank of Baroda on Montieth Rd, near the *Ambassador Pallava* hotel. There's also an increasing number of 24hr ATMs popping up around town, such as at Citibank, 766 Anna Salai.

Bookshops Higginbothams, on Anna Salai, is Chennai's oldest bookshop, with a vast assortment of Indian and Western titles, and a few maps at rupee rates. Landmark, on the 1st floor of Spencer Plaza on Anna Salai, has a huge selection of books, stationery and music. The hole-in-the-wall Giggles in the *Taj Connemara* hotel grounds has a matchless stock of novels, academic tomes on the region and coffee-table books piled precariously high. Unlike other bookstores in the city, this one takes credit cards and will post purchases abroad for you for a nominal charge.

Cinemas The Abhirami and Lakshmi along Anna Salai show English-language films, but for the full-on Tamil film experience, take in a show at the Shanti, off the top of Anna Salai, which boasts the city's biggest screen and a digital stereo soundsystem. Nearby, the equally massive Devi hosts the latest Bollywood blockbusters.

Consulates Canada, 3rd Floor Dhun Bldg, 827 Anna Salai ☎ 044/2852 0918; Sri Lanka, 196 TTK Rd ☎ 044/2498 7896; UK, 20 Anderson Rd, Nungambakkam ☎ 044/2825 7422; USA, Anna Salai ☎ 044/2811 2000.

Hospitals Chennai's best-equipped private hospital is the Apollo, 21/22 Greams Rd ☎ 044/2829 3333. For an ambulance, try ☎ 044/102, but it's usually quicker to jump in a taxi.

Internet Internet access is widely available in cybercafés for around Rs30–40 per hour, or for a bit more in hotel business centres. The snazziest option is the pricier than average Net Café at 101/1 Kanakasri Nagar, down an alleyway off Cathedral Rd (daily 7am–midnight) – look for the neon @ sign. SRIS Netsurfing Café on the first floor of Spencer Plaza is a cheaper, though smaller, alternative. Gee Gee Net in Triplicane, next door to the *Hotel Comfort*, is open 24hr. Egmore options include the 24hr service at the *Pandian* hotel.

Left luggage Counters at Egmore and Central railway stations store bags for Rs10 per day; they usually require you to chain and padlock your baggage, and you must also show your train ticket. Some hotels also guard luggage at a daily rate.

Music shops Musee Musical, 67 Anna Salai, stocks sitars, percussion instruments, flutes and the usual shoddy selection of Hofner/Gibson-copy guitars. For the best range of concert-quality Indian instruments, including *vinas*, check out Saptaswara Music Store, on Raipetha Rd, Mylapore. Music World, on the first floor of Spencer Plaza, has the best selection of contemporary Indian and Western music CDs in the city.

Photographic equipment Dozens of stores around town offer film and developing services on modern machines (Konica studios are particularly reliable), but the only Kodak-approved Q-Lab in the city (recommended for transparency processing) is Image Park, GEE Plaza, 1 Craft Rd. Nungambakkam Reliance Opticals, at 136 Anna Salai, stocks Fuji Provia and Sensia II. For camera repairs, try Camera Crafts, 325/8A Quaide Milleth Salai, Triplicane, near *Broadlands Hotel*. Delhi Photo Stores, in an arcade directly behind the big Konica shop on Wallajah Rd, is crammed with spare parts and other useful Indian-made bits and bobs for cameras.

Postal services Chennai's main post office is opposite the Shanti Theatre on Anna Salai (Mon–Sat 8am–8pm, Sun 10am–5pm). If you're using it for poste restante, make sure that anyone writing to you marks the envelope "Head Post Office, Anna Salai", or your letters could well end up across town at the GPO, north of Parry's Corner on Rajaji Salai (same hours). The post office on Quaide Milleth Salai, in Triplicane (Mon–Sat 7am–3pm) is convenient if you're staying at *Broadlands*.

Souvenirs Spencer Plaza, on Anna Salai, has an excellent selection of boutiques, clothes shops and small souvenir stalls. Across the road, The Indian Arts Emporium, 152 Anna Salai, has a good selection of handicrafts, furniture and metalwork.

Tax clearance To get a tax clearance certificate (see Basics, p.34) take exchange documents and passport to 121 Uttamar Gandhi Rd, and allow for 3–4hr of tedious form-filling.

Travel agents Reliable travel agents include American Express Travels, Phase 2, 5th Floor, Spencer Plaza, Anna Salai ☎ 044/2849 3592; PL World Way, G-11 Ground Floor, Spencer Plaza ☎ 044/2822 6853; Surya Travels, F-14 1st Floor, Spencer Plaza ☎ 044/2852 3934; Thomas Cook, Eldorado Building, 112 Nungambakkam High Rd ☎ 044/2827 4941; Welcome Tourrs and Travels, 150 Anna Salai ☎ 044/2846 0908, ⓔ welcome@md2.vsnl.net.in.

Yoga Chennai may seem like an insalubrious place to study yoga, but some of South India's most renowned schools are based here. The following offer short courses: Adyar Yoga Research Institute, 15 III Main Rd, Kasturba Nagar, Adyar, near the

Theosophical Society Headquarters; Bharatiya Vidya Bhavan, East Mada St, Mylapore; Prof T. Krishnamacharya's Yoga Mandiram, 103 St Mary's Rd (☎044/2499 7602), Yoga Brotherhood, Geetha Bhavan, 233, Avvai Shanmugam Salai, Lloyd's Rd, Gopalapuram (☎044/2825 4213).

Moving on from Chennai

Transport connections between Chennai and the rest of India are summarized on p.468. If you're short of time, consider employing one of the **travel agents** listed on p.465 to book your plane, train or bus ticket for you. This doesn't apply to boat tickets for the Andaman Islands, which have to be booked in person (see below).

By air

Chennai's domestic airport is next to the international terminal, 16km southwest of the centre at Trisulam in **Meenambakkam** district. The easiest way to get there is by taxi or auto-rickshaw, but if you're not too weighed down with luggage you can save money by jumping on a suburban train to **Trisulam station**, 500m from the airport.

Indian Airlines flies from here to fifteen destinations around the country, including several daily flights to Mumbai, Delhi and Hyderabad, two to Kolkata (Calcutta) and one or two to Bangalore. In addition, Jet Airways operates services to Bangalore, Coimbatore, Delhi, Hyderabad, Madurai, Mumbai and Pune. Both airlines fly daily to Port Blair. Some of these destinations are also served by Air Deccan and Air Sahara.

By train

Trains to Tiruchirapalli (Trichy), Thanjavur, Pudukottai, Kodaikanal Road, Madurai, and most other destinations in south Tamil Nadu leave from **Egmore Station**, with the occasional service leaving from the suburban **Tambaram** station. All other trains leave from **Chennai Central** where, left of the main building on the first floor of the Moore Market Complex, the efficient **tourist reservation counter** (Mon–Sat 8am–8pm, Sun 8am–2pm; no phone) sells "tourist quota" tickets for trains from either station, which you can pay for in dollars, sterling, travellers' cheques or rupees (providing you have a recent encashment certificate). The booking office at Egmore, up the stairs left of the main entrance (same hours), also handles bookings for both stations, but has no tourist counter.

If you're arriving in Chennai by plane, note that Southern Railways also has a **reservation counter** (daily 10am–5pm) outside the domestic terminal at the airport.

By boat

Boats leave Chennai every week for **Port Blair**, capital of the **Andaman Islands**. However, getting a ticket can be a rigmarole, even though the schedule is now more regular. The first thing you'll need to do is head up to the Chennai Port Trust, next to the Directorate of Shipping on Rajaji (North Beach) Salai, George Town, where a small hut houses the Andaman Administration Office. A chalkboard on the wall advertises details of the next sailing, and you buy a ticket from the hatch around the corner, at the front of the main building. There are no ticket sales on the day of sailing. You no longer have to get a **permit** on the

Recommended trains from Chennai

Destination	Name	No.	From	Departs	Total time
Bangalore	Shatabdi Express*	#2007	Central	6am**	4hr 50min
	Chennai–Bangalore Express	#6523	Central	1pm	7hr 5min
Bhubaneswar	Coromandel Express	#2842	Central	9.05am	20hr 10min
	Howrah Mail	#6004	Central	10.30pm	22hr 55min
Coimbatore	Kovai Express	#2675	Central	6.15am	7hr 40min
	Cheran Express	#2673	Central	10.10pm	8hr 5min
Delhi	Tamil Nadu Express	#2621	Central	10pm	33hr 30min
	Grand Trunk Express	#2615	Central	4.30pm	36hr 30min
Hyderabad	Charminar Express	#2759	Central	6.10pm	14hr 15min
Kanniyakumari	Kanniyakumari Express	#2633	Egmore	5.30pm	13hr
Kochi/ Ernakulam	Chennai–Alleppey Express	#6041	Central	8.30pm	11hr 40min
	Trivandrum Mail	#2623	Central	7.30pm	11hr
Kodaikanal Road	Pandyan Express	#2637	Egmore	9.30pm	8hr
Kolkata (Calcutta)	Coromandel Express	#2842	Central	9.05am	28hr
	Chennai–Howrah Mail	#6004	Central	10.30pm	31hr 10min
Madurai	Vaigai Express	#2635	Egmore	12.25pm	7hr 50min
Mettuppalayam (for Ooty)	Nilgiri Express	#2671	Central	9pm	9hr 20min
Mumbai	Mumbai Express	#6012	Central	11.45am	26hr
	Chennai–Dadar Express	#1064	Central	6.50am	23hr 15min
Mysore	Shatabdi Express*	#2007	Central	6am**	7hr
	Mysore Express	#6222	Central	9.30pm	10hr 55min
Rameshwaram	Sethu Express	#6713	Tambaram	1pm	17hr 50min
	Rameshwaram Express	#6701	Tambaram	8.15pm	17hr 5min
Thanjavur	Rock Fort Express	#6177	Egmore	10.30pm	8hr 20min
Thiruvanantha-puram	Trivandrum Mail	#2623	Central	7.30pm	16hr 20min
Tirupati	Saptagiri Express	#6057	Central	6.25am	3hr 5min
Varanasi	Ganga Kaveri Express***	#6039	Central	5.30pm	38hr 40min

*A/c only
**Except Tues
***Mon & Sat only

mainland, as they are available on arrival in Port Blair. For more details, see the Andaman Islands chapter p.615.

By bus

All long-distance buses leave from the new **Moffussil bus stand**, the largest bus stand in South Asia. The stand is clean and well organized, although it's also rather inconveniently located 10km west of the centre in the suburb of Koyambedu – local buses (see "Arrival", p.446) and auto-rickshaws ply the route. From Mofussil there are frequent services to destinations throughout Tamil Nadu and neighbouring states. The first stop beyond Chennai for many people is **Mamallapuram**, for which the fastest services are #188, #188A and anything marked "East Coast Express" (every 15–30min; less than 2hr); #19A, #19C, #119 and #119A all take rather longer, and the 108B (via the airport and Chengalpattu) much longer.

Travel details

Trains

The following services leave from different stations including Egmore (marked *), Tamabaram (**) and Egmore and Tambaram (***); Egmore and Central (****); all others leave from Central.

Chennai to: Bangalore (7 daily; 4hr 50min–8hr 50min); Bhubaneswar (3–4 daily; 20–23hr); Chengalpattu (9 daily***; 1hr); Coimbatore (2 daily; 8hr); Delhi (2–4 daily; 33hr 30min–41hr); Dindigul (6–7 daily*; 6hr 30min–8hr); Hyderabad (2 daily; 14hr–14hr 30min); Kanniyakumari (1–2 daily; 13hr–16hr 55min); Kochi (2–3 daily; 11hr 40min–14hr 35min); Kodaikanal Road (3–4 daily*; 8hr–8hr 30min); Kolkata (Calcutta) (2–4 daily; 28hr–31hr 10min); Kumbakonam (2 daily***; 7hr 30min–9hr 15min); Madurai (6–8 daily*; 7hr 50min–10hr 40min); Mettuppalayam (1 daily; 9hr 20min); Mumbai (3 daily; 23hr 15min–28hr 45min); Mysore (1–2 daily; 7hr–10hr 55min); Pune (3 daily; 19hr–24hr 15min); Rameshwaram (2 daily**; 17hr 5min–17hr 50min); Salem (10 daily; 4hr 30min–5hr 45min); Thanjavur (1 daily*; 8hr 20min); Thiruvananthapuram (2–3 daily****; 15hr 20min–18hr 50min); Tiruchirapalli (9–10 daily*; 5hr 10min–6hr 35min); Tirupati (3 daily; 3hr–3hr 35min); Vijayawada (10–11 daily; 6hr 20min–9hr).

Buses

Chennai to: Bangalore (every 15–30min; 8–11hr); Chengalpattu (every 5–10min; 1hr 30min–2hr); Chidambaram (22 daily; 5–7hr); Coimbatore (9 daily; 11–13hr); Dindigul (10 daily; 9–10hr); Kanchipuram (every 20min; 1hr 30min–2hr); Kanniyakumari (10 daily; 16–18hr); Kodaikanal (1 daily; 14–15hr); Kumbakonam (33 daily; 7–8hr); Madurai (every 20–30min; 10hr); Mamallapuram (every 20–30min; 2–3hr); Pondicherry (every 20–30min; 4–5hr); Rameshwaram (1 daily; 14hr); Salem (21 daily; 5–7hr); Thanjavur (20 daily; 8hr 30min); Thiruvananthapuram (6 daily; 20hr); Tindivanam (every 30min; 3–4hr); Tiruchirapalli (every 15–30min; 8–9hr); Tirupati (9 daily; 4–5hr); Tiruvannamalai (every 20min; 4–6hr); Udhagamandalam (Ooty) (2 daily; 15hr).

Flights

Chennai to: Bangalore (11–12 daily; 50min); Bhubaneswar (3 weekly; 2hr 30min); Coimbatore (3–4 daily; 55min–1hr 55min); Delhi (11 daily; 2hr 30min); Hyderabad (7–8 daily; 1hr); Kochi (1–3 daily; 1hr–2hr 15min); Kolkata (Calcutta) (5 daily; 2hr 5min); Madurai (4 daily; 55min–1hr 20min); Mumbai (14–17 daily; 1hr 45min–3hr 40min); Port Blair (2 daily; 2hr); Thiruvananthapuram (1–2 daily; 1hr 10min); Tiruchirapalli (1–2 daily; 50min).

Tamil Nadu

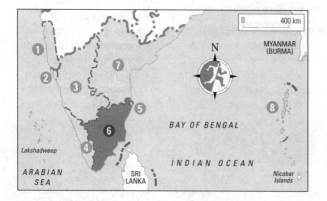

CHAPTER 6

Highlights

✳ **Mamallapuram** Stone-carvers' workshops, a long sandy beach and a bumper hoard of Pallava monuments have made Mamallapuram the state's principal tourist attraction. See p.475

✳ **Pondicherry** A former French colony which has retained the ambience of a Gallic seaside town: croissants, a promenade and gendarmes wearing *képis*. See p.496

✳ **Thanjavur** Dominated by the colossal shrine tower of the Brihadishwara Temple and home to some of the world's finest Chola bronzes. See p.515

✳ **Madurai** This major temple, the love-nest of Shiva and his consort Meenakshi, hosts a constant round of festivals. See p.530

✳ **Kanniyakumari** Sacred meeting point, at the southern tip of the subcontinent, of the Bay of Bengal, Indian Ocean and Arabian Sea. See p.551

✳ **The Ghats** The spine of southern India, with trekking through forested mountains and tea plantations from the refreshingly cool hill stations of Ooty, Coonoor and Kodaikanal. See p.555

△ Krishna's Butter Ball, Mamallapuram

Tamil Nadu

hen Indians refer to "the South", it's usually **TAMIL NADU** they're talking about. While Karnataka and Andhra Pradesh are essentially cultural transition zones buffering the Hindi-speaking north, and Kerala and Goa maintain their own distinctively idiosyncratic identities, the peninsula's massive Tamil-speaking state is India's Dravidian Hindu heartland. Traditionally protected by distance and the military might of the southern Deccan kingdoms, the region has, over the centuries, been less exposed to northern influences than its neighbours. As a result, the three powerful dynasties dominating the South – the Cholas, the Pallavas and the Pandyans – were able, over a period of more than a thousand years, to develop their own unique religious and political institutions, largely unmolested by marauding Muslims. The most visible legacy of this protracted cultural flowering is a crop of astounding **temples**, whose gigantic gateway towers, or *gopuras*, still soar above just about every town large enough to merit a railway station. It is the image of these colossal wedge-shaped pyramids, covered with garishly painted gods, goddesses and mythological creatures – described by Edward Lear as "stupendous and beyond belief" – which linger in the memory of most travellers.

The great Tamil temples are merely the largest landmarks in a vast network of **sacred sites** – shrines, bathing places, holy trees, rocks and rivers – interconnected by a web of ancient pilgrims' routes. Tamil Nadu harbours 274 of India's holiest Shiva temples, and 108 of its most sacred Vishnu temples. In addition, five shrines devoted to the five Vedic elements (Earth, Wind, Fire, Water and Ether) are to be found here, along with eight to the planets, as well as other places revered by Christians and Muslims. These sites were celebrated in the hymns of the Tamil saints, composed between one and two thousand years ago, and so little has changed since then that the same devotional songs are still widely sung and understood in the region today.

The Tamils' living connection with their ancient Dravidian past has given rise to a strong **nationalist movement**. With a few fleeting lapses, one or other of the pro-Dravidian parties have been in power here since the 1950s, spreading their anti-brahmin, anti-Hindi proletarian message to the masses, principally through the medium of movies (indeed, since Independence, the majority of Tamil Nadu's political leaders have been drawn from the state's prolific **cinema** industry). Indians from elsewhere in the country love to caricature their southern cousins as "reactionary rice growers" led by "fanatical film stars". While such stereotypes should be taken with a pinch of salt, it is undeniable that the Tamil way of life, which has evolved along a distinctive and unbroken path since prehistoric times, sets it apart from the rest of the subcontinent. This remains,

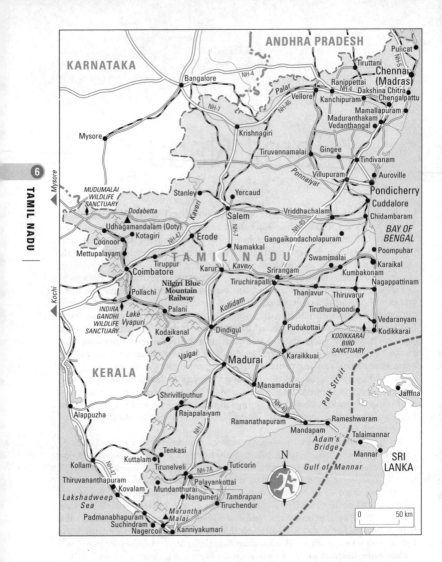

after all, one of the last places in the world where a classical culture has survived into the present – "India's Holy Land", described by Marco Polo as "the most splendid province in the world".

Visiting Tamil Nadu

Despite its seafront fort, grand mansions and excellence as a centre for the performing arts, the state capital **Chennai** (covered in the previous chapter) is probably its least appealing destination: a scruffy, dusty, noisy city that still carries faint echoes of the Raj. Much the best place to start a temple tour is nearby **Mamallapuram** (also known as **Mahabalipuram**), a seaside village which boasts exquisite Pallava rock-cut architecture (fifth–ninth centuries) and a long stretch of white-sand beach. Inland, the pilgrimage town of **Kanchipuram** is filled with reminders of an illustrious past under successive dynastic rulers, while further down the coast is one of India's rare French colonial possessions, **Pondicherry**, and the "New Age" centre of **Auroville**. The road south from Pondicherry puts you back on the temple trail, leading to the tenth-century Chola kingdom and the extraordinary architecture of **Chidambaram**, **Gangaikondacholapuram**, **Kumbakonam** and **Darasuram**. For the best Chola bronzes, however, and a glimpse of the magnificent paintings that flourished under Maratha rajas in the eighteenth century, travellers should head for **Thanjavur**. Chola capital for four centuries, the city boasts almost a hundred temples and was the birthplace of Bharatanatyam dance, famous throughout Tamil Nadu.

In the very centre of Tamil Nadu, just northwest of Thanjavur, the commercial town of **Tiruchirapalli** held some interest for the Cholas but reached its heyday under later dynasties, when the temple complex in neighbouring **Srirangam** became one of South India's largest. Among its patrons were the Nayaks of **Madurai**, whose erstwhile capital further south, bustling with pilgrims, priests, peddlers, tailors and tourists, is an unforgettable destination. Further south are two of the region's main pilgrimage centres: **Rameshwaram**, situated on the long spit of land stretching towards Sri Lanka, and **Kanniyakumari**, at India's southern tip and the auspicious meeting place of the Bay of Bengal, Indian Ocean and Arabian Sea, where cool breezes and sea vistas are added attractions.

While Tamil Nadu's temples are undeniably its major attraction, it would take months to see them all, and there are plenty of other distractions for even the most ardent architecture buff. In the west of the state the hill stations of **Kodaikanal** and **Ootacamund** (**Ooty**) are the premier attractions, set amidst verdant hills offering mountain views and a network of trails winding through forests and tea and coffee plantations. Nearby, the **Mudumalai Wildlife Sanctuary** and the **Indira Gandhi** or **Anamalai Sanctuary** have both been closed to visitors for several years due to local terrorist activities. To get close to any real wildlife you'll have to head for the coast, where areas of wetland provide perfect resting places for migratory birds, whose numbers soar during the winter monsoon at **Vedanthangal**, near Chennai, and **Point Calimere**.

Temperatures in Tamil Nadu usually hover around 30°C and peak in May and June, when they often soar above 40°, and the overpowering heat makes anything all but sitting in a shaded café exhausting. The state is barely affected by the southwest monsoon that pounds much of India from June to September: it receives most of its **rain** between October and January. Cooler, rainy days bring their own problems; widescale flooding can disrupt road and rail links and imbue everything with an all-pervasive dampness.

Accommodation prospects are good; all but the smallest towns and villages have something for every budget. Most hotels have their own dining halls which, together with local restaurants, sometimes serve sumptuous thalis, tinged with tamarind and presented on banana leaves. **Indigenous dishes** are almost exclusively vegetarian; for North Indian or Western alternatives, head for the larger hotels or more upmarket city restaurants.

Some history

Since the fourth century BC, Tamil Nadu has been shaped by its majority **Dravidian** population, a people of uncertain origins and physically quite different from north Indians. Their language developed separately, as did their social organization; the difference between high-caste brahmins and low-caste workers has always been more pronounced here than in the north – caste divisions that continue to dominate the state's political life. The influence of the powerful *janapadas*, the small republics and monarchies established in the north by the fourth and third centuries BC, extended as far south as the Deccan, but they made few incursions into **Dravidadesa** (Tamil country). Incorporating what are now Kerala and Tamil Nadu, Dravidadesa was ruled by three dynasties: the **Cheras**, who held sway over much of the Malabar coast (Kerala), the **Pandyas** in the far south, and the **Cholas**, whose realm stretched along the Coromandel Coast in the east. Indo–Roman trade in spices, precious stones and metals flourished at the start of the Christian era, when **St Thomas** arrived in the South, but dwindled when trade links began with Southeast Asia.

The prosperity of the early kingdoms having faded by the fourth century AD, the way was clear for the **Pallavas**, who emerged in the sixth century as leaders of a kingdom centred around Kanchipuram. By the seventh century, the successors of the first Pallava king, Simhavishnu, were engaged in battles with the southern Pandyas and the forces of the **Chalukyas**, based further west in Karnataka. However, the centuries of Pallava dominion were not marked simply by battles and territorial expansion; this was also an era of social development. **Brahmins** became the dominant community, responsible for lands and riches donated to temples. The emergence of *bhakti*, devotional worship, placed temples firmly at the centre of religious life, and the inspirational *sangam* literature of saint-poets fostered a tradition of dance and music that has become Tamil Nadu's cultural hallmark.

In the tenth and eleventh centuries, the Cholas experienced a period of profound expansion and revival; they soon held sway over much of Tamil Nadu, Andhra Pradesh, and even made inroads into Karnataka and Orissa. In the spirit of such glorious victories and power, the Cholas ploughed their new wealth into the construction of splendid and imposing temples, such as those at Gangaikondacholapuram, Kumbakonam and Thanjavur.

The **Vijayanagars**, who gained a firm footing in Hampi (Karnataka) in the fourteenth century, resisted Muslim incursions from the north and spread to cover most of South India by the sixteenth century. This prompted a new phase of architectural development in the building of new temples, the expansion of older ones and the introduction of colossal *gopuras*, or towers. In Madurai, the Vijayanagar governors, **Nayaks**, set up an independent kingdom whose impact spread as far as Tiruchirapalli.

Simultaneously, the South experienced its first significant wave of **Europeans**. First came the Portuguese, who landed in Kerala and monopolized Indian trade for about a century before being joined by the British, Dutch and French. Though mostly on cordial terms with the Indians, the Western powers soon found themselves engaged in territorial disputes. The most marked were between the French, based in **Pondicherry**, and the British, whose stronghold since 1640 had been Fort St George in **Madras** (Chennai). After battles at sea and on land, the French were confined to Pondicherry, while British ambitions reached their apex in the eighteenth century, when the East India Company occupied Bengal (1757) and made firm its bases in Bombay and Madras.

As well as rebellions against colonial rule, Tamil Nadu also saw anti-brahmin protests, in particular those led by the Justice Party in the 1920s and 1930s. **Independence** in 1947 signalled the need for state boundaries to be reorganized, and by 1956 they had been demarcated on a linguistic basis. Andhra Pradesh and Kerala were formed, along with Mysore state (later Karnataka) and the **Madras Presidency**, a slightly smaller area than that governed from Madras by the British, where Tamil was the predominant language. In 1965

Madras Presidency became **Tamil Nadu**, the latter part of its name coming from the Chola agrarian administrative units known as *nadus*.

Since Independence, Tamil Nadu's industrial sector has mushroomed. The state was a Congress stronghold until 1967, when the **DMK** (Dravida Munnetra Kazhagam), championing the lower castes and reasserting Tamil identity, won a landslide victory. The DMK flourished until the film star "**MGR**" (M.G. Ramachandran) broke away to form the **All India Anna Dravida Munnetra Kazhagam** (AIADMK), and won an easy victory in the 1977 elections. Virtually deified by his supporters, MGR remained in power until his death in 1987, when the Tamil government fell back into the hands of the DMK. Soon after, the AIADMK were back in power, led by **Sri Jayalalitha Jayaram**, an ex-film star and dancer closely associated with MGR (see p.456), who is currently enjoying her second term as the state's chief minister.

The northeast

Fazed by the fierce heat and air pollution of Chennai, most visitors escape as fast as they can, heading down the Coromandel coast to India's stone-carving capital, **Mamallapuram**, whose ancient monuments include the famous Shore Temple and a batch of extraordinary rock sculptures. En route, it's well worth jumping off the bus at the artists' village of **Cholamandal**, just beyond the city limits, and at **Dakshina Chitra**, a superb folk museum 30km south of Chennai, where traditional buildings from across South India have been beautifully reconstructed. Further inland, **Kanchipuram** is an important pilgrimage and silk-sari-weaving town, from where you can loop west towards the Andhran border on the way to **Tiruvannamalai**, a wonderfully atmospheric temple town clustered at the base of the sacred mountain, Arunachala. The sprawling ruins of **Gingee** fort stand midway between here and the coast, where you can breakfast on croissants and espresso coffee in the former French colony of **Pondicherry**. A short way north, **Auroville**, the utopian settlement founded by followers of the Sri Aurobindo Ghose's spiritual successor, The Mother, provides a New Age haven for soul-searching Westerners and an economy for the local population.

Both Mamallapuram and Pondicherry are well connected to Chennai by nail-bitingly fast bus services along the smooth coastal highway. Take care to use state buses where possible; their safety record is far better than the private ones. You can also get to Pondicherry by train, but this involves a change at the junction town of **Villupuram**, from where services are slow and relatively infrequent.

Mamallapuram (Mahabalipuram)

Scattered around the base of a colossal mound of boulders on the Bay of Bengal, **MAMALLAPURAM** (aka Mahabalipuram), 58km south of Chennai, is dominated less by the sea, as you might expect, than by the smooth volcanic rocks surrounding it. From dawn till dusk, the rhythms of chisels chipping granite resound through its sandy lanes – evidence of a stone-carving tradition that has endured since this was a major port of the Pallava dynasty, between the fifth and ninth centuries. Little is known about life in the ancient city, and it is only possible to speculate about the purpose of much of the boulder sculpture, which includes one of India's most photographed monuments, the **Shore Temple**. It does appear, however, that the friezes and shrines were not made for worship at all, but rather as a permanent showcase for the talents of local artists. Due in no small part to the maritime activities of the Pallavas, their style of art and architecture had wide-ranging influence, spreading from South India as far north as Ellora, as well as to Southeast Asia. This international cultural importance was recognized in 1995 when Mamallapuram was granted World Heritage Site status by UNESCO.

Given the location of so many stunning archeological remains right next to a long white-sand **beach**, it was almost inevitable that Mamallapuram would become a major destination for Western travellers. Over the past two decades, the town has oriented its economy to the needs of tourists, with the inevitable Kashmiri trinket sellers, bus-loads of city dwellers at the weekends, massage-wallahs and hawkers on the beach, and lots of backpacker-style budget hotels and little fish restaurants. The Shore Temple, now protected from the corrosive effects of the salt spray by a wall of fir trees and stone blocks, is a shadow of the exotic spectacle it used to be when the waves lapped its base. However, the atmosphere generated by the busy fishermen on the beach, the steady hammering of the stone carvers and the mesmerizing ancient rock-art backdrop is unique in India. Mamallapuram is worth at least a couple of days if you're heading to or from Chennai; many people actually prefer to stay here and travel into the city for the day to book tickets or pick up mail.

Mamallapuram was badly hit by the **tsunami** of December 26, 2004, though fortunately the death-toll here was very low compared to other stretches of the Tamil Nadu coastline. The beach restaurants bore the brunt of the waves, and it was these structures that saved the fishing village and hundreds of families living in the palm houses just behind. Many of the damaged cafés reopened remarkably quickly, though unfortunately many of the owners were not eligible for compensation since, according to the law, their properties had been built too close to the sea, and therefore infringed insurance regulations.

Arrival, information and getting around

Numerous daily **buses** ply to and from Chennai, Thiruvannmalai, Kanchipuram and Pondicherry. The bus stand is in the centre of the village. The nearest **railway station**, at Chengalpattu (Chingleput), 29km northeast on the bus route to Kanchipuram, is on the main north–south line, but not really a convenient access point. A **taxi** from Chennai costs around Rs1000 (or Rs600–800 from the airport); book through the tourist office here or in Chennai, or the prepaid taxi booth at Chennai airport. If you're travelling to Mamallapuram by night in a taxi, make sure the price is clearly agreed before setting off. There have been recent reports of the driver stopping short of the village and demanding more money, or claiming that the fare was per person, rather than per vehicle, as it should have been.

The **Government of Tamil Nadu Tourist Office** on Kovalam Road (Mon–Sat 10am–5.45pm; ☎04114/242232) is one of the first buildings you see in the village; it's on your left as you arrive from Chennai and is a good place to find out about local festivals, pukka hotels and bus times. Unless you're staying at one of the upmarket hotels, there are only two official places to **change money** in the village: the Indian Overseas Bank, on TK Kunda Road, or the more efficient LKP Forex on East Raja Street, a few metres down from Othavadai Street. The most reputable **travel agents** in the village are Welcome Tourrs and Travels (℡044/2846 0908) on Othavadai Street, Hi-Tours (℡04114/243260) and J.R.S. Travels (℡04114/242285), both on East Raja Street.

You will notice that almost every hotel advertises an "in-house" **masseur** – although some women have reported that the massage experience was not at all relaxing. If you want to avoid any potentially problematic situations, B. Kamaraj at *Hotel Daphne*, 17 Othavadai Cross Street (℡04114/242811) has a good reputation. Mr M. Kumar and his wife at 7/A Thirukula Street (℡04114/242112) are also highly recommended; both are fully qualified in Ayurveda and a range of massage techniques, and there's the option of a steam bath at the end of the session. Book at both places in advance; full body massages are around Rs300. The *Sea Breeze Hotel* (℡04114/243035) on Othavadai Cross Street also offers Ayurvedic massage.

Mamallapuram itself comprises little more than a few sandy roads and the sights are all within easy strolling distance. You can hire **bicycles** from shops on East Raja Street and the M.K. Cycle Centre, 28 Othavadai Street, for around Rs20 per day. **Scooters** and Enfield **motorcycles** are also available for Rs150–300 a day from Poornima Travels, next to *Moonraker's* restaurant, and through some guesthouses. **Net facilities** in the village have mushroomed; rates hover around Rs30–40 per hour, though connection speed and reliability may vary somewhat. If you need **medical treatment**, visit the Suradeep Hospital on Thirukula Street (℡04114/242390).

Accommodation

Mamallapuram is not short of **accommodation**, and bargaining is the order of the day. The bulk of cheap and mid-range lodges are within the village, a short stroll from the beach, which is the preserve of the more expensive places. Large resort hotels of varying standards sit side by side along the six-kilometre stretch of coast north of the village; they tend to be booked out by tour groups, so reserve a room well in advance. Without a taxi or bike, getting to these can prove a bit of a hassle; it's easy enough to take a rickshaw out there from the village, but not in the other direction. However, the walk back into Mamallapuram along the beach is pleasant.

Greenwoods Resort Othavadi Cross St ℡04114/243318, ℮greenwoods_resort@yahoo .com. A very friendly family-run place set in a lush garden, lovingly tended by the numerous ladies of the house. There are a/c and non-a/c rooms a stone's throw from the beach, some with private balcony, plus a pleasant balcony restaurant with street views. Extremely good value. ❷–❺
GRT Temple Bay Beach Resort ℡04114/242251, ℠www.grttemplebay.com. Great location on the beach near the village, with views of the Shore Temple. The thatched, beachside cottages have sea-facing balconies, and there are also huge rooms in the main building, plus a swimming pool and restaurant. Rates start at $130. ❾

Ideal Beach Resort 5km from town, Kovalam Rd ℡04114/242240, ℠www.idealresort.com. Comfortable cottages near the Tiger Cave, and a large pool and pleasant alfresco restaurant on site. Popular with overland tour groups, so book well ahead during the high season. ❼–❾
Mamalla Beach Resort 108 Kovalam Rd, 2.5km north of town ℡04114/242375, ℮mbresort@vsnl .net. Good-value resort with spacious, well-decorated chalets with attached bathrooms and verandas. There's a choice of a/c and non a/c rooms, plus a decent restaurant and games area, but no pool. ❺–❻
Mamalla Heritage 104 East Raja St ℡04114/242060, ℻242160. Efficient modern hotel on the main drag through the village, with

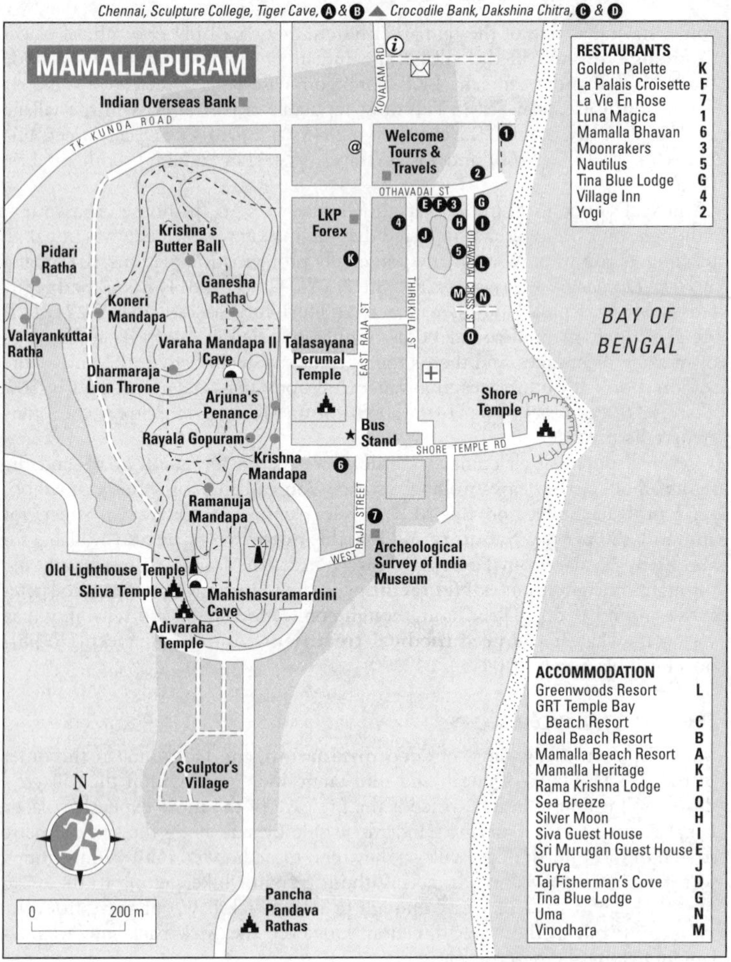
Chennai, Sculpture College, Tiger Cave, A & B
Crocodile Bank, Dakshina Chitra, C & D
MAMALLAPURAM
Indian Overseas Bank
TK KUNDA ROAD
KOVALAM RD
Welcome Tourrs & Travels
OTHAVADAI ST
LKP Forex
Krishna's Butter Ball
Pidari Ratha
Ganesha Ratha
Koneri Mandapa
Valayankuttai Ratha
Varaha Mandapa II Cave
Talasayana Perumal Temple
EAST RAJA ST
THIRUKULA ST
OTHAVADAI CROSS ST
BAY OF BENGAL
Dharmaraja Lion Throne
Arjuna's Penance
Shore Temple
Bus Stand
Rayala Gopuram
SHORE TEMPLE RD
Krishna Mandapa
Ramanuja Mandapa
WEST RAJA STREET
Archeological Survey of India Museum
Old Lighthouse Temple
Shiva Temple
Mahishasuramardini Cave
Adivaraha Temple
Sculptor's Village
Pancha Pandava Rathas
N
0 200 m
Pondicherry & Tirukalikundram (14 km)
RESTAURANTS
Golden Palette K
La Palais Croisette F
La Vie En Rose 7
Luna Magica 1
Mamalla Bhavan 6
Moonrakers 3
Nautilus 5
Tina Blue Lodge G
Village Inn 4
Yogi 2
ACCOMMODATION
Greenwoods Resort L
GRT Temple Bay Beach Resort C
Ideal Beach Resort B
Mamalla Beach Resort A
Mamalla Heritage K
Rama Krishna Lodge F
Sea Breeze O
Silver Moon H
Siva Guest House I
Sri Murugan Guest House E
Surya J
Taj Fisherman's Cove D
Tina Blue Lodge G
Uma N
Vinodhara M

spotless and comfortable a/c rooms (with fridge and TV) overlooking a courtyard, and a very good restaurant. 5

Rama Krishna Lodge 8 Othavadai St ⓣ04114/242331. Clean, well-maintained rooms in the heart of the village, all with bathrooms (but no a/c), set round a courtyard filled with pot plants; the newest ones are on the top storey and have sea views. There's a back-up generator, too, and they often have vacancies when everywhere else is full. 1

Sea Breeze Othavadai Cross St ⓣ04114/243035, ⓔmbresort@hotmail.com. The only bona fide beach resort in town, featuring comfy and spacious rooms (singles are particularly good value) with a choice of a/c or non a/c and a smart new pool (open to non-residents for Rs150). 4–6

Silver Moon 2/A Othavadai Cross St ⓣ04114/243644, ⓔsilver_moonguesthouse@yahoo.com. Very clean and friendly lodge with cosy attached rooms and a small leafy courtyard. 2

Siva Guest House 2 Othavadai Cross Rd ⓣ04114/243234, ⓔsivaguesthouse@hotmail.com. Clean, tidy and good-value rooms in a new guest-house with choice of a/c and non a/c rooms. 2–4

Sri Murugan Guest House 42 Othavadai St ⓣ04114/242552. Small and peaceful place, with courteous service, clean non a/c rooms and a rooftop restaurant. One of the nicest options in the area. 1–2

Surya Thirukula St ☏04114/242292, ℱ242492. Lakeside hotel set in a leafy compound next to a sculpture school and gallery. There's a range of rooms, some with a/c and balconies (mosquito nets are available) and a small pool (non-guests Rs100). ❸–❺

Taj Fisherman's Cove Covelong Beach, 30min drive north of Mamallapuram ☏04114/272304, ◉www.tajhotels.com. Large, immaculate hotel with swimming pool, spa, tennis courts and several dining options. Accommodation is either in rooms in the main building (from $180); luxury detached circular cottages dotted around the gardens ($219); or similar cottages but closer to the beach (from $247). ❾

Tina Blue Lodge Othavadai St ☏04114/242319, ℮stevesan@yahoo.com. Established family guest-house with simple turquoise and whitewashed rooms (all en suite with mosquito nets) and a good rooftop restaurant (see p.483). ❷

Uma Guest House 11 Othavadai Cross St ☏04114/242697. Quiet and immaculate hotel with a choice of good-value a/c and non a/c rooms. Some have sea views, and the pricier ones come with breezy private balconies and swing chairs (but no sea view). ❷–❺

Vinodhara 4 Othavadai Cross St ☏04114/242694, ℮vinodhara@yahoo.com. Large place with a range of immaculately tiled, good-value rooms (some with a/c) cooled by sea breezes. You can see the Shore Temple from the top floor. ❷–❺

The Monuments

Mamallapuram's monuments divide into four categories: open-air **bas-reliefs**, **temples**, man-made **caves** and **rathas** ("chariots", carved in situ from single boulders to resemble temples or the chariots used in temple processions). The famous bas-reliefs, **Arjuna's Penance** and the **Krishna Mandapa**, adorn massive rocks near the centre of the village, while the beautiful **Shore Temple** presides over the beachfront. Sixteen man-made caves in different stages of completion are scattered through the area; the most complete of the nine *rathas* are in a group, named after the five Pandava brothers of the Mahabharata.

The **entrance fee** for the Shore Temple and the Pancha Pandava Rathas is now $5 [Rs10], payable at the ticket booth outside either monument. The ticket is valid for one day only (sunrise–sunset), and will give you access to both sites. Alternatively, you can peek through the wire-mesh fence at all the restricted access sights, and the bas-reliefs are free.

The Shore Temple

East of the village, a distinctive silhouette above the crashing ocean, Mamal-lapuram's **Shore Temple** (see above for entrance details) dates from the early eighth century and is considered to be the earliest stone-built temple in South India. The design of its two finely carved towers was profoundly influential: it was exported across South India and eventually abroad to Southeast Asia. Today, due to the combined forces of wind, salt and sand, much of the detailed carving has eroded, giving the whole temple a soft, rounded appearance.

The taller of the towers is raised above a cell that faces out to sea – don't be surprised to see mischievous monkeys crouching inside. Approached from the west through two low-walled enclosures lined with small Nandi (bull) figures, the temple comprises two *lingam* shrines (one facing east, the other west), and a third shrine between them housing an image of the reclining Vishnu. Recent excavations, revealing a tank containing a structured stone column thought to have been a lantern, and a large Varaha (boar incarnation of Vishnu) aligned with the Vishnu shrine, suggest that the area was sacred long before the Pallavas chose it as a temple site.

The Krishna Mandapa and Arjuna's Penance

A little to the west of the village centre, off Shore Temple Road, the enormous bas-relief known as the **Krishna Mandapa** shows Krishna raising Mount

Govardhana aloft in one hand. The sculptor's original intention must have been for the rock above Krishna to represent the mountain, but the seventeenth-century Vijayanagar addition of a columned *mandapa*, or entrance hall, prevents a clear view of the carving. Krishna is also depicted seated milking a cow, and standing playing the flute. Other figures are *gopas* and *gopis*, the cowboys and girls of his pastoral youth. Lions sit to the left – one with a human face – and above them is a bull.

Another bas-relief, **Arjuna's Penance** (also referred to as the "Descent of the Ganges") is a few metres north, opposite the modern Talasayana Perumal Temple. The surface of this rock erupts with detailed carving, most notably the endearing and naturalistic renditions of animals. A family of elephants dominates the right side, with tiny offspring asleep beneath a great tusker. Further still to the right, separate from the great rock, is a freestanding sculpture of an adult monkey grooming its young.

On the left-hand side, Arjuna, one of the Pandava brothers and a consummate archer, is shown standing on one leg. He is looking at the midday sun through a prism formed by his hands, meditating on Shiva, who is represented by a nearby statue, fashioned by Arjuna himself. The *Shiva Purana* tells that Arjuna made the journey to a forest on the banks of the Ganges to do penance, in the hope that Shiva would part with his favourite weapon, the *pashupatashastra*, a magic staff or arrow. Shiva eventually materialized in the guise of Kirata, a wild forest-dweller, and picked a fight with Arjuna over a boar they both claimed to have shot. Arjuna only realized he was dealing with the deity after his attempts to drub the wild man proved futile; narrowly escaping death at the playful hand of Shiva, he was finally rewarded with the weapon. Not far away, mimicking Arjuna's devout pose, an emaciated (presumably ascetic) cat stands on its hind legs, surrounded by mice.

To the right of Arjuna, a natural cleft represents the **Ganges**, complete with *nagas* – water spirits in the form of cobras. Near the bottom, a fault in the rock that broke a *naga* received a quick fix of cement in the 1920s. Evidence of a cistern and channels remain at the top, which at one time must have carried water to flow down the cleft, simulating the great river. It's not known if there was some ritual purpose to all this, or whether it was simply an elaborate spectacle to impress visitors. You may see sudden movements among the carved animals: lazing goats often join the permanent features.

Ganesh ratha and Varaha Cave

Just north of Arjuna's Penance a path leads west to a single monolith, the **Ganesh ratha** – some say that its image of Ganesh was installed at the instigation of England's King George V. The sculpture at one end, of a protecting demon with a tricorn headdress, is reminiscent of the Indus Valley civilization's 4000-year-old horned figure known as the "proto-Shiva".

Behind Arjuna's Penance, southwest of the Ganesh *ratha*, is the **Varaha Mandapa II Cave**, whose entrance hall has two pillars with horned lion-bases and a cell flanked by two *dvarpalas*, or guardians. One of four **panels** shows the boar-incarnation of Vishnu, who stands with one foot resting on the *naga* snake-king as he lifts a diminutive Prithvi – the earth – from the primordial ocean. Another is of Gajalakshmi, the goddess Lakshmi seated on a lotus being bathed by a pair of elephants. Trivikrama, the dwarf brahmin who becomes huge and bestrides the world in three steps to defeat the demon king Bali, is shown in another panel, and finally a four-armed Durga is depicted in another.

A little way north of Arjuna's Penance, precipitously balanced on the top of a ridge, is a massive, natural, almost spherical boulder called **Krishna's Butter Ball**. Picnickers and goats often rest in its perilous-looking shade.

The lighthouses and the Mahishasuramardini Cave

South of Arjuna's Penance at the highest point in an area of steep paths, unfinished temples, ruins, scampering monkeys and massive rocks, the **New Lighthouse** affords fine views east to the Shore Temple and west across paddy fields and flat lands littered with rocks. Next to it, the **Olakanesvara** ("flame-eyed" Shiva), or **Old Lighthouse Temple**, used as a lighthouse until the beginning of the twentieth century, dates from the Rajasimha period (674–800 AD) and contains no image.

Nestling between the two lighthouses is the **Mahishasuramardini Cave**, whose central image portrays Shiva and Parvati with the child Murugan seated on Parvati's lap. Shiva's right foot rests on the back of the bull Nandi, and Parvati sits casually, leaning on her left hand. On the left wall, beyond an empty cell, a panel depicts Vishnu reclining on the serpent, his attitude of repose contrasted with the weapon-brandishing demons, Madhu and Kaithaba. Other figures seek Vishnu's permission to chase them. Opposite, in one of the most celebrated sculptures in Indian art, an intricately carved panel shows the eight-armed goddess Durga as Mahishasuramardini, the "crusher" of the buffalo demon Mahishasura. The story goes that Mahishasura became so powerful that he took possession of heaven, causing great misery to its inhabitants. To deal with such a dangerous foe, Vishnu and Shiva hit upon the idea of combining all the gods' powers into a single entity. This done, fiery jets appeared, from which emerged the terrifying "mother of the universe", Durga. In the ensuing battle, Durga caught Mahishasura with a noose, and he changed into a lion; she beheaded the lion, and he transformed into a human wielding a sword. Then she fired off a flight of arrows, only to see him turn into a huge trumpeting elephant; she cut off his trunk, whereupon the buffalo returned. Now furious, Durga partook of her favourite beverage: blood, "the supreme wine". Climbing on top of the buffalo, she kicked him about the neck and stabbed him with her trident. The impact of her foot forced him halfway out of his own mouth, only to be beheaded by his own sword, at which point he fell. The panel shows Durga riding a lion, in the midst of the struggle. Accompanied by dwarf *ganas*, she wields a bow and other weapons; Mahishasura, equipped with a club, can be seen to the right, in flight with fellow demons.

The tiny **Archeological Survey of India Museum** (daily 9am–5.30pm; Rs2, camera Rs10) on West Raja Street, near the lighthouse, has a rather motley collection of unlabelled Pallava sculpture found in and around Mamallapuram.

Pancha Pandava rathas

In a sandy compound 1.5km south of the village centre stands the stunning group of monoliths known – for no historical reason – as the **Pancha Pandava rathas** (see p.479 for entrance details), the five chariots of the Pandavas. Dating from the period of Narasimhavarman I (c.630–670 AD), the *rathas* consist of five separate free-standing sculptures built in imitation of traditional temples, set alongside some beautifully carved life-size animals.

The "architecture" of the *rathas* reflects the variety of styles employed in temple building of the time, and stands almost as a model for much subsequent development in the **Dravida**, or southern, style. The Arjuna, Bhima and Dharmaraja *rathas* show strong affinities with the Dravidian temples at Pattadakal in Karnataka. Carving was always executed from top to bottom, enabling the artists to work on the upper parts with no fear of damaging anything below. Any unfinished elements there may be are always in the lower areas. Intriguingly, it's thought that the *rathas* were never used for worship. A Hindu temple is only complete when the essential pot-shaped finial, the *kalasha*, is put in place

– which would have presented a physical impossibility for the artisans, as the *kalasha* would have had to have been sculpted first. *Kalashas* can be seen next to two of the *rathas* (Dharmaraja and Arjuna), but as part of the base, as if it was intended to put them in place at a later date.

The southernmost and tallest of the *rathas*, named after the eldest of the Pandavas, is the pyramidal **Dharmaraja**. Set on a square base, the upper part comprises a series of diminishing storeys, each with a row of pavilions. Four corner blocks, each with two panels and standing figures, are broken up by two pillars and pilasters supported by squatting lions. Figures on the panels include Ardhanarishvara (Shiva and female consort in one figure), Brahma, the king Narasimhavarman I, and Harihara (Shiva and Vishnu combined). The central tier includes sculptures of Shiva Gangadhara holding a rosary with the adoring river goddess Ganga by his side and one of the earliest representations in Tamil Nadu of the dancing Shiva, Nataraja, who became all-important in the region. Alongside, the **Bhima** *ratha*, the largest of the group, is the least complete, with tooling marks all over its surface. Devoid of carved figures, the upper storeys, as in the Dharmaraja, feature false windows and repeated pavilion-shaped ornamentation. Its oblong base is very rare for a shrine.

The Arjuna and Draupadi *rathas* share a base. Behind the **Arjuna**, the most complete of the entire group and very similar to the Dharmaraja, stands a superb unfinished sculpture of Shiva's bull Nandi. **Draupadi** is unique in terms of rock-cut architecture, with a roof that appears to be based on a straw thatched hut (a design later copied at Chidambaram; see p.505). There's an image of Durga inside, but the figure of her lion vehicle outside is aligned side-on and not facing the image, a convincing reason to suppose this was not a real temple. To the west, close to a life-size carving of an elephant, the *ratha* named after the twin brothers **Nakula** and **Sahadeva** is, unusually, apsidal ended. The elephant may be a visual pun on this, as the Sanskrit technical name for a curved ended building is *gajaprstika*, "elephant's backside".

The road out to the *rathas* resounds with incessant hammering and chiselling from sculptors' workshops. Much of their work is excellent, and well worth a browse – the sculptors produce statues for temples all over the world and are used to shipping large-scale pieces. Some of the artists are very young; children often do the donkey work on large pieces, which are then completed by master craftsmen.

Eating

Mamallapuram is crammed with small restaurants, most of which specialize in **seafood** – tiger prawns, pomfret, tuna, shark and lobster – usually served marinated and grilled with chips and salad. The upmarket hotels charge a lot more for the same variety of dishes, and lack the atmosphere of the village. Wherever you eat, avoid a nasty shock at the end of your meal by establishing exactly how much your fish, or lobster, is to cost in advance, as the price quoted is often just the cost per kilo.

As this is a traveller's hangout, there also are numerous places offering the usual array of pasta, pancakes, brown bread and bland Indian dishes. If you want to enjoy real Indian food – including full-on fiery fish curry – head over to the bus stand where there are some good joints serving excellent, spicy thalis and *dosas*. Likewise, for breakfast you can get a plate of steaming *iddlis* from the carts at the station for less than Rs10. **Beer** is widely available, but it's on the pricey side (Rs80–90).

Golden Palette *Mamalla Heritage Hotel*, 104 East Raja St. Blissfully cool café with a/c and tinted windows, serving possibly the best veg food in the village – Rs55 thalis at lunchtime, north Indian tandoori in the courtyard in the evenings, and wonderful ice-cream sundaes. Worth popping in just for a coffee to beat the heat.

La Palais Croisette *Rama Krishna Hotel*, 8 Othavadai St. A popular Nepali-run rooftop restaurant with variations on noodles, salads and seafood, plus a range of pancakes.

La Vie En Rose West Raja St, next to the sculpture museum at the south end of the village. Pleasant garden location offering a Western-oriented menu, plus a few unusual salads, pasta dishes (the spaghetti's great) and chicken specialities.

Luna Magica On the beach, 100m north of Othavadai St. Top-notch seafood, including tiger prawns and lobster which are kept alive in a tank before being served up in a rich tomato, butter and garlic sauce. There are also plenty of less expensive dishes – including a good fish curry and "sizzlers" – cold beer, and a passable sangria made with sweet Chennai red wine.

Mamalla Bhavan Shore Temple Rd, opposite the bus stand. Popular pure-veg joint, and usually very busy. Equally good for *iddli-wada* breakfasts, evening *dosas* and other snacks, and there are unlimited lunchtime thalis for Rs22–32. Open in evening 6.30pm–9.30pm.

Moonrakers Othavadai St. Cool jazz and blues sounds, great fresh seafood, chess sets and slick service ensure this place is filled year round with foreign tourists.

Nautilus Othavadai Cross St. High-quality but reasonably priced eatery, run by an amiable French chef who turns out fine soups, meat, seafood and veg dishes, grilled or with an array of sauces, plus the usual travellers' favourites. Also does a good espresso.

Tina Blue Lodge Othavadai St. Reasonable Indian and continental food – try the excellent honey-banana pancakes – served on a sociable rooftop terrace.

Village Inn Thirukula Street. This tiny thatched eatery (with a couple of outdoor tables) serves grilled seafood and a superb butter-fried chicken in a tomato-garlic sauce.

Yogi Othavadai St. Run by a French and Indian couple, this welcoming and relaxed place is a good spot to sit and chill, with good coffee, lassis, salads and a small range of main courses.

Around Mamallapuram

The sandy hinterland and flat estuarine paddy fields around Mamallapuram harbour a handful of worthwhile sights. A short way north along the main highway, the **Government College of Sculpture** and elaborately carved **Tiger Cave** can easily be reached by bicycle. The **Crocodile Bank**, where rare reptiles from across South Asia are bred for release into the wild, and **Dakshina Chitra**, a museum devoted to South Indian architecture and crafts, are a bus ride away, or you could hire a moped for the day. Further north still, the **Cholamandal Artists' Village** is a showcase for less traditional arts that's best visited en route to or from Chennai. Finally, a good target for a day-trip inland is the hilltop temple at **Tirukalikundram**, west of Mamallapuram across a swathe of unspoilt farmland.

Government College of Sculpture and the Tiger Cave

A visit to the **Government College of Sculpture**, 2km north of Mamallapuram on the Kovalam (Covelong) Road (℡04114/242261; free) gives a fascinating insight into the processes of sculpture training. You can watch anything from preliminary drawing, with its strict rules regarding proportion and iconography, through to the execution of sculpture, both in wood and stone, in the classical Hindu tradition. Contact the college office to make an appointment.

A further 3km north along Kovalam Road from the college, set amid trees close to the sea, the extraordinary **Tiger Cave** (sunrise–sunset; free) contains a shrine to Durga, approached by a flight of steps that passes two subsidiary cells. Following the line of an irregularly shaped rock, the cave is remarkable for its elaborate exterior, which features multiple lion heads surrounding the entrance to the main cell. If you sit for long enough, the section on the left with seated figures in niches above two elephants begins to resemble an enormous owl.

Crocodile Bank

The **Crocodile Bank** (Tues–Sun 8am–6pm; Rs20, camera Rs10, video Rs75) at Vadanemmeli, 14km north of Mamallapuram on the road to Chennai, was set up in 1976 by the American zoologist Romulus Whittaker to protect and breed indigenous crocodiles. The bank has been so successful (expanding from fifteen crocs to five thousand in the first fifteen years) that its remit now extends to saving endangered species, such as turtles and lizards, from around the world.

Low-walled enclosures in its garden compound house hundreds of inscrutable crocodiles, soaking in ponds or sunning themselves on the banks. Breeds include the fish-eating, knobbly-nosed gharial, and the world's largest species, the saltwater *crocodylus porosus*, which can grow to 8m in length. You can watch feeding time at about 4.30pm on Monday or Thursday or have your own brief feeding session anytime for a fee of Rs20. The temptation to take photos is tempered by the sight of those hungry saurians clambering over each other to snap up the chopped flesh, within inches of the top of the wall.

Another important field of work is conducted with the collaboration of local Irula people, whose traditional expertise is with snakes. Cobras are brought to the bank for **venom collection**, to be used in the treatment of snakebites. Elsewhere, snakes are repeatedly "milked" until they die, but here at the bank only a limited amount is taken from each snake, enabling them to return to the wild. This section costs an extra Rs5.

Coastal route buses #117 and #118 stop at the entrance.

Dakshina Chitra

Occupying a patch of sun-baked sand dunes midway between Chennai and Mamallapuram, **Dakshina Chitra** (daily except Tues 10am–6pm; Rs50), literally "Vision of the South", is one of India's best-conceived folk museums, devoted to the rich architectural and artistic heritage of Kerala, Karnataka, Andhra Pradesh and Tamil Nadu. The museum was set up by the Chennai Craft Foundation with support from local government and American sponsors. Apart from giving you the chance to look around some immaculately restored old buildings, a permanent display exposes visitors to many disappearing traditions of the region, from tribal fertility cults and *Ayyannar* field deities to pottery and leather shadow puppets.

Visits kick off with a short introductory video, followed by a **guided tour** of the campus, where a selection of traditional buildings from across India have been painstakingly reconstructed using authentic materials. Highlights include an airy Tamil brahmins' dwelling; a Chettinad merchant's mansion filled with Burmese furniture and Chinese lacquerware; a Syrian Christian home from the backwaters of Kerala with a fragrant jackwood interior; and a north Keralan house with separate rooms for the women – a unique feature reflecting the area's strongly matrilineal society. Exhibitions attached to the various structures convey the environmental and cultural diversity of the south, most graphically expressed in a wonderful textile collection featuring antique silk and cotton saris from various castes and regions. There is also a pottery demonstration, where you can try your hand at throwing clay on a

Tamil wheel, and a memorable slapstick shadow puppet (*tolu bommalaatam*) display, as well as a separate restaurant with fixed price meals (Rs175).

Cholamandal Artists' Village

Tucked away on the scruffy southern edge of Chennai, the **Cholamandal Artists' Village** (daily 10am–7pm; free) was established in the mid-1960s to encourage contemporary Indian art. In a country where visual culture is so comprehensively dominated by convention, fostering innovation and artistic experimentation proved no easy feat. Despite an initially hostile response from the Madrasi establishment (who allegedly regarded the tropical storm that destroyed the artists' first settlement as an act of nemesis), the village has prospered. Today, Cholamandal's thirty-strong community has several studios and a large gallery filled with paintings, sketches, sculpture and metalwork, and a shop selling work produced here. For those with more than a passing interest in the village, there's also a small **guesthouse** (T044/2492 6092; ❷).

Tirukalikundram

The village of **TIRUKALIKUNDRAM**, 16km west of Mamallapuram on the road to Kanchipuram, is locally famous for its hilltop Shiva temple. A pair of white Egyptian vultures (*Neophron percnopterus*), believed to be reincarnated saints on their way between Varanasi and Rameshwaram, used to swoop down at noon to be fed by the temple priests. No one knew how long these visits had been going on, nor why the vultures suddenly stopped coming in 1994. Their absence, however, was taken as a bad omen and, sure enough, that year massive cyclones ravaged the Tamil Nadu coast.

Four hundred hot stone steps need to be scaled to reach the top, but don't let that – or the effort required to disabuse various individuals, including the priests, of the impression that you need their multifarious services and paid company – deter you. Once on the hilltop, the views are sublime, especially at sunset. The temple is closed between 1pm and 4pm.

Regular **buses** run to Tirukalikundram from Mamallapuram, en route to Kanchipuram, but it's more fun to rent a moped or motorcycle for the trip (see p.477). You could conceivably pedal out here, too (the route is flat all the way), but you'll need to start out early in the day to avoid the worst of the heat.

Kanchipuram

Ask any Tamil what **KANCHIPURAM** (aka "Kanchi") is famous for, and they'll probably say silk saris, shrines and saints – in that order. A dynastic capital throughout the medieval era, it remains one of the seven holiest cities in the subcontinent, sacred to both Shaivites and Vaishnavites, and among the few surviving centres of goddess worship in the south. Year round, pilgrims pour through for a quick puja stop on the Tirupati tour circuit and, if they can afford it, a spot of shopping in the sari emporia. For non-Hindu visitors, however, Kanchipuram holds less appeal. Although the temples are undeniably impressive, the town itself is unremittingly hot and dusty, although there's some reasonable accommodation if you want to stay overnight. Alternatively, it's possible to visit as a rather long **day-trip** from either Chennai or Mamallapuram, both a two-hour bus ride east.

The Town and temples

Established by the **Pallava** kings in the fourth century AD, Kanchipuram served as their capital for five hundred years, and continued to flourish throughout the Chola, Pandya and Vijayanagar eras. Under the Pallavas, it was an important scholastic forum, and a meeting point for Jain, Buddhist and Hindu cultures. Its **temples** dramatically reflect this enduring political prominence, spanning the years from the peak of Pallava construction to the seventeenth century, when the ornamentation of the *gopuras* and pillared halls was at its most elaborate (for more on Tamil Nadu's temples, see p.685). All can be easily reached by foot, bike or rickshaw, and are closed daily between noon and 4pm. You'll be offered a panoply of services – from sanctuary priests, shoe bearers, guides, women giving out food for fish in the temple tanks, and well-trained temple elephants that bless you with their trunks – so go prepared with a pocketful of change. Always animated, the temples really come alive during major festivals such as the **Car Festival** (May) and **Navaratri** (Oct/Nov).

Ekambareshvara Temple

Kanchipuram's largest temple and most important Shiva shrine, the **Ekambareshvara Temple** (daily 6am–noon & 4pm–8pm; camera Rs10, video Rs20) – also known as Ekambaranatha – on the north side of town, is easily identified by its colossal whitewashed *gopuras*, which rise to almost 60m. The main temple contains some Pallava work, but was mostly constructed in the sixteenth and seventeenth centuries, and stands within a vast walled enclosure beside some smaller shrines and a large fish-filled water tank.

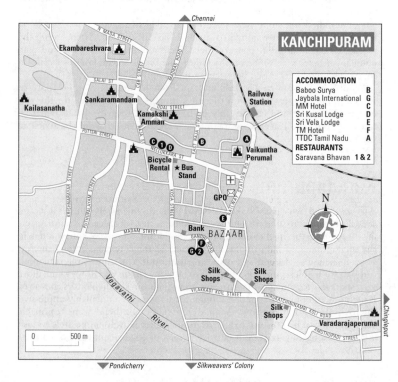

The entrance is through a high-arched passageway beneath an elaborate *gopura* in the south wall. It leads to an open courtyard and a majestic "thousand-pillared hall" (*kalyan mandapa*), whose slightly decaying grey stone columns are modelled as nubile maidens, animals and deities. This hall faces the tank to the north and a sanctuary to the west protecting an "earth" *lingam* (one of five types of *lingam* in Tamil Nadu that represent the elements), the emblem of Shiva here in his form as **Kameshvara**, or "Lord of Desire". Legend connects it with the goddess **Kamakshi** (Shiva's consort, "Wanton-Eyed"), who angered Shiva by playfully covering his eyes and plunging the world into darkness. Shiva reprimanded her by sending her to fashion a *lingam* from the earth in his honour; once it was completed, Kamakshi found she could not move it. Local myths tell of a great flood that swept over Kanchipuram and destroyed the temples, but did not move the *lingam*, to which Kamakshi clung so fiercely that marks of her breasts and bangles were imprinted upon it.

Behind the sanctum, accessible from the covered hallway around it, an eerie bare hall lies beneath a profusely carved *gopura*, and in the courtyard a venerable **mango tree** represents the tree under which Shiva and Kamakshi were married. This union is celebrated during a festival each April, when many couples are married in the *kalyan mandapa*. The four branches of the tree are supposed to yield different-tasting fruit, believed to symbolize the four Vedas, which are collected by the temple priests and given to women coming here to petition for fertility. For Rs50 you can perform a special problem-solving puja: walk three times around the tree to sort out financial difficulties or to find a husband for your daughter. Finally, don't miss the temple's other "thousand-pillared" *mandapa*, beneath the *gopura* on the west wall, which houses the extraordinary **Pictorial Depication of Historical Episodes in Sound and Light by Electronic Meriods** (sic), a collection of bizarre gizmos elucidating the basic tenets of Hinduism. One involves thrusting your head into a contraption to hear electronically triggered excerpts from the *Vedas*.

The somewhat neglected twelfth-century **Jvaraheshvari temple**, in leafy gardens to the south, is the only Chola (tenth–twelfth centuries) structure in Kanchipuram not to have been modified and overshadowed by later buildings. Unlike the Pallava constructions, it is built of hard grey stone and its sculpted pyramidal roof is an early form of the *gopuras* used extensively by the Pandyas.

Sankaramandam

Kanchipuram is the seat of a line of holy men bearing the title **Acharya**, whose lineage dates back to the saint Adi Sankaracharya. The 68th Acharya, the highly revered Sri Chandrasekharendra Sarasvati Swami, died in January 1994 at the age of 101. Buried in the sitting position, as is the custom for great Hindu sages, his mortal remains are enshrined in a *samadhi* at the **Sankaramandam**, a *math* (monastery for Hindu renunciates) down the road from the Ekambreshvara Temple. The present incumbent, the 69th Acharya, has his quarters on the opposite side of a marble meditation hall to the shrine, and gives *darshan* to the public during the morning and early evening, when the *math*'s two huge elephants are given offerings. Lined with old photographs from the life of the former swami, with young brahmin students chanting Sanskrit verses in the background, it's a typically Tamil blend of simple sanctity and garish modern glitz.

Kailasanatha Temple

The **Kailasanatha Temple**, the oldest structure in Kanchipuram and the finest example of Pallava architecture in South India, is situated among several low-roofed houses just over 1km west of the town centre. Built by the Pallava king Rajasimha early in the eighth century, its intimate size and simple carving distinguish it from the town's later temples. Usually quieter than its neighbours, the shrine becomes the focus of vigorous celebrations during the **Mahashivar-atri festival** each March. Like its contemporary, the Shore Temple at Mamallapuram, it is built of soft sandstone, but its relatively sheltered position inland has spared it from wind and sand erosion, and it remains remarkably intact, despite some rather clumsy recent renovation work.

Topped with a modest pyramidal spire, the small temple stands within a rectangular courtyard, enclosed by a wall inlaid with tiny meditation chambers and sculpted with images of Shiva, Parvati and their sons, as well as rearing mythical lions (*yalis*). On the south side of the spire Shiva is depicted as a begging ascetic (Bhikshatana); on the north he's in the pose of the dance of destruction (Samhara–Tandava). Walls in the dim interior bear traces of frescoes, and the ceilings are etched with religious verses written in Pali. The sanctum, inaccessible to non-Hindus, shelters a sturdy sixteen-sided black *lingam,* guarded by elephant-headed Ganesh and Shiva's other son, Skanda, the god of war, with whom Rajasimha was closely associated. Double walls were built round the sanctuary to support the weighty tower above; the passage between them is used as a circumambulatory path as part of the ritual worship of Shiva.

Kamakshi Amman Temple

Built during Pallava supremacy and modified in the fourteenth and seventeenth centuries, the **Kamakshi Amman Temple**, northwest of the bus stand, combines several styles, with an ancient central shrine, gates from the Vijayanagar period, and high, heavily sculpted creamy *gopuras* set above the gateways in a later period. To the right of the central shrine, inaccessible to non-Hindus, a raised *mandapa* is now an art gallery, housing many pictures of the recent **Acharyas** (see p.487). This is one of India's three holiest shrines to Shakti, Shiva's cosmic energy depicted in female form, usually as his consort. The goddess Kamakshi, a local form of Parvati, shown with a sugar-cane bow and arrows of flowers, is honoured as having lured Shiva to Kanchipuram, where they were married, and thus having forged the connection between the local community and the god. Inside the gate a couple of temple elephants bestow gentle blessings with their trunks upon the bowed heads of pilgrims in exchange for donations to the mahout.

In February or March, deities are wheeled to the temple in huge wooden "cars", decked with robed statues and swaying plantain leaves – the intricately carved "cars" are kept behind bars on Gandhi Road during the rest of the year.

Vaikuntha Perumal Temple

Built shortly after the Kailasanatha temple at the end of the eighth century, the smaller **Vaikuntha Perumal Temple**, a few hundred metres south of the railway station, is dedicated to Vishnu. Its lofty carved *vimana* (towered sanctuary) crowns three shrines containing images of Vishnu, stacked one on top of the other. Unusual scenes carved in the walls enclosing the temple yard depict events central to Pallava history, among them coronations, court gatherings and battles with the Chalukyas who ruled the regions to the northwest. The temple's pillared entrance hall was added by Vijayanagar rulers five centuries later, and is very different in style, with far more ornate sculpting.

Varadarajaperumal Temple

The Vaishnavite **Varadarajaperumal Temple** stands within a huge walled complex in the far southeast of town, guarded by high gates topped with

△ Temple detail, Chennai

gopuras. The inner sanctuary boasts superb carving and well-preserved paintings, but non-Hindus only have access to the outer courtyards and the elaborate sixteenth-century pillared hall close to the Western entrance gate. The outer columns of this *mandapa* are sculpted as lions and warriors on rearing horses, to celebrate the military vigour of the Vijayanagars, who believed their prowess was inspired by the power of Shakti.

Practicalities

Flanked on the south by the Vegavathi River, Kanchipuram lies 70km southwest of Chennai and about the same distance from the coast. **Buses** from Chennai, Mamallapuram and Chengalpattu stop at the stand in the town centre on Raja Street. The sleepy **railway station** in the northeast sees just four daily passenger services from Chengalpattu (two of them originating in Chennai) and two from Anakkonam.

As most of the main roads are wide and traffic rarely unmanageable, the best way to **get around** Kanchi is by **bicycle** – available for minimal rates (Rs2/hr) at stalls west and northeast of the bus stand. The town's vegetable markets, hotels, restaurants and bazaars are concentrated in the centre of town, near the bus stand. The nearest official **foreign exchange** places are in Chennai and Mamallapuram, though a couple of hotels accept payment by credit card or cash dollars.

Accommodation and eating

There's not a great choice of **accommodation** in Kanchipuram, though the recent addition of a couple of mid-range places has improved matters. Most places are reasonably clean and comfortable and some have their own **restaurants**. The best place to eat in town is *Saravana Bhavan* (daily 6am–10pm), an offshoot of the famous Chennai chain of pure veg restaurants. There are branches on Gandhi Road and Nellukkara Street, both of which offer superb Rs30 "meals" at lunch time, a long list of delicious South Indian snacks and good Coorg coffee the rest of the day and are marginally less bedlam-like than the other "meals" joints in the centre, which tend to get swamped by shaven-headed pilgrims from Tirupati.

Baboo Surya 85 East Raja St ☎04112/222556, ⓦwww.hotelbaboosoorya.com. One of Kanchi's top hotels: large and modern with immaculate a/c and non-a/c rooms, glass lift, a good veg/tandoori restaurant and a chill a/c bar. Ask for a room with temple view. ❸–❹

Jaybala International 504 Gandhi Rd (just off the road at the end of a short narrow drive), ☎04112/224348, www.hoteljaybala.com. Slightly more old-fashioned than the *Baboo Surya*, with large clean rooms (some with a/c) and lower tariffs. They also offer good-value single rates, and the good *Saravana Bhavan* restaurant is on the doorstep. ❸–❹

MM Hotel 65/66 Nellukkara St ☎04112/230032, ⓔinfo@mmhotels.com. New, very clean mid-range option, with good-sized and good-value rooms. It's also next to a branch of the *Saravana Bhavan* restaurant, who provide room-service food. Credit cards accepted. ❸–❹

Sri Kusal Lodge 68C Nellukkara St ☎04112/223342. Very friendly lodge, though the rooms (some with TV) open onto a rather dismal corridor. Good English spoken. ❶–❸.

Sri Vela Lodge Railway Station Rd ☎04112/221504. Cheap but slightly grubby lodge offering larger-than-average rooms with attached shower-toilets and fans, but still airless. Busy "meals" restaurant downstairs. ❶–❷

TM Hotel 487 Gandhi Rd, ☎04112/225250, ⓕ224263. Centrally a/c hotel with clean, decent-sized rooms. There are also two restaurants and a bar. Credit cards accepted. ❺

TTDC Tamil Nadu Railway Station Rd ☎04112/222553, ⓔttdc@md3.vsnl.net.in. Friendly state-run hotel with large rooms, although the place is looking slightly shabby and the restaurant is dingy. ❸–❹

Vedanthangal

One of India's most spectacular bird sanctuaries lies roughly 1km east of the village of **VEDANTHANGAL**, a cluster of squat, brown houses set in a patchwork of paddy fields 30km from the east coast and 86km southwest of Chennai. It's a tiny, relaxed place, bisected by one road and with just two chai stalls.

The **sanctuary** (daily dawn–dusk), a low-lying area less than half a kilometre square, is at its fullest between December and February, when it's totally flooded. The rains of the northeast monsoon, sweeping through in October or November, bring indigenous water birds here to nest and settle until the dry season (usually April), when they leave for wetter areas. Abundant trees on mounds above water level provide perfect nesting spots, alive by January with fledglings. Visitors can watch the avian action from a path at the water's edge, or from a watchtower (fitted out with strong binoculars). Try to come at sunset, when the birds return from feeding. Common Indian species to look out for are openbill storks, spoonbills, pelicans, black cormorants and herons of several types. You may also see ibises, grey pelicans, migrant cuckoos, sandpipers, egrets, which paddle in the rice fields, and tiny, darting bee-eaters. Some migrant birds pass through and rest on their way between more permanent sites; swallows, terns and redshanks are common, while peregrine falcons, pigeons and doves are less frequently spotted.

Practicalities

Getting to Vedanthangal can present a few problems. The nearest town is **Maduranthakam**, 8km east, on NH-45 between Chengalpattu and Tindivanam. Hourly buses run from Maduranthakam to the sanctuary. Alternatively, catch one of the four direct daily services from Chengalpattu to the sanctuary. Taxis make the journey from Maduranthakam for Rs250–300, but cannot be booked from Vedanthangal.

Vedanthangal's only accommodation is the four-room **forest lodge** (❸) near the bus stand, school and chai stall. The spacious, comfortable en-suite rooms (a/c or non-a/c) should be booked through the Wildlife Warden, 4th floor, No. 259, 3rd Rd Block, DMS Compound, Teynampet, Chennai (☎044/2432 1471 or ☎954115 200006). They'll prepare food if given enough notice. Often full in December and January.

Tiruvannamalai

Synonymous with the fifth Hindu element of fire, **TIRUVANNAMALAI**, 100km south of Kanchipuram, ranks, along with Madurai, Kanchipuram, Chidambaram and Trichy, as one of the five holiest towns in Tamil Nadu. Its name, meaning "Red Mountain", derives from the spectacular extinct volcano, **Arunachala**, which rises behind it, and which glows an unearthly crimson at dawn. This awesome natural backdrop, combined with the presence in the centre of town of the colossal Arunchaleshvara temple, make Tiruvannamalai one of the region's most memorable destinations. Far removed from the tourist trail, it's a perfect place to get to grips with life in small-town Tamil Nadu. For those searching for the spiritual south, the countless shrines, sacred tanks, ashrams and paved pilgrim paths scattered around the sacred mountain (not to mention the legions of dreadlocked *babas* who line up for alms outside the main sites) will keep anyone who is interested in Hinduism absorbed for weeks.

Pradakshana

During the annual **Karttigai festival**, Hindu pilgrims are supposed to perform an auspicious circumambulation of Arunachala, known as the **Pradakshana** (*pra* signifies the removal of all sins, *da* the fulfilment of desires, *kshi* freedom from the cycle of rebirth and *na* spiritual liberation). Along the way, offerings are made at a string of shrines, tanks, temples, *lingams*, pillared meditation halls, sacred rocks, springs, trees and caves related to the Tiruvannamalai legends. Although hectic during the festival, the paved path linking them all together is quiet for most of the year and makes a wonderful day-hike, affording fine views of the town and its environs.

An even more inspiring prospect is the **ascent of Arunachala** itself, which can be completed in two to three hours if you're fit and can cope with the heat (if you can't, don't attempt this hike). The path is less easy to follow than the Pradakshana, and you may feel like employing one of the guides who offer their services at the trailhead, just above the Shri Ramanasram ashram. At the summit, where you can see remnants of the annual Deepam blaze, sits Swami Narayana, a renunciate who has been performing an austerity of silence here for more than sixteen years.

Mythology identifies Arunachala as the place where Shiva asserted his power over Brahma and Vishnu by manifesting himself as a *lingam* of fire, or **agnilingam**. The two lesser gods had been disputing their respective strengths when Shiva pulled this primordial pyro-stunt, challenging his adversaries to locate the top and bottom of his blazing column. They couldn't (although Vishnu is said to have faked finding the head) and collapsed on their knees in a gesture of supreme submission. The event is commemorated each year at the rising of the full moon in November/December, when the **Deepam ceremony**, bringing to an end the ten-day **Karttigai festival**, culminates with the illumination of gallons of camphor in the temple courtyard. This acts as a signal for brahmins stationed on the summit of Arunachala to light a vast vat of ghee and paraffin, which blazes for days and can be seen from a radius of more than 20km. It represents the fulfilment of Shiva's promise to reappear each year to vanquish the forces of darkness and ignorance with firelight. The massive *agnilingam* attracts tens of thousands of pilgrims, who rush from the temple below to the summit in time to fuel the inferno with their own offerings. The whole event, best enjoyed from the relative safety of a rooftop in town, is one of the great spectacles of sacred India. The latest incarnation of a prehistoric fire-worshipping cult, it has probably been performed here in some form or another, without interruption, for four thousand years.

The alleged regenerative and healing powers of the sacred Red Mountain also explain why the famous twentieth-century saint **Shri Ramana Maharishi** chose this as the site for his 23-year meditation retreat in a cave on the side of the hill. Shri Ramana's subsequent teachings formed the basis of a worldwide movement, and his former ashram on the edge of Tiruvannamalai attracts a stream of Western devotees. A crop of other smaller ashrams have mushroomed alongside it, some of them more authentic than others, and the ranks of white-cotton-clad foreigners floating between them have become a defining feature of the area south of town over the past years.

Arunachaleshvara Temple

Known to Hindus as the "Temple of the Eternal Sunrise", the enormous **Arunachaleshvara Temple**, built over a period of almost a thousand years and incorporating several distinct styles, consists of three concentric courtyards whose gateways are topped by tapering *gopuras*, the largest of which cover the east and north gates. The best spot from which to view the precinct, a breathtaking spectacle against the sprawling plains and lumpy, granite Shevaroy hills, is the path up to Sri Ramana Maharishi's meditation cave, Virupaksha (see p.494), on the lower slopes of Arunachala. To enter the temple, however, head for the huge eastern gateway, which leads through the thick outer wall carved with images of deities, local saints and teachers, to a paved inner courtyard. The large stepped Shivaganga tank to the left originally lay outside the temple precincts; on the right stands a vast "thousand-pillared" *mandapa*, where the temple elephant lives when not taking part in rituals. In the basement of a raised hall to the right before entering the next courtyard is the Parthala *lingam*, where Shri Ramana Maharishi is said to have sat in a state of Supreme Awareness while ants devoured his flesh.

The second enclosure, built a couple of centuries earlier, in the 1200s, is much smaller, with a large Nandi bull facing the sanctuary and a shrine to the goddess (Shiva's consort) on its northern edge. In the temple kitchens in its southeastern corner, food is prepared for the gods. A nineteenth-century roof shelters the central courtyard, surveyed by numerous deities etched into its outer walls, among them Shiva, Parvati, Venugopala (Krishna), Lakshmi, Ganesh and Subrahmanya. In the dim interior, arcaded cloisters supported by magnificently carved columns lead to the main shrine dedicated to Shiva (and

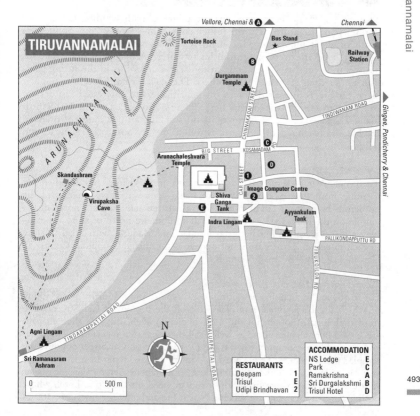

accessible to non-Hindus): a *lingam* raised on a platform bearing tenth-century inscriptions. This is the location of six daily puja, or acts of worship, when the *lingam* is bathed, clothed and strewn with flower garlands amid the heady smell of incense and camphor and the sound of bells and steady chanting.

In one of the outer courtyards on the north side, drenched devotees – mostly women – circumambulate an ancient hybrid *neem* and *bodhi* tree, draping it with offerings for the health of offspring and the success of married life.

Virupaksha and Skandashram caves

Opposite the western entrance of the temple complex, a path leads up a holy hill (15min) to the **Virupaksha cave**, where Shri Ramana Maharishi stayed between 1899 and 1916. He personally built the bench outside and the hill-shaped *lingam* and platform inside, where all are welcome to meditate in peace. When this cave became too small, constantly crowded with relatives and devotees, Ramana shifted to another, hidden away in a clump of trees a few minutes further up the hill. He named this one, and the small house built onto it, **Skandashram**, and lived there between 1916 and 1922. The inner cave here is also set aside for meditation, and the front patio affords splendid views across the temple, town and surrounding plains.

Sri Ramanasram ashram

The caves can also be reached via the pilgrims' path winding uphill from the **Sri Ramanasram ashram** (office daily 8am–11am & 2pm–5pm), 2km south of the temple along the main road. This simple complex is where the sage lived after returning from his retreat on Arunachala, and where his body is today enshrined (Hindus customarily bury saints in the sitting position rather than cremate their bodies). The *samadhi* has become a popular place for Sri Ramana's devotees on pilgrimage, but interested visitors are welcome to stay in the dorms here. There's also an excellent **bookshop** (daily 7.30am–11am & 2.30pm–6.30pm) stocking a huge range of titles on the life and teachings of the guru, as well as quality postcards, calendars and religious images.

Practicalities

Tiruvannamalai is served by regular **buses** from Vellore and Pondicherry. Coming from the coast, it's easiest to make your way there on one of the numerous buses from Tindivandum. The town bus stand is 2km north of the temple on the main road to Gingee. Half a kilometre north of there, the **railway station** is on the line between Tirupati and Madurai, with a daily service in each direction. There's **Internet access** at the Image Computer Centre, 52 Car Street (daily 9.30am–9.30pm; Rs20/hr).

Accommodation and eating

For **food**, you've a choice of a dozen or so typical South Indian "meals" joints, of which the *Udipi Brindhavan Hotel*, just off the bottom of Car Street, is the most traditional (though not the most hygienic). Delicious hot ghee chapatis are served here all afternoon, as well as all the usual rice specialities. The other commendable restaurant in town is the *Deepam*, also on Car Street opposite the temple's east entrance, which boasts a cooler "deluxe" wing next door where you can order ice creams and milkshakes; both branches serve excellent *parotas*. If you feel like a change from South Indian, head for the *Trisul* hotel, whose posh ground-floor restaurant serves a North Indian buffet for around Rs100, as well as a full tandoori menu. The *Ramakrishna* also serves a range of north (and south) Indian food in the evenings, as well as decent lunchtime thalis.

For such an important pilgrimage place, Tiruvannamalai has surprisingly few decent **hotels**.

NS Lodge 47 Thiruvoodal Street ℡ 04175/225388. Facing the Arunachaleshvara Temple's south entrance, this good-value place has clean en-suite rooms, some with a/c and all with cable TV; there's also a great view of the temple towers from the roof. ❷–❸

Park 26 Kosmadam Street, just northeast of the main temple entrance ℡ 04175/222471. Another reliable option, boasting a range of rooms from basic but clean to a/c and comfortable. There's a busy vegetarian canteen on the ground floor. ❷–❹

Ramakrishna 34-F Polur Road, a three-minute walk north of the bus stand. Follow Chinnakadai Street to the main fork just north of

the bus stand and take the left fork; the hotel is 100m along on the right ℡ 04175/250005, ℯ info@hotelramakrishna.com. One of the best places in town, with large en-suite rooms (a/c or non-a/c) and a decent restaurant. ❸–❹

Sri Durgalakshmi 73 Chinnakadai Street, just west of the bus stand ℡ 04175/226041. The pick of the budget lodges. ❷

Trisul 6 Kanakaraya Mudali Street ℡ 04175/222219, ℯ tact@vsnl.com. A couple of minutes' walk from the main temple entrance, with huge, immaculately clean rooms (some with a/c), courteous staff and a good restaurant. Its only drawback is that it gets booked up for long periods by Westerners studying at the ashrams. ❹–❺

Gingee

An epic landscape of huge boulder hills, interspersed by lush splashes of rice paddy and banana plantations, stretches east of Tiruvannamalai towards the coast. The scenery peaks at **GINGEE** (pronounced "*Shinjee*"), 37km east of the Red Mountain along the Pondicherry highway, where the ruins of Tamil Nadu's most spectacular **fort** (whole complex, including palace: daily 9am–5pm; $2 [Rs5]) sprawl over a vast swathe of sun-scorched granite. If this were anywhere except India, you wouldn't be able to move for interpretative panels and Walkman posts, but here the miles of crumbling ramparts and temple masonry have been left to the mercy of the weeds and tropical weather. Only on weekends, when bus parties pour around the most accessible monuments, does the site receive more than a trickle of visitors. Come here in the week, and you may well have the place to yourself, save for the odd troupe of monkeys and inquisitive tree squirrels.

Bisected by the main Tiruvannamalai–Pondicherry road, Gingee fort comprises three separate citadels, crowning the summits of three dramatic hills: Krishnagiri to the north, Rajagiri to the west and Chandrayandur to the southeast. Connecting them to form an enormous triangle, 1.5km from north to south, are twenty-metre-thick walls, punctuated by bastions and gateways giving access to the protected zones at the heart of the complex. It's hard to imagine such defences ever being overrun, but they were, on numerous occasions following the fort's foundations by the Vijayanagars in the fifteenth century. The Muslim Adil Shahis from Bijapur, Shivaji's Maharatas and the Moghuls all conquered Gingee, using it to consolidate the vulnerable southern reaches of their respective empires. The French also took it in 1750, but were ousted by the British after a bloody five-week siege eleven years later.

A network of raised, paved paths links the site's principal landmarks. From the road, head south to the main **east gate**, where a snaking passage emerges, after no fewer than four changes of direction, inside the **palace** enclave. Of the many structures unearthed by archeologists here, the most distinctive is the square seven-storey **Kalyana Mahal tower**, focal point of the former governor's residence; featuring an ingenious hydraulic system that carried water to the uppermost levels, it is crowned by a tapering pyramidal tower. Continue west through a gateway, and you'll pick up the path to **Rajagiri**, Gingee's loftiest citadel; at 165m above the surrounding plain it's a very stiff climb in the heat, but the views are well worth the effort.

The other ruins worth exploring lie a short way beyond the east gate. Typifying Gingee's position at the interface between the warring powers of north and South India is the **mosque of Sadat Ullah Khan I**, built in the early years of the eighteenth century. It stands a stone's throw from the sixteenth-century **Venkatarama temple**, dedicated to an aspect of Vishnu known as "Lord of the Venkata Hills". A dilapidated seven-storey *gopura* caps the east entrance, its passageway carved with scenes from the Ramayana.

Practicalities

Gingee is easily accessible by **bus** from Tiruvannamalai, 37km west, and Pondicherry, 68km southeast. You can either alight at the site itself, 2km west of Gingee town, or, if you intend to spend the night there, dump your bags at the hotel and continue to the ruins by auto-rickshaw. The only **accommodation** to speak of (and the only dependable place to leave luggage while you visit the fort) is the *Shivasand* hotel, on MG Road, opposite the main bus stand (⊕04145/222218; ❷–❹), whose *Vasantham* South Indian restaurant is Gingee's classiest place to eat. From the town centre, auto-rickshaws charge Rs40–60 for the return trip to the fort; you'll have to settle an additional fee for waiting time. Note that there are no refreshments, not even drinking water, available at the site, so take your own, or wander 500m back down the road towards town to the small roadside chai stall in the village.

Pondicherry and Auroville

First impressions of **PONDICHERRY**, the former capital of French India, can be unpromising. Instead of the leafy boulevards and *pétanque* pitches you might expect, its messy outer suburbs and bus stand are as cluttered and chaotic as any typical Tamil town. Closer to the seafront, however, the atmosphere grows tangibly more Gallic as the bazaars give way to rows of houses whose shuttered windows and colourwashed facades wouldn't look out of place in Montpellier. For anyone familiar with the British colonial imprint, it can induce culture shock to see richly ornamented Catholic churches, French road names and policemen in De Gaulle-style *képis*. Even today, it is common to hear French spoken in the street and to see elderly men playing a late afternoon game of *boules* in the dusty squares around Ambour Salai and Gingee Salai.

Known to Greek and Roman geographers as "Poduke", Pondicherry was an important staging post on the second-century maritime trade route between Rome and the Far East (a Roman amphitheatre has been unearthed at nearby Arikamedu). When the Roman empire declined, the local Pallava and Chola kings took control, followed by a succession of colonial powers, from the Portuguese in the sixteenth century to the French, Danes and British. The enclave was exchanged several times between them during the various battles and treaties of the Carnatic Wars in the early eighteenth century, finally leaving the small territory in the hands of the French. Finally left in peace, Pondicherry's heyday dates from the arrival of **Dupleix**, who accepted the governorship in 1742 and immediately set about rebuilding a town decimated by its former British occupants. It was he who instituted the street plan of a central grid encircled by a broad oblong boulevard, bisected north to south by a canal dividing the "Ville Blanche", to the east, from the "Ville Noire", to the west.

Although relinquished by the French in 1954 – when the town became the headquarters of the **Union Territory of Pondicherry**, administering the three other former colonial enclaves scattered across South India – Pondicherry's split personality still prevails. West of the canal stretches a bustling Indian market town, while to the east, towards the sea, the streets are emptier, cleaner and decidedly European. The seaside promenade, **Goubert Salai** (formerly Beach Road), has the forlorn look of an out-of-season French resort, complete with its own white Hôtel de Ville. Tanned sun-worshippers share space with grave Europeans in white Indian costume, busy about their spiritual quest. It was here that **Sri Aurobindo Ghose** (1872–1950), a leading figure in the freedom struggle in Bengal, was given shelter after it became unwise to live close to the British in Kolkata (Calcutta). His **ashram** attracts thousands of devotees from all around the world, but particularly from Bengal.

Ten kilometres north, the utopian experiment-in-living **Auroville** was inspired by Aurobindo's disciple, the charismatic Mirra Alfassa, a Parisian painter, musician and mystic better known as "The Mother". Today this slightly surreal place is populated by numbers of expats and visited by long-stay Europeans eager to find inner peace. Nearby are two beaches – Auroville and Serenity – that are suitable for sunbathing and swimming.

Arrival, information and getting around

All buses – local and long distance – pull into **New Bus Stand** on the western edge of town; for a summary of routes, see the Travel Details on p.576. From here, a ride into the main hotel district should cost about Rs20 by cycle-rickshaw, or Rs30 by auto-rickshaw. Pondicherry's **railway station** is on the south side of town, five minutes' walk from the sea but sees few trains.

The **Pondicherry Tourism Development Corporation** (PDTC) office is at 40 Goubert Salai (daily 8.45am–5pm; ☎0413/233 9497). The staff are extremely helpful, providing leaflets and a city map, and information about Auroville; they can also book you onto their **city tours** (full-day tours 9.30am–5.30pm, Rs100; half-day tours 2pm–5.30pm, Rs80) and arrange **car rental** (Rs650 per day plus fuel at Rs2.5 per km). Recommended places to **change money** include: the Indian Overseas Bank, in the Hôtel de Ville; the State Bank of India on Surcouf Street; and UCO Bank, Rue Mahe de Labourdonnais. The **GPO** is on Ranga Pillai Street (Mon–Sat 10am–7.30pm). There are plenty of **Internet** places in Pondicherry along Rue Nehru, Ranga Pillai Street and Mission Street; most are open daily from around 9am to 11pm and charge Rs20 per hour.

Pondicherry is well served with both auto- and cycle-rickshaws, but for **getting around** most tourists rent a **cycle** from one of the many stalls dotted around town (Rs20 per day plus Rs200 refundable deposit). If you're staying at the *Park Guest House*, use one of theirs (they're all immaculately maintained). For trips further afield (to Auroville, for example) you may want to rent a **moped** or **scooter**. Of the rental firms operating in town, Sri Ganesh Cycle Store, 39 Mission Street (☎0413/222 2801), has new Honda Kinetics for Rs100 per day, plus a Rs300 deposit and passport or driving licence as security.

Accommodation

Pondicherry's **basic lodges** are concentrated around the main market area, Ranga Pillai Street and Rue Nehru. Throughout Pondicherry, guesthouses belonging to the **Sri Aurobindo Ashram** (ⓦ www.sriaurobindosociety.org.in)

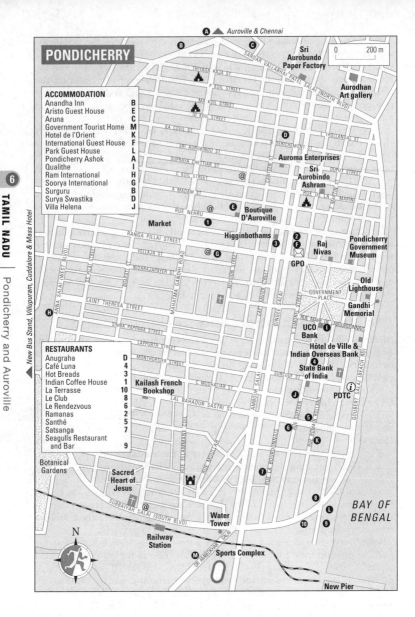

PONDICHERRY

A ▲ Auroville & Chennai

Sri Aurobundo Paper Factory

Aurodhan Art gallery

0   200 m

ACCOMMODATION
Anandha Inn   B
Aristo Guest House   E
Aruna   C
Government Tourist Home   M
Hotel de l'Orient   K
International Guest House   F
Park Guest House   L
Pondicherry Ashok   A
Qualithe   I
Ram International   H
Soorya International   G
Surguru   B
Surya Swastika   D
Villa Helena   J

THIYAGA RAJA ST

P KOIL STREET

MA KOIL STREET

ID KOIL STREET

KA COVIL ST

SRI AUROBINDO ST

SUPRAYA CHETTIAR ST

C KOIL STREET

A MADAM ST

RUE NEHRU

Market

Higginbothams

L THOLLANDAL ST

B DERICHEMONT ST

Auroma Enterprises

Sri Aurobindo Ashram

DUPUY STREET

RUE DE LA MARINE

Boutique D'Auroville

Raj Nivas

GPO

Pondicherry Government Museum

Old Lighthouse

GOVERNMENT PLACE

Gandhi Memorial

UCO Bank

Hôtel de Ville & Indian Overseas Bank

State Bank of India

PDTC

RESTAURANTS
Anugraha   D
Café Luna   4
Hot Breads   3
Indian Coffee House   1
La Terrasse   10
Le Club   8
Le Rendezvous   6
Ramanas   2
Santhé   5
Satsanga   7
Seagulls Restaurant
  and Bar   9

ANNA SALAI (WEST BLVD)

NSC BOSE STREET

SAINT THERESA STREET

SINNA PAPPARA STREET

LAPPORTH STREET

MONTHORSIER STREET

VELLAJA ST

NIDARAJAPAYER SANTHI ROAD

MAHATMA GANDHI ROAD

MISSION STREET

KAP XAVIER STREET

GINGEE SALAI

SUFFREN STREET

RUE MAHE DE LABOURDONNAIS

Kailash French Bookshop

C MUDHALIAR ST

LAL BAHADUR SASTRI ST

AMBOUR SALAI

SURCOUT ST

RUE SUFFREN

RUE ROMAN ROLLAND

RUE LA BOURDONNAIS

RUE ELLAIMMANE

RUE ELLAMMANE COIL

RUE AMOUDOU

GOUBERT SALAI (BEACH RD)

Botanical Gardens

Sacred Heart of Jesus

Water Tower

SUBBAIAH SALAI (SOUTH BLVD)

BAY OF BENGAL

N

Railway Station

DR AMBEDKAR SALAI

Sports Complex

New Pier

offer fantastic value for money, but come with a lot of baggage apart from your own (regulations, curfews and overpowering "philosophy of life" notices). Although supposedly open to all, they are not keen on advertising, or on attracting misguided individuals indulging in "spiritual tourism".

Anandha Inn 154 Sardar Vallabhai Patel Salai ☎0413/233 0711, ©checkin@anandhain.com. Seventy luxurious rooms, two restaurants and a

cocktail lounge in a gleaming white building. Good value and popular with tour groups, so book well in advance. ⑦–⑧

Aristo Guest House 124 Mission St ☎ 0413/233 6728, ⓕ 233 0057. Budget rooms arranged around a raised courtyard above a shop. It's a bit dingy and not advised for single women, but fine for a short stay. ❷

Aruna 3 Zamindar Garden, off Sardar Vallabhai Patel Salai ☎ 0413/233 7756. Situated on a quiet side street, with clean en-suite doubles of varying sizes. Some have a/c, some have TV, and all have balconies. ❸–❹

Government Tourist Home Dr Ambedkhar Salai, Uppalam ☎ 0413/235 8276. Charmless neon-lit concrete block at the bottom end of town and within earshot of the railway line, but fairly cheap. All rooms have attached shower-toilets, and two also have a/c. ❷–❸

Hotel de l'Orient 17 Rue Romain Rolland ☎ 0413/234 3067, ⓕ 222 7829. A beautiful, UNESCO heritage-listed French house with sixteen rooms, individually decorated with French antiques, tiled balconies and long shuttered windows over-looking a leafy courtyard restaurant. Wonderfully romantic. ❽–❾

International Guest House 47 Gingee Salai, near the GPO ☎ 0413/233 6699, ⓔ ingh@vsnl.net. The largest Aurobindo establishment, with dozens of very large, clean rooms, some with a/c. One of the best budget options in town, and safe for single women. ❷–❸

Park Guest House Goubert Salai ☎ 0413/233 4412, ⓔ parkgh@sriaurobindoashram.org. A Sri Aurobindo Society pad, with strict rules (no alcohol or TVs) and an 10.30pm curfew. Rooms are spot-less and very comfortable, however, and are right on the seafront, with new mozzie nets and "sit-outs" overlooking a well-watered garden. There's also bike rental, laundry and restaurant. ❸

Pondicherry Ashok Chinnakalapet, 12km from Pondicherry on the old coastal road to Mamallapuram, near Auroville ☎ 0413/265 5160, ⓔ itdcpa@satyam.net.in. Comfortable rooms in a quiet, breezy location on the seashore. There's a children's park, restaurant, barbecue and bar, plus generous discounts for stays of three days or more. ❽–❾

Qualithe 3 Rue Mahe de Labourdonnais ☎ 0413/233 4325, ⓔ rajarathnam@engineer .com. Pondy's most characterful budget lodge, in a slightly rickety old French building. Upstairs, big, spotless rooms that fit four lead off a pleasant balcony with wicker chairs and great views over Government Place. Just one cheap single. ❹

Ram International 398 Anna Salai ☎ 0413/233 7230, ⓕ 233 7230. Very good-value, efficient, modern place on the western edge of town. Advance booking recommended. ❸–❺

Soorya International 55 Ranga Pillai St ☎ 0413/233 6856, ⓔ hotelsooryainternational @hotmail.com. Central hotel with very large, immaculate rooms. Prices are reasonable, despite the ostentatious exterior. ❸–❺

Surguru 104 Sardar Vallabhai Patel Salai (North Blvd) ☎ 0413/233 9022, www.hotelsurguru.com. The best value mid-range place in town, with spruce, spacious rooms, brisk service and most mod cons, including an excellent veg restaurant (see p.501). ❹–❺

Surya Swastika 11 ID Koil St ☎ 0413/234 3092, ⓔ suryaswastika@sify.com. Traditional Tamil guest-house in a quiet corner of town, with nine basic rooms around a central courtyard that doubles as a pilgrims' canteen at lunchtime. Incredibly cheap, and cleaner than most of the bazaar lodges. ❶–❸

Villa Helena 14 Suffren St ☎ 0413/222 6789, ⓔ villahelena@satyam.net.in. Four rooms in an old colonial house with tasteful French–Thai interior, including antique furniture. Price includes break-fast. ❻

The Town

Pondicherry's beachside promenade, **Goubert Salai**, is a favourite place for a stroll, with cafés and bars to idle in and cooling breezes blowing in off the sea. There's little to do, other than watch the world go by, but the Hôtel de Ville, today housing the municipal offices, is still an impressive spectacle, and a four-metre-high Gandhi memorial, surrounded by ancient columns, dominates the northern end of the promenade. Nearby, a French memorial commemorates Indian soldiers from French territories who lost their lives in World War I.

Just north of the Hôtel de Ville, a couple of streets back from the promenade, is the leafy old French-provincial-style square now named **Government Place**. A fountain stands at the centre, while among the square's paths and lawns are a number of sculptures carved in nearby Gingee. On its northern side, guarded by policemen in red *képis*, the impressive, gleaming white **Raj Nivas**, official home to the present lieutenant governor of Pondicherry Territory, was built late in the eighteenth century for Joseph Francis Dupleix, who became governor of French India. Unfortunately, the home of Ananda Ranga Pillai (1709–61), *dubash*, or close adviser of Dupleix – once one of the highlights of a visit to Pondicherry – is now closed to the public.

The **Pondicherry Government Museum** (Tues–Sun 10am–5pm; Rs2), on Ranga Pillai Street opposite Government Place, has an archeological collection comprising Neolithic and 2000-year-old remains from Arikamedu, a few Pallava (sixth–eighth centuries) and Buddhist (tenth-century) stone sculptures, bronzes, weapons and paintings. Alongside these are displayed a bizarre collection of French salon furniture and bric-a-brac from local houses, including a velvet S-shaped "conversation seat".

The **Sri Aurobindo Ashram**, 300m north of Government Place on Rue de la Marine (daily 8am–noon & 2–6pm; no children under 3; Ⓦwww .sriaurobindosociety.org.in), is one of the best known and wealthiest ashrams in India, founded in 1926 by the Bengali philosopher-guru Aurobindo Ghose and his chief disciple, personal manager and mouthpiece, "The Mother". It now serves as the headquarters of the Sri Aurobindo Society (or SAS) which today owns most of the valuable property and real estate in Pondicherry, and wields what many consider to be a disproportionate influence over the town. A beautifully maintained small rockery, cactus and flower garden greet you as you enter the compound. The **samadhi**, or mausoleum, of Sri Aurobindo and "The Mother" is covered daily with flowers and usually surrounded by supplicants with their hands and heads placed on the tomb. Inside the main building is an incongruous and very bourgeois-looking Western-style room, complete with three-piece suite, where "The Mother" and Sri Aurobindo used to chill out. Avoid treading on the Persian carpet, as devotees prostrate themselves here. The bookshop next door has Aurobindo literature and details of the various cultural programmes put on in the building opposite.

The **Aurodhan Art Gallery**, at 11 Thillai Nattar Street, just off SV Patel Salai (Mon–Sat 9am–1pm, 3–6pm; free), is a peaceful sanctuary dedicated to contemporary Indian art. The permanent exhibition showcases the talent of local artists, who have produced a prodigious amount of work – pictures and sculptures line the rooms and corridors over several floors. Many of the exhibits reflect the influence of Sri Aurobino or the environment of Auroville, and there are some excellent portraits. Five minutes' walk away is the **Sri Aurobindo Paper Factory**, on SV Patel Salai (Mon–Sat 8.30am–5pm; free), where you can watch the fascinating and laborious process of making the handmade paper that is sold in tourist spots all over India.

In the southwest of town, near the railway station, is the huge cream and brown **Sacred Heart of Jesus**, one of Pondicherry's finest Catholic churches, built by French missionaries in the 1700s. Nearby, the shady **Botanical Gardens** (daily 9.30am–6pm; free), established in 1826, offer many quiet paths to wander. The French planted nine hundred species of imported trees, shrubs and flowers here, experimenting to see how they would fare in Indian conditions; one, the *khaya senegalensis*, has grown to a height of 25m.

Eating

If you've been on the road for a while and are hankering for healthy salads, fresh coffee, crusty bread, cakes and real pastry, you'll be spoilt for choice in Pondicherry. Unlike the traveller-oriented German-bakery-style places elsewhere in the country, the Western **restaurants** here cater for a predominantly expatriate clientele with discerning palettes and fat French-franc pay cheques. Cheap **beer** is available just about everywhere except the SAS-owned establishments, and indeed some travellers maintain that this is the only reason to visit Pondy. The ubiquitous presence of the restaurant-cum-bar and predominance of male drinkers can be off-putting to some female travellers. Many mid-range hotels have their own bars, which may feel less seamy than some of the downtown joints.

Anugraha *Hotel Surguru*, 104 SV Patel Salai (North Blvd). Widely rated as the best lunchtime "meals" restaurant in town, but also serving superb *dosa-iddli* breakfasts and filter coffee, and a full tandoori menu in the evening.

Café Luna Rue Suffren, near the State Bank of India. A little hole in the wall where old men gather to drink coffee and pass the time of day. The coffee is prepared with great pomp and style, and the lunch-time plate of lemon rice and *vada* (Rs5) is absolutely superb.

Hot Breads 42 Ambour Salai. Crusty croissants, fresh baguettes, and delicious savoury pastry snacks, served in a squeaky-clean French *boulangerie*-café full of French expats.

Indian Coffee House Rue Nehru. Not their cleanest branch, but the coffee is good, and the prices are unbeatable.

La Terrasse 5 Subbiah Salai. The most popular French restaurant amongst European backpackers, who hang out here to devour croissants and cappuccino al fresco. Excellent prawn dishes start at Rs80, pizzas go for Rs70–175, and there's also a range of Indian, Chinese and French food. Daily except Wed 8.30am–10pm.

Le Club 33 Dumas St (closed Mon). Far and away the town's top place to eat, although beyond the pocket of most travellers, not to mention locals. The predominantly French menu features their famous coq au vin, steak au poivre, plenty of seafood options and a full wine list, rounded off with cognac at Rs200 a shot. Count on Rs300 per head (if you forsake the shorts). There's also a cheaper bistro that is great for Sunday brunch, a tapas and cocktail bar, and

a Vietnamese and Southeast Asian restaurant which is open daily.

Le Rendezvous 30 Rue Suffren. Filling seafood sizzlers, fantastic pizza and tandoori brochettes are specialities of this popular expat-oriented restaurant. They also serve fresh croissants and espresso for breakfast, indoors or up on the more romantic rooftop, where there are jazz sounds and chilled beer in discreet ceramic jugs in the evenings. Most main dishes Rs100–150.

Ramanas Corner of Rue Nehru and Gingee Salai. Filled with a hard-core *iddli*-eating office crowd; service is fast, and the South Indian food is cheap and good. Open from 7am.

Santhé Romain Roland St. Friendly and atmospheric roof terrace serving a mixture of French, Indian and Chinese for less than Rs100, though service is rather chaotic.

Satsanga 30 Labourdonnais St. If you only eat once in Pondy, it should be here. Served on the colonnaded veranda of an old colonial mansion, the menu (devised by the French patron) is carefully prepared and exactly the kind of thing you dream about elsewhere in India: organic salads with fresh herbs, tzatziki and garlic bread, sauté potatoes, *tagliatelle alla carbonara* and mouthwatering pizzas washed down with chilled Kingfisher. Check their *plat du jour* for fresh fish dishes. Around Rs300 per head for three courses, with drinks.

Seagulls Restaurant and Bar Damas St. Reasonably priced, open-air rooftop restaurant in breezy spot right next to the sea, new pier and cargo harbour. Huge, inexpensive menu, with veg dishes, meat, seafood, Indian, Chinese and even some Italian (pizza and spaghetti). Open 11am–11pm.

Auroville

The most New Age place anywhere in India must surely be **AUROVILLE**, the planned "City of Dawn", 10km north of Pondicherry, just outside the Union Territory in Tamil Nadu. Founded in 1968, Auroville was inspired by "The Mother", the spiritual successor to Sri Aurobindo. Around 1350 people live in communes here (two-thirds of them non-Indians), with names such as Fertile, Certitude, Sincerity, Revelation and Transformation, in what it is hoped will eventually be a city with a population of 50,000 people. Architecturally experimental buildings, combining modern Western and traditional Indian elements, are set in a rural landscape of narrow lanes, deep red earth and lush greenery. Income is derived from ecofriendly agriculture, handicrafts and home-made foodstuffs, alternative technology, educational and development projects and Aurolec, a computer software company. The entire complex is run on natural energy generated by solar panels and windmills, and water is drawn using wind turbines.

The avowed aim of the commune is harmony, leading a life made meaningful through hard physical work backed up by a spiritual discipline of inner consciousness, rather than dogma, rule or ritual behaviour. Nonetheless, the place has had its ups and downs, not least of which have been the **disputes** between the community and the Sri Aurobindo Society (SAS) over ownership since the death of "The Mother" in 1973. Rejecting the Aurovillians' calls for self-determination, the SAS cut off funds to the community, forcing its members to become financially self-sufficient. The power struggle intensified in the mid-1970s, erupting into full-blown violence on a couple of occasions before the police were called in. At one stage, the war of attrition got so tough that some Western countries had to provide aid to the Aurovillians. Eventually, however, the High Court ruled in their favour, and in 1988 the Auroville Foundations Act was passed, placing responsibility for the administration of the settlement in the hands of a seven-member council, with representatives from the state government, the SAS and Auroville itself.

One of the accusations levelled at the settlers around this time was that, although Auroville was supposedly an egalitarian community, most of the Indians involved were being relegated to the status of labourers. Aurovillians countered these attacks by pointing to the numerous ways they had worked to improve the lives of low-caste Tamils in the surrounding villages, many of whom had been given full-time jobs manufacturing textiles, software and non-polluting unbaked bricks. The site also has a school for local Tamil children, started by a retired policeman from Essex in England.

Considering how little there is to see here, Auroville attracts a disproportionately large number of day-trippers – much to the chagrin of its inhabitants, who rightly point out that you can only get a sense of what the settlement is all about if you stay a while. Interested visitors are welcomed as paying guests in most of the communes, where you can work alongside permanent residents (see opposite).

The Matri Mandir

The various conflicts of the past two decades have inevitably spawned divisions among the Aurovillians themselves. While some still treat the teachings of "The Mother" with the same uncritical devotion as the Pondicherry ashramites, others have strayed from the orthodoxy. One thing, however, unites the whole community: the **Matri Mandir**, or "dwelling place of The Mother", a gigantic hi-tech meditation centre at the heart of the site, 36m in diameter (information booth open daily 8.30am–5.15pm). Begun in 1970, the space-age structure was conceived as "a symbol of the Divine's answer to man's inspiration for perfection". Soil from 126 countries was symbolically placed in an urn, and is kept in a concrete cone in the amphitheatre adjacent to Matri Mandir, from where a speaker can address an audience of 3000 without amplification. In accordance with the instructions of "The Mother", this is open to all (daily 4–4.45pm; arrive at least one hour in advance; the Mandir is closed if there is rain), although the Aurovillians' reluctance to admit outsiders is palpable. After a long wait for tickets to be issued, accompanied by strict instructions on how to behave while inside, visitors are ushered in silence to the Matri Mandir's ramped entrance. You are allowed a fleeting glimpse of the seventy-centimetre crystal ball that forms its focal point, made by the German optical company, Karl Zeiss, which is believed to be the largest of its kind in the world. Contrary to the intentions of the architects, the whole experience can leave a bad taste in your mouth: the Aurovillians clearly hate having to herd day-trippers through what most of them regard as the soul of their community. However, you'll get a different response if you express more than a passing interest; your original entry ticket allows you to return later for an hour of silent meditation. If you are keen to come back again after this, you may be granted permission for a visit out of normal hours (apply at the information booth between 3.30pm & 4.30pm). Only then, Aurovillians claim, will you appreciate the real significance of the place.

Practicalities

Auroville lies 10km north of Pondicherry on the main Chennai road; you can also get there via the new coastal highway, turning off at the village of Chinna Mudaliarchavadi. **Bus** services are frequent along both routes but – as Auroville is so spread out, covering some fifty or so square kilometres – it's best to come with your own transport, at the very least a bike. Most people rent a scooter or **motorcycle** from Pondicherry and ride up. Alternatively, there's Tamil Nadu Tourism's daily **tour** from Pondicherry (depart 2pm, return 5.30pm; Rs60); book at the Pondy office (see p.497).

For a pre-visit primer, call in at the **visitor centre** (daily 9am–5.30pm; ☎0413/262 2239), bang in the middle of the site near the Bharat Niwas, which holds a permanent exhibition on the history and philosophies of the settlement. Free passes to enter the grounds are issued here (Mon–Sat 9.45am–12.45pm & 1.45pm–4pm; Sun 9.45am–12.30pm), but visitors are first requested to watch a short video about Auroville. You can also pick up some inexpensive literature on Auroville in the adjacent bookshop and check out a notice board for details of **activities** in which visitors may participate (these typically include yoga, reiki and Vipassana meditation, costing around Rs100 per session). In addition, there are a couple of quality handicraft outlets and several pleasant little vegetarian cafés serving snacks, meals and cold drinks.

The information desk at the visitor centre is also the place to enquire about **paying guest accommodation** in Auroville's thirty or so communes. Officially there's no lower limit on the time you have to stay, but visitors are encouraged to stick around for at least a week, helping out on communal projects; tariffs range from Rs100–500 per day, depending on levels of comfort. Alternatively, you can arrange to stay in one of the four **guesthouses**, which offer a/c rooms for Rs1500. It's advisable to book well in advance (c/o Auroville Guest Programmes, Auroville 605 101, Tamil Nadu, ☎0413/262 2704, ℮avguests@auroville.org.in), especially during the peak periods from December to March and from July to August, as accommodation is in short supply. Otherwise, the only rooms in the area are just outside Auroville in the village of Chinna Mudaliarchavadi. The *Palm Beach Cottage Centre* (no phone; ❶) is nothing of the kind (the sea is fifteen minutes' walk away), but has passably clean rooms with shared toilets and a small garden, where meals are served. Nearby, the *Cottage Guest House* (no phone; ❷–❸) offers a little more comfort in thatched huts or in a block of en-suite rooms. For **food**, you won't do better than the excellent vegetarian meals served in Auroville itself.

Central Tamil Nadu

To be on the banks of the Cauvery listening to the strains of Karnatic music is to
have a taste of eternal bliss

Tamil proverb

Continuing south of Pondicherry along the Coromandel coast you enter the
flat landscape of the **Kaveri** (aka Cauvery) **Delta**, an intensely green world of
paddy fields cut by thirty major rivers, canals, dams, dykes and rivulets that has
been intensively farmed since ancient times. Only a hundred miles in diameter,
it forms the rice bowl of Tamil Nadu. The **Kaveri** is the largest river, known
in Tamil as Ponni, "The Lady of Gold" (a form of the Mother Goddess), and is
revered as a conduit of liquid *shakti*, the primordial female energy that nurtures
the millions of farmers who live on her banks and tributaries. Three bumper
crops each year are coaxed from the giant patchwork of paddy, which Colonel
Fullarton in his *View of English Interests in India* (1785) described as "teeming
with an industrious race expert in agriculture". Amid the stifling heat of mid-
July, on the eighteenth day of the solar month Adi, villagers have for hundreds,
possibly thousands, of years gathered in vast numbers to mark the rising of the
river. During the festival, money, cloth, jewellery, food, tools and household
utensils are thrown into the river as offerings, so that the goddess will have
all she needs for the coming year. From October until December the delta is
washed with the powerful second annual monsoon, bringing a rich harvest of
rainwater for the paddy. This is one of the most beautiful periods of the year, as
diagonal swathes of rain sweep across the endless green fields between bursts of
dazzling sunshine, and the sunrise is pure and clear after stormy nights.

This mighty delta formed the heartland of the **Chola** empire, which reached
its apogee between the ninth and thirteenth centuries, an era often compared
to classical Greece and Renaissance Italy both for its cultural richness and the
sheer scale and profusion of its architectural creations. Much as the Cholas
originally intended, every visitor is immediately in awe of their huge temples,
not only in cities such as **Chidambaram**, **Kumbakonam** and **Thanjavur**, but
also out in the countryside at places like **Gangaikondacholapuram**, where
the magnificent temple is all that remains of a once-great city. Exploring the
area for a few days will bring you into contact with the more delicate side of
Chola artistic expression, such as the magnificent **bronzes** of Thanjavur, and
the incantatory **saints' hymns** of the *Sangam* and *Tevaram* – bodies of oral
poetry that emerged in the delta more than a thousand years ago. Its composers were wandering poets who travelled the length and breadth of the South,
singing, dancing and spreading a new devotional brand of Hinduism known
as **bhakti**. Phrased in classical Tamil and with a richness rarely equalled since,
their verses praise the beauty of the delta's natural landscape and recall the
significance of the countless shrines and sacred sites (more than half of the 274
holy Shaivite places in Tamil Nadu are found here). Considering many were
not set down in Sanskrit until centuries after they were composed, it's a miracle
that the hymns have survived at all. But today they form the basis of a thriving oral tradition, sung in temples, *maths* (religious institutions), pilgrims' buses
and homes wherever Tamil is the lingua franca. The poems have also provided
the raw material for many a hit mythological movie, and you'll hear modern
versions of the better-known ones, jazzed up with electric guitars and synthe-
sizers, blaring out of audio-cassette stores.

Nowhere else in the world has a classical civilization survived till the twenty-first century, and the knowledge that the ancient culture of the Cholas endures here alongside their awesome monuments lends a unique resonance to any journey across the Kaveri Delta.

Chidambaram

CHIDAMBARAM, 58km south of Pondicherry, is so steeped in myth that its history is hard to unravel. As the site of the *tandava*, the cosmic dance of Shiva as **Nataraja**, King of the Dance, it is one of the holiest Hindu sites in South India. A visit to the **Sabhanayaka Nataraja temple** affords a fascinating glimpse into ancient Tamil religious practice and belief. The legendary king **Hiranyavarman** is said to have made a pilgrimage here from Kashmir, seeking to rid himself of leprosy by bathing in the temple's Shivaganga tank. In thanks for a successful cure, he enlarged the temple. He also brought in 3000 brahmins, of the Dikshitar caste, whose descendants, distinguishable by top-knots of hair at the front of their heads, are the ritual specialists of the temple to this day.

Few of the fifty *maths*, or monasteries, that once stood here remain, but the temple itself is still a hive of activity and hosts numerous **festivals**. The two most important are ten-day affairs, building up to spectacular finales: on the ninth day of each, temple chariots process through the four Car streets in the **Car festival**, while on the tenth day, **abhishekham**, the principal deities in the Raja Sabha (thousand-pillared hall) are anointed. For exact dates (one is in May/June, the other in Dec/Jan), contact any TTDC tourist office and plan well ahead, as they are very popular. Other local festivals include fire-walking and *kavadi* folk dance (dancing with decorated wooden frames on the head) at the Thillaiamman Kali (April/May) and Keelatheru Mariamman (July/Aug) temples.

The town also has a hectic market and a large student population, based at Annamalai University's centre of Tamil studies in the east. Among the simple thatched huts in the flat, sparsely populated surrounding countryside, which becomes very dry and dusty in summer, the only solid-looking structures are the small roadside temples, most of which are devoted to Aiyannar, the village deity who protects borders, and whose shrines are flanked with *kudirais*, brightly painted terracotta or wooden figures of horses.

Arrival and information

Chidambaram revolves around the Sabhanayaka Temple and the busy market area that surrounds it, along North, East, South and West Car streets. Though little more than a country halt, the **railway station**, just over 1km southeast of the centre, has good connections both north and south, and boasts retiring rooms and, on platform 1, a **post office** (Mon–Sat 9am–1pm & 1.30–5pm). Frequent buses from Chennai, Thanjavur, Mamallapuram and Madurai pull in at the **bus stand**, also in the southeast, but nearer the centre, about 500m from the temple.

Staff at the TTDC **tourist office** (Mon–Fri 9.45am–5.45pm; ℡04144/238739), next to the *Vandayar Gateway Inn* hotel on Railway Feeder Road, are charming and helpful, but only have a small pamphlet to give visitors. None of the **banks** in Chidambaram change money, although the *Saradharam* hotel, near the bus stand, will change cash, and there's an ICICI Bank ATM in the forecourt. They also have an **Internet** café where you can get online for Rs30 per hour.

Accommodation and eating

Chidambaram abounds in budget **accommodation** aimed at the influx of tourists and pilgrims, but there are also a few decent mid-range options. As for **eating**, there are plenty of basic, wholesome "meals" places on and around the Car streets – the *Sri Ganesa Bhavan*, on West Car Street, gets the locals' vote. For quality, inexpensive South Indian food you can't beat the *Pallavi*, at the *Saradharam* hotel, which is packed at lunchtimes for its good-value thalis. The *Anupallavi* behind it is an equally commendable, though somewhat dingy, non-veg alternative. There's also a small *Indian Coffee House* on Venugopal Pillai Street – a pleasant breakfast venue or place to peruse the papers over coffee.

Akshaya 17/18 East Car St ☏04144/222592, ✉akshayhotel@hotmail.com. Pleasant, clean mid-range hotel with a lawn backing onto the temple wall. There is a range of a/c and non a/c , though the latter are better value. ❷–❺

Mansoor Lodge 91 East Car St ☏04144/221072. A friendly and good-value cheapie. Rooms have spotless tiled floors and clean bathrooms, all freshly painted, and TVs are available. ❶–❷

Railway retiring rooms The best deal in town, with huge clean rooms, though the bathrooms are a little dilapidated. Ask at the Station Master's Office on platform 1. ❶–❷

Raja Rajan 162 West Car St ☏04144/222690. Close to the west gate of the temple, this place has clean rooms with tiled bathrooms and low tariffs; the a/c ones are good value. ❶–❸

Ritz 2 Venu Gopal Pillai St, near the bus stand ☏04114/223312, ℻221098. One of the best places in town, this comfortable hotel boasts a convenient location and big rooms (all with TV, and some with a/c) plus a good restaurant. ❹–❺

Sabanayagam 22 East Sannathi St, off East Car St ☏04144/220896. Despite its flashy exterior, this is just a run-of-the-mill budget place. Rooms have a choice of Indian or Western loos, and some have a/c; ask for one with a window, preferably on the second floor overlooking the temple entrance. There's also a good veg restaurant. ❷–❹

Saradharam 19 Venu Gopal Pillai St, opposite the bus stand ☏04144/221336, ✉hsrcdm@vsnl.com. Large, clean and well-kept rooms (some with a/c) in modern buildings, with two decent restaurants (including one serving pizzas), a small garden, bar, laundry and foreign exchange. ❸–❹

Vandayar Gateway Inn Railway Feeder Rd, located between the railway station and bus stand ☏04144/238056. Very clean, decent-sized rooms with tiled floors, plus two restaurants and an a/c bar. Also home to the TTDC tourist Office. ❷–❺

Sabhanayaka Nataraja Temple

For South India's Shaivites, the **Sabhanayaka Nataraja Temple** (daily 4am–noon & 4pm–10pm), where Shiva is enthroned as Lord of the Cosmic Dance (Nataraja), is the holiest of holies. Its huge *gopuras*, whose lights are used as landmarks by sailors far out to sea in the Bay of Bengal, soar above a 55-acre complex, divided by four concentric walls. The oldest parts now standing were built under the Cholas, who adopted Nataraja as their chosen deity and crowned several kings here. Four gates on each side of the rectangular outermost wall afford entry, so if you have the time the best way to tackle the complex is to work slowly inwards from the third enclosure in clockwise circles. **Guides** are readily available but tend to shepherd visitors towards the central shrine too quickly. Frequent devotional (puja) **ceremonies** take place at the innermost sanctum, the most popular being at noon and 6pm, when a fire is lit, great gongs are struck and devotees rush forward to catch a last glimpse of the *lingam* before the doors are shut. On Friday nights before the temple closes, during a particularly elaborate puja, Nataraja is carried on a palanquin accompanied by music and attendants carrying flaming torches and tridents. At other times, you'll hear ancient devotional hymns from the *Tevaram*.

Unfortunately, the temple has acquired a bad reputation due to **hassle** from aggressive priests, including forceful demands for hundreds of rupees even for the simple act of applying a tikka dot to the forehead. Unlike most major temples in Tamil Nadu, which are funded by the state, Chidambaram is a private temple and is dependent solely upon pilgrims' donations. Recent attempts to rein in aggressive priestly demands for cash seem to have been successful, but you might still want to avoid potential hassle by taking an official temple guide (arrange one through your hotel or the tourist office). It's also a good idea to resist being tikka'ed by any of the priests, and to take plenty of small change for smaller donations.

The third enclosure

Four gigantic *gopura* towers rise out of the irregular third wall, each with a granite base and a brick-built superstructure of diminishing storeys covered in a profusion of carved figures. The western *gopura* is the most popular entrance, as well as being the most elaborately carved and probably the oldest (c.1150 AD). Turning north (left) from here, you come to the colonnaded **Shivaganga tank**, the site of seven natural springs. From the broken pillar at the tank's edge, all four *gopuras* are visible.

Facing the tank, on the left side, is the **Shivakamasundari Temple**, devoted to Parvati, consort of Shiva. Step inside to see the Nayak (sixteenth-century) ceiling paintings arranged in cartoon-like frames in muted reds and yellows. On the right as you enter, the story of the leper king Hiranyavarman is illustrated and, at the back, frames form a map of the temple complex. Next door, in the northwest corner, a shrine to Subrahmanya, the son of Shiva, is adorned with paintings illustrating stories from the *Skanda Purana*. Beyond this, in front of the northern *gopura*, stands a small shrine to the Navagraha (nine planets).

In the northeast corner, the largest building in the complex, the **Raja Sabha** (fourteenth to fifteenth century) is also known as "the thousand-pillared hall"; tradition holds that there are only nine hundred and ninety-nine actual pillars, the thousandth being Shiva's leg. During festivals the deities Nataraja and Shivakamasundari are brought here and mounted on a dais for the anointing ceremony, *abhishekha*.

The importance of **dance** at Chidambaram is underlined by the reliefs of dancing figures inside the east *gopura* demonstrating 108 *karanas* (a similar set is to be found in the west *gopura*). A *karana* (or *adavu* in Tamil) is a specific point in a phase of movement prescribed by the extraordinarily comprehensive Sanskrit treatise on the performing arts, the *Natya Shastra* (c.200 BC–200 AD) – the basis of all classical dance, music and theatre in India. A caption from the *Natya Shastra* surmounts each *karana* niche. Four other niches are filled with images of patrons and *stahapatis* – the sculptors and designers responsible for the iconography and positioning of deities.

A pavilion at the south *gopura* houses an image of Nandi, Shiva's bull. Although not accessible from here, the central Nataraja shrine faces south; as with all Shiva temples, Nandi sits opposite the god. In the southwest corner, a shrine contains one of the largest images in India of the elephant-headed son of Shiva, Ganapati (Ganesh). If you stand inside the entrance (*mandapa*), with your back to Ganapati, you'll see at the base of the two pillars nearest the shrine, carvings of the two important devotees of Nataraja at Chidambaram (see box on p.508). To the right is the sage Patanjali, with a snake's body, and on the left Vyaghrapada, with a human body and tiger's feet.

The second enclosure

To get into the square **second enclosure**, head for its western entrance (just north of the west *gopura* in the third wall) which leads into a circumambulatory passageway. Once beyond this second wall it's easy to become disorientated, as the roofed inner enclosures see little light and are supported by a maze of colonnades. The atmosphere is immediately more charged, reaching its peak at the very centre.

On the north side, the **Mulasthana** houses the *svayambhulingam* worshipped by Patanjali and Vyaghrapada. The **Deva Sabha**, or "hall of the gods", on the east, shelters as many as a hundred bronze images used in processions and is a meeting place for members of the three hundred Dikshitar brahmin families who own and maintain the temple. Beyond it lies the other, eastern entrance to the second enclosure.

The **Nritta Sabha**, or "dance hall", stands on the site where Shiva outdanced Kali (see box below), now the southwest corner of the second enclosure. Probably the oldest surviving structure of the two inner areas, its raised platform was fashioned in stone to resemble a wooden temple chariot, or *ratha*. Before they were inexplicably concreted over in the mid-1950s, the east and west sides of the base were each adorned with a wheel and a horse; all that can be seen now are fragments.

The innermost enclosure

Passing through the southern entrance (marked by a gold flagstaff) to the **innermost enclosure** brings you immediately into a hallway which leads west to the nearby **Govindaraja shrine**, dedicated to Vishnu – a surprise in this most Shaivite of environments. The deity is attended by non-Dikshitar brahmins, who, it is said, don't always get along with the Dikshitars. From outside the shrine, non-Hindus can see through to the most sacred part of the temple, the **Kanaka Sabha** and the **Chit Sabha**, adjoining raised structures, roofed with copper and gold plate and linked by a hallway. Two huge bells and extremely loud *nagaswarams* (double-reed wind instruments), *tavils* (drums) and *nattuvangams* (cymbals) call worshippers for ceremonies. The only entrance – closed to non-Hindus – is up five silver-plated steps into the Chit Sabha, guarded by the devotees Vyaghrapada and Patanjali and lit by an arc of flickering oil lamps.

The Chit Sabha houses bronze images of Nataraja and his consort Shivakamasundari. Behind and to the left of Nataraja, a curtain, sacred to Shiva and strung with rows of leaves from the bilva tree, demarcates the most potent area

---

Shiva and Kali's dance

The thousand-headed cosmic serpent, **Adisesha**, upon whose coiled body Vishnu reclines in the primordial ocean, once expressed a wish to see Shiva's famed dance. Having arranged time off from his normal duties with Vishnu, Adisesha prayed to Shiva, who was so impressed by the serpent's entreaties that he promised to dance in the forest of Tillai (the site of Chidambaram). Adisesha was reborn as the human sage **Patanjali** (represented as half-man, half-snake) and made straight for Tillai. There he met another sage who shared his wish to see Shiva dance, **Vyaghrapada** – "Tiger Feet", who had been granted the claws of a tiger to help him climb trees and pluck the best flowers to offer Shiva. Together, they worshipped a *svayambhulingam*, a *shivalingam* that had "self-manifested" in the forest, now housed in the Mulasthana shrine of Sabhanayaka temple. However, the guardian of the forest, who turned out to be the goddess **Kali**, refused to allow Shiva to dance when he arrived. In response, he challenged her to a **dance competition** for possession of the forest. Kali agreed but, perhaps due to modesty, she could not match a pose of Shiva's – it involved raising the right foot above the head. Defeated, Kali was forced to move off a little way north, where a temple now stands in her honour.

of all. Within it lies the **Akashalingam**, known as the *rahasya*, or "secret", of Chidambaram; made of the most subtle of the elements, Ether (*akasha*) – from which Air, Fire, Water and Earth are born – the *lingam* is invisible. This is said to signify that God is nowhere, only in the human heart.

A crystal *lingam*, said to have emanated from the light of the crescent moon on Shiva's brow, and a small ruby Nataraja are worshipped in the Kanaka Sabha. They are ritually bathed in the flames of the priests' camphor fire or oil lamps six times a day. This inner area is where you're most likely to hear **oduvars**, hereditary singers from the middle, non-brahmin castes, intoning verses of ancient Tamil poetry. The songs with which they regale the deities at puja time, drawn from compilations such the *Tevaram* or earlier *Sangam*, are believed to be more than a thousand years old.

Gangaikondacholapuram

Devised as the centrepiece of a city built by the Chola king Rajendra I (1014–42 AD) to celebrate his conquests, the magnificent **Brihadishwara temple** stands in the tiny village of **GANGAIKONDACHOLAPURAM**, in Trichy District, 35km north of Kumbakonam. The tongue-twisting name means "the town of the Chola who took the Ganges". Under Rajendra I, the Chola empire did indeed stretch as far as the great river of the north, an unprecedented achievement for a southern dynasty. Aside from the temple and the rubble remains of Rajendra's palace, 2km east at Tamalikaimedu, nothing of the city remains. Nonetheless, this is among the most extraordinary archeological sites of South India, outshone only by Thanjavur, and devoid of visitors most of the time, which gives it a memorably forlorn feel.

Buses run here from Kumbakonam every five minutes, and Gangaikonda-cholapuram is also served by some between Trichy and Chidambaram; to move on, buses back to Kumabakonam pass through the village every ten minutes. Be sure not to get stuck here between noon and 4pm when the temple is closed. Parts of the interior are extremely dark, and a torch is useful. Facilities in the surrounding village are minimal; there's little more than a couple of chai shops.

Brihadishwara Temple

Dominating the village landscape, the **Brihadishwara Temple** (daily 6am–noon & 4–8pm; free) is enclosed by a rectangular wall; visitors enter through a gateway to the north, separated from the main road by a car park. You must remove your shoes and leave them at the hut in the corner of the car park, to the right of the main gateway entrance. From the gateway, you arrive at a well-maintained, grassy courtyard, flanked by a closed hall-way (*mandapa*). Over the sanctuary, to the right, a massive pyramidal tower (*vimana*) rises 55m in nine diminishing storeys. Though smaller than the one at Thanjavur, the tower's graceful curve gives it an impressive refinement. At the entrance you're likely to meet an ASI caretaker, who can act as a guide to all the deities sculpted on the temple; you will also be shown the lovingly tended gardens.

Turning right (north) inside the courtyard, before you reach a small shrine to the goddess **Durga**, containing an image of Mahishasuramardini (the slaying of the buffalo demon), you come across a small well guarded by a lion statue known as Simha-kinaru and made from plastered brickwork. King Rajendra is said to have had Ganges water placed in the well to be used for the ritual anointing of the *lingam* in the main temple. The lion, representing Chola kingly power, bows to the huge Nandi respectfully seated before the eastern entrance of the temple, in line with the *shivalingam* contained within.

Directly in front of the eastern entrance to the temple stands a small altar for offerings. Two parallel flights of stairs ascend to a porch, the *mukhamandapa*, where a large pair of guardian deities flank the entrance to the long pillared hallway.

Immediately inside the temple a guide can show you the way to the tower, up steep steps. On either side of the temple doorway, sculptures of Shiva in his various benevolent (*anugraha*) manifestations include him blessing Vishnu, Devi, Ravana and the saint Chandesha. In the northeast corner an unusual square stone block features carvings of the nine planets (*navagraha*). A number of **Chola bronzes** (see p.689) stand on the platform; the figure of Karttikeya, the war god, carrying a club and a shield, is thought to have had particular significance.

The base of the main temple sanctuary is decorated with lions and scrollwork. Above this decoration, running from the southern to the northern entrance of the *ardhamandapa*, a series of sculpted figures in plastered niches, portray different images of Shiva. The most famous is at the northern entrance, showing Shiva and Parvati garlanding the saint Chandesha, who here is sometimes identified as Rajendra I.

Two minutes' walk northeast along the main road (turn right from the car park), the tiny **Archeological Museum** (daily except Fri 10am–1pm & 2–5.45pm; free) contains locally discovered Chola odds and ends including terracotta lamps, coins, weapons, tiles, bronze, bangle pieces, palm-leaf manuscripts and an old Chinese pot.

Kumbakonam and around

Sandwiched between the Kaveri (Cauvery) and Arasalar Rivers is the busy town **KUMBAKONAM**, 74km southwest of Chidambaram and 38km northeast of Thanjavur. Kumbakonam is believed by Hindus to be the place where the water pot (*kumba*) of *amrita*, the ambrosial beverage of immortality, was washed up by a great deluge from atop sacred Mount Meru in the Himalayas. Shiva, who just happened to be passing the pot in the guise of a wild forest-dwelling hunter, for some reason fired an arrow at the pot, causing it to break. From the shards, he made the *lingam* that is now enshrined in the **Kumbareshwara Temple**, whose *gopuras* tower over the town, along with those of some seventeen other major shrines. A former capital of the Cholas, who are said to have kept a high-security treasury here, Kumbakonam is today the chief commercial centre for the Thanjavur region. The main bazaar, **TSR Big Street**, is especially renowned for its quality costume jewellery.

The main reason to stop in Kumbakonam is to admire the exquisite sculpture of the **Nageshwara Swami Shiva Temple**, which contains the most refined Chola stone carving still in situ. The town also lies within easy reach of the magnificent Darasuram and Gangaikondacholapuram temples, both spectacular ancient monuments that see very few visitors. In addition, the village of **Swamimalai**, only a bike ride away, is the state's principal centre for traditional **bronze-casting**. As is usually the case, all the temples close soon after noon and reopen around 4pm.

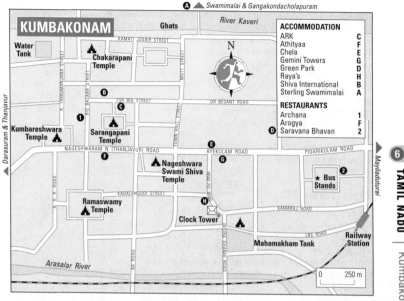

Arrival and information

Kumbakonam's small **railway station**, in the southeast part of town, 2km from the main bazaar, is well served by trains from both north and south, and has a left-luggage office (24hr) and decent **retiring rooms** (non a/c ❶, a/c ❷). The hectic **Moffussil** (local) and **Aringannar** (long-distance) bus stands are opposite each other in the southeast of town, five minutes' walk from the railway station. All the timetables are in Tamil, but there's a 24hr enquiry office with English-speaking staff. Buses leave for Gangaikondacholapuram, Pondicherry and Thanjavur every few minutes, many via Darasuram. Frequent services run to Chennai and Trichy, and several daily to Bangalore. There are a few small **Internet** places on TSR Big Street, plus an ICICI ATM machine, 100m east of the *Siva International*.

Accommodation

Kumbakonam is not a major tourist location, and has limited **accommodation**, with only one upper-range hotel, the *Sterling Swamimalai*, 10km southeast of town on the outskirts of Swamimalai village (see p.514). The good news for budget travellers is that most of the inexpensive places are clean and well maintained.

ARK 21 TSR Big St ☎0435/242 1234. Fifty large, clean rooms (some a/c) on five floors, all with windows, and TVs on request. Bland, but comfortable enough, with an a/c bar serving snacks. ❸–❺

Athityaa Nageshwaram N (Thanjavur) Rd ☎0435/242 1794, ✉hotathi_kmb@sancharnet .in. Rather worn and grubby place, especially for

the price, although the rooms are spacious – ask for one on the west side, facing the temple. ❸–❹

Chela 9 Ayikulam Rd ☎0435/243 0336, ✆243 1592. Large mid-range place between the bus stand and centre, distinguished by its horrendous mock-classical facade. Soap, fresh towels and TVs are offered as standard, and there are also two restaurants and a bar. ❸–❺

Gemini Towers 18 Ayikulam Rd ☏0435/243 1559. Across the road from the *Chela*; a grand name for a very run-of-the-mill budget lodge, but it's welcoming and all the rooms are tidy and good value (though non-a/c). ❷

Green Park 10 Lakshmi Vilai St ☏0435/240 3912, ✉greenpark_hotel@rediffmail.com. Excellent-value business-oriented hotel with spotless doubles, all with TV, and some with a/c. There's also a coffee shop (5am–10pm) and the *Peacock* non-veg restaurant. ❹–❺

Raya's 18 Head Post Office Rd ☏0435/242 3170, ⓦwww.hotelrayas@yahoo.co.in. A well-maintained

hotel near the sights with clean and comfortable, albeit smallish, rooms; there's also some traffic noise. ❹–❺

Shiva International 101/3 TSR Big St ☏0435/242 4013, ✉hotelsiva@rediff.com. After the temple *gopuras*, this huge hotel complex is the tallest building in town. Their standard non-a/c is a bargain (ask for #301, which has great views on two sides) and all the spacious, airy doubles are decent value. You can climb up on the roof for incredible views of sunset and dawn behind the *gopuras*. ❸–❹

The Town

Surmounted by a multicoloured *gopura*, the eastern entrance of Kumbakonam's seventeenth-century **Kumbareshwara temple**, home of the famous *lingam* from which the town derived its name, is approached via a covered market selling a huge assortment of cooking pots (a local speciality), as well as the usual glass bangles and trinkets. As you enter you'll pass the temple elephant, Manganal, with painted forehead and necklace of bells. Beyond the flagstaff, a *mandapa* houses a fine collection of silver *vahanas* (vehicles of the deities, used in festivals) and *pancha loham* (compound of silver, gold, brass, iron and tin) figures of the 63 Nayanmar poet-saints (see p.643).

The principal and largest of the Vishnu temples in Kumbakonam is the thirteenth-century **Sarangapani Temple**, entered through a ten-storey pyramidal *gopura* gate more than 45m high. The **central shrine** dates from the late Chola period, with many later accretions. Its entrance, within the innermost court, is guarded by huge *dvarpalas*, identical to Vishnu whom they protect. Between them are carved stone *jali* screens, each different, while in front of them stands the sacred, square *homam* fireplace. During the day, rays of light from tiny ceiling windows penetrate the darkness around the sanctum, designed to resemble a chariot with reliefs of horses, elephants and wheels. A painted cupboard contains a mirror for Vishnu to see himself when he leaves the inner sanctum.

The small **Nageshwara Swami Shiva Temple**, in the centre of town, is Kumbakonam's oldest temple, founded in 886 AD and completed a few years into the reign of Parantaka I (907–c.940 AD). First impressions are unpromising, as much of the original building has been hemmed in by later Disney-coloured accretions, but beyond the main courtyard, occupied by a large columned *mandapa*, a small *gopura*-topped gateway leads to an inner enclosure where the earliest Chola shrine stands. Framed in the main niches around its sanctum wall are a series of exquisite stone figures, regarded as the finest surviving pieces of **ancient sculpture** in South India. With their languid stance and mesmeric, half-smiling facial expressions, these modest-sized masterpieces far outshine the more monumental art of Thanjavur and Gangaikondacholapuram. The figures show Dakshinamurti (Shiva as a teacher, on the south wall), Durga and a three-headed Brahma (north wall) and Ardanari, half-man, half-woman (west wall). Joining them are near-life-size voluptuous maidens believed to be queens or princesses of King Aditya's court.

The most famous and revered of many sacred **water tanks** in Kumbakonam, the **Mahamakham** in the southeast of town, is said to have filled with ambrosia (*amrit*) collected from the pot broken by Shiva. Every twelve years, when Jupiter passes the constellation of Leo, it is believed that water from the Ganges and eight other holy rivers flows into the tank, thus according it the status of *tirtha*, or sacred river crossing. At this auspicious time, as many as four million pilgrims come here for an absolving bathe. On February 18, 1992, these pilgrims included Jayalalitha Jayaraman (see box on p.456). As Jayalalitha was being showered with sacred water in a specially reserved corner of the tank, the crowds pressed forward to get a closer look, provoking a *lathi* charge from her police bodyguard. In the ensuing stampede, 48 pilgrims were crushed to death. Newspaper reports over the following weeks ascribed the accident to "collapsing walls" and "general mayhem". The most recent gathering, in 2004, passed without incident.

Eating

There's nothing very exciting about **eating out** in Kumbakonam, and most visitors stick to their hotel restaurant. For a change of scene, though, a few places stand out.

Archana Big Bazaar St. Right in the thick of the market, and popular among shoppers for its good-value South Indian "meals" and great *uttapams*, although it can get hot and stuffy inside. Foreigners cause quite a stir here, but are made very welcome.

Arogya *Athityaa* hotel (ground floor), Nageshwaram N (Thanjavur) Rd. The best veg restaurant in town.

No surprises on the menu, but their lunchtime "unlimited meals" (Rs25–35) are excellent, and they serve North Indian tandoori in the evenings. No alcohol.

Saravana Bhavan Just east of bus stand. South Indian veg restaurant serving *iddlis*, vegetable dishes, lunchtime thalis with chai and coffee, and early breakfasts.

Around Kumbakonam

The delta lands around Kumbakonam are scattered with evocative vestiges of the Cholas' golden age, but the most spectacular has to be the crumbling Airavateshwara temple at **Darasuram**, 6km southwest. Across the fields to the north, the bronze-casters of **Swamimalai** embody a direct, living link with the culture that raised this extraordinary edifice, using traditional "lost wax" techniques, unchanged since the time when Darasuram was a thriving medieval town, to create graceful Hindu deities. You can combine the two sights in an easy half-day trip from Kumbakonam. The route is flat enough to cycle, although you should keep your wits about you when pedalling the main Thanjavur highway, which sees heavy traffic. To reach Swamimalai from Darasuram, return to the main road from the temple and ask for directions in the bazaar. Swamimalai is only 3km north, but travelling between the two involves several turnings, so expect to have to ask someone to wave you in the right direction at regular intervals. From Kumbakonam, the route is more straightforward; cross the Kaveri at the top of Town Hall Street (north of the centre), turn left and follow the main road west through a ribbon of villages.

Darasuram

The **Airavateshwara Temple**, built by King Rajaraja II (c.1146–73 AD), stands in the village of **DARASURAM**, an easy five-kilometre bus or cycle ride (on the Thanjavur route) southwest of Kumbakonam. This superb, if little-visited, Chola monument ranks alongside those at Thanjavur and Gangaikondacholapuram; but while the others are grandiose, emphasizing heroism and conquest, this is far smaller, exquisite in proportion and detail and said to have been decorated with *nitya-vinoda*, "perpetual entertainment", in mind. Shiva is here known as Airavateshwara, because he was worshipped in this temple by Airavata, the white elephant belonging to the king of the gods, Indra.

The entrance is through a large *gopura* gateway a metre below ground level in the main wall, which is topped with small reclining bull figures. Inside, the main building is set in a spacious courtyard. Next to the inner sanctuary, fronted by an open porch, the steps of the closed *mandapa* feature elegant, curled balustrades decorated with elephants and *makaras* (mythical crocodiles with floriate tails). At the corners, rearing horses and wheels make the whole into a chariot. Elsewhere, clever sculptural puns include the head of an elephant merging with that of a bull.

Darasuram's finest pieces of sculpture are the Chola black basalt images adorning wall niches in the *mandapa* and inner shrine. These include images of Nagaraja, the snake-king, with a hood of cobras, and Dakshinamurti, the "south-facing" Shiva as teacher, expounding under a banyan tree. One rare image shows Shiva as Sharabha, part man, beast and bird, destroying the man-lion incarnation of Vishnu, Narasimha – indicative of the animosity between the Shaivite and Vaishnavite cults.

Outside, a unique series of somewhat gruesome panels, hard to see without climbing onto the base, form a band along the top of the basement of the closed *mandapa* and the sanctum sanctorum. They illustrate scenes from Sekkilar's *Periya Purana*, one of the great works of Tamil literature. The poem tells the stories of the Tamil Shaivite saints, the Nayanmars, and was commissioned by King Kulottunga II, after the poet criticized him for a preoccupation with erotic, albeit religious, literature. Sekkilar is said to have composed it in the Raja Sabha at Chidambaram; when it was completed the king sat every day for a year to hear him recite it.

Each panel illustrates the lengths to which the saints were prepared to go to demonstrate devotion to Shiva. The boy Chandesha, for example, whose job it was to tend the village cows, discovered one day that they were involuntarily producing milk. He decided to bathe a *lingam* with the milk as part of his daily worship. Appalled by this apparent waste, the villagers complained to his father, who went to the field, cursed the boy, and kicked the *lingam* over. At this affront to Shiva, Chandesha cut off his father's leg with an axe; he is shown at the feet of Shiva and Parvati, who have garlanded him. Another panel shows a man who frequently gave food to Shiva devotees. When his wife was reluctant to welcome and wash the feet of a mendicant who had previously been their servant, he cut off her hands. Elsewhere, a Pallava queen has her nose cut off for inadvertently smelling a flower, rendering it useless as an offering to Shiva. The last panel shows the saint **Sundara** who sang a hymn to Shiva, in return for which Shiva rescued a child who had been swallowed by a crocodile.

Swamimalai

SWAMIMALAI, 8km west of Kumbakonam, is revered as one of the six sacred abodes of Lord Murugan, Shiva's son, whom Hindu mythology records became his father's religious teacher (*swami*) on a hill (*malai*) here. The site of this epic role reversal now hosts one of the Tamils' holiest shrines, the **Swaminatha Temple**, crowning the hilltop of the centre of the village, but of more interest to non-Hindus are the hereditary **bronze-casters'** workshops dotted around the bazaar and the outlying hamlets.

Known as **sthapathis**, Swamimalai's casters still employ the "lost wax" process (*madhuchchishtavidhana* in Sanskrit) perfected by the Cholas to make the most sought-after temple idols in South India. Their finished products are displayed in numerous showrooms along the main street, from where they are exported worldwide, but it can be more memorable to watch the *sthapathis* in action, fashioning the original figures from beeswax and breaking open the moulds to expose the mystical finished metalwork inside. One of most welcoming workshops lies 2km south of the village, sheltered under a coconut coppice along the main road to Darasuram (look out for it on the right if you're coming from this direction). At any one time, you can see most stages of the manufacturing process, and they keep a modest selection of souvenir pieces for sale. For more on Tamil bronze-casting, see p.689.

The nearby hamlet of **Thimmakkudy**, 2km back towards Kumbakonam, is home to the area's grandest **hotel**, the *Sterling Swamimalai* (☏0435/248 0044, ℮sterling_kmb@sancharnet.in; rooms from $93.50; ❾) a beautifully restored nineteenth-century brahmins' mansion with resident yoga teacher, Ayurvedic massage room, and lively culture shows in the evenings.

Thanjavur

One of the busiest commercial towns of the Kaveri delta, **THANJAVUR** (aka "Tanjore"), situated 55km east of Tiruchirapalli and 35km southwest of Kumbakonam, is often overlooked by travellers. However, its history and treasures – among them the breathtaking **Brihadishwara Temple**, Tamil Nadu's most awesome Chola monument – give it a crucial significance to South Indian culture. The home of the world's finest Chola bronze collection, it holds enough of interest to keep you enthralled for at least a couple of days, and is the most obvious base for trips to nearby Gangaikondacholapuram, Darasuram and Swamimalai.

Thanjavur is roughly split in two by the east–west **Grand Anicut Canal**. North of the canal and once entirely enclosed by a fortified wall, the **old town** was, between the ninth and the end of the thirteenth centuries, chosen as the capital of their extensive empire by all the Chola kings save one. None of their secular buildings survives, but you can still see as many as ninety temples, of which the Brihadishwara most eloquently epitomizes the power and patronage of Rajaraja I (985–1014), whose military campaigns spread Hinduism to the Maldives, Sri Lanka and Java. Under the Cholas, as well as the later Nayaks and Marathas, literature, painting, sculpture, Karnatic classical music and Bharatanatyam dance all thrived here. Quite apart from its own intrinsic interest, the Nayak **Royal Palace compound** houses an important library and museums including the aforesaid collection of bronzes.

Of major local **festivals**, the most lavish celebrations at the Brihadishwara Temple are associated with the birthday of King Rajaraja, in October. An eight-day celebration of **Karnatic classical music** is also held each January at the Panchanateshwara temple at **Thiruvaiyaru**, 13km away, to honour the great Karnatic composer-saint, Thyagaraja.

Arrival and information

Buses from Chennai pull in at the long-distance State Bus Stand, opposite the City Bus Stand just south of the walled old town. Most other services, including buses from Madurai, Tiruchirapalli and Kumbakonam, stop at the New Bus Stand, inconveniently located 4km southwest of the centre in the middle of nowhere. Rickshaws into town from here cost Rs40–50,

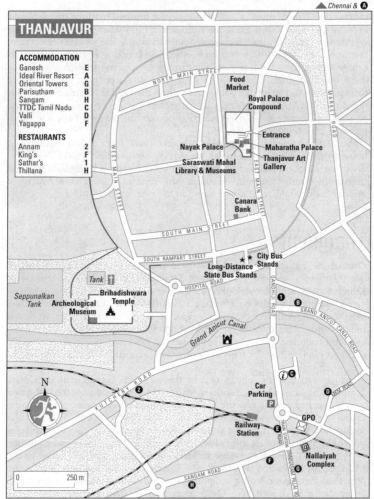

▼ *New Bus Stand, Rajaraja Cholan Museum & Tiruchirapalli*

or you can jump on one of the very frequent shuttle buses #74 for just Rs3. The **railway station** is just south of the centre and has a reservation office (Mon–Sat 8am–2pm & 2.15–8pm; Sun 10am–2pm & 3–5pm) for booking trains to Chennai, Tiruchirapalli, Rameshwaram and other destinations. There are also several fast passenger services daily to Thiruvarur, Nagapattinam and Nagore. Luggage can be left in the parcel office for a small baksheesh.

The **GPO** and most of the hotels and restaurants lie on or around **Gandhiji Road** (aka Train Station Road), which crosses the canal and leads to the railway station in the south. The **TTDC Tourist Office** (Mon–Fri 10am–5.45pm; ☏04362/230984) is next to the *TTDC Tamil Nadu* hotel on Gandhiji Road. You can **change money** at Canara Bank on South Main Street and, with a bit of gentle persuasion, at the *Parisutham* hotel – useful out of banking hours, although the rates are not always favourable. The government **hospital** is on Hospital Road, and there are plenty of pharmacies on Gandhiji Road. For **Internet** access, head for Gemini Soft (daily 9am–10pm; Rs30 per hour), on the first floor of the *Oriental Towers* hotel, Srinivasam Pillai Road.

Accommodation

Most of Thanjavur's **hotels** are concentrated in the area between the railway station and bus stands. They tend to be more expensive than elsewhere in the state, and there's very little choice at the bottom of the market; if you're travelling on a tight budget, this may be somewhere to consider treating yourself to an upgrade.

Ganesh 314 Srinivasam Pillai Rd ☎04362/231113, ⓔhotel_ganesh2004@hotmail .com. Very close to the railway station, but also on a very noisy road. The rooms (some with a/c) are clean, however, and there's a good veg restaurant. ❷–❹

Ideal River Resort Vennar Bank, Palli Agrharam ☎04362/250833, ⓔresortsindia@satyam.net.in. Luxurious chalet-rooms in a self-contained resort 7km from the centre in a very pleasant riverside location complete with swimming pool and very good restaurant. Free drop-offs and pick-ups from town for guests. Popular with tour groups, so book in advance. ❼–❾

Oriental Towers 2889 Srinivasam Pillai Rd ☎04362/230724, ⓔtnj_hottowers@sancharnet .in. Huge hotel-cum-shopping complex with a small swimming pool on the fourth floor and luxurious rooms. Good value for the price, with a business centre, Internet access and three restaurants. ❼

Parisutham 55 Grand Anicut Canal Rd ☎04362/231801, ⓔhotel.parisutham@vsnl.com. Plush hotel with spacious a/c rooms (from $119), a large palm-fringed pool (residents only), multi-cuisine restaurant, craft shop, foreign exchange and a travel agent. Popular with tour groups, so book ahead. ❾

Railway Retiring Rooms Contact Matron on the first floor of the railway station. Six big clean

doubles opening out onto a large communal veranda overlooking the station approach. Great value. ❶

Sangam Trichy Rd ☎04362/234151, ⓦwww .hotelsangam.com. Thanjavur's newest luxury hotel, about 1km southwest of the station. Comfortable a/c rooms (from $102), an excellent restaurant, pool (Rs150 for non-residents), health club and beautiful Tanjore paintings – the one in the lobby is worth a trip here in itself. ❾

TTDC Tamil Nadu Gandhiji Rd, 10min from the bus and railway stations ☎04362/231325, ⓕ231970. Once the raja's guesthouse, but now a typically dilapidated state-run hotel, albeit with more character than modern alternatives. Rooms, set around a leafy enclosed garden, are large, comfortable and carpeted; some have a/c. ❷–❺

Valli 2948 MKM Rd ☎04362/231580. The best budget option in town, this exceptionally friendly place has super-clean rooms (some with a/c) opening onto bright green corridors, plus a roof terrace and a popular restaurant downstairs. ❷–❹

Yagappa 1 Trichy Rd ☎04362/230421. Spacious, well-appointed rooms with sit-outs, large, tiled bathrooms, friendly staff and a bar and restaurant. Reception features intriguing picture frames made from coffee roots. The King's Bar is friendly, but the "20% discount for foreigners" is strictly ignored. ❸

Brihadishwara Temple

Thanjavur's skyline is dominated by the huge tower of the **Brihadishwara Temple** (daily 6am–noon & 4–8pm; free), which for all its size lacks the grandiose excesses of later periods. The site has no great significance; the temple was constructed as much to reflect the power of its patron, King Rajaraja I, as to facilitate the worship of Shiva. Profuse **inscriptions** on the base of the main shrine provide incredibly detailed information about the organization of the temple, showing it to have been rich, both in financial terms and in ritual activity. Among recorded **gifts** from Rajaraja, from booty acquired in conquest, are the equivalent of 600lb of silver, 500lb of gold and 250lb of assorted jewels, plus income from agricultural land throughout the Chola empire, set aside for the purpose. No fewer than four hundred female dancers, **devadasis** (literally "slaves to the gods", married off to the deity), were employed, and each provided with a house. Other staff – another two hundred people – included dance teachers, musicians, tailors, potters, laundrymen, goldsmiths, carpenters, astrologers, accountants and attendants for all manner of rituals and processions.

Entrance to the complex is on the east, through two **gopura** gateways some way apart. Although the outer one is the larger, both are of the same pattern: massive rectangular bases topped by pyramidal towers with carved figures and vaulted roofs. At the core of each is a monolithic sandstone lintel, said to have been brought from Tiruchirapalli, over 50km away. The outer facade of the inner *gopura* features mighty fanged *dvarpala* door guardians, mirror images of each other, and thought to be the largest monolithic sculptures in any Indian temple. Panels illustrating scenes from the *Skanda Purana* decorate the base, including the marriage of Shiva and Parvati.

Once inside, the gigantic **courtyard** gives plenty of space to appreciate the buildings. A sixteenth-century pavilion, fronted by a tall lamp column and facing the main temple, holds the third largest Nandi (Shiva's bull-vehicle) in India. The **main temple**, constructed of granite, consists of a long pillared *mandapa* hallway, followed by the *ardhamandapa*, or "half-hall", which in turn leads to the inner sanctum, the *garbha griha*. The plinth of the central shrine measures 46 square metres; above it, the pyramidal *vimana* tower (at just under 61m high, the largest and tallest in India when it was built in 1010) rises in thirteen diminishing storeys, the apex being exactly one-third of the size of the base. Such a design is quite different from later temples, where the *vimanas* become smaller as the *gopura* entranceways increasingly dominate – a desire to protect the sanctum sanctorum from the polluting gaze of outsiders. The long pillared *mandapa* from the Vijayanagar period (sixteenth century) has been roughly adjoined to the *ardhamandapa*; you can see the mouldings do not match. Inside, the walls are decorated with eighteenth-century Maratha portraits. The *vimana* is an example of a "structured monolith", a stage removed from the earlier rock-cut architecture of the Pallavas, in which blocks of stone are assembled and then carved. The profusion of carvings, aside from the inscriptions, include the *dvarpala* door guardians, Shiva, Vishnu, Durga, Ganapati (Ganesh), Bhu-devi (the female goddess Earth) and Lakshmi, arranged on three sides in two rows. As the stone that surmounts the *vimana* is said to weigh eighty tonnes, there is considerable speculation as to how it got up there; the most popular theory is that the rock was hauled up a six-kilometre-long ramp. Others have suggested the use of a method comparable to the Sumer Ziggurat style of building, in which logs were placed in gaps in the masonry and the stone raised by leverage. The simplest answer, of course, is that perhaps it's not a single stone at all.

Over 3.5m high, the black *shivalingam* in the **inner sanctum** is called Adavallan, "the one who can dance well" – a reference to Shiva as Nataraja, the King of the Dance, who resides at Chidambaram and was the *ishtadevata*, chosen deity, of the king. The *lingam* is not always on view, but during puja ceremonies (8 & 11am, noon & 7.30pm) a curtain is pulled, revealing the god to the devotees.

Surrounding the *garbha griha*, an **ambulatory passage** contains some of South India's greatest art treasures, including a frieze of beautiful **frescoes** dating from the reign of Rajaraja I, though unfortunately the passage was closed to the public at the time of writing to protect the paintings. These were only recovered in the 1930s, having remained hidden for nearly one thousand years behind layers of inferior murals from the seventeenth century. Featuring uncannily lifelike portraits of the royals, deities, celestials and dancing girls – naked save for their

Shopping in Thanjavur

In an old house in the suburb of Karanthattangudi, ten minutes by auto-rickshaw from the centre of Thanjavur, V.R. Govindarajan's **shop** at 31 Kuthirakkatti Street contains an amazing array of **antiques**, including brass pots, betel nut boxes, oil lamps, coins and Tanjore paintings. Small, modern and simple examples of Tanjore paintings cost around Rs500, while large, recently made pictures with 24-carat gold decoration may cost as much as Rs20,000, and for a fine hundred-year-old painting you can expect to part with Rs80,000 or more. Upstairs, seven artists work amid a chaotic collection of clocks and bric-a-brac, and you can watch the various stages in the process of Tanjore painting.

The **Chola Art Galerie**, two minutes' walk south of the palace entrance at 78/799 East Main Street, opposite the Sharja Building, has a good selection of handicrafts including some excellent bronzes and woodwork. The owner of the **Parishutham hotel craft shop** is very knowledgeable about local craftsmen, Tanjore paintings, copper "art plates" and musical instruments such as the classical *vina*. A branch of the government chain, **Poompuhar Handicrafts**, on Gandhiji Road (next to the *TTDC Tamil Nadu Hotel*), stocks copper Thanjavur "art plates", brass oil lamps and sandalwood carvings, and there's also a **cooperative handicrafts shop** above the Sangeeta Mahal concert hall in the Royal Palace compound.

For more background on Tanjore paintings, see Contexts, p.691.

jewellery and ornate hairstyles – the frieze is a swirl of rich pigments made from lapis lazuli, yellow and red ochre, lime and lamp soot. In the upper ambulatory, also kept under lock and key, a sculpted series of reliefs showing the 108 classical dance poses predates the famous sets at Chidambaram (see p.505).

Outside, the walls of the courtyard are lined with **colonnaded passageways** – the one along the northern wall is said to be the longest in India. The one on the west, behind the temple, contains 108 *lingams* from Varanasi and (heavily graffitied) panels from the Maratha period. At the centre stands a small shrine to Varuna (the Vedic god associated with water and the sea), next to an image of the goddess Durga, usually kept clothed.

Other **shrines** in the enclosure include one behind the main temple to a devotee-saint, Karuvurar, supposedly able to cure barrenness. To the northwest, a seventeenth-century temple to Subrahmanya (a son of Shiva) has a base finely decorated with sculptures of dancers and musicians. Close to the figure of Nandi is a thirteenth-century Devi shrine; in the northeast corner, a *mandapa* houses images of Nataraja, his consort and a devotee, and is also used for decorating icons prior to processions. A **path** leads from between the two *gopuras* the length of the main wall where, behind the temple, the manicured lawn lined with benches is a haven of quiet. The temple water tank lies just beyond, next to the northwest corner.

In the southwest corner of the courtyard, the small **Archeological Museum** (daily 9am–1pm & 4–6pm; free) houses an interesting collection of sculpture, including an extremely tubby, damaged Ganesh, before-and-after photos detailing restoration work to the temple in the 1940s and displays about the Cholas. You can also buy the excellent ASI booklet, *Chola Temples*, which gives detailed accounts of Brihadishwara and the temples at Gangaikondacholapuram and Darasuram.

The Royal Palace Compound and around

Members of the erstwhile royal family still reside at the **Royal Palace Compound**, on East Main Street (a continuation of Gandhiji Road), 2km northeast of Brihadishwara Temple. Dotted around the compound are several reminders of Thanjavur's past under the Nayaks and the Marathas, including an exhibition of oriental manuscripts and a superlative museum of **Chola bronzes**. Just south, the dusty and run-down **Tamil University Museum** contains coins and musical instruments, while near the entrance to the complex the rambling **Royal Museum** (daily 9am–6pm; Rs1, Rs20 extra for camera) houses a modest collection of costumes, portraits, musical instruments, weapons, manuscripts and courtly accessories. Just after the ticket office for the Royal Museum, in a damp upper room of the palace, is a new collection, the **H.H. Raja Serfoji II Memorial Hall and Museum** (daily 9am–6pm; Rs1, camera Rs20). In the eighteenth century, the youthful Serfoji II was a victim of a violent feud between two regional ruling families, the Pandayas and Haysalas, and ended up in a pitch-black prison cell for years. Despite several attempts to suffocate him by burning red chillies in his cell, Serfoji survived and was eventually rescued by a Danish missionary in 1789. He then accepted his rightful position as Maharajah of Thanjvaur, and never forgot his debt to the missionary, who remained a close adviser and taught the ruler about Christianity, a religion he grew to hold in great respect. The museum's collection is the outcome of a lifetime investigation into the turbulent life and reign of Serfoji II by his grandson, though sadly it doesn't do much to illuminate his life. The permanent exhibition comprises a clutter of ivory desk sets, silverware, newspaper cut-outs, royal portraits and decaying royal finery.

The palace buildings have been in a sorry state for years. Work on the palace began in the mid-sixteenth century under Sevappa Nayak, the founder of the Nayak kingdom of Thanjavur; other sections were added by the Marathas from the end of the seventeenth century onwards. Remodelled by Shaji II in 1684, the **Durbar Hall**, or hall of audience, houses a throne canopy decorated with the mirrored glass distinctive of Thanjavur. Although damaged, the ceiling and walls are elaborately painted. Five domes are striped red, green and yellow, while the wall friezes showing leaf and pineapple designs, plus trumpeting angels in a night sky, show European influence. Wall niches house sculptures of deities, including the figure of Shiva devotee Patanjali (see box on p.508) with a snake winding around his leg, and an Englishman said to be in the unlikely position of learning classical dance from a young woman, to whom he is presenting a gift. Visible on the left wall, as you face the throne, are traces of a Nayak mural of deer in a forest. Next to this, two holes in the floor, once entrances to a secret passageway, are allegedly home to cobras and not recommended for exploration. Some of the later paintings portray the entertainers who, as recently as the 1960s, performed in the now overgrown square outside: fighters, circus performers and wrestlers.

The **courtyard** outside the Durbar Hall was the setting for one of the more poignant moments in Thanjavur's turbulent history when, in 1683, the last of the Nayak kings gave himself up to the king of Madurai, whose forces were swarming through the city after a long siege. Legend has it that the attackers gained the upper hand after the Raja of Madurai's chief guru-magician filled the Kaveri with rotten pumpkins, casting a spell to ensure that whoever drunk its water would defect to their side. Finding himself deserted by his troops, the Nayak king is said to have donned his ceremonial gem-studded robes, pinned his bushy eyebrows back with gold wires and marched to his death intoning Vaishnavite verses. As he did so, a massive explosion behind him signalled the destruction of the palace harem, along with all its inhabitants, whose honourable deaths the king had ensured by packing the ground floor with gunpowder.

Saraswati Mahal Library Museum

The **Saraswati Mahal Library**, one of the most important Oriental manuscript collections in India, is closed to the public, but used by scholars from all over the world. Over eighty percent of its 44,000 manuscripts are in Sanskrit, many on palm-leafs, and some are very rare or even unique. The Tamil works include treatises on medicine and commentaries on works from the Sangam period, the earliest literature of the South. A small **museum** (daily except Wed 10am–1pm & 2–5pm; free) displays a bizarre array of books and pictures from the collection. Among the palm-leaf manuscripts is a calligrapher's *tour de force* in the form of a visual mantra, where each letter in the inscription "Shiva" comprises the god's name repeated in microscopically small handwriting. Most of the Maratha manuscripts, produced from the end of the seventeenth century, are on paper; they include a superbly illustrated edition of the Mahabharata. Sadists will be delighted to see that the library managed to hang onto its copy of the explicitly illustrated **Punishments in China**, published in 1804. Next to it, full rein is given to the imagination of French artist, **Charles Le Brun** (1619–90), in a series of pictures on the subject of physiognomy. Animals such as the horse, bullock, wolf, bear, rabbit and camel are drawn in painstaking care above a series of human faces which bear an uncanny, if unlikely, resemblance to them. You can buy postcards of this and exhibits from the other palace museums in the **shop** next door.

Thanjavur Art Gallery

A magnificent collection of **Chola bronzes** – the finest of them from the Tiruvengadu hoard unearthed in the 1950s – fills the **Thanjavur Art Gallery** (daily 9am–1pm & 3–6pm; Rs15, camera Rs30, video Rs200), a high-ceilinged audience hall with massive pillars, dating from 1600. The elegance of the figures and delicacy of detail are unsurpassed. A tenth-century statue of Kannappa Nayannar (#174), a hunter-devotee, shows minutiae right down to his embroidered clothing, fingernails and the fine lines on his fingers. The oldest bronze, four cases left of the main doorway (#58), shows Vinadhra Dakshinamurti ("south-facing Shiva") who, with a deer on one left hand, would have originally been playing the *vina* – though the musical instrument has long since gone. However, the undisputed masterpiece of the collection shows Shiva as Lord of the Animals (#86), sensuously depicted in a skimpy loin-cloth, with a turban made of snakes. Next to him stands an equally stunning Parvati, his consort (#87), but the cream of the female figures, a seated, half-reclining Parvati (#97), is displayed on the opposite side of the hall.

Rajaraja Cholan Museum

The **Rajaraja Cholan Museum** (daily 10am–1pm & 2–5.30pm; Rs1), in the basement of the modern Mandimandapam, about 2km southwest of town on the Trichy Road, houses Chola stone sculpture and small objects excavated at Gangaikondacholapuram (see p.509) such as tiny marbles, games boards, bangles and terracotta pieces. Two illuminated maps show the remarkable extent of the Chola empire under the great kings Rajaraja I and his son, Rajendra I, but otherwise the rest of the collection is rather uninspiring and poorly labelled, with practically no English at all.

Eating and drinking

For **food**, there's the usual crop of busy and cheap "meals" canteens dotted around town, the best of which are *Annantha Bhavan* and the *Sri Venkantan*, both

For more on **Chola bronzes**, see Contexts p.689.

The best **train** service for Chennai is the Rockfort Express #6178 (departs 8.30pm; 8hr 30min), which terminates at Egmore Station in Chennai. There are also trains from Thanjavur to Bangalore, Chengalpattu and Madurai, but to other places in Tamil Nadu there are more frequent connections from Trichy and Thiruvarur, both a one-hour journey from Thanjavur by **bus**. There are very frequent departures from the New Bus Stand, 4km southwest of the centre, for both Trichy and Kumbakonam (roughly every 10min) and Madurai (roughly every 30min).

on Gandhiji Road near the textile stores. Of Thanjavur's dingy bars, *King's* in the *Yagappa* hotel is the best choice for a quiet beer.

Annam *Pandiyar Residency*, 14 Kutchery Rd. Small, inexpensive and impeccably clean veg restaurant that's recommended for its cut-above-the-competition lunchtime thalis (Rs25) and evening South Indian snacks (especially the delicious cashew *uttapams*). A safe option for women travellers.

King's *Yagappa*, Trichy Rd. Seven kinds of beer are served in the usual dimly lit room, or on the "lawn" (read: "sandy back yard"), where decor includes stuffed lizards and plastic flowers in fish tanks. They also serve tasty chicken and *pakora* plate snacks.

Sathar's Gandhiji Rd. This is the town's most popular non-veg restaurant (mains Rs60–80), and a pretty safe place to eat chicken, thanks to the constant turnover. Seating is downstairs, or on a covered terrace, and there's a mostly male clientele.

Thillana *Sangam*, Trichy Rd. Swish multi-cuisine restaurant that's renowned for its superb South Indian thalis at lunchtime (11am–3pm; Rs105), while evenings (7.30pm–10pm) feature an extensive à la carte menu, including superb *chettinad* specialities. Worth a splurge just for the live Carnatic music (*veena*, flute and vocals on alternate days). Count on Rs250–300 per head.

Thiruvarur

Often bypassed by visitors travelling between Thanjavur and the coast, **THIRUVARUR**, 55km east of Thanjavur, is famed as the birthplace of the musical saint **Thyagaraja**, to whom the town's huge temple is dedicated. According to Hindu myth, the first temple was built on this spot after Shiva and Parvati, at rest in a garden at the foot of Mount Kailash, were disturbed by a handful of bilva leaves scattered over them by a playful monkey. Shiva, delighted, blessed the beast, who was reincarnated as the kindly King Muchukunda of the Manu dynasty. The king built many temples but later got involved in a fight with the demon Vala, who was finally killed by the god Indra. Muchukunda was offering puja in thanks for his salvation when Shiva appeared and instructed him to build a temple at Thiruvarur. The current **Thyagarajaswamy temple**, on the north side of town, dates mainly from the fourteenth and fifteenth centuries, and its three successive enclosed courtyards contain a number of shrines, including one to Thyagaraja with an unusual line of the nine *navagrahas* (planet deities) peering in at the saint's image. The outer walls and ceilings are brightly painted with vivid images of Shiva and accompanying deities, while the inner sanctum houses a bronze *lingam* crowned with a seven-headed cobra.

In March the town hosts the **Arulmigu Thyagarajaswamy car festival**, when for ten days animated crowds pull and push the great temple car (the largest in Tamil Nadu) and its smaller companions on a laborious path around the surrounding streets. Ask at regional tourist offices for specific dates.

Practicalities

Frequent **buses** and **trains** run to Thiruvarur from Thanjavur and Nagappattinam; there are also a few trains from Mayiladuturai in the north. The
railway station and bus stand are five minutes' walk apart in the south of town.
To reach the temple, cross the bridge just north of the bus stand, and carry
straight on for ten minutes or so. It's not difficult to find **accommodation**,
even during the car festival. Several adequate lodges (all ❶) are situated close to
the bus stand on Thanjavur Road: try the *President* (☎04366/222748) or *Sekar*
(☎04366/222525), which is next to the post office. If you're not on a rock-
bottom budget, the best option by far, though, is the *Royal Park Hotel*, just over
1km out of the centre on By-Pass Road (☎04366/221020, ℉221024; ❸–❺),
which has a choice of a/c and non-a/c rooms, and two decent **restaurants**
serving South and North Indian cuisine.

Kodikkarai Bird Sanctuary

On a small knob of land jutting out into the sea, 65km south of Nagappattinam and 80km southeast of Thanjavur, **KODIKKARAI BIRD SANCTU-
ARY** plays host to around 250 avine species in a mix of dry evergreen forest
and swampland. On the way to the sanctuary, you pass through fifty thousand
acres of salt marshes around **Vedaranyam**, the nearest town, 11km north.
Traditionally the mainstay of the local economy, vast salt fields line the road,
the salt drying in thatched mounds. During the struggle for Independence this
was an important site for demonstrations in sympathy with Gandhi's famous
salt protest. Over the last few years, however, salt has been pushed into second
place by prawn cultivation, which brings in a good income but has necessitated
widespread forest clearance and has reduced the numbers of birds visiting
Kodikkarai.

The **best time** to visit the sanctuary is between November and February,
when migratory birds arrive, mostly from Iran, Russia and Poland, to spend the
winter. The rarest species include black bittern, barheaded goose, ruddy shelduck,
Indian black-crested baza and eastern steppe eagle. During December and January the swamps host spotted billed pelicans and around ten thousand flamingos,
who live on tiny shrimps (the source of the lurid pink colouring of their plumage); their numbers have dropped from the 30,000 that wintered here in the days
before prawn production took off. The deep forest is also the home of one of the
most colourful birds in the world, the Indian pitta (*pitta brachyura*).

Well-informed local **guides** equipped with powerful binoculars can take
you to key birdspotting sites. The Forest Department works with the Mumbai
Natural History Society to ring birds and trace their migrating patterns, and the
MNHS occasionally organizes **field trips** around the area.

From the jetty, you might be lucky enough to spot schools of **dolphins**,
although to get access to the jetty you'll need to seek permission from the Navy
Command – Kodikkarai is only 40km across the Palk Strait from Jaffna, and
the navy monitors all seaborne activity between Sri Lanka and the Indian coast
from the grounds of the *Thambuswamy Lodge*.

Practicalities

Regular **buses** run to Kodikkarai via Vedaranyam, which is connected by
bus to Nagappattinam, Thanjavur, Trichy, Chennai and Ramanathapuram (for

Rameshwaram). Chennai buses can be booked in advance in a house next door to Shitharthan Medical Stores on Vedaranyam's East Main Street (over the road from the bus stand). The nearest **railway station** is 30km away at Tiruthuraipondi.

The only **accommodation** in the area is at the *Thambuswamy Lodge*, near the lighthouse (reserve through the wildlife warden in Nagapattinam ☏04365/253092; ●), which has en-suite rooms for just Rs100. The lodge is invariably full during January, but at other times it's possible to turn up without a reservation. **Food** is limited to a couple of chai shops outside the gate of the sanctuary, although staff can bring meals in if asked. If you need to eat in Vedaranyam, the simple *Karaivani*, near the bus station in the main bazaar on Melai Street, serves vegetarian banana-leaf meals.

Tiruchirapalli and around

TIRUCHIRAPALLI – usually referred to as **Trichy** – stands in the plains between the Shevaroy and Palani hills, just under 100km north of Madurai. Dominated by the dramatic Rock Fort, it's a sprawling commercial centre with a modern feel; the town itself holds little attraction, but pilgrims flock through en route to the spectacular **Ranganathaswamy Temple** in **Srirangam**, 6km north, the work of the Chola kings who gained supremacy here in the eleventh century. In the twelfth century, the Cholas were ousted by the Vijayanagar kings of Hampi, who then stood up against Muslim invasions until 1565, when they succumbed to the might of the sultans of the Deccan. Less than fifty years later the Nayaks of Madurai came to power, constructing the fort and establishing Trichy as a trading city. After almost a century of struggle against the French and British, who both sought lands in southeast Tamil Nadu, the town came under British control until it was declared part of Tamil Nadu state in 1947.

Arrival and information

Trichy's **airport**, 8km south of the centre, has Indian Airline flights to Chennai (Mon, Wed, Fri & Sun), Kozhikode (Tues & Sat) and Thiruvananthapurum (Tues, Thur, Sat & Sun). There are also daily flights to **Colombo** with SriLankan Airlines (☏0431/246 0844; office at the *Femina* hotel). The journey into town by taxi (Rs200) or bus (#7, #28, #59, #63 and #K1) takes less than half an hour; for airport enquiries and bookings go to Indian Airlines, 4A Dindigul Road (☏0431/248 0233).

Trichy's main railway station, **Trichy Junction** – which has given its name to the southern district of town – provides frequent rail links with Chennai, Madurai and the eastern coastline. From here you're within easy reach of most hotels, restaurants and banks, as well as the **bus stands**. There are two stands – **Central** and **State Express** – but no fixed rules about where a particular bus will depart from; you just have to keep asking. State Express buses run frequently to major towns such as Madurai, Kodaikanal and Pondicherry right around the clock. **Private buses**, if you really want to risk the manic and dangerous driving, line up along Rockins Road, between the two bus stands. The efficient local city service (#1) that leaves from the platform on Rockins Road, opposite the *Shree Krishna* restaurant, is the most convenient way of getting to the Rock Fort, the temples and Srirangam. **Rickshaws** are also widely available.

The **tourist office** (Mon–Fri 10am–5.45pm; ☏0431/246 0136) is opposite the Central Bus Stand, just outside the *Tamil Nadu* hotel, and offers helpful

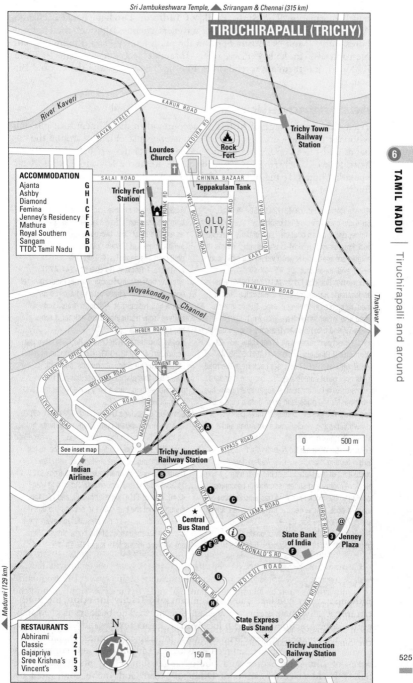

Sri Jambukeshwara Temple, ▲ Srirangam & Chennai (315 km)

TIRUCHIRAPALLI (TRICHY)

River Kaveri

NAVAB STREET

KARUR ROAD

MADURA RD

Trichy Town
Railway
Station

Lourdes
Church ✝

Rock
Fort

SALAI ROAD

Trichy Fort
Station

CHINNA BAZAAR

Teppakulam Tank

SHASTRI RD

MADRAS TRUNK RD

WEST BOULEVARD ROAD

BIG BAZAAR ROAD

OLD
CITY

EAST BOULEVARD ROAD

BOULEVARD ROAD

ACCOMMODATION
Ajanta	G
Ashby	H
Diamond	I
Femina	C
Jenney's Residency	F
Mathura	E
Royal Southern	A
Sangam	B
TTDC Tamil Nadu	D

Woyakondan Channel

THANJAVUR ROAD

Thanjavur ▲

MUNICIPAL OFFICE RD

HEBER ROAD

COLLECTOR'S OFFICE ROAD

WILLIAMS ROAD

CONVENT RD

MADURAI ROAD

RACE COURSE ROAD

CLEVELAND ROAD

DINDIGUL ROAD

See inset map

Ⓐ

BYPASS ROAD

0   500 m

Indian
Airlines

Trichy Junction
Railway Station

Ⓑ

Ⓞ ①

Ⓒ

ROYAL RD

WILLIAMS ROAD

BIRDS ROAD

@ ②

RACQUET COURT LANE

★ Central
Bus Stand

ⓘ

Ⓞ ⑤ E @ ④

Ⓞ D

MCDONALD'S RD

State Bank
of India

Ⓕ

③ Jenney
Plaza

Ⓖ

ROCKINS RD

DINDIGUL ROAD

MADURAI ROAD

Ⓗ

Ⓘ ①

State Express
Bus Stand ★

Trichy Junction
Railway Station

N

0   150 m

RESTAURANTS
Abhirami	4
Classic	2
Gajapriya	1
Sree Krishna's	5
Vincent's	3

▲ Madurai (129 km)

▼ Airport (6km)

travel information. The **State Bank of India** on Dindigul Road exchanges American Express and Thomas Cook travellers' cheques, although the Highway Forex office (Mon–Sat 10am–6pm) in the plush Jenney Plaza is more efficient. Netpark, also in Jenney Plaza, offers **Internet** access (daily 8am–10.30pm; Rs20/hr), and there are several other Internet places opposite the Central Bus Stand.

Accommodation

Trichy has no shortage of **hotels** to accommodate the thousands of pilgrims who visit the town; dozens of pretty characterless places cluster around the bus stands and offer good value for money, keeping tariffs just below the Rs200 mark to avoid incurring luxury taxes. There are also a few more comfortable upmarket hotels. Traffic noise is a real problem in this area, so ask for a room at the back of any hotel you check into.

Ajanta Rockins Rd ☎0431/241 5504. A huge, 85-room complex centred on its own Vijayanagar shrine, and with an opulent Tirupati deity in reception. Popular with middle-class pilgrims; rooms (the singles are particularly good value) are plain and clean, and some have a/c. ❸–❺

Ashby 17A Rockins Rd ☎0431/246 0652. This atmospheric Raj-era place is great value, and is most foreign tourists' first choice. The rooms are large and impeccably clean, with fresh towels, soap, cable TV and mozzie coils. There's a decent bar and a little courtyard restaurant. Great value. ❸–❺

Diamond 2 Dindigul Rd ☎0431/241 5858. A jaded, offbeat 1960s hotel, set back from the road in its own quiet compound. The bargain standard rooms have a fair amount of superficial grime, but are huge for the price, and open onto a veranda and lawn. The cosier "cottages" have pebble-strewn verandas, wacky colour schemes and mouldy bathrooms. ❷–❸

Femina 109 Williams Rd ☎0431/241 4501, ✉try_femina@sancharnet.in. Well-maintained place east of the state bus stand with a sprawling block of rooms and suites, some with balconies looking to the Rock Fort. Also has plush restaurants, a pool, fitness centre, travel services, shops and a 24hr coffee bar. ❹–❼

Jenney's Residency 3/14 McDonald's Rd ☎0431/241 4414, ✉jenneys@satyam.net.in.

A slightly jaded marble-and-mirrors place with comfortable rooms, featuring all mod cons, as well as a "Wild West" bar, two good restaurants (including an upmarket Chinese place) and swimming pool (non-residents Rs100). ❼–❽

Mathura 1 Rockins Rd ☎0431/241 4737, ⊛www.hotelmathura.com. Large, modern hotel opposite the bus stand with big a/c rooms and a veg restaurant – though it also but suffers from traffic noise, so ask for a room at the back. ❸–❹

Royal Southern Race Course Rd, 3km from the centre ☎0431/242 1303, ✉royalsouthern@eth .net. Set in five acres of grounds, and with its own pool, this places has spacious a/c rooms in a peaceful setting, plus a very good restaurant and Internet access. ❻–❼

Sangam Collector's Office Rd ☎0431/241 4700, ⊛www.hotelsangam.com. Trichy's top hotel boasts all the facilities of a four-star, including an excellent pool (Rs75 for non-residents) and the top-notch *Chembian* multi-cuisine restaurant, with live Carnatic music at weekends. Rooms from $125. ❾

TTDC Tamil Nadu McDonald's Rd ☎0431/241 4346. One of TTDC's better hotels, and just far enough from the bus stand to escape the din. Best value are the non-a/c doubles, though even these are dowdier than most of the competition. There are also a/c rooms with cable TV. ❷–❺

The Town

Although Trichy conducts most of its business in **Trichy Junction**, the southern district, the main sights are at least 4km north. The **bazaars** immediately north of the Junction heave with locally made cigars, textiles and fake diamonds made into inexpensive jewellery and used for dance costumes. Thanks to the town's frequent, cheap air connection with Sri Lanka, you'll also come across boxes of smuggled Scotch and photographic film. Head north along Big Bazaar Road (a continuation of Dindigul Road) and you're confronted by the dramatic profile of the **Rock Fort**, topped by the seventeenth-century Vinayaka (Ganesh) Temple.

North of the fort, the River Kaveri marks a wide boundary between Trichy's crowded streets and its more serene temples; the **Ranganathaswamy Temple** is so large it holds much of the village of Srirangam within its courtyards. Also north of the Kaveri is the elaborate **Sri Jambukeshwara Temple**, while several British **churches** dotted around town make for an interesting contrast. The **Shantivanam Ashram**, a bus ride away, is open to visitors year round.

The Rock Fort

Looming incongruously above the bazaars in the north of town, Trichy's **Rock Fort** (daily 6am–8pm; Rs1, camera Rs10, video Rs50) is best reached by bus (#1) from outside Trichy Junction railway station or from Dindigul Road; auto-rickshaws will try to charge you Rs50 or more for the five-minute ride to the rock fort.

The massive sand-coloured rock on which the fort rests towers to a height of more than 80m, its irregular sides smoothed by wind and rain. The Pallavas were the first to cut into it, but it was the Nayaks who grasped the site's potential as a fort, adding a few walls and bastions as fortifications. From the entrance, at the north end of Chinna Bazaar, a long flight of red-and-white painted steps cuts steeply uphill, past a series of Pallava and Pandya rock-cut temples (closed to non-Hindus), to the **Ganesh Temple** crowning the hilltop. The views from its terrace are spectacular, taking in the Ranganathaswamy and Jambukeshwara temples to the north, their *gopuras* rising from a sea of palm trees, and the cubic concrete sprawl of central Trichy to the south.

Shri Jambukeshwara Temple

By the side of the Chennai-bound road north out of Trichy, the **Shri Jambukeshwara Temple**, dedicated to Shiva, is smaller and later than the Ranganathaswamy Temple. Much of it is closed to non-Hindus, but the sculptures that adorn the walls in its outer courts, of an extravagance typical of the seventeenth-century Nayak architects, are worth the short detour.

Srirangam: Ranganathaswamy Temple

The **Ranganathaswamy Temple** at **Srirangam**, 6km north of Trichy, is among the most revered Vishnu shrines in South India, and also one of the largest and liveliest, engulfing homes, shops and markets within its outer walls. Enclosed by seven rectangular walled courtyards, and covering more than 120 acres, it stands on an island defined by a tributary of the Kaveri River. This location symbolizes the transcendence of Vishnu, housed in the sanctuary reclining on the coils of the snake Adisesha, who in legend formed an island for the god, resting on the primordial Ocean of Chaos.

Frequent **buses** from Trichy pull in and leave from outside the southern gate; bus #1 from the Central Bus Stand in Trichy is the most regular. The temple is approached from the south. A gateway topped with an immense and heavily carved *gopura*, plastered and painted in bright pinks, blues and yellows, and completed as recently as 1987, leads to the outermost courtyard, the latest of seven built between the fifth and seventeenth centuries. Most of the present structure dates from the late fourteenth century, when the temple was renovated and enlarged after a disastrous sacking by the Delhi armies in 1313. The **outer three courtyards**, or *prakaras*, form the hub of the temple community, housing ascetics, priests and musicians, and the streets are lined with food stalls and shops selling souvenirs, ritual offerings and fresh flower garlands to be presented to Vishnu in the inner sanctuary. You can people-watch for hours here as the narrow streets are filled with pilgrims and locals going about their daily business and devotional activities.

The **entrance** to the temple proper at the wall enclosing the **fourth courtyard**, is where visitors remove footwear and purchase camera and video tickets (Rs50 and Rs100) before passing through a high gateway which is topped by a magnificent *gopura* and lined with small shrines to teachers, hymn-singers and sages. In earlier days, this fourth *prakara* would have formed the outermost limit of the temple, and was the closest members of the lowest castes could get to the sanctuary. It contains some of the finest and oldest buildings of the complex, including a temple to the goddess **Ranganayaki** in the northwest corner, where devotees worship before approaching Vishnu's shrine. On the eastern side of the *prakara*, the heavily carved "thousand pillared" *kalyan mandapa*, or hall, was constructed in the late Chola period. During the month of Margali (Dec/Jan) Tamil hymns are recited from its southern steps as part of the Vaikuntha Ekadasi festival. South of the *kalyan mandapa*, the pillars of the outstanding **Sheshagiriraya Mandapa** are decorated with rearing steeds and hunters armed with spears. These are splendid examples of **Vijayanagar** style, which depicts chivalry defending the temple against Muslim invaders, and represents the triumph of good over evil. On the southern side of the *prakara*, the Venugopala shrine, dedicated to Krishna, probably dates from the Nayak period (late sixteenth century).

To the right of the gateway into the fourth courtyard, a small **museum** (daily 10am–noon & 3–5pm; free) houses a modest collection of stone and bronze sculptures, and some delicate ivory plaques. For Rs10, you can climb to the roof of the fourth wall from beside the museum and take in the view over the temple rooftops and *gopuras*, which increase in size from the centre outwards. The central tower, crowning the holy sanctuary, is coated in gold and carved with images of Vishnu's incarnations, on each of its four sides.

Inside the gate to the **fifth courtyard** – the final section of the temple open to non-Hindus – is a pillared hall, the **Garuda Mandapa**, carved throughout in typical Nayak style. Maidens, courtly donors and Nayak rulers feature on the pillars that surround the central shrine to Garuda, the man-eagle vehicle of Vishnu. Other buildings in the third courtyard include the vast kitchens, which emanate delicious smells as *dosas* and *vadas* are prepared for the deity, while devotees ritually bathe in the tanks of the moon and the sun in the northeast and southeast corners.

The dimly lit **sixth** (and innermost) **courtyard**, the most sacred part of the temple, shelters the image of Vishnu in his aspect of Ranganatha, reclining on the serpent Adisesha. The shrine is usually entered from the south, but for one day each year, during the **Vaikuntha Ekadasi festival**, the north portal is opened; those who pass through this "doorway to heaven" can anticipate great merit. Most of the temple's daily festivals take place in this enclosure, beginning each morning with *vina*-playing and hymn-singing, as Vishnu is awakened in the presence of a cow and an elephant, and ending just after 9pm with similar ceremonies.

Eating

To **eat** well in Trichy, you won't have to stray far from the bus stand, where the town's most popular "meals" joints do a roaring trade throughout the day.

Abhirami 10 Rockins Rd, opposite the bus stand. Trichy's best-known South Indian restaurant serves up unbeatable value lunchtime "meals" (Rs20), along with the standard range of snacks during the rest of the day. They also have a fast food counter where you can get *dosas* and *uttapams* at any time. It opens at 6.30am for piping hot *wada-pongal* breakfasts.

Classic 4 Madurai Rd, down the road from Jenney's Plaza. This bakery-cum-snack bar is *the* place to buy fresh bread, cream cakes, biscuits, cinnamon rolls and filled sandwiches. You can choose from a seemingly limitless variety of ice-cream sundaes, served up by a gaggle of giggling girls.

Gajapriya Royal Rd, on the ground floor of the *Gajapriya* hotel. Non-veg North Indian and noodle dishes are specialities of this small but blissfully cool and clean a/c restaurant. A good place to chill out over coffee.

Sree Krishna's 1, Rockins Rd, opposite the bus stand. Delicious and very filling American (Rs55) or South Indian (Rs25) "set breakfasts", specialities from all over the South after 6.30pm, and unlimited Rs35 banana leaf thalis served between 11am and 3pm.

Vincent's Dindigul Rd, next to the bakery. An "Oriental" theme restaurant, set back from the road on its own terrace, with mock pagodas, concrete bamboo, and a multi-cuisine menu that includes tasty chicken tikka and other tandoori dishes. A bit shabby now, but it's an escape from the hectic bus stand area. No alcohol; opens at 6.30pm.

Shantivanam Ashram

Situated on the banks of the sacred river Kaveri, the peaceful **Shantivanam Ashram** (T 04323/222262, E saccidananda@hotmail.com) is located in the small village of **THANNEEPALLI**, forty minutes northwest of Trichy by bus (towards Kullithalai). Its Sanskrit name literally means "Forest of Peace", an appropriate title for this small haven of ecumenical study. Founded by a Benedictine monk, Father Bede Griffiths (who died in 1993 and is buried in the ashram grounds), the ashram is based on a fusion of Christianity and Hinduism – lines from the Bhagavad Gita and *Om* symbols share space in the chapel with crosses and Biblical verses. Visitors can participate in as much or as little of the ashram's programme as they wish, and are free to make use of the extensive library. **Accommodation** in rooms and dorms is available (suggested donation Rs200 daily, including all food), and visitors are expected to share in simple chores such as food preparation. Note that the ashram is usually full during Christian celebrations.

The far south

The **far south** of Tamil Nadu comprises the broad sweep of the Vaigai plains, enfolded in the west by the bare brown Alagar Hills, which arch south from the edge of the Kaveri Delta to the tip of peninsular India. Studded with massive outcrops of pink and pale-brown granite, the region is rich in ancient myths: daredevil Shiva is said to have turned evil elephants into stone boulders, and rivers were formed to quench the thirst of giant pot-bellied dwarfs. Many of these stories probably predate the earliest traces of human settlement, but most were set down when this was the heartland of the mighty **Pandyans**, the southernmost of South India's three great warring dynasties. Their former capital, **Madurai**, is today the state's second city and, as the site of the famous Meenakshi-Sundareshwarar temple, the region's spiritual root, often dubbed "The Varanasi of the South". Further east, **Rameshwaram**, occupying a narrow spit that fractures into dozens of islets as it nears the north coast of neighbouring Sri Lanka, is equally sacred to Hindus. It forms the eastern point of a sacred triangle whose apex, at **Kanniyakumari**, combines the heady intensity of an age-old pilgrimage place with all the gimcrackery you'd expect from India's own Land's End.

Madurai and around

... a city gay with flags, waving over homes and shops selling food and drinks; the streets are broad rivers of people, folk of every race, buying and selling in the bazaars, or singing to the music of wandering bands and musicians ... amid the perfume of ghee and incense [are stalls] selling sweet cakes, garlands of flowers, scented powder and betel paan ... [while nearby are] men making bangles of conch shells, goldsmiths, cloth dealers, tailors making up clothes, coppersmiths, flower sellers, vendors of sandalwood, painters and weavers.

The Garland of Madurai, traditional Tamil poem, second century AD

One of the oldest cities in south Asia, **MADURAI**, on the banks of the River Vaigai, has been an important centre of worship and commerce for as long as there has been civilization in south India – indeed, it has long been described as "the Athens of the East". Not surprisingly, then, when the Greek ambassador Megasthenes came here in 302 BC, he wrote of its splendour, and described its queen, Pandai, as "a daughter of Herakles". Meanwhile, the Roman geographer Strabo complained that the city's silk, pearls and spices were draining the imperial coffers of Rome. It was this lucrative trade, meticulously detailed in the Alexandrian mariner's manual *The Periplus of the Erythraean Sea*, dating from the first century AD, that enabled the **Pandyan** dynasty to erect the mighty **Sri Meenakshi-Sundareshwarar Temple**. Although today surrounded by a sea of modern concrete cubes, the massive *gopuras* of this vast complex, writhing with multicoloured mythological figures and crowned by golden finials, remain the greatest man-made spectacle of the south. Any day of the week no less than 15,000 people pass through its gates; increasing to over 25,000 on Friday (sacred to the goddess Meenakshi), while the temple's ritual life spills out into the streets in an almost ceaseless round of festivals and processions. The chance to experience sacred ceremonies that have persisted largely unchanged since the time of the ancient Egyptians is one that few travellers pass up.

Madurai is the subject of an extraordinary number of **myths**. Its origins stem from a *sthala* (a holy site where legendary events have taken place) where Indra, the king of the gods, bathed in a holy tank and worshipped Shiva. Hearing of this, the Pandyan king Kulashekhara built a temple on the site and installed a *shivalingam*, around which the city grew. The name Madurai is popularly derived from the Tamil word *madhuram*, meaning "sweetness"; according to legend, Shiva shook his matted locks over the city, coating it with a fine sprinkling of *amrita*, the nectar of immortality.

Madurai's urban and suburban sprawl creates traffic jams to rival India's very worst. Chaos on the narrow, potholed streets is exacerbated by political demonstrations and religious processions, wandering cows – demanding right of way with a peremptory nudge of the haunch – and put-upon pedestrians forced onto the road by ever-increasing numbers of street traders. Open-air kitchens extend from chai-shops, where competing *parota*-wallahs literally drum up custom for their delicious fresh breads with a tattoo of spoon-on-skillet signals. Given the traffic problems, it's just as well that Madurai, with its profusion of markets and intriguing corners, is an utterly absorbing city to walk around.

Some history

Although invariably interwoven with myth, the recorded history of Madurai stretches back well over 2000 years. Numerous natural **caves** in local hills and boulders, often modified by the addition of simple rock-cut beds, were used both in prehistoric times and by ascetics, such as the Ajivikas and Jains, who practised withdrawal and penance. Madurai appears to have been the capital of the **Pandyan empire** without interruption for at least a thousand years. It became a major commercial city, trading with Greece, Rome and China through the Pandyan seaports along the Tamil coastline. Some *yavanas* (a generic term for foreigners) were employed in Madurai as palace guards and police-men; the Tamil epics describe them walking around town with their eyes and mouths wide open with amazement, much as foreign tourists still do when they first arrive. Under the Pandya dynasty, Madurai also became an established seat of Tamil culture, credited with being the site of three **sangams**, "literary academies", said to have lasted 10,000 years and to have supported some 8000 poets; despite this fanciful reckoning, the most recent of these academies does have a historical basis. The "sangam period" is generally taken to mean the first three to four centuries of the Christian era.

The Pandyas' capital finally fell in the tenth century, when the **Chola** king Parantaka took the city. In the thirteenth century, the Pandyas briefly regained power until the early 1300s, when the notorious **Malik Kafur**, the Delhi Sultanate's "favourite slave", made an unprovoked attack during a plunder-and-desecration tour of the south and destroyed much of the city. Forewarned of the raid, the Pandya king, Sundara, fled with his immediate family and treasure, leaving his uncle and rival, Vikrama Pandya, to repel Kafur. Nevertheless, the latter returned to Delhi with booty said to consist of "six hundred and twelve elephants, ninety-six thousand *mans* of gold, several boxes of jewels and pearls and twenty thousand horses".

Shortly after this raid Madurai became an independent Sultanate; in 1364, it joined the Hindu **Vijayanagar** empire, ruled from Vijayanagar/Hampi (see p.308) and administered by governors, the **Nayaks**. In 1565, the Nayaks asserted their own independence. Under their supervision and patronage, Madurai enjoyed a renaissance, being rebuilt on the pattern of a lotus centring on the Meenakshi Temple. Part of the palace of the most illustrious of the Nayaks, **Thirumalai** (1623–55), survives today. The city remained under Nayak control until the mid-eighteenth century when the **British** gradually took over. A hundred years later the British de-fortified Madurai, filling its moat to create the four Veli streets that today mark the boundary of the old city.

Arrival and information

Madurai's small domestic **airport** (℡0452/269 0433), 12km south of the city, is served by flights to and from Chennai, Mumbai and Thiruvananthapuram. Theoretically you should be able to get information at the **Government of Tamil Nadu Tourist Information Centre** booth by the exit, but it's not always open to meet flights. There's also a bookshop and a branch of Indian Bank, which changes travellers' cheques only. **Taxis** charge fixed rates of around Rs200 for journeys within the city. **City Bus** #10A leaves frequently from near the exit and will drop you at Periyar Bus Stand in town.

Arriving in Madurai by **bus**, you come in at one of two stands. The new **Central Bus Stand** is 7km east from the centre: it's connected to the centre by, among others, city bus #700. This stand is the arrival point for all services except those from towns in the west, including Kodaikanal and Coimbatore,

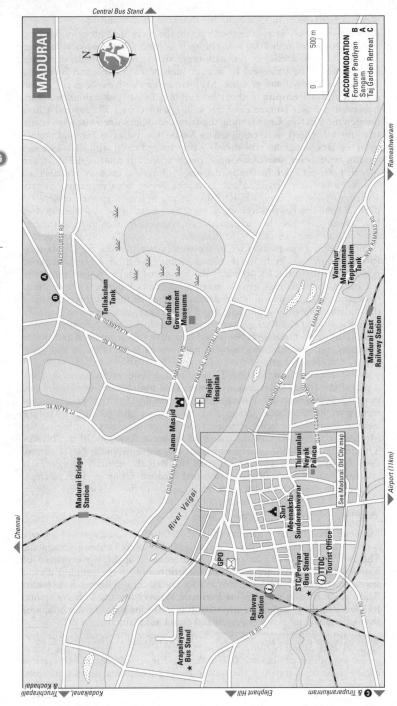

MADURAI

Central Bus Stand

N

0   500 m

ACCOMMODATION
Fortune Pandiyan   B
Sangam   A
Taj Garden Retreat C

Rameshwaram

RACECOURSE RD

Tallakulam
Tank

Gandhi &
Government
Museums

ALAGARKOIL RD

GOKALE RD

TAMUKKAN RD

PANJAL HOSPITAL RD

NEW RAMNAD RD

RAMNAD RD

Vandiyur
Mariamman
Teppakulam
Tank

Madurai East
Railway Station

PT RAJIN RD

KODAIKANAL RD

Jama Masjid

Rajaji
Hospital

MUNICHALAI RD

KALANKI RD

OLD KUSAVAR

Airport (11km)

Madurai Bridge
Station

River Vaigai

Thirumalai
Nayak
Palace

See Madurai: Old City map

Chennai

Shri
Meenakshi-
Sundareshwar

GPO

STC/Periyar
Bus Stand

TTDC
Tourist Office

Railway
Station

TPK RD

Arapalayam
Bus Stand

TB RD

Kodaikanal, Tiruchirapalli

Elephant Hill

Tiruparankunram

C & Tiruparankunram

Trichirapalli & Kochadai

and Kerala, which terminate at the **Arapalayam Bus Stand** in the northwest corner of town, about 2km from the railway station. In the centre, local city buses operate from either the **STC bus stand**, or **Periyar stand** next door.

Both are on West Veli Street in the west of the old city, and are very close to the railway station and most accommodation. Madurai's clean and well-maintained **railway station** is just west of the centre off West Veli Street. You can leave your luggage at the 24-hour cloakroom (Rs10 per 24hr) in the main hall, where you'll also find a very helpful branch of the **Tourism Department Information Centre** (daily 6.30am–8.30pm). The **reservations office** (Mon–Sat 8am–2pm & 2.15–8pm, Sun 8am–2pm) is in a new building to the left of the main station hall. There's a small veg **canteen** on Platform 1 and a **prepaid auto-rickshaw** and **taxi booth** outside the main entrance, which opens to coincide with train arrivals.

Information

The **TTDC** Tourist office is on West Veli Street (Mon–Fri 10am–5.45pm, plus most Saturdays 10am–1pm; ☎0452/233 4757) and staff are very helpful, as are those at the railway station tourist office (see above). Both offices offer general information and maps about Madurai and the surrounding areas, and provide details of **car rental**. They will also arrange, with a little notice, **city tours** (7am–noon or 3–8pm; Rs100 per head) in a minibus with one of the government-approved **guides**, who can otherwise usually be found at the southern entrance to the temple. If you're hiring a guide at the temple entrance, get a list of names first from the tourist office; government-approved guides usually speak far better English than private operators and are reliable. If you want to rent a **taxi** to see the outlying sights, the rank at the main railway station abides by government set rates; a five-hour city tour will cost Rs550.

Madurai's **GPO** is at the corner of West Veli Street. and North Veli Street. For postal services, enter on the Scott Road side (Mon–Sat 8am–7.30pm, Sun 9am–4.30pm; speedpost 10am–7pm). For **poste restante** (Mon–Sat 9.30am–7pm), go to the Philatelic Bureau on the southwest corner of the building. **Internet access** is offered at many places around town – try Net Tower, 13/8 Kaka Thoppu Street, beside the *Hotel International* (daily 8am–10pm; Rs30 per hr), or Friends (daily 9am–11pm; Rs20 per hr), just around the corner from it.

The best place to **change money** is Alagendran Forex Services at 168 North Veli St, opposite the post office (Mon–Sat 9am–6.30pm). The State Bank of India is at 6 West Veli St. There are several 24hr ATMs in town, including those at the Canara Bank on West Perumal Maistry Street and the UTI Bank on Station Road. Cheap **bike rental** is available at SV, West Chitrai Street, near the west entrance to the temple, or at the stall on West Veli Street, opposite the *Tamil Nadu* hotel.

Accommodation

Madurai has a wide range of **accommodation**, from rock-bottom lodges to good, clean mid-range places that cater for the flocks of pilgrims and tourists. There's a cluster of hotels on **West Perumal Maistry Street**; upmarket options lie a few kilometres out of the town centre, north of the Vaigai. Unless otherwise stated, the hotels listed below are marked on the Old City map (p.534).

Aarathy 9 Perumal Kovil, West Mada St ☎0452/233 1571. Great location near the Periyar bus stand, overlooking the Kundalagar Temple. All rooms have TV, and some have a/c and a balcony.

Good a/c restaurant and a courtyard restaurant which gets especially popular when the temple elephant is led through each morning and afternoon. It's usually full of foreigners so book ahead,

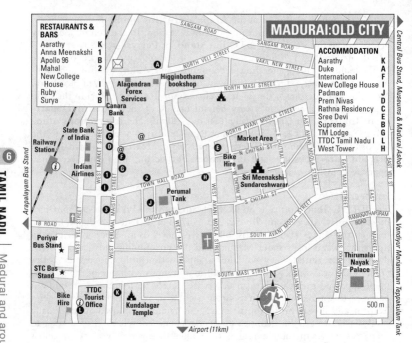

RESTAURANTS & BARS

Aarathy	K
Anna Meenakshi	1
Apollo 96	B
Mahal	2
New College House	I
Ruby	3
Surya	B

MADURAI:OLD CITY

ACCOMMODATION

Aarathy	K
Duke	A
International	F
New College House	I
Padmam	J
Prem Nivas	D
Rathna Residency	C
Sree Devi	E
Supreme	B
TM Lodge	G
TTDC Tamil Nadu I	L
West Tower	H

Central Bus Stand, Museums & Madurai Ashok

Vandiyur Mariamman Teppakulam Tank

Arapalayam Bus Stand

▼ Airport (11km)

but ask to see your room before checking in, as not all of them are up to standard. ③–④

Duke 6 North Veli St, close to the junction with West Veli St ☎0452/234 1154. Good-value modern hotel with its own rooftop restaurant and larger-than-average non-a/c rooms (plus smaller a/c rooms); ask for one with a window. ③–④

Fortune Pandiyan Racecourse Rd, north of the river (see main Madurai map, p.532) ☎0452/253 7090, ℮mail@fortunepandiyan.com. Smart, centrally a/c hotel with large comfortable rooms. It's quiet and relaxed, if a little way out of town, and there's a good restaurant, bar, exchange facilities and a travel agency. Rooms from $75. ⑨

International 46/80 West Perumal Maistry St ☎0452/537 7463. Recently renovated lodge with laid-back service, but the rooms are decent and all have cable TV. ②–④

New College House 2 Town Hall Rd ☎0452/234 2971, ℮info@newcollegehouse.com. Recently spruced up, this huge, maze-like place has more than 200 rooms (a few with a/c), and one of the town's best "meals" canteens on the ground floor (see p.542). The very cheapest rooms are grubby, but there are likely to be vacancies here when everywhere else is full. ②–⑤

Padmam 1 Perumal Tank West St ☎0452/234 0702. Modern, clean, comfortable and central

hotel, with a small rooftop restaurant – although it's popular with the foreign crowd, so book in advance. The views from the front rooms, overlooking the ruined Perumal tank, are worth paying extra for. ④–⑤

Prem Nivas 102 West Perumal Maistry St ☎0452/234 2532, ℮premnivas@eth.net. From the outside this place looks a lot swankier than it is, but the spacious rooms are among the best deals in the city. ③–④

Railway Retiring Rooms First floor of the station via the stairway on platform 1 (turn right from the main entrance hall). Huge and cleanish rooms, some with a/c, though they often get booked up. ②

Rathna Residency 109 West Perumal Maistry St ☎0452/537 4444, ℮hotelrathna@eth.net. Decent, clean a/c and non a/c rooms (the latter are better value), plus two restaurants, one on the rooftop. ④–⑥

Sangam Alagar Koil Rd (see main Madurai map, p.532) ☎0452/253 7531, ⊛www.hotelsangam .com. Situated in its own grounds on the northern outskirts of town, this plush, centrally a/c hotel has very comfortable rooms (from $125), 24hr room service, bar, currency exchange, swimming pool and pleasant gardens. ⑨

Sree Devi 20 West Avani Moola St ☎0452/234 7431. Always filled with foreigners thanks to its good-value, spotless non-a/c doubles right next to the temple. The deluxe a/c rooftop room has matchless views over the western *gopura*. No restaurant, but they will order in food and beer for you. ②–③

Supreme 110 West Perumal Maistry St ☏0452/234 3151, ✉hsupreme@sancharnet.in. A large, swish and centrally located hotel, with a great rooftop restaurant (see p.542) for sundowners as well as a 24hr forex desk, Internet facilities and travel counter. Book in advance. ③–⑥

Taj Garden Retreat 40 TPK RD, Pasumalai Hills, 6km from town (see main Madurai map, p.532) ☏0452/237 1601, ⊛www.tajhotels .com. Madurai's most exclusive hotel, occupying a beautifully refurbished colonial house set in 63 acres of landscaped grounds in the hills overlooking Madurai. There are three kinds of rooms: standard rooms in the new block ($146), superior period rooms ($174), and modern deluxe cottages ($190) dotted around the delightful gardens with great views over the Vaigai plain.

Facilities include a gourmet restaurant, pool, bar and tennis court. ⑨

TM Lodge 50 West Perumal Maistry St ☏0452/234 1651, ✉tmlodge@maduraiinfo .com. One of the best budget options on this street (despite the rather unfriendly reception and institutional atmosphere), offering immaculately clean rooms with spotless attached bathrooms; the top-floor rooms are the airiest. ③–④

TTDC Hotel Tamil Nadu I West Veli St ☏0452/233 7471, ✉ttdc@md3.vsnl.net.in. Set somewhat out on a limb, away from the temples and bazaar, but therefore pleasantly quiet, with spacious rooms overlooking a leafy courtyard. The smaller non a/c rooms are especially good value. ②–④

West Tower 42/60 West Tower St ☏0452/234 6908. Close to the temple, and with the great views from the rooftop (but not from the rooms), where there's a pleasant little thatched terrace. The cheaper rooms are fairly basic, though some rooms have a/c. It's overpriced, but you're paying for the views. ③–⑤

The City

Although considerably enlarged and extended over the years, the overall layout of Madurai's **old city**, south of the River Vaigai, has remained largely unchanged since the first centuries AD. It comprises a series of concentric squares, centred on the massive Sri Meenakshi-Sundareshwarar Temple and aligned with the cardinal points. The intention of the ancient architects was clearly to follow the dimensions of an auspicious mandala, or sacred diagram, set down in canonical texts known as the *Vastu Shastras*. These provided the blueprints for the now-lost cities of the Vedic age, 3000 years ago, and were believed to represent the laws governing the universe; they are also abstract depictions of the Hindu creator god, Brahma, in the form of the primeval being, Parusha. Whereas rectangular grid plans symbolize temporal or royal power, squares are used by Hindus to indicate the Absolute, which is why the streets boxed around Madurai's temple, each named after the different Tamil months, are of even lengths. The reason many of the city's mass rituals involve circuits of these streets in a strictly clockwise direction is because circumambulation of a powerful shrine, such as the Meenakshi Temple, is believed to activate the sacred properties of the giant mandala.

North of the river, Madurai becomes markedly more mundane and irregular. You're only likely to cross the Vaigai to reach the city's more expensive hotels or the Gandhi Museum.

Sri Meenakshi-Sundareshwara Temple

Enclosed by a roughly rectangular six-metre-high wall, in the manner of a fortified palace, the **Sri Meenakshi-Sundareshwara Temple** (daily 6am–12.30pm & 4–9.30pm; camera permit Rs30) is one of the largest temple complexes in India. Much of it was constructed during the Nayak period between the sixteenth and eighteenth centuries, but certain parts are very much older. The principal shrines (closed to non-Hindus) are those to Sundareshwarar (Shiva)

Date	Name	No. of days
Jan/Feb	Teppa	12
Feb/March	Machi Mantala	10
March/April	Kotaivasanta	9
April/May	Chittirai	12
May/June	Vasanta	10
June/July	Unchal	10
July/Aug	Ati Mulaikkottu	10
Aug/Sept	Avani Moola	12
Sept/Oct	Navaratri	9
Oct/Nov	Kolatta	6
Nov/Dec	Tirukkarttikai	10
Dec/Jan	Ennai Kappu	9

The date of each of the Madurai temple's **annual festivals** varies each year; check with a tourist office when you plan your visit. The principal and most exciting component of most of them is the **procession** (*purappatu*, or "setting forth"), held on the morning and evening of every day. Each procession is accompanied by officiating brahmins, temple employees bearing royal insignia, umbrellas, silver staffs and, at night, flaming torches. The entourage is invariably preceded by the penetrating orchestra of *tavil* (barrel drum), hand cymbals and the distinctive *nagaswaram*, a double-reed, oboe-like wind instrument for which the Madurai area is particularly famous.

Processions circumambulate clockwise inside the temple, and many leave its precincts, starting from the east entrance, passing along the Chitrai, Avani Moola or Masi streets and, on special occasions such as the floating festival (days ten and eleven of the Teppa ceremonies), leave the centre of the city altogether. Locals and visiting pilgrims crowd the streets for *darshan*, a view of the deities. The evening processions, weaving through the starlit night, are undoubtedly the most atmospheric.

Icons from the temple, special movable images, are taken out and lavishly clothed in silk and ornaments of rubies, sapphires, pearls, silver and gold. When the festival celebrates both Meenakshi and Sundareshwarar (Shiva in his form as Meenakshi's bridegroom), the contingent is usually led by Vinayaka (Ganesh, son of Shiva), as the "remover of obstacles", followed in succession by Subrahmanya (another son of Shiva), Sundareshwarar, Meenakshi and Chandeshwarar (another form of Shiva). On some occasions, the deities may be enshrined on a simple canopy, but on others, they ride on silver or gold vehicles (*vahanas*) such as horses, elephants or, most auspiciously, huge silver bulls.

At the **Avani Moola** festival, the coronation of Shiva is celebrated and his Maduran miracles are enacted in a series of plays (*lilas*). During the greatest festival of all, **Chittirai**, more plays are staged, telling the story of Meenakshi. The eighth day sees the goddess crowned as queen of the Pandyas and, on the tenth, her marriage to Shiva draws as many as fifty thousand people to the temple. Out in the streets the next morning, mayhem ensues when the most elaborate transport is brought into use for procession. The god and goddess travel in fifteen-metre-high **chariots**, with giant wooden wheels, hauled through the streets by hundreds of devotees, all tugging on long ropes. Rising from a wooden platform, the massive pyramidal bamboo superstructures are decorated in colourful appliqué and fronted by a row of rearing wooden horses.

The god and goddess are taken to the banks of the River Vaigai to meet Meenakshi's brother who, in southern mythology, is Lord Kallalagar (Vishnu). The icon of Vishnu is brought from the forested hilltop temple at Alagarkovil, 20km northeast of Madurai. Vishnu travelled to Madurai to give his sister away at the wedding, only to find on reaching the river that the ceremony had already occurred. Because of this, to appease the deity, the festivities always take place on the northern bank of the river.

and his consort Meenakshi (a form of Parvati); unusually, the goddess takes precedence and is always worshipped first.

For the first-time visitor, confronted with a confusing maze of shrines, sculptures and colonnades, and unaware of the logic employed in their arrangement, it's very easy to get disorientated. However, if you're not in a hurry, this should not deter you. Quite apart from the estimated thirty-three million sculptures to arrest your attention, the life of the temple is absolutely absorbing, and many visitors find themselves drawn back at several different times of the day. There's always plenty of activity: endless rounds of puja ceremonies; loud *nagaswaram* and *tavil* music; weddings; brahmin boys being instructed in the *Vedas*; devotees prostrating themselves; glittering market stalls inside the east entrance; and the occasional festival procession, all making this one of the most compelling places in Tamil Nadu.

Approximately fifty priests work in the temple, and live in houses close to the north entrance. They are easily identified – each wears a white *dhoti* (*veshti* in Tamil) tied between the legs; on top of this, around the waist, is a second, coloured cloth, usually of silk. Folded into the cloth, a small bag contains holy white ash. The bare-chested priests invariably carry a small towel over the shoulder. Most wear earrings and necklaces including *rudraksha* beads, sacred to Shiva. As Shaivite priests, they place three horizontal stripes of white ash on the forehead, arms, shoulders and chest and a red powder dot, sacred to the goddess, above the bridge of the nose. Most also wear their long hair tied into a knot, with the forehead shaved. Inside the temple they also carry brass trays holding offerings of camphor and ash.

The Meenakshi Temple takes the **gopura**, so prominent in other southern temples, to its ultimate extreme. The entire complex has no fewer than twelve such towers; set into the outer walls, the four largest reach a height of around 46m, and are visible for miles outside the city. Each is covered with a profusion of gaily painted stucco gods and demons, with the occasional live monkey scampering and chattering among the divine images. After a referendum in the 1950s, the *gopuras*, which had become monochrome and dilapidated, were repainted in the vivid greens, blues and bright reds you can see today; they have to be completely redone every ten years or so (the last repaint was in the mid-1990s). It is sometimes possible, for a small fee, to climb the southern, and tallest, tower to enjoy superb views over the town; for permission, enquire with the guards at one of the gateways.

The most popular **entrance** is on the eastern side and leads directly to an auspicious Shiva shrine. Another entrance nearby, parallel to this, leads through a towerless gate to the Meenakshi shrine deep inside. In the **Ashta Shakti Mandapa** ("Eight Goddesses Hallway"), a market sells puja offerings and souvenirs, from fat garlands of flowers to rough-hewn, sky-blue plaster deities. Sculpted pillars illustrate different aspects of the goddess Shakti, and Shiva's 64 miracles at Madurai. Behind this hall, to the south, are stables for the temple elephants and camels.

If you continue straight on from here and go through the seven-storey **Chitrai gopura**, you enter a passageway leading to the eastern end of the **Pottamarai Kulam** ("Tank of Golden Lotuses"), where Indra bathed before worshipping the *shivalingam*. From the east side of the tank you can see the glistening gold of the Meenakshi and Sundareshwarar *vimana* towers. Steps lead down to the water from the surrounding colonnades, and in the centre stands a brass lamp column. People take a ritually cleansing bath here, prior to entering the inner shrines, or just sit, gossip and rest on the steps.

The ceiling paintings in the open corridors are modern, but Nayak murals around the tank illustrate scenes from the *Gurur Vilayadal Puranam*, which describe Shiva's Madurai miracles. Of the two figures located halfway towards the Meenakshi shrine on the north side, one is the eighth-century king Kulashekhara Pandyan, said to have founded the temple; opposite him is a wealthy merchant patron.

On the western side of the tank is the entrance to the **Meenakshi shrine** (closed to non-Hindus), popularly known as **Amman Kovil**, literally the "mother temple". The immoveable green stone image of the goddess is contained within two further enclosures forming two ambulatories. Facing Meenakshi, just past the first entrance and in front of the sanctum sanctorum, stands Shiva's bull-vehicle, Nandi. At around 9pm, the moveable images of the god and goddess are carried to the **bed chamber**. Here the final puja ceremony of the day, the **lalipuja**, is performed, when for thirty minutes or so the priests sing lullabies (*lali*), before closing the temple for the night.

The corridor outside Meenakshi's shrine is known as the **Kilikkutu Mandapa** ("Parrot Cage Hallway"), due to the parrots which are kept here as offerings to Meenakshi. Sundareshwarar and Meenakshi are brought every Friday (6–7pm) to the sixteenth-century **Oonjal Mandapa** further along, where they are placed on a swing (*oonjal*) and serenaded by members of a special caste, the Oduvars. The black and gold, almost fairground-like decoration of the *mandapa* dates from 1985.

Across the corridor, the small **Rani Mangammal Mandapa**, next to the tank, has a detailed eighteenth-century ceiling painting of the marriage of

Meenakshi the fish-eyed goddess

The goddess **Meenakshi** of Madurai emerged from the flames of a sacrificial fire as a 3-year-old child, in answer to the Pandyan king Malayadvaja's prayer for a son. The king, not only surprised to see a female, was also horrified that she had three breasts. In every other respect, she was beautiful, as her name, Meenakshi ("fish-eyed"), suggests – fish-shaped eyes are classic images of desirability in Indian love poetry. Dispelling his concern, a mysterious voice told the king that Meenakshi would lose the third breast on meeting her future husband.

In the absence of a son, the adult Meenakshi succeeded her father as Pandyan monarch. With the aim of world domination, she then embarked on a series of successful battles, culminating in the defeat of Shiva's armies at the god's Himalayan abode, Mount Kailash. Shiva then appeared at the battlefield; on seeing him, Meenakshi immediately lost her third breast. Fulfilling the prophecy, Shiva and Meenakshi travelled to Madurai, where they were married. The two then assumed a dual role, firstly as king and queen of the Pandya kingdom, with Shiva assuming the title Sundara Pandya ("King Shiva"), and secondly as the presiding deities of the Madurai temple, into which they subsequently disappeared.

Their shrines in Madurai are today the focal point of a hugely popular fertility cult, centred on the gods' coupling, which temple priests maintain ensures the preservation and regeneration of the universe. Each night, the pair are placed together in Sundareshwarar's bedchamber, but not before Meenakshi's nose ring has been carefully removed so that it won't cut her husband in the heat of passion. Their celestial lovemaking is consistently earth-moving enough to ensure that Sundareshwarar remains completely faithful to his consort (exceptional for the notoriously promiscuous Shiva). Nevertheless, this fidelity is never taken for granted, and has to be ritually tested each year when the beautiful goddess Cellattamman is brought to Sundareshwarar "to have her powers renewed". After she is spurned, she flies into a fury that can only be placated with the sacrifice of a buffalo – one among the dozens of arcane ceremonies that make up Madurai's round of temple rituals.

Meenakshi and Sundareshwarar, surrounded by lions and elephants against a blue background. Sculptures in the hallway portray characters such as the warring monkey kings from the Ramayana, the brothers Sugriva (Sukreeva) and Bali (Vahli), and the indomitable Pandava prince, Bhima, from the Mahabharata, who was so strong that he uprooted a tree to use as a club.

Walking back north past the Meenakshi shrine, through a towered entrance, leads you to the area around the Sundareshwarar shrine. Just inside, is the huge monolithic figure of Ganesh, **Mukkuruni Vinayaka**, believed to have been found during the excavation of the Mariamman Teppakulam tank (see below). Chubby Ganesh is well known for his love of sweets, and during his annual **Vinayaka Chaturthi festival** (Sept) a special *prasad* (gift offering of food) is concocted from ingredients including 300 kilos of rice, 10 kilos of sugar and 110 coconuts. Around a corner, a small image of the monkey god **Hanuman**, covered with *ghee* and red powder, stands on a pillar. Devotees take a little with their finger for a *tillak*, to mark the forehead. A figure of Nandi and two gold-plated copper flagstaffs face the entrance to the **Sundareshwarar shrine** (closed to non-Hindus). From here, outsiders can just about see the *shivalingam* beyond the blue-and-red neon "Om" sign (in Tamil).

North of the flagstaffs are figures of Shiva and Kali in the throes of a dance competition. A stall nearby sells tiny **butter balls** from a bowl of water, which visitors throw at the god and goddess "to cool them down". If you leave through the gateway here, on the east, you'll find in the northeast corner the fifteenth-century **Ayirakkal Mandapa**, or thousand-pillared hall, now transformed into the temple's **Art Museum** (daily 10am–5.30pm; Rs2, camera Rs5) – disappointingly, screens and dusty educational displays now prevent visitors getting a clear view of this gigantic hall. However, there's a fine, if rather dishevelled, collection of wood, copper, bronze and stone sculpture, and an old nine-metre-high teak temple door. Throughout the hall, large sculptures of guardians and cosmic deities rear out at you from the broad stone pillars; many of these columns when tapped, produce different, and startlingly metallic, musical tones.

Vandiyur Mariamman Teppakulam Tank

At one time, the huge **Vandiyur Mariamman Teppakulam Tank** in the southeast of town (bus #4 or #4A; 15min) was full with a constant supply of water, flowing via underground channels from the Vaigai. Nowadays, however, it is only filled during the spectacular Teppam **Floating Festival** (Jan/Feb), when pilgrims take boats out to the goddess shrine in the centre. Before their marriage ceremony, Shiva and Meenakshi are brought in procession to the tank, where they are floated on a raft decorated with lights, which devotees pull by ropes three times, encircling the shrine. The boat trip is believed to be the overture to a seduction that reaches its passionate conclusion later that night in the temple. This traditionally makes the Teppam the most auspicious time of year to get married.

During the rest of the year the tank and the central shrine remain empty. Accessible by steps, the tank is most often used as an impromptu cricket green, and the shade of the nearby trees makes a popular gathering place. Tradition states that the huge image of Ganesh, Mukkuruni Vinayaka, in the Meenakshi Temple, was uncovered here when the area was originally excavated to provide bricks for the Thirumalai Nayak Palace.

Thirumalai Nayak Palace

Only a quarter of the seventeenth-century **Thirumalai Nayak Palace** (daily 9am–1pm & 2–5pm; Rs10 [Rs50], includes Palace Museum), 1.5km southeast of the Meenakshi Temple, now survives. Much of it was dismantled by

Thirumalai's grandson, Chockkanatha Nayak, and the materials used for a new palace at Tiruchirapalli. What stands here today is a result of the restoration and renovation in 1858 by the governor of Chennai, Lord Napier, and of further work done in 1971 for the Tamil World Conference. The palace originally consisted of two residential sections, plus a theatre, private temple, harem, band-stand, armoury and gardens.

The remaining building, the **Swargavilasa** ("Heavenly Pavilion"), is a rectan-gular courtyard, flanked by eighteen-metre-tall colonnades. As well as occa-sional live performances of music and dance, the Tourism Department arranges a nightly **Sound and Light Show** (in English 6.45–7.30pm; Rs10), which relates the story of the Tamil epic, *Shilipaddikaram*, and the history of the Nayaks. Some find the spectacle edifying, and others soporific. In an adjoining hall, the **Palace Museum** (same hours as the palace) includes unlabelled Pandyan, Jain and Buddhist sculpture, terracottas and an eighteenth-century print showing the palace in a dilapidated state.

Tamukkam Palace: the Gandhi Library and Government Museum

Across the Vaigai, 5km northeast of the centre near the Central Telegraph Office, stands **Tamukkam** (bus #1, #2, #11, #17 or #24; 20min), the

---

Shopping and markets in Madurai

Old Madurai is crowded with **textile and tailors' shops**, particularly in West Veli, Avani Moola and Chitrai streets and Town Hall Road. If you're looking to have some tailoring done, the locally produced textiles are generally good value, and the tailors pride themselves on turning out faithful copies of favourite clothes in a matter of hours. Unfortunately, most of the **souvenir shops** in the vicinity of the temple employ touts who invite tourists to "come and enjoy temple view free of charge only looking". It's worth doing once as the views are impressive, but getting back down to street level without making a purchase at hugely inflated prices is quite a challenge.

South Avani Moola Street is packed with **jewellery**, particularly gold shops, while at 10 North Avani Moola St, you can plan for the future at the Life & Lucky Number Numerology Centre. Madurai is also a great place to pick up South Indian **crafts**. Among the best outlets are All India Handicrafts Emporium, 39–41 Town Hall Road; Co-optex, West Tower Street, and Pandiyan Co-op Supermarket, Palace Road (for handwoven textiles); and Surabhi, West Veli Street, for Keralan handicrafts. For souvenirs such as sandalwood, temple models, carved boxes and oil lamps head for Poompuhar, 12 West Veli Street, or Tamilnad Gandhi Smarak Nidhi Khadi Gramodyog Bhavan, West Veli Street, opposite the railway station, which sells crafts, oil lamps, Meenakshi sculptures and *khadi* cloth and shirts.

The old purpose-built, wooden-pillared **fruit and vegetable market**, between North Chitrai and North Avani Moola streets, provides a slice of Madurai life that can't have changed for centuries. Beyond it, on the first floor of the concrete building at the back, the **flower market** (24hr) is a riot of colour and fragrance; weighing scales spill over with tiny white petals and plump pink garlands hang in rows. Varieties such as orange, yellow or white marigolds (*samandi*), pink jasmine (*arelli*), tiny purple spherical *vanameli* and holy *tulsi* plants come from hill areas such as Kodaikanal and Kumily. These are bought in bulk and distributed for use in temples or to wear in the hair; some are made into elaborate wedding garlands (*kalyanam mala*). The very friendly traders will show you each and every flower, and if you've got a camera will more than likely expect to be recorded for posterity. It's a nice idea to offer to send them a copy of any photograph you take.

seventeenth-century palace of Queen Rani Mangammal. Built to accommodate regal entertainments such as elephant fights, Tamukkam was taken over by the British and used as a courthouse and collector's office, and in 1955 became home to the Gandhi and Government museums. The **Gandhi Memorial Museum** (daily 10am–1pm & 2–5.30pm; free), far better organized than most of the species, charts the history of India since the landing of the first Europeans, viewed in terms of the freedom struggle. Generally the perspective is national, but where appropriate reference is made to the role played by Tamils. It is wholeheartedly critical of the British, quoting the Englishman John Sullivan: "We have denied to the people of the country all that could raise them in society, all that could elevate them as men; we have insulted their caste; we have abrogated their laws of inheritance; we have seized the possessions of their native princes and confiscated the estates of their nobles; we have unsettled the country by our exactions, and collected the revenue by means of torture." One chilling artefact, kept in a room painted black, is the bloodstained *dhoti* the Mahatma was wearing when he was assassinated. Next door to the museum, the **Gandhi Memorial Museum Library** (daily except Wed 10am–1pm & 2–5.30pm; free) houses a reference collection, open to all, of 15,000 books, periodicals, letters and microfilms of material by and about Gandhi.

Opposite, the small **Government Museum** (daily 9am–5pm; Rs100) displays stone and bronze sculptures, musical instruments, paintings (including examples of Tanjore and Kangra styles) and folk art such as painted terracotta animals, festival costumes and hobby-horses. There's also a fine collection of shadow puppets said to have originated in the Thanjavur area and probably exported to Southeast Asia during the Chola period – though the admission price will deter all but the most ardent afficionados. A small house in which **Gandhi** once lived stands in a garden within the compound.

Kochadai Aiyannar Temple

The village of **KOCHADAI**, a northwestern suburb of Madurai, has a beautifully maintained temple dedicated to **Aiyannar**, the Tamil village deity and guardian of borders. Travelling through Tamil Nadu, you often see such shrines from the road, but it may not always be possible, or appropriate, to investigate them. Here, however, they are accustomed to visitors. Flanked by two huge garish *dvarpalas* (doorkeepers), the entrance opens directly onto two sculptures of gigantic horses with riders and furious-looking armed attendants. The shrine on the left houses the god Rama and his brother Lakshmana, while facing the entrance is the shrine to Aiyannar. To the right, the *alamaram* tree, also a shrine, apparently houses a **cobra**, fed with eggs and milk; according to the priests, it only comes out during full moon. During a big **festival** in the Tamil month of Panguni (March/April), Aiyannar is taken around the village to the accompaniment of music and fireworks.

Kochadai is served by frequent buses (#68 or #54) en route to Solavandan.

Eating

As with accommodation, the range of **places to eat** in Madurai is gratifyingly wide, and standards are generally high whether you're eating at one of the many utilitarian-looking "meals" places around the temple, or in an upscale hotel – though to make the most of Madurai's exotic skyline you'll have to seek out a **rooftop restaurant** – another of the modern city's specialities. Rock-bottom-budget travellers should try the street-side stalls at the bottom of West Perumal Maistry Street, where old ladies dish up filling leaf plates of freshly steamed *iddli* and spicy fish masala for Rs10 per portion and delicious melt-in-the-mouth flaky *parotas*. When the afternoon heat gets too much, head for one of the **juice bars** dotted around the centre, where you can order freshly squeezed pomegranate, pineapple, carrot or orange juice for around Rs15 per glass.

Restaurants and bars

Aarathy *Aarathy Hotel*, 9 Perumal Kovil, West Mada St. Tasty tiffin (*dosas, iddlis* and hot *wada sambar*), served on low tables in a hotel forecourt, where the temple elephant turns up at various times of day. The blissfully cool a/c restaurant is very popular with locals and serves excellent food including great lunchtime thalis for just Rs40.

Anna Meenakshi West Perumal Maistry St. Arguably the most hygienic and best-value food in the centre, this upmarket branch of *New College House*'s more traditional canteen (see below) serves top tiffin to a discerning, strictly vegetarian clientele. Absolutely delicious coconut or lemon "rice meals" and cheap banana-leaf thalis are served daily 11.30am–4pm.

Apollo 96 *Supreme Hotel*, 110 West Perumal Maistry St. Boasting 75,000 flashing diodes and a punchy sound system, South India's most hi-tech bar looks like the set from a low-budget 1970s sci-fi movie – an altogether surreal experience. Closes at 11pm sharp.

Mahal 21 Town Hall Rd. Nicely decorated street level restaurant serving small but tasty portions of fish and chips, plus tandoori items and South Indian veg snacks.

New College House 2 Town Hall Rd. Huge meals-cum-tiffin hall in old-style hotel. Lunch-time, when huge piles of pure veg food are served on banana leaves to long rows of locals, is a real deep-south experience; and the coffee's pure Coorg.

Ruby 94 West Perumal Maistry St. This popular meeting place for foreign travellers is primarily a bar. Cold beers are served in a leafy courtyard or in the more claustrophobic interior, and they also serve hot snacks and dishes, including a fiery "Chicken 65", noodles and biriyani.

Surya *Supreme Hotel*, 110 West Perumal Maistry St. Possibly Madurai's best and breeziest rooftop restaurant, with sweeping views of the city and temple, and an eclectic multi-cuisine menu; the ideal venue for a sundowner. Open 4pm–midnight.

Around Madurai

Stretching west towards the blue haze of the Alagar Hills, the Vaigai plains **around Madurai** are broken by colossal outcrops of granite, some of them weathered into weird forms like petrified monsters. Each occupies a place in the mythological landscape of the Pandyan heartland. To the northeast of the city is "Elephant Hill", said to have been created by Shiva to punish a rampaging pachyderm. The holiest rock hereabouts, however, looms over the southwest fringes of the city, where the Muslim conquerors of the early fourteenth century consolidated their fleeting colonization of the far south by founding a capital at the foot of an ancient Hindu site. Referred to by Islamic historians as "City of Ma'bar", the orderly grid-planned town served as the headquarters of the **Madurai Sultanate**, whose origins remain obscure. The sultanate endured for eight generations until the army of the mighty Hindu Vijayanagar empire swept south to mop up the remnants of Muslim rule left after Malik Kafir's bloody sack of 1311. The last sultan, **Sikander Shah**, allegedly died defending the town, and his tomb crowns the top of the 365-metre-monolith, known to Muslim pilgrims throughout India as **Sikandermalai**, "Hill of Sikander" at the village of **TIRUPARANKUNDRAM**, 8km southwest of Madurai (buses #4A and #32 from the STC bus stand).

For Hindus, however, the sheer-sided rock is revered as **Sikandermalai**, one of the six abodes of Shiva's son and the Tamils' favourite god, Lord Murugan. Identified in mythology as the site of Murugan's marriage to Indra's daughter, Deivani, it is one of the most sacred shrines in Tamil Nadu. At the auspicious time of Murugan's wedding anniversary in early February, thousands of newly-weds come here to be blessed. In the summer, the god's birthday is celebrated with displays of fire-walking and body-piercing, along with other acts of ostentatious masochism, such as devotees dragging ox carts along with chains embedded in the flesh of their shoulders.

Outside festival time, however, Tiruparankundram is a peaceful spot offering a welcome respite from the frenzy of Madurai. Its **temple**, built around an eighth-century shrine cut into the rock 35m above the town's rooftops, comprises a series of huge terraces and halls, interconnected by stone staircases. At ground

Moving on from Madurai

By air
Indian Airlines flies daily at 1.20pm to **Mumbai** via **Chennai**; their office, at 7a West Veli Street near the post office (℡0452/234 1234), is efficient and helpful. Jet Airways (office at the airport; ℡0452/234 1234) also has two daily flights (9am & 8.55pm) to Chennai. To get to the airport, catch a taxi (around Rs200), or take city bus #10A from the Periyar Bus Stand.

By bus
Services to Chennai, Bangalore, Mysore, Thanjavur, Tiruchirapalli, Kumbakonam, Rameshwaram, Kanniyakumari and Thiruvananthapuram (in Kerala) all leave from the **Central Bus Stand**. From the **Arapalayam Stand**, buses depart to Coimbatore, Kodaikanal, Kumily (for Periyar Wildlife Sanctuary), Palakaad and Ernakulam/Kochi via Kottayam. There are no direct services from Madurai to Ooty.

By train
Madurai is well connected by train to most major towns and cities in south India. To make a **reservation**, ask for a form at the enquiry counter, then join the long queues in the forecourt at the station; the best time to book trains is in the evening or early morning. For **timetable** details, ask the Tourism Department Information Centre, to the right of the ticket counters.

It's possible to reach the railhead for **Kodaikanal** by train, but the journey is much faster by express bus. For **Thiruvananthapuram, Ernakulam** and **Quilon**, head over to **Coimbatore** (see table below), and then catch the super-fast Kerala Express #2626 (daily at 5.40am). For **Ooty**, catch any train to Coimbatore, where you can spend the night in order to pick the early morning Nilgiri Express (daily at 5.15am) to Mettapalayam, departure point for the Blue Mountain Railway (see p.567), or connect with it via the overnight express given below. The daily Chennai–Kanniyakumari Express #2633 passes through Madurai at the rather unsociable hour of 1.55am, while the #6803/6355 Howrah–Kanniyakumari Express departs at the friendlier time of 7.15am on Tuesday, Wednesday and Saturday (5hr 50min).

For more on transport out of Madurai, see "Travel Details", p.576.

Recommended trains from Madurai
The following daily express trains are recommended, although conversion work on the line will adversely affect some main-line services; check the current situation when booking.

Destination	Name	No.	Departs	Total time
Bangalore	Tuticorin–Mysore Express	#6731	7.40pm	10hr 55min
Chennai	Vaigai Express	#2636	6.45am	7hr 45min
	Pandiyan Express	#2638	8.30pm	9hr
Coimbatore (Ooty)	Madurai–Coimbatore Express	#6716	10.45pm	6hr 15min
Trichy	Vaigai Express	#2636	6.45am	2hr 20min

level, the main colonnaded *mandapa*, adorned with brightly painted horses and *yalis*, served as a field hospital for British soldiers in the 1760s, when the temple was badly defaced (one local priest allegedly burned himself to death in protest at the British vandalism). Perhaps as a consequence of this, non-Hindus are not always allowed to visit the upper levels (if you're refused entry, seek permission at the temple office). It's definitely worth making the climb to see the ancient rock-carvings in, around and below the walls of the central shrine, where Murugan's vehicle (*vahana*) the peacock, features prominently; these are some of the best surviving examples of Pallava rock art in the South.

Crowning the windswept summit of the hill, amid gnarled old umbrella trees that cling to the bare rock, the **Dargah of Sikander Shah** is the region's holiest Muslim shrine. The ruler – whose heroic death on this spot failed to save his capital from the Vijayanagar reconquest – is today revered as a saint. His tomb complex, made up of a domed mosque and covered colonnade dating from the fifteenth century, attracts pilgrims from across the country. Sikander's reputation for piety, however, doesn't square with the account of the Madurai Sultanate featured in the chronicles of Shams Siraj of Delhi, in which Sikander is accused of having succumbed to the decadence of neighbouring Madurai:

He began to perform acts of indecency in public . . . when he held court in the audience hall he wore women's ornaments on his wrists and ankles, and his neck and fingers were adorned with feminine decorations. His indecent acts with pederasts were performed openly . . . (and) the people of Ma'bar were utterly and completely weary and out of patience with him and his behaviour.

Given the paucity of other historical sources relating to this brief period of Muslim supremacy in South India, it's hard to know which version of the story – Sikander as valiant sage or as sybaritic sultan – is the more apocryphal. The **views** of Madurai and the surrounding plains from the tomb, however, are unambiguously impressive.

Rameshwaram and around

The sacred island of **RAMESHWARAM** – 163km southeast of Madurai and less than 20km from Sri Lanka across the Gulf of Mannar – is, along with Madurai, South India's most important pilgrimage site. Hindus tend to be followers of either Vishnu or Shiva, but Rameshwaram brings them together, being the place where the god Rama, an incarnation of Vishnu, worshipped Shiva in the Ramayana. The **Ramalingeshwara temple** complex, with its magnificent pillared walkways, is the most famous on the island, but there are several other small temples of interest, such as the **Gandhamadana Parvatam**, sheltering Rama's footprints, and the **Nambunayagi Amman Kali temple**, frequented for its curative properties. **Danushkodi**, "Rama's bow", at the eastern end of the peninsula, is where Rama is said to have bathed, and the string of tiny islands and sandbanks known as "Adam's Bridge", peppering the sea between here and Sri Lanka are believed to be the stepping stones used by Hanuman in his search for Rama's wife, Sita, after her abduction by Ravana, the demon king of Lanka.

Rameshwaram, whose streets radiate out from the vast block enclosing the Ramalingeshwara, is always crowded with day-trippers, and ragged mendicants who camp outside the Ramalingeshwara and the **Ujainimahamariamman**, the small goddess shore temple. An important part of their pilgrimage is to bathe in the main temple's sacred tanks and in the sea; the narrow strip of beach is shared by groups of bathers, relaxing cows and mantra-reciting *swamis* sitting next to sand *lingams*. As well as fishing – prawns and lobsters for packaging and export to Japan – the coastal villages make a lot of money selling shells to pilgrims – a symbol that they have been to Rameshwaram and worshipped Vishnu (he is always portrayed as holding a conch).

Arrival and information

The NH-49, the main road from Madurai, connects Rameshwaram with Mandapam on the mainland via the impressive two-kilometre-long Indira Gandhi Bridge, originally built by the British in 1914 as a railway link. **Buses** from Madurai (via Ramnad), Trichy, Thanjavur, Kanniyakumari and Chennai pull in at the bus stand, 2km west of the centre. The **railway station**, 1km southwest of the centre, is the end of the line for trains from Chennai, Thiruvarur and Trichy, and boasts decent retiring rooms, a veg restaurant and a left-luggage office (daily 5.30am–10pm). There are two daily express trains to and from Chennai, and one (the Rameshwaram–Coimbatore Express #6716) for Coimbatore, via Madurai. Buses run half-hourly to Madurai (4hr) and four times daily to Kanniyakumari (9–10hr). Travel agents around the temple run faster and more comfortable **minibuses** around South India.

Red-and-white city buses run every ten minutes from the bus stand to the main temple; otherwise, **local transport** consists of unmetered cycle- and auto-rickshaws that gather outside the bus stand. Jeeps are available for rent near the railway station, and bicycles from shops in the four Car streets around the temple.

The main TTDC **tourist office** at the bus stand (daily 10am–5.45pm; ℡04573/221371) gives out information about guides, accommodation and

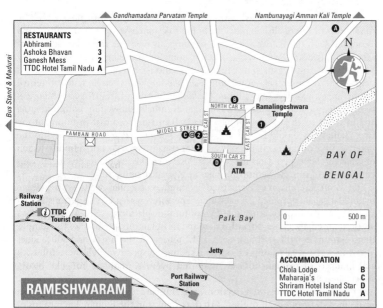

RAMESHWARAM

RESTAURANTS
Abhirami 1
Ashoka Bhavan 3
Ganesh Mess 2
TTDC Hotel Tamil Nadu A

ACCOMMODATION
Chola Lodge B
Maharaja's C
Shriram Hotel Island Star D
TTDC Hotel Tamil Nadu A

Gandhamadana Parvatam Temple
Nambunayagi Amman Kali Temple
Ramalingeshwara Temple
NORTH CAR ST
MIDDLE STREET
WEST CAR ST
EAST CAR ST
SOUTH CAR ST
PAMBAN ROAD
ATM
BAY OF BENGAL
Railway Station
TTDC Tourist Office
Palk Bay
Jetty
Port Railway Station
Bus Stand & Madurai
0   500 m
N
Adam's Bridge (18 km)

boat trips. TTDC also have a counter at the railway station (open to coincide with arriving trains; ☎04573/221373). The best source of information, however, is friendly official guide R. Kannan (☎04573/221277), who can also be contacted through the *TTDC Hotel Tamil Nadu*; he's happy to give advice even if you don't use his services. The **post office** is on Pamban Road.

Accommodation

Most of the **accommodation** in Rameshwaram is restricted to basic lodges in and around the Car streets around the temple. The temple itself has a range of rooms for pilgrims; ask at the Devasthanam Office, East Car Street (☎04573/221223).

Chola Lodge North Car St ☎04573/221307. Basic but adequate pilgrim place in the quietest of the Car streets, with a couple of more expensive a/c rooms. Some rooms have TV. ❷–❹
Maharaja's 7 Middle St ☎04573/221271, ✉hotelmaharajas@sancharnet.com. Located next to the temple's west gate, this place has good clean and comfortable rooms with attached bathrooms and TV (some also have a/c), plus temple views from balconies. There's no restaurant, although management will bring restaurant food in. ❷–❹
Railway Retiring Rooms Six large doubles and three triples – generally cleaner and quieter than those in the town lodges, but at similar prices – plus a dorm (Rs30). ❶

Shriram Hotel Island Star 41a South Car St ☎04573/221472, ℻239332. Large, clean hotel with pleasantly appointed a/c and non-a/c rooms, most with sea views. The non a/c rooms are particularly good value, but the most expensive a/c rooms are a little overpriced. ❷–❻
TTDC Hotel Tamil Nadu Near the beach, 700m northeast of main temple ☎04573/221277, ℻221070. The nicest place in Rameshwaram, in a pleasant location and with a bar, restaurant and comfortable sea-facing rooms (some a/c); the best are actually the cheaper ones in the new block, with pleasant sit-outs ❸–❺

Ramalingeshwara Temple

The core of the **Ramalingeshwara** (or Ramanathaswamy) **Temple** was built by the Cholas in the twelfth century to house two much-venerated **shivalingams** associated with the Ramayana. After rescuing his wife Sita from the clutches of the demon Ravana, Rama was advised to atone for the killing of the demon king – a brahmin – by worshipping Shiva. Rama's monkey lieutenant, Hanuman, was despatched to the Himalayas to fetch a *shivalingam*, but when he failed to return by the appointed day, Sita fashioned a *lingam* from sand (the *Ramanathalingam*) so the ceremony could proceed. Hanuman eventually showed up with his *lingam* and in order to assuage the monkey's guilt Rama decreed that in future, of the two, Hanuman's should be worshipped first. The *lingams* are now housed in the inner section of the Ramalingeshwara, not usually open to non-Hindus. Much of what can be visited dates from the 1600s, when the temple received generous endowments from the Sethupathi rajas of Ramanathapuram.

The Ramalingeshwara is enclosed by high rectangular walls with a huge pyramidal *gopura* entrance on each side. The gateways lead to a spacious closed ambulatory, flanked to either side by continuous platforms with massive pillars set on their edges. These **corridors** are the most famous attribute of the temple, their extreme length – 205m, with 1212 pillars on the north and south sides – giving a remarkable impression of receding perspective. Delicate scrollwork and brackets of pendant lotuses supported by *yalis*, mythical lion-like beasts, adorn the pillars.

Before entering the inner sections, pilgrims are expected to take a ritual bathe in water from each of the 22 **tirthas** (tanks) in the temple. The groups of dripping-wet pilgrims, most of them fully clothed, make their way from one tank to the next to be doused in a bucket of water by a temple attendant. Each tank is said to have special benefits: the Rama Vimosana Tirtha provides relief from debt, the Sukreeva Tirtha gives "complete wisdom" and the attainment of *Surya Loka*, the realm of the Sun, and the Draupadi Tirtha ensures long life for women and "the love of their spouses".

Monday is Rama's auspicious day, when the Padilingam puja takes place. **Festivals** of particular importance at the temple include **Mahashivaratri** (ten days during Feb/March), **Brahmotsavam** (ten days during March/April) and **Thirukalyanam** (July/Aug), celebrating the marriage of Shiva to Parvati.

Minor temples

On a hill 2km north of Rameshwaram town centre, the **Gandhamadana Parvatam** (daily 6–11am & 3.30–6.30pm) is a venerable shrine housing Rama's footprints. On some days, ceremonies are conducted here after the 5.30am puja at the Ramalingeshwara temple, encouraging pilgrims to climb the hill to continue their devotions. From the roof, fine views extend over the surrounding country – on clear nights you can see the lights of Jaffna.

Three kilometres east of town towards the old fishing village of **Dhanush-kodi**, the small **Nambunayagi Amman Kali temple**, set in a quiet sandy grove 200m off the main road, attracts people in search of cures for illnesses. Inside a banyan tree next to it is a shrine dedicated to the spirit Retatalai, "the two-headed". A pair of wooden sandals with spikes, said to belong to the spirit, is left in the shrine and locals say they can hear them clip-clopping at night when Retatalai chooses to wander. Pieces of cloth are tied to the branches of the tree to mark thanks for such boons as pregnancy after barrenness and the healing of family feuds. The bus terminates at Dhanushkodi, from where you can walk along the ever-narrowing spit of sand until the sea finally closes in and the island peters out, tantalizingly short of Sri Lanka.

Eating

Eating in Rameshwaram is more about survival than delighting the taste buds. Most places serve up fairly unexciting "meals" for Rs50–100.

Abhirami Shore Rd, near the east entrance to the temple. Reasonably clean South Indian vegetarian joint with street views en route to the seashore.
Ashoka Bhavan West Car St. Offers cheap, regional varieties of thalis.
Ganesh Mess Middle St. One of the better "meals" joints, which also does classic South Indian snacks at other times of day.

TTDC Hotel Tamil Nadu Near the beach. Gigantic, noisy, high-ceilinged glasshouse near the sea, serving good South Indian snacks and "meals" – some items on the menu may be unavailable, however. There is also a bar in the main hotel building.

Around Rameshwaram

RAMANATHAPURAM (aka Ramnad) offers a possible break on the bus or train between Madurai (120km northwest) and Rameshwaram (36km east). It's worth stopping here to see the neglected but atmospheric **Ramalinga Vilasam**, palace of the Sethupati rajas, who by tradition were guardians of the mythical Sethu bridge built by Rama to cross to Lanka. The entrance to the **palace** (daily except Fri 9am–1pm & 2–5pm; Rs5 [Rs50]), 2km from the bus stand, takes you into the big and dusty **Durbar Hall**, whose central aisle is hung with oil portraits of the rajas of the last few hundred years. Throughout the building, ceilings and walls are decorated with early eighteenth-century murals, depicting subjects such as business meetings with the English, battles with the Maratha king Sarabhoji, and scenes from the epics; one battle scene shows soldiers fighting with boomerangs, and there's a real Indian boomerang on display. Also on show are palm-leaf manuscripts, a Ravi Varma painting (see p.351) with appliquéd brocade and sculptures of Vishnu from the eighth and thirteenth centuries.

From the **throne room**, a secret passageway once gave an escape route to a local temple. The raja's throne, supported on carved elephant legs, is decorated with a coat of arms, given by the British, featuring a lion and unicorn. As further proof of the royal family's compliance with the foreign power, the raja, at the end of the eighteenth century, allowed them to use the bedchambers upstairs – decorated with erotic murals – as a meeting hall. This cosy relationship did not find unanimous approval among his subjects. Influential local landowners showed their contempt for the British by responding to tax demands with bags of stones and, in 1798 and 1801, rebellions took place, sometimes dubbed the "South Indian War of Independence". In 1803, at the request of the British, the Ramnad raja was obliged to accept the lesser rank of *zamindar* (feudatory chieftain). On the roof is a stone bed on which the raja would lounge in the evenings to enjoy panoramic views of the town and surrounding country. The buildings immediately below were royal guesthouses; a descendant of the rajas now lives in one of them.

Tirunelveli and around

Separated by the only perennial river in the far south, the Tambraparni, **TIRUNELVELI** and its modern counterpart **PALAYANKOTTAI** together form the largest conurbation in the densely populated red-soil region south of Madurai. Aside from the huge **Nellaiyappa temple**, built by the Pandyas in the thirteenth century with a towering pyramidal *gopura*, situated 2km west of the river, neither holds much of specific interest. However, you may want to use Tirunelveli as a base for day-trips to nearby **Thiruppudaimarudur**, 25km west, whose old riverside temple is famed for its wood-carvings, or further west to **Kuttalam**, in the foothills of the Ghats, where a series of dramatic waterfalls attract streams of day-trippers. An hour or so east on the Coromandel Coast, the traditional Tamil pilgrimage town of **Tiruchendur** has the region's most spectacular shore temple, dominating an appropriately impressive sweep of surf-lashed beach. The sea between the Coromandel and Sri Lanka is rich enough to support a string of fishing settlements, but the most lucrative harvest yielded by the Gulf of Mannar are the pearls gathered by divers from the port of **Tuticorin**, an hour north of Tiruchendur. The Portuguese founded one of their first colonies in India here.

Tirunelveli's **bus stand**, in the town centre just across the river from Palay-ankottai, has services to and from Madurai (3hr), Nagercoil (1hr 30min), Tuticorin (1hr), Tiruchendur (1hr) and Kollam (5hr). For Kuttalam, you have to head to Tenkasi (1hr) and change onto a local bus. **Trains** from Chennai, Madurai, Nagercoil and Kollam pull in at the main-line station, five minutes' walk west on the opposite side of Madurai Road.

Most of the **accommodation** in town is lined up outside the bus stand, on Madurai Road. Pick of the bunch is the *Sri Jankiran* (℡0462/233 1941, ⒺSjh_tvl@sancharnet.in; ❸–❺), which has some a/c rooms, a cosy **restaurant** and roof terrace. Next door, the *Barani* (☎0462/233 3234, ℗233 0170; ❸–❺) is marginally cheaper but dependably clean, as is the extremely good-value *Balaji Mansion* (☎0462/233 3302; ❶–❷), just off Madurai Road near the station, whose rooms have TVs.

Thiruppudaimarudur

THIRUPPUDAIMARUDUR, a small riverside village 25km west of Tirunelveli, is the site of a temple renowned throughout the region for its splendid medieval wood-carvings and murals. The best-preserved of these murals line the interior of the temple's east tower, which you can scale via flights of precariously steep wooden steps. Pillars and brackets propping up a succession of ceilings have been sumptuously decorated, while the walls (which you'll need a flashlight to see clearly) are covered with vibrant paintings, depicting scenes from the Ramayana, Vishnu's various incarnations and mythical battles.

Buses to Thiruppudaimarudur leave more or less hourly from Tirunelveli, and take fifty minutes. The village doesn't have any hotels or guesthouses.

Kuttalam

An image familiar to collectors of exotic prints and engravings in Victorian Britain was that of the great waterfalls at **KUTTALAM** (**Courtalam**), 136km northwest of Kanniyakumari, where the River Chittar plunges down a sheer cliff on the very edge of the Western Ghats. A couple of centuries ago, when the famous Raj-era artist Thomas Daniells came to sketch the falls, this was still a remote spot, overgrown with vegetation and frequented only by wandering *sadhus* and the odd party of sickly Brits. A hydro project upstream has somewhat diminished the falls' splendour, and the barrage of film music and hoardings in the modern concrete village that has sprung up at their feet does little to enhance the overall atmosphere, but it's still worth coming here for an invigorating bathe. Bussing in from all over the state, thousands of Tamils do just that each day, especially at weekends and between July and late September, when water levels are at their highest. From late January until May, the falls can dry up completely.

In all, nine major cascades are dotted around Kuttalam, but only one, known for obvious reasons as **Main Falls**, is located in the village proper. This is where the largest crowds congregate – with ladies to the left, fully dressed in soaking saris; old folk and kids to the right; and men, in regulation voluminous underpants, taking the full force of the central flow. It's worth pointing out that few foreigners come to Kuttalam, so expect to create a bit of a stir if you strip off; for a little more privacy, try jumping onto one of the minibuses that run throughout the day to smaller waterfalls around Kuttalam.

To reach Kuttalam by bus, you first have to head for **Tenkasi**, which is well connected to Tirunelveli (2hr) and Madurai (3hr), from where local buses run the final twenty minutes to the falls. The limited **sleeping** and **eating** options in Kuttalam include the *TTDC Hotel Tamil Nadu I,* opposite Parasakthi Women's college (☎04633/221 0003; ❷–❺), with overpriced and uniformly shabby double rooms, some with a/c; next door, the *TTDC Hotel Tamil Nadu II* (☎04633/232 2263; ❷–❺) and has the same range of rather dilapidated a/c and non-a/c rooms but at a slightly cheaper rate. Both offer good off-season (Sept–May).

Tuticorin

TUTICORIN, 51km east of Tirunelveli on the NH-7 or 130km northeast of Kanniyakumari, developed as a flourishing Portuguese colony in the sixteenth century and later expanded under the Dutch and British. Eclipsed by Madras in the late 1700s, it is nowadays the state's second port and would be an entirely forgettable, gritty Tamil town were it not for the prodigious quantities of **pearl**-bearing saltwater molluscs, *pinctada martensi*, that grow in the shark-infested shallows offshore. These are harvested for one month each year (normally in March–April) by divers equipped with little more than antiquated face masks. The pearls they collect are said to rank among the finest in the world, on a par with those found in the Persian Gulf, which is presumably why you won't easily find any for sale in the bazaar; all but a tiny proportion are exported.

Tuticorin is largely industrial and not a particularly appealing place to stay, but if you find yourself in need of a hotel, head for VE Road, a short rickshaw ride from the centre of town. The business-traveller-orientated *Jony International* (☎0461/232 8350; ❺–❼) has decent rooms with a/c and cable TV; nearby, the *Sugam* (☎0461/232 8172; ❸–❺) is a clean and dependable budget option.

Tiruchendur

TIRUCHENDUR, some 60km southeast of Tirunelveli, means "beautiful holy town" in Tamil, and for once the epithet fits, thanks to the awesome presence on its shoreline of the mighty **Subrahmanya Temple**. The shrine – one of the six sacred abodes of the Tamils' favourite god, **Lord Murugan** (Shiva's son, Subrahmanya), here in the form of the Ascetic ("renouncer of the transitory and illusory"), presides over a spectacular sandy beach, with breakers crashing in off the Gulf of Mannar. Corrosive salt winds have taken their toll on the original building erected by the Pallavas in the ninth century, and large sections of what you see today are modern, dating from 1941. However, references to the deity inside occur in some of the Tamils' oldest scriptures, while archeological digs conducted in the 1890s on the banks of the River Tambraparni nearby yielded evidence of a three-thousand-year-old religious cult focused on a spear-wielding deity very similar to Murugan. More extraordinary still were the prehistoric mouth locks that came to light at the same time, identical to those worn by more fervent devotees at Murugan festivals in Tamil Nadu today.

The Subrahmanya temple is approached via a long colonnaded walkway, running 700m through a sacred precinct lined with shops selling puja paraphernalia and pilgrims' souvenirs. Non-Hindus are permitted to enter the central shrine on payment of a small donation. The deity inside is among the most revered in South India, attracting crowds of more than a million during the temple's annual festival, just before the monsoon, when 108 different herbs and auspicious preparations are offered to the god, symbolizing the renewal of the earth. The ritual is accompanied by the chanting of some of the oldest Sanskrit verses surviving in India. In his 1995 travelogue *The Smile of Murugan*, the British historian Michael Wood speculates that these may even predate human speech; scholars have shown their nearest analogue is birdsong, lending credence to the theory that ritual came before verbal language in human evolution.

Tiruchendur is well connected by **bus** to Tirunelveli (1hr), Madurai's Arapalayam bus stand (4hr), Tuticorin (40min) and Nagercoil (2hr), and there are four daily trains to and from Tirunelveli. Apart from a handful of spartan pilgrims' hostels in the sacred precinct, the best **accommodation** in town is the *TTDC Hotel Tamil Nadu* (☎04639/242268; ❷–❹), a typically lacklustre government-run place, with a/c and non a/c options, five minutes' walk northeast of the temple, but in a setting by the sea. Nearer the temple, on Kovil Street, there's a cluster of small but adequate hotels including the *Rathina Lodge* (☎04639/242383; ❶–❸), also with a/c and non a/c options. The *Ashoka Bhavan*

During the month of *Thai* (February) in the Tamil calendar, the usual intensity of the devotional activities among the thousands of Shaivite pilgrims trailing around Tamil Nadu reaches a fanatical peak on the occasion of **Thaipusam**, the full-moon festival in honour of Lord Murugan (aka Lord Subrahmanya), son of Shiva and Parvati, who represents the triumph of good over evil. Thaipusam recalls the day that Parvati gave Murugan the *vel*, a magical weapon that destroys all wickedness, sins and banishes negativity from the soul.

The archaic rituals seen today are rooted in myth and legend. The most popular version is that there was a devotee, Idumban, who, on the night of the full moon in the month of *Thai*, was instructed in a dream to go to Shivagiri hill to worship Lord Murugan. Idumban dutifully set off, taking with him two pots of milk as an offering, and along the way he sang devotional hymns.

Today, the practice continues as **Shaivite pilgrims** from all over India congregate to venerate Lord Murugan; there are temples dedicated to Murugan throughout Tamil Nadu, and a few in Kerala. Each pilgrim has to take an offering, called a **kavadi**, meaning "sacrifice at each step", to remind them of their previous sin and their personal vow to Lord Murugan. In accordance with the tradition set by Idumban, most devotees carry a milk *kavadi* (a pot filled with milk), which is covered in fruit and flowers and carried on the head in a long and winding procession. The pilgrims sing hymns as they wander from temple to temple to do puja to Murugan.

A *kavadi*, however, can also be a huge metal or wooden structure. These *kavadis* are strung with razor-sharp hooks and lavishly decorated with flowers, bells and peacock feathers. In an extreme act of personal penance and homage to Murugan, a devotee may volunteer to be hooked up to one of these frames. Before they can be pierced, volunteers have to undergo a whole month of inner cleansing, with a strict vegetarian diet, celibacy and spiritual nourishment to give them strength. On the day of *Thaipusam*, with the help of the frantic drumming and the chanting by the crowds, the devotee enters a deep trance to make the pain disappear, then spears and hooks are pushed through the flesh. Alternatively, a devotee may pull a wagon or chariot by a set of hooks pierced in the skin of their back.

The tradition of bringing milk *kavadis* remains very popular in Tamil Nadu – it is not uncommon for up to 20,000 people to gather at a shrine to offer their *kavadi* on Thaipusam. The most famous Murugan temples are at Palani (see p.560) and Tiruchendur (see opposite); ask at a TTDC tourist office to find out exact places and dates (which change each year). The act of piercing, however, is now officially prohibited in India, although the practice may still be witnessed on extremely rare occasions in the very rural areas. Piercing continues unabated in those countries, such as Thailand, Sri Lanka, Singapore and Malaysia, where there are significant populations of Tamil Hindus.

on Kovil Street is the best of the cheap snacks and "meals" joints, and caters for a constant stream of pilgrims.

Kanniyakumari and around

KANNIYAKUMARI, at the southernmost extremity of India, is almost as compelling for Hindus as Rameshwaram. It's significant not only for its association with a virgin goddess, Kanya Devi, but also as the meeting point of the Bay of Bengal, Indian Ocean and Arabian Sea. Watching the sun rise and set from here is the big attraction, especially on full moon day in April, when it's possible

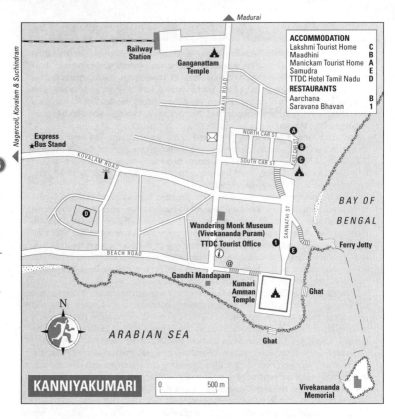

Within the map:

Madurai

Railway Station

Ganganattam Temple

MAIN ROAD

Nagercoil, Kovalam & Suchindram

Express Bus Stand

KOVALAM ROAD

NORTH CAR ST

SOUTH CAR ST

EAST CAR ST

SANNATHI ST

BAY OF BENGAL

Ferry Jetty

Wandering Monk Museum (Vivekananda Puram)

TTDC Tourist Office

BEACH ROAD

@

Gandhi Mandapam

Kumari Amman Temple

Ghat

Ghat

N

ARABIAN SEA

KANNIYAKUMARI

0   500 m

Vivekananda Memorial

ACCOMMODATION
Lakshmi Tourist Home   C
Maadhini   B
Manickam Tourist Home   A
Samudra   E
TTDC Hotel Tamil Nadu   D
RESTAURANTS
Aarchana   B
Saravana Bhavan   1

---

to see both the setting sun and rising moon on the same horizon. Although Kanniyakumari is in the state of Tamil Nadu, most foreign visitors arrive on day-trips from Thiruvananthapuram (Trivandrum), the capital of Kerala, 86km northwest. While the place is of enduring appeal to pilgrims, other visitors may find it bereft of atmosphere, its magic obliterated by ugly concrete buildings and hawkers selling shells and trinkets – although anyone with completist tendencies will regard it as *de rigeur* to visit India's own "Land's End".

Kanniyakumari was seriously affected by the **tsunami** of December 26, 2004. The town's seafront and jetty were devastated and around a thousand people were killed, many of them pilgrims on tours of Tamil Nadu's sacred places. In one of the tsunami's most dramatic rescue operation, more than five hundred people were airlifted to safety after being stranded on the Vivekananda Memorial for around ten hours. The enormous statue on its tiny rocky isle was sufficiently distant from the shore to escape the ferocity of the breaking waves.

The Town

The seashore **Kumari Amman Temple** (daily 4.30–11.30am & 4–8pm) is dedicated to the virgin goddess **Kanya Devi**, who may originally have been the local guardian deity of the shoreline, but was later absorbed into the figure of Devi, or Parvati, consort of Shiva. One version of Kanya Devi's story relates how she did penance to win the hand of Shiva. The god was all in favour and set out from Suchindram for the wedding, due to take place at midnight. The celestial *devas*, however, wanted Kanya Devi to remain a virgin, so that she could retain her full quota of *shakti*, or divine power, and hatched a plot. Narada the sage assumed the form of a cock and crowed; on hearing this, Shiva, thinking that it was dawn and that he had missed the auspicious time for the ceremony, went home. The image of Kanya Devi inside the temple wears a diamond nose-stud of such brilliance that it's said to be visible from the sea. Male visitors must be shirtless and wear a *dhoti* before entering the temple; non-Hindus are not allowed in the inner sanctum. It is especially auspicious for pilgrims to wash at the bathing *ghat* here.

Resembling a prewar British cinema, the **Gandhi Mandapam** (daily 7am–7pm; free), 300m northwest of the Kumari Amman Temple, was actually conceived as a modern imitation of an Orissan temple. It was designed so that the sun strikes the auspicious spot where the ashes of Mahatma Gandhi were laid, prior to their immersion in the sea, at noon on his birthday, October 2.

Possibly the original sacred focus of Kanniyakumari are two rocks, about 60m apart, half-submerged in the sea 500m off the coast, which came to be known as the Pitru and Matru *tirthas*. In 1892 they attracted the attention of the Hindu reformer **Vivekananda** (1862–1902), who swam out to the rocks to meditate on the syncretistic teachings of his recently dead guru, Ramakrishna Parama-hamsa. Incorporating elements of architecture from around the country, the 1970 **Vivekananda Memorial** (daily except Tues 7–11am & 2–5pm), reached by the Poompuhar ferry service from the jetty on the east side of town (every 30min; same hours), houses a statue of the saint. The footprints of Kanya Devi can also be seen here, at the spot where she performed her penance. The other rock features an imposing forty-metre-high statue of the ancient Tamil saint Thiruvalluva.

For more on the life and teachings of Vivekananda, visit the **Wandering Monk Museum** (or **Vivekananda Puram**), just north of the tourist office at the bottom of town (daily 8am–noon & 4–8pm; Rs2). A sequence of 41 panels (in English, Tamil and Hindi) provide a meticulously detailed account of the *swami*'s odyssey around the subcontinent at the end of the nineteenth century. Born in Bengal, Vivekananda received a Western education, which he subsequently rejected. Vivekananda countered the traditional Hindu dogma that the universe is a delusion beyond the sole reality of Brahma, and attempted to replace this philosophy with a proactive ethos based on social work and reform – a kind of early Indian *engagement* without Jean-Paul Sartre's baggy suits and strong coffee.

Practicalities

Trains from Thiruvananthapuram, Mumbai, Bangalore – and even Jammu (at 86hr the longest rail journey in India) – stop at the **railway station** in the north of town, 2km from the seafront. **From Madurai** the best train service is the fast passenger train which leaves at 3pm and takes just over four hours. You can leave **luggage** in the generator room behind the ticket office for Rs10 per item.

The well-organized **Express Bus Stand**, near the lighthouse on the west side of town, is served by regular buses from Thiruvananthapuram (hourly; 2hr), Kovalam (12 daily; 1hr 30min–2hr), Madurai (13 daily; 6hr), Rameshwaram (4 daily; 9–10hr via Madurai) and Chennai (11 daily; 14–16hr). Auto-rickshaws and taxis provide **local transport**.

The main **tourist office** is on Main Road (Mon–Fri 10am–5.30pm); there's **Internet** access just around the corner on Beach Road.

Accommodation

As Kanniyakumari is a "must-see" for Indian tourists and pilgrims, **hotels** can fill up early. However, recent developments have raised standards, and relieved the pressure on space.

Lakshmi Tourist Home East Car St ☎04652/246333, ℱ246627. Smart rooms, some sea-facing, with swish a/c. Also has an excellent non-veg restaurant. ②–④

Maadhini East Car St ☎04652/246787, ℱ246657. Large hotel right on the seafront above the fishing village, with fine sea views, comfortably furnished rooms and one of the best restaurants in town. ③–⑥

Manickam Tourist Home North Car St ☎04652/246387. Spacious and modern rooms with sea views facing the sunrise and the Vivekananda rock. Good value. ②–③

Samudra Sannathi St ☎04652/246162, ℱ246627. Smart hotel near the temple entrance, with well-furnished deluxe rooms facing the sunrise plus satellite TV and a veg restaurant. ③–⑥

TTDC Hotel Tamil Nadu On the seafront ☎04652/346257, ℮ttdc@md3.vsnl.net.in. A range of accommodation in cottages (some a/c) and clean rooms (a/c on the first floor), most with sea view, along with cheaper and very basic "mini" doubles at the back and a dorm (Rs50). Good square meals are served in functional surroundings. ②–⑥

Eating

Aside from the usual "meals" places and hotel dining rooms, there are a few popular veg and non-veg **restaurants** in the centre of town, most attached to one of the hotels. The *Archana*, at the *Maadhini Hotel* on East Car Street, has an extensive veg and non-veg multi-cuisine menu served either inside a well-ventilated dining hall or alfresco in a courtyard (evenings only). They also have the town's widest selection of ice cream. *Saravana Bhavan*, north of the Kumari Amman Temple, on the main bazaar, is arguably Kanniyakumari's best "meals" restaurant, serving all the usual snacks, cold drinks, and huge Tamil thalis at lunchtime, to hoards of hungry pilgrims. Their coffee is good, too.

Around Kanniyakumari

Construction of the **Stanunathaswami Temple** at **SUCHINDRAM**, 12km northwest of Kanniyakumari, extended over a period of at least six hundred years. Parts date back as far as the ninth or tenth century, others are from the fifteenth, and a huge seven-storey pyramidal *gopura* was erected during the sixteenth. Its oldest and most remarkable feature, however, is a series of beautifully preserved **epigraphs** carved on a huge boulder in the main *mandapa*. Some are in the ancient Pali language, dating from the third century BC when this was the most southerly outpost of the Mauryan empire. Later inscriptions in classical Tamil are the first known references to the three traditional dynasties of the South, the Cholas, the Pandyas and the Pallavas. Although its main sanctuary houses a *shivalingam*, the temple is jointly dedicated to Brahma, Vishnu and Shiva. Its proudest boasts, aside from the epigraphs and some remarkably extravagant stone sculpture, are **musical pillars**, which emit a chime when struck, and an extraordinary three-metre-high figure of Hanuman. A special puja takes place at sunset (around 6pm) every Friday, with music and a procession. The temple is open to non-Hindus and all castes, although male visitors must remove their shirts before entering.

As you head along the NH-47 towards Kerala, the spectacular crags of the Travancore Hills encroach upon the flats of iridescent rice paddy lining the coastal strip, completely dominating the landscape to Thiruvananthapuram. The most prominent peak in the area is the pyramidal **Maruntha Malai** (aka "Maruval Malai"), 13km from Kanniyakumari, renowned among Tamils as "Medicine Mountain". During the monsoon, its steep green slopes sprout a profusion of medicinal herbs. Local healers must have been aware of this fact for thousands of years because the hill crops up time and again in Hindu mythology, most famously in the Ramayana. According to the epic, Hanuman had been dispatched to Mount Kailash in the Himalayas to look for herbs for Laxmana, who had been wounded by a poisoned arrow during the battle with the evil demon Ravana's army in Lanka. Instead of picking the plants, however, Hanuman ripped up the whole mountain to keep them fresh. On his way back to Rama, Hanuman dropped a piece of Mount Kailash at this spot on his way. Today, the Maruntha Malai remains an important source of curative herbs used in the preparation of Ayurvedic medicines. It's also home to a scattering of *sadhus* who, when they aren't away wandering, live in a string of caves that dot the pilgrim path to the *shivalingam* crowning the summit. Taking around six hours, the **hike** to it is especially popular with pilgrims who have walked to Kanniyakumari in fulfilment of a vow. It should not be attempted without a guide as the route is hard to follow; the best place to find a guide is in the village of **Pothayadi**, near the trailhead.

The Southern Ghats

Sixty or more million years ago, what we know today as peninsular India was a separate land mass drifting northwest across the ocean towards central Asia. Current geological thinking has it that this mass must originally have broken off the African continent along a fault line that is today discernible as a north–south ridge of volcanic mountains, stretching 1400km down the west coast of India, known as the **Southern Ghats**. The range rises to a height of around 2500m, making it India's second-highest mountain chain after the Himalayas.

Forming a natural barrier between the Tamil plains and coastal Kerala and Karnataka, the *ghats* (literally "steps") soak up the bulk of the southwest monsoon, which drains east to the Bay of Bengal via the mighty Kaveri and Krishna river systems. The massive amount of rain that falls here between June and October (around 2.5m) allows for an incredible **biodiversity**. Nearly one-third of all of India's flowering plants can be found in the dense evergreen and mixed deciduous forests cloaking the *ghats*, while the woodland undergrowth supports the subcontinent's richest array of wildlife, from jungle civets, muntjac and the rare tahr antelope to gaur (Indian bison), herds of wild Asian elephant and tigers.

It was this abundance of game, and the cooler temperatures of the range's high valleys and grasslands, that first attracted the sun-sick British, who were quick to see the economic potential of the temperate climate, fecund soil and plentiful rainfall. As the forests were felled to make way for tea plantations, and the region's many tribal groups – among them the Todas – were forced deeper into the mountains, permanent **hill stations** were established. Today, as in the days of the Raj, these continue to provide welcome escapes from the fierce summer heat for the middle-class Tamils, and foreign tourists, who can afford the break.

Much the best known of the hill resorts – in fact better known and more visited than it deserves – is **Udhagamandalam** (formerly Ootacamund, and usually known just as "**Ooty**"), in the **Nilgiris** (from *nila-giri*, "blue mountains"– named after the profusion of blue gum trees). The ride up to Ooty, on the **miniature railway** via Coonoor, is fun, and the views breathtaking, but in general (unless you have the means to stay in the best hotels), the grey and concrete centre of town comes as a rude shock. The other main hill station, founded by American missionaries, is leafy and quiet **Kodaikanal**, further south near Madurai.

Accessed via the hill stations, the forest areas lining the state border harbour Tamil Nadu's principal wildlife sanctuaries, **Annamalai** and **Mudumalai** which, along with Wayanad in Kerala and Nagarhole and Bandipur in Karnataka, form the vast **Nilgiri Biosphere Reserve**, the country's most extensive tract of protected forest. Road building, illegal felling, hydroelectric projects and overgrazing have gradually whittled away large tracts of this huge wilderness area over the past two decades. In recent years a more pressing threat has been the posed by the infamous sandalwood smuggler and brigand **Veerappan** (see p.574), whose activities led to the parks being indefinitely closed to the public. Although Veerappan was killed in late 2004, the area has yet to be reopened. However, as the main route between Mysore and the cities of the Tamil plains wriggles through the Nilgiris, you may well find yourself pausing for a night or two along the way, if only to enjoy the cold air and serene landscape of the tea terraces. Whichever direction you're travelling in, a brief stopover at the dull and congested textile-producing city of **Coimbatore** is hard to avoid.

The **best time to visit** the ghats is between late November and early March. At other times, either the weather is too cloudy and wet, or the hill stations are swarming with hoards of summer tourists. Winter is also the optimum period for **trekking** in the Nilgiris, which allows you to visit some of the region's most unspoilt forest areas, the traditional homeland of the Todas.

Kodaikanal

Perched on top of the Palani range, around 120km northwest of Madurai, **KODAIKANAL**, also known as **Kodai**, owes its perennial popularity to its hilltop situation, which at an altitude of more than 2000m, affords breathtaking views over the blue-green reaches of the Vaigai plain. Raj-era bungalows and flower-filled gardens add atmosphere, while short walks out of the centre lead to rocky outcrops, waterfalls and dense *shola* forest. With the more northerly wildlife sanctuaries and forest areas of the *ghats* closed to visitors, Kodai's outstandingly scenic hinterland also offers South India's best **trekking** terrain. Even if you're not tempted by the prospect of the open trail and cool air, the jaw-dropping **bus ride** up here from the plains makes the detour into this easternmost spur of the *ghats* an essential one.

Kodaikanal's **history** has been uneventful, and the only monuments to its past are the neat British bungalows that overlook the lake and Law's Ghat Road on the eastern edge of town. The British first moved here in 1845, to be joined later by members of the American Mission, who set up schools for European children. One remains as the Kodai International School; despite the name, almost all its students are Indian. The school occasionally holds concerts on the green just east of the lake.

After a while in the South Indian plains, a retreat to Kodai's cool heights is more than welcome. However, in the height of summer (June–Aug), when temperatures compete with those in the lowlands, it's not worth the trip – nor is it a good idea to come during the monsoon (Oct–Dec), when the town is shrouded in mists and drenched by heavy downpours. In late February and early

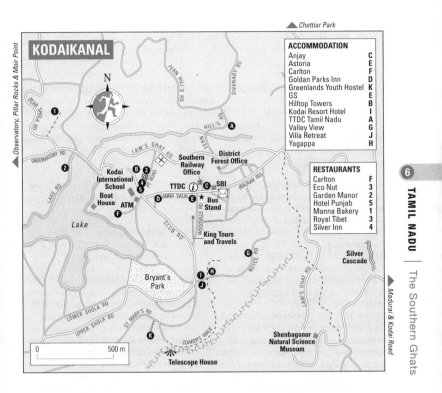

KODAIKANAL

ACCOMMODATION	
Anjay	C
Astoria	E
Carlton	F
Goldan Parks Inn	D
Greenlands Youth Hostel	K
GS	E
Hilltop Towers	B
Kodai Resort Hotel	I
TTDC Tamil Nadu	A
Valley View	G
Villa Retreat	J
Yagappa	H

RESTAURANTS	
Carlton	F
Eco Nut	3
Garden Manor	2
Hotel Punjab	5
Manna Bakery	1
Royal Tibet	3
Silver Inn	4

Southern Railway Office

District Forest Office

Kodai International School

Boat House

ATM

Lake

TTDC

SBI

Bus Stand

King Tours and Travels

Silver Cascade

Bryant's Park

Shenbaganur Natural Science Museum

COAKER'S WALK

Telescope House

0   500 m

► Madurai & Kodai Road

March the nights are chilly; the **peak tourist season**, therefore, is from April to June, when prices soar.

Arrival, information and getting around

Buses from Madurai and Dindigul pull in at the **bus stand** in the centre of town. Unless you're coming from as far as Chennai or Tiruchirapalli, the bus is much more convenient than the train: the nearest **railhead**, Kodaikanal Road – also connected to Dindigul (30min) and Madurai (50min) – is three hours away by bus. There are two roads to Kodaikanal: that **from Palani** is by far the more spectacular approach, although the less travelled, except during the monsoons, when the other route, from Dindigul, is invariably blocked.

Tickets for onward rail journeys from Kodaikanal Road can be booked at the Southern Railway office, down a lane beside the *Anjay Hotel* (Mon–Sat 8am–noon & 2.30–5pm, Sun 8am–noon). King Tours and Travels on Wood-ville Road can reserve seats on trains, buses and planes across South India. The **TTDC Tourist Office** (Mon–Fri 10am–5.45pm; ☎04542/241675) on Anna Salai (Bazaar Road) can arrange **treks** (5hr with a guide costs Rs300 per group); longer routes such as the three-day trek to Munnar in Kerala can also be negoti-ated. For **Internet** access, try Alpha Net (daily 9am–9pm; Rs40 per hour), next to the *Royal Tibet* restaurant on PT Road.

Taxis line Anna Salai in the centre of town, offering sightseeing at high fixed rates. Most tourists, however, prefer to amble around at their own pace. Kodaikanal is best explored on foot, or by **bicycle**, which you can rent for around Rs10 per day from numerous stalls around the lake. If you need to **change money**, head for the State Bank of India or the Canara Bank, both on Anna Salai near the *Anjay* hotel; there is also a State Bank of India ATM near the *Carlton Hotel*.

Accommodation

Kodaikanal's inexpensive **lodges** are grouped at the lower end of Anna Salai; many are dim and poky, however, so hunt around. Always ask whether blankets and hot water are provided (this should be free in the moderate to expensive places, but you may be charged in budget hotels). **Mid-range hotels** are usually good value, especially if you get a room with a view, but they hike their prices drastically during high season (April–June). The codes below reflect rates outside April–June.

Anjay Anna Salai ☎04542/241089. Simple budget lodge slap in the centre. Rooms are smarter than you'd expect from the outside, and many have views, although those at the front suffer some traffic noise. If they're full, check out the similarly good-value *Jaya* behind. ②–③

Astoria Anna Salai ☎04542/240524, @astoria1 @eth.net. Well-kept hotel opposite the bus stand, with homely rooms and a good, mid-priced restaurant. Hardly any views, but comfortable enough. ③–④

Carlton Off Lake Rd ☎04542/240056, @carlton @krahejahospitality.com. The most luxurious hotel in Kodaikanal, set in a spacious, tastefully renovated and well-maintained colonial house overlooking the lake, with a bar and comfortable lounge. Rooms in the house start at $100, and further accommodation is available in cottages within the grounds (from $187) – attractive if a little overpriced; all rates include meals. ⑨

Goldan Parks Inn Anna Salai ☎04542/246181, @goldanparksinn@sify.com. This friendly and central hotel has sixty clean and spacious carpeted rooms with TVs, though it lacks character. There's a decent veg restaurant attached, plus an Ayurvedic massage service. ⑤–⑦

Greenlands Youth Hostel St Mary's Rd ☎04542/241099, @greenlandsyh@rediffmail.com. Attractive old stone house offering unrivalled views and sunsets from its deep verandas. The rooms are basic, with wooden beds, open fireplaces (wood Rs50) and attached bathrooms. Book ahead. Dorm beds Rs80, rooms ③–④

GS Woodville Rd ☎04542/240456, @hotelgsin@yahoo.com. Small comfy rooms in a compact modern block by the bus stand, all with TV and tiny balconies, but no real views. ③

Hilltop Towers Club Rd ☎04542/240413, @httowers@sancharnet.in. Very near the lake

and school, with comfortable modern rooms, three restaurants and attentive service. ④–⑤

Kodai Resort Hotel Noyce Rd ☎04542/241301, @kodairesort@eth.net. Large complex of fifty incongruous-looking but very pleasant chalets situated at the top of the hill, with good views of the town, a health club and a rather dull restaurant. ⑤–⑥

TTDC Tamil Nadu Fern Hill's Rd ☎04542/241336. Large government-run hotel block northwest of town, primarily aimed at Indian family groups. Three types of room are available: standard mid-range rooms with TVs; family cottages sleeping several people; and a cheap dorm (Rs125). There's also a restaurant, bar and large child-friendly gardens with swings and slides. Good off-season discounts. ④–⑤

Valley View Post Office Rd ☎04542/240181, @hotelsivapriya@vsnl.net.in. Swish modern place on the eastern side of town, popular with honeymooners. All the rooms are warm, comfortable and have satellite TV; #308 and #309 have good views over the valley below. Also has a good pure veg restaurant. ④–⑤

Villa Retreat Coaker's Walk, off Club Rd ☎04542/240940, @villaretreat@yahoo.com. Comfortable and characterful old stone house, set in lovely gardens with superb views. All rooms have attached hot-water bathrooms, and wood and electric heaters are available on request. There's a range of rooms of various sizes and prices – a touch overpriced, but compensated for by the sunrise views. ④–⑦

Yagappa Noyce Rd ☎04542/241235. The best budget deal in town, this small, clean lodge is set in old buildings ranged around a lawn-cum-courtyard and has good views. Rooms are modest but clean, and there's a great little bar with wicker chairs and a tiny whitewashed restaurant serving veg meals and breakfasts. ②–③

The Town

Kodai's focal point is its **lake**, sprawling like a giant amoeba over a full 24 hectares just west of the town centre. This is a popular place for strolls, or bike rides along the five-kilometre path that fringes the water's edge, and pedal boats or rowing **boats** can be rented from the Boat House on the eastern shore (Rs20–100 for 30min, plus Rs20–40 if you require an oarsman). Horse riding is also an option down by the lake; it costs Rs80 to be led along the lakeside or Rs240 for a five-kilometre ride. Shops, restaurants and hotels are concentrated in a somewhat congested area of brick, wood and corrugated iron buildings east and downhill from the lake. To the south is **Bryant's Park** (daily 8.30am–6.30pm, last entry 6pm; Rs5, camera Rs25, video Rs500), with tiered flowerbeds against a backdrop of pine, eucalyptus, rhododendron and wattle which stretches southwards to Shola Road, less than 1km from the point where the hill drops abruptly to the plains. A path, known as **Coaker's Walk** (Rs2), skirts the hill, winding from the *Villa Retreat* to *Greenland's Youth Hostel* (10min), offering remarkable views that on a clear day stretch as far as Madurai, and fantastic sunsets.

One of Kodai's most popular natural attractions is **Pillar Rocks**, 7km south of town, where a series of granite cliffs rise more than 100m above the hillside. To get there, follow the westbound Observatory Road from the northernmost point of the lake (a steep climb) until you come to a crossroads. The southbound road passes the gentle **Fairy Falls** on the way to Pillar Rocks. Observatory Road continues west to the **Astrophysical Observatory**, perched at Kodai's highest point (2347m), although it's closed to visitors. Closer to the north shore of the lake, **Bear Shola Falls** are at their strongest early in the year, just after the second annual monsoon.

Southeast of the town centre, about 3km down Law's Ghat Road (towards the plains), the **Shenbaganur Natural Science Museum** (Mon–Sat 9am–noon & 2–5pm; Rs2.50) has a far from inviting collection of stuffed animals. However, the orchid house is spectacular, and well worth a look on the way to **Silver Cascade** waterfalls, a further 2km along the road.

Chettiar Park, on the very northwest edge of town, around 3km from the lake at the end of a winding uphill road, flourishes with trees and flowers all year round, and every twelve years is flushed with a haze of pale-blue **Kurinji blossoms** (the next flowering will be in 2006). These unusual flowers are associated with the god Murugan, the Tamil form of Karttikeya (Shiva's second son), and god of Kurinji, one of five ancient divisions of the Tamil country. A temple in his honour stands just outside the park.

Eating

If you choose not to eat in any of the **hotel restaurants**, head for the food stalls along **PT Road** a five-minute walk from the bus stand. Menus include Indian, Chinese, Western and Tibetan dishes, and some places cater specifically for vegetarians. Look out, too, for the **bakeries**, with their wonderful, fresh, warm bread and cakes each morning.

Carlton *Carlton Hotel*, off Lake Rd. Splash out on a buffet spread (Rs330) at Kodai's top hotel, rounded off with a *chhota* peg of IMFL scotch in the bar.

Eco Nut J's Heritage Complex, PT Rd. One of South India's few bona fide Western-style wholefood shops and a great place to stock up on trekking supplies: muesli, home-made jams, breads, pickles and muffins, high-calorie "nutri-balls" and delicious cheeses from Auroville.

Garden Manor Pleasant lakeside garden restaurant, featuring a wide menu of Indian, Chinese and continental cuisine, all at fairly inexpensive prices.

Hotel Punjab PT Rd. Top North Indian cuisine and reasonably priced tandoori specialities; try their great butter chicken and hot naan.

Manna Bakery Bear Shola Rd. The fried breakfasts, pizzas and home-baked brown bread and cakes served in this eccentric, self-consciously ecofriendly café-restaurant are great, though the bare concrete dining hall is a bit dingy.

Royal Tibet PT Rd. One of three small Tibetan joints in town, with dishes ranging from thick home-made bread to particularly tasty *momos* and noodles, and some Indian and Chinese options.

Silver Inn PT Rd. Western favourites like porridge, lasagne, mashed potato and apple crumble are all adequately served at this hole-in-the-wall place.

Palani

Few sacred sites in South India enjoy as dramatic a location as **PALANI**, just over 100km northwest of Madurai. Crowning a smooth-sided, perfectly dome-shaped outcrop of granite, the town's principal shrine overlooks a vast lake, **Vyapuri**, enfolded by the pale yellow crags of the Palani Hills, rising sheer to the south. During the monsoons, the tortuous road that scales the mountains from here provides the only dependable access to Kodaikanal. At other times, relatively few travellers are aware of its existence, but the views outstrip those from the busier southern approach to the hill station, while Palani itself, a busy little Tamil pilgrimage town, warrants at least a day-trip or stopover between Kodai and Ooty.

Praised for over two thousand years in the songs of the wandering Tamil saints, Palani's red-and-white-striped **Malaikovil Temple** attracts thousands of Hindu pilgrims each day. Each visitor is expected to perform two important rituals. The first involves an auspicious circuit of the base of the hill, via a two-kilometre-long sandy path known as the **Giri–Veedhi**, which is punctuated with shrines and stone-carved peacocks (Murugan's *vahana*, or vehicle). The second is an ascent of the sacred walkway via its 704 steps, illuminated from dusk onwards with tiny camphor lamps left by the devotees (and interrupted by more prosaic billboards advertising the names of the temple's corporate sponsors), to the hilltop shrine itself. During Palani's main festival in April/May, thousands of devotees – mostly male and clad in black *dhotis* – pour up the winding flight to worship the image, said to be formed from an aggregate of poisonous minerals, that, if mixed with coconut milk, fruits and flowers, produces medicinal herbs. Some carry pails of milk on yokes as offerings for Lord Murugan, while the more fervent among them perform austerities (cheek-piercing with metal leaf-shaped skewers is a favourite). Those unable to climb the steps can ascend in a carriage pulled slowly up the steep incline by electric winch (Rs10), but it can take a lot of queuing to get on (although you can fast-track yourself by paying Rs50). The summit **views** across Vyapuri lake and the Vaigai plain to the distant ghats are unforgettable.

Apart from the numerous simple *choultries* – pilgrims' hostels owned by various caste associations from all over South India – Palani has two proper **hotels**. The *TTDC Tamil Nadu* on West Giri Street, opposite the Winch Station (℡04545/241156; ❸–❺), has decent a/c and non-a/c doubles with attached bathrooms and hot water, as does the smart *Subam Hotel*, 7 North Giri Street near the main temple entrance (℡04545/242672, ℮hotelsubam@sancharnet.in; ❸–❺). **Buses to Palani** from Kodaikanal (every 1hr 30min; 3hr) often fill up, so it's wise to reserve a seat a day in advance. The town is also well connected by train and bus to Coimbatore, via Pollachi (for the Indira Gandhi wildlife sanctuary), and Madurai via Dindigul.

Indira Gandhi (Anamalai) Wildlife Sanctuary

Indira Gandhi (Anamalai) Wildlife Sanctuary is a 958-square-kilometre tract of forest on the southern reaches of the Cardamom Hills, southwest of the

Kodaikanal has become something of a low-key **trekking** centre in recent years. As you wander around town, **guides** continually approach offering their services on day hikes to local view points and beauty spots, or for longer trips involving night halts in villages. Scrutinize their recommendation books for comments by other tourists, and before you employ anyone go for a coffee to discuss possible routes, costs and the nature of the walks they're offering. While most are relatively straightforward, some tackle unstable paths and steep climbs for which you'll need sturdy footwear. You should also clarify accommodation and food arrangements, transport costs and also their fees, in advance.

Generally, simple meals and tiffin are available at villages along the routes of longer hikes, so you don't need to carry much more than a sleeping bag, water, emergency food supplies and warm clothes for the evening. **Maps** of the area tend to be hopelessly inaccurate, but the one featured in the booklet *Beauty in Wilderness* (Rs10), available from the DFO (District Forest Office) near the *Hotel Tamil Nadu*, gives you a rough idea of distances, if not the lie of the land. While at the DFO, get permission to stay in the **Forest Rest Houses**, which provide rudimentary accommodation for around Rs25–50 per night; most have fireplaces, but bear in mind that any wood you might burn contributes to the overall **deforestation** of the Palanis. Local environmental groups are concerned about the potential long-term impact of trekking on the economy and ecology of the range, and as a result encourage walkers to carry all rubbish, bury their faeces where toilets are not available and use purification tablets rather than bottled water.

If you'd prefer to hike without a guide, the following route is worth considering; most of it follows forest roads, and there are settlements at regular intervals, many of them connected to Kodai by daily bus services. You don't get to explore the wild tops of the range, but the views and countryside throughout are beautiful, with patches of indigenous *shola* forest accessible at various points.

First head out of town on the **Pillar Rocks** road towards Berijam; if you can hitch a ride, you'll avoid the horn beeping that otherwise accompanies your progress as far as the end of the road at **Moir Point**. **Berijam** (23km), a picturesque lake surrounded by dense pine and acacia forest, is little more than an outpost for forest wardens. From here, however, you can follow quiet back-country roads, taking local herders' and wood gatherers' paths that cut between the bends, to **Kavunji**, which is served by six daily buses to Kodai – handy if you're short of time. This sleepy Palani village is the home of a small NGO that promotes children's health projects, run by S.A. Iruthyaraj (look for the house with a white chicken painted on the wall), who is highly knowledgeable about local *shola* forests and off-track routes in the area. Further along the trail at **Polur** (8km) are some spectacular **waterfalls**. The locals say it is impossible to get close to them, but you can, by scrambling down the hillside via a muddy overgrown cattle path – and it's well worth it for the refreshing shower.

For more information on environmentally friendly trekking in the Kodai area, contact the **Palani Hills Conservation Council (PHCC)**, Amarville House, Lower Shola Road, Kodaikanal 62410 (℡04542/240711). This excellent environmental organization also welcomes foreign volunteer workers to help with their various campaigns and grass-roots projects in the Palanis.

busy junction town of **Pollachi**.Vegetation ranges from dry deciduous to tropical evergreen, and the sanctuary is home to lion-tailed macaques (black-maned monkeys), wild elephants, crocodiles, *sambhar*, spotted- and barking deer, as well as fifteen tigers at the last count.

The sanctuary has been at the centre of several water and land rights disputes over the past few years, mostly between local tribal people and the government, which has been developing major hydroelectric and irrigation projects in the area. Access to visitors was always strictly limited, but since 1998 the park has been closed altogether, ostensibly due to the activities of the infamous brigand Veerappan (see p.574). Veerappan was killed in late 2004, though it remains to be seen whether the Indira Gandhi Wildlife Sanctuary will now reopen.

Coimbatore

Visitors tend only to use the busy industrial city of **COIMBATORE** as a stopover on the way to Ooty, 90km northwest. Once you've climbed up to your hotel rooftop to admire the blue, cloud-capped haze of the Nilgiris in the west, there's little to do here other than kill time wandering through the

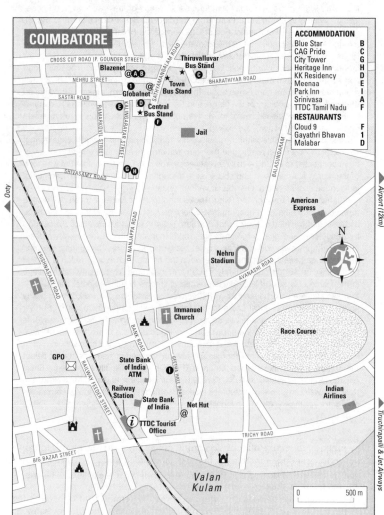

COIMBATORE

CROSS CUT ROAD (P. GOUNDER STREET)
NEHRU STREET
Blazenet
SASTRI ROAD
Globalnet
CROSS CUT ROAD (P. GOUNDER STREET)
Thiruvalluvar
Bus Stand
Town
Bus Stand
BHARATHIYAR ROAD
Central
Bus Stand
Jail
SHIVASAMY ROAD
RAMAKKOVIL STREET
KALINGARAYAN STREET
DR NANJAPPA ROAD
BALASUNDARAM
American
Express
Ooty
KRISHNASAMY ROAD
Nehru
Stadium
AVANASHI ROAD
N
BANK ROAD
Immanuel
Church
Race Course
GPO
State Bank
of India
ATM
Railway
Station
State Bank
of India
TTDC Tourist
Office
Net Hut
GEETHA HALL ROAD
Indian
Airlines
RAILWAY FEEDER STREET
BIG BAZAR STREET
TRICHY ROAD
Valan
Kulam
0   500 m

ACCOMMODATION
Blue Star   B
CAG Pride   C
City Tower   G
Heritage Inn   H
KK Residency   D
Meenaa   E
Park Inn   I
Srinivasa   A
TTDC Tamil Nadu   F
RESTAURANTS
Cloud 9   F
Gayathri Bhavan   1
Malabar   D

Airport (12km)

Tiruchirapalli & Jet Airways

Ukkadam Bus Stand, Pollachi, Kodaikanal & Palani

nuts-and-bolts bazaars, lined with lookalike textile showrooms, "General Traders" and shops selling motor parts.

Coimbatore earned its reputation as the "Manchester of South India" in the 1930s, when the nearby **Pykara Falls** hydroelectric project was built to provide cheap power for its huge **textile mills** and spin-off industries. Since then, the city has never looked back. If you arrive here from more traditional corners of Karnataka or the deep south, you'll find it distinctly prosperous, modern and orderly: new office buildings and business hotels dominate the skyline, while in the street, trousers far outnumber *lunghis* and virtually every man sports a pen in his shirt pocket.

Practicalities

Coimbatore has three main **bus stands** all fairly near each other in the northern part of town, a couple of kilometres north of the railway station. Thiruvalluvar Bus Stand is the main state and interstate station. Buses to Ooty, Coonoor and Mettupalayam leave from Central Bus Stand, while the busy Town Bus Stand is sandwiched in between. A fourth bus stand, Ukkadam, in the south of town, has departures to Palani, Pollachi, Madurai and towns in northern Kerala. The **railway station** is in the southern part of town and there are daily services to and from Chennai, Bangalore and Ernakulam. Coimbatore's **airport** is 12km northeast of town and served by buses to and from Town Bus Stand; a taxi will charge around Rs175.

You can **change money** at the State Bank of India and Bank of Baroda, near the railway station, or at the American Express Foreign Exchange on Avanashi

---

Moving on from Coimbatore

By air

Coimbatore **airport** is 12km northeast of town and served by buses to and from Town Bus Stand (taxis charge around Rs175). There are daily flights to Bangalore, Chennai, Delhi, Kozhikode and Mumbai. The Indian Airlines office is 2km east of the railway station on Trichy Road (☏ 0422/239 9833); Jet Airways is 4km along the same road (☏ 0422/221 2034).

By train

Coimbatore is well connected to major southern destinations by train. To catch the Nilgiri Blue Mountain Railway (see p.567) to **Ooty**, join the #2671 Nilgiri Express from Chennai, which leaves Coimbatore at 5.15am (1hr), and change onto the Blue Mountain Railway line at **Mettupalayam**, from where a train departs at 7.10am. Should you get stuck in Mettupalayam, try the *EMS Maruya Hotel* at 212 Coimbatore Rd (☏ 04254/227 936; ❹), which has en-suite a/c doubles. Overnight services from Coimbatore to **Chennai** include the Cheran Express #2674 (daily 10pm; 8hr 35min) and the Nilgiri Express #2672 (daily 9pm; 8hr 15min). For **Kochi**, catch the daily #2626 New Delhi–Trivandrum Kerala Express (daily at 5.40am; 4hr 35min). The best train for **Mangalore** is the #6667 Tiruchirapalli–Mangalore Express (daily 7.45pm; 9hr 45min).

By bus

Buses leave for Ooty every fifteen minutes from Central Bus Stand. Buses to Bangalore and Mysore from Central can be booked in advance at the **reservation office** (9am–noon & 1–8pm). There are also frequent services to and from Madurai, Chennai and Tiruchirapalli. Ukkadam Bus Stand, in the southwest of the city next to the lake, serves local towns and destinations in northern Kerala, such as Pollachi, Palakkad, Thrissur, Trissur and Kannur.

Road, a five-minute auto-rickshaw ride northeast of the railway station. **Internet** access is available all over Coimbatore for around Rs30 per hour. Options include Globalnet, on the first floor of Krishna Towers, on Sathyamangalam Road, just north of the Central Bus Stand; the smaller Blazenet, on Nehru Street next to the *Blue Star* hotel; and Net Hut, on Geetha Hall Road near the *Park Inn*.

Accommodation and eating

Most of Coimbatore's **accommodation** is concentrated around the bus stands. The cheapest places line Nehru Street and Shastri Road, but whatever you do avoid the rock-bottom places facing the bus stand itself, which are plagued with traffic noise from around 4am onwards.

As for **eating**, your best bets are the bigger hotels such as the *City Tower*, whose excellent rooftop restaurant, *Cloud 9*, serves a top-notch multi-cuisine menu to a predominantly business clientele; mains are around Rs100. The *Malabar*, on the first floor of the *KK Residency*, is a less pricey option, popular with visitors from across the Ghats for its quality non-veg Keralan cuisine. For vegetarian South Indian food, however, you won't do better than the ultramodern *Gayathri Bhavan*, opposite the *Blue Star* hotel on Nehru Street, which has a squeaky clean "meals" restaurant, open-air terrace, and an excellent little juice bar. The food here is superb, and only marginally pricier than average.

Hotels and guesthouses

Blue Star 369 Nehru St ☎0422/223 0635. The best mid-price place in this area, with impeccably clean rooms, some with balconies, quiet fans and bathrooms, in a modern multistorey building five minutes' walk from the bus stands. ③–④

CAG Pride 312 Bharathiar Rd ☎0422/252 7777, ✉sales@cagpride.com. One of the best hotels in town, fully a/c with comfortable rooms, health club, garden restaurant, cocktail bar and foreign exchange. ⑦–⑧

City Tower Sivasamy Rd, just off Dr Nanjappa Rd, a two-minute walk south of the Central Bus Stand ☎0422/223 0681, ⓦwww .hotelcitytower.com. Smart a/c city centre hotel with decent-sized rooms with modern interiors (heavy on leatherette and vinyls) and marble flooring; the "Executive" rooms are slightly more luxurious. ⑥–⑦

Heritage Inn 38 Sivasamy Rd ☎0422/223 1451, ✉heritageinn@vsnl.com. Coimbatore's top hotel, featuring more than sixty very comfortable a/c rooms, a couple of quality restaurants (veg and non-veg) and foreign exchange. Credit cards accepted. ⑦–⑧

KK Residency 7 Shastri Rd ☎0422/223 2433. Large tower-block hotel with very clean rooms and a couple of good restaurants. ③–④

Meenaa 109 Kalingarayan St ☎0422/223 5420. This good budget option is tucked away off the main drag, but handy for the bus stand. The rooms are clean, with attached shower-toilets and small balconies. ②–③

Park Inn 37 Geetha Hall Rd ☎0422/230 1284, ✉parkinn_cbe@sify.com. The smartest option along a street of hotels near the railway station – immaculate, quiet and good value (especially the non a/c rooms). Rates include breakfast. ⑤

Srinivasa 365 Nehru St, next door to the *Blue Star* ☎0422/223 2901. Near the bus stands and the cleanest of the cheap lodges in this area, though that isn't saying much. ①–②

TTDC Tamil Nadu Dr Nanjappa Rd ☎0422/230 2176. Opposite the Central Bus Stand, this convenient, clean and reliable place is one of the TTDC's better hotels, with a/c and non-a/c rooms. ③–⑤

Coonoor and Kotagiri

COONOOR, a scruffy bazaar and tea-planters' town on the Nilgiri Blue Mountain Railway (see box on p.567), lies at the head of the Hulikal ravine, 27km north of Mettupalayam and 19km south of Ooty, at an altitude of 1858m, on the southeastern side of the Dodabetta mountains. Often considered second best to its more famous neighbour, Coonoor has luckily avoided Ooty's over-commercialization, and can make a pleasant place for a short stop. In addition to an atmospheric little hill market specializing in leaf tea and fragrant essential oils, there are also plenty of rejuvenating strolls to be taken in the outlying hills and valleys. Accommodation in the town is in short supply, so most tourists visit on a day-trip, although there are a few reasonable places to stay

Coonoor loosely divides into two sections, with the bus stand (regular services to Mettupalayam, Coimbatore and elsewhere in the Nilgiris), railway station and market huddled together in **Lower Coonoor**. In **Upper Coonoor**, **Sim's Park** is a fine botanical garden on the slopes of a ravine, with hundreds of rose varieties (daily 8am–6.30pm; Rs5).

Visible from miles away as tiny orange or red dots amid the green vegetation, **tea-pickers** work the slopes around Coonoor, carrying wicker baskets of fresh leaves and bamboo rods that they use like rulers to ensure that each plant is evenly plucked. Once the leaves reach the factory, they're processed within a day, producing seven grades of tea. **Orange Pekoe** is the best and most expensive; the seventh and lowest grade, a dry dust of stalks and leaf swept up at the end of the process, is used to make teabags. To visit a tea or coffee plantation, contact UPASI (United Planters' Association of Southern India), "Glenview", Coonoor.

Around the town, rolling hills and valleys, carpeted with spongy green tea bushes and stands of eucalyptus and silver oak, offer some of the most beautiful scenery in the Nilgiris, immortalized in many a Hindi movie dance sequence. Cinema fans from across the south flock here to visit key locations from their favourite blockbusters, among them **Lamb's Rock** (5km) and **Dolphin's Nose** (9km), former British picnicking spots with paved pathways and dramatic views of the Mettupalayam plains. Buses to both from Coonoor leave every two hours, but it's a good idea to catch the first one at 7am, which gets you to Dolphin's Nose before the mist starts to build up. It's possible to walk the 9km back into town via Lamb's Rock – an enjoyable amble that takes you through tea estates and dense forest.

The only other major settlement hereabouts, **KOTAGIRI**, lies a winding one-hour bus ride from Coonoor at an altitude of just under 2000m. High on the cloudy hilltops, it's even more given over to tea planting than Coonoor, and as a result has little to recommend it as a tourist destination. The one reason you might want to venture up here is to shop at the **Women's Cooperative** off Ramchand Square, which stocks the region's best selection of locally made handicrafts, including traditional red-and-black **Toda embroidery** (see box on p.570). Hand-woven woollen shawls are the most expensive items on offer, but they also keep smaller souvenir items such as spectacle cases and wallets, all at very fair fixed prices. Income from the shop is used to fund women's development projects in the area, principally among the Todas; they've an interesting frieze of photos on the wall showing where the money goes.

Kotagiri is connected to Coonoor (every 15min; 1hr) and Mettupalayam (every 30min; 2hr) by regular and reliable **bus** services. You can also get here from Ooty, 28km west (hourly; 2hr), via one of the highest motorable roads in the Nilgiris.

Practicalities

There isn't much choice of places to **stay** or **eat** in Coonoor, and it's not a good idea to leave looking for a room until too late in the day. By and large the hotels are dotted around Upper Coonoor, within 3km of the station; you'll need an auto-rickshaw to find most of them. As ever, ignore any rickshaw-wallahs who tell you the hotel you want to go to is "full" or "closed". The fare from the bus stand to Bedford Circle or the *YWCA* is around Rs25.

If you're staying at the *YWCA* or one of the upmarket hotels your best bet is to eat there. In the bazaar, the only commendable **restaurants** are *Hotel Tamizhamgam* (pronounced "Tamirangum"), on Mount Road near the bus stand, which is Coonoor's most popular vegetarian "meals"-cum-tiffin joint. For good-value non-veg North Indian tandoori and Chinese food, try the *Greenland* hotel, up the road.

The Travancore Bank, on Church Road in Upper Ooty, near Bedford Circle, **changes currency**, but not always travellers' cheques. Otherwise, the nearest place is the State Bank of India in Ooty (see p.569).

Accommodation

The tariffs included here are for the low season, as high-season prices may increase by anywhere between twenty and a hundred percent, depending on the tourist influx.

La Barrier Inn Coonoor Club Rd ☎0423/223 2561. Comfortable mid-range option located way up above the bazaar, with great views of surrounding hills. The rooms are spotless and very large, opening onto flower-filled balconies. **❹**

Taj Garden Retreat Church Road, Upper Coonoor ☎0423/223 0021, ⓦwww.tajhotels.com. This luxurious but very overpriced colonial-era hotel offers cottage accommodation, a tea-garden, lawns and spectacular views, plus a good range of sports and activities, including freshwater fishing. The restaurant serves spectacular lunchtime buffets (around Rs300). Rooms from $120. **❾**

Velan (Ritz) Ritz Rd, Bedford Circle ☎0423/223 0784, ⓕ223 0606. Recently refurbished, this luxury hotel is in a great location on the outskirts

of town. Very spacious carpeted rooms with deep balconies and fine views – much better value than the *Taj Garden Retreat* but lacking its charm. **❻–❼**

Vivek Tourist Home Figure of Eight Rd, nr Bedford Circle ☎0423/223 0658. Managed by a very amiable lady, with clean rooms (some with tiny balconies overlooking the tea terraces) and a great value dorm (Rs60). Just beware of the monkeys. **❷–❸**

YWCA Guest House Near the hospital, Upper Coonoor ☎0423/223 4426. Five double rooms and two singles in a characterful Victorian-era house on a bluff overlooking town, with flower garden, tea terraces and fine views from relaxing verandas. There are also superb home-cooked meals at very reasonable rates. No alcohol. **❸**

Udhagamandalam (Ootacamund) and around

British *burra-sahib* John Sullivan is credited with "discovering" **UDHAGA-MANDALAM**, still more commonly referred to as **Ooty**, a shortened version of its anglicized name, Ootacamund. When he first clambered into this corner of the Nilgiris through the Hulikal ravine in the early nineteenth century, the territory was the traditional homeland of the pastoralist **Toda** hill tribe. Until then, the Todas had lived in almost total isolation from the cities of the surrounding plains and Deccan plateau lands. Sullivan quickly realized the agricultural potential of the area, acquired tracts of land for Rs1 per acre from the Todas, and set about planting flax, barley and hemp, as well as potatoes, soft fruit and, most significantly of all, **tea**, which all flourished in the mild climate. Within twenty years, the former East India Company clerk had made himself a fortune and drawn the attention of British residents sweating it out on the southern plains. Sullivan and his business cronies planned and founded Ootacamund, a town complete with artificial lake, churches and stone houses that wouldn't have looked out of place in Surrey or the Scottish Highlands. Ootacamund quickly become the most popular hill retreat in peninsular India, known fondly by the *burra-* and *memsahibs* of the south as "Ooty", the "Queen of Hill Stations".

The Nilgiri Blue Mountain Railway

The famous narrow-gauge **Nilgiri Blue Mountain Railway** climbs up from Mettupalayam on the plains, via Hillgrove (17km) and Coonoor (27km) to Udhagamandalam, a journey of 46km passing through sixteen tunnels, eleven stations and nineteen bridges. It's a slow haul of four-and-a-half hours or more – sometimes the train moves little faster than walking pace, and always takes at least twice as long as the bus – but the **views** are absolutely magnificent, especially along the steepest sections in the Hulikal ravine.

The line was built between 1890 and 1908, paid for by tea-planters and other British inhabitants of the Nilgiris. It differs from India's two comparable narrow-gauge lines, to Darjeeling and Shimla, in that it uses the so-called **Swiss rack system**, by means of which the tiny locomotives are able to climb gradients of up to 1 in 12.5. Special bars were set between the track rails to form a ladder, which cogs of teeth, connected to the train's driving wheels, engage like a zip mechanism. Because of this novel design, only the original locomotives can still run the steepest stretches of line, which is why the section between Mettupalayam and Coonoor has remained one of South Asia's last functioning **steam routes**. The chuffing and screeching whistles of the tiny train, echoing across the valleys as it pushes its blue-and-cream carriages up to Coonoor (where a diesel locomotive takes over) rank among the most romantic sounds of South India, and evoke the determined gentility of the Raj era even more strongly than Ooty's faded colonial monuments.

Timetable details for the line appear in the account of Coimbatore (see p.563) and in the "Moving on from Ooty" box on p.573.

Of the Todas, little further note was made beyond a couple of anthropological monographs, references to their *munds*, or settlements, in the *Madras Gazette*, and the financial transactions that deprived them of the traditional lands. Christianized by missionaries and uprooted by tea-planters and forest clearance, they retreated with their buffalo into the surrounding hills and wooded valleys where, in spite of hugely diminished numbers, they continued to preserve a more or less traditional way of life (see box on p.570).

By a stroke of delicious irony, the Todas outlived the colonists whose cash crops originally displaced them – but only just. Until the mid-1970s, "Snooty Ooty" (as the notoriously snobby town became known) was home to some of the subcontinent's last British inhabitants, those who chose to "stay on" after Independence, living out their last days on tiny pensions that only here allowed them to continue living in their accustomed style. Over the past two decades, travellers have continued to be attracted by Ooty's cool climate and peaceful green hills, forest and grassland. However, if you come in the hope of finding quaint vestiges of the Raj, you're likely to be disappointed; what with indiscriminate development and a deluge of holiday-makers, they're few and far between.

The **best time to come** is between January and March, thereby avoiding the high-season crowds (April–June & Sept–Oct). In May, the summer festival brings huge numbers of people and a barrage of amplified noise; worlds away from the peaceful retreat envisaged by the *sahibs*. From June to September, and during November, it'll be raining and misty, which appeals to some. The skies are clear between October or November until February, when it can get really cold at night – but it's pleasantly warm in the midday sunshine.

Arrival, information and local transport

Most visitors arrive in Ooty either by bus from Mysore in Karnataka (the more scenic, if steeper, route goes via Masinagudi), or on the miniature **Nilgiri Blue**

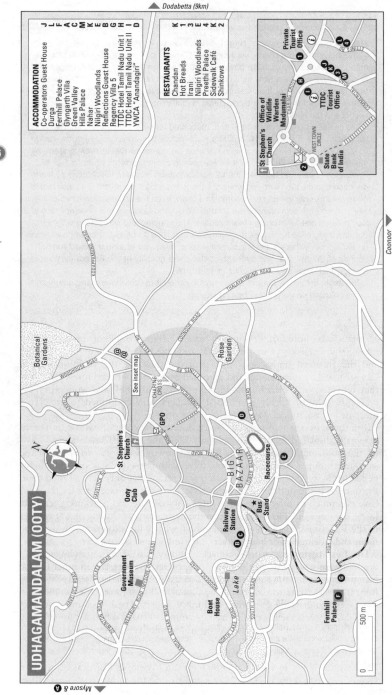

UDHAGAMANDALAM (OOTY)

▲ Dodabetta (9km)

▲ Mysore & A

Coonoor ▶

ACCOMMODATION

Co-operators Guest House	J
Durga	L
Fernhill Palace	F
Glyngarth Villa	A
Green Valley	C
Hills Palace	M
Nahar	K
Nilgiri Woodlands	E
Reflections Guest House	B
Regency Villa 5	G
TDDC Hotel Tamil Nadu Unit I	H
TDDC Hotel Tamil Nadu Unit II	I
YWCA "Anandagiri"	D

RESTAURANTS

Chandan	K
Hot Breads	1
Irani	3
Nilgiri Woodlands	E
Preethi Palace	4
Sidewalk Café	K
Shinkows	2

Botanical Gardens

WOODHOUSE ROAD

HAVELOCK RD

See inset map

CHARING CROSS

COMMERCIAL RD

FINGERT'S ROAD

Rose Garden

THE OSTER

GPO

St Stephen's Church

Ooty Club

Government Museum

Railway Station

Bus Stand

BIG BAZAAR

Racecourse

Boat House

Lake

Fernhill Palace

500 m

N

Inset map

Private Tourist Office

St Stephen's Church

Office of Wildlife Warden Madumalai

WEST TOWN CIRCLE

State Bank of India

TTDC Tourist Office

ETTINES RD

Mountain Railway (see p.567) from Coonoor and Mettupalayam. The **bus stand** and **railway station** are fairly close together, at the western end of Big Bazaar and racecourse. **Local transport** consists of auto-rickshaws and taxis, which meet incoming trains and gather outside the bus stand and on Commercial Road around Charing Cross. You can **rent bikes** (no gears), but the steep hills make cycling very hard work.

The **TTDC Tourist Office** (Mon–Sat 10am–5.45pm; ☎0423/244 3977), at the *TTDC Hotel Tamil Nadu II*, is eager to help, but their information is not always reliable. You can book tours here, among them one that takes in Ooty, Pykara and Mudumalai (daily 9.30am–7pm; Rs200), plus calls at Pykara dam, falls and boathouse and Mudumalai Wildlife Sanctuary, making a very long day. There's a less strenuous tour of just Ooty and Coonoor (daily 9.30am–5.30pm; Rs125), which goes to Sim's Park, the Botanical Gardens, the lake, Dodabetta Peak, Lamb's Rock and Dolphin's Nose. The private **tourist information centre** (daily 10am–7pm), in the clocktower building on Charing Cross, can help with hotels, sightseeing and restaurants.

Ooty's **post office**, northwest of Charing Cross at West Town Circle, off Spencers Road and near St Stephen's Church, has a **poste restante** counter (enquiries and stamps Mon–Fri 9am–5pm; parcels Mon–Fri 9am–3pm & Sat 9am–2pm). **Internet access** is widely available, especially around Charing Cross, with most places charging around Rs30 per hour. The only **bank** in Ooty that changes travellers' cheques and currency is the very *pukka* State Bank of India, on West Town Circle. While you're waiting for your cash, check out the photos in the hallway connecting the old and new blocks, dating from the era when this was the "Imperial Bank of India": stalwart, stiff-backed *burra-sahibs* pose with pipes, wives and mandatory Scottish terriers in front of the old bank building. There's also a State Bank of India ATM near the *Hotel Nahar* on Commercial Road.

Accommodation

Accommodation in Ooty is a lot more expensive than many places in India; during April and May the prices given below can rise by thirty to a hundred percent. It also gets very crowded, so you may have to hunt around to find what you want. The best by far are the grand old Raj-era places; otherwise, the choice is largely down to average hotels at above-average prices. In **winter** (Nov–Feb), when it can get pretty cold, most hotels provide extra blankets and buckets of hot water on request, but a few sharks may quietly add a charge for these services onto your final bill, so check beforehand.

Co-operators Guest House Charing Cross ☎0423/244 4046. Cheap and central guest house in an L-shaped Raj-era building with clean rooms and turquoise balconies looking down to a courtyard; it's set slightly back from the main road so is relatively quiet. Unfortunately the place has become somewhat cramped by a large concrete block next door. ❷

Durga Ettines Rd ☎0423/244 3837, ✉hotel_durga@thenilgiris.com. The best deal among the many mid-range places around Charing Cross. It's clean, comfortable and central, but the constant noise of buses stopping outside creates a lot of noise and dust. ❹–❺

Fernhill Palace Behind *Regency Villas*

☎0423/244 3097, ✉regency@sancharnet.in. Occupying the Maharajah of Mysore's palace, this luxury hotel is scheduled to open in summer 2005. The immaculate refurbishment has preserved the palace's antique furniture and old world charm whilst adding modern bathrooms complete with jacuzzis. The rooms are huge, with fireplaces and central heating, with prices ranging from $85 to $250. ❾

Glyngarth Villa Golf Club Rd, 4.5km out of town on the Mysore Rd ☎0423/ 244 5754, ✉glyngarthvilla@rediffmail.com. Set in a 150-year-old colonial villa in four acres of greenery with valley views. The five double-rooms, comfortable and with wooden interiors, give the

Until the arrival of the British, the **Todas** of the Nilgiri Hills maintained their own language and customs in villages (*munds*) of wagon-shaped huts made from bamboo, thatch and reeds. Today the Toda tribal community still exists, albeit in depleted numbers. Some wear traditional costume: plain white waistcloths under thick white woven shawls (*puthikuzhi*) striped with red and black. Once, all adult women had their upper body tattooed and their hair oiled and curled into long ringlets at the front; feminine beauty is judged by the narrowness of the feet and facial hair is admired. Men keep their hair and beards long.

Toda culture centres around the **buffalo**, which is held sacred; the only product the Todas use is its milk, consuming it in vast quantities. Toda temples are dairies, off-limits to everyone save the officiating priests. The community is divided into fourteen patriarchal clans, though its polyandrous social system is fast breaking down. "Marriages" were arranged at birth with partners from another clan; at the age of fifteen the female moved in with the husband's family and automatically became the wife of his younger brothers too. She could also seek further partners from other families, with the permission of her principal partner, who would generally assume the paternal role for any resultant offspring.

Traditionally, the Todas lived in interdependence with four other tribal groups, based on a barter system under which their main responsibility was to supply the others with dairy products. Of these, the **Irulus** – Vishnu-worshipping tool-makers and ritual specialists who are regarded by the Todas as caste inferiors – are today the most numerous, with a population of around seven thousand. Fears of caste pollution also determine relations between the Todas and the **Kotas**, ironsmiths and potters who provide music for rituals. The jungle-dwelling **Kurumbas**, known for their aptitude in magic, gathered honey and wood, while the **Badagas**, who arrived in the fourteenth century after being displaced by Muslim invasions, kept the others supplied with grain and beans.

At present there are about seventeen hundred Todas, of whom a quarter are Christian. Due to high infant mortality and the introduction of life-threatening diseases by the British, their population had dwindled to little more than six hundred by the 1940s. This alarming situation was dramatically reversed, however, largely through the efforts of an exceptional Toda woman, **Evam Piljain-Wiedemann**, who trained as a nurse in England and succeeded in winning the confidence of other Todas to take advantage of a mobile medical clinic. She continues to work to secure rights for the Todas, and to protect the natural environment.

Blame for the threat to the survival of the Nilgiris cannot simply be laid at the door of colonial exploitation, though the story does begin with the arrival of the British in

place a charming atmosphere. Rates include breakfast. **7**

Green Valley North Lake Rd ☎0423/244 4219. A little grubby but friendly and a good fallback if *Reflections* next door is full. Sizeable en-suite rooms, some with lake views, some with TV, all painted in wild colours. **2**–**3**

Hills Palace Commercial Rd, Charing Cross ☎0423/244 6483, ✉hillspalace@sify.com. Modern place that's just below the main bazaar, but secluded, quiet and spotlessly clean inside. Great value in low season. **3**

Nahar Commercial Rd, Charing Cross ☎0423/244 2173, ✉nahar@mds.vsnl.net.in. One of Ooty's smartest hotels, offering spacious, well-furnished

rooms (the best are in the modern building at the back) and two veg restaurants. A favourite with large Indian family holiday parties, so book ahead. **6**–**9**

Nilgiri Woodlands Racecourse Rd, 1km from bus stand and railway station ☎0423/244 2451, ✉nilgiris_woodlands@yahoo.com. A grand Raj-era building, with a wood-panelled lobby, hunting trophies and bare, clean rooms that are particularly good value in winter. The little cottages around the garden are worth the extra cost. Staff are friendly and helpful, and there's a good restaurant. **3**–**6**

Reflections Guest House North Lake Rd ☎0423/244 3834, ✉reflectionsin@yahoo.co.in. Homely, relaxing guesthouse by the lake, five minutes' walk from the railway station, with rooms

1821. Despite the British penchant for hunting (panther, tiger and deer) and fishing, they were aware, within the vision of the time, of protecting the natural landscape. The most destructive period came after Independence. From 1952, a series of five-year plans were implemented involving the widespread planting of exotic trees, principally eucalyptus, wattle and pine – they provided a generous income for the government, but had far-reaching effects on local ecology. A synthetic fibre industry, established in the foothills, requires huge amounts of pulp to make fibre. Despite local fears and protests, including a *satyagraha*-style public fast, land is still being cleared in order to feed factories.

Traditional *shola* forest, once destroyed, takes thousands of years to replace, and newly planted eucalyptus trees draw water from miles around – for the first time in its history, this once swampy region suffers from **water shortages**. The Todas can no longer get enough thatching grass to build houses and temples, and their traditional homes are being replaced by concrete. Nothing grows under eucalyptus and pine, and the sacred buffalo have nowhere to graze. Many Todas have been forced to sell their stock, and barely enough are left to perform the ceremonies at the heart of Toda life.

Visiting the Todas

In recent years, the Todas have become something of a tourist curiosity, and numerous trekking agencies and guides offer day-trips, or longer treks, to their settlements from Ooty. Although nothing on the scale of Thailand's Hill Tribe tourist circuit, the experience has to be a hollow one, consisting of a brief visit, and possibly a meal, followed up with the inevitable photo session. That said, the Todas in the more commonly visited villages do little to discourage foreigners from coming; on the contrary, they seem only too happy to pose in traditional costume for the pre-arranged fee handed over to them by the tour leaders.

A recommended **guide** for trips to Toda settlements around Ooty is R. Seniappan (aka "Sinni"), contactable through the official guides' office on the corner between the bus stand and railway station. He has been running tours into the area for years, is highly knowledgeable about local customs and etiquette and enjoys cordial relations with Toda people in the villages visited. Count on around Rs250 per day for his fee, and additional costs for meals and transport. You'll probably learn just as much, however, if not more, about the Todas' way of life by reading Anthony Walker's definitive anthropological study, *The Todas of South India: A New Approach*, researched in the 1970s.

opening onto a small terrace. Easily the best budget option in Ooty, but it's small and fills up quickly, so book in advance. ❷–❸
Regency Villas ☏ 0423/244 3097, Ⓔregency@sancharnet.in. The maharaja of Mysore's former guesthouse, now a rather run-down, though atmospheric, old hotel. If you're here for faded traces of the Raj, this is the place. The palatial suites (❼) in the main block are locked in a time warp, with frayed nineteenth-century furniture, original bathtubs, and old sepia photos of the Ooty hunt. By contrast, the cottages (❻) are cheerless and not such good value. Even if you can't afford to stay here, come out for a nose around and coffee on the lawn. ❻–❼

TTDC Hotel Tamil Nadu, Unit I & II Unit I is in the northwest corner of the complex above Charing Cross, reached by a flight of stairs, and Unit II in the northeast corner ☏ 0423/244 4370, Ⓕ 244 4369. Two identical large, characterless complexes in the centre of town, but with good-value restaurants, a bar and billiards rooms. ❸–❺
YWCA "Anandagiri" Ettines Rd ☏ 0423/244 2218. Charming 1920s building, set in spacious grounds near the racecourse. Seven varieties of rooms and chalets are on offer, all immaculate, with bucket hot water and bathrooms. There is a dining room and you can while away the evening in the cosy "English parlour" or by the piano. Excellent value. An inexpensive laundry facility is available. Book ahead. ❷–❹

The Town

Ooty sprawls over a large area of winding roads and steep climbs. The obvious focal point is **Charing Cross**, a busy road junction on dusty **Commercial Road**, the main, relatively flat, shopping street that runs south to the Big Bazaar and municipal vegetable market. Goods on sale range from fat plastic bags of cardamom and Orange Pekoe tea to presentation packs of essential oils (among them natural mosquito repellent citronella). A little way northeast of Charing Cross, the **Botanical Gardens** (daily 8.30am–6.30pm; Rs10, camera Rs30, video Rs500), laid out in 1847 by gardeners from London's Kew Gardens, consist of forty acres of immaculate lawns, lily ponds and beds, with more than a thousand varieties of shrubs, flowers and trees. There's a refreshment stand inside, shops outside selling snacks and souvenirs, and a small Tibetan market.

Northwest of Charing Cross, the small Gothic-style **St Stephen's Church** was one of Ooty's first colonial structures, built in the 1820s on the site of a Toda temple; timber for its bowed teak roof was taken from Tipu Sultan's palace at Srirangapatnam and hauled up here by elephant. The area around the church gives some idea of what the hill station must have looked like in the days of the Raj. To the right of the church is the rambling and rather dilapidated **Spencer's store**, which opened in 1909 and sold everything a British home in the colonies could ever need; it's now a computer college.

South of here, in the same compound as the post office, gowned lawyers buzz around the red-brick **Civil Court**, a quasi-Gothic structure with leaded diamond-shaped windows, corrugated iron roofs and a clock tower capped with a weather vane. Over the next hill (west), the snootiest of Ooty's institutions, the **Club**, dates from 1830. Originally the house of Sir William Rumbold, it became a club in 1843 and expanded thereafter. Its one claim to fame is that the rules for snooker were first set down here (although the members of Jabalpur Club in Madhya Pradesh are supposed to have originated the game in the first place). Entry is strictly restricted to members and their guests, or members of affiliated clubs. Further along Mysore Road, the modest **Government Museum** (daily except Fri & second Sat of month 10am–5.30pm; free) houses a few paltry tribal objects, sculptures and crafts.

West of the railway station and racecourse (races mid-April to mid-June), the **lake**, constructed in the early 1800s, is one of Ooty's main tourist attractions, despite being heavily polluted (most of the town's raw sewage gets dumped here – worth bearing in mind if you're tempted to venture out on it). Boats are available for hire (daily 9am–6pm; rowing & paddle boats Rs60–100, charter motor boats seating 8–15 people Rs200–375), and you can also go horse riding here (short rides Rs50–75, or Rs100 per hour).

Not far from the southeast end of the lake lies **Fernhill Palace**, once the summer residence of the Maharaja of Mysore and now a smart hotel (see p.569). It's an extraordinary place, built in the fullest expression of Ooty's characteristic Swiss-chalet style, with carved wooden bargeboards and ornamental cast-iron balustrades. *Regency Villas*, the Maharajah's guesthouse, located just behind the palace, is also a hotel and well worth a stop for a cup of tea on the lawn. Snacks and meals are also available at both places.

Eating

Many of the mid-range hotels serve up good South Indian food, but Ooty has yet to offer a gourmet **restaurant**, unless you want to take a taxi out to *Fernhill Palace*. The *Regency Villa*, however, is well worth checking out for its colonial ambience. For an inexpensive *udipi* breakfast, just head for one of the "meals" restaurants around Charing Cross serving *iddli-dosa* and filter coffee.

Chandan *Nahar Hotel*, Commercial Rd, Charing Cross. Inexpensive, carefully prepared North Indian specialities (their *paneer kofta* is particularly good), and a small selection of tandoori vegetarian dishes, served inside a posh restaurant or on a lawnside terrace. They also do a full range of lassis and milkshakes.

Hot Breads Charing Cross. French-established franchise selling the usual range of quality pastries, cheesy and plain breads and savouries from a bakery outlet downstairs, as well as pizzas and other tasty snacks in a rather dull first-floor café.

Irani Commercial Rd. A gloomy old-style Persian joint run by Baha'ís. Uncompromisingly non-veg (the menu's heavy on mutton, liver and brains), but an atmospheric coffee stop, and a popular hang-out for both men and women.

Nilgiri Woodlands *Nilgiri Woodlands* hotel, Race-course Rd, 1km from bus stand and railway station. Has a limited à la carte menu of Indian and Western dishes and inexpensive lunchtime and evening thalis (Rs45). No alcohol.

Preethi Palace Ettines Rd. Excellent lunchtime thalis (north and south Indian) and a range of superb pure veg food in the evenings.

Shinkows 42 Commissioners Rd. Authentic Chinese restaurant serving up good-sized portions on the spicy side. It's more expensive than the downtown restaurants but still good value – main meat courses cost around Rs120–150, veg dishes are cheaper (Rs50–80).

Sidewalk Cafe *Nahar Hotel*, Commercial Rd. Bright, modern café offering soups, sandwiches, pizza, cakes and fresh fruit juices.

Around Ooty

Regular local bus services to outlying villages and plantations allow you to reach the less developed regions **around Ooty**. The most popular destination for a day-trip is the Nilgiris' second highest mountain, **Dodabetta** (2638m), 10km east along the Kotagiri road. Sheltering Coonoor from the southwest monsoon (and, conversely, Ooty from the reach of the northwest monsoon of October and November), the peak is the region's most prominent landmark. It's also easily accessible by road: buses run every couple of hours from Ooty (10am–3.30pm) to the summit, where a viewing platform and telescope make the most of a stunning panorama. To enjoy it, however, you'll have to get here before the daily deluge of bus parties.

Moving on from Ooty

Ooty **railway station** has a reservation counter (daily 8am–12.30pm & 2.30–4.30pm) and a booking office (6.30am–7pm) where you can buy tickets for the Nilgiri Blue Mountain Railway (see p.567), as well as onward services to most other destinations in the south. Four trains daily (9.15am, 12.15pm, 3pm & 6pm) pootle down the narrow-gauge line to Coonoor, but only one (3pm) continues down to Mettupalayam, on the main broad-gauge network. If you're heading to Chennai, the 3pm train should get you to Mettupayalam to connect with the daily #2672 Nilgiri Express (depart 7.45pm; 9hr 30min).

You can also book **buses** in advance, at the reservation offices for both state buses (daily 9am–12.30pm & 1.30–5.30pm) and the local company, Cheran Transport (daily 9am–1pm & 1.30–5.30pm), at the bus stand. A combination of stop-start local and express "super-deluxe" state buses serve Bangalore and Mysore (half-hourly buses to both pass through Mudumalai), Kodaikanal, Thanjavur, Thiruvananthapuram and Kanniyakumari, as well as Kotagiri, Coonoor and Coimbatore. **Private buses** to Mysore, Bangalore and Kodaikanal can be booked at hotels, or agents in Charing Cross; even when advertised as "super-deluxe", many turn out to be cramped minibuses.

Sandalwood smuggling

The delicate scent of **sandalwood** – *chandan* in Hindi – is one of the quintessential fragrances of South India, particularly around Mysore in Karnataka, where specialist craftsmen carve combs, beads, elephants and gods and use its oil to make incense and soap. Mashed into a paste, the valuable heartwood of the tree is regarded as a powerful antiseptic capable of curing migraine and skin ailments. Vaishnavites also smear their foreheads with sandalwood powder before performing puja, a practice recorded in the Ramayana, as well as the poetry of the sage Kalidasa, dating from the third century BC.

Sandalwood may be an essential element in traditional Indian culture, but it is fast becoming a rare commodity due to demand from foreign markets, which has forced the price skywards in recent years (a kilo of sandalwood oil will now fetch around US$14,000). The largest importer is the US perfume industry, which uses vast quantities of the oil as a base and fixative, followed by the Gulf states, where sandalwood (along with myrrh, jasmine and amber) ranks among the few fragrances permitted by Islamic law.

The vast bulk of India's sandalwood comes from mixed, dry deciduous forests of the southern Deccan Plateau, around Bangalore, where trees – if allowed to grow for at least thirty years – reach an average height of 20m. Extraction and oil-pressing are strictly controlled by the Indian government, in accordance with a law passed by the Sultan of Mysore in 1792, who declared that no individual other than himself could own a sandalwood tree, even if it grew on private land. This law is still enforced, although these days foresters receive seventy percent of the sale value if they can prove they have grown and protected the wood.

However, in spite of having the law on their side, the Indian government has been failing miserably in its attempts to control sandalwood stocks and trade over the past decade or so. Their difficulties have largely been due to the activities of the notorious smuggler **Veerappan**, whose cartel handled an estimated seventy percent of Karnataka's total export, amounting to billions of rupees of lost revenue each year. South India's most infamous brigand, Veerappan began his career at the age of 14, when he poached his first elephant. Two thousand pachyderm carcasses later, he jacked in ivory smuggling for the sandalwood racket, was imprisoned in 1986, but escaped soon after, remaining at large until October 18, 2004, when he was tracked down and shot dead in the Dharmapuri district.

Mudumalai Wildlife Sanctuary

Set 1140m up in the Nilgiri Hills, the **MUDUMALAI WILDLIFE SANCTUARY** covers 322 square kilometres of deciduous forest, split by the main road from Ooty (64km to the southeast) to Mysore (97km to the northwest). It boasts one of the largest populations of elephants in India, along with wild dogs, gaur (Indian bison), common and Nilgiri langur and bonnet macaques (monkeys), jackal, hyena and sloth bear, and even a few tigers and panthers. Unfortunately, most of the park has been off-limits to visitors for the past few years, due to the activities of sandalwood smuggler **Veerappan** (see box above). You can, however, still stay here en route to or from Mysore to sample the peace and fresh air of the Nilgiri forest after the bus parties of day-trippers from Ooty have all gone home.

Until the Forest Department (☎0423/252 6235) relaxes restrictions on trekking in the remote woodland areas around the Mudumalai, you can only reach the park by road. The main route from Ooty to Mudumalai, taken by most Mysore- and Bangalore-bound buses, goes via Gudalur and takes 2hr

Moving continually between sixty camps in the dense jungle lining the Karnataka–Tamil Nadu border, Veerappan and his men, sporting green army fatigues and ostentatious moustaches, kept one step ahead of the crack army forces sent out to arrest them, managing their lucrative operation over a massive area. Because of the sums his smuggling generated, Veerappan was able to pay local villagers Rs30 per day to cut and transport wood – more than double what the Forest Service was paying for the same work. This, combined with rumours of extravagant gifts to poor people and temples, earned him a near-mythical, Robin Hood-like status across a 6000-square-kilometre swathe of forest, despite the policy of systematic and violent intimidation which he employed to discourage informers and punish those who crossed him – although it was an informer who ultimately betrayed him.

Veerappan's treatment of Forest Service and government officials who fell into his clutches was brutal, with regular murders, kidnappings and incidents of torture enhancing his already fearsome reputation. His worst atrocity took place in April 1993, when 21 policemen were lured into an ambush and killed by landmines. The Indian government responded swiftly by launching the largest manhunt in history: six hundred border security troops were flown in for the operation, but somehow Veerappan still managed to slip through the net. In 2000, Veerappan made the headlines again when he kidnapped and held hostage an ageing but still popular Tami film actor, **Rajkumar**. As the weeks went by questions were asked by the public when mediators and journalists managed to meet Veerappan, yet a crack squad of National Security Force officers failed again and again to corner the brigand and free Rajkumar. The eventual release of the film star after 107 days was arranged by the mysterious Dr Banu, a female doctor who appeared from nowhere and was suspected of having connections with the illegal local quarrying business.

Veerappan and his band were the main reason given for the government closure to tourists of huge tracts of protected forest in the Western Ghats. It is hoped that the forests and wildlife reserves may now be reclaimed and reopened for tourism and wildlife projects, though this will ultimately depend on whether the sandalwood mafia is able to continue its operations without the guidance and influence of Veerappan himself.

30min to reach **Theppakkadu**, the main access point to the sanctuary. The alternative route is a tortuous journey of very steep gradients and hairpin bends, which can only be attempted by smaller vehicles such as the Cheran transport minibuses. These take around one hour and end up at **Masinagudi**, from where there are regular bus and jeep connections to Theppakkadu, 8km away.

At Theppakkadu, the big event of the day is the **Elephant Camp** show (daily 6pm; free), during which put-upon pachyderms perform puja or play soccer to Boney M songs. There is a reasonable selection of fairly luxurious jungle lodges dotted around the park perimeter, including the *Wilds* at **Northern Hay**, 5km from Masinagudi (☎0423/244 9490, ✉thewildstay@tahoo.com; ❼), where you can enjoy bathtubs, four-poster beds and local coffee. A cheaper and more convenient option is the *TTDC Hotel Tamil Nadu* in Theppakkadu (☎0423/252 6580) with a choice of dormitory accommodation (Rs75), double rooms (❷) and four-bed family rooms (Rs400). Officially, you should book in advance at the TTDC office in Ooty (see p.569), but if rooms are available there should be no problem.

Travel details

Trains

Chidambaram to: Chengalpattu (4 daily; 4hr 45min–6hr); Kumbakonam (1 daily; 2hr 12min); Rameshwaram (2 daily; 11hr 35min–12hr 16min).
Coimbatore to: Bangalore (2–3 daily; 6hr 45min–9hr); Chennai (5–6 daily; 7hr 20min–8hr 55min); Delhi (1–2 daily; 43–47hr 30min); Hyderabad (1 daily; 21hr 15min); Kanniyakumari (1 daily; 11hr 55min); Kochi (7–8 daily; 2hr 15min–5hr 30min); Kolkata (Calcutta; 7 weekly; 38hr 45min); Madurai (1–2 daily; 6hr 15min–6hr 35min); Mettupalayam, for Ooty (1 daily; 1hr 5min); Mumbai (2 daily; 31hr 10min–32hr 50min); Salem (10–11 daily; 2hr 35min–3hr 15min); Thiruvananthapuram (4–5 daily; 9hr 30min–10hr 25min); Tiruchirapalli (2 daily; 5hr 15min–5hr 40min).
Kanniyakumari to: Bangalore (1 daily; 19hr 40min); Chennai (2–3 daily; 13hr–15hr 25min); Coimbatore (1 daily; 11hr 55min); Delhi (Wed only; 53hr 10min); Kochi (2 daily; 6hr 15min–6hr 30min); Madurai (1–2 daily; 4hr 25min–5hr 15min); Mumbai (1 daily; 44hr 10min); Thiruvananthapuram (2 daily; 1hr 35min–2hr); Tiruchirapalli (1–2 daily; 7hr 10min–8hr 15min).
Madurai to: Bangalore (1 daily; 10hr 55min); Chengalpattu (6–7 daily; 6hr 45min–8hr 55min); Chennai (7–9 daily; 7hr 45min–10hr 15min); Coimbatore (1–2 daily; 6hr 15min); Kanniyakumari (1–2 daily; 4hr 35min–5hr 50min); Kodaikanal Road (2–4 daily; 33min–43min); Tiruchirapalli (6–8 daily; 2hr 20min–3hr 10min); Tirupati (2 weekly; 11hr 30min).
Tiruchirapalli to: Bangalore (1 daily; 10hr); Chengalpattu (6–7 daily; 4hr–5hr 28min); Chennai (7–9 daily; 5hr 20min–7hr); Coimbatore (2 daily; 4hr 55min–5hr 10min); Kanniyakumari (1–2 daily; 7hr 40min–9hr 5min); Kochi (1 daily; 9hr 30min); Kodaikanal Road (2–4 daily; 1hr 50min–2hr 18min); Madurai (7–9 daily; 2hr 35min–3hr 35min); Thanjavur (2 daily; 1hr 10min–1hr 25min).

Buses

Chidambaram to: Chengalpattu (22 daily; 4hr 30min–5hr); Chennai (22 daily; 5–6hr); Coimbatore (6 daily; 7hr); Kanchipuram (8–10 daily; 7–8hr); Kanniyakumari (3 daily; 10hr); Kumbakonam (every 10min; 2hr 30min); Madurai (5 daily; 8hr); Pondicherry (every 20min; 2hr); Thanjavur (every 20min; 4hr); Tiruchirapalli (every 30min; 5hr); Tiruvannamalai (16 daily; 3hr 30min).
Coimbatore to: Bangalore (10 daily; 8–9hr); Chennai (9 daily; 10–12hr); Kanchipuram (3 daily; 9–10hr); Kanniyakumari (3 daily; 14hr); Kodaikanal (2 daily; 6hr); Madurai (25 daily; 5–6hr); Mysore (3 daily; 6hr); Ooty (every 15mins; 3hr 30min–4hr); Pondicherry

(8 daily; 9hr); Rameshwaram (2 daily; 14hr); Salem (every 15mins; 3hr 30min); Thiruvananthapuram (10–15 daily; 12hr); Tiruchirapalli (every 30min; 5hr).
Kanchipuram to: Chennai (every 10min; 1hr 30min–2hr); Coimbatore (3 daily; 9–10hr); Madurai (4 daily; 10–12hr); Pondicherry (8 daily; 3-4hr); Tiruchirapalli (2 daily; 7hr); Tiruvannamalai (15–20 daily; 3–4hr).
Kanniyakumari to: Chennai (10 daily; 16–18hr); Kovalam (10–12 daily; 2hr); Madurai (every 30min; 6hr); Pondicherry (10–12 daily; 12–13hr); Rameshwaram (via Madurai; 4 daily; 10hr); Thiruvananthapuram (20 daily; 2hr 45min–3hr 30min); Tiruchirapalli (every 30min; 10–12hr).
Madurai to: Bangalore (21 daily; 8–9hr); Chengalpattu (every 20–30min; 9hr); Chennai (every 20–30min; 11hr); Chidambaram (5 daily; 8hr); Coimbatore (every 30min; 5–6hr); Kanchipuram (4 daily; 10–12hr); Kanniyakumari (every 30min; 6hr); Kochi (8 daily; 10hr); Kodaikanal (10 daily; 4hr); Mysore (5 daily; 10hr); Pondicherry (14 daily; 11–13hr); Rameshwaram (every 30min–1hr; 4hr); Thanjavur (every 30 min; 4–5hr); Thiruvananthapuram (15 daily; 7hr); Tiruchirapalli (every 30min; 4–6hr); Tirupati (daily; 15hr).
Pondicherry to: Bangalore (4 daily; 10–12hr); Chennai (every 10–20min; 2hr 30min–3hr); Chidambaram (every 20min; 2hr); Coimbatore (8 daily; 9hr); Kanchipuram (8 daily; 3–4hr); Kanniyakumari (10–15 daily; 12–13hr); Madurai (hourly; 11–13hr); Mamallapuram (every 10–20min; 3hr); Thanjavur (20 daily; 5hr); Tiruchirapalli (every 30min; 5–6hr); Tiruvannamalai (every 20min; 2hr).
Tiruchirapalli to: Chengalpattu (every 20min; 7–8hr); Chennai (hourly; 8–9hr); Coimbatore (every 30min; 5hr); Kanchipuram (2 daily; 7hr); Kanniyakumari (15–20 daily; 10–12hr); Kodaikanal (8–10 daily; 5hr); Madurai (every 30min; 4–6hr); Pondicherry (every 30min; 5–6hr); Thanjavur (every 10min; 1hr–1hr 30min); Tiruvannamalai (5 daily; 6hr).

Flights

In the following IA = Indian Airlines; DA = Deccan Airlines; JA = Jet Airways; and SA = Sahara Airlines.
Coimbatore to: Bangalore (DA; 2 daily; 40–55min); Chennai (DA, IA, JA, SA; 3–4 daily; 1hr 5min–1hr 55min); Delhi (IA, SA; 1 daily; 4hr 45min); Kochi (JA; 2 weekly; 30 min); Kozhikode (IA; daily; 30min); Mumbai (IA, JA, SA; 3 daily; 1hr 45min).
Madurai to: Chennai (DA, IA, JA; 4 daily; 55min–1hr 20min); Mumbai (IA; 1 daily; 3hr 20min).
Tiruchirapalli to: Chennai (IA; 4 weekly; 50 min); Kozhikode (IA; 2 weekly); Thiruvananthapuram (IA; 4 weekly).

Andhra Pradesh

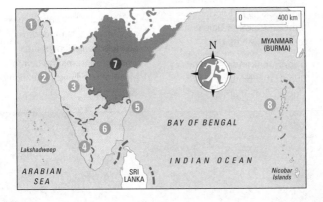

CHAPTER 7

Highlights

* **Hyderabad** A predominantly Islamic city offering a compelling combination of monuments, museums and lively bazaars. See p.581

* **Golconda Fort** Set in a lush landscape just west of Hyderabad, the capital of the Qutb Shahi dynasty boasts a dramatic fort. See p.589

* **Warangal** Features two important Hindu monuments: the medieval fort and a thousand-pillared Shiva temple. See p.594

* **Nagarjunakonda** Ancient Buddhist sculptures and stupas, dotted around an island in Nagarjuna Sagar lake. See p.595

* **Amaravati** Fine carvings surround the remains of a great Buddhist stupa at this village on the banks of the Krishna. See p.597

* **Tirumala Hill, Tirupati** The most visited pilgrimage centre in the world, Tirumala Hill is crowned by the Venkateshwara Vishnu Temple. See p.600

* **Puttaparthy** Sai Baba's main ashram attracts modern pilgrims from all over the world, and forms the centrepiece of a thriving community. See p.604

△ Tirupati

Andhra Pradesh

lthough **ANDHRA PRADESH** is the largest state in South India and occupies a great swathe of land, stretching for over 1200km along the coast from Orissa to Tamil Nadu and reaching far inland from the fertile deltas of the Godavari and Krishna rivers to the semi-arid Deccan Plateau, it's not a place that receives many tourists. Most foreign travellers pass through en route to its more attractive neighbours, which is understandable as places of interest are few and far between. However, the sights that Andhra Pradesh does have to offer are absorbing and well enough connected to warrant at least a few stops on a longer tour of South India.

The state capital, **Hyderabad**, is an atmospheric city, dating from the late sixteenth century, which is now thriving as a hi-tech hub. Its endless bazaars, eclectic Salar Jung museum and the mighty **Golconda Fort** nearby make it an enticing place to spend a day or two. By contrast, the adjacent twin city of **Secunderabad** excels only in characterlessness. **Warangal**, 150km northeast of Hyderabad, has both Muslim and Hindu remains from the twelfth and thirteenth centuries, while the region's Buddhist legacy – particularly its superb sculpture – is preserved in museums at sites such as **Nagarjunakonda** (south of Hyderabad) and **Amaravati**, the ancient Satavahana capital. In the east, the big cities of **Vishakapatnam** and **Vijayawada** have little to recommend them, though the latter makes a convenient access point for Amaravati. The temple town of **Tirupati** in the far southeast – best reached from Chennai in Tamil Nadu – is one of India's great Hindu phenomena, a fascinating and impossibly crowded pilgrimage site, said to attract more pilgrims than Mecca. In the southwest of the state, the small town of **Puttaparthy** attracts a more international pilgrim crowd, drawn here by the prospect of *darshan* from spiritual leader Sai Baba.

Although modern industries have grown up around the capital, and shipbuilding, iron and steel are important on the coast, most people in Andhra Pradesh remain poor. Away from the Godavari and Krishna deltas, where the soil is rich enough to grow rice and sugar cane, the land is in places impossible to cultivate.

Some history

Earliest accounts of the region, dating back to the time of **Ashoka** (third century BC), refer to a people known as the Andhras. The **Satavahana dynasty** (second century BC–second century AD), also known as the Andhras, came to control much of central and southern India from their second capital at Amaravati on the Krishna. They enjoyed extensive international trade with both eastern Asia and Europe, and were great patrons of Buddhism. Subsequently,

the Pallavas from Tamil Nadu, the Chalukyas from Karnataka, and the Cholas all held sway. By the thirteenth century, the Kakatiyas of Warangal were under constant threat from Muslim incursions, while later on, after the fall of their city at Hampi, the Hindu Vijayanagars transferred operations to Chandragiri near Tirupati.

The next significant development was in the mid-sixteenth century, with the rise of the Muslim **Qutb Shahi dynasty**. In 1687, the son of the Moghul emperor Aurangzeb seized Golconda. Five years after Aurangzeb died in 1707, the viceroy of Hyderabad declared independence and established the Asaf Jahi dynasty of **Nizams**. In return for allying with the British against Tipu Sultan of Mysore, the Nizam dynasty was allowed to retain a certain degree of autonomy even after the British had come to dominate all India.

During the struggle for Independence, harmony between Hindus and Muslims in Andhra Pradesh disintegrated, and **Partition** brought matters to a bloody climax (see box on p.582). Andhra Pradesh state was created in 1956 from Telugu-speaking regions (although Urdu is widely spoken in Hyderabad) that had previously formed part of the Madras Presidency on the east coast and the princely state of Hyderabad to the west. Today almost ninety percent of the population is Hindu, with Muslims largely concentrated in the capital. In 2004 Congress regained control of the state government, easing lingering sectarian tensions, although the minority TRS party is pushing for northwestern Andhra Pradesh, known as Telangana, to split off as a separate state.

Hyderabad/Secunderabad

A melting-pot of Muslim and Hindu cultures, the capital of Andhra Pradesh comprises the twin cities of **HYDERABAD** and **SECUNDERABAD**, with a combined population of around six million. Secunderabad, of little interest to visitors, is the modern administrative city founded by the British, whereas Hyderabad, the old city, with its teeming **bazaars**, **Muslim monuments** and **Salar Jung Museum**, has far more character. Hyderabad went into decline after Independence, with tensions often close to the surface due to lack of funding – the old city only received 25 percent of the budget despite having 45 percent of the population. Recently Hyderabad has overtaken Bangalore as the South's hi-tech capital, and is now India's foremost computer and information technology centre, bringing much revenue into the city and giving rise to the nickname "Cyberabad".

Hyderabad was founded in 1591 by **Mohammed Quli Shah** (1562–1612), beside the River Musi, 8km east of Golconda, the fortress capital of the

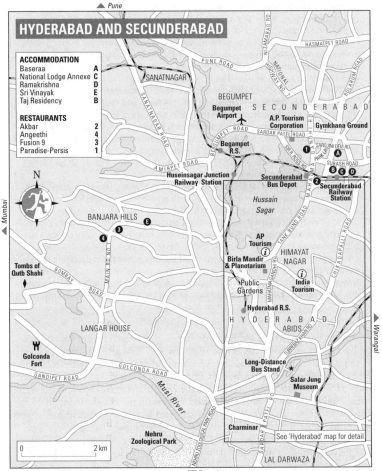

HYDERABAD AND SECUNDERABAD

ACCOMMODATION
Baseraa	A
National Lodge Annexe	C
Ramakrishna	D
Sri Vinayak	E
Taj Residency	B

RESTAURANTS
Akbar	2
Angeethi	4
Fusion 9	3
Paradise-Persis	1

The last Nizam

Picking your way through the sprawl of modern Hyderabad, it's hard to imagine that only sixty years ago this was the capital of a vast and powerful state, whose sumptuous palaces, mosques and ornamental gardens made it among the most splendid cities ever seen in south Asia. That the last outpost of living Moghul grandeur in the subcontinent could be so quickly and so thoroughly reduced hints at the terrible events surrounding the demise of the state's last ruler. Direct descendants of the prophet Mohammed on one side, and the prophet's right-hand man, the Khalifa, on the other, the Asaf Shah dynasty of Hyderabad – known since the seventeenth century by its honorific Moghul title, **Nizam** – rose to pre-eminence in the twilight of Muslim rule in India. Feuds of succession nearly consumed the family, but it survived the colonial incursions of the French, East India Company and Marathas, and by the twentieth century presided over the premier princely state in British India, home to a population of between fifteen and twenty thousand.

Marooned amid the vast ocean of Hindu India, the state capital, Hyderabad, emerged from the collapse of the Moghul empire and Deccan Sultanates as a lone outpost of courtly Muslim culture in India. Its nobles, merchants, craftsmen and artists, drawn from as far afield as Turkey, Persia and Central Asia, as well as the fading Indo-Islamic capitals of the north, lived in a splendid isolation epitomized by the extravagant lifestyles of the Nizams. Behind the high walls of the King Kothi palace, some 10,000 people – ranging from the Arab mercenaries and Abyssinian amazons who guarded the harem, to the legions of wives, courtesans and servants who attended on the ruler – lived an increasingly anachronistic, introverted life, regulated by complex medieval etiquette and old-world courtly manners.

When he ascended to the throne in 1911, the tenth and last Nizam, **Mir Osman Ali**, was reputedly the richest man in the world. Memoirs of former British diplomats and local aristocrats describe his collection of 300 vintage Daimlers and Rolls-Royce cars; of the famously huge, 185-carat "Jacobi" diamond, thought to be the largest ever found, which the Nizam used as a paperweight; and of trucks stacked with pearls, precious stones and gold ingots – a portable fortune that could be spirited away in the event of revolution or attack.

Taciturn, paranoid and addicted to opium, the last Nizam grew progressively more eccentric as British rule waned. The city was as rife with rumours of his extreme stinginess as of his unsurpassed wealth. Visitors, it was said, were limited to one biscuit when they called for tea, while the Nizam wore the same threadbare clothes for thirty or more years. One British resident mistook him for "a snuffly old clerk too old to be sacked". He even reputedly knitted his own socks, and ate all his meals off a tin plate on his bedroom floor, surrounded by the contents of overspilling wastepaper baskets. Perhaps the most surprising facet of the last Nizam's eccentricity, however, was his prodigious sexual appetite; he is said to have fathered more than one hundred illegitimate children. Hidden cameras installed inside the guest quarters

Golconda empire which by that time had begun to suffer from overcrowding and a serious lack of water. Unusually, this new city was laid out on a grid system, with huge arches and stone buildings that included Hyderabad's most famous monument, **Charminar**. At first it was a city without walls; these were only added in 1740 as defence against the Marathas. Legend has it that a secret tunnel linked the spectacular **Golconda Fort** with the city, dotted with dome-shaped structures at suitable intervals to provide the unfortunate messengers who had to use it with the opportunity to come up for fresh air.

For the three hundred years of Muslim reign, there was harmony between the predominantly Hindu population and the minority Muslims. Hyderabad was the most important focus of Muslim power in South India at this time; the of his palaces also enabled him to compile what is thought to be India's largest collection of pornographic photographs.

When the end of the Raj finally came in 1947, Mir Osman Ali was given one year in which to decide whether to throw his lot in with India or faraway Pakistan. In the event, much to the amazement of Prime Minister Nehru and Home Affairs minister Patel, he chose instead to tough it out alone, declaring himself ruler of a fully autonomous **Hyderabad State**. The decision, symptomatic of the Nizam's introversion and bull-headed cupidity, was an act of hubris that would cost the lives of hundreds of thousands of this former subjects.

Often glossed over by historians as a bloodless formality, the ensuing assault on Hyderabad ordered by Nehru in 1948 – in which a fully mechanized Indian army attacked a feudal force armed with little more than 300 rifles – turned into one of the ugliest episodes in the history of Independent India. After being held at bay for four days, Nehru's troops rampaged through Hyderabad state, looting and leaving a trail of destruction in their wake. Taking advantage of the mayhem, gangs of Hindu *goondas* also ran amuck, slaughtering their Muslim neighbours and systematically raping the women. Although outwardly unruffled, Nehru was privately outraged by reports of the atrocities committed by the Indian army in "**Operation Polo**", and commissioned an official enquiry once the dust had settled. The report, entitled *Hyderabad: After the Fall*, concluded that as many as 200,000 Muslims were massacred in the wake of the army action.

While tens of thousands of his former supporters, staff and nobles fled to escape execution and imprisonment, Nizam Mir Osman Ali was accorded the usual princely rights, along with privy purse amounting to Rs5 million per year. He was also allowed to retain income derived from his estates and keep his treasure. Nevertheless, he died in 1967 complaining that the annexation of Hyderabad had reduced him to poverty.

Among the Nizam's surviving assets being squabbled over by his heirs is a mysterious million, deposited in a London bank account shortly before the 1948 debacle. Following Partition, both the Indian and Pakistani governments laid claim to the sum, along with a several of the Nizam's descendants and an Indian Princess called Tahera, who told the High Court of Andhra Pradesh that a stake of the money was owed to her as a *mehr*, the dowry given by a Muslim woman's family upon marriage which is traditionally returned in the event of divorce. So far the only beneficiary of the unending legal wrangle over the lost million has been the UK's Natwest bank. Since it was deposited in 1947, the £1,007,940 and nine shillings are estimated to have grown to anything from £25 to £80 million. The bank insists it cannot relinquish the money until all the parties involved in the dispute are in agreement – an unlikely prospect indeed, given the perennially turbulent state of Indo–Pakistani relations, and the refusal of the various protagonists involved to recognize each others' claims.

princes' fabulous wealth derived primarily from the fine gems mined in the Kistna Valley at Golconda, which during the 1600s was the diamond centre of the world. The famous **Koh-i-Noor** diamond was found here – the only time it was ever captured was by Moghul emperor Aurangzeb, when his son seized the Golconda Fort in 1687. It is now set in a British royal crown.

Arrival and information

The old city of **Hyderabad** straddles the River Musi. Most places of interest lie south of the river, while much of the accommodation is to the north. Further north, separated from Hyderabad by Hussain Sagar Lake, is the modern twin city

APTDC operates a number of **guided tours** (bookable through their two offices; see below). Times quoted below are for when tours set off from the Secunderabad office; pick-up time in Hyderabad is 45min later. The better of the two APTDC **city tours** (daily 8am–5.45pm; Rs190) includes Hussain Sagar, the Birla Mandir and Planetarium, Qutb Shahi tombs (not Fri), Salar Jung Museum (not Fri), Charminar and Golconda. There are also shorter morning and afternoon city tours and one to **Golconda Fort's sound and light show** (daily 2–9pm; Rs170 including entrance fee), which also stops at the Botanical Gardens and drives past Hi-Tech City. Andhra Pradesh Tourism hits most of the principal sights twice a day (9am–1pm & 2–6pm; Rs125) and offers an evening tour (daily 7–9pm), though these tours only run when there's sufficient demand. **Ramoji Film City**, a 2000-acre site full of wild and wonderful film sets, 35km from Hyderabad, also has its own tour (daily 7.45am–6pm; Rs375 including entry).

APTDC's **Nagarjuna Sagar** tour (Sat & Sun 7am–9.30pm; Rs310, excluding entry fees) covers 360km in total, and is rather rushed, but is a convenient way to get to this fascinating area (see p.595). The longer tours to **Tirupati/Tirumala**, more conveniently reached from Chennai and further afield in south India, are not worth considering.

of **Secunderabad**, where some long-distance trains terminate, and where all through trains deposit passengers. If you do have to get off at Secunderabad, your ticket is valid for any connecting train to Hyderabad; if none is imminent, many buses including #5, #8 and #20 ply between both stations. **Hyderabad railway station** (also known as Nampally) is close to all amenities and offers a fairly comprehensive service to major destinations. The well-organized **long-distance bus stand** occupies an island in the middle of the River Musi, 3km southeast of the railway station. Hyderabad **airport**, 8km north of the city at Begumpet, is served by auto-rickshaws, taxis and buses #9M or #10 via Nampally station, and a number of routes including #10, #45, #47 and #49 from Secunderabad.

The main **tourist office** in Hyderabad is the **AP Tourism office** (daily 7am–7pm; ☎040/2345 3110, ⓦwww.aptourism.com) on Secretariat Road just before it becomes Tank Bund Road, near the start of the flyover. The **APTDC office** next door (daily 7am–8pm; ☎040/2345 3036, ⓦwww.tourisminap .com) and the other APTDC office, at Yatri Nivas, Sardar Patel Road, Secunderabad (☎040/2781 6375), are useful principally if you want to book one of their tours (see box above). The **India Tourism office**, Sandozi Buildings, Himayatnagar Road, Hyderabad (Mon–Fri 9am–5pm; ☎040/2763 1360), offers a few brochures. However, the best source of local information is the monthly listings **magazine**, *Channel 6* (Rs15; ⓦwww.channel6magazine.com), available from most bookstalls. It lists airlines, hospitals, rail enquiries, as well as body-freezing boxes and eye banks.

Accommodation

The area in front of **Hyderabad railway station** (Nampally) has the cheapest accommodation, but you're unlikely to find even a basic room for less than Rs250. The grim little enclave of five lodges with "Royal" in their name is usually full and best avoided. The real **bargains** are in the mid- to upper-range hotels, which offer better facilities for lower rates than in other big cities. Little over 1km north of Secunderabad railway station, decent mid-range places can be found on **Sarojini Devi Road**, near the Gymkhana Ground. Most hotels operate a 24-hour checkout system.

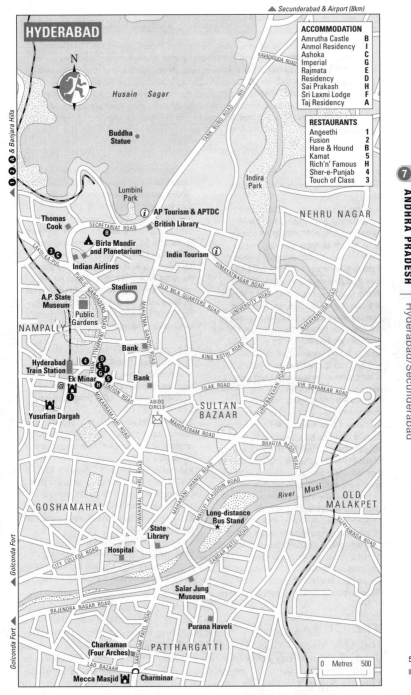

HYDERABAD

Secunderabad & Airport (8km)

ACCOMMODATION
Amrutha Castle	B
Anmol Residency	I
Ashoka	C
Imperial	G
Rajmata	E
Residency	D
Sai Prakash	H
Sri Laxmi Lodge	F
Taj Residency	A

RESTAURANTS
Angeethi	1
Fusion	2
Hare & Hound	B
Kamat	5
Rich'n' Famous	H
Sher-e-Punjab	4
Touch of Class	3

Husain Sagar

Buddha Statue

Lumbini Park

Indira Park

NEHRU NAGAR

Thomas Cook

AP Tourism & APTDC
British Library

Birla Mandir and Planetarium

India Tourism

Indian Airlines

Stadium

A.P. State Museum

Public Gardens

NAMPALLY

Bank

Bank

Hyderabad Train Station

Ek Minar

Yusufian Dargah

ABIDS CIRCLE

SULTAN BAZAAR

GOSHAMAHAL

River Musi

OLD MALAKPET

Long-distance Bus Stand

State Library

Hospital

Salar Jung Museum

Purana Haveli

Charkaman (Four Arches)

PATTHARGATTI

Mecca Masjid   Charminar

0   Metres   500

Golconda Fort
Golconda Fort

KAVADIGUDA ROAD
TANK BUND ROAD
SECRETARIAT ROAD
LAKDI-KA-PUL
PUBLIC GARDENS ROAD
NAMPALLY HIGH
MAHATMA GANDHI ROAD
OLD MLA QUARTERS ROAD
HIMAYATNAGAR ROAD
UNIVERSITY ROAD
NARAYANGUDA ROAD
KING KOTHI ROAD
TILAK ROAD
VIR SAVARKAR ROAD
TURBA BAKHAN ROAD
STATION ROAD
MUKARAMJAHI ROAD
MAHIPATRAM ROAD
BHAGYA REDDI ROAD
JAWAHARLAL NEHRU ROAD
MAHARANI JHANSI ROAD
MAULVI ALAUDDIN ROAD
SARDAR PATEL ROAD
VIJAYWADA ROAD
CITY COLLEGE ROAD
RAJENDRA NAGAR ROAD
SARDAR PATEL ROAD
LAD BAZAAR

Secunderabad, Airport & Banjara Hills

Hyderabad addresses

Hyderabadis appear to have a deep mistrust of logical, consistent road-naming, mapping and **addresses**. One road merges into another, some addresses refer to nothing more specific than a locality and others identify themselves as being opposite buildings that no longer exist. Just as confusing are those that have very specific addresses consisting of a string of hyphenated numbers referring to house and plot numbers, incomprehensible to anybody other than town surveyors. All this is somewhat ironic in a city that is home to one of the major sections of the Survey of India.

Hyderabad

The following places are marked on the map on p.585.

Amrutha Castle 5-9-16 Saifabad, opposite the Secretariat ☎040/5663 3888, ⓦwww .amruthacastle.com. Affiliated to the Best Western chain, this extraordinary hotel, designed like a fairy castle with round turret rooms, offers international facilities at fair prices. With its rooftop swimming pool, it's a good place to splash out. ⑧–⑨

Anmol Residency Next to the Ek Minar Mosque, Nampally ☎040/2460 8116. Great-value and friendly lower mid-range place, handily placed for the station. The deluxe corner rooms have a lot more space and windows covering two walls. ③–④

Ashoka 6-1-70 Lakdi-ka-Pul ☎040/2323 0105, ⓕ5551 0220. Standard mid-range hotel with a variety of clean en-suite rooms with cable TV (some also have a/c). ④–⑤

Imperial 5-8-107 Nampally Station Rd ☎040/5582 7777, ⓕ2320 9089. Reasonably well-kept lodge a three-minute walk from the station. Some of the rooms have a/c and/or TV. ②–④

Rajmata Nampally High Rd, opposite the railway station ☎040/5566 5555, ⓕ2320 4133. Set back from the road in the same compound as the various *Royal* lodges, with large and clean non-a/c deluxe rooms. The adjacent *Lakshmi* restaurant offers good south Indian veg food. ④

Residency Nampally High Rd ☎040/2320 4060, ⓦwww.theresidency-hyd.com. Swish, modern hotel belonging to the Quality Inn group; the most upmarket option near the station but overcharges foreigners at $72–120. Good veg restaurant. ⑨

Sai Prakash Station Rd ☎040/2461 1726, ⓔhotelsaiprakash@rediffmail.com. A five-minute walk from the station, this modern hotel has comfortable carpeted rooms, all with cable TV, plus good restaurants and a bar. The non-a/c rooms are good value and very popular. ⑤–⑥

Sri Laxmi lodge Gadwal Compound, Station Rd ☎040/5563 4200. Quiet place down a small lane opposite the *Sai Prakash*, with reasonably clean rooms. Good value, especially for singles. ②

Taj Residency Road No. 1, Banjara Hills, 4km from the centre ☎040/2666 3939, ⓦwww.tajhotels .com. The least expensive ($140–160) of the three Taj Group hotels in the vicinity, with the usual top-notch facilities including a quality multi-cuisine restaurant and 24hr coffee shop. ⑨

Secunderabad

Baseraa Sarojini Devi Rd ☎040/2770 3200, ⓦwww.baseraa.com. The comfiest hotel within fifteen minutes' walk of the station, with 77 modern rooms and suites boasting all mod cons. ⑦–⑧

National Lodge Annexe Opposite Secunderabad Railway Station ☎040/2770 5572. No-frills lodge amongst the motley cluster of hotels opposite the railway station. ②

Ramakrishna St John's Rd ☎040/2783 4567, ⓕ2782 0933. Comfy mid-range option in a large concrete block opposite the railway reservation complex 400m from station. Some a/c rooms, and it's the smartest place in the immediate vicinity of the station. ④–⑥

Sri Vinayak Off Regimental Bazaar ☎040/2771 0146, ⓕ2780 2146. Decent lower mid-range lodge tucked away in a quiet lane only a few minutes from the station. Has some a/c and air-cooled rooms. ③–⑤

The City

Hyderabad has three fairly distinct sectors: **Hyderabad**, the old city; **Secunderabad**, the new city (originally called Hussain Shah Pura); and **Golconda**, the old fort. The two cities are basically one big sprawl, separated by a lake, **Hussain Sagar**, which was created in the 1500s and named after Hussain Shah

Wali, who had helped Ibrahim Quli Qutb Shah recover from a serious illness. A large stone Buddha stands on an island in the lake.

The most interesting area, south of the River Musi, holds the **bazaars**, **Charminar** and the **Salar Jung Museum**. The river itself is just a trickle, even after the rains, and most of the riverside is grassed over and planted with palms and rice. North of the river, the main shopping malls are found around **Abids Circle** and the **Sultan Bazaar** (ready-made clothes, fruit, veg and silk), ten minutes' walk east of the railway station. Abids Circle is connected to MG Road, which runs north to join Tank Bund Road at Hussain Sagar and continues to Secunderabad, while to the south it metamorphoses into Nehru Road. Trendy new shops, restaurants and bars are also springing up in the posh **Banjara Hills** district, on the west side of the city.

Salar Jung Museums

The unmissable **Salar Jung Museum** (daily except Fri 10am–5pm; Rs150 [Rs10]), on the south bank of the Musi, houses part of the huge collection of Salar Jung, one of the Nizam's prime ministers, and his ancestors. A wealthy and well-travelled man with an eye for objets d'art, he bought whatever took his fancy from both the East and West, and ranging from the sublime to the ridiculous. His extraordinary hoard includes Indian jade, miniatures, furniture, lacquer-work, Moghul opaque glassware, fabrics, bronzes, Buddhist and Hindu sculpture, manuscripts and weapons. There are also good examples of *bidri*, decorated metalwork cast from an alloy of zinc, copper and tin, that originated in Bidar in northern Karnataka. Avoid visiting the museum at the weekend, when it gets very crowded.

Charminar, Lad Bazaar and the Mecca Masjid

At the heart of the old city's crowded maze of bazaars is the **Charminar**, or Four Towers, a triumphal arch built at the centre of Mohammed Quli Shah's city in 1591 to commemorate an epidemic. As its name suggests, it features four graceful minarets, each 56m high, housing spiral staircases to the upper storeys. The (now defunct) mosque on the roof is the oldest in Hyderabad, built to teach the royal children the Koran. The yellowish colour of the building is due to a special stucco made of marble powder, gram (a local pulse) and egg yolk.

Charminar marks the beginning of the fascinating **Lad Bazaar**, as old as the town itself, which leads to **Mahboob Chowk**, a market square featuring a mosque and Victorian clocktower. Lad Bazaar specializes in everything you could possibly need for a Hyderabadi marriage, full of old stores selling jewellery, rosewater, herbs and spices, and cloth, including *lunghis*. You'll also find silver filigree jewellery, antiques and *bidri* ware, as well as boxes, plates, *hookah*-paraphernalia and the like, delicately inlaid with silver and brass. Hyderabad is the centre of the national trade in **pearls** – so beloved of the Nizams (see p.582) that they not only wore them but apparently liked to have them ground into powder to eat as well. Pearls can be bought, for good prices, in the markets near the Charminar. Southeast of Lad Bazaar, the complex of **Royal Palaces** includes Chaumahalla, four palaces set around a central courtyard.

Just a stone's throw from the Charminar stands **Mecca Masjid**, the sixth largest mosque in India, constructed in 1598 by the sixth king, Abdullah Qutb Shah, from locally hewn blocks of black granite and small red bricks from Mecca, which are slotted over the central arch. The mosque can hold 3000 worshippers with up to 10,000 more in the courtyard; on the left of the courtyard are the tombs of the Nizams.

The **Charkaman**, or "Four Arches", north of Charminar, were built in 1594 and once led to the parade ground of royal palaces to the south (now long gone). The surrounding narrow streets spill over with interesting small shops; through **Doulat-Khan-e-Ali** – the western arch, which originally led to the palace – stores sell lustrous brocade and antique saris. The arch itself is said to have been once hung with rich gold tapestries.

The **Nizam's Museum** at Purana Haveli (daily except Fri 10am–5pm; Rs50) houses the longest wardrobe in the world, with built-in changing rooms where the Nizams would consider which of his innumerable costumes to don for the

The fish miracle

In a land of a thousand-and-one holy healers, miracle cures and all-round weird phenomena, one stands out as the fishiest. Each year from the 6th to the 8th of June, on "mrigasira karti", the traditional arrival of the monsoon in Andhra, more than half a million asthmatics wheeze their way across India to Hyderabad on a quest to solve their breathing problems. With the summer heat at its fiercest and most humid, they stand for hours in the sun clutching little plastic bags containing a live merrel fish. Once patients reach the head of the mile-long queue, the fish, together with a nut-sized pellet of marzipan-coloured paste, is rammed wriggling down their throats.

The secret recipe for the wonder seafood cure is jealously guarded by the three brothers of a family of Hyderabadi toddy tappers, the **Bathini Gouds**. It was revealed in 1845 to one of their ancestors, Veerana Goud, by a *rishi* (saint) returning after a pilgrimage to the Himalayas, to thank the Gouds for their hospitality and kindness. The holy man, however, insisted the fish cure would only be efficacious if administered once each year, free of charge and using the exact ingredients prescribed by him, among them "holy water" from the so-called "Milk-well" (*Doodhbaowli*) in the toddy tappers' back yard.

Over the century and a half or so since the first fish cure, the treatment's fame has grown to such an extent that the Gouds are now unable to host the annual dispensary at their home, in the cramped confines of the old bazaar, 2km from the Charminar. Instead, the local municipality has set aside the city's vast Exhibition Ground in Gandhinagar to accommodate the hundreds of thousands of asthmatics and their families who pour in. Indian Railways lays on several special trains from Delhi, Guwahati and Thiruvananthapuram, and extra divisions of police are drafted in to cope with the crowds, who usually number well over half a million.

To keep up with the ever increasing demand, the Gouds employ a team of dozens to prepare the paste in the months leading up to the break of the monsoon. But none of the old *rishi*'s provisos are ignored. The expense of making and administering the cure – roughly Rs20,000 annually – is still met entirely by the three brothers, although patients are these days required to bring their own fish (unless they're vegetarian, in which case bananas may be used).

If you're tempted to take the treatment, it's a good idea to contact the Goud family in advance by post (128, State Bank of India Colony, Gandhinagar, Kavadiguda, Hyderabad 500038). Get to Hyderabad a couple of days in advance, and they will issue you with a pass that will save you having to queue for hours in the heat. Bear in mind, too, that to benefit fully from the fish cure you should have the treatment three times on successive years, and stick to a special Ayurvedic diet for 45 days after each one.

Finally, watch out for the crop of soundalike Goud impostors trying to cash in on the fish cure, who prey on unsuspecting new arrivals at the railway station. Not only do these fly-by-nights charge for the treatment, but none are likely to have mastered the deft finger-down-the-throat stab required to shove the merrel speedily on its wiggly way.

For a vivid account of what the fish cure actually feels like, hunt out a copy of Tahir Singh's *The Sorcerer's Apprentice* (see "Books", p.721).

day. There is also an impressive display of gold, silver, pearls, precious jewels and artefacts as well as family portraits and newspaper cuttings that chart the history of the Nizam's family and lineage.

North of the river

The **Yusufian Dargah**, with its striking bulbous yellow dome, is set in a leafy courtyard not far south of the railway station (follow the road that runs down from the Ek Minar Mosque and look for an alley on the right). It's the shrine of a seventeenth-century Sufi saint of the venerable Chisti order, and you can enter (with covered head) to view the flower-decked tomb. About a kilometre north of the station, set in Hyderabad's tranquil public gardens, the **AP State Museum** (daily except Fri and every other Sat 10.30am–5pm; Rs10) displays a modest but well-labelled collection of bronzes, prehistoric tools, copper inscription plates, weapons, household utensils and even an Egyptian mummy. There's a gallery of modern art in the extension.

The **Birla Venkateshwara Temple** (daily 7am–noon & 3–9pm), on Kalapahad ("black mountain") Hill, north of the Public Gardens, was constructed in Rajasthani white marble in 1976 by the Birla Trust, set up by the wealthy industrialist Birla family. Although the temple itself is not of great interest, it affords fine views over the whole city. Nearby, and built by the same organization, is the **planetarium** (shows in English daily except Thurs at 11.30am, 4pm & 6pm; Rs17) and a **science centre** (daily 10.30am–8pm; Rs15) with lots of satellite hardware and photos, machines demonstrating sensory perceptions and a small dinosaur display.

Hussain Sagar

Hussain Sagar, the large expanse of water separating Hyderabad from Secunderabad, offers a welcome area of tranquillity within the busy conurbation. People come here to stroll along Tank Bund, the road that runs around the eastern side of the lake, and to relax in the small parks dotted along the water's edge. The parks contain numerous statues of prominent local figures from the last few centuries, and comes alive with ice-cream and snack stalls, particular as sunset approaches and people gather to watch the glowing red reflections in the lake.

In the centre of the lake stands a large stone statue of the **Buddha Purnima** or "Full Moon Buddha". The huge figure measures 55ft high, weighs 350 tons and took five years to build – tragically, during the first attempt to install it in 1990 the barge carrying it sank, killing eight people. After spending two years underwater it was finally placed on its plinth by a salvage company in 1992. **Boats** chug out to the statue from Lumbini Park, just off Secretariat Road, every hour from 9am to 6pm; the half-hour round trip costs Rs25.

Two luxury boats – the *Bhageerathi* and the *Bhagmati* – operated by APTDC tourism offer hour-long **cruises** of the lake (11am–3pm, Rs50; 6–8pm, Rs60). Both boats can also be chartered for special functions – check with APTDC for details.

Golconda Fort and the tombs of the Qutb Shahi kings

Eleven kilometres west of old Hyderabad, **Golconda** was the capital of the seven Qutb Shahi kings from 1518 until the end of the sixteenth century, when the court moved to Hyderabad. Set on rock outcrop which rises imposingly above the surrounding plain, the well-preserved fort is one of the most impressive in India, though large portions of its battlements are draped in grasses, lending it a soft, natural air. Its outer wall was formerly 18m high in places and the citadel boasted 87 semicircular bastions and eight mighty gates, four of which are still in use, complete with gruesome elephant-proof spikes.

To get **to the fort**, bus #119 runs from Nampally. Both the #66G direct bus from Charminar and #80D from the railway station in Secunderabad stop outside the main entrance. **For the tombs**, take #123 and #142S from Charminar. From Secunderabad the #5, #5S and #5R all go to Mehdipattanam, where you can hop onto #123. Or, of course, you could take a rickshaw and spare yourself the bother (agree a waiting fee in advance). Set aside a day to explore the fort, which covers an area of around four square kilometres; it's well worth hiring one of the many guides who gather at the entrance, or at least buying one of the handy little pamphlets, including a map, sold by vendors.

Entering the **fort** (daily 9am–5pm; $2 [Rs5]) by the Balahisar Gate, you come into the Grand Portico, where guards clap their hands to show off the fort's acoustics; the claps can be clearly heard at the Durbar Hall. To the right is the **mortuary bath**, where the bodies of deceased nobles were ritually bathed prior to burial. If you follow the arrowed anticlockwise route, you pass along a straight, walled path before coming to the two-storey residence of ministers Akkana and Madanna, and start the proper ascent to the Durbar Hall. Halfway along the steps, which pass assorted water channels and wells that supplied the fort's water system, you come to a small, dark cell named after the court cashier **Ramdas**, who during his incarceration here produced the clumsy carvings and

The Qutb Shahi

Quli, destined to become the first king of the Qutb Shahi dynasty, came from Persia with his uncle to sell horses to the Bahmani kingdom at Gulbarga and Bijapur. After a spell as a popular governor, he was titled **Quli Qutb Shah** by the Bahmani ruler Mamu Shbahmani who had appointed him. By 1518 the power of the Bahmanis was waning and Quli Qutb Shah raised an army and established independence for his state, ruling for 25 years and making Golconda his dynastic capital. When he was in his nineties, his eldest son Jamshed – who had briefly succeeded to the throne – attempted to have his father beheaded while praying in the mosque and his brothers exiled. However, an outraged people prevented Jamshed's coup by forcibly deposing him. Quli Qutb Shah preferred, thereafter, one of his younger sons, Ibrahim, to inherit his throne.

Ibrahim Quli Qutb Shah returned from exile to take over the kingdom at the age of eighteen. He was a learned man who wrote poetry in both Urdu and Telugu and oversaw the construction of many of Golconda's most important buildings, including the stone fort. His reign saw the dynasty reach the height of its power, despite occasional conflicts with the neighbouring states of Bijapur and Ahmadnagar. These three kingdoms later formed an alliance to defeat the powerful Vijayanagars in 1565.

The reigns of Ibrahim's only son, **Muhammad Quli Qutb Shah** (1580–1612), and grandson, **Muhammad Qutb Shah** (1612–26), both cultured men, saw the expansion of Golconda and foundation of Hyderabad after a bridge had been built over the River Musi in 1578. Despite the growing threat from the Moghuls to the north, these were peaceful times, and prosperous trade was established with the European merchants on the coast, including diamonds. Rumour has it that a mine still exists in the fort, its exact location known only to the government.

Increasing pressure came from the Moghuls during the long reign of **Abdullah Qutb Shah** (1626–72), and the dynasty finally ended with the surrender of his son, **Abdul Hasan Qutb Shah**, in 1687 to the forces of Aurangzeb. This followed an eight-month battle, which, as the story goes, only ended when Aurangzeb bribed a doorman to allow his troops in to secure victory.

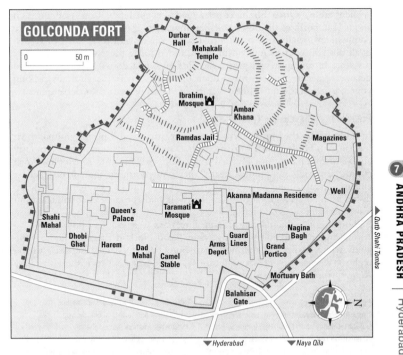

GOLCONDA FORT

0   50 m

Durbar Hall
Mahakali Temple
Ibrahim Mosque
Ambar Khana
Ramdas Jail
Magazines
Akanna Madanna Residence
Well
Shahi Mahal
Queen's Palace
Taramati Mosque
Nagina Bagh
Dhobi Ghat
Harem
Dad Mahal
Camel Stable
Arms Depot
Guard Lines
Grand Portico
Mortuary Bath
Balahisar Gate

Qutb Shahi Tombs

N

Hyderabad   Naya Qila

paintings that litter the gloomy room. Nearing the top, you come across the small, pretty mosque of Ibrahim Qutb Shah; beyond this, set beneath two huge granite stones, is an even smaller temple dedicated to Durga in her manifestation as Mahakali.

The steps are crowned by the three-storey **Durbar Hall** of the Qutb Shahs. The lower level of the hall has vaulted bays and the rooftop pavilion gave the monarchs uninterrupted views over their domain. Their accompaniment was the lilting strains of court musicians, as opposed to the cacophony of incessant clapping heard today from far below. As you head back down to the palaces and harems, you pass the tanks that supplied the fort's water system.

The ruins of the **Queen's Palace**, once elaborately decorated with multiple domes, stand in a courtyard centred on an original copper fountain that used to be filled with rosewater. You can still see traces of the "necklace" design on one of the arches, at the top of which a lotus bud sits below an opening flower with a cavity at its centre that once contained a diamond. Petals and creeper leaves are dotted with tiny holes that formerly gleamed with rubies and diamonds; parrots, long gone, had rubies for their eyes. Today visitors can only speculate how splendid it must all have looked, especially at night, when flaming torches illuminated the glittering decorations. At the entrance to the **palace** itself, four chambers provided protection from intruders. Passing through two rooms, the second of which is overgrown, you come to the **Shahi Mahal**, the royal bedroom. Originally it had a domed roof and niches on the walls that sheltered candles or oil lamps. It is said that the servants used silver ladders to get up there to light them. Golconda's **sound and light show** (in English daily March–Oct 7pm; Nov–Feb 6.30pm; Rs40) is suitably theatrical.

There are 82 **Qutb Shahi tombs** (daily except Fri 9.30am–4.30pm; Rs5) about 1km north of the outer wall. Set in peaceful gardens, they commemorate commanders, relatives of the kings, dancers, singers and royal doctors, as well as all but two of the Qutb Shahi kings. Faded today, they were once brightly coloured in turquoise and green; each has an onion dome on a block, with a decorative arcade. You can reach them by road or, more pleasantly, by picking your way across the quiet grassy verges and fields below the fort's battlements.

Eating and drinking

In addition to the hotel restaurants, plenty of "meals" places around town specialize in **Hyderabadi cuisine**, such as authentic biriyanis, or the famously chilli-hot Andhra cuisine. Hyderabadi cooking is derived from Moghul court cuisine, featuring sumptuous meat dishes with northern ingredients such as cinnamon, cardamom, cloves and garlic, and traditional southern vegetarian dishes with an array of flavourings like cassia buds, peanuts, coconut, tamarind leaves, mustard seeds and red chillies.

Though not as abundant as in Bangalore, **bars** welcoming to both sexes have started cropping up, mostly along Main Road No.1 in Banjara Hills: try the plush white leather couches and Indo-Euro pop at *Liquids*, the disco theme nights at *Cinnabar Redd* (above *Fusion 9*), or the basement rock sounds at *Easy Rider*, further down the road.

Hyderabad

Angeethi Main Rd No. 1, Banjara Hills. Highly rated and rather pricey north Indian restaurant, with excellent Punjabi and tandoori dishes.

Fusion 9 Main Rd No. 1, Banjara Hills. Expensive but quality global cuisine from regions as diverse as Mexico, Europe, the Middle East and Southeast Asia served in a smart modern lounge overlooking the street through tinted windows.

Hare and Hound *Amrutha Castle* hotel, Secretariat Rd, Saifabad. The *Amrutha Castle* hotel's multi-cuisine restaurant and bar, presided over by suits of armour, has a wide-ranging à la carte menu, while there's a great-value lunchtime buffet (12.30–3pm; Rs175) in the section outside the restaurant next to the reception and foyer.

Kamat Station Rd, opposite *Sai Prakash* hotel. Conveniently located branch of the extremely inexpensive and clean veggie chain.

Rich 'n' Famous Station Rd. The posher and pricier of the *Sai Prakash* hotel's two restaurants, with comfy chairs and imaginative daily specials

including crab, prawns and specialities from both Hyderabad and further afield; the veg *Sukha Sagara* downstairs serves cheaper south Indian snacks and north Indian dishes.

Sher-e-Punjab Corner of Nampally High Rd and station entrance. Popular basement restaurant with good tasty north Indian veg and non-veg food at bargain prices.

Touch of Class Lakdi-ka-Pul. The *Central Court* hotel's restaurant offers good Hyderabadi non-veg cuisine, plus some veg options and barbecue kebabs, Mughlai, Western and Chinese food, and good-value lunch (Rs175) and late-night (Rs125) buffets.

Secunderabad

Akbar 1-7-190 MG Rd, Secunderabad. A fine range of Hyderabadi dishes at moderate prices.

Paradise-Persis MG Rd, Secunderabad. Very popular multi-restaurant complex bashing out fine and inexpensive Hyderabadi cuisine.

Listings

Airlines Air Canada, see Gulf Air; Air France, Gupta Estate 1st floor, Basheerbagh ☎040/2323 0947; Air India, 5-9-193 HACA Bhavan, opposite Public Garden Saifabad ☎040/2338 9719; Bangladesh Biman, see Gulf Air; British Airways, Nijhawan Travel Services, 5-9-88/4 Ainulaman Fateh Maidan Rd ☎040/2324 1661; Delta/Swissair/Singapore

Airlines, Aviation Travels, Navbharat Chambers, 6-3-1109/1 Raj Bhavan Rd ☎040/2340 2664; Emirates, Floor F, Reliance Classic Bldg 3 & 4, Main Rd No.1, Banjara Hills ☎040/2332 1111; Gulf Air/Bangladesh Biman/Air Canada/Royal Jordanian, Jet Air Flat 202, 5-9-58 Gupta Estate, Basheerbagh ☎040/2324 0870; Indian Airlines, opposite

Assembly Saifabad ☎040/2329 9333; Jet Airways, 6-3-1109/1 GF Nav Bharat Chambers, Raj Bhavan Rd ☎040/2340 1222; Lufthansa, 3-5-823 Shop #B1–B3, Hyderaguda ☎040/2323 5537; Qantas, Transworld Travels, 3A Ist floor, 5-9-93 Chapel Rd ☎040/2329 8495; Qatar Airways, Reliance Krishna 5-10-197197/A, B & C Hillfort Rd, Nowbat Pahad ☎040/5536 7333; Royal Jordanian, see Gulf Air; Sabena, see Delta Airlines; Sahara, 15 Sahara Manzil opp Secretariat, Saifabad ☎040/2321 2767; Singapore Airlines, see Delta Airlines; Swissair, see Delta Airlines.

do foreign exchange, two exceptions being the State Bank of Hyderabad, MG Rd, and Federal Bank, 1st floor, Orient Estate, MG Rd (both open Mon–Fri 10.30am–2.30pm, the latter also Sat 10.30am–12.30pm). It's better to head for an agency such as Thomas Cook ☎040/2329 6521 at Nasir Arcade, Secretariat Rd; or L.K.P. Forex ☎040/2321 0094 on Public Gardens Rd, only ten minutes' walk north of Nampally station; both open Mon–Sat 9.30am–5.30pm. There are an increasing number of ATMs around town, however, including

Moving on from Hyderabad

See "Travel details" at the end of this chapter for more information on journey frequencies and durations.

By train

Daily **train** services from **Hyderabad Railway Station (Nampally)** include: the Charminar Express #2760 to Chennai (20.10pm; 14hr 10min); the Hyderabad–Ernakulam Express #7030 (noon; 26hr); the Andhra Pradesh Express #2723 to Delhi (6.40am; 26hr 20min); the Hyderabad–Mumbai Express #7032 (8.40pm; 16hr 15min); the East Coast Express #7046 to Kolkata (Calcutta; 6.50am; 31hr 25min) via Vijayawada (6hr 16min), Vishakapatnam (12hr 55min) and Bhubaneswar (22hr 25min); and the Rayasaleema Express #7429 to Tirupati (5.25pm; 15hr 35min). Almost all northeast-bound services call at Warangal and at Vijayawada. **From Secunderabad**, there are some originating services and many through trains in all directions. Useful services include the Konark Express #1020 to Mumbai (11.45am; 16hr 10min); the Secunderabad–Bangalore Express #7085 (6.40pm; 12hr 35min); and the Secunderabad–Rajendranagar Express #7091 via Varanasi (Mon & Wed 10.30pm; 30hr 10min).

The **railways reservations office** at Hyderabad (Mon–Sat 8am–2pm & 2.30–8pm, Sun 8am–2pm) is to the left as you enter the station. Counter #211 (next to enquiry counter) is supposedly for tourist reservations, but it's also used for group bookings and lost tickets. Foreign visitors can make bookings at the Chief Reservation Inspector's Office on platform 1 for same-day journeys (daily 9am–5pm). The **Secunderabad reservation complex** is by the major junction with St John's Road over 400m to the right as you exit the station. Counter #34 is for foreigners.

By bus

From the Central Bus Stand, **regular bus services** run to Amaravati, Bangalore, Bidar, Chennai, Mumbai, Nagarjuna Sagar, Tirupati, Vijayawada and Warangal. Various **deluxe and video buses** depart for Bangalore, Chennai, Mumbai and other major destinations from outside Nampally station, where you'll find a cluster of private agencies, such as National Travels (☎040/2320 3614).

By air

Between them, Indian Airlines, Jet Airways and Sahara offer five **daily flights** to Bangalore, nine to Mumbai, seven to Delhi, seven or eight to Chennai, two to Visakhapatnam and three to Kolkata (Calcutta), via Bhubaneswar on three of those days. There are also once-daily flights to Panjim in Goa, Pune, Varanasi and Mangalore, four weekly to Tirupati and five weekly to Ahmedabad. Indian Airlines runs one flight daily to Dubai, as well as other destinations in the Gulf, while Air India has flights to Mumbai and twice-weekly departures to Singapore (2hr 30min). Silk Air, the regional wing of Singapore Airlines (☎040/2340 2644), also flies three times a week to Singapore.

at the State Bank of India on Nampally High Rd, Syndicate Bank on Station Rd, and Oriental Bank at Secunderabad railway station.

Bicycle hire Bikes can be rented for Rs20 per day at a friendly stall on the right as you approach Hyderabad station from Nampally High Rd.

Bookshops A.A. Hussain & Co., 5-8-551 Arastu Trust Building, Abid Rd, Hyderabad; Akshara, 8-2-273 Pavani Estate, Road no. 2, Banjara Hills, Hyderabad; Higginbothams, 1 Lal Bahadur Stadium, Hyderabad; Gangarams, 62 DSD Rd, near *Garden Restaurant* in Secunderabad; and Kalaujal, Hill Fort Rd, opposite the Public Gardens, which specializes in art books.

Car rental Air Travels in Banjara Hills (⊕040/2335 3099, ⊕2335 5088) and Classic Travels in Secunderabad (⊕040/2775 5645) both provide a 24hr service, with or without driver.

Crafts Lepakshi, the AP state government emporium at Gunfoundry on MG Rd, stocks a wide range of handicrafts, including *bidri* metalwork, jewellery and silks. Utkalika (Government of Orissa handicrafts), House no. 60-1-67, between the Ravindra Bharati building and *Hotel Ashoka*, has a modest selection of silver filigree jewellery, handloom cloth, *ikkat* tie-dye, Jagannath papier-mâché figures and buffalo bone carvings. Cheneta Bhavan is a modern shopping complex a little south of the railway station, stuffed with hand-loom cloth shops from various states. For silks and saris, try Meena Bazaar, Pochampally Silks and Sarees, and Pooja Sarees, all on Tilak Rd.

Dentist Kakade's Dentistree, opposite *Taj Banjara*, Rd No. 1 ⊕040/ 2330 2633.

Hospitals The government-run Gandhi Hospital is in Secunderabad ⊕040/2770 2222; the private CDR Hospital is in Himayatnagar ⊕040/2322 1221; and there's a Tropical Diseases Hospital in Nallakunta ⊕040/2766 7843.

Internet access Internet outlets abound throughout both cities: try Modi Xerox opposite Ek Minar mosque (Rs20 per hr). Net2phone facilities can be found behind the large Medwin Hospital on Nampally High Rd.

Library The British Library, Secretariat Rd (Tues–Sat 11am–7pm; ⊕040/2323 0774) has a wide selection of books and recent British newspapers. Officially you must be a member or a British citizen to get in, but if you look western you're unlikely to be asked to prove it.

Pharmacies Apollo Pharmacy ⊕040/2323 1380 and Health Pharmacy ⊕040/2331 0618 are both open 24hr.

Police ⊕040/2323 0191. In an emergency call ⊕100.

Travel agents General agents for airline and private-bus tickets include: Travel Club Forex ⊕040/2323 4180, Nasir Arcade, Saifabad, close to Thomas Cook; and Kamat Travels in the *Hotel Sai Prakash* complex ⊕040/2461 2096. There's a host of private-bus agents on Nampally High Rd outside Hyderabad railway station. Check prices as they vary from agent to agent.

Around Hyderabad

As you head north from Hyderabad towards the borders of Maharashtra and Madhya Pradesh, the landscape becomes greener and more hilly, sporadically punctuated by photogenic black-granite rock formations. There is little to detain visitors here except the small town of **Warangal**, situated on the main railway line, worth a stop to visit the nearby medieval fort and Shiva temple. South of the capital, vast swathes of flat farmland stretch into the centre of the state, where the Nagarjuna Sagar dam has created a major lake with the important Buddhist site of **Nagarjunakonda**, now an island in its waters.

Warangal

WARANGAL – "one stone" – 150km northeast of Hyderabad, was the Hindu capital of the Kakatiyan empire in the twelfth and thirteenth centuries. Like other Deccan cities, it changed hands many times between the Hindus and the Muslims – something that is reflected in its architecture and the remains you see today.

Warangal's **fort** (daily 9am–5pm; $2 [Rs5]), 4km south, is famous for its two circles of fortifications: the outer made of earth with a moat, and the inner of stone. Four roads into the centre meet at the ruined temple of **Svayambhu** (1162), dedicated to Shiva. At its southern, freestanding gateway, another Shiva temple, from the fourteenth century, is in a much better shape; inside, the remains of an enormous *lingam* came originally from the Svayambhu shrine. Also inside the citadel is the **Shirab Khan**, or audience hall, an early eleventh-century building very similar to Mandu's Hindola Mahal.

The largely basalt Chalukyan-style **"thousand–pillared" Shiva temple** (daily 10am–6pm; Rs5), just off the main road, beside the slopes of Hanamkonda Hill (6km north), was constructed by King Rudra Deva in 1163. A low-roofed building on several stepped stages, it features superb carvings and shrines to Vishnu, Shiva and Surya the sun god. These lead off the *mandapa*, whose numerous finely carved columns give the temple its name. In front sits a polished Nandi bull, carved out of a single stone. A Bhadrakali temple stands at the top of the hill.

Practicalities

If you make an early start, it's just about possible to visit Warangal in a day-trip from Hyderabad. Frequent buses and trains run to the town (roughly 3hr). Warangal's **bus stand** and **railway station** are opposite each other, served by local buses, auto- and cycle rickshaws. The easiest way to cover the site is to **rent a bicycle** from one of the stalls on Station Road. To reach the fort, follow Station Road from the station and turn left just beyond the post office, under the railway bridge, and left again at the next main road. For Hanamkonda turn right onto JPN Road at the next main junction after the post office, left at the next major crossroads onto MG Road, and right at the end onto the Hanamkonda main road. The temple and hill are on the left.

Accommodation is limited: the *Hotel Ashok* on Main Road, Hanamkonda, 6km from the railway and bus stand (☎08712/285491; ❸–❺), has a/c rooms, a restaurant and bar, and is rather more upmarket than *Hotel Ratna* (☎08712/260645, ℱ260096; ❷–❹), 2km from the station on MG Road. Basic lodges nearer the station include the *Vijaya* (☎0870/225851; ❷–❸) on Station Road, which is the closest and best value, and *Urvasi* (☎08712/261760; ❷–❹), at the junction of Station and JPN roads, which has some a/c rooms. Several decent **eating places** line Station Road – the upstairs *Titanic*, halfway along on the right, serves good tandoori and other non-veg dishes. **Internet** facilities are available at Grace@Net on JPN Road (Rs30 per hr).

Nagarjunakonda

NAGARJUNAKONDA, or "Nagarjuna's Hill", 166km south of Hyderabad and 175km west of Vijayawada, is all that now remains of the vast area, rich in archeological sites, submerged when the huge Nagarjuna Sagar Dam was built across the River Krishna in 1960. Ancient settlements in the valley were first discovered in 1926; extensive excavations carried out between 1954 and 1960 uncovered more than one hundred sites dating from the early Stone Age to late medieval times. Nagarjunakonda was once the summit of a hill, where a fort towered 200m above the valley floor; now it's just a small oblong island near the middle of Nagarjuna Sagar Lake, accessible by boat from the mainland. Several Buddhist monuments have been reconstructed, in an operation reminiscent of that at Abu Simbel in Egypt, and a **museum** exhibits the more remarkable ruins of the valley. **VIJAYAPURI**, the village on the shore of the lake, overlooks the colossal dam itself, which stretches for almost 2km. Torrents of water flushed through its 26 floodgates produce electricity for the whole region and irrigate an area of almost 800 square kilometres. Many villages had to be relocated to higher ground when the valley was flooded.

The island and the museum

Boats arrive on the northeastern edge of **Nagarjunakonda island** (daily 9am–5pm; $2 [Rs5]), unloading passengers at what remains of one of the gates of the fort, built in the fourteenth century and renovated by the Vijayanagar kings in the mid-sixteenth century. Low, damaged, stone walls skirting the island mark the edge of the fort, and you can see ground-level remains of the Hindu temples that served its inhabitants. Well-kept gardens lie between the jetty and the museum, beyond which nine Buddhist monuments from various sites in the valley have been rebuilt. West of the jetty, there's a reconstructed bathing *ghat*, built entirely of limestone during the reigns of the Ikshvaku kings (third century AD), with a series of steps leading down to the water's edge. Boards etched into some of the slabs were probably used for dice games.

The **maha-chaitya**, or stupa, constructed at the command of King Chamtula's sister in the third century AD, is the earliest Buddhist structure in the area. It was raised over relics of the Buddha – said to include a tooth – and has been reassembled in the southwest of the island. Nearby, a towering **statue** of the Buddha stands draped in robes beside a ground plan of a monastery that enshrines a smaller stupa. Other **stupas** stand nearby; the brick walls of the *svastika chaitya* have been arranged in the shape of swastikas, common emblems in early Buddhist iconography.

In the **museum** (daily except Fri 9am–5pm; Rs3), **Buddhist sculptures** include large stone friezes decorated with scenes from the Buddha's life: his birth; his mother's vision of an elephant and a lotus blossom; his renunciation; and his subversion of evil as he meditated and realized enlightenment under the *bodhi* tree. Twelve statues of standing Buddhas – one of which reaches 3m – show the Buddha in various postures of teaching or meditation. Many of the pillars are profusely carved with Buddha images, bowing devotees, elephants and lotus medallions.

Earlier **artefacts** include stone tools and pots from the Neolithic age (third millennium BC), and metal axe heads and knives (first millennium BC). Among later finds are several inscribed pillars from Ikshvaku times, recording in Prakrit or Sanskrit the installation of Buddhist monasteries and statues. The final phase of art at Nagarjunakonda is represented by **sculptures**: a thirteenth-century *tirthankara* (Jain saint), a seventeenth-century Ganesh and Nandi, and a set of eighteenth-century statues of Shiva and Shakti, his female consort. Also on display is a model showing the excavated sites in the valley.

Practicalities

Organized **APTDC tours** from Hyderabad to Nagarjunakonda at weekends (see p.584) – taking in the sites and museum, the nearby Ethiopothala waterfalls (entry Rs20) and an engraved third-century Buddhist monolith known as the Pylon – can be a bit rushed; if you want to spend more time in the area you can take a bus from the Central Bus Stand in Hyderabad (4hr; all the regular Macherla services stop at Vijayapuri) or Vijayawada (6hr; a direct service runs daily at 11am and frequent services leave from Guntur).

Accommodation at Vijayapuri is limited, and you need to decide in advance where you are going to stay to know where to get off the bus, as there are two distinct settlements 6km apart on either side of the dam. For easy access to the sites it's better to stay near the jetty on the right bank of the dam. Ask the bus to leave you at the launch station. The drab-looking concrete *Nagarjuna Motel Complex* (☎08642/278188; ❷–❹) has adequate rooms and some a/c. Five hundred metres away in the village, the *Golden Lodge* (☎08642/278148; ❶) is much more basic. APTDC run two hotels, both on the other side of the dam as you approach the lake form Hyderabad – the *Punnami Vihar* (☏08680/277361; ④–⑤) and the *Punnami Hill Colony* (☏08680/276540; ②–④) – both have a/c and non-a/c rooms, while the latter also has a dorm (Rs100).

Tickets for **boats** to the island (daily 9am & 1.30pm; 45min) go on sale 25 minutes before departure (Rs45). Each boat leaves the island ninety minutes after it arrives, which allows enough time to see the museum and walk briskly round the monuments, but if you want to take your time and soak up the atmosphere, take the morning boat and return in the afternoon. A cafeteria on the island serves drinks and occasionally biscuits, but only opens when the boat is in, so take provisions. At weekends there are three-hour luxury cruises (Rs150) aboard a twin-deck boat.

Eastern Andhra Pradesh

Perhaps India's least visited area, **eastern Andhra Pradesh** is sandwiched between the Bay of Bengal in the east and the red soil and high peaks of the Eastern Ghats in the north. Its one architectural attraction is the ancient Buddhist site of **Amaravati**, near the city of **Vijayawada**, whose sprinkling of historic temples is completely overshadowed by impersonal, modern buildings. The region's other major city, the bustling port of **Vishakapatnam**, is really only worth stopping at if you want to get a boat to the Andamans or are intent on exploring the nearby caves.

If you want to explore an area well off the beaten track, however, there are rewarding pockets of natural beauty along the coast and in the hills of eastern Andhra Pradesh. In this sleepy landscape, little affected by modernization, bullocks amble between swaying palms and the rice fields are iridescent against rusty sands. However, unless you have the patience to endure the excruciatingly slow public transport system, your own vehicle is essential.

Vijayawada and around

Almost 450km north of Chennai, **VIJAYAWADA** is a bustling commercial centre on the banks of the Krishna delta, hemmed in by bare granite outcrops 90km from the coast. This mundane city, alleviated by the mountain backdrop and some urban greenery, is seldom visited by tourists, but does make the obvious stopoff point for visits to the third-century Buddhist site at **Amaravati**, 60km west.

A handful of temples in Vijayawada merit a quick look. The most important, raised on the low Indrakila Hill in the east, is dedicated to the city's patron goddess **Kanaka Durga** (also known as Vijaya). Though it is believed to be thousands of years old, what you see today, with the exception of a few pillared halls and intricate carvings, is largely renovated. Some 3km out of town across the river there's an ancient cave temple at **Undavalli**, a tiny rural village set off the main road, easily reached on any Guntur-bound bus or the local #13 service. The temple is cut out of the granite hillside in typical Pallava style: simple, solid and bold. Each of its five levels contains a deep low-roofed hall, with small rock-cut shrines to Vishnu, Shiva and Parvati, and pillared verandahs guarded by statues of deities, saints and lions. Views from the porches take in a sublime patchwork of rivulets, paddy fields and banana plantations.

Practicalities

The city is bisected by **Ryes Canal**, which flows through the heart of town. Vijayawada's **railway station**, on the main Chennai–Kolkata (Calcutta) line, is in the centre of town. Buses arriving from Guntur, Amaravati and as far afield as Hyderabad and Chennai pull into the **Pandit Nehru Bus Stand**, 1.5km further west, on the other side of the canal. Specific ticket offices cater for each service, while a **tourist office** (℡0866/252 3966) has details on local hotels and sights. APTDC also has an office in the centre of town at *Hotel Ilapuram* complex, Gandhi Nagar (℡0866/257 0255), and they run local sightseeing tours (daily 8am–5.45pm; Rs160). You can **change money** at Zen Global Finance, 40–6–27 Krishna Nagar in Labbipet, or use the State Bank of India.

Vijayawada is a major business centre, with a good selection of mid-range **hotels**, all within 1km of the railway station and bus stand. *Monika Lodge* (℡0866/257 1334; ②), just off Elluru Road about 300m northeast of the bus stand, is one of the cheapest but a bit grubby. Two better-value places, both on Atchutaramaiah Street, which links the railway station to Elluru Road, are the *Hotel Narayana Swamy* (℡0866/257 1221; ③–④) and the *Sri Ram* (℡0866/257 9377; ③–④), both with spotless rooms (some a/c) and cable TV. *Raj Towers* (℡0866/257 1311, ℻556 1714; ③–⑥) on Elluru Road is a tall modern block with good mid-range rooms and a decent **restaurant**. The fourth-floor *Palace Heights* restaurant at the *Hotel Swarna Palace*, where Atchutaramaiah St meets Elluru Rd, also provides large portions of Indian, Chinese and continental food with city views and has a bar. Cheap Andhra thali joints abound.

Guntur

Another sprawling and bustling commercial city, 30km southwest of Vijayawada, **GUNTUR** has no merits of its own but makes an even more convenient jump-ing-off point for Amaravati than Vijayawada, especially if you are coming from Nagarjuna Sagar. There are buses every ten to fifteen minutes to Vijayawada (45min–1hr) and every half-hour to Amaravati from the old bus stand (adjacent to the main bus stand). If you decide to spend the night here, try the **lodges** opposite the bus stands. *Annapurna Lodge* (℡0863/235 6493; ②–④) has decent-sized clean rooms and some a/c; *Padmasri Lodge* (℡0863/222 3813; ②–④) also has a/c and cheaper singles.

Amaravati

AMARAVATI, a small village on the banks of the Krishna 30km west of Vijayawada, is the site of a Buddhist settlement, formerly known as Chintapalli, where a stupa was erected over relics of the Buddha in the third century BC, during the reign of Ashoka. The stupa no longer stands, but its size is evident from the mound that formed its base. There was a gateway at each of the cardinal points, one of which has been reconstructed in an open courtyard. Its decoration, meticulously carved and perfectly preserved, shows the themes represented on all such Buddhist monuments: the Buddha's birth, renunciation and life as an emaciated ascetic, enlightenment under the *bodhi* tree, his first sermon in the Deer Park, and *parinirvana*, or death. Several foundation stones of the monastic quarters remain on the site. A two-week **Kalachakra initiation programme** (a special form of Buddhist meditation) will be conducted by the Dalai Lama here from January 2 to 18, 2006, to commemorate 2550 years since the Buddha's birth; it is reckoned the Buddha himself held such a ceremony at the same spot.

Exhibits at the small but fascinating **museum** (daily except Fri 10am–5pm; $2 [Rs5]) range in date from the third century BC to the twelfth century AD and include Buddha statues with lotus symbols on his feet, tightly curled hair, and long ear lobes – all traditional indications of an enlightened teacher. Other stone carvings include symbols such as the *chakra* (wheel of *dharma*), a throne, a stupa, a flaming pillar, a *bodhi* tree and the lotus flower. The lotus motif is connected with a dream the Buddha's mother had shortly after conception, and represents purity. Later sculptures include limestone statues of the goddess Tara and *bodhisattva* Padmapani, both installed at the site in medieval times when the community had adopted Mahayana teachings in place of the earlier Theravada doctrines. Some of the best excavations are on display here – other remains are now in the Chennai Government Museum and the British Museum in London.

Practicalities

Theoretically **buses** run hourly from Vijayawada to Amaravati but the service seems to be unreliable, so it's best to take a bus to Guntur (every 15min; 45min–1hr), where you can pick up a connection to Amaravati (1hr–1hr 30min). Buses return to Guntur every half-hour, while during the monsoon **boats** gather at the jetty in Amaravati and follow the River Krishna all the way to Vijayawada. The excavated site and museum are roughly 1km from the bus stand. Trishaws – miniature carts attached to tricycles and brightly painted with chubby film stars – take tourists to the site and the riverbank, where there are several drink stalls. The APTDC *Punnami*, on the bank of the Krishna (T08645/255332; ❷), has reasonable rooms and a dorm (Rs50). Their canteen provides basic meals and snacks.

Vishakapatnam and around

One of India's most rapidly growing industrial cities, and its fourth largest port, **VISHAKAPATNAM** (aka Vizag), 350km north of Vijayawada, is a big, unpleasant city choked with the smells and dirt of a busy shipbuilding industry, an oil plant and a steel factory. Such is its sprawl that it has overtaken and polluted much of the neighbouring town of **Waltair**, once a health resort. Although there's little to warrant a stop at Vishakapatnam, the district of Waltair, with its uncrowded treelined roads and attractive seafront, makes for a pleasant stroll and is also home to a modest collection of art and sculpture at the **Vishaka Museum** (Tues–Sun 4–8pm; Rs3) on Beach Road near the *Hotel Park*. The beach around here is far enough from the port for the sea to be reasonably clean, though the best beach for swimming is at Kalshagiri, further north, reached by regular buses from the RTC complex.

Various traces of older civilizations lie within a day's journey of the city. At **Bheemunipatnam**, 30km north, you can see the remains of a Dutch fort and a peculiar cemetery with slate-grey pyramidal tombs. **Borra**, 70km inland on a minor road that winds through the Eastern Ghats and the Araku forests, boasts a set of eerie limestone **caves** whose darkness is pierced with age-old stalactites and stalagmites (daily 10am–12.30pm & 2–5pm; Rs25). You'll need a car to get to **Mukhalingam**, 100km north of Bheemunipatnam, where three Shaivite temples, built between the sixth and twelfth centuries, rest in low hills. Their elaborate carvings and well-preserved towering *shikharas* display slight local variations from the otherwise standard Orissan style. There's nowhere to stay in Mukhalingam.

Practicalities

Vishakapatnam's **railway station**, on the Chennai–Kolkata (Calcutta) coastal route, is in the old town, towards the port. The **bus stand**, known as RTC Complex, is 1km away in a newer area, while the beach is a further 4km on, reached by bus #28. There's an **airport**, 12km west of town, with daily connections to Hyderabad and Mumbai, and several weekly to Kolkata (Calcutta) and Bhubaneswar. Bus #38 runs from the airport to the centre. Irregular **ships** make the three-day crossing from here to Port Blair on the Andaman Islands, although it's planned to improve the service and add a ferry from Vishakapatnam to Chennai.

The **India Tourism** office (Mon–Sat 10am–5pm; ☎0891/275 4716) is situated in the Vuda complex, Sitapura, 3km from the RTC Complex; there's also a new **APTDC office** (daily 6am–10pm; ☎0891/274 6446) in the RTC complex, which is useful for booking **tours** of the city (daily 8am–8pm; Rs280, including lunch) and the Borra caves (daily 7am–9pm; Rs300 or Rs400 by train; includes breakfast & lunch). The Andhra Bank near the RTC complex will **change money**. There are also several places around the complex offering **Internet** access.

If you arrive late by bus, head for the well-maintained **retiring rooms** (❶) in the bus stand. Otherwise, most **hotels** are in the old town, near the railway station: turn right out of the station and walk for a few minutes. The best is *Hotel Karanths*, 33-1-55 Patel Marg (☎0891/256 0347, ℱ256 0416; ❷–❸), whose spotless rooms have balconies, pressed sheets, cable TV and attached bathrooms. The downstairs restaurant serves unbeatable thalis and tiffin at low prices. Just further on at Ramachandra Circle, the *Hotel Ramachandra* (☎0891/556 8610; ❷–❹) comes a good second. Vishakapatnam's nicest upmarket hotel, the *Park* on Beach Road (☎0891/275 4488, ⓦwww.theparkhotels .com; ❾), has luxurious rooms starting at $80, a swimming pool, a bar, restaurant, and access to the beach. Adjacent to the *Park* is the pleasant but far more modest *Palm Beach* (☎0891/255 4026, ℮palm_beach_vzg@yahoo.com; ❹–❺), which also offers good amenities.

Southern Andhra Pradesh

The further south you travel from the fertile lands watered by the great Krishna and Godavari rivers, the less hospitable the terrain becomes, especially in the rocky southwest of the state. For Hindus, the main attraction in southern Andhra Pradesh is the tenth-century **Shri Venkateshvara Temple**, outside **Tirupati**, the most popular Vishnu shrine in India, where several thousand pilgrims come each day to receive *darshan*. **Puttaparthy**, the home town of the spiritual leader Sai Baba, is the only other place in the region to attract significant numbers of visitors, mostly devotees of the guru from many parts of India and the world. Both Tirupati and Puttaparthy are closer to Chennai in Tamil Nadu and Bangalore in Karnataka than to other points in Andhra Pradesh, and for many tourists constitute their only foray into the state.

Tirupati and Tirumala Hill

Set in a stunning position, surrounded by wooded hills capped by a ring of vertical red rocks, the **Shri Venkateshvara temple** at **Tirumala Hill**, 170km northwest of Chennai, is said to be the richest and most popular place of pilgrimage in the world, drawing more devotees than either Rome or Mecca. With its many shrines and *dharamshalas*, the whole area provides a fascinating insight into contemporary Hinduism. Most practical services and accommodation are at the town of **TIRUPATI**, 11km away as the crow flies, but double that by road.

Arrival and information

The best way of **getting to Tirupati** is by train from Chennai; the trip can be done in a day if you get the earliest of the three daily services (3hr 30min). Frequent express buses run from Chennai (4hr), but the train is far more comfortable. From Hyderabad it's a gruelling 13- to 15-hour journey by bus or train.

The main APTDC **tourist office** is at 139 T.P. Area, 3rd Choultry (daily 6.30am–9pm; ☎0877/225 5385), and there's also an APTDC counter at the **railway station** accessible from the entrance hall and platform 1, where there's a 24hr left-luggage office and a self-service veg refreshment room. Stands sell English copies of TKT Viraraghava Charya's *History of Tirupati*, and there's a Vivekananda religious bookshop next door. Tirupati's APSRTC Central **bus station** – also with 24-hour left-luggage – is about 1km east of the railway station. Beautifully decorated cycle-rickshaws and auto-rickshaws ply the city streets looking for custom.

A special section at the back of the bus stand has services every few minutes **to Tirumala** and the Venkateshvara temple, although you can also reach the hill from a separate local bus stand outside the railway station. You shouldn't have to wait too long for a bus unless it's a weekend or festival. An easier option is to take a **taxi**, best organized through the APTDC counter at the railway station; avoid the unlicensed taxis outside the station as they could be stopped by the Tirumala police. If you're climbing the hill on foot, take any of the temple buses and alight at Alipiri where the trail starts. The tourist office runs **tours** which takes in **Chandragiri Fort** (except Fri) and a number of temples (10am–5.30pm; Rs165 or Rs190 including Chandragiri sound & light show), but doesn't include the Venkateshvara Temple because of the queues.

There are a few **Internet** places in Tirupati, including Q Net N Play, 340 Netaji Road, one minute from the railway station (turn left as you exit), and Net Hill in the shopping complex at the corner of the bus stand. The Syndicate and ICICI banks both have **ATMs** on Netaji Road, and there are even a couple up on Tirumala Hill.

Accommodation

Unless you're a pilgrim seeking accommodation in the *dharamshalas* near the temple, all the decent **places to stay** are in Tirupati, near the railway and bus stand; there's a vast array of hotels and lodges to suit all budgets. **Eating** is almost exclusively vegetarian, even in the hotels, and cheap "meals" places abound in town and on Tirumala Hill. If you're in need of meat and booze, head for the *Yalamuri* beer garden, off the traffic circle opposite the bus stand.

Apsara 213 TP Area ☎0877/557 8062. Basic but clean en-suite rooms on the street almost opposite the bus station. ❷

Balaji Bhavan 189 Railway Station Rd ☎0877/222 5930. Newish place with clean, fair-sized rooms (some a/c), all en suite. ❷–❺

Bhimas Deluxe 34–38 G Car St, near the railway station ☎0877/222 5521, ⓦ www.bhimas.com. Decent, comfortable rooms with central a/c, with 12hr "transit rooms" available at half price. The *Maya* veg restaurant serves north and south Indian food plus some Chinese dishes in the evenings. ❺

Indira Rest House Tiruchanur Rd ☎0877/222 7479. Basic no-nonsense lodge, a few minutes'

walk behind the railway lines from the bus stand, 100m beyond the *Poojith Residency*. Also has some new a/c rooms, though these are also fairly basic. ❷–❸

Mayura 209 TP Area ☎0877/222 5925, ⓔ mayura@nettlink.com. The best – and most expensive – of a host of hotels opposite the bus station. ❹–❺

Raghunadha 191 Railway Station Rd ☎0877/222 3130. One of the better cheap places, this good, simple and clean lodge has cable TV in all rooms and some inexpensive a/c. ❷–❸

Sindhuri Park Beside the bathing tank ☎0877/225 6430, ⓦ www.hotelsindhuri.com.

The smartest place in the centre, this all-a/c hotel has excellent facilities and great views of the tank and temple. The basement *Vrinda* restaurant serves quality veg food, including a range of thalis, and has a Rs99 buffet on weekend evenings. ⑤–⑦

Govindarajaswamy temple

Just a five-minute walk from the railway station and with a modern grey *gopura* visible from many points in town, Govindarajaswamy is the town's main temple and the one temple in Tirupati itself which is definitely worth a visit. Begun by the Nayaks in the sixteenth century, it's an interesting complex with large open courtyards decorated with lion sculptures and some ornately carved wooden roofing. The temple's **inner sanctum** is open to non-Hindus and contains a splendid large black reclining Vishnu, coated in bronze armour and bedecked in flowers. A visit during the *sanadarsanan* (daily 10am–8.45pm; Rs5) will let you in to glimpse the deity and participate in fire blessings at the main and subsidiary shrines.

Tucked away at the side of the complex, not far from the south *gopura*, is the fine little **Venkateshvara Museum of Temple Arts** (daily 8am–8pm; Rs1). Set in a colonnaded compound, the bulk of the displays of old stone and bronze statues and more modern paintings and dolls are arranged around the perimeter of the courtyard. The shrine in the middle of the compound is supported by some beautifully carved pillars and contains cases displaying scenes from mythology portrayed by colourful dolls. The temple's impressive **bathing tank** lies 200m to the east.

Tiruchanur Padmavati temple

Between Tirupati and Tirumala Hill, the **Tiruchanur Padmavati temple** (no photography; a Rs20 ticket allows you to jump the queue to enter the sanctuary) is another popular pilgrimage halt. A gold *vimana* tower with lions at each corner surmounts the sanctuary, which contains a black stone image of Lakshmi with one silver eye – you can donate a sari to the goddess for Rs1200.

Tirumala Hill, the Venkateshvara temple and Kapilateertham

There's good reason for the small shrine to Ganesh at the foot of **Tirumala Hill**. The journey up is hair-raising and it's worth saying a quick prayer when embarking on it, but at least separate routes up and down preclude head-on crashes. Overtaking is strictly forbidden, but drivers do anyway; virtually every bend is labelled "blind" and every instruction to drive slowly is blithely ignored. The fearless sit on the left for the best views.

The most devout pilgrims, of course, climb the hill **on foot**. The **trail** starts at **Alipuri**, 4km from the centre of Tirupati (all the pilgrim buses pass through) – look out for a large Garuda statue and the soaring *gopura* of the first temple. The first hour consists of a flight of knee-crunching concrete steps, covered in yellow, orange and red *tikka* daubed by pilgrims as they ascend. The path then mercifully levels out before the final assault some two hours on. Allow at least four hours to the top – fitter pilgrims might do it half an hour quicker. The trail is covered over for most of the way, affording protection from the blistering sun, and there are drinks stalls all along the route. An early start is recommended. When you get to the top, you will see barbers busying themselves giving pilgrims tonsures as part of their devotions.

The **Venkateshvara Temple** (aka Sri Vari), dedicated to **Vishnu** and started in the tenth century, is surrounded by a rabbit warren of passages and waiting rooms which wind their way around the complex and in which pilgrims interminably shuffle towards the inner sanctum (weekends, public holidays and festivals are even busier). Non-Hindus are permitted to enter the inner sanctum, but for everyone *darshan*, a view of the god, is the briefest of experiences. Unless your visit is intended to be particularly rigorous, on reaching the temple you should follow the signs for the special *darshan* costing Rs50 (daily 6–10am & noon–9pm) as this may reduce the time it takes to get inside by quite a few hours; you have to sign a declaration of faith in Lord Venkateshvara and give your passport number. Alternatively you can obtain tickets with a *darshan* time printed on at the temple tourism office near the temple bus stand on Station Road.

Once inside the temple, you'll see the somewhat incongruous sight of brahmins sitting at video monitors, observing the goings-on in the inner sanctum; the constant to-ing and fro-ing includes temple attendants bringing in supplies, truckloads of oil and other comestibles, and huge cooking pots being carried across the courtyard. You may also see deities being hauled past on palanquins to the accompaniment of *nageswaram* (a South Indian oboe-like double-reed wind instrument) and *tavil* drum, complete with an armed guard. At the entrance is a colonnade, lined with life-sized statues of royal patrons, in copper or stone. The *gopura* gateway leading to the inner courtyard is decorated with sheets of embossed silver; a gold *stambha* (flagstaff) stands outside the inner shrine next to a gold upturned lotus on a plinth. Outside, opposite the temple, is a small museum, the **Hall of Antiquities** (daily 8am–8pm). Your special *darshan* ticket entitles you to enter the museum via a shorter queue opposite the exit and to pick up two free *laddu* sweets. Temple funds support a university, hospital, orphanages and schools at Tirupati as well as providing cheap, and in some cases free, accommodation for pilgrims.

At the bottom of the hill, the **Sri Kapileswaraswami** temple at **Kapilateertham** is the only Shiva temple amongst the many Vaishnavite temples in Tirupati. It has a small Hindu pleasure garden at the entrance and a sacred waterfall which crashes into a large tank surrounded by colonnades, where pilgrims pile in for a bath.

Chandragiri Fort

In the sixteenth century, **Chandragiri**, 11km southwest of Tirupati, became the third capital of the Vijayanagars, whose power had declined following

---

Moving on from Tirupati

Buses to Chennai run frequently and take 3hr 30min–4hr. However, if you're travelling south and want to avoid Chennai, there are hourly buses to Kanchipuram (3hr 30min), three of which continue to Mamallapuram (5hr 30min). There are also frequent ordinary and deluxe buses (approx every hour) to Bangalore (around 4hr). There is only one direct bus to Puttaparthy (8pm; 10hr); otherwise change at Madanapalli or Bangalore.

Useful **trains** include the #7405 Tirupati–Hyderabad Krishna Express (departs daily 5.30am; 16hr 10min); the #7480 Tirupati–Howrah Express (departs daily 9.45am; 38hr 30min); and the #7494 Tirupati–Mumbai Express (departs Mon & Fri 10pm; 23hr 25min). The fastest trains for Chennai are the #6204 Tirupati–Chennai Intercity Express (daily at 6.45am; 2hr 55min) and the #6054 Tirupati–Chennai Express (daily at 10.05am; 3hr 10min). In addition, the useful #6351 Tirupati–Nagercoil Express (daily at 12.45pm) stops at the Tamil Nadu temple towns of Kanchipuram (2hr 40min), Tiruchchirapalli (8hr 35min) and Madurai (12hr 20min).

If you're in a mad rush to get to Hyderabad note that Indian Airlines operate **flights** on Monday, Thursday, Friday and Saturday (departs 1.05pm; 55min).

the fall of the city of Vijayanagar (Hampi) in Karnataka. It was here that the British negotiated the acquisition of the land to establish Fort St George, the earliest settlement at what is now Chennai. The original fort (daily except Fri 10am–5pm; $2 [Rs5]), thought to date from c.1000 AD, was taken over by Haider Ali in 1782, followed by the British in 1792. A small **museum** of sculpture, weapons and memorabilia is housed in the main building, the Indo-Saracenic Raja Mahal. Another building, the **Rani Mahal**, stands close by, while behind that is a hill with two freestanding boulders that was used as a place of public execution during Vijayanagar times. A little temple from the Krishna Deva Raya period and a freshwater tank stand at the top of the hill behind the Raja Mahal. In the evening there is a 45-minute **sound and light show** (English version daily: Nov–Feb 7.30pm, March–Oct 8pm; Rs30) – a good way of glimpsing the fort without having to pay the admission price.

Puttaparthy

Deep in the southwest of the state, amid the arid rocky hills bordering Karnataka, a thriving community has grown up around the once insignificant village of **PUTTAPARTHY**, birthplace of spiritual leader **Sai Baba**, whose followers believe him to be the new incarnation of God. Indeed, you will not be in the town long before being greeted by the oft-heard salutation of "Sai Ram". Centring on **Prasanthi Nilayam** ("Abode of Peace") the ashram where Sai Baba resides from July to March, the town has schools, a university, a hospital

Shri Satya Sai Baba

Born **Satyanarayana Raju** on November 23, 1926, in Puttaparthy, then an obscure village in the Madras Presidency, Satya is reported to have shown prodigious talents and unusual purity and compassion from an early age. His apparently supernatural abilities initially caused some concern to his family, who took him to Vedic doctors and eventually to be exorcized. Having been pronounced to be possessed by the divine rather than the diabolical, at the age of 14 he calmly announced that he was the new incarnation of **Sai Baba**, a saint from Shirdi in Maharashtra who had died eight years before Satya was born.

Gradually his fame spread, and a large following grew. In 1950 the **ashram** was inaugurated and a decade later Sai Baba was attracting international attention; today he has millions of devotees worldwide, a considerable number of whom turn out for his birthday celebrations in Puttaparthy, when he delivers a message to his devotees. Just 5ft tall, with a startling Hendrix-style Afro, his smiling, saffron-clad figure is seen on posters, framed photos and murals all over South India. Though his **miraculous powers** reportedly include the ability to materialize *vibhuti* – sacred ash – with curative properties, Sai Baba claims this to be an unimportant activity, aimed at those firmly entrenched in materialism, and emphasizes instead his message of **universal love**. Indeed, he prefers the ash to be seen as a representation of the final condition of worldly things and the desire to give them up in search of the divine.

In recent years a number of ex-followers, some of whom had obtained high positions, have made serious allegations of coercion and even sexual abuse on the part of the guru himself, which have been vehemently denied. Whatever your feelings about the divinity of Sai Baba, the atmosphere around the ashram is undeniably peaceful, and the growth of such a vibrant community in this once-forgotten backwater is no small miracle in itself.

For more on the guru, visit ⓦ www.saibabalinks.com.

and sports centre which offer up-to-date and free services to all. There's even a small airport. The **ashram** itself is a huge complex that can accommodate thousands of pilgrims, with its own canteens, shops, a museum and library, and a vast assembly hall where Sai Baba gives *darshan* twice a day (6.40am & 3pm). Queues start more than an hour before the appointed time, and a lottery decides who gets to sit near the front.

The **museum** (daily 10am–noon), situated up a small hill to the left after entering the main gates, is undoubtedly the most interesting place for the casual visitor. The ground floor contains a fascinating display on the world's major faiths with illustrations and quotations from their sacred texts, punctuated by Sai Baba's comments which are invariably intended to point out the underlying unity of the different belief systems. The first floor has more colourful exhibits, focusing on various places of worship and one dedicated to Sai Baba's predecessor, the Shirdi Sai Baba (see box opposite). Finally, the third floor displays bring the animistic tribal religions of Africa into the universal fold, as well as the beliefs and philosophy of the ancient Greeks – it's noteworthy that the divinity of Socrates is accorded special emphasis.

Practicalities

The nearest major city to Puttaparthy is Bangalore in Karnataka (see p.242), from where seven daily **buses** (4hr) run to the stand outside the ashram entrance. The town is also connected to Hyderabad (3 daily; 10hr) and Chennai (1 nightly; 11hr). Regular buses make the 42-kilometre run to **Dharmavaram**, the nearest **railhead**, which has good services north and south. There are also three Indian Airlines **flights** a week from Bangalore (Mon, Thurs & Sat; departs 2pm; 30min), though the short distance hardly justifies the expense.

Accommodation in the ashram is strictly segregated by sex, except for families, as are meals and *darshan*. Overt socializing is discouraged and there is a strict policy of lights-out at 9pm. Costs are minimal and, though you can't book in advance, you can enquire about availability at the secretary's office (☎08555/287583). Space is only usually a problem around the time of Sai Baba's birthday in late November. If you do want to stay, you have to register by filling out forms and surrendering your passport at the office before being allocated a bed by the Public Relations Officer. Your passport is returned after attending the first orientation session. Outside the ashram, many of the basic **lodges** are rather overpriced, but a good cheap option is the friendly *Sai Ganesh Guest House* near the police station (☎08555/287079; ❷). The *Sri Sai Sadan* at the far end of the main street (☎08555/287507; ❷–❹) is also great value; all rooms have fridges, TV and a balcony with views of the countryside or the ashram, and there's a meditation room and rooftop restaurant. At the top end, the *Sai Towers* near the ashram entrance (☎0855/287270, ⓦwww.saitowers.com; ❺–❽), charges a lot for its smallish non-a/c and a/c rooms, but has a good **restaurant** downstairs. The ashram also has a canteen which is open to non-residents and there are simple snack stalls along the main street outside the ashram. Or you could try the delicious Tibetan grub at the *Bamboo Nest* on Chitravathi Road.

Travel details

Trains

Hyderabad/Secunderabad to: Aurangabad (1 daily; 12hr 15min); Bangalore (2–4 daily; 12hr–15hr 55min); Bhubaneswar (4 daily; 18hr 40min–22hr 25min); Chennai (2 daily; 14hr 10min); Delhi (3–4 daily; 22hr 20min–32hr); Kolkata (Calcutta; 2–3 daily; 26hr 45min–31hr 25min); Mumbai (3 daily; 16hr 10min–17hr); Tirupati (3–4 daily; 13hr 30min–15hr 35min); Varanasi (2 weekly; 30hr 10min); Vijayawada (12–13 daily; 5hr 30min–7hr 45min); Vishakapatnam (5–6 daily; 11hr 15min–19hr 30min); Warangal (11–13 daily; 2hr 14min–3hr 13min).

Tirupati to: Chennai (3 daily; 2hr 55min–3hr 15min); Hyderabad (3–4 daily; 12hr 50min–17hr 10min); Kolkata (Calcutta; 1 daily; 38hr 30min; Varanasi (1 weekly; 39hr 40min); Vijayawada (4–6 daily; 7hr–8hr 45min); Vishakapatnam (2–3 daily; 13hr 10min–18hr 45min).

Vijayawada to: Chennai (7–12 daily; 6hr 35min–8hr 50min); Delhi (4–6 daily; 23hr 10min–32hr 40min); Hyderabad/Secunderabad (12–13 daily; 5hr 20min–8hr 15min); Kolkata (Calcutta; 5–7 daily; 21hr 15–33hr 20min); Tirupati (4–6 daily; 6hr 30min–8hr 15min); Vishakapatnam (13–16 daily 6hr 5min–11hr 45min).

Vishakapatnam to: Bhubaneswar (5–7 daily; 6hr 45min–9hr 40min); Chennai (3–6 daily; 12hr 50min–15hr 55min); Delhi (1–2 daily; 34hr 30min–39hr 45min); Hyderabad/Secunderabad (5–6 daily; 11hr 50min–16hr 20min); Kolkata (Calcutta: 5–7 daily; 15hr 15min–22hr 50); Tirupati (2–3 daily; 14hr 15min–16hr 45min); Vijayawada (13–16 daily; 5hr 55min–11hr 20min).

Buses

Hyderabad to: Amaravati (2 daily; 7hr); Bangalore (hourly; 13hr); Bidar (1–2 hourly; 4hr); Chennai (1 daily; 16hr); Mumbai (7 daily; 17hr); Puttaparthy (3 daily; 10hr); Tirupati (8 daily; 12hr); Vijayapuri (hourly; 4hr); Vijayawada (every 15min; 6hr); Warangal (every 15–30min; 3hr).

Tirupati to: Bangalore (hourly; 4hr); Chennai (every 15–30min; 3hr 30min–4hr); Hyderabad (8 daily; 12hr); Kanchipuram (hourly; 3hr 30min); Mamallapuram (3 daily; 5hr 30min); Puttaparthy (1 daily at 8pm; 10hr).

Vijayawada to: Amaravati (hourly; 2hr); Guntur (every 15min; 1hr–1hr 30min); Hyderabad (every 15min; 6hr).

Flights

Hyderabad to: Ahmedabad (5 weekly; 1hr 40min); Bangalore (5 daily; 1hr–1hr 30min); Chennai (7–8 daily; 1hr–1hr 30min); Delhi (7 daily; 2hr–4hr 15min); Kolkata (Calcutta; 3 daily; 2–2hr 55min); Mangalore (1 daily; 3hr 10min); Mumbai (9 daily; 1hr 15min–3hr 45min); Panjim (1 daily; 3hr); Pune (1 daily; 1hr); Tirupati (4 weekly; 55min); Varanasi (1 daily; 5hr 30min).

Puttaparthy to: Bangalore (3 weekly; 30min).

Tirupati to: Hyderabad (4 weekly; 55min).

Vishakapatnam to: Bhubaneswar (3 weekly; 55min); Chennai (1 daily; 1hr 5min); Delhi (4 weekly; 3hr); Hyderabad (1 daily; 1hr); Kolkata (Calcutta; 3 weekly; 2hr 15min); Mumbai (1 daily; 1hr 45min).

The Andaman Islands

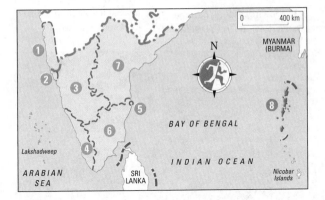

CHAPTER 8

Highlights

✱ **Port Blair** The Cellular Jail stands as a stark reminder of the Andaman capital's bleak colonial past. See p.615

✱ **Wandoor** The white sandy beach and islets of the Mahatma Gandhi National Marine Park are the archipelago's most popular day-trip destination, and a good appetizer for more remote areas. See p.622

✱ **Scuba diving** Plunge into the islands' beautiful coral reefs, which teem with vivid underwater life. See p.624

✱ **Havelock and Neill islands** Cruise by boat to the Andamans' most popular holiday hang-outs, both laid-back, friendly and great for snorkelling or diving. See p.625

✱ **North Andaman** The long haul up the road from Port Blair is worth it for North Andaman's dazzling tropical beaches, set against a backdrop of thick rainforest. See p.629

△ Coral reef, Andaman Islands

The Andaman Islands

T he **ANDAMAN ISLANDS** – India's most remote state – are situated 1000km off the east coast in the middle of the Bay of Bengal, connected to the mainland by flights and ferries from Kolkata, Chennai and Vishakapatnam. Thickly covered by deep green tropical forest, the archipelago supports a profusion of wildlife, including some extremely rare species of bird, but the principal attraction for tourists lies offshore, around the pristine reefs ringing most of the islands. Filled with colourful fish and kaleidoscopic corals, the crystal-clear waters of the Andaman Sea feature some of the world's richest and least spoilt marine reserves – perfect for **snorkelling** and **scuba diving**. Potential visitors have long been faced by the quandary as to whether the expense and effort required in getting there, the lack of infrastructure and certain increased health risks, as well as ethical concerns about ecological and tribal issues, outweigh the benefits of a trip. On the other hand, more islanders are becoming dependent on tourism and industry, which was decimated by the tsunami (see box on p.611).

For administrative purposes, the Andamans are grouped with the **Nicobar Islands**, 200km further south and separated from the Andamans by the deep Ten Degree Channel. Foreign tourists are only permitted to visit certain parts of the Andaman group, while the Nicobar Island remain strictly off-limits to foreigners. There are approximately 200 islands in the Andaman group and nineteen in the Nicobar. The islands are of varying sizes, being the summits of a submarine mountain range stretching 755km from the Arakan Yoma chain in Burma (Myanmar) to the fringes of Sumatra in the south. All but the most remote of these are populated in parts by **indigenous tribes** whose numbers fell dramatically as a result of nineteenth-century European settlement and, more recently, rampant **deforestation**. New felling is now supposed to be strictly controlled, but how closely this is adhered to is a matter for conjecture, and there is the additional problem of timber poachers from Burma and Thailand.

The point of arrival for boats and planes is **South Andaman**, where the predominantly Tamil and Bengali community in the small but busy capital, **Port Blair**, accounts for almost half the islands' total population. The most beautiful beaches and coral reefs are found on **outlying islands**, and a healthy get-up-and-go spirit is essential if you plan to explore these, as connections and transport can be erratic, frequently uncomfortable and severely limited, especially on the smaller islands. Once away from the settlements, you enter a Coca-Cola-free zone where you'll need your own camping supplies and equipment. It's also worth pointing out that a surprising number of travellers fall sick in the Andamans. The dense tree cover, marshy swamps and high rainfall combine to

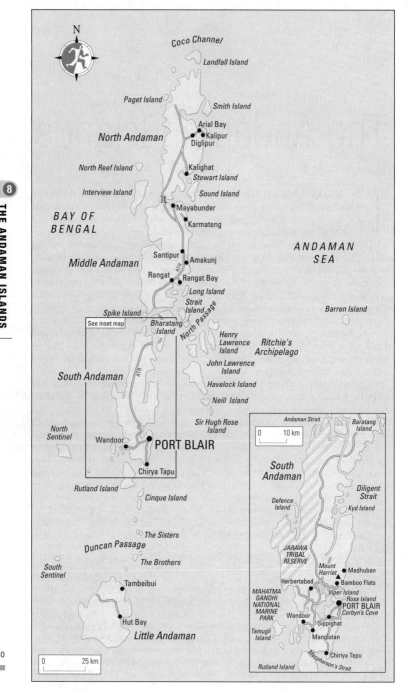

provide the perfect breeding ground for mosquitoes, and **malaria** is endemic in even the most remote settlements. Sandflies are also ferocious in certain places and **tropical ulcer** infections from scratching the bites is a frequent hazard.

The **climate** remains tropical throughout the year, with temperatures ranging from 24°C to 35°C and humidity levels never fall below seventy percent. By far the best time to visit is between January and May. From mid-May to October, heavy rains flush the islands, often bringing violent cyclones that leave west-coast beaches strewn with fallen trees, while in November and December less severe rains arrive with the northeast monsoon. Despite being so far east, the islands run on Indian time, so the sun rises as early as 4.30am in summer and darkness falls soon after 5pm.

Some history

The earliest mention of the Andaman and Nicobar islands is found in **Ptolemy's** geographical treatises of the second century AD. Other records from the Chinese Buddhist monk I'Tsing some five hundred years later and Arabian travellers who passed by in the ninth century describe the inhabitants as fierce and cannibalistic. **Marco Polo** arrived in the thirteenth century and could offer no more favourable description of the natives: "The people are without a king and are idolaters no better than wild beasts. All the men of the island of Angamanian have heads like dogs . . . they are a most cruel generation, and eat everybody they catch . . ." It is unlikely, however, that the Andamanese were cannibals, as the most vivid reports of their ferocity were propagated by Malay pirates who held sway over the surrounding seas, and needed to keep looters well away from trade ships that passed between India, China and the Far East.

During the eighteenth and nineteenth centuries, **European missionaries** and trading companies turned their attention to the islands with a view to colonization. A string of unsuccessful attempts to convert the Nicobarese to

---

The tsunami in the Andamans

Contrary to the half-baked rumours that emerged from the region in the days following the devastating **tsunami** of December 26, 2004, the Andamans did not suffer the total destruction which had at first been feared. Most of the damage occurred in the Nicobars, which lie much closer to the earthquake's epicentre off Indonesia, especially the islands of Car Nicobar, Katchall and Great Nicobar. The only island in the Andamans to suffer extensively was **Little Andaman** (see p.632). In all, around three thousand people were confirmed dead in the two island chains, with a further four and a half thousand declared missing, presumed dead.

The handful of fatalities and the only structural damage in the Port Blair area – mainly to a few old buildings around the town and quay, and the water sports complex at Aberdeen Jetty – were caused by the **earthquake** itself rather than the ensuing tsunami. Elsewhere, the Austin Bridge connecting Middle to North Andaman also had to be closed for repairs, but no foreigners suffered anything more serious than the loss of a few belongings. The worst effect was that the flow of visitors to the islands diminished almost to nothing in the months following the disaster, leaving those whose livelihood depends on tourism high and dry.

Remarkably, in both the Andamans and Nicobars there was not a single reported fatality amongst those indigenous natives who are still allowed to live in the traditional way, even on islands which were badly battered. Tribal people are said to have been alerted to the impending tragedy by observing the agitation amongst the wildlife, and quickly shifted to higher ground. Such a powerful testament to the benefits of living so close to nature provides a sobering lesson to more "civilized" folk.

Native people of the Andaman and Nicobar islands

Quite where the **indigenous population** of the Andaman and Nicobar islands originally came from is a puzzle that has preoccupied anthropologists since Radcliffe-
Brown conducted his famous field work among the Andamanese at the beginning
of the twentieth century. Asian-looking groups such as the Shompen may have
migrated here from the east and north when the islands were connected to Burma,
or the sea was sufficiently shallow to allow transport by canoe, but this doesn't
explain the origins of the black populations, whose appearance suggests African
roots. Wherever they came from, the survival of the islands' first inhabitants has been
threatened by traders and colonizers, who introduced disease and destroyed their
territories by widespread felling. Thousands also died from addiction to alcohol and
opium, which the Chinese, Japanese and British exchanged for valuable shells. Of
perhaps 5000 aborigines in 1858, from six of the twelve native tribal groups, only five
percent remain. For more information, visit Survival International's excellent website
(⊛www.survival-international.org).

The indigenous inhabitants of the Andamans, divided into *eramtaga* (those living in
the jungle) and *ar-yuato* (those living on the coast), traditionally subsisted as hunter-
gatherers living on fish, turtles, turtle eggs, pigs, fruit, honey and roots. The largest
surviving population is of 30,000 or so **Nicobarese** – being horticulturalists, they
assimilated more readily than other tribes to modern culture, and many converted
to Christianity.

Although they comprised the largest group when the islands were first colonized,
only 43 **Great Andamanese** now survive. In the 1860s, the Rev. H. Corbyn set up
a "home" for them to learn English on Ross Island, insisting that they wear clothes
and attend reading and writing classes. Five children and three adults from Corbyn's
school were taken as curiosities to Kolkata in 1864, where they were shown around
the sights. The whole experience, however, proved more fascinating for the crowds
who'd come to ogle the "monkey men" than for the Andamanese themselves, who,
one of the organizers of the trip ruefully remarked, ". . . never evinced astonishment
or admiration at anything which they beheld, however wonderful in its novelty we
might suppose it would appear to them". From the foreign settlers the Andamanese
tragically contracted diseases such as syphilis, measles, mumps and influenza, and
fell prey to opium addiction. Within three years almost the entire population had died.
In recent years the surviving Great Andamanese were forcibly settled on Strait Island,
north of South Andaman, as a "breeding centre", where they were forced to rely on
the Indian authorities for food and shelter. In the aftermath of the tsunami they were
relocated to Port Blair, though for how long remains uncertain.

The **Jarawas**, who were shifted from their original homes when land was cleared
to build Port Blair, currently number around 270 and now live on the remote western
coasts of Middle and South Andaman, hemmed in by the Andaman Trunk Road
(ATR), which since the 1970s has cut them off from hunting grounds and freshwater
supplies. During the 1980s and 1990s, encroachments on their land by loggers,
road builders and Bengali settlers met with fierce resistance, and dozens, possibly

Christianity was made by the French, Dutch and Danish, all of whom were
forced to abandon their plans in the face of hideous diseases and a severe lack
of food and water. Though the missionaries themselves seldom met with any
hostility, several fleets of trading ships which tried to dock on the islands were
captured, and their crews murdered, by the Nicobarese.

In 1777, the British Lieutenant Blair chose the South Andaman harbour now
known as **Port Blair** as the site for a **penal colony**, based on the system of
deporting of criminals that had proved successful in Sumatra, Singapore and
Penang. Both this scheme, and an attempt to settle the Nicobar Islands in 1867,

hundreds, of people died in **skirmishes**. In one incident a party of Burmese were caught poaching on Jarawa land; of the eleven men involved, six limped out with horrific injuries, two were found dead, and the other three were never seen again. Most incidents occurred on or near the ATR, which is why armed escorts board buses at several points during the journey north from Port Blair to Mayabunder. Some **contact** between settlers and tribals was made for a while through gift exchanges at each full moon, when consignments of coconuts, bananas and red cloth were taken to a friendly band of Jarawas on a boat, but the initiative was later cancelled. These meetings nevertheless led to some Jarawas becoming curious about what "civilization" had to offer, and they started to hold their hands out for goodies to passing vehicles and even visiting Indian settlements near their territory. When the initially generous reception waned, their visits evolved into surreptitious raids culminating in an attack on a police outpost in March 1998. Since then the authorities have tried to minimize contact, and conflicts have ceased. The government has also increased Jarawa land by 180 square kilometres, but has dragged its feet over enforcing a 2002 Indian Supreme Court order to close the ATR which was passed following protests by international pressure groups such as Survival International.

Aside from a couple of violent encounters with nineteenth-century seamen (seventy were massacred on first contact in 1867), relations with the **Onge**, who call themselves the **Gaubolambe**, have been relatively peaceful. Distinguished by their white-clay and ochre body paint, they continue to live in communal shelters (*bera*) and construct temporary thatched huts (*korale*) on Little Andaman. The remaining population of around one hundred retain their traditional way of life on two small reserves. The Indian government has erected wood and tin huts for them, dispatched a teacher to instruct them in Hindi, and encouraged coconut cultivation, but to little avail. Contact with outsiders is limited to an occasional trip into town to purchase liquor, and visits from rare parties of anthropologists. The reserves are strictly off limits to foreigners, but you can learn about the Onge's traditional hunting practices, beliefs and rituals in Vishvajit Pandya's wonderful ethnography study, *Above the Forest*.

Only very limited contact is ever had with the isolated **Shompen** tribe of Great Nicobar, whose population of around 380 manage to lead a traditional hunting-and-gathering existence. The most elusive tribe of all, the **Sentinelese**, live on North Sentinel Island west of South Andaman. Some contact was made with them in 1990, after a team put together by the local administration had left gifts on the beaches every month for two years, but subsequent visits have invariably ended in a hail of arrows. Since the early 1990s, the AAJVS, the government department charged with tribal welfare, has effectively given up trying to contact the Sentinelese, who are estimated to number anywhere between fifty and two hundred and fifty. Flying in or out of Port Blair, you pass above their island, ringed by a spectacular coral reef. It's reassuring to think that the people sitting at the bottom of the plumes of smoke drifting up from the forest canopy have for so long resisted contact with the outside world.

were thwarted by the harsh climatic conditions of the forests. However, the third go at colonization was more successful, and in 1858 Port Blair finally became a penal settlement where political activists who had fuelled the Mutiny in 1857 were made to clear land and build their own prison. Out of 773 prisoners, 292 died, escaped or were hanged in the first two months. Many also lost their lives in attacks by Andamanese tribes who objected to forest clearance, but the settlement continued to fill with people from mainland India, and by 1864 the number of convicts had grown to 3000. In 1896, work began on a jail made up of hundreds of tiny solitary cells, which was used to confine political prisoners until 1945. The prison still stands and is one of Port Blair's few tourist "attractions".

In 1919, the British government in India decided to close down the penal settlement, but it was subsequently used to incarcerate a new generation of freedom fighters from India, Malabar and Burma. During World War II, the islands were occupied by the **Japanese**, who tortured and murdered hundreds of indigenous islanders suspected of collaborating with the British, and bombed the homes of the Jarawa tribe. British forces moved back in 1945, and at last abolished the penal settlement.

After **Partition**, refugees, mostly low-caste Hindus from Bangladesh and Bengal, were given land in Port Blair and North Andaman, where the forest was clear-felled to make room for rice paddy, cocoa plantations and new industries. Since 1951, the population has increased more than ten-fold, further swollen by repatriated Tamils from Sri Lanka, thousands of Bihari labourers, ex-servicemen given land grants, economic migrants from poorer Indian states, and the legions of government employees packed off here on two-year "punishment postings". This replanted population greatly outnumbers the Andamans' indigenous people, who currently comprise around half of one percent of the total. Contact between the two societies is limited, and not always friendly. In addition, there exists within Port Blair a clear divide between the relatively recent incomers and the so-called "**pre-42s**" – descendants of the released convicts and freedom fighters whose families settled here before the major influx from the mainland. This small but influential minority, based at the exclusive Browning Club in the capital, has been calling for curbs on immigration and new property rules to slow down the rate of settlement. While doubtless motivated by self-interest, their demands nevertheless reflect growing concern for the future of the Andamans, where rapid and largely unplanned development has wreaked havoc on the natural environment, not to mention on the indigenous population.

With the days of logging now firmly numbered, the hope is that **tourism** will replace tree felling as the main source of revenue. However, the extra visitor numbers envisaged are certain to overtax an already inadequate infrastructure, aggravating seasonal water shortages and sewage disposal problems. Given India's track record with tourism development, it's hard to be optimistic. Delhi has already given the go-ahead for services from Southeast Asia – and eventually charter flights from Europe – to land on the recently extended airport runway; indeed the first flights from Bangkok would have touched down in January 2005 but for the tsunami. If even a small percentage of the tourist traffic between Thailand and India is diverted through the Andamans, the impact on this culturally and ecologically fragile region could be catastrophic.

Getting to the Andaman Islands

Port Blair, on South Andaman, is served by Indian Airlines **flights** from Kolkata (1–2 daily) and daily flights from Chennai on both IA and Jet Airways. Tickets for the two-hour flights cost around $200 one way. It's also possible to get to Port Blair by **ship**. Services to and from Chennai can be reasonably relied upon to leave in each direction once a week. Those from Kolkata (departing every two weeks) and Vishakapatnam (once every month) are still somewhat erratic. Although far cheaper than flying, the crossings are long (3–5 days), uncomfortable and often delayed by bad conditions.

However you arrive, thirty-day **permits** are obtainable on arrival in Port Blair. Permits are usually extendable for fifteen days but the authorities sometimes only allow you to stay in Port Blair for that period – not an appealing prospect.

South Andaman: Port Blair and around

South Andaman is today the most heavily populated of the Andaman Islands – particularly around the capital, **Port Blair** – thanks in part to the drastic thinning of tree cover to make way for settlement. Foreign tourists can only visit the island's southern and east central reaches – including the beaches at **Corbyn's Cove** and **Chiriya Tapu**, the fine reefs on the western shores at **Wandoor**, 35km southwest of Port Blair and the environs of **Madhuban** and **Mount Harriet** on the east coast across the bay from the capital. With your own transport it's easy to find your way along the narrow bumpy roads that connect small villages, weaving through forests and coconut fields, and skirting the swamps and rocky outcrops that form the coastline.

Port Blair

PORT BLAIR is a refreshingly leafy but ultimately characterless cluster of tin-roofed buildings tumbling towards the sea in the north, east and west and petering out into fields and forests in the south. There's little to see here – just the **Cellular Jail** and a few small **museums** – but as the point of arrival for the islands, and the only place with a bank, tourist offices and hotels, it can't be avoided. If you plan to head off to more remote islands, this is also the best place to stock up on supplies and buy necessary equipment.

Arrival and information

Port Blair has two jetties: **boats** from the mainland moor at **Haddo Jetty**, nearly 2km northwest of **Phoenix Jetty**, arrival point for inter-island ferries. The Director of Shipping Services at Phoenix Jetty has the latest information on boats and ferries, but you can also check the shipping news column of the local newspaper, the *Daily Telegrams* (Rs1.50), for details of forthcoming departures. Advice on booking ferry tickets appears in the box on p.620.

The smart **Veer Sarvakar airport** terminal is 4km south of town at Lamba Line. Free entry **permits** are issued to foreigners from the immigration counters as you enter the arrivals hall. **Taxis** and **auto-rickshaws** are on hand for short trips into town (Rs40–50), but if you have booked a room in any of the middle- or upper-range hotels (or do so at the counter in the airport), you should find a shuttle bus waiting outside. Local **buses** also frequently ply the route to town from the main road about 300m from the terminal building.

The **A&N Directorate of Tourism** counter at the **airport** (☎03192/232414) hands out a useful brochure, but trying to get more than basic tour and hotel info from the desk in the lobby of their **main office** (Mon–Fri 10am–5pm, Sat 10am–1pm; ☎03192/232747, ⓦ www.andaman.nic.in), situated in a modern building diagonally opposite Indian Airlines on the southern edge of the town, can be frustrating – try to talk to someone in the hierarchy upstairs. Further southwest, on Junglighat Main Road, the **India Tourism office** (Mon–Fri 8.30am–5pm; ☎03192/233006) isn't much cop either. Note that if you intend to visit Interview Island (see p.629), you must first obtain a free permit from the **Chief Wildlife Warden**, whose office (☎03192/233270) is next to the zoo in Haddo.

Road names are not used much in Port Blair, with most establishments addressing themselves simply by their local area. The name of the busiest and most central area is **Aberdeen Bazaar**, where you'll find the superintendent of police (for permit extensions), the SCI office, for onward bookings by sea

(☎03192/233590) and the State Bank of India (Mon–Fri 9am–1pm, Sat 9–11am). Some hotels will change travellers' cheques, but you'll get faster service and better rates at Island Travels (☎03192/233034; Mon–Sat 9am–6pm), which has a licence to change money, and is just up the road from the clocktower in Aberdeen Bazaar. There's an ICICI Bank **ATM** at the lower end of Moulana Azad Road and a UTI Bank ATM near Netaji Stadium. **Internet** access is available at Cyber Point on Moulana Azad Road; Samsuras, next to the post office; and at the *Holiday Resort* (see opposite; all Rs30 per hr).

Local transport and tours

Walking is tiring and time-consuming in hilly Port Blair – even taking into account the minimal amount of sightseeing the place offers – making transport essential. Yellow-top **taxis** gather opposite the bus stand. They all have meters, but negotiating the price before leaving is usual practice. Expect to pay Rs50 for a trip from the centre of town to Corbyn's Cove. The islands' **auto-rickshaws**, tend to charge just as much as taxis.

Local **buses** run infrequently from the bus stand in central Port Blair to Wandoor and Chiriya Tapu, and can be used for day-trips, though it's best to have your own transport to get around South Andaman. **Bicycles** can be rented from Aberdeen Bazaar, at Rs5 per hour, but the roads to the coasts are most easily covered on a **motorbike** or **scooter**, available for rent at TSG Travels (☎03192/232894) and GDM Tours (☎03192/232999), both of which are on Moulana Azad Road, behind Phoenix Bay. Bikes and scooters cost Rs120–150 per day; you'll need to show a licence and leave a Rs500 deposit. There are petrol pumps on the crossroads west of the bus stand and on the road towards the airport. Fill up before you leave town, as petrol is hard to come by elsewhere.

Most of the ANIIDCO **tours** – cramming the island's few interesting sights together with a string of dull destinations – are a complete waste of time; you're better off renting a scooter or taxi and taking in the jail and museums at your own pace. More worthwhile are the the ANIIDCO **harbour cruises** (daily 3–5pm; Rs65) which depart from Phoenix Jetty for fleeting visits to the floating docks and **Viper Island**, and excursions to **Ross Island** (daily 8.30 & 10.30am and 12.30pm; Rs65). They also run day-trips to **Wandoor** and the **Mahatma Gandhi National Marine Park**: the bus tour to Wandoor (8am; Rs104) connects with the 10am boat to the islands of Red Skin (Rs100) and Jolly Buoy (Rs150).

Accommodation

Port Blair boasts a fair selection of places to stay. Concentrated mainly in the centre of town, the bottom-range **accommodation** can be as dour as any port town on the mainland. More comfortable hotels occupy correspondingly more salubrious locations on the outskirts. The abundance of places means it's rarely a problem finding a room.

Andaman Teal House Delanipur ☎03192/234060. High on the hill above Haddo port, this Directorate of Tourism place offers great views, spacious and pleasant rooms, and is very good value, although the location can be inconvenient without your own transport. ❸–❺

Hotel Blair HSKP Complex, 5min from the bus stand ☎03192/238109, ✉hotelblair@yahoo.com. Rather over-priced modern hotel with large clean rooms in a fairly quiet and central location. Airy rooftop restaurant. ❹–❼

Central Lodge Middle Point ☎03192/233634. Rock-bottom option occupying a ramshackle wooden building situated in a quiet and secluded corner of town. Accommodation is in either basic rooms or a dorm (Rs60), and there's also garden space for hammocks. ❶

Fortune Resort Bay Island Marine Hill

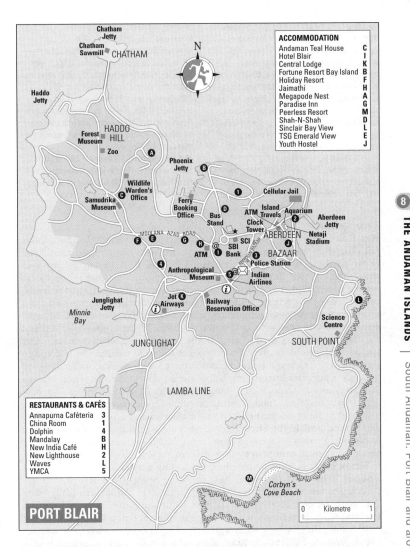

ACCOMMODATION

Andaman Teal House	C
Hotel Blair	I
Central Lodge	K
Fortune Resort Bay Island	B
Holiday Resort	F
Jaimathi	H
Megapode Nest	A
Paradise Inn	G
Peerless Resort	M
Shah-N-Shah	D
Sinclair Bay View	L
TSG Emerald View	E
Youth Hostel	J

RESTAURANTS & CAFÉS

Annapurna Caféteria	3
China Room	1
Dolphin	4
Mandalay	B
New India Café	H
New Lighthouse	2
Waves	L
YMCA	5

PORT BLAIR

☎03192/234101, ⊛www.fortuneparkhotels
.com. Port Blair's swishest hotel: elegant and airy
with polished dark wood. All rooms have carpets
and balconies overlooking Phoenix Jetty (the less
expensive ones are a little cramped), and there's
also a quality restaurant, gardens and an open-air
sea-water swimming pool. The steep tariff (from
\$134) includes full board. **❾**

Holiday Resort Premnagar, a fifteen-minute
walk from the centre ☎03192/230516,
ⓔholidayresort88@hotmail.com. Only a little more
expensive – and much better value – than most

budget places with clean and spacious rooms with
TV, plus a bar and Internet access. **❸**

Hotel Jaimathi Moulana Azad Rd
☎03192/230836. Popular with both Westerners
and Indians, this place has large and fairly clean
rooms with communal balconies. **❷**

Megapode Nest Haddo Hill ☎03192/232380,
⊛www.aniidco.nic.in. ANIIDCO's upmarket option
offers comfortable rooms along with pricier self-
contained "cottages" ranged around a central lawn
with good views. There's also a quality restaurant.
❻–❼

Paradise Inn Moulana Azad Rd ☏ 03192/245772, ℱ 233479. Compact and great-value modern lodge, offering rooms with TV and phone. Off-season (May–Oct) discounts available. ❸

Peerless Resort Corbyn's Cove ☏ 03192/229263, ℮ pblbeachinn@sancharnet.in. Lovely setting amid gardens of palms, jasmine and bougainvillea opposite a white sandy beach, but the balconied a/c rooms and cottages are a bit tatty given the starting price of Rs3650. There's a bar and mid-range restaurant with an average evening buffet. ❾

Shah-N-Shah Mohanpura ☏ 03192/233696. Set between the bus stand and Phoenix Jetty, this basic but friendly and comfortable place has en-suite rooms, a sociable terrace and a restaurant. ❸

Sinclair Bayview On the coast road to Corbyn's Cove ☏ 03192/227824, ℮ pblsinbview@sancharnet.in. Clifftop hotel offering spotless carpeted rooms (from Rs3240) with balconies, en-suite bathrooms, dramatic views, bar and restaurant and airport shuttle bus. ❾

TSG Emerald View 25 Moulana Azad Rd ☏ 03192/246488, ⓦ www.andamantsghotels.com. Smart new upper mid-range place with spacious, colourfully furnished rooms (some a/c) boasting all mod cons. ❸–❻

YHA Opposite Netaji Stadium ☏ 03192/232459. Run-down and predictably institutional place, but dorm beds are only Rs50 and there are two doubles. Often full of students or itinerant workers. ❶

The Town

Port Blair's only firm reminder of its gloomy past, the sturdy brick **Cellular Jail** (Tues–Sun 9am–noon & 2–5pm; Rs5), overlooks the sea from a small rise in the northeast of town. Built between 1896 and 1905, its tiny solitary cells were quite different and far worse than the dormitories in other prison blocks erected earlier. Only three of the seven wings that originally radiated from the central tower now remain. Visitors can peer into the cells (3m by 3.5m) and imagine the grim conditions under which the prisoners existed. Cells were dirty and ill-ventilated, drinking water was limited to two glasses per day, and the convicts were expected to wash in the rain as they worked clearing forests and building prison quarters. Food, brought from the mainland, was stored in vats where the rice and pulses became infested with worms; more than half the prison population died long before their twenty years' detention was up. Protests against conditions led to hunger strikes in 1932, 1933 and 1937, resulting in yet more deaths, and frequent executions took place at the gallows that still stand in squat wooden shelters in the courtyards, in full view of the cells. The **Sound and Light Show** (daily except during the rainy season May–Sept & Nov: in English 7.15pm; in Hindi 6pm; Rs20) outlines the history of the prison, and a small **museum** by the entrance gate (same hours as the jail) exhibits lists of convicts, photographs and grim torture devices.

About 300m south of the jail, near the Water Sports Complex, you can see tanks full of fish and coral from the islands' reefs at the **Aquarium** (daily 9am–1pm & 2–4.45pm; Rs5). Three kilometres out along the coast road towards Corbyn's Cove, Port Blair's newest attraction is the **Science Centre** (Mon–Sat 9am–5.30pm; free), which displays an array of equipment and has some interactive displays on different scientific subjects. There's also a **planetarium** within the complex, with shows on demand (Rs5).

On the west side of town, close to the Directorate of Tourism, the **Anthropological Museum** (Mon–Sat 9am–noon & 1–4pm; free) has exhibits on the Andaman and Nicobar tribes, including weapons, tools and rare photographs of the region's indigenous people taken in the 1960s. Among the most striking of these is a sequence featuring the Sentinelese, taken on April 26, 1967, when a party of Indian officials made the first contact with the tribe. After scaring the aborigines, the visitors marched into one of their hunting camps and made off with the bows, arrows and other artefacts now displayed in the museum. The anthropologist charged with documenting the expedition noted afterwards that "the whole atmosphere was that of conquering hordes over-running conquered territory".

Further northwest in Delanipur opposite ANIIDCO's *Teal House* hotel, the **Samudrika Naval Maritime Museum** (Tues–Sun 8.30am–noon & 2–5pm; Rs10) is an excellent primer if you're heading off to more remote islands, with a superlative shell collection and informative displays on various aspects of local marine biology. One of the exhibits features a cross-section of the different corals you can expect to see on the Andamans' reefs, followed by a rundown of the various threats these fragile plants face, from mangrove depletion and parasitic starfish to clumsy snorkellers.

Wildlife lovers are advised to steer clear of the grim little **zoo** (Tues–Sun 8am–5pm; Rs2), further down towards Haddo, whose only redeeming feature is that it has successfully bred rare crocodiles and monkeys for release into the wild. The adjoining **Forest Museum** (Mon–Sat 8am–noon & 2–5pm; free) is an equally dismal spectacle, feebly attempting to justify the Indian Forest Service's wholesale destruction of the Andamans' forests with a series of lacklustre photographs of extraction methods. However, if you really want to confront the grim reality of the local timber industry, press on north to **Chatham Sawmill** (daily 7am–2.30pm; free), at the end of the peninsula marking the northernmost edge of Port Blair. One of the oldest and largest wood-processing plants in Asia, it seasons and mills rare hardwoods taken from various islands – a sad testimony to the continued abuse of international guidelines on tropical timber production. Photography is prohibited.

Eating

Between them, Port Blair's **restaurants** offer dishes from north and south India, Burmese specialities and a wide variety of seafood. Roadside stalls sell plates of grilled fish at Rs15–20, in addition to the usual crop of cheap but run-of-the-mill "meals" cafés in the main bazaar: of these, the *Majestic, Gagan* and *Milan* on AB Road are the best, but steer clear of the *Dhanalakshmi*'s notoriously dreadful canteen. **Alcohol** is becoming increasingly easy to come by, either in the upscale hotels or a smattering of less salubrious bars such as the one underneath the *Jaimathi*.

Annapurna Caféteria Aberdeen Bazaar, towards the post office. Far and away Port Blair's best south Indian joint, serving the usual range of huge crispy *dosas*, north Indian and Chinese plate meals, delicious coffee, and wonderful *pongal* at breakfast. The lunchtime thalis are also great. Closed Sundays.

China Room On the hill above the Phoenix Jetty ℡03192/230759. The most tourist-oriented restaurant in town, run by a Burmese–Punjabi couple whose roots are vividly reflected in the chilli-and-ginger-rich cuisine (which also shows some Chinese influence). Particularly recommended for seafood, which comes in a range of tasty sauces. There's a roomy courtyard, but reserve a table inside if it's rainy.

Dolphin Marthoma Church Complex, Golghar. Pleasantly decorated new restaurant with cane chairs and blinds and a menu of carefully prepared dishes, mostly Indian and Chinese, but also featuring some European dishes and a few house chicken and seafood specialities.

Mandalay *Fortune Resort*, Marine Hill. Airy open restaurant with great bay views dishing up over-priced à la carte dishes and a reasonable Rs350 dinner buffet of mixed Indian, Chinese and Western food, though service can be a bit lax for its class. The adjacent *Nico Bar* is good for a drink.

New India Cafe Moulana Azad Rd. In the basement of *Jaimathi* lodge, this cheap restaurant is popular with Westerners and Indians alike. Wide menu of veg and meat dishes, but expect to wait if you order anything that's not already prepared.

New Lighthouse Near Aberdeen Jetty. Popular place with outdoor seating where you can catch the sea breeze while feasting on some of the cheapest lobster and other seafood in India.

Waves *Peerless Resort*, Corbyn's Cove. Slightly pricey but very congenial alfresco hotel restaurant under a shady palm grove, and one of the few places in town you can order a beer with your meal. Most dishes around Rs100–150.

YMCA Near Post Office. North and south Indian standards served on a pleasant covered terrace. The pure veg thalis are especially good.

Port Blair is the departure point for all flights and ferry crossings to the **Indian mainland**; it is also the hub of the Andamans' inter-island bus and ferry network. Unfortunately, booking tickets (especially back to Chennai, Kolkata or Vishakapatnam) can be time-consuming, and many travellers are obliged to come back here well before their permit expires to make reservations, before heading off to more pleasant parts again.

To the mainland

If you've travelled to the Andamans **by ship**, you'll know what a rough ride the three-day (or more) crossing can be in bunk class, and how difficult tickets are to come by (see p.466). It's also a good idea to talk to fellow travellers about current conditions, which vary from year to year and vessel to vessel. The one factor you can be sure about is that, at around Rs1500, the ship offers the cheapest route back. The downside is that schedules can be erratic, and accurate information about them difficult to obtain – annoying when you only have a one-month permit. For **Chennai**, whose weekly service run by the DSS is the most reliable, you'll have to head down to the ticket office at Phoenix Jetty. Basically, the only sure way of finding out when the next ship is leaving and securing a ticket to **Kolkata** and **Vishakapatnam** is to join the "queue" outside the SCI office (℡03192/233590), opposite the *Dhanalakshmi* hotel in Aberdeen Bazaar. Tickets are supposed to go on sale a week in advance of departure, but don't bank on it. Bear in mind, too, if you're reading this a couple of days' journey from the capital, and with only a week or less left on your permit, that the local police can get heavy with foreigners who outstay their allotted time.

Returning to the mainland by **plane** in just two hours instead of seventy-two can save lots of time and hassle, but at $205 one-way ($157 student or under 30), air tickets to **Chennai** and **Kolkata** are far from cheap. With Jet Airways and Indian Airlines now both running daily flights, tickets to Chennai are usually easy to obtain at short notice apart from peak times like Diwali or Christmas. The situation has also eased in the case of Kolkata, as Indian Airlines operates a daily flight (plus a second flight four days a week). The Indian Airlines office (℡03192/234744) is diagonally opposite the

Around Port Blair

At some point, you're almost certain to find yourself killing time in Port Blair, waiting for boats to show up or tickets to go on sale. Rather than wasting days in town, it's worth exploring the **coast** of South Andaman which, although far more densely populated than other islands in the archipelago, holds a handful of easily accessible beauty spots and historic sites. Among the latter, the ruined colonial monuments on **Viper** and **Ross islands** can be reached on daily harbour cruises or regular ferries from the capital. For **beaches**, head southeast to **Corbyn's Cove**, or cross South Andaman to reach the more secluded **Chiriya Tapu**, both of which are easily accessible on day-trips if you rent a moped or taxi. By far the most rewarding way to spend a day out of town, however, is to catch the tourist boat from **Wandoor** to **Jolly Buoy** or **Red Skin islands** in the **Mahatma Gandhi National Marine Park** opposite, which boasts some of the Andamans' best snorkelling. The other area worth visiting is **Mount Harriet** and **Madhuban** on the central part of South Andaman, north across the bay from Port Blair.

Viper and Ross islands

First stop on the harbour cruise from Port Blair (daily 3–5pm; Rs65) is generally **Viper Island** (entry Rs16), named not after the many snakes that doubtless

ANIIDCO office, while Jet Airways (☎03192/236922) is on the first floor at 189 Main Road, Junglighat, next to the GITO office.

Travellers intending to catch onward **trains** from their port of arrival on the mainland should note that Port Blair has an efficient computerized Southern Railways reservation office near the Secretariat (Mon–Sat 8.30am–1pm & 2–4pm).

Inter-island services

Buses connect Port Blair with most major settlements on South and Middle Andaman, mainly via the Andaman Trunk Road. From the mildly chaotic bus stand at the bottom of town, one daily government service at 5am runs via **Rangat** (6hr) and **Mayabunder** (9hr) to **Diglipur** (11hr) and **Ariel Bay**. There's another daily service to Rangat at 6am. Several private companies including Geetanjali Travels (tickets at *Tillai* teashop by the bus stand) and the cheaper Ananda (☎03192/233252) run deluxe or video coach (ear-plugs essential) services, which leave from the road outside the bus stand also at 5am.

Most of the islands open to foreign tourists, including **Neill**, **Havelock**, **Middle** and **North Andaman**, are also accessible by **boat** from Phoenix Jetty. Details of forthcoming departures are posted in the shipping news columns of the local newspapers, but the only way to gurantee a passage is to book tickets in advance at the office by the quay between 9am and 11am the day before – this can turn into quite a scrum. Note that there are three separate queues: the left one for Hut Bay, the middle one for Diglipur and the right-hand one for Neill, Havelock, Long and Rangat. Schedules change frequently but you can expect at least one boat daily to Havelock, Neill and Rangat, four weekly to Long, three to Diglipur and every other day to Hut Bay. If possible, try to travel on a newer vessel like the *Ramanujam* or *Long Island*. The journeys on older boats can be a lot longer and more uncomfortable than you might expect. From 9am onwards, the heat on board is intense, with only corrugated plastic sheets for shade, while the benches are highly uncomfortable and the toilets generally dismal. You should take adequate supplies of food and water with you; only biscuits and simple snacks are sold on the boats. More details of boat services to destinations outside the capital appear in the relevant accounts.

inhabit its tangled tropical undergrowth, but a nineteenth-century merchant vessel that ran aground on it during the early years of the colony. Lying a short way off Haddo Wharf, it served as an isolation zone for the main prison, where escapees and convicts (including hunger strikers) were sent to be punished. Whipping posts and crumbling walls, reached from the jetty via a winding brick path, remain as relics of a torture area, while occupying the site's most prominent position are the original gallows.

No less eerie are the decaying colonial remains on **Ross Island** (entry Rs16), at the entrance to Port Blair harbour, where the British sited their first penal settlement in the Andamans. Originally cleared by convicts wearing iron fetters (most of them sent here in the wake of the 1857 Mutiny, or First War of Independence), Ross witnessed some of the most brutal excesses of British colonial history, and was the source of the prison's infamy as **Kalapani**, or Black Water. Of the many convicts transported here, distinguished by their branded foreheads, the majority perished from disease or torture before the clearance of the island was completed in 1860. Thereafter, it served briefly as the site of Rev. Henry Corbyn's "**Andaman Home**" – a prison camp created with the intention of "civilizing" the local tribespeople – before becoming the headquarters of the revamped penal colony, complete with theatre hall, tennis courts, swimming pool, hospitals and grand residential bungalows. Rather ambitiously dubbed "the Paris of the East", the settlement typified the stiff-upper-lipped spirit of the Raj at its most cruel: while the *burra-* and *memsahibs* dressed for dinner and sang hymns in church, convicts languished in the most appalling conditions only a kilometre away. In the end, the entry of the Japanese into World War II, hot on the heels of a massive earthquake in 1941, forced the British to evacuate, and in the coming years most of the buildings were dismantled by the new overlords, who themselves founded a POW camp here.

Little more than the hilltop Anglican church, with its weed-infested graveyard, has survived the onslaught of tropical creepers and vines, but the island makes a peaceful break from Port Blair. To get here, jump on one of the regular launches from Phoenix Jetty (daily; departing 8.30am, 10.30am & 12.30pm and returning 8.45am, 10.45am & 12.40pm; Rs65).

Corbyn's Cove and Chiriya Tapu

The best beach within easy reach of the capital lies 10km southeast at **Corbyn's Cove**, a small arc of smooth white sand backed by a swaying curtain of palms. There's a large hotel here (*Sinclairs Bay View*, see p.618), but the water isn't particularly clear, and bear in mind that lying around scantily clothed will bring you considerable attention from crowds of local workers.

For more isolation, rent a moped or take a taxi 30km south to **Chiriya Tapu** ("Bird Island"), at the tip of South Andaman. The motorable track running beyond this small fishing village leads through thick jungle overhung with twisting creepers to a large bay, where swamps give way to shell-strewn beaches. Other than at lunchtime, when it often receives a deluge of bus parties, the beach offers plenty of peace and quiet, forest walks on the woodcutters' trails winding inland from it, and easy access to an inshore reef. However, the water here is nowhere near as clear as at some spots in the archipelago, and serious snorkellers and divers should enquire if any boats are going out from the big hotels to volcanic **Cinque Island** (see p.632), a couple of hours' further south. It's also possible to charter your own fishing boat here; ask around the bar in the village, and expect to pay around Rs3000 per boat for the return trip to Cinque.

Wandoor and the Mahatma Gandhi National Marine Park

Much the most popular excursion from Port Blair is the boat ride from **Wandoor**, 30km southwest, to one or other of the fifteen islets comprising the **Mahatma Gandhi National Marine Park**. Although set up purely for tourists, the trip is worth considering, as it gains you access to one of the richest coral reefs in the region. The downside is that entry into the park for foreigners now costs Rs500 (Indians Rs50). Boats depart at 10am (daily except Mon; Rs100–150) from Wandoor, which you can reach on A&N Tourism's **tour** (Rs104) or by local bus, but it is more fun to rent a moped and ride down to meet the boat yourself.

The long white **beach** at Wandoor is littered with the dry, twisted trunks of trees torn up and flung down by annual cyclones, and fringed not with palms, but by dense forest teeming with bird life. The water's very shallow, so you should only snorkel here at high tide. From the jetty, the boats chug through broad creeks lined with dense mangrove swamps and pristine forest to either **Red Skin Island** or, more commonly, **Jolly Buoy**. The latter, an idyllic deserted island, boasts an immaculate shell-sand beach, ringed by a bank of superb coral. The catch is that the boat only stops for around an hour, which isn't nearly enough time to explore the shore and reef. Beware of **strong currents** while snorkelling off the edges of the reef.

Mount Harriet and Madhuban

The richly forested slopes of **Mount Harriet** can easily be visited as a day-trip from Port Blair. You can either take one of the passenger ferries (every 30min–1hr) from Chatham to **Bamboo Flats** or, if you want to have your own transport on the other side, there are eight daily vehicle ferries from Phoenix Bay between 5.30am and 8.30pm. From Bamboo Flats it's a pleasant seven-kilometre stroll east along the coast and north up a path through trees hung with thick vines and creepers to the 365-metre summit, which affords fine views back across the bay. An intermittent bus service runs between Bamboo Flats and Hope Town, where the path starts, and saves you 3km. Alternatively, Jeeps and taxis are available to take you all the way to the top but they charge at least Rs300. There's a charge of Rs250 (Indians Rs25; students/teachers Rs5) to enter Mount Harriet National Park, but the checkpost is on the road so you probably won't be asked to pay if you take the path. It's 2.5km from the checkpost up to the resthouse and viewing tower at the summit. If you have strong legs you can reach **Madhuban** on the coast northeast of the mountain by the sixteen-kilometre round route via Kala Patthar (Black Rock) and back via the coast. There's a decent beach at Madhuban and the area is still used for training logging **elephants**, so you stand a good chance of seeing them learning their trade.

Islands north of Port Blair

Printed on the permit card you receive on arrival in the Andamans is a list of all the other **islands** you're allowed to visit in the archipelago. The majority of them are north of Port Blair. Given the distances involved, not to mention the sometimes erratic connections between them (and the time limit imposed by the one-month permit), it definitely pays to know where to head for as soon as you arrive, rather than drift off on the first promising ferry out of Phoenix Jetty. The best way of doing this is to talk to fellow travellers arriving back in the capital. The following accounts will give you a good idea of what to expect upcountry, but new islands are opened up to tourists (and occasionally one goes off-limits again) each year, and these may well offer the kind of wilderness experience you're here for.

Having travelled all the way to the Andamans, it is surprising how many visitors make a beeline for the only two developed islands in the group, **Neill** and **Havelock**, both within easy reach of Port Blair. To get further north, where tourism of any kind has thus far had very little impact, you can take a bus or ferry from Havelock to ramshackle **Rangat**, at the south end of **Middle Andaman**, or bypass the whole east coast by catching a bus or boat from Port Blair direct to **Diglipur**'s port of Arial Bay, at the top of **North Andaman**. Either way, you'll be lucky not to be marooned from time to time in some truly grim little settlements, interspersed with a few long hard slogs up the infamous **Andaman Trunk Road** (or "ATR"). On Middle and North Andaman, and their satellite islands, **accommodation** is scarce, to say the least. Aside from a handful of ANIIDCO hotels (bookable in advance in Port Blair), the only places to stay are a few basic (and occasionally) grim lodges or, preferably, APWD *Rest Houses* (see box p.627).

To escape the settled areas you have to be prepared to rough it, travelling on inshore fishing dugouts, sleeping on beaches and cooking your own food. The rewards, however, are great. Backed by dense forest filled with colourful birds and insects, the beaches, bays and reefs of the outer Andamans teem with wildlife, from gargantuan crabs, pythons and turtles, to dolphins, sharks, giant rays and the occasional primeval-looking dugong. Essential **kit** for off-track wanderings includes a sturdy mosquito net, mats to sleep on (or a hammock), a large plastic container for water, some strong antiseptic for cuts and bites (sand flies are a real problem on many of the beaches) and, most important of all, **water purification** tablets or a water purifier, since bottled water is virtually

Scuba diving in the Andaman Islands

The seas around the Andaman and Nicobar islands are some of the world's most unspoiled. Marine life is abundant, with an estimated 750 species of fish existing on one reef alone. Parrot, trigger and angel fish live alongside manta rays, reef sharks and loggerhead turtles. Many species of fish and coral are unique to the area and fascinating life-systems exist in ash beds and cooled lava based around the volcanic Barren Island (see p.632).

For a quick taste of marine life, you could start by **snorkelling**; most hotels can supply masks and snorkels, though some equipment is in dire need of replacement. The only way to get really close, however, and venture out into deeper waters, is to **scuba dive**. The experience of weaving in and out of coral beds, coming eye to eye with fish or swimming with dolphins and barracudas is unforgettable.

Dive operations have come and gone more frequently than the rains in recent years and the picture is constantly changing. At the time of writing the only fully operational and certified schools were the following two based on Havelock, but it's always worth checking if any have opened up in Port Blair or elsewhere. Based at the *MS Lodge* near the jetty, the British–Indian **Andaman Dive Club** (℡03192/282002, or in London on ℡020/7538 4643, ⓦwww.andamandiveclub.com) has a smart boat, brand new equipment and offers two-dive trips (including food) for $80 as well as PADI open water courses for $340 and BSAC ocean diver certfication for $400; more advanced courses are also available. Further down the coast at *Wild Orchid* on beach #5, **Dive India** (℡03192/282472, ⓦwww.diveindia.com) is run by friendly divemasters from the Karen community around Mayabunder; single dives cost Rs2000, while a PADI course will set you back Rs15,500. The **Jungle Resort** over on Radhnagar beach has also invested in scuba equipment and was just about to bring groups from Thailand when the tsunami put things on hold. Permit difficulties made the affable Swiss duo of the **Andaman Scuba Club** suspend operations some time back, but you can check ⓦwww.andamanscubaclub.com to see if they are up and running again.

Underwater in the Andamans, it is not uncommon to come across schools of reef sharks, which rarely turn hostile, but one thing to watch out for and avoid is the **black-and-white sea snake**. Though the snakes seldom attack – and, since their fangs are at the back of their mouths, they find it difficult to get a grip on any human – their bite is twenty times more deadly than that of the cobra.

Increased tourism inevitably puts pressure on the delicate marine ecosystem, and poorly funded wildlife organizations can do little to prevent damage from insensitive visitors. You can ensure that your presence in the sea around the reefs does not harm the coral by observing the following **Green Coral Code** while diving or snorkelling:

• Never touch or walk on living coral – it will die.
• Try to keep your feet away from reefs while wearing fins; the sudden sweep of water caused by a flipper kick can be enough to destroy coral.
• Always control the speed of your descent while diving; enormous damage can be caused by divers landing hard on a coral bed.
• Never break off pieces of coral from a reef, and remember that it is illegal to export dead coral from the islands, even fragments you may have found on a beach.

nonexistent. Wherever you end up, preserve the goodwill of local people by packing your rubbish out – carrying it in your backpack – or burning it, and being sensitive to scruples about dress and nudity, especially in areas settled by conservative Bengali or Tamil Hindus.

Neill

Tiny, triangular-shaped **Neill** is the most southerly inhabited island of **Ritchie's Archipelago**, barely two hours northeast of Port Blair on a fast ferry. The source of much of the capital's fresh fruit and vegetables, its fertile centre, ringed by a curtain of stately tropical trees, comprises vivid patches of green paddy dotted with small farmsteads and banana plantations. The beaches are mediocre by the Andamans' standards, but worth a day or two en route to or from Havelock. **Boats** leave Port Blair's Phoenix Jetty for Neill (1–2 daily; 2hr–3hr 30min); all services connect with Havelock, and some also with Rangat.

Neill boasts three **beaches**, all of them within easy cycling distance of the small bazaar just up the lane from the jetty (you can rent **cycles** from one of several stallholders from Rs20–30 per day). The best place to swim is **Neill Kendra**, a gently curving bay of white sand, which straddles the jetty and is scattered with picturesque wooden fishing boats. This blends into **Lakshmangar**, which continues for 3km north: to get there by road, head right at the ANIIDCO hotel (see below) and follow the road for around twenty minutes until it dwindles into a surfaced track, then turn right. Wrapped around the headland, the beach is a broad spur of white shell sand with shallow water offering good snorkelling, but that makes entry into the water tough at any time other than high tide. Exposed to the open sea and thus prone to higher tides, **Sitapur** beach, 6km south at the tip of the island, is also appealing and has the advantage of a sandy bottom extending into the sea. The ride there, by hourly bus or bicycle, across Neill's central paddy land is pleasant, but there are no facilities when you get there, so stock up for the day.

The island has four **accommodation** places. From the jetty, a two-minute walk brings you to the ANIIDCO *Hawabill Nest* (☎03192/282630; ❺), where there are a dozen or so clean, carpeted rooms with sitouts ranged around a central courtyard and restaurant, best booked in advance from Port Blair. The three private options are all at Lakshmangar or en route to it: the best of the bunch is *Tango Beach Resort* (☎03192/282634, ✉tangobeachresort@rediffmail .com; ❶–❸), a friendly place right on the beach, with two deluxe and ten much more basic bamboo huts. Before *Tango*, a little over 500m from the jetty, you pass *Cocon Huts* (☎03192/282528, ✉coconhuts@yahoo.com; ❶–❸), which has a similar range of huts, although the bar can attract rowdy revellers from the village. The furthest option, 1km north of *Tango*, is *Pearl Park Hotel* (☎03192/282510; ❶–❻), which has some small huts and posher but hugely overpriced a/c bungalows. Although many people stick to the **restaurants** at these three establishments, far and away the best place to eat is the delightful and welcoming *Gyan Garden*, opposite the football pitch 500m along the road to Lakshmangar, where fresh fish and home-grown veg dishes are a speciality. Of the few tiny eateries in the bazaar, *Hotel Chand* serves up the tastiest, albeit somewhat oily, food.

Havelock

Havelock is the largest island in Ritchie's Archipelago, and the most intensively cultivated, settled like many in the region by Bengali refugees after Partition. Thanks to its regular ferry connection (1–2 daily; 2hr–4hr 30min) with the capital, it is also visited in greater numbers than anywhere else in the Andamans. In recent peak seasons, well over three hundred tourists could be holed up here, making Havelock's much-photographed Radhnagar beach, often touted as the most beautiful in India, feel overwhelmed, but the tsunami just about stemmed the flow of visitors and it may take two or three years for numbers to recover; bad for locals but a bonus for travellers. The boat journey here from Neill, skirting a string of uninhabited islets with shadowy views of South Andaman to the west, is wonderful, and wildlife – both on land and in the sea – remains abundant, despite intensive settlement and deforestation.

Havelock's main **jetty** is on the north side of the island, at the village known as **Havelock #1**. There are three small **lodges** as you turn right from the jetty, on the mangrove-lined outskirts of the village. Best of these is the seafront *M.S. Guest House* (☏03192/282439; ❸), but just about everyone heads for a more picturesque place to stay. You'll also find a handful of basic **restaurants** and **stalls** dotted around the settlement. Otherwise, rent a **moped** (Rs150 per day) or **cycle** (Rs50 per day) for a few days and head straight inland to the bazaar, 2km to the south. Here there are more stalls and shops, plus the island's only place to change money, the State Co-operative Bank (Mon–Fri 9am–1pm, Sat 9–11am). Further **accommodation** listed below is available at **beaches #2 to #5**, really one long unbroken strand, which you get to by turning left at the main junction, or at **Radhnagar** (aka #7 beach), 12km southwest, reached by turning right. An intermittent bus service also covers the east coast between beaches #3 and #5, but you could find yourself waiting all day for it and missing out on a room; buses to Radhnagar are more reliable.

The first proper place to stay on the **east coast** is *Eco Villa* (☏03192/282072; ❶), at **beach #2** – the ten huts are only average value but the food is tasty. On the other side of the bazaar at **beach #3** is the relaxed *Café del Mar* (☏03192/282343; ❶–❻), followed by the friendly and peaceful *Pristine Beach Resort* (☏03192/282344; ❶–❸) – both offer a friendly atmosphere and have the advantage of lockable huts, as well as some sturdier bungalows. Next up are half a dozen places backing onto **beach #5**; the best of these, in order of appearance, are *Sunrise* (☏03192/282408; ❶), with basic huts set in a picturesque palm grove; *Wild Orchid* (☏03192/282472; ⓦwww.wildorchidandaman.com; ❼), by far the plushest resort on this side of the island, with superbly furnished rooms, landscaped gardens and a great split-level multi-cuisine restaurant-bar – they have also opened the more budget-orientated *Emerald Gate* (❸–❺), a few hundred metres down the road past the adequate but institutional ANIIDCO *Dolphin Resort* (☏03192/282411; ❸–❼); and *Coconut Grove* (☏03192/282427; ❶–❷), another sociable hangout with sturdy huts of varying sizes. Beyond these the road carries on for about 3km before petering out behind disappointing **beach #6**.

Heading past a string of thatched villages hemmed in by banana groves and paddy fields, the road towards **Radhnagar** drops through some spectacular woodland to a kilometre-long arc of perfect white sand, backed by stands of giant *mowhar* trees. The water is a sublime turquoise colour and, although the coral is sparse, marine life here is diverse and plentiful, especially among the rocks around the corner from the main beach (to get there on foot, back-track along the road and follow the path through the woods and over the bluff). The main drawback, which can make sunbathing uncomfortable, is a preponderance of pesky sandflies. Radhnagar has few **places to stay**: behind the beach are ANIIDCO's *Tent Camp* (no phone; ❶–❸), rows of canvas tents of varying size and comfort and a toilet block, and the upmarket *Jungle Resort*

(☎03192/237656, ☯www.barefootindia.com; ❶–❷), recently taken over by a large conglomerate who have revamped the luxurious wood-and-thatch cottages. A kilometre inland, the new *Harmony Resort* (☎03192/282421; ❸) is the only real budget-hut venture on this side of the island but overpriced nonetheless. The *Jungle Resort* has a good **restaurant** or you can try the tree-house-like *Golden Sands*, next to *Tent Camp* – both serve a standard mixture of Indian, Chinese and Western dishes. A string of basic food shacks lines the road down to the beach, of which *Arati* is the best. As the nesting site for a colony of Olive Ridley **turtles**, Radhnagar is strictly protected by the Forest Department, whose wardens ensure tourists don't light fires or sleep on the beach. Elephant "jolly rides" are available for Rs20 per person from a podium en route to the beach. Five buses daily (7.30am–5.30pm) run between Radhnagar and the jetty.

Long Island

Just off the southeast coast of Middle Andaman, **Long Island** is dominated by an unsightly plywood mill, but don't let this put you off. Served by just four boats per week from the capital and Rangat (5–8hr), plus two daily launches from Yeratta (7am & 2pm; 1hr), around 10km from Rangat, it sees far fewer visitors than either Neill or Havelock, but boasts a couple of excellent beaches, at **Marg Bay** and **Lalaji Bay**. Both are most easily reached by chartering a fisherman's dinghy from the jetty, as they are a good couple of hours' hike from where the boat docks. The **main settlement** by the jetty has the island's only facilities, including a couple of tatty lodges – try *Kaniappa* (☎03192/278529; ❶). Most foreigners head for the beaches with tents, hammocks and supplies; mercifully, plans to develop the beaches into an upscale resort have been shelved, so the Robinson Crusoe experience remains.

Middle Andaman

For most travellers, **Middle Andaman** is a charmless rite of passage to be endured en route to or from the north. The sinuous Andaman Trunk Road, hemmed in by walls of towering forest, winds through miles of jungle; drivers cross the strait that separates the island from its neighbour, Baratang Island, by

THE ANDAMAN ISLANDS | Middle Andaman

APWD rest houses

Though theoretically set aside for government officials and engineers, travellers are often allowed to stay at **APWD rest houses**, frequently the best – and sometimes the only – accommodation in Middle and North Andaman. To stay at these rest houses it's best to get a free **letter of recommendation** from the APWD office (☎03192/232294), just up the road from the *Hotel Blair* in Port Blair, but you'll have to give specific dates. Theoretically they'll reserve a room for you, but you'll still get bumped if a pukka VIP shows up in the meantime. Just turning up at a rest house isn't guaranteed to meet with success even if rooms are free, but you'll stand a much better chance of getting in if you can provide them with photocopies of your permit and the Indian visa and personal details pages from your passport. Details of particular rest houses are given throughout the text, but all have standardized prices despite varying standards of comfort; all rooms are doubles, but costs are per bed (Rs200 for non-a/c, Rs400 for a/c).

means of rusting flat-bottomed ferry. The island's frontier feeling is heightened by the presence on the buses of armed guards, and the knowledge that the impenetrable forests west of the ATR comprise the **Jarawa Tribal Reserve** (see p.612). Of its two main settlements, the more northerly **Mayabunder**, the port for alluring **Interview Island**, is slightly more appealing than characterless inland **Rangat** because of its pleasant setting by the sea, but neither town gives any reason to dally for long.

Rangat and around

At the southeast corner of Middle Andaman, **RANGAT** consists of a ramshackle sprawl ranged around two rows of insanitary chai shops and general stores divided by the ATR, which in the monsoon degenerates into a fly-infested mud slick, churned at regular intervals by overladen buses. However, as a major staging post on the journey north, it's impossible to avoid – just don't get stranded here if you can help it.

Daily **ferries** to and from Port Blair (6–9hr) dock at **Rangat Bay** (aka **Nimbutala**), 8km east; all stop at Havelock Island and most at Long Island (4 weekly), and there are also two daily launches to Long Island from nearby **Yeratta**. In addition, Rangat is served by two daily government **buses** to Port Blair (6–7hr) as well as some private services, which pass through in the morning en route from further north. The APWD *Rest House* (☎03192/274237; ❸–❺), pleasantly situated up a winding hill from the bazaar with views across the valley, is the best place to stay and eat, providing good filling fish thalis. The newish *RG Lodge* (☎03192/274237; ❷–❸), just off the main road, is a decent fallback. The town's best restaurant is the *Hotel Vijay*, whose amiable proprietor serves up copious thalis and, if the boat is in, crab curry.

If you do get stuck here, rather than staying put in Rangat, jump on a bus heading north, or find a Jeep to take you to **Amakunj beach**, aka Cuthbert Bay, 9km along the road to Mayabunder. On the right of the road just beyond the helipad, a Forest Department signboard saying "Sand Collection Point" marks the start of a track running the remaining 500m to the sea. The beach has little shade to speak of, but the snorkelling is good and, best of all, there's the very comfortable ANIIDCO *Hawksbill Nest* (☎03192/279022; ❶–❷) **hotel** on the main road, which is invariably empty.

Mayabunder

Only 70km north of Rangat by road (a bus journey of three hours or more), perched on a long promontory right at the top of the island and surrounded by mangrove swamps, is **MAYABUNDER**, springboard for the remote northern Andaman Islands. The village, which is home to a large minority of former Burmese **Karen** tribal people who were originally brought here as cheap logging labour by the British, is more spread out and more appealing than Rangat, but again there is little to hold your interest for long.

At the brow of the hill, before it descends to the jetty, a small hexagonal wooden structure houses the **Forest Museum/Interpretation Centre** (Mon–Sat 8am–noon & 1–4pm; free), which holds a motley collection of turtle shells, snakes in formaldehyde, dead coral, a crocodile skull and precious little information. Next door, the APWD *Rest House* (☎03192/273211; ❸–❺) is large and very comfortable, with a pleasant garden and gazebo overlooking the sea, and a dining room serving good set meals. The only other reasonable accommodation nearby is back in the centre of the bazaar at the *Anmol Lodge* (☎03192/262695; ❷–❸), some of whose attached rooms have TV, and the nearby *S&S Lodge* (☏03192/273449; ❶), which has clean rooms with shared bathrooms; the dilapidated and cockroach-infested *Lakshminarayan Lodge* should be avoided at all costs. Further afield at **Karmateng beach**, 14km southeast, there's another ANIIDCO hotel, the *Swiftlet Nest* (☏03192/273495; ❸–❹) but nothing else. Two buses are supposed to go there daily, failing which there are taxis or auto-rickshaws.

Buses from Port Blair now continue over the new bridge to Diglipur on North Andaman at least twice a day. Heading back towards the capital, there are a couple of private services, such as Geetanjali Travels, as well as one government bus, all departing very early in the morning.

Interview Island

Mayabunder is the jumping-off place for **Interview Island**, a windswept nature sanctuary off the remote northwest coast of Middle Andaman. Only opened to tourists in 1997, it's large, mainly flat and completely uninhabited save for a handful of unfortunate forest wardens, coast guards and policemen, posted here to ward off poachers. Foreigners aren't permitted to spend the night on the island, and to visit you must first obtain permission from the Chief Wildlife Warden in Port Blair. If you've come to the Andamans to watch **wildlife**, a visit here should be top of your list.

The only way to reach Interview is to charter a private fishing dingy from Mayabunder jetty for around Rs500. Arrange one the day before and leave at first light. Approaching the island, you'll be struck by its wild appearance, particularly noticeable on the northwest, where the monsoon storms have wrecked the shoreline forest. If you can, however, get your boatman to pull up on to the **beach** at the southern tip of the island, which has a perennial freshwater pool inside a low cave; legend has it that the well, a nesting site for white-bellied **swifts**, has no bottom. At the forest post, where you have to sign an entry ledger, ask the wardens about the movements of Interview's feral **elephants**, descendants of trained elephants deserted here by a Kolkata-based logging company after its timber operation failed in the 1950s. When food (or potential mates) are scarce, the elephants take to the sea and swim to other islands (sometimes, it is said, all the way to Mayabunder).

North Andaman

Shrouded in dense jungle, **North Andaman** is the least populated of the region's large islands, crossed by a single road linking its scattered Bengali settlements. Timber extraction is proceeding apace here, though the authorities claim they are sticking to new regulations. The total absence of motorable roads into northern and western areas of the island has ensured blanket protection for a vast stretch of convoluted coastline, running from Austin Strait in the southeast to the northern tip, Cape Price. There is concern, however, that the completion of the ATR so close to this wilderness may herald the start of a new settlement influx, with the same disastrous consequences for the environment seen elsewhere.

There is no reason to spend more time in **Kalighat**, where the boat arrives from Mayabunder, than it takes to get a bus out, nor longer in North Andaman's ugly main town of **Diglipur** than it takes to get a connection down to **Arial Bay** for **Smith** and **Ross** islands or on to the attractive coastal area round **Kalipur**.

Kalighat and around

Although you can now proceed directly to Diglipur by road across the Austin Bridge, a small ferry still runs once daily (departs 9.30am; returns 12.30pm) from Mayabunder to **KALIGHAT**, a more relaxed, if slower, point of entry, as it chugs through a narrowing, mangrove-lined estuary. A cluttered little bazaar unfolds from the top of the slipway, hemmed in by dense mangrove swamps, and when you arrive you should hope a bus is standing here to take you to Diglipur. If there isn't, head for one of the village's dismal little chai stalls and dig in for a wait, or turn right to see if there's a **room** in the three-roomed APWD *Rest House* (☏03192/273360; ❸–❺) on the hill overlooking the end of the street. The only **food** is at chai stalls in the bazaar.

The one worthwhile place to visit in this area is **Ramnagar**, 10km northeast of town and served by hourly buses, where there's a beautiful sandy beach backed by unspoilt forest in which it's possible to camp. Try to rent a **cycle** from one of the stalls in Kalighat, though, as the beach is 2km from Ramnagar bazaar, the nearest source of refreshments. In principle, four **buses** per day run north from Kalighat to **Diglipur**; they get crammed full, but the trip takes only 45 minutes. Look out for logging elephants beside the road shortly after leaving Kalighat.

Diglipur, Arial Bay and around

Known in the British era as Port Cornwallis, **DIGLIPUR**, North Andaman's largest settlement, is another disappointing market settlement where you're only likely to pause long enough to pick up a local bus further north to the coast. On the hill above the main road, the APWD *Rest House* (☏03192/272203; ❸–❺) offers the village's nicest **accommodation**; the *Maa Yashoda Lodge* (☏03192/272258; ❶) is a cheaper alternative. Reasonable veg and non-veg fare can be found at the central *Ganga Devi* **restaurant**, while *Ice Cube*, on the road north, serves Chinese and tandoori cuisine. It's better, however, to head 9km on to **ARIAL BAY**, where an APWD *Rest House* (☏03192/271230; ❸–❺) stands on a hillock overlooking the settlement's tiny bazaar. The best place to while away time with a snack or beer while waiting for a boat is the Annu General Store. From Arial Bay, the **boat** that has made its way up from the capital returns direct to Port Blair overnight (3 weekly; 13–14hr).

Better still, continue another 9km to **Kalipur**, served by several daily buses, where the ANIIDCO *Turtle Resort* (☏03192/272553; ❸–❹), occupies a perfect spot on a hilltop with superb views inland and out to sea. It's an unfeasibly large hotel for such a remote location, with spacious, clean rooms with fans and a restaurant (residents only). Recently there has even been competition in the shape of the *Pristine Beach Resort Resort* (☏03192/2722 0603; ❶–❸), whose simple bamboo huts lie on the opposite side of the road below. Just five minutes' walk down the path by the sharp bend in the road there's an excellent deserted **beach**, backed by lush forest and covered in photogenic driftwood. Swimming is best at high tide before the water recedes across rocky mudpools.

It's possible to walk from here to **Saddle Peak**, at 737m the highest mountain in the Andamans, which rises dramatically to the south, swathed in lush jungle. Permission to make the three- to four-hour climb must be obtained from the Range Officer at the Forest Check Post, but don't attempt it without a guide and plenty of drinking water.

Many of the tourists who make it up here do so in order to explore the various **islands** dotted around the gulf north of Arial Bay, particularly **Smith** and **Ross** (not to be confused with its namesake near Port Blair), where you'll find

△ Kalipur beach through driftwood

splendid white sand bars, coral reefs and flora. Neither island is officially listed on the arrival permit, but day-trips can be sanctioned on payment of Rs500 at the Forestry Dept in Arial Bay; you will need to charter a dinghy for Rs400 to reach the islets.

Other islands

The remaining islands open to foreign tourists in the Andaman group are all hard to get to and, with the exception of **Little Andaman** – where a vestigial population of Onge tribespeople has survived a massive influx of Indian Tamils and native Nicobarese – uninhabited. Two hours' boat ride south of Chiriya Tapu on South Andaman, **Cinque Island** offers superlative diving, outshone only by distant **Barren Island**, whose volcanic sand beds teem with marine life.

Cinque Island

Cinque Island actually comprises two islets, joined by a spectacular sand isthmus, with shallow water either side that covers it completely at high tide. The main incentive to come here is the superlative diving and snorkelling around the reefs. However, heaps of dead coral on the beach attest to damage wreaked by the Indian navy during the construction of the swish "cottages" overlooking the beach. Rumour has it that these were built for the visit of a Thai VIP in 1996, but local government officials now use them as bolt holes from Port Blair. Although there are no **ferries** to Cinque, it is possible to arrange dinghies from Chiriya Tapu village on South Andaman (see p.622). Currently, your permit only allows you to spend the day on the island; overnights stays are prohibited.

Barren Island

The furthest flung island open to tourists in the Andaman group is **Barren Island**, a ten-hour sea voyage northeast of Port Blair, though a fast boat can do it much quicker. India's only active **volcano**, the arid brown mountain blew its top in May 1991 after lying dormant for 188 years, and repeated the performance twice more in the mid-Nineties. The only living creatures on Barren are a herd of **goats**, released in 1891 by the British to provide sustenance for any shipwrecked sailors. There are no ferries to the island, but diving expeditions sometimes make the trip, as the seas around Barren are the richest in the region.

Little Andaman

Little Andaman is the furthest point south in the archipelago you can travel to on a standard one-month tourist permit. Located ten hours by sea from Port Blair, most of the island has been set aside as a tribal reserve for the **Onge** (see p.613) and is thus off limits. Little Andaman was also the only island open to foreigners to sustain extensive damage in the 2004 **tsunami**, and at the time of writing it was unclear how much was left standing along the coastal strip surrounding the main port of **Hut Bay** and the attractive beach at **Butler Bay**, some 15km north. Boats from the capital leave for the island every other day, but given the current uncertainties it isn't possible to give reliable accommodation details. The island also has a chronic problem with **malaria** and **sandflies**. If you're still intent on visiting and providing the locals with some much-needed tourist cash, check thoroughly at the tourist office in Port Blair or, better still, with returning fellow travellers before you set off.

Travel details

Flights

Port Blair to: Chennai (2 daily; 2hr); Kolkata (Calcutta; 1–2 daily; 2hr).

Boats

Arial Bay to: Port Blair (3 weekly; 13–14hr).
Havelock to: Long Island (3 weekly; 2–3hr); Neill Island (5–6 weekly; 1hr–1hr 30min); Port Blair (1–2 daily; 2hr–4hr 30min); Rangat Bay (4 weekly; 3–5hr).
Mayabunder to: Kalighat (1 daily; 2hr 30min).
Port Blair to: Arial Bay (3 weekly; 13–14hr; 3–4 days); Chennai (1 weekly; 60–72hr); Havelock Island (1–2 daily; 2hr–4hr 30min); Kolkata (Calcutta; every 2 weeks; 3–4days) Little Andaman (3–4 weekly; 9–10hr); Long Island (4 weekly; 5–8hr); Neill Island (1–2 daily; 2hr–3hr 30min); Rangat Bay (1 daily; 6–9hr); Vishakapatnam (1 monthly; 3–3.5 days).

Rangat Bay to: Havelock Island (4 weekly; 3–5hr); Long Island (2–3 daily; 1hr–1hr 30min); Neill Island (2–3 weekly; 4–6hr); Port Blair (1 daily; 6–9hr).

Buses

Diglipur to: Arial Bay (every 1–2hr; 20min); Kalighat (4 daily; 45min); Kalipur (5 daily; 40min); Port Blair (2–3 daily; 11–12hr).
Mayabunder to: Karmateng beach (2 daily; 30min); Port Blair (2–4 daily; 9–10hr); Rangat (5 daily; 2hr 30min–3hr 30min).
Port Blair to: Chiriya Tapu (3 daily; 1hr 15min); Diglipur (2–3 daily; 11–12hr); Mayabunder (2–4 daily; 9–10hr); Rangat (5 daily; 6–7hr); Wandoor (4 daily; 1hr 15min).
Rangat to: Mayabunder (5 daily; 2hr 30min–3hr 30min); Port Blair (5 daily; 6–7hr).

Contexts

Contexts

History

South India – the vast triangular-shaped peninsula beyond the River Narmada – is separated from the North by the Vindhya Range, a barren band of sheer-sided table mountains. For many centuries, this geographical obstacle discouraged the movement of peoples between the two regions, and the South remained largely isolated from the changes imported by successive waves of invaders who swept across the Gangetic plains from the northwest. Tracing the progress of these newcomers, written histories of the subcontinent have tended to focus on the impact of North upon South. Influences did traverse the Vindhyas and Deccan Plateau, but they invariably did so slowly, by a process of gradual assimilation rather than conquest, enabling the societies of the peninsula to develop in their own way. Moreover, some of India's most defining cultural traits and traditions originated in the deep Dravidian south, from where they spread northwards.

Prehistory

Compared to the extraordinary wealth of archeological finds in northwestern India, evidence of **prehistoric settlement** in the South is scant – although one of the oldest human artefacts ever unearthed in Asia was discovered at Pallavaram, near Chennai (Madras), in 1863, by British archeologist Bruce Foote, who found an oval-shaped hand-axe which he surmised must have originated in the Lower Paleolithic era. Since this initial discovery, similar tools have come to light as far south as the Kaveri River delta, indicating that the region was inhabited by **nomadic hunter-gatherers** at the same time as similar groups emerged in the distant north, between 400,000 and 10,000 years ago.

The first archeologist to establish a sequence for the various stone implements discovered in the South was **Mortimer Wheeler**, whose work on the Coromandel Coast near Pondicherry in 1945 showed that metal was introduced comparatively late to the region. Fixing the date-spans of upper strata with the Roman coins he found in them, Wheeler showed how copper made its first appearance midway through the second millennium BC, by which time rudimentary **agriculture** and the **domestication of animals** were widespread along open coastal areas and river deltas.

It has never been proven, but new technologies, including metal, were probably imported into South India from the northwest, where the sophisticated urban civilizations of the Indus Valley – the region straddling the present-day India–Pakistan border – were already well established by 3000 BC. Recent paleo-botanical studies have shown that a sharp rise in rainfall occurred around this time, which probably explains why agriculture was able to flourish and cities emerge. The inhabitants of **Harappa** and **Mohenjo Daro**, large urban centres which reached their peaks between 2300 and 1800 BC, were certainly experts in the management of water. Amid the ruins of their well-organized cities, remnants of elaborate sewerage and irrigation systems have been found, along with scales and weights, metal jewellery, weapons, precious stones, seals and delicate pottery. Huge communal granaries stored the surplus grain that underpinned a flourishing foreign trade, and the existence of palaces and spacious houses show that this was a highly stratified society, with its own script and formalized religion.

After the sensational rediscovery of the Harappan ruins in the 1920s, it was long assumed that invasions from the northwest brought about the eventual demise of the Indus Valley civilizations, but it now seems more likely that prolonged drought caused the decline. The same climatic changes may also explain how **metal** technology and knowledge of **rice cultivation** first found their way south: as rainfall decreased, the corresponding drop in agricultural output impoverished the once-thriving cities of the Indus Valley, forcing its inhabitants to flee south in search of more fertile land.

The Dravidians

Some historians have advanced this migration theory to account for the origins of the so-called **Dravidians**, who are believed to have colonized the South around the same time as the Indus Valley civilization went into decline in the second millennium BC. However, the most compelling evidence that the Dravidians originated in the northwest is linguistic. Kannada, Telegu, Malayalam and Tamil – the principal modern languages of South India – have a completely different root from the main languages of the North, which derive from the so-called Indo-Aryan group, and are based principally on Sanskrit. Over the years, some wild comparisons have been made between Dravidian and other Asian tongues (most notably Japanese), but the only surviving Asian language with definite Dravidian antecedents is Brahui, spoken by the nomadic people of the Baluchistan uplands on the Iran–Pakistan border. This fact suggests that the Dravidians almost certainly came from the Baluchi grasslands in the fourth or third millennium BC, via the Indus Valley, where they would have acquired the metalwork and farming techniques that subsequently allowed them to establish permanent settlements in the far south.

Although far less technologically advanced than the Indus Valley civilizations, the Dravidian tribes – based around fertile riverine lands separated by densely wooded hills and mountain ranges – forged a strong agrarian base and gradually evolved into distinct chiefdoms. Like the Harappans, their essentially agricultural economies were supplemented by trade in luxury goods such as shells, precious stones and pearls (the Old Testament records that King Solomon sent ships every three years to South India to buy silver, gold, ivory, monkeys and peacocks). This maritime trade expanded steadily over the centuries, enabling the region's chiefs to extend their rule inland and create larger settlements away from the coast.

The Aryans

For most of the twentieth century, archeologists believed the dramatic demise of the Indus Valley cities, between 1800 and 1700 BC, was precipitated by the arrival of invaders from the northwest. Recent carbon-dating techniques, however, have shown that the decline occurred between two and three centuries before the first appearance on the northern plains of a fairer-skinned nomadic people, who called themselves the *Aryas*, or **Aryans**.

The precise route of this migration remains a moot point among historians. Some argue that the newcomers travelled southeast through Persia, while others claim they came via Afghanistan. There is, however, a general consensus that they originated in a region around the Caucasus Mountains, and were part of an ancient diaspora that spread as far as western Europe (their language, an antiquated form of Sanskrit, has astonishingly close affinities with Latin, Greek and Celtic).

The main historical source for this era is the **Rig Veda**, a vast body of 1028 hymns, epic chants, spells, songs and instructions for religious rituals equal in length to the *Iliad* and *Odyssey* combined. Phrased in 10,600 elaborate metered verses, this laboriously sophisticated work includes sections composed between 1400 and 1500 BC, transmitted orally and only set down in writing in the modern era. The Aryans' sacred scriptures contain a wealth of detail about their daily life, philosophical ideas and religious practices. Frequent references to Agni, the "God of Fire", and Indra, the "Fort Breaker", are indicative of violent encounters with the dark-skinned indigenous inhabitants of northern India, known as *Dasa* or *Dasyus*, whom the warrior bands swept aside in their slow expansion eastwards over the middle of the second millennium BC. These conquests were facilitated by the Aryans' use of horse-drawn, spoke-wheeled **chariots**, an incomparably fast and effective way of crossing the dry plains.

By the dawn of the **Iron Age** early in the first millennium BC, the dominion of the Aryans, by now a loose confederacy of tribes who fought each other as much as their indigenous enemies, stretched south as far as the Vindhya Range and the rich soils of the Deccan Plateau. Beyond lay the wild unexplored territory of **Dakshinapatha**, "the Way South", blocked by dense forests and ravine-scarred hills.

Sanskritization of the South

The Rig Veda records the reluctance of the Ayrans to press south along this route, but it is clear that some of their priests (brahmins) and wandering ascetics (*rishis*) did, probably in search of patronage. Along with their sacred verses, Vedic philosophies and knowledge of iron, they took with them concepts of racial discrimination derived from centuries of war with the Dasyus, who by this time seem to have become a sub-class below the three existing grades in Aryan society: priests (brahmins), warriors (*kshatriyas*) and artisans (*vaishyas*). A product of the transition from nomadic to settled society, the **caste** system – based on notions of **varna**, or colour, and ritual pollution – seemed to have found favour among the tribal chiefs of southern India, who deployed the new ideas and scriptures of the brahmins to legitimize their rule.

The transmission of cultural influences from north to south was slow but pervasive. By the sixth century BC, brahmanical philosophies formed the religious bedrock of the many petty chiefdoms and larger principalities that had proliferated in the South, where village culture had by now firmly taken root under the tutelage of the brahmins – a way of life that would remain largely intact in the region for another two thousand years.

The Mauryan era

In the Gangetic basin, meanwhile, small tribal kingdoms (*janapadas*) were beginning to merge with others to form larger confederacies (*mahajanapadas*) governed by single rulers from fortified capitals. Two new reforming religious movements were also gaining ground in the North. The first, **Buddhism** (see p.677), arose from the teachings of a young prince from the Nepalese foot-hills, Siddharta, or **Gautama Buddha** (563–483 BC). In addition, **Jainism**, founded by the prophet **Mahavira** (599–527 BC) around the same time, began to attract followers, most notably among the ruling elite of a dynasty that was destined to become the most powerful in the subcontinent.

Stepping into the vacuum left by the departure of **Alexander the Great** from the northwest, the **Mauryans**, who ruled the region southeast of the

Ganges, usurped the throne of their arch-adversaries, the Nandas, in 320 BC to make their king, **Chandragupta Maurya**, the first *de facto* emperor of India, with control of an area stretching from the Punjab to Karnataka. A strict Jain, he eventually renounced his throne and starved himself to death on a hilltop at Sravanabelgola (still an important South Indian pilgrimage centre), thereby achieving the status of a saint.

From their capital at Pataliputra (in Bihar, near present-day Patna), the Mauryans ruled over a vast swathe of the subcontinent, greatly enlarged during the reign of Chandragupta's grandson, **Ashoka**, who defeated the mighty Kalingas on the east coast (modern Orissa). It was the bloody aftermath of that battle, in which 100,000 people were killed and 150,000 abducted, that the emperor embraced Buddhism and the path of non-violence. Edicts proclaiming the tenets of the new imperial faith were erected throughout the empire, and missionaries and ambassadors dispatched to spread the message of "right conduct", or *dhamma*, abroad. No such edicts, however, have so far come to light further south than the goldfields around Mysore, and it seems likely that most of the Deccan and peninsular India, including all of modern Andhra Pradesh, Kerala and Tamil Nadu, remained outside Mauryan influence.

The Mauryans may never have conquered the far south, but their way of life and system of government strongly influenced developments in the region. Through trade and interaction with Jain and Buddhist monk-missionaries, concepts of statehood gradually filtered south, encouraging the dominant powers in the peninsula to expand their realms.

Dravidadesa: the early kingdoms

Inscribed on the eight rock-cut edicts that Ashoka raised on the frontiers of his empire in the third century BC are verses expressing goodwill towards his "undefeated neighbours" (*avijita*). The list includes the earliest known references to the three ancient ruling clans who dominated the far south in the final centuries of the first millennium BC: the **Cholas** of the Coromandel region and Kaveri basin; the **Pandyas**, whose capital was at Madurai; and the **Cheras**, from southwest Kerala. Collectively, the kingdoms of these three dynasties comprised a domain known to northerners as **Dravidadesa**, "Land of the Tamils".

A wealth of historical detail relating to the early kingdoms of the South has survived, most of it in a remarkable body of classical Tamil poetry known as the **Sangam**, composed between the first and third centuries AD in the literary academies (*sangam*) of Madurai. The texts, which were only rediscovered in the nineteenth century, refer to an era when the indigenous Dravidian culture of the deep south was being transformed by Sanskritic influences from the North. Nevertheless, they vividly demonstrate that some of the most distinctive characteristics of Indian civilization – including yoga, *tantra*, the cult of the god Murugan and goddess worship – were almost certainly indigenous to the South, and widespread well before the Aryans came to dominate the region completely.

The Sangam also records the stormy political relations between the three dynasties, who were frequently at war with each other, or with the rulers of neighbouring Sri Lanka. Ultimately, however, all three seem to have succumbed to an enigmatic fourth dynasty, the **Kalabhras**, about whom the Sangam poems say very little other than that they were "bad kings" (*kaliarasar*). Buddhist texts from a later period suggest the Kalabhras were originally hill tribes who swept down from the Deccan Plateau to harass the inhabitants of the river valleys and coastal areas, and later took up Jainism and Buddhism, deposing the Dravidian kings and persecuting the brahmins.

The expansion of trade

The cultural flowering of the Sangam era in the south, during the first two centuries AD, was stimulated by a rapid growth in **maritime trade** throughout the region. As well as Arab merchants, the ports of the Malabar and Coromandel coasts now began to welcome **Roman** ships. After a century of relentless civil war, peace had returned to Rome, bringing with it renewed demand in the imperial capital for luxury goods such as pearls, spices, perfumes, precious stones and silk. When Augustus conquered Egypt to open up the Red Sea, and Hippalus discovered that the monsoon winds would blow a ship from there across the Arabian Sea in around a fortnight, the means to supply this appetite for exotic oriental merchandise was within the Romans' grasp.

A vivid picture of the boom that ensued has survived in an extraordinary mariners' manual entitled the *Periplus of the Erythraean Sea*, written by an anonymous Alexandrian merchant-adventurer. Featuring meticulous descriptions of the trade, ports and capital cities of the far south, it reveals that the region was an entrepôt for valuable foreign goods – notably Chinese silk and oil from the Gangetic basin – and that the Coromandel was gradually eclipsing the Malabar as peninsular India's principal trade platform.

This fact was borne out by Mortimer Wheeler's discovery of the Romans' main trading post at **Arikamedu**, just south of modern Pondicherry in Tamil Nadu, where large brick buildings, water reservoirs, baths and a huge number of artefacts – including shards of pre-Christian ceramics from Arezzo and hoards of coins – suggest it was largely the lust for Roman gold that fuelled the ancient trade in the South. Indeed, the Roman chronicler, Strabo, famously complained that the Indian merchants were threatening to completely empty the treasuries of Rome of gold coins. Prodigious quantities of these have been unearthed in recent times, especially in the area around the ancient port of **Muziris**, near present-day Kannur in northern Kerala.

The Satavahanas

Coupled with the advances in knowledge of state administration made by the Mauryans, the vast trade wealth pouring into South India around the turn of the millennium enabled the region's rulers to create larger and more organized kingdoms, backed by well-equipped armies. Conditions were ripe for the rise of a major power, and this came in the first century BC with the advent of the **Satavahanas**, an obscure tribal dynasty from the Deccan who, in the space of a hundred years, assumed the imperial mantle of the Mauryans. By the time Ptolemy was writing his *Geography*, midway through the second century AD, the empire, based in **Pratisthana** (near modern Paithan in Maharashtra), comprised thirty fortified cities and stretched from coast to coast. Administered by a network of noblemen, it was upheld by semi-autonomous military garrisons, with an army said by the Roman chronicler Pliny to consist of 30,000 cavalry and 9000 war elephants.

Thanks to their control of the region's lucrative foreign trade, the Satavahanas (or Andhras, as they are referred to in some ancient texts) were also prolific patrons of the arts, responsible for the greatest monuments in India at that time, notably the famous ornamental gateways (*toranas*) of the Buddhist stupa at **Sanchi** (in Madhya Pradesh) and many of the most accomplished rock-cut caves of the northwest Deccan. However, the crowning glory of Andhran art was to be the Great Stupa complex at **Amaravati**, in Andhra Pradesh (see p.597), whose exquisite bas-reliefs (some of which are now housed in the Government Museum, Chennai; see p.455) are considered by many scholars to be the finest ancient Indian sculpture.

The Early Middle Ages: 600–1200 AD

The history of the early middle ages in South India, from the time of the Satavahanas' demise to the arrival of the Muslims, revolves around the rise and fall of a mosaic of **regional dynasties**. These invariably fought each other to gain supremacy for short periods, and then found their rule usurped by one or other of their adversarial neighbours. Not until the sword of Islam descended on the Deccan in the thirteenth century did the peninsula succumb to a single overlord.

Various theories have been advanced to explain this, but the most convincing is that the warring kingdoms were generally too small to exert control over large territories for long. Bringing rebellious chiefdoms to heel meant costly military expeditions, which would inevitably render the ruler's own region vulnerable to attack. Despite this, the ongoing power balance mitigated against the rise of an empire and the long-term political stability it afforded allowed for the development of distinct regional cultures. The wealth of historic monuments scattered across South India today graphically exemplifies the differences between these cultures, and the way in which they interacted over the centuries.

Chalukyas, Pallavas and Cholas

Foremost among the states of the southern Deccan were the **Chalukyas**, who had been underlings of the Kadambas (Hindu rulers of the region that later became Goa) until **Pulakeshin I** broke away and founded a capital at Vatapi (**Badami**; see p.318). Here, atop a rocky escarpment overlooking a lake, the king and his descendants erected a series of magnificent stone temples. From simple rock-cut excavations, these evolved into more sophisticated free-standing structures, embellished with elaborate iconographic sculpture, which were among the first buildings in the region to fuse indigenous architectural styles with those of northern India. The Chalukyas' conspicuous wealth inevitably attracted the attentions of their neighbours. After fending off two invasions, they eventually succumbed in 753 AD to the **Rashtrakutas**, whose domain extended most of the way across the Deccan.

The Chalukyas' southern enemies, the **Pallavas**, emerged after defeating the Kalabhras, the "bad kings" who originally routed the region's three early dynasties. Originally Buddhists, they converted to brahmanism sometime in the fifth century and thereafter carved out a kingdom that would spread from the mouth of the River Krishna to the edge of the Kaveri basin in the South. From the outset, the Pallavas seem to have been keen seafarers, trading with Greeks, Satavahanas and Romans, whose coins have all been found amid the ruins of ancient **Mamallapuram** (see p.475), just south of Chennai. The extraordinary crop of stone temples, open-air bas-reliefs and finely carved caves dotted around this fishing and stone-carving village recall the era when it ranked among the busiest ports in Asia.

The majority of Mamallapuram's monuments were begun in the mid-seventh century, during the reign of Narasimha Varman I (aka Mamalla, "the Great

Wrestler"), and completed over the following two generations. Of them all, the best known is the **Shore Temple**, overlooking the beach and thought to be the first shrine built of loose stone blocks in the subcontinent. Surmounted by a steep pyramidal tower (*vimana*), it closely resembles the better preserved Kailasanatha temple in the Pallavas' former capital, **Kanchipuram**, where, in the mid-seventh century, the Chinese pilgrim Hsiuen-Tsang reported seeing one hundred Buddhist monasteries as well as eighty major Hindu temples.

The Shore Temple at Mamallapuram provided the main architectural inspiration for the **Cholas**, an offshoot of the ancient dynasty of the same name who asserted their independence from the Pallavas in 897 AD, when the latter had their hands full fighting off the Rashtrakutas. During their 250-year rule, the Cholas expanded out of their royal capital, **Thanjavur**, in the Kaveri basin, defeating both the Pandyas and Cheras, and later conquering Sri Lanka, the Maldives and the Andamans, in addition to enclaves in Java and Sumatra, which they captured in order to control trade with Southeast Asia.

Combined with the huge sums in plunder yielded by their military campaigns, the Cholas' trade monopoly financed an awesome building spree. The dynasty's most visionary ruler was **Rajaraja I** (985–1014), who erected the colossal Brihadishwara temple, in its day the largest in India. Decorating the walls of the shrine, beneath its soaring tower, exquisite frescoes recall the opulence and sophistication of the Chola court, where keen patronage of the arts – most famously bronze-casting, but also Carnatic music, sculpture, dance and literature – produced works that have never been surpassed since.

Bhakti and the Tamil poets

From the eighth century onwards, the devotional form of Hinduism known as **bhakti**, which first blossomed in Tamil Nadu, spread north into the rest of India to become, as it still is, the dominant strain of Hinduism throughout the country. This was essentially a popular movement which encouraged individual devotees to form a highly personal relationship with a chosen god (*ishtadevata*), an approach which revolutionized Hindu practice by offering a religious path and goal open to all castes.

The great champions of *bhakti* were the **poet–saints** of Tamil Nadu, often said to have "sung" the religions of Jainism and Buddhism out of South India. Although in practice a variety of deities was worshipped, the movement had two strands: the **Nayanmars**, devoted to Shiva, and the **Alvars**, faithful to Vishnu. Collections of their poetry, the greatest literary legacy of South India, remain popular today, and the poets themselves are almost deified, featuring in carvings in many temples.

The four most prominent of the 63 Nayanmar poet-saints were **Campantar**, who converted the king of Madurai from Jainism and had a great cult centre at Chidambaram; **Cuntarar**, a brahmin who had two low-caste wives; **Appar**, himself a convert from Jainism; and **Manikkavachakar**, whose mystical poems are still sung in homes and temples throughout Tamil Nadu. The Vaishnavite movement centred on Srirangam (near Trichy), its poets including men and women of all social classes. The most celebrated Alvar was **Nammalvar**, a *shudra* who spent his life in fasting and meditation. **Antal**, the most popular female Alvar, is said to have married Vishnu's statue at Srirangam, and was thereafter regarded as an incarnation of Vishnu's consort, Shri.

All the poems tell of the ecstatic response to intense experiences of divine favour, an emotion frequently described in terms of conjugal love, and expressed in verses of great tenderness and beauty. They stress selfless love between man and god, claiming that such love alone can lead to everlasting union with the divine. Devotees travelled the South, singing, dancing and challenging opponents to public debates.

Among the most significant consequences of the *bhakti* revolution in Hinduism was the emergence of **temple cities**. By stressing the importance of the individual's devotion to a particular god or goddess, *bhakti* inspired a massive upsurge in popular worship and, inevitably, a proliferation of shrines to accommodate worshippers. This process went hand in hand with the assimilation of important regional deities into the Hindu pantheon. Thus, trees, rocks, caves or bodies of water held sacred in a given place began to be "legitimized" through identification with Shiva or Vishnu. Notable examples include the deities of Chidambaram and Madurai, two of South India's most important religious centres, whose importance was firmly established well before the Sanskritization that associated them with Shiva in the sixth century.

In time, the same happened to lesser local gods and village deities, until innumerable cult centres across the South became bound in a complex web of interconnections. The institution of **pilgrimage**, linking local and distant deities, emerged as an essential element of Hinduism for the first time during the era of the Tamil saints, and has remained an important unifying force in India ever since. It is no coincidence that some of the most defining texts of the *bhakti* movement are the *Mahatmyas*, oral chants intoned by brahmins that elucidate the significance of individual temples and their relationship to other shrines.

Muslim incursions

At the start of the eleventh century, a new player appeared on the political map of northern India. **Mahmud**, a Turkish chieftain who had established a powerful kingdom at Ghazni, near Kabul in Afghanistan, made seventeen plundering raids into the plains of northern India between 1000 and 1027 AD. His was the first of many Muslim incursions from the northwest that would, after two hundred years of constant infighting and wars with local rulers, lead to the creation of an Islamic empire based in Delhi.

Founded in 1206 AD, the **Delhi Sultanate** made little impact on the South during its formative years. In 1309, however, the redoubtable Sultan **Allauddin Khilji** set his sights southwards. Having heard rumours of the treasures stored in the great Tamil temples (Rajaraja had not long before donated 880kg of gold to the Brihadishwara temple), he took advantage of the Cholas' decline to mount a raid. It is recorded that his general, the ruthless military genius and former Hindu slave **Malik Kafur**, returned with a thousand camels bearing booty, including the famous Kohinoor diamond.

This, however, was merely a prelude to the Sultanate's second expedition of 1310–11, in the course of which Allauddin's army pressed into the deep south itself. Raiding towns and desecrating the splendid Chola temples of the Kaveri Delta, it reached Madurai on April 10, 1311, and mercilessly sacked the Pandyas' capital, massacring the few of its inhabitants who had not fled. Forewarned of Kafur's approach, many temples had hidden or buried their treasures. Some, like the eighty priceless Chola bronzes that came to light in Chidambaram in the 1960s, were rediscovered; others remain lost.

Aside from the wholesale destruction of art treasures, the main legacy of Allauddin's plunder was the creation of a short-lived **Muslim Sultanate** at Tirupparakunram (see p.542), near Madurai. Overlooking the town from the top of a huge sandstone outcrop, the tomb of its eighth and last Sultan, **Sikander Shah**, remains one of the far south's few bona fide Muslim shrines.

The Deccan Sultanates

The Delhi Sultanates possessed sufficient military strength to subdue most of India, but time and again showed themselves incapable of consolidating their territorial gains with strong administrations. In the end, the despot **Muhammed-bin-Tughluq**'s incessant wars, together with his crackpot plan to relocate the capital from Delhi to Daulatabad, 1000km south on the Deccan, saw the sultanates' reign degenerate into one of terror and profligacy. Forced by drought, famine and the threat of Moghul invasion to abandon Daulatabad and return to Delhi, Tughluq struggled until his death to hold onto power. By the mid-fourteenth century, his successor, **Feroz Shah**, had completely lost control of the Deccan.

In the wake of the Daulatabad debacle, one of Tughluq's former generals, **Zafar Shah**, aka **Bahman Shah**, saw his chance to found his own dynasty, which he located at a safe distance south of the old capital, at **Gulbarga** (in present-day northern Karnataka). The **Bahmanis'** rule lasted around two hundred years, and was as bloody as the old Delhi Sultanate's; Zafar Shah's son, Mohammed Shah (1358–73), is said to slaughtered half a million people in his wars with neighbouring states, which included the Vijayanagars, who founded their empire at around the same time (see below).

In the fifteenth century AD, the Bahmanis shifted their capital further northeast to **Bidar**, constructing a massive fortress that still survives. Under the careful stewardship of **Mahmud Gawan**, a talented prime minister who served several successive sultans, the dynasty flourished, but went into a dramatic decline after his death. The ensuing power struggle saw the governors of the four largest districts in the kingdom – Bijapur, Ahmadnagar, Bidar and Golconda – declare independence, with Bijapur eventually emerging as the major power by the sixteenth century. Their rule, however, was bedevilled by conflict with both Vijayanagar and the Portuguese; they lost the port of Goa to the latter in 1510.

The power balance between the Deccan kingdoms was decisively turned in the Muslims' favour after 1565 when, following years of fighting each other, the sultanates formed a pact to wage war on their common Hindu enemies, the **Vijayanagars** (see p.308). At the battle of Talikota that year, the alliance crushed the Hindu army and set about the most destructive sack of a city the subcontinent had ever seen. Within 21 years, however, the Deccan sultanates had succumbed completely to the might of the Moghuls.

Vijayanagar: 1346–1565

To the south of the Bahmanis' territory, the River Krishna formed the border with the mighty Hindu kingdom of **Vijayanagar**, which emerged in response to the threat of Muslim invasions. Its founders were two brothers from Andhra Pradesh, **Harihara** and **Bukka**, who were allegedly captured by Tughluq during his sack of Kampili in 1327 AD and taken as prisoners to Delhi, where they converted to Islam before being dispatched as governors to their native town to restore order after an uprising. Legend has it that the sage Vidyaranya then reconverted the brothers to Hinduism and encouraged them to defect (although some Indian historians have disputed this, claiming Harihara and Bukka were actually offshoots of the Hoysalas).

Whatever its roots, the dynasty the brothers founded on the banks of the River Tungabhadra (at modern-day Hampi; see p.308) quickly flourished. Following a series of short wars with the Hoysalas, Madurai and the Gajapatis of eastern India, the rulers of the southern kingdoms pragmatically threw in their lot with the ambitious newcomers, realizing their best chance of protection from marauding Muslims lay in a strong Hindu front to the north. This proved to be the case. At a time when the influence of Turkish, Persian and Afghan culture on northern India was most marked, the South, insulated by Vijayanagar, remained outside the sway of Islam – a fact that accounts perhaps better than anything else for the striking cultural differences that still exist between the north and the south of the subcontinent.

Vijayanagar's golden period was during the reign of **Krishna Deva Raya** (1509–29), before its monopoly over the trade in spices and Arabian horses had been undermined by the Portuguese and other European powers. While the Bijapuris were a constant and costly source of irritation, the king's well-organized administration, together with his control of some thirty or so rich ports, ensured a steady flow of wealth.

The dynastic capital, Vijayanagar ("City of Victory"), became, for an all too brief period, among the most splendid in the world. Travellers such as Domingo Paes, who stayed there between 1522 and 1524, marvelled at the opulence of its royal court, the richness of its bazaars and the sumptuousness of its festivals. Krishna Deva Raya's rule was also the period when the South acquired some of its most impressive **temple towers** (**gopuras**), erected by the king to foster loyalty among brahmins and inhabitants of distant regions over which Vijayanagar's hold was precarious.

After Krishna Deva Raya's death in 1529, internal struggles and conflicts with the Portuguese weakened the empire. However, it was the Vijayanagars' old foe, the Bijapuris, who eventually brought their glorious rule to an abrupt and bloody end. Having benefited from the Deccan Sultanates' constant feuding for more than a century, the Vijayanagars made a fatal mistake when they desecrated mosques during campaigns in the 1550s. This finally galvanized the sultans to set aside their differences and march on Vijayanagar. The armies met at Talikota in 1565. At first, the battle seemed to be going the Hindus' way, but suddenly turned against them when two of their Muslim generals defected. The Vijayanagar regent, Rama Raya, was captured and beheaded, while his brother, Tirumala, fled with what was left of the army, leaving the capital defenceless.

The ensuing sack lasted six months and reduced Asia's most illustrious city to rubble. Predictably, the Deccan sultans squabbled over the spoils and spent the next century fighting each other, leaving the region vulnerable to invasion by the Moghuls.

The Portuguese

Around the same time as Vijayanagar was enjoying its period of greatest prosperity, the harbinger of a new regional power appeared on the horizon of the Arabian Sea. Driven by the lust for "Christians and Spices", **Vasco da Gama**'s arrival on the Malabar Coast in 1498 (see box on p.648) blazed a trail that would, after only fifteen years, result in the creation of Europe's first bona fide colony in the East.

Formerly a Vijayanagar port, **Goa** had been taken by the Bahmanis, whom the Portuguese, under **Admiral Afonso de Albuquerque**, expelled in 1510. Thereafter, despite repeated attempts by the Muslims to regain their possession, the colony expanded at a breathless pace. At the height of its power, the city was the linchpin of a trade network extending from the Philippines to the north Atlantic, with cathedrals to rival Rome's and a population that at one time was greater even than Lisbon's.

Yet, despite enjoying an early monopoly on maritime trade in Asia, ruthlessly enforced by their insurmountable naval supremacy, the Portuguese were unable to sustain an early lead over their European rivals. Repeated outbreaks of disease depleted the population of Goa, while the defeat in 1565 of Vijayanagar, which by that time accounted for a significant portion of the city's trade, had a disastrous effect on the whole Portuguese economy. Unable to maintain control of the sea lanes, Portugal gradually saw its trade empire whittled away, first by the Dutch, and later by the French and British. Goa actually survived as a Portuguese colony until 1961, but was effectively a spent force by the end of the seventeenth century.

The Moghul Empire

Descendants of Timur and Genghis Khan's Mongols from Samarkhand in Central Asia, the **Moghuls** staked their claim to North India with Babur's defeat of the Delhi Sultan, Ibrahim Lodi, in 1526. Through the revolutionary deployment of small arms and mobile artillery, the invaders routed an army ten times their size. The victory inaugurated an empire that would, by the time of its demise two hundred years later, become the largest and most powerful since Ashoka's, eighteen centuries earlier. Keen patrons of the arts as well as fearsome military strategists, successive emperors blended Persian and Indian culture to create some of the subcontinent's greatest treasures, including the Red Fort in Delhi and the Taj Mahal in Agra.

Aurangzeb and the Marathas

The Moghuls' influence, however, had little impact on the South until the reign of **Shah Jahan** (1627–58), when the northernmost of the Deccan Sultanates, Ahmadnagar, was annexed. A hundred years after their sack of Vijayanagar, Bijapur and Golconda also succumbed, this time to the last of the Great Moghuls, **Aurangzeb** (1658–1707).

The most expansionist ruler of the dynasty, Aurangzeb was also a devout Sunni, notorious for his rough treatment of Hindus, and for reinstating the much-hated *jizya* tax on non-Muslims that his great-grandfather, Akbar, had repealed. Aurangzeb's arch-adversaries in the Deccan region were a confederacy of low-caste Hindu warriors called the **Marathas**. Unlike the Moghuls, they attacked not with large, formal armies, but by mounting guerrilla-style raids, retreating to the safety of impregnable fortresses perched on the top of table mountains.

Under their most audacious and gifted leader, **Shivaji**, whom Aurangzeb named "The Mountain Rat", the Marathas managed on numerous occasions to

Quincentennial controversy

On May 18, 1498, three Portuguese *caravelas* dropped anchor off the coast of northern Kerala at a beach called Kappad, having sailed from Lisbon via the Cape of Good Hope in a little over ten months. Five hundred years later, to the day, groups of angry protesters gathered on the same beach to burn effigies of the explorer who had led that expedition, **Vasco da Gama**. By rounding the tip of Africa and opening up a maritime route to the spice markets of western India, da Gama would change the pattern of world history, for which he has been feted as a national hero ever since by the Portuguese public. In India, however, he is reviled as a pirate and looter, who committed acts of appalling barbarism out of greed for "black gold" – the pepper of the Malabar Coast.

While the ramifications of da Gama's voyages remain a subject of heated debate, the essential facts of his three expeditions to India have survived, thanks to the diaries of Alvaro Velho, one of da Gama's soldiers. These describe in detail how the small fleet of five ships set sail from Lisbon in July 1497, with an aura of messianic resolve as the sacred symbol of Christ billowed in their sails. Their route took them around the islands of Cabo Verde (Cape Verde) and four thousand miles southeast to round the Cape of Good Hope at the beginning of November.

At Malindi, da Gama was granted the services of an expert navigator, an Arab sea captain called **Ibn' Masjid**, who piloted the three remaining *caravelas* across the Indian Ocean to Calicut. However, news of atrocities committed by the Portuguese en route had preceded their arrival, and the local *zamorin*, Mana Vikrama, briefly imprisoned da Gama before he was allowed to fill his holds with pepper and leave – an insult the proud Portuguese admiral would never forget.

Four years later he returned to Calicut, this time bent on revenge. In addition to what he perceived as his own "contumely treatment" at the hands of the Hindu ruler, he intended to avenge the murder of 53 Portuguese killed during a previous expedition in 1500. As a prelude to the onslaught, da Gama waylaid a Muslim ship en route from Mecca and burned alive all 700 of its passengers and crew. Then he set about

outwit the Moghul's superior forces, and over time came to dominate a large chunk of western India. The year of Shivaji's death in 1680, Aurangzeb's son, Akbar, slipped south from Delhi to form an alliance with his opposite number, with whose help he hoped to overthrow his father. But the plot ended in a heavy defeat for the usurper and his Hindu allies. Soon afterwards, Aurangzeb moved his court from Delhi to Aurangabad in order to personally supervise the subjugation of the Marathas. It was from there, too, that he mounted the victorious campaigns against Bijapur and Golconda which would extend Moghul rule to its eventual highwater mark.

Aurangzeb may have pushed the empire's boundaries further south than any of his predecessors, but his policies ultimately brought about the dynasty's downfall. To win over the nobles of his new acquisitions in the Deccan, the emperor demanded lower taxes from them, which left an administrative shortfall that he subsequently made up for by over-taxing his farmers. This duly provoked **peasant uprisings**, made more deadly by the proliferation of small arms at that time, which Aurangzeb's cumbersome, elephant-based army was ill suited to quell. In addition, the burden on the shattered Deccan states of reprovisioning an army whose annual losses were calculated at 100,000 men and around 300,000 animals was enormous. In 1702–3, famine and pestilence wiped out an estimated two million people in the region.

After the last Great Moghul's death in 1707, half a century of gradual decay was presided over by a succession of eight incompetent emperors. The final bombarding the city. While the cannonade decimated Calicut's temples and houses, da Gama ordered the crews of a dozen or so trade ships anchored in the harbour to be rounded up. Before killing them, he had the prisoners' hands, ears and noses hacked off and the pieces sent ashore piled in a small boat.

This horrific act set the precedent, and genocide became a hallmark of early Portuguese colonialism in Asia, as the Europeans extended their trade links up the South Indian coast to Goa. And so it was with some astonishment that, five centuries later, Goan nationalist politicians and journalists greeted Portugal's invitation to participate in the festivities marking the quincentennial of Vasco da Gama's voyage. Quite apart from those original atrocities, Goan freedom fighters, who had struggled to oust the Portuguese, found it particularly absurd that they should now be expected to celebrate the start of their rule. An organization called **Deshpremi Samiti** was duly formed to campaign against the celebrations, stirring up acrimonious debate in the Goan press.

The controversy eventually came to a head with the Kerala Tourism Development Corporation's announcement that they were intending to stage a full-blown re-enactment of da Gama's landing, complete with wooden replicas of the three *caravelas* and tourists acting the parts of Portuguese mariners. The plans provoked large protest marches in Goa, and the Delhi government was forced to issue a statement saying India would not under any circumstances participate in the so-called "celebrations" of 1498.

In the event, the anniversary passed off peacefully, though clearly the raking over of da Gama's unsavoury conduct did little to enhance relations between India and its first colonizer. Significantly, however, the controversy did serve to fix in Indian minds a parallel between the exploitation of colonial times and the activities of today's multinationals, who use current trade agreements to open up emerging markets in India. It is no coincidence that alongside the effigies of Vasco da Gama being burned on Kappad beach were others of Coca-Cola and Pepsi bottles.

blow to the Moghul dynasty came in 1779, when the Persian Nadir Shah raided Delhi and made off with a vast loot that included the Peacock Throne itself. "The streets", wrote one eyewitness, "were strewn with corpses like a garden with weeds. The city was reduced to ashes and looked like a burnt plain."

Dutch, British and French

The Portuguese domination of the Indian Ocean was complete by the time Babur descended on Delhi, and neither he nor his Moghul successors felt in the least threatened by the presence of foreign powers on their coastal borders. In fact, they welcomed the traders as providers of silver and gold which they could use to mint money. In the course of the seventeenth and eighteenth centuries, however, the European powers would become a force to be reckoned with, eventually replacing the Moghuls as India's rulers.

The first challengers of the Portuguese trade supremacy were the **Dutch**, whose cheaper and more manoeuvrable *fluyt* ships easily outsailed the more old-fashioned, ungainly *caravelas* from Lisbon. Determined not to allow Asia to be carved up by the proselytizing Roman Catholics, the Protestant Dutch East India Company – founded in 1602, only a couple of decades after Holland's victorious war of independence over Spain – systematically took control of the international spice trade, relieving the Portuguese of the strategically essential Molaccas in 1641, Ceylon in 1663 and their chief ports on the Malabar Coast soon after.

Although established two years before its Dutch counterpart, the British East India Company lagged behind initially, operating on a more modest scale with a fleet of smaller, privately run ships. Following the example of the Dutch, they set up a string of trading posts, or **factories**, around the coast, where goods – mostly **textiles** – could be stored awaiting annual shipment. Its first head-quarters (from 1612), in Surat, Gujarat, was relocated to Bombay (Mumbai) in 1674, and by the mid-seventeenth century the British possessed 27 such outposts, the largest being **Fort St George** on the Coromandel Coast – the forerunner of Madras (modern Chennai). Over time, as the nature of the textile trade in India changed, the factories evolved from mere warehouses into large financial centres whose influence spread far inland. Gradually, communities of weavers settled around them, while growing numbers of recruits arrived to staff ever-expanding administrations and the military apparatus required to protect them.

The greatest threat to Britain's early Indian colonies was not local rulers, but rival Europeans. In the case of Fort St George, the **French** – whose own East India Company, started in 1664, was based further south on the Coromandel Coast at **Pondicherry** – were to prove the most troublesome. Initially, agree-ments between the two rival companies forestalled any armed encounters. But with the outbreak of the War of the Austrian Succession in 1740, Britain and France found themselves members of opposing coalitions in a conflict which, although rooted in central Europe, proved a turning point in the history of South Asia.

The first clash between France and Britain came in 1746 when the French governor of Pondicherry, wily diplomat **Joseph François Dupleix**, captured Fort St George with the help of a French fleet commanded by **Admiral La Bourdonnais**. Among those imprisoned during the short French occupation (the fort was handed back two years later) was a young East India Company clerk whose humiliation at the hands of the French is often used to explain his sudden career change from pen-pushing to soldiering. Considered one of the founders of the British Raj, **Robert Clive** cut his military teeth in the politi-cally unstable Carnatic region around Madras.

Dupleix had long since learned that the best way to extend French influence, and trade, was to forge alliances with whichever local ruler looked likely to emerge victorious from the furious in-fighting that wracked the South during the break-up of the Moghul empire. In this way, the British and the French were drawn into the conflicts of regional rulers, often facing each other from opposite ends of a battlefield.

In one such encounter, where the European powers pitched in to support rival sons of the Nawab of **Arcot** in 1751, Clive, then only 26 years old, distinguished himself by holding a breached and sprawling fortress for fifty days with only two hundred men against a vastly superior force of 15,000 French and their Indian allies. The first great triumph of British arms in the history of India, this feat made Clive a hero, a reputation he consolidated soon afterwards by marching through the monsoons to intervene decisively at the siege of **Trichinopoly**. The French lost half their army in this second battle, and saw their protégé, Chandra Sahib, captured and killed. Dupleix's reputation never recovered; he was recalled two years later and died destitute.

The British went on to defeat the French again at Wandiwash in 1760, and finally took Pondicherry after an eight-month siege, effectively bringing to an end the French bid for power in India. For Robert Clive, the Carnatic war was but a local skirmish compared to the significance of his later achievements in Bengal, where his victory at **Plassey** in 1757 laid the foundations of a British rule that would last for two hundred years. It did, however, teach him and his compatriots lessons that would serve them well in the future: not least of all, how effective a relatively small number of highly disciplined troops could be against a far larger, but undisciplined, army.

Haider Ali and Tipu Sultan of Mysore

After the heavy defeats in the Carnatic, the French were certainly down, but they were not yet quite out, thanks to the one remaining thorn in the side of British territorial ambitions: **Haider Ali**. A former general of the Maharaja of Mysore, Haider Ali had usurped his master's throne in 1761 and within a short time ruled over virtually the entire South. The secret of his dramatic success lay in his readiness to learn from the Europeans, in particular the French, whose military tactics he emulated, and who provided him with officers to train his infantry. Between 1767 and 1769, he fought a series of battles with the British, whom he had always, unlike other Indian rulers, regarded as a threat to India as a whole, and whom he eventually coerced into a highly favourable treaty after threatening to attack Madras.

Held back by corrupt officials in both Madras and Calcutta, the British failed to provide a robust response, but rallied during the governorship of **Warren Hastings**. In 1778, they were once again at war with the French, and fending off Marathas in the west, which Haider Ali took as his cue to launch a major offensive. Assisted by the French, who landed troops by sea to join the battle, Haider again forced the British to sue for peace.

This was far from the most honourable period in the imperial history of France and Britain. During their various marches and skirmishes across the Carnatic, temples were regularly desecrated and massacres were commonplace; in all, a million Tamils were killed. On one occasion, four hundred wounded Hindu women were raped by rioting British soldiers, while in the Kaveri region, the French general, Lally, fired brahmin priests from his cannons for refusing to tell him where their temple treasure was hidden.

After Haider's death in 1782, his son **Tipu Sultan**, aka "the Tiger of Mysore", carried on his father's campaigns, but did so with diminished support from the French, who had by this time begun to wind down their Indian operations. In the end, Tipu Sultan was let down badly by his father's former allies. In 1799, they failed to dispatch troops to reinforce him when an army, led by Lord Wellesley and his brother Arthur (later the Duke of Wellington, of Waterloo fame) marched on **Srirangapatnam**. Tipu Sultan died defending a breach in his capital's walls (a story that later inspired Wilkie Collins's novel, *The Moonstone*), and Mysore was returned to the old Hindu dynasty Haider Ali had deposed. After more than a century of continual conflict between the European powers and their various allies, the struggle for control of India was finally won by the British.

British rule in the South

Following their victory at Srirangapatnam, the British, under Hastings' successor, **Lord Cornwallis**, annexed the coastal areas and interior plains that had been under Tipu Sultan's sway, settling down to a period of relatively trouble-free rule. Stretching from the Telegu-speaking region of present-day Andhra Pradesh to the Malabar Coast, the **Madras Presidency** was a notoriously "hands-off" regime, with vast administrative districts on which colonial officers could make very little impact. Life basically continued as it had before the advent of the British Raj. Unlike in the North, where the economic changes brought about by the Industrial Revolution in Britain had a huge impact, the South's output was geared towards domestic consumption; when the Lancashire mills forced the bottom out of the cotton industry in Bengal, the weavers of Madras were largely unaffected.

Nevertheless, resentment at British rule was not confined to the northern plains, where the so-called **Indian Mutiny** (redubbed "the First War of Independence" by nationalist politicians) broke out in Lucknow in 1857. **Uprisings** also occurred in forest regions of Andhra Pradesh, and the Mopilah Muslims of the Malabar mounted small insurrections. Generally, however, opposition to the British came not from low-caste or tribal populations, but ironically from members of the English-speaking, university-educated elite in Madras, where the nineteenth century saw the emergence of a nascent **nationalist movement**. Based at the Theosophical Society's headquarters in Adyar, Annie Besant's Home Rule League openly objected to the colonial regime, while publications such as *The Hindu* spread the nationalist message among the literate classes.

The South since Independence

Independence passed off relatively peacefully in South India in 1947, as the North succumbed to the horrors of Partition. With the exception of the Nizam of Hyderabad, who tried to retain his dominions and had to be ousted by the new Indian army (see box on p.582), the Princely States – namely Cochin, Travancore and Mysore – acceded gracefully to the Indian Union. Although deprived of their privy purses and most of their land, many of the former rulers used their privileged backgrounds to secure powerful roles in their new states, becoming members of parliament or industrialists.

The dissolution of British rule also generated an upsurge in regional sentiments. In the South, calls to restructure state boundaries along linguistic lines gained pace, culminating in the 1956 **State Reorganization Act**, when the region was divided into four main states: the Kannada-speaking area became Mysore (later changed to Karnataka); the Telegu zone made up Andhra Pradesh; the former Tamil region of the Madras Presidency became Madras (subsequently renamed Tamil Nadu); and Kerala was created from the Malayalam-speaking Malabar coastal zone. Goa, meanwhile, remained under Portuguese control until 1961, when India's first prime minister, **Jawaharlal Nehru**, lost his patience with the Portuguese dictator Salazar and sent in the troops.

From the start, Nehru vociferously opposed the creation of language-based states, predicting such a move would lead to fragmentation, schisms and regionalism. The political upheavals of the past fifty years have proved him right. With the rise in popularity of the pro-Dravidian **DMK** in Tamil Nadu and the **Telegu Desam** in Andhra Pradesh, the South's political scene has been completely dominated by **regional parties** in one guise or another, reflecting widespread mistrust of central government rule from Delhi. This has been most vehemently expressed in resistance to the imposition of Hindi – the most widely spoken language in northern India – as the medium of education and law. As these parties gained larger shares of the vote, state-specific issues and calls for greater regional autonomy have increasingly dominated the political agendas of all four states.

Caste and communal conflict

The period since Independence has also seen a marked rise in **caste conflict**. Caste (see p.669) has always been more firmly rooted in South Indian society than the more Muslim-influenced north, but political legislation passed over the previous two decades to encourage greater participation in government and education of low, tribal and "Other Backward Castes" (OBCs) has does little to erase these age-old social divisions. Adopted in 1950, the Constitution of India paved the way for laws to combat caste discrimination, with clauses obliging the states to implement policies of "positive discrimination". "Untouchables" and OBCs were given **quotas** in educational institutions, parliament, regional assemblies and state sector jobs.

The Mandal Commission, set up in 1979 to look at the impact of quotas, came out strongly in favour of positive discrimination, and in August 1990 Prime Minister **V.P. Singh** announced that his party would implement its recommendations. Cynics accused him of trying to poach the Muslim and low-caste vote blocks from the opposition Congress Party, but the ensuing backlash was a strong contributory factor in the downfall of V.P. Singh's Janata Dal coalition in the elections of 1991.

The issue of quotas remains a contentious one in the South. "Affirmative action" policies, as quotas have been euphemistically dubbed, have certainly increased the level of scheduled caste participation in government, but they have had some negative effects too. Inevitably, sought-after university places and public sector jobs are often granted to unqualified people instead of better qualified members of higher castes, creating sectarian resentment that has increasingly spilled into violence. Several times in the past decade, violent clashes between brahmins and low-caste farmers have led to whole districts of Tamil Nadu being placed under martial law.

The other harmful repercussion of positive discrimination has been the **politicization** of caste. In order to be elected or to form power-wielding coalitions, Indian politicians these days have to galvanize **vote banks** – blocks of support from specific caste or ethnic groups. In return, these vote banks look to their leaders to advance their agendas in government, a process that all too often results in national or state interests being subordinated to the demands of minority groups.

With the expansion of the quota system under Prime Minister **Narasimha Rao** in 1994 to include disadvantaged Muslims and other "ethnic" minorities, state and national politics have become increasingly dominated not only by caste, but by communal issues – precisely the kind of sectarianism that the Mandal report and India's resolutely secular constitution sought to eradicate.

The South has traditionally been spared the kind of **communal conflict** that has so often plagued the North. Over the past five years, however, the steady rise of communal parties, such as the far right pro-Hindu BJP, has been accompanied by violent confrontations between Hindus and Muslims, particularly in Tamil Nadu. The spiralling violence came to a head on February 14, 1998, when fifteen bombs exploded in crowded districts of Coimbatore, killing sixty people. The Home Affairs Minister and BJP leader at that time, L.K. Advani, was due to address a rally in the city, which the Islamic extremist organization **Al-Umma** decided to use as a pretext to settle communal scores for earlier attacks on Muslims in the region.

Tamil nationalism and the war in Sri Lanka

The highest profile victim of communal violence in India since the assassination of Mahatma Gandhi by Hindu extremists in 1948 was the former prime minister **Rajiv Gandhi** (son of Indira), killed while electioneering in Tamil Nadu on May 21, 1991 in reprisal for his role in the civil war in neighbouring Sri Lanka – a conflict that has dominated foreign policy in the south over the past eighteen years and made a lasting impression on the coastal regions of Tamil Nadu.

The **ethnic conflict** between the majority (Buddhist) Sinhalese and minority Tamil populations of Sri Lanka erupted into full-scale war in 1987. Following several years of escalating clashes between Sri Lankan government forces and the Liberation Tigers of Tamil Eelam (LTTE – popularly known as the Tamil Tigers), Sri Lankan president J. R. Jayawardene sent the Sri Lankan Army in against the LTTE stronghold on the Jaffna peninsula in the north of the island. Prime Minister Rajiv Gandhi, under pressure from Indian Tamils concerned at the treatment of their fellow Tamils in Sri Lanka, began talks with the Jayawardene government, and in July 1987 the two countries signed a peace accord, part of which permitted the Indian army to intervene and disarm the LTTE. In the event, however, India became bogged down in a messy war with the LTTE, with high casualties on both sides – it was this debacle, with Indian troops fighting Tamil guerillas, which led to Rajiv Gandhi's assassination. Millions of Tamil refugees, meanwhile, poured across the Palk Straits to settle in camps around Rameshwaram, Tamil Nadu, where they remain, despite the end to hostilities on the island in 2002.

India was only able to extricate itself after the defeat of Rajiv Gandhi in the 1989 elections, following which, in March 1990, the new government withdrew all troops from the island. It was during the campaign for the following elections, in May 1991, that Rajiv and sixteen others were **assassinated** by a female suicide bomber. Seven years later, an Indian court convicted 26 people for the killing – all were Sri Lankan militants or Indian allies of the LTTE conspirators.

Ripples from the war in Sri Lanka have also had a marked influence on political life in the Tamil Nadu, home to an estimated 60 million Tamil speakers. Following its resounding defeat in the wake of Rajiv's assassination, when it was accused of harbouring and training **separatist guerrillas** to fight the war, the **DMK**, the then dominant (Tamil nationalist) party, has had to distance itself from the LTTE. Its increasingly high profile within central government also required it to adhere to New Delhi's "hands off" line. In the background, however, DMK ministers and parliament representatives in the capital were able to exert influence over foreign policy, keeping Indian troops out of the war and banning pro-Tiger demonstrations. Tamil Nadu's previous Chief Minister, M. Karunanidhi, had an additional reason to downplay his party's connections with the LTTE. Through the late 1990s, he made several speeches insisting that the Tigers should not be seen as the only legitimate representatives of the Tamil people, hinting that he saw himself as a potential pan-Tamil leader if and when the north of Sri Lanka ever gained independence. At the same time, Tamil nationalist leaders such as Karunanidhi could not afford to overtly oppose the LTTE, who command huge popular support in Tamil Nadu, and thus considerable influence at election time. The other main party to have ruled the state, the **AIADMK**, led by the maverick ex-film starlet **Jayalalitha** (see p.457), have consistently exploited this fact to kindle support, forming coalitions with more openly pro-Tiger nationalist parties and leaders.

The rise of the BJP

With the demise of the Congress Party (and corresponding rise of the pro-Hindu, nationalist BJP) throughout the 1990s, politics at national level became increasingly fragmented. No longer dominated by a single party, the succession of short-lived governments in New Delhi tended to be formed by shaky coalitions, brought together by political expediency more than any common agenda. Thus regionalist parties such as the pro-Tamil DMK and AIADMK, who had for decades enjoyed massive support in their home state but wielded disproportionately little influence at national level, emerged as a potent new force.

The strength of this new political element was dramatically demonstrated in the wake of the 1998 national elections, won by a BJP-led coalition. To bring it down, Congress – now led by Sonia Gandhi, the Italian-born widow of the former prime minister Rajiv Gandhi – collaborated with Jayalalitha, leader of the AIADMK. When she pulled out of the BJP-led coalition, Prime Minister Vajpayee lost a vote of no confidence and was forced to call yet another general election in April 1999 – the third in three years.

At the start of the campaign, Congress hopes were high that with a Gandhi once again as party leader, it could revive the popular support lost after years of in-fighting and corruption scandals. Moreover, to compound the BJP's problems, Vajpayee's caretaker government was saddled with a worsening financial deficit and a welter of domestic difficulties. Events took an unexpected turn following a sudden and dramatic flare up in the long-standing **border war** between India and Pakistan in Kashmir.

While the world was preoccupied with NATO's bombing of Belgrade, at least 800 Pakistani fighters crept across the so-called Line of Control (the de facto border) overlooking the Srinagar–Leh road near **Kargil**. India's response was to move thousands of troops and heavy artillery into the area, swiftly followed up with an aerial bombardment. Within days the two countries were poised on the brink of all-out war, only months after both had successfully tested long-range nuclear missiles. In the event the conflict was contained, but Pakistan took a bloody nose from the encounter, and by July 1999 the Indian army had retaken all the ground previously lost to the militants. An estimated 700 Pakistani and 330 Indian soldiers died before the Pakistani premier, Nawaz Sharif, bowed to international pressure and withdrew his forces.

The wave of patriotism that swept India after the 1998 nuclear tests and then the Kargil victory was a godsend for Vajpayee (cynics argued it may well have been the hidden policy behind the army's uncompromising response to the crisis). Riding high on the feel-good factor, his party inflicted the biggest defeat Congress had sustained since it first came to power in 1947. Vajpayee's majority was far from as large as he might have hoped, and the BJP-led **National Democratic Alliance** (**NDA**) coalition was fractured and tenuous. But those who gleefully interpreted Sonia's second election defeat as the end of dynastic politics in India were to be proved wrong in the most dramatic fashion only five year later.

Having betrayed the former BJP government, Jayalalitha, meanwhile, was capitulated into something of a political wilderness, with her party soundly beaten by a BJP-led coalition that included the DMK, led by her arch rival, the then chief minister of Tamil Nadu, **M. Karunanidhi**. No longer a minister, she lacked protection against the raft of **corruption** charges dating from the period when she was the state's chief minister (1991–96). Finally, in October 2000, the High Court in Chennai (Madras) found her guilty of accepting bribes from businessmen to permit illegal construction projects, and issued a three-year suspended prison sentence. In the riots that followed 5000 demonstrators were arrested, as Jayalalitha's supporters set fire to a bus full of students, killing three innocent women – an incident filmed and broadcast by Star TV news.

The new millennium

To rub salt in Jayalalitha's wounds, her appeal against the conviction was quashed by the High Court of Chennai in April 2001, casting doubts on whether she would be able to run in the state assembly **elections** the following month (Indian electoral law debars candidates who've been sentenced to a prison term of more than two years). However, the ruling only seems to have intensified her desire to get even with her arch adversary, Karunanidhi. Despite having her nomination papers rejected by the election officials, "Jaya", as the redoubtable ex-starlet is known to her fans, announced she would run anyway, expecting that the corruption charges could be overturned at a later date. In the build up to the election, her AIADMK-led coalition comprised the Tamil Maanila Congress, the (overtly pro-Tamil Tiger) Pattali Makkal Katchi (or PMK), two communist parties and two Muslim parties.

From the outset, the thrust of Jayalalitha's campaign was to personally target Karunanidhi, now heading a sixteen-party coalition dominated by the DMK and BJP. Speeches appealing to the memory of her former lover, matinee idol and charismatic chief minister, the late M.G. Ramchandran (aka "MGR"; see p.456), depicted her as a lone woman persecuted by a regime hell-bent on keeping her out of public life. On several occasions she even vowed that if she were re-elected she would incarcerate Karunanidhi in the same cell she'd been locked up in, and make him eat off the same tin plate. Jayalalitha's **vendetta** seemed to capture the imagination of Tamil voters, who returned her coalition with a landslide majority. The new chief minister wasted no time in settling scores with her opponents, ordering Karunanidhi's arrest on corruption charges, along with that of around one thousand of his supporters. Television audiences across the country were shocked by film footage of the then 78-year-old former chief minister being roughly pulled down the stairs of his house by police and bundled into a van by police. The indignity of the arrest, followed by that of two federal cabinet ministers who tried to intervene, caused a political storm in Delhi. The governor of the state, who had been criticized for allowing Jayalalitha to run despite her criminal record, was sacked and pressure applied to secure Karunanidhi's release.

This came a few days later (having been allegedly granted "on humanitarian grounds"), but the ageing former premier had to face the charges that he accepted bribes from road constructors in Chennai while in power. Violent protests accompanied the dispute. One Tamil farmer burned himself to death in protest at Karunanidhi's arrest, and a purge of Jayalalitha's political opponents followed her election. A high-ranking BJP government official, despatched by prime minister Vajpayee from New Delhi to investigate the situation, reported that "no law of the land prevails in Tamil Nadu".

To the brink of war

Political life in early years of the new millennium may have been dominated by the power struggle between Jayalalitha and Karunanidhi, but the foreign media was at the time more enthralled by the exploits of the sandalwood bandit **Veerappan** (see p.574) who demonstrated his legendary elusiveness by kidnapping South India's most famous living matinee idol, **Rajkumar**, in 2000. Despite a massive manhunt, the luxuriantly mustachioed brigand remained at large in the forests lining the Karnatakan, Keralan and Tamil Nadu borders, and held on to his hostage for 107 days, during which time protest riots by fans brought Bangalore to a standstill on several occasions. Following Rajkumar's release, secured in a shady deal involving payment of undisclosed sums by state politicians to the bandit, Veerappan and his band slipped back into the jungle. The hunt for him was stepped up in December 2002, after the decomposing body of another of his hostages, a senior politician, was discovered, but the failure of the crack National Security Squad to bring him to justice only fed rumours that Veerappan had somehow managed to bribe or intimidate the state's most powerful players into protecting him. It wasn't until October 20, 2004, that police finally caught up with the bandit. By then wanted for killing 130 people and 2000 elephants, Veerappan had been suffering from acute ill health, which undercover agents who had infiltrated his gang exploited to lure him into an ambush. En route to hospital in a nearby town, he and his entourage were gunned down on a deserted jungle road – the end of a manhunt which had, by its conclusion, cost the government a stagging Rs1.5 billion (£19 million).

Meanwhile, in rural South India, the start of the third millennium was marked by catastrophic **tropical storms** which ripped across the region during the monsoons. In 2000, record rainfalls wrought havoc in the southern state of Andhra Pradesh. An estimated 12 million were left marooned or homeless as river levels rose by as much as four metres in places. With transport and communications at a standstill for weeks, food distribution and rescue efforts all but ground to a halt. Riots broke out in camps set up by the army for **flood** victims, as supplies of food and plastic sheets ran out.

Ironically, only the previous year the chief ministers of Tamil Nadu and Karnataka had been locked in a bitter dispute about **water shortages** – a debate that has been rumbling on ever since. Karnataka had repeatedly withheld supplies of water on the River Kaveri, guaranteed by the terms of an accord forged by Prime Minister Vajpayee (a treaty which his party waived as a vote winner in the 1999 elections, and whose failure was a huge source of embarrassment for the BJP generally and the prime minister in particular).

Many commentators at the time regarded the fallout from the "**River Dispute**", as the Kaveri controversy has become known, as symptomatic of the **regionalism** that had long been on the rise in the South. The growth of parties such as the DMK, AIADMK and Telegu Desam has been accompanied by a marked weakening of New Delhi's grip. Incapable of forming a majority government, Atal Bihari Vajpayee's ruling BJP had to forge coalitions with, and yield concessions to, its political partners in the NDA (or National Democratic Alliance) government, which markedly increased the power of the southern states at the centre.

Domestic politics, however, took a backseat to foreign affairs in late 2001, as India entered one of the tensest periods in its troubled **relations with Pakistan**. Following the collapse of talks on **Kashmir** at a summit in Agra, a series of major terrorist attacks brought the two countries once again to the brink of full-scale war. First, the car bombing of the State Assembly building in Srinagar provoked a furious tirade from Delhi about "Pakistani-sponsored cross-border terrorism". Then, in December 2001, three Muslim gunmen mounted an **attack on the Parliament Building** in New Delhi. Having killed several police guards they were picked off by army marksmen, but the sense of outrage grew in the days afterwards. Pakistani involvement was inevitably suspected, and Vajpayee announced he was in favour of declaring war immediately. Only after some deft US and British diplomacy, and some conciliatory remarks from Islamabad, were New Delhi's ruffled feathers temporarily smoothed.

A more heated confrontation was about to erupt, though. Its catalyst was the suicide attack by *fedayin* Islamicists on an army cantonment near Jammu in April 2002; women and children numbered among the dead. This time Vajpayee was in no mood for diplomacy. Bowing to the hawks on the right of his own party, he called for a "decisive battle", initiating a massive build up of troops on the western border. An estimated million men at arms were involved in the ensuing stand-off, which was only diffused after concerted diplomacy by the US (who sent Colin Powell to lead negotiations) diffused the crisis and the armies had stood down by the end of the monsoons.

Also in the spring of 2002, India was wracked by **communal tension**, after 38 Hindu pilgrims returning by train from the disputed temple site of Ayodhya were brutally murdered by Muslim mobs in Godhra, Gujarat. The atrocity sparked off terrible reprisal massacres across the country, in which an estimated 2000 died, but the troubles did not spread to the south. Around the same time, killings of Hindus in Kashmir further strained communal relations, as did an attack in September by Islamist gunmen on the headquarters of the Swami-narayan sect, Akshardam, in Gujarat (in which 33 people were killed and 72 more injured). Yet none of these events managed to derail the peace talks over Kashmir that followed, as their perpetrators intended.

Peace talks and the Mumbai bombings

Indo-Pak negotiations over Kashmir lasted until March 2003, but were suspended by India after Islamabad announced the successful testing of its Shaheen missile, capable of delivering nuclear warheads over a distance of 750km (as far as Delhi). The talks, however, resumed in May, when Vajpayee made a **declaration of peace**, announcing that the Delhi–Lahore bus connec-tion would recommence and that hundreds of Pakistanis detained in Indian prisons since the Kargil war would be released. Pakistan responded with more "confidence-building measures", announcing that it would ease trade restric-tions, improve travel and sporting links and, later, by declaring a ceasefire along the Line of Control.

These moves paved the way for a full-blown **summit**, eventually held in Islamabad in early 2004. Watched by the world's press, President Pervez Musharaf and Atul Bihari Vajpayee posed for a historic handshake and even managed an hour-long discussion in which plans to strengthen diplomatic ties and re-open the Kashmir Highway (between Srinagar and Muzaffarabad) were mooted. In tandem with these formal dialogues, Indian officials also held behind-the-scenes talks with Kashmiri separatist leaders. Both sides emerged optimisitic and committed to a non-violent "Road Map". Not since the start of the troubles had a rapprochement between the subcontinent's old foes looked so likely to result in a definitive end to hostilities.

Neverthless, relations between Hindus and Muslims in some parts of India remained at crisis point. As the first trials of suspects accused of atrocities in the wake of the Godhra massacres reached court in Ahmedabad, the Archeologi-cal Survey of India released its long-awaited **report on Ayodhya**. Since the destruction of the Babri Masjid by Hindu extremists in 1992, debate had raged as to whether there had in fact ever been a Rama temple beneath the mosque. To no one's surprise, the ASI panel of "experts" appointed by the right-wing BJP government (prominent members of which had incited the Babri Masji destruction in the first place), declared they'd found evidence to show there had been a temple, in effect condoning the tearing down of the mosque by Hindu activists.

Opening up old wounds, the ruling did little to quel post-Godhra tensions; and when, on August 25, 2003 (the day after the Ayodhya report was published) two bombs ripped through the centre of downtown **Mumbai**, commentators were quick to identify the Babri Masjid dispute as the provocation. One of the bombs exploded in a taxi next to the Gateway of India, Mumbai's main tourist hub, killing 107 people. No one claimed responsibility, but four suspects believed to have links with Islamic militant groups were arrested soon after.

The 2004 elections

With India booming as never before and peace on the horizon in Kashmir, Prime Minister Vajpayee and his BJP-led coalition decided to cash in the perceived "feel good" factor and call a snap **election** in May 2004. "India Shining" was their slogan, but the campaign strategy boomeranged badly. True, India was experiencing a period of unparallelled economic growth, but the boom was based largely on information technology, benefiting urban professional classes, and had had little impact on the vast majority of India's population. Congress leader Sonia Gandhi was quick to seize the initiative and appealed directly to rural, poor voters to show the government what they thought of Vajpayee's vision of the country. She also played the dynastic card, introducing her son Rahul and daughter Priyanka to the campaign, which caught the imagination of younger voters (one in two of the Indian electorate is aged under 35).

Far from increasing his majority, as he had expected, Vajpayee and his government were thrown out in the most dramatic political turnaround of recent times. Congress gained the largest share of the vote and **Sonia Gandhi** was duly invited to form a government. However, she stunned supporters by "humbly declining" the invitation and stepped down. The announcement caused clamorous scenes in parliament, provoking the worst losses ever seen in the 129-year history of India's stock market. Eventually, former finance minister, 71-year-old **Manmohan Singh**, stepped into the breach and was named as prime minister, the first Sikh to lead the country.

One of the casualties of the national elections in the south was Andhran chief minister **Chandrababu Naidu**. The darling of the World Bank, Naidu had come to power vowing to stamp out corruption, curb the power of bureact, make state government more transparent and efficient, and transform the region's economy. He aimed to do this following a blueprint drawn up by international management consultants MacKinsey's. In "Vision 2020" **IT** was given a leading role. Up until the late 1990s, Bangalore had remained the unchallenged info-tech capital of India, but spurred on by Naidu's reforms, the Andhra capital Hyderabad soon caught up with and overtook its rival as the country's leading software enclave. Subsidies of Rs20,000 were granted to companies for every job created in "**Cyberabad**", as the new development was nicknamed. Big players persuaded to relocate to there included Microsoft and Dell, and when Bill Clinton came to see India's IT miracle in action, it was Hyderabad he chose to visit and Chandrababu Naidu who showed him around.

Naidu passionately believed that the answer to Andhra's problems was to shift its economy from a rural, agricultural base into the service sector and IT. Call centres not fields would henceforth form the basis of future prosperity in the state, and "E-Government" would make its leaders more accountable to the people. Needless to say, although the World Bank loved Naidu's revolution, it was far from popular with farmers. While Hyderabad's professional classes surged ahead, Andhra's rural poor were suffering the worst economic crisis in

Over the past decade, a mounting agricultural crisis in South India has had a massive impact on rural populations. Hundreds of thousands of farming families have been forced off their land by debt and crop failure; many have chosen to take their own lives in protest against the policies of governments they feel are to blame.

The roots of the crisis lie in the so-called **Green Revolution**. From the 1960s, encouraged by Western governments and aid donors, India introduced modern farming techniques to intensify wheat and rice production. Based on the use of new high-yield varieties of seed, together with chemical fertilizers, the new methods led to a dramatic increase in agricultural output (India survived a severe drought in 1988 and even managed to contribute grain to famine-stricken farmers in the African Sahel at around the same time). Their longer-term impact, however, remains under scrutiny.

One of the major drawbacks of the Green Revolution has been a growing disparity between the wealthy land-owning farmers and their landless share-cropping tenants. Unable to afford the expensive seeds and accompanying chemicals, poor farmers and their families have been forced, by mounting debts, to leave the countryside in search of waged employment. The majority end up living on the streets, or in the vast slum encampments that have sprung up on the edges of all South Indian cities over the past two decades.

Recent global economic trends have also been felt in the South Indian countryside. The General Agreement on Tariffs and Trade, or **GATT**, is potentially the most significant of these. Signed in 1994, the treaty aims to promote free trade by defending foreign investors from economic protectionism. While popular with the business community, GATT and other policies like it have proved controversial in a country as sensitive to its colonial history as India (particularly one brought up on the Gandhian ideals of *svadeshi*, or small-scale, non-polluting self-reliance).

A component of the treaty that has come in for particular criticism in India is its promotion of **genetic patenting**. This enables the large multinationals who manufacture seed used by South Indians to patent their products, making it illegal for farmers to replant them – no matter that the seeds may have originated in developing countries such as India, where generations of peasant farmers have painstakingly experimented to create pest- and drought-resistant strains. If a company can prove that it has modified the seed in any way, it is entitled by GATT to patent it.

The issue prompted indignation in India, but little more than that until it transpired the expensive seeds didn't even produce the promised increased yields – their one redeeming feature in the eyes of small farmers. In 1993, on the anniversary of Gandhi's birthday, half a million farmers issued "Quit India" notices to the US company Cargill, whose genetically modified sunflower seeds had been used by many farmers in northern Karnataka. Angry protesters succeeded in dismantling the company's plant in Bangalore within half an hour. The police, most of whom had family in the countryside, did not offer any significant resistance.

The **Seed Satyagraha**, as this grassroots farmers' movement became known, makes explicit the connection with the anticolonial struggle by using the name chosen by Gandhi for his campaign of non-violent civil disobedience, or *satyagraha*. Replacing the spinning wheel with a seed as the movement's symbol, it has been seen by many as a second freedom struggle and its ideas have spread from Karnataka through Andhra Pradesh, Tamil Nadu and Kerala in recent years.

Government support for the Seed Satyagraha, however, did not materialize until the late 1990s, following rumours that the giant corporation Monsanto planned to unleash the new so-called **"Terminator Gene"** on the region. Designed to protect the company's patents, the new genetically modified gene produces plants that yield sterile seeds (i.e. ones that cannot be re-sown, and thus forces farmers to purchase new ones – and the accompanying fertilizers – each season). Moreover, it is widely feared that cross-pollination would render other crops sterile, resulting in complete dependence on foreign companies. To draw attention to this risk, a coalition of ten million Karnatakan farmers, the KRSS, mounted **"Operation Cremate Monsanto"**, pulling up cotton crops at test sites and organizing mass rallies against the WTO. Its leader, the maverick **Professor Najundasmamy**, also staged a much publicized laugh-in, when 6000 farmers laughed all day outside the town hall in Bangalore at their elected representatives, for "subverting democracy". To diffuse the crisis, and the prospect of a full-scale rural uprising, the Indian government banned the technology and required all exporting countries to guarantee that seeds entering India are "terminator free". It then spent hundreds of thousands of dollars unsuccessfully fighting a US decision to grant a Texan company patents on basmati rice in 1997. Meanwhile, Monsanto, the world's largest genetically modified seed producer, was awarded patents on the wheat used for making chapatis, even though the strain had been developed over centuries of experimentation by India farmers.

Another change that has had serious implications for millions of Indian farmers over the past decade or so has been the government's relationship with the International Monetary Fund (IMF) and its sister organization, the World Bank. In order to qualify for a £90 billion loan in the late 1980s, India was obliged to end its programme of **subsidies** to farmers, who for years had been entitled to free or cheap electricity, diesel, fertilizers and pesticides. According to the World Trade Organization, such state aid constituted "interference with the free market" and was illegal. Farmers were instead encouraged by a raft of incentives and publicity drives to grow **cash crops** such as cotton, which offered the additional benefit of generating foreign currency (needed to repay the IMF loans). Using specially developed high-yield seeds and chemicals, improved harvests and profits were assured, and within a couple of years, huge chunks of the country (as much as sixty percent of farm land in Andhra Pradesh) had been given over to the "White Gold".

The advertising campaigns mounted by the multinational agri-manufacturers, however, failed to warn that cotton prices might suddenly drop; that pests might develop immunities to the chemicals; that the new hybrid seeds didn't always grow; or that much greater quantities of water would be needed to cultivate them. When all these disasters struck at once, as they did in 1999–2000, millions of farmers in South India were ruined. Their only option was to borrow money from the *aarthis*, or "money lenders", who had sold them the seeds and chemicals in the first place.

In **Andhra Pradesh** alone, around 500 farmers committed suicide by drinking the useless insecticide, lying down to die amid their failed crops. Despite such obvious drawbacks, field trials of GM cotton continued in 2001–2, with results published the following year showing an eighty percent increase in yields. The findings increased pressure on the central government to relax laws preventing the introduction of GM crops – music to the ears of the then chief minister of Andhra Pradesh, **Chandrababu Naidu**, who had long championed the GM cause in his bid to squeeze the state's rural-based economy into the more lucrative "service sector". Famous as the go-ahead leader responsible for bringing Dell and Microsoft to Hyderabad, Naidu had earlier enraged farmers (and delighted the World Bank) by slashing rice subsidies. Despite his popularity among the professional classes, however, he fell victim to a rural backlash in the elections of May 2004 when he and his party were wiped out. This dramatic electoral upset served notice to leaders throughout the region that they could ignore the plight of the south Indian farmers only at their peril.

C

CONTEXTS | History

decades. Crop failure and debt caused primarily by the government's policies led to the suicides of thousands of farmers across the south in the early 2000s. Yet in the face of what the press dubbed "the Digital Divide", Naidu continued to slash subsidies to agriculture and denied farmers the **free electricity** they'd previously been promised (see box on p.660).

The tsunamis in South India

Although southeast India was 2000km away from the epicentre of the Indonesian earthquake, much of its coast lay in the direct path of the **tsunamis**, and on the morning of December 26, 2004, three giant waves, between nine and twelve metres high, swept ashore from the Bay of Bengal. The areas worst hit, in order of severity, were the Andaman and Nicobar Islands, the Nagappattinam–Karaikal and Cuddalore districts of Tamil Nadu, Kanyakumari at the southern extremity of the peninsula, and a small stretch of coastline west of the Kollam–Allapuzha backwaters in Kerala. Official estimates placed the death toll at around 11,000, with as many as ten times that made homeless. The real figure, however, is probably much higher and will never be known.

A massive clear-up operation ensued, with rehabilitation efforts focusing on the subsistence fishing communities who lost their homes and livelihoods in the disaster. Countless houses, boats, nets and tools were destroyed, and few of their owners can afford replacements. Inland, vast swaths of formerly fertile paddy were badly salinated; it is unclear as yet whether much of this land will ever be productive again.

Lying less than 1000km from the coast of Sumatra, the **Andaman and Nicobar Islands** ranked among some of the most severely stricken regions in the entire disaster zone. Whole chunks of land, beaches and forests were swept away, coral reefs pulled apart, lighthouses submerged and towns flattened. Estimates of the death toll range from 818 to 10,000. **Little Andaman** was the worst hit of the islands open to visitors.

More than two-thirds (4363) of India's total official dead were from **Nagapatinam** and its satellite fishing villages, at the mouth of the Kaveri (Cauvery) Delta, halfway down the **Tamil Nadu** coast. Densely populated, the district hosts a cluster of important pilgrimage sites. At the Christian Basilica of **Velankanni**, 650 worshippers lost their lives and a thousand more went missing; the Muslim Dargah of **Nagur**, further north, suffered a further thousand fatalities. Another blackspot was Marina Beach, fronting the state capital, **Chennai** (formerly Madras), from which more than one hundred adults and children were washed away. Nearby **Mamallapuram** (Mahabalipuram) was also hit but saw only a handful of deaths. Most of the damage sustained was to the beach shacks, which have since been rebuilt.

Kannyakumari, at the southernmost tip of India, was the other place in Tamil Nadu seriously affected. More than a thousand tourists were trapped here on the Vivekananda Memorial Rock. Palk Bay and the northern part of the Gulf of Mannar – including the Hindu temple town of **Rameshwaram** – were largely spared, as they were protected by Sri Lanka.

Although the waves were felt on the southwest coast in **Kerala**, severe damage and loss of life were limited to the stretch west of the backwaters, between Kollam (Quilon) and Allapuzha (Allepey), where around six hundred villagers are said to have been killed. Beach shacks and other temporary structures were swept away at **Kovalam**, but the resort quickly recovered.

Goa's busy beaches, packed on Boxing Day morning, experienced unseasonally hide tides and waves during the tsunamis and their aftermath, which damaged some shacks in **Palolem**. Otherwise, the state was unaffected, save for much higher visitor numbers than normal as tourists from other parts of India fled disaster areas further south and east.

The 2004 elections finally gave Andhra's rural populations the opportunity to express their opinion of Naidu's experiment: the party suffered a resounding defeat and its reforms were halted. A similar pattern repeated itself across the South, as voters in the countryside registered their dissatisfaction with economic policies that had benefited the urban middle classes but not in the least alleviated poverty in the villages. Having pinned its colours to the BJP-led coalition in Delhi, **Jayalalitha**'s AIADMK also crashed at the polls in Tamil Nadu after her government had cut free electricity to farmers and introduced other measures penalizing rural populations.

Visiting India, the ironies resulting from decades of poor governance are all too evident. The country chosen by Bill Gates as the site of a new Microsoft complex, capable of launching satellites, nuclear rockets and manned-space programmes, is unable to provide clean drinking water, adequate nutrition and basic education for millions of its citizens. As Goldman Sachs recently observed, India is home to 'nearly a third of the world's software engineers and a quarter of the world's undernourished'. Its capacity to close this yawning gap will depend on the extent to which India's leaders are, over the coming years, able to deliver stable government and curb the self-interest that has come to dominate public life, particularly in the South.

Religions

This great and ancient nation was once the fountain of human light, the apex of human civilization, the exemplar of courage and humanity, the perfection of good government and settled society, the mother of all religions, the teacher of all wisdom and philosophy.

Shri Aurobindo (1907)

Long regarded as the bastion of Hindu values, South India boasts many of the finest, oldest and most extravagant temples in the country. The devotion displayed by the millions of pilgrims is just the most obvious aspect of the fact that Hinduism permeates every element of life here, from social structures to education and politics. The vast pantheon of Hindu deities is manifest everywhere, from soaring temple gateways to *beedi* packets and the little mobile shrines erected in houses, buses, cars and shops. The South is also home to a substantial Muslim community; since the twelfth century, Muslims have settled in the South as traders and rulers, constructing pearl-domed mosques throughout the region. Today, Muslims are largely concentrated in the major cities and Kerala. Christians, believed to have been living in South India since the first century AD, have developed distinct denominations, and worship in buildings that range from simple thatched huts to the grand basilicas and churches erected by the Portuguese, French and British. Although Jains and Buddhists are now a minute fraction of the southern population, several magnificent temples stand testament to an impressive presence in the past. The once influential Keralan Jews are now a pitifully small group, originally attracted here from both the Arab world and Europe by the rich pickings of the Malabar Coast and its spice belts, but their influence can still be strongly felt in Fort Cochin (Kochi). Mumbai features a rapidly dwindling society of Zoroastrian Parsis (see p.681); both groups continue to intermarry to preserve their unique heritage and identity.

Hinduism

Contemporary **Hindu society** – which represents over 85 percent of South Indians – is the product of several thousand years of evolution and assimilation. The South has played a vital role in the development of Hinduism in the subcontinent, producing reformers like **Shankara**, who travelled throughout India in the ninth century, bringing about sweeping reforms by utilizing Buddhist models to establish a revitalized Hindu monastic order that is still in use today. Later, in the thirteenth century, in the face of a Muslim onslaught on Hindu institutions, South Indian **Vaishnavas** (worshippers of Vishnu and his incarnations) were pivotal in the development of Krishna worship, establishing centres in Krishna's mythological homeland of Braj, to the south of Delhi. Ever since, Vaishnavism has been at the heart of South Indian Hindu life.

The Hindu religion boasts no founder or prophet, no single creed and no single prescribed practice or doctrine; it takes in hundreds of gods, goddesses, beliefs and practices, and widely variant cults and philosophies. Some Hindu deities are recognized by only two or three villages; others, such as Vishnu and Shiva, are popular right across the subcontinent, with devotion tending to border on fanaticism in the South. Hindus (from the Persian word for Indians) call their beliefs and practices **dharma**, which embraces natural and moral law to define a way of living in harmony with a natural order, while achieving personal goals and meeting the requirements of society.

Early developments

In the second millennium BC, the foundations of Hinduism as a religion and way of life were laid down by the Aryans, semi-nomads who had wandered into the Indus Valley in the North. They brought a belief in gods associated with the elements, including **Agni**, the god of fire and sacrifice, **Surya**, the sun god, and **Indra**, the chief god. Most of these deities faded in importance in later times, but Indra is still regarded as the father of the gods, and Surya was widely worshipped until the medieval period.

Aryan beliefs were set out in the **Vedic** scriptures as they had been "heard" (*shruti*) by "seers" (*rishis*). Transmitted orally for centuries, they were finally written, in Sanskrit, between 1000 BC and 500 AD. The earliest were the *Samhitas*, or hymns; the *Brahmanas*, sacrificial texts, and *Aranyakas*, or "forest treatises" came later.

The earliest and most important *Samhita*, the **Rig Veda**, contains hymns to deities and *devas* (divine powers), and is supplemented by other books detailing rituals and prayers for ceremonial use. The **Brahmanas** stress correct ritual performance, drawing heavily on concepts of **purity and pollution** which persist today and concentrating on sacrificial rites. Pedantic attention to ritual soon supplanted worship of the *devas*, whose importance was further undermined by a search for a single cosmic power thought to be their source, eventually conceived of as **Brahma**, the absolute creator, personified from earlier mentions of Brahman, an impersonal principle of cosmic unity.

The **Aranyakas** focused on this all-powerful godhead, and reached their final stage in the **Upanishads**, which describe in beautiful and emotive verse the mystic experience of unity of the soul (*atman*) with Brahma, ideally attained through asceticism, renunciation of worldly values and meditation. In the *Upanishads* the concepts of **samsara**, a cyclic round of death and rebirth characterized by suffering and perpetuated by desire, and **moksha**, liberation from *samsara*, became firmly rooted. Fundamental aspects of the Hindu world view, both are accepted by all but a handful of Hindus today, along with the belief in **karma**, the belief that one's present position in society is determined by the effect of one's previous actions in this and past lives.

Philosophical trends

The complications presented by Hinduism's view of deities, *samsara, atman* (the human soul) and *moksha* naturally encouraged philosophical debate, and led eventually to the formation of six schools of thought, known as the **Darshanas**. Each presented a different exposition of the true nature of *moksha* and how to attain it.

Foremost among these was the **Advaita Vedanta** school of **Shankara** (c.788–850 AD), who interpreted Hinduism as pure monotheism verging on monism (the belief that all is one: in this case, one with God). Drawing on Upanishadic writings, he claimed that they identified the essence of the human soul with that of God (*tat tvam asi*, "that thou art"), and that all else – the phenomenal world and all *devas* – is an illusion (*maya*) created by God. Shankara is revered as saint-philosopher at the twelve **jyotirlingas**, the sacred Shaivite sites associated

Vishnu

The chief function of **Vishnu**, the "pervader", is to keep the world in order, preserving, restoring and protecting it. With four arms holding a conch, discus, lotus and mace, Vishnu is blue-skinned, and often shaded by a serpent, or resting on its coils, afloat on an ocean. He is usually seen alongside his half-man-half-eagle vehicle, Garuda.

Vaishnavites, often distinguishable by two vertical lines on their foreheads, recognize Vishnu as the supreme lord, and hold that he has manifested himself on earth nine times. These incarnations, or *avatars*, have been as fish (Matsya), tortoise (Kurma), boar (Varaha), man-lion (Narsingh), dwarf (Vamana), axe-wielding brahmin (Parasuram), Rama, Krishna and Balaram (though some say that the Buddha is the ninth *avatar*). Vishnu's future descent to earth as Kalki, the saviour who will come to restore purity and destroy the wicked, is eagerly awaited.

The most important *avatars* are Krishna and Rama, star of the epic Ramayana (see p.738). **Krishna** is the hero of the Bhagavad Gita, in which he proposes three routes to salvation (*moksha*): selfless action (*karmayoga*), knowledge (*jnana*) and devotion to god (*bhakti*), and explains that *moksha* is attainable in this life, even without asceticism and renunciation. This appealed to all castes, as it denied the necessity of ritual and officiating brahmin priests, and evolved into the popular *bhakti* cult that legitimized love of God as a means to *moksha*, and also found expression in emotional songs of the quest for union with God. Through *bhakti*, Krishna's role was extended, and he assumed different faces: most popularly he is the playful cowherd who seduces and dances with cowgirls (*gopis*), giving each the illusion that she is his only lover. He is also pictured as a small, chubby, mischievous baby, known for his butter-stealing exploits, who inspires tender motherly love in women. Like Vishnu, Krishna is blue, and is often shown dancing and playing the flute.

Vishnu is worshipped especially in the form of Lord Venkateshvara at Tirumala in Andhra Pradesh, and the huge popularity of this pilgrimage centre is largely due to his role as the granter of wishes, leading many thousands to his shrine daily to pray for favours.

Shiva

Shaivism, the cult of **Shiva**, was also inspired by *bhakti*, requiring selfless love from devotees in a quest for divine communion, but Shiva has never been incarnate on earth. He is presented in many different aspects, such as **Nataraja**, "Lord of the Dance", **Mahadev**, "Great God", and **Maheshvar**, "Divine Lord", source of all knowledge. Though he does have several terrible forms, his role extends beyond that of destroyer, and he is revered as the source of the whole universe.

Shiva is often depicted with four or five faces, holding a trident, draped with serpents, and bearing a third eye in his forehead. In temples, he is identified with the *lingam*, or phallic symbol, resting in the *yoni*, a representation of female sexuality. Whether as statue or *lingam*, Shiva is guarded by his bull-vehicle, Nandi, and often accompanied by a consort, who also assumes various forms and is looked upon as the vital energy, *shakti*, that empowers him. Their erotic exploits were a favourite sculptural subject between the ninth and twelfth centuries.

Shiva is the object of popular veneration all over India; devotees are identifiable by the horizontal lines (between one and three) painted on their foreheads. In particular, Shaivite **ascetics** worship Shiva in the aspect of the terrible **Bhairav**. The ascetics renounce family and caste ties and perform extreme meditative and yogic practices. Many, though not all, smoke *ganja*, Shiva's favourite herb; all see renunciation and realization of God as the key to *moksha*. Some ascetic practices enter the realm of **tantrism**, in which confrontation with all that is impure, such as alcohol, death and sex, is used to merge the sacred and the profane, and bring about the profound realization that Shiva is omnipresent.

Ganesh

Tubby and smiling, elephant-headed **Ganesh**, the first son of Shiva and Parvati, is invoked before every undertaking (except funerals). Seated on a throne or lotus, his image is often placed above temple gateways, in shops and in houses. In his four arms he holds a conch, discus, bowl of sweets (or club) and a water lily, and he's always attended by his vehicle, a rat. Credited with writing the Mahabharata as it was dictated by the sage Vyasa, Ganesh is regarded by many as the god of learning, the lord of success, prosperity and peace. In the South he is often known as Vinayaka and as such there is a huge festival, Vinayakapuja, in his honour in late monsoon, when he is thrown into the sea; the celebration in Mumbai is the most ostentatious and famous.

Other gods and goddesses

Shiva's consort, **Parvati** (also known as Uma), is remarkable only for her beauty and fidelity, although in another aspect, as **Durga**, she is the fiercest of the female deities. In whatever form, Shiva's consort is *shakti*, the fundamental energy that spurs him into action. Among Durga's many aspects, each a terrifying goddess eager to slay demons, are Chamunda, Kali and Muktakeshi, but in all her forms she is **Mahadevi** (Great Goddess). Statues show her with ten arms, holding the head of a demon, a spear, and other weapons; she tramples demons underfoot, or dances upon Shiva's body. A garland of skulls drapes her neck, and her tongue hangs from her mouth, dripping with blood – a particularly gruesome sight on pictures of **Kali**. In all her temples, animal sacrifices are a crucial element of worship, to satisfy her thirst for blood and deter her ruthless anger.

The comely goddess **Lakshmi**, usually shown sitting or standing on a lotus flower, and sometimes called Padma (lotus), is the embodiment of loveliness, grace and charm, and the goddess of prosperity and wealth. Vishnu's consort, she appears in different aspects alongside each of his *avatars*; the most important are Sita, wife of Rama, and Radha, Krishna's favourite *gopi*. In many temples she is shown as one with Vishnu, in the form of Lakshmi Narayan.

Pictured as a triumphant youth, bedecked with flowers, images of **Murugan**, son of Shiva and his consort Parvati, are particularly common in Tamil Nadu and rural Kerala (see box on p.551). He provides protection from evil and negative actions, which makes him a popular family deity. It is possible that he derives from a pre-Aryan fertility god.

Though some legends claim that his mother was Ganga, or even Agni, **Karttikeya** is popularly believed to be the second son of Shiva and Parvati. Primarily a god of war, he was popular among the northern Guptas, who worshipped him as Skanda, and the southern Chalukyas, for whom he was Subrahmanya. Usually shown with six faces, and standing upright with bow and arrow, Karttikeya is commonly petitioned by those wishing for male offspring.

Another son of Shiva, this time from a peculiar mythological union with Vishnu (see box on p.393), **Ayappa** is also associated with the role of protection, and his shrine in northern Kerala is a huge magnet to pilgrims, making the black-clad, mostly male, devotees a familiar sight. The common depiction of Ayappa riding a tiger with an entourage of leopards denotes his victory over evil.

India's great monkey god **Hanuman** features in the Ramayana as Rama's chief aide in the fight against the demon king of Lanka. Depicted as a giant monkey clasping a mace, Hanuman is the deity of acrobats and wrestlers, but is also seen as Rama and Sita's greatest devotee, and an author of Sanskrit grammar. As his representatives, monkeys find sanctuary in temples across southern India.

The most beautiful Hindu goddess, **Saraswati**, the wife of Brahma – with her flawless milk-white complexion – sits or stands on a water lily or peacock, playing a lute, *sitar* or *vina*. Associated with the River Saraswati, mentioned in the *Rig Veda*, she is seen as a goddess of purification and fertility, but is also revered as the inventor of writing, the queen of eloquence and goddess of music.

Closely linked with the planet Saturn, **Sani** is feared for his destructive powers. His image, a black statue with protruding blood-red tongue, is often found on street corners; strings of green chillies and lemon are hung in shops and houses each Saturday (*Saniwar*) to ward off his evil influences.

Mention must also be made here of the sacred cow, **Khamdenu**, who receives devotion through the respect shown to all cows, who are allowed to amble through streets and temples all over southern India. The origin of the cow's sanctity is uncertain; some myths record that Brahma created cows at the same time as brahmins, to provide *ghee* (clarified butter) for use in priestly ceremonies. To this day cow dung and urine are used to purify houses (in fact the urine keeps insects at bay), and the killing or harming of cows by any Hindu is a grave offence. The cow is often referred to as mother of the gods, and each part of its body is significant: its horns symbolize the gods, its face the sun and moon, its shoulders Agni (god of fire) and its legs the Himalayas. Hindus touch the hip of a cow to give them fertility and prosperity.

C

CONTEXTS | Religions

with the unbounded *lingam* of light, which as a manifestation of Shiva once persuaded both Brahma and Vishnu to acknowledge Shiva's supremacy.

Another important *Darshana* centred around the age-old practice of **yoga** (literally "the action of yoking [to] another"), elucidated by **Patanjali** (second century BC) in his *Yoga Sutras*. Interpreting yoga as the yoking of mind and body, or the yoking of the mind with God, Patanjali detailed various practices, which used in combination may lead to an understanding of the fundamental **unity** of all things. The most common form of yoga known in the West is *hatha-yoga*, whereby the body and its vital energies are brought under control through physical positions and breathing methods, with results said to range from attaining a calm mind to being able to fly through the air, enter other bodies or become invisible. Other practices include *mantra-yoga*, the recitation of formulas and meditation on mystical diagrams (mandalas), *bhakti-yoga* (devotion), *jnana-yoga* (knowledge) and *raja-yoga* (royal) – the highest form of yoga when the mind is absorbed in God.

Popular deities

Alongside the *Dharma Shashtras* and *Dharma Shutras*, the most important works of the *smriti* tradition, thought to have been completed by the fourth century AD at the latest, were the **Puranas**, long mythological stories focused on the Vedic gods and their heroic actions, and Hinduism's two great epics, the **Mahabharata** and the **Ramayana** (see boxes on pp.737–738). Through these texts, the main gods and goddesses became firmly embedded in the Hindu religion. Alongside **Brahma**, the creator, **Vishnu** was acknowledged as the preserver, and **Shiva** ("auspicious, benign"), referred to in the *Rig Veda* as Rudra, was recognized for his destructive powers. The three are often depicted in a trinity, *tri-murti*, but in time Brahma's importance declined, and Shiva and Vishnu became the most popular deities. Nearly all Hindus belong to sects that actively worship Shiva or Vishnu in one form or another (see box on p.666).

Other gods and goddesses who came alive in the mythology of the *Puranas* – each depicted in human or semi-human form and accompanied by an animal **"vehicle"** – are still venerated across South India. River goddesses, ancestors, guardians of particular places and protectors against disease and natural disaster are as central to village life as the major deities.

Caste and social structure

The stratification of Hindu society is rooted in the **Dharma Shashtras** and **Dharma Shutras**, scriptures written from "memory" (*smriti*) at the same time as the *Vedas*. These defined four hierarchical classes, or **varnas**, each assigned specific religious and social duties known as **varnashradharma**, and established Aryans as the highest social class. The **Aryans** already had a class system in place before reaching the subcontinent; their nobility was known as the *kshatra* and the ordinary tribesman as the *vish*. However, their contact with darker-skinned people known as the **Dasas** caused them concern about racial purity, resulting in a division of society based on **varna** – literally "colour" – a unique institution of **racism** that has lasted over three thousand years. In descending order the *varnas* are: **brahmins** (priests and teachers), **kshatryas** (rulers and warriors), **vaishyas** (merchants and cultivators) and **shudras** (menials). The first three classes, known as "twice-born"– initially to distinguish those born in their native place and then born again during their induction as an Aryan – are distinguished by a sacred thread worn from the ceremony of initiation, and are granted full access to religious texts and rituals. Below all four categories, groups whose jobs involve contact with dirt or death (such as undertakers, leather workers and cleaners) were classified as **Untouchables**. Though discrimination against Untouchables is now a criminal offence, in part thanks to the campaigns of Gandhi – who renamed Untouchables *Harijans*, "Children of God" – the lowest stratum of society has by no means disappeared. Today, the word "**dalit**" is the politically correct term to use when talking about this class. Children, widows and ascetics remained outside the *varna* system.

When at the end of the Vedic age new ideas threatened the absolute power of the priesthood, and religions such as Buddhism and Jainism preached equality, the brahmins responded with the manuscript **Manu-smriti** (the words of Manu, the original man, remembered). Composed by a succession of authors some time around the third century BC, *Manu-smriti* laid out the *varna* system in detail and defined the role and tasks of each *varna*, as well as the strict interaction between each group. The moral grounds laid out for the system of division was that one should perform every task well and with pride rather than to try and take on someone else's tasks. This argument, combined with **karma** (the result of one's deeds), and the concept of rebirth which developed from the late Vedic period onwards, proposes that you are what you are born. Through good deeds you may have the fortune of being reborn at a higher level in the next life.

These ethics also carried through to the **Bhagavad Gita**, where Aryan beliefs are protected against reformers and non-believers by singing the virtues of each of the four divisions – wisdom for the brahmin, valour for the *kshatriya*, industry for the *vaishya* and service for the *shudra*. Interaction between the divisions had become clearly defined. *Manu-smriti*, which continues to act as the foundation of **Hindu law**, lays down the rules of purity – for example, a *shudra*'s shadow may never cross a brahmin, and if it does the brahmin will have to perform a ritual to purify himself.

Within the four *varnas*, social status is further defined by **caste**, which refers to numerous social groupings within Hindu society. When the Portuguese first came to India in the sixteenth century, they came across these divisions and referred to them as "*castas*" (tribes, clans or families), a term which led to the

The left hand versus the right

Literature suggests that caste came late to Tamil country, in about the ninth century. As Tamil society was fundamentally agrarian, there were few families who could claim to be *kshatriyas* (warriors) and so most of the population was divided between brahmins, *shudras* and untouchables. The largest group among the Tamils, the *shudras*, divided itself into a further two groups, the **left-handed** and the **right-handed** castes – the **Idangai** and the **Valangai**. The left and right hands allude to which hand was considered pure by either group (in most of Hindu India, the right hand is the pure hand while the left is menial). These two seemingly innocuous divisions have been at odds with each other ever since their inception, leading to bitter conflict and rivalry. The left-hand group includes craftsmen, weavers, some cultivators, cowherds and leather workers; the right-hand one includes traders, most cultivators, some weavers, musicians, barbers, washermen, potters and labourers.

word "caste". Caste lays restrictions on all aspects of life from food consumption, religious obligations and contact with other castes, to the choice of marriage partners. Those that belong to other faiths have been given a caste status to clarify their position in the general social hierarchy; Christians in Kerala have actually adopted this system of classification and developed a caste system of their own.

Within the broader caste identity, there are sub-groups known as **jati**, which classify individuals by family and precise occupation (for example, a *vaishya* may be a jewellery-seller, cloth merchant, cowherd or farmer). There are almost three thousand *jatis*; the divisions and restrictions they have enforced have become, time and time again, the substance of reform movements and the target of critics. Whereas *varna* and caste is fixed from birth to death, there is a degree of flexibility to a *jati* identity, and some have a tendency to be upwardly mobile, in which case the members try to assume the ethics, manners and ways of the *jati* group they aspire to. Their tenure at this new rung in the hierarchy depends solely on whether the other *jatis* are willing to accept their new position. Despite this, Hindus still tend to marry members of the same caste and *jati* – marrying someone of a different caste often results in ostracism from both family and caste, leaving the couple stranded in a society where caste affiliation takes primacy over all other aspects of individual identity.

Castes have distinctive patterns of intra–caste relationships within themselves while at the same time interacting with other castes along strict rules of behaviour. Although castes maintain their structural place in society through both interaction and segregation, there is an element of fraternity, especially with castes close to each other in the hierarchy. Horizontal caste relations are limited by the diversity of India's geography and culture; while *varna* has its roots in theology, caste and *jati* is able to adapt itself to its local environment. Each region has such strong ritual and linguistic traits that a brahmin in Goa is unable to relate directly to a brahmin in Tamil Nadu.

Practice

A Hindu has three aims in life: **dharma**, fulfilling one's duty to family and caste and acquiring religious merit (*punya*) through right living; **artha**, the lawful making of wealth; and **karma**, desire and satisfaction. The primary concern of most Hindus is to reduce bad *karma* and acquire merit (*punya*), by honest and charitable living within the restrictions imposed by caste and worship, in the hope of attaining a higher status in rebirth.

These goals are linked with the four traditional **stages in life**. The first is as a child and student, devoted to learning from parents and a guru. Next comes the stage of householder, expected to provide for a family and raise sons. That accomplished, he or she may then take up a life of celibacy and retreat into the forest to meditate alone, and finally renounce all possessions to become a home-less ascetic, hoping to achieve the ultimate goal of *moksha*. According to ancient custom, the life of a high-class Hindu man progressed through four distinct phases – *brahmachari* (celibate) following his initiation or "thread ceremony", *grhastha* (householder), *vanaprashta* (forest dweller) following middle age and after his children have grown up, and finally, *sanyasi* (a renunciate). However, in practice, few follow this course in life and the *vanaprashta* is no more; in general, life is meant to progress along ordered lines from initiation (for high-caste Hindus) through education, career and marriage. A small number of Hindus who follow this ideal life, including some women, assume the final stage as **sanyasis**, saffron-clad **sadhus** who wander throughout India, begging for food and retreating to isolated caves, forests and hills to meditate. They are a common feature in most Indian towns, and many stay for long periods in particular temples. Not all have raised families: some assume the life of a *sadhu* at an early age as a *chella* (pupil or disciple) to an older *sadhu*.

However, strict rules still address the dharmic principles of **purity** and **pollu-tion**, the most obvious of them requiring high-caste Hindus to limit their contact with potentially polluting lower castes. All bodily excretions are pollut-ing (hence the strange looks Westerners receive when they blow their noses and return the handkerchief to their pocket or request toilet paper). Above all else, **water** is the agent of purification, used in ablutions before prayer, and revered in all rivers, especially Ganga (the Ganges).

In most Hindu homes and businesses, a small shrine is set up with pictures of chosen deities, and scriptures are read. Outside the home, worship takes place in temples, and consists of **puja**, or devotion to God. This may be a simple act of prayer, but more commonly it is a complex process when the god's image is circumambulated, offered flowers, rice, sugar and incense, and anointed with water, milk or sandalwood paste (which is usually done on behalf of the devotee by the temple priest, the *pujari*). The aim in puja is **darshan** – to glimpse the god – and thus receive his or her blessing. Whether devotees simply worship the deity in prayer, or make requests – for a healthy crop, a son, good results in exams, a vigorous monsoon or a cure for illness – they always leave the temple with *prasad*, an offering of food or flowers from the holy sanctuary, given to them by the *pujaris*.

Communal worship and get-togethers en route to pilgrimage sites are celebrated with *kirtan* or *bhajan*, singing of hymns, perhaps verses in praise of Krishna taken from the *Bhagavad Purana*, or repetitive cries of "Jay Shankar!" (Praise to Shiva). Temple ceremonies are conducted in Sanskrit by *pujaris* who tend the image in daily rituals that symbolically wake, bathe, feed and dress the god, and finish each day by preparing the god for sleep. The most elaborate is the evening ritual, **aarti**, when lamps are lit, blessed in the sanctuary, and passed around devotees amid the clanging of drums, gongs and cymbals. In many villages, shrines to *devatas*, village deities who function as protectors and may bring disaster if neglected, are more important than temples.

Each of the great stages in life – birth, **initiation** (when boys of the three twice-born castes are invested with a sacred thread, and a mantra is whispered into their ear by their guru), marriage, death and cremation – are marked by fervent prayer, energetic celebration and feasting. The most significant event in a Hindu's life is **marriage**, which symbolizes ritual purity, and for women is so important that it takes the place of initiation. Feasting, dancing and singing among the bride and groom's families, usually lasting for a week or more before and after the marriage, are the order of the day all over India. The actual marriage is consecrated when the couple walks seven times round a sacred fire, accompanied by sacred verses read by an officiating brahmin. Relatives pour in from all over the country and abroad to witness not just the union of man and wife, but also to reaffirm the group's social standing. Today, most Hindu marriages traditionally involve the parents, who negotiate the match; love marriages are increasingly common, especially in urban areas, but still tend to depend on parental consent and collusion.

The age-old Indian tradition of giving **dowry**, a gift of money, jewellery and goods from the bride's family to the groom's, is now officially illegal, but still widely demanded and invariably given, for fear that a daughter's welfare will be in jeopardy if it is withheld. Dowry is prevalent in both Hindu and Christian communities, and is as much practised by the upper and middle classes as it is by the poor, but for the latter it can represent an endless cycle of saving and debt with each new generation. Among more wealthy and cosmopolitan families, scooters, TVs and holidays are now the essential elements of a modern dowry. As it is a "gift", dowry is undeclared income, and the groom's family can place relentless pressure on the bride's family to continue providing "gifts" long after the wedding. The abuse, torture and burning of wives whose family provides a dowry that is below expectations is still all too common, especially in rural areas where there is little female literacy and brides are not aware of their rights under the constitution. Despite active opposition by progressive women's groups, dowry is a practice that is too deeply ingrained in Indian culture to easily eradicate, and the government seems unable to put a stop to it.

As a rule, Hindu society frowns upon **divorce**, but with increasing modernization, especially among the middle classes, it has become more common. Hindu law does not recognize divorce, and the legal procedure is relatively complicated.

For Hindus, **death** is an essential process in an endless cycle of rebirth in the grand illusion (*maya*) until the individual attains enlightenment and freedom (*moksha*) from *samsara* (transmigration). Hindus cremate their dead (except for young children, who they bury or cast into a river). The eldest son is entrusted to light the funeral pyre and the ashes are scattered, usually on a sacred river, such as the Ganges in northern India. Rites after death can be lengthy and complicated according to each Hindu community, and the role of the *purohit* (priest) is indispensable. **Widows** traditionally wear white and, according to ancient Hindu belief, are considered to be outside society.

Pilgrimage

The Hindu calendar is jam-packed with **festivals** devoted to deities, re-enacting mythological stories and commemorating holy sites. The grandest festivals are held at places made holy by association with gods, goddesses, miracles and great teachers, or at sacred rivers and mountains; throughout the year these are all important **pilgrimage** sites, visited by devotees eager to receive *darshan*, glimpse the world of the gods, and attain merit. The journey, or *yatra*, to a pilgrimage site is every bit as significant as reaching the sacred location, and bands of Hindus (particularly *sadhus*) often walk from site to site. Modern transport, however, has made things easier, and every state lays on pilgrimage tours, when buses and jeeps full of chanting families roar from one temple to another, filling up with religious souvenirs as they go.

South India has many important sites. The Venkateshvara temple atop Tirumala Hill in Andhra Pradesh claims to draw more pilgrims than any other holy place in the world. Every year, another two million or so devotees head up to the Ayappa Forest Temple at Sabarimala in Kerala. At Kanniyakumari, the southern tip of India, the waters of the Indian Ocean, the Bay of Bengal and the Arabian Sea are thought to merge at an auspicious point. Pilgrimages here are often combined with visits to the great temples of Tamil Nadu, where Shaivite and Vaishnavite saints established cults and India's largest temples were constructed. Madurai, Thanjavur, Chidambaram and Srirangam are major pilgrimage centres, representing the pinnacle of the architectural development that began at Mamallapuram. Their festivals often involve the pulling of deities on vast wooden chariots through the streets, lively and noisy affairs that make for an unforgettable experience. As well as specific temples sacred to particular gods, historical sites, such as the former Vijayanagar capital at Hampi, remain magnets for pilgrims. More than a common ideology, it is this map of sacred geography, entwined with popular mythology, that unites hundreds of millions of Hindus, who have also been brought together in nationalistic struggles, particularly in response to Christian missionaries and Muslim and British domination.

Islam

Across South India, **Muslims** – some ten percent of the total population – form a significant presence in almost every town, city and village. In most of the southern states, the percentage is slightly lower, the exception being Kerala, where nearly a quarter of the populace are Muslims, concentrated in fishing and trading communities right along the Malabar Coast. The only major southern city with a distinctly Islamic flavour is Hyderabad in Andhra Pradesh, although Mumbai and Chennai also boast well-established Muslim quarters.

The belief in only one god, **Allah**, the condemnation of idol worship and the observance of strict dietary laws and specific festivals sets Muslims apart from their Hindu neighbours, with whom they have coexisted for centuries, although not always peaceably. Such differences have helped fuel communal tensions, most notably during Partition in 1947, and more recently in the violent wake of the destruction of the Babri Masjid in Ayodhya in Uttar Pradesh in 1992. Although most of southern India managed to avoid the worst excesses of the early 1990s, Mumbai turned into a bloodbath, an experience documented in the magnificent film, *Bombay*, directed by M. Ratnam.

Origins and development

Islam, "submission to God", was founded by **Mohammed** (570–632 AD), who is regarded as the last in a succession of prophets and who transmitted God's final and perfected revelation to mankind through the writings of the divinely revealed "recitation", the **Koran** (Qur'an). The Koran is the authoritative scripture of Islam that sets down the basics of Islamic belief: that there is one god, Allah (though he is also attributed with 99 other beautiful names), and that Mohammed is his prophet. The beginning of Islam is dated at 622 AD, when Mohammed and his followers, exiled from Mecca, made the **hijra**, or migration, north to Yathrib, later known as Medina, "City of the Prophet". The *hijra* marks the start of the Islamic lunar calendar; the Gregorian year 2006 is for Muslims 1427 AH (*Anno Hijra*).

From Medina, Mohammed ordered raids on caravans heading for Mecca, and led his community in battles against the Meccans, inspired by *jihad*, or "striving" on behalf of God and Islam. This concept of holy war was the driving force behind the incredible expansion of Islam – by 713 Muslims had settled as far west as Spain, and as far east as the banks of the Indus. When **Mecca** surrendered peacefully to Mohammed in 630, he cleared the sacred shrine, the Ka'ba, of idols, and proclaimed it the pilgrimage centre of Islam.

Mohammed was succeeded as leader of the *umma*, the Islamic community, by Abu Bakr, the prophet's representative, or caliph, the first in a line of caliphs who led the orthodox community until the eleventh century AD. However, a schism soon emerged when the third caliph, Uthman, was assassinated by followers of Ali, Mohammed's son-in-law, in 656 AD. This new sect, calling themselves **Shi'as**, "partisans" of Ali, looked to Ali and his successors, infallible *imams*, as leaders of the *umma* until 878 AD, and thereafter replaced their religious authority with a body of scholars, the *ulema*.

By the second century after the *hijra* (ninth century AD), orthodox, or **Sunni**, Islam had assumed the form in which it survives today. A collection of traditions about the prophet, **Hadith**, became the source for ascertaining the **Sunna**, customs, of Mohammed. From the Koran and the Sunna, seven major **articles of belief** were laid down: belief in one God; in angels as his messengers; in prophets (including Jesus and Moses); in the Koran; in the doctrine of predestination by God; in the Day of Judgement; and in the bodily resurrection of all people on this day. Religious practice was also standardized under the Muslim law, **Sharia**, in the **Five Pillars of Islam**. The first "pillar" is the confession of faith, *shahada*, that "There is no god but God, and Mohammed is his messenger." The other four are: prayer (*salat*) five times daily, almsgiving (*zakat*), fasting (*saum*), especially during the month of Ramadan and, if possible, pilgrimage (*hajj*) to Mecca, the ultimate goal of every practising Muslim.

Islam in South India

The first Muslims to settle in India were traders who arrived on the south coast in the seventh century, probably in search of timber for shipbuilding. Later, in 711, Muslims entered Sind, in the northwest, to take action against Hindu pirates, and dislodged the Hindu government. Their presence, however, was short-lived. Much more significant was the invasion of North India, first under **Mahmud of Ghazni**, then under the Turkish **sultanates** from the twelfth century on. It was the powerful **Moghuls** (see p.647) who succeeded them and pushed Islam deep into central and northern India, although the South remained largely unconquered.

The Muslims of the Malabar Coast, and especially Kerala, owe their roots not to migration from central Asia but to the long history of trade and interaction with the Arab world. These Muslims of the **Moplah** community have nurtured a unique heritage alongside their Hindu and Christian neighbours. More recently, returning expatriate workers from the Gulf have helped to inject new wealth into the Moplah community and provide a facelift for towns like Kozhikode.

Many of the Muslims who settled in South India intermarried with Hindus, Buddhists and Jains, and the community spread. A further factor in its growth was the arrival of the **Sufis**, whose proselitizing missions in what is now northern Karnataka intensified with the rise of the Deccani sultans in the fourteenth century. Their teachings emphasized abstinence and self-denial in service to God, and stressed the attainment of inner knowledge of God through meditation and mystical experience. Sufi teachings particularly appealed to Shaivites and Vaishnavites, who shared their passion for personal closeness to God. This similarity meant that Sufis were more easily able to adapt to the cultural landscape of medieval India – although not all groups of Sufis were benign; some took to the task of spreading the word with zeal and with the occasional use of force.

For sufis, music (particularly *qawwali* singing) and dance is a significant medium of expression, and for this reason they have always been shunned by orthodox Muslims. However, this devotional music appealed to Hindus, for whom *kirtan* (singing) has played an important role in religious practice. One *qawwali*, relating the life of the Sufi saint Waris Ali Shah, draws parallels between his early life and the childhood of Krishna – an outrage for hardline Muslims, but attractive to Hindus. Sufi shrines, or *dargahs*, all over India bridge the gap between Islam and Hinduism. The most important in the region are Hazrat Gesu Daraz in Gulbarga, northern Karnataka; the hilltop shrine of Sikander Shah near Madurai; and the Golgumbaz in Bijapur.

Practice

Muslims are enjoined to pray five times daily. They may do this at home or in a **mosque**; the latter are always full at noon on Friday for communal prayer (although the Druze, an esoteric sect based in Mumbai, hold communal prayers on Thursdays). All mosques are distinguishable by their bulbous white domes and minarets, from which a *muezzin* calls the faithful to prayer, although they range in scale from the grand edifices of Hyderabad to those in rural areas of Karnataka, for example, where the landscape is scattered with mosques that are no more than a simple wall between two minarets, standing in a field outside the village. All mosques also feature a *mihrab*, or niche indicating the direction of prayer (to Mecca), and some may also include a *mimbar* or pulpit, from which the Friday sermon is read, a source of water for ablutions, and a separate balcony for women.

The position of **women** in Islam is a subject of great debate. It is customary for women to be veiled, and in strictly orthodox communities most wear a *burqa*, usually black, that covers them from head to toe. In larger cities, however, many women do not cover their head. Like other Indian women, Muslim women take second place to men in public, but in the home, where they are often shielded from men's eyes in an inner courtyard, they wield great influence. In theory, **education** is equally available to boys and girls, but girls tend to forgo learning soon after they are 16, encouraged instead to assume the traditional role of wife and mother.

On **marriage**, a woman *receive*s a **dowry** from her husband as financial security and a sign of respect. Contrary to popular belief, polygamy is not widespread; while it does occur, and Mohammed himself had several wives, many Muslims prefer monogamy, and several sects actually stress it as the duty of Muslims.

In Islam, **divorce** may occur through the Indian court, or according to Muslim law, but a woman can only divorce her husband if there is mutual consent.

Christianity

Around fifteen million of India's 22 million **Christians** live in the South, practising in one or another of the largely indigenized versions of established

Church denominations. There has also been a spread of alternative experiments, including ashrams in which devotees practise a synthesis of Hindu and Christian elements, following a programme of retreat and meditation not so different from that in traditional monasteries in the West.

Christianity in South India

The Christian presence in South India goes back a long way – the **Apostle Thomas** ("Doubting Thomas") is said to have arrived in Kerala, in 54 AD, to convert itinerant Jewish traders living in the flourishing port of Muziris. There are many tales of the miracles performed by **Mar Thoma**, as St Thomas is known in Malayalam. One legend tells of how he approached a group of Hindu brahmins of Palur (now Malabar) who were trying to appease the gods by throwing water into the air; if the gods accepted the offerings, the droplets would hang above them. St Thomas also threw water in the air, which miraculously remained suspended, leading the brahmins to convert to Christianity there and then. It is customarily believed in the South that St Thomas was martyred and buried on December 21, 72 AD, at Mylapore in Chennai, whose former name, Madras, comes from the Syriac, "*madrasa*" meaning "monastery". His tomb has since been a major place of pilgrimage and, in recognition of this, in the late nineteenth century the Portuguese built the San Thome Cathedral on the site. By oral tradition, this is the **oldest Christian denomination** in the world, but actual documentary evidence of Christian activity in the subcontinent can only be traced back to the sixth century, when immigrant Syrian communities were granted settlement rights along the Malabar coastline by royal charter. Ever since, Christianity has flourished in Kerala, aided by magnanimous Hindu rulers.

Christianity then spread across the South by attracting indigenous congregations; the concept of a godhead and soul, simplicity and prayer, was not dissimilar to traditional Indian mysticism and spirituality. In the pre-colonial era, the manner in which Christianity developed was largely affected by the local cultural environment and retained Indian customs, with congregations bringing their social beliefs and habits to church. The Syrian Christians, especially, developed a social hierarchy that had overtones of the Hindu caste system.

The history of **foreign domination** from the sixteenth century in India is closely affiliated to the spread of Christianity across the whole subcontinent. **St Francis Xavier** arrived in the Portuguese trading colony of Goa in 1552 to convert and establish missions to reach out to the Hindu "untouchables"; his tomb and alleged relics are retained in the Basilica of Bom Jesus in Old Goa. In 1559, the bloody and brutal Inquisition in Goa by Portuguese Jesuit missionaries, at the behest of their king, marked the height of a campaign to "cleanse" the small colony of Hindu and Muslim religious practice, although it was actually set up primarily to purge the colony of Jews.

The **British** initially took the attitude that the subcontinent was a heathen and polytheistic civilization waiting to be proselytized. By the nineteenth century, conversion to Christianity was particularly appealing to those of the lower and sub-castes, and in the South mass conversions took place in Andhra Pradesh. Later, the British realized that conversion did not necessarily incur a change in moral and educational standards; they gradually became less zealous in their missionary efforts and content to provide social welfare among the more established Christian communities and to build very English-looking churches in their cantonments.

Christian society

Today, Christians in Goa and Kerala number nearly a third and a fifth of the population respectively. While most in Goa follow the **Catholicism** of their former Portuguese rulers, Kerala is home to an array of denominations, ranging from Catholic through Syrian and Malankara **Orthodox** to the Church of South India, modelled on **Anglicanism**; see p.386 for more on this.

As Christianity, based on the equality and brotherhood expounded by its founder Jesus Christ, is intended to be free of caste stigmas, it is attractive to those seeking social advancement and consequently there have always been conversions among disaffected tribal peoples and untouchables. Although the syncretic nature of Christianity in southern India has meant that it has largely avoided the situation in some of the northern states, where there has recently been a rise in tension between Christian communities and Hindu extremists.

Practice

Christian practice in South India has, over the centuries, absorbed many elements of Hindu worship. In Tamil Nadu, Christian **festivals** are highly structured along "caste" lines and, like their Hindu brethren, Tamil Christians never eat beef or pork as it is considered polluting. In many churches across the South, you will see devotees offering the Hindu *arati*-plate of coconut, sweets and rice, and women wearing a *tilak* dot on their forehead. Christians carry plates of food to the graves of their ancestors to honour their dead, on the anniversary of their death, in much the same manner that a Hindu family will share a feast on such a day.

In the same way that Hindus and Muslims consider the **pilgrimage** to be an integral part of life's journey, Indian Christians tend to visit churches where there is a relic, such as a shard of finger bone alleged to have belonged to St Thomas. Most churches in Kerala and Goa claim to hold at least one part of the saint's body, especially his fingers and toes. These relics are brought out on special feast days, and huge crowds will jostle to catch a rare sight of the tiny bit of yellowing bone lying in a casket.

Christians in India have never adopted the practice of giving or receiving **dowry** on the occasion of marriage, although in an arrangement similar to Hindu practice, a Christian **marriage** tends to take place between a man and woman who are members of the same denomination or sect. In most cases, the parents of the couple play a central role in the selection process, paying particular attention to the social status and education of the prospective bride or groom. If a woman becomes a **widow**, she is not socially ostracized as a Hindu woman would be, but is instead encouraged to remarry.

Buddhism

For several centuries **Buddhism** dominated India, with adherents in almost every part of the subcontinent. However, having reached its height in the fifth century, it was all but eclipsed by the time of the Muslim conquest. Today, Buddhists constitute a minute fraction of the population in South India, but a collection of superb monuments offer firm reminders of the previous importance of the faith, and its central role in southern India's cultural legacy.

Origins and development

The founder of Buddhism, **Siddhartha Gautama**, known as the **Buddha**, "the awakened one", was born into a wealthy *kshatrya* family in Lumbini, north of the Gangetic plain in present-day Nepal, around 566 BC. Brought up in luxury as a prince and a Hindu, he married at an early age but renounced family life when he was 30. Unsatisfied with the explanations of worldly suffering proposed by Hindu gurus, and convinced that asceticism did not lead to spiritual awakening, Siddhartha spent years in meditation, wandering through the ancient kingdom of Magadha. His enlightenment (*bodhi*) is said to have taken place under a *bodhi* tree in **Bodhgaya** (Bihar), after a night of contemplation during which he resisted the worldly temptations set before him by the demon, Mara. Soon afterwards he gave his first sermon in **Sarnath**, just outside Varanasi, now a major pilgrimage centre. For the rest of his life he taught, expounding **Dharma**, the true nature of the world, human life and spiritual attainment. Before his death (c.486 BC) in Kushinagara (Uttar Pradesh, North India), he established the **sangha**, a community of monks and nuns, who continued his teachings.

The Buddha's view of life incorporated the Hindu concepts of *samsara* and karma, but remodelled the ultimate goal of religion, calling it **nirvana** (literally "no wind"). Indefinable in worldly terms, *nirvana* is represented by clarity of mind, pure understanding and unimaginable bliss. Its attainment signals an end to rebirth, but no communion of a "soul" with God; neither has independent existence. The most important concept outlined by the Buddha was that all things, subject to change and dependence, are characterized by **impermanence**, and there is **no self**, no permanent ego, so **attachment** to anything (possessions, emotions, spiritual attainment and *devas*) must be renounced before impermanence can be grasped, and *nirvana* realized.

Disregarding caste and priestly dominance in ritual, the Buddha formulated a teaching open to all. His followers took refuge in the three jewels – the Buddha, Dharma, and Sangha – and his teachings became known as **Theravada**, or "Doctrine of the Elders". By the first century BC the **Tripitaka**, or "Three Baskets" (a Pali canon in three sections), had set out the basis for early Buddhist practice. *Dana* (selfless giving) and *sila* (precepts which aim at avoiding harm to oneself and others), were presented as the most important guidelines for all Buddhists, and the essential code of practice for the lay community.

Carried out with good intentions, *dana* and *sila* maximize the acquisition of good karma, and minimize material attachment, thus making the individual open to the more religiously oriented teachings, the **Four Noble Truths**. The first of these states that all is suffering (*dukkha*), not because every action is necessarily unpleasurable, but because nothing in the phenomenal world is permanent or reliable. The second truth states that *dukkha* arises through attachment, the third refers to *nirvana*, the cessation of suffering, and the fourth details the path to *nirvana*. Known as the **Eightfold Path** – right understanding, thought, speech, action, livelihood, effort, mindfulness and concentration – it aims at reducing attachment and ego and increasing awareness, until all four truths are thoroughly comprehended, and *nirvana* is achieved. Even this should not be clung to – those who experience it are advised by the Buddha to use their understanding to help others to achieve realization.

The Sanskrit word **bhavana**, referred to in the West as **meditation**, translates literally as "bringing into being". Traditionally meditation is divided into two categories: **Samatha**, or calm, which stills and controls the mind, and **Vipassana**, or insight, during which thought processes and the noble truths are investigated, leading ultimately to a knowledge of reality. Today, both methods are taught.

At first, Buddhist iconography represented the Buddha by symbols such as a footprint, *bodhi* tree, parasol or vase. These can be seen on stupas (domed monuments containing relics of the Buddha) built throughout India from the time of the Buddhist emperor Ashoka (see p.640), and in ancient Buddhist caves, which served as meditation retreats and *viharas* (monasteries). Though the finest examples are to be found in the North, there are interesting sites in the South, such as the stupas at Amaravati and Nagarjunakonda in Andhra Pradesh and caves at Aihole and Badami in Karnataka.

This artistic development coincided with an increase in the devotional side of Buddhism, and the recognition of **bodhisattvas** – those bound for enlightenment who delayed their self-absorption in *nirvana* to become teachers, spurred by selfless compassion and altruism. The importance of the *bodhisattva* ideal grew as a new school, the **Mahayana**, or "Great Vehicle", emerged. By the twelfth century it had become fully established and, somewhat disparagingly, renamed the old school **Hinayana**, or "Lesser Vehicle". Mahayanists proposed emptiness (*sunyata*) as the fundamental nature of all things, taking to extremes the belief that nothing has independent existence. The **wisdom** necessary to understand *sunyata*, and the **skilful means** required to put wisdom into action in daily life and teaching, and interpret emptiness in a positive sense, became the most important qualities of Mahayana Buddhism. Before long *bodhisattvas* were joined in both scripture and art by female consorts who embodied wisdom.

Theravada Buddhism survives today in Sri Lanka, Burma, Thailand, Laos and Cambodia. Mahayana Buddhism spread from India to China, Japan, Korea and Vietnam, where it incorporated local gods and spirits into a family of *bodhisattvas*. In many places further evolution saw the adoption of magical methods, esoteric teachings and the full use of sense experience to bring about spiritual transformation, resulting in a separate school known as **Mantrayana** or **Vajrayana** based on texts called *tantras*. Mantrayana encouraged meditation on *mandalas* (symbolic diagrams representing the cosmos and internal spiritual attainment), sexual imagery and sometimes sexual practice, in which the female principle of wisdom could be united with skilful means.

Practice

For Buddhist monks and nuns, and some members of the lay community, meditation is an integral part of religious life. Most lay Buddhists concentrate on *dana* and *sila*, and on auspicious days, such as *Vesak* (marking the Buddha's birth, enlightenment and death), make **pilgrimages** to Bodhgaya, Sarnath, Lumbini and Kushinagar (all in northern India). After laying offerings before Buddha statues, devotees gather in silent meditation, or join in chants taken from early Buddhist texts.

Uposathas, full moon days, are marked by continual **chanting** through the night. Temples are lit by glimmering butter lamps, often set afloat on lotus ponds, among the flowers that represent the essential beauty and purity to be found in each person in the thick of the confusing "mud" of daily life.

Jainism

The **Jain** tradition has been tremendously influential for at least 2500 years, though there is now only a tiny Jain population in South India, with most families involved in commerce and trade. This dwindling community represents a tradition that has been tremendously influential for at least 2500 years.

Similarities to Hindu worship, and a shared respect for nature and non-violence, have contributed to the decline of the Jain society through conversion to Hinduism, but there is no antagonism between the two faiths.

Origins and development

The Jain doctrine is based upon the teachings of **Mahavira**, or "Great Hero", the last in a succession of 24 **tirthankaras** ("crossing-makers") said to appear on earth every 300 million years. Mahavira (c.599–27 BC) was born as Vardha-mana Jnatrputra into a *kshatrya* family near modern Patna, in northeast India. Like the Buddha, Mahavira rejected family life at the age of 30, and spent years wandering as an ascetic, renouncing all possessions in an attempt to conquer attachment to worldly values. Firmly opposed to sacrificial rites and caste distinctions, after gaining complete understanding and detachment, he began teaching others, not about Vedic gods and divine heroes, but about the true nature of the world, and the means required for release, *moksha*, from an endless cycle of rebirth.

His teachings were written down in the first millennium BC, and Jainism prospered throughout India, under the patronage of kings such as Chandragupta Maurya (third century BC). Not long after, there was a schism, in part based on linguistic and geographical divisions, but mostly due to differences in monastic practice. On the one hand the **Digambaras** ("sky-clad") believed that nudity was an essential part of world renunciation, and that women are incapable of achieving liberation from worldly existence. The ("white-clad") **Svetambaras**, however, disregarded the extremes of nudity, incorporated nuns into monastic communities and even acknowledged a female *tirthankara*.

In an incredibly complicated process of philosophical analysis known as **Anekanatavada** (many-sidedness), Jainism approaches all questions of exist-ence, permanence and change from seven different viewpoints, maintaining that things can be looked at in an infinite number of valid ways. Thus it claims to remove the intellectual basis for violence, avoiding the potentially damaging result of holding a one-sided view. In this respect Jainism accepts other religious philosophies, and it has adopted, with a little reinterpretation, several Hindu festivals and practices.

Focusing on the practice of **ahimsa** (non-violence), Jains follow a rigorous discipline to avoid harm to all **jivas**, or "souls", which exist not only in animals and humans, but also in plants, water, fire, earth and air. They assert that every *jiva* is pure, omniscient and capable of achieving liberation, or *moksha*, from existence in this universe. However, *jivas* are obscured by **karma**, a form of subtle matter that clings to the soul, is born of action, and binds the *jiva* to physical existence. For the most orthodox Jain, the only way to dissociate karma from the *jiva*, and thereby escape the wheel of death and rebirth, is to follow the path of asceticism and meditation, rejecting passion, wrong view, attachment, carelessness and impure action.

Practice

Today the two Jain sects worship at different temples, but the number of naked Digambaras is minimal. Many Svetambara monks and nuns wear white masks to avoid breathing in insects, and carry a "fly-whisk", sometimes used to brush their path; none will use public transport, and they often spend days or weeks walking barefoot to a pilgrimage site. Practising Jain householders vow to avoid injury, falsehood, theft (which includes cheating in commerce), infidelity and worldly attachment.

Jain **temples** are wonderfully ornate, with pillars, brackets and spires carved by *silavats* into voluptuous maidens, musicians, saints and even Hindu deities; the swastika symbol commonly set into the marble floors is central to Jainism, representing the four states of rebirth as gods, humans, "hell beings", or animals and plants. Worship in temples consists of prayer and puja before images of the *tirthankaras*; the devotee circumambulates the image, chants sacred verses and makes offerings of flowers, sandalwood paste, rice, sweets and incense. It's common to fast four times a month on *parvan* (holy) days, the eighth and fourteenth days of the moon's waxing and waning periods. While reducing attachment to the body, this emulates the fast to death (while in meditation), or *sallekhana*, accepted by Jain mendicants as a final rejection of attachment, and a relatively harmless way to end worldly life.

To enter a monastic community, lay Jains must pass through eleven *pratimas*, starting with right views, the profession of vows, fasting and continence, and culminating in the renunciation of family life. Once a monk or nun, a Jain aims to clarify understanding through meditation, hoping to extinguish passions and sever the ties of karma and attachment, entering fourteen spiritual stages (*gunasthanas*) to emerge as a fully enlightened, omniscient being. Whether pursuing a monastic or lay lifestyle, however, Jains recognize the rarity of enlightenment, and religious practice is, for the most part, aimed at achieving a state of rebirth more conducive to spiritual attainment.

Pilgrimage sites are known as **tirthas**, but this does not refer to the literal meaning of "river crossing", sacred to Hindus because of the purificatory nature of water. One of the foremost Svetambara *tirthas* is **Shatrunjaya**, in Gujarat in northern India, where over nine hundred temples crown a single hill. There is also an important Digambara *tirtha* at **Sravanabelgola** in Karnataka, where an eighteen-metre-high image of Bahubali (recognized as the first human to attain liberation) stands at the summit of a hill, and is anointed in the huge *abhishekha* festival every twelve years.

Zoroastrianism

Of all South India's religious communities, Western visitors are least likely to come across – or recognize – **Zoroastrians**, who have no distinctive dress and few houses of worship. Most live in Mumbai, where they are known as **Parsis** (Persians) and are active in business, education and politics. Today, the most famous Parsis are the Tata family – leading industrialists who have long held an unprecedented monopoly over a vast range of commercial interests that range from trucks, cars and scooters to several major steel and chemical factories, tea plantations and even lipsticks. Nonetheless, economic successes aside, Zoroastrian numbers (roughly 90,000) are dwindling rapidly, mainly due to the strict rule of intermarriage and a sharp decline in the birth rate; Parsis are increasingly forced to marry into the wider community and their distinct identity is slowly becoming diluted.

Origins and development

The religion's founder, **Zarathustra** (Zoroaster), who lived in Iran in 6000 BC (according to Zoroastrians), or between 1700 and 1400 BC, was the first religious prophet to expound a dualistic philosophy, based on the opposing powers of good and evil. For Zarathustra, the absolute, wholly good and wise god, **Ahura Mazda**, together with his holy spirit and six emanations present in earth, water, the sky, animals, plants and fire, is constantly at odds with an evil power, **Angra Mainyu**, who is aided by **daevas**, or evil spirits.

Mankind, whose task on earth is to further good, faces judgement after death, and depending on the proportion of good and bad words, thoughts and actions will find a place in heaven or suffer the torments of hell. Zarathustra looked forward to a day of judgement, when a saviour, **Saoshyant**, miraculously born of a seed of the prophet and a virgin maiden, will appear on earth, restoring Ahura Mazda's perfect realm and expelling all impure souls and spirits to hell.

The first Zoroastrians to enter India arrived on the Gujarati coast in the tenth century, soon after the Arabian conquest of Iran, and by the seventeenth century most had settled in Mumbai.

Practice

Zoroastrian practice is based on the responsibility of every man and woman to choose between good and evil and to respect God's creations. Five daily prayers, usually hymns (*gathas*), uttered by Zarathustra and standardized in the main Zoroastrian text, the **Avesta**, are said in the home or in a temple, before a fire, which symbolizes the realm of truth, righteousness and order. For this reason, Zoroastrians are often, incorrectly, called "fire-worshippers".

No Ruz, or "New Day", which celebrates the creation of fire and the ultimate triumph of good over evil, is the most popular Zoroastrian festival.

Members of other faiths may not enter Zoroastrian temples, but one custom that is evident to outsiders is the method of disposing of the dead. A body is laid on a high open rooftop (or isolated hill) known as *dakhma* (often referred to as a "tower of silence"), for the flesh to be eaten by vultures, and the bones cleansed by the sun and wind. Recently, some Zoroastrians, by necessity, have adopted more common methods of cremation or burial; in order not to bring impurity to fire or earth, they only use electric crematoria, and shroud coffins in concrete before laying them in the ground.

Sacred art and architecture

It's often said that South India is the most religious place on earth, and if the region's vast storehouse of sacred art and architecture is anything to go by, this is probably true. For thousands of years, successive chieftains, emperors, nawabs and nizams – whether Hindu, Buddhist, Jain or Muslim – have assigned huge sums of money and human resources towards raising religious structures, as much to symbolize the power of their earthly rule as the super-human power of the gods and natural forces. Some, like the towering temple *gopuras* of Tamil Nadu and the gigantic Golgumbaz tomb at Bijapur, were conceived on an awesome scale; others, such as the rock-cut Pallava shrines in Mamallapuram and the meticulously crafted architecture of the Hoysalas in Karnataka, were more intimate. Yet the South's religious monuments have one thing in common: nearly all of them testify to the Indians' enduring love of elaboration. Even the most austere Muslim sultans of the Deccan couldn't resist decorating their tombs and mosques with exquisite geometric shapes, while the attention to fine detail demonstrated by the sculptors of the Cholas is astonishing when juxtaposed with the sheer size of the buildings.

Another common feature of South Indian religious art and architecture is the extent to which the various mediums have, over the centuries, been governed by **convention**. In the same way as ritual follows precise rules passed through generations, buildings and their decor conform to the most exacting specifications, set down in ancient canonical texts. This is particularly true of **iconography** – the complex language of symbols used to represent gods, goddesses and saints, in their many and diverse forms. Even nowadays, the stone-carvers of Mamallapuram spend years learning how to render the exact size and lines of their subjects. Without such exactitude, an icon or religious building is deemed to be devoid of its essential power. If the proportions are incorrect, the all-important sequence of auspicious numbers through which the magical power of the gods become manifest is disrupted, and the essential order of the universe compromised.

Such rigorous adherence to tradition would seem to leave little scope for innovation, but somehow South Indian artists have devised an amazing variety of **regional styles**. One of the most absorbing aspects of travelling around the peninsula is comparing these. After a while, you'll begin to be able to differentiate between them and, in the process, gain a more vivid sense of the people and period that created them. The following descriptions are intended as a primer; for more in-depth explorations, hunt out some of the titles listed on p.724.

Stupas

Among the very earliest sacred structures built in India were hemispherical mounds known as **stupas**, which have been central to Buddhist worship since the sixth century BC, when the Buddha himself modelled the first prototype. Asked by one of his disciples for a symbol to help disseminate his teachings after his death, the master took his begging bowl, teaching staff and a length of cloth – his only worldly possessions – and arranged them into the form of a stupa, using the cloth as a base, the upturned bowl as the dome and the stick as the projecting finial, or spire.

Originally, stupas were simple burial mounds of compacted earth and stone containing relics of the Buddha and his followers. As the religion spread, however, the basic components multiplied and became imbued with **symbolic significance**. The main dome, or *anda* – representing the sacred mountain, or axis, linking heaven and earth – grew larger, while the wooden railings, or *vedikas*, surrounding it were replaced by massive stone ones. A raised ambulatory terrace, or *medhi*, was added to the vertical sides of the drum, along with two flights of stairs and four ceremonial entrances, carefully aligned with the cardinal points. Finally, crowing the tip of the stupa, the single spike evolved into a three-tiered umbrella, or *chhattra*, representing the Three Jewels of Buddhism: the Buddha, the Law and the community of monks, or *Sangham*.

The *chhattra*, usually enclosed within a low square stone railing, or *harmika* (a throwback to the days when sacred *bodhi* trees were surrounded by fences), formed the topmost point of the axis, directly above the reliquary in the heart of the stupa. Ranging from bits of bone wrapped in cloth to fine caskets of precious metals, crystal and carved stone, the reliquaries were the "seeds" and their protective mounds the "egg". Excavations on the estimated eighty-four thousand stupas scattered around the subcontinent have shown that the solid interiors were also sometimes built as elaborate **mandalas** – symbolic patterns that exerted a beneficial influence over the stupa and those who walked around it. The ritual of **circumambulation**, or *pradakshina*, which enabled the worshipper to tap into a magical force-field and be transported from the mundane to the divine realms, was always carried out in a clockwise direction from the east, in imitation of the sun's passage across the heavens.

In South India, the **Satavahana** (or Andhra) dynasty, who ruled a vast tract of the country towards the end of the first millennium (see History, p.641), erected stupas across the region, among them the Great Stupa at **Amaravati** in Andhra Pradesh (see p.597). Little of this once-impressive monument remains in situ, but you can admire some of the outstanding sculpture that decorated its ornamental gateways (*toranas*) in the Government Museum at Chennai (see p.455). To see a stupa in action, however, you have to follow in the footsteps of the emperor Ashoka's missionaries southwards to Sri Lanka, where stupas are still revered as repositories of sacred energy.

Temples

To make sense of Hindu **temples**, you need to be able to identify their common features. Many of these conventions are recorded in the **Shilpa Shastras** – Sanskrit manuals that set out, in meticulous detail, ancient building specifications and their symbolic significance.

Unlike Christian churches or Muslim mosques, temples are not simply places of worship, but are objects of worship in themselves – re-creations of the "Divine-Cosmic-Creator-Being" or the particular deity enshrined within them. For a Hindu, to move through a temple is akin to entering the very body of the god, and to glimpse the deity in the shrine-room during the moment of *darshan*, or ritual viewing, is the culmination of an act of worship. In South India, this concept also finds expression in the technical terms used in the

Shastras to designate different parts of the structure: the foot, shin, torso, neck, head and so forth.

The temples of Tamil Nadu

No Indian state is more dominated by its **temples** than Tamil Nadu, whose huge temple towers dominate most towns and villages. The majority were built in honour of Shiva or Vishnu and their consorts; all are characterized not only by their design and sculptures, but by constant activity – devotion, dancing, singing, pujas, festivals and feasts. Each is tended by brahmin priests, recognizable by their *dhotis* (loincloths), a sacred thread draped over the right shoulder and marks on the forehead. One to three horizontal (usually white) lines distinguish Shaivites; vertical lines (yellow or red), often converging into a near-V shape, are common among Vaishnavites.

Dravida, the temple architecture of Tamil Nadu, first took form in the **Pallava** port of **Mamallapuram**. A step up from the cave retreats of Hindu and Jain ascetics, the earliest Pallava monuments were **mandapas**, shrines cut into rock-faces and fronted by columns. The magnificent **bas-relief** at Mamallapuram, **Arjuna's Penance**, shows the fluid carving of the Pallavas at its most exquisite. This sculptural skill was transferred to free-standing temples, **rathas**, carved out of single rocks and incorporating the essential elements of Hindu temples: the dim inner sanctuary, the *garbhagriha*, capped with a modest tapering spire featuring repetitive architectural motifs. In turn, the Shore Temple was built with three shrines, topped by a *vimana* similar to the towering roofs of the *rathas*; statues of Nandi, Shiva's bull, later to receive pride of place, surmount its low walls. In the finest structural Pallava temple, the Kailasanatha Temple at **Kanchipuram**, the sanctuary, again crowned with a pyramidal *vimana*, stands within a courtyard enclosed by high walls. The projecting and recessing bays of the walls, carved with images of Shiva, his consort and ghoulish mythical lions, *yalis*, were the prototype for later styles.

Pallava themes were developed in Karnataka by the Chalukyas and Rashtrakutas, but it was the Shaivite **Cholas** who spearheaded Tamil Nadu's next architectural phase, in the tenth century. In **Thanjavur**, Rajaraja I created the Brihadeshwara temple principally as a status symbol. Its proportions far exceed any attempted by the Pallavas. Set within a vast walled courtyard, the sanctuary, fronted by a small pillared hall (*mandapa*), stands beneath a sculpted *vimana* that soars over sixty metres high. Most sculptures once again feature Shiva, but the **gopuras**, or towers, each side of the eastern gateway to the courtyard, were a new innovation, as were the lions carved into the base of the sanctuary walls, and the pavilion erected over Nandi in front of the sanctuary. The second great Chola temple was built in **Gangaikondacholapuram** by Rajendra I. Instead of a mighty *vimana*, he introduced new elements, adding subsidiary shrines and placing an extended *mandapa* in front of the central sanctuary, its pillars writhing with dancers and deities.

By the time of the thirteenth-century **Vijayanagar** kings, the temple was central to city life, the focus for civic meetings, education, dance and theatre. The Vijayanagars extended earlier structures, adding enclosing walls around a series of *prakaras*, or courtyards, and erecting free-standing *mandapas* for use as meeting halls, elephant stables, stages for music and dance, and ceremonial marriage halls. Raised on superbly decorated columns, these *mandapas* became known as **thousand-pillared halls** (*kalyan mandapas*). **Tanks** were added, doubling as water stores and washing areas, and used for festivals when deities were set afloat in boats surrounded by glimmering oil lamps.

Under the **Vijayanagars**, the *gopuras* were enlarged and set at the cardinal points over the high gateways to each *prakara*, to become the dominant feature. Rectangular in plan, and embellished with images of animals and local saints or rulers as well as deities, *gopuras* are periodically repainted in pinks, blues, whites and yellows, a sharp and joyous contrast with the earthy browns and greys of halls and sanctuaries below. **Madurai** is the place to check out Vijayanagar architecture, and experience the timeless temple rituals. Dimly lit halls and sun-drenched courtyards hum with murmured prayers, and regularly come alive for festivals in which Shiva and his "fish-eyed" consort (see p.538) are hauled through town on mighty wooden chariots tugged by hordes of devotees. Outside Tiruchirapalli, the temple at **Srirangam** was extended by the Vijayanagar Nayaks to become South India's largest. Unlike that in Madurai, it incorporates earlier Chola foundations. The ornamentation, with pillars formed into rearing horses, is superb.

ⓒ Hoysala temples

The Hoysala dynasty ruled southwestern Karnataka between the eleventh and thirteenth centuries. From the twelfth century, after the accession of King Vishnu Vardhana, they built a series of distinctive temples centred primarily at three sites: **Belur** (see p.272) and **Halebid** (see p.270) close to modern Hassan, and **Somnathpur** (see p.265), near Mysore.

At first sight, and from a distance, Hoysala temples appear to be modest structures, compact and even squat. On closer inspection, however, their profusion of fabulously detailed and sensuous sculpture, covering every inch of the exterior, is astonishing. Detractors are prone to class Hoysala art as decadent and overly fussy, but anyone with an eye for craftsmanship is likely to marvel at these jewels of Karnatakan art.

The intricacy of the carvings was made possible by the material used in construction: a soft **steatite soapstone** which on oxidization hardens to a glassy, highly polished surface. The level of detail, similar to that seen in sandalwood and ivory work, became increasingly freer and fluid as the style developed, and reached its highest point at Somnathpur. Beautiful bracket figures, often delicate portrayals of voluptuous female subjects, were placed under the eaves, fixed by pegs top and bottom. A later addition (except possibly in the Somnathpur temple), these serve no structural function.

Another technique more usually associated with wood is the unusual treatment of the massive stone pillars: lathe-turned, they resemble those of the wooden temples of Kerala. They were probably turned on a horizontal plane, pinned at each end, and rotated with the use of a rope. It may be no coincidence that, to this day, wood-turning is still a local speciality. Only the central shaft of each pillar seems to have been turned; in the base and capitals, a less precise, presumably handworked, imitation of turning is evident.

The architectural style of the Hoysala temples is commonly referred to as **vesara**, or "hybrid" (literally "mule"), rather than belonging to either the northern, nagari, or southern, Dravidian styles. However, they show great affinity with nagari temples of western India, and represent another fruit of contact, like music, painting and literature, facilitated by the trade routes between the North and the South. All Hoysala temples share a star-shaped plan, built on high plinths (*jagati*) which follow the shape of the sanctuaries and *mandapas* to provide a raised surrounding platform. Such northern features may have been introduced by the designer and artists of the earliest temple at Belur, who were imported by Vishnu Vardhana from further north in Andhra Pradesh. Also characteristic of the Hoysala style is the use of ashlar masonry, without mortar. Some pieces of stones are joined by pegs of iron or bronze, or mortice and tenon joints. Ceilings inside the *mandapas* are made up of corbelled domes, looking similar to those of the Jain temples of Rajasthan and Gujarat; in the Hoysala style they are only visible from inside.

Keralan temples

As you'd expect from one of India's most culturally distinct regions, **Kerala**'s temples are quite unlike those elsewhere in the South. Their most striking features are the sloping tiled roofs – built to defend against torrential downpours – that crown the sanctuaries, colonnades and gateways. In addition, the innermost shrines are invariably circular, or apsidal – perhaps in imitation of earlier indigenous styles.

In the corner of the spacious temple courtyards (which are often very broad to make room for the annual elephant processions) stands a covered hall with beautiful lathe-turned pillars and wooden panels, where performances of Kathakali and other forms of ritualized theatre are held (see p.714). In some older temples, **murals** also adorn the inner faces of the high enclosing walls (see p.690).

Keralan temples are generally closed to non-Hindus, but many make exceptions during festivals, when drum bands, tuskers and ritual dances comprise some of the most compelling spectacles in all of South India (see "Thrissur Puram", p.420).

Goan temples

Stick to the former Portuguese heartland of Goa, and you'd be forgiven for thinking the state was exclusively Christian. It isn't, of course, as the innumerable brightly painted Hindu temples hidden amid the lush woodland and areca groves of the more outlying areas confirm. The oldest-established and best known lie well away from the coastal resorts, but are worth hunting out.

Goa's first stone temples date from the rule of the Kadamba dynasty, between the fifth and fifteenth century AD. From the few fragments of sculpture and masonry unearthed at the ruins of their old capital, it is clear that these were as skilfully constructed as the famous monuments of the neighbouring Deccan region. However, only one, the richly carved Mahadeva temple at **Tamdi Surla** in east Goa, has survived. The rest were systematically destroyed, first by Muslim invaders, and later by the Portuguese.

Goan temples incorporate the main elements of Hindu architecture, but boast some unusual features of their own – some developed in response to the local climate or the availability of building materials, others the result of outside influences. The impact of European-Portuguese styles (inevitable given the fact that the majority of Goan temples were built during the colonial era, but ironic considering that the Portuguese destroyed the originals) is most evident on the exterior of the buildings. Unlike conventional Hindu temple towers, which are curvilinear, Goan *shikharas*, taking their cue from St Cajetan's church in Old Goa (see p.184), consist of octagonal drums crowned by tapering copper domes. Hidden inside the top of these is generally a pot of holy water called a **poornakalash**, drawn from a sacred Hindu river or spring. The sloping roofs of the *mandapas*, with their projecting eves and terracotta tiles, are also distinctively Latin, while the glazed ceramic Chinese dragons often perched above them, originally imported from Macau, add to the colonial feel. Embellished

CONTEXTS | Sacred art and architecture

with Baroque-style balustrades and pilasters, Islamic arches and the occasional bulbous Moghul dome, the sides of larger temples also epitomize Goan architecture's flair for fusion.

Always worth looking out for inside the main assembly halls are **wood-carvings** and panels of **sculpture** depicting mythological narratives, and the opulently embossed solid silver **doorways** around the entrance to the shrines, flanked by a pair of guardians, or **dvarpalas**. The most distinctively Goan feature of all, however, has to be the **lamp tower**, or *deepmal*, an addition introduced by the Marathas, who ruled much of Goa during the seventeenth and eighteenth centuries. Also known as *deep stambhas*, literally "pillars of light", these five- to seven-storey whitewashed pagodas generally stand opposite the main entrance. Their many ledges and windows hold tiny oil lamps that are illuminated during the *devta*'s weekly promenade, when the temple priests carry the god or goddess around the courtyard on their shoulders in a silver sedan chair known as a **palkhi**.

Near the deepmal you'll often come across a ornamental plant pot called a **tulsi vrindavan**. The straggly sacred shrub growing inside it, tulsi, represents a former mistress of Vishnu whom his jealous consort Lakshmi turned into a plant after a fit of jealous pique.

Hindu sculpture

Hindu sculpture has traditionally been an integral part of temple architecture. Masons and stone-carvers often laboured for decades, even a whole lifetime, on the same site, settled in camps with their families, in much the same style as modern construction workers live around what they are building in India today. Each grade of artisan – from the men who cut the stone blocks or etched bands of decorative friezes, to the master-artists who fashioned the main idols – was a member of a **guild** that functioned along the same lines as caste, determining marriages and social relations. Guilds also controlled the handing down of tools, specialist knowledge and techniques to successive generations, through years of rigorous apprenticeship.

Another role of the guilds was to apply the rules of iconography set in the *Shilpa Shastras*, still followed today. Measurement always begins with the proportions of the artist's own hand and the image's resultant face-length as the basic unit. Then follows a scheme which is allied to the equally scientific rules applied to classical music, and specifically *tala* or rhythm. Human figures total eight face-lengths, eight being the most basic of rhythmic measures. Figures of deities are *nava-tala*, nine face-lengths.

Like their counterparts in medieval Europe, South Indian sculptors remained largely anonymous. Even though the most talented artists may have been known to their peers – in some rare cases earning renown in kingdoms at opposite ends of the subcontinent – their names have become lost over time. An explanation often advanced for this is the *Shastras*' insistence that the personality of an individual artist must be suppressed in order for divine inspiration to flow freely. For this reason, only a tiny number of stone sculptures in India bear inscriptions that preserve the identity of their creators.

With the entry of Indian religious sculpture into the international art market, the old conventions of anonymity are beginning to break down. A handful of sculptors at South India's stone-carving capital, **Mamallapuram** in Tamil Nadu (see p.475), have become well known, as the demand for pieces to adorn temples and shrines in the homes of expatriate Indians has increased. However, age-old guidelines governing iconographic sculpture are still applied here as rigorously as they have been for more than a thousand years, which makes it somewhat difficult to differentiate between the work of masters and less experienced apprentices.

You can watch sculptors in action, and buy their work, at innumerable workshops around Mamallapuram, while the Government Sculpture College nearby welcomes visitors, offering you the chance to see how students learn to measure out the proportions of the sculpture with their hands, and memorize the extraordinary body of iconographic lore that must be fully internalized before they graduate.

Chola bronzes

Originally sacred temple objects, **Chola bronzes** are another art form from Tamil Nadu that has become highly collectable (even if their price tags are considerably higher than stone sculptures). The most memorable bronze icons are the **Natarajas**, or dancing Shivas. The image of Shiva, standing on one leg encircled by flames, with wild locks caught in mid-motion, has become almost as recognizably Indian as the Taj Mahal, and few Indian millionaires would feel their sitting rooms were complete without one.

The principal icons of a temple are usually stationary and made of stone. Frequently, however, ceremonies require an image of the god to be led in procession outside the inner sanctum, and even through the streets. According to the canonical texts known as *Agamas*, these moving images should be made of metal. Indian bronzes are made by the **cire perdu** ("lost-wax") process, known as *madhuchchistavidhana* in Sanskrit. Three layers of clay mixed with burned grain husks, salt and ground cotton are applied to a figure crafted in bees' wax, with a stem left protruding at each end. When that is heated, the wax melts and flows out, creating a hollow mould into which molten metal – a rich five-metal alloy (*panchaloha*) of copper, silver, gold, brass and lead – can be poured through the stems. After the metal has cooled, the clay shell is destroyed, and the stems filed off, leaving a unique completed figure, which the caster-artist, or *sthapathi*, remodels to remove blemishes and add delicate detail.

Knowledge of bronze-casting in India goes back at least as far as the Indus Valley civilization (2500–1500 BC), and the famous "**Dancing Girl**" from Mohenjo Daro. The earliest produced in the South were made by the Andhras, whose techniques were continued by the Pallavas, the immediate antecedents of the Cholas. The few surviving **Pallava** bronzes show a sophisticated handling of the form; figures are characterized by broad shoulders, thick-set features and an overall simplicity that suggests all the detail was completed at the wax stage. The finest bronzes of all, however, are from the **Chola** period, from the late ninth to early eleventh centuries. As the Cholas were predominantly Shaivite, Nataraja, Shiva and his consort Parvati (frequently in a family group with son Skanda) and the 63 Nayanmar poet-saints are the most popular subjects. Chola bronzes display more detail than their predecessors. Human figures are invariably slim-waisted and elegant, with the male form robust and muscular and the female graceful and delicate. As with stone sculpture, the design, iconography and proportions of each figure are governed by the strict rules laid down in the *Shilpa Shastras*, which draw no real distinction between art, science and religion.

Those bronzes produced by the few artists practising today invariably follow the Chola model; the chief centre is now **Swamimalai**, 8km west of Kumbakonam (see p.514). Original Chola bronzes are kept in many Tamil temples, but

CONTEXTS | Sacred art and architecture

as temple interiors are often dark it's not always possible to see them properly. Important **public collections** include the Nayak Durbar Hall Art Museum at Thanjavur, the Government State Museum at Chennai and the National Museum, New Delhi.

Murals

Fragments of paint indicate that **murals** adorned the walls and ceilings of India's oldest rock-cut prayer halls, dating from the third century BC. Only a couple of hundred years later, the art form reached its peak in the sumptuous Satavahana paintings at Ajanta, in the northwest Deccan, where the walls of huge caves were covered in the most exquisite images, rendered in muted reds, greens and blues. For the most part, these show religious scenes – episodes from the life of the Buddha (*jatakas*) – but they also incorporate pictures of courtly life, battles and a host of secular detail. However, remnants of ancient murals in the far south are scant, limited to a few patches at **Badami** in Karnataka (see p.318), and the Kailasanatha temple at **Kanchipuram** (see p.485).

Not until the resurgence of the Tamil Cholas in the ninth and tenth centuries did mural painting flourish again in the region. The finest examples – showing sensuously detailed vignettes from life at the royal court of Rajaraja I – are those decorating the interior of the main sanctum of the Brihadishwara temple at **Thanjavur** (see p.512). Sadly, these are closed to the public, but you can still enjoy the wonderful ceiling paintings of the Nayak rulers at the Shivakamasundari temple in **Chidambaram** (see p.505), which illustrate Shaivite myths and legends.

Keralan murals

One of the best-kept secrets of South Indian art are the unique Keralan murals found at Mattancherry Palace in old Kochi (see p.405) and at around sixty other locations in the state. Most are on the walls of functioning temples; they are not marketable, transportable, or indeed even seen by many non-Hindus. Few date from before the sixteenth century, though their origins may go back to the seventh century, probably influenced by the Pallava style of Tamil Nadu, but only traces in one tenth-century cave temple survive from the earliest period. Castaneda, a traveller who accompanied Vasco da Gama on the first Portuguese landing in India, described how he strayed into a temple, supposing it to be a church, and saw "monstrous looking images with two inch fangs" painted on the walls, causing one of the party to fall to his knees exclaiming, "if this be the devil, I worship God".

Technically classified as **fresco-secco**, Kerala murals employ vegetable and mineral colours, predominantly ochre reds and yellows, white and blue-green, and are coated with a protective sheen of pine resin and oil. Their ingenious design incorporates intense detail with clarity and dynamism in the portrayal of human (and celestial) figures; subtle facial expressions are captured with the simplest of lines, while narrative elements are always bold and arresting. In common with all great Indian art, they share a complex iconography and symbolism.

Non-Hindus can see fine examples in Kochi, Padmanabhapuram (see p.362), Ettumanur (see p.385) and Kayamkulam (see p.373). Visitors interested in how they are made should head for the Mural Painting Institute at Guruvayur. A paperback book, *Murals of Kerala*, by M.G. Shashi Bhooshan serves as an excellent introduction to the field.

Tanjore (Thanjavur) painting

The name **Tanjore painting** is given to a distinctive form of southern picture-making that came to prominence in the eighteenth century, encouraged by the Maratha Raja of Thanjavur, Serfoji. The term "painting", however, is misleading, and inadequate to describe work of the Tanjore school. It is distinctive because – aside from a painted image – details such as clothing, ornaments and any (typically Baroque) architectural elements are raised in low plaster relief from the surface, which is then decorated by the sumptuous addition of glass pieces, pearls, semi-precious or precious stones and elaborate gold-leaf work. Other variations include pictures on mica, ivory and glass. Figures are delineated with simple outlines; unmixed primary colours are used in a strict symbolic code, similar to that found in the make-up used in the classical dramas of Kerala, where each colour indicates qualities of character. Other schools of painting normally show Krishna with blue-black skin; in the Tanjore style, he is white.

Traditionally, most Tanjore paintings depicted Vaishnavite deities, with the most popular single image probably being that of **Balakrishna**, the chubby baby Krishna. In the tenth-century Sanskrit *Bhagavata Purana*, Balakrishna was portrayed as a rascal who delighted in stealing and consuming milk, butter balls and curd. Despite his naughtiness, all women who came into contact with him were seized with an overflowing of maternal affection, to the extent that their breasts spontaneously oozed milk. Thanks to such stories, Krishna as a child became the chosen deity par excellence of mothers and grandmothers. Tanjore paintings typically show him eating, accompanied by adoring women.

Although Tanjore painting went into decline after the nineteenth century, in recent years there has been new demand for works, though intended for domestic, rather than temple, shrines. High-quality work is produced in Thanjavur (see p.515), Kumbakonam (see p.510) and Tiruchirapalli (see p.524).

Kalam ezhuttu

The tradition of **kalam ezhuttu** (pronounced "kalam-erroo-too") – detailed and beautiful ritual drawings, in coloured powder, of deities and geometric patterns (*mandalas*) – is very much alive all over **Kerala**, although few visitors to the region even know of its existence. The designs usually cover an area of around thirty square metres, often outdoors and under a *pandal* – a temporary shelter made from bamboo and palm fronds. Each colour, made from rice flour, turmeric, ground leaves and burnt paddy husk, is painstakingly applied using the thumb and forefinger as a funnel. Three communities produce *kalams*; two come from the temple servant (*amblavasi*) castes, whose rituals are associated with the god Ayappa (see p.393) or the goddess Bhagavati; the third, the *pullavans*, specialize in serpent worship. Iconographic designs emerge gradually from the initial grid lines and turn into startling figures, many of terrible aspect, with wide eyes and fangs. Noses and breasts are raised, giving the whole a three-dimensional effect. As part of the ritual, the significant moment when the powder is added for the iris or pupil, "opening" the eyes, may well be marked by the accompaniment of *chenda* drums and *elatalam* hand-cymbals.

Witnessing the often day-long ritual is an unforgettable experience. The effort expended by the artist is made all the more remarkable by the inevitable destruction of the picture shortly after its completion; this truly ephemeral art cannot be divorced from its ritual context. In some cases, the image is destroyed by a fierce-looking *vellichapad* ("light-bringer"), a village oracle who can be recognized by shoulder-length hair, red *dhoti*, heavy brass anklets and the hooked sword he brandishes either while jumping up and down on the spot (a common sight), or marching purposefully about to control the spectators. At the end of the ritual, the powder, invested with divine power, is thrown over the onlookers. *Kalam ezhuttu* rituals are not widely advertised, but check at tourist offices.

Islamic architecture

South India may be best known for its Hindu monuments, but the southern **Deccan** region, encompassed by the modern states of Karnataka and western Andhra Pradesh, is littered with wonderful Muslim **mosques** and **tombs**, dating from an era when this was the buffer zone between the ancient Indian cultures of the Dravidian south and the dynasties who succeeded the Delhi sultans.

The buildings that survive from this era illustrate the extraordinary cross-fertilization that took place between indigenous art forms and Islamic styles from distant Central Asia. Thus, some of the oldest Muslim constructions at **Bidar** (see p.331) and **Gulbarga** (see p.330) look Afghan, whereas the later masterpieces of the Bahmani dynasty, such as the Ibrahim Rauza at **Bijapur** (see p.329), incorporate motifs that wouldn't have looked out of place on a temple. This fusion occurred both because of a certain stylistic tolerance on the part of later Muslim rulers in southern India, and because the craftsmen they employed were often Hindus, to whom lotus flowers and fancy floral scrollwork came more easily than Persian geometric patterns.

The most famous Muslim monument in the South is the **Golgumbaz** at **Bijapur** (see p.327) – India's largest domed structure – but there are enough superb buildings in the same town, and in the other old capitals of the former Deccan sultans, dotted along the northern border of Karnataka between Bijapur and Hyderabad, to keep enthusiasts of Islamic architecture occupied for weeks.

Wildlife

A fast-growing population and the rapid spread of industries have inflicted pressures on the rural landscape of South India, but the region still supports a wealth of distinct flora and fauna. Although many species have been hunted out over the past fifty years, enough survive to make a trip into the countryside well worthwhile. Walking on less frequented beaches or through the rice fields of the coastal plain, you'll encounter dozens of exotic birds, while the hill country of the interior supports an amazing variety of plants and trees. The majority of the peninsula's larger mammals keep to the dense woodland of the Western Ghat mountains, where a string of contiguous reserves affords them some protection from the hunters and loggers who have wrought such havoc on India's fragile forest regions over the past few decades.

Flora

Something like 3500 species of flowering plants have been identified in South India, as well as countless lower orders of grasses, ferns and brackens. The greatest diversity of flora occurs in the Western Ghats, where it is not uncommon to find one hundred or more different types of trees in an area of just one hectare. Many species were introduced by the Portuguese from Europe, South America, Southeast Asia and Australia, but there are also a vast number of indigenous varieties which thrive in the moist climate.

Along the coast, the rice **paddy** and **coconut** plantations predominate, forming a near-continuous band of lush foliage. Spiky **spinifex** also helps bind the shifting sand dunes behind the miles of sandy beaches lining both the Malabar and Coromandel coasts, while **casuarina** bushes form striking splashes of pink and crimson during the winter months.

In towns and villages, you'll encounter dozens of beautiful **flowering trees**. The Indian **laburnum**, or cassia, throws out masses of yellow flowers and long seed pods in late February before the monsoons. This is also the period when mango and Indian **coral trees** are in full bloom; both produce bundles of stunning red flowers.

One of the region's most distinctive trees, found in both coastal and hill areas, is the stately **banyan**, which propagates by sending out roots from its lower branches. The largest specimens spread out over an area of two hundred metres. The banyan is revered by Hindus, and you'll often find small shrines at the foot of mature trees. The same is true of the *peepal*, which has distinctive spatula-shaped leaves. Temple courtyards often enclose large *peepals*, which usually have strips of auspicious red cloth hanging from their lower branches.

The Western Ghats harbour a bewildering wealth of flora, from flowering trees and plants, to ferns and fungi. **Shola** forests, lush patches of moist evergreen woodland which carpet the deeper mountain valleys, exhibit some of the greatest biodiversity. Sheltered by a leafy canopy, which may rise to a height of twenty metres or more, buttressed roots and giant trunks tower above a luxuriant undergrowth of brambles, creepers and bracken, interspersed by brakes of bamboo. Common tree species include the kadam, sisso or martel, kharanj and teak, while rarer sandalwood thrives on the higher, drier plateaux south of Mysore. There are dozens of representatives of the fig family, too, as well as innumerable (and ecologically destructive) eucalyptus and rubber trees, planted as cash crops by the Forest Department.

Mammals

Although peninsular India boasts more than fifty species of wild mammals, visitors who stick to populated coastal areas are unlikely to spot anything more inspiring than a monkey or squirrel. During a field expedition to Goa in the 1970s, the eminent Indian naturalist, Salim Ali, complained that the only animal he spotted was a lone leopard cat, dead at the roadside. Most of the larger animals have been hunted to the point of extinction; the few that remain roam the dense woodland lining the Western Ghats, in the sparsely populated forest zones of the **Nilgiri Biosphere Reserve**.

The largest Indian land mammal is, of course, the Asian **elephant**, stockier and with much smaller ears than its African cousin, though no less venerable. Travelling around Kerala and Tamil Nadu, you'll regularly see elephants in temples and festivals, but for a glimpse of one in the wild, you'll have to venture into the mountains where, in spite of the huge reduction of their natural habitat, around six and a half thousand still survive. Among the best places for sightings are Periyar in Kerala (see p.387) and Nagarhole in Karnataka (see p.268). In the era when it was a maharaja's hunting reserve, the latter became infamous as the place where the British hunter, G.P. Sanderson, devised the brutal *khedda* system for trapping elephants: herds were driven into lethal stockades and captured, or killed. Between 1890 and 1971, 1536 elephants were allegedly caught in this way, of which 225 died – a figure that probably only represents the tip of the iceberg. Today, wild elephants, which are included under the Endangered Species Protection Act, are under increasing threat from villagers: each adult animal eats roughly two hundred kilos of vegetation and drinks one hundred litres of water a day, and their search for sustenance inevitably brings them into conflict with rural communities.

Across India, local villagers displaced by wildlife reserves have often been responsible for the poaching that has reduced **tiger** populations to such fragile levels (see box on p.696). These days, in South India sightings are very rare indeed, though several kinds of big cat survive. Among the most beautiful is the **leopard**, or panther (*Panthera panthus*). Prowling the thick forests of the Ghats, these elusive cats prey on monkeys and deer, and occasionally take domestic cattle and dogs from the fringes of villages. Their distinctive black spots make them notoriously difficult to see amongst the tropical foliage, although their mating call (reminiscent of a saw on wood) regularly pierces the night air in remote areas. The **leopard cat** (*Felis bengalensis*) is a miniature version of its namesake, and more common. Sporting a bushy tail and round spots on soft buff or grey fur, it is about the same size as a domestic cat and lives around villages, picking off chickens, birds and small mammals. Another cat with a penchant for poultry, and one which villagers occasionally keep as a pet if they can capture one, is the docile Indian **civet** (*Viverricual indica*), recognizable by its lithe body, striped tail, short legs and long pointed muzzle.

Wild cats share their territory with a range of other mammals unique to the subcontinent. One you've a reasonable chance of seeing is the **gaur**, or Indian bison (*Bos gaurus*). These primeval-looking beasts, with their distinctive sleek black skin and knee-length white "socks", forage around bamboo thickets and shady woods. The bulls are particularly impressive, growing to an awesome height of two metres, with heavy curved horns and prominent humps.

With its long fur and white V-shaped bib, the scruffy **sloth bear** (*Melursus ursinus*) – whose Tamil name (*bhalu*) inspired that of Rudyard Kipling's character in *The Jungle Book* – ranks among the weirder-looking inhabitants of the region's forests. Sadly, it's also very rare, thanks to its predilection for raiding sugar-cane plantations, which has brought it, like the elephant, into direct conflict with man. Sloth bears can occasionally be seen shuffling along woodland trails, but you're more likely to come across evidence of their foraging activities: trashed termite mounds and chewed-up ants' nests. The same is true of both the portly Indian **porcupine** (*Hystrix indica*), or *sal*, which you see a lot less often than the mounds of earth it digs up to get at insects and cashew or teak seedlings; and the **pangolin** (*Manis crassicaudata*), or *tiryo*, a kind of armour-plated anteater whose hard, grey overlapping scales protect it from predators.

Full-moon nights and the twilight hours of dusk and dawn are the times to look out for nocturnal animals such as the **slender loris** (*Loris tardigradus*). This shy creature – a distant cousin of the lemur, with bulging round eyes, furry body and pencil-thin limbs – grows to around twenty centimetres in length. It moves as if in slow motion, except when an insect flits to within striking distance, and is a favourite pet of forest people. The **mongoose** *(Herpestes edwardsi)* is another animal sometimes kept as a pet to keep dwellings free of scorpions, mice, rats and other vermin. It will also readily take on snakes – you might see one writhing in a cloud of dust with king cobras during performances by snake charmers.

Late evening is also the best time for spotting **bats**. South India boasts four species, including the fulvous fruit bat (*Rousettus leshenaulti*), or *vagul* – so-called because it gives off a scent resembling fermenting fruit juice; Dormer's bat (*Pipistrellus dormeri*); the very rare rufous horseshoe bat; and the Malay fox vampire (*Magaderma spasma*), which feeds off the blood of live cattle. **Flying foxes** (*Pteropus gigantus*), the largest of India's bats, are also present in healthy numbers. With a wingspan of more than one metre, they fly in cacophonous groups to feed in fruit orchards, sometimes falling foul of electricity cables on the way: frazzled flying foxes dangling from live cables are a common sight in the interior.

Other species to look out for in forest areas are the Indian **giant squirrel** (*Ratufa indica*), or *shenkaro*, which has a coat of black fur and red-orange lower parts. Two and a half times larger than its European cousins, it lives in the canopy, leaping up to twenty metres between branches. The much smaller three-striped squirrel (*Funambulus palmarum*), or *khadi khar*, recognizable by the three black markings down its back, is also found in woodland. The five-striped palm squirrel (*Funambulus pennanti*) is a common sight all over the state, especially in municipal parks and villages.

Forest clearings and areas of open grassland are grazed by four species of deer. Widely regarded as the most beautiful is the **cheetal** (*Axis axis*), or spotted axis deer, which congregates in large groups around water holes and salt licks, occasionally wandering into villages to seek shelter from its predators. The plainer buff-coloured **sambar** (*Cervus unicolor*) is also common, despite being affected by diseases spread by domestic cattle during the 1970s and 1980s. Two types of deer you're less likely to come across, but which also inhabit the border forests, are the **barking deer** (*Muntiacus muntjak*), whose call closely resembles that of a domestic dog, and the timid **mouse deer** (*Tragulus meminna*), a speckled-grey member of the *Tragulidae* family that is India's smallest deer, growing to a mere

The Indian tiger: survival or extinction?

Feared, adored, immortalized in myth and used to endorse everything from breakfast cereals to petrochemicals, few animals command such universal fascination as the **tiger**. Only in India, however, can this rare and enigmatic big cat still be glimpsed in the wild, stalking through the teak forests and terai grass to which it is uniquely adapted. A solitary predator at the apex of the food chain, it has no natural enemies save one.

As recently as the turn of the century, up to 100,000 tigers still roamed the subcontinent, even though **shikar** (tiger hunting) had long been the "sport of kings". An ancient dictum held it auspicious for a ruler to notch up a tally of 109 dead tigers, and nawabs, maharajas and Moghul emperors all indulged their prerogative to devastating effect. But it was the trigger-happy British who brought tiger hunting to its most gratuitous excesses. Photographs of pith-helmeted, bare-kneed *burrasahibs* posing behind mountains of striped carcasses became a hackneyed image of the Raj. Even Prince Philip (now president of the Worldwide Fund for Nature) couldn't resist bagging one during a royal visit.

In the years following Independence, **demographic pressures** nudged the Indian tiger perilously close to extinction. As the human population increased in rural districts, more and more forest was cleared for farming – thereby depriving large carnivores of their main source of game and of the cover they needed to hunt. Forced to turn on farm cattle as an alternative, tigers were drawn into direct conflict with humans; some animals, out of sheer desperation, even turned man-eater and attacked human settlements.

Poaching has taken an even greater toll. The black market has always paid high prices for live animals – a whole tiger can fetch up to $100,000 – and for the various body parts believed to hold magical or medicinal properties. The meat is used to ward off snakes, the brain to cure acne, the nose to promote the birth of a son and the fat of the kidney – applied liberally to the afflicted organ – as an antidote to male impotence.

By the time an all-India moratorium on tiger shooting was declared in the 1972 Wildlife Protection Act, numbers had plummeted to below 2000. A dramatic response geared to fire public imagination came the following year, with the inauguration of **Project Tiger**. At the personal behest of then prime minister Indira Gandhi, nine areas of pristine forest were set aside for the last remaining tigers. Displaced farming communities were resettled and compensated, and armed rangers employed to discourage poachers. Demand for tiger parts did not end with Project Tiger, however, and the poachers remained in business, aided by organized smuggling rings. Undercover investigators repeatedly come across huge hauls of tiger bones and skins, and over the past few years the discovery of tiger carcasses rotting in several reserves indicate that poachers have been resorting to new, more random killing methods: four tigers (a tigress and three cubs) were killed in May 2003 after they stumbled across a live electricity cable laid for the purpose in the jungles of Kerala, while three more tiger bodies were found in northern Maharashtra the previous year after a water hole had been poisoned.

Today, even though there are 23 Project Tiger sites, numbers continue to fall. Official figures optimistically claim a **population** of up to 3000–3500, but independent evidence is more pessimistic, putting the figure at under 2000. The population rise indicated by counts based on pug marks – thought to be like human fingerprints, unique to each individual – that gave such encouragement in the early 1990s has been declared inaccurate. Poorly equipped park wardens are still fighting a losing battle: in 1996 it was estimated that one tiger was being poached every eighteen hours, and the situation is believed to be as depressing today. The most pessimistic experts even claim that at the present rate of destruction, India's most exotic animal could face extinction within two decades.

thirty centimetres in height. Both of these are highly secretive and nocturnal; they are also the preferred snack of Goa's smaller predators: the **striped hyena** (*Hyaena hyaena*), **jackal** (*Canis aureus*), or *colo*, and **wild dog** (*Cuon alpinus*), which hunt in packs.

Long-beaked **dolphins** are regular visitors to the shallow waters of South India's more secluded bays and beaches. They are traditionally regarded as a pest by local villagers, who believe they eat scarce stocks of fish. However, this long-standing antipathy is gradually eroding, as local people realize the tourist-pulling potential of the dolphins: Palolem beach, in Goa (see p.227), is a dependable dolphin-spotting location.

Finally, no rundown of South Indian mammals would be complete without some mention of **monkeys**. The most ubiquitous species is the mangy pink-bottomed **macaque** (*Macaca mulatta*), or *makad*, which hangs out anywhere scraps may be scavenged or snatched from unwary humans: temples and picnic spots are good places to watch them in action. The black-faced Hanuman **langur**, by contrast, is less audacious, retreating to the trees if threatened. It is much larger than the macaque, with pale grey fur and long limbs and tail. In forest areas, the langur's distinctive call is an effective early-warning system against big cats and other predators, which is why you often come across herds of cheetal grazing under trees inhabited by large colonies of them.

Reptiles

Reptiles are well represented in the region, with more than forty species of snakes, lizards, turtles and crocodiles recorded. The best places to spot them are not the interior forests, where dense foliage makes observation difficult, but open, cultivated areas: paddy fields and village ponds provide abundant fresh water, nesting sites and prey (frogs, insects and small birds).

Your hotel room, however, is where you are most likely to come across tropical India's most common reptile, the **gecko** (*Hemidactylus*), which clings to walls and ceilings with its widely splayed toes. Deceptively static most of the time, these small yellow-brown lizards will dash at lightning speed for cracks and holes if you try to catch one, or if an unwary mosquito, fly or cockroach scuttles within striking distance. The much rarer chameleon is even more elusive, mainly because its constantly changing camouflage makes it virtually impossible to spot. They'll have no problem seeing you, though: independently moving eyes allow them to pinpoint approaching predators, while prey is slurped up with their fast-moving forty-centimetre-long tongues. The other main lizard to look out for is the **Bengal monitor**. This giant brown speckled reptile looks like a refugee from *Jurassic Park*, growing to well over a metre in length. It used to be a common sight in coastal areas, basking on roads and rocks. However, monitors are often killed and eaten by villagers, and have become increasingly rare. Among the few places you can be sure of sighting one is South Andaman, in the Andaman archipelago.

The monsoon period is when you're most likely to encounter **turtles**. Two varieties paddle around village ponds and wells while water is plentiful: the flap-shell (*Lissemys punctata*) and black-pond (*Melanochelys trijuga*) turtles, neither of which are endangered. Numbers of Olive Ridley marine turtles (*Lepidochely olivacea*), by contrast, have plummeted over the past few decades as a result of villagers raiding their nests when they crawl onto the beach to lay their eggs.

This amazing natural spectacle occurs each year at a number of beaches in the region, notably Morgim in north Goa and Havelock Island in the Andamans (see p.625). Local coastguards and scientists from the Institute of Oceanography in Goa monitor the migration, patrolling the beaches to deter poachers, but the annual egg binge remains a highlight of the local gastronomic calendar, eagerly awaited by fisher families, who sell the illegal harvest in local markets. Only in Orissa, in eastern India, where a special wildlife sanctuary has been set up to protect them, have the sea turtles survived the seasonal slaughter to reproduce in healthy numbers.

An equally rare sight nowadays is the **crocodile**. Populations have dropped almost to the point of extinction, although the Cambarjua Canal near Old Goa, and more remote stretches of the Mandovi and Zuari estuaries, support vestigial colonies of saltwater crocs, which bask on mud flats and river rocks. Dubbed "salties", they occasionally take calves and goats, and will snap at the odd human if given half a chance. The more ominously named mugger crocodile, however, is harmless, inhabiting unfrequented freshwater streams and riversides. You can see all of India's indigenous crocodiles at the wonderful Crocodile Bank near Mamallapuram (see p.484).

Snakes

Twenty-three species of snake are found in South India, ranging from the gigantic **Indian python** (*Python molurus*, or *har* in Konkani) – a forest-dwelling constrictor that grows up to four metres in length – to the innocuous worm snake (*Typhlops braminus*), or *sulva*, which is tiny, completely blind and often mistaken for an earthworm.

The eight **poisonous snakes** present in the region include India's four most deadly species: the cobra, the krait, Russel's viper and the saw-scaled viper. Though these are relatively common in coastal and cultivated areas, even the most aggressive snake will slither off at the first sign of an approaching human. Nevertheless, ten thousand Indians die from snake bites each year, and if you regularly cut across paddy fields or plan to do any hiking, it makes sense to familiarize yourself with the following four or five species, just in case; their bites nearly always prove fatal if not treated immediately with anti-venom serum – available at most clinics and hospitals.

Present in most parts of the state and an important character in Hindu mythology, the Indian **cobra** (*Naja naja*), or *naga*, is the most common of the venomous species. Wheat-brown or grey in colour, it is famed for the "hood" it unfurls when confronted and whose rear side usually bears the snake's characteristic spectacle markings. Its big brother, the **king cobra** (*Naja hannah*), or *Naga raja*, is much less often encountered. Inhabiting the remote forest regions along the Karnataka border, this beautiful brown, yellow and black snake, which grows to a length of four metres or more, is very rare, although the itinerant snake charmers who perform in markets occasionally keep one. Defanged, they rear up and "dance" when provoked by the handler, or are set against mongooses in ferocious (and often fatal) fights. The king cobra is also the only snake in the world known to make its own nest.

Distinguished by their steel-blue colour and faint white cross markings, **kraits** (*Bungarus coerulus*) are twice as deadly as the Indian cobra: even the bite of a newly hatched youngster is lethal. **Russel's viper** (*Viperi russeli*) is another one to watch out for. Distinguished by the three bands of elliptical markings that extend down its brown body, the Russel hisses at its victims before darting at them and burying its centimetre-long fangs into their flesh. The other common poisonous snake in South India is the **saw-scaled viper** (*Echis carinatus*). Grey with an arrow-shaped mark on its triangular head, it hangs around in the cracks between stone walls, feeding on scorpions, lizards, frogs, rodents and smaller snakes. They also hiss when threatened, producing the sound by rubbing together serrated scales located on the side of their head. Finally, **sea snakes** (*Enhdrina schistosa*) are common in coastal areas and potentially lethal (with a bite said to be twenty times more venomous than a cobra's), although rarely encountered by swimmers, as they lurk only in deep water off the shore.

Harmless snakes are far more numerous than their killer cousins and frequently more attractive. The beautiful **golden tree snake** (*Chrysopelea ornata*), for example, sports an exquisitely intricate geometric pattern of red, yellow and black markings, while the **green whip snake** (*Dryhopis nasutus*), or *sarpatol*, is a stunning parakeet-green with a whip-like tail extending more than a metre behind it. The ubiquitous **Indian rat snake**, often mistaken for a cobra, also has beautiful markings, although it leaves behind a foul stench of decomposing flesh. Other common non-poisonous snakes include the wolf snake (*Lycodon aulicus*), or *kaidya*; the Russel sand boa (*Eryx conicus*), or *malun*; the kukri snake (*Oligodon taeniolatus*), or *pasko*; and the cat snake (*Boiga trigonata*), or *manjra*.

Birds

You don't have to be an aficionado to enjoy South India's abundant **birdlife**. Travelling around the region, you can see breathtakingly beautiful birds regularly flash between the branches of trees or appear on overhead wires at the roadside.

Thanks to the internationally popular brand of Goan beer, the **kingfisher** has become that state's unofficial mascot: it's not hard to see why the brewers chose it as their logo. Three common species of kingfisher frequently crop up amid the paddy fields and wetlands of the coastal plains, where they feed on small fish and tadpoles. With its enormous bill and pale green-blue wing feathers, the stork-billed kingfisher (*Perargopis capensis*) is the largest and most distinctive member of the family, although the white-breasted kingfisher (*Halcyon smyrnensis*) – which has iridescent turquoise plumage and a coral-red bill – and the common, or small, blue kingfisher (*Alcedo althis*) are more alluring.

Other common and brightly coloured species include the grass-green, blue and yellow **bee-eaters** (*Merops*), the stunning **golden oriole** (*Oriolus oriolus*), and the **Indian roller** (*Coracias bengalensis*), famous for its brilliant blue flight feathers and exuberant aerobatic mating displays. **Hoopoes** (*Upupa epops*), recognizable by their elegant black-and-white tipped crests, fawn plumage and distinctive "*hoo...po...po*" call, also flit around fields and villages, as do **purple sunbirds** (*Nectarina asiatica*) and several kinds of **bulbuls**, **babblers** and **drongos** (*Dicrurus*), including the fork-tailed black drongo (*Dicrurus adsimilis*) – a winter visitor that can often be seen perched on telegraph wires. If you're lucky, you may also catch a glimpse of the **paradise flycatcher** (*Tersiphone paradisi*), which is widespread and among the region's most exquisite birds, with a thick black crest and long silver tail-streamers.

Paddy fields, ponds and saline mudflats usually teem with water birds. The most ubiquitous of these is the snowy white **cattle egret** (*Bubulcus ibis*), which can usually be seen wherever there are cows and buffalo, feeding off the grubs, insects and other parasites that live on them. The large egret (*Ardea alba*) is also pure white, although lankier and with a long yellow bill, while the third member of this family, the little egret (*Egretta garzetta*), sports a short black bill and, during the mating season, two long tail feathers. Look out too for the mud-brown **paddy bird**, India's most common heron. Distinguished by its pale green legs, speckled breast and hunched posture, it stands motionless for hours in water, waiting for fish or frogs.

The hunting technique of the beautiful **white-bellied fish eagle** (*Haliaetus leucogaster*), by contrast, is truly spectacular. Cruising twenty to thirty metres above the surface of the water, this black and white osprey stoops at high speed to snatch its prey – usually sea snakes and mackerel – from the waves with its fierce yellow talons. More common birds of prey such as the **brahminy kite** (*Haliastur indus*) – recognizable by its white breast and chestnut head markings – and the **pariah kite** (*Milvus migrans govinda*) – a dark-brown buzzard with a fork tail – are widespread around towns and fishing villages, where they vie with raucous gangs of house **crows** (*Corvus splendens*) and **white-eyed jackdaws** (*Corvus monedula*) for scraps. Gigantic pink-headed **king vultures** (*Sarcogyps clavus*) and the **white-backed vulture** (*Gyps bengalensis*), which has a white ruff around its bare neck and head, also show up whenever there are carcasses to pick clean.

Other birds of prey to keep an eye open for, especially around open farmland, are the **white-eyed buzzard** (*Butastur teesa*), the **honey buzzard** (*Pernis ptilorhyncus*), the **black-winged kite** (*Elanus caeruleus*) – famous for its blood-red eyes – and the **shikra** (*Accipiter badius*), which closely resembles the European sparrowhawk.

Forest birds

The region's forests may have lost many of their larger animals, but they still offer exciting possibilities for bird-watchers. One species every enthusiast hopes to glimpse while in the woods is the magnificent **hornbill**, of which three species have been spotted: the grey hornbill (*Tockus birostris*), with its blue-brown plumage and long curved beak, is the most common, although the Indian pied hornbill (*Anthracoceros malabaricus*), distinguished by its white wing and tail tips and the pale patch on its face, often flies into villages in search of fruit and lizards. The magnificent great pied hornbill (*Buceros bicornis*), however, is more elusive, limited to the most dense forest areas, where it may occasionally be spotted flitting through the canopy. Growing to 130 centimetres in length, it has a black-and-white striped body and wings, and a huge yellow beak with a long curved casque on top.

South Indian wildlife sanctuaries and national parks

The South Indian states covered in this book harbour a total of 96 **wildlife sanctuaries and national parks** – if you include the various protected islets of the Andaman and Nicobar Islands, and the many minor reserves dotted around the region. What follows is a selection (listed in alphabetical order) of the most rewarding, both in terms of their wildlife and the natural environment.

Cotigao Wildlife Sanctuary (Goa). Tucked away in the extreme south of Goa, near Palolem beach, its extensive mixed deciduous forest and hilly backdrop make up for a relative paucity of wildlife. Best time: November to March. See p.232.

Eravikulam National Park (Kerala). Located 17km northeast of Munnar in the lap of the Western Ghats. Famous for its thriving population of Nilgiri tahr, a rare antelope that lives only here, on the high rolling grasslands. See them on the hard hike up Anamudi, South India's highest mountain. Best time: January to April. See p.396.

Indira Gandhi (Anamalai) Wildlife Sanctuary (Tamil Nadu). On the southernmost reaches of the Cardamom Hills, this park is more remote than Mudumalai, and consequently less visited, but encompasses some beautiful mountain scenery as well as abundant fauna. Best time: January to March. See p.560.

Kodikkarai (Point Calimere) (Tamil Nadu). On a promontory jutting into Palk Bay, some 250 species of bird, mostly migrants, descend on a swathe of mixed swampland and dry deciduous forest in the wake of the monsoon. Best time: November to February. See p.523.

Mahatma Gandhi National Marine Park (Andaman Islands). The islets in this reserve, encircled by vivid coral reefs, rise out of crystal-clear water that teems with tropical fish, turtles and other marine life. Can be reached by daily excursion boats, via bus links, from the capital Port Blair. Best time: January to March. See p.622.

Mudumalai Wildlife Sanctuary (Tamil Nadu). Set 1140m up in the Nilgiri Hills, Mudumalai is one of the most easily reached reserves in the South. It offers a full range of accommodation and trails and gives access to huge areas of protected forest. Best time: January to March. See p.622.

Periyar Wildlife Sanctuary (Kerala). A former Maharaja's hunting reserve, centred on an artificial lake high in the Cardamom Hills. Occasional tiger sightings, but you're much more likely to spot an elephant. Well placed for trips into the mountains and tea plantations, with good accommodation, including remote observation towers which you have to trek to. Best time: October to March. See p.387.

Vadanemmeli Crocodile Bank (Tamil Nadu). Endangered species of indigenous crocodiles, lizards and turtles are bred here, 15km north of Mamallapuram, for release into the wild. Local Irula tribes people collect venom from poisonous snakes to make serum. Open year round. See p.484.

Vedanthangal Bird Sanctuary (Tamil Nadu). A wonderful mixed sanctuary, 86km southwest of Chennai, where you can sight 250 species of migrant wetland birds, blown in by the northwest monsoon. Best time: December and February. See p.491.

Several species of **woodpecker** also inhabit the interior forests, among them two types of goldenback woodpecker: the lesser goldenback (*Dinopium bengalensis*) is the more colourful of the pair, with a crimson crown and bright splashes of yellow across its back. The Cotigao sanctuary in south Goa (see p.232) is one of the last remaining strongholds of the Indian great black woodpecker, which has completely disappeared from the more heavily deforested hill areas further north. In spite of its bright red head and white rump, this shy bird is more often heard than seen, making loud drumming noises on tree trunks between December and March.

A bird whose call is a regular feature of the Western Ghat forests, particularly in teak areas, is the wild ancestor of the domestic chicken – the **jungle fowl**. The more common variety is the secretive but vibrantly coloured, red junglefowl (*Gallus gallus*), which sports golden neck feathers and a metallic black tail. Its larger cousin, the grey or Sommerat's jungle fowl (*Galolus sommeratii*), has darker plumage scattered with yellow spots and streaks. Both inhabit clearings, and are most often seen scavenging for food on the verges of forest roads.

Wildlife viewing

Although you can expect to come across many of the species listed above on the edge of towns and villages, a spell in one or other of South India's nature reserves offers the best chance of viewing wild animals. Although these reserves are a far cry from the well-organized and -maintained national parks you may be used to at home, at the larger and more easily accessible wildlife reserves – such as Periyar and Mudumalai – a reasonable infrastructure exists to transport visitors around, whether by jeep, minibus, coach or, in the case of the former, boat. Don't, however, expect to see much if you stick to these standard excursion vehicles laid on by the park authorities. Most of the rarer animals keep well away from noisy groups of trippers. Wherever possible, try to organize **walking safaris** with a reliable, approved guide in the forest, while bearing in mind that not all guides may be as knowledgable and experienced as they claim, and that an untrained guide may even lead you into dangerous situations. Ask to see recommendation books before parting with any money.

Music

One who is an expert in playing the veena, well versed in shruti and other forms of musical sound, and has a deep understanding of thaalam, will attain enlightenment with ease.

Tyagaraja (1767–1847)

Industani music from North India may be better known internationally, but the classical music of the South – called Carnatic – is by far the more ancient. Its tenets, once passed on only orally, were codified in Vedic literature between 4000 and 1000 BC, long before Western classical music was even in its infancy. Visiting the region, you'll have ample opportunity to attend Carnatic recitals, a key feature of cultural life in major cities such as Chennai, while religious rituals in South Indian temples invariably feature some kind of musical accompaniment. Styles of music – whether secular or religious – vary greatly from state to state, but among the most singular South Indian idioms are Keralan percussion, and the heavily Portuguese-accented music of Goa, both of which convey the cultural distinctiveness of these two regions more vividly than anything else.

Carnatic instrumental music

The **Carnatic music** of South India might be labelled "classical", but it's nothing like classical music anywhere else in the world. Rather than being the province of an urbane elite, it's an explosion of colour, sound and Hindu worship. While Hindustani music developed close associations with court and palace, Carnatic music remained part of the warp and weft of South Indian culture, both religious and secular. The other major difference is that Carnatic music, lacking written notation, is taught by demonstration and learned by ear or – in the case of its highly sophisticated rhythmic system – taught by a marvellous, mathematical structure of "finger computing" which enables a percussionist to break down a complex *thaalam* (rhythmic cycle) into manageable units. Indian percussion maestros readily admit the supremacy of Carnatic concepts of rhythm, and increasing numbers of Hindustani percussionists have studied in the South.

The music and the faith which inspired Carnatic music have remained inseparable. Visitors to the vast temples of South India are much more likely to encounter music than in the North. It's usually the piercing sound of the *nagaswaram* (shawm) and the *tavil* (barrel drum). More than likely it accompanies flaming torches and a ceremonial procession of the temple deity.

While devotional and religious in origin, Carnatic music is as much a vehicle for education and entertainment as for spiritual elevation. **Kritis**, a genre of Hindu hymn, are hummed and sung as people go about their daily business. In their tunefulness and recognizability, they hold a similar position in popular culture to the Christian hymn in Western societies.

The association of music and **dance** with Hindu thought has a long heritage, beginning with Shiva himself as Nataraja, the Cosmic Dancer, whose potent image is ever present in Hindu iconography. His temple at Chidambaram, for example, is rich with sculptures of *natya* dance poses, music-making and musical instruments, and the *devadasis*, the servants of God, were traditionally temple dancers.

Carnatic composers, too, are looked upon with some reverence. Indeed, the music's three great composers – **Tyagaraja** (1767–1847), **Muttuswamy Dikshitar** (1776–1835) and **Syama Sastri** (1762–1827) – are known as the *Trimurti* or "Holy Trinity" and are regarded as saint-composers. Between them, the trinity were responsible for hundreds of compositions: Tyagaraja alone is credited with some six hundred kritis.

Indians compare the music of the Trimurti to the grape, the coconut and the banana. Tyagaraja can be consumed and enjoyed immediately; appreciating Muttuswamy Dikshitar is like cracking open a shell to get to the contents; and with Syama Sastri you have to remove the soft outer layer to get to the fruit. Their era has become known as the **Golden Period**, and their music is revered and celebrated year in, year out, at various music conferences (festivals) and on a never-ending stream of recordings.

In performance

In concert, Carnatic music often seems to lack Hindustani music's showmanship and flamboyance. But neither does it require the same sustained level of

---

A glossary of southern music

bansuri Transverse bamboo flute (*venu* in Sanskrit), typically shorter than its Hindustani counterpart of the same name. The *venu* is Lord Krishna's instrument, and therefore holds a special place in Indian music.

bharatanatyam Literally "Dance of India", the classical dance of South India formerly known as *dasi attam* or the dance of the *devadasis*.

clarionet An alternative local name for the Western clarinet; its introduction into *chenda melam* (see box on p.710) is attributed to the nineteenth-century musician Madadeva Nathamuni.

devadasi Female temple- or courtesan-dancers, trained in music and dance.

ghatam Tuned clay pot played with the hands or, for effect, by bouncing off the belly.

jalatarangam A half-ring of water-filled china bowls tuned so the biggest vessel produces the deepest note. Musicians such as M.S. Chandrasekharian (also a renowned vina player), Krishnarajapuram Dhanam, the instrument's first female player, and Seeta Doraiswamy (featured on *An Anthology of South Indian Classical Music*) are amongst its exponents.

javali Type of composition, often playfully erotic in content.

kanjira Tambourine-like hand drum, lacking the Western tambourine's side jingles.

morsing Jew's harp.

mridangam Double-headed barrel drum, termed the "king of percussion and the queen of melody".

mukhavina Soft-toned, double-reed woodwind instrument.

tanpura Four- or sometimes five-stringed drone instrument; some "modernists" substitute an electronic version called a shruti box or a sur peti.

tavil Double-headed barrel drum, closely associated with *nagaswaram* ensembles and the Pillai caste.

tillana Type of composition, associated with the bharatanatyam style of classical dance.

vina or **veena** Fretted seven-string instrument, the southern equivalent of the sitar.

violin The European violin, tuned to suit Indian tastes.

concentration from both performer and audience. A Carnatic **ragam** (raga) might be said to resemble a miniature beside a large-scale Hindustani canvas.

Carnatic musicians will distil the essence of a ragam into six to eight minutes. In part this is because a *kriti*, the base of many performances, is a fixed composition without improvisation. Carnatic musicians' creativity lies in their ability to interpret that piece faithfully while shading and colouring the composition appropriately. The words of a *kriti* affect even non-vocal compositions: instrumentalists will colour their interpretations as if a vocalist were singing along; the unvoiced lyric determines where they place an accent, a pause or melodic splash.

Improvisation has its place too, most noticeably in a sequence known as **ragam-thanam-pallavi**. This is a full-scale flowering of a Carnatic ragam and is every bit the equal of a Hindustani performance, although it is employed more sparingly, tending to be the centrepiece or climax of a Carnatic concert.

Whereas Carnatic music tends to break down into three strands: temple music, temple dance-accompaniment, and music for personal and private devotional observance, **sabha**, or paying concert performances, have somewhat blurred these distinctions. During the 1890s, the sabha associations in **Madras** (now Chennai) took an innovative path, moving from music performances to dance recitals. Chennai remains a centre of excellence and its music conferences, especially around December and January, attract devout audiences each year.

Concert-giving led to other changes: **microphones** came into use during the 1930s. They lent soft-voiced instruments such as members of the vina family (see below) a new lease of life, and replaced full-tilt vocal power with greater subtlety. Nowadays, concerts will typically feature a named principal soloist (either vocal or instrumental) with melodic and rhythmic accompaniment and a *tanpura* or drone player. Percussionists of standing are often included in concert announcements and advertising as they are attractions in their own right. Female musicians involved in a principal role tend to be vocalists, vina players or violinists. Male musicians have access to a wider range of musical possibilities as well as outnumbering female principal soloists or accompanists by roughly three to one.

Traditional Carnatic instruments

The **vina** (or *veena*) is the foremost Carnatic **stringed instrument**, the southern equivalent (and ancestor) of the sitar. A hollow wooden fingerboard with 24 frets is supported by two resonating gourds at each end. The vina has seven strings, four used for the melody and the other three for rhythm and drone. Current leading players include V. Doreswamy Iyengar, Chitti Babu, S. Balachandar and Sivasakti Sivanesan. The **chitra vina** (or *gotuvadyam*) is an unfretted 21-string instrument with sets for rhythm and drone as well as sympathetic strings. It has a characteristically soft voice which, before amplification, meant it was best suited to intimate surroundings. The best-known player is the young N. Ravikiran, who has switched to a hollow cylinder of teflon for his slide.

As in the North, the transverse bamboo flute goes under the name of **bansuri** or **venu**, although it is typically shorter and higher in pitch than the Hindustani instrument. Watch out for recordings by N. Ramani and the younger S. Shashank. The **nagaswaram** (or *nadaswaram*) is a piercing double-reed shawmlike instrument. It's longer and more deep-toned than the Hindustani *shehnai* and is associated with weddings, processions and temple ceremonies. It's often paired with a drone nagaswaram or *ottu*. Besides its ceremonial functions – and it is perhaps best heard in the open air – it is sometimes employed in formal

Compilations

An Anthology of South Indian Classical Music (Ocora, France). A substantial work compiled by the eminent violinist Dr L. Subramaniam. This four-CD primer gathers many of Carnatic music's vocal and instrumental giants with detailed descriptions of the music they make and the instruments they play. M.S. Subbulakshmi (vocals), T.R. Mahalingam (flute), A.K.C. Natarajan (clarinet), Raajeshwari Padmanabhan (*vina*), N. Ravikiran (*chitra vina*), Subashchandran (*morsing*), V.V. Subrahmanyam (violin) and T.H. Vinayakram (*ghatam*) are among the concentration of virtuosi.

Vocal artists

M. Balamuralikrishna Born in 1930 into a musical family, Balamuralikrishna was a child prodigy. He is also credited as a composer of new ragam formulations and some four hundred classical compositions.

Vocal (Moment, US). A *kriti* in Lathangi lasting nearly an hour, followed by a spectacular *tillana* performance using four different ragams in succession to create a *tillana ragamalika* (garland of ragams). Zakir Hussain (tabla) and T.H. Vinayakram (*ghatam*) provide rhythmic support.

Sudha Ragunathan Since her debut, Sudha Ragunathan (b.1958) has proved to be one of the most illuminating female singers in Carnatic music. Although she has recorded for labels such as EMI India and Inreco, her prime work is to be found on Winston Panchacharam's New York-based Amutham label.

Kaleeya Krishna (Amutham, US). Released in 1994, this album of devotional music finds Ragunathan in the company of a full Indian orchestra conducted by Vazhuvoor R. Manikkavinayakam. The record celebrates the work of the composer Venkatasubbaiyar (1700–65), whose muse was Krishna. An uplifting performance, even for non-Hindus. The more intimate, violin, *mridangam* and *ghatam* instrumentation on *San Marga* (Amutham, US) is similarly recommended.

M.S. Subbulakshmi M.S. Subbulakshmi (b. 1916) is a cultural ambassador for Indian arts on a par with Ravi Shankar, though unlike Ravi Shankar she did not support her recording career with constant touring. Even so, she has been heaped with honours, and is considered a national treasure.

M.S. Subbulakshmi at Carnegie Hall (Gramophone Company of India, India). This double CD captures Subbulakshmi in New York in October 1977 with her daughter Radha Viswanathan, the violinist Kandadevi Alagiriswami and the percussionist Guruvayur Dorai.

Instrumental artists

S. Balachander The *vina* maestro S. Balachander (1927–90) was one of the best known Carnatic instrumentalists, having been one of the influential World Pacific label's major artists with groundbreaking issues such as *Sounds of the Veena* (featuring the flute of N. Ramani) and *The Magic Music of India*. His recorded interpretations of ragams tend to be longer than average.

The Virtuoso of Veena (Denon, Japan). An interpretation of ragam chakravaakam forms the centrepiece of this disc. Taeko Kusano's touching notes marvellously capture the spirit of this maverick musician.

Kadri Gopalnath Gopalnath's father started on his father's instrument, the *nagaswaram*, but got turned on to the saxophone after hearing the palace band at Mysore. Pioneering the use of the saxophone in a Carnatic classical setting, his work typifies the duality of Carnatic music in playing a modern instrument in a tradition that goes back centuries.

Gem Tones: Saxophone Supreme, South Indian Style (Globestyle, UK). A fervent and thrilling collection with accompaniment by A. Kanyakumari on her low-tuned violin, sounding for all the world like a tenor sax, plus *mridangam* (M. R. Sainatha) and *morsing* (B. Rajasekhar).

Lalgudi Jayaraman Violin may only be a relatively recent South Indian import – just a few centuries old – but it is difficult to imagine Carnatic music without it and Jayaraman is one of the finest contemporary violinists.

Violin (Moment, US). An interesting North–South excursion with a *kriti*, a *bhajan* (a Hindu devotional song form) and a *tillana* (a light dance-derived form using drum syllables as well as lyrics proper). Percussion accompaniment is from Vellore Ramabhadran (*mridangam*) and Zakir Hussain (tabla).

The Karnataka College of Percussion The Karnataka College has worked with German fusionists Dissidenten on their Germanistan and Jungle Book albums, and has made a number of records in its own right. Despite the ensemble's percussive-sounding identity, KCP also features the voice of Ramamani and melody instruments such as *vina* (played by leader Raghavendra), violin (M.S. Govindaswamy) and flute (V.K. Raman).

River Yamuna (Music of the World, US). This 1997 album is an edited, reworked and reordered version of *Shiva Ganga*, the 1995 album produced by Dissidenten's Marlon Klein. An accessible introduction for beginners testing the heat of Carnatic water.

N. Ramani The flautist Dr N. Ramani (b. 1934) was born in Tiruvarur in Tamil Nadu, the birthplace of Tyagaraja, and by the age of 12 was accomplished enough to be appearing on All India Radio.

Classical Carnatic Flute (Nimbus, UK). A recording with a great deal of presence dating from 1990. Ramani is accompanied on the violin by T.S. Veeraraghhavan, *mridangam* by Srimushnam Rajarao and *ghatam* by E.M. Subramaniam in pieces by Tyagaraja and Ramani himself.

N. Ravikiran The magisterial Ravikiran (b. 1967), who gave his first recital at the age of 5, is the foremost exponent of the *chitra* vina, making it an instrument capable of arcane and ethereal sounds. Ravikiran is also the author of the first-rate introductory guide, *Appreciating Carnatic Music* (Ganesh & Co., Madras, 1997). Log on to ⒲www.ravikiranmusic.com for more information.

Young Star of Gottuvadyam (Chhanda Dhara, Germany). Mesmerizing performances, accompanied on *mridangam* by Trichur R. Mohan and on *ghatam* by T.H. Subashchandran – the nearly nineteen-minute long performance of Shankara Bharanam is especially good.

Shankar L. Shankar (b. 1953) played in a violin trio with his brothers L. Vaidyanathan and L. Subramaniam before embarking on a solo career, and founding the Indo-Jazz fusion group Shakti with guitarist John McLaughlin. He is renowned for creating his own ten-string double violin with its startling extended range.

Raga Aberi (Music of the World, US). A spectacular *ragam-thanam-pallavi* performance growing out the growling low notes of Shankar's extraordinary violin. The performance also features spectacular vocal percussion and solos by Zakir Hussain (tabla) and Vikku Vinayakram (*ghatam*).

U. Srinivas Mandolin-player U. Srinivas (b. 1969) uses a five-string, solid body instrument, akin to a cut-down electric guitar, rather than the eight-string Western mandolin, which he claims is ideally suited to the ragas of South Indian music. Like many Carnatic musicians he was a child prodigy and has excited listeners the world over, notably in the West with a successful fusion album, *Dream* (1995 – see below), with Michael Brook. He sometimes performs mandolin duets with his brother U. Rajesh.

Rama Sreerama (RealWorld, UK). An inspiring introduction to Srinivas's music, including pieces by Srinivas himself and Tyagaraja. Strongly devotional in character, with violin, *mridangam* and *ghatam* accompaniment.

L. Subramaniam L. Subramaniam (b. 1947) is from a dynasty of violinists (his brothers are L. Vaidyanathan and Shakti-founder L. Shankar). One of the most recorded Carnatic artists in the West, he has regularly played in non-Carnatic contexts – with Hindustani musicians, jazz-fusion groups, Western orchestras and in films (including Mira Nair's *Salaam Bombay* and *Mississippi Masala*).

Electric Modes (Water Lily Acoustics, US). A two-CD set, one volume of which consists of original compositions, the second of which focuses on traditional ragams. The album's title recalls Muddy Waters' album *Electric Mud*.

Fusion

Michael Brook Toronto-born composer and producer Michael Brook has had an eclectic career, with early stints in rock bands (Martha and the Muffins) leading to ambient/minimalist-influenced soundtrack work. But he is perhaps best known as a producer, working on albums for Peter Gabriel's Realworld label with U. Srinivas and Nusrat Fateh Ali Khan amongst others.

Dream (Realworld, UK). An album that began with the idea of Brook producing Srinivas and turned into a full-blown East–West collaboration, including contributions from Canadian singer Jane Siberry.

John McLaughlin/Shakti Guitarist John McLaughlin has been a linchpin of East–West fusion since introducing Miles Davis to Indian music back in the 1960s, moving through solo work, the jazz-rock Mahavishnu Orchestra and, most impressively, the all-acoustic group Shakti, formed in 1974 with tabla player Zakir Hussain, L. Shankar (violin) and T.H. Vinayakram (*ghatam*). Shakti toured and recorded to great acclaim through until 1977, when Columbia, used to massive-selling albums from McLaughlin, withdrew support. The group has since continued to perform in various permutations, including the Remember Shakti revival in 1997 with musicians such as Selvaganesh (percussion), Debashish Bhattacharya (guitar) and U. Srinivas (mandolin) in place of L. Shankar.

Remember Shakti *The Believer* (Verve, UK). In this wonderful live recording, made during a tour in 2000, McLaughlin teams up with mandolin maestro U. Srinivas and percussion virtuosos Zakir Hussain and V. Selvaganesh, to rework the successful Shakti formula. The result is some of the most inspired improvisation ever captured on disc.

classical concert settings. Leading players include Sheik Chinnamoulana and the brothers M.P.N. Sethuraman and M.P.N. Ponnuswamy.

The Carnatic counterpart to the tabla is the **mridangam**, a double-headed, barrel-shaped drum made from a single block of jackwood. Both heads are made from layers of hide and can be tuned according to the ragam being performed. Vellore Ramabhadran and Mysore Rajappa Sainatha are two of the top players. Other percussion instruments include the **tavil**, a folk-style barrel drum commonly found in ceremonial nagaswaram ensembles, and the **ghatam**, a clay pot tuned by firing. The latter is frequently found in South Indian ensembles and, unlikely as it may seem, in the hands of a top player like T.H. "Vikku" Vinayakram it can contribute some spectacular solos. The **morsing** (or *morching*) is a Jew's harp, often part of the accompanying ensemble (but frequently dropped when groups tour to save on the air fare). The **jalatarangam** (or *jalatarang*) is something of a curiosity: a melodic percussion instrument comprising a semicircle of water-filled porcelain bowls. It can create a sound of extraordinary beauty as the lead melody instrument in a typical Carnatic ensemble with violin, *mridangam* and *ghatam*. Players include Mysore's M.S. Chandrasekharian and the brothers Anayampatti S. Dhandapani and Anayampatti S. Ganesan.

New instruments

Both the subcontinent's two classical systems give pride of place to the voice, while melodic instruments, to some degree, are played to mimic it. Nevertheless, Carnatic music makes use of a fascinating array of stringed, wind and percussion instruments, many unique to the subcontinent.

From the nineteenth century, Carnatic music began to appropriate **Western instruments**, notably the violin and clarinet. More recent additions include the mandolin and saxophone. In the South – where the northern *sarangi* is a stranger – the **violin**'s fluidity, grace, speed and penetrative volume guaranteed it a complement of converts during the nineteenth century, most notably **Tanjore Vadivelu** of the Tanjore Quartette. Nowadays, Carnatic music without the violin is inconceivable. Credit for introducing it and adapting its Western tuning is given to **Balaswamy Dikshitar** (1786–1859), younger brother of the saintly composer – though some traditionalist scholars claim it as really a descendant of the earlier *dhanur vina*. Maestros such as Lalgudi G. Jayaraman, V.V. Subrahmanyam and L. Subramaniam are major artists, while A. Kanyakumari typifies the female violinists who are coming to the fore. In South India, the violin is played sitting on the floor with the body of the violin against the upper chest and the scroll wedged against the ankle leaving the left hand free to slide more freely up and down the strings. **Shankar**, brother of L. Subramaniam, has devised his own electric double violin with an extended bottom range and dark tone.

The introduction of the **clarinet**, or to give it its local name *clarionet*, is credited to Mahadeva Nattuvanar, in around 1860. Until around 1920 the clarinet was mostly used as an ensemble instrument in *cinna melam*, a dance accompaniment form. Thereafter, it was gradually established as a soloist's instrument. Balaraman of the Nadamuni Band was one of the twentieth century's first *clarionet* maestros and his work has been continued by musicians like A.K.C. Natarajan.

The **mandolin** has gained acceptance thanks to another of South India's child prodigies, **U. Srinivas**, often known as Mandolin Srinivas. He started playing the instrument aged 6 and has since toured worldwide and proved that the mandolin (albeit heavily modified) is highly effective at spinning gossamer webs of Tyagaraja improvisations. He is a very devout musician and his performances usually have a devotional ingredient.

The **saxophone** is another recent import, and its champion, Kadri Gopalnath, is one of South India's most popular musicians, with dozens of recordings to his credit. Gopalnath demonstrates Carnatic music's particular ability to be ancient and modern at the same time. When he plays the Carnatic ragams, the powerful sound of the saxophone echoes the ancient *nagaswaram*, but with a distinctively contemporary tone and attitude.

Ken Hunt

Goan music

With reggae and techno blaring out of so many beach bars, you'd be forgiven for thinking **Goa's music and dance scene** started with the invention of the synthesizer. However, the state boasts a vibrant musical tradition of its own: a typically syncretic blend of east and west that is as spicy and distinctive as the region's cuisine. You won't hear the calypso-like rhythms of Konkani pop or haunting Kunbi folk songs at the full-moon parties, though. Rooted in village and religious life, Goan music is primarily for domestic consumption, played at temple festivals, harvest celebrations, as an accompaniment to popular theatre and, most noticeably, on the crackly cassette machines of local buses.

Wander into almost any Hindu village on the eve of an important puja, particularly around harvest time after the monsoons, and you'll experience Goan roots music and dance at its most authentic. The torchbearers of the region's thriving **folk tradition** are the Kunbi class of landless labourers, most often seen bent double in rice paddy, the women with garish coloured cotton saris tied *dhoti*-style around their legs. Agricultural work – planting, threshing and grinding grain, raking salt pans, and fixing fishing nets – provide the essential rhythms for Konkani songs, known as **Kunbi geet**. More rehearsed performances take place

Chenda Melam: Keralan ritual percussion

The noisiest, rowdiest and most intense phase of any Keralan temple festival is the one presided over by the local drum orchestra, or **chenda melam**, whose ear-shattering performances accompany the procession of the deity around the sacred precinct and into the shrine. As impressive for their mental arithmetic as percussion technique and sheer bodily stamina in the intense heat, the musicians play an assortment of upright barrel drums (**chenda**) supported over the shoulder, bronze cymbals and wind instruments – the oboe-like **kuzhal** and the spectacular C-shaped brass trumpets (**kombu**), which emphasize and prolong the drum beating.

Performances invariably begin with an impressive "ghrr" and "dhim" produced on the drums. This is said to symbolize a lion's roar and was probably once performed in support of a lion hunt. After this mighty introduction, the drums drop the tempo and the music builds up like a pyramid. It starts slowly with long-lasting musical cycles and works up to a short, fast, powerful climax. During the performance, an elephant, musicians and crowd process round the temple precinct – after more than two hours, the excited crowd and sweating musicians celebrate the conclusion and follow the elephant and deity into the inner temple.

The first stage broadly symbolizes the ordinary life of men, while the peak of the last stage shows the ideal human or divine aspect of reality. The music must please the god on top of the elephant and, of course, the assembled temple crowd. While the main beats are provided by hitting the underside of the *chenda*, the skilled solo *chenda* players create intricate patterns over the top. Different players may gather for each event, but they are capable of playing together perfectly with no rehearsal. The concept is more like a big jazz band than a European classical orchestra.

A typical setup for a medium-sized temple festival kicks off with a turn from the **panchavadyam** orchestra, comprising three types of drums, cymbals and the *kombu* trumpets. A conch is blown three times, symbolizing the holy syllable "Om", and the performance begins its first stage with a slow, 1792-beat rhythmic cycle. The next cycle has 896 beats, half that number, then 448, half again, then 224 and so on. The speed increases until fast 56-beat cycles round it off. Fireworks, a large crowd and elephants trumpeting support the ecstatic climax.

For the evening, performances of **tayambaka**, **keli** and **kuzhal pattu** are announced. Each is a solo performing style, with players from the *chenda melam* and *panchavadyam* orchestras. *Tayambaka* is the main attraction, an improvised *chenda* solo played with a small ensemble of accompanying treble and bass *chenda* and cymbals. The other solo styles, *keli* (with a soloist on the *maddalam*, horizontally slung barrel drum) and *kuzhal pattu* (oboe), precede the midnight performance of the last *chenda melam*.

Rolf Killius

during the Hindu month of Paush (late Feb), when groups of women gather in the village square-cum-dance ground (*mannd*) to sing *dhalos* and *fugdis*. The singing may run over seven or more nights, culminating with outbreaks of spirit possession and trances.

The most famous Goan folk song and dance form, though, has to be the **mando**. Originally, this slow and expressive dance (whose name derives from the Sanskrit mandala, meaning circular pattern) was traditionally performed in circles, but these days tends to be danced by men and women standing opposite each other in parallel lines, waving fans and coloured handkerchiefs. *Mandos* gather pace as they progress and are usually followed by a series of **dulpods**, quick-time tunes whose lyrics are traditionally satirical, exposing village gossip about errant housewives, lapsed priests and so on. *Dulpods*, in turn, merge into the even jauntier rhythms of **deknis**, bringing the set dances to a tumultuous conclusion.

The basic rhythmic cycles, or *ovis*, of Goan folk songs were exploited by early Christian missionaries in their work. Overlaid with lyrics inspired by Bible stories, many were eventually assimilated into the local Catholic tradition: today, the *mando*, for example, is usually danced by Christians on church festivals and wedding days. It also became the favourite dance of the Goan gentry who, dressed in ball gowns and dinner suits with fans and flamboyant handkerchiefs, used to perform it during the glittering functions held in the reception rooms of the territory's top houses.

Fado

The most European-influenced of all the Goan folk idioms is the **fado**. Rendered in a turgid mock operatic style, these melancholic songs epitomize the colonial predilection for nostalgia or longing for the home country, known in Portuguese as *saudade*. Ironically, though, few *fadistas* actually laid eyes on the fabled lights of Lisbon or Coimbra they eulogized in their lyrics, and today the fado is a dying art form. However, a couple of renowned folk singers, notably the band leader **Oslando** and singer-guitarist **Lucio Miranda**, invariably include a couple of old fado numbers on their albums. Lucio, the greatest living exponent of the form, also gives the odd performance in the five-star hotels around Panjim.

Konkani pop

Rave music aside, most of the sounds you hear around Goa these days are either *filmi* hits from the latest blockbuster Hindi movies, or a mishmash of folk tunes and calypso rhythms known as **Konkani pop**. Backed by groups of women singers and fanfaring mariachi-style brass sections, Konkani lead vocalists croon away with the reverb cranked up against a cacophony of electric guitar and keyboard accompaniment.

Konkani pop is best experienced live (the costumes tend to be as lurid as the music), but if you don't manage to get to a gig, every roadside cassette-wallah stocks a range of popular tapes. No particular artist is worth singling out – nor are many likely to find fans among Western visitors. However, world-music aficionados should definitely check out a couple of cassettes to sample the sometimes surreal blend of musical influences. Underpinning the Portuguese-style melodies are conga-driven African and Caribbean rhythms, Brazilian syncopations, and almost Polynesian-sounding harmonies. The only part of the world Konkani pop sounds like it doesn't come from is India.

Dance

A mong the most magical experiences a visitor to South India can have is to see one of the dances that play such an important part in the cultural life of the region. India's most prevalent classical dance style, **bhara-tanatyam**, originated in the South and still fills concert halls in Tamil towns, while other types of ritualized theatre, such as **kathakali**, **kuttiyattam** and **theyyam**, remain integral to temple worship in Kerala. If you're lucky enough to catch an authentic performance in situ, you'll never forget it: the stamina of the performers and the spectacle of an audience sitting up all night to see the finale of a dance drama at dawn is utterly remarkable.

The Natya Shastra

All forms of Indian dance share certain broad characteristics and can be traced back to principles enshrined in the **Natya Shastra**, a Sanskrit treatise on drama-turgy dating from the first century BC. The text covers every aspect of the origin and function of **natya**, the art of dance-drama, which combines music, stylized speech, dance and spectacle, and characterizes theatre throughout South Asia. The spread of this art form occurred during the centuries of cultural expansion from the second century BC to the eighth century AD, when South Indian kings sent trade missions, court dancers, priests and conquering armies all over the region. Even in countries that later embraced Buddhism or Islam, dances continue to show evidence of Indian forms, and Hindu gods and goddesses still feature, mixed with indigenous heroes and deities.

Indian dance is divided into two temperaments: **tanava**, which represents the fearful male energy of Shiva, and **lasya**, representing the grace of his wife Parvati. Dances can fall into one or other category (kathakali is *tanava* and bharatanatyam is *lasya*), or combine the two elements. Equally, they include in differing degrees the three main components of classical dance: **nritta**, pure dance in which the music is reflected by decorative movements of the body; **natya**, which is the dramatic element of the dance and includes the portrayal of character; and **nritya**, the interpretive element, in which mood is portrayed through hand and facial gestures and the position of the feet and legs.

The term **abinaya** describes the resources at the disposal of a performer in communicating the meaning of a dance; they include costume and make-up, speech and intonation, psychological understanding and, perhaps the most distinctive and complex element, the language of gestures. Stylized gestures are prescribed for every part of the body – there are seven movements for the eyebrows, six for the nose and six for the cheeks, for example – and they can take a performer years of intensive training to perfect.

Once complete control of the body has been mastered, a performer will have a repertoire of several thousand meanings. In combination with other move-ments, a single hand gesture, with the fingers extended and the thumb bent for example, can be used to express heat, rain, a crowd of men, the night, a forest, a flight of birds or a house. Similarly, up to three characters can be played by a single performer by alternating facial expressions.

Despite frequent feats of technical brilliance, performers are rarely judged by their skill in executing a particular dance, but by their success in communicating

Dance recitals take place throughout the winter, building up to fever pitch during April and May before pausing for the monsoon (June, July & Aug). Finding them requires a little perseverance, and a certain amount of luck, but it's well worth the effort.

Bharatanatyam is performed at concert halls in most major cities and towns in the South. In addition, it is always well represented at the annual dance festivals held at Mamallapuram (see p.475), Hampi (see p.308) and Thiruvananthapuram (see p.344). Wherever you are, it's always worth enquiring at tourist offices. If you're in Chennai, check out the Listings pages of the regional press, such as *The Hindu*, for details of forthcoming events.

In Kerala, buy a copy of the Malayalam daily paper *Mathrabhumi* and ask someone to read the listings for you. **Temple festivals**, where most of the action takes place, are invariably announced. Tourist **kathakali** is staged in Kochi (see p.408), but to find authentic performances, contact performing arts schools such as Thiruvananthapuram's Margi (see p.348) and Cheruthuruthy's Kerala Kalamandalam (see p.427). **Kutiyattam** artists work at both, as well as at Natana Kairali at Irinjalakuda (see p.423). A good source of information on more obscure Keralan rituals, festivals and dance forms is the privately run tourist desk at Main Boat Jetty, Ernakulam (see p.413).

certain specific emotions, or **bhava**, to the audience. This can only be measured by the quality of **rasa**, a mood or sentiment, one for each of the nine bhavas, which the audience experiences during a performance.

Bharatanatyam

The best-known Indian classical dance style, **bharatanatyam**, is a graceful, gestural form performed by women. A popular subject for temple sculptures throughout South India (especially Tamil Nadu), it originated in the dances of the **devadasis**, temple dancing girls who originally performed as part of their devotional duties in the great Tamil shrines. Usually "donated" to a temple by their parents, the young girls were formally "wedded" to the deity and spent the rest of their lives dancing or singing as part of their devotional duties. Later, however, the *devadasis* system became debased, and the dancers, who formerly enjoyed high status in Hindu society, became prostitutes controlled by the brahmins, whom male visitors to the temple would pay for sexual services.

In the latter half of the nineteenth century, four brothers set themselves the task of saving the dance from extinction and pieced together a reconstruction of the form through study of the *Natya Shastra*, the images on temple friezes and through information gleaned from former *devadasis*. Although the dance today is largely based on their findings, this was only the first step in its revival, as *bharatanatyam* continued to be confined to the temples and was danced almost exclusively by men – the only way, as the brothers saw it, of preventing its moral decline. Not until the 1930s, when **Rukmini Devi**, a member of the Theosophical Society, introduced the form to a wider middle-class audience, did *bharatanatyam* begin to achieve popularity as a secular art form.

As ward of the nineteenth-century British rebel **Annie Besant**, Devi had greater exposure to foreign arts than many women of her generation. She

C

CONTEXTS | Dance

developed an interest in Western dance while accompanying her husband, George Arundale, former principal of the Theosophical Society's school in Adyar, Chennai, on lecture tours and had studied under Pavlova, among others. In 1929, however, after witnessing a performance of the dance she later named "*bharatanatyam*", she dedicated her life to its revival. The dance school she founded at Adyar is now known as Kalakshetra and continues to develop some of the world's most accomplished exponents.

In her determination to make the art form socially respectable, Devi eliminated all erotic elements and was known to be rigid and authoritarian in her views about how *bharatanatyam* should be danced. Many ex-pupils have gone on to develop their own interpretations of the style, but the form continues to be seen as an essentially spiritual art. Its theme is invariably romantic love, with the dancer seen as a devotee separated from the object of her devotion. In this way, she dramatizes the idea of **sringara bhakti**, or worship through love.

As with other classical dance forms, training is rigorous. Performers are encouraged to dissolve their identity in the dance and become instruments for the expression of divine presence. The order in which the phases of the dance are performed and practised is considered to be the one best suited to this goal. A recital usually lasts about two hours and consists of the following phases: *alarippu, jatiswaram, sabdam, varnam, padams, javalis, tillana* and *mangalam*.

All performances are preceded by a *namaskaram*, a salutation to the gods, offered by the stage, musicians and audience; a floral offering is made to a statue of the presiding deity, which stands at the right of the stage. The pivotal part of the performance is **varnam**, which the preceding three phases build up to through *nritta* (pure dance based on rhythm), adding melody and then lyrics. In *varnam*, every aspect of the dancer's art is exercised through two sections, the first slow, alternating *abinhaya* with rhythmic syllables, and the second twice the pace of the first, alternating *abinhaya* with melodic syllables. In the following two phases the emphasis is on the expression of mood through mime, and in the penultimate phase, the *tillana*, the dancer reverts again to the pure rhythm which began the dance. A *mangalam*, or short prayer, marks the end of a performance.

Kathakali

Here is the tradition of the trance dancers, here is the absolute demand of the subjugation of body to spirit, here is the realization of the cosmic transformation of human into divine.

Mrinalini Sarabhai, classical dancer

The image of a **kathakali** actor in a magnificent costume with extraordinary make-up and a huge gold crown has become Kerala's trademark, seen on anything from matchboxes to TV adverts for detergents. Traditional performances, of which there are still many, usually take place on open ground outside a temple, beginning at 10pm and lasting until dawn, illuminated solely by the flickers of a large brass oil lamp centre stage. Virtually nothing about kathakali is naturalistic, because it depicts the world of gods and demons. Both male and female roles are played by men.

Standing at the back of the stage, two musicians play driving rhythms, one on a bronze gong, the other on heavy bell-metal cymbals; they also sing the dialogue. Actors appear and disappear from behind a handheld curtain and never utter a sound, save the odd strange cry. Learning the elaborate hand gestures, facial expressions and choreographed movements, as articulate and precise as any sign language, requires rigorous training that can begin at the age of eight and last ten years. At least two more drummers stand left of the stage; one plays the upright **chenda** with slender curved sticks, the other plays the **maddalam**, a horizontal barrel-shaped hand drum. When a female character is "speaking", the chenda is replaced by the hourglass-shaped *ettaka*, a "talking drum" on which melodies can be played. The drummers keep their eyes on the actors, whose every gesture is reinforced by their sound, from the gentlest embrace to the gory disembowelling of an enemy.

Although it bears the unmistakable influences of *kutiyattam* and indigenous folk rituals, kathakali, literally "story-play", is thought to have crystallized into a distinct theatre form during the seventeenth century. The plays are based on three major sources: the Mahabharata, Ramayana and the Bhagavata Purana. While the stories are ostensibly of god-heroes such as Rama and Krishna, the most popular characters are those that give the most scope to the actors – the villainous, fanged, red-and-black-faced *katti* ("knife") anti-heroes. These types, such as the kings Ravana and Duryodhana, are dominated by lust, greed, envy and violence. David Bolland's handy paperback *Guide to Kathakali*, widely available in Kerala, gives invaluable scene-by-scene summaries of the most popular plays and explains in simple language a lot more besides.

When attending a performance, arrive early to get your bearings before it gets dark, even though the first play will not begin much before 10pm. Members of the audience are welcome to visit the dressing room before and during the performance, to watch the **masks** and **make-up** being applied. The colour and design of these, which specialist artists take several hours to apply, signify the personality of each character. The principal characters fall into the following seven types.

Pacca ("green" and "pure") characters, painted bright green, are the noble heroes, including gods such as Rama and Krishna.

Katti ("knife") are evil and clever characters such as Ravana. Often the most popular with the audience, they have green faces to signify their noble birth, with upturned moustaches and white mushroom knobs on the tips of their noses.

Chokannatadi ("red beard") characters are power-drunk and vicious, and have black faces from the nostrils upwards, with blood-red beards.

Veluppatadi ("white beard") represents Hanuman, monkey son of the wind god and personal servant of Rama. He always wears a grey beard and furry coat, and has a black and red face and green nose.

Karupputadi ("black beard") is a hunter or forest-dweller and carries a sword, bow and quiver. He has a coal-black face with a white flower on his nose.

Kari ("black") characters, the ogresses and witches of the drama, have black faces, marked with white patterns, and huge breasts.

Minnukku ("softly shaded") characters are women, brahmins and sages. The women have pale yellow faces sprinkled with mica and the men wear orange *dhotis*.

Once the make-up is finished, the performers are helped into their costumes – elaborate wide skirts tied to the waist, towering head-dresses and long silver talons fitted to the left hand. Women, brahmins and sages are the only characters with a different style of dress: men wear orange, and the women wear saris and cover their heads. The transformation is completed with a final prayer before the performance begins.

Visitors new to kathakali will undoubtedly get bored during such long programmes, parts of which are very slow indeed. If you're at a village performance, you may not always find accommodation, so you can't leave during the night. Be prepared to sit on the ground for hours, and bring some warm clothes. Half the fun is staying up all night to witness, just as the dawn light appears, the gruesome disembowelling of a villain or a demon *asura*.

Kuchipudi

Kuchipudi originated in Andhra Pradesh and is considered to follow the *Natya Shastra* more closely than any other form – though despite this it was until recently seen essentially as a folk idiom and a means of presenting scenes from mythology and the Hindu epics to relatively unsophisticated audiences. Similar in form to *bharatanatyam*, it also shares a history of decline and regeneration. Its present form is thought to date back to the seventeenth century when a local man capsized his boat while on the way to his wedding and prayed that his life might be saved. On finding his prayers answered, he wrote, in his new incarnation as **Siddhappa Yogi**, a dance drama in praise of Krishna, and gathered a troupe of brahmin men to perform it. When presented at court in 1675, it so impressed the resident *nawab* that he granted the village of Kuchipudi to the artists so that they might pass on their art to future generations. Taking its name from the village, the dance has been practised by the same fifteen brahmin families ever since.

Traditionally performed only by groups of men, *kuchipudi* requires seven years of rigorous training, with parallel education in music, Sanskrit, the ancient scriptures and mythology. Since the turn of the century, however, there has been an increase in solo performances, as well as those by women dancing.

Like *bharatanatyam*, *kuchipudi* follows a fixed sequence of phases and uses similar techniques and costumes, but is distinguished by the important role given to dialogue and song. It also differs from other forms in that the dancers sing for themselves, usually in Telugu. Humour and spectacle are other important elements that distinguish it from the more restrained mood of *bharatanatyam*: the highlight of most performances is a scene in which one dancer carries a pot of water on her head while balancing on the edge of a brass plate.

Mohiniyattam

A semiclassical form originating in Kerala, **mohiniyattam**, like *bharatanatyam*, grew out of the temple dances of the *devadasis*. It, too, was revived through the efforts of enthusiastic individuals, first in the nineteenth century by Swati Thirunal, the king of Travancore, and again in the 1930s, after a period of disrepute, by the poet Vallathol. Mohiniyattam ("the dance of the enchantress") takes its name from the mythological maiden **Mohini**, who evoked desire and had the ability to steal the heart of the onlooker. Usually a solo dance performed by women, it is dominated by the mood of *lasya*, with graceful movements distinguished by a rhythmic swaying of the body from side to side. The central theme is one of love and devotion to god, with Vishnu or Krishna appearing most frequently as the heroes.

Dancers of *mohiniyattam* wear realistic make-up and the white, gold-bordered Kasavu sari of Kerala. The music which accompanies the dancer is classical Carnatic, with lyrics in Malayalam.

Kutiyattam

Three families of the Chakyar caste and a few outsiders perform the Sanskrit drama **kutiyattam**, the oldest continually performed theatre form in the world. Until recently, it was only performed inside temples, and then only in front of the uppermost castes. Visually, it is very similar to its offspring, kathakali, but its atmosphere is infinitely more archaic. The actors, eloquent in sign language and symbolic movement, speak in the bizarre, compelling intonation of the local brahmins' Vedic chant, unchanged since 1500 BC.

A single act of a *kutiyattam* play can require ten full nights; the entire play forty. A great actor, in full command of the subtleties of gestural expression, can take half an hour to do such a simple thing as murder a demon, berate the audience, or simply describe a leaf falling to the ground. Unlike kathakali, *kutiyattam* includes comic characters and plays. The ubiquitous Vidushaka, narrator and clown, is something of a court jester, and traditionally has held the right to criticize openly the highest in the land without fear of retribution.

Teyyattam

In northern Kerala, a wide range of ritual "performances", loosely known as **teyyattam**, are extremely localized, even to particular families. They might include *bhuta* (spirit or hero worship), trance dances, the enactment of legendary events and oracular pronouncements. Performers are usually from low castes, but during the ritual, a brahmin will honour the deities they represent, so the status of each individual is reversed.

Although *teyyattam* can nowadays be seen in government-organized cultural festivals, the powerful effect is best experienced in the courtyard of a house or temple, in a village setting. Some figures, with painted faces and bodies, are genuinely terrifying; costumes include headgear metres high, sometimes doubling as a mask, and clothes of leaves and bark.

The only place you can be sure of seeing *teyyattam* is at **Parassinikadavu**, a small village 20km north of Kunnur, in the far north of Kerala, where the head priest of the local temple dances each day. This is an extraordinary spectacle that shouldn't be missed if you're in the area. For more typical village *teyyattam*, you have to be in the right place at the right time. First, head for Kunnur and ask the local tourist officer to point you in the right direction; after a few days' of waiting around, someone will hear you're looking for *teyyattam* and take you back to their village if a performance is planned – an experience anyone with more than a passing interest in ritual theatre and costume definitely shouldn't miss.

Vicki Maggs

Books

Appropriately for a part of the world with a written history dating back nearly two and a half thousand years, South India has spawned an extraordinary wealth of books – what follows is merely a small selection. Most are available in the UK and US, and frequently in India, too, where they tend to be much cheaper. Where separate editions exist in the UK and US, publishers are detailed below in the form "UK publisher/US publisher", unless the publisher is the same in both countries. Where books are published in India only, this follows the publisher's name. O/p signifies an out-of-print book (sometimes available through ⊛www.amazon.com or ⊛www.amazon .co.uk). Titles marked with a ⊡ are particularly recommended.

History

Jad Adams and Phillip Whitehead *The Dynasty: the Nehru-Gandhi Story* (Penguin). A brilliant and intriguing account of India's most famous – or infamous – family and the way its various personalities have shaped post-Independence India, although Sonia Gandhi's recent prominence rather begs an update.

A.L. Basham *The Wonder that was India* (South Asia Books, India). A veritable encyclopedia by India's foremost authority on his country's ancient history. Every page of this masterpiece bristles with the author's erudition. A companion volume, by S.A. Rizvi, brings it up to the arrival of the British.

Larry Collins and Dominique Lapierre *Freedom at Midnight* (HarperCollins). Readable, if shallow, account of Independence, highly sympathetic to the British and, particularly, to Mountbatten, who was the authors' main source of information.

⊡ **William Dalrymple** *White Mughals* (HarperCollins). In the course of five years' research into the lives of early European colonials who adopted "native" customs and married Indian women, William Dalrymple stumbled upon the forgotten story of James Achilles Kirkpatrick, British Resident at Hyderabad at the end of the eighteenth century, who fell in love with, and subsequently married, the great niece of the Nizam's prime minister. Both it, and the author's account of how he pieced the picture together, make an extraordinary tale, told with relish, erudition and an impeccable sense of pace in a book that grips like a great nineteenth-century novel.

Charles Dellon *L'Inquisition de Goa* (Editions Chandeigne, Paris). The only surviving first-hand account of the Goan Inquisition, by a French traveller who survived it in the seventeenth century. Dellon's chilling narrative, in this French edition illustrated with the original engravings, was the *Papillon* of its day, and remains a shocking indictment of the genocide perpetrated by the colonial clergy – at least, if you can read French (its English translation is out of print and extremely rare).

Patrick French *Liberty or Death* (HarperCollins). The definitive account of the last years of the British Raj. Material from hitherto unreleased intelligence files shows how Churchill's "florid incompetence" and Atlee's "feeble incomprehension" contributed to the debacle that was Partition, which French concludes was doomed through "confusion, human frailty and neglect". All in all, a damning indictment of Britain's role, that debunks many myths.

Dilip Hiro *The Rough Guide History of India* (Rough Guides). No other book crams so much background material on India into such a small format as this pocket history, which fleshes out a bare-bones time line with contextual boxes, literary extracts, potted biographies, quotations and black and white photos. An ideal travelling companion.

Lawrence James *Raj: the Making and Unmaking of British India* (Abacus, UK). A door-stopping 700-page history of British rule in India, drawing on recently released official papers and private memoirs. The most up-to-date, erudite survey of its kind, and unlikely to be bettered as a general introduction.

★ **John Keay** *India: a History* (HarperCollins). In this, the most recent of his five consistently excellent books on India, John Keay manages to coax clear, impartial and highly readable narrative from 5000 years of fragmented events. Arguably the best single-volume history currently in print.

John Keay *The Honourable East India Company* (HarperCollins). In characteristically fluent style, Keay strikes the right balance between those who regard the East India Company as a rapacious institution with malevolent intentions, and those who present its acquisition of the Indian empire as an unintended, almost accidental process.

Bhermann Kulke and Dietmar Rothermund *A History of India* (Routledge). Among the few complete histories of India to give adequate coverage to the South (one of the authors' specialist subjects), from the Mesolithic era (100,000 BC) to the war in Sri Lanka.

Geoffrey Moorhouse *India Britannica* (HarperCollins; Academy Chicago). A balanced, lively survey of the rise and fall of the British Raj, with lots of illustrations. Recommended if this is your first foray into the period, as it's a lot more concise and readable than Lawrence James' *Raj.*

Robert Sewell *A Forgotten Empire* (reprinted in facsimile by Asian Educational Services, New Delhi). The definitive history of the Vijayanagars, supplemented with the translated chronicles of Domingo Paes and Fernao Nuniz, two Portuguese travellers who visited in the royal city at the height of its splendour. Essential reading if you want to get to grips with the history behind Hampi's ruins.

Percival Spear's *History of India* Volume II (Penguin/Viking). Covers the period from the Moghul era to the death of Gandhi. Among the most readable offerings of its kind, and the most widely available.

Romila Thapar *History of India* Volume I (Penguin/Viking). Concise paperback account of early Indian history, ending with the Delhi Sultanate.

Gillian Tindall *City of Gold* (Penguin, India). Definitive, if rather dry biography of Mumbai, from colonial trading post to modern metropolis.

Society

★ **William Dalrymple** *The Age of Kali* (HarperCollins). This collection of stylish essays from ten years of journalistic assignments is rich with insights drawn from encounters and interviews with a vast range of personalities. Madurai's Meenakshi temple and the extraordinary history of the Nizam of Hyderabad comprise the South India content. Published in India as *In the Court of the Fish-Eyed Goddess*.

Gita Mehta *Karma Cola: Marketing the Mystic East* (Minerva/Fawcett Books). Satirical look at the psychedelic 1970s freak scene in India, with some hilarious anecdotes, and many a wry observation on the wackier (US) excesses of spiritual tourism. Her latest book, *Snakes and Ladders* (Vintage/Fawcett Books), is a brilliant overview of contemporary urban India in the form of a pot-pourri of essays, travelogues and interviews. It covers issues from Bollywood and the sex industry, to caste, gender, ecology and the contradiction between Indian poverty and the country's multi-million-dollar arms and business sector.

V.S. Naipaul *India: a Wounded Civilisation* (Penguin). This bleak political travelogue, researched and written during and shortly after the Emergency, gained Naipaul, an Indian Trinidadian, a reputation as one of India's harshest critics. Two decades later, he returned to see what had happened to the country his parents left. The result, *A Million Mutinies Now*, is an altogether more sympathetic and rounded portrait – a superbly crafted mosaic of individual lives from around the subcontinent, including a memorable portrait of a staunchly traditional Tamil brahmin.

One of the best books on India ever written.

Christopher Pinney *Photos of the Gods* (Reaktion Books). This history of the printed image in Indian popular culture focuses on political, cultural and religious themes and traces the importance that the visual arts – in the form of posters, postcards and other printed images – have had on India's history since the 1870s. A fascinating book illustrated with 80 colour and 87 black-and-white pictures

Mark Tully *No Full Stops in India* (Penguin/Viking). Crystallizing a lifetime's experience as the BBC's man in India, Tully's thesis – that Indians should seek inspiration for their future in their own great traditions rather than those of the West – provoked widespread scorn from the country's Westernized elite. Yet this remains among the best-informed critiques on India of its generation. Most of the ten essays in it refer to the North, but the issues tackled are equally relevant to the South. His latest book, *India in Slow Motion*, covers a similarly diverse range of subjects, from Hindu extremism, child labour and Sufi mysticism to the crisis in South Indian agriculture and the persistence of political corruption to the problem of Kashmir. Both challenge preconceptions foreigners often hold about India, and those held by Indians about their own country.

Travel

Rachel Dwyer and Divia Patel *Cinema India: The Visual Culture of Hindi Film* (Reaktion Books). Definitive guide to Bollywood from 1913 until the present, charting the changes in costumes, sets and advertising trends, with lots of illustrations.

Alexander Frater *Chasing the Monsoon* (Penguin). Frater's wet-season

jaunt down the west coast and across the Ganges plains took him through an India of muddy puddles and grey skies: an evocative account of the country as few visitors see it, and now something of a classic of the genre.

Justine Hardy *Bollywood Boy* (John Murray). Sassy, chick-lit-style travelogue through the larger-than-life world of the Bombay film industry, following the author's quest to interview heartthrob Hrithik Roshan at the height of his fame. Along the way, Justine brushes shoulders with a lurid cast of has-been movie stars, Grant Road prostitutes, gangsters and some formidable regulars at her local beauty salon. Much of the book's appeal lies in the fact that its author finds the glamour as seductive as she does shallow.

Geoffrey Moorhouse *Om* (Sceptre). Not Moorhouse's best, but nevertheless an absorbing account of his 1992 journey to South India's key spiritual centres, following the death of his daughter, with typically well informed asides on history, politics, contemporary culture and religion.

Dervla Murphy *On a Shoestring to Coorg* (Flamingo/Overlook Press). Murphy stays with her young daughter in the little-visited tropical mountains of Coorg, Karnataka. Arguably the most famous modern Indian travelogue, and a manifesto for single-parent budget travel.

François Pryard *Voyage to the East Indies, the Maldives, the Moluccas and Brazil* (Hakluyt Society, India). Goa was Pryard's first port of call after being shipwrecked in the Maldives in 1608, and Albert Gray's translation of the famous French chronicler's travelogue includes a vivid first-hand description of the Portuguese colony during its decadent heyday.

Tahir Shah *Sorcerer's Apprentice* (Weidenfeld & Nicolson). A journey through the weird underworld of occult India. Travelling as apprentice to a master conjurer and illusionist, Shah encounters hangmen, baby renters, skeleton dealers, *sadhus* and charlatans. If it were set anywhere else in the world, this would be an unbelievable story.

David Tomory *Hello Goodnight* (Lonely Planet). An upbeat account of Goa through the ages, enlivened with a seamless bricolage of anecdotes, experiences and encounters distilled from over thirty years of visiting and reading about the region. It's all in here: from Albuquerque to Wendell Rodricks and Jungle Barry to the Nine Bar, crammed into 23 chapters of poppy prose that faithfully capture Goa's essential quirkiness. Some will find it short on analysis, but the book's depiction of contemporary tourist culture, in particular, is spot on.

⭐ **Michael Wood** *The Smile of Murugan* (Viking). A supremely well-crafted and affectionate portrait of Tamil Nadu and its people in the mid-1990s, centred on a video-bus pilgrimage tour of the state's key sacred sites. Indispensable if you plan to explore the deep southeast.

Fiction

⭐ **Anita Desai** *Feasting and Fasting* (Vintage). This novel by one of India's leading female authors eloquently portrays the frustration of a sensitive young woman stuck in the stifling atmosphere of home while her spoilt brother is packed off to study in America.

Clive James *The Silver Castle* (Picador/Random House). A delightful story of a street urchin's rise from the roadside slums of outer Mumbai to the bright lights of Bollywood. James succeeds in balancing his witty celebration of the Hindi film world with an earnest attempt to dissect the ironies of the Maharashtran capital.

Rohinton Mistry *A Fine Balance* (Faber/Vintage). Two friends seek promotion from their low-caste rural lives to the glitz of the big smoke. A compelling and savage triumph-of-the-human-spirit novel exposing the evils of the caste system and of Indira Gandhi's brutal policies during the Emergency years. Mistry's *Such a Long Journey* (Faber/ Vintage) is a highly acclaimed account of a Mumbai Parsi's struggle to maintain personal integrity in the face of betrayals and disappointment.

R.K. Narayan *Gods, Demons and Others* (Minerva/University of Chicago Press). Many of Narayan's beautifully crafted books, full of subtly drawn characters and good-natured humour, are set in the fictional South Indian territory of Malgudi. This one tells classic Indian folktales and popular myths through the voice of a village storyteller.

★ **Arundhati Roy** *The God of Small Things* (Flamingo/HarperCollins). Haunting Booker Prize-winning novel about a well-to-do South Indian family caught between the snobberies of high-caste tradition, a colonial past and the diverse personal histories of its members. Seen through the eyes of two children, the assortment of scenes from Keralan life are as memorable as the characters themselves, while the comical and finally tragic turn of events says as much

about Indian history as the refrain that became the novel's catchphrase: "things can change in a day."

★ **Salman Rushdie** *The Moor's Last Sigh* (Jonathan Cape/ Pantheon). Set in Kerala and Mumbai, Rushdie's follow-up to *The Satanic Verses*, a characteristically lurid and spleen-ridden evocation of the Maharashtran capital's paradoxes, caused a stir in India, and was the subject of a defamation case brought by Shiv Sena leader Bal Thackeray.

Manohar Shetty (ed) *Ferry Crossing: Short Stories From Around Goa* (Penguin, India). This long-awaited anthology of Goan fiction, compiled by a local poet, comprises broadly themed short stories woven around the local landscape and people. Translated from Konkani, Marathi and Portuguese, none are what you might call world-class, but they offer fresh perspectives on Goan life, particularly the impact of modernization on villages.

William Sutcliffe *Are You Experienced?* (Penguin). Easy-read send up of a "typical" backpacker trip around India.

Biography and autobiography

Charles Allen *Plain Tales from the Raj* (Abacus). First-hand accounts from erstwhile sahibs and memsahibs of British India.

James Cameron *An Indian Summer* (Penguin). Affectionate and humorous description of the veteran British journalist's visit to India in 1972, and his marriage to an Indian woman. An enduring classic.

★ **Louis Fischer** *The Life of Mahatma Gandhi* (HarperCollins). First published in 1950, this biography has been re-issued several times since, and quite rightly

– veteran American journalist Louis Fischer knew his subject personally, and his book provides an engaging account of Gandhi as a man, politician and propagandist.

M.K. Gandhi *Experiments with Truth* (Penguin/Dover). Gandhi's fascinating records of his life, including the spiritual and moral quests, changing relationship with the British Government in India, and gradual emergence into the forefront of politics.

★ **Robert Harvey** *Clive: The Life and Death of a British Emperor* (Sceptre). The most recent biography of the man often dubbed the "founding father" of the British empire. Although more famous for his role in the battle of Plassey, he pulled off some extraordinary military feats during a formative early spell in the South, based in Madras, which are recounted here in engaging style.

Women

Chantal Boulanger *Saris: An Illustrated Guide to the Indian Art of Draping* (Shakti Press International). The fruit of six years' fieldwork by a French anthropologist, this astonishingly comprehensive book catalogues the numerous styles of sari tying, and their sociocultural significance (check out their site at ⑩www.devi.net).

★ **Elizabeth Bumiller** *May You Be the Mother of a Hundred Sons* (Fawcett Books/Penguin India). Lucid exploration of the Indian woman's lot, drawn from dozens of first-hand encounters, by an American journalist. Subjects tackled include dowries, arranged marriages, *sati*, magazines and film stars.

Shashi Deshpande *The Binding Vine* (Virago). Disturbing story of one woman's struggle for independence, and her eventual acceptance of the position of servitude traditionally assumed by an Indian wife.

Anees Jung *The Night of the New Moon* (Penguin UK/India).

Revealing and poetic stories woven around interviews with Muslim women from all sectors of Indian society. Jung's *Unveiling India* is a compelling account of the life of a Muslim woman who has chosen to break free from orthodoxy.

Vrinda Nabar *Caste as Woman* (Penguin India). Conceived as an Indian counterpart to Greer's *The Female Eunuch*, this is a wry study of the pressures brought to bear during the various stages of womanhood. Drawing on scripture and popular culture, Nabar looks at issues of identity and cultural conditioning.

Viramma, Josiane Racine and Jean-Luc Racine *Viramma: Life of an Untouchable* (Verso). Unique autobiography of an untouchable woman told in her own words (transcribed by French anthropologists), over a fifteen-year period, offering frank, often humorous insights into life in rural Tamil Nadu, the universe and everything.

Development and the environment

Julia Cleves Mosse *India: Paths to Development* (Oxfam). Concise analysis of the economic, environmental and political changes affecting India, focusing on the lives of ordinary poor people and the exemplary ways some have succeeded in shaping their own future. The best country brief on the market; only available through Oxfam.

★ **Jeremy Seabrook** *Notes from Another India* (Pluto Press). Life histories and interviews – compiled over a year's travelling and skilfully

contextualized. They reveal the everyday problems faced by Indians from a variety of backgrounds, and how grassroots groups have tried to combat them. One of the soundest and most engaging overviews of Indian development issues ever written.

Paul Sinath *Everybody Loves a Good Drought* (Review). A classic report on India's poorest districts, telling the stories of individual villages that are usually lost in a maze of development statistics.

Wildlife

Salim Ali, Dillon and Ripley *The Handbook of the Birds of India and Pakistan* (OUP, UK). Covers all of South Asia's birds in a single volume, with plates and maps: the definitive work, although hard to come by.

Claude Alvares (ed) *Fish Curry and Rice: a Citizens' Report on the Goan Environment* (Ecoforum, India). A comprehensive overview of Goan green issues, giving a region-by-region rundown of the state's natural habitats, followed by articles outlining the principal threats to the environment from tourism, transport policy, changes in local farming practices and a host of other eco-evils.

P.V. Bole and Yogini Vaghini *Field Guide to the Common Trees of India* (OUP, UK/US). A handy-sized, indispensable volume for tree-spotters.

★ **Bikram Grewal** *Birds of India, Bangladesh, Nepal, Pakistan and Sri Lanka* (Odyssey). Five hundred species are detailed in this glossy and practical field guide – most with excellent colour photographs. Based on Salim Ali & Co's authoritative work, and the best of the bunch

available in UK and US high-street bookshops.

Insight Guides *Indian Wildlife* (APA Publications, UK). An excellent all-round introduction to India's wildlife, with scores of superb colour photographs, features on different animals and habitats and a thorough bibliography. Recommended.

S. Prater *The Book of Indian Animals* (OUP/Bombay Natural History Society, India). The most comprehensive single-volume reference book on the subject, although only available in India.

Romulus Whitaker *Common Indian Snakes* (Macmillan, UK). A detailed illustrated guide to the subcontinent's snakes, with all the main species included.

Martin Woodcock *Handguide to the Birds of the Indian Subcontinent* (Collins, UK). For years the market leader, although now superseded by Grewal's guide. Available in light-weight, pocket-sized paperback form, and very user-friendly, with nearly every species illustrated (some in black and white).

The arts and architecture

Roy Craven *Indian Art* (Thames & Hudson). Concise general introduction to Indian art, from Harappan seals to Moghul miniatures, with lots of illustrations.

Mohan Khokar *Traditions of Indian Classical Dance* (Clarion Books, India). Detailing the religious and social roots of Indian dance, this lavishly illustrated book, with sections on regional traditions, is an excellent introduction to the subject.

George Michell *The Hindu Temple* (University of Chicago Press). The

definitive primer, introducing Hindu temples, their significance, and architectural development.

George Michell and Antonio Martinelli *The Palaces of India* (Thames & Hudson) Now available in affordable paperback, this over-view of India's royal architecture is a recommended coffee-table tome for serious India buffs, memorable less for its lacklustre prose than magnifi-cent images of India's decaying architectural treasures. Photographer Antonio Martinelli's genius is his ability to frame the buildings from novel perspectives, highlighting their natural backdrops and revealing the interiors in natural light.

Bonnie C. Wade *Music in India: the*

Classical Traditions (Manmohar, India). A scrupulous catalogue of Indian music, outlining the most commonly used instruments, with illustrations and musical scores.

Religion

Dorf Hartsuiker *Sadhus: Holy Men of India* (Inner Traditions International). The weird world of India's itinerant ascetics exposed in glossy colour photographs and erudite but accessible text.

J.R. Hinnelle (ed) *A Handbook of Living Religions* (Penguin). The beliefs, practices, iconography and historical roots of all India's major faiths explained in accessible language, with full bibliographies to back up each chapter. Deservedly the most popular book of its kind in print, and an ideal introduction.

Roger Hudson *Travels through Sacred India* (o/p). Knowledgeable and accessible introduction to religious India, with a gazetteer of holy places, listings of ashrams and lively essays on temples, *sadhus*, gurus and sacred sites. Hudson derives much of his material from personal encounters, which bring the subjects to life. Includes sections on all of India's main faiths, and an excellent bibliography.

★ **Stephen P. Huyler** *Meeting God* (Yale). This acclaimed introduction provides an unrivalled overview of the beliefs and practices of contemporary Hinduism. Accompanied by text that evokes general principles by focusing on individual acts of worship, Huyler's photographs are in a class of their own, suffused with sublime colours, magical light, and an intimate sense of spirituality.

Sarah McDonald *Holy Cow* (Bantam/Broadway). Very readable account of how a young Aussie journalist grew to love India, concentrating particularly on her personal brushes with the various spiritual traditions of the country. Prone to hyberbole at times, but consistently perceptive and occasionally hilarious.

★ **Wendy O'Flaherty** (transl) *Hindu Myths* (Penguin). Translations of key myths from the original Sanskrit texts, providing an insight into the foundations of Hinduism.

Yoga

B.K.S. Iyengar *Yoga: the Path to Holistic Health* (Dorling Kindersley). The definitive guide to yoga by the world's leading teacher, and the only book of its kind recommended by practitioners from across the yoga spectrum. Some 1900 colour photos illustrate step-by-step instructions on how to achieve the postures, and there's a copious introduction giving

the philosophical background and history. Too heavy to cart around India with you, but indispensable as a reference tool. A lighter (and much less expensive) version – fully endorsed by the great man, though modelled and written by three of his senior pupils – is *Yoga: the Iyengar Way*, by Silva, Mira and Shyan Mehta (also Dorling Kindersley).

Language

Language

Language

No fewer than seventeen major languages officially recognized by the constitution, numerous minor ones and over a thousand dialects are spoken across India. When Independent India was organized, the present-day states were largely created along linguistic lines, which helps the traveller at least make some sense of the complex situation. Considering the continuing prevalence of English, there is rarely any necessity to speak a local language but some theoretical knowledge of the background and having at least a few words of one or two can only enhance your visit.

While the main languages of northern India are all Indo-Aryan, in South India the picture changes completely. The four most widely spoken languages, Tamil (Tamil Nadu), Telugu (Andhra Pradesh), Kannada (Karnataka) and Malayalam (Kerala), all belong to the **Dravidian** family, the world's fourth largest group. These and related minor languages grew up quite separately among the non-Aryan peoples of southern India over thousands of years. The exact origins of the Dravidian group have not been established but it is possible that proto-Dravidian was spoken further north in prehistoric times before the people were driven south by the Aryan invaders.

The earliest written records of **Tamil**, the most dominant and oldest language of the family, date back to the second century AD, while **Malayalam** is the most closely related to Tamil but also the newest, dating from the tenth century.

Indian English

Over the period of the British Raj, Indian English developed its own characteristics, which have survived to the present day. The lilting stress and intonation patterns are the result of crossover from the Indian languages, as is the sometimes bewildering pace of delivery. Likewise, certain vowel sounds, for example the lack of distinction between the pronunciation of "cot" and "caught", and the utterance of some consonants, such as the common retroflex nature of "d", "t" and "r" with the tongue touching the soft palate, are also due to strong local linguistic features.

Indian languages have contributed a good deal of vocabulary to everyday English as well, including words like veranda, bungalow, sandal, pyjamas, shampoo, jungle, turban, caste, chariot, chilli, cardamom and yoga. The traveller to India soon becomes familiar with other terms in common usage that have not spread so widely outside the subcontinent: *dacoit, dhoti, bandh, panchayat, lakh* and *crore* are but a few (see Glossary, p.740, for definitions).

Perhaps the most endearing aspect of Indian English is the way it has preserved forms now regarded as highly old-fashioned in Britain. Addresses such as "Good sir" and questions like "May I know your good name?" are commonplace, as are terms like "tiffin", "cantonment" or "top-hole". This type of usage reaches its apogee in the more flowery expressions of the media which regularly feature in the vast array of daily newspapers published in English. Thus headlines often appear such as "37 perish in mishap", referring to a train crash, or passages like this splendid report of a bank robbery: "The miscreants absconded with the loot in great haste. They repaired immediately to their hideaway, whereupon they divided the iniquitous spoils before vanishing into thin air."

In between those two in age, **Telugu** (seventh century) has the second most speakers and **Kannada** (fourth century) follows closely on the heels of Tamil in terms of both antiquity and literary tradition. The beautiful flowing **scripts**, especially the exquisite curls of Kannada, add a constant aesthetic quality to any tour of the South. They developed that way thanks to the *palmyra* and *talipot* palm leaves prevalent in the South, which were turned under a firmly held hard stylus – a technique also adopted in Southeast Asian scripts like Burmese, Thai and Khmer.

Of the non-Dravidian languages, two have a substantial number of speakers: **Konkani**, only recognized as the official language of Goa in 1992, is Indo-Aryan and closely related to Marathi; while **Dakhani**, an old form of Urdu, dates back to the fourteenth century and remains the first language in the Muslim communities of Karnataka and Andhra Pradesh, especially noticeable in Hyderabad. Of course, the trained ear may catch numerous **minor languages** or dialects while travelling in South India – indigenous peoples, such as the tribes of the Andaman Islands, all have their own languages, some of very uncertain linguistic origins.

Useful words and phrases

Tamil

Basic words

Aamaam	Yes
Illai	No
Varavaanga	Goodbye (will return again)
Koncham dhayavuseydhu	Please
Nauri	Thanks
Romba nanringa	Thank you very much
Enga	Excuse me
Mannikkavum	Pardon
Idhu	This
Adhu	That
Idhu/adhu ennaanga?	What is this/that?
Romba nallayirukkudhu	Very good
Paravaayillai	Not bad
Vaanaga	Come (inviting someone in)
Neruthu	Stop
Evaikal	These
Pareya	Big
Sarreya	Small
Athekam	Much
Kuvrairu	Little

Time

Enrru	Today
Naalai	Tomorrow
Neerru	Yesterday
Pakal/kezhamai	Day
Eravu	Night
Athekaalai	Early morning
Kaalai	Morning
Matiyam	Afternoon
Maalai	Evening
Thengal	Monday
Chavvaay	Tuesday
Buthan	Wednesday
Veyaacha	Thursday
Valle	Friday
Chane	Saturday
Gnaayetrru/ Kezhama	Sunday

Communicating

I don't understand	Enakku puriya-villaiye
I understand	Enakku puriyudhu
I don't know Tamil	Enakku thamizh theriyaathunga

Do you know someone who knows English?	Inge aangilam therinchavanga yaaraavadhu irukkiraangalaa?
Could you speak slowly?	Koncham methuvaa pesuveengalaa?
Could you speak loudly?	Koncham balamaa pesunga?
What does he say?	Avar enna sollugiraar?

Food and shopping

I am hungry	Enakku pasikkudhul
I am thirsty	Enakku dhaga maayirukkudhu
How much is it?	Athanudaiya vilaienna?
I want only coffee	Enakku kapi maththi-ram than vendum
Please show me	Koncham kan-pikkireengalaa
Coffee	Kapi
Tea	Teyneer
Milk	Paal
Sugar	Sakkaray
Water	Neer
Rice	Arese
Cooked Rice	Satham
Vegetables	Kaaykarikal
Cooked vegetables	Kane
Curd/yoghurt	Thayer
Coconut	Thaenkaay

Directions

Far	Turam
Near	Arukkil
Where is... ?	Enge iruk-kuthunga...?
Is it near here?	Athu ingeyirundhu pakkam thaane?
How far is it from here?	Athu ingeyirundhu evvalavu dhoora-mayirukkunga?
Where can I get an auto?	Enga auto enga kidaikunga?

What is the charge to get there?	Empaa, anga povad hukku evvalavu?
Where is the bank?	Vangi enge irukkuthunga?
Where is the bus stand?	Bas staandu enge irukki radhu?
Where is the train station?	Tireyn staashan enge iruk-kuthunga?
Where is the restroom?	Kakkoos enge irukkudhu?
Where is the enquiries (information) office?	Visaranai enge irukki radhu?
Where is... road?	... theru enge irukkiradhu?
Post office	Anja lagam
Temple	Kohvil

Numbers

1	onru
2	eranndu
3	mundru
4	naangu
5	iyendhu
6	aaru
7	aezshu
8	ayttu
9	nbathu
10	patthu
11	pathenonrru
12	panereynndu
13	pathemoonrru
14	pathenaangu
15	pathenainthu
16	pathenaaru
17	pathnaezshu
18	pathenayttu
19	pathenthonbathu
20	erapathu
30	muppathu
40	naarpathu
50	iymbathu
60	arupathu
70	azhupathu

80	aennapathu
90	thonnoorru
100	noorru

1000	aayeram
100,000	latcham

Malayalam

Basic words

Yes	Aanaate
No	Alla
Hello	Namaste
Please	Dayavuchetu
Thank you	Nanni
Excuse me	Ksamikkuu
How much is it?	Etra?
I don't understand	Enikka arriyilla
Do you speak English?	Ninal englisha samsaarik-kumo?
My name is...	Ente pero...
Where is... ?	Eviteyaannaa...?
How much is it?	Etra?
Coffee	Kaappi
Tea	Chaaya
Milk	Paalu
Sugar	Panchasara
Medicine	Marunnu
Water	Vellam
Vegetables	Pachakkari
Fish	Meen
Curd	Tairu
Rice	Ari
Banana	Eyttappalam
Coconut	Teynna

Numbers

1	onnu
2	randu
3	muunu
4	naalu
5	anchu
6	aaru
7	eylu
8	ettu
9	ombatu
10	pattu
11	pationnu
12	pantrantu
13	pati-muunu
14–18	pati-...
19	pattonpattu
20	irupatu
21	irupattonnu
22	irupatti-randu
30	muppatu
31	muppati-yonnu
40	nalpatu
50	anpatu
60	arupatu
70	elapatu
80	enpatu
90	tonnuru
100	nuura
1000	aayiram
100,000	laksham

Telugu

Basic words

Yes	Awunu
No	Kaadu
Goodbye	Namaskaram
Please	Dayatesi
Thank you	Dhanyawadalu
Excuse me	Ksamiynchannddi

How much is it?	Enta?
What is your name?	Ni peru eymitti?
My name is...	Naa peru...
I don't understand	Naadu artham kaawattamleydu
Do you speak English?	Miku angalam vaacha?
Where is... ?	Ekkada undi... ?

How far is… ?	… Enta duram?	6	aaru
Big	Pedda	7	eyddu
Small	Tsinna	8	enimidi
Today	Iroju	9	tommidi
Day	Pagalu	10	padi
Night	Raatri	11	pada-kondu
Coffee	Kaafii	12	pad-rendu
Tea	Tti	13–19	pad-…
Milk	Palu	20	iruvay
Sugar	Chakkera	21	iruvay-okatti
Salt	Uppu	30	muppay
Water	Nillu	31	muppay-okati
Rice	Biyyamu	40	nalapay
Fish	Chepa	50	yaabay
Vegetables	Kuragayalu	60	aruvay
		70	debbay

Numbers

		80	enabay
1	okatti	90	tombay
2	renddu	100	nuru/wanda
3	muddu	200	renddu-wanda
4	naalugu	1000	veyi
5	aaydu	100,000	laksha

Kannada

Basic words

		Tea	Tea
		Milk	Haalu
Yes	Havdu	Sugar	Sakkare
No	Illa	Water	Neeru
Hello	Namaskara	Rice	Akki
Please	Dayavittu	Vegetables	Tarakari
Thank you	Vandanegallu	Fish	Massali
Excuse me	Kshamisi	Coconut water	Yella-neeru
Stop	Nillisu		

Numbers

How much is it?	Eshttu?
What is your name?	Nimma hesaru eynu?

1	ondu
My name is…	Nanna hesaru…
Where is… ?	Ellide… ?
2	eradu
I don't understand	Nanage artha aagalla
3	mooru
4	naalku
5	aydu
Do you speak English?	Neevu english mataaddtiiraa?
6	aaru
7	eylu
Day	Hagalu
8	entu
Night	Raatri
9	ombhattu
Today	Ivattu
10	hattu
Coffee	Kaafi
11	hannondu

12	hanneradu	50	aivattu
13	hadi-mooru	60	aravattu
14–18	hadi-…	70	eppattu
19	hattombhattu	80	embattu
20	ippattu	90	tombattu
21	ippattondu	99	tombattombattu
30	muvattu	100	nooru
31	muvattondu	1000	ondu saavira
40	naalvattu	100,000	laksha

Konkani

Basic words

Yes	Hoee	Water	Oodak
No	Na	Coconut	Nal
Hello	Paypadta	Tender coconut	Adzar
Goodbye	Miochay		

Please	Upkar kor
Thank you	Dio borem korunc
Excuse me	Upkar korkhi
How much?	Kitlay?
How much does it cost?	Kitlay poisha lakthele?
I don't want it	Mhaka naka tem
I don't understand	Mhaka kay samzona na
Where is… ?	Khoy aasa… ?
Beach	Prayia
Road	Rosto
Coffee	Kaafi
Tea	Chai
Milk	Dudh
Sugar	Shakhar
No sugar	Shakhar naka
Rice	Tandul

Numbers

1	ek
2	dohn
3	teen
4	char
5	paanch
6	soh
7	saht
8	ahrt
9	nou
10	dha
20	vees
30	tees
40	cha-ees
50	po-nas
100	chem-bor
1000	ek-azaar
100,000	laakh

Hindi/Urdu

(Not spoken in Tamil Nadu, Kerala, Karnataka [except in the northeast] or much of Andhra Pradesh)

Basic words and phrases

Namaste (said with palms together at chest height as in prayer – not used for Muslims)	Greetings
Aslaam alequm	Greetings (to a Muslim)
Ale qum aslaam	Greetings (in reply)
Phir milenge	We will meet again (goodbye)
Khudaa Haafiz (may god bless you)	Goodbye (to a Muslim)

Aap kaise hain?	How are you? (formal)	Kaan	Ear
Kya hal hai?	How are you? (familiar)	Piit	Back
Bhaaii/bhaayaa	Brother (a common address to a stranger)	Paao	Foot

Didi	Sister
Saaheb	Sir (Sahib)
Haan	Yes
Achhaa	OK/good
Nahiin	No
Kitna?	How much?
Kharaab	Bad
Mera nam… hai	My name is…
Aapka naam kya hai?	What is your name? (formal)
Yumhara naam kya hai	What is your name? (familiar)
Samaj nahin aayaa	I don't understand
Thiik hai	It is OK
Kitna?	How much?
… Kahaan hai?	Where is the… ?
Kitnaa duur?	How far?
Ruko	Stop
Thero	Wait
Dawaaii	Medicine
Dard	Pain
Pet	Stomach
Aankh	Eye
Naakh	Nose

Literary traditions

The rich will make temples for Shiva,
What shall I, a poor man, do?
My legs are pillars, the body the shrine,
The head a cupola of gold.
Listen, O lord of the meeting rivers,
Things standing shall fall, but the moving shall stay forever

Basavanna (Kannada poet, tenth century AD)

Of South India's main languages, **Tamil** boasts a literary tradition that goes back to pre-Pallava times. According to popular belief, three literary academies or **Sangam** met at Madurai, the earliest of which was attended by the gods and is no longer in existence. The Second Sangam is supposed to have been responsible for the **Tolkappiyam** – a treatise on Tamil grammar – but on close examination this would seem to have appeared later than the **Ettutogai**, the

"Eight Anthologies" ascribed to the Third Sangam. Although in archaic Tamil, and barely readable by ordinary Tamils today, the Eight Anthologies, consisting of over 2000 poems composed by around two hundred authors, and the **Pattuppattu**, or "Ten Songs", represent the greatest works of ancient Tamil literature. Even from this early stage, literature was subject to the Tamil love of classification, and the poems were divided into two main categories: *agam* (internal), dealing with love, and *puram* (external), laudatory poems in praise of the kings.

Although the Aryan influence on Tamil culture was already evident in Sangam literature, the influence of northern civilization grew and, in the sixth century, Hindu, Buddhist and Jain practices were widespread in the far south. Sanskrit left an indelible impression on Tamil literature, and the epic style of Sanskrit was emulated by long narrative poems such as **Shilappadigaram** (*The Jewelled Anklet*). Unlike the Sanskrit epics, however, Tamil poems such as the *Shilappadigaram* deal with the lives of ordinary people – in this case the hapless couple, Kovalan and Kannagi – and provide an invaluable insight into everyday life of the time. Shortly after the *Shilappadigaram* was written, Sattan, a poet from Madurai, composed the **Manimegalai**, a sort of anthology to the *Shilappadigaram*, but with a philosophical bent and a Buddhist message. The **Shivaga Shidamani**, another great early Tamil epic, was written by the Jain author Tiruttakkadevar and emulates Sanskrit court poetry, but concerns itself with the fantastic heroics of Shivaga (aka Jivaka) who eventually embraces the faith and becomes a monk.

Perhaps the greatest of all Tamil epics is Kamban's **Ramayanam**, composed in the ninth century – not just a translation from the Sanskrit *Ramayana* (see p.738) but a reinterpretation, with additional story lines, and, on occasion, markedly different interpretations of the main characters. Rama is not always shown as heroic, while Ravana, the demon king, occasionally is. During this period, inspired by the *Bhagavad Purana*, Vaishnavism became a predominant force in Tamil literature, promoting the new-found hero and man-god, Krishna.

In terms of antiquity, **Kannada**, the language of Karnataka, comes second only to Tamil amongst the Dravidian languages, with its earliest literature dating back to the ninth century AD and evidence from inscriptions that traces the language back to the fourth century. The golden age of Kannada literature was between the tenth and the twelfth centuries, when the poet-saints of the **Virashaiva** sect composed their **Vacanas** or "sayings". Also known as the **Lingayatas**, or "those who wear the *linga*", the Virashaiva poets dedicated their lives to the god Shiva. Although the sect, distinguished by the *lingam* encased in a small stone casket and worn around the neck, is still in existence, and *vacanas* are still composed, the four greatest poet-saints – **Basvanna**, **Dasimayya**, **Allama** and **Mahadeviyakka** – all flourished in the early medieval period. Basvanna, the most illustrious of all, epitomized the spirit of Virashaiva, with an uncompromising view of life and society and a single-minded devotion to the pursuit of truth through homage to Shiva. Basvanna and the Virashaivas rejected caste and believed the true path was open to all; they believed in the equality of women and the right of widows to remarry. They also rejected the highly structured poetic devices of classical Sanskrit poetry and composed simple free verse with a direct and universal philosophical wisdom which has caused some to refer to their work as the **Kannada Upanishads**.

The Lingayatas also composed their *vacanas* in Telugu, the language of Andhra Pradesh and parts of northern Tamil Nadu and southeast Karnataka. Telugu literature did not really develop until the twelfth century, and not as strongly as those of Tamil and Kannada until the sixteenth century, when it was adopted

The Mahabharata

Eight times as long as the *Iliad* and *Odyssey* combined, the **Mahabharata** is the most popular of all Hindu texts. Written around 400 AD, it tells of a feuding *kshatrya* family in upper India (Bharata) during the fourth millennium BC. Like all good epics, the *Mahabharata* recounts a gripping tale, using its characters to illustrate moral values. In essence it attempts to elucidate the position of the warrior castes, the *kshatryas*, and demonstrate that religious fulfilment is as accessible for them as it is for brahmins.

The chief character is **Arjuna**, a superb archer, who with his four brothers – Yudhishtra, Bhima, Nakula and Sahadeva – represents the **Pandava** clan, upholders of righteousness and supreme fighters. Arjuna won his wife **Draupadi** in an archery contest, but wishing to avoid jealousy she agreed to be the shared wife of all five brothers. The Pandava clan is resented by their cousins, the evil **Kauravas**, led by Duryodhana, the eldest son of Dhrtarashtra, ruler of the Kuru kingdom.

When Dhrtarashtra handed his kingdom over to the Pandavas, the Kauravas were far from happy. Duryodhana challenged Yudhishtra (known for his brawn but not his brain) to a gambling contest. The dice game was rigged; Yudhishtra gambled away not only his possessions, but also his kingdom and his shared wife. The Kauravas offered to return the kingdom to the Pandavas if they could spend thirteen years in exile, together with their wife, without being recognized. Despite much scheming, the Pandavas succeeded, but on return found that the Kauravas would not fulfil their side of the bargain.

Thus ensued the great battle of the Mahabharata, told in the sixth book, the **Bhagavad Gita** – immensely popular as an independent story. Vishnu descends to earth as **Krishna**, and steps into battle as Arjuna's charioteer. The Bhagavad Gita details the fantastic struggle of the fighting cousins, using magical weapons and brute force. Arjuna is in a dilemma, unable to justify the killing of his own kin in pursuit of a rightful kingdom for himself and his brothers. Krishna consoles him, reminding him that his principal duty, his *varnashradharma*, is as a warrior. What is more, Krishna points out, each man's soul, or *atman*, is eternal, and transmigrates from body to body, so Arjuna need not grieve the death of his cousins. Krishna convinces Arjuna that by fulfilling his *dharma* he not only upholds law and order by saving the kingdom from the grasp of unrighteous rulers, he also serves God in the spirit of devotion (*bhakti*), and thus guarantees himself eternal union with the divine in the blissful state of *moksha*.

The Pandavas finally win the battle, and Yudhishtra is crowned king. Eventually Arjuna's grandson, Pariksit, inherits the throne, and the Pandavas trek to Mount Meru, the mythical centre of the universe and the abode of the gods, where Arjuna finds Krishna's promised *moksha*.

---

at the court of the Vijayanagar empire at Hampi (see p.308). Telugu-speaking brahmins – most dedicated Vaishnavas (devotees of the god Vishnu and his incarnations) – were attracted to the court of King Krishna Deva Raya, who was also an accomplished composer of Sanskrit and Telugu verse. After the fall of Vijayanagar, the cultural centre shifted to the court of Tanjore where, despite its location in the heart of Tamil country, Telugu continued to enjoy its privileged status, partly due to the high calibre of religious poets who travelled to Tanjore and the surrounding country. In its heyday Tanjore was home to the merging of devotional literature with theatre, music and dance – nowhere better seen than in the work of the saint, poet and songwriter Tyagaraja (1767–1847), another Telugu-speaking brahmin, who was to leave an indelible impression on Carnatic music (see p.703).

Post Independence issues

With **Independence** it was decided by the government in Delhi that Hindi should become the **official language** of the newly created country. Interestingly, the idea of using Hindustani, a more recent colloquial hybrid of Hindi and Urdu, popular with Gandhi and others in an effort to encourage communal unity during the fight for freedom, was never pursued; this was due to a mixture of political reasons following Partition and the fact that the language lacked the necessary refinement. A drive to teach Hindi in all schools followed and over half the country's population are now reckoned to have a decent working knowledge of the language. However, the **Tamil-led** Dravidian

The Ramayana

Rama is the seventh of Vishnu's ten incarnations and the story of his life unfolds in the epic *Ramayana*. Although possibly based on a historic figure, Rama is seen rather more as a representation of the qualities of Vishnu. Rama was the oldest of four sons born to Dasaratha, King of Ayodhya, by his three wives and was heir to the throne. At the time of the coronation one of the king's wives, Kaikeya, seized the moment to ask for the two favours he had previously promised her in a moment of rash appreciation. Her first request was that her oldest son Bharata be anointed king instead of the rightful Rama. Her second request was that Rama be banished to the forest for fourteen years.

Rama in an exemplary show of filial piety accepted his father's unfortunate request and left the city together with his wife **Sita** and brother **Laksmana**. From their place of exile they continued their long battle against the demon forces led by **Ravana**, the evil king of Lanka. One day Ravana's sister Suparnakhi spotted Rama in the woods and immediately fell in love with him. Being a faithful and ideal husband Rama rebuffed her advances; Suparnakhi as a result tried to kill Sita, seeing her as the obstacle to Rama's heart. Laksmana intervened and cut off her nose and ears in retaliation. Suparnakhi fled to her brother, who mobilized fourteen giants to dispose of Rama. Rama destroyed them single-handedly and then similarly killed 14,000 warriors. Ravana was furious but heeded his advisers who suggested they should no more fight Rama but just kidnap his beloved, hinting that he would then quickly die of a broken heart. Sita was thus captured and flown by chariot to one of Ravana's palaces on the island of Lanka.

Determined to find Sita, a distraught Rama enlisted the help of **Hanuman**, lord of the monkeys. Rama and Laksmana then start their search for Sita, which leads to the discovery that she is being held on the island of Lanka. Hanuman leaps across the strait and makes his way surreptitiously into Ravana's palace where he hears the evil king trying to persuade Sita to marry him instead of the squeaky clean Rama – offering her the choice of consummation or consumption – become my bride or "My cooks shall mince thy limbs with steel and serve thee for my morning meal." Hanuman reports back to Rama who gathers an army and prepares to attack. This time the monkeys form a bridge across the straits allowing the army to cross and after much fighting Sita is rescued and reunited with the victorious Rama.

During the long journey back to Ayodhya Sita's honour was brought into question. To verify her innocence she asks Laksmana to build a funeral pyre. She prays to **Agni** before stepping into the flames and asks for protection before walking through them. Agni walks her through the fire to a delighted Rama. They march into Ayodhya guided by a trail of lights put there by the local people and this enlightened homecoming has long since been celebrated as **Divali** – the festival of lights. Soon after, Rama is finally crowned as rightful king, his younger brother gladly stepping down.

South has always been at the forefront of a strong **resistance** to the imposition of Hindi, which has even led to riots over the issue on occasions. The practical outcome of this southern distaste for Hindi is that the vast majority of people living below the Deccan plateau have little or no knowledge of it.

This is where English, the language of the ex-colonists, becomes an important means of communication. Not surprisingly, given India's rich linguistic diversity, **English** remains a **lingua franca** for many people (see box on p.729). It is still the preferred language of law, higher education, much of commerce and the media, and to some degree political dialogue. For many educated Indians, not just those living abroad, it is actually their first language. All this explains why the Anglophone visitor can often soon feel surprisingly at home despite the huge cultural differences. It is not unusual to overhear everyday contact between Indians from different parts of the country being conducted in English, and surprisingly stimulating conversations can often be had, not only with students or businesspeople, but also with chai-wallahs or shoeshine boys.

Glossary

ACHARYA religious teacher

ADIVASI official term for tribal person

AGARBATI incense

AHIMSA non-violence

AMRITA nectar of immortality

ANDA literally "egg": the spherical part of a stupa

ANICUT irrigation dam

ANKUSHA elephant goad

ANNA coin, no longer minted (Sixteen annas to one rupee)

APSARA heavenly nymph

ARAK liquor distilled from rice or coconut

ARATI evening temple puja of lights

ASANA yogic seating posture; small mat used in prayer and meditation

ASHRAM centre for spiritual learning and religious practice

ASURA demon

ATMAN soul

AVATAR reincarnation of Vishnu on earth, in human or animal form

AYURVEDA ancient system of medicine employing herbs, minerals and massage

BABA respectful term for a *sadhu*

BAGH garden, park

BAKSHEESH tip, donation, alms, occasionally meaning a corrupt backhander

BANDH general strike

BANDHANI tie-and-dye

BANIYA another term for a *vaishya*; a money lender

BANYAN vast fig tree, used traditionally as a meeting place, or shade for teaching and meditating; also, in South India, a cotton vest

BASTEE slum area

BASTI Jain temple

BAZAAR commercial centre of town; market

BEGUM Muslim princess; Muslim women of high status

BETEL leaf chewed in paan, with the nut of the areca tree; loosely applies to the nut

BHAJAN song

BHAKTI religious devotion expressed in a personalized or emotional relationship with the deity

BHANG pounded marijuana, often mixed in lassis

BHAWAN (also *bhavan*) palace or residence

BHUMI earth, or earth goddess

BHUMIKA storey

BEEDI tobacco rolled in a leaf; the "poor man's puff"

BIDRI inlaid metalwork as produced in Bidar

BINDU seed, or the red dot (also *bindi*) worn by women on their foreheads as decoration

BARADARI summer house, pavilion

BODHI enlightenment

BODHI TREE/BO TREE peepal tree, associated with the Buddha's enlightenment (*Ficus religiosa*)

BODHISATTVA Buddhist saint

BRAHMIN a member of the highest caste group; priest

BUNDH (also *bandh*) general strike

BURKHA body-covering shawl worn by orthodox Muslim women

BURRA-SAHIB colonial official, boss or a man of great importance

CANTONMENT area of town occupied by military quarters

CASTE social status acquired at birth

CELLA chamber in temple, often housing the image of a deity

CENOTAPH ornate tomb

CHAAT snack

CHADDAR large head-cover or shawl

CHAITYA Buddhist temple

CHAKRA discus; focus of power; energy point in the body; wheel, often representing the cycle of death and rebirth

CHANDAN sandalwood paste

CHANDRA moon

CHAPPAL sandals or flip-flops (thongs)

CHARAS hashish

CHARBAGH garden divided into quadrants (Moghul style)

CHARPOI string bed with wooden frame

CHAUMUKH image of four faces placed back to back

CHAURI fly whisk, regal symbol

CHELA pupil

CHERUVU lake

CHHATRI tomb; domed temple pavilion

CHILLUM cylindrical clay or wood pipe for smoking *charas* or *ganja*

CHITAL spotted deer

CHOLI short, tight-fitting blouse worn with a sari

CHOR robber

CHOULTRY quarters for pilgrims adjoining South Indian temples

CHOWGAN green in the centre of a town or village

CHOWK crossroads or courtyard

CHOWKIDAR watchman, caretaker

COOLIE porter, labourer

CRORE ten million

CUPOLA small delicate dome

DACOIT bandit

DALIT "oppressed", "out-caste"; the term, introduced by Dr Ambedkar, is preferred by so-called "untouchables" as a description of their social position

DANDA staff or stick

DARGAH sufi shrine

DARSHAN vision of a deity or saint; receiving religious teachings

DARWAZA gateway, door

DAWAN servant

DEG cauldron for food offerings, often found in *dargahs*

DEVA god

DEVADASI temple dancer

DEVI goddess

DHABA food hall selling local dishes

DHAM important religious site, or a theological college

DHARAMSHALA rest house for pilgrims

DHARMA sense of religious and social duty (Hindu); the law of nature, teachings, truth (Buddhist)

DHOBI laundry

DHOLAK double-ended drum

DHOLI sedan chair carried by bearers to hilltop temples

DHOOP thick pliable block of strong incense

DHOTI white ankle-length cloth worn by males, tied around the waist, and sometimes hitched up through the legs

DHURRIE woollen rug

DIGAMBARA literally "sky-clad": a Jain sect, known for the habit of nudity among monks, though this is no longer commonplace

DIKPALAS guardians of the four directions

DIWAN (*dewan*) chief minister

DIWAN-I-AM public audience hall

DIWAN-I-KHAS hall of private audience

DOWRY payment or gift offered in marriage

DRAVIDIAN of the southern culture

DUKKA tank and fountain in courtyard of mosque

DUPATTA veil worn by Muslim women with *salwar kamise*

DURBAR court building; government meeting

DVARPALA guardian image placed at sanctuary door

EVE-TEASING sexual harassment of women, either physical or verbal

FAKIR ascetic Muslim mendicant

FENI Goan spirit, distilled from coconut or cashew fruits

FINIAL capping motif on temple pinnacle

GADA mace (the weapon)

GADI throne

GANDHARVAS Indra's heavenly musicians

GANJ market

GANJA marijuana buds

GARBHA GRIHA temple sanctuary, literally "womb-chamber"

GARH fort

GARI vehicle, or car

GAUR Indian bison

GHAT mountain, landing platform, or steps leading to water

GHAZAL melancholy Urdu songs

GHEE clarified butter

GIRI hill

GODOWN warehouse

741

GOMPA Tibetan, or Ladakhi, Buddhist monastery

GOONDA ruffian

GOPI young cattle-tending maidens who feature as Krishna's playmates and lovers in popular mythology

GOPURA towered temple gateway, common in South India

GUMBAD dome on mosque or tomb

GURU teacher of religion, music, dance, astrology etc

GURUDWARA Sikh place of worship

HAJ Muslim pilgrimage to Mecca

HAJJI Muslim engaged upon, or who has performed, the *haj*

HAMMAM sunken hot bath, Persian-style

HARIJAN title – "Children of God" – given to "untouchables" by Gandhi

HARTAL one-day strike

HAVELI elaborately decorated (normally wooden) mansion

HIJRA eunuch or transvestite

HINAYANA literally "lesser vehicle": the name given to the original school of Buddhism by later sects

HOOKAH water pipe for smoking strong tobacco or marijuana

HOWDAH bulky elephant saddle, sometimes made of pure silver, and often shaded by a canopy

IDGAH area laid aside in the west of town for prayers during the Muslim festival Id-ul-Zuhara

IMAM Muslim leader or teacher

IMAMBARA tomb of a Shi'ite saint

IMFL Indian-made foreign liquor

INAM baksheesh in Tamil

INDO-SARACENIC overblown Raj-era architecture that combines Muslim, Hindu, Jain and Western elements

ISHWARA God; Shiva

IWAN the main (often central) arch in a mosque

JAGHIDAR landowner

JALI lattice work in stone, or a pierced screen

JANGHA the body of a temple

JATAKAS popular tales about the Buddha's life and teachings

JATI sub-caste, determined by family and occupation

JAWAN soldier

JHUTA soiled by lips: food or drink polluted by touch

-JI suffix added to names as a term of respect

JIHAD striving by Muslims, through battle, to spread their faith

JINA another term for the Jain *tirthankara*

JOHAR old practice of self-immolation by women in times of war

JYOTIRLINGA twelve sites sacred by association with Shiva's unbounded *lingam* of light

KABUTAR KHANA pigeon coop

KAILASA or KAILASH Shiva's mountain abode

KALAM school of painting

KALASHA pot-like capping stone characteristic of South Indian temples

KAMA satisfaction

KAMISE women's knee-length shirt, worn with *salwar* trousers

KARAN *wallah* in Tamil

KARMA weight of good and bad actions that determine status of rebirth

KATCHA the opposite of pukka, unacceptable

KATHAKALI traditional Keralan dance-drama

KAVAD small decorated box that unfolds to serve as a travelling temple

KHADI home-spun cotton; Gandhi's symbol of Indian self-sufficiency

KHAN honorific Muslim title

KHOL black eyeliner, also known as *surma*

KHUD valley side

KIRTAN hymn-singing

KOT fort

KOTHI residence

KOTLA citadel

KOVIL term for a Tamil Nadu temple

KSHATRYA the warrior and ruling caste

KUMKUM red mark on a Hindu woman's forehead (widows are not supposed to wear it)

KUND tank, lake, reservoir

KURTA men's long shirt worn over baggy pyjamas

LAKH one hundred thousand

LAMA Tibetan Buddhist monk and teacher

LATHI heavy stick used by police

LINGAM phallic symbol in places of worship representing the god Shiva

LIWAN cloisters in a mosque

LOKA realm or world, eg *devaloka*, world of the gods

LUNGHI male garment; long wrap-around cloth, like a *dhoti*, but usually coloured

MADRASA Islamic school

MAHA- common prefix meaning great or large

MAHADEVA literally "Great God", a common epithet for Shiva

MAHAL palace; mansion

MAHARAJA (*Maharana*, *Maharao*) king

MAHARANI queen

MAHATMA great soul

MAHAYANA literally "great vehicle": a Buddhist school that has spread throughout Southeast Asia

MAHOUT elephant driver or keeper

MAIDAN large open space or field

MAKARA crocodile-like animal featuring on temple doorways, and symbolizing the River Ganges; also the vehicle of Varuna, the Vedic god of the sea

MALA necklace, garland or rosary

MANDALA religious diagram

MANDAPA hall, often with many pillars, used for various purposes, eg *kalyan(a) mandapa* for wedding ceremonies and *nata mandapa* for dance performances

MANDI market

MANDIR temple

MANTRA sacred verse or word

MAQBARA Muslim tomb

MARG road

MASJID mosque

MATAJI female *sadhu*

MATH Hindu or Jain monastery

MAUND old unit of weight (roughly 20kg)

MAYUR peacock

MEDHI terrace

MELA festival

MEMSAHIB respectful address to European woman

MIHRAB niche in the wall of a mosque indicating the direction of prayer (to Mecca); in India the *mihrab* is in the west wall

MIMBAR pulpit in a mosque from which the Friday sermon is read

MINARET high slender tower, characteristic of mosques

MITHUNA sexual union, or amorous couples in Hindu and Buddhist figurative art

MOKSHA blissful state of freedom from rebirth aspired to by Hindus and Jains

MOR peacock

MUDRA hand gesture used in Vedic rituals, featuring in Hindu, Buddhist and Jain art and dance, and symbolizing teachings and life stages of the Buddha

MUEZZIN man behind the voice calling Muslims to prayer from a mosque

MULLAH Muslim teacher and scholar

MUND village

MUNDA male garment like *lunghi*

MUTT Hindu or Jain monastery

NADI river

NAGA mythical serpent

NALA stream gorge in the mountains

NATAK dance

NATYA drama

NAUTCH performance by dancing girls

NAWAB Muslim landowner or prince

NILGAI blue bull

NIRVANA Buddhist equivalent of *moksha*

NIWAS building or house

NIZAM title of Hyderabad rulers

NULLAH stream gorge in the mountains

OM (aka *AUM*) symbol denoting the origin of all things, and ultimate divine essence, used in meditation by Hindus and Buddhists

PAAN betel nut, lime, calcium and aniseed wrapped in a leaf and chewed as a digestive; it is mildly addictive

PADA foot, or base, also a poetic metre

PADMA lotus; another name for the goddess Lakshmi

PAGODA multistoreyed Buddhist monument

PAISE small unit of currency (100 paisa = 1 rupee)

PALANQUIN enclosed sedan chair, shouldered by four men

PALI original language of early Buddhist texts

PALLI old mosque or church in Kerala

PANCHAYAT village council

Owing to the very distinct languages of South India, an effective glossary of food terms is almost impossible, but the following list represents a highlight of food and the terms you are likely to come across as a visitor.

apa de camarão	spicy prawn pie with a rice and semolina crust (Goa)
appam	wok-cooked rice pancake speckled with holes, soft in the middle; a speciality of the Malabar coast of Kerala (Kerala)
assado	a spicy pan-cooked beef preparation (Goa)
bagheri baingan	small aubergine cooked with peanut paste and spices (Hyderabad)
bebinca	custard made with *gram* (chickpea) flour, eggs and coconut juice (Goa)
biriyani	rice baked with saffron or turmeric, whole spices and meat (sometimes vegetables), and often hard-boiled egg (North India and Hyderabad)
Bombay duck	dried bummelo fish (Mumbai)
caldeen	fish marinated in vinegar and cooked in a spicy sauce of coconut and chillies (Goa)
chapati	unleavened bread made of wholewheat flour and baked on a round griddle-dish called a *tawa* (universal)
chop	minced meat or vegetable surrounded by breaded mashed potato (universal)
cutlet	cutlet – often minced meat or vegetable fried in the form of a flat cake (universal)

dahi rice	a pleasant and light preparation – sometimes lightly spiced – of boiled rice with yoghurt (*dahi*)
dhal	lentils, pronounced "da'al" and found in one form or another throughout India; in the South often replaced by *sambar* (universal)
dhansak	meat and lentil curry, a Parsi speciality; medium-hot (Mumbai)
dosa	rice pancake – should be crispy; when served with a filling it is called a masala dosa and when plain, a *sada dosa* (Andhra Pradesh, Karnataka, Tamil Nadu, universal)
eshtew	a stew, usually made with chicken, cooked with potatoes in a creamy white sauce of coconut milk (Kerala)
ghee	clarified butter sometimes used for festive cooking, and often sprinkled onto food before eating (universal)
iddli	steamed rice cake, usually served with *sambar*; *malligi* (jasmine) *iddlis* around Mysore are exceptionally fluffy and so named because of their lightness – the scent of jasmine is said to waft on the breeze (Andhra Pradesh, Karnataka,

Kerala, Tamil Nadu, universal)

jaggery   unrefined sugar made from palm sap (universal)

jeera rice   rice cooked with cumin seeds (*jeera*) (universal)

karhi leaf   a type of laurel from which the leaf and the seeds are widely used as a spice throughout South India (universal)

keema   minced meat (Hyderabad)

khichari   rice cooked with lentils in various ways, from plain, to aromatic and spicy (Hyderabad, universal)

kofta   balls of minced vegetables or meat in a curried sauce (Hyderabad)

korma   meat braised in yoghurt sauce, mild (Hyderabad)

kulcha   fried flat bread to accompany curries (Hyderabad)

molee   curry with coconut, usually fish, originally Malay (hence the name), now a speciality of Kerala; hot (Kerala)

mulligatawny   curried vegetable soup, a classic Anglo-Indian dish rumoured to have come from "Mulligan Aunty" but probably South Indian; medium-strength (universal)

naan   white, leavened bread kneaded with yoghurt and baked in a *tandoor* (universal)

papad   crisp, thin chickpea flour *poppadu* cracker (universal)

paratha   wholewheat bread made with butter, rolled thin and griddle-fried; a little bit like a chewy pancake, sometimes stuffed with meat or vegetables (universal)

pomfret   a flatfish popular in Bombay and Calcutta (universal)

pulau   also known as *pilaf* or *pullao*, rice, gently spiced and pre-fried (universal)

puri   crispy, puffed-up, deep-fried wholewheat bread (universal)

rasam   spicy, pepper water often drunk to accompany "meals" in the South

roti   loosely used term; often just another name for *chapati*, though it should be thicker, chewier and baked in a *tandoor* (universal)

sambar   soupy lentil and vegetable curry with asafoetida and tamarind; used as an accompaniment to *dosas*, *iddlis* and vadas (universal)

sarpotel   pork dish with liver and heart, cooked in plenty of vinegar and spices (Goa)

uppma   popular breakfast cereal made from semolina, spices and nuts, and served with *sambar* (Kerala, Tamil Nadu)

uttapam   thick rice pancake often cooked with onions (Karnataka, Tamil Nadu, Kerala, universal)

vada	also known as *vadai*, a doughnut-shaped deep-fried lentil cake, which usually has a hole in its centre	– (sometimes fish) curry, originally pork; very hot (but not as hot as the kamikaze UK version) (Goan, universal)
vindaloo	Goan meat – seasoned with vinegar	

PANDA pilgrims' priest

PARIKRAMA ritual circumambulation around a temple, shrine or mountain

PARSI Zoroastrian

PIR Muslim holy man

POLE fortified gate

PRADAKSHINA PATHA processional path circling a monument or sanctuary

PRAKARA enclosure or courtyard in a South Indian temple

PRANAYAMA breath control, used in meditation

PRASAD food blessed in temple sanctuaries and shared among devotees

PRAYAG auspicious confluence of two or more rivers

PUJA worship

PUJARI priest

PUKKA correct and acceptable, in the very English sense of "proper"

PUNYA religious merit

PURDAH seclusion of Muslim women inside the home, and the general term for wearing a veil

PURNIMA full moon

PUROHIT priest

QABR Muslim grave

QAWWALI devotional singing popular among sufis

QILA fort

RAGA or **RAAG** series of notes forming the basis of a melody

RAJ rule; monarchy; in particular the period of British imperial rule 1857–1947

RAJA king

RAKSHASA demon (demoness: *rakshasi*)

RANGOLI geometrical pattern of rice powder laid before houses and temples

RATH processional temple chariot of South India

RAWAL chief priest (Hindu)

RISHI "seer"; philosophical sage or poet

RUDRAKSHA beads used to make Shiva rosaries

SADHU Hindu holy man with no caste or family ties

SAGAR lake

SAHIB respectful title for gentlemen; general term of address for European men

SALABHANJIKA wood nymph

SALWAR KAMISE long shirt and baggy ankle-hugging trousers worn by Muslim women

SAMADHI final enlightenment; a site of death or burial of a saint

SAMSARA cyclic process of death and rebirth

SANGAM sacred confluence of two or more rivers, or an academy

SANGEET music

SANNYASIN homeless, possessionless ascetic (Hindu)

SARAI resting place for caravans and travellers who once followed the trade routes through Asia

SARI usual dress for Indian women: a length of cloth wound around the waist and draped over one shoulder

SAROVAR pond or lake

SATI one who sacrifices her life on her husband's funeral pyre in emulation of Shiva's wife; no longer a common practice, and officially illegal

SATSANG teaching given by a religious figurehead

SATYAGRAHA literally "grasping truth": Gandhi's campaign of non-violent protest

SCHEDULED CASTES official name for "untouchables"

SEPOY an Indian soldier in European service

SETH merchant or businessman

SEVA voluntary service in a temple or community

SHAIVITE Hindu recognizing Shiva as the supreme god

SHANKHA conch, symbol of Vishnu

SHASTRA treatise

SHIKAR hunting

SHIKHARA temple tower or spire

SHISHYA pupil

SHLOKA verse from a Sanskrit text

SHRI respectful prefix; another name for Lakshmi

SHUDRA the lowest of the four castes or *varnas;* servant

SINGHA lion

SOMA medicinal herb with hallucinogenic properties used in early Vedic and Zoroastrian rituals

STAMBHA pillar, or flagstaff

STHALA site sacred for its association with legendary events

STUPA large hemispherical mound, representing the Buddha's presence, and often protecting relics of the Buddha or a Buddhist saint

SURMA black eyeliner, also known as *kohl*

SURYA the sun, or sun god

SUTRA (*sutta*) literally "thread": verse in Sanskrit and Pali texts

SVETAMBARA "white-clad" sect of Jainism, that accepts nuns and shuns nudity

SWAMI title for a holy man

SWARAJ "self-rule"; synonym for independence, coined by Gandhi

TALA rhythmic cycle in classical music; in sculpture a *tala* signifies one face-length; in architecture a storey

TALUKA district

TANDAVA vigorous, male form of dance; the dance of Shiva Nataraja

TANDOOR clay oven

TAPAS literally "heat": physical and mental austerities

TEMPO three-wheeled taxi

THALI combination of vegetarian dishes, chutneys, pickles, rice and bread served, especially in South India, as a single meal; the metal plate on which a meal is served

THERAVADA "Doctrine of the Elders": the original name for early Buddhism, which persists today in Sri Lanka and Thailand

TIFFIN light meal

TIFFIN CARRIER stainless steel set of tins used for carrying meals

TIKA devotional powder-mark Hindus wear on forehead, usually after puja

TILAK red dot smeared on the forehead during worship, and often used cosmetically

TIRTHA river crossing considered sacred by Hindus, or the transition from the mundane world to heaven; a place of pilgrimage for Jains

TIRTHANKARA "ford-maker" or "crossing-maker": an enlightened Jain teacher who is deified – 24 appear every 300 million years

TOLA the weight of a silver rupee: 180 grains, or approximately 116g

TONGA two-wheeled horse-drawn cart

TOPI cap

TORANA arch, or free-standing gateway of two pillars linked by an elaborate arch

TRIMURTI the Hindu trinity

TRISHULA Shiva's trident

TUK fortified enclosure of Jain shrines or temples

TULKU reincarnated teacher of Tibetan Buddhism

UNTOUCHABLES members of the lowest strata of society, considered polluting to all higher castes

URS Muslim saint's day festival

VAHANA the "vehicle" of a deity; the bull Nandi is Shiva's *vahana*

VAISHYA member of the merchant and trading caste group

VARNA literally "colour": one of four hierarchical social categories – brahmins, *kshatryas, vaishyas* and *shudras*

VEDAS sacred texts of early Hinduism

VEDIKA railing around a stupa

VIHARA Buddhist or Jain monastery

VILASA hall or palace

VIMANA tower over temple sanctuary

WADA mansion or palace

WALLAH suffix implying occupation, eg dhobi-wallah, rickshaw-wallah

WAZIR chief minister to the king

YAGNA Vedic sacrificial ritual

YAKSHA pre-Vedic folklore figure connected with fertility and incorporated into later Hindu iconography

YAKSHI female *yaksha*

YALI mythical lion

YANTRA cosmological pictogram, or model used in an observatory

YATRA pilgrimage

YATRI pilgrim

YOGI *sadhu* or priestly figure possessing occult powers gained through the practice of yoga (female: *yogini*)

YONI symbol of the female sexual organ, set around the base of the *lingam* in temple shrines

YUGA aeon: the present age is the last in a cycle of four *yugas*, *kali-yuga*, a "black age" of degeneration and spiritual decline

ZAMINDAR landowner

ZENANA women's quarters; segregated area for women in a mosque

Travel store

Rough Guides travel...

TRAVEL STORE

UK & Ireland
Britain
Devon & Cornwall
Dublin DIRECTIONS
Edinburgh DIRECTIONS
England
Ireland
Lake District
London
London DIRECTIONS
London Mini Guide
Scotland
Scottish Highlands &
  Islands
Wales

Europe
Algarve DIRECTIONS
Amsterdam
Amsterdam
  DIRECTIONS
Andalucía
Athens DIRECTIONS
Austria
Baltic States
Barcelona
Barcelona DIRECTIONS
Belgium & Luxembourg
Berlin
Brittany & Normandy
Bruges DIRECTIONS
Brussels
Budapest
Bulgaria
Copenhagen
Corfu
Corsica
Costa Brava
  DIRECTIONS
Crete
Croatia
Cyprus
Czech & Slovak
  Republics
Dodecanese & East
  Aegean
Dordogne & The Lot
Europe
Florence & Siena
Florence DIRECTIONS
France

French Hotels & Restos
Germany
Greece
Greek Islands
Hungary
Ibiza & Formentera
  DIRECTIONS
Iceland
Ionian Islands
Italy
Italian Lakes
Languedoc &
  Roussillon
Lisbon
Lisbon DIRECTIONS
The Loire
Madeira DIRECTIONS
Madrid DIRECTIONS
Mallorca & Menorca
Mallorca DIRECTIONS
Malta & Gozo
  DIRECTIONS
Menorca
Moscow
Netherlands
Norway
Paris
Paris DIRECTIONS
Paris Mini Guide
Poland
Portugal
Prague
Prague DIRECTIONS
Provence & the Côte
  d'Azur
Pyrenees
Romania
Rome
Rome DIRECTIONS
Sardinia
Scandinavia
Sicily
Slovenia
Spain
St Petersburg
Sweden
Switzerland
Tenerife & La Gomera
  DIRECTIONS
Turkey
Tuscany & Umbria

Venice & The Veneto
Venice DIRECTIONS
Vienna

Asia
Bali & Lombok
Bangkok
Beijing
Cambodia
China
Goa
Hong Kong & Macau
India
Indonesia
Japan
Laos
Malaysia, Singapore &
  Brunei
Nepal
The Philippines
Singapore
South India
Southeast Asia
Sri Lanka
Taiwan
Thailand
Thailand's Beaches &
  Islands
Tokyo
Vietnam

Australasia
Australia
Melbourne
New Zealand
Sydney

North America
Alaska
Boston
California
Canada
Chicago
Florida
Grand Canyon
Hawaii
Honolulu
Las Vegas DIRECTIONS
Los Angeles
Maui DIRECTIONS

Miami & South Florida
Montréal
New England
New Orleans
  DIRECTIONS
New York City
New York City
  DIRECTIONS
New York City Mini
  Guide
Orlando & Walt Disney
  World DIRECTIONS
Pacific Northwest
Rocky Mountains
San Francisco
San Francisco
  DIRECTIONS
Seattle
Southwest USA
Toronto
USA
Vancouver
Washington DC
Washington DC
  DIRECTIONS
Yosemite

Caribbean
& Latin America
Antigua & Barbuda
  DIRECTIONS
Argentina
Bahamas
Barbados DIRECTIONS
Belize
Bolivia
Brazil
Cancùn & Cozumel
  DIRECTIONS
Caribbean
Central America
Chile
Costa Rica
Cuba
Dominican Republic
Dominican Republic
  DIRECTIONS
Ecuador
Guatemala
Jamaica

...music & reference

Mexico
Peru
St Lucia
South America
Trinidad & Tobago
Yúcatan

Africa & Middle East
Cape Town & the
   Garden Route
Egypt
The Gambia
Jordan
Kenya
Marrakesh
   DIRECTIONS
Morocco
South Africa, Lesotho
   & Swaziland
Syria
Tanzania
Tunisia
West Africa
Zanzibar

Travel Theme guides
First-Time Around the
   World
First-Time Asia
First-Time Europe
First-Time Latin
   America
Travel Online
Travel Health
Travel Survival
Walks in London & SE
   England
Women Travel

Maps
Algarve
Amsterdam
Andalucia & Costa
   del Sol
Argentina
Athens
Australia
Baja California
Barcelona
Berlin
Boston

Brittany
Brussels
California
Chicago
Corsica
Costa Rica & Panama
Crete
Croatia
Cuba
Cyprus
Czech Republic
Dominican Republic
Dubai & UAE
Dublin
Egypt
Florence & Siena
Florida
France
Frankfurt
Germany
Greece
Guatemala & Belize
Hong Kong
Iceland
Ireland
Kenya
Lisbon
London
Los Angeles
Madrid
Mallorca
Marrakesh
Mexico
Miami & Key West
Morocco
New England
New York City
New Zealand
Northern Spain
Paris
Peru
Portugal
Prague
Rome
San Francisco
Sicily
South Africa
South India
Sri Lanka
Tenerife
Thailand

Toronto
Trinidad & Tobago
Tuscany
Venice
Washington DC
Yucatán Peninsula

Dictionary Phrasebooks
Croatian
Czech
Dutch
Egyptian Arabic
European Languages
   (Czech, French,
   German, Greek,
   Italian, Portuguese,
   Spanish)
French
German
Greek
Hindi & Urdu
Hungarian
Indonesian
Italian
Japanese
Latin American
   Spanish
Mandarin Chinese
Mexican Spanish
Polish
Portuguese
Russian
Spanish
Swahili
Thai
Turkish
Vietnamese

Music Guides
The Beatles
Bob Dylan
Cult Pop
Classical Music
Elvis
Frank Sinatra
Heavy Metal
Hip-Hop
Jazz
Opera
Reggae

Rock
World Music (2 vols)

Reference Guides
Babies
Books for Teenagers
Children's Books, 0–5
Children's Books, 5–11
Comedy Movies
Conspiracy Theories
Cult Fiction
Cult Football
Cult Movies
Cult TV
The Da Vinci Code
Ethical Shopping
Gangster Movies
Horror Movies
iPods, iTunes & Music
   Online
The Internet
James Bond
Kids' Movies
Lord of the Rings
Macs & OS X
Muhammad Ali
Music Playlists
PCs and Windows
Poker
Pregnancy & Birth
Sci-Fi Movies
Shakespeare
Superheroes

Unexplained
   Phenomena
The Universe
Weather
Website Directory

Football
Arsenal 11s
Celtic 11s
Chelsea 11s
Liverpool 11s
Newcastle 11s
Rangers 11s
Tottenham 11s
Man United 11s

Rough Guides maps

Rough Guide Maps, printed on waterproof
and rip-proof Yupo™ paper, offer an
unbeatable combination of practicality,
clarity of design and amazing value.

ROUGH GUIDES

not just travel

THE ROUGH GUIDE TO

Superheroes

THE COMICS ✻ THE COSTUMES ✻ THE CREATORS ✻ THE CATCHPHRASES

The Rough Guide to

The Corner Bookstore

India's Only National Bookstore Chain

Ahmedabad: Darpana Academy

Bangalore: St. Marks Rd, Kemp Fort, ITPL, Star Mall

Bhilai: New Civic Centre

Chennai: Abhiramapuram, Kadar Nawaz Khan Rd, Chottabhai Centre

Chandigarh: Sector17C

Delhi: defence Colony, Green Park, GK II, GK I, New Friends Colony, Janak Place
Connaught Place, India Habitat Centre, Humayun Road, South Ex

Gurgaon: DT Megamall, Sahara Mall, Scottish High School

Indore: Palasia Tower

Jaipur: Mall 21, Jal Mahal

Ludhiana: Saraba Nagar

Mumbai: Santa Cruz, Breach Candy, Prithvi Theatre, President Hotel

Pune: MG Road, Koregaon Park.

Raipur: Shankar Nagar

Vizag: Waltair Uplands

Vijaywada: MG Road

• Wide range • Exquisite Collection • Cozy and Comfortable ambience

STANF RDS

EXPLORE DISCOVER INSPIRE

The world's finest map and travel bookshops

Explore   Discover   Inspire

Maps   **Stanfords Flagship Store**
                     12-14 Long Acre
Travel Guides   **Covent Garden**
                     London
Illustrated Books   **WC2 9LP**
                     (T) 020 7836 1321
Travel Literature

World Atlases

Globes   **39 Spring Gardens**
                     Manchester
World Wall Maps   **M2 2BG**
                     (T) 0161 831 0250
Climbing Maps & Books

Maritime Maps & Books **29 Corn Street**
                      Bristol
Historical Maps   **BS1 1HT**
                      (T) 0117 929 9966
Instruments

Children's

                     International Mail Order
                     Department
                     +44 (0)20 7836 1321

                     www.stanfords.co.uk

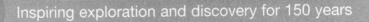

Inspiring exploration and discovery for 150 years

Travel Insurance

*Wherever you are, wherever you are going,
we ve got you covered!*
Visit our website at
www.roughguides.com/insurance
or call:

- UK: 0800 083 9507
- Spain: 900 997 149
- Australia: 1300 669 999
- New Zealand: 0800 55 99 11
- Worldwide: +44 870 890 2843
- USA, call toll free on: 1 800 749 4922

Please quote our ref: *Rough Guides Newsletter*
Cover for over 46 different nationalities and available in
4 different languages.

small print and

Index

A Rough Guide to Rough Guides

In the summer of 1981, Mark Ellingham, a recent graduate from Bristol University, was travelling round Greece and couldn't find a guidebook that really met his needs. On the one hand there were the student guides, insistent on saving every last cent, and on the other the heavyweight cultural tomes whose authors seemed to have spent more time in a research library than lounging away the afternoon at a taverna or on the beach.

In a bid to avoid getting a job, Mark and a small group of writers set about creating their own guidebook. It was a guide to Greece that aimed to combine a journalistic approach to description with a thoroughly practical approach to travellers' needs – a guide that would incorporate culture, history, and contemporary insights with a critical edge, together with up-to-date, value-for-money listings. Back in London, Mark and the team finished their Rough Guide, as they called it, and talked Routledge into publishing the book.

That first *Rough Guide to Greece*, published in 1982, was a student scheme that became a publishing phenomenon. The immediate success of the book – with numerous reprints and a Thomas Cook Prize shortlisting – spawned a series that rapidly covered dozens of destinations. Rough Guides had a ready market among low-budget backpackers, but soon also acquired a much broader and older readership that relished Rough Guides' wit and inquisitiveness as much as their enthusiastic, critical approach. Everyone wants value for money, but not at any price.

Rough Guides soon began supplementing the "rougher" information about hostels and low-budget listings with the kind of detail on restaurants and quality hotels that independent-minded visitors on any budget might expect, whether on business in New York or trekking in Thailand.

These days the guides – distributed worldwide by the Penguin Group – offer recommendations from shoestring to luxury and cover more than 200 destinations around the globe, including almost every country in the Americas and Europe, more than half of Africa, and most of Asia and Australasia. Our ever-growing team of authors and photographers is spread all over the world, particularly in Europe, the USA, and Australia.

In 1994, we published the *Rough Guide to World Music* and *Rough Guide to Classical Music*, and a year later the *Rough Guide to the Internet*. All three books have become benchmark titles in their fields – which encouraged us to expand into other areas of publishing, mainly around popular culture. Rough Guides now publish:

- Travel guides to more than 200 worldwide destinations
- Dictionary phrasebooks for 22 major languages
- History guides ranging from Ireland to Islam
- Maps printed on rip-proof and waterproof Polyart™ paper
- Music guides running the gamut from Opera to Elvis
- Restaurant guides to London, New York, and San Francisco
- Reference books on topics as diverse as the Weather and Shakespeare
- Sports guides from Formula 1 to Man Utd
- Pop culture books from Lord of the Rings to Cult TV
- World Music CDs in association with World Music Network

Visit **www.roughguides.com** to see our latest publications.

Rough Guide credits

Text editors: Gavin Thomas, Polly Thomas
Layout: Amit Verma
Cartography: Rajesh Mishra
Picture editor: Kate Noble, Harriet Mills
Production: Julia Bovis
Proofreader: Susannah Wight
Editorial: **London** Kate Berens, Claire
Saunders, Geoff Howard, Ruth Blackmore,
Richard Lim, Clifton Wilkinson, Alison Murchie,
Sally Schafer, Karoline Densley, Andy Turner,
Ella O'Donnell, Keith Drew, Edward Aves,
Nikki Birrell, Helen Marsden, Joe Staines,
Duncan Clark, Peter Buckley, Matthew Milton;
New York Andrew Rosenberg, Richard Koss,
Steven Horak, AnneLise Sorensen, Amy
Hegarty, Hunter Slaton
Design & Pictures: **London** Simon Bracken,
Dan May, Diana Jarvis, Mark Thomas, Jj Luck,
Chloë Roberts; **Delhi** Madhulita Mohapatra,
Umesh Aggarwal, Ajay Verma, Jessica
Subramanian, Amit Verma, Ankur Guha
Production: Sophie Hewat, Katherine Owers
Cartography: **London** Maxine Repath,
Ed Wright, Katie Lloyd-Jones; **Delhi** Manish
Chandra, Rajesh Chhibber, Jai Prakash
Mishra, Ashutosh Bharti, Jasbir Sandhu,
Karobi Gogoi, Animesh Pathak
Online: **New York** Jennifer Gold, Suzanne
Welles, Kristin Mingrone; **Delhi** Manik Chauhan,
Narender Kumar, Shekhar Jha, Rakesh Kumar,
Lalit Sharma, Chhandita Chakravarty
Marketing & Publicity: **London** Richard
Trillo, Niki Hanmer, David Wearn, Demelza
Dallow, Louise Maher; **New York** Geoff
Colquitt, Megan Kennedy, Milena Perez;
Delhi Reem Khokhar
Custom publishing and foreign rights:
Philippa Hopkins
Manager India: Punita Singh
Series editor: Mark Ellingham
Reference Director: Andrew Lockett
PA to Managing and Publishing Directors:
Megan McIntyre
Publishing Director: Martin Dunford
Managing Director: Kevin Fitzgerald

Publishing information

This 4th edition published October 2005 by
Rough Guides Ltd,
80 Strand, London WC2R 0RL
345 Hudson St, 4th Floor,
New York, NY 10014, USA
14 Local Shopping Centre, Panchsheel Park,
New Delhi 110017, India.
Distributed by the Penguin Group
Penguin Books Ltd,
80 Strand, London WC2R 0RL
Penguin Putnam, Inc.,
375 Hudson St, NY 10014, USA
Penguin Group (Australia)
250 Camberwell Road, Camberwell,
Victoria 3124, Australia
Penguin Books Canada Ltd,
10 Alcorn Avenue, Toronto, ON,
M4V 1E4 Canada
Penguin Group (New Zealand),
Cnr Rosedale and Airborne Roads,
Albany, Auckland, New Zealand

Typeset in Bembo and Helvetica to an original
design by Henry Iles.
Printed in Italy by LegoPrint S.p.A
© David Abram, Nick Edwards, Mike Ford,
Devdan Sen and Beth Wooldridge 2005

776pp includes index
A catalogue record for this book is available from
the British Library.
ISBN-13: 978-1-84353-502-7
ISBN-10: 1-84353-502-5

The publishers and authors have done their best
to ensure the accuracy and currency of all the
information in **The Rough Guide to South India**,
however, they can accept no responsibility for
any loss, injury, or inconvenience sustained by
any traveller as a result of information or advice
contained in the guide.

1 3 5 7 9 8 6 4 2

Help us update

We've gone to a lot of effort to ensure that the
fourth edition of **The Rough Guide to South
India** is accurate and up to date. However,
things change – places get "discovered,"
opening hours are notoriously fickle,
restaurants and rooms raise prices or lower
standards. If you feel we've got it wrong or
left something out, we'd like to know, and if
you can remember the address, the price, the
time, the phone number, so much the better.

We'll credit all contributions, and send a
copy of the next edition (or any other Rough
Guide if you prefer) for the best letters.
Everyone who writes to us and isn't already
a subscriber will receive a copy of our full-
colour thrice-yearly newsletter. Please mark
letters: **"Rough Guide South India update"**
and send to: Rough Guides, 80 Strand,
London WC2R 0RL, or Rough Guides, 4th
Floor, 345 Hudson St, New York, NY 10014.
Or send an email to **mail@roughguides.com**.
    Have your questions answered and tell
others about your trip at
www.roughguides.atinfopop.com.

Acknowledgements

David Abram: Thank you to Rohinton Commissariat and the Taj Group; Denzil Sequeira; Sarah Britto and family; Nick Edwards; and Ruth French.

Nick Edwards: Thanks for invaluable help in making a smooth trip to: Rohinton Commissariat in Mumbai; the Taj hotel staff in Nasik and Pune; all those at the tourist offices of Maharashtra, Karnataka, Kerala, AP and the Andamans, especially Mr Yadav in Aurangabad and Mr Varghese in Kochi; the good folk at the following establishments: Anand of *Classic Tours and Hotel*, Aurangabad; Arjun at the *Shree Maya*, Aurangabad; all at the *Plaza, Jalgaon, Costa Malabari* and *Pachyderm Palace*, Kerala; Benny and Linda of *Wild Orchid*, Havelock Island; kindly Gyan on Neill Island; Johnson of *The Nest*, Allepey; scholarly Mr Walton in Fort Kochi. Cheers to Antonia and Jemila for company in Munnar; Kathleen and Bethany for high times in Hampi; and Noam for making the Arial Bay to Port Blair boat trip a pleasure. Fair play to Paul and Jess for Xmas frolics and them plus Graham (completing his hat-trick) for the Kerala tour; yiasou to Sylvia for the last few days in Mamallapuram; thanks to Ashok and Anita for Madras hospitality. Last but not least, much love to Maria for enduring another long absence and not changing the locks! Finally, a prayer for all those lost and affected by the tsunami.

Mike Ford: A very big thank you to the following: Mr Karunanidhi of Welcome Tourrs and Travels in Chennai for your help with transport in Tamil Nadu; to my fearless and excellent driver Mr Ramesh; to Mrs Anu John at TTDC Kerala Office in Chennai for information, connections, friendship and a wonderful Keralan meal; to Mr Varghese at the Tourist Desk in Ernakulam for contacts; to the *Taj Connemara* in Chennai, *Greenwoods* in Mamallapuram and the *Sangam* hotel in Trichy; to Polly Thomas for excellent editing. Finally, a very big thank you to friends in Bristol – too many to name – for inspiration, support, drinks and technical support during computer traumas; and heartfelt sympathy for those in Tamil Nadu who suffered during the tsunami.

Devdan Sen: Thanks to everyone who assisted, especially Vivek Angra and India Tourism; Jai Chand, Bunny Mahtab and family; Sangela and Norbu Dekevas; Norden, Thinley Pempahishey and family; Norden's father Karma; Neil Law; Thendup and Pema; and Nima and Dorji Bhutia.

Readers' letters

Thanks to all the readers for taking the trouble to write and email in with comments and suggestions (and apologies to anyone whose name we might have inadvertently misspelt or omitted):

Florence Acworth; Kate Allen; Andreas Augustin; Wendy Backhouse; Michael Bastow; Lucy Beck; Hugh Begbie; Chris Berger; Anna Bibra; Ujjwal Borkataki; Heather Bowen; Jon Braham; Diana Care; David Carle-Ellis; Howard Carter; Heather and Michael Carver; Terrie Chilvers; Annie Clark; Antonio Claver; Paul Compton; Joy Cook; Clive Collins; James Coupland; Joel Cranshaw; Liz Curran; Jacqueline Deley; Roos Derks; Vanessa Dupin; Tina Ealovega; Ceryn Evans; Ms D. Faithfull; Faiz Farooqi; Raphael Fasko; Betty Gardiner; Amorey Gethin; Jennifer Gold; Tony Gomm; Mark Goodman; Don Grisbrook; Evelin Grofield; Gavin and Samantha Gross; Yorsten Haggenmiller; Bridget Hauserman; Alan Hickey; Jeffrey Hobbs; Sally Holmes; Mr Howell; Benjamin Hughes; Rohin S. Jaisinghani; Rafael Kampel; Vinod Kaistha; Thomas Keenan; Katja Kerl; Dr Sandeep Kesavan; Andy Kiley; Sarah Kline; Michael Knowles; Josh Krinsky; Philipe Labbey; Cari Lawley; Leanne and Mark; Marie Lippens; Chris Lucas; Nadine Maddaford; Geerdt Magiels; Tony Maisnam; Sandra Markow; Linde Maroudi; Curtis Marr; Craig McAvinue; Asha Rani Mathur; Les Medcroft; Thorsten Meyer; Patricia Moore; Julie Morrisey; Peter Nelson; Bill New; Amar Niwas; Barbara O'Callayhan; Yumi Onishi; I.H. Page; Sarah Parker; Margie Parsons; Victoria Peacock; Matthys de Pee; Remy Pigois; Pirashanthie; Martin Pitcher; Bettina Preussler; Singh Prithviraj; Robin Ray; Dominique Renn; Daniella Reif; Anita Reinhardt; Asya Reznikov; Wayne Richardson; Blair Robertson; Nikki Robilliard; Jenny Ross; Yair Sagi; Sajid Sait; Nicholas Sardi; Andrew Savage; Mr P.A. Shah; Edward Simpson; Professor Rana P.B. Singh; Trevor Skingle; David Smithson; Carol Smurthwaite; Natasha and Sven Sommer; See Stanley; Daniele Stewart; Dr Birender Thakur; Marie Thureau; Colin Todhunter; Michael Tsan; Uma; Lisa Verity and Kelly; Brenda Walker; Darren Walker; Joanna Westcombe; Julie White; Mike White; Kelly Woods; Isabel Wright; Melanie J. Wynne; Martin York; Randy Yuen; Kira Zielinski.

Photo credits

Cover

Main front picture: Kerala backwaters © Alamy
Small front top picture: Bullock, Madurai
© Alamy
Small front lower picture: Red flower, Kerala
© Alamy
Back top picture: Men outside temple, Karnataka
© Getty
Back lower picture: Brihadesvara Temple,
Thanjavar © Alamy

Title page

Taxi canoe, Kerala backwaters © Nikhilesh
Haval/Alamy

Full page

Bazaar, Mumbai © Peter Adams/Corbis

Introduction

Auto Rickshaw, Tamil Nadu © Petr Svarc/Alamy
Kailasanatha temple, Kanchipuram
© Bob Kirst/Corbis
Stuffing Peppers © Paul Harris
Elephant, Thanjavur © David Abram
Kodaikanal © Reuben Knutson
Movie poster © Jerry Dennis
Pouring saffron and vermillion over Bahubali
Statue © Chris Lisle/Corbis
Teyyattam © LinkIndia
Pao Bhaji breakfast © David Abram
North Goa beach © David Abram
Thrissur Elephant Festival © Blaine Harrington the
Third/Corbis
View from Palani temple © Reuben Knutson

Things Not To Miss

01 Jog falls, Karnataka © LinkIndia
02 Srirangam's Ranganathaswamy shrine
© Colin Pantall
03 Toddy-tapper in tree © Andrew Morris
04 Colonial architecture, Old Goa
© David Abram
05 Cricket at the Oval Maidan © LinkIndia
06 Boating in Kerala © Mike Ford
07 Palolem beach © Dave Abram
08 Golgumbaz tomb © ArkReligion.com/J
Sweeney/Art Directors and Trip
09 Kathakali performer © David Abram
10 Goats relaxing at Arjuna's Penance
© David Abram

11 Scuba diving © Louise Murray/Robert
Harding Picture Library
12 Temple drummers, Kerala © Simon Broughton
13 Periyar Wildlife Sanctuary © Paul Harris
14 Vizhinjam village © Andrew Morris
15 Nilgiri Blue Mountain Railway © LinkIndia
16 Ayurvedic massage © Michael Freeman/
Corbis
17 Madurai Temple, Tamil Nadu © Mike Ford
18 Indian elephants © Jagdeep Rajput/Getty
19 Fishing nets, Kochi © Andrew Morris
20 Worshippers at altar, Kerala © Robert Harding
21 Ashram sign © Art Directors and Trip
22 Temple chariot festival, Thiruvarur © LinkIndia
23 Fishing boats, Gokarna, Karnataka
© S. Reddy/Art Directors and Trip
24 Chola bronze © Colin Pantall
25 Dusshera festival © Dinodia/LinkIndia
26 Sravanabeloga © Devdan Sen
27 Achyutaraya temple at dawn, Hampi
© Andrew Morris
28 Golconda Fort, vaulted ceiling © Neil
McAllister/Alamy
29 Keralan Art © Mike Ford
30 Kalarippayat martial art © Remi Benali
31 Elephant Caves © LinkIndia
32 Tirumala pilgrims © ArkReligion.com/F. Good
/Art Directors and Trip

Black and whites

p.106 Gateway of India © Alamy
p.130 Ganesh Chaturthi © LinkIndia
p.168 Arambol beach © Mike Jones
p.228 Boat, Palolem beach © Greg Evans
p.238 The Maharaja's Palace © Amar Grover/
John Warburton-Lee Photography
p.295 Stone Statue at Shravanbelgola, Karnataka
© Dinodia Photo Library/Alamy
p. 338 Billboard advertising Kathakali dance
show, Fort Cochin © Sue Carpenter/Axiom
p.400 Holy Cross Church. Kochi © Monica Wells/
Pictures Colour Library
p.442 Chennai railway station, Madras © Alamy
p.470 Krishna's Butterball © David Abram
p.489 Parathasarathy temple © Steve Davey
p.578 Tirupati © LinkIndia
p.608 School of Moorish Idol fish © Jane Gould/
Alamy
p.631 Kalipur beach driftwood © Nick Edwards

Index

Map entries are in colour

Map symbols

Maps are listed in the full index using coloured text

--·-·-	International boundary	⋀⋁	Spring
--·-··	State boundary	⛫	Mosque/Muslim monument
-- --	Chapter boundary	⚶	Hindu/Jain temple
▬▬▬	Motorway	⊙	Statue
═══	Main road	♈	Fort
───	Minor road	◉	Accommodation
⬝⬝⬝	Steps	▣	Restaurant
━━━	Railway	ⓘ	Tourist office
= =	Track/trail	⊠	Post office
-----	Path	@	Internet access
───	Coastline/river	★	Public transport stop
— —	Ferry	Ⓗ	Helipad
▪▪▪	Wall	🅿	Parking
峚	Mountains	🛢	Fuel station
▲	Peak	⊞	Hospital
⋔ⱴ	Rocks	⛳	Golf course
⌂	Cave	▮	Building
) (	Pass	⊟	Church
⚱	Waterfall	◯	Stadium
⚸	Viewpoint	▦	Park
✈	International airport	▦	Beach
✗	Domestic airport	▩	Mudflats
◆	Point of interest	▨	Marshland
⚲	Lighthouse	▦	Forest
⸸⸸	Palm trees	⬜	Muslim cemetery

MAP SYMBOLS